PC Cumulative Title Index, Vols. 1-116

"A***" (Char) **56**:128
"A" (Zukofsky) **11**:337-40, 345-46, 351, 356-58, 361-67, 369-73, 383, 385-93, 395-99
"A" 1-9 (Zukofsky) **11**:380
"A" 1-12 (Zukofsky) **11**:343-44, 367-68
"A, a, a, DOMINE DEUS" (Jones) **116**:132-33, 148
"A. B." (Whitney)
See "To Her Sister Misteris A. B."
"The A.B.C.'s" (Baraka) **113**:4-5, 7
"À l'Abbé Eustache Barbe" (Sainte-Beuve) **110**:56
À Alfred de Musset (Sainte-Beuve) **110**:39
"À celle qui est trop gaie" (Baudelaire) **1**:44, 60-62; **106**:26, 139, 141-42, 145-46, 150, 172-76
"A Colón" (Darío) **15**:84, 115
"À David statuaire" (Sainte-Beuve) **110**:57, 65
"A. E." (de la Mare) **77**:60
"À Félix Guiliemardet" (Lamartine) **16**:284
"A Francisca" (Darío) **15**:107, 111
"A Janne impitoyable" (Ronsard) **105**:199
"A Jean de la Peruse, Poete" (Ronsard) **105**:215
"À Jenn de la Peruse, poète dramatique" (Ronsard) **11**:246
"A la forest de Gastine" (Ronsard)
See *See "Elégie XXIIII"*
"À la gloire d'un ami" (Ponge) **107**:142
À la lumière d'hiver (Jaccottet) **98**:181-86, 191, 195, 198
"À la lumière d'hiver" (Jaccottet) **98**:186-87
"À La Lune" (Williams) **109**:236
"À la nue accablante tu . . ." (Mallarmé) **102**:98, 101
"À la petite Adèle" (Sainte-Beuve) **110**:45
"À la promenade" (Verlaine) **32**:349, 390
À la rime (Sainte-Beuve) **110**:37, 58, 65
"A la Royne Mere" (Ronsard) **105**:272
"À la santé" (Apollinaire) **7**:44, 46-7
"A las estatuas de los dioses" (Cernuda) **62**:248-53
"À l'intérieur de l'armure" (Péret) **33**:203
"À l'Italie" (Apollinaire) **7**:22
"A lo lejos" (Jiménez) **7**:199
"A los poetas risueños" (Darío) **15**:95
A lune spento (Pound) **95**:114
"A.M. Viguier" (Sainte-Beuve) **110**:53
"A. M. Villemain" (Sainte-Beuve) **110**:56-57
"À Madame V. H." (Sainte-Beuve) **110**:55
À Manuel (Béranger) **112**:9-10
"A mi alma" (Jiménez) **7**:194
"À mon ami V. H. . . ." (Sainte-Beuve) **110**:65
"À Philippes des-Portes Chartrain" (Ronsard) **11**:269-70
"¡A probiña qu' esta xorda . . . !" (Castro) **41**:89
"À quatre heures du matin" (Rimbaud) **3**:274
"À quel psaume de nul antique antiphonaire" (Mallarmé) **102**:20-21, 23
"À Quoi Bon Dire" (Mew) **107**:25, 27-28, 30, 36
"À Ronsard" (Sainte-Beuve) **110**:65
"A Roosevelt" (Darío) **15**:77, 81, 90, 106, 115
"A sa lyre" (Ronsard) **105**:213, 249, 251
"À son ame" (Ronsard) **11**:244
"À Terre" (Owen) **19**:327, 331, 336, 339-40, 357, 359, 368; **102**:217, 225, 232, 263, 265-66
"A ti" (Darío) **15**:99
À travers un verger (Jaccottet) **98**:191, 194
"À une heure du matin" (Baudelaire) **1**:59, 72
"À une Malabaraise" (Baudelaire) **1**:49
"À une passante" (Baudelaire) **1**:45, 73; **106**:11-20, 79-81, 83-85, 101-2, 104, 147-48
"A une raison" (Rimbaud) **3**:260; **57**:282
"A Verlaine" (Darío) **15**:93
"À Victor Hugo" (Sainte-Beuve) **110**:65-69
"Aaron" (Herbert) **4**:102, 114, 130
"Aaron Hatfield" (Masters) **36**:184, 191
"Aaron Stark" (Robinson) **1**:460, 467; **35**:367
"Abacus" (Seifert)
See "Počitadlo"
"Abandon" (Li Po) **29**:177
"The Abandoned" (Abse) **41**:9
"The Abandoned Newborn" (Olds) **22**:329
"The Abandoned Observatory" (Yau) **61**:329
"The Abbey Mason" (Hardy) **92**:254, 256
"Abbey Theatre Fire" (Clarke) **112**:55
"Abbey Theatre, 1951" (Montague) **106**:336
"Abbeylara" (Montague) **106**:312
ABC of Economics (Pound) **4**:328
"ABCs" (Olson) **19**:267, 271, 316
"Abdala" (Martí) **76**:78, 99
"The Abduction" (Kunitz) **19**:181-82
"The Abduction of Saints" (Walker) **30**:354
"L'abeille" (Valéry) **9**:353, 387-88, 393-94
"L'Abeille, la couleur" (Bonnefoy) **58**:167-68
"Abel" (Stein) **18**:316
"Abel and Cain" (Baudelaire)
See "Abel et Caïn"
"Abel et Caïn" (Baudelaire) **1**:68; **106**:96
"Abel's blood" (Vaughan) **81**:306
"Abel's Bride" (Levertov) **11**:175
"Abend" (Stramm) **50**:170-71, 174, 198, 201, 207, 221
"Der Abend" (Trakl) **20**:237-38, 244, 251, 258
"Abendgang" (Stramm) **50**:171, 175-76, 202
"Ein Abendgesang" (Werfel)
See "An Evening Song"
"Abendland" (Trakl) **20**:231-32, 235, 240-44, 251, 269
"Abendländisches Lied" (Trakl) **20**:231, 236, 248-49, 251, 258, 269
"Abendlied" (Trakl) **20**:239, 269
"Abendmahl, Venezianisch, 16. Jahrhundert" (Enzensberger) **28**:165
"Abercuawg" (Thomas) **99**:259
"abgelegenes haus" (Enzensberger) **28**:140
Abhorrences (Dorn) **115**:157, 161-62, 199-200, 202, 215, 222, 230
"Abigail" (Silverstein) **49**:333
"Abiruna fi Kalamin 'Abir" (Darwish) **86**:19
"Abishag" (Glück) **16**:126, 141
"Abnegation" (Rich) **5**:365
"Aboard the Santa Maria" (Illyés) **16**:248
"Abode" (Milosz) **8**:215
"The Abominable Lake" (Smith) **12**:353
"Abomnewcast . . . On the Hour . . ." (Kaufman) **74**:261
"Abomunist" (Kaufman) **74**:260
Abomunist Manifesto (Kaufman) **74**:180, 194, 199-200, 211-12, 225, 230-31, 250, 259, 272
"Abomunist Rational Anthem" (Kaufman) **74**:211, 240
Abondance viendra (Char) **56**:127-28, 187
"Aboriginal Themes" (Gilmore) **87**:301
"The Aboriginals" (Gilmore) **87**:301
"Abortion" (Ai) **72**:28-29
"An Abortion" (O'Hara) **45**:162
"The Abortion" (Sexton) **2**:349; **79**:204, 257, 262, 264-67, 318, 323-24
"Abou Ben Adhem" (Hunt) **73**:137-38, 141, 155, 162
"About Almonds and Ambergis" (Goodison) **36**:158
"About Money" (Ignatow) **34**:273
"About Opera" (Meredith) **28**:195, 206
"About Poetry" (Meredith) **28**:193-94
"About the Dead Man and Sin" (Bell) **79**:37
"About the House" (Auden) **1**:21, 24
"About the Phoenix" (Merrill) **28**:239
"About These Verses" (Pasternak) **6**:251
Above the Barriers (Pasternak)
See *Poverkh barierov*
"Above the Gaspereau" (Carman) **34**:225
Above the River: The Complete Poems of James Wright (Wright) **36**:360-61, 370-71, 379, 391, 397-400
"Above These Cares" (Millay) **6**:235
"Abra; or, The Georgian Sultana" (Collins) **72**:80
"Abraham" (Sachs) **78**:115
"Abraham and Orpheus, Be with Me Now" (Schwartz) **8**:306, 308-09
"Abraham and the Fire Worshippers" (Hunt) **73**:138
"Abraham Davenport" (Whittier) **93**:239, 251, 275
"Abraham Lincoln Walks at Midnight" (Lindsay) **23**:275, 280, 284, 288, 294-95
"Abram Morrison" (Whittier) **93**:238-39, 252
"L'Abri rudoyé" (Char) **56**:152
"L'abricot" (Ponge) **107**:79, 169
"Abril sus flores abría" (Guillén) **23**:125
Abrojos (Darío) **15**:94
Absalom and Achitophel (Dryden) **25**:82-3, 88, 106-08, 113-14
"Abschied" (Benn) **35**:82, 83, 85
"Abschied—" (Sachs) **78**:164
"Der Abschied" (Sarton) **39**:338
"abschied von einem mittwoch" (Enzensberger) **28**:136
"Absence" (Borges)
See "Ausencia"
"Absence" (Gozzano) **10**:178
"Absence" (Hughes) **89**:104
"Absence" (Mew) **107**:36
"Absence" (Sarton) **39**:369
"The Absence" (Thomas) **99**:263, 319, 358-59

"L'absence, ny l'oubly, ny la course du jour" (Ronsard) **11**:246
"The Absence of Little Wesley" (Riley) **48**:340, 360
"An Absence of Slaves" (Jacobsen) **62**:315, 318, 324
"Absence Proves Nothing" (Stone) **53**:247-48, 257
"Absences" (Justice) **64**:252, 259, 271, 276
"Absences" (Larkin) **21**:249-51
"Absences I" (Éluard) **38**:70-71
"Absences II" (Éluard) **38**:70-71
"L'Absent" (Char) **56**:153
"Absent from Thee" (Wilmot) **66**:266, 324
"The Absent Girl" (Ní Chuilleanáin) **34**:357
"The absent One" (Senghor)
See "L'Absente"
"Absent With Official Leave" (Jarrell) **41**:201
"L'Absente" (Senghor) **25**:255, 258
"Absentia animi" (Ekeloef) **23**:59-60, 63, 76, 86
"The Absent-Minded Beggar" (Kipling) **91**:61, 67-68, 73, 173-74
"Absent-minded Nocturne" (Cernuda)
See "Nocturno entre las musarañas"
"Absent-Minded Professor" (Nemerov) **24**:266
"Absolute Clearance" (Ashbery) **26**:124
"The Absolute Explains" (Hardy) **92**:212, 229
"Absolute Retreat" (Finch)
See "The Petition for an Absolute Retreat"
"Absolute Zero" (Parra) **39**:308-10
"Absolution" (Brooke) **24**:52
"Absolution" (Sassoon) **12**:241, 250, 252, 261, 276, 278, 280
"Absolution" (Thomas) **99**:234
"Abstinence" (Traherne) **70**:322
"Abstract" (Creeley) **73**:97
"Absurd Prayer" (Cohen) **109**:56
"Abt Vogler" (Browning) **2**:37, 75, 80, 88, 95; **97**:13
"Abu" (Randall) **86**:329, 337
"El abuelo" (Guillén) **23**:134-37
"Abundance" (Traherne) **70**:323
"Abur Don Pepe" (Guillén) **23**:126
"Abyss" (Kennedy) **93**:145
"The Abyss" (Roethke) **15**:270
"The Abyss of Mr. Cogito" (Herbert) **50**:19
"The Abyss of War" (Owen) **19**:343
"Abzählreime" (Celan) **10**:124-25
"Academic" (Roethke) **15**:246
"Academic Discourse at Havana" (Stevens) **110**:216
Academic Squaw: Reports to the World from the Ivory Tower (Rose) **13**:233, 238
"Accelerating Frame" (Waldrop) **109**:158
"Acceptance" (Sassoon) **12**:259
"Accepted" (Patmore) **59**:230
"Accès" (Tzara) **27**:229-31
"Accesse" (Traherne) **70**:321
"The Accident" (Strand) **63**:153, 160
"Accident" (Traherne) **70**:321
"The Accident" (Williams) **109**:207
"Accidentally on Purpose" (Frost) **1**:213
"Accomplishment" (Gallagher) **9**:59
"The Account" (Cowley) **90**:15
"An Account of a Visit to Hawaii" (Meredith) **28**:171, 189
An Account of a Weatherbeaten Journey (Matsuo Basho)
See *Nozarashi kikō*
"Account of the Family of the DeBerghams" (Chatterton) **104**:4
"Accountability" (Dunbar) **5**:133, 146
"The Accounte of W. Canyges Feast" (Chatterton) **104**:7, 10-11, 13
"An Accounting of All Her Men" (Ríos) **57**:325
"Les accroupissements" (Rimbaud) **3**:284; **57**:203, 253, 289, 293-95
"The Accusation" (Wright) **36**:343
"The accused" (Hughes) **89**:194
"Accused Cherub" (Rimbaud)
See "L'Angelot maudit"
"The Accuser" (Milosz) **8**:204
Ace (Raworth) **107**:278, 299, 310, 324-25, 327-28, 336
"The Ace of Spades" (Péret)
See "As de Pique"
"Acevedo" (Borges) **32**:88
"Ach das Erhabene" (Benn) **35**:36
"Ach, um deine feuchten Schwingen" (Goethe) **5**:247
"The Ache of Marriage" (Levertov) **11**:169
"Achieving a Poem while Drinking Alone" (Tu Fu) **9**:327
"The Achill Woman " (Boland) **58**:7, 15-16, 27, 30, 55, 57-58, 66, 68
"Achilles and Deidamia" (Gower) **59**:98-99
Achilles Shield (Chapman) **96**:36
"Achille's Song" (Duncan) **2**:115; **75**:159, 256
"Achronos" (Blunden) **66**:7-8
"Ackneystadt" (Kipling) **91**:71
"Acknowledgment" (Lanier) **50**:55
"Acon" (H. D.) **5**:273
Aconsejo beber hilo (Fuertes) **27**:10-12
"El acorde" (Cernuda) **62**:221
"Acquainted with the Night" (Frost) **1**:197, 205-06, 208; **39**:246
"Acquamorta" (Quasimodo) **47**:285-86
Acque e terre (Quasimodo) **47**:270, 274-75, 300-302
"An Acre of Grass" (Yeats) **51**:142, 152
An Acre of Land (Thomas) **99**:239
"Across America" (Hall) **70**:32
"Across Kansas" (Stafford) **71**:276, 288, 295
"Across Lamarck Col" (Snyder) **21**:288
"Across the Bay" (Davie) **29**:110
"An Acrostic" (Poe) **1**:446
"The Act of Love" (Creeley) **73**:91
"The act of madness" (Char)
See "L'Extravagant"
"Act of Union" (Clarke) **112**:140
"Act of Union" (Heaney) **18**:196; **100**:224
"Act Sederunt of the Session—A Scots Ballad" (Burns) **114**:129
"Act III, Sc. 2" (Graham) **59**:175
"Acta de independecia" (Parra) **39**:277
Actaeon (Clough) **103**:52
"Actaeon: Eleven Glosses on an Alibi" (Waldrop) **109**:120
"Acteon" (Gower) **59**:88, 92
"Acteon" (Hughes) **89**:129
"Actfive" (MacLeish) **47**:191-92, 259
Actfive, and Other Poems (MacLeish) **47**:176, 178-79, 191, 197, 246, 260
"Acting" (Thomas) **99**:304
"The Action of the Beautiful" (Sarton) **39**:325, 333, 365
"L'Action restreinte" (Mallarmé) **102**:116
Actions and Reactions (Kipling) **91**:135
"Active Night" (Corso) **108**:8, 38
"Acto completo'" (Guillén) **35**:227
"Actors, Middle East" (Seferis) **66**:210
"Actors waiting in the wings of Europe" (Douglas) **106**:187
"Acts and Monuments" (Ní Chuilleanáin) **34**:359, 363, 380-81
Acts and Monuments (Ní Chuilleanáin) **34**:348, 350-51, 355, 359, 363
"Acts passed beyond the boundary of mere wishing" (Spender) **71**:181, 217
"Acuteness" (Traherne) **70**:323
"Ad Alessandro d'Ancona" (Carducci) **46**:52
"Ad amicos cum aegrotaret" (Campion) **87**:4
"Ad Angelo Mai quand'ebbe trovato i libri di Cicerone della Repubblica" (Leopardi) **37**:111, 147-49
"A.D. Blood" (Masters) **36**:170, 230
"Ad C: Favonium Aristium" (Gray) **80**:136, 138, 235
"Ad C: Favonium Zephyrinum" (Gray) **80**:136, 235
"Ad Cambricum" (Campion) **87**:35
"Ad Castitatem" (Bogan) **12**:117
"Ad Corvinum" (Campion) **87**:5
"Ad Daphnin" (Campion) **87**:4
"Ad Deum in afflictione: Elegia" (Southwell)
See "To God in Affliction: An Elegy"
"Ad Dianam" (Campion) **87**:4
"Ad Ed. Spencerum" (Campion) **87**:5
"Ad Ge. Chapmannum" (Campion) **87**:5
"Ad Graios" (Campion) **87**:3
"Ad Io. Davisium" (Campion) **87**:5
"Ad Io. Dolundum" (Campion) **87**:4
"Ad Lectorem" (Campion) **87**:4
"Ad Libitum" (Elytis) **21**:132-33
"Ad Mariam" (Hopkins) **15**:159, 164, 166
"Ad Nashum" (Campion) **87**:4-5
"Ad Nassum" (Campion)
See "Ad Nashum"
"Ad Patrem" (Milton) **29**:241
"Ad Ricardum Savage" (Johnson) **81**:119, 170
"Ad sanctam Catherinam, virginem et martyrem" (Southwell)
See "To Saint Catherine, Virgin and Martyr"
"Ad Thamesin" (Campion) **87**:4, 11, 63
"Ad Urbanum" (Johnson) **81**:119
"Adam" (Brathwaite) **56**:62
"Adam" (Hecht) **70**:108
"Adam" (Tomlinson) **17**:316, 342
"Adam" (Traherne) **70**:223, 237
"Adam" (Williams) **7**:350, 354
"Adam and Eve" (Clough) **103**:55, 57, 79-80, 82-83, 135, 137
"Adam and Eve" (Shapiro) **25**:284-85, 287, 290-91, 301, 320
Adam & Eve & the City (Williams) **7**:350, 402
Adam and the Sacred Nine (Hughes) **89**:124, 130, 150
"Adam and the Sacred Nine #11" (Hughes) **89**:130
"Adam Is Your Ash" (Borges)
See "Adán es tu ceniza"
The Adam of Two Edens: Selected Poems (Darwish) **86**:26-28
"adam thinking" (Clifton) **17**:30, 36
"Adam II" (Traherne) **70**:323
"The Adamant" (Roethke) **15**:272, 291
"Adamas and Eva" (Masefield) **78**:51
"Adams" (Douglas) **106**:199
"The Adams Cantos" (Pound) **95**:206-8
"Adam's Curse" (Yeats) **20**:338
"Adam's Dream" (Muir) **49**:260-61
"Adam's Way" (Duncan) **2**:103
"Adán es tu ceniza" (Borges) **32**:67
"Add This to Rhetoric" (Stevens) **110**:201
"The Addict" (Sexton) **2**:364; **79**:227, 229
"Addition" (Cavafy) **36**:53
Additional Poems (Housman) **2**:176-77, 190; **43**:221, 243, 258-61
"address" (Alurista) **34**:32
"Address" (Dorn) **115**:83
"Address for a Prize-Day" (Auden) **1**:8, 37
"An Address for the First Woman to Face Death in Havana—Olga Herrara Marcos" (Dorn) **115**:82
"Address of Beelzebub" (Burns) **6**:83-4, 88-9; **114**:34, 45, 52-53, 58, 64, 68, 135, 147-48
"Address to a Haggis" (Burns) **114**:42
"Address to a Lark" (Clare) **23**:39
"Address to a Louse" (Burns)
See "To a Louse, on Seeing One on a Lady's Bonnet at Church"
"Address to an Old Wooden Gate" (Kavanagh) **105**:129, 155
"Address to Kilchurn Castle" (Wordsworth) **67**:269
An Address to Miss Phillis Wheatly (Hammon) **16**:179, 187-89
"Address to My Soul" (Wylie) **23**:303, 305, 310, 313, 322, 333
"Address to Saxham" (Carew) **29**:7-8, 41-43
"Address to the Angels" (Kumin) **15**:204
"Address to the Beasts" (Auden) **92**:98
"Address to the De'il" (Burns) **6**:49, 78, 83-4, 87; **114**:8, 20, 54, 60, 65, 119, 155-56

"The Address to the Evening Sun" (Macpherson) **97**:177, 205
"An Address to the Muse" (Abse) **41**:8
"Address to the Scholars of New England" (Ransom) **61**:289
"Address to The Steam-Washing Company" (Hood) **93**:116
"Address to the Unco' Guild" (Burns) **114**:70, 129
"An Address to Weyerhauser, the Tree-Growing Company" (Wagoner) **33**:352
"Addressed to a Lady, Who Was Affected at Seeing the Funeral of a Nameless Pauper" (Smith) **104**:207, 325
Addressed to Haydon (Keats) **96**:349
"Adelaide Abner" (Smith) **12**:310, 326
"Adelaide Crapsey" (Sandburg) **41**:241
The Adi Granth (Kabīr) **56**:343-46
"L'adieu" (Apollinaire) **7**:48
"L'adieu" (Lamartine) **16**:277, 299
"Adieu" (Rimbaud) **3**:273; **57**:172, 247, 249, 251-52, 254, 276, 279
"Adieu á Charlot" (Ferlinghetti) **1**:181-82, 188
"Adieu, Farewell Earths Blisse" (Nashe) **82**:280, 282
"Adieu, ma redoubtee Dame" (Christine de Pizan) **68**:192
"Adieu, Mlle. Veronique" (Brodsky) **9**:2, 5
"Adieu to Norman, Bon Jour to Joan and Jean-Paul" (O'Hara) **45**:133, 138, 141, 145, 147, 160-61, 219
"Adieux a la poesie" (Lamartine) **16**:273
"Adieux à la poésie" (Sainte-Beuve) **110**:65
"Adieux à Marie Stuart" (Swinburne) **24**:313
"The Adirondacs" (Emerson) **18**:76-77, 111, 113
"Adivinanzas" (Guillén) **23**:106
"Adler" (Stern) **115**:279
"Adlestrop" (Thomas) **53**:338-41, 344
"Administrator" (Kinsella) **69**:132, 135, 137
"The Admiral and the Snake" (Espada) **74**:138
"The Admiral's Ghost" (Noyes) **27**:121, 134
"Admonition" (Spicer) **78**:285
"Admonition" (Wagoner) **33**:369-70
"Admonition to a Special Person" (Sexton) **79**:245
"admonitions" (Clifton) **17**:31
Admonitions (Spicer) **78**:240, 250, 256-57, 259, 268-70, 292, 301, 304-6, 308
"Adolescence" (Dove) **6**:106
"Adolescence—III" (Dove) **6**:109
"Adolescencia" (Jiménez) **7**:183, 209
"The Adolescent" (Jiménez)
See "Adolescencia"
"Adolescent" (Seferis) **66**:144
"Adolescent" (Tsvetaeva)
See "Otrok"
"Adolfo and Lucía" (Espada) **74**:139
"Adonais" (Arnold) **5**:7
"Adonais" (Wylie) **23**:323
Adonais (Shelley)
See *Adonais: An Elegy on the Death of John Keats*
Adonais: An Elegy on the Death of John Keats (Shelley) **14**:164, 171, 174, 178, 183, 186-89, 197, 211, 218, 233-34, 236-37, 239-40; **67**:138, 145, 148, 158, 169, 180, 222
"Adonis" (H. D.) **5**:269, 304, 308
"Adonis" (Ronsard) **11**:251
"Adonis in Summer" (Rexroth) **95**:259
"Adonis in Winter" (Rexroth) **95**:259
"La adoración de los magos" (Cernuda) **62**:169-70
"The Adoration of the Magi" (Cernuda)
See "La adoración de los magos"
"Adorations, Requests, Buzzings in the Ears" (Zanzotto)
See "Adorazioni, richieste, acufeni"
"Adorazioni, richieste, acufeni" (Zanzotto) **65**:312
"Adore te'" (Crashaw) **84**:93-94, 96, 103
"Adowa" (Brathwaite) **56**:12
Adrastea (Herder) **14**:171, 173, 178, 192, 211-12, 217, 221-24, 233-37, 239
"Adult Bookstore" (Shapiro) **25**:306-307, 322
"Adultery" (Dickey) **40**:181, 197, 226-27, 232, 258
"Adulthood" (Giovanni) **19**:110, 139
"Adulto? Mai" (Pasolini) **17**:261
"Adults Only" (Stafford) **71**:299, 320
"Advance your choral motions now" (Campion) **87**:7, 12
"An Advancement of Learning" (Heaney) **18**:187, 190, 200; **100**:215
"The Advantages of Learning" (Rexroth) **95**:271
"El advenimiento" (Borges) **32**:49-50
"Advenimiento" (Guillén) **35**:187
"Advent" (Kavanagh) **33**:72, 85, 94, 134, 138, 161; **105**:152
"Advent" (Merton) **10**:340
"Advent" (Rexroth) **95**:259
"Advent" (Rossetti) **7**:290, 297
Advent (Rilke) **2**:280
"Advent 1955" (Betjeman) **75**:96
"Advent, 1966" (Levertov) **11**:176
"Advent Calendar" (Schnackenberg) **45**:338, 341
"Adventure in an Antique Shop" (Akhmadulina)
See "Prikljucenie v antikvarnom magazine"
"Advent Meditation" (Meynell) **112**:299
"Adventures" (Pavese) **13**:205
"Adventures in the Bohemian Jungle" (Kavanagh) **33**:86, 95, 117-8, 121; **105**:120, 144, 173
"Adventures of a Frisbee" (Silverstein) **49**:331
"Adventures of Isabel" (Nash) **21**:265
Adventures While Preaching the Gospel of Beauty (Lindsay) **23**:278, 295
"Adventures While Singing These Songs" (Lindsay) **23**:282
"Adversity" (Gray)
See "Ode to Adversity"
"Advertencia" (Fuertes) **27**:26
"Advertencia al lector" (Parra) **39**:296, 305-8
"Advertisement" (Jackson) **44**:13
"Advertisement for the Waldorf-Astoria" (Hughes) **53**:115
"Advertisement to Lyrical Ballads" (Wordsworth) **67**:282-83, 285, 289, 294, 308, 330, 334-38, 340, 345-46, 349-51, 357, 361
"Advice" (Crabbe) **97**:148, 152
"Advice" (Lovelace) **69**:168-72, 239, 243
"The Advice" (Raleigh) **31**:212, 214, 236
"The Advice" (Roethke) **15**:274
"The Advice" (Wilmot) **66**:329, 339
"Advice about Roses" (Stein) **18**:313
"Advice to a First Cousin" (Ríos) **57**:323
"Advice to a Girl" (Teasdale) **31**:332, 341, 349
"Advice to a Hamilton (Ont.) Laby About to Travel Again" (Birney) **52**:16, 36, 96
"Advice to a Prophet" (Wilbur) **51**:208, 218, 227, 229, 231, 237, 248, 287
Advice to a Prophet and Other Poems (Wilbur) **51**:202, 214, 232, 235, 273-74, 287, 289, 291, 293, 301
"Advice to the Girls" (Harper) **21**:207, 216
"Advice to the Orchestra" (Wagoner) **33**:327
"Advice to Young Ladies" (Hope) **56**:303
"Advocate" (Traherne) **70**:322
"An Advocate with the Father" (Taylor) **63**:333
"Advocates" (Graves) **6**:144
"AE" (Clarke) **112**:93
"Ae Fond Kiss" (Burns) **6**:97
"Aedh Hears the Cry ofthe Sedge" (Yeats) **20**:347
Aeginetan Odes (Pindar) **19**:406
"Aella" (Chatterton) **104**:5, 28, 38, 51, 68-70, 73
"Aeneas and Dido" (Brodsky) **9**:7
"Aeneas at New York" (Tate) **50**:322
"Aeneas at Washington" (Tate) **50**:231, 244, 250-51, 270, 272, 274, 280, 295, 304, 306-7, 321-22
"Aenigma Christi" (Meynell) **112**:223
The Aeneid (Vergil) **12**:358, 361, 364-68, 371-73, 375-78, 380-99, 401-08
"The Aeolian Harp" (Coleridge) **11**:51, 63, 73-74, 81-82, 88, 91, 97, 106-7, 109; **39**:180, 221; **67**:281
"The Aeolian Harp" (Melville) **82**:73, 86, 103, 144, 163-64
"Aesthetic" (Tomlinson) **17**:327, 344
"The Aesthetic Point of View" (Auden) **1**:12, 15
"Aesthetics after War" (Eberhart) **76**:8, 66
"Aesthetics of Being Glorious" (Koch) **80**:342
"Aesthetics of the Shah" (Olds) **22**:314
"Aesthetics II" (Ignatow) **34**:204
"Aeterna Poetae Memoria" (MacLeish) **47**:145
"Aether" (Ginsberg) **4**:81
"Aetna and the Moon" (Patmore) **59**:201, 228, 233
"Afar" (Reese) **29**:336
"Afelpado" (Storni) **33**:260
"Affairs" (Traherne) **70**:321-23, 335
"Affection" (Traherne) **70**:322
"Affinity" (Thomas) **99**:241
"Affinity" (Traherne) **70**:321
"The Affinity" (Wickham) **110**:311
"Affliction" (Herbert) **4**:118, 131
"Affliction" (Mistral)
See "Tribulación"
"Affliction" (Vaughan) **81**:331-32, 341, 370
"Affliction I" (Herbert) **4**:111-12, 128, 131-32
"Affliction IV" (Herbert) **4**:112, 120
"The Affliction of Margaret—of—" (Wordsworth) **4**:402
"The Affliction of Richard" (Bridges) **28**:88
"Afflictions Sanctified by the Word" (Cowper) **40**:84
"Afforestation" (Thomas) **99**:253
"Affres, détonation, silence" (Char) **56**:155, 190-91
"Afin qu'àtout jamais" (Ronsard) **11**:242
"Afinamiento" (Storni) **33**:271
"Afoot" (Carman) **34**:197, 217
"Afraid" (Hughes) **53**:83-84
"Afraid of the Dark" (Silverstein) **49**:347
"Africa" (Angelou) **32**:28
"Africa" (Giovanni) **19**:141
"Africa" (McKay) **2**:221
Africa (Blake) **12**:13
Africa (Petrarch) **8**:239-42, 246, 258, 260, 266-68, 278
"Africa and My New York" (Viereck) **27**:278, 282
"Africa on the Mind Today" (Goodison) **36**:158
"The African Chief" (Bryant) **20**:4
"African Dream" (Kaufman) **74**:181, 240
"An African Elegy" (Duncan) **2**:103; **75**:173-74, 225-26, 228
"African Images: Glimpses from A Tiger's Back" (Walker) **30**:347
African Revolution (Baraka)
See *Afrikan Revolution: A Poem*
"African Suite" (Randall) **86**:291, 302, 339
"Africa's Dark Face" (Hughes) **53**:85
Afrikan Revolution: A Poem (Baraka) **113**:73
"Afro-American Fragment" (Hughes) **53**:84, 121
"After" (Reese) **29**:330
"After 1984" (Muir) **49**:223, 256
"After a Childhood Away from Ireland" (Boland) **58**:53
"After a Death" (Tomlinson) **17**:336
"After a Departure" (Abse) **41**:3, 12
"After a Flight" (Montale) **13**:158
"After a Flight" (Sebag-Montefiore)
See "Dopa una fuga"
"After a Hypothetical War" (Muir) **49**:223, 258
"After a Journey" (Hardy) **8**:88, 93, 118, 135; **92**:259, 305, 307-8, 310, 327

"After a Killing" (Heaney) **100**:233
"After a Long Illness" (Duncan) **2**:119; **75**:233
"After a Parting" (Meynell) **112**:157, 189, 286
"After a Phrase Abandoned by Wallace Stevens" (Justice) **64**:280, 282, 284-85
"After a Rain" (Pasternak) **6**:271
"After a Tempest" (Bryant) **20**:37-8
"After a Train Journey" (Sarton) **39**:290
"After a Visit (At Padraic Colum's Where There Were Irish Poets)" (Cullen) **20**:60, 69
"After an Accident" (Davie) **29**:129
"After an Illness, Walking the Dog" (Kenyon) **57**:6
After and Before the Lightning (Ortiz) **17**:245
"After Another Reading of Dante" (Corso) **33**:37
"After Apple-Picking" (Frost) **1**:193, 221-22; **39**:230, 235, 237, 246-47
"After Aspromonte" (Carducci)
See "Dopo Aspromonte"
"After Auschwitz" (Sexton) **79**:215-16
"After Beckett" (Mahon) **60**:225
"After Catullus" (Hacker) **47**:80
"After Consulting My Yellow Pages" (Wagoner) **33**:327
"After Dark" (Rich) **5**:364
"After Death" (Rossetti) **7**:269, 280, 287
"After Death" (Teasdale) **31**:325, 336
"After Dinner" (Curnow) **48**:20
"After Drinking All Night with a Friend, We Go Out in a Boat at Dawn to See Who Can Write the Best Poem" (Bly) **39**:75-6
After Every Green Thing (Abse) **41**:6, 10, 33
"After Everything" (Cisneros) **52**:148
After Experience (Snodgrass) **74**:282, 291-93, 312-13, 319, 323, 326
"After Experience Taught Me . . ." (Snodgrass) **74**:314, 326
"After Forty Years of Age" (Kavanagh) **33**:121, 162
"After Grace" (Merrill) **28**:234, 250
"After great stormes the cawme retornes" (Wyatt) **27**:311
After Hearing a Waltz by Bartok (Lowell) **13**:84
"After Jericho" (Thomas) **99**:266
"After Keats" (Levine)
See "Having Been Asked 'What Is a Man?' I Answer"
"After Kent State" (Clifton) **17**:17, 35
"After Long Silence" (Yeats) **20**:328-29; **51**:106, 136
"After Lorca" (Creeley) **73**:36
"After Lorca" (Hughes) **89**:100
After Lorca (Spicer) **78**:237-38, 250-52, 255-58, 263-64, 266, 268, 270, 276, 278-79, 283, 288, 294, 303-4, 314-15, 323-24, 335, 347-50, 353-54, 363
"After Love" (Teasdale) **31**:321
"After Making Love We Hear Footsteps" (Kinnell) **26**:259, 292
"After Many Days" (Dunbar) **5**:137
"After Mass" (Montague) **106**:257, 259-60
"After May" (Kavanagh) **33**:117
"After Mecca" (Brooks) **7**:63, 81
"After Moonless Midnight" (Hughes) **89**:134-35
"After My Chronology by Peter Lorre" (Yau) **61**:337
"After My Last Paycheck from the Factory" (Chin) **40**:3
"After Nerval" (Mahon) **60**:136, 139
"After Paradise" (Milosz) **8**:209
"After Parting" (Teasdale) **31**:363
After Parting (Bely)
See *Posle razluki*
"After Peire Vidal, & Myself" (Berrigan) **103**:36
"After Rain" (Page) **12**:168, 178, 190
"After Rain" (Thomas) **53**:268
"After Reading Barely and Widely" (Duncan) **75**:187-88
"After Reading H. D.'s Hermetic Definitions" (Duncan) **75**:199, 245
"After Reading Mickey in the Night Kitchen for the Third Time before Bed" (Dove) **6**:121
"After Reading Sylvia Plath" (Clampitt) **19**:99
"After Reading Two Towns in Provence" (Carver) **54**:12
After Russia (Tsvetaeva)
See *Posle Rossii*
"After School" (Carman) **34**:224
"After Smiling" (Jackson) **44**:6
"After success, your little afternoon, success" (Spender) **71**:219
"After the Agony" (Atwood) **8**:6
"After the Alphabets" (Merwin) **45**:94
"After the Ball" (Baraka) **113**:13-14
"After the Ball" (Merrill) **28**:270
"After the Battle" (Gilmore) **87**:302
After the Bombing and Other Short Poems (Blunden) **66**:9
"After the Cleansing of Bosnia" (Kumin) **15**:224
"After the Crash" (MacNeice) **61**:179
"After the Cries of the Birds" (Ferlinghetti) **1**:173-74, 176
"After the Dancing" (Cruz) **37**:11
"After the Deluge" (Rimbaud)
See "Après le déluge"
"After the Dinner Party" (Kenyon) **57**:13, 40
"After the Dinner Party" (Warren) **37**:377
"After the Ducks Went In" (Bell) **79**:14, 25
"After the Fire" (Merrill) **28**:221-22, 225, 258, 263-64
"After the first fright" (Hughes) **89**:199
"After the Flood, We" (Atwood) **8**:12
"After the Funeral" (Abse) **41**:14
"After the Funeral: In Memory of Anne Jones" (Thomas) **2**:390; **52**:213, 217, 226, 235, 255, 265, 269, 271, 273, 276, 281, 314
"After the Gentle Poet Kobayashi Issa" (Hass) **16**:196
"After the Harvests" (Merwin) **45**:74
"After the Illness" (Das) **43**:74, 90
After the Killing (Randall) **86**:285, 291, 295, 302, 333-34, 339-41
"After the Killing" (Randall) **86**:339-40
"After the Last Bulletins" (Wilbur) **51**:187, 206, 212-13, 220, 222, 297
"After the Last Dynasty" (Kunitz) **19**:179
"After the Lecture" (Thomas) **99**:246
"After the Opera" (Lawrence) **54**:238-39
"After the Persian" (Bogan) **12**:107, 118, 124-25, 129
"After the plague, the city-wall caked with flies, the smoke's amnesia" (Walcott) **46**:258
"After the Pleasure Party" (Melville) **82**:75, 86, 97, 104-5, 145-46
"After the Release of Ezra Pound" (Abse) **41**:16
"After the Sabbath Prayers" (Cohen) **109**:52
"After the Sentence" (Brutus) **24**:106
"After the Service" (Kinsella) **69**:129
"After the Shipwreck" (Gilmore) **87**:298
"After the Solstice" (Merwin) **45**:20
"After the Storm" (Sarton) **39**:367
"After the Storm" (Stryk) **27**:203
"After the stubbornly cheerful day" (Brutus) **24**:118
"After the Surprising Conversions" (Lowell) **3**:202-03
"After the Visit" (Hardy) **92**:213
"After the Winter" (McKay) **2**:228
"After they have tired of the brilliance of cities" (Spender) **71**:145, 180, 221, 242-44
"After Troy" (H. D.) **5**:268
"After Twenty Years" (Rich) **5**:384
"After Waking" (Bly) **39**:7
"After wards" (Stein) **18**:313
"After Whistler" (Mueller) **33**:176-77
"After Work" (Snyder) **21**:288
"After Working" (Bly) **39**:4, 76, 84
"After Working Long on One Thing" (Kenyon) **57**:45
"After You Speak" (Thomas) **53**:271
"An After-Dinner Poem" (Holmes) **71**:115
"Afterglow" (Carver) **54**:19
"Afterimages" (Lorde) **12**:155
"Afterlives" (Mahon) **60**:132, 134-35, 140, 142-43, 153, 168, 178, 185-86, 192, 234
"Aftermath" (Longfellow) **30**:42
"Aftermath" (Plath) **1**:389; **37**:177
"Aftermath" (Sassoon) **12**:269, 289
Aftermath (Longfellow) **30**:47
"An Afternoon" (Carver) **54**:21-22
"Afternoon" (Parker) **28**:362
"Afternoon" (Spicer) **78**:256, 303
"An Afternoon in June" (Bly) **39**:115
"Afternoon in the House" (Kenyon) **57**:13, 17, 26, 39
Afternoon of a Faun (Mallarmé)
See *L'après-midi d'un faune*
"Afternoon of Sand" (Wagoner) **33**:365-66
"Afternoon on a Hill" (Millay) **6**:235-36; **61**:213
"Afternoon Rain in State Street" (Lowell) **13**:79
"Afternoon Service at Mellstock" (Hardy) **92**:235
"Afternoon Sleep" (Bly) **39**:79
"The Afternoon Sun" (Cavafy) **36**:42
"Afternoon Tea" (Service) **70**:130
"Afternoons with Allen" (Chappell) **105**:21
"Aftersong" (Carman) **34**:225
"The After-thought" (Smith) **12**:329-32, 341
"An Afterward" (Heaney) **18**:243
"Afterward" (Schuyler) **88**:212, 225
"Afterward" (Warren) **37**:326
"Afterwards" (Hardy) **8**:101, 131; **92**:210, 319, 322; **92**:210, 319, 322
"Afterwards, They Shall Dance" (Kaufman) **74**:182, 194, 212, 217, 231
Afterwhiles (Riley) **48**:290, 322
"Afterword" (Atwood) **8**:11
"Afterword" (Brodsky) **9**:25
"Afterword" (Carruth) **10**:71
"(Afterword)" (Graham) **59**:136
"An Afterword: For Gwen Brooks" (Madhubuti) **5**:346
"Afton Water" (Burns)
See "Sweet Afton"
"Again" (Kavanagh) **33**:151
"Again" (Nemerov) **24**:291
"Again Again" (Viereck) **27**:265
"Again and Again and Again" (Sexton) **2**:353
"Again at Zima Station" (Yevtushenko) **40**:340, 347
"Again I Visited" (Pushkin)
See "Vnov' Ya Posetil"
"Again, Kapowsin" (Hugo) **68**:252
"Again, the River" (Hacker) **47**:118-19
"Against a comely Coistroun" (Skelton)
See *Agaynste a Comely Coystrowne*
"Against Absence" (Suckling) **30**:123
"Against Botticelli" (Hass) **16**:198
"Against Bourgeois Art" (Baraka) **113**:26
"Against Constancy" (Wilmot) **66**:339
"Against Dullness" (Szirtes) **51**:158
"Against Elegies" (Hacker) **47**:103, 105-7, 116
"Against Fruition" (Cowley) **90**:35, 115, 117
"Against Fruition II" (Suckling) **30**:123, 129, 140-41, 147
"Against Hope" (Cowley) **90**:6, 14, 113-14
"Against Irresolution and Delay in Matters of Religion" (Crashaw) **84**:30
"Against Larks" (Hughes) **89**:259-60, 264
"Against System Builders" (Goethe) **5**:229
"Against That Day" (Brown) **55**:74, 114
Against the Evidence: Selected Poems 1934-1994 (Ignatow) **34**:341-43
"Against the Love of Great Ones" (Lovelace) **69**:185
"Against the Transcendentalists" (Spark) **72**:213, 217, 226, 229, 234, 251, 255
"Against War, Against Watchtower" (Chin) **40**:29
"Against Whatever It Is That's Encroaching" (Simic) **69**:366

"Agamemnon" (Cavafy) **36**:54
"Aganis the Solistaris in Court" (Dunbar) **67**:38
"Agape" (Enright) **93**:29
"Agape" (Kinnell) **26**:287
"Agatha" (Eliot) **20**:101, 123
"Agatha" (Valéry)
See "Agathe; ou, La sainte du sommeil"
"The Agatha Christie Books by the Window" (Ondaatje) **28**:335
"Agathe; ou, La sainte du sommeil" (Valéry) **9**:357, 400-01
Agaynste a Comely Coystrowne (Skelton) **25**:339
"Age" (de la Mare) **77**:94
"Age" (Larkin) **21**:227, 236, 248
"The Age" (Mandelstam) **14**:121
"Age" (Teasdale) **31**:380
"Age" (Thomas) **99**:233
"Age and Youth" (Deloney) **79**:57
L'Age cassant (Char) **56**:112, 115, 117-18
"L'Age de la vie" (Éluard) **38**:65
"The Age Demanded" (Pound) **4**:320
"Age d'or" (Rimbaud) **57**:243, 250, 253
The Age of Anxiety: A Baroque Eclogue (Auden) **1**:14, 23, 33-4, 39; **92**:14, 64-65, 94, 117-23
Age of Bronze (Byron) **95**:14
"The Age of Innocence" (Hope) **56**:266
"The Age of Reason" (Graham) **59**:147, 155-56, 179, 187
The Age of Reason (Hope) **56**:290-91, 297
"The Age of the Antonines" (Melville) **82**:145, 147
"The Aged Aged Man" (Carroll) **74**:94, 100
"The Aged Lover Discourses in the Flat Style" (Cunningham) **92**:169, 177
"Aged Man Surveys the Past Time" (Warren) **37**:275, 284, 288, 331
"The Agent" (Jones) **116**:167
"The Agent" (Wilbur) **51**:215, 231
"The Ages" (Bryant) **20**:4, 35
"The Ages of Man" (Bradstreet)
See "The Four Ages of Man"
The Ages of the Year (Cassian) **17**:6
"Ages I" (Traherne) **70**:322
"Ages II" (Traherne) **70**:322
"Aggression" (O'Hara) **45**:223
The Aggressive Ways of the Casual Stranger (Waldrop) **109**:167, 177, 180
"Aghlaqu al-Mashhad" (Darwish) **86**:20
"Agib and Secander; or, the Fugitives" (Collins) **72**:81
Agincourt (Drayton)
See *The Battaile of Agincourt*
"Aging Refugee from the Old Country" (Viereck) **27**:280
"The Aging Whore" (Randall) **86**:347
"Agitato ma non troppo" (Ransom) **61**:269, 280
"Agli amici della Valle Tiberina" (Carducci) **46**:51, 70-71, 74, 80
"Agli Italiani" (Carducci) **46**:51
"Agnes" (Holmes) **71**:73
"Agnosco Veteris Vestigia Flammae" (Cunningham) **92**:133, 135, 169, 182
"An Agnostic" (Smith) **12**:352
"Agnostoi Theo" (Hardy) **92**:221
"The Agonie" (Herbert) **4**:100
"The Agony" (Herbert)
See "The Agonie"
"An Agony. As Now" (Baraka) **4**:16, 24; **113**:40, 99, 150
"An Agony in the Garret" (Eliot) **90**:300
"Agora que conmigo" (Juana Inés de la Cruz) **24**:187
"Agosta the Winged Man and Rasha the Black Dove" (Dove) **6**:109
"Agraphon" (Sikelianos) **29**:366, 374-75
"The Agreement" (Vaughan) **81**:307, 338, 340, 343, 368
"Les Agréments et l'utilité" (Éluard) **38**:91
"Agrigente" (Jaccottet) **98**:172
"Agrio está el mundo" (Storni) **33**:246
"Agrippina in the Golden House of Nero" (Lowell) **3**:222
"Agua" (Mistral) **32**:161
"Agua sexual" (Neruda) **4**:306
"Aguadilla" (Cruz) **37**:33-34
"El águila" (Cernuda) **62**:213, 267, 269
"Aguila blanca" (Martí) **76**:96-97
Águila o sol? (Paz) **1**:354, 359; **48**:229-30, 244
"Ah, Are You Digging on My Grave?" (Hardy) **8**:131; **92**:248-49, 286
"Ah Deus, ecce tuli" (Southwell) **83**:229
"Ah, God, the Way Your Little Finger Moved" (Crane) **80**:80
"Ah, ken ye what I met the day" (Keats) **96**:284
"Ah, me!" (Storni)
See "¡Ayme!"
"Ah, Momotombo" (de la Mare) **77**:148
"Ah Natercia cruel" (Camões) **31**:29
"Ah pox upon they needful scorn" (Behn)
See "A pox upon thy needful scorn"
"Ah! Sun-Flower" (Blake) **12**:34; **63**:68, 70, 105, 108
"Ah, 'Tis Vain the Peaceful Din" (Thoreau) **30**:254
"Ah Yes, Columbus Day, No Mail" (Dorn) **115**:230
Ahad Ashar Kawkaban (Darwish)
See *Ahada 'Ashara Kawkaban*
Ahada 'Ashara Kawkaban (Darwish) **86**:20, 26
"Ahasuerus" (Nemerov) **24**:257, 295
"Ahí nomás" (Paredes) **83**:31
"Ahmad" (Thumboo) **30**:305, 333
"Ahmad al-Za'tar" (Darwish) **86**:20
"Ahora habla Dios" (Fuertes) **27**:28
"Ahvan" (Tagore) **8**:415
"Ai critici cattolici" (Pasolini) **17**:258
"Ai fratelli Carvi, alla loro Italia" (Quasimodo) **47**:287
"Aigeltinger" (Williams) **7**:370
"L'aigle du casque" (Hugo) **17**:56
"Aiguevive" (Char) **56**:152, 156
Aika (Nishiwaki) **15**:238
"Aim" (Randall) **86**:290
"The Aim, The Best that Can be Hoped For: The Magician" (Piercy) **29**:325
"The Aim Was Song" (Frost) **1**:194
"Aimless Journey" (Tagore)
See "Niruddesh yatra"
"Ainu Child" (Blunden) **66**:22
"Air" (Baraka) **113**:15
"Air" (Merwin) **45**:15
"Air" (Toomer) **7**:333
"Air" (Walcott) **46**:321, 325
"Air and Angels" (Rexroth) **95**:254, 258, 274
"Air and Fire" (Berry) **28**:11
L'air de l'eau (Breton) **15**:51-52
"Air de sémiramis" (Valéry) **9**:365, 391-92
"Air Hostess" (Amichai) **38**:19
"Air Liner" (Shapiro) **25**:296
Air mexicain (Péret) **33**:220, 231
"The Air of June Sings" (Dorn) **115**:57, 79, 81, 109, 119, 126
Air Raid (MacLeish) **47**:148-49, 152, 164, 210-11, 242, 257
"The Air Raid Across the Bay" (Spender) **71**:139
"Air Raid Over Harlem" (Hughes) **53**:114
"Air: 'The Love of a Woman'" (Creeley) **73**:39
"El aire" (Guillén) **35**:231
"El aire" (Mistral) **32**:161, 168
"Aire and Angels" (Donne) **1**:130, 149
Aire nuestro (Guillén) **35**:185, 186, 187-88, 225-32, 234, 237, 238, 239
"Airen" (Hagiwara) **18**:167, 180
"Los aires" (Guillén) **35**:157
"Airman's Virtue" (Meredith) **28**:182-83
"Airone morto" (Quasimodo) **47**:278
"Airoplain" (Cruz) **37**:36
Airs & Tributes (Brutus) **24**:110-11, 117
Airs: Poèmes, 1961-1964 (Jaccottet) **98**:147, 149-51, 167-68, 182, 184-89, 191, 195-96, 198
"An Airstrip in Essex, 1960" (Hall) **70**:32
"The Airy Christ" (Smith) **12**:295, 330-31, 333
"The Airy Tomb" (Thomas) **99**:240, 245, 258
"Aisling" (Clarke) **112**:79, 138-39
"Aisling" (Heaney) **100**:224
"Aix-en-Provence" (Rexroth) **20**:209
"Ajanta" (Rukeyser) **12**:204, 214, 219, 224
"Ajedrez II" (Borges) **22**:84-5
"Ajudah" (Mickiewicz) **38**:166
"Akatsuki no kane" (Ishikawa) **10**:214
"Akbar's Dream" (Tennyson) **101**:145
"Akerman Steppes" (Mickiewicz)
See "Stepy Akermańskie"
Akhshav bara'ash (Amichai) **38**:23, 26
'Akhshav 'vayamim ha'aherim (Amichai) **38**:33
"Akiko San" (Enright) **93**:20, 33-34
Akogare (Ishikawa) **10**:194, 212-16
"The Akond of Swat" (Lear) **65**:165
"Al Aaraaf" (Poe) **1**:437, 449
"Al adquirir una Enciclopedia" (Borges) **32**:91
"Al amor cualquier curioso" (Juana Inés de la Cruz) **24**:184, 234
"Al Capone in Alaska" (Reed) **68**:333
"Al Conte Carlo Pepoli" (Leopardi) **37**:112
"Al coronel Francisco Borges" (Borges) **32**:57
"Al extranjero" (Martí) **76**:106
"Al iniciar el estudio de la gramática anglosajona" (Borges) **22**:99
"Al lector" (Darío) **15**:105
"Al maragen de mis libros de estudios" (Guillén) **23**:97
"Al margen de Mallarmé" (Guillén) **35**:202
"Al margen de un cántico" (Guillén) **35**:201
"Al margen de un contacto" (Guillén) **35**:229
"Al mio grillo" (Montale) **13**:138
"Al Mio Primore Amore" (Peacock) **87**:341
"Al mismo individuo" (Guillén) **23**:126
"Al mondo" (Zanzotto) **65**:315
"Al oído de Cristo" (Mistral) **32**:155, 174
"Al pintor Swaminathan" (Paz) **1**:354
"Al poeta español Rafael Alberti, entregándole un jamón" (Guillén) **23**:134
"Al que ingrato me deja, busco ama" (Juana Inés de la Cruz) **24**:183
Al que quiere! (Williams) **7**:344-45, 348-49, 377-79, 387-88, 398, 405-10; **109**:191, 236, 238, 240-41, 287, 290
"Al soneto con mi alma" (Jiménez) **7**:192
"Al tuo lume naufrago" (Quasimodo) **47**:278
"Ala bāb al-haykal" (Gibran) **9**:78
"Alaba los ojos negros de Julia" (Darío) **15**:114
"Alabama Poem" (Giovanni) **19**:140
Alabanza: New and Selected Poems, 1982-2002 (Espada) **74**:163, 167-69
"Alabaster" (Merrill) **28**:283
Al-ajnihah (Gibran) **9**:78
"Alakanak Break-Up" (Berssenbrugge) **115**:36
"Las alamedas" (Guillén) **35**:193
Alameim to Zem Zem (Douglas) **106**:181, 198-200, 202, 204-5, 209
"The Alarmists" (Peacock) **87**:322
"Alas, a Prince" (Tu Fu) **9**:317
"Alas! How Weary Are My Human Eyes" (Tennyson)
See "Sonnet"
"Alas the While" (Wyatt) **27**:318
"Alas, when he laughs it is not he" (Spender) **71**:219
"Alaska" (Benn) **35**:45, 46
"Alaska" (Snyder) **21**:300
"Alaska: In Two Parts" (Dorn) **115**:134
"Alaska Passage" (Birney) **52**:28, 82
"Alastor; or, The Spirit of Solitude" (Shelley) **14**:171, 173, 178, 192, 211-12, 217, 221-24, 233-37, 239
Alastor; or, The Spirit of Solitude, and Other Poems (Shelley) **67**:136, 167, 169, 209, 229, 237
"Alatus" (Wilbur) **51**:249
Al-'awāsif (Gibran) **9**:79-81
"Alba" (Creeley) **73**:107
"Alba" (Spicer) **78**:253

"Alba for Hecate" (Winters) **82**:315, 318
"Al-bahr" (Gibran) **9**:80
"Albaniad" (Elytis) **21**:115
"Albany" (Collins) **68**:226
"Albâtre" (Pound) **95**:95
"L'albatros" (Baudelaire) **1**:65; **106**:60, 62, 104, 134
"The Albatross" (Baudelaire)
See "L'albatros"
"Albero" (Quasimodo) **47**:272
"À Albert Durer" (Hugo) **17**:94-95
"Albert Schirding" (Masters) **36**:170, 182
Albertine Disparue (Enzensberger) **28**:156
"Albertus" (Gautier) **18**:142-43, 151-54, 160-64
Albertus, ou l'âme et le péché: légende théologique (Gautier) **18**:147, 149-51, 154
"Albi, a Day Trip" (Dorn) **115**:231
"The Albigenses" (Duncan) **75**:176
"Albino" (Komunyakaa) **51**:29
"Albinus and Rosemund" (Gower) **59**:88, 108
"Album" (Szymborska)
See "Album Rodzinny"
Album de vers anciens, 1890-1900 (Valéry) **9**:363, 365, 386-87, 390-91, 395
Album de vers et de prose (Mallarmé) **102**:135
"Album Rodzinny" (Szymborska) **44**:269
Album zutique (Rimbaud) **57**:204, 246, 252-53
"Alceste in the Wilderness" (Hecht) **70**:69
"Alcestis" (Gower) **59**:58
"The Alchemist" (Bogan) **12**:98, 103, 114
"The Alchemist" (Meredith) **28**:187
"The Alchemist" (Pound) **95**:95, 219
"The Alchemists" (Hogan) **35**:259
The Alchemist (Donne) **43**:125
"Alchemy" (Corso) **33**:37
"Alchemy of the Logos" (Rimbaud)
See "Alchimie du verbe"
"Alchemy of the Word" (Rimbaud)
See "Alchimie du verbe"
"L'Alchimie de la douleur" (Baudelaire) **106**:128
"Alchimie du verbe" (Rimbaud) **3**:261, 267, 274; **57**:174, 227, 238, 243, 245, 247-49, 254, 273, 280
"Alcohol" (MacNeice) **61**:141
"The Alcoholic Love Poems" (Alexie) **53**:30
"An Alcoholic's Death" (Hagiwara)
See "Death of an Alcoholic"
Alcools (Apollinaire) **7**:6, 9-10, 12, 14-15, 38-46, 48-9
"Aldershot Crematorium" (Betjeman) **75**:34, 97
"Alegorí a de la primavera" (Storni) **33**:294-96
"Alegría de la soledad" (Cernuda) **62**:178
"Alejamiento" (Borges) **22**:92
"Aleksandru" (Pushkin) **10**:421
"Aleluja" (Pasolini) **17**:256
"Alessandria" (Carducci) **46**:9, 24, 64
"Alessandrina" (Carducci)
See "Alessandria"
"Alewives Pool" (Kinnell) **26**:238
"Alex Katz Paints a Picture" (Schuyler) **88**:179, 181
"Alexander" (de la Mare) **77**:61
"Alexander Jannaeus and Alexandra" (Cavafy) **36**:22
"Alexander Throckmorten" (Masters) **36**:221
"Alexander's Feast; or, The Power of Musique. An Ode, in Honour of St. Cecilia's Day" (Dryden) **25**:72-5, 88
"Alexandra" (Serote) **113**:283, 293-95
"Alexandria" (Carducci)
See "Alessandria"
"Alexandria" (Doty) **53**:52
"Alexandria" (Shapiro) **25**:295
"Alexandrian Kings" (Cavafy) **36**:3, 8, 29-32, 40, 50
"An Alexandrite Pendant for My Mother" (Hacker) **47**:119
"Alexis und Dora" (Goethe) **5**:240
"Alf Burt, Tenant Farmer" (Warren) **37**:319, 331
"Alfansa" (Forché) **10**:134, 169-70
"Alfonso" (McKay) **2**:205
"Alfred the Great" (Smith) **12**:296, 316
"Algae" (Wagoner) **33**:356
"Algernon, Who Played with a Loaded Gun, and, on Missing His Sister, Was Reprimanded by His Father" (Belloc) **24**:26
Algiers in Wartime (Viereck) **27**:265
"Al-hurūf al-nāriyah" (Gibran) **9**:78
Alí dagli occhi azzurri (Pasolini) **17**:264-65
"Alice" (Graves) **6**:139
"Alice Du Clos" (Coleridge) **11**:106
"Alice Fell" (Wordsworth) **4**:404, 415; **67**:248
"Alice ffoster-Fallis" (Waldrop) **109**:179
"An Alien Craft" (Akhmadulina)
See "Cuzoe remeslo"
"Alien Winds" (Kaufman) **74**:259
"Aliénés" (Char) **56**:137, 157
"Alive" (Harjo) **27**:56
Alive: Poems, 1971-1972 (Wright) **14**:372, 375
"Alive Together" (Mueller) **33**:175
Alive Together: New and Selected Poems (Mueller) **33**:195, 197
"Al-jamāl" (Gibran) **9**:81
"Alki Beach" (Hugo) **68**:238
"All, All Are Gone the Old Familiar Quotations" (Nash) **21**:273
"All Alone Along the Road I Am Walking" (Lermontov)
See "Alone I Go along the Road"
"All along the Watchtower" (Dylan) **37**:49, 56, 61
"All and Some" (Ashbery) **26**:124, 127, 135
"All But Blind" (de la Mare) **77**:111
"All Choice is Error" (Cunningham) **92**:165, 177
"All Clowns Are Masked and All Personae" (Schwartz) **8**:305
"All Comes" (Ignatow) **34**:318
"All Elegies are Black and White" (Guest) **55**:185, 212
"All Erdly Joy Returnis in Pane" (Dunbar) **67**:12, 128
"All for You" (Ní Chuilleanáin) **34**:369
"All God's Children" (Brathwaite) **56**:19
"All Gone" (Char)
See "Tous partis"
"All Gray-Haired My Sisters" (Guest) **55**:208, 213, 218
"All Guilt and Innocence Turned Upside Down" (Schwartz) **8**:285
"All Hallows" (Glück) **16**:126-27, 132, 140-43, 148-49
"All Hallows, Jack O'Lantern Weather, North of Time" (Kaufman) **74**:215
"All I Gotta Do" (Giovanni) **19**:108, 112
"All I Want of Love Is a Beginning" (Darwish) **86**:28
"All in All" (Traherne) **70**:322
"All in Green Went My Love Riding" (Cummings) **5**:87
"All in the Street" (Baraka) **113**:23, 79
"All is Emptiness and I Must Spin" (Kinsella) **69**:72
"All Is Mine" (Guillén)
See "Tengo"
All Is Mine (Guillén)
See *Tengo*
"All Kinds of Caresses" (Ashbery) **26**:139
"All kings and all their favourites" (Donne)
See "The Anniversarie"
"All Lands Are Ready to Rise" (Sachs) **78**:227, 233
All Legendary Obstacles (Montague) **106**:215, 218, 270, 276, 298, 302, 328
"All Life in a Life" (Masters) **1**:326, 328, 335-36, 342; **36**:175
"All Life Is a Rotary Club" (Corso) **33**:48
All Love (Seifert)
See *Samá láska*
"All Men to Women" (Wickham) **110**:270
"All Morning" (Roethke) **15**:271
"All Mountain" (H. D.) **5**:305
"All my circling a failure to return" (Montague) **106**:227
"All my past life is mine no more" (Wilmot) **66**:266
"All My Pretty Ones" (Sexton) **79**:187, 211, 253
All My Pretty Ones (Sexton) **2**:346-47, 349-50, 353, 355, 360-61, 370; **79**:203-4, 208, 210-11, 216-17, 226-27, 229, 231, 248, 257-58, 261-62, 267, 310
"All Nearness Pauses, While a Star Can Grow" (Cummings) **5**:109
"All Night Long" (Benét) **64**:22
"All of Us Always Turning Away for Solace" (Schwartz) **8**:305
All of Us: The Collected Poems (Carver) **54**:25-29
"All Our Yesterdays" (Borges) **32**:90
"All Out" (Hecht) **70**:95
"All Over Again" (MacNeice) **61**:125
"All over Minnesota" (Stevens) **110**:93
"All over Whitneyville" (Hall) **70**:32
"All Quiet" (Ignatow) **34**:277, 207, 323
"All Reaction Is Doomed" (Baraka) **113**:36
"All Revelation" (Frost) **39**:233
"All Right" (Thomas) **99**:304
"All Souls" (Sarton) **39**:326
"All Souls' Day" (Sassoon) **12**:258
"All Souls' Night" (Yeats) **51**:151
"All Sounds Have been as Music" (Owen) **19**:336
All That Is Lovely in Men (Creeley) **73**:3, 6, 27
"All That Was Mortal" (Teasdale) **31**:341
"All the Beautiful Are Blameless" (Wright) **36**:282, 396
All: The Collected Short Poems, 1923-1958 (Zukofsky) **11**:348-49, 351, 354-56, 393-94
All: The Collected Shorter Poems, 1956-64 (Zukofsky) **11**:349, 353, 356, 383, 390
"All the Dead Dears" (Plath) **1**:388, 407; **37**:186, 199, 214, 245
"All the Earth, All the Air" (Roethke) **15**:286
"All the Fancy Things" (Williams) **7**:394
All the Poems (Spark) **72**:264
"All the Spirit Powers Went to Their Dancing Place" (Snyder) **21**:291
"All the World Moved" (Jordan) **38**:119
"All There Is to Know about Adolph Eichmann" (Cohen) **109**:74, 89, 92
"All These Birds" (Wilbur) **51**:188, 305
"All Things" (Traherne) **70**:321, 323
"All Things Are Current Found" (Thoreau) **30**:181, 204, 213-14
"All Things Conspire" (Wright) **14**:338
"All Things Were Made in Seven Days" (Kipling) **91**:169
"All Those Ships That Never Sailed" (Kaufman) **74**:215-16, 239
"All We" (Muir) **49**:200, 250
"All Worlds Have Halfsight, Seeing Either With" (Cummings) **5**:111
"allá ajüera" (Alurista) **34**:32-3
"Alla città di Ferrara" (Carducci) **46**:52
"Alla croce di Savoia" (Carducci) **46**:51, 56
"Alla Francia" (Pasolini) **17**:295
"Allá lejos" (Darío) **15**:93
"Allá lejos" (Guillén) **23**:126
"Alla Libertà rileggendo le opere di Vittorio Alfieri" (Carducci) **46**:51
"Alla Luna" (Leopardi) **37**:82, 84, 102, 109, 124-34
"Alla memoria di D.C." (Cannan) **46**:64
"Alla mia terra" (Quasimodo) **47**:301-02
"Alla primavera o delle favole antiche" (Leopardi) **37**:141, 165, 167
"Alla Regina d'Italia" (Carducci) **46**:52
"Alla rima" (Carducci) **46**:74, 80-81
"Alla stagione" (Zanzotto) **65**:311, 316
"Alla Stazione in una Mattina d'Autunno" (Carducci) **46**:6-7, 25, 51, 56, 86

"Alla sua donna" (Leopardi) **37**:144-45
"Alla Tha's All Right, but" (Jordan) **38**:118, 125
"Alla Vittoria" (Carducci) **46**:52
"All'amor suo" (Leopardi) **37**:144
"All'Aurora" (Carducci) **46**:54
"All-destroyer" (Tagore)
See "Sarvaneshe"
"an alle fernsprechteilenhmer" (Enzensberger) **28**:134, 136, 140
"Alle fonti del Clitumno" (Carducci) **46**:7, 16, 29, 37, 39, 42, 54, 65, 76, 81-84, 88
"Alle fronde dei salici" (Quasimodo) **47**:281
"Alle Valchirie" (Cannan) **46**:26
"L'allée" (Verlaine) **32**:348-49
"Allégeance" (Char) **56**:155
"Allegiance" (Montague) **106**:243, 327
Allegiances (Stafford) **71**:265, 275, 278, 283, 288, 297, 302, 320-21, 328, 333, 349, 377, 379
"Allégorie" (Baudelaire) **1**:56; **106**:24, 26-27
"Allegory of the Adolescent and the Adult" (Barker) **77**:29-30, 38, 40
"Allegre" (Walcott) **46**:272
L'Allegria di Naufragi (Ungaretti) **57**:335, 338-39, 342-43, 347, 373, 375, 377
"L'Allegro" (Milton) **19**:201-02, 226, 228-34, 249, 254-56; **29**:220, 232, 239
"Allelujah" (Werfel) **101**:324
"Die alles Vergessende" (Sachs) **78**:201-02
"Alley Rats" (Sandburg) **2**:304
"The All-Golden" (Riley) **48**:289
"Allí despacio" (Martí) **76**:105
"Alliance of Education and Government" (Gray)
See "Essay on the Alliance of Education and Government"
"Allie" (Graves) **6**:141
"The Allies" (Lowell) **13**:76, 78
"The Alligator Bride" (Hall) **70**:32
The Alligator Bride: Poems, New and Selected (Hall) **70**:9, 26, 32
"Allison Beals and Her Twenty-Five Eels" (Silverstein) **49**:341
"All'Italia" (Leopardi) **37**:81, 98-104, 107, 150
"Allmacht" (Stramm) **50**:169, 175, 189, 192-93, 198, 206
"Allô" (Péret) **33**:201, 206, 214, 231
"Allons adieu messieurs tachez de revenir" (Apollinaire) **7**:22
"Allora e Ora" (Carducci) **46**:5
"Alloy" (Rukeyser) **12**:210
"All's Well" (Baraka) **113**:15
"Allurement" (Traherne) **70**:322
"Allusion to Horace" (Wilmot) **66**:244, 249, 257, 260, 262, 264
"The Ally" (Cervantes) **35**:116
"Alma" (Storni) **33**:251
"Alma desnuda" (Storni) **33**:237
"Alma Mater" (Robinson) **35**:367
"Alma minha gentil" (Camões) **31**:24-25
Alma: or, the Progress of the Mind (Prior) **102**:281-84, 286-90, 294-96, 299, 317, 320-21
"Alma pocha" (Paredes) **83**:30, 34
"Almanac" (Sandburg) **41**:308
"Almanac" (Swenson) **14**:268
"Almanach pour l'année passée" (Verlaine) **32**:399-402, 405
Almansor (Heine) **25**:145, 160
"Almas de Duralex" (Fuertes) **27**:23
Almas de violeta (Jiménez) **7**:199
Al-mawakib (Gibran) **9**:79-81
"Almond" (McGuckian) **27**:92-93, 105
"Almond Blossom" (Lawrence) **54**:220
"The Almond of the World" (Elytis) **21**:132
"The Almond Trees" (Walcott) **46**:284-85
"Almost a Fantasy" (Montale) **13**:151
"Almost a Song" (Montague) **106**:298
Almost Everything (Kavanagh) **33**:74
"Almost Last Judgement" (Borges)
See "Casi Juicio Final"
"Almost Perfect" (Silverstein) **49**:333
"Alms" (Storni)
See "Limosna"
"Almswomen" (Blunden) **66**:5, 26
"Almuerzo al sol" (Mistral) **32**:185
"Alone" (Bly) **39**:71
"Alone" (Niedecker) **42**:100, 121, 127, 138
"Alone" (Poe) **1**:442-44
"Alone" (Teasdale) **31**:360
"Alone" (Winters) **82**:334-35, 339
"Alone for a Week" (Kenyon) **57**:15
"Alone I Go along the Road" (Lermontov) **18**:281, 298, 303
"Alone I Wander" (Smith)
See "Sonnet 66"
"Alone in a Shower" (Hongo) **23**:197
"Along Highway 40" (Stafford) **71**:267
"Along History" (Rukeyser) **12**:228
"Along the Field as We Came By" (Housman) **2**:183; **43**:245
"Along the Grand Canal" (Kavanagh) **105**:164
"Alonso Quijano Dreams" (Borges) **32**:66
"Alpha" (Brathwaite) **56**:50, 96
"Alpha" (Tolson) **88**:235, 256, 263, 267, 304, 315, 325
"The Alphabet" (Shapiro) **25**:283, 291, 298-99
Alphabet (Cage)
See *Marcel Duchamp, James Joyce, Erik Satie: An Alphabet*
"Alphabet of Ahtt" (Mackey) **49**:57
"Alphabets" (Heaney) **18**:230-31, 237; **100**:297
"alphabirney" (Birney) **52**:32
"Alphonso of Castile" (Emerson) **18**:71
Alpine (Oppen) **35**:311
"Alpine Noontime" (Carducci)
See "Mezzogiorno alpino"
"Alpuhara" (Mickiewicz)
See "Alpujarra"
"Alpujarra" (Mickiewicz) **38**:174
"Alquimia" (Borges) **22**:94
"Als mich dein Wandeln an den Tod verzückte" (Werfel) **101**:346, 356
"Al-shā'ir" (Gibran) **9**:79
"Altar" (Chin) **40**:12-13
"The Altar" (Herbert) **4**:114, 120, 130
"The Altar" (MacLeish) **47**:182
"The Altar" (Pound) **95**:122
"The Altar of Righteousness" (Swinburne) **24**:350-54
The Altar of the Past (Gozzano)
See *L'altare del Passato*
L'altare del Passato (Gozzano) **10**:177
"Altarwise by Owl-light" (Thomas) **2**:388-89, 403, 406; **52**:237, 240-41, 245, 247, 296-301, 304, 314, 331
"Eine alte Frau geht" (Werfel) **101**:346, 357
Der Alte Matrose (Coleridge)
See *The Rime of the Ancient Mariner*
"Einem alten Architekten in Rom" (Brodsky) **9**:2, 4
"Alternate Thoughts from Underground" (Atwood) **8**:40
"An Alternative Life" (Duncan) **75**:190, 208
"Althea" (Lovelace)
See "To Althea: From Prison"
"Although I had a check" (Surrey) **59**:297
"Altitude: 15,000" (Meredith) **28**:173
"L'alto veliero" (Quasimodo) **47**:303
"Altri papaveri" (Zanzotto) **65**:338-39
"Altrui e mia" (Zanzotto) **65**:275
Alturas de Macchu Picchu (Neruda) **4**:282, 284-85, 292-93; **64**:293-353
"Al-umm wa wahīduha" (Gibran) **9**:78
"Aluroid" (Birney) **52**:85
"Ałushta at Night" (Mickiewicz)
See "Ałuszta w nocy"
"Ałushta in Daytime" (Mickiewicz)
See "Ałuszta w dzień"
"Ałuszta at Day" (Mickiewicz)
See "Ałuszta w dzień"
"Ałuszta at Night" (Mickiewicz)
See "Ałuszta w nocy"
"Ałuszta w dzień" (Mickiewicz) **38**:166
"Ałuszta w nocy" (Mickiewicz) **38**:166
"Always a Rose" (Lee) **24**:247-48, 251
"Always and always the amaranth astir" (Villa) **22**:346
"Always Between Hope and Fear" (Spender) **71**:179
"Always I did want more God" (Villa) **22**:352
"Always the Mob" (Sandburg) **2**:302; **41**:240, 274, 329
"Always to Love You America" (Viereck) **27**:279-80
"The Alyscamps at Arles" (Swenson) **14**:255
"Alysoun" (Snyder) **21**:288
"Am I My Brother's Keeper?" (Eberhart) **76**:31
"am or" (Bissett) **14**:14
"Am Rand Eines alten Brunes" (Trakl) **20**:265
"Am Saum des nordischen Meers" (Benn) **35**:23-25
"Am/Trak" (Baraka) **4**:39; **113**:25-26
"am was. are leaves few this. is this a or" (Cummings) **5**:107
"Ama tu ritmo..." (Darío) **15**:101
"Amabel" (Hardy) **92**:241, 244, 248
Amadis of Gaul (Southey)
See *Amados de Gaula*
"Amado dueño mío" (Juana Inés de la Cruz) **24**:181
Amados de Gaula (Southey) **111**:250
"Amām 'arsh al-jamāl" (Gibran) **9**:79
"Amanda Barker" (Masters) **36**:181
"Amando en el tiempo" (Cernuda) **62**:201, 264-67, 269
"Amanece, amanezco" (Guillén) **35**:195
"Amanecer" (Borges) **32**:81, 124
"Amang thir freiris" (Dunbar) **67**:18-19
"Amante dulce del alma" (Juana Inés de la Cruz) **24**:189
"Los amantes" (Guillén) **35**:180, 183
Amantes (Brossard) **80**:6-9, 12, 16
"Los amantes viejos" (Aleixandre) **15**:5-7
"Les Amants de Montmorency" (Vigny) **26**:391, 411-12
"Amaranth" (H. D.) **5**:305
Amaranth (Robinson) **1**:477-78, 482-83; **35**:368
"Amazing Grace" (Mueller) **33**:174-75
"Amazing Grace in the Back Country" (Warren) **37**:312, 336
"The Amazons" (Barker) **77**:4
"Ambarvalia" (Nishiwaki) **15**:238
Ambarvalia (Clough) **103**:51, 53, 58, 92, 111-12, 116, 148
Ambarvalia (Nishiwaki) **15**:228-29, 232-41
"The Ambassador" (Smith) **12**:330, 339
"Ambassadors of Grief" (Sandburg) **2**:308
Ambit (Aleixandre)
See *Ambito*
"Ambition" (Kennedy) **93**:150-51
"Ambition" (Thomas) **53**:287-88
Ambito (Aleixandre) **15**:9, 16, 27, 29-32
Ambitus (Cassian) **17**:6
"Ambulances" (Larkin) **21**:229-30, 234
"Ambush" (Mickiewicz)
See "Czaty"
"Ame" (Nishiwaki) **15**:228
Amelia (Patmore) **59**:213, 215-16, 218, 222-23, 257
"Amelia Garrick" (Masters) **36**:188
"Amen!" (Rossetti) **7**:268
"Amen" (Thomas) **99**:245
"Amen" (Trakl) **20**:248
Amen (Amichai)
See *Me-horei Kol Zeh Mistater Osher Gadol*
"El amenazado" (Borges) **22**:80-1
"Amendment" (Traherne) **70**:175, 191, 253, 274, 316-17, 322, 331
"Amends" (Dunbar) **67**:16
Amenities of Stone (Wright) **36**:389, 391
"America" (Angelou) **32**:28
"America" (Ginsberg) **47**:3, 5, 8, 10, 38, 66
"America" (McKay) **2**:212

"America" (Melville) **82**:92, 135, 138, 145
"America" (Merrill) **28**:267
"America" (Wheatley) **3**:363
America: A Prophecy, 1793 (Blake) **12**:13, 25-7, 63; **63**:107
"America America" (Ignatow) **34**:318
"AMERICA BUILDS MORE / buildbores to bill more—" (Birney) **52**:79
"America Historia Politica" (Corso) **33**:27
"America, I Do Not Invoke Your Name in Vain" (Neruda)
See "América, no invoco tu nombre en vano"
"América, no invoco tu nombre en vano" (Neruda) **4**:292
"America Politica Historia, in Spontaneity" (Corso) **33**:35, 49
America Was Promises (MacLeish) **47**:158, 165, 167, 191, 201, 237, 243, 245, 257
"The American" (Kipling) **3**:161; **91**:83-84
"The American Aloe" (Melville) **82**:77
"The American Cemetery" (Yevtushenko) **40**:345
"American Change" (Ginsberg) **4**:53, 84
"The American Dream" (Wright) **36**:390
"American Heartbreak" (Hughes) **53**:150
"The American Hegemony" (Corso) **33**:44
"American Indian Songs" (Rexroth) **95**:340
"American Journal" (Hayden) **6**:188-89, 191-92, 195
American Journal (Hayden) **6**:194-96
"American Letter" (MacLeish) **47**:126, 135, 145-46, 188
"American Milk" (Stone) **53**:253
"American Miscellany" (H. D.) **5**:268
"American Names" (Benét) **64**:20, 53-54
"American Politica Historica, in Spontaneity" (Corso) **108**:10
"American Portrait, Old Style" (Warren) **37**:312, 337
American Primitive: Poems (Oliver) **75**:282-88, 295, 299, 302, 305, 317, 321, 329
American Scenes and Other Poems (Tomlinson) **17**:309, 317-18, 325-26, 333, 335, 337, 341-42, 348, 352
"American Sketches" (Justice) **64**:280
"American Triptych" (Kenyon) **57**:14, 39, 43
"American Twilights, 1957" (Wright) **36**:337
"The American Way" (Corso) **33**:27, 44, 49; **108**:10
Americana (Viereck) **27**:263
Americana, and Other Poems (Updike) **90**:359
Amers (Perse) **23**:217, 221, 223, 233, 237-47, 249-56
"Ametas and Thestylis Making Hay-Ropes" (Marvell) **10**:269, 271, 294, 304
"L'Ami" (Sainte-Beuve) **110**:54
"L'amica di nonna speranza" (Gozzano) **10**:177, 181-82
"L'amico che dorme" (Pavese) **13**:229
Les amies (Verlaine) **2**:432
"L'Amiral" (Péret) **33**:210
"The Amish" (Updike) **90**:357
L' Amitié du Prince (Perse) **23**:217, 246
Amitié d'un Prince (Perse) **23**:211, 221, 230, 249-50
L'Amitié se succède (Char) **56**:115-16
"Amnaid" (Dafydd ap Gwilym) **56**:225-29
"Amnesia in Memphis" (Corso) **33**:40
"Amnesiac" (Plath) **37**:256
"Amo amor" (Mistral) **32**:152
"Among all lovely Things my Love had been" (Wordsworth) **67**:248
"Among My Friends Love Is a Great Sorrow" (Duncan) **75**:225
"Among Ourselves" (Meredith) **28**:216
"Among School Children" (Hall) **70**:9
"Among School Children" (Yeats) **20**:316, 326, 328, 330, 332, 336-38, 340-42; **51**:76, 120, 128, 143, 151
"Among Sunflowers" (Wright) **36**:370
"Among the Coffee Cups and Soup Tureens Walked Beauty" (Spicer) **78**:302
"Among the Gods" (Kunitz) **19**:149, 173
Among the Hills, and Other Poems (Whittier) **93**:175-76, 230, 238-39, 267, 345, 349
"Among the Red Guns" (Sandburg) **41**:339
"Among the Tombs" (Kinnell) **26**:256
"Among the Trees" (Bryant) **20**:14, 47
"Among the Worst of Men" (Thoreau) **30**:233, 235-36
"Among Those Killed in the Dawn Raid Was a Man Aged a Hundred" (Thomas) **2**:388; **52**:278
"Amor a Silvia" (Guillén) **35**:201
"Amor de ciudad grande" (Martí) **76**:141-43
"Amor e'l cor gentil" (Dante) **21**:73
"Amor mundi" (Rossetti) **7**:282
"El amor que calla" (Mistral) **32**:152, 176
"Amore e Morte" (Leopardi) **37**:92, 111, 123, 125, 138, 171
Amores (Lawrence) **54**:162, 231, 233-35, 240
Amores (Ovid) **2**:234-35, 237-38, 242-43, 245, 251, 253-54, 258-59, 261
Amoretti (Spenser) **8**:329, 388-89
Amoretti and Epithalamion (Spenser) **8**:388
The Amorous Zodiacke (Chapman)
See *Ovids Banquet of Sense. A Coronet for His Mistresse Philosophie, and His Amorous Zodiacke. With a Translation of a Latine Coppie, Written by a Fryer, Anno Dom. 1400*
"Amos (Postscript 1968)" (Walker) **20**:278-79
"Amos Sibley" (Masters) **36**:182
"Amos-1963" (Walker) **20**:278-79
"Amour 8" (Drayton) **98**:120
"Amour 48" (Drayton) **98**:72
"L'amour" (Char) **56**:168
"L'Amour" (Éluard) **38**:96
Amour (Verlaine) **2**:416-17, 425; **32**:359, 370, 386
"L'amour et le crâne" (Baudelaire) **1**:45; **106**:24, 30
"Amour et les fleurs ne durent qu'un Printemps" (Ronsard) **105**:201
"L'Amour la mort la vie" (Éluard) **38**:79
L'amour la poésie (Éluard) **38**:61, 67, 80, 83-6
"L'amour par terre" (Verlaine) **32**:351, 390, 393
"Amour parcheminé" (Breton) **15**:52
"L'amoureuse" (Éluard) **38**:69, 73
"L'amoureuse en secret" (Char) **56**:171
"Les amours" (Laforgue) **14**:74
Amours (Ronsard) **11**:220-21, 246, 250, 254, 256, 258, 275, 277-78, 293
Amours de Marie (Ronsard)
See *See Les amours de P. de Ronsard vandomois, ensemble le cinqiesme de ses odes*
Les amours de P. de Ronsard vandomois, ensemble le cinqiesme de ses odes (Ronsard) **11**:247-48, 270; **105**:184-85, 197, 205-6, 208, 214-19, 221, 225, 242-44, 246-47, 274, 279, 288, 301-2, 315-16, 325-26, 334-35, 337-39, 343, 346-47
Amours de Voyage (Clough) **103**:51-52, 54, 57-59, 63-66, 71-72, 74, 92, 103, 105-6, 108-9, 111, 116-17, 119, 137-38, 145-46, 157, 161-63, 166
"Amours d'Eurymedon et de Calliree" (Ronsard) **11**:241; **105**:241-42, 244, 247
Amours Diverses (Ronsard)
See *See Les amours de P. de Ronsard vandomois, ensemble le cinqiesme de ses odes*
"Amours Diverses 45" (Ronsard)
See *See "Sonnet 45"*
"Amphibian" (Browning) **2**:80
"Amplifier" (Enright) **93**:4
Amplitude: New and Selected Poems (Gallagher) **9**:57-62
"Ampolla (cisti) e fuori" (Zanzotto) **65**:268-69
"Amravan" (Tagore) **8**:416
"Amsterdam" (Merrill) **28**:223
Amubaruwaria (Nishiwaki)
See *Ambarvalia*
"Amusing Stanzas to Don Juan" (Storni)
See "Divertidas estancias a don Juan"
"Amy Lowell Thoughts" (Schuyler) **88**:207
"Amy Wentworth" (Whittier) **93**:175, 247-48, 250, 266-67
"Amyntor from beyond the Sea to Alexis. A Dialogue" (Lovelace) **69**:232
"Amyntor's Grove" (Lovelace) **69**:200, 232, 234
"Amy's Cruelty" (Barrett Browning) **6**:23, 28, 32
"An Afterwards" (Heaney) **100**:274
"An den Knaben Elis" (Trakl) **20**:226, 234-35, 246
"An den Leser" (Werfel) **101**:299, 317, 345, 354, 357
"An den Wassern Babels" (Celan) **10**:127-28
"An einen Frühverstorbenen" (Trakl) **20**:230
"L'an se rejeunissoit" (Ronsard) **105**:199
"L'an trentiesme de mon eage" (MacLeish) **47**:125, 127, 156, 186, 197
"Ana María" (Guillén) **23**:102
Anabase (Perse) **23**:209-14, 216-18, 221-23, 225-28, 230-31, 233-34, 241-43, 246, 248, 250, 253, 256-59, 261
"Anabasis" (Merwin) **45**:23-4, 74
Anabasis (Perse)
See *Anabase*
"Anacona" (Tennyson) **101**:142
"Anacreontic" (Winters) **82**:310
"Anacreontica romantica" (Carducci) **46**:78
Anacreontiques (Cowley) **90**:22, 59, 61
"Anactoria" (Swinburne) **24**:308, 310-11, 322, 325-26, 343, 360-61
"Anahorish" (Heaney) **18**:201-2, 241, 251; **100**:196-97, 336
"The Anamalai Hills" (Das) **43**:82
Anamalai Poems (Das) **43**:81-84
"Ananse" (Brathwaite) **56**:47, 69, 86, 100
"Ananta jivan" (Tagore) **8**:406
"Ananta maran" (Tagore) **8**:406
"Anaphora" (Bishop) **3**:37, 56; **34**:124, 127-28
"L'anapo" (Quasimodo) **47**:278
"Anasazi" (Snyder) **21**:295-96
"Anashuya and Vijaya" (Yeats) **20**:343
The Anathemata: Fragments of an Attempted Writing (Jones) **116**:77-80, 83-84, 86, 88-91, 95-97, 100-108, 110, 112-13, 115, 117-20, 123, 129-32, 136-37, 141-48, 158-59, 164, 166-69, 171-73, 177-79, 182, 192-94, 196-97, 199-202, 210-16, 218-21, 224-28, 232, 234-37, 239
An Anatomie of the World (Donne)
See *The First Anniversarie. An Anatomie of the World. Wherein By Occasion of the untimely death of Mistris Elizabeth Drury, the frailtie and decay of this whole World is represented*
"The Anatomist's Hymn" (Holmes) **71**:63
"Anatomy" (Barker) **91**:11, 17
"Anatomy" (Muir) **49**:237
"An Anatomy of Migraine" (Clampitt) **19**:92
"Ancestor" (Berryman) **64**:81
"Ancestors" (Pavese) **13**:204
"Ancestors" (Randall) **86**:290, 299, 337, 343
"The Ancestors" (Tate) **50**:255, 257, 280
"The Ancestors" (Wright) **14**:353
Ancestors (Brathwaite) **56**:100
"Ancestral Houses" (Yeats) **20**:349
"Ancestral Photograph" (Heaney) **18**:200; **100**:263
"Ancestry" (Corso) **33**:50; **108**:3
"Anchar" (Pushkin) **10**:373
"Anchor" (Montague) **106**:240-41, 287-88, 311
"Anchor Song" (Kipling) **91**:86
"Anchorage" (Harjo) **27**:55, 58, 63, 65-66
"The Anchored Angel" (Villa) **22**:348-49
The Ancient Acquaintance (Skelton)
See *Auncient Aqueyntaunce*
"The Ancient Art of Wooing" (Berrigan) **103**:34
"An Ancient Ballet" (Kinsella) **69**:118
"The Ancient Briton Lay Ynder His Rock"

(Hughes) **7**:147
Ancient Days (Cavafy) **36**:53
"Ancient discipline" (Pavese)
See "Disciplina antica"
"An Ancient Gesture" (Millay) **6**:232, 240
"The Ancient Heroes and the Bomber Pilot" (Hughes) **7**:132
"Ancient History" (Sassoon) **12**:258
"Ancient Lament" (Carducci)
See "Pianto antico"
Ancient Lights (Clarke) **112**:31, 34, 37, 47, 50-51, 53-54, 62, 65, 80, 88, 91-92, 102-3, 113, 117
"Ancient Lights" (Clarke) **112**:39, 53-54, 66-70, 92, 103-4, 115
"the ancient lord laydee un th univers" (Bissett) **14**:27
"The Ancient Mansion" (Crabbe) **97**:106
"The Ancient Mariner" (Coleridge)
See *The Rime of the Ancient Mariner: A Poet's Reverie*
The Ancient Mariner (Coleridge)
See *The Rime of the Ancient Mariner: A Poet's Reverie*
"The Ancient Mystic" (Tennyson)
See "The Ancient Sage"
"Ancient One" (Montale)
See "Antico, sono ubriacato della tua voce"
"The Ancient Rain" (Kaufman) **74**:202, 249, 251-54, 259, 272
The Ancient Rain: Poems, 1956-1978 (Kaufman) **74**:179, 181-85, 194-95, 203, 210, 214-17, 219, 236, 239-41, 249, 252, 254, 271-72, 275-76
"The Ancient Sage" (Tennyson) **6**:407; **101**:199, 233
The Ancient Sage and Other Poems (Tennyson) **101**:232-33, 236
"An Ancient Song" (Muir) **49**:237
"An Ancient to Ancients" (Hardy) **8**:121; **92**:254, 295, 297
"Ancient tragedy" (Cavafy) **36**:54
"Ancient Tuscan Poetry" (Carducci)
See "L'Anitca Poesia Toscana"
"Ancient Wisdom Speaks" (H. D.) **5**:307
"Ancora ad Annecy" (Montale) **13**:138
"Ancora dell'inferno" (Quasimodo) **47**:289
And (Cummings)
See *&*
& (Cummings) **5**:75, 92-3, 95, 104-05
"And a Few Negroes Too" (Madhubuti)
See "A Message All Blackpeople Can Dig (& A Few Negroes Too)"
"And a Wisdom as Such" (Duncan) **2**:115
"And All I Have is Tu Fu" (Chin) **40**:30-1, 33-4
"And Another Thing" (Giovanni) **19**:118
"& Co." (Shapiro) **25**:295
"And Daughters with Curls" (Stevens) **6**:292
"And Death Shall Have No Dominion" (Thomas) **2**:379, 385, 389-90, 397
"And did those feet in ancient time" (Clough) **103**:84
"And Did Those Feet in Ancient Time Walk upon England's Mountains Green?" (Blake) **12**:45
"And do they so?" (Vaughan) **81**:331
"And Forty-second Street" (MacLeish) **47**:126, 145
"And God a Me" (Goodison) **36**:158
"And How Do You See Yourself, Mrs. Waldrop?" (Waldrop) **109**:166
"And I" (Abse) **41**:19
"And I Lounged and Lay on their Beds" (Cavafy) **36**:76
"And I Must Go" (Owen) **102**:144
"And if an eye may save or slay" (Wyatt) **27**:354
"And in the Hanging Gardens" (Aiken) **26**:24
And in the Human Heart (Aiken) **26**:22
And No One Knows Where to Go (Sachs)
See *Und Niemand weiss weiter*
"And now a soft commentaries from Angelo Solimann Africanus the Neumann" (Brathwaite) **56**:54
"And One for My Dame" (Sexton) **2**:363
"And Pass" (Toomer) **7**:332
"And So Goodbye to Cities" (Merton) **10**:334, 344
"And So Today" (Sandburg) **2**:307-08; **41**:249, 255, 260, 271
"And Socializing" (Ashbery) **26**:163
"And Step" (Ignatow) **34**:318
And Still I Rise (Angelou) **32**:2-3, 11, 23, 28
"And the Children of Birmingham" (Merton) **10**:334, 341
". . .And the Clouds Return after the Rain" (Smith) **12**:331
"And the Earth Grow Young Again" (Birney) **52**:37
"and the green wind is mooving thru the summr trees" (Bissett) **14**:33
"And the Head Began to Burn" (Storni)
See "Y la cabeza comenzó a arder"
"And The Land Is Just As Dry" (Ortiz) **17**:227
"And the Mother-Norm" (Zanzotto)
See "E la madre-norma"
"And the Stars Were Shining" (Ashbery) **26**:164-166
And the Stars Were Shining (Ashbery) **26**:164-166
"And the Trains Go On" (Levine) **22**:224
"And Their Winters and Their Nights in Disguise" (Oppen) **35**:337
"And then you said the words" (Shvarts) **50**:145
"And There Was a Great Calm" (Hardy) **8**:119; **92**:231, 328
"And They Call This Living!" (Stryk) **27**:203
"And This is Your Praise" (Amichai)
See "Vehi tehillatekha"
"And Thus" (Dorn) **115**:125
"and Tuesday III" (Hacker) **47**:94
"And Ut Pictura Poesis Is Her Name" (Ashbery) **26**:118, 123, 135
"And What About the Children" (Lorde) **12**:139
"And with What Bodies Do They Come?" (Dickinson) **1**:102
"And You as Well Must Die" (Millay) **6**:211
"And You, Helen" (Thomas) **53**:290-91, 293
Æneid (Surrey) **59**:284-87, 289, 298, 312, 339, 341, 343-44, 347-49, 353
"Æstivation" (Holmes) **71**:66, 68, 118
"El andaluz universal" (Jiménez) **7**:205
"&" (Wilbur) **51**:295
"The Andean Flute" (Mahon) **60**:148
"Andenken" (Hölderlin) **4**:172, 178
"der andere" (Enzensberger) **28**:139
"Andraitix, Pomengranate Flowers" (Lawrence) **54**:172
"André Masson" (Éluard) **38**:71
"Andrea del Sarto" (Browning) **2**:37, 86, 88, 95; **61**:5, 88;
"Andrée Rexroth" (Rexroth) **20**:206-07
"Andrew Jones" (Wordsworth) **67**:328
"Andromeda" (Hopkins) **15**:134, 148
"Andromeda Chained to Her Rock the Great Nebula in her Heart" (Rexroth) **20**:196; **95**:255, 259
Andromeda Liberata. Or the Nuptials of Perseus and Andromeda (Chapman) **96**:34, 55, 113
"Ane Ballat of the Abbot of Tungland" (Dunbar) **67**:109
"Ane Blak-Moir" (Dunbar)
See "Of Ane Blak-Moir"
"Ane Murlandis Man of Uplandis Mak" (Dunbar) **67**:3
"Ane Orisoun" (Dunbar) **67**:19, 25
"Anecdote" (Parker) **28**:360
"Anecdote for Fathers" (Wordsworth) **4**:425-28; **67**:277, 286, 300, 310, 313-17, 338, 368
Anecdote of Rain (Zagajewski) **27**:389, 399
"Anecdote of the Jar" (Stevens) **6**:309, 326-27; **110**:106-8, 138, 140, 159, 216
"Anecdote of the Prince of Peacocks" (Stevens) **6**:309
"Anelida and Arcite" (Chaucer) **19**:10, 74
"Aneurin's Harp" (Meredith) **60**:250
"Anew" (Ignatow) **34**:335
Anew (Zukofsky) **11**:342, 347, 382-83
"L'ange du méridien" (Rilke) **2**:275
"L'ange, fragment épique" (Lamartine) **16**:266
"Das angebrochene Jahr" (Celan) **10**:124
"The Angel" (Blake) **63**:4, 16-17, 28, 107
"The Angel" (Hughes) **89**:123
"Angel" (Lermontov) **18**:274, 276, 279
"Angel" (Merrill) **28**:248
"The Angel" (Spender) **71**:189
"The Angel" (Wright) **36**:280, 289
Angel (Graham) **59**:166
"Angel Atrapado XXI" (Yau) **61**:336
"Angel Atrapado XXII (The Elements)" (Yau) **61**:336
"Angel Boley" (Smith) **12**:352
"Angel Butcher" (Levine) **22**:222-23
"Angel/Engine" (Brathwaite) **56**:70, 97
"An Angel in Plaster" (Carman) **34**:226
"An Angel in the House" (Hunt) **73**:162
The Angel in the House (Patmore) **59**:200, 203-6, 209-14, 218-19, 221-27, 229-30, 232-35, 237, 239-40, 243-45, 247-51, 253-55, 258-62, 264-65, 267, 269, 271, 274
The Angel in the House, Book I: The Betrothal (Patmore) **59**:227, 244
The Angel in the House, Book II: The Espousals (Patmore) **59**:204, 220, 227, 239, 244
"The Angel of Death" (Lermontov)
See "Angel smerti"
The Angel of History (Forché) **10**:160, 169
"Angel smerti" (Lermontov) **18**:300
"The Angel Sons" (Lindsay) **23**:281
"Angel Surrounded by Paysans" (Stevens) **6**:304
"Los Angeles Poems" (Davie) **29**:99
"Angelic Love" (Meredith) **60**:244
"L'angelo nero" (Montale) **13**:134
Angelos Sikelianos: Selected Poems (Sikelianos) **29**:368
"L'Angelot maudit" (Rimbaud) **57**:253
"The Angels" (Updike) **90**:356
Angels and Earthly Creatures (Wylie) **23**:303-304, 307, 309, 313-14
"The Angels at Hamburg" (Jarrell) **41**:195-96
"The Angels of Fate" (Amichai)
See "Mal'akhei goral"
"Angels of the Love Affair" (Sexton) **2**:365, 367; **79**:217
"Angels Surrounded by Paysans" (Paz) **48**:261; **110**:97, 216
"Angelus" (Fuertes) **27**:39
"Angel-Volk" (Shvarts) **50**:135
"The Angel-Wolf" (Shvarts)
See "Angel-Volk"
"Anger" (Creeley) **73**:46-48, 122
"The Anger of the Sea" (Ishikawa)
See "Umi no ikari"
"Anger's Freeing Power" (Smith) **12**:295, 311, 330
"Les anges sont blancs" (Seferis) **66**:165, 168, 170-71, 207
"Angina" (Dickey) **40**:196, 213-14, 256
"Anglais Mort à Florence" (Stevens) **6**:311
"Angle Land" (Jones) **116**:101
Angle of Ascent (Hayden) **6**:188, 190, 194
Angle of Geese, and Other Poems (Momaday) **25**:187, 188-89, 193
"An Anglican Lady" (Davie) **29**:116
"Angling A Day" (Kinnell) **26**:260
"Anglo-Irish" (Melville) **82**:35, 38
"Anglo-Mongrels and the Rose" (Loy) **16**:316, 322
"Anglosaxon Street" (Birney) **52**:8-10, 14, 21, 27, 37, 44, 46, 56, 79
"Angoisse" (Rimbaud) **57**:178, 246, 275, 285-86, 293

"L'Angoisse" (Verlaine) **32**:386-87
"L'Angolo Franciscano" (Seferis) **66**:115
"Angriff" (Stramm) **50**:208, 218
"The Angry God" (Ferlinghetti) **1**:183
"Angry Love" (Aleixandre) **15**:19
"Angry Samson" (Graves) **6**:151
"The Angry Woman" (Wickham) **110**:270, 272, 310
"Angry Young Men" (Yevtushenko) **40**:345
"Angststurm" (Stramm) **50**:172, 205, 208-9, 222
"L'anguilla" (Montale) **13**:111
"The Anguish" (Millay) **6**:217
"Anguish" (Rimbaud)
See "Angoisse"
"Anguish" (Vaughan) **81**:366
"Anillo" (Guillén) **35**:179, 180, 181, 183
"Anima" (Carruth) **10**:85
"Anima" (Eberhart) **76**:15
"De Anima" (Nemerov) **24**:289
"Anima hominis" (Yeats) **20**:327
"Anima mundi" (Yeats) **51**:151
"Anima Sola" (Pound) **95**:117
Animadversions upon the Remonstrants Defence (Milton) **29**:238
Animal de fondo (Jiménez) **7**:183-84, 203, 211, 214
"Animal de luz" (Neruda) **4**:289
The Animal Inside (Jacobsen) **62**:300, 308, 312, 320
Animal of Depth (Jiménez)
See *Animal de fondo*
Animal of Inner Depths (Jiménez)
See *Animal de fondo*
"Animal of Light" (Neruda)
See "Animal de luz"
Animal Poems (Hughes) **89**:212
"The Animal That Drank Up Sound" (Stafford) **71**:272, 287, 304, 321, 339
"The Animal Trainer" (Berryman) **64**:82
"The Animal Trainer (2)" (Berryman) **64**:78
"Animal Tranquility and Decay" (Wordsworth)
See "Animal Tranquillity and Decay"
"Animal Tranquillity and Decay" (Wordsworth) **67**:312
"Animal, Vegetable, and Mineral" (Bogan) **12**:92, 99, 107, 125
"Animal-Flower" (Shvarts)
See "Zver'-tsvetok"
"The Animals" (Merwin) **45**:21, 25, 42
"The Animals" (Muir) **49**:196, 271, 273
"Animals Are Passing from Our Lives" (Levine) **22**:213
The Animals in That Country (Atwood) **8**:3-4, 12, 15-16, 23
"Animula" (Oppen) **35**:343
Animula (Eliot) **5**:194, 197-98, 203; **31**:120; **90**:303
Animula (Masefield) **78**:62
"Animus" (Shvarts) **50**:135, 142
"L'Anitca Poesia Toscana" (Carducci) **46**:52
Ankh (Corso) **108**:16-17
"Anklage" (Goethe) **5**:248
"Ankor Wat" (Ginsberg) **4**:61
"Ann Arbor Elegy" (Berrigan) **103**:40
"Ann Arbor Song" (Berrigan) **103**:4
"Anna" (Wyatt) **27**:345
"Anna Akhmatova" (Akhmadulina) **43**:32
"Anna Comnena" (Cavafy) **36**:33, 90, 93
"Anna Comnene" (Cavafy)
See "Anna Comnena"
"Anna Imroth" (Sandburg) **41**:239, 243, 336
"Anna Liffey" (Boland) **58**:20, 22, 28, 37-38, 50
"anna speaks of the childhood of mary her daughter" (Clifton) **17**:37
"Annabel Lee" (Poe) **1**:425, 429, 434, 438, 441, 444, 447-48
"Annandale Again" (Robinson) **1**:476
"Anne" (Valéry) **9**:374, 392
"Anne Boleyn's Song" (Sitwell) **3**:315
"Anne Hay" (Carew)
See "Obsequies to the Lady Anne Hay"
"Anne Rutledge" (Masters) **1**:334, 348; **36**:174, 183, 191-92, 199
"The Annealing" (Piercy) **29**:314
"L'anneau de la licorne" (Char) **56**:138
L'année terrible (Hugo) **17**:55-56, 65, 97-99, 101
Les Années funestes (Hugo) **17**:65
"Anne's First Exercise in Adverbs" (Wickham) **110**:266
"Annetta" (Montale) **13**:138
"The Anniad" (Brooks) **7**:53, 58, 61, 80, 102, 104
Annie Allen (Brooks) **7**:53-4, 56-8, 60-2, 68, 75, 78, 80-1, 85, 91, 96, 102, 104-05
"Annie Hill's Grave" (Merrill) **28**:248
"Annie Pengelly" (Goodison) **36**:155
"Annie's Arctic Snake" (Wakoski) **15**:334
"Annihilation" (Aiken) **26**:24
"The Anniversarie" (Donne) **1**:130; **43**:132-33
"Anniversaries" (Justice) **64**:276, 280
The Anniversaries (Donne) **1**:145-48, 155-56, 158; **43**:118-19, 122, 179
"Anniversario" (Montale) **13**:110
"Anniversary" (Abse) **41**:8
"An Anniversary" (Berry) **28**:12-13
"Anniversary" (Elytis) **21**:118-19, 134
"Anniversary" (Hughes) **89**:217
"The Anniversary" (Lowell) **13**:66, 97
"Anniversary" (Marvell)
See "The First Anniversary of the Government under O. C."
"Anniversary" (Montale)
See "Anniversario"
"The Anniversary" (Stryk) **27**:204
"Anniversary" (Thomas) **99**:312
"Anniversary Poem" (Oppen) **35**:286, 295, 339
"Anniversary Poem" (Whittier) **93**:315
"Anniversary Verses for My Oldest Wife" (Snodgrass) **74**:332
"Anniversary Words" (Randall) **86**:290, 338, 343
Anno Domini (Barker) **77**:49
"Anno domini MCMXLVII" (Quasimodo) **47**:284
Anno Domini MCMXXI (Akhmatova) **2**:3, 13-14, 18
"Announcement" (Hugo) **68**:255
"Annual" (Swenson) **14**:284
The Annual Anthology (Southey) **111**:244
"The Annunciation" (Merton) **10**:339
"The Annunciation" (Merwin) **45**:11-12, 14, 16, 29
"The Annunciation" (Mueller) **33**:180
"The Annunciation" (Muir) **49**:196, 200, 205, 273, 298
"Annunciation" (Sarton) **39**:326, 328, 323, 342-43
"The Annunciation Altered from That before" (Southwell) **83**:279
"Annunciation Eve" (Tsvetaeva)
See "Kanun Blagoveshchen'ia"
"Annunciation with a Bullet in It" (Graham) **59**:137-38
Annunciations (Tomlinson) **17**:359-60
"Annus Mirabilis" (Larkin) **21**:237
"Annus Mirabilis, 1789" (Cowper) **40**:97-8, 120
"Annus Mirabilis: The Year of Wonders, 1666" (Dryden) **25**:90-1, 93, 95, 99, 115-16
"Annus Mirabilis: The Year of Wonders, 1666. An Historical Poem: Containing the Progress and Various Successes of our Naval War with Holland, under the Conduct of His Highness Prince Rupert, & His Grace the Duke of Albamarl" (Dryden)
See "Annus Mirabilis: The Year of Wonders, 1666"
"El año lírico" (Darío) **15**:95, 117
"anodetodalevy" (Bissett) **14**:31
"Anodyne" (Komunyakaa) **51**:52, 55
"Anointed" (Traherne) **70**:322
"Anon. Poster" (Reed) **68**:332
"Anonymous" (Ciardi) **69**:24
"Anonymous Signature" (MacLeish) **47**:126
"Anorexic" (Boland) **58**:37, 72-75, 77
"Another" (Chappell) **105**:51
"Another" (Cowley) **90**:15
"Another" (Lovelace) **69**:167, 183, 239-41, 250, 256
"Another" (Prior) **102**:306
"Another" (Traherne) **70**:192, 317
"Another Animal" (Swenson) **14**:284
Another Animal (Swenson) **14**:246, 251-52, 260, 264, 267, 274, 277, 282-83
"Another August" (Merrill) **28**:221
"Another Birthday" (Das) **43**:81
"Another Dark Lady" (Robinson) **35**:368
"Another dreadful job about Mother Ireland" (Kavanagh) **33**:77
"Another (II)" (Bradstreet) **10**:35-6
"Another Early Morning Exercise" (Rexroth) **95**:257, 259, 270
"Another Journey from Béthune to Cuinchy" (Blunden) **66**:36
"Another Letter to My Husband" (Bradstreet) **10**:28
Another Life (Walcott) **46**:232, 235-36, 239-42, 244-45, 259, 266-67, 269, 271, 273, 276-80, 287-89, 308, 321-22
"Another Mystery" (Carver) **54**:18
"Another Nameless Prostitute Says the Man Is Innocent" (Espada) **74**:148
"Another New-yeeres Gift; or song for the Circumcision" (Herrick) **9**:118, 120
"Another on Fame" (Keats) **96**:354
"Another Poem for Me—After Recovering from an O.D." (Knight) **14**:39, 43, 53
"Another Poem of Gifts" (Borges) **32**:58, 66
"Another Poem of Thanksgiving" (Borges) **32**:131
"Another Ride from Ghent to Aix" (Riley) **48**:340
"Another Room" (Cohen) **109**:25, 69
"Another September" (Kinsella) **69**:119
Another September (Kinsella) **69**:65, 75, 80, 84-85, 97, 115-16, 119-22
Another Side of Bob Dylan (Dylan) **37**:60
"Another Son" (McGuckian) **27**:100
Another Song (Cage) **58**:201
"Another Space" (Page) **12**:180, 190, 197-98
"Another Spring" (Levertov) **11**:169-70
"Another Spring" (Rexroth) **20**:207; **95**:259
"Another Sunday Morning" (Mahon) **60**:147-48
"Another Time" (Auden) **1**:18-19, 30, 34
"Another Time" (Soto) **28**:402
Another Time (Auden) **92**:51, 74
"Another Version" (Mueller) **33**:188
"Another Week-end at the Beach" (Curnow) **48**:39
"Another Word on the Scientific Aspiration" (Lindsay) **23**:269
"Another Year" (Williams) **7**:370
"Anoukis and later Jeanne" (Char)
See "Anoukis et plus tard Jeanne"
"Anoukis et plus tard Jeanne" (Char) **56**:157, 171, 177
A'nque (Alurista) **34**:15, 26
"anrufung des fisches" (Enzensberger) **28**:136
"Anselmo" (Riley) **48**:300
"The Answer" (Behn) **88**:148
"Answer" (Blake)
See "Earth's Answer"
"Answer" (Burns) **114**:89, 155
"Answer" (Finch)
See "Ardelia's Answer to Ephelia"
"Answer!" (Guillén)
See "Responde tú"
"The Answer" (Herbert) **4**:130
"The Answer" (Jeffers) **17**:129, 131
"The Answer" (Montague) **106**:297
"The Answer" (Sandburg) **41**:242, 314
"The Answer" (Teasdale) **31**:321-22, 325

"The Answer" (Thomas) **99**:263, 359
The Answer (Montagu) **16**:340-41, 346
"Answer to a consul" (Paz)
See "Respuesta a un cónsul"
"An Answer to an Invitation to Cambridge" (Cowley) **90**:3
"An Answer to Another Perswading a Lady to Marriage" (Philips) **40**:297
"Answer to Cloe Jealous, in the Same Stile. The Author Sick" (Prior) **102**:316
"An Answer to Comfort Her" (Whitney) **116**:290
"An Answer to Lerone Bennett's Questionnaire on a Name for Black Americans" (Randall) **86**:298, 329
"An Answer to Some Verses Made in His Praise" (Suckling) **30**:156-57
"Answer to the Platonics" (Cowley) **90**:14
"An Answer to the Rebus" (Wheatley) **3**:363
"Answer to Voznesensky and Evtushenko" (O'Hara) **45**:118, 165
"Answering a Layman's Question" (Li Po) **29**:142
"Answering a Question in the Mountains" (Ashbery) **26**:129
"Answering Magistrate Chang" (Wang Wei) **18**:364-65
"The Ant" (Johnson) **81**:218
"The Ant" (Lovelace) **69**:168-69, 171, 174, 239-42, 244, 250, 255-57
"Ant" (Traherne) **70**:321
"Ant Trap" (Kennedy) **93**:139
"Antaeus" (Heaney) **18**:203, 207-9; **100**:211-12, 298
"Antaeus: A Fragment" (Owen) **19**:354
"Antarctica" (Mahon) **60**:217
Antarctica (Mahon) **60**:192-94, 196, 199
"Antaryami" (Tagore) **8**:408
"Ante Aram" (Brooke) **24**:62
"Ante Lucem" (Blok) **21**:2, 23
"Ante Mortem" (Jeffers) **17**:117, 141
"An Antebellum Sermon" (Dunbar) **5**:120, 123, 133, 147
"Antecedents" (Tomlinson) **17**:302-04, 306, 311, 323, 338
Antechinus: Poems, 1975-1980 (Hope) **56**:282
"Antediluvian" (Ní Chuilleanáin) **34**:351
"Antelación de amor" (Borges) **32**:83
"Ante-Natal Dream" (Kavanagh) **33**:147; **106**:296
"Antenati" (Pavese) **13**:217, 220, 225-26
"Antéros" (Nerval) **13**:181, 191-92, 194, 198
"Anthem" (Cohen) **109**:103
"Anthem for Doomed Youth" (Hughes) **89**:146
"Anthem for Doomed Youth" (Owen) **19**:326, 332, 336, 346, 360-63, 365-67, 369-70; **102**:142-43, 157-58, 161-62, 171, 181, 225, 228, 246, 265, 275
"Anthem for Man" (Wagoner) **33**:326
"The Anthill" (Cervantes) **35**:114, 134
Anthology (Jiménez)
See *Antolojía poética (1898-1953)*
Anthology for a Thousand Ages (Yakamochi)
See *Man'yōshū*
The Anthology of Magazine Verse (Braithwaite) **52**:106-7
"L'anthracite" (Ponge) **107**:130
"An Anthropological Guide to the Customs of the Country" (Shvarts)
See "Antropologicheskoe stranovedenie"
"The Anthropology of Water" (Carson) **64**:200, 202-4
"Antichrist" (Traherne) **70**:320, 322
"Anticipated Elegy" (Cernuda)
See "Elegía anticipada"
"The Anticipation" (Traherne) **70**:192, 232, 275, 277, 299, 317-18
"Antico inverno" (Quasimodo) **47**:275
"Antico, sono ubriacato della tua voce" (Montale) **13**:115, 141
"Anti-Desperation" (Arnold) **5**:7
"Antigone" (Arnold) **5**:8
"The Antigone Riddle" (Mahon) **60**:150, 192
"Antigone, This Is It" (Reed) **68**:348
"Antigua casa madrileña" (Aleixandre) **15**:34, 36
The Antihead (Tzara)
See *L'Antitête*
The Antilles: Fragments of Epic Memory (Walcott) **46**:260
"Antilógica" (Guillén) **35**:146
"Antinous" (Pessoa) **20**:165, 169
"Antiphon" (Herbert) **4**:103
"The Antiphon" (Levertov) **11**:198
L'Anti-Platon (Bonnefoy) **58**:119, 150
"Anti-poem" (Shapiro) **25**:316, 321
"Antipoema?" (Fuertes) **27**:48
Antipoems: New and Selected (Parra) **39**:291-92, 306-9
"Antipolis" (Dickey) **40**:176, 178
"Antique" (Rimbaud) **57**:230, 254
"Antique Harvesters" (Ransom) **61**:268-69, 275
"Antiquitie" (Traherne) **70**:322
"The Antiquity of Freedom" (Bryant) **20**:43, 47
L'Antitête (Tzara) **27**:234-37
Anti=Thelyphthora (Evans) **40**:71
"Anti-Vietnam War Peace Mobilization" (Ginsberg) **4**:76
Antología mayor (Guillén) **23**:142
Antología personal (Borges) **32**:93
Antología poética (Storni) **33**:235, 245
Antología total (Aleixandre) **15**:32
Antología y poemas (Fuertes) **27**:10-1
Antología y poemas del suburbio (Fuertes) **27**:10, 18
Antolojía poética (1898-1953) (Jiménez) **7**:183-84
"Antonio Machado" (Guillén) **35**:201
"Antrim" (Jeffers) **17**:117
"Antropologicheskoe stranovedenie" (Shvarts) **50**:162
"The Ants" (Empson) **104**:122
"Anvil" (Brathwaite) **56**:12
The Anxiety of the Rose (Storni)
See *La inquietud del rosal*
"Any Human to Another" (Cullen) **20**:60
"Any Porch" (Parker) **28**:353-54
"Any Time" (Stafford) **71**:283
"Any Time Now" (Curnow) **48**:38-39
"Any where out of the world" (Baudelaire) **106**:108
"anyone lived in a pretty how town" (Cummings) **5**:81
"Anything Can Happen" (Heaney) **100**:330
"Anyway" (Berryman) **64**:102
"Anywhere is a Street into the Night" (Momaday) **25**:202, 212
"Aodh Ruadh Ó Domhnaill" (Melville) **82**:10, 12, 29, 34-36, 38-40, 49, 54-55
Aoneko (Hagiwara) **18**:170, 172-73, 175-77, 181-83
"Ap Huw's Testament" (Thomas) **99**:271-72, 308
"Apá" (Alurista) **34**:28
"Apache Love" (Ortiz) **17**:224
"Apache: Miss Treavle Pursues W. D." (Snodgrass) **74**:333
"Apache Red" (Ortiz) **17**:228
"El aparecido" (Guillén) **35**:187
"Apart and Yet Together" (Service) **70**:150, 152
"The Apartment Is as Silent as Paper" (Mandelstam) **14**:149
"Apathy and Enthusiasm" (Melville) **82**:130, 132, 207
"Apegado a mí" (Mistral) **32**:200-02
"El apellido" (Guillén) **23**:131
"The Apennines" (Bryant) **20**:16-17
"Apes and Ivory" (Noyes) **27**:114
"Aphasia" (Mueller) **33**:192
"Aphorisms" (Randall) **86**:290
"Aphorisms, I" (Villa) **22**:355
"Aphorisms, II" (Villa) **22**:353, 355
"Aphorisms, III" (Villa) **22**:355
"Aphorisms on Futurism" (Loy) **16**:311-13, 316, 322, 324
"Aphrodite" (Glück) **16**:150
"Aphrodite Goes Away for Saturday Night" (Shvarts) **50**:143
"Aphrodite Ode" (Sappho)
See "Ode to Aphrodite"
"Aphrodite Rising" (Sikelianos) **29**:367, 369
"Aplauso humano" (Cernuda) **62**:175
"Apocalipsis" (Cardenal) **22**:112, 125, 129
"Apocalypse" (Cardenal)
See "Apocalipsis"
"Apocalypse: Umbrian Master, about 1490" (Enzensberger) **28**:151
"Apocalyptic Harvest" (Winters) **82**:314
"Apogee of Celery" (Neruda)
See "Apogeo del apio"
"Apogeo del apio" (Neruda) **4**:277
"Apollo" (Dickey) **40**:189, 199-200, 220, 237
"Apollo and Daphne" (Winters) **82**:338, 340, 342-43
"Apollo and Marsyas" (Herbert)
See "Apollo i marsjasz"
"Apollo at Pheræ" (Masters) **1**:329; **36**:176
"Apollo i marsjasz" (Herbert) **50**:3, 5, 34
"Apollo in New York" (Viereck) **27**:278
"Apollo of the Physiologists" (Graves) **6**:152-53
"Apollo Sends Seven Nursery Rhymes to James Alexander" (Spicer) **78**:241, 306, 308-9
"An Apollonian Elegy" (Duncan) **2**:105; **75**:225
Apollonius of Tyana (Olson) **19**:282, 298
"Apollonius of Tyre" (Gower)
See *Confessio Amantis*
"Apollo's Edict" (Swift) **9**:252
"Apologia por vita sua" (Cernuda) **62**:214, 268-71
"Apologia pro poemate meo" (Owen) **19**:329, 334-35, 344, 348, 353-55, 370; **102**:145, 148, 168, 170-71, 173, 208-9, 226, 267
"Apologie for the Fore-Going Hymne" (Crashaw) **84**:32-33, 52, 121, 177
"Apologies to All the People in Lebanon" (Jordan) **38**:127, 145
"Apologies to the Federal Bureau of Investigation" (Giovanni) **19**:108
"Apology" (Benét) **64**:22
"Apology" (Chappell) **105**:52
"Apology" (Hardy) **92**:245
"Apology" (Morris) **55**:242, 253, 285, 291-97, 325, 329
"Apology" (Wilbur) **51**:188
"Apology for Bad Dreams" (Jeffers) **17**:129-30, 142, 147
"An Apology for Not Invoking the Muse" (Ciardi) **69**:57
"The Apology of Demetrius" (Masters) **1**:343
"Apology of Genius" (Loy) **16**:308, 321
"An Apology to the Lady Cartaret" (Swift) **9**:296
Apophoreta (Martial) **10**:230, 241
"The Apostacy" (Traherne) **70**:222, 245, 247-50, 302, 322
"The Apostacy of One, and But One Lady" (Lovelace) **69**:239
"Apostle" (Traherne) **70**:321
"Apostle of Hope" (Kinsella) **69**:82, 129, 131
"Apostrophe to a Dead Friend" (Kumin) **15**:218-20
"The Apostrophe to Vincentine" (Stevens) **6**:309; **110**:94
"apoteos" (Ekeloef) **23**:75
"The Apotheosis of the Garbagemen" (Wagoner) **33**:337
"The Apotheosis of Tins" (Mahon) **60**:136, 138, 149, 155, 174, 189-90
"Apparent Failure" (Browning) **2**:68; **61**:49
"The Apparition" (Berryman) **64**:81
"The Apparition" (Donne) **1**:130, 152
"The Apparition" (Melville) **82**:76, 102, 134-35, 138, 150, 200

"The Apparition of His Mistress Calling Him to Elizium" (Herrick) **9**:93, 103, 133, 138-39
"Apparition of Splendor" (Moore) **49**:126-28, 131, 136, 139, 161
"The Apparitions" (Yeats) **20**:351
"Apparuit" (Pound) **95**:96, 102
"The Appeal" (Kipling) **91**:153
"Appeal" (Spender) **71**:179, 215
"Appeal to a Lady with a Diaper" (Birney) **52**:28, 63, 79
"Appeal to Dwynwen" (Dafydd ap Gwilym) See "Galw ar Ddwynwen"
"An Appeal to the American People" (Harper) **21**:190
"Appearances" (Glück) **16**:157, 161
"Appearances" (Melville) **82**:50
"The Appeasement of Demeter" (Meredith) **60**:330
Appendice (Pasolini) **17**:279
"Appendix Form in Poetry" (Viereck) **27**:287
"Appendix to the Anniad Leaves from a Loose-Leaf War Diary" (Brooks) **7**:61
"L'Appennino" (Pasolini) **17**:270
"Appetite" (Smith) **12**:310
"Appetite" (Traherne) **70**:322
"The Apple" (Kinnell) **26**:261
"The Apple" (Page) **12**:168, 170
"Apple" (Soto) **28**:398
Apple (Yevtushenko) See *Yabloko*
"The Apple Blossom Snow Blues" (Lindsay) **23**:264
"Apple Dropping into Deep Early Snow" (Kenyon) **57**:35
An Apple from One's Lap (Seifert) See *Jablko z klína*
An Apple From the Lap (Seifert) See *Jablko z klína*
An Apple from Your Lap (Seifert) See *Jablko z klína*
"The Apple Garths of Avalon" (Rexroth) **95**:271
"An Apple Gathering" (Rossetti) **7**:260-1, 280
"Apple Peeler" (Francis) **34**:255
The Apple That Astonished Paris (Collins) **68**:203, 205, 208
"Apple Tragedy" (Hughes) **7**:143, 159
"The Apple Tree" (Berry) **28**:5
"The Apple Tree" (Parker) **28**:364
"The Apple Trees" (Glück) **16**:126-27, 132, 140, 142
"The Apple Woman's Complaint" (McKay) **2**:210
"Apples" (Hall) **70**:32
"Apples" (Merwin) **45**:87, 95-7
"Apples and Water" (Graves) **6**:141
"Appleton House" (Marvell) See "Upon Appleton House"
The Applewood Cycles (Viereck) **27**:286, 289
"The Applicant" (Plath) **1**:394, 400-01; **37**:232, 255
"Applies" (Reese) **29**:335
"The Appointment" (Kenyon) **57**:17
"The Appointment Card" (Ignatow) **34**:318
"The Appology" (Finch) **21**:140, 159, 162, 167, 178
"Appraisal" (Teasdale) **31**:349
"The Apprehension" (Traherne) **70**:318
"Apprehensions" (Duncan) **2**:110, 112; **75**:123, 250, 256, 259, 261, 263-66
"Apprehensions" (Hecht) **70**:65, 86-87, 92
"Apprehensions" (Hughes) **89**:177
"An Apprentice Angel" (MacDiarmid) **9**:155
"l'Appressamento della morte" (Leopardi) **37**:170, 172
"The Approach" (Traherne) **70**:189, 248, 268, 271, 314-15
"Approach to Thebes" (Kunitz) **19**:156, 161, 168, 173-74
"The Approaches" (Merwin) **45**:45
"Approaching Prayer" (Dickey) **40**:163, 175, 192, 208-9, 248
"The Approaching Silence" (Illyés) **16**:248
"Approaching the Castle" (Hugo) **68**:253
"Approaching Winter" (Bly) **39**:7, 85
Approximate Man (Tzara) See *L'homme approximatif*
Approximate Man and Other Writings (Tzara) See *L'homme approximatif*
"Appuldurcombe Park" (Lowell) **13**:84
"Aprendiendo olvido" (Cernuda) **62**:195
"Après le déluge" (Péret) **33**:230
"Après le déluge" (Rimbaud) **3**:261; **57**:173, 177, 221, 236, 239, 249, 275, 282, 285, 293
"Après une lecture d'Adolphe" (Sainte-Beuve) **110**:48
"Après une lecture de Dante" (Hugo) **17**:96-97
L'après-midi d'un faune (Mallarmé) **4**:186, 188, 190, 197, 207-08; **102**:19, 23, 29, 31, 51, 55-57, 59, 64, 74, 87, 109-10
"April" (Glück) **16**:171
"April" (Kavanagh) **33**:109, 162
"April" (Merwin) **45**:20
"April" (Ransom) **61**:294
"April" (Smith) **104**:227, 230-31
"April" (Winters) **82**:319, 323
"April 5, 1974" (Wilbur) **51**:284
"April 1885" (Bridges) **28**:83
April Airs (Carman) **34**:205, 211, 228
"April and Its Forsythia" (Schuyler) **88**:206
"April Asylum" (Jacobsen) **62**:309
"April Byeway" (Blunden) **66**:21
"April Fables" (Nishiwaki) **15**:231
April Galleons (Ashbery) **26**:162, 174
"April in November" (MacLeish) **47**:210
"April in Paris" (Komunyakaa) **51**:33
April in Sydney (Komunyakaa) See *February in Sydney*
April Interval (Hacker) **47**:112
"April Inventory" (Snodgrass) **74**:284-86, 293, 295-96, 307-8, 320
"April Is the Saddest Month" (Williams) **7**:351, 354, 400
"April Mood" (Randall) **86**:338
"April on Toronto Island" (Mahon) **60**:195
"April Treason" (Ransom) **61**:272
"April Walk" (Kenyon) **57**:45
"April was Opening its Flowers" (Guillén) See "Abril sus flores abría"
"April Weather" (Carman) **34**:223
"Aprilian" (Carman) **34**:202
"Aquarelles" (Verlaine) **2**:415
"L'aquarium" (Laforgue) **14**:72
"An Aquarium" (Lowell) **13**:79
"Aquatic Park" (Spicer) **78**:254-55, 264
"Aquél" (Borges) **32**:56
"Aqui" (Paz) **48**:248
"Aquí estoy expuesta como todos" (Fuertes) **27**:25
"Aqui Nomas" (Alurista) **34**:47
Ara Vos Prec (Eliot) **90**:338
"Arab Music" (Enright) **93**:32
"Arabel" (Masters) **1**:328; **36**:175
"Arabella" (Crabbe) **97**:95, 103-5
"Arabia" (de la Mare) **77**:73, 105
"Arachne" (Empson) **104**:84, 89, 98, 133
"L'Araignée" (Ponge) **107**:73, 100, 108, 161-62, 208
L'Araignée mise au mur (Ponge) **107**:157-62
"Aramantha" (Lovelace) See "To Amarantha, That She Would Dishevell Her Hair"
"Aran" (Mahon) **60**:198
Arap Petra Velikogo (Pushkin) **10**:394
Ararat (Glück) **16**:157-64, 168, 170
"Araucanian and Latin" (Parra) **39**:277
"El árbol" (Aleixandre) **15**:22
"El árbol" (Cernuda) **62**:196, 215
Arbol adentro (Paz) **1**:374, 376-77; **48**:192, 261
"Arbol muerto" (Mistral) **32**:178
"Arboreal Cathedral" (Shvarts) **50**:147
Arbre des voyageurs (Tzara) **27**:234
"L'arbre, la lampe" (Bonnefoy) **58**:118, 167-68
"Les Arbres" (Bonnefoy) **58**:170
"Arbres III" (Jaccottet) **98**:150
Arbuthnot (Pope) See *An Epistle to Dr. Arbuthnot*
"L'Arc" (Perse) **23**:228
"The Arc Inside and Out" (Ammons) **16**:12, 61
"L'arca" (Montale) **13**:113
Arcadia (Sidney) See *The Countess of Pembroke's Arcadia*
"La Arcadia perdida" (Cardenal) **22**:132
"Arcady Unheeding" (Sassoon) **12**:240, 275
"An Archaeological Picnic" (Betjeman) **75**:66
Archaeologist of Morning (Olson) **19**:268, 282, 306, 308
"Archaic Figure" (Clampitt) **19**:92
Archaic Figure (Clampitt) **19**:91-3
"Archaics" (Guest) **55**:212
"The Archbishop and Gil Blas" (Holmes) **71**:65, 68
"Archduchess Anne" (Meredith) **60**:251, 262-63
"The Arched Instant" (Shvarts) **50**:132
"Archeology" (Auden) **92**:71
The Archeology of Movies and Books (Wakoski) **15**:372-73
Archer (Viereck) **27**:285, 288-89, 291-92
Archer in the Marrow (Viereck) See *Archer in the Marrow: The Applewood Cycles 1967-1987*
Archer in the Marrow: The Applewood Cycles 1967-1987 (Viereck) **27**:285-88, 292
"Archibald Higbie" (Masters) **1**:333
"The Archipelago" (Melville) **82**:77, 151
"Der Archipelagus" (Hölderlin) **4**:147-8, 164
"Architects" (Benét) **64**:23
"Architectural Image" (Sarton) **39**:320
"The Architectural Metaphor" (Ní Chuilleanáin) **34**:368-69
"Architecture" (Alexie) **53**:40
"An Architecture" (Berry) **28**:4, 7
"Architecture" (Stevens) **6**:293
"The Architecture: Passages 9" (Duncan) **2**:107
"An Archival Print" (Stafford) **71**:370
"El arco-iris" (Mistral) **32**:169
"The Arctic Ox (or Goat)" (Moore) **49**:143
"Arcturus" (Teasdale) **31**:360
"Arcturus in Autumn" (Teasdale) **31**:338
"Ardelia to Melancholy" (Finch) **21**:146, 150, 152, 157, 165, 168, 177-80
"Ardelia's Answer to Ephelia" (Finch) **21**:148, 154-55, 163, 165
The Ardent Slingsman (Neruda) See *El hondero entusiasta, 1923-1924*
"Ardilla de los tunes de un katu" (Cardenal) **22**:131
Ardor: The Book of the Dead Man, Volume 2 (Bell) **79**:38-40
"Are They Dancing" (Dorn) **115**:109
"Are you what your faire lookes expresse?" (Campion) **87**:72
"La arena traicionada" (Neruda) **4**:292-93
"Arethusa" (Shelley) **14**:167
"The Argonauts" (Lawrence) **54**:199
"The Argument" (Aiken) **26**:24
"Argument" (Char) **56**:114, 190
"The Argument" (Kenyon) **57**:27, 37
"Argument" (Lawrence) **54**:173, 207, 212
"Argument" (Ponge) **107**:79
"The Argument Is" (Dorn) **115**:125
"Argument 1" (Hughes) **53**:115
"The Argument of His Book" (Herrick) **9**:85, 95, 97, 101, 105, 107-10, 116, 132-34, 138-39, 141
"Ariadne" (H. D.) **5**:304
Arias tristes (Jiménez) **7**:199, 209
"Ariel" (Plath) **1**:381, 409, 413; **37**:234, 240-41, 260
Ariel (Plath) **1**:379-80, 383-84, 387, 389-91, 393-96, 405-07, 410-11; **37**:175-76, 187, 193, 196-98, 260-61, 263-65
Ariel Poems (Eliot) **31**:156
"Ariettes oubliées" (Verlaine) **2**:431
"Arion" (Eliot) **20**:123, 125, 134-35, 145
"Arion" (Herbert) **50**:3

"Arion on a Dolphin to his Marjestie in his passadge into England" (Philips) **40**:318
"Ariosto" (Carducci) **46**:52
"Ariosto" (Mandelstam) **14**:144
"Ariosto and the Arabs" (Borges) **22**:92
"Ariosto's (or The Lover's) Prison" (Hunt) **73**:138
"Arisbe" (Howe) **54**:119-21, 149-50
"Arisen at Last" (Whittier) **93**:211
"Ariso" (Ishikawa) **10**:215
"Aristoboulos" (Cavafy) **36**:34
"Aristocrats" (Douglas) **106**:203, 210
Aristophanes' Apology (Browning) **2**:96
"Aristotle's Philosophy" (Traherne) **70**:320-21
"Arizona Desert" (Tomlinson) **17**:331, 341
"Arizona Highways" (Welch) **62**:337, 345-47, 370-71
"The Ark" (Montale)
See "L'arca"
The Arkansas Testament (Walcott) **46**:259, 266, 323
The Arm and the Flame (Seifert)
See *Ruka a plamen*
"The Armada" (Swinburne) **24**:312
"Armada Ballads" (Deloney) **79**:57
"The Armada Song" (Berryman)
See "Dream Song 361"
"The Armadillo" (Bishop) **34**:78, 80
"Armageddon" (Ransom) **61**:308, 324
"Armageddon" (Tennyson) **6**:407-08, 413, 415-18; **101**:140-41, 237, 246
Armand Schwerner (Schwerner) **42**:204
"Armed with the vision of narrow wasps" (Mandelstam)
See "Vooruzhennyi zren'em uzkikh os"
"Armenia" (Mandelstam) **14**:118
"Les armes miraculeuses" (Césaire) **25**:8, 29
Les Armes Miraculeuses (Césaire) **25**:15, 18, 21, 29-30, 44
"Armgart" (Eliot) **20**:101, 116, 124, 131, 133-36, 144
"Armies in the Fire" (Stevenson) **84**:316-17, 344
"The Armies of the Wilderness" (Melville) **82**:84, 94, 133, 137, 191, 196, 204, 270
"Una armonía" (Guillén) **35**:181
"Armor" (Dickey) **40**:150, 175
"Armor's Undermining Modesty" (Moore) **4**:267; **49**:126, 128, 132, 134, 157
"Arms" (Tagore)
See "Bahu"
"Arms and the Boy" (Owen) **19**:336, 354, 358; **102**:181, 189, 205, 263
The Arms of Venus (Seifert)
See *Ruce Venušiny*
"Army" (Corso) **33**:25, 47-8; **108**:31
"Army Song" (Wang Wei) **18**:367
"Arnold, Master of the Scud" (Carman) **34**:202
Ārogya (Tagore) **8**:424, 426
Aromates chasseurs (Char) **56**:130, 136-38, 140, 145, 173, 184, 187-89
Aromatic Hunters (Char)
See *Aromates chasseurs*
"Aromos" (Parra) **39**:285
"Around Pastor Bonhoeffer" (Kunitz) **19**:158
"Arp" (Éluard) **38**:71
"El arpa" (Cernuda) **62**:177, 197
"Arrabal" (Borges) **32**:126
"Arrabal en que pesa el campo" (Borges) **32**:84
"Arracombe Wood" (Mew) **107**:34, 57
"Arrangement in Gray and Black" (Melville) **82**:35, 37
"Arrangements with Earth for Three Dead Friends" (Wright) **36**:336
"Arras" (Page) **12**:168, 170, 178, 180, 189-90, 197
"Arremba sulla strinata proda" (Montale) **13**:116
"Arrest of Antoñito the Camborio" (García Lorca)
See "Prendimiento de Antoñito el Camborio"
"The Arrest of Oscar Wilde at the Cadogan Hotel" (Betjeman) **75**:46, 78
Arrière-histoire du poème pulvérisé (Char) **56**:112
"Arrival" (Brathwaite) **56**:7, 49, 86
"Arrival" (Guillén) **23**:105
"The Arrival" (Merwin) **45**:52, 55, 86
"Arrival and Departure" (MacLeish) **47**:197
"The Arrival and Departure of Adam and Eve at Dover" (Abse) **41**:33
"Arrival at Santos" (Bishop) **3**:44; **34**:78, 94, 116, 189
"The Arrival of the Bee Box" (Plath) **1**:410-13; **37**:233
"Arrivals" (Birney) **52**:16, 45
"Arrivals and Departures" (Stone) **53**:228
"Arrivals, Departures" (Larkin) **21**:236
"Arrivals Wolfville" (Birney) **52**:34, 36
The Arrivants (Brathwaite)
See *The Arrivants: A New World Trilogy*
The Arrivants: A New World Trilogy (Brathwaite) **56**:26, 32-33, 36, 41, 43-45, 49-51, 53, 59, 61, 65-66, 72-77, 82, 84, 86, 88-89, 94-96, 98-100
"Arrivée des voyageurs" (Éluard) **38**:91
"Arriving at the Frontier on a Mission" (Wang Wei) **18**:367, 389
"Arriving in the Country Again" (Wright) **36**:326
"An Arrogant Bagpiper" (Castro)
See "Un arrogante gaitero"
"Un arrogante gaitero" (Castro) **41**:110
"El arrorró elquino" (Mistral) **32**:180
"The Arrorró of Elqui" (Mistral)
See "El arrorró elquino"
"Arrow" (Dove) **6**:123
"The Arrow That Flieth by Day" (O'Hara)
See "Ode (to Joseph LeSueur) on the Arrow That Flieth by Day"
"The Arrow That Flieth by Night" (O'Hara) **45**:154
"Arrows of Flowers" (Bissett) **14**:7
"Arrullo patagón" (Mistral) **32**:180
Ars Amandi (Ovid)
See *Ars amatoria*
Ars amatoria (Ovid) **2**:233-34, 238-39, 241-47, 253-55, 261
"Ars Amoris" (Cunningham) **92**:136-37, 168, 182
"Ars poetica" (Borges) **32**:42, 62, 65
"Ars Poetica" (Cavafy) **36**:112
"Ars poetica" (Dove) **6**:121-22
"Ars poetica" (Kennedy) **93**:138, 145
"Ars Poetica" (MacLeish) **47**:125, 181, 186, 195, 212-14
"Ars poetica?" (Milosz) **8**:197, 201
"Ars Poetica" (Spicer) **78**:302
Ars Poetica (Cavafy) **36**:54, 55-56
Ars Poetica (Horace) **46**:97, 99, 101, 104-5, 114, 124-25, 132, 138, 140-42, 145-47, 157, 159, 222
"Ars Poetica: A Found Poem" (Kumin) **15**:216
"Ars Poetica: Some Recent Criticism" (Wright) **36**:317, 373, 377
"Ars vivendi" (Guillén) **35**:197-98
Arsenal (Char) **56**:112, 126-27, 168
"The Arsenal at Springfield" (Longfellow) **30**:21, 27, 46
"Arsenio" (Montale) **13**:107, 120, 124-25, 147, 164
"Arsinoë" (Ekeloef) **23**:59, 61
"Art" (Emerson) **18**:98
"L'art" (Gautier) **18**:128, 156-57, 164
"Art" (Melville) **82**:74, 86, 98, 105, 145, 148
"An Art Called Gothonic" (Olson) **19**:305
L'Art d'être grand-père (Hugo) **17**:65, 86
"Art for the Sake of Something Very Misty Indeed" (Enright) **93**:4
"Art Is Either A Complaint Or Do Something Else" (Cage) **58**:220
"Art is the Farthest Retreat from Boredom" (Raworth) **107**:316
"Art McCooey" (Kavanagh) **33**:81, 94-95, 102, 152-4, 157; **105**:99, 101, 126
The Art of Drowning (Collins) **68**:203, 205-6, 215, 217-19, 223
"The Art of Forgetting" (Mueller) **33**:193
"The Art of Love" (Koch) **80**:312, 322, 341
The Art of Love (Koch) **80**:290-91, 303, 308-9, 327, 339
Art of Love (Ovid)
See *Ars amatoria*
"The Art of Modern Drama" (Peacock) **87**:326
"Art of Poetry" (Bonnefoy)
See "Art poétique"
"The art of poetry" (Dalton) **36**:137
"The Art of Poetry" (Hugo) **68**:253-54, 315
"The Art of Poetry" (Koch) **80**:303, 325-27, 334
"Art of Poetry" (Verlaine)
See "L'Art poètique"
The Art of Poetry (Horace)
See *Ars Poetica*
"The Art of Response" (Lorde) **12**:140
The Art of Worldly Wisdom (Rexroth) **20**:179, 181-83, 192, 198, 203, 211, 213; **95**:248, 255-58, 269, 306
"Art poétique" (Bonnefoy) **58**:132
"L'Art poètique" (Verlaine) **2**:416-18, 428, 430-34; **32**:340-43, 353, 355, 360, 363, 368-69, 374, 376, 385-86, 396, 398-99, 401-04, 412
"Art the Herald" (Noyes) **27**:140
"An Art Worker" (Masefield) **78**:44, 47
"Arte poética" (Guillén) **23**:128
De Arte Poetica liber (Horace)
See *Ars Poetica*
"L'arte povera" (Montale) **13**:138
"Artémis" (Nerval) **13**:173, 179, 181, 184-87, 195-96, 198
"Artemis Orthia" (Sikelianos) **29**:367
"Artemis Prologuises" (Browning) **2**:26
"Arterial" (Kipling) **91**:154
"An Artesian Well" (Sarton) **39**:321, 339
"Arthur Mitchell" (Moore) **49**:146
"Article" (Traherne) **70**:320, 322
"The Articles of War" (Francis) **34**:243
"Articulation of Sound Forms in Time" (Howe) **54**:38, 41, 43, 45-48, 51-52, 54, 59-62, 64, 66-69, 87, 93-95, 97, 100-1, 110, 112, 114-16, 124-25, 128-30, 133
"Artificer" (Kennedy) **93**:139
"Artificer" (Milosz) **8**:191
"Artificial Flowers" (Cavafy) **36**:105
Artificial Paradises (Baudelaire)
See *Les paradis artificiels: Opium et haschisch*
"Artificial Populations" (Stevens) **110**:95, 230
"Artillerie" (Herbert) **4**:101, 129
"Artillery" (Herbert)
See "Artillerie"
Artine (Char) **56**:126-27
"The Artist" (Blok) **21**:16
"An Artist" (Heaney) **18**:215
"An Artist" (Jeffers) **17**:141
"The Artist" (Koch) **80**:318
"The Artist" (Kunitz) **19**:161, 168, 173-75
"The Artists' and Models' Ball" (Brooks) **7**:107
"Artists' Letters" (Kinsella) **69**:77
"An Arundel Tomb" (Larkin) **21**:229-30, 234, 238-39, 258
"Der Arzt" (Benn) **35**:50
"As a Child, Sleepless" (Snodgrass) **74**:334
"As a Possible Lover" (Baraka) **4**:16; **113**:96
"As a World Would Have It" (Robinson) **1**:460
"As Any (Men's Hells Having Wrestled with)" (Cummings) **5**:108
"As Bad as a Mile" (Larkin) **21**:233-34
"As by the streames of Babilon" (Campion) **87**:65
"As Children Together" (Forché) **10**:144, 156-57, 168-69
"As Chloris full of harmless thought" (Wilmot)
See "Song to Chloris"
"As Created" (Riley) **48**:302

"As de Pique" (Péret) **33**:217
As Does New Hampshire (Sarton) **39**:338-9, 342, 360
"As due by many titles I resigne" (Donne) **43**:160
"As Eagles Soar" (Toomer) **7**:340
"As Envoy to the Barbarian Pass" (Wang Wei) **18**:362
As Fine As Melanctha (Stein) **18**:327
"As Flowers Are" (Kunitz) **19**:155, 162
"As for Fame I've Had It" (Ammons) **16**:44
"As for me, I sing and sing" (Castro)
See "Yo cantar, cantar, canté"
"As He Draws Away" (Darwish) **86**:34
"As Hermes Once" (Keats) **1**:279
"As I Ebb'd with an Ebb of the Ocean of Life" (Whitman) **91**:312-17, 319-21
"As I Ebb'd with the Ocean of Life" (Whitman) **3**:396-97, 421
"As I Grow Older" (Hughes) **1**:251; **53**:122
"As I Lay with My Head on Your Lap Camarado" (Whitman) **3**:379
"As I Remember" (Stone) **53**:222
"As I Sat Alone by Blue Ontario's Shore" (Whitman) **3**:377, 387
"As I Step over the Puddle at the End of Winter, I Think of an Ancient Chinese" (Wright) **36**:340, 374
"As I Was Saying" (Parra) **39**:310-11
"As I Went Down to Havre de Grace" (Wylie) **23**:305, 310, 324
"As I Went Out One Morning" (Dylan) **37**:55-6
"As I Would Wish You Birds" (Ciardi) **69**:13
"As if a Phantom Caress'd Me" (Whitman) **91**:312, 319-20
As If: Poems New and Selected (Ciardi) **69**:25, 27, 31, 33, 35-36, 40, 50, 55
"As If We Didn't Have to Talk" (Waldrop) **109**:177
"As in a rose the true fire moves" (Villa) **22**:351
"As in their Time" (MacNeice) **61**:177
"As Is the Sea Marvelous" (Cummings) **5**:104
"As It Should Be" (Mahon) **60**:142, 152, 183
"As It Was Written" (Sexton) **79**:245
"As John to Patmos" (Walcott) **46**:272
"As kingfishers catch fire" (Hopkins) **15**:169
"As Lovers Do" (MacDiarmid) **9**:156
"As Loving Hind" (Bradstreet)
See "Another (II)"
"As Many Questions As Answers" (Jackson) **44**:6
"As Miracles Go" (Stone) **53**:223
"As My Blood Was Drawn" (Hayden) **6**:194
"As My Uncle Ust to Say" (Riley) **48**:300
"As on a Holiday" (Hölderlin)
See "Wie wenn am Feiertage ..."
"As One Does Sickness Over" (Dickinson) **1**:94
"As One Put Drunk into the Packet Boat" (Ashbery) **26**:120
"As one who hath sent forth on bold emprise" (Belloc) **24**:10
"As Pippa Lilted" (Stafford) **71**:299
"As Plato Said" (Hecht) **70**:89
"As Seen by Disciples" (Brooks) **7**:63
As Ten, as Twenty (Page) **12**:163-64, 167, 173, 193
"As the Dead Prey upon Us" (Olson) **19**:321, 323
"As the Mist Leaves No Scar" (Cohen) **109**:68
"As the Team's Head-Brass" (Thomas) **53**:298, 305, 308, 346, 350
"As the Wind" (Cernuda) **62**:171
"As Thyself" (Lawrence) **54**:249
"As virtuous men pass mildly away" (Donne)
See "A Valediction: forbidding mourning"
"As viudas d'os vivos e as viudas d'os mortos" (Castro) **41**:88
"As We Desired" (Guillén)
See "Como quisimos"
"As We Know" (Ashbery) **26**:136-138, 141, 156, 172
As We Know: Poems (Ashbery) **26**:131-132, 135-137, 140
"As We Sit" (Creeley) **73**:117-18
"As We with Sappho" (Rexroth)
See "When We with Sappho"
"As Weary Pilgrim" (Bradstreet) **10**:8, 15, 28, 34, 36-7
"As Well as Any Other" (Jackson) **44**:73, 103-4
"As Ye Sow, So Shall Ye Reap" (Very) **86**:166
"As You Leave Me" (Knight) **14**:41, 43, 52
"As You Leave the Room" (Stevens) **110**:210
"As Your Sweet Ways Enraptured Me to Death" (Werfel)
See "Als mich dein Wandeln an den Tod verzückte"
"Asa Gray wrote Increase Lapham:" (Niedecker) **42**:152
"Asahya bhalobasa" (Tagore) **8**:405
"Ascending the Mountain on Double Nine" (Li Po) **29**:183-84, 186
"Ascensão de Vasco da Gama" (Pessoa) **20**:155
"Ascension" (Traherne) **70**:322
"Ascension Day" (Vaughan) **81**:306, 348, 351
"Ascension-Hymn" (Vaughan) **81**:348, 351
"Ascent" (Merwin) **45**:90-1
"The Ascent" (Randall) **86**:289, 334
"Ascent into Hell" (Hope) **56**:266, 271, 278, 288
"Ascetic" (Kavanagh) **33**:69, 92, 96, 120, 161; **105**:156, 163
"aschermittwoch" (Enzensberger) **28**:134
"The Ash Grove" (Thomas) **53**:310
"The Ash Plant" (Heaney) **100**:320
"Ash Snow or Moonlight" (Lee) **24**:240
"The Ash Tree" (Marie de France)
See "Le Fraisne"
"Ash Wednesday" (Seifert) **47**:323
"Ashar nairashya" (Tagore) **8**:405
"Ashes" (Teasdale) **31**:335
Ashes (Bely)
See *Pepel'*
"Ashes, ashes, all fall down" (Piercy) **29**:315, 318, 320
"The Ashes of Gramsci" (Pasolini) **17**:258, 284, 288-89
The Ashes of Gramsci (Pasolini)
See *Le ceneri di Gramscí*
"Ashes of Life" (Millay) **6**:206; **61**:212
"Ashes on Saturday Afternoon" (O'Hara) **45**:167, 231
Ashes: Poems New and Old (Levine) **22**:218-19, 223-24
"Ashurnatsirpal III" (Sandburg) **2**:323
Ash-Wednesday (Eliot) **5**:162-64, 170, 174, 186, 192, 194, 197-206, 209-10; **31**:119, 156
"Asia" (Carver) **54**:23
"Asian Birds" (Bridges) **28**:51, 85
"Asian Figures" (Merwin) **45**:61
Asian Figures (Merwin) **45**:62
"Asian Peace Offers Rejected Without Publication" (Bly) **39**:91
"The Asians Dying" (Merwin) **45**:9, 23, 34, 43, 49, 52
"Aside" (Shapiro) **25**:295
"Aside" (Thomas) **99**:241
"Asides on the Oboe" (Stevens) **110**:192, 226
"Ask Me" (Stafford) **71**:363, 373
"Ask Me No More" (Tennyson) **6**:366; **101**:151-53, 155
"Ask me no more where Jove bestows" (Carew) **29**:5
Ask the Bloody Horse (Abse) **41**:31
"Ask the Roses" (Levine) **22**:224
"Ask Your Mama" (Hughes) **53**:115
Ask Your Mama: 12 Moods for Jazz (Hughes) **1**:249, 251-53, 261, 268, 270; **53**:94, 108, 145, 164, 178
"The Asking" (Soto) **28**:400-01
"Asking for a Reconciliation" (Dafydd ap Gwilym)
See "Gofyn Cymod"
"Asleep" (Owen) **19**:336, 354, 359, 368; **102**:156-57, 167, 222, 224
"L'Asne au Molin" (Scève) **111**:9
Asolando: Fancies and Facts (Browning) **2**:66-67, 88, 96
"L'asparagus" (Ponge) **107**:79, 140
"Aspasia" (Leopardi) **37**:92, 103, 109, 123
"An Aspect of Love, Alive in the Fire and Ice" (Brooks) **7**:82, 88, 91, 94
"Aspecto" (Storni) **33**:237
"The Aspen and the Stream" (Wilbur) **51**:220, 229, 231
"Aspen Tree" (Celan) **10**:112-13
"Aspens" (Thomas) **53**:275, 294-96, 330
"Aspen's Song" (Winters) **82**:319, 343
Asphalt Georgics (Carruth) **10**:77, 91
"An Asphodel" (Ginsberg) **47**:6
"Asphodel, That Greeny Flower" (Williams) **7**:371, 375, 390-92, 402-03; **109**:218, 276, 290, 327-31, 336
"Aspic Surmise" (Mackey) **49**:75-76
"Aspiration" (Traherne) **70**:322
"An Aspiration of the Spirit" (Dobell) **100**:139
"Aspirations" (Verlaine) **32**:384
"Aspiring to Music" (Stern) **115**:285
"Ass" (Cisneros) **52**:162
"The Ass" (Smith) **12**:302-6, 319
"The Assabet" (Thoreau) **30**:195
"The Assassin" (Hall) **70**:32
"Assassin" (Hass) **16**:195
"The Assassin" (Sexton) **2**:365
"Assassin" (Tomlinson) **17**:318, 322, 325-27, 341, 345-46
"The Assassination" (Justice) **64**:251
"Assassination Raga" (Ferlinghetti) **1**:173
"Assault" (Millay) **6**:236, 238
"Assay of the Infinite Man" (Neruda)
See *Tentativa del hombre infinito*
"An Assent to Wildflowers" (Meredith) **28**:192
"The Assertion" (Day Lewis) **11**:146
"The Assignation" (Wright) **36**:280, 343
"Assimilation" (Traherne) **70**:321
"Les assis" (Rimbaud) **57**:184, 203, 210, 212, 216, 293-94, 289289
"The Assistant Draper's Petition" (Hood) **93**:43, 83
"Assommons les pauvres" (Baudelaire) **1**:59
"The Assumption" (Noyes) **27**:136
"The Assumption of Our Lady" (Southwell) **83**:227, 282, 284
"De Assumptione" (Southwell)
See "The Assumption of Our Lady"
Assumptions (Hacker) **47**:80-81, 105, 119
"Assunta" (Pound) **95**:235-36
"Astern" (Benn) **35**:67
"Astigmatism" (Lowell) **13**:84
"Astonishment" (Szymborska)
See "Zdumienie"
"Astræa" (Holmes) **71**:70-71
"Astrea at the Capital" (Whittier) **93**:207
"Astrea Brokage" (Chatterton) **104**:58
"Astrea Redux. A Poem on the Happy Restoration and Return of His Sacred Majesty Charles the Second" (Dryden) **25**:99-101, 103-06
"the astrologer predicts at mary's birth" (Clifton) **17**:37
"Astrometaphysical" (Frost) **39**:233
"Astronauts" (Hayden) **6**:194
"The Astronomer Poems" (Wakoski) **15**:348, 365
"Astrono-mía" (Cervantes) **35**:132
"Astrophel" (Swinburne) **24**:313
"Astrophel: A Pastoral Elegy" (Spenser) **8**:365, 367, 387
Astrophel and Stella (Sidney) **32**:216-17, 224, 227, 231-34, 237-44, 248-53, 267-68, 270, 272-93, 298, 303, 307, 310-11, 315, 318, 320-26, 329-34
Astrophil and Stella (Sidney)
See *Astrophel and Stella*
"The Asylum" (Carruth) **10**:71, 82-4

"At a Bach Concert" (Rich) **5**:352, 387, 393
"At a Bridal" (Hardy) **92**:241, 247
"At a Calvary near the Ancre" (Owen) **19**:334, 341, 362-63; **102**:146, 167, 181
"At a Concert of Music" (Aiken) **26**:24, 72
"At a Country Funeral" (Berry) **28**:16, 29
"At a Country Hotel" (Nemerov) **24**:260
"At a Glance" (Tomlinson) **17**:333
"At a Hasty Wedding" (Hardy) **8**:85
"At a House in Hampstead" (Hardy) **92**:236, 255-56
"At a Loose End" (Lawrence) **54**:244
"At a Lunar Eclipse" (Hardy) **8**:89; **92**:207
"At a March against the Vietnam War" (Bly) **39**:12
"At a Motel near O'Hare Airport" (Kenyon) **57**:46
"At a Party" (Bogan) **12**:106
"At a Party" (Spicer) **78**:302
"At a Poet's Grave" (Meynell) **112**:156, 288
"At a Potato Digging" (Heaney) **18**:200; **100**:195, 211, 231-32, 292
"At a Rehearsal of Uncle Vanya" (Justice) **64**:270
"At a Solemn Music" (Milton)
See "On a Solemn Music"
"At a Solemn Musick" (Schwartz) **8**:289
At A Vacation Exercise (Milton) **29**:241
"At a Wayside Shrine" (Owen) **19**:362
"At a Window" (Sandburg) **2**:300; **41**:225, 243, 268
"At Algeciras—A Meditation upon Death" (Yeats) **20**:342
"at any hour" (Alurista)
See "a cualquier hora"
"At Auden's Grave" (Shapiro) **25**:322
"At Baia" (H. D.) **5**:267
"At Barstow" (Tomlinson) **17**:353, 355
"At Bickford's" (Stern) **115**:249, 253, 277, 293
"At Candle-Lightin' Time" (Dunbar) **5**:122
"At Castellon" (Spender) **71**:202, 204, 227
"At Castle Boterel" (Hardy) **8**:118; **92**:259
"At Cedar Creek" (Wright) **14**:375
"At Chinese Checkers" (Berryman) **64**:82-83
"At Colonus" (Kennedy) **93**:143
"At Cooloolah" (Wright) **14**:344, 371
"At Cove on the Crooked River" (Stafford) **71**:264, 266, 287, 332
"At Darien Bridge" (Dickey) **40**:191
"At Darragh's, I" (Schuyler) **88**:190
"At Dawn" (Milosz) **8**:210
"At Dawn" (Williams) **109**:236
"At Daybreak" (Sassoon) **12**:247
"At Daybreak" (Zagajewski) **27**:389
"At Day-Close in November" (Hardy) **92**:370
"At Dead Low Water" (Curnow) **48**:6
At Dead Low Water, and Sonnets (Curnow) **48**:3, 12
"At Delphi" (Sarton) **39**:339, 341
"At Dusk" (Cummings) **5**:93, 106
"At Easterly" (Clampitt) **19**:100
"At First" (Walker) **30**:355
"At First, at Last" (Swenson) **14**:262, 288
"At Grass" (Larkin) **21**:229, 238-39, 244, 251, 257
"At Hanratty's" (Tomlinson) **17**:361
"At His Execution" (Kipling) **91**:137
"At Holwell Farm" (Tomlinson) **17**:326, 341, 349, 352, 354
"At Home in Heaven" (Southwell) **83**:239, 267, 281, 286, 337
"At It" (Thomas) **99**:261, 286, 297, 299
"At Ithaca" (H. D.) **5**:268
"At Joan's" (O'Hara)
See "Poem Read at Joan Mitchell's"
"At Keats's Grave" (Meynell) **112**:288
"At Lake Desolation" (Rexroth) **95**:259, 270
"At Last" (Montague) **106**:326
"At Last" (Walcott) **46**:236, 248, 274, 278, 289
"At Last" (Whittier) **93**:169, 275
"At Lenin's Tomb" (Service) **70**:144
"At Liberty School" (Stafford) **71**:275-76, 289
"At Lindos" (Sarton) **39**:343
"At Loxahatchie" (Oliver) **75**:293, 302
"At Luca Signorelli's Resurrection of the Body" (Graham) **59**:148, 155-56
"At Lulworth Cove a Century Back" (Hardy) **92**:255
"At McDonald's in Rutland" (Stone) **53**:258
"At Melville's Tomb" (Crane) **3**:90, 103 **99**:53, 75, 89, 107, 133;
"At Middle-Field Gate in February" (Hardy) **92**:326
"At Midnight" (Teasdale) **31**:360, 370
"At Midnight's Hour I Raised my Head" (Thoreau) **30**:254
"At Moonrise and Onwards" (Hardy) **92**:207
"At Muzot" (Sarton) **39**:326, 342
"At My Father's Grave" (MacDiarmid) **9**:156
"At My Hospital Window" (Viereck) **27**:294, 296
"At Night" (Ekeloef) **23**:85
"At Night" (Spender) **71**:188
"At Night the Salmon Move" (Carver) **54**:28
"At Noon" (Kavanagh) **105**:163
"At North Farm" (Ashbery) **26**:159-160
"At Odd Moments" (Brutus) **24**:116
"At One O'Clock in the Morning" (Baudelaire)
See "À une heure du matin"
"At Penshurst" (Waller) **72**:340
"At Rest in the Blast" (Moore) **49**:112, 126, 129, 136
"At Rugmer" (Blunden) **66**:59
"At School" (Smith) **12**:330, 333
"At Sea" (Carman) **34**:199
"At Sea" (Teasdale) **31**:360
"At Sea" (Toomer) **7**:336
"At Sea" (Wagoner) **33**:357
"At Senlis Once" (Blunden) **66**:58
"At Shag's Heath" (Hardy) **92**:268, 277
"At Su Terrace Viewing the Past" (Li Po) **29**:145
At Sundown (Whittier) **93**:345
"At Sunset" (Simic) **69**:305
At Terror Street and Agony Way (Bukowski) **18**:23
"At That Hour" (Joyce)
See "III"
"At the Atlantic Dinner" (Holmes) **71**:93
"At the Ball Game" (Williams) **7**:368, 385; **109**:296
"At the Big A" (Corso) **108**:24
"At the Birth of an Age" (Jeffers) **17**:111, 130, 141-42, 144
"At the Bomb Testing Site" (Stafford) **71**:281-82, 286, 293, 299, 325, 331
"At the Bottom of the Green field She Lies" (Sarton) **39**:323
"At The Brink" (Curnow) **48**:24
"At the Cabaret-Vert, 5 p.m." (Rimbaud)
See "Au caberet-vert cinq heures du soir"
"At the Caberet-Vert" (Rimbaud)
See "Au caberet-vert cinq heures du soir"
"At the Café Door" (Cavafy) **36**:67
"At the Carnival" (Spencer) **77**:341, 344, 346
"at the cemetary walnut grove plantation south carolina 1989" (Clifton) **17**:30
"At the Center" (Stone) **53**:230
"At the Centre" (Gunn) **26**:226
"At the Chairman's Housewarming" (Stafford) **71**:294-95
"At the Chelsea Arts Club" (Mahon) **60**:237
"At the Close" (Meredith) **60**:250
"At the Corner of the Field" (Amichai) **38**:22
"At the Crossroads" (Kinsella) **69**:71
"At the Custer Monument" (Stafford) **71**:326
"At the Désespérade" (Char)
See "À la désespérade"
"At the Dime Store" (Kenyon) **57**:45
"At the Edge" (Tomlinson) **17**:343, 345
"At the End of Sirmione" (Wright) **36**:378
"At the end of two months' holiday there came a night" (Spender) **71**:167, 219
"At the End of War" (Eberhart) **76**:8, 24, 33, 67
"At the Entering of the New Year" (Hardy) **92**:269
"At the Executed Murderer's Grave" (Wright) **36**:291, 303, 315, 324, 337, 353, 362, 373-74, 399
"At the Fair" (Stafford) **71**:286
"At the Fall of an Age" (Jeffers) **17**:141, 144
"At the Faucet of June" (Williams) **7**:382-83, 387-89, 410
"At the Feeder" (Kenyon) **57**:39
"At the feet of others I did not forget" (Lermontov)
See "U nog drugikh ne zabyval"
"At the Ferocious phenomenon of 5 O'clock I find Myself" (Cummings) **5**:93
"At the Fillmore" (Levine) **22**:224
"At the Fishhouses" (Bishop) **3**:42, 46, 48; **34**:57-8, 61, 97, 101, 105-05, 133-34, 144, 181-85, 189
"At the Frick" (Hecht) **70**:94
"At the Funeral of Great-Aunt Mary" (Bly) **39**:11
"At the Gare Bruxelles-Midi" (Ferlinghetti) **1**:183
"At the Gate of the Valley" (Herbert) **50**:34
"At the Gates of the Tombs" (Sandburg) **2**:307; **41**:271, 314
"At the German Meetingplace" (Éluard)
See "Au Rendez-vous allemand"
At the German Meetingplace (Éluard)
See *Au rendez-vous allemand*
"At the German Writers Conference in Munich" (Dove) **6**:109
"At the Granite Gate" (Carman) **34**:213
"At the Grave of Eloisa and Abelard, in Père la Chaise" (Howe) **81**:22
"At the Grave of Henry James" (Auden) **92**:38, 58
"At the Grave of Henry Vaughan" (Sassoon) **12**:246-47
"At the Grave of Virgil Campbell" (Chappell) **105**:27, 30, 32, 50, 74, 81, 83
"At the Great Release" (Carman) **34**:226
"At the Hairdresser's" (Brooks) **7**:58, 68, 86, 102
"At the Head of This Street a Gasping Organ is Waving Moth-" (Cummings) **5**:93
"At the Head Table" (Kinsella) **69**:79, 138, 142
"At the Hemingway Memorial" (Wagoner) **33**:348
"At the Hour of the Breaking of the Rocks" (Warren) **37**:331
"At the IGA: Franklin, New Hampshire" (Kenyon) **57**:45
"At the Indian Killer's Grave" (Lowell) **3**:202
"At the Klamath Berry Festival" (Stafford) **71**:341
"At the Last Rites for Two Hotrodders" (Kennedy) **93**:131
"At the Lincoln Monument in Washington, August 28, 1963" (Walker) **20**:277-78
"At the Loom" (Duncan) **75**:120, 189, 215
"At the Loom: Passages 2" (Duncan) **2**:107
"At the Mouth of a Creek" (Wagoner) **33**:374
"At the Museum, 1938" (Stone) **53**:257
"At the Museum of Modern Art" (Swenson) **14**:265
"At the National Black Assembly" (Baraka) **4**:28, 38; **113**:24
"At the Old Place" (O'Hara) **45**:115, 126
"At the Pantomime" (Holmes) **71**:93
"At the Park Dance" (Snodgrass) **74**:284, 298, 300-301, 310-11
"At the Piano" (Hardy) **8**:93
"At the Playground" (Stafford) **71**:322
"At the Pool" (Mahon) **60**:190
"At the Public Market Museum: Charleston, South Carolina" (Kenyon) **57**:6, 23
"At the Pyramid of Cestius" (Hardy) **92**:236

"At the Railroad Station on an Autumn Morning" (Carducci)
See "Alla Stazione in una Mattina d'Autunno"
"At the River Charles" (Viereck) **27**:282
"At the round earths imagin'd corners, blow" (Donne) **43**:160, 163
"At the Salt Marsh" (Stafford) **71**:257
"At the Saturday Club" (Holmes) **71**:117, 120
"At the Screen Door" (Komunyakaa) **51**:24-25
"At the Sea-Side" (Stevenson) **84**:346
"At the Slackening of the Tide" (Wright) **36**:281-82, 299, 324
"At the Sources of the Clitumnus" (Carducci)
See "Alle fonti del Clitumno"
"At the Station on an Autumn Morning" (Carducci)
See "Alla Stazione in una Mattina d'Autunno"
"At the Stilli's Mouth" (Hugo) **68**:270
"At the Stoplight by the Paupers' Graves" (Kennedy) **93**:141
"At the Summer Solstice" (Kenyon) **57**:4
"At the Summit" (Holmes) **71**:96
"At the Summit" (Stafford) **71**:267
"At the Theatre" (Cavafy) **36**:41, 42
"At the Tomb of the Czech Kings" (Seifert) **47**:326
"At the Tombs of the Medicis" (Barker) **77**:20
"At the Tourist Centre in Boston" (Atwood) **8**:5, 23
"At the Town Dump" (Kenyon) **57**:39-40
"At the Vacancy Sign" (Simic) **69**:305
At the Very Edge of the Sea (Akhmatova)
See *U samovo morya*
"At the Voice of a Bird" (Carman) **34**:210
"At the Wake of Dylan Thomas" (Barker) **77**:18
"At the Well" (Piercy) **29**:300
"At the Wellhead" (Heaney) **100**:245, 247
"At the Western Ocean's Edge" (Kinsella) **69**:97, 132
"At The-Place-of-Sadness" (Gallagher) **9**:64
"At This Point" (Montale)
See "A questo punto"
"At Tintagel" (Teasdale) **31**:335
"At Toomebridge" (Heaney) **100**:243, 327
"At Utter Loaf" (Riley) **48**:334
"At Waking" (Hardy) **8**:104
"At Washington" (Whittier) **93**:207
"At Welsh's Tomb" (Wakoski) **15**:353
"At Zime Junction Once More" (Yevtushenko) **40**:351-52
Atalanta in Calydon (Swinburne) **24**:340
"Atalanta in Camden Town" (Carroll) **74**:29
"Atalanta's Race" (Morris) **55**:242, 249
Atarashiki yokujō (Hagiwara) **18**:175
"Atardeceres" (Borges) **32**:60, 102-03, 124
"Atavism" (Stafford) **71**:317, 336
"Atavism" (Wylie) **23**:301, 307
"Atavismo" (Pavese) **13**:209, 214
Atemwende (Celan) **10**:96-7, 105, 110
"Atheist" (Traherne) **70**:321
"Athena in the front lines" (Piercy) **29**:313, 317
"Athene's Song" (Boland) **58**:42
"Atherton's Gambit" (Robinson) **1**:466
"Ations" (Silverstein) **49**:331, 335
"Atlanta in Camden Town" (Carroll) **18**:46
Atlanta Offering Poems (Harper) **21**:189
"The Atlantic" (Tomlinson) **17**:333
"Atlantic City Waiter" (Cullen) **20**:52, 64
"Atlantic Coast Reggae" (Jordan) **38**:132
"Atlantic Door" (Birney) **52**:35, 92
"The Atlantic Monthly, December 1970" (Reed) **68**:333
"Atlantic Oil" (Pavese) **13**:223
"The Atlantides" (Thoreau) **30**:203
"Atlantis" (Crane) **3**:90, 97, 106, 110-11
"Atlantis" (Szymborska) **44**:300
Atlantis (Doty) **53**:47, 49, 51, 53-55, 61, 63, 65-66
"An Atlas of the Difficult World" (Rich) **5**:398
An Atlas of the Difficult World: Poems, 1988-1991 (Rich) **5**:398-99
"Atom" (Traherne) **70**:320-22
"Atonement" (Traherne) **70**:321
Atta Troll (Heine)
See *Atta Troll: Ein Sommernachtstraum*
Atta Troll: Ein Sommernachtstraum (Heine) **25**:132-34, 137-38, 164
"Attack" (Sassoon) **12**:266, 283-84, 286
"An Attempt at a Room" (Tsvetaeva)
See "Popytka komnaty"
"An Attempt at Jealousy" (Tsvetaeva)
See "Popytka revnosti"
"Attempt to Discover Life" (Stevens) **110**:86-87
L'Attente (Sainte-Beuve) **110**:37
"Attention, Attention" (Baraka) **4**:24; **113**:75
"Attibon Legba" (Brathwaite) **56**:75
"The Attic" (Mahon) **60**:141, 155, 187, 228
"Attic" (Sikelianos) **29**:368
"The Attic Landscape" (Melville) **82**:74, 150
"The Attic Which Is Desire" (Williams) **7**:351, 399; **109**:278, 335
"Attis" (Tennyson) **6**:363
"Attoniti, amanti" (Zanzotto) **65**:269
"Atumpan" (Brathwaite) **56**:100
"Atys the Enthusiast" (Hunt) **73**:138
"Atys, the Land of Biscay" (Housman) **2**:179, 181
"Au cabaret-vert" (Rimbaud)
See "Au caberet-vert cinq heures du soir"
"Au caberet-vert cinq heures du soir" (Rimbaud) **3**:283; **57**:203, 241, 244, 253
"Au Clair de la lune" (MacDiarmid) **9**:191
"Au Comte d'Orsay" (Lamartine) **16**:267
"Au cœur de mon amour" (Éluard) **38**:70
"Au Jardin" (Pound) **95**:122-23
"Au lecteur" (Baudelaire) **1**:46, 57, 67, 70; **106**:23-24, 28, 80, 88, 92-93, 97-98, 125, 127, 137-39, 152, 172
"Au Loisir" (Sainte-Beuve) **110**:65
"Au platane" (Valéry) **9**:365, 394-96
"Au Rendez-vous allemand" (Éluard) **38**:63
Au rendez-vous allemand (Éluard) **38**:79
"Au revoir" (Éluard) **38**:67
"Au Rossignol" (Lamartine) **16**:280
"Au Roy" (Ronsard)
See "Discours au Roy"
"Au Salon" (Pound) **4**:364; **95**:122
"Aubade" (Chappell) **105**:50
"Aubade" (Empson) **104**:84-86
"Aubade" (Glück) **16**:133
"Aubade" (Larkin) **21**:259
"Aubade" (Lowell) **13**:93
"Aubade" (Sitwell) **3**:297
"Aubade" (Smith) **12**:331
"Aubade for Hope" (Warren) **37**:282-84, 366, 377
"Aubade: Harlem" (Merton) **10**:340
"Aubade: Lake Erie" (Merton) **10**:333, 340, 350
"Aubade: Opal and Silver" (Doty) **53**:54
"Aubade—The Annunciation" (Merton) **10**:339
"Aube" (Rimbaud) **3**:261-62, 264; **57**:174, 228, 239, 244, 250, 275, 284
"L'Aube a l'envers" (Verlaine) **32**:378
"Aube, fille des larmes, rétablis" (Bonnefoy) **58**:167
"L'aube spirituelle" (Baudelaire) **1**:56, 63
"Aubépine" (Char) **56**:120
"L'Auberge" (Verlaine) **32**:375-76
"The Auction" (Kinnell) **26**:286
"Auction at Stanbury" (Hughes) **89**:190
"The Auctor to the Reader" (Whitney) **116**:271-72, 277, 287, 290, 311
"Audacity of the Lower Gods" (Komunyakaa) **51**:30
"Auden Aetat XX, LX" (Spender) **71**:191
"Auden and MacNeice: their Last Will and Testament" (MacNeice) **61**:171
"Audenesque" (Heaney) **100**:240
Au-Dessus du vent (Char) **56**:117
"Auditors In" (Kavanagh) **33**:62, 99, 121-2, 137, 148, 161; **105**:96, 110, 156
"Audley Court" (Tennyson) **6**:365
"Audubon" (Carson) **64**:221
"Audubon" (Niedecker) **42**:152
Audubon, A Vision (Warren) **37**:307-8, 310, 313, 326-28, 330, 334, 340, 345-50, 358-59, 361, 363, 366, 371, 373, 381, 384
"Auf dem See" (Goethe) **5**:255
"Aufblick" (Benn) **35**:50
"Aufschwung" (Werfel) **101**:355
"The Augean Stables" (Heaney) **100**:242-44
"The Augsburg Adoration" (Jarrell) **41**:180, 197
"Auguri per Proprio Compleanno" (Ungaretti) **57**:376
"Auguries of Innocence" (Blake) **12**:35-6; **63**:5, 7
"Augurios" (Paz) **1**:361
"Augury for an Infant" (Randall) **86**:288
"August" (Belloc) **24**:29
"August" (Oliver) **75**:295
"August" (Rich) **5**:371
"August" (Riley) **48**:309
"August" (Wylie) **23**:319, 322, 332
"August 9th 1" (Thumboo) **30**:332
"August 9th 2" (Thumboo) **30**:333
"August 19th..." (Hughes) **53**:114
"August 22, 1939" (Rexroth) **20**:195; **95**:260, 270, 305, 309, 311, 315, 333
"August, 1914" (Masefield) **78**:8-9, 35-36, 54-55, 64, 71-72
"August, 1968" (Auden) **92**:70
"August Evening" (Hughes) **89**:135
"August First" (Carruth) **10**:91
"August first, 1974" (Schuyler) **88**:200
"August Hail" (Cunningham) **92**:140, 189
"August Journal" (Hacker) **47**:104, 106, 116
"An August Midnight" (Hardy) **8**:112; **92**:197-201, 254, 258, 261, 319, 328
"August Night" (Swenson) **14**:266, 284
"August Night" (Teasdale) **31**:335
"August on Sourdough, A Visit from Dick Brewer" (Snyder) **21**:288
"August Rain, After Haying" (Kenyon) **57**:11, 41, 43
"August Revival: Crosby Junction" (Warren) **37**:331
"An August Salmon" (Hughes) **89**:135
"August Sun" (Bly) **39**:70
August Thoughts (Sainte-Beuve)
See *Pensées d'août*
"August Was Foggy" (Snyder) **21**:288
Aujourd'hui (Hugo) **17**:80
"Aul Bastundzi" (Lermontov) **18**:300
"The Auld Farmer's New Year Morning Salutation" (Burns)
See "The Auld Farmer's New Year's Day Address to His Auld Mare Maggie"
"The Auld Farmer's New Year's Day Address to His Auld Mare Maggie" (Burns) **6**:78; **114**:42, 101-2
"Auld Lang Syne" (Burns) **6**:59, 75, 98-9; **114**:29, 87, 168
"AÚN" (Darío) **15**:98
Aún (Neruda) **4**:289
Auncient Aqueyntaunce (Skelton) **25**:345, 351
"Aunque cegué de mirarte" (Juana Inés de la Cruz) **24**:187
"Aunt Chloe's Politics" (Harper) **21**:200, 202, 213
"Aunt Leaf" (Oliver) **75**:292
"Aunt Mabel" (Stafford) **71**:286, 380
"Aunt Sue's Stories" (Hughes) **53**:82, 118
"Aunt Tabitha" (Holmes) **71**:68
"The Auntie Otherside" (Serote) **113**:292
"Auntie's Skirts" (Stevenson) **84**:299, 314
"Aunts" (McGuckian) **27**:95
"La aurora" (García Lorca) **3**:141
"Aurora Borealis" (Dove) **6**:110
Aurora Leigh (Barrett Browning) **6**:2, 6-7, 10-13, 21-3, 25-6, 31-2, 34-8, 40, 44, 46; **62**:3-11, 13-17, 23-24, 26-28, 30, 34-37, 39-40,

42-44, 48-51, 53-54, 59-64, 68-69, 72-73, 75-76, 79-80, 84, 93-97, 100, 102-3, 105-9, 111-16, 122-25, 128-32, 134-36, 140-41, 143-45, 154-61
"The Auroras of Autumn" (Justice) **64**:282
"The Auroras of Autumn" (Roethke) **15**:280
"The Auroras of Autumn" (Stevens) **6**:338; **110**:96, 156, 158, 193, 225-26, 228-29, 231
The Auroras of Autumn (Stevens) **6**:303, 335; **110**:226-27, 229
"Aurore" (Valéry) **9**:356, 363, 365, 367-68, 371, 394, 396
"Aus dem Traum einer Hölle" (Werfel) **101**:337
"Aus der Harzreise" (Heine) **25**:139
"Aus einer Sturmnacht" (Rilke) **2**:277
"Auschwitz" (Quasimodo) **47**:287
"Auschwitz, mon Amour" (Montague) **106**:276
"Ausencia" (Borges) **22**:94; **32**:60, 82
Ausgewahlte gedichte (Celan) **10**:102
"Auspice of Jewels" (Jackson) **44**:12
"Auspices" (Hecht) **70**:100
"Aussenminister" (Benn) **35**:58
"Aussi bien que les cigales" (Apollinaire) **7**:18, 22
"Aussöhnung" (Goethe) **5**:250-51
Austerities (Simic) **69**:311, 313, 318
"Australia" (Hope) **56**:266, 283
"Australia to Abraham Lincoln" (Gilmore) **87**:303
"Authentic Edens in a Pagan Sea" (Melville) **82**:142
"Author of light" (Campion) **87**:54-56
"The Author of the Jesus Papers Speaks" (Sexton) **79**:218
"The Author to her Book" (Bradstreet) **10**:7, 18, 27, 34
"The Author to the Critical Peruser" (Traherne) **70**:205, 235, 258, 263, 301, 303, 2139
"The Author to the Reader" (Southwell)
See "To the Reader"
"The Author upon Himself" (Swift) **9**:295-96, 304, 306, 308-09
"Authoris Emblema" (Vaughan)
See "The Author's Emblem"
The Authors Dreame to the Ladie Marie the Countesse Dowager of Pembrooke (Lanyer) **60**:5, 79, 97, 111-12, 115
"The Author's Earnest Cry and Prayer, to the Right Honorable, the Scotch Representatives in the House of Commons" (Burns) **6**:78-9; **114**:28, 115, 135, 138, 140-46
"The Author's Emblem" (Vaughan) **81**:317-18, 323, 366
"The Author's Last Words to His Students" (Blunden) **66**:18, 24, 31, 51
"The Author's Manner of Living" (Swift) **9**:295
"Author's Note on Marabouts and Planted Poets" (Viereck) **27**:259, 262
"Author's Prologue" (Thomas) **52**:226, 237, 263, 277, 290, 303-4
"The Auto Ride" (Williams) **109**:286
"Auto Wreck" (Shapiro) **25**:279, 288, 297, 312, 319, 325
"Autobiografía" (Fuertes) **27**:49
"Autobiographia literaria" (O'Hara) **45**:177
"Autobiographies" (Mahon) **60**:160
"Autobiography" (Ferlinghetti) **1**:177-80, 183-84, 187
"Autobiography" (Gunn) **26**:205, 208
"Autobiography" (Harjo) **27**:71
"Autobiography" (MacLeish) **47**:193
"Autobiography" (MacNeice) **61**:110, 135, 168-69
"Autobiography" (Thomas) **99**:271
Autobiography (Zukofsky) **11**:365
"Autobiography in 5 Parts" (Berrigan) **103**:35
"Autobiography of a Comedian" (Ciardi) **69**:9, 14
Autobiography of Red: A Novel in Verse (Carson) **64**:217-19, 221, 236-39, 241-42, 244-45
"Autobiography of the Present" (Jackson) **44**:96
"Autochthon" (Masters) **1**:333; **36**:177
"Automatism of Taste" (Tzara) **27**:235
"The Automaton" (Jarrell) **41**:127
"Automne" (Apollinaire) **7**:42
"L'automne" (Lamartine) **16**:277, 290, 298, 301
"Automne" (Verlaine) **32**:400-02, 404-06
"Automne malade" (Apollinaire) **7**:39, 42-3
"Automobile" (Seferis) **66**:119, 123-25
"Autoprólogo" (Fuertes) **27**:23
"Autopsicografia" (Pessoa) **20**:172
"The Autopsy" (Elytis) **21**:123
"The Autopsy Room" (Carver) **54**:14
"Autopsychography" (Pessoa)
See "Autopsicografia"
"Autoretrato" (Parra) **39**:270, 300
"Autorretrato barroco" (Storni) **33**:293-94, 296
"Autre complainte de Lord Pierrot" (Laforgue) **14**:62, 81, 88, 97
"Autre complainte de l'orgue de barbarie" (Laforgue) **14**:81, 98
"Autre éventail" (Mallarmé) **102**:101
"L'autre nuit je veillais dans mon lit sans humière" (Sainte-Beuve) **110**:69
"Autre sonnet" (Mallarmé) **102**:66
"Une autre voix" (Bonnefoy) **58**:174
Autrefois (Hugo) **17**:80
Autres balades (Christine de Pizan) **68**:11, 22, 76, 192
Autres Balades 7 (Christine de Pizan) **68**:73
Autres Balades 17 (Christine de Pizan) **68**:74
"Autumn" (Cunningham) **92**:140, 182
"Autumn" (Dickey) **40**:186
"Autumn" (Hood)
See "Ode to Autumn"
"Autumn" (Ignatow) **34**:322
"The Autumn" (Lamartine)
See "L'automne"
"Autumn" (Lowell) **13**:97
"Autumn" (Neruda)
See "Otoño"
"Autumn" (Pasternak) **6**:266
"Autumn" (Paz)
See "Otoño"
"Autumn" (Smith) **12**:345
"Autumn" (Thoreau) **30**:286
"Autumn" (Tomlinson) **17**:339
"Autumn Begins in Martins Ferry, Ohio" (Wright) **36**:324, 339-40, 374, 389-90
"The Autumn Bleat of the Weathervane Trombone" (Chappell) **105**:24, 44-45, 59, 72-74
"An Autumn Burning" (Berry) **28**:9
"Autumn Cellars" (Montale) **13**:149-50
"Autumn Cove Song #5" (Li Po) **29**:145
"Autumn Equinox" (Rich) **5**:351-52, 393
"Autumn Evening" (Merwin) **45**:88
"Autumn Forest" (Pasternak) **6**:267
"Autumn Gold: New England Fall" (Ginsberg) **4**:54
"Autumn I" (Ignatow) **34**:306
"Autumn in California" (Rexroth) **20**:194, 214; **95**:257, 270, 310, 332
"Autumn in Funland" (Abse) **41**:30
"Autumn in Non-Yuch" (Empson)
See "Autumn on Nan-Yueh"
"Autumn in Tarusa" (Akhmadulina)
See "Osen' v Taruse"
Autumn Journal (MacNeice) **61**:106-7, 109-10, 115, 123-26, 134, 144-45, 148-55, 161, 163-66, 172-73, 175, 180-82, 185-86
"Autumn Lament" (Mallarmé)
See "Plainte d'automne"
"The Autumn Leaf" (Very) **86**:68-69
"Autumn Leaves" (Schuyler) **88**:176
"Autumn Meditation" (Wang Wei) **18**:343
"Autumn Movement" (Sandburg) **41**:313
"Autumn Nature Notes" (Hughes) **89**:125
"Autumn near Prague" (Muir) **49**:228, 238
"Autumn 1980" (Hacker) **47**:105
"Autumn, 1922" (Melville) **82**:8
"The Autumn of Many Years" (Rexroth) **95**:275
"Autumn on Nan-Yueh" (Empson) **104**:85, 89, 94
"Autumn on the Land" (Thomas) **99**:242, 258
"Autumn (Parc Monceau)" (Teasdale) **31**:339
"Autumn Scene" (Snodgrass) **74**:313
Autumn Sequel (MacNeice)
See *Autumn Sequel: A Rhetorical Poem*
Autumn Sequel: A Rhetorical Poem (MacNeice) **61**:127-28, 162-66, 181-82
"Autumn Sequence" (Rich) **5**:363, 382
"Autumn Song" (Darío)
See "Canción otoñal"
"Autumn Song" (Verlaine)
See "Chanson d'automne"
"Autumn Song" (Werfel)
See "Herbstlied"
"The Autumn Sonnets" (Sarton) **39**:340, 360-1
"Autumn Valentine" (Parker) **28**:365
"Autumn Variations" (Snodgrass) **74**:332
"Autumnal" (Darío) **15**:117
"Autumnal" (Eberhart) **76**:9, 45
"Autumnal" (Owen) **102**:226
Autumnal Leaves (Hugo) **17**:44
"The Autumnall" (Donne) **43**:134
"Autunno romantico" (Carducci) **46**:48, 77, 80
"Auvergnat" (Belloc) **24**:34
"Aux arbres" (Bonnefoy) **58**:130-33
"Aux Chrétiens" (Lamartine) **16**:280
"Aux Ecluses du vide" (Césaire) **25**:12
"Aux ruines de Montfort-L'Amaury" (Hugo) **17**:89
"Avant-dernier mot" (Laforgue) **14**:95
"L'avant-Glanum" (Char) **56**:177
"Avanti! Avanti!" (Carducci) **46**:28, 50
"Avarice" (Herbert) **4**:102, 130
"Avarice" (Traherne) **70**:322
"The Avatar" (Melville) **82**:77-78
"Ave" (Rossetti) **44**:207-8
"Ave atque Vale" (Swinburne) **24**:321, 330-35, 337
"Ave Imperatrix!" (Kipling) **3**:190
"Ave Maria" (Crane) **3**:84, 86
"Ave Maria" (O'Hara) **45**:115, 147, 171-74, 207-8, 218
"'Avec Ardeur'" (Moore)
See "Occasionem Cognosce"
"Avec la Mécanique sous les Palmes" (Berrigan) **103**:36
"Avenel Gray" (Robinson)
See "Mortmain"
"Avenue" (Pinsky) **27**:175
"The Avenue Bearing the Initial of Christ into the New World" (Kinnell) **26**:236-37, 239, 241, 257, 262, 264, 289
"Avenue of Limes" (Pasternak) **6**:267
"The Avenue of Poplars" (Williams) **7**:382
"The Average Egyptian Faces Death" (Updike) **90**:357
"Averroes' Search" (Borges)
See "La busca de Averroes"
"Averroes's Search" (Borges)
See "La busca de Averroes"
"L'Aveu dans l'obscurité" (Jaccottet) **98**:176-77
"L'Aveugle Prédestiné tourne de lex dos aux passants" (Éluard) **38**:91
"Les Aveugles" (Baudelaire) **106**:80
"Aviary" (McGuckian) **27**:81, 98
"Avila 1" (Yau) **61**:333
"Avila 4" (Yau) **61**:331
"Avis de tirs" (Césaire) **25**:29
"Aviso" (Parra) **39**:272
"Aviso a los gobernantes del mundo" (Fuertes) **27**:2
"Avisos" (Pessoa) **20**:162
"Avocado Lake" (Soto) **28**:375, 379
"Avoiding News by the River" (Merwin) **45**:21, 60
"Avon" (Carman)
See "Low Tide on Avon"
"Avondale" (Smith) **12**:352
"Avondall" (Smith) **12**:352

Avon's Harvest (Robinson) **1**:465-66, 468-69, 483
"Avtobus" (Tsvetaeva) **14**:325, 327
"Awake, awake, thou heavy spright" (Campion) **87**:55-56, 66
Awake in the Red Desert (Bissett) **14**:12, 14, 18-19
"Awake, my heart, to be loved: awake, awake" (Bridges) **28**:53, 63, 87
"Awake, thou spring of speaking grace" (Campion) **87**:13, 58, 70
"Awakening" (Bly) **39**:11, 84, 90
"The Awakening" (Brathwaite) **56**:8
"The Awakening" (Creeley) **73**:10-11, 104
"Awakening" (Herbert) **50**:19
"Awakening" (Stryk) **27**:184, 186-87, 189, 206, 213
Awakening (Stryk) **27**:181, 195-98, 202-3, 213-16
"Awakening of the Waterfall" (Tagore)
See "Nirjharer svapnabhanga"
"Awakening to Music" (Chappell) **105**:18, 38
Awakening to Music (Chappell) **105**:37-38
"Away!" (Frost) **39**:237
"Away" (Riley) **48**:289, 325
Away (Creeley) **73**:54-55
"Away! Away! Away! Away!" (Thoreau) **30**:203, 240, 265
"Away Go We" (de la Mare) **77**:112
"Away; Let Nought to Love Displeasing" (Gray) **80**:137
"Away, Melancholy" (Smith) **12**:333
"Awe and Devastation of Solomos" (Elytis) **21**:135
"Awful Music" (Merton) **10**:337
The Awful Rowing Toward God (Sexton) **2**:360, 367-68, 371-73; **79**:200, 202, 209-12, 214-17, 219-20, 223, 225, 232-34, 236-39, 244, 251-52, 254, 257, 298, 310, 336
"Awkward Bridge" (Spicer) **78**:310
"AWOL" (Abse) **41**:31
"The Awthorn" (Clare) **23**:46-7
"Ax" (Simic) **69**:314
"Axe Handles" (Snyder) **21**:308
Axe Handles (Snyder) **21**:299-302, 307-10, 320
"The Ax-Helve" (Frost) **1**:215; **39**:235
The Axion Esti (Elytis) **21**:118, 120-30, 133
"Axis" (Paz) **48**:188
"Axum" (Brathwaite) **56**:29
"Ay negra, si tu supiera" (Guillén) **23**:111, 142
"Ay qué tristeza que tengo!" (Guillén) **23**:119-20, 127
"Aye, Black Lover, If You Only Knew" (Guillén)
See "Ay negra, si tu supiera"
"Ayer Biru" (Thumboo) **30**:321
"Ayer me dijeron negro" (Guillén) **23**:142
"Ayianapa II" (Seferis) **66**:167
"Ayíasma" (Ekeloef) **23**:64
"Aylmer's Field" (Tennyson) **6**:362; **101**:161
"¡Ayme!" (Storni) **33**:276
"Aymerillot" (Hugo) **17**:58
"The Azalea" (Patmore) **59**:209, 215, 239
"AZEGBEQUX" (Corso) **108**:8
Ázma iroikó ke pénthimo yia ton haméno anthipolohaghó tis Alvanías (Elytis) **21**:115, 120, 124, 127-29
"Azrail" (Lermontov) **18**:300
"Azucena" (Alurista) **34**:22
Azul . . . (Darío) **15**:78, 86-7, 91-2, 94-6, 102-03, 105-07, 115, 117-18, 120
"L'azur" (Mallarmé) **4**:199-200, 208, 213; **102**:95, 110
"The Azure" (Mallarmé)
See "L'azur"
"Azure and Gold" (Lowell) **13**:60
"B Negative" (Kennedy) **93**:138
"Babbitry" (Stryk) **27**:211
"The Babe" (Olson) **19**:319-20
"Babe" (Traherne) **70**:322
"Babel" (Traherne) **70**:322
"Babette" (Service) **70**:141
"Babi Yar" (Yevtushenko) **40**:339, 343-46, 350, 352, 356, 359, 365, 368, 370
"The Babies" (Strand) **63**:158
"Babii Yar" (Yevtushenko)
See "Babi Yar"
"Babočka" (Brodsky) **9**:29
"Babord pour tous" (Péret) **33**:230
"Babushka" (Akhmadulina) **43**:32-33
"Babushka" (Yevtushenko) **40**:340
"The Baby" (Nash) **21**:278
"Baby" (Sexton) **2**:367; **79**:194
"Baby Boom Che" (Alexie) **53**:16
"The Baby Carriage Forgotten near a Shop" (Shvarts)
See "Koliaska, zabytaia u magazina"
"Baby Face" (Sandburg) **41**:296
"Baby Marigold" (Wickham) **110**:259
"Baby Picture" (Sexton) **2**:370; **79**:217
"Baby song" (Gunn) **26**:210
"Baby Tortoise" (Lawrence) **54**:187
"Baby V" (Levine)
See "Baby Villon"
"Baby Villon" (Levine) **22**:213
"Babyhood" (Swinburne) **24**:323
"Babylon" (Tennyson) **101**:193
"Babylon" (Tolson) **88**:344
"Babylon Revisited" (Baraka) **4**:18; **113**:47, 49, 51-52
"Bacardi Spreads the Eagle's Wing" (Crane) **99**:111, 114, 123
"Baccalaureate" (MacLeish) **47**:182
"The Bacchae" (H. D.) **5**:305
"The Bacchae Sonnets" (Schwerner) **42**:196
"Bacchanales" (Ronsard) **11**:230-32, 234
"Bacchanalia" (Pasternak) **6**:267
"Bacchic" (Cavafy) **36**:52
"Bacchus" (Emerson) **18**:85, 99, 103, 106
"Bacchus" (Empson) **104**:84, 91-92, 94, 97, 122
"Bacchus and Ariadne" (Hunt) **73**:148-49
"Bacchus and his crew" (Cavafy) **36**:57
"Bacchus and the Pirates" (Noyes) **27**:121, 124-25, 133
"Bacchus in Tuscany" (Hunt) **73**:136
"Bachelor" (Meredith) **28**:189
"Bachelor Uncle" (Wright) **14**:348
"Back" (Kenyon) **57**:36
"Back Again, Home" (Madhubuti) **5**:324, 329, 338
The Back Country (Snyder) **21**:288, 291-92, 296, 300
"Back Door" (Montague) **106**:328
"Back from a Walk" (García Lorca)
See "Vuelta de paseo"
"Back from Australia" (Betjeman) **75**:32
"Back from the City" (Kenyon) **57**:4, 39
"Back Home" (Stafford) **71**:378
"Back Home in Pompeii" (Ciardi) **69**:56
"back in th city" (Bissett) **14**:30
"The Back Lane" (Kinsella) **69**:79, 135-37, 143
"The Back o' Beyond" (MacDiarmid) **9**:196
"Back of Gino's Place" (Hugo) **68**:275
"Back Then" (Komunyakaa) **51**:30
"Back Then" (Sexton)
See "Where It Was Back Then"
"Back to Life" (Gunn) **26**:192, 212
"Back to the Mother Breast" (Jackson) **44**:61
"The Back-Again" (MacNeice) **61**:121
"Backdrop Addresses Cowboy" (Atwood) **8**:4, 16, 41
"Background Noises" (Szirtes) **51**:171
"Background with Revolutionaries" (MacLeish) **47**:189, 240-41, 255
"The Backlash Blues" (Hughes) **1**:251, 257
Backpack Notes (Matsuo Basho)
See *Oi no kobumi*
"The Backside of the Academy" (Rukeyser) **12**:236
"Backtracking" (Wagoner) **33**:339
"Backward Bill" (Silverstein) **49**:327
"A Backward Glance o'er Travel'd Roads" (Whitman) **91**:345
"The Backward Look" (Heaney) **100**:196, 214, 295, 336
"The Backward Look" (Nemerov) **24**:287, 301
"Backyard" (Ignatow) **34**:306, 309
"Backyard" (Wright) **14**:377
"The Bacterial War" (Nemerov) **24**:298
"Bad Baby" (Enright) **93**:34
"A Bad, Bad Man" (Brown) **55**:102, 104, 122
"Bad Blood" (Rimbaud)
See "Mauvais sang"
Bad Boys (Cisneros) **52**:156
The Bad Child's Book of Beasts (Belloc) **24**:12, 23-6, 35
"Bad Company" (Collins) **68**:217-18
"Bad Dreams" (Browning) **2**:59
"Bad Dreams" (Pinsky) **27**:145
"Bad Faith" (Cavafy) **36**:86, 117
"The Bad Glazier" (Baudelaire)
See "Le mauvais vitrier"
"The Bad Host" (Wickham) **110**:259
"Bad Man" (Hughes) **1**:270; **53**:82, 138-39
"Bad Morning" (Hughes) **1**:241
"Bad Ol' Stagolee" (Walker) **20**:287
"The Bad Old Days" (Rexroth) **20**:218; **95**:250, 258, 260, 273, 306, 308-9, 317
The Bad Parents' Garden of Verse (Nash) **21**:264-65
"Bad Penny" (Levine) **22**:218
"The Bad Season Makes the Poet Sad" (Herrick) **9**:89, 103, 109, 115
"Bad Times" (Oppen) **35**:289
"Bad Vision at the Skagit" (Hugo) **68**:236
"Bad War: a New Year's Card" (Warren) **37**:306
"Badger" (Clare) **23**:7
"The Badgers" (Heaney) **18**:219, 244
"The Badlands" (Hughes) **89**:160, 162
"Badman of the Guest Professor " (Reed) **68**:321, 323-24, 329, 332-33, 348
"Bad-Man Stagolee" (Walker)
See "Bad Ol' Stagolee"
"Badon Hill" (Masefield) **78**:47
"Bag Woman" (Randall) **86**:347
"Bagabonds" (Rimbaud) **57**:191
"The Bagel" (Ignatow) **34**:204, 207, 305, 308
"Bagel Shop Jazz" (Kaufman) **74**:181, 208, 224-26, 228-32, 240
"Baggot Street Deserta" (Kinsella) **69**:66, 81, 85, 95, 98, 109, 120, 122, 135, 138
"Bagpipe Music" (MacNeice) **61**:133-34, 137, 157
"Baha'u'llah in the Garden of Ridwan" (Hayden) **6**:185-86, 196, 198
"Bahia, Brazil" (Carver) **54**:22, 24
"Bahnhofstrasse" (Joyce) **22**:137
"Bahu" (Tagore) **8**:407
"Baie des Anges, Nice" (Enright) **93**:16
"Baignée" (Valéry) **9**:392
"La bailarina española" (Martí) **76**:101
"La bailerina de los pies desnudos" (Darío) **15**:80
"Le baiser" (Char) **15**:138, 144, 171
"Le Baiser" (Éluard) **38**:62
"Bajdary" (Mickiewicz) **38**:166
Bajo tu clara sombra y otros poemas sobre España (Paz) **48**:179-81, 244
"Bakche-Sarai" (Mickiewicz)
See "Bakczysaraj"
The Bak-Chesarian fountain: A Tale of the Tauride (Pushkin)
See *Bakhchisaraiski Fontan*
"Bakczysaraj" (Mickiewicz) **38**:149
"The Baker's Island Light" (Very) **86**:91, 139
The Bakhchisarai Fontan (Pushkin)
See *Bakhchisaraiski Fontan*
Bakhchisaraiski Fontan (Pushkin) **10**:358, 365, 386-88, 411, 417, 419, 421
"Bakhchisaray by Night" (Mickiewicz) **38**:223
"Le Bal" (Vigny) **26**:410-11
"Bal des pendus" (Rimbaud) **3**:281, 283; **57**:243, 289, 291-92
"Balaam's Ass" (Jones)
See "The Book of Balaam's Ass"

"Balada" (Mistral) **32**:152, 176
"Balada arrítmica para un viajero" (Storni) **33**:268
"La balada azul" (Guillén) **23**:100, 140
"Balada de los dos abuelos" (Guillén) **23**:103, 132, 138
"Balada del güje" (Guillén) **23**:131-32
Baladas de primavera (Jiménez) **7**:184
"Balade" (Chatterton)
See "An Excelente Balade of Charitie"
Balākā (Tagore) **8**:413-15, 418, 427
"Balakhana" (McGuckian) **27**:82, 93
"Balance" (Thomas) **99**:274, 359
"The Balance" (Wagoner) **33**:369
"Balance der Welt" (Werfel) **101**:346
"Balance of the World" (Werfel)
See "Balance der Welt"
"Balance Sheet" (Montague) **106**:258, 262-63, 310
"A Balanced Bait in Handy Pellet Form" (Curnow) **48**:16, 18, 38
"Balanchine's" (Merrill) **28**:254
Balaustion's Adventure, Including a Transcript from Euripedes (Browning) **97**:36
"Balboa, the Entertainer" (Baraka) **113**:99, 150
"Le balcon" (Baudelaire) **1**:45, 63; **106**:86
"Los balcones del Oriente" (Guillén) **35**:233, 234
"The Balcony" (Baudelaire)
See "Le balcon"
"Balcony Scene" (Shapiro) **25**:316
"Balder Dead" (Arnold) **5**:35, 37, 58-9, 62
Balder: Part the First (Dobell) **100**:137-39, 141, 144, 147-48, 150, 152, 154, 159-60, 172, 174-76, 179, 186
"Balin and Balan" (Tennyson) **101**:206, 228-29, 231-33, 235-36
"Balkan Ballad" (Shvarts) **50**:148
"Ball" (Benn) **35**:50
"The Ball Game" (Creeley) **73**:7
"The Ball Poem" (Berryman) **64**:78, 80, 88, 90, 142, 154-55, 160
"Ballad" (Ammons) **16**:25
"Ballad" (Mistral)
See "Balada"
"Ballad" (Oppen) **35**:324
"Ballad" (Pasternak) **6**:270
"A Ballad" (Suckling)
See "A Ballade. Upon a Wedding"
"A Ballad about Benkendorf, Chief of Gendarmerie, and Lermontov's Poem 'Death of a Poet'" (Yevtushenko) **40**:352
"Ballad Air and Fire" (Baraka) **113**:60
"Ballad Fourth: The Trogger" (Burns) **6**:78
"Ballad from a Fairy Tale" (Hughes) **89**:123
"Ballad of a Sweet Dream of Peace" (Warren) **37**:332
"Ballad of a Thin Man" (Dylan) **37**:51
"Ballad of a Willful Woman" (Lawrence) **54**:204-5
The Ballad of Agincourt (Drayton) **98**:44, 59, 64-65, 69, 73, 79, 83
"Ballad of Army Wagons" (Tu Fu) **9**:330
"The Ballad of Ballymote" (Gallagher) **9**:42
"The Ballad of Beautiful Words" (Nash) **21**:273
"A Ballad of Beauty and Time" (Boland) **58**:45, 98-99
"The Ballad of Billie Potts" (Warren) **37**:286-89, 312, 324-25, 331-34, 340, 348, 370, 376, 379-80, 382
"Ballad of Birmingham" (Randall) **86**:285-86, 288, 306, 326, 333, 349
"The Ballad of Blasphemous Bill" (Service) **70**:116, 153-54
"A Ballad of Boding" (Rossetti) **7**:271
"The Ballad of Boh Da Thone" (Kipling) **91**:134
"Ballad of Carmilhan" (Longfellow) **30**:25
"The Ballad of Chocolate Mabbie" (Brooks) **7**:57, 68, 102, 104
"Ballad of Delusion and Death" (Werfel)
See "Ballade von Wahn und Tod"
"The Ballad of East and West" (Kipling) **3**:157, 182-83, 188
"The Ballad of Eternal Life" (Muir) **49**:214-15, 217, 228, 238
"The Ballad of Everyman" (Muir) **49**:257
"Ballad of Faith" (Williams) **7**:363
"The Ballad of Father Hudson" (Carman) **34**:225
"The Ballad of Father O'Hart" (Yeats) **20**:349
"the ballad of Francie Canoye, proofreader" (Niedecker) **42**:101
"A Ballad of François Villon" (Swinburne) **24**:324
"The Ballad of Frankie Lee and Judas Priest" (Dylan) **37**:55
"Ballad of Goldenhair" (Hall) **70**:32
"The Ballad of Gregorio Cortez" (Paredes)
See "El Corrido de Gregorio Cortez"
"The Ballad of Hank the Finn" (Service) **70**:140140
"The Ballad of Hard-Luck Harry" (Service) **70**:115
"Ballad of Hector in Hades" (Muir) **49**:204, 213-14, 228-29, 234, 237, 264, 277, 287
"The Ballad of Jakko Hill" (Kipling) **3**:187
"The Ballad of Jesse Helms" (Snodgrass) **74**:332, 334
"The Ballad of Joe Meek" (Brown) **55**:101, 113, 121-23, 150, 154-55
"A Ballad of John Silver" (Masefield) **78**:94
"The Ballad of Kind Kittock" (Dunbar)
See "Kynd Kittok"
"The Ballad of Late Annie" (Brooks) **7**:102-04
"The Ballad of Launcelot and Elaine" (Masters) **1**:328; **36**:175
"The Ballad of Margie Polite" (Hughes) **1**:241, 243, 247
"The Ballad of Missing Lines" (Rukeyser) **12**:228
"Ballad of Mister Dutcher and the Last Lynching in Gupton" (Warren) **37**:305, 384
"The Ballad of Moll Magee" (Yeats) **20**:337
"Ballad of Mr. Chubb" (Birney) **52**:8, 22, 25, 27-28
"The Ballad of Nat Turner" (Hayden) **6**:176, 178-80, 186-87, 194-95, 198
"A Ballad of Negro History" (Hughes) **53**:115
"Ballad of Oedipus Sex" (Abse) **41**:22
"The Ballad of One-Eyed Mike" (Service) **70**:117
"Ballad of Oriana" (Tennyson) **6**:359; **101**:240-41, 243
"A Ballad of Past Meridian" (Meredith) **60**:252, 279-80, 330, 334
"The Ballad of Peace and War" (Owen) **102**:149
"Ballad of Pearl May Lee" (Brooks) **7**:57, 68, 86, 103-04
"The Ballad of Pious Pete" (Service) **70**:116
"The Ballad of Reading Gaol" (Wilde) **111**:283-324
"Ballad of Rebirth" (Muir) **49**:237-38
"A Ballad of Remembrance" (Hayden)
See *A Ballad of Remembrance*
A Ballad of Remembrance (Hayden) **6**:183, 188, 194-95, 200
"Ballad of Roosevelt" (Hughes) **53**:115
"The Ballad of Rudolph Reed" (Brooks) **7**:62, 96
"The Ballad of Sally Brown and Ben the Carpenter" (Hood)
See "Faithless Sally Brown"
"A Ballad of Sark" (Swinburne) **24**:313
"Ballad of Simón Caraballo" (Guillén) **23**:106
"The Ballad of Sir Bors" (Masefield) **78**:5
"Ballad of Sleeping Somewhere Else" (Spicer) **78**:255
The Ballad of St. Barbara and Other Verses (Chesterton) **28**:96-97
"The Ballad of Sue Ellen Westerfield" (Hayden) **6**:196
"Ballad of the Attendants" (Werfel)
See "Ballade von den Begleitern"
"The Ballad of the Big Stamp" (Yevtushenko) **40**:369-70
"The Ballad of the Black Fox Skin" (Service) **70**:117
"Ballad of the Black Sorrow" (García Lorca)
See "Romance de la pena negra"
"The Ballad of the Bold Bohemian and the Philistine Maid" (Service) **70**:153
"The Ballad of the Bolivar" (Kipling) **3**:164
"A Ballad of the Boston Tea-Party" (Holmes) **71**:91
"The Ballad of the Brand" (Service) **70**:117
"Ballad of the Brown Girl" (Walker) **30**:347, 365
The Ballad of the Brown Girl: An Old Ballad Retold (Cullen) **20**:55, 61, 64, 77, 79, 85-86
"The Ballad of the Children of the Czar" (Schwartz) **8**:302, 305, 309
"Ballad of the Dark Trouble" (García Lorca)
See "Romance de la pena negra"
"The Ballad of the Dead Woodcutter" (Spicer) **78**:253
"Ballad of the Despairing Husband" (Creeley) **73**:5, 29-30, 104
"The Ballad of the Enamord Mage" (Duncan) **75**:256
"The Ballad of the Fanfarlo" (Spark) **72**:213, 215, 217, 220, 227, 229-30, 232, 246-47, 255-56, 258-61, 264
"Ballad of the Five Senses" (MacDiarmid) **9**:157, 193
"Ballad of the Flood" (Muir) **49**:211-12, 217, 224, 228, 237, 287
"Ballad of the Free" (Walker) **20**:276, 284, 292
"Ballad of the Girl Whose Name Is Mud" (Hughes) **53**:124
"Ballad of the Güije" (Guillén)
See "Balada del güje"
"The Ballad of the Harp-Weaver" (Millay) **6**:211, 225, 233
"Ballad of the Hoppy Toad" (Walker) **20**:290-92
"Ballad of the Icondic" (Ciardi) **69**:57
"Ballad of the Jollie Gleeman" (Viereck) **27**:259
"The Ballad of the King's Jest" (Kipling) **3**:182
"Ballad of The Ladies of Past Times" (Villon)
See "Ballade des Dames du Temps Jadis"
"Ballad of the Landlord" (Hughes) **1**:258, 267; **53**:191
"Ballad of the Little Square" (García Lorca)
See "Ballada de la Placeta"
"The Ballad of the Lonely Masturbator" (Sexton) **2**:352, 370
"The Ballad of the Long-Legged Bait" (Thomas) **2**:382, 393, 402; **52**:255
"Ballad of the Moon, the Moon" (García Lorca)
See "Romance de la luna, luna"
"Ballad of the Muse at Sea" (Barker) **77**:21
"The Ballad of the Northern Lights" (Service) **70**:115-16
"Ballad of the Oysterman" (Holmes) **71**:68, 85, 92, 123
"The Ballad of the Red Earl" (Kipling) **3**:181-82
"Ballad of the River Spirit" (Guillén)
See "Balada del güje"
"Ballad of the Seven Passages" (Spicer) **78**:252
"Ballad of the Seven Songs: A Poem for Emancipation Day" (Hughes) **53**:114
"Ballad of the Sixties" (Sarton) **39**:344
"Ballad of the Soul" (Muir)
See "The Ballad of Eternal Life"
"Ballad of the Spanish Civil Guard" (García Lorca)
See "Romance de la Guardia Civil Española"
"Ballad of the Summoned Man" (García Lorca) **3**:147
"The Ballad of the True Beast" (Hayden) **6**:196-97

"Ballad of the Two Grandfathers" (Guillén)
See "Balada de los dos abuelos"
The Ballad of the White Horse (Chesterton) **28**:93, 100, 105-08, 119-28
"Ballad of the World Extinct" (Celan)
See "Ballade von der erloschenen Welt"
"The Ballad of Trees and the Master" (Lanier) **50**:56, 81, 93, 101
"The Ballad of Valès-Dunes" (Belloc) **24**:11
"The Ballad of Weeping" (Spicer) **78**:303
"The Ballad of Wild Children" (Barker) **77**:19-20
"The Ballad of William Sycamore, 1790-1880" (Benét) **64**:19
"A Ballad on Mr. J. H. to Amoret" (Behn) **88**:147-48, 152
"Ballad on the American War" (Burns) **114**:43, 45-46
"Ballad upon a Wedding" (Suckling)
See "A Ballade. Upon a Wedding"
"A Ballad Upon a Wedding" (Suckling)
See "A Ballade. Upon a Wedding"
"Ballad Written in a Clinic" (Montale)
See "Ballata scritta in una clinica"
"Ballada de la Placeta" (García Lorca) **3**:125
"Ballade I" (Christine de Pizan) **68**:181
"Ballade III" (Christine de Pizan) **68**:181
"Ballade IV" (Christine de Pizan) **68**:181, 183
"Ballade V" (Christine de Pizan) **68**:181-82
"Ballade VI" (Christine de Pizan) **68**:181
"Ballade VII" (Christine de Pizan) **68**:181-82
"Ballade VIII" (Christine de Pizan) **68**:36, 100, 181
"Ballade IX" (Christine de Pizan) **68**:181-82
"Ballade X" (Christine de Pizan) **68**:34
"Ballade XII" (Christine de Pizan) **68**:22, 182
"Ballade XV" (Christine de Pizan) **68**:182
"Ballade XVI" (Christine de Pizan) **68**:35
"Ballade XXI" (Christine de Pizan) **68**:35
"Ballade XXV" (Christine de Pizan) **68**:179
"Ballade XXVI" (Christine de Pizan) **68**:100
"Ballade XXXII" (Christine de Pizan) **68**:179, 183
"Ballade XXXIII" (Christine de Pizan) **68**:179-80
"Ballade XXXIV" (Christine de Pizan) **68**:179
"Ballade XXXVIII" (Christine de Pizan) **68**:180
"Ballade XXXIX" (Christine de Pizan) **68**:180, 183, 191
"Ballade XLIII" (Christine de Pizan) **68**:35, 97, 180
"Ballade XLVI" (Christine de Pizan) **68**:180, 182
"Ballade XLVII" (Christine de Pizan) **68**:180, 183
"Ballade XLVIII" (Christine de Pizan) **68**:100
"Ballade XLIX" (Christine de Pizan) **68**:183
"Ballade L" (Christine de Pizan) **68**:97, 183
"Ballade LII" (Christine de Pizan) **68**:183
"Ballade LIII" (Christine de Pizan) **68**:183
"Ballade LIV" (Christine de Pizan) **68**:183
"Ballade LIX" (Christine de Pizan) **68**:183
"Ballade LV" (Christine de Pizan) **68**:182
"Ballade LVI" (Christine de Pizan) **68**:22
"Ballade LVII" (Christine de Pizan) **68**:180, 182-83
"Ballade LVIII" (Christine de Pizan) **68**:100, 183
"Ballade LXII" (Christine de Pizan) **68**:183
"Ballade LXIV" (Christine de Pizan) **68**:180
"Ballade LXV-LXXXVI" (Christine de Pizan) **68**:97-98
"Ballade LXXXVI" (Christine de Pizan) **68**:1
"Ballade XCI" (Christine de Pizan) **68**:183
"Ballade XCIV" (Christine de Pizan) **68**:184
"Ballade XCVII" (Christine de Pizan) **68**:34
"Ballade" (Dunbar) **5**:139-40
"Ballade" (Gautier) **18**:348-51
"Ballade" (Koch) **80**:327
"Ballade" (Stryk) **27**:191
The Ballade (Suckling)
See "A Ballade. Upon a Wedding"
"Ballade de bon conseil" (Villon) **13**:394-95
"Ballade de bonne doctrine à ceux de mauvaise vie" (Villon) **13**:394-95, 404-05
"Ballade de conclusion" (Villon) **13**:417
"Ballade de la Grosse Margot" (Villon) **13**:389-90, 393
"Ballade de mercy" (Villon) **13**:399, 413
"Ballade des contre verites" (Villon) **13**:414
"Ballade des Dames du Temps Jadis" (Villon) **13**:374, 405, 409-10
"Ballade des femmes de Paris" (Villon) **13**:380, 390, 413
"Ballade des Langues Envieuses" (Villon) **13**:404
"Ballade des menus propos" (Villon) **13**:409
"Ballade des Pendus" (Villon)
See "Epitaphe Villon"
"Ballade des proverbes" (Villon) **13**:404, 414
Ballade des seigneurs du temps jadis (Villon) **13**:410
"Ballade du concours de Blois" (Villon) **13**:392, 414
"La ballade du Mal Aimé" (Apollinaire)
See "La chanson du mal-aimé"
"Ballade d'une grande dame" (Chesterton) **28**:117
"Ballade for the Duke of Orleans" (Wilbur) **51**:221-22, 262, 273, 293, 301, 311
"Ballade of a Talked-off Ear" (Parker) **28**:363
"Ballade of Big Plans" (Parker) **28**:354
"Ballade of Dead Ladies" (Villon) **13**:387, 390-91
"Ballade of Fat Margot" (Villon)
See "Ballade de la Grosse Margot"
"Ballade of Hell and Mrs Roebeck" (Belloc) **24**:49
"A Ballade of Interesting News" (Belloc) **24**:42
"The Ballade of Lord Bernard Stewart, Lord of Aubigny" (Dunbar) **67**:21, 44
"A Ballade of Suicide" (Chesterton) **28**:99
"Ballade of the Critic" (Shapiro) **25**:281
"Ballade of the Hanged" (Villon)
See "Epitaphe Villon"
"Ballade of the Women of Paris" (Villon)
See "Ballade des femmes de Paris"
"Ballade of Unfortunate Mammals" (Parker) **28**:351, 363
"Ballade pour prier Nostre Dame" (Villon) **13**:403, 405, 413
"Ballade pour Robert d'Estouteville" (Villon) **13**:395, 415
"Ballade to Our Lady" (Villon) **13**:390-91
"A Ballade. Upon a Wedding" (Suckling) **30**:119-20, 122, 148, 151-53, 155-56
"Ballade vom Auszug der drei" (Celan) **10**:126
"Ballade von den Begleitern" (Werfel) **101**:338, 340-41
"Ballade von der erloschenen Welt" (Celan) **10**:125
"Ballade von Wahn und Tod" (Werfel) **101**:349
"Ballades III, V, VII" (Christine de Pizan) **68**:181
"Ballades III-IX" (Christine de Pizan) **68**:181
"Ballades V-VI" (Christine de Pizan) **68**:181
"Ballades XIV-XLII" (Christine de Pizan) **68**:35
"Ballades XLV-LXI" (Christine de Pizan) **68**:183
"Ballades XLV-LXII" (Christine de Pizan) **68**:182
"Ballades LXV-LXXXVIII" (Christine de Pizan) **68**:36
"Ballades LXXIV-LXXVI" (Christine de Pizan) **68**:180
"Ballades LXXV and LXXVI" (Christine de Pizan) **68**:180
"Ballades LXXVI-LXXX" (Christine de Pizan) **68**:183
"Ballades XCVII" (Christine de Pizan) **68**:183
Ballades d'Estrange Façon (Christine de Pizan) **68**:96
Ballades en Jargon (Villon) **13**:404, 406
Ballades in a Curious Form (Christine de Pizan)
See *Ballades d'Estrange Façon*
"Ballads" (Hughes) **53**:101
Ballads (Coleridge)
See *Lyrical Ballads*
Ballads (Kipling)
See *Barrack-Room Ballads*
Ballads (Masefield) **78**:8, 68, 96
Ballads (Stevenson) **84**:325, 331-32
Ballads, and Other Poems (Longfellow) **30**:107
Ballads and Poems (Masefield) **78**:8, 20, 70, 95
Ballads and Poems of Tragic Life (Meredith) **60**:263, 292, 294, 327
Ballads and Romances (Mickiewicz)
See *Ballady i Romanse*
Ballads for Sale (Lowell) **13**:76, 84-5
Ballads of a Bohemian (Service) **70**:118, 121, 129, 132, 153, 158-60
Ballads of a Cheechako (Service) **70**:113-14, 129, 153-54, 157-60
Ballads of Lost Haven (Carman) **34**:205, 207, 211-13
Ballads of New England (Whittier) **93**:349
Ballads of Spring (Jiménez)
See *Baladas de primavera*
"Ballads of the Traveler" (Sarton) **39**:345-46
Ballady i Romanse (Mickiewicz) **38**:157, 162, 164, 189
"De Ballaigues à Orbe, Jura" (Sainte-Beuve) **110**:56
"Ballat of Our Lady" (Dunbar) **67**:37, 43
"Ballata Dolorossa" (Carducci) **46**:23
"Ballata scritta in una clinica" (Montale) **13**:108, 131, 167
"A Ballet" (Douglas) **106**:186, 197
"The Ballet" (Meredith) **28**:193, 215
"Ballet" (Pavese)
See "Balletto"
"Ballet" (Stone) **53**:228
"The Ballet of the Buffoon" (Sexton) **79**:218
"Ballet-Drama in One Act" (Cohen) **109**:58
"Ballets" (Mallarmé) **102**:66-67, 125, 129
"Balletto" (Pavese) **13**:205, 226
"Balloon" (Ní Chuilleanáin) **34**:350
"Balloon Faces" (Sandburg) **41**:276
"Balloons" (Plath) **1**:391; **37**:258
"The Ballpark at Moiese" (Hugo) **68**:291
"The Ballroom at Sandover" (Merrill) **28**:235
"Ball's Bluff" (Melville) **82**:94, 194
"Ballydavid Pier" (Kinsella) **69**:84-85, 89, 99
"Ballynahinch Lake" (Heaney) **100**:237
"Balsa Wood" (Carver) **54**:12
"Baltasar Gracián" (Borges) **32**:132
"Baltazar" (Alurista) **34**:22
Balustion's Adventure (Browning) **2**:85-6, 95
"Bamberg" (Jarrell) **41**:197
"Bamboo" (Hagiwara)
See "Take"
"The Bamboo Flute" (Hope) **56**:291
"Bamboo Lodge" (Wang Wei) **18**:382
Banabani (Tagore) **8**:416
"Banane" (Benn) **35**:8, 50
"Banaphul" (Tagore) **8**:405
"Le Banc d'ocre" (Char) **56**:155
"Band Concert" (Sandburg) **41**:240
"The Bandaged Shoulder" (Cavafy) **36**:39, 41, 42
"La Bande Noire" (Hugo) **17**:87-88
"Bandi" (Tagore) **8**:407, 412
"The Bandit" (Hood) **93**:114
"The Bandog" (de la Mare) **77**:73
"Bandot" (Stryk) **27**:204-5
"The Bands and the Beautiful Children" (Page) **12**:169, 177
Bandusia Ode (Horace) **46**:127
"Banga bir" (Tagore) **8**:407
"Bangkok Boy" (Birney) **52**:60-61, 69
"The Bangkok Gong" (Kumin) **15**:213
"The Bangs" (Montale)
See "La frangia dei capelli"

"The Banished Gods" (Mahon) **60**:151, 190, 207
"Banishment" (Sassoon) **12**:267, 288
"Banist if he made Loue" (Waller) **72**:339
"A Banjo Song" (Dunbar) **5**:146
"A Banjo Song" (Johnson) **24**:136, 141
"The Bank" (Thomas) **99**:266
"Bankashi" (Yakamochi) **48**:133, 137-39
"The Banker's Daughter" (Lowell) **3**:218, 221
"The Banker's Secret" (Holmes) **71**:94
"Banking Coal" (Toomer) **7**:333
"Banking Potatoes" (Komunyakaa) **51**:23
"The bankrupt Peace Maker" (Lindsay) **23**:269
"Bankruptcy" (Carver) **54**:29
"Banks of a Stream Where Creatures Bathe" (Merrill) **28**:223, 255
"Bann Valley Eclogue" (Heaney) **100**:239, 327-28
"Banneker" (Dove) **6**:105, 109
"The Banner Bearer" (Williams) **7**:389-90
"The Banners" (Duncan) **2**:102
"Bannières de mai" (Rimbaud) **57**:174, 238, 250
"Bannockburn—A Song—Robert Bruce's Address to His Army" (Burns)
See "Bruce to His Men at Bannockburn"
"Banquet" (Gozzano) **10**:183
"The Banquet" (Herbert) **4**:134
The Banquet (Dante)
See *Convivio*
Banquet of Sense (Chapman)
See *Ovids Banquet of Sense. A Coronet for His Mistresse Philosophie, and His Amorous Zodiacke. With a Translation of a Latine Coppie, Written by a Fryer, Anno Dom. 1400*
"Bantams in Pine-Woods" (Stevens) **6**:293, 303, 327; **110**:95, 187, 189
"Banyan" (Swenson) **14**:273
"The Banyan Tree, Old Year's Night" (Walcott) **46**:279
"Baptême funèbre" (Ponge) **107**:143-46, 148-49
"Baptism" (Erdrich) **52**:191
"Baptism" (Herbert) **50**:24
"Baptism" (Herbert) **4**:100
"Baptism" (McKay) **2**:211
Baptism of Desire (Erdrich) **52**:186-87, 189-90, 193-94
"The Baptist" (Hughes) **89**:195, 197
"A Baptist Childhood" (Davie) **29**:101, 112
"Bar" (Benn) **35**:71
"A Bar in Manhattan" (Mahon) **60**:146
"Bar Orient" (Yau) **61**:334
"Bar Time" (Collins) **68**:220
Barabajan Poems (Brathwaite) **56**:62
"Barbara Frietchie" (Whittier) **93**:167, 174, 184, 232, 239, 247, 280, 348
"Barbare" (Césaire) **25**:10, 23-25, 28, 31, 37
"Barbare" (Rimbaud) **3**:261; **57**:175, 228, 232, 240, 247, 253, 284
"Barbarian" (Rimbaud)
See "Barbare"
Barbaric Odes (Carducci)
See *Odi barbare*
Barbarous Odes (Carducci)
See *Odi barbare*
"Barbecue" (Stryk) **27**:208
"The Barberry Bush" (Very) **86**:161
"Barclay of Ury" (Whittier) **93**:221, 245
"El barco" (Paz) **48**:179-80, 183
"Barco de refugiados" (Cervantes) **35**:108, 130, 132
"The Bard" (Gray) **2**:134-35, 139, 143-44, 146, 148, 151-54; **80**:207, 236-37, 283
"The Bard of Addis Ababa" (Tolson) **88**:344
Barddoniaeth Dafydd ab Gwilym (Dafydd ap Gwilym) **56**:232
"Bardic Dust" (Kavanagh) **105**:173
"The Bards" (Graves) **6**:140, 144
"A Bard's Epitaph" (Burns) **114**:70, 144
"Bards of Passion and of Mirth" (Keats) **1**:312
"Bard's Song" (Blake) **12**:6
"Bare Almond-Trees" (Lawrence) **54**:187
"The Bare Deal Board" (Ní Chuilleanáin) **34**:360
"Bare Fig-Trees" (Lawrence) **54**:187, 194
The Bare Hills (Winters) **82**:312-16, 320-23, 334-35
"Barefoot" (Sexton) **2**:352; **79**:245
"The Barefoot Boy" (Whittier) **93**:172, 232-33, 239, 252, 266-67
A Barefoot Boy (Riley) **48**:340
"The Barefoot Dancer" (Darío)
See "La bailerina de los pies desnudos"
Barely and Widely, 1956-1958 (Zukofsky) **11**:348
"The Bargain" (Cowley) **90**:13
"Bargain" (Stone) **53**:229
"The Bargeman's Inns" (Masefield) **78**:30
"The Barges" (Masefield) **78**:30
Barking at the Moon (Hagiwara)
See *Tsuki ni hoeru*
"Barking Hall: A Year After" (Swinburne) **24**:318-19
"Barmaids Are Diviner than Mermaids" (Nash) **21**:265
"The Barn" (Blunden) **66**:4
"The Barn" (Heaney) **18**:194, 200; **100**:212
"The Barn" (Thomas) **53**:329
"Barney Hainsfeather" (Masters) **36**:182
"Barnsley, 1966" (Davie) **29**:102
"Barnsley and District" (Davie) **29**:111
"The Barnyard" (Winters) **82**:317
"The Baron of St. Castine" (Longfellow) **30**:62
The Barons Warres (Drayton)
See *Mortimeriados. The Lamentable Civell Warres of Edward the Second and the Barrons*
"Baroque Comment" (Bogan) **12**:90, 92, 97, 101
"A Baroque Sunburst" (Clampitt) **19**:90
"A Baroque Wall-Fountain in the Villa Sciarra" (Wilbur) **51**:192, 195, 217, 250, 300, 314
"Barrabas. Eine Phantasie" (Trakl) **20**:239
Barrack Room Ballads and Other Verses (Kipling) **3**:155-56, 159-60, 163, 165, 167-69, 177, 182, 187-89
"Barrack Street" (Ní Chuilleanáin) **34**:349, 381
Barrack-Room Ballads (Kipling) **91**:63, 68-69, 81-82, 84-85, 87-88, 97-98, 100, 102, 134, 148, 152, 170-71, 173
"Barrancas del Plata en Colonia" (Storni) **33**:261, 294
"Barranquilla Bridge" (Birney) **52**:18
"A Barred Owl" (Wilbur) **51**:336
"The Barrel Organ" (Noyes) **27**:115-16, 133, 136-38
"Barren Spring" (Rossetti) **44**:173
"Barrenness" (Traherne) **70**:323
"The Barrier" (McKay) **2**:212
The Barrons Wars in the Raigne of Edward the Second (Drayton)
See *Mortimeriados. The Lamentable Civell Warres of Edward the Second and the Barrons*
"Bar-Room Matins" (MacNeice) **61**:139
"Barry Holden" (Masters) **36**:230
"Barter" (Teasdale) **31**:332, 340, 356, 388
"Barthélémon At Vauxhall" (Hardy) **92**:255
"Bartok" (Illyés) **16**:231
"Baruch Spinoza" (Borges) **32**:68-72
"Basaleg" (Dafydd ap Gwilym) **56**:233
"Basant" (Kabīr) **56**:342, 346
"Base Details" (Sassoon) **12**:268, 277, 280
"The Base Stealer" (Francis) **34**:246, 255
"Baseball and Writing" (Moore) **4**:242, 256, 259-60; **49**:146-47
"Baseball Canto" (Ferlinghetti) **1**:183
"The Baseball Players" (Hall) **70**:19
"Basement Apartment" (Shapiro) **25**:316
The Basement Tapes (Dylan) **37**:60
"Baseness" (Traherne) **70**:321
"Básežn nejpokornější" (Seifert) **47**:330
Basic Work (Parra)
See *Obra gruesa*
"A Basin of Eggs" (Swenson) **14**:250
"The Basket" (Lowell) **13**:84, 95-6
"A Basket of Chestnuts" (Heaney) **100**:322
"Baskets" (Glück) **16**:152
"The Basket-Weaver's Companion" (Char)
See "La compagne du vannier"
"Bas-Relief" (Sandburg) **41**:285
"A Bastard Peace" (Williams) **7**:369
"The Bastille" (Brooke) **24**:66, 80, 84, 89
"The Bat" (Kenyon) **57**:4, 37
"Bat" (Lawrence) **54**:170, 225
"Bat" (Sexton) **79**:240, 245
"Le Bateau a rames froisées" (Scève) **111**:5
"Bateau ivre" (Hugo) **17**:65
"Le bateau ivre" (Rimbaud) **3**:249, 257-58, 268-70, 272-74, 282, 286; **57**:171-72, 197, 199, 202, 214, 216, 235, 239, 245-47, 249, 251-52, 299-300
"The Bath" (Ríos) **57**:325
"Bath" (Sandburg) **41**:365
"The Bath" (Snyder) **21**:292, 297
"A Bather" (Lowell) **13**:93-6
"The Bathers" (Shapiro) **25**:304
"Bathing in the River" (Cowley) **90**:115
"Bathos" (Pope) **26**:357
"Batjushkov" (Mandelstam) **14**:118
"Batouque" (Césaire) **25**:29
"Bats" (Jarrell) **41**:208
The Battaile of Agincourt (Drayton) **98**:64, 73-75, 77, 79-82
"Battalion-Relief" (Sassoon) **12**:269
"Batter my heart, three person'd God" (Donne)
See "Holy Sonnet XIV: Batter my heart, three-person'd God"
"Battersea Park" (Barker) **77**:38
"The Battle" (Brooks) **7**:67
"The Battle Autumn of 1862" (Whittier) **93**:185, 213
"The Battle for the Bay" (Melville) **82**:202
"The Battle for the Mississippi" (Melville) **82**:92, 133, 201
"The Battle Hymn" (Crane) **80**:52, 69, 83
"The Battle Hymn of the Republic" (Howe) **81**:3, 5-7, 9-11, 30, 62-63
"The Battle of Brunanburh" (Tennyson) **6**:363, 369
"The Battle of Hastings" (Chatterton) **104**:3, 12, 49, 69-70, 72
"The Battle of Hastynges" (Chatterton)
See "The Battle of Hastings"
"The Battle of Lora" (Macpherson) **97**:178, 230, 355
"The Battle of Lowell's Pond" (Longfellow) **30**:20
The Battle of Marathon: A Poem (Barrett Browning) **6**:19; **62**:106, 112
"Battle of Murfreesboro (1862-1922)" (Tate) **50**:306
"The Battle of Osfrontalis" (Hughes) **7**:123, 142, 160-61; **89**:137, 141
"Battle of Stone River, Tennessee" (Melville) **82**:133, 202
"The Battle of the School-books" (Collins) **72**:44
"The Battle of the Summer Islands" (Waller) **72**:298
"Battle Problem" (Meredith) **28**:172, 189
"Battle Report" (Kaufman) **74**:174-75, 240, 259, 273-74
"Battle Song" (Elliott) **96**:162, 180
"The Battlefield" (Bryant) **20**:5
Battlefields (Gilmore) **87**:302
Battle-Pieces (Melville)
See *Battle-Pieces and Aspects of the War*
Battle-Pieces and Aspects of the War (Melville) **82**:71-73, 82-85, 90-94, 100-102, 104, 113, 117, 129-32, 134-39, 141, 145, 156, 158, 164, 182, 190-92, 198-212, 216-17, 266, 269-70, 272, 276
"Battlewagon" (Meredith) **28**:174

Battre tout bas (Char) **56**:115
"Baudelaire" (Schwartz) **8**:311, 319
"Baudelaire Irritates Nietzsche" (Char)
See "Baudelaire mécontente Nietzsche"
"Baudelaire mécontente Nietzsche" (Char) **56**:196, 198-202
"Bauxit" (Benn) **35**:70
"Bavaria" (Schnackenberg) **45**:342, 345
"Bavarian Gentians" (Lawrence) **54**:168-69, 172, 179, 181, 186-87, 197-202, 220, 226-27
"Bawdry Embraced" (Hughes) **89**:139, 188
Bay (Lawrence) **54**:173, 238
"Bay of Recovery" (Hugo) **68**:261
"Bayn al-kharā'ib" (Gibran) **9**:79
"Bayonet" (Sexton) **79**:240
"Bayonet Charge" (Hughes) **89**:208
"Bayonne Turnpike to Tuscarora" (Ginsberg) **4**:54
"Bayou Afternoon" (Clampitt) **19**:102
"Bazook" (Stone) **53**:228-29, 236
"B.C." (Stafford) **71**:258
"B. W." (Whitney)
See "To her Brother. B. W."
Be Angry at the Sun and Other Poems (Jeffers) **17**:123, 135
"Be Grave, Woman" (Jackson) **44**:29-30
"Be Nobody's Darling" (Walker) **30**:339, 353, 365
Be Seated, Thou: Poems, 1989-1998 (Abse) **41**:32
"Be Still, My Soul, Be Still" (Housman) **2**:184, 192
"Be thou then my beauty named" (Campion) **87**:69
"The Beach" (Hughes) **89**:191
"Beach at Versilia" (Montale)
See "Proda di Versilia"
"Beach Glass" (Clampitt) **19**:88
"The Beach Head" (Gunn) **26**:218
"The Beach Hotel" (Strand) **63**:188
"The Beach Women" (Pinsky) **27**:162
"The Beachcomber" (Stryk) **27**:185-86
"Beachhead" (Walcott) **46**:247
"Beachy" (Sandburg) **2**:300; **41**:225
Beachy Head, with Other Poems (Smith) **104**:151-53, 156, 161, 166, 168-71, 174, 179-84, 196, 219-31, 233, 238, 240, 256-65, 293, 295-302, 305-12, 314-15, 328-33, 338, 353
"The Beacon" (Cunningham) **92**:134, 140, 143, 182
"The Beacon" (Wilbur) **51**:187
"Beaded Balustrade" (Schuyler) **88**:183, 216
"The Beaks of Eagles" (Jeffers) **17**:145
"Beale Street Love" (Hughes) **1**:269
"The Bean Eaters" (Brooks) **7**:55-6, 62, 69, 100
The Bean Eaters (Brooks) **7**:56-8, 62-3, 67, 81, 86, 95-6, 98-9, 101-02, 105, 107
Bean Spasms (Berrigan) **103**:33
"Bean Spasms" (Berrigan) **103**:5-6, 33
"Beans with Garlic" (Bukowski) **18**:23
"The Beanstalk" (Millay) **6**:237, 239
"The Bear" (Frost) **1**:203-04
"The Bear" (Hughes) **89**:106
"The Bear" (Kinnell) **26**:241-42, 244, 252, 257, 262-63, 273, 291
"The Bear" (Momaday) **25**:185-86, 188, 191, 193-95, 201-202, 209-10, 220
"Bear" (Wagoner) **33**:373
"The Bear and the Garden-Lover" (Moore) **4**:261
"Bear Fat" (Hogan) **35**:259
"The Bear on the Delhi Road" (Birney) **52**:44-46, 60-61, 87
"Bear Paw" (Hugo) **68**:288
"Bearded Oaks" (Warren) **37**:276, 288, 301, 307, 322, 332
"The Bearer of Evil Tidings" (Frost) **1**:202
"Bears" (Herbert)
See "Niedzwiedzie"
"The Beast and Burden" (Komunyakaa) **51**:34
Beast in View (Rukeyser) **12**:231-32
"Beasts" (Randall) **86**:339-40
"Beasts" (Wilbur) **51**:206, 221, 331
"The Beast's Confession to the Priest" (Swift) **9**:281, 295
"Beat! Beat! Drums!" (Whitman) **91**:197
"The Beaters" (Gunn) **26**:198, 201, 220
"Beato sillón" (Guillén) **35**:156, 228
"La Béatrice" (Baudelaire) **106**:9-10, 24, 26-27
"Beatrice" (Carroll) **74**:65
"Beatrice" (Teasdale) **31**:343
"Le beau navire" (Baudelaire) **1**:60; **106**:100
"Le Beau Navire" (Char) **56**:197
"Beau sang giclé" (Césaire) **25**:44-5
"La beauté" (Baudelaire) **1**:61, 65; **106**:22, 27, 47, 86, 118, 122, 172
"Beauté de femmes, leur faiblesse, et ces mains pâles" (Verlaine) **2**:416
"The Beautiful American Word, Sure" (Schwartz) **8**:302, 315
"Beautiful and Kind" (Ignatow) **34**:277, 287
"Beautiful Are the Delights of Early Years" (Yevtushenko) **40**:347
"Beautiful Black Men (with compliments and apologies to all not mentioned by name)" (Giovanni) **19**:106-7, 112
"Beautiful Black Women" (Baraka) **113**:77
"The Beautiful Changes" (Wilbur) **51**:193, 198, 204, 214, 242
The Beautiful Changes and Other Poems (Wilbur) **51**:203-4, 226, 237, 254, 257, 263-64, 267, 269, 289-90, 292-93, 295-96, 314, 324, 330, 333
"Beautiful Girl in Bed" (Koch) **80**:342
"Beautiful Lofty Things" (Yeats) **20**:307
"The Beautiful Man—France" (Cisneros) **52**:162
"Beautiful Ohio" (Wright) **36**:321, 360, 368
"The Beautiful Pauses" (Sarton) **39**:309
"The Beautiful Train" (Empson) **104**:133
"A Beautiful Young Nymph Going to Bed. Written for the Honour of the Fair Sex" (Swift) **9**:257, 262, 267-69, 279, 281, 283-84, 286, 291, 295, 298, 301-03
"A beautifull Mistris" (Carew) **29**:9
"Beauty" (Cowley) **90**:15, 117
"Beauty" (Masefield) **78**:63, 69
"The Beauty" (Pushkin) **10**:371
"Beauty" (Storni)
See "La belleza"
"Beauty" (Teasdale) **31**:359
"Beauty" (Thomas) **53**:284, 286, 288-89, 292
"Beauty" (Very) **86**:45, 58, 72-73, 134
"Beauty" (Wylie) **23**:300, 313, 327, 333
Beauty (Jiménez)
See *Belleza*
Beauty (Zanzotto)
See *La Beltà*
"Beauty and Beauty" (Brooke) **24**:56, 62
"Beauty and Sadness" (Song) **21**:341, 347
"Beauty and the Beast" (Dove) **6**:108
"Beauty and the Beast" (Tomlinson) **17**:323
"Beauty and the Illiterate" (Elytis) **21**:123
"The Beauty Fades" (Very)
See "Thy Beauty Fades"
"The Beauty of Holiness" (Howe) **81**:4
"The Beauty of the Head" (Swenson) **14**:281
The Beauty of the Husband: A Fictional Essay in 29 Tangos (Carson) **64**:224-26, 230-31
"Beauty Shoppe" (Brooks) **7**:59, 102
"Beauty, since you so much desire" (Campion) **87**:71, 97
"Beauty Who Took Snuff" (Pushkin) **10**:407
"Beaver People" (Stafford) **71**:338
"The Beaver Pool in December" (Kenyon) **57**:14
"Beaver Talk" (Stafford) **71**:318, 338
"Bebop Boys" (Hughes) **1**:267; **53**:192
"Becalmed" (Longfellow) **30**:31
"Because" (Teasdale) **31**:356, 369, 388
"Because" (Thomas) **99**:246
"Because Clemente Means Merciful" (Espada) **74**:147-48
"Because I Could Not Stop for Death" (Dickinson) **1**:84, 86
"Because I Deeply Praised" (Sikelianos) **29**:368
"Because I Love You (Last Night)" (Cummings) **5**:105
"Because I Sit Here So" (Jackson) **44**:29-30
"Because I Was Not Able to Restrain Your Hands" (Mandelstam) **14**:114, 118
"Because la Raza is Tired" (Alurista) **34**:23
"Because of Clothes" (Jackson) **44**:6
"Because One Is Always Forgotten" (Forché) **10**:138, 142, 144, 153, 155
"Because What I Want Most is Permanence" (Sarton) **39**:323, 338, 365
"Because,thy,smile,is,primavera" (Villa) **22**:356, 358
Beckonings (Brooks) **7**:84, 94
"Becoming new" (Piercy) **29**:301
"Becoming Strangers" (Piercy) **29**:309
"The Bed" (Creeley) **73**:11, 30
"The Bed" (Hope) **56**:287
The Bed and the Table (Éluard)
See *Le lit la table*
"The Bed by the Window" (Jeffers) **17**:131
"Bed in Summer" (Stevenson) **84**:346
"The Bed in the Sky" (Snyder) **21**:289
Bed of the Stranger (Darwish)
See *Sarir al-Ghariba*
"Bed Time" (Hughes) **1**:255
"Bedazzled" (Komunyakaa) **51**:65
"Bedfordshire" (Davie) **29**:116
Bedlam (Sexton)
See *To Bedlam and Part Way Back*
"Bedlam and the Girle, the Grandsire and the Boy" (Drayton) **98**:68
"The Bedouin" (Riley) **48**:323
"The Bed-Post" (Graves) **6**:141
"Bedrock" (Wagoner) **33**:367
"Bedspread" (Goodison) **36**:141-42, 148, 153
"Bedtime Prayers" (Chappell) **105**:52
"A Bedtime Story" (Hughes) **7**:159
"Bedtime Story" (Mueller) **33**:193
"Bedtime Story" (Stone) **53**:218
"Bedtime Story" (Yamada) **44**:333-34, 346
"The Bee" (Dickey) **40**:229, 253
"The Bee" (Lanier) **50**:77
"The Bee" (Vaughan) **81**:366
"The Bee God" (Hughes) **89**:179
"The Bee Meeting" (Plath) **1**:394, 410-13; **37**:211
Bee Time Vine (Stein) **18**:316-34, 336, 341-42, 344, 349-54
"Beech" (Frost) **1**:197
"Beech, Pine, and Sunlight" (Lowell) **13**:64
Beechen Vigil and Other Poems (Day Lewis) **11**:148
"Beehive" (Toomer) **7**:311, 320, 334
"The Beekeeper Speaks" (Nemerov) **24**:262, 274
"The Beekeeper's Daughter" (Plath) **1**:389, 410-12; **37**:220, 241, 246, 248
"Beeny Cliff" (Hardy) **8**:136; **92**:203, 328
"Beerhall Queen" (Serote) **113**:291-93, 296
"The Bees and the Flies" (Kipling) **91**:153
"Bees Stopped" (Ammons) **16**:46
"Beethoven Attends the C Minor Seminar" (Tomlinson) **17**:320
"Beethoven Opus 111" (Clampitt) **19**:82, 85, 89
"Beethoven Triumphant" (Berryman) **64**:159
"Beethoven's Death Mask" (Spender) **71**:179-80, 218, 225
"The Beetle" (Cohen) **109**:24
"Beetles" (Cervantes) **35**:119
"Before a Blue Light" (Kumin) **15**:211
"Before a Cashier's Window in a Department Store" (Wright) **36**:341, 345, 365, 375
"Before a Midnight Breaks in Storm" (Kipling) **3**:183
"Before an Old Painting of the Crucifixion"

(Momaday) **25**:186, 188, 190, 197-98, 211, 219
"Before and After Summer" (Hardy) **92**:370, 373-74
"Before Dawn" (de la Mare) **77**:64, 75
"Before Disaster" (Winters) **82**:311
Before Disaster (Winters) **82**:333
"Before Glanum" (Char)
See "L'avant-Glanum"
"Before I Knocked and Flesh Let Enter" (Thomas) **2**:383, 402; **52**:227, 237, 290, 293-95, 302, 309-10, 313
"Before, If I Remember Well . . ." (Rimbaud)
See "Jadis, si je me souviens bien . . ."
"Before Knowledge" (Hardy) **8**:89
"Before Leaving" (Cernuda) **62**:169
"Before March" (MacLeish) **47**:190
"Before San Guido" (Carducci)
See "Davanti San Guido"
"Before Sleep" (Kinsella) **69**:97
"Before That" (Merwin) **45**:64
"Before the Altar" (Lowell) **13**:69, 83
"Before the Anaesthetic" (Betjeman) **75**:8, 66, 83, 89, 92, 97-98
"Before the Battle" (Sassoon) **12**:262
"Before the Big Storm" (Stafford) **71**:264, 287
"Before the Birth of one of her Children" (Bradstreet) **10**:12, 18
"Before the Dance" (Tomlinson) **17**:319, 328, 330
"Before the Feast of Shushan" (Spencer) **77**:328-29, 341, 345-46
"Before the Flesh in Bones" (Alurista) **34**:25, 47
Before the Flood (Dylan) **37**:63
"Before the Judgment" (Duncan) **2**:116
"Before the Lecture" (Betjeman) **75**:40
"Before the Look of You" (Reese) **29**:331
"Before the Old Castle of Verona" (Carducci)
See "Davanti il castel vecchio di Verona"
"Before the Statue of Endymion" (Cavafy) **36**:73
"Before the Storm" (Lowell) **13**:60-1
"Before the Story" (Cohen) **109**:18
"Before the Trip" (Montale)
See "Prima del viaggio"
"Before Time Altered Them" (Cavafy) **36**:74
"Before We Mothernaked Fell" (Thomas) **2**:402
"Before We Sinned (Incarnate Devil)" (Thomas) **2**:402
"Before You Go" (Cervantes) **35**:104
"Begat" (Sexton) **2**:366
"Begegnung" (Stramm) **50**:175, 189
"Begegnungen" (Benn) **35**:69
"The Begetting of Arthur" (Masefield) **78**:92
"The Beggar to Mab, the Fairies' Queen" (Herrick) **9**:86
"The Beggars" (Wordsworth) **4**:377
"The Beggar's Valentine" (Lindsay) **23**:286
"The Beginner" (Kipling) **3**:183
"Beginner's Guide" (Nemerov) **24**:285
"Beginning" (Brathwaite) **56**:23-24, 88
"The Beginning" (Brooke) **24**:56, 82
"The Beginning" (Glück) **16**:164, 167
"Beginning" (Wright) **36**:286, 399-400
"Beginning a Poem of These States" (Ginsberg) **4**:81
"The Beginning and the End" (Jeffers) **17**:128, 132, 141
"The Beginning and the End" (Very) **86**:98
The Beginning and the End and Other Poems (Jeffers) **17**:114-15, 123, 128, 136
"The Beginning of September" (Hass) **16**:199, 210
"The Beginning of the End of the World" (Clifton) **17**:29
Beginning With 1914 (Mueller) **33**:197
"Beginnings" (Hayden) **6**:190
"The Beginnings" (Kipling) **3**:192
"Behaving Like a Jew" (Stern) **115**:249, 254, 269-70, 278, 281, 293
"Behaviour of Fish in an Egyptian Tea Garden" (Douglas) **106**:203
"Behind the Arras" (Carman) **34**:202
"Behind the Arras" (Dunbar) **5**:133
Behind the Arras: A Book of the Unseen (Carman) **34**:200, 205, 211-13, 218, 237-38
"Behind the Façade" (Stone) **53**:252
Behind the Landscape (Zanzotto)
See *Dietro il paesaggio*
"Behind the Mirror" (Gunn) **26**:210-213
Behold Mama, Flowers! (Serote) **113**:286, 288, 297-98
"Behold the Brand of Beauty Tossed" (Waller) **72**:334
"Behold the Lilies of the Field" (Hecht) **70**:78, 81, 84, 86
"Bei Hennef" (Lawrence) **54**:187, 195, 206-8, 224
"Beijing Spring" (Chin) **40**:9
"Beiname" (Goethe) **5**:248
"Being a Person" (Stafford) **71**:373
"Being a Woman" (Stone) **53**:231-32, 236
"The Being as Memory" (Carruth) **10**:71
"The Being as Moment" (Carruth) **10**:71
"The Being as Prevision" (Carruth) **10**:71
"Being Beauteous" (Rimbaud) **3**:261, 263-64; **57**:234, 248, 282, 286-87
Being Here: Poetry, 1977-80 (Warren) **37**:313, 325, 329, 335-36, 345, 350, 357, 359-60, 365-67, 373, 380, 382
"Being of Beauty" (Rimbaud) **3**:263
"Being Shot" (Wagoner) **33**:337, 339, 345
"Being Young and Green" (Millay) **6**:236
"The Beirut Poem" (Darwish)
See "Qasidat Beirut"
"The beistly lust the furius appetyt" (Dunbar) **67**:25
"Un Bel di Vedremo" (Rexroth) **95**:259, 271, 309
"Le Bel oiseau déchiffrant l'inconnu au couple d'amoureux" (Breton) **15**:49
Belaia staia (Akhmatova)
See *Belaya staya*
Belaia staja (Akhmatova)
See *Belaya staya*
Belaya staya (Akhmatova) **2**:3, 6, 11-12, 18
"Beldams of Tepoztlán" (Birney) **52**:97
"Belderg" (Heaney) **18**:203; **100**:212-14
"Belfast" (MacNeice) **61**:106, 124, 170
"Belfast Lough" (Montague) **106**:297
"Belfast on a Sunday Afternoon" (Davie) **29**:106-8, 119
"Belfast Tune" (Brodsky) **9**:28
The Belfry of Bruges (Longfellow) **30**:21, 27, 46
"Belgravia" (Guest) **55**:227
"Beli" (Kabīr) **56**:342
"Believe History" (Jeffers) **17**:141
"Believer" (Stafford) **71**:321
"Bell" (Brathwaite) **56**:51, 96
"The Bell" (Kinsella) **69**:137
"La bell au bois dormant" (Valéry) **9**:392
"Bell Buoy" (Merwin) **45**:7
"The Bell of Atri" (Longfellow) **30**:62
"Bell Paints a Picture" (Schuyler) **88**:179, 181
"Bell Speech" (Wilbur) **51**:187
Bella adrede (Guillén) **35**:175, 176, 177
"La Bella Bona Roba" (Lovelace) **69**:223, 228
"La Belle Angèle" (Thomas) **99**:305-6
"La Belle au Bois Dormant" (Jarrell) **41**:145, 175, 208
"La belle dame sans merci" (Keats) **1**:279, 282, 304-05; **96**:209-10, 213, 236, 245, 260, 284, 299-300, 352
"La belle Dorothée" (Baudelaire) **1**:49; **106**:100
"La belle époque" (Milosz) **8**:211
"La Belle Hequmière aux filles de joie" (Villon) **13**:389
"Belle Isle" (Randall) **86**:348
"Belle lecon aux enfants perdus" (Villon) **13**:394-95
"Bellerophon in Argos" (Morris) **55**:336
"Bellerophon in Lycia" (Morris) **55**:329, 331
"La belleza" (Storni) **33**:279, 300
Belleza (Jiménez) **7**:202
"The Bell-ringers" (Masefield) **78**:100
"The Bells" (Holmes) **71**:66
"The Bells" (Poe) **1**:430-31, 439, 441; **54**:276, 321
"The Bells" (Sexton) **2**:359
"Bells" (Traherne) **70**:198, 243, 326
Bells and Pomegranates (Browning) **61**:11; **97**:10
Bells and Pomegrantes (Browning) **2**:27, 70
"The Bells at Bray" (Spark) **72**:263
"Bells for John Whiteside's Daughter" (Ransom) **61**:261, 263, 267-69, 287, 296, 301, 307, 318, 320
"Bells I" (Traherne) **70**:302
"Bells in the Rain" (Wylie) **23**:328-29
"Bells in Winter" (Milosz) **8**:189, 205
Bells in Winter (Milosz) **8**:174
Bells of Lombardy (Stryk) **27**:214-15, 218
"The Bells of San Blas" (Longfellow) **30**:47
"Bells of Winter" (Milosz)
See "Bells in Winter"
"The Bells that Signed" (Day Lewis) **11**:144
"Belly Song" (Knight) **14**:46, 48
Belly Song and Other Poems (Knight) **14**:41-2, 48, 52
"A Beloved" (Lawrence) **54**:237
"Beloved" (Schnackenberg) **45**:338
"Beloved, Sleep" (Yevtushenko) **40**:347
"Below" (Celan) **10**:118
"Below Tintern" (Tomlinson) **17**:334, 336
"Belsazar" (Heine) **25**:140
"Belsen, Day of Liberation" (Hayden) **6**:194
La Beltà (Zanzotto) **65**:263-71, 273, 276-79, 287-88, 292, 300-301, 308-12, 315, 318-20, 327, 338
"Belts" (Kipling) **3**:162
"Ben Jonson Entertains a Man from Stratford" (Robinson) **1**:462, 468, 487; **35**:362
"Ben uinei ogni durezza" (Michelangelo) **103**:198
"Benares" (Borges) **22**:72; **32**:80-1
"The Bench of Boors" (Melville) **82**:76, 148
"Bending the Bow" (Duncan) **2**:107; **75**:231
Bending the Bow (Duncan) **2**:104, 107, 113-116, 119, 125, 127; **75**:113-20, 126-27, 131-35, 140, 149, 156-60, 171, 181, 189-90, 203-4, 215-17, 221, 231-33, 250, 253-56, 258, 260, 273-77
"Bendita Suerte" (Alurista) **34**:45
"Bendito sea tu Vientre" (Alurista) **34**:46
"Beneath a Cool Shade" (Behn) **13**:15
"Beneath My Hand and Eye the Distant Hills, Your Body" (Snyder) **21**:288
Beneath the Fortinaria (Bukowski) **18**:21
"Beneath the Shadow of the Freeway" (Cervantes) **35**:104, 106, 108, 110, 112, 117, 124, 133, 134, 135
"Bénédiction" (Baudelaire) **1**:54, 70; **106**:5-6, 60, 122, 125
"Benediction" (Kaufman) **74**:194, 212, 260-61, 269, 275
"Benediction" (Kunitz) **19**:148
"Bengali Heroes" (Tagore)
See "Banga bir"
"Benjamin Pantier" (Masters) **1**:347; **36**:169, 182, 230
"Benjamin Peirce" (Holmes) **71**:68
"Benn and Becht" (Corso) **108**:6
"Bennie's Departure" (McKay) **2**:225
"Ben's Last Fight" (Merton) **10**:345
"An Beo" (O'Flaherty)
See "Life"
"Beowulf" (Wilbur) **51**:189
Beowulf (Anonymous) **22**:1-65; **85**:1-179
Beowulf: A New Verse Translation (Heaney) **100**:237, 254, 261-62, 281, 288-89, 313, 340

Beppo (Byron)
See *Beppo: A Venetian Story*
Beppo: A Venetian Story (Byron) **16**:83, 115-20; **95**:51
"Bequests" (Clarke) **112**:53
"Berck-Plage" (Plath) **1**:390; **37**:198-205, 232
"Bereavement" (Smith) **12**:351
"Bereft" (Frost) **39**:232
"Bereft" (Hardy) **8**:131
"The Berg" (Melville) **82**:73, 103, 143-44, 163
"Bergerie" (Ronsard) **105**:272
"Bergidylle" (Heine) **25**:145
"Berkeley Eclogue" (Hass) **16**:217
"Berlin" (Ferlinghetti) **1**:167
"Berlin: First Night and Early Morning" (Creeley) **73**:54
"Berlin in ruins" (Gunn) **26**:211-212
"Berlin Is Hard on Colored Girls" (Lorde) **12**:142
The Berlin Songbook (Bely)
See *Berlinsky pesennik*
"Berlin Zoo" (Corso) **108**:25, 40
Berlinsky pesennik (Bely) **11**:7
"Bermudas" (Marvell) **10**:268-69, 271, 275, 289, 311, 313-14
"Berrathon" (Macpherson) **97**:183, 231-32, 315, 324
"Berry Holden" (Masters) **1**:324
Berryman's Sonnets (Berryman) **64**:77, 79, 88, 90, 99, 106, 126, 168, 170, 176
"Bert Kessler" (Masters) **36**:182
"Bertha in the Lane" (Barrett Browning) **6**:17
"Bertolt Brecht's Testimony Before a Military Court" (Darwish) **86**:33
Beschwörungen (Werfel) **101**:301, 308, 319, 323-24, 336, 349-50, 360
"Beside the Bed" (Mew) **107**:35, 56
Beside the River Sar (Castro)
See *En las orillas del Sar*
"Beside the Seaside" (Betjeman) **75**:21
"Beside the Shepherd" (Cohen) **109**:51
"The Besieged" (Paz) **48**:273
"Los besos" (Aleixandre) **15**:38
"Bess" (Stafford) **71**:379
"Bessey of the Glen" (Clare) **23**:25
"Bessy and Her Spinning Wheel" (Burns) **114**:18
The Best American Poetry (Graham) **59**:184
"The Best Daddy" (Silverstein) **49**:349
"The Best Days" (Wright) **36**:360
"The Best of It" (Sassoon) **12**:248, 260
The Best of Leonard Cohen (Cohen) **109**:35
The Best of Robert Service (Service) **70**:148, 161
"The Best She Could" (Hardy) **92**:291
"Best Year's" (Soto) **28**:398-99
Le bestiaire; ou, Cortège d'Orphée (Apollinaire) **7**:48
A Bestiary (Wilbur) **51**:189-91
Bestiary/Bestiario (Neruda) **4**:286-87
"A Bestiary for My Daughters Mary and Katharine" (Rexroth) **20**:187, 190, 195, 218; **95**:247, 250, 254, 258, 260, 274
"Bestiary U.S.A." (Sexton) **2**:367
"Besuch bei Ingres" (Enzensberger) **28**:150
"Besy" (Pushkin) **10**:413
"Beta" (Tolson) **88**:236, 317, 332
"Betancourt" (Baraka) **4**:15; **113**:131
Betäubung (Benn) **35**:5, 8, 68
"Bête Noire" (Douglas) **106**:185-87, 201
Bethlehem in Broad Daylight (Doty) **53**:47, 62
"Betraktelse" (Ekeloef) **23**:76
"Betrayal" (Lanier) **50**:56, 67
"Betrayal" (Muir) **49**:228, 237, 248, 297
"Betrayal" (Pavese)
See "Tradimento"
"The Betrothal" (Apollinaire)
See "Les fiançailles"
"The Betrothal" (Millay) **6**:211
The Betrothal (Patmore)
See *The Angel in the House, Book I: The Betrothal*
"The Betrothal of Cavehill" (Heaney) **100**:224, 269, 271
"Betrothed" (Bogan) **12**:127-28
"A Better Answer" (Prior) **102**:316
"Better is an handfull with quietness" (Kinsella) **69**:138
"A Better Resurrection" (Rossetti) **7**:290
"The Better Self" (Very) **86**:136
"Betty's Ball Blues" (Reed) **68**:329-30
"Betuix twell houris and ellevin" (Dunbar) **67**:16
"Between" (Corso) **108**:18
"Between" (Montague) **106**:327
"Between" (Waldrop) **109**:167, 177, 185
"Between Going and Staying" (Paz) **48**:273
Between Here and Now (Thomas) **99**:248, 256, 259-60, 274, 282, 304-7, 360
"Between Myself and Death" (Rexroth) **95**:260
Between Our Selves (Lorde) **12**:137, 156
"Between Ourselves" (Lorde) **12**:139
Between Stone and Flower (Paz)
See *Entre la piedra y la flor*
"Between the Porch and the Altar" (Lowell) **3**:200, 203-04, 206
"Between the Worlds" (Sandburg) **41**:330
"Between Two Hills" (Sandburg) **41**:243
"Between Two Prisoners" (Dickey) **40**:175, 258
"Between Two Wars" (Rexroth) **95**:271
Between Two Worlds (Paredes) **83**:27-29, 34, 44, 56-57, 63, 66
"Between Us" (Merrill) **28**:252
"Between Walls" (Williams) **7**:399, 402; **109**:241, 279
"Between What I See and What I Say" (Paz)
See "Entre Lo Que Veo y Digo..."
"Beucolicks" (Herrick) **9**:89
"Beverly Hills, Chicago" (Brooks) **7**:81
"Beware!" (Wylie) **23**:322
"Beware, Madam!" (Graves) **6**:163
"Bewick Finzer" (Robinson) **1**:467
"The Bewildered" (Rimbaud)
See "Les effarés"
"Bewty and the Presoneir" (Dunbar) **67**:25, 38, 57-58
"Beyond" (Guillén)
See "Más allá"
"Beyond" (Jackson) **44**:103
"Beyond Delinquency" (Corso) **33**:25; **108**:18
"Beyond Even Faithful Legends" (Bissett) **14**:6, 24, 31
Beyond Even Faithful Legends (Bissett)
See *Selected Poems: Beyond Even Faithful Legends*
"Beyond Harm" (Olds) **22**:325, 341
"Beyond Howth Head" (Mahon) **60**:133-34, 142, 147, 164-65, 168, 196, 203-9, 214, 233
"Beyond Sharp Control" (Brutus) **24**:116
"Beyond the Alps" (Lowell) **3**:205, 211, 218, 221
"Beyond the Gamut" (Carman) **34**:202, 212
"Beyond the Hunting Woods" (Justice) **64**:274
"Beyond the Last Lamp" (Hardy) **8**:125; **92**:201-3
Beyond the Mountains (Rexroth) **20**:185-86; **95**:249, 262, 275, 284
"Beyond the Pale" (Clarke) **112**:90
"Beyond the Pleasure Principle" (Nemerov) **24**:260
"Beyond the Question" (Sarton) **39**:328-29, 342, 365, 367
"Beyond What" (Niedecker) **42**:147
"Beyond You" (Merwin) **45**:48
"Bez nazvaniya" (Pasternak) **6**:288
"Bezverie" (Pushkin) **10**:409, 411
"Bhagna mandir" (Tagore) **8**:415
"Bhairavi gan" (Tagore) **8**:407
"Bhakti" (Kabīr) **56**:331
Bhanu Singha (Tagore)
See *Bhanusinga Thakurer Padavali*
Bhānu singha (Tagore)
See *Bhanusinga Thakurer Padavali*
Bhanusinga Thakurer Padavali (Tagore) **8**:403
Bhanusingh Thakurer padavali (Tagore) **8**:405
"Bhar" (Tagore) **8**:412
Bhauda, Nepal '70 (Berssenbrugge) **115**:9
"Biafra" (Levertov) **11**:176, 194
"Bianca among the Nightingales" (Barrett Browning) **6**:23-4, 28, 32, 38, 40
"Bianca's Dream" (Hood) **93**:80
Biathanatos (Donne) **43**:119
"The Bible" (Traherne) **70**:204, 244, 325
"The Bible Business" (Dalton) **36**:127
"The Bible Defense of Slavery" (Harper) **21**:190, 208, 217
"Bible Stories" (Reese) **29**:330
"bibliographie" (Enzensberger) **28**:137
"A Bibliography of the King's Book, or, Eikon Basilike" (Howe) **54**:89, 106, 125
A Bibliography of the King's Book or, Eikon Basilike (Howe) **54**:72-73, 76, 102, 105
La Bibliothèque est en feu (Char) **56**:113-14
"Bickford's Buddha" (Ferlinghetti) **1**:186-87
"Bicocca di San Giacomo" (Carducci) **46**:52
"The Bicycles and the Apex" (Oppen) **35**:321
"Biddy McGuire, Her Certainty" (Gilmore) **87**:302
"Bien loin d'ici" (Baudelaire) **1**:49
"Bien pudiera ser" (Storni) **33**:252, 276, 311
"Bien que le trait de vostre belle face" (Ronsard) **11**:250
"Biens égaux" (Char) **56**:150
"Bienvenue" (Char) **56**:154
"Bi-Focal" (Stafford) **71**:278, 296, 333, 361, 374
"Bifurcation" (Tzara) **27**:229-31
"The Big Baboon" (Belloc) **24**:24
"Big Bastard with a Sword" (Bukowski) **18**:13
"Big Bessie" (Tolson) **88**:258-59
"Big Bessie Throws Her Son into the Street" (Brooks) **7**:63, 81
"The Big Boots of Pain" (Sexton) **79**:215, 241
"Big Buttons, Cornets: the Advance" (Berryman)
See "Dream Song 2"
Big City Primer (Yau) **61**:330-31
"The Big Coverup" (Simic) **69**:334
"Big Elegy" (Brodsky)
See "The Great Elegy for John Donne"
"Big Fat Hairy Vision of Evil" (Ferlinghetti) **1**:167
"The Big Game Hunter" (Tolson) **88**:348-49, 351
"The Big Graveyard" (Viereck) **27**:262
The Big Green Day (Raworth) **107**:275, 309, 316
"The Big Heart" (Sexton) **2**:368; **79**:215, 222
"Big Island Notebook 11" (Yau) **61**:331
"Big John Henry" (Walker) **20**:287
"Big Momma" (Madhubuti) **5**:326, 344
"Big Steamers" (Kipling) **91**:115
"Big Terror Descends" (Hughes) **89**:195
"The Big Timer" (Hughes) **53**:114
"Big Wind" (Roethke) **15**:276, 279
"The Biggest Killing" (Dorn) **115**:125
"The Bight" (Bishop) **3**:50, 52-4; **34**:97, 116, 118, 130, 158
"Biglia" (Zanzotto) **65**:263
"Big-Time Wrestling" (Simic) **69**:362
Bījak (Kabīr) **56**:341-42, 344-46
The Bijak of Kabir (Kabīr) **56**:342-43
"Les bijoux" (Baudelaire) **1**:61; **106**:6, 26, 47-48, 51-52
"Bilbea" (Sandburg) **41**:240, 312
"Bi-Lingual Education" (Cruz) **37**:35
"Bill" (Masefield) **78**:68, 95
"Bill of Fare" (Enzensberger) **28**:142
"The Billboard Painters" (Ferlinghetti) **1**:183
"Billboards" (Ondaatje) **28**:328, 331
"Billboards and Galleons" (Lindsay) **23**:287
"Billboards Build Freedom of Choice" (Birney) **52**:16, 21, 25, 63, 79
"Billet à Whistler" (Mallarmé) **102**:10
"Billet-Doux" (Hughes) **89**:138-39
"Billy" (Spicer) **78**:249

"Billy in the Darbies" (Melville) **82**:97, 103, 156
Billy the Kid (Ondaatje) **28**:293-94, 296-97
Billy the Kid (Spicer) **78**:240, 247-50, 253, 258, 272, 279, 285, 305, 308, 328, 336, 354, 363
"Bimini" (Heine) **25**:167
"Binding the Dragon" (Sarton) **39**:365
"Bingu mondo no uta" (Yakamochi) **48**:102-3, 111-12, 129, 136
"Bío-Bío" (Mistral) **32**:166
Biograph (Dylan) **37**:59, 64-5
"The Biographer's Mandate" (Nemerov) **24**:289
"Biography" (Birney) **52**:58
"Biography" (Ciardi) **69**:25
"Biography" (Masefield) **78**:5, 8-9, 27-28, 31, 34, 40, 43, 54-55, 72, 88, 90
"The Biography of a Myth" (Jackson) **44**:74, 89
"Biology for Breakfast" (Wickham) **110**:265
"The Biology of Art" (Merwin) **45**:98
"Il Biondomoro" (Pasolini) **17**:264
"Biotherm (for Bill Berkson)" (O'Hara) **45**:120, 127, 131, 166-70, 245
"Birahulì" (Kabīr) **56**:342
"Birchbrook Hill" (Whittier) **93**:239, 251
"Birches" (Frost) **1**:196, 221, 225, 227-28, 230; **39**:230, 253, 256
"Birches" (Wylie) **23**:326
"Bird" (Brathwaite) **56**:45, 75
"Bird" (Harjo) **27**:72
"The Bird" (Hughes) **89**:180
"The Bird" (Muir) **49**:232
"The Bird and the Arras" (Finch) **21**:157, 160, 172
"The Bird Auction" (McGuckian) **27**:94
"Bird Ave" (Cervantes) **35**:134
"Bird Call Valley" (Wang Wei) **18**:381-82, 391
"Bird-Cherry Tree the Last but One" (Akhmadulina)
See "Ceremuxa predposlednjaja"
"The Bird Frau" (Dove) **6**:108
"Bird of Air" (H. D.) **5**:287
"Bird Sanctuary" (Mahon) **60**:166-67
"Bird Watching" (Ciardi) **69**:56
"The Bird with the Coppery, Keen Claws" (Stevens) **6**:293, 304
"Birdbrain!" (Ginsberg) **4**:62, 76
"Birdcage Walk" (Merton) **10**:351
"The Bird-Catcher's Boy" (Hardy) **92**:270
"Birdcries Stream" (Wang Wei)
See "Bird-Singing Stream"
"The Birdnesters" (Szirtes) **51**:157
"The Birds" (Belloc) **24**:5, 8
"Birds" (Césaire) **25**:46
"The Birds" (Jacobsen) **62**:320
"Birds" (Jeffers) **17**:147
"Birds" (Wright) **14**:347, 349, 353, 366
Birds (Perse)
See *Oiseaux*
Birds (Wright) **14**:348-49, 354
Birds, Beasts, and Flowers (Lawrence) **54**:170, 173, 187, 189, 191, 197, 200-201, 207, 212, 218, 227-28, 232, 236
"Birds Caught, Birds Flying" (Snodgrass) **74**:330, 332, 334
"The Bird's Companion" (Williams) **109**:193
"Birds for Janet" (Ondaatje) **28**:318, 332
"Birds in the Night" (Cernuda) **62**:267-68
"Birds in the Night" (Verlaine) **2**:415; **32**:396, 408-09, 411
"Birds in Winter" (Ignatow) **34**:306
"Birds' Nests" (Thomas) **53**:328
"The Birds of Killingworth" (Longfellow) **30**:62
"Birds of Passage" (Longfellow) **30**:27
The Birds of Pompeii (Ciardi) **69**:56
"Birds of Prey" (McKay) **2**:212
"The birds that sing on Autumn eves" (Bridges) **28**:84
"Birds Walking" (Merwin) **45**:28
"Birds without Descent" (Aleixandre)
See "Pajaros sin descenso"
"Bird-Singing Stream" (Wang Wei) **18**:360, 376, 380-81, 386, 390
"Birdsong of the Lesser Poet" (Jacobsen) **62**:324, 328
"Bird-Watching" (Thomas) **99**:326
"Bird-Witted" (Moore) **49**:101
"The Biretta" (Heaney) **18**:256
"Birmingham" (MacNeice) **61**:116-17, 119-20, 124, 131, 138
"Birmingham" (Walker) **20**:283, 287
"Birmingham Sunday" (Hughes) **1**:252; **53**:150
"A Birth" (Dickey) **40**:181
"Birth and Death" (Eberhart) **76**:5
"Birth and Death" (Jeffers) **17**:141
"Birth and Death" (Swinburne) **24**:324
"The Birth in a Narrow Room" (Brooks) **7**:54, 80
"Birth of a Fascist" (Viereck) **27**:280
"Birth of a Genius among Men" (MacDiarmid) **9**:153
"Birth of a Smile" (Mandelstam)
See "Rozhdenie ulybki"
"The Birth of Christ" (García Lorca)
See "Nacimiento de Cristo"
"The Birth of Flattery" (Crabbe) **97**:73
"The Birth of John Henry" (Tolson) **88**:274
The Birth of Kumara (Kālidāsa)
See *Kumārasambhava*
"Birth of Love" (Warren) **37**:308, 360
"The Birth of Potchikoo" (Erdrich) **52**:193
The Birth of the Prince (Kālidāsa)
See *Kumārasambhava*
"Birth of the Sun" (Randall) **86**:348
"Birth of the Virgin" (Swenson) **14**:285
The Birth of the War-God (Kālidāsa)
See *Kumārasambhava*
"Birth on Range 18" (Welch) **62**:370
"Birth Report" (Kennedy) **93**:140
"Birthday" (Aleixandre) **15**:16
"Birthday" (Benn)
See "Der Geburtstag"
"Birthday" (Ciardi) **69**:54
"A Birthday" (Creeley) **73**:12, 44, 46, 48
"Birthday" (Jeffers) **17**:141
"A Birthday" (Muir) **49**:233, 250-51
"A Birthday" (Rossetti) **7**:276, 278, 280
"Birthday" (Stern) **115**:276
"Birthday" (Szymborska)
See "Urodziny"
Birthday (Corso)
See *The Happy Birthday of Death*
The Birthday (Merrill) **28**:270
"A Birthday Cake for Lionel" (Wylie) **23**:321-22
"The Birthday Dream" (Dickey) **40**:154, 158
"A Birthday Kid Poem" (Ortiz) **17**:228
Birthday Letters (Hughes) **89**:159-60, 162, 176-83, 187, 189-91, 193, 206, 208, 212-14, 217, 226-27, 230, 232-35, 238-39, 242-45, 251, 254, 261-62, 265-67, 269-75
"Birthday Ode" (Burns)
See "Ode for General Washington's Birthday"
"Birthday on the Acropolis" (Sarton) **39**:327, 341
"Birthday on the Beach" (Nash) **21**:270
"The Birthday Party" (Jacobsen) **62**:324
"A Birthday Poem" (Hecht) **70**:84
"Birthday Poem" (Shapiro) **25**:263
"A Birthday Poem" (Tapahonso) **65**:253
"A Birthday Present" (Plath) **37**:232, 255
"Birthday Sonnet" (Wylie) **23**:315
"Birthday 35" (Chappell) **105**:16, 25, 27-28, 30-31, 42, 54-56, 59, 71
"A Birthday Tribute to James Freeman Clarke" (Holmes) **71**:66
"Birthmarks" (Song) **21**:341
"Birthplace" (Corso) **108**:21
"The Birthplace" (Heaney) **18**:214
"Birthplace" (Oppen) **35**:297
"Birthplace Revisited" (Corso) **33**:23, 41; **108**:31
"Bisclavret" (Marie de France) **22**:258, 260, 268, 272, 282-84, 286, 298-99
"Biscuit" (Kenyon) **57**:41
"La bise se rue à travers" (Verlaine) **32**:363
"Bishop Blougram" (Browning) **2**:37
"Bishop Blougram's Apology" (Browning) **2**:43, 73; **97**:54
"The Bishop Orders His Tomb at St. Praxed's" (Browning) **2**:37, 48, 82, 94; **97**:11-13
"Bison" (Winters) **82**:319
"El bisonte" (Borges) **32**:90
"Bitaqat Huwiyya" (Darwish) **86**:14, 20, 29
"The Biting Insects" (Kinnell) **26**:288
"The Bitter Moon" (Winters) **82**:319, 321, 326, 336-37
"The Bitter River" (Hughes) **1**:251
"Bitter Thoughts" (Stern) **115**:277
"Bituminous?" (Silverstein) **49**:342
Bixby Canyon to Jessore Road (Ginsberg) **4**:89
Black and Beautiful: Soul and Madness (Baraka) **113**:26
Black & Blues (Brathwaite) **56**:34, 54, 60-62, 88-89
"The Black Angel" (Montale)
See "L'angelo nero"
Black Armour (Wylie) **23**:301-302, 307, 309-10, 324, 332
Black Art (Baraka) **113**:12, 17, 19-20, 55, 74-75, 77-78
"Black Art" (Baraka) **4**:10, 19, 25, 40; **113**:13-14, 17, 26, 29-30, 32-33, 35, 41-42, 45, 52, 75, 104, 152
"The Black Art" (Sexton) **2**:373; **79**:253
Black Art (Baraka) **4**:18
"Black Bourgeoisie" (Baraka) **113**:47
"Black Bill's Honeymoon" (Noyes) **27**:123, 134
"A Black Birch in Winter" (Wilbur) **51**:283
"Black Blood" (Blok) **21**:5
"Black Boy in the Dark" (Hecht) **70**:99
"Black Buttercups" (Clampitt) **19**:83, 86, 91
"The Black Christ" (Hughes) **53**:94
"The Black Christ" (Madhubuti) **5**:339-40
The Black Christ and Other Poems (Cullen) **20**:59, 62, 64, 68
"The Black Christ (Hopefully Dedicated to White America)" (Cullen) **20**:59, 64-66, 68, 71, 73-75, 87
"The Black Clown" (Hughes) **53**:114
"Black Coat" (Hughes) **89**:272
"Black Cock" (Montale)
See "Gallo cedrone"
"The Black Cock" (Reed) **68**:323
"The Black Cottage" (Frost) **1**:193, 198
"BLACK DADA NIHILISMUS" (Baraka) **4**:9, 14; **113**:9, 61, 148
"Black Dancer in the Little Savoy" (Hughes) **1**:246
"The Black Day" (MacLeish) **47**:246, 260
"Black Eagle Returns to St. Joe" (Masters) **1**:344
"Black Earth" (Mandelstam)
See "Chernozem"
"Black Earth" (Moore)
See "Melancthon"
"Black Easter" (Shvarts)
See "Chernaia Paskha"
"Black Eyed Susan" (Williams) **109**:286, 294
"The Black Faced Sheep" (Hall) **70**:28, 34
Black Feeling, Black Talk (Giovanni) **19**:133, 135, 139
Black Feeling, Black Talk, Black Judgement (Giovanni) **19**:107-8, 110-11, 114, 118, 120-22, 124, 128, 136
"The Black Fox" (Whittier) **93**:243
"The Black Goddess" (Graves) **6**:154
"Black Hair" (Hughes) **89**:188
"Black Hair" (Soto) **28**:379-80
"Black Harmonium" (Hagiwara)
See "Kuroi fūkin"
"Black Hawk held: In reason" (Niedecker) **42**:151
"The Black Hood" (Francis) **34**:254

Black Hosts (Senghor)
See *Hosties noires*
"Black Jackets" (Gunn) **26**:201
"A Black Job" (Hood) **93**:99-100
Black Judgement (Giovanni) **19**:135, 139, 143
"The Black Knight" (Thoreau)
See "Independence"
"The Black Labour Advocate" (Gilmore) **87**:300
"Black Leather Because Bumblebees Look Like It" (Wakoski) **15**:326
"Black Love" (Madhubuti) **5**:342
"Black Magdalens" (Cullen) **20**:56, 62, 64
Black Magic (Baraka) **113**:12, 14, 18, 31, 55, 57, 61, 73-75, 126, 132, 141, 145, 148, 152
"Black Magic" (Randall) **86**:289
"Black Magic" (Sanchez) **9**:223, 234
Black Magic: Sabotage, Target Study, Black Art; Collected Poetry, 1961-1967 (Baraka) **4**:6, 8, 16-18, 24, 26
"Black Mail" (Walker) **30**:339, 352
"Black Majesty" (Cullen) **20**:64
"The Black Mammy" (Johnson) **24**:142
"The Black Man Is Making New Gods" (Baraka) **4**:19; **113**:75
"Black Maps" (Strand) **63**:177
"Black March" (Smith) **12**:300-01, 308, 319, 326
A Black Mass (Baraka) **113**:26
"Black Mesa" (Baca) **41**:47
"The Black Mesa" (Merrill) **28**:223, 255
Black Mesa Poems (Baca) **41**:47, 61, 63
"Black Money" (Gallagher) **9**:36, 53
"Black Mother Woman" (Lorde) **12**:154, 156-57
Black Music (Baraka) **113**:61
"A Black November Turkey" (Wilbur) **51**:218
"Black Nude" (Tomlinson) **17**:311
"Black Oaks" (Oliver) **75**:321
"Black Panther" (Hughes) **1**:251-52; **53**:111, 151
"Black People!" (Baraka) **4**:19, 25-6; **113**:18-19, 35, 74
"The Black Pit" (Hayden) **6**:187
"Black Poet, White Critic" (Randall) **86**:324, 327
Black Power Chant (Baraka) **4**:19
"Black Power Poem" (Reed) **68**:337, 347, 349
Black Pride (Madhubuti) **5**:321, 336, 338-41, 346
"Black Pudding" (Gallagher) **9**:64
"The Black Rhino" (Hughes) **89**:146
The Black Riders, and Other Lines (Crane) **80**:39-40, 44-50, 56-59, 65-69, 71, 74-85, 93-97, 100-103, 106-8, 110, 112-14
"Black Riders Came from the Sea" (Crane) **80**:52, 101
"Black Riders Rode Forth" (Crane) **80**:101
"Black Rook in Rainy Weather" (Plath) **37**:237-38, 241
"Black Sampson of Brandywine" (Dunbar) **5**:129, 131, 138
"The Black Sheep" (Service) **70**:117
"Black Shit" (Serote) **113**:295
"Black Shroud" (Ginsberg) **4**:90
"Black Silk" (Gallagher) **9**:50, 59, 62
"Black Sketches" (Madhubuti) **5**:337
"Black Snake Visitation" (Mackey) **49**:3
"Black Snakes" (Oliver) **75**:292
"Black Song" (Guillén)
See "Canto negro"
"Black String of Days" (Komunyakaa) **51**:35
"The Black Swan" (Jarrell) **41**:171, 173, 179, 191-92
"Black Tambourine" (Crane) **3**:98; **99**:17, 80
The Black Unicorn (Lorde) **12**:137-38, 141-42, 144, 148, 151, 153-55, 157-58, 160
"Black Velvet Art" (Kennedy) **93**:151
"The Black Virginity" (Loy) **16**:322
"Black/White" (Wright) **14**:366
Black white (Illyés)
See *Fekete feher*
"The Black Winds" (Williams) **7**:383-85, 388-89; **109**:283
"Black Woman" (Senghor) **25**:224-30
"Blackberries" (Ponge)
See "Les mûres"
"Blackberries Sweet" (Randall) **86**:306
"Blackberrying" (Plath) **1**:407-09; **37**:238-39
"Blackberry-Picking" (Heaney) **18**:192; **100**:263
"The Blackbird" (Hughes) **89**:273
The Blackbird (Zagajewski) **27**:396
"The Blackbird of Derrycairn" (Clarke) **112**:54, 71, 101, 117
"Black-Eyed Bess" (Cowley) **90**:15
"Blackfeet, Blood and Piegan Hunters" (Welch) **62**:339, 346, 373
"Blackgirl Learning" (Madhubuti) **5**:344
"Blacklash Blues" (Hughes) **53**:111, 151
"Blackman/An Unfinished History" (Madhubuti) **5**:326, 343, 345
Blackout of the Stars (Sachs)
See *Sternverdunkelung*
Blacks (Brooks) **7**:105
"Black-Shouldered Kite" (Wright) **14**:344
"Blacksmith" (Rimbaud)
See "Le forgeron"
"The Blacksmith's Serenade" (Lindsay) **23**:264
"The Blackstone Rangers" (Brooks) **7**:88, 90-1
"Blackstudies" (Lorde) **12**:147, 158
"Blake" (Borges) **22**:97
"Blake" (Moore) **49**:114
"Blame not my cheeks" (Campion) **87**:32-33, 63-64
"Blame not my lute" (Wyatt) **27**:315, 324
"Blanc" (Valéry) **9**:392
"Blanco" (Soto) **28**:375
"Lo blanco" (Storni) **33**:272
Blanco (Paz) **1**:355-56, 358, 363, 368-69, 372, 374, 376-77; **48**:181, 194, 206, 214-16, 228, 232, 267, 274
"Blank" (Baraka) **113**:16
The Blasted Pine (Birney) **52**:17
"Blasting from Heaven" (Levine) **22**:223
"Blaubeuren" (Tomlinson) **17**:360
"Bleeding" (Swenson) **14**:269-70, 285
"Blenheim Oranges" (Thomas) **53**:294, 318, 326
"Blessèd Accident" (Warren) **37**:337
"Blessed are They that Mourn" (Bryant) **20**:6
"Blessed be the Paps" (Crashaw) **84**:76-77, 99, 115, 140-45, 147, 153, 155
"Blessed, Cursed Memory" (Tennyson) **101**:249
"The Blessed Damozel" (Rossetti) **44**:164-65, 173, 184, 195, 202-3, 205, 236, 238
"The Blessed Damozele" (Rossetti) **44**:164-65, 173, 184, 195, 202-3, 205, 236, 238
"Blessed Is the Man" (Moore) **49**:126, 134, 139
"Blessed Sleep" (Johnson) **24**:159
"The Blessed Virgin, Compared to the Air We Breathe" (Hopkins) **15**:166
"The Blessed Virgin Mary Compared to a Window" (Merton) **10**:330, 338
"Blessing" (Clarke) **112**:83
"Blessing" (Montague) **106**:243
"A Blessing" (Wright) **36**:285, 294, 325, 327-28, 334, 344, 350, 352, 356-57, 364, 369, 372, 374, 392, 394-96, 398, 403
"A Blessing in Disguise" (Ashbery) **26**:129, 143
"Blessing Myself" (Ignatow) **34**:276, 318
Blew Ointment (Bissett) **14**:5
blew trewz (Bissett) **14**:7-8
"Blighters" (Sassoon) **12**:263, 277, 282
"Blind Bartimeus" (Longfellow) **30**:13, 64
"The Blind Child's Story" (Dickey) **40**:177
"Blind Curse" (Ortiz) **17**:246
"The Blind Doge at 83" (Viereck) **27**:280
Blind Fireworks (MacNeice) **61**:180
"The Blind Leading the Blind" (Mueller) **33**:197
"Blind Man" (Alurista)
See "Hombre Ciego"
"Blind Man" (Seferis) **66**:208
"The Blind Man" (Wright) **14**:337, 369
"Blind Man's Holiday" (Curnow) **48**:60
"Blind Panorama of New York" (García Lorca)
See "Panorama ceigo de Nueva York"
"Blind Spring" (Shvarts) **50**:148
"Blind William's Song" (Merwin) **45**:18
"Blind Willie and the Talking Dog" (Silverstein) **49**:349
"Blind Willie McTell" (Dylan) **37**:59, 65-66
"Der blinde junge" (Loy) **16**:309, 316
"Der blinde Sänger" (Hölderlin) **4**:147
"The Blinded Bird" (Hardy) **8**:98
Blindenschrift (Enzensberger) **28**:133-35, 138-40, 143, 150
Blindsight (Waldrop) **109**:175
"Bliss" (Pushkin) **10**:407
"Blisse" (Traherne) **70**:194-95, 238, 275, 318
Bliznets v tuchakh (Pasternak) **6**:263, 275
"Blizzard" (Sarton) **39**:368
Blizzard of One (Strand) **63**:187, 194-99
"blk/chant" (Sanchez) **9**:204, 225, 234
"blk / wooooomen / chant" (Sanchez) **9**:225
"Block 4 Barrack 4 'Apt' C" (Yamada) **44**:340, 342
"Block City" (Stevenson) **84**:315, 328, 345-47
"Blockade Portrait Via Genre, Still Life, and Landscape Painting" (Shvarts)
See "Portret blokady cherez zhanr, natiurmort, i peizazh"
"Blocks" (O'Hara) **45**:114, 160
"Blödigkeit" (Hölderlin) **4**:148
"The Blond Road" (Hugo) **68**:315
Blonde on Blonde (Dylan) **37**:44, 47, 50-52, 54
"Blood" (Das) **43**:80, 87-88
Blood (Quintana)
See *Sangre*
Blood & Family (Kinsella) **69**:80-81
"Blood and Innocence" (Hughes) **89**:182
"Blood and the Moon" (Yeats) **20**:313; **51**:106
"Blood Feud" (Wylie) **23**:301
Blood for a Stranger (Jarrell) **41**:127-28, 139, 146, 159, 179, 184
"Blood from a Stone" (Oppen) **35**:320, 321, 342
"Blood Money" (Whitman) **91**:275
"Blood on a Dead World" (Rexroth) **95**:249
Blood on the Tracks (Dylan) **37**:54, 56, 58-60
"Blood Orange" (Simic) **69**:303
"Blood Precious Blood" (Randall) **86**:341
"The Blood Thinks, and Pauses" (Raworth) **107**:274
"Bloodbirth" (Lorde) **12**:157
"Bloodfire" (Chappell) **105**:5, 27, 43, 70
Bloodfire (Chappell) **105**:24, 30, 34-36, 39-40, 43-44, 47, 53, 58, 60, 67-68, 72
"Bloodfire Garden" (Chappell) **105**:24, 26-27, 59, 63
"The Blood-Red Fourragère" (Service) **70**:132
"Bloodsmiles" (Madhubuti) **5**:337
"Bloody Absurdities" (Rimbaud)
See "Conneries"
"The Bloody Sire" (Jeffers) **17**:139
"The Bloom of Creed" (Barker) **77**:7
The Bloomingdale Papers (Carruth) **10**:78-84
"Bloomingdale's I" (Hacker) **47**:94, 97
"The Blossom" (Blake) **12**:7, 23, 33; **63**:24-26, 30, 68, 100, 125
"The Blossom" (Donne)
See "The Blossome"
"Blossom" (Oliver) **75**:286
"The Blossome" (Donne) **1**:126, 130, 147
"The Blow" (Hardy) **8**:94
"The Blow" (Neruda)
See "El golpe"
"Blow and Counterblow" (Montale)
See "Botta e riposta"
"Blow Up Tight to Fly" (Alurista) **34**:42
"Blowin' in the Wind" (Dylan) **37**:49-50, 56, 71
"Blowing Boy" (Page) **12**:177
"Blown Hilcote Manor" (Masefield) **78**:91
"Blue" (Brathwaite) **56**:55
"Blue" (Schuyler) **88**:216

Blue (Darío)
See *Azul . . .*
"Blue and White Lines after O'Keeffe" (Song) **21**:331, 334, 336, 340-41
"Blue Bag" (Moore) **49**:146
"The Blue Battalions" (Crane) **80**:52-53, 65, 70
"Blue Bayou" (Hughes) **53**:108
"The Blue Birds" (Thoreau) **30**:192, 194-95, 242, 257
"The Blue Bouquet" (Paz)
See "El ramo azul"
"The Blue Cat" (Hagiwara) **18**:181
Blue Cat (Hagiwara)
See *Aoneko*
Blue Chicory (Niedecker) **42**:98, 101, 106
"The Blue Closet" (Morris) **55**:238, 240, 279-84, 301-3, 323
"Blue Cockerel" (Merwin) **45**:6
The Blue Estuaries: Poems, 1923-1968 (Bogan) **12**:96-7, 100-03, 107, 112, 120-21
"Blue Evening" (Brooke) **24**:57-8, 76
"Blue Farm" (McGuckian) **27**:95
"The Blue Flannel Suit" (Hughes) **89**:181
"The Blue from Heaven" (Smith) **12**:302, 304, 319, 331, 333
"Blue Gem Creeper" (Tagore)
See "Nilamanilata"
"Blue Girls" (Ransom) **61**:271, 288, 307, 313, 321-22
"Blue Guitar" (Stevens)
See "The Man with the Blue Guitar"
"Blue Horses Rush In" (Tapahonso) **65**:233-34, 244, 258
Blue Horses Rush In: Poems and Stories (Tapahonso) **65**:235, 252-53
Blue Iris: Poems and Essays (Oliver) **75**:342
"Blue Lantern" (Song) **21**:331, 338-40, 343
"Blue Light Lounge Sutra for the Performance Poets at Harold Park Hotel" (Komunyakaa) **51**:14, 63
"Blue Like Death" (Welch) **62**:337, 346
"Blue Lizard Lounge" (Yau) **61**:334-35
"The Blue Meridian" (Toomer) **7**:309, 311-12, 324-26, 328-29, 336,-37, 340
"Blue Moles" (Plath) **1**:389; **37**:188, 190
"Blue Monday" (Wakoski) **15**:325, 348
Blue Notes (Komunyakaa)
See *Blue Notes: Essays, Interviews, and Commentaries*
Blue Notes: Essays, Interviews, and Commentaries (Komunyakaa) **51**:62-64
"Blue O'Clock" (Kaufman) **74**:195
The Blue Pencil (Bishop) **34**:95
"A Blue Ribbon at Amesbury" (Frost) **1**:196
Blue Screen (Raworth) **107**:307, 325, 336
"The Blue She Brings with Her" (McGuckian) **27**:81-82
"Blue Skies, White Breasts, Green Trees" (Stern) **115**:247, 270
"Blue Sky Rain" (McGuckian) **27**:82, 93
"Blue Slanted Into Blueness" (Kaufman) **74**:216
"Blue Squills" (Teasdale) **31**:358
The Blue Stairs (Guest) **55**:213, 217-19
"The Blue Swallows" (Nemerov) **24**:300
The Blue Swallows (Nemerov) **24**:260-63, 274, 277, 281, 289, 291
"The Blue Taj" (Berssenbrugge) **115**:37, 41, 44
"The Blue Tower" (Stryk) **27**:214
"Blue Umbrellas" (Enright) **93**:11
"Blue Winter" (Francis) **34**:259
"A Blue Woman with Sticking out Breasts Hanging" (Cummings) **5**:99, 103
"Bluebeard" (Millay) **6**:205
"Bluebell among the Sables" (Spark) **72**:226, 229
"Bluebells" (MacNeice) **61**:119
The Bluebells and Other Verse (Masefield) **78**:41, 49, 73, 85, 91
"Bluebells for Love" (Kavanagh) **33**:102, 157
"Blueberries" (Frost) **1**:225
"The Blue-Bird" (Melville) **82**:107, 153
"A Bluebird in March" (Carman) **34**:203
"The Blue-Eyed Exterminator" (Jacobsen) **62**:323, 329
"The Blue-Flag in the Bog" (Millay) **6**:233
"The Blue-Fly" (Graves) **6**:163
"Bluejay" (Francis) **34**:256-57
"Blues" (Meredith) **28**:187
"Blues" (Walcott) **46**:230, 285
"Blues at Dawn" (Hughes) **1**:266; **53**:158
A Blues Book for Blue Black Magical Women (Sanchez) **9**:207, 211-16, 218-20, 228-29, 234, 238-41, 243
"Blues Chant Hoodoo Revival" (Komunyakaa) **51**:34, 46
"Blues for Hal Waters" (Kaufman) **74**:217
"Blues for Ladies" (Hughes) **53**:101
"Blues for Men" (Hughes) **53**:101
"Blues for Ruby Matrix" (Aiken) **26**:24, 29
"Blues Note" (Kaufman) **74**:262, 270, 274
"Blue-Stocking Revels; or, The Feast of the Violets" (Hunt) **73**:137, 140, 151-52, 169
"The Bluet" (Schuyler) **88**:199
"Blüte" (Stramm) **50**:170, 189, 208
"Boa Constrictor" (Silverstein) **49**:310
"Boädicea" (Tennyson) **6**:360, 363
"Boadicea. An Ode" (Cowper) **40**:115-16
"Board of Selection" (Enright) **93**:33
"Boast of Quietness" (Borges)
See "Jactancia de quietud"
"Boasting of stillness" (Borges)
See "Jactancia de quietud"
"The boat" (Paz)
See "El barco"
"The Boat" (Sexton) **2**:365
"The Boat of Life" (Ishikawa)
See "Inochi no fune"
The Boat of Quiet Hours (Kenyon) **57**:3-4, 6, 9, 11, 19, 22-24, 35-37, 39-40, 45
"The Boat of the White Feather Bird" (Ishikawa)
See "Shiraha no toribune"
"Boat Ride" (Gallagher) **9**:50-1, 58-60
"Boatman" (Thomas) **99**:272, 308
"Boats" (Montague) **106**:243, 277
"Boats on the Marne" (Montale) **13**:146
Bob Dylan at Budokan (Dylan) **37**:64
"The Bobby to the Sneering Lady" (McKay) **2**:226
"Bobo's Metamorphosis" (Milosz) **8**:187
"Bob's Lane" (Thomas) **53**:305
"Bobsled" (Kennedy) **93**:135
Le Bocage (Ronsard) **11**:246; **105**:215
"Boccaccio: The Plague Years" (Dove) **6**:109
"Bodies and Souls" (Heaney) **100**:329
"THE BODY" (Bissett) **14**:9, 34
"Body" (Creeley) **73**:96
"Body" (Tagore)
See "Tanu"
"Body and Soul: A Mediation" (Kumin) **15**:206
"The Body as Braille" (Cervantes) **35**:132
"Body Fished from the Seine" (Corso) **108**:11, 16
Body Image (Waldrop) **109**:179
"The Body in Smoke through the Air" (Sachs)
See "Dein Leib im Rauch durch die Luft"
"Body in Torment" (Cernuda)
See "Cuerpo en pena"
"The Body of God" (Lawrence) **54**:199, 250
"Body of Summer" (Elytis) **21**:115
Body of This Death (Bogan) **12**:85-7, 103-04, 116, 119-20, 126-28
"Body of Waking" (Rukeyser) **12**:217, 220
Body of Waking (Rukeyser) **12**:217, 219-21, 224
Body Rags (Kinnell) **26**:240-42, 244, 246, 257, 261, 290-91, 293
"Body, Remember" (Cavafy) **36**:74, 75
"Body's Beauty" (Rossetti) **44**:253
"Boeotian" (Frost) **39**:254
"'Boes" (Sandburg) **41**:347
"Bog Oak" (Heaney) **18**:201; **100**:194-95
"Bog Poems" (Heaney) **100**:308
"Bog Queen" (Heaney) **18**:188, 195, 211; **100**:219, 224, 308-9
"Bog Royal" (Montague) **106**:320, 327
"Bogland" (Heaney) **18**:188, 195, 201, 205, 209, 211; **100**:209, 231, 349
"Bogumil" (Dorn) **115**:231
"Bohemia" (Parker) **28**:363
"The Bohemian" (Dunbar) **5**:125
"Bohémiens en voyage" (Baudelaire) **106**:59
Boiarin Orša (Lermontov) **18**:279, 300
"Boiling the desperate coffee" (Spender) **71**:216
"The Boiling Water" (Koch) **80**:313
"Boire" (Éluard) **38**:71
"Le bois amical" (Valéry) **9**:391
"Le bois de l'epte" (Char) **56**:108, 113, 182
"La Boîte aux lumières" (Péret) **33**:230
Bojarin Orša (Lermontov)
See *Boiarin Orša*
"Bokardo" (Robinson) **1**:468; **35**:367
"A Boke" (Berrigan) **103**:32-33, 43
Boke of Phyllyp Sparowe (Skelton) **25**:330, 332-33, 335, 343-44, 346, 348, 353-54, 356-60, 367, 369, 374, 380-82, 384, 393-94, 396-400
"Bolezn" (Akhmadulina) **43**:7
Bolivia: Another End of Ace (Raworth) **107**:325
"Bologna: A Poem about Gold" (Wright) **36**:367
"Bolshevik Epic" (Borges) **32**:121
"Bomb" (Corso) **33**:5-6, 9, 36, 43-4, 47-8; **108**:17, 22-24, 31, 49-50, 52-57
"Bomba" (Fuertes) **27**:39, 45
"Bomba atómica" (Guillén) **23**:124
"Bombardment" (Lowell) **13**:78
"Une bombe aux Feuillantines" (Hugo) **17**:100
"The Bombed Happiness" (Spender) **71**:227
"Bombed Train Station, 80 Killed" (Corso) **33**:50
"Bombinations of a Chimera" (MacDiarmid) **9**:193
"Bombings" (Niedecker) **42**:151
"Bon Vin et Fillette" (Béranger) **112**:21
"Bon Voyage" (Robinson) **35**:368
"Bonaparte" (Lamartine) **16**:277, 291
"Bond and Free" (Frost) **39**:233
"Bone Dreams" (Heaney) **18**:188, 204; **100**:214-16, 224-25
"Bone Poem" (Oliver) **75**:287
"Bonehead Bill" (Service) **70**:118
"The Bones" (Merwin) **45**:7, 9
"Bones" (Sandburg) **41**:360
"The Bones of My Father" (Knight) **14**:43, 52
Bones of the Cuttlefish (Montale)
See *Ossi di seppia*
"The Bones of the Dead" (Mistral)
See "Los huesos de los muertos"
"The Bones Speak" (Wright) **14**:337, 339
"Bonfire" (Gallagher) **9**:61-62
"Bongo Song" (Guillén)
See "La canción del bongo"
Bonheur (Verlaine) **2**:417; **32**:386
"Bonheur champêtre" (Sainte-Beuve) **110**:39, 51, 65
"Bonie Mary" (Burns) **114**:129
La bonne chanson (Verlaine) **2**:413-14, 419, 431-32; **32**:353, 368, 375, 385, 393-94, 396, 399, 401, 407
"The Bonnie Broukit Bairn" (MacDiarmid) **9**:156, 160, 187
"Bonr" (Rimbaud) **57**:247, 251
"Les bons chiens" (Baudelaire) **1**:58-9
"Bonsai Poems" (Kaufman) **74**:259
"Bonsal" (Guillén) **23**:126
"Boogie 1 a.m." (Hughes) **53**:92; **53**:123
"Boogie Segue to Bop" (Hughes) **53**:190
"The Book" (Darío)
See "El libro"
"A Book" (Stein) **18**:325, 348
"The Book" (Vaughan) **81**:339, 343, 351, 370
"Book Buying in the Tenderloin" (Hass) **16**:195
The Book of Ahania (Blake) **12**:13

A Book of Airs (Campion)
See *A Booke of Ayres, Set foorth to be song to the Lute, Orpherian, and Base Violl*
A Book of Americans (Benét) **64**:22-23, 53
"Book of Ancestors" (Atwood) **8**:28-9, 42
"The Book of Annandale" (Robinson) **1**:460-61
"The Book of Balaam's Ass" (Jones) **116**:88-89, 100, 108-9, 172-73
"The Book of Beginnings" (Hunt) **73**:151-52
The Book of Earth (Noyes) **27**:130, 132-3, 135
The Book of Elizabethan Verse (Braithwaite) **52**:106, 124
"The Book of Ephraim" (Merrill) **28**:224-25, 227-31, 235-37, 243, 245, 260-61, 263, 266, 271-75, 278
The Book of Exercises (Seferis) **66**:90, 184-86, 209
The Book of Exercises II (Seferis) **66**:125, 208-9
Book of Fame (Chaucer)
See *House of Fame*
The Book of Folly (Sexton) **2**:355-56, 360, 365, 368; **79**:190, 192-93, 199, 202, 207, 213-14, 216-19, 230-31, 233, 242-43, 250-51
The Book of Georgian Verse (Braithwaite) **52**:106
The Book of Gods and Devils (Simic) **69**:278-79, 300, 302, 305, 307, 309-11, 316, 318
Book of Gypsy Ballads (García Lorca)
See *Primer romancero gitano*
The Book of Hours (Rilke)
See *Das Stundenbuch*
"The Book of Hours of Sister Clotilde" (Lowell) **13**:84
The Book of Images (Rilke)
See *Buch der Bilder*
"The Book of Isaiah" (Carson) **64**:198, 232, 235
"Book of Joyous Children" (Riley) **48**:296, 303
The Book of Light (Clifton) **17**:31
Book of Longing (Cohen) **109**:97-98, 101-2, 104
The Book of Los (Blake) **12**:62-4
Book of Magazine Verse (Spicer) **78**:241, 245, 253, 285, 288, 294, 310-12, 339, 363
The Book of Medicines (Hogan) **35**:259, 265, 276, 277, 279
Book of Mercy (Cohen) **109**:16, 19, 32, 35, 111
A Book of Music (Spicer) **78**:240, 253, 257, 261-62, 270-72, 305, 354
"The Book of Myths" (Harjo) **27**:66-67
"The Book of Nature" (Eberhart) **76**:29, 31
The Book of Nightmares (Kinnell) **26**:241-45, 247-49, 252-58, 261, 264-67, 271-75, 283, 291-93
Book of Nonsense (Lear) **65**:135-36, 139, 141-44, 166, 168-69, 202
Book of Pictures (Rilke)
See *Buch der Bilder*
Book of Poems (García Lorca)
See *Libro de poemas*
The Book of Purgatory (Marie de France)
See *L'Espurgatoire Saint Patrice*
Book of Questions (Neruda)
See *Libro de las preguntas*
A Book of Resemblances: Poems 1950-1953 (Duncan) **75**:261
The Book of Restoration Verse (Braithwaite) **52**:106
Book of Saint Valentines Day of the Parlement of Briddes (Chaucer)
See *Parlement of Foules*
"The Book of Sand" (Borges)
See "El reloj de arena"
Book of Songs (García Lorca)
See *Canciones*
Book of Songs (Heine)
See *Buch der Lieder*
Book of Sparrows (Bécquer)
See *El Libro de los Gorriones*
"The Book of the Dead" (Rukeyser) **12**:203, 207, 210, 213
The Book of the Dead Man (Bell) **79**:34-42
Book of the Duchess (Chaucer) **19**:6, 10, 13, 21, 23, 38, 64-9, 71-4, 76; **58**:352
Book of the Duchesse (Chaucer)
See *Book of the Duchess*
The Book of the Duke of True Lovers (Christine de Pizan)
See *Le livre du duc des vrais amans*
Book of the Five and Twenty Ladies (Chaucer)
See *Legend of Good Women*
The Book of the Long Road of Learning (Christine de Pizan)
See *Le livre du chemin de long estude*
The Book of the Mutation of Fortune (Christine de Pizan)
See *Le livre de la mutacion de fortune*
Book of the path of long study (Christine de Pizan)
See *Le livre du chemin de long estude*
"A Book of the Unseen" (Carman) **34**:212
The Book of Thel (Blake) **12**:19, 33-5, 37, 51; **63**:6, 89, 115, 125
The Book of Three Judgments (Christine de Pizan)
See *Le Livre des Trois jugemens*
Book of Troilus (Chaucer)
See *Troilus and Criseyde*
The Book of Urizen (Blake) **12**:15, 19, 35, 38, 60, 62; **63**:110, 112
Book of Vagaries (Neruda)
See *Extravagario*
Book of Verse (Masters)
See *A Book of Verses*
Book of Verse (Morris) **55**:340
A Book of Verses (Masters) **1**:332, 342; 200, 221
"The Book of Yolek" (Hecht) **70**:87, 102-3, 105, 108-9
Book One (Tolson)
See *Harlem Gallery: Book One, The Curator*
A Booke of Ayres, Set foorth to be song to the Lute, Orpherian, and Base Violl (Campion) **87**:4, 11-12, 23-26, 32, 50, 54, 57, 62-68, 71-72, 77, 84-85, 88, 93, 96-99, 101-3, 108-9, 111, 117
"Booker T. and W. E. B." (Randall) **86**:288, 301, 306, 317-18, 341
"Booker T. Washington" (Dunbar) **5**:131
The Books of the Polish Nation and the Polish Pilgrimage (Mickiewicz)
See *Księgi narodu polskiego i pielgrzymastwa polskiego*
"Boom" (Hughes) **89**:101
"Boom!" (Nemerov) **24**:266, 278
"Boom" (Stone) **53**:257
"Boom Town" (Stafford) **71**:293
"A Boon" (Meredith) **28**:174
"Boone" (Berry) **28**:28, 38
"Boone Children" (Stafford) **71**:292, 299
"A Boone County Pastoral" (Riley) **48**:332
"Boop-Boop-Adieup Little Group!" (Nash) **21**:265
"A Boor" (Bukowski) **18**:15
"Boot Hill" (Ondaatje) **28**:304
The Bootleg Series Volumes 1-3 (Dylan) **37**:65
"Boots" (Kipling) **3**:192; **91**:174
"Boots of Spanish Leather" (Dylan) **37**:54, 58
"Booz endormi" (Hugo) **17**:65, 85
"Bora Ring" (Wright) **14**:335, 340, 374
"Border Blues" (Thomas) **99**:252-53
"The Border Campaign" (Heaney) **100**:242
"Border Line" (Hughes) **53**:122
Border Sick Call (Montague) **106**:308, 310, 314, 324-25, 328
The Borderers (Wordsworth) **4**:416
The Borderland (Tagore)
See *Prāntik*
Borderland (Tagore)
See *Prāntik*
"Bords de mer" (Ponge) **107**:224
"Bored" (Silverstein) **49**:330
"Bored on a Greyhound" (Stone) **53**:228
"Borges and I" (Borges)
See "Borges y yo"
"Borges and Myself" (Borges)
See "Borges y yo"
"Borges y yo" (Borges) **32**:61, 77, 95, 133
"Boris Karloff in The Mummy Meets Dr. Fu Manchu" (Yau) **61**:346
Born in Brooklyn (Montague) **106**:352-57
"Born in December" (Rukeyser) **12**:224
"Born of a Shade" (Meredith) **60**:330
Born of a Woman: New and Selected Poems (Knight) **14**:37-9, 41-42, 46, 49, 51-52
"Borodinó" (Lermontov) **18**:278, 283, 290, 297, 304
The Borough: A Poem, in Twenty-Four Letters (Crabbe) **97**:71-72, 74, 76, 81-83, 85, 88, 101, 103, 107, 109-10, 113, 116-22, 124, 128, 135-36, 149, 151-53
Borrowed Love Poems (Yau) **61**:337, 348, 357-58
"Bosque y bosque" (Guillén) **35**:155
"The Boss" (Ignatow) **34**:286
"Boston" (Moore) **49**:142
"Boston" (Stryk) **27**:203
"A Boston Ballad" (Whitman)
See "Poem of Apparitions in Boston in the 73rd Year of These States"
"Boston Common" (Berryman) **64**:79, 81, 85-86, 90
"The Boston Evening Transcript" (Eliot) **5**:153; **90**:294
"The Boston Hymn" (Emerson) **18**:77, 113, 119-20
"Boston to Florence" (Holmes) **71**:100
"The Botanic Garden" (Noyes) **27**:129
"The Botanic Gardens" (Boland) **58**:43
"Botanical Gardens" (Masters) **1**:330
"Botanical Gardens" (Wright) **14**:341
"A Botanical Trope" (Meredith) **28**:190
"Botanist on Alp (No. 1)" (Stevens) **6**:297; **110**:167
"Botany Bay Eclogues" (Southey) **111**:193
"Bothering Me at Last" (Ignatow) **34**:273
The Bothie of Tober-na-Vuolich (Clough)
See *The Bothie of Toper-na-Fuosich: A Long-Vacation Pastoral*
The Bothie of Toper-na-Fuosich: A Long-Vacation Pastoral (Clough) **103**:51-55, 58, 71, 82, 92, 102, 109, 114, 118-22, 124-29, 135, 138, 144-52, 161, 163, 166
"Bothwell" (Elliott) **96**:157, 161, 183
"Boticelli's Spring" (Corso) **33**:26, 41
"Botta e riposta" (Montale) **13**:129, 131, 134, 147, 165
"The Botticellian Trees" (Williams) **109**:193
"The Bottle in the Sea" (Vigny)
See "La bouteille à la mer"
"A Bottle of 1848 Vintage Valtellina" (Carducci)
See "A una Bottiglia di Valtellina del 1848"
"Bottled Water" (Stone) **53**:257
"Bottleneck" (MacNeice) **61**:141
"Bottles and Bottles and Bottles" (Crane) **80**:52
"Bottom" (Rimbaud) **57**:234, 254, 285
"The Bottom of the Sea Is Cruel" (Crane) **99**:89
"Bouche usée" (Éluard) **38**:70
"Boudaries" (Wright) **14**:374
"Boudicca" (Tennyson) **101**:188
"Le Bouge de l'historien" (Char) **56**:134
The Bouge of Court (Skelton)
See *The Bowge of Courte*
"La Bougie" (Ponge) **107**:192
"Bound No'th Blues" (Hughes) **1**:254; **53**:82, 119, 136-37
"A Boundless Moment" (Frost) **1**:218
The Bounty (Walcott) **46**:258-59
"Bouquet" (Darío) **15**:113
"The Bouquet" (Stevens) **110**:155, 160, 162-63
"Bouquet of Belle Scavoir" (Stevens) **110**:94
The Bourgeois Poet (Shapiro) **25**:287-90, 292-94, 297, 299, 301-302, 308-11, 314-17, 321-22, 325

"Bournemouth" (Verlaine) **2**:416
"La bouteille à la mer" (Vigny) **26**:367, 371, 380-83, 391-92, 397, 402-404
"Bova" (Pushkin) **10**:407
"The Bow" (Bell) **79**:32
The Bow and the Lyre (Yevtushenko) **40**:341
"Bow St. Cases" (Owen) **102**:149
The Bowge of Court (Skelton)
See *The Bowge of Courte*
The Bowge of Courte (Skelton) **25**:329, 336-37, 340, 343, 349-50, 352, 361-62, 364-65, 367
"Bowing to the Empress" (Oliver) **75**:296
"The Bowl and the Rim" (Graves) **6**:128
"The Bowl of Blood" (Jeffers) **17**:123, 144
"Bowled Over" (Hughes) **89**:99, 102
"Bowls" (Moore) **4**:265; **49**:90
"Box" (Creeley) **73**:46
"A Box" (Stein) **18**:320-31, 349-50, 353
"A Box and Its Contents" (Ashbery) **26**:133
"A Box Comes Home" (Ciardi) **69**:12
"The Box of Beads" (Kenyon) **57**:46
"Box Score" (Dorn)
See "The World Box-Score Cup of 1966"
"Boy" (Ciardi) **69**:14, 53
"The Boy" (Hacker) **47**:117
"The Boy" (Tagore) **8**:417
"The Boy and the Doom" (Wickham) **110**:267
"The Boy and the Dream" (Wickham) **110**:267
The Boy and the Stars (Seifert) **47**:326
"Boy at the Window" (Wilbur) **51**:230, 243, 266
"Boy by the Waterfall" (Sarton) **39**:323, 331
"Boy Driving his Father to Confession" (Heaney) **18**:243
"A Boy Drowns" (Thumboo) **30**:332
"The Boy from Pauntley" (Masefield) **78**:49-50
"A Boy Named Sue" (Silverstein) **49**:346-48
"Boy Riding Forward Backward" (Francis) **34**:242, 257
"Boy Wandering in Simms' Valley" (Warren) **37**:336
"Boy with a Sea Dream" (Page) **12**:168, 170
"Boy with Book of Knowledge" (Nemerov) **24**:287
"Boy with His Hair Cut Short" (Rukeyser) **12**:223
The Boyar Orsha (Lermontov)
See *Boiarin Orša*
"The Boyg, Peer Gynt, The One Only One" (Jarrell) **41**:174
"Boyhood in Tobacco Country" (Warren) **37**:318
"Boy-Man" (Shapiro) **25**:279, 297, 319
"The Boys" (Holmes) **71**:65, 68
"Boys. Black." (Brooks) **7**:84
"The Boy's Dream" (Very) **86**:54
"Boys in Dresses" (Komunyakaa) **51**:23
"The Boys of Summer" (Thomas)
See "I See the Boys of Summer"
"A Boy's Summer Song" (Dunbar) **5**:138
"The Boy's Tale" (Thomas) **99**:271-72, 308
A Boy's Will (Frost) **1**:192, 195, 197, 207, 213-14, 223-24; **39**:230-32, 235, 240, 246, 256; **71**:41, 54
"The Bracelet" (Donne) **43**:126, 181-84, 186, 192-98
"Bracken Hills in Autumn" (MacDiarmid) **9**:197
Bradstreet (Berryman)
See *Homage to Mistress Bradstreet*
"The Braggart" (Tolson) **88**:349-50
"Brahma" (Emerson) **18**:83, 85, 88
Braided Apart (Stafford) **71**:329
"Braiding" (Lee) **24**:247
"The Brain Cells" (Hall) **70**:33
"The brainsick race that wanton youth ensues" (Raleigh) **31**:201
"Brainstorm" (Nemerov) **24**:257, 268
"Braly Street" (Soto) **28**:375, 378-79, 384-85
"A Branch from Palestine" (Lermontov) **18**:298
A Branch of May (Reese) **29**:330, 335-337, 339, 345-346, 351-352
The Branch Will Not Break (Wright) **36**:283, 292-96, 298, 300, 302-5, 307-8, 313-14, 316-17, 319, 325-31, 338, 341-42, 344-45, 348, 350-52, 355, 362, 364-65, 371, 373-75, 378-79, 385-86, 389-91, 396, 399
"La branche d'amandier" (Lamartine) **16**:278
"Branches" (McGuckian) **27**:105
"Brancusi's Golden Bird" (Loy) **16**:321
"A Brand" (Johnson) **24**:160
"The Branded Hand" (Whittier) **93**:210, 317
"Brandons Both" (Rossetti) **7**:271
"A Brash of Wowing" (Dunbar) **67**:128
"Le brasier" (Apollinaire) **7**:47
"Brasilia" (Hughes) **89**:274
"Brasilia" (Plath) **37**:204, 230, 233
"Brass Keys" (Sandburg) **2**:329
"Brass Spittoons" (Hughes) **1**:241, 263, 265; **53**:82, 143
Brats (Kennedy) **93**:133-35
"Bratsk Hydroelectric Station" (Yevtushenko) **40**:347, 350-53, 368
Bratsk Hydroelectric Station (Yevtushenko)
See *Bratskaya G.E.S.*
The Bratsk Power Station (Yevtushenko)
See *Bratskaya G.E.S.*
The Bratsk Station (Yevtushenko)
See *Bratskaya G.E.S.*
Bratskaya G.E.S. (Yevtushenko) **40**:356, 364
Bratya Razboiniki (Pushkin) **10**:358, 365, 386
"Bravado" (Frost) **39**:233
"A Brave and Startling Truth" (Angelou) **32**:30
"The brave combatants keep on falling" (Castro)
See "Cayendo van los bravos combatientes"
"Brave New World" (MacLeish) **47**:191, 246, 260
"Bravely deckt" (Campion) **87**:55-56
A Bravery of Earth (Eberhart) **76**:5, 9, 11-12, 20, 33, 35-36, 38, 57
Braving the Elements (Merrill) **28**:220-23, 228-29, 244, 254, 256, 258-59, 281
"Brawl" (García Lorca)
See "Reyerta"
The Brazen Serpent (Ní Chuilleanáin) **34**:361-63, 367-69, 373, 383-84
"The Brazier" (Apollinaire)
See "Le brasier"
"Brazil, January 1, 1502" (Bishop) **3**:56; **34**:109, 139
"Brazil-Copacabana" (Guillén) **23**:117
"Brazilian Fazenda" (Page) **12**:178, 183, 190
"Brazzaville 22 Feb 72" (Brutus) **24**:123
"Bread" (Olds) **22**:328
"Bread" (Pasternak) **6**:267
"Bread Alone" (Wylie) **23**:311, 324
"Bread and Apples" (Mueller) **33**:197
"Bread and Music" (Aiken) **26**:24, 72
"Bread and Wine" (Cullen) **20**:62
"Bread and Wine" (Hölderlin)
See "Brot und Wein"
"Bread at Midnight" (Merwin) **45**:22, 49
The Bread God (Montague) **106**:216-17, 244, 251, 253-66, 340
Bread in the Wilderness (Merton) **10**:352
The Bread of Time (Levine) **22**:231
The Bread of Truth (Thomas) **99**:232, 235, 237, 269-72, 280
Bread Rather Than Blossoms (Enright) **93**:4, 6
Bread without Sugar (Stern) **115**:270-71, 285
"Bread without Sugar" (Stern) **115**:253
"The Break" (Pasternak) **6**:280-82
"The Break" (Sexton) **2**:352-53
"The Break Away" (Sexton) **79**:241
"Break, Break, Break" (Tennyson) **6**:358
"A Break from the Bush" (Komunyakaa) **51**:41, 60
"Break of Day" (Brown) **55**:102, 105-6, 120, 122
"Break of Day" (Sassoon) **12**:244, 277
"Breake now my heart and dye" (Campion) **87**:71
"Breake of Day" (Donne) **1**:152; **43**:166, 168-70, 176
"Breakfast" (Duncan) **75**:175
"Breakfast" (Stauffer) **18**:322-23
Breaking and Entering (Kennedy) **93**:130, 142-43, 148, 152
"Breaking Camp" (Piercy) **29**:308
"Breaking Camp" (Wagoner) **33**:335, 344
Breaking Camp (Piercy) **29**:307
"Breaking Green" (Ondaatje) **28**:331
"The Breaking of Nations" (Hardy) **92**:197
"The Breaking of the Rainbows" (Nemerov) **24**:288
"Breaking Open" (Rukeyser) **12**:221, 224, 230
Breaking Open (Rukeyser) **12**:220, 224-25, 230
"Breaking Out" (Ammons) **16**:45, 63
"Breaklight" (Clifton) **17**:35
"Breast" (Hall) **70**:32
"The Breast" (Sexton) **2**:352, 364
"Breasts" (Simic) **69**:269
"Breasts" (Tagore)
See "Stan"
"the breath" (Bissett) **14**:19, 24, 29, 34
"Breath" (Strand) **63**:191-92
"The Breath of Life" (Lawrence) **54**:250
"The Breath of Night" (Jarrell) **41**:137
"The Breathing" (Levertov) **11**:171
Breathing Exercises (Parra)
See *Ejercicios respiratorios*
"Breathing Landscape" (Rukeyser) **12**:209
"The Breathing Lesson" (Wagoner) **33**:327
"The Breathing, the Endless News" (Dove) **6**:122
Breathing the Water (Levertov) **11**:200, 202-05, 209-10
Breathing Tokens (Sandburg) **41**:322-24
Breath-Turning (Celan)
See *Atemwende*
"Brebeuf and His Brethren" (Birney) **52**:36
"Brecht in Svendborg" (Mahon) **60**:177-78
"Bredfield Hall" (FitzGerald) **79**:70, 108
"Bredon Hill" (Housman) **2**:160, 182-83, 185
"The Breeze and I" (Hafiz) **116**:15-16, 18-21, 23-24
"A Breeze Swept Through" (Tapahonso) **65**:215, 249, 258
A Breeze Swept Through (Tapahonso) **65**:240
"The Breeze's Invitation" (Thoreau) **30**:258
"Brendel Playing Schubert" (Mueller) **33**:197
"Brennan" (Wright) **14**:375
"Brennende liebe, 1904" (Glück) **16**:128
"Brer Rabbit, You's de Cutes' of 'Em All" (Johnson) **24**:142, 163
"Breton Oracles" (Melville) **82**:38-39, 50, 55
"Breton Walks" (Mahon) **60**:163
"Breton Walks, 1: Early Morning" (Mahon) **60**:191
"Breton Walks, 2: Man and Bird" (Mahon) **60**:191
"Brevity" (Wright) **14**:375-76
"Brewing of Soma" (Whittier) **93**:169, 239, 345
"El brezal" (Cernuda) **62**:178, 215
"Brian Age 7" (Doty) **53**:69
"Brian the Still-Hunter" (Atwood) **8**:19
"The Briar Rose" (Boland) **58**:92
"Briar Rose" (Sexton) **79**:191, 205, 211, 327, 329-30
"Briar Rose (Sleeping Beauty)" (Sexton) **2**:354, 365, 368
"The Bridal Ballad" (Poe) **1**:428, 432, 445, 447
"Bridal Birth" (Rossetti) **44**:169, 203
"The Bridal Nightmare I" (Barker) **77**:8
"The Bridal Nightmare II" (Barker) **77**:9-10
"The Bridal Nightmare III" (Barker) **77**:10
"Bridal Nightmares" (Barker) **77**:8, 13, 32
"Bridal of Pennacook" (Whittier) **93**:171, 224
The Bridal of Triermain (Scott) **13**:297, 301-02, 311-12, 314, 317, 320
"Bridal Photo" (Ciardi) **69**:9, 51
"Bridal Piece" (Glück) **16**:127
"The Bride" (Lawrence) **54**:167, 245
"The Bride" (Very) **86**:58

"Bride and Groom Lie Hidden for Three Days" (Hughes) **7**:165, 168; **89**:142, 144, 150, 200-201
"The Bride in the Country" (Montagu) **16**:338
The Bride of Abydos: A Turkish Tale (Byron) **16**:91, 109
"Bride Song" (Rossetti) **7**:264
"The Bridegroom" (Hardy) **92**:266
"The Bridegroom" (Kipling) **3**:183
"Bridegroom Dick" (Melville) **82**:71-72, 82, 97, 142-44, 160-61
"The Bride-Night Fire" (Hardy) **8**:99; **92**:241
"The Brides" (Hope) **56**:266, 303
Brides of Reason (Davie) **29**:92-95, 107, 111, 116-17
"Bridestones" (Hughes) **89**:123
"Bridge" (Ammons) **16**:40-1, 54
"The Bridge" (Baraka) **113**:5, 148-50
"The Bridge" (Heaney) **100**:243
"The Bridge" (Longfellow) **30**:18, 26, 46
"The Bridge" (Paz) **48**:273
"The Bridge" (Walcott) **46**:237
The Bridge (Crane) **3**:84-5, 87-90, 93-8, 100-01, 105-10; **99**:3-8, 10-13, 17, 19, 28-31, 41, 47, 49, 52, 57, 59, 71-72, 74, 77, 85, 95, 98-99, 103-4, 106, 108-16, 118-19, 123-24, 126-29, 132, 134-37, 141, 146
"Bridge Narrative" (Chatterton) **104**:11
"The Bridge of Cloud" (Longfellow) **30**:18
"The Bridge of Estador" (Crane) **3**:100; **99**:8, 71, 73, 84
"Bridge of Knaves" (Jacobsen) **62**:302
"The Bridge of Sighs" (Hood) **93**:44, 61, 69, 81, 87-88, 102, 105, 118-19, 123-24
"Bridge Passage" (Szirtes) **51**:169
Bridge Passages (Szirtes) **51**:167, 171
"Bridge-Guard in the Karroo" (Kipling) **91**:174-75
"Bridging" (Piercy) **29**:302
"Brief Account of William Cannings from the Life of Thomas Rowlie Preeste" (Chatterton) **104**:27
"Brief Elegy" (Ignatow) **34**:272, 276
"Briefings" (Ammons) **16**:31
Briefings: Poems Small and Easy (Ammons) **16**:10, 21-23, 28, 45-6
"Briefly It Enters, and Briefly Speaks" (Kenyon) **57**:37, 40
The Brigand Brothers (Pushkin) See *Bratya Razboiniki*
"A Bright Day" (Montague) **106**:277, 296, 299, 313
"Bright and Morning Star" (Baraka) **113**:25
"The Bright Field" (Thomas) **99**:266, 339
"The Bright Field" (Walcott) **46**:233-34
"Bright star" (Keats) **96**:236
"Bright Star! Would I Were Steadfast as Thou Art" (Keats) **1**:279
"Bright Sunlight" (Lowell) **13**:64
"Bright-Cut Irish Silver" (Boland) **58**:24
"Brighton Beach" (Mahon) **60**:147, 210
"The Brigs of Ayr" (Burns) **6**:78; **114**:88-90, 135, 144, 147-49, 176, 182
"Brilliant Sad Sun" (Williams) **7**:396, 409
"Brindis cotidiano" (Fuertes) **27**:39
"Brindisi funebre" (Carducci) **46**:23, 69
"Bring Down the Beams" (Bukowski) **18**:4
"Bring in the Wine" (Li Po) **29**:145
"Bring the Day" (Roethke) **15**:252, 273-74, 301-02
"Bring Your Own Victim" (Curnow) **48**:16-17, 49
The Bringer of Water (Berry) **28**:35
"Bringers" (Sandburg) **2**:316-17, 324; **41**:261
"bringing home th bacon" (Bissett) **14**:34
"Bringing in New Couples" (Hughes) **7**:166
Bringing It All Back Home (Dylan) **37**:44, 50
"Bringnal Banks are Wild and Fair For a' That" (Scott) **13**:278
"Brise marine" (Mallarmé) **4**:208; **102**:54, 100
"Bristol" (Betjeman) **75**:20, 77
"Bristowe Tragedie" (Chatterton) **104**:69
"The British Church" (Herbert) **4**:100
"The British Museum Reading Room" (MacNeice) **61**:116, 138-39
"Britons, Guard Your Own" (Tennyson) **101**:269, 287
"The Brittish Church" (Vaughan) **81**:298, 312, 314, 337
"Brittle Beauty" (Wyatt) **27**:302
"Broadcast" (Larkin) **21**:237
"The broad-leaved Arrow-head" (Niedecker) **42**:98, 102, 152
Broadside Memories: Poets I Have Known (Randall) **86**:286
"The Broadstone" (Jeffers) **17**:117
"Broadway" (Sandburg) **41**:248, 340
"Broadway" (Teasdale) **31**:331
"A Broadway Pageant" (Whitman) **91**:344
"Broagh" (Heaney) **18**:202, 241; **100**:196, 198, 336, 352
"Broceliande" (Hacker) **47**:119
"Brod und Wein" (Hölderlin) See "Brot und Wein"
"Broke" (Hughes) **53**:114
"A Broken Appointment" (Hardy) **8**:88, 110
"The Broken Balance" (Jeffers) **17**:144
"The Broken Bowl" (Very) **86**:91
"Broken Chord Sequence" (Chin) **40**:36
"The Broken Dark" (Hayden) **6**:181, 193-95
"Broken Dreams" (Yeats) **20**:328
Broken English (McHugh) **61**:207
"Broken Fingernails" (Enright) **93**:18, 35
The Broken Ground (Berry) **28**:2-5, 14, 31
"The Broken Home" (Merrill) **28**:221, 227, 230, 253
"Broken Jar" (Paz) See "El cántaro roto"
"The Broken Man" (Wylie) **23**:321
"The Broken Oar" (Longfellow) **30**:51
"Broken Off By The Music" (Yau) **61**:329
"The Broken Pitcher" (Paz) See "El cántaro roto"
"Broken Promise" (MacLeish) **47**:190
"The Broken Tower" (Crane) **3**:90, 103, 111; **99**:3, 12, 32-33, 48-50, 68, 71, 102, 145-51
"The Broken Window of Rosa Ramos" (Espada) **74**:150
"The Broken Wings" (Gibran) **9**:75
"Broken-Face Gargoyles" (Sandburg) **41**:313-14
"The Broncho That Would Not Be Broken" (Lindsay) **23**:269, 273, 286
Bronwen, the Traw, and the Shape-Shifter (Dickey) **40**:233-34
"Bronz Trumpets and Sea Water" (Wylie) **23**:301, 315
"Bronze" (Walcott) **46**:273, 322
Bronze (Merrill) **28**:247-68, 272
"The Bronze Buckaroo" (Baraka) **113**:16
"The Bronze David of Donatello" (Jarrell) **41**:208
"bronze fruit" (Alurista) See "fruto de bronce"
"A Bronze Head" (Yeats) **20**:332
The Bronze Horseman (Pushkin) See *Medny Vsadnik*
"The Bronze Horses" (Lowell) **13**:60, 62, 64, 73, 80, 82
"Bronze Rape" (Alurista) **34**:46
"Bronze Tablets" (Lowell) **13**:76, 78
"Bronzes" (Sandburg) **41**:314
"Bronzeville Man with a Belt in the Back" (Brooks) **7**:106
"A Bronzeville Mother Loiters in Mississippi. Meanwhile a Mississippi Mother Burns Bacon" (Brooks) **7**:56, 62, 81, 86, 96, 98-9
"Bronzeville Woman in a Red Hat" (Brooks) **7**:58, 62
"Brooding" (Ignatow) **34**:282
"The Brook" (Tennyson) **6**:357, 359; **101**:215, 251
"The Brook" (Thomas) **53**:327-28
"Brook Farm" (Toomer) **7**:323
"The Brooklyn Bridge" (Martí) **76**:110-11
"Brooklyn Bridge Nocturne" (García Lorca) See "Ciudad sin sueño"
"The Broom, the Shovel, the Poker, and the Tongs" (Lear) **65**:152-53
"Broom Weed" (Goodison) **36**:142
"The Broomstick Train" (Holmes) **71**:85, 88, 121, 127
"Brot und Wein" (Hölderlin) **4**:146-51, 161, 166, 169, 171, 176
"Brother" (Stafford) **71**:324
"A Brother" (Thumboo) **30**:300
"The Brother" (Walcott) **46**:278, 291
"Brother and Sister" (Carroll) **74**:68
"Brother and Sister" (Eliot) **20**:102, 124
"Brother and Sisters" (Wright) **14**:336, 340, 351
"Brother Burke" (Kinsella) **69**:87
"Brother, Do Not Give Your Life" (Yosano) See "Kimi Shinitamô koto nakare"
"Brother Fire" (MacNeice) **61**:160-61
"Brother Jonathan's Lament for Sister Caroline" (Holmes) **71**:93
Brother to Dragons (Warren) **37**:290-92, 294, 300, 304, 310, 312, 326-29, 332-33, 339-40, 348, 361, 369-70, 377, 380, 382-83
"Brother Where Dost Thou Dwell" (Thoreau) **30**:180
"Brotherhood in Pain" (Warren) **37**:309
"The Brotherhood of Men" (Eberhart) **76**:15, 50, 59, 67
"Brotherly Love: A Little Letter to the White Citizens of the South" (Hughes) **53**:115
"Brothers" (Hughes) **53**:193
"Brothers" (Johnson) **24**:130-31, 138, 142, 161, 170
"The Brothers" (Muir) **49**:219, 296
"Brothers" (Thomas) **99**:268
"The Brothers" (Whittier) **93**:193
"The Brothers" (Wordsworth) **4**:374, 380, 381, 393, 402, 414; **67**:328
The Brothers Highwaymen (Pushkin) See *Bratya Razboiniki*
Brothers, I Loved You All: Poems, 1969-1977 (Carruth) **10**:69-70, 72-3, 91
"Brothers in the Craft" (Kinsella) **69**:131
"Brothers, Who When the Sirens Roar" (Auden) **92**:127
"Brought from Beyond" (Clampitt) **19**:102
"A Brown" (Stein) **18**:3312
"Brown Boy to Brown Girl" (Cullen) **20**:64
"The Brown Dwarf of Rügen" (Whittier) **93**:249
"A Brown Girl Dead" (Cullen) **20**:55, 62
"The Brown Menace or Poem to the Survival of Roaches" (Lorde) **12**:154-55, 158
"The brown muskrat, noiseless" (Niedecker) **42**:151
"Brown of Ossawatomie" (Whittier) **93**:280-81
"Brown River, Smile" (Toomer) **7**:324
"The Brown Woman's Husband" (Gilmore) **87**:300
"Browning resuelve ser poeta" (Borges) **22**:98; **32**:50-1
"Brown's Descent" (Frost) **1**:195
"Browser" (Stafford) **71**:373
"Bruce to His Men at Bannockburn" (Burns) **114**:47, 94, 115-16, 162
"Bruce's Address" (Burns) **6**:55
"Brueghel's Two Monkeys" (Szymborska) See "Dwie malpy Bruegla"
"A Bruised Reed Shall He Not Break" (Rossetti) **7**:290
"Una brújula" (Borges) **32**:75
"Brush Fire" (Wright) **36**:365, 369
"Brussels: Merry-Go-Round" (Verlaine) **32**:370
"Bruto Minore" (Leopardi) **37**:79, 102, 118
"Brutus" (Cowley) **90**:70, 104-5
"Bruxelles" (Rimbaud) **57**:252
"Bruxelles: Simple fesques" (Verlaine) **32**:411
"Bryan, Bryan, Bryan, Bryan" (Lindsay) **23**:265, 270, 273-74, 279, 287-88, 294-95
"Bryant's Seventieth Birthday" (Holmes) **71**:98

"Bubba" (Sanchez) **9**:240
Buch der Bilder (Rilke) **2**:266-67
Das Buch der Bilder (Rilke)
See *Buch der Bilder*
"Buch der Lieder" (Bridges) **28**:88
Buch der Lieder (Heine) **25**:129-131, 139-41, 143, 145-46, 153-54, 157-58, 161, 164
"The Buck in the Snow" (Millay) **6**:238
The Buck in the Snow, and Other Poems (Millay) **6**:213-14
"Buck Lake Store Auction" (Ondaatje) **28**:335
"Buckdancer's Choice" (Dickey) **40**:213
Buckdancer's Choice (Dickey) **40**:151, 155, 157, 160, 187, 192-97, 200, 212, 215-16, 231-32, 257, 261-62
"Buckin' Bronco" (Silverstein) **49**:335
Buckthorn (Akhmatova)
See *Podorozhnik*
Bucolic Comedies (Sitwell) **3**:293, 302-04, 307-08, 319, 322
"Bucolics" (Auden) **1**:23
Bucolics (Vergil)
See *Georgics*
"The Bud" (Waller) **72**:373
The Budapest File (Szirtes) **51**:173, 175-79
"Buddha" (Melville) **82**:148, 240, 242
"The Buddhist Painter Prepares to Paint" (Carruth) **10**:89
"Budgie" (MacNeice) **61**:178, 182
"The Buds Now Stretch" (Roethke) **15**:288
"Buenos Aires" (Borges) **32**:57-8
"Buenos Aires" (Lowell) **3**:214
"Buenos Aires: 1962" (Birney) **52**:42, 97, 100
"La bufera" (Montale) **13**:113, 131
La bufera e altro (Montale) **13**:103-04, 107, 113-14, 117-18, 122, 125, 131-33, 141, 148-49, 156, 160, 165-67
"The buffalo" (Borges)
See "El bisonte"
"Buffalo. 12.7.41" (Howe) **54**:45
"Buffalo Bill" (Sandburg) **41**:259
"Buffalo Bill's Defunct" (Cummings) **5**:93
"Le buffet" (Rimbaud) **3**:271, 283; **57**:253
"The Bugler-Boy" (Hopkins) **15**:138
"The Bugler's First Communion" (Hopkins) **15**:136, 144
"Buick" (Shapiro) **25**:288, 295, 297, 319, 322, 325
"Build Soil: A Political Pastoral" (Frost) **1**:196, 199, 203, 217
"Builder Kachina" (Rose) **13**:236-37
"Builders" (Cavafy) **36**:53, 57
"Builders of Ruins" (Meynell) **112**:153, 247, 260
"The Building" (Larkin) **21**:255
"The Building of the Long Serpent" (Longfellow) **30**:20
"The Building of the Ship" (Longfellow) **30**:20, 27, 37, 48-50, 82
"The Building of the Skyscraper" (Oppen) **35**:309
"The Building of the Trophy" (Rose) **13**:235
"Building the Library, Tokyo University Night Scene" (Blunden) **66**:18, 24
"Buildings" (Birney) **52**:28, 46
"Build-Up" (Montague) **106**:318
"Buildings" (Schuyler) **88**:216
"The Bull" (Wright) **14**:333, 359
"The Bull Moses" (Hughes) **7**:131, 140, 158
"Bull of Bandylaw" (Plath) **37**:260-65
"The Bull of Bendylaw" (Plath)
See "Bull of Bandylaw"
"Bull Song" (Atwood) **8**:25
"The Bullfinches" (Hardy) **92**:323
"Bullfrog" (Hughes) **7**:165
"Bullocky" (Wright) **14**:336, 340, 345, 349, 351, 357, 360, 368
"The Bull-Roarer" (Stern) **115**:272, 293
"Bully" (Espada) **74**:124, 129-30, 153, 160
Bulsh (Kennedy) **93**:142-43, 148
"Bulwarked Against Fate" (Moore) **49**:136
"Bum Series" (Scalapino) **114**:333, 336
"Bumming" (McKay) **2**:226
"Bums, on Waking" (Dickey) **40**:255
"The Bunch of Grapes" (Herbert) **4**:123, 125
"Buques" (Storni) **33**:239
"Burbank with a Baedeker: Bleistein with a Cigar" (Eliot) **90**:217
"Burbles" (Mahon) **60**:225
"The Burden" (Kipling) **3**:183
"A Burden" (Rossetti) **7**:286
"Burden" (Tagore)
See "Bhar"
"The Burden of Ninevah" (Rossetti) **44**:204, 260-61
"The Burden of Nineveh" (Rossetti) **44**:204, 260-61
"The Burghers" (Hardy) **8**:99
"The Burghers' Battle" (Morris) **55**:340
"Burghers of Petty Death" (Stevens) **110**:96
"The Burglar of Babylon" (Bishop) **3**:48, 56; **34**:78, 82, 116, 188
"The Burial" (Kipling) **91**:144
"Burial" (Vaughan) **81**:272
"Burial" (Walker) **30**:340, 349, 365
"Burial of an Irish President" (Clarke) **112**:63-64, 97
"Burial of Barber" (Whittier) **93**:211
"The Burial-place" (Bryant) **20**:3
Burials (Crabbe) **97**:129, 138, 144
"Buried at Springs" (Schuyler) **88**:179, 195
"The Buried Bride or True Love Finds a Way" (Masefield) **78**:49
"The Buried City" (Chesterton) **28**:101
"The Buried Lake" (Tate) **50**:281, 290, 292, 294-96, 329, 332-34, 336
"The Buried Life" (Arnold) **5**:37-8, 41-5, 47, 49-50, 59, 64
"Buried Love" (Teasdale) **31**:336, 387-88
The Buried Port (Ungaretti)
See *Il Porto Sepolto*
"Burliuk" (Shvarts) **50**:132, 153
"The Burly Fading One" (Hayden) **6**:196
"The Burn" (Kinnell) **26**:290
"Burn and burn and burn" (Bukowski) **18**:24
"Burned" (Levine) **22**:220-21, 227-28, 232
"The Burning" (Momaday) **25**:200-201
"The Burning Babe" (Southwell) **83**:251, 257, 259, 262, 270, 276, 278, 286-89, 309, 326, 341
"The Burning Baby" (Barker) **77**:51
"The Burning Child" (Clampitt) **19**:83
"Burning Cigarette" (Serote) **113**:292
Burning City (Benét) **64**:6-8, 13-16, 24-26
Burning City: New Poems (Benét)
See *Burning City*
"A Burning Desire to Be Explicit" (Moore) **49**:144
"The Burning General" (Baraka) **113**:13
The Burning Glass, and Other Poems (de la Mare) **77**:92
"Burning Hills" (Ondaatje) **28**:327, 332-33
Burning in Water Drowning in Flame: Selected Poems 1955-1973 (Bukowski) **18**:21
"Burning Mountain" (Merwin) **45**:8
The Burning Mystery of Anna in 1951 (Koch) **80**:290
"The Burning of Paper Instead of Children" (Rich) **5**:371, 393-95
"The Burning of the Books" (Enright) **93**:21
"Burning Oneself Out" (Rich) **5**:360
"The Burning Passion" (MacDiarmid) **9**:153
The Burning Perch (MacNeice) **61**:110, 125, 175-79, 182
"Burning River" (Ortiz) **17**:233
"Burning the Christmas Greens" (Williams) **7**:360; **109**:275
"Burning the Frankenstein Monster" (Chappell) **105**:36, 40, 47
"Burning the Holly" (Hardy) **92**:276-77
"Burning the Letters" (Jarrell) **41**:137-38, 171, 173-74, 177-79
"Burning the Letters" (Plath) **37**:260-65
"Burning the Tomato Worms" (Forché) **10**:132, 134, 142
"Burns" (Whittier) **93**:259
"The Burnt Bridge" (MacNeice) **61**:128
"The Burnt Dancer" (Eliot) **90**:298
"Burnt Lands" (Pavese) **13**:205
"Burnt Norton" (Eliot) **5**:164, 166-68, 171, 174, 177-85, 201, 210
"The Burnt-Out Spa" (Plath) **1**:389; **37**:185-87
"Burque" (Baca) **41**:42
Burr Oaks (Eberhart) **76**:5, 8, 30, 40, 42, 58
"Burr Oaks: The Barn" (Eberhart) **76**:12
"Bury Me In a Free Land" (Harper) **21**:185, 187, 190, 192
"Burying an Animal on the Way to New York" (Stern) **115**:253-54, 270
"Burying Ground by the Ties" (MacLeish) **47**:146, 189
"Burza" (Mickiewicz) **38**:149
"A Bus along St. Clair: December" (Atwood) **8**:40
"Bus Fare" (Duncan) **75**:175
"Bus Stop" (Silverstein) **49**:349
"Busby Berkeley in the Soviet Union" (Szirtes) **51**:172
"La busca de Averroes" (Borges) **32**:48, 50
"Búscate plata" (Guillén) **23**:142
"The Buses Headed for Scranton" (Nash) **21**:271
"Bush" (Jacobsen) **62**:309, 317
"Bush Christmas Eve" (Jacobsen) **62**:312
"The Bush Garden" (Atwood) **8**:38-9
"Bushed" (Birney) **52**:22, 32, 44-45, 47-48
"Busie old foole" (Donne)
See "The Sunne Rising"
"The Business" (Creeley) **73**:29, 36, 39, 59, 63-64
"The Business Life" (Ignatow) **34**:273, 305, 316, 323
"The Business Man of Alicante" (Levine) **22**:213
The Business of Fancydancing (Alexie) **53**:4, 10-11, 23, 25-26, 29-31, 34, 39-40
"Busker" (Stryk) **27**:208
"A bust of Janus speaks" (Borges)
See "Habla un busto de Jano"
"Buster Keaton Rides Again: A Sequel" (Spicer) **78**:255, 304
"The Busy Man Speaks" (Bly) **39**:14, 94
"Busybody under a Cherry Tree" (Enright) **93**:6
"But Also" (Warren) **37**:326
"But at Last" (Blunden) **66**:7, 9-10
"But Born" (Aleixandre) **15**:5
"But for the Grace of God" (Robinson) **35**:367
"But He Was Cool; or, He Even Stopped for Green Lights" (Madhubuti) **5**:329, 341
"But I Do Not" (Corso) **108**:21
"But I Do Not Need Kindness" (Corso) **33**:41, 43
"But I say unto you: love one another" (Lawrence) **54**:249
"But Not Forgotten" (Parker) **28**:362
"But Not to Me" (Teasdale) **31**:379
"But One Talent" (Holmes) **71**:96
"But We've the May" (Cummings)
See "Song"
"'Butch' Weldy" (Masters) **1**:324
"Butcher Shop" (Simic) **69**:263
"Butcher's Dozen" (Kinsella)
See "Butcher's Dozen: A Lesson for the Octave of Widgery"
"Butcher's Dozen: A Lesson for the Octave of Widgery" (Kinsella) **69**:123-25, 127, 129, 133-34
"The Butcher's Wife" (Erdrich) **52**:172, 174-77, 189
"Buteo Regalis" (Momaday) **25**:186, 188, 193, 195, 199, 210, 220
"The Butler and the Gentleman" (Wickham) **110**:271
Butterflies (Gozzano)
See *Le farfalle*

"Butterflies Over the Map" (Warren) **37**:332
"The Butterfly" (Akhmadulina) **43**:26
"The Butterfly" (Brodsky)
See "Babočka"
"The Butterfly" (Giovanni) **19**:112
"Butterfly" (Lawrence) **54**:200
"Butterfly" (Sachs) **78**:115, 227, 232
"Butterfly Piece" (Hayden) **6**:194, 198
"Butterflyweed" (Ammons) **16**:4
"Buttons" (Sandburg) **41**:236, 269, 351
"Buveuse" (Char) **56**:137
"Buy Braw Troggin'" (Burns) **114**:146
"Buying Loveliness" (Teasdale) **31**:356
"Buying the Dog" (Ondaatje) **28**:335
"Buying the Whore" (Sexton) **79**:244
"Buzz" (Spicer) **78**:332
"Buzzard" (Hughes) **89**:189
"by 3/6/51" (Olson) **19**:316
"By a Lost Riverside" (Wagoner) **33**:361
"By a Reactionary" (Chesterton) **28**:114
"By a River" (Wagoner) **33**:374
"By all love's soft, yet mighty powers" (Wilmot) **66**:278-80
By Avon River (H. D.) **5**:302
"By Coming to New Jersey" (Stern) **115**:249
"By Disposition of Angels" (Moore) **49**:102, 126-27, 129
"By God I Want above Fourteenth" (Cummings) **5**:94
"By IS. W. to Two of Her Yonger Sisters Servinge in London" (Whitney)
See "A Modest Meane for Maides"
"By Lamplight" (Kunitz) **19**:171
By Lingual Wholes (Cruz) **37**:10-13, 16, 25, 35
"By Moonlight" (Sarton) **39**:325
"By Night When Others Soundly Slept" (Bradstreet) **10**:62
"By Nilus Once I Knew" (Crane) **99**:81
"By Now This Waiting So Has Wearied Me" (Stampa) **43**:296
"By Rugged Ways" (Dunbar) **5**:131
By the Aurelian Wall, and Other Elegies (Carman) **34**:205, 211, 220
"By the Boyne" (Barker) **77**:46
"By the Century's Deathbed" (Hardy) **92**:228
"By the Cloud Path" (Merwin) **45**:48
"By the Deschutes Shore" (Stafford) **71**:317, 335-36
By the Earth's Corpse (Hardy) **8**:121
"By the Fireside" (Browning) **2**:76, 78-9, 88; **97**:36
"By the Hoof of the Wild Goat" (Kipling) **3**:186
"By the Lake" (Sitwell) **3**:325
"By the North Sea" (Swinburne) **24**:313-17, 319, 327, 329, 343
By the Rivers Dark (Cohen) **109**:79
"By the Road" (Williams) **7**:382-83
"By the Road to the Contagious Hospital" (Williams) **109**:274, 292
"By the Rosanna" (Meredith) **60**:250
"By the Ruins of a Gun Emplacement: Saint-Benoît" (Wright) **36**:313
"By the Same. To the North Star" (Smith)
See "Sonnet 23"
"By the Sea" (Teasdale) **31**:358
By the Seashore (Akhmatova)
See *U samovo morya*
"By the Snake River" (Stafford) **71**:295, 297
"By The Stream" (Dunbar) **5**:127
"By the Waters of Babylon" (Celan)
See "An den Wassern Babels"
"By Twilight" (Swinburne) **24**:317
"By Wauchopeside" (MacDiarmid) **9**:197, 199
"By Way of Explanation" (Cisneros) **52**:162-64
"Bye-Child" (Heaney) **100**:203, 205
"By-pass" (Wright) **14**:373
"Bypassing Rue Descartes" (Milosz) **8**:200
"The Byrnies" (Gunn) **26**:186
"Byron. Written after a perusal of his works" (Whittier) **93**:195
Byron's Letters & Journals (Byron) **95**:20
Býti básníkem (Seifert) **47**:320, 323, 326-27, 340
"A Byzantine Nobleman in Exile Composing Verses" (Cavafy) **36**:94, 96, 98-99
"Byzantium" (Yeats) **20**:308, 310, 316, 327, 334-35; **51**:71, 77-80, 82, 86-87, 90, 93-94, 97-100, 105, 108, 115, 150
"C 33" (Crane) **99**:68-69, 133, 135
"a C." (Montale) **13**:138
"C Minor" (Wilbur) **51**:283
C: Poems (Chappell) **105**:47-53
"Ça ira" (Carducci) **46**:47, 55
"Ça le creux" (Césaire) **25**:33
"Ca' the Yowes to the Knowes" (Burns) **6**:76
"The Cabal at Nickey Nackeys" (Behn)
See "Our Cabal"
"Cabala" (Swenson) **14**:288
"Cabaret" (Brown) **55**:71, 76, 95, 102, 114, 151
"Cabaret" (Hughes) **1**:237
"Cabaret Girl Dies on Welfare Island" (Hughes) **1**:247
Cabbage Gardens (Howe) **54**:40, 52, 107
"Cabellera" (Paz) **48**:175, 243
"A Cabin in the Clearing" (Frost) **1**:212
"A Cabin Tale" (Dunbar) **5**:120
Cables to Rage (Lorde) **12**:140
"Cables to Rage, or I've Been Talking on This Street Corner a Hell of a Long Time" (Lorde) **12**:155
"Cables to the Ace" (Merton) **10**:337
Cables to the Ace; or, Familiar Liturgies of Misunderstanding (Merton) **10**:338, 345, 348, 351, 354
"Caboose Thoughts" (Sandburg) **2**:302; **41**:240, 270, 280, 282
"Cabra" (Joyce) **22**:149
"Le cacot" (Lamartine) **16**:284
Cadastre (Césaire) **25**:12, 15, 17, 30-2, 35-6, 38-9
"Cadenas rotas" (Alurista) **34**:27, 38
"Cadenus and Vanessa" (Swift) **9**:253-55, 296
"A Cadenza" (Clampitt) **19**:102
"Cadenza" (Hughes) **7**:159; **89**:103
"Cadore" (Carducci) **46**:52
Caelo tonantem (Horace) **46**:97
"Caerulei Oculi" (Gautier) **18**:125
"Caesar" (Merwin) **45**:22, 49
"Caesar when that the traytour of Egipt" (Wyatt) **27**:339
"Caesarion" (Cavafy) **36**:20, 75, 86, 87-89
Caesar's Camp; or, St. George's Hill (Duck) **89**:67
Caesar's Gate (Duncan) **2**:101
Caesar's Gate: Poems, 1949-1950 (Duncan) **75**:122, 125-29, 156-59, 162, 179-80, 228, 261
"Café" (Milosz) **8**:175
"Café: 3 A.M." (Hughes) **53**:115, 127, 177, 192
"Café at Rapallo" (Montale) **13**:148
"Cafe Atarah" (Amichai) **38**:27
"Cafe du neant" (Loy) **16**:312-13, 328
"Café Tableau" (Swenson) **14**:275
"The Cage" (Montague) **106**:277-78, 356
A Cage of Spines (Swenson) **14**:247-48, 252, 260, 277, 284
"Caged Bird" (Angelou) **32**:7
"The Caged Bird" (Sarton) **39**:324
"The Caged Fortuneteller" (Simic) **69**:367
"Caged Rats" (Elliott) **96**:163
"The Caged Thrush Freed and Home Again" (Hardy) **92**:323
"Le cageot" (Ponge) **107**:133, 252
"Cages" (Kenyon) **57**:3
Cahier de verdure (Jaccottet) **98**:193, 201
Cahier d'un retour au pays natal (Césaire) **25**:2-3, 5-7, 10-11, 13-16, 18-19, 29-33, 41-4, 47-9, 51-6, 58-61, 63, 65
"Caída de Europa" (Mistral) **32**:188
"Cain" (Byron) **95**:55
"Cain" (Coleridge)
See "The Wanderings of Cain"
"Cain" (Nemerov) **24**:261
"Cain" (Thomas) **99**:257
Cain (Byron) **16**:86, 88, 90, 103-05, 108, 111
"Caino" (Ungaretti) **57**:369
"Cairn Maker" (Heaney) **100**:320
"Cairo Jag" (Douglas) **106**:200, 203-4, 209
"La cajita de Olinalá" (Mistral) **32**:179
"Cake" (Stein) **18**:322
Calafia: The California Poetry (Reed) **68**:340, 347
Calamiterror (Barker) **77**:29, 38, 51
"Calamus" (Whitman) **91**:198, 238, 241, 243, 245-49, 251-52, 296, 302-3, 305, 307, 309, 311-12, 314, 318, 321
"A Calder" (Shapiro) **25**:291
"Calendar" (Warren) **37**:331
The Calender (Spenser)
See *The Shepheardes Calender: Conteyning Twelve Æglogues Proportionable to the Twelve Monethes*
"Calendrier" (Char) **56**:154, 157
"Calendrier lagunaire" (Césaire) **25**:33, 45
"The Calf" (Hardy) **92**:322
"Caliban" (Brathwaite) **56**:87, 100
"Caliban upon Setebos" (Browning) **2**:58-9, 88, 95
"The Calico Cat" (Lindsay) **23**:281
"Calico Pie" (Lear) **65**:147, 151, 160-61
Calidore (Keats) **96**:241, 346
"Calidus Juventa?" (Tate) **50**:306, 319, 325
"California" (Oppen) **35**:284
"California Oaks" (Winters) **82**:319
"The California Water Plan" (Snyder) **21**:291
Californians (Jeffers) **17**:134-35, 138
"The Call" (Akhmatova)
See "Zov"
"The Call" (Brooke) **24**:57, 82
"The Call" (Dickey) **40**:175-77, 184
"The Call" (Herbert) **4**:130
"The Call" (Kenyon) **57**:47
"Call" (Lorde) **12**:139, 141
"The Call" (Very) **86**:98, 112
"The Call Across the Valley of Not-Knowing" (Kinnell) **26**:251, 269, 273-75
"Call for Faith" (Wickham) **110**:276
"Call It Fear" (Harjo) **27**:54, 61
"Call it love" (Enzensberger) **28**:139
"Call Me Back Again" (Tagore)
See "Ebar phirao more"
"Call me Ishmael" (Cage) **58**:219
"The Call of the Wild" (Service) **70**:115
"The Call of the Wild" (Snyder) **21**:292-93, 297
"A Call to Arms" (Tennyson) **101**:269
"Call to Arms" (Welch) **62**:340, 374
Call Yourself Alive? (Cassian) **17**:4, 6, 13
"La calle" (Paz) **48**:230
"Calle" (Storni) **33**:239, 246, 283
"Calle con almacén rosado" (Borges) **32**:83, 124
"Las Calles" (Borges) **22**:68; **32**:38, 80-1, 124
"Callie Ford" (Brooks) **7**:62, 69
Calligrammes (Apollinaire) **7**:3, 9-10, 12, 35-6, 42, 44, 46, 48-9
"A Calling" (Kumin) **15**:210
"The Calling" (Thomas) **99**:260, 264, 275
"Calling Cards" (Hughes) **53**:109
"Calling Collect" (Jacobsen) **62**:323, 331
"Calling Lucasta from Her Retirement" (Lovelace) **69**:159
Calling Myself Home (Hogan) **35**:247, 248, 250, 252, 253, 257, 258
"The Calling of Names" (Angelou) **32**:13
"Calling on All Silent Minorities" (Jordan) **38**:137, 141
Calling Out to Yeti (Szymborska)
See *Wołanie do Yeti*
"Calling To Minde Mine eie Long Went About" (Raleigh) **31**:201, 295-97, 312
"Callinge To Minde" (Raleigh)
See "Calling To Minde Mine eie Long Went About"
"Calliope" (H. D.) **5**:304

"Callow Captain" (Graves) **6**:133
"The Calls" (Owen) **19**:336; **102**:144, 151, 275
"The Calm" (Donne) **1**:122
"The Calm" (Gallagher) **9**:58
"The Calme" (Donne) **43**:128-29
Le Calme (Sainte-Beuve) **110**:39, 51
"Calming Kali" (Clifton) **17**:24
"Calmly We Walk Through This April's Day" (Schwartz) **8**:305-06
"Calthon and Colmal" (Macpherson) **97**:182, 246, 310
"La Calunnia e un Venticello" (Melville) **82**:49-50
"Calverly's" (Robinson) **1**:466; **35**:362, 363
"Calvinistic Evensong" (Betjeman) **75**:69
"Calypso" (Brathwaite) **56**:43, 96
"Calypso" (H. D.) **5**:306
"Calypso's Island" (MacLeish) **47**:196
"Camberley" (Betjeman) **75**:20
"Cambios de nombre" (Parra) **39**:278, 294, 305, 307
"Cambridge" (Borges) **32**:43
"The Cambridge Churchyard" (Holmes) **71**:68, 70, 91
"Cambridge, First Impressions" (Corso) **33**:35; **108**:31
"The Cambridge Ladies Who Live in Furnished Souls" (Cummings) **5**:94
"Cambridge Sky" (Corso) **108**:13
"Cambridge, Spring 1937" (Schwartz) **8**:301
"Cambridge Thirty Years Since" (Holmes) **71**:85
Camcar (Kabīr) **56**:342, 346
"Camden 1892" (Borges) **32**:100, 113
"The Camel" (Nash) **21**:278
"Camelia" (Tagore) **8**:417
"Camellia Sabina" (Moore) **49**:98, 119, 134
"El camello (auto de los Reyes Magos)" (Fuertes) **27**:8, 15, 31
"Cameo Appearance" (Simic) **69**:308-9
"Camilo" (Guillén) **23**:128
"Caminata" (Borges) **32**:81, 125
"Camino blanco, viejo camino" (Castro) **41**:99
"Caminos" (Darío) **15**:82
"La camisa de fuerza" (Parra) **39**:271-72
La camisa de fuerza (Parra) **39**:279, 288
"Camoens" (Melville) **82**:104
"Camouflage" (Heaney) **100**:264
"Camouflaging the Chimera" (Komunyakaa) **51**:6
"Camp" (Fuertes) **27**:23
"Camp 1940" (Senghor) **25**:235
"Camp and Cloister" (Browning) **2**:26
"A Camp in the Prussian Forest" (Jarrell) **41**:135-38, 173-74, 195-96
"Camp Notes" (Yamada) **44**:346
Camp Notes and Other Poems (Yamada) **44**:323, 325-26, 329-35, 337-46, 348-49
"Campau Bun" (Dafydd ap Gwilym) **56**:208
"The Campbells are Coming" (Burns) **114**:62
"Campeón Finlandés" (Mistral) **32**:188
"The Camperdown Elm" (Moore) **49**:150
"Camping at Split Rock" (Wright) **14**:366
"Camping Out" (Empson) **104**:91, 119, 122, 124
"Campions" (Lawrence) **54**:227-31, 234-36
"El campo, la ciudad, el cielo" (Guillén) **35**:156
"Camps of Green" (Whitman) **3**:378
"The Campus on the Hill" (Snodgrass) **74**:285-86, 306
"campus theatre steps" (Birney) **52**:34
"Can Cranes Cogitate" (Stone) **53**:258
Can Grande's Castle (Lowell) **13**:60, 62-3, 65-6, 72-4, 79-83, 93
"Can I See Arcturus from Where I Stand?" (Warren) **37**:330, 333, 367, 378
"Can I Tempt You to the Pond Walk?" (Schuyler) **88**:188
"Caña" (Guillén) **23**:98
"Canaan" (Spark) **72**:214, 217, 252
Canaans Calamitie, or the Dolefull Destruction of faire Jerusalem (Deloney) **79**:53, 57-58
"Canace and Machaire" (Gower) **59**:6
"canada" (Bissett) **14**:25, 34
"Canada: Case History, 1945" (Birney) **52**:8, 25, 42, 58
Canada Gees Mate for Life (Bissett) **14**:26
"The Canadian" (Bissett) **14**:10, 25
"Canadian Pacific" (Mahon) **60**:140, 213-15
"Canadians and Pottawatomies" (Sandburg) **41**:302
"Canal" (Tomlinson) **17**:313, 343
"The Canal at Rye" (Bell) **79**:27, 29
"Canal Bank Sonnets" (Kavanagh) **33**:145, 147
"Canal Bank Walk" (Kavanagh) **33**:95-6, 103, 115, 119, 138; **105**:95, 110, 153, 155, 172
"The Canal Garden" (Seifert) **47**:328
"The Canal's Drowning Black" (Hughes) **7**:148; **89**:122
"The Canary Bird" (Very)
See "To the Canary Bird"
"Cancarì" (Kabīr)
See *Camcar*
"The Cancer Cells" (Eberhart) **76**:50, 60
"The Cancer Match" (Dickey) **40**:191, 199-200
"Cancer Winter" (Hacker) **47**:104, 107, 116-17
"Canción" (Parra) **39**:284
"Canción de la Muerte" (Mistral) **32**:179
"Canción de la mujer astuta" (Storni) **33**:299-300
"Canción de otoño en primavera" (Darío) **15**:96, 107, 109-11
"Canción de taurus" (Mistral) **32**:181
"Canción de virgo" (Mistral) **32**:181
"La canción del bongo" (Guillén) **23**:106, 111-14, 132, 136, 139
"Canción otoñal" (Darío) **15**:82
"La canción que chua" (Mistral) **32**:180
"Canción tonta" (García Lorca) **3**:136
"Cancionero sin nombre" (Parra) **39**:292
Cancionero sin nombre (Parra) **39**:260, 266-67, 270, 272, 292, 295
Canciones (García Lorca) **3**:118-19, 148-49
"Canciones de cuna" (Mistral) **32**:161
Canciones rusas (Parra) **39**:271-72, 278, 285, 295
"Candelabro" (Guillén) **35**:201
The Candidate (Crabbe) **97**:78-79, 162-63
"Candidate's Prayer before Master's Oral" (Birney) **52**:17
"candide" (Enzensberger) **28**:134, 136
Candle (Akhmadulina)
See *Svecha*
"Candle Hat" (Collins) **68**:219
The Candle in the Cabin (Lindsay) **23**:286
"Candle, Lamp, and Firefly" (Gallagher) **9**:59
"Candle Shuffle" (Alurista) **34**:24, 41
"Candle-Lightin' Time" (Dunbar) **5**:122
"Candles" (Cavafy) **36**:54, 57, 88
"Candles at Three Thirty" (McGuckian) **27**:91
Candles in Babylon (Levertov) **11**:198-201, 209
"The Candlestick" (Brodsky) **9**:3
"The Candlestick" (Guillén)
See "Candelabro"
"Cane" (Brathwaite) **56**:76
Cane (Toomer) **7**:309-11, 319, 323-24, 326, 330, 332-33, 335, 339-41
"la canería y el sol" (Alurista) **34**:5-6
"El cangrejo" (Guillén) **23**:124
"las canicas y mis callos" (Alurista) **34**:11, 36
"Canicula di Anna" (Carson) **64**:204-5
"Canis Major" (Frost) **39**:233
"The Cannery" (Stryk) **27**:211
"Cannery Town in August" (Cervantes) **35**:116, 121
"canoe" (Bissett) **14**:23
"The Canoe Speaks" (Stevenson) **84**:300
"Canonica" (Stevens) **110**:201-4
"The Canonization" (Amichai) **38**:43
"The Canonization" (Bridges) **28**:73
"The Canonization" (Donne) **1**:126, 130, 132-34; **43**:125, 132, 199
"Canon's Yeoman's Prologue" (Chaucer) **19**:26
"Canon's Yeoman's Tale" (Chaucer) **19**:13, 19; **58**:266, 351
"Canso" (Merwin) **45**:24, 91
"Canst Thou Draw Out Leviathan With An Hook?" (Curnow) **48**:36
"Canta el sinsonte en el Turquino" (Guillén) **23**:124
"Cantares 1" (Castro) **41**:109
"Cantares 2" (Castro) **41**:109
"Cantares 3" (Castro) **41**:89, 109
"Cantares 4" (Castro) **41**:109
"Cantares 5" (Castro) **41**:90, 109
"Cantares 7" (Castro) **41**:109
"Cantares 8" (Castro)
See "Un arrogante gaitero"
"Cantares 9" (Castro) **41**:110
"Cantares 10" (Castro) **41**:109
"Cantares 11" (Castro) **41**:110
"Cantares 12" (Castro) **41**:109
"Cantares 13" (Castro) **41**:109-10
"Cantares 14" (Castro) **41**:109
"Cantares 16" (Castro) **41**:93, 110
"Cantares 17" (Castro) **41**:110
"Cantares 18" (Castro) **41**:109-10
"Cantares 19" (Castro) **41**:110
"Cantares 20" (Castro) **41**:110
"Cantares 21" (Castro) **41**:110
"Cantares 24" (Castro) **41**:109
"Cantares 26" (Castro) **41**:109
"Cantares 27" (Castro) **41**:110
"Cantares 28" (Castro) **41**:110
"Cantares 29" (Castro) **41**:110
"Cantares 30" (Castro) **41**:109
"Cantares 31" (Castro) **41**:109
"Cantares 32" (Castro) **41**:109
"Cantares 33" (Castro) **41**:110
"Cantares 37" (Castro) **41**:110
Cantares gallegos (Castro) **41**:79, 87-9, 93, 97, 106-9, 111, 115-16
Cantares Mexicanos I (Cardenal) **22**:127-28, 129, 132
Cantares Mexicanos II (Cardenal) **22**:127-28, 129, 132
"Cantares mexicanos (II)" (Cardenal) **22**:128, 130
"Cantares mexicanos(I)" (Cardenal) **22**:127, 130
"El cántaro roto" (Paz) **1**:361
"A Cantata" (Lanier) **50**:75
"Cantata" (Spicer) **78**:270
"Cantate meco, Progne e Filomena" (Stampa) **43**:319
Canterburie-Tales (Chaucer)
See *Canterbury Tales*
Canterbury Tales (Chaucer) **19**:3, 6, 13, 16, 18, 20, 22, 24, 26-7, 34, 37, 43-50, 52-4, 60, 64; **58**:237, 277, 281, 283-86, 288, 299-300, 322, 325, 342, 352, 361, 363, 365, 367
"Canthara" (Williams) **7**:367
Canti (Leopardi) **37**:91-92, 118, 122-23, 125-32, 134, 141, 165, 169
Canti postumi (Pound) **95**:167-71
"Canti Romani" (Ferlinghetti) **1**:183
"Canticle" (Berry) **28**:3-4
"A Canticle" (Melville) **82**:134, 207
"Canticle" (Sarton) **39**:357
Canticle (Guillén)
See *Cántico*
Cántico (Guillén) **35**:139, 145, 152-153, 154, 155, 156, 157, 158, 159, 160, 169, 170, 174, 175, 179, 180, 181, 182, 183, 184, 185, 186, 187, 188, 189, 191, 192-93, 194-97, 200-2054, 207, 210, 211, 212, 213, 214-19, 225-32, 233, 235-40, 241
"Cantilena londinese" (Zanzotto) **65**:268, 325-30
"Cantina Iannini" (Hugo) **68**:283
"Cantique des colonnes" (Valéry) **9**:366, 394
"Le Cantique de Saint Jean" (Mallarmé) **102**:20, 22
"Canto CII" (Pound) **95**:188

"Canto I" (Pound) **4**:334, 357; **95**:129, 154, 184, 186
"Canto II" (Pound) **95**:162-63, 165, 184
"Canto III" (Pound) **95**:184
"Canto IV" (Pound) **95**:184, 186-87
"Canto IX" (Pound) **95**:127
"Canto LII" (Pound) **95**:131
"Canto LIII" (Pound) **95**:131, 185
"Canto LIV" (Pound) **95**:131
"Canto LIX" (Pound) **95**:131
"Canto LV" (Pound) **95**:131
"Canto LVI" (Pound) **95**:131
"Canto LVII" (Pound) **95**:131
"Canto LVIII" (Pound) **95**:131
"Canto LX" (Pound) **95**:131
"Canto LXI" (Pound) **95**:131, 206
"Canto LXII" (Pound) **95**:187, 207
"Canto LXIII" (Pound) **95**:223
"Canto LXIV" (Pound) **95**:185
"Canto LXXI" (Pound) **95**:156
"Canto LXXII" (Pound) **95**:129-30, 151-56, 234
"Canto LXXIII" (Pound) **95**:151-54, 234, 240
"Canto LXXIII: Cavalcanti—Corrispondenza Republicana" (Pound)
See "Canto 73"
"Canto LXXVII" (Pound) **95**:185, 190
"Canto LXXXVII" (Pound) **95**:128
"Canto LXVII" (Pound) **95**:188
"Canto LXVIII" (Pound) **95**:185
"Canto VII" (Pound) **95**:82
"Canto VIII" (Pound) **4**:353; **95**:127, 185, 187
"Canto XC" (Pound) **95**:171, 184, 196
"Canto XCII" (Pound) **95**:171, 196-97
"Canto XCIII" (Pound) **95**:171, 196-98
"Canto XCIV" (Pound) **95**:169, 171, 196
"Canto XCV" (Pound) **95**:171, 196
"Canto XCVI" (Pound) **95**:186, 189
"Canto XII" (Pound) **95**:187
"Canto XIII" (Pound) **95**:187, 204
"Canto XIV" (Pound) **4**:328, 358; **95**:153
"Canto XLIX" (Pound) **95**:168-69, 171, 175
"Canto XV" (Pound) **4**:358; **95**:153
"Canto XVI" (Pound) **4**:328; **95**:129, 187
"Canto XVII" (Pound) **95**:129, 187
"Canto XX" (Pound) **95**:175, 197
"Canto XXI" (Pound) **95**:188
"Canto XXIII" (Pound) **95**:127
"Canto XXV" (Pound) **95**:188
"Canto XXVI" (Pound) **4**:324
"Canto XXVII" (Pound) **4**:325, 345
"Canto XXX" (Pound) **95**:130
"Canto XXXI" (Pound) **95**:130, 132, 204
"Canto XXXII" (Pound) **95**:130, 204
"Canto XXXIII" (Pound) **95**:130, 204
"Canto XXXIX" (Pound) **95**:169
"Canto XXXVI" (Pound) **95**:220, 223, 230
"Canto XLI" (Pound) **4**:357; **95**:140
"Canto XLVII" (Pound) **4**:346-47, 349; **95**:169
"Canto L" (Pound) **4**:360, 362
"Canto LI" (Pound) **4**:326
"Canto LXXIV" (Pound) **4**:345-49, 352, 354; **95**:80, 170, 180, 235, 238-40
"Canto LXXV" (Pound) **4**:347, 349; **95**:235
"Canto LXXVI" (Pound) **4**:352-53; **95**:155, 184, 197, 239
"Canto LXXVIII" (Pound) **4**:349; **95**:155, 189
"Canto LXXIX" (Pound) **4**:349; **95**:186
"Canto LXXX" (Pound) **4**:345, 349; **95**:128, 169
"Canto LXXXI" (Pound) **4**:349, 352; **95**:238-40
"Canto LXXXII" (Pound) **4**:349, 352
"Canto LXXXIII" (Pound) **4**:345, 348; **95**:175
"Canto LXXXIV" (Pound) **4**:345, 348; **95**:170-71
"Canto LXXXVI" (Pound) **4**:347
"Canto XCI" (Pound) **4**:354; **95**:171, 196, 198
"Canto C" (Pound) **4**:360-62
"Canto CI" (Pound) **4**:353
"Canto CIV" (Pound) **4**:357; **95**:188
"Canto CX" (Pound) **4**:353
"Canto CXIII" (Pound) **4**:353-54
"Canto CXV" (Pound) **4**:354
"Canto CXVI" (Pound) **4**:353-54; **95**:191, 198
"Canto CXVIII" (Pound) **4**:353
"Canto CXX" (Pound) **4**:354
"Canto a Bolivar" (Neruda) **4**:279-80
"Canto à la Argentina" (Darío) **15**:82, 115
"Canto a las madres de los milicianos muertos" (Neruda) **4**:278
"Canto a Stalingrado" (Neruda) **4**:279
"Canto amor" (Berryman) **64**:81, 88
"Canto de la sangre" (Darío) **15**:91-2, 96, 105
"Canto di Apòllion" (Quasimodo) **47**:277
"Canto di marzo" (Carducci) **46**:55, 65
"Canto di Primavera" (Carducci) **46**:18
Canto general (Neruda)
See *Canto general de Chile*
Canto general de Chile (Neruda) **4**:279-82, 291-96; **64**:298-99, 306, 312-13, 316-17, 322, 324, 326-30, 333, 343-44, 347-50, 352
"Canto nacional" (Cardenal) **22**:103
"Canto negro" (Guillén) **23**:134
"Canto notturno di un pastore errante dell'Asia" (Leopardi) **37**:83, 92, 102, 116, 121, 123-24, 126, 129, 131-32, 140-41, 165
"Canto notturno di un pastore errante nell'Asia" (Montale) **13**:109
"Canto of Signs Without Wonders" (Curnow) **48**:32-38
"Canto popolare" (Pasolini) **17**:294
"Canto Primo" (Campion) **87**:11, 62
"Canto primo" (Ungaretti) **57**:347
"Canto Quarto" (Campion) **87**:62
"Canto Quinto" (Campion) **87**:62
"Canto Secundo" (Campion) **87**:11, 62
"Canto sobre unas ruinas" (Neruda) **4**:309
"Canto Tertio" (Campion) **87**:62
Cantos (Pound) **4**:332, 343-45, 350-54; **95**:73, 77, 80, 82, 91, 100, 102-3, 109-11, 118, 126, 128-32, 140-41, 148-49, 151-52, 156, 162, 164-65, 167-68, 170-71, 174, 176, 183-93, 195-96, 198-99, 203-8, 218-19, 223, 230, 234
Cantos de adolescencia (Paredes) **83**:39-40, 56
Cantos de vida y esperanza (Darío) **15**:78, 80, 87, 89, 91-2, 96, 103-05, 107, 109, 115, 117, 120
Cantos LII-LXXI (Pound) **95**:77
Cantos para soldados y sones para turistas (Guillén) **23**:99, 101, 131, 133, 140
"Canvas" (Zagajewski) **27**:387-88, 393, 395
Canvas (Zagajewski) **27**:389, 393, 399
"Canvass" (Niedecker) **42**:146-49
"Canyon de Chelly" (Ortiz) **17**:225
"Canzona" (Seferis) **66**:208
"Canzone" (Auden) **92**:81-83, 85-89
"Canzone" (Mandelstam) **14**:138
"Canzone" (Ungaretti) **57**:339, 374, 376
"La Canzone di Legnano" (Carducci) **46**:53
"Canzone on an Old Proverb" (Stryk) **27**:198
"Canzone 22" (Michelangelo) **103**:296
"Canzones" (Okigbo)
See "Four Canzones"
Canzones (Okigbo)
See "Four Canzones"
Canzoni (Leopardi) **37**:123
Canzoni (Pound) **4**:317; **95**:111-12, 117-20, 220
Canzoniere (Petrarch) **8**:218, 220, 224-40, 242-5, 247-9, 251-65, 268-73, 276-8
Canzoniere (Stampa) **43**:341
"Cap" (Brathwaite) **56**:93
"The Cap and Bells" (Keats) **1**:279, 311
The Cap and Bells; or, The Jealousies (Keats) **96**:298, 305
"Cap on Head" (Masefield) **78**:42, 49-50, 62
"Capacity" (Updike) **90**:351
"Cape Alava" (Hugo) **68**:234
"Cape Breton" (Bishop) **3**:39, 58-9; **34**:104-105, 108
"Cape Cod" (Brodsky)
See "A Cape Cod Lullaby"
"A Cape Cod Lullaby" (Brodsky) **9**:7, 19
"Cape Dread" (Merwin) **45**:7
"Cape Hatteras" (Crane) **3**:86-7, 90, 96, 106-10
"Cape Horn Gospel I" (Masefield) **78**:6, 69, 95
"Cape Horn Gospel II" (Masefield) **78**:69
"Cape Mootch" (Pasternak) **6**:251
"Caperucita Roja" (Mistral) **32**:179
"The Capital" (Rilke)
See "Das Kapitäl"
"Capital del invierno" (Guillén) **35**:154
Capital of Pain (Éluard)
See *Capitale de la douleur*
"Capital Punishment" (Alexie) **53**:21
Capitale de la douleur (Éluard) **38**:60, 64, 66, 68, 70, 76-7, 80, 99, 101-5, 107
"Capitol Air" (Ginsberg) **4**:62, 76, 83
"Cappadocian Song" (Carruth) **10**:89
"Capri" (Teasdale) **31**:322
Capriccio (Hughes) **89**:188, 190, 193, 234
"Capriccios" (Hughes) **89**:234-35
"Caprice" (Betjeman) **75**:61
"Caprice" (Cullen) **20**:55
"Caprice" (Wright) **36**:372
"Capricho" (Storni) **33**:275, 307
"Capricorn Rising" (Mackey) **49**:6, 22
"Captain Carpenter" (Ransom) **61**:275, 311, 313, 320, 324-25
"Captain Cook" (Birney) **52**:21
"Captain Cook's Last Voyage" (Thomas) **99**:310
"Captain Craig" (Robinson) **1**:460, 467, 483, 486
Captain Craig and Other Poems (Robinson) **1**:462-63, 470-72, 474, 490; **35**:362, 367
"Captain Haddock" (Szirtes) **51**:158
Captain Jack's Chaps, or Houston/MLA (Dorn) **115**:120, 124
Captain Lavender (McGuckian) **27**:104-106
"A Captain of the Press Gang" (Carman) **34**:207
"Captain Samuel Cook" (Very) **86**:54
"Captain Stratton's Fancy" (Masefield) **78**:20
Captain Sword and Captain Pen (Hunt) **73**:137, 139, 144, 152-54, 168-69, 200
"Captivating the Soul with Immortality" (Akhmadulina) **43**:56
"Captive" (Das) **43**:73, 87
"The Captive" (Morris) **55**:344-45
"Captive" (Stafford) **71**:263
The Captive of the Caucasus (Pushkin)
See *Kavkazsky plennik*
"A Captive of the Khan" (Tsvetaeva)
See "Khansky polon"
"Captivity" (Erdrich) **52**:174, 176, 195-97, 202
"Captivity" (Mueller) **33**:196
"The Captivity and Restoration of Mrs. Mary Rowlandson" (Howe) **54**:96
"Captivity of the Fly" (MacLeish) **47**:192
"The Capture of Mr. Moon" (Snodgrass) **74**:324, 334
"The Capture of Mr. Sun" (Snodgrass) **74**:324, 334
"Captured by the Khan" (Tsvetaeva)
See "Khansky polon"
"Capturing Animals" (Hughes) **89**:158
"Car Journeys" (Abse) **41**:13-14
"Car Poem" (Shvarts) **50**:148
"Car Song" (Spicer) **78**:295-97
"Car Wreck" (Shapiro) **25**:205
"Cara a cara" (Guillén) **35**:157, 227
"Cara joven" (Cernuda) **62**:271
"Les carabosses" (Hacker) **47**:86
"Caracas" (Birney) **52**:41
"A Carafe That Is a Blind Glass" (Stein) **18**:318, 334
"Caravanserai" (Goodison) **36**:143
Carcari (Kabīr)
See *Camcar*
"The Card Party" (Spark) **72**:217
"The Card Players" (Larkin) **21**:237
"A Card Skull in Atlantis" (Szirtes) **51**:159
"Cardigan Bay" (Masefield) **78**:95
"A Cardinal" (Snodgrass) **74**:284-85, 290, 305-6
"A Career" (Yevtushenko) **40**:343-44
"A Careful Passion" (Walcott) **46**:230, 273

"A carefull complaynt by the unfortunate Auctor" (Whitney) **116**:312
"Careless Water" (Stein) **18**:334
"Caress" (Mistral)
See "Caricia"
"Cargoes" (Masefield) **78**:5, 20, 68, 74, 97
"Caribbean Kingdoms" (Birney) **52**:16, 18, 103
"Caribbean Sunset" (Hughes) **1**:236
"Caribbean Wind" (Dylan) **37**:64-65
"Caribou" (Warren) **37**:367, 376
"Caribou Girl" (Cervantes) **35**:104, 107, 112, 117
"Caricia" (Mistral) **32**:179
"Carico d'anni e di peccati pieno" (Michelangelo) **103**:306
"Caritas" (Cummings) **5**:94
"Carl Hamblin" (Masters) **36**:183
"Carlo Goldoni" (Carducci) **46**:52
"Carlos" (Ríos) **57**:312
"Carlos among the Candles" (Stevens) **6**:295
"The Carmelites" (Berssenbrugge) **115**:8, 12, 25
"Carmelites" (Erdrich) **52**:186
"Carmen" (Blok) **21**:26
Carmen (Horace)
See *Carmen Saeculare*
Carmen Deo Nostro (Crashaw) **84**:8-9, 20, 31-32, 52-53, 69, 72, 75, 113, 151, 167
Carmen Saeculare (Horace) **46**:97, 99, 108, 211, 222
"Carmen Seculare" (Prior) **102**:309
"Carmen Triumphale, for the Commencement of the Year 1814" (Southey) **111**:250-51
"Carnal Knowledge" (Gunn) **26**:182, 188, 199-200, 207, 210, 218
"Carnales el amor nos pertenece" (Alurista) **34**:23, 29
"el carnalismo nos une" (Alurista) **34**:31
"Carnaval" (Gautier) **18**:125
"La Carne de tus Labios" (Alurista) **34**:46
"Carnegie Hall: Rescued" (Moore) **4**:242; **49**:148
"The Carnegie Library" (Jarrell)
See "The Carnegie Library, Juvenile Division"
"The Carnegie Library, Juvenile Division" (Jarrell) **41**:159, 165, 167, 177, 194
"Carnegie, Oklahoma, 1919" (Momaday) **25**:221
Le Carnet des bois de pin (Ponge) **107**:73, 118, 124
"Carnevale" (Carducci) **46**:5, 51
"Carnevale di Gerti" (Montale) **13**:117
"Carney Elegy" (Jacobsen) **62**:325
"Carnival" (Carducci)
See "Carnevale"
"The Carnival Girl Darkly Attracts W. D." (Snodgrass) **74**:334-35
"Caro m'è 'l sonno, e più l'esser di sasso" (Michelangelo) **103**:317
"Carol" (Merton) **10**:340
"Carol" (Nemerov) **24**:258
"A Carol for Children" (Nash) **21**:275
"Carolina Cabin" (Hughes) **53**:116
Carolina Said Song (Ammons) **16**:19
"Caroline Branson" (Masters) **36**:188
Carols of an Old Codger (Service) **70**:140, 143-44
La Carona (Donne) **43**:123
"Carousing Students" (Pushkin) **10**:407
The Carpentered Hen and Other Tame Creatures (Updike) **90**:346-48, 350-53, 357
"The Carpenter's Son" (Housman) **2**:192
"A Carpet Not Bought" (Merrill) **28**:253
"Le carreau" (Char) **56**:171, 173
"Carrefour" (Lowell) **13**:85
"A Carriage from Sweden" (Moore) **49**:100
"Carrick Revisited" (MacNeice) **61**:112-13
"Carrickfergus" (MacNeice) **61**:118, 120, 131, 137, 144
"Carric-thura" (Macpherson) **97**:246, 265
"Carrier" (Meredith) **28**:174, 186
"Carrier Bag" (Enright) **93**:34
"Carrier Letter" (Crane) **99**:70-71
The Carrier of Ladders (Merwin) **45**:10, 16, 18-19, 26-30, 32-3, 35, 37-8, 40-2, 45-7, 51, 57, 59, 66, 73-4, 77, 84, 90, 94-6, 98
The Carrier Pigeon (Seifert)
See *Poštovní holub*
"Carriers of the Dream Wheel" (Momaday) **25**:199, 217
"A Carrion" (Baudelaire)
See "Une charogne"
"Carrion Comfort" (Hopkins) **15**:144
"Carro del cielo" (Mistral) **32**:169
Carrying a Torch (Berrigan) **103**:31, 35
"Carrying Mission to the Frontier" (Wang Wei)
See "Arriving at the Frontier on a Mission"
"The Carrying Ring" (McGuckian) **27**:105
"The Cart Horse" (Das) **43**:82
"Carta a Miguel Otero Silva, en Caracas, 1948" (Neruda) **4**:293
"Carta de creencia" (Paz) **1**:376; **48**:232
"Carta de la eme" (Fuertes) **27**:37
"Carta de la Habana" (Guillén) **23**:127
"Carta explicatoria de Gloria" (Fuertes) **27**:17, 48-9
"Carta lírca a una mujer" (Storni) **33**:254, 277-78
"Carta lírica a otra mujer" (Storni) **33**:254, 277-78
"Cartagena de Indias" (Birney) **52**:15, 21, 23, 34, 41, 44-45, 60-62, 80, 96-98
"Cartas a una desconocida" (Parra) **39**:285-86
"Cartas del poeta que duerme en una silla" (Parra) **39**:286
"Carte du 8 novembre" (Char) **56**:154
Des Cartes à l'Amazone (Wickham) **110**:262, 301, 303
"Carthon" (Macpherson) **97**:175, 240, 319
"The Cartographer of Meadows" (Ciardi) **69**:33, 55
"Cartographies of Silence" (Rich) **5**:378-79, 394-95
"Cartoons of Coming Shows Unseen Before" (Schwartz) **8**:291
"The Cartridges" (Levine) **22**:213
"La cartuja" (Darío) **15**:102
"Caru Merch Fonheddig" (Dafydd ap Gwilym) **56**:245, 247
"Caru yn y Gaeaf" (Dafydd ap Gwilym) **56**:225, 227-33
"The Caruso Poem" (Bissett) **14**:4, 19
"Caryatid" (Benn) **35**:9
"Caryatids *1*" (Hughes) **89**:180
"Caryatids *2*" (Hughes) **89**:273
"Caryl Chessman Interviews the PTA (from his swank gas chamber)" (Kaufman) **74**:212, 241
"La casa dei doganieri" (Montale) **13**:114
La casa dei doganieri e altri versi (Montale) **13**:106, 138
"Casa Elena" (Borges) **22**:92
Casa Guidi Windows: A Poem (Barrett Browning) **6**:2, 6-9, 16, 36, 38, 41, 46; **62**:26, 35
"Casa in costruzione" (Pavese) **13**:226
"Casa mia" (Ungaretti) **57**:346
"Casa sul mare" (Montale) **13**:137, 147, 164
"Casabianca" (Bishop) **3**:37, 56, 67; **34**:122, 149
"La casada infiel" (García Lorca) **3**:119, 132, 134
"Cascada en sequedal" (Mistral) **32**:161
Case d'armons (Apollinaire) **7**:21-22
"Case in Point" (Jordan) **38**:123, 126, 139
"The Case of Conscience" (Burns) **114**:129
"A Case of Murder" (Hagiwara)
See "Satsujin jiken"
"The Case of the Assassinated Bird" (Cernuda)
See "El caso del pájaro asesinado"
"Case-moth" (Wright) **14**:374
"Casi Juicio Final" (Borges) **32**:38
"El caso del pájaro asesinado" (Cernuda) **62**:187, 189-91, 254
"Caso vocativo" (Zanzotto) **65**:274
"Caspar Hauser Song" (Trakl) **20**:226, 259-60, 267, 269
"Cassandra" (Bogan) **12**:110
"Cassandra" (Heaney) **100**:340-41, 343
"Cassandra" (Jeffers) **17**:139
"Cassandra" (Robinson) **1**:487
"Cassandra Southwick" (Whittier) **93**:198, 244-45
"Cassandra's Answer" (Montague) **106**:286, 289, 313
"Cassandre CLX" (Ronsard) **105**:185, 189
"Cassandre LVII" (Ronsard) **105**:185
"Cassandre XIX" (Ronsard) **105**:184-85
"Cassandre XXIX" (Ronsard) **105**:184
"Cassandre XXVIII" (Ronsard) **105**:184
"Cassinus and Peter, a Tragic Elegy" (Swift) **9**:262, 270, 274, 279, 286, 288, 298, 302-03
"The Cassis River" (Rimbaud)
See "La Rivière de Cassis"
"Castástrofe en Sewell" (Neruda) **4**:294
"The Castaway" (Cowper) **40**:44-6, 98, 126
"Castaway" (Thomas) **99**:272
"The Castaway" (Walcott) **46**:230, 274, 283-84, 290
The Castaway, and Other Poems (Walcott) **46**:229-31, 238, 259, 272, 274-75, 283-85, 322
"The Castaways" (McKay) **2**:221
"Castel Saint' Angelo" (Hugo) **68**:237
"Castilian" (Wylie) **23**:310, 312
"Casting a Spell" (Duncan) **75**:127
"Casting and Gathering" (Heaney) **18**:257
The Casting of Bells (Seifert)
See *Odlévání ní zvonů*
The Casting of the Bells (Seifert)
See *Odlévání ní zvonů*
Casting the Bells (Seifert)
See *Odlévání ní zvonů*
"The Castle" (Graves) **6**:131, 135, 142, 144
"The Castle" (Muir) **49**:232, 245, 248-49, 255-56
"The Castle" (Silverstein) **49**:343
"The Castle" (Tomlinson) **17**:308, 311
"Castle Boterel" (Hardy) **92**:318
"Castle Childbirth" (Heaney) **100**:243
"Castle Gordon" (Burns) **114**:120
"The Castle of Thorns" (Winters) **82**:338, 341-43
Castle Tzingal (Chappell) **105**:6, 9-10, 14-17, 37, 47, 65
"Castles and Distances" (Wilbur) **51**:187-88, 207-9, 236
"Casual" (Hughes) **53**:115
"Casualty" (Heaney) **18**:198, 211, 240, 246; **100**:206, 233, 274, 352
"The Casualty" (Hughes) **7**:114
"The Casualty" (MacNeice) **61**:126, 128, 141
"Casualty" (Service) **70**:132
"Cat" (Brathwaite) **56**:49
"The Cat" (Kinnell) **26**:286-7
"A Cat, a Kid, and a Mom" (Silverstein) **49**:342
"The Cat and I Dream Away the Days and Nights" (Shvarts)
See "My s koshkoi dremlem den' i noch"
"The Cat and the Moon" (Yeats) **20**:304
The Cat and the Moon (Yeats) **51**:108
"The Cat and the Saxophone" (Hughes) **1**:236; **53**:79
"Cat in an Empty Apartment" (Szymborska)
See "Kot w pustym mieszkaniu"
"cat walked in" (Alurista) **34**:32, 33
Catacoustics (Raworth) **107**:305, 307, 309-10, 325, 328
"Cataldo Mission" (Hugo) **68**:288
"Catalina Macaw" (Doty) **53**:69
"Catalina Parra" (Parra) **39**:285
"A Catalogue of the Heroicall Loves" (Drayton) **98**:127
"The Catalpa Tree" (Bogan) **12**:129, 131

"Catarina to Camoens" (Barrett Browning) **6**:16-17, 38
"Catastrophe at Sewell" (Neruda)
See "Castástrofe en Sewell"
"Cat-Boat" (Oppen) **35**:327
"the catch" (Bukowski) **18**:25
"Catch" (Francis) **34**:255
"The Catch" (Wilbur) **51**:335
"A Catch of Shy Fish" (Brooks) **7**:105
"The Catching Ballet of the Wedding Clothes" (Hardy) **92**:277
"Catching Frogs" (Kenyon) **57**:12
"Catchment" (Kumin) **15**:209, 211, 223
"Catechism of d Neoamerican Hoodoo Church" (Reed) **68**:323-24, 326, 328-30, 332-33, 338, 348
catechism of d neoamerican hoodoo church: Poems (Reed) **68**:321, 337
"Catedral" (Borges) **22**:92
"Categories" (Giovanni) **19**:110-12, 116
"Categories" (Kennedy) **93**:149
"Catering For The People" (Thumboo) **30**:301, 329, 333
"The Caterwauling Beast at Last Has Utterance" (Barker) **77**:20
Cathay (Pound) **4**:317, 364, 366
Cathay: Translations by Ezra Pound for the Most Part from the Chinese of Rihaku, From the Notes of the Late Ernest Fenollosa, and the Decipherings of the Professors Mori and Ariga (Pound) **95**:123, 171
"Cathedral" (Ciardi) **69**:25
"The Cathedral" (Rilke)
See "Die Kathedrale"
"The Cathedral Close" (Patmore) **59**:228
"Catherine Lloyd" (Crabbe) **97**:138-40, 142-44
"Catherine of Alexandria" (Dove) **6**:107, 109
"Catherine of Siena" (Dove) **6**:107, 109
"Cathlin of Clutha" (Macpherson) **97**:182, 233, 252
"Cath-loda" (Macpherson) **97**:174, 230, 233
"The Catholic Bells" (Williams) **109**:286
"Cato Braden" (Masters) **1**:33, 343
"The Cats" (Baudelaire)
See "Les chats"
"Cats" (Hagiwara)
See "Neko"
"Cats and a Cock" (Rukeyser) **12**:209
Cats and Bats and Things with Wings (Aiken) **26**:24, 30
"The Cats of St. Nicholas" (Seferis) **66**:200, 204, 212
"Catterskill Falls" (Bryant) **20**:14-16, 43
"Cattle Gredo" (Milosz) **8**:207
"Cattle Show" (MacDiarmid) **9**:160, 176
"The Cattledrive in Connaught" (Clarke) **112**:28, 105
The Cattledrive in Connaught and Other Poems (Clarke) **112**:27-29, 33, 40, 44, 66, 72, 74-76, 78
"Catullus" (Nishiwaki) **15**:238
"Catullus: Carmina" (Carson) **64**:223, 228
The Caucasian Captive (Pushkin)
See *Kavkazsky plennik*
"Cauchemar" (Gautier) **18**:142, 164
"Cauchemar" (Verlaine) **32**:387
"The Caucuses: A Romance" (Carver) **54**:28
"Caught" (Montague) **106**:311
"Caupolicán" (Darío) **15**:95
"Cause & Effect" (Swenson) **14**:264
"Causerie" (Baudelaire) **1**:45, 66; **106**:103
"Causerie" (Tate) **50**:230-31, 243, 250, 255, 316
"Causerie au bal" (Sainte-Beuve) **110**:57, 65, 68
"Causerie II" (Tate) **50**:316
"The Causes" (Borges) **32**:58, 66-7
Cautionary Tales for Children (Belloc) **24**:21, 26, 49
Cautionary Verses (Belloc)
See *Cautionary Verses: The Collected Humorous Poems*
Cautionary Verses: The Collected Humorous Poems (Belloc) **24**:13-15, 17-18, 23, 27
"Le Cavalier poursuivi" (Gautier) **18**:142-43
"Cavalier Tunes" (Browning) **2**:26, 36
Cave Birds (Hughes) **89**:119, 124, 130, 142, 149, 151, 193-201, 212, 232-33
Cave Birds: An Alchemical Cave Drama (Hughes) **7**:153-58, 162-65, 171
Cave Birds: An Alchemical Drama (Hughes)
See *Cave Birds*
"Cave Canem" (Millay) **6**:233
"The Cave of Making" (Auden) **92**:67
"The Cave of Night" (Montague) **106**:243-44, 246-47
Cavender's House (Robinson) **1**:471-72, 475, 479, 483
"Caves" (Wakoski) **15**:363
"The Caves of Dahra" (Patmore) **59**:240
"Cawdor" (Jeffers) **17**:107-08, 110
Cawdor, and Other Poems (Jeffers) **17**:110, 135
"Cayendo van los bravos combatientes" (Castro) **41**:116
"Ce n'est pas la poésie qui" (Éluard) **38**:69
"Ce n'est plus Lisette" (Béranger) **112**:22
"Ce que dit la bouche d'ombre" (Hugo) **17**:66, 83-84, 90
"Ce que dit l'homme de peine est toujours hors de propos" (Éluard) **38**:68
"Ce qui est à moi" (Césaire) **25**:43
Ce qui fut sans lumière (Bonnefoy) **58**:137, 139, 141, 150, 156-59, 165-66, 170
"Ce qu'on dit au poète à propos de fleurs" (Rimbaud) **57**:177, 202, 208, 210, 212, 214, 237, 247, 250, 255-56, 258, 261-62, 293
"Ce qu'on entend sur la montagne" (Hugo) **17**:91
"Ce siècle est grand et fort" (Hugo) **17**:94
"Cease, Cease, Aminta to Complain" (Behn) **13**:7
"Cebula" (Szymborska) **44**:320
"The Cedars" (Wright) **14**:339, 346
"La ceinture" (Valéry) **9**:372, 374, 387, 396
"Celandine" (Thomas) **53**:318
"Celebration" (Cohen) **109**:4
"The Celebration" (Dickey) **40**:185
"A Celebration" (Williams) **7**:345
"Celebration: Birth of a Colt" (Hogan) **35**:258
A Celebration of Charis in Ten Lyric Pieces (Jonson) **17**:169-70, 180, 194-96, 207, 214
"Celebration of the trees and the hunter" (Char)
See "Fête des arbres et du chasseur"
"Celebrations" (Clarke) **112**:37-39, 51, 91, 103, 117
"Celebrations" (Sarton) **39**:322, 356
Celebrations after the Death of John Brennan (Kennedy) **93**:143
Celebrations of Patience (Rimbaud)
See *Fête de la patience*
"Célébrer Giacometti" (Char) **56**:119
"Celestial Freedom" (Aleixandre) **15**:19
"Celestial Globe" (Nemerov) **24**:263, 274
Celestial Hoyden (Lowell) **3**:199
"Celestial Music" (Glück) **16**:158
"The Celestial Poets" (Neruda)
See "Los poetas celestes"
"Celestials at the Board of Projects" (Milosz) **8**:214
"Celia singing" (Carew) **29**:25
"Celia's Birthday Poem" (Zukofsky) **11**:342
"Celibacy" (Clarke) **112**:34-35, 113, 116, 119
"Celibacy at Twenty" (Olds) **22**:338
"Célibat, célibat, tout n'est que célibat" (Laforgue) **14**:76
The Cell (Hejinian) **108**:267, 288, 310
"Cell Song" (Knight) **14**:40, 52-3
"Celladon" (Behn)
See "A Farewell to Celladon"
"The Cellar" (Soto) **28**:371
"Cellar Hole in Joppa" (Kumin) **15**:190
"The Cellar of Memory" (Akhmatova) **2**:20
"Celle de toujours, toute" (Éluard) **38**:77
"A Celle dont its rêvent" (Éluard) **38**:64
"Celle qui n'a pas la parole" (Éluard) **38**:70, 86
"Celle qui sort de l'onde" (Valéry) **9**:392
"Celles" (Hacker) **47**:87
"Cells" (Kipling) **3**:163
"The Celtic Fringe" (Smith) **12**:339
A Celtic Miscellany (Dafydd ap Gwilym) **56**:221
"El Cementerio" (Cernuda) **62**:197
"Un cementerio que mira al mar" (Storni) **33**:246, 254
"Cemetery, Stratford Connecticut" (Rose) **13**:239
"La cena triste" (Pavese) **13**:205, 208
"Le Cénacle" (Sainte-Beuve) **110**:38, 65
"The Cenci" (Carducci) **46**:26
The Cenci (Shelley) **14**:165, 171-75, 182-83, 196, 202-03, 205, 208-10, 213; **67**:187
The Cenci: A Tragedy in Five Acts (Shelley)
See *The Cenci*
"La Cène" (Péret) **33**:210
Ceneri (Pasolini) **17**:294-95
"Le ceneri di Gramscí" (Pasolini) **17**:263, 265, 271, 284-85, 289-92, 294-95
Le ceneri di Gramscí (Pasolini) **17**:255, 263-67, 269-70, 272, 286-87, 293
"The Cenotaph" (Mew) **107**:63
"Census" (Szymborska) **44**:300
"The Census-Taker" (Frost) **1**:194; **39**:235
Cent balades (Christine de Pizan) **68**:8, 11, 15, 34-37, 60, 69, 73, 76, 80-88, 96-98, 132, 173, 179-83, 192
Cent balades d'amant et de dame (Christine de Pizan) **68**:9-11, 15, 19, 21, 26, 35-36, 97, 99-100, 132, 138, 145, 153, 179, 181-84, 191
"The Centaur" (Swenson) **14**:248, 252, 255, 262-63, 281-82, 288
"The Centaur" (Thoreau) **30**:189
"The Centenarian" (Whitman) **91**:278
"A Centenary Tribute" (Clarke) **112**:123
"Centennial Cantata" (Lanier) **50**:112-15, 118-19
The Centennial Edition of the Works of Sidney Lanier (Lanier) **50**:94, 97
"Centennial for Walt Whitman" (Eberhart) **76**:9
"The Centennial Meditation of Columbia" (Lanier) **50**:74-75, 77, 112
"El centinela" (Borges) **22**:79; **32**:61, 89
"Centipede Sonnet" (Villa) **22**:350-51
"Central Europe" (Zagajewski) **27**:398
"Central Heat" (Kennedy) **93**:147
The Central Motion: Poems, 1968-1979 (Dickey) **40**:219, 222-23, 241
"Central Park" (Lowell) **3**:226
"Central Park at Dusk" (Teasdale) **31**:363
"Central Park West" (Spicer) **78**:302
Le Centre blanc (Brossard) **80**:3-4, 6, 10, 18
"Centre of Free Enterprise" (Birney) **52**:38
Centuries of Meditations (Traherne) **70**:189, 195, 198, 201, 205, 219, 238-39, 244-45, 261-64, 266-68, 270-71, 275-78, 280-81, 285, 287-92, 295, 298, 312, 314, 320, 325-27, 329-31, 334
A Century of Roundels (Swinburne) **24**:313, 322-27
"The Century's Decline" (Szymborska)
See "Schylek wieku"
"Ceras eternas" (Mistral) **32**:176
"Cercanías" (Borges) **32**:81
"Cerdick" (Chatterton) **104**:71
Cerebro y corazón (Guillén) **23**:104, 133-34
"Ceremonies for Candlemasse Eve" (Herrick) **9**:99
"Ceremonies for Christmasse" (Herrick) **9**:99, 104
"Ceremony" (Stafford) **71**:297-98, 355, 369
"Ceremony" (Wilbur) **51**:188, 192-93

Ceremony (Wilbur) **51**:236-37, 269, 291, 293, 296, 323, 330
"Ceremony after a Fire Raid" (Thomas) **2**:382, 388; **52**:258, 278, 290-91, 299-303
"A Ceremony for One of My Dead" (O'Hara) **45**:173
"Ceremony for the Banishment of the King of Swords" (Goodison) **36**:147-48, 151
"Ceremuxa predposlednjaja" (Akhmadulina) **43**:19
"Le Cerf" (Scève) **111**:4
A Certain Distance (Francis) **34**:251
"Certain familier Epistles and friendly Letters by the Auctor: with Replies" (Whitney)
See "Famyliar and friendly Epistles"
"Certain Mercies" (Graves) **6**:152
"A Certain Morning Is" (Villa) **22**:350
"Certain Phenomena of Sound" (Stevens) **110**:106, 202
"Certain Poets" (MacLeish) **47**:182
A Certain Slant of Sunlight (Berrigan) **103**:23-24, 26, 28, 31, 36-37
"A Certain Slant of Sunlight" (Berrigan) **103**:30, 42
Certain Sonnets (Sidney)
See *Certaine Sonets*
Certaine Sonets (Sidney) **32**:235, 239-40, 244, 247, 249, 250, 273, 282, 286
"Certainty" (Paz)
See "Certeza"
"Certainty before Lunch" (Berryman) **64**:96
"Certeza" (Paz) **1**:355; **48**:269
"A certi Censori" (Carducci) **46**:51
"El César" (Cernuda) **62**:203
"César" (Valéry) **9**:391
"Cet amour à tous retiré" (Char) **56**:173-74
Cette fumée qui nous portait (Char) **56**:115
"Ceux qui luttent" (Smith) **12**:333
"Cezanne at Aix" (Tomlinson) **17**:304, 306, 335
"Cézanne 'The Bridge at Maincy'" (Thomas) **99**:339
"Chaadayevu" (Pushkin) **10**:408
"Chacun en sa beauté vante ce qui le touche" (Sainte-Beuve) **110**:65-66
"Chacun sa chimère" (Baudelaire) **1**:58
"Chad" (Brathwaite) **56**:6, 29
"Chahinkapa Zoo" (Erdrich) **52**:172, 192
"La chaine a mille anneaux" (Lamartine) **16**:284
"Chains" (Apollinaire)
See "Liens"
"A Chair" (Stein) **18**:319, 349
"Chair Gallows" (Komunyakaa) **51**:29
Chaitāli (Tagore) **8**:403, 409-10
"Le Chaitivel" (Marie de France) **22**:248-49, 255, 258, 260, 267-73, 295
"Chaka" (Senghor) **25**:241, 255
"Chalice" (Alurista) **34**:28, 41
"The Chalk Pit" (Thomas) **53**:286, 288, 291, 324
"Chalk White" (Szirtes) **51**:172
"Challenge" (Brown) **55**:110, 114, 118, 124-30
"The Challenge" (Graves) **6**:137
"The Challenge" (Longfellow) **30**:42
"The Chamber over the Gate" (Longfellow) **30**:42
"The Chambered Nautilus" (Holmes) **71**:60, 66, 68, 72-73, 82, 88, 94-95, 110, 117-18
"La chambre" (Bonnefoy) **58**:118
"La Chambre dans l'Espace" (Char) **56**:108
"La Chambre dorée" (Ronsard) **105**:273
"La chambre double" (Baudelaire) **1**:54, 58
"Chameli-vitan" (Tagore) **8**:416
"Chamfort" (Sandburg) **41**:339
The Champion (Tsvetaeva)
See *Molodets*
"Les Champs" (Béranger) **112**:22
Les Champs Magnétiques (Breton) **15**:58, 68, 73
"Chance" (H. D.) **5**:304
"Chance Meeting" (H. D.) **5**:304
"Chance Topic" (Tu Fu) **9**:324, 327
"The Chances" (Owen) **19**:334, 344, 347
"The Chances of Rhyme" (Tomlinson) **17**:333, 240
"Chanchal" (Tagore) **8**:415
"The Change" (Cohen) **109**:24-25
"The Change" (Cowley) **90**:120
"The Change" (Dickey) **40**:186
"The Change" (Finch) **21**:175
"The Change" (Hardy) **8**:93; **92**:235
"Change" (Kunitz) **19**:147
"Change" (Pasternak)
See "Peremena"
"Change" (Teasdale) **31**:347
"Change" (Wright) **14**:379
"Change and Fate" (Rossetti) **44**:254
"Change in Recurrence" (Meredith) **60**:299
"Change Is Not Always Progress" (Madhubuti) **5**:344
"The Change: Kyoto-Tokyo Express" (Ginsberg) **4**:50, 63, 81; **47**:17
"Change of Season" (Lorde) **12**:154, 157
A Change of World (Rich) **5**:352-53, 358, 360, 362, 369, 375, 387-88, 392
"Change upon Change" (Barrett Browning) **6**:32
"The Changed Woman" (Bogan) **12**:94, 103
"The Changeful World" (MacDiarmid) **9**:183
"The Changeling" (Curnow) **48**:12
"The Changeling" (Mew) **107**:9, 41, 49-50
"The Changeling" (Whittier) **93**:176, 250
"Changes" (Kenyon) **57**:19
"Changes at Meridian" (Hugo) **68**:273, 291
"Changes; or, Reveries at a Window Overlooking a Country Road with Two Women Talking Blues in the Kitchen" (Komunyakaa) **51**:31-32
"Changing Diapers" (Snyder) **21**:300
The Changing Light at Sandover (Merrill) **28**:259-60, 262-63, 265-79, 281
Changing Mind (Aiken) **26**:14
"Changing the Children" (Kumin) **15**:215
"Changing the Subject" (Enright) **93**:7
Ch'ang-ku (Li Ho) **13**:44
"Channel 13" (Merrill) **28**:267
"Channel Firing" (Hardy) **8**:119-21; **92**:291
"A Channel Passage" (Brooke) **24**:53-4, 63, 83
"A Channel Passage" (Swinburne) **24**:313, 317-18
"Channels" (Silverstein) **49**:330
"Chanon's Yeoman's Tale" (Chaucer)
See "Canon's Yeoman's Tale"
"Chanson" (Creeley) **73**:7
"Chanson" (Hugo) **17**:80
Chanson complète (Éluard) **38**:79
"Chanson d'après-midi" (Baudelaire) **106**:130
"Chant d'automne" (Baudelaire) **106**:76, 117
"Chanson d'automne" (Verlaine) **32**:362, 368, 387
"Chanson de la plus haute tour" (Rimbaud) **57**:175, 251
La Chanson de Roland (Anonymous) **83**:70-220
Chanson de Roland (Anonymous)
See *La Chanson de Roland*
"La chanson des ingénues" (Verlaine) **2**:431; **32**:353, 385, 388
"La chanson du mal-aimé" (Apollinaire) **7**:3, 7-9, 11, 15, 22, 44, 46-9
"Chanson du petit hypertrophique" (Laforgue) **14**:66, 93
"Chanson du Présomptif" (Perse) **23**:230
"Chanson du velours à côtes" (Char) **56**:157
Le Chanson du vieux marin (Coleridge)
See *The Rime of the Ancient Mariner*
"Chanson Juive" (Celan) **10**:127-28
"Chanson of a Lady in the Shade" (Celan) **10**:112
"Chanson un peu naïve" (Bogan) **12**:86, 90, 92, 101, 103
"Chanson without Music" (Holmes) **71**:64, 68
"Chansons bas" (Mallarmé) **102**:10
Chansons des rues et des bois (Hugo) **17**:55, 65, 67, 72
Chansons inédites (Béranger) **112**:12-14
Chansons intimes (Béranger) **112**:3
Chansons morales et autres (Béranger) **112**:17
Chansons nouvelles (Béranger) **112**:12-14
Chansons pour elle (Verlaine) **2**:417; **32**:407
"Chant d'amour" (Lamartine) **16**:291-92
"Chant d'automne" (Baudelaire) **1**:60, 62-3
"Chant de guerre parisien" (Rimbaud) **3**:255, 284; **57**:205
"Chant de l'horizon en champagne" (Apollinaire) **7**:22
Chant de liesse, au Roy (Ronsard) **105**:232
"Chant de Printemps" (Senghor) **25**:258
"Le Chant de sauvegarde" (Bonnefoy) **58**:125
Le chant du sacre (Lamartine) **16**:279
"Chant for Dark Hours" (Parker) **28**:352, 360
"Chant for May Day" (Hughes) **53**:114
"A Chant for Young/Brothas and Sistuhs" (Sanchez) **9**:218, 225
"Chant to Be Used in Processions around a Site with Furnaces" (Merton) **10**:334, 337
"Chant You Loud Punishments" (Crane) **80**:82
"The Chanterelles" (Jacobsen) **62**:320, 322
"Chanteuse" (Doty) **53**:47, 52
Chanting at the Crystal Sea (Howe) **54**:107-8
"Chant-Pagan" (Kipling) **91**:70, 136, 142-43, 175-76
"Chantre" (Apollinaire) **7**:48
Les chants de Crépuscule (Hugo) **17**:43, 45, 52, 63, 91-94
Chants de la balandrane (Char) **56**:185-87, 189
Chants de la Balandrane: Poèmes (Char)
See *Chants de la balandrane*
"Chants Democratic and Native American 2" (Whitman)
See "Song of the Broad-Axe"
"Chants Democratic and Native American 3" (Whitman)
See "A Song for Occupations"
Chants d'en bas (Jaccottet) **98**:151, 168, 182-85, 198
Chants d'ombre (Senghor) **25**:224, 227, 230-33, 236, 238, 241, 243-44, 255
Chants for Socialists (Morris) **55**:251, 329, 340
"Les chants lyriques de Saül" (Lamartine) **16**:277, 290
Chants pour Naëtt (Senghor) **25**:225, 227, 232, 238-40
Chants pour signare (Senghor)
See *Chants pour Naëtt*
"Chaos" (Benn) **35**:33, 50, 58, 75, 77
"Chaos and Poetry" (Lawrence) **54**:215
"Chaos in Motion and Not in Motion" (Stevens) **6**:307-10, 313; **110**:181
"Chaos Poem" (Atwood) **8**:24
"Chaos Staggered" (Ammons) **16**:46
"Chapel Deacon" (Thomas) **99**:232
"A Chapel Further West than Most" (Hugo) **68**:234
"The Chapel in Lyoness" (Morris) **55**:238, 299-300, 302, 348-49
"The Chapel of the Hermits" (Whittier) **93**:170, 172, 222
The Chapel of the Hermits, and Other Poems (Whittier) **93**:266
"Chapelle Brancacci" (Bonnefoy) **58**:130
"The Chapel-Organist" (Hardy) **8**:100, 124; **92**:256
"Chaplinesque" (Crane) **3**:98-100; **99**:17, 80
Chapman's Homer (Chapman) **96**:12-13;
"Chapman's Homer" (Keats)
See "On First Looking Into Chapman's Homer"
"Chapter 51.61: The Patient's Bill of Rights" (Espada) **74**:113
"Chapters From a Poem" (Akhmadulina) **43**:54
"A Character" (Montagu) **16**:338
"A Character" (Snodgrass) **74**:291
"Character/Jeu de lettres" (Brossard) **80**:15
Character/Jeu de lettres (Brossard) **80**:14-15
"The Character of Holland" (Marvell) **10**:271
"The Character of the Happy Warrior" (Wordsworth) **4**:377

Characters of Women (Pope) **26**:239
"Charcutons charcutez" (Péret) **33**:203
"The Charge of the Light Brigade" (Tennyson) **6**:359; **101**:241, 271-72
"The Chariot" (Dickinson)
See "Because I Could Not Stop for Death"
"Charioteer" (H. D.) **5**:268
"The Charioteer of Delphi" (Merrill) **28**:241
"Charitas Nimia" (Crashaw) **84**:20-21, 33, 37, 51, 69-72
"La charite" (Ronsard) **11**:236, 243, 263-64
"Charity" (Cowper) **40**:49-50, 105, 116-17, 127, 139
"Charity" (Prior) **102**:331
"Charity Never Faileth" (Prior) **102**:331
"Charity Overcoming Envy" (Moore) **49**:145
"Charivari" (Atwood) **8**:38
"Charlemagne" (Brathwaite) **56**:93
"Charleroi" (Verlaine) **32**:361, 378, 411
"Charles Augustus Fortescue, Who always Did what was Right, and so accumulated an Immense Fortune" (Belloc) **24**:26
"Charles on Fire" (Merrill) **28**:253
"Charles Summer" (Longfellow) **30**:50
"Charleston in the 1860s" (Rich) **5**:383
"Charleston Plantations" (Sarton) **39**:321, 332
"Charlie Howard's Descent" (Doty) **53**:62
"Charlie is My Darling" (Burns) **114**:168
"Charlotte Corday" (Tomlinson) **17**:345-46, 350
Charlotte Mew: Collected Poems and Prose (Mew) **107**:10, 32
"Charlotte's Delivery" (McGuckian) **27**:105
"A Charm" (Dickinson) **1**:112
The Charm (Creeley) **73**:38-39, 41
Charmes; ou, Poèmes (Valéry) **9**:355, 358, 365-67, 371, 374, 386-88, 390-96
"Charms" (Snyder) **21**:294, 297
"The Charnel Rose" (Aiken) **26**:11, 15, 37
The Charnel Rose (Aiken) **26**:6, 22, 70, 72
"Une charogne" (Baudelaire) **1**:48; **106**:6, 25, 74-78, 84, 146, 165, 172
"Charon" (MacNeice) **61**:125, 176-77
"Charon's Cosmology" (Simic) **69**:269
Charon's Cosmology (Simic) **69**:264, 302, 311, 317
"The Chart" (de la Mare) **77**:93
"Chartres" (Oppen) **35**:321
"The Chase" (Cunningham) **92**:135, 166
"The Chase" (Merwin) **45**:48
"The Chase" (Toomer) **7**:338, 340
"Chasing the Paper-Shaman" (Rose) **13**:238
"Chasse à courre" (Péret) **33**:231
"La Chasse, à Jean Brinon" (Ronsard) **105**:247
"Chassidische Schriften" (Sachs) **78**:122
"Chast' rechi" (Brodsky) **9**:7, 19
Chast' rechi: Stikhotvoreniia 1972-76 (Brodsky) **9**:6-8, 13-15, 26-7, 29-31
"A Chastel" (Éluard) **38**:86
"Le chat" (Ronsard) **11**:280, 282
"chat bilingual" (Birney) **52**:32-33, 77
"Chateau de Muzot" (Tomlinson) **17**:315, 324
"Le Château du souvenir" (Gautier) **18**:125, 129, 157
"Le châtiment de Tartuff" (Rimbaud) **3**:283; **57**:172, 289-90
Les Châtiments (Hugo) **17**:45, 53-54, 65, 74, 78-80, 91
"Les chats" (Baudelaire) **106**:118, 123-24, 126, 130, 146
"Les chats blancs" (Valéry) **9**:391
"Chattanooga" (Melville) **82**:203
"Chattanooga" (Reed) **68**:328
Chattanooga (Reed) **68**:325, 328-30, 332, 335, 340, 348-49
"Chatyrdah" (Mickiewicz) **38**:166
"Chaucer" (Hughes) **89**:162
"Chaucer" (Longfellow) **30**:42
"Chaume des Vosges" (Char) **56**:150
"The Chaunty of the Nona" (Belloc) **24**:6, 31
"El Che en Praga en 1965" (Dalton) **36**:129
"Che fece ... il gran rifiuto" (Cavafy) **36**:57
"Che Guevara" (Guillén) **23**:127
"Che sotto l'alta guida" (Zanzotto) **65**:277
A che valse? Versi, 1938-1942 (Zanzotto) **65**:273, 276, 289
Cheap (Stone) **53**:220, 228-29, 239, 258
"Checkers" (Brown) **55**:155
"Cheddar Pinks" (Bridges) **28**:80-1, 85
"The Cheek" (Hope) **56**:306
"The Cheer" (Meredith) **28**:205, 217
The Cheer (Meredith) **28**:177, 179-82, 197-200, 202, 205-09, 215
"A Cheerful Alphabet" (Updike) **90**:352
Cheerleader for the Funeral (Cassian) **17**:13
"Chekhov in Nice" (Stryk) **27**:187
"Chekhov on Sakhalin" (Heaney) **18**:214
"Chekhov's Story" (Kenyon) **57**:15
"Cheltenham" (Betjeman) **75**:20
"Chelyuskintsy" (Tsvetaeva) **14**:328
"Chemin de fer" (Bishop) **34**:146, 160, 164
Le Chemin de Long Estude (Christine de Pizan)
See *Le livre du chemin de long estude*
"La Cheminée d'usine" (Ponge) **107**:112
"Les chemins" (Bonnefoy) **58**:118, 167
"Chemo du Jour: The Impeachment on Decadron" (Dorn) **115**:215, 232
Chemo Sábe (Dorn) **115**:218, 223, 230-33, 235
"Le chêne" (Lamartine) **16**:293
"Chenille" (Dickey) **40**:191, 196
"Les chercheuses de poux" (Rimbaud) **3**:271, 276; **57**:191, 249
"Cherepki" (Akhmatova) **55**:52
"Les chères, mains qui furent miennes" (Verlaine) **2**:416
"Chérir Thouzon" (Char) **56**:156
"Cherish You Then the Hope I Shall Forget" (Millay) **6**:211
"Cherkesy" (Lermontov) **18**:278, 299
"Chernaia Paskha" (Shvarts) **50**:131-32, 139-41, 160
"Chernozem" (Mandelstam) **14**:150-51, 154
"Cherries" (Brathwaite) **56**:34, 51
"Cherry Blossoms" (Gallagher) **9**:65
"The Cherry Robbers" (Lawrence) **54**:166-67
"The Cherry Tree" (Gunn) **26**:205
"The Cherry-Blossom Wand" (Wickham) **110**:268, 275, 277, 301, 309
"Cherrylog Road" (Dickey) **40**:161, 168-69, 189, 191-92
"Cheshire Lines" (Betjeman) **75**:83
"The Chestnut Casts His Flambeaux" (Housman) **2**:199; **43**:250, 261
Chetki (Akhmatova)
See *Chyotki*
"Un cheval de race" (Baudelaire) **1**:59
"The Cheval-Glass" (Hardy) **8**:100
Les chevaliers (Lamartine) **16**:269
"Chevaux de bois" (Verlaine) **32**:382
"La chevelure" (Baudelaire) **1**:45, 66-7, 69; **106**:7, 70, 86, 88, 103, 114-19, 121-22, 126, 129, 153
"Chevelure" (Césaire) **25**:10, 17
"La Chevelure" (Char) **56**:197
"La Chevelure" (Mallarmé) **102**:126
"La chèvre" (Ponge) **107**:74, 90, 118, 192-94
"Chevrefoil" (Marie de France) **22**:248, 255, 257-58, 262-64, 266-67, 269, 272, 274, 301
"Chez Jane" (O'Hara) **45**:135
"Chhabi" (Tagore) **8**:414
"Chi" (Tolson) **88**:244, 273, 304, 316, 324, 326
"Chi è questa che vèn" (Cavalcanti) **114**:219, 228, 255-57, 259-60
"Chi vuol veder" (Petrarch) **8**:256
"Chiare fresche e dolci acque" (Petrarch) **8**:221, 230, 232-33, 235-36
"Chiasmadon" (Hughes) **89**:129
"Chic Freedom's Reflection" (Walker) **30**:347, 359
"Chicago" (Sandburg) **2**:317, 322-23, 333, 335, 339; **41**:225, 229, 232-34, 237, 242, 248, 257, 261, 267, 271-74, 277, 279, 281, 295, 301, 304, 318, 326, 334, 336, 346, 356-58, 360-62, 364-65
"The Chicago Defender Sends a Man to Little Rock" (Brooks) **7**:62
"Chicago Morning" (Berrigan) **103**:34
"The Chicago Picasso" (Brooks) **7**:82
Chicago Poems (Sandburg) **2**:300-2, 307-8, 312, 314, 316-18, 321, 333, 335-36, 338-39; **41**:225-27, 229, 233-34, 236-37, 239, 242-43, 246-48, 250, 252, 254-55, 257, 261, 269, 272-75, 277, 285, 287, 289, 293, 295-96, 298, 306, 308-10, 312-15, 318, 322, 325-29, 334, 339-41, 343, 347-52, 358-65, 367
"Chicago Poet" (Sandburg) **2**:339; **41**:244, 270, 278, 344
"The Chicago Train" (Glück) **16**:149, 153
"Chicano Heart" (Alurista) **34**:11, 46
"chicano infante" (Alurista) **34**:13, 38
"Chicken" (de la Mare) **77**:114
"Chicken" (Stein) **18**:313
Chicken, Shadow, Moon & More (Strand) **63**:198-200
"The Chicken's Foot" (Enright) **93**:10
"Chickens the Weasel Killed" (Stafford) **71**:263, 293
"Chicory" (Updike) **90**:359
"Chicory and Daisies" (Williams) **7**:373, 407
Chief Joseph of the Nez Perce (Warren) **37**:325-27, 334, 342-45, 350, 358, 377, 381-82
"Chief Standing Water" (Tomlinson) **17**:309
"La chiesa di Polenta" (Carducci) **46**:54, 76, 81, 84, 88-89
"Chievrefueil" (Marie de France)
See "Chevrefoil"
"Chiffres et constellations amoureux d'une femme" (Breton) **15**:49
"Chilblain" (Wright) **36**:348
"The Child" (Carruth) **10**:71
"The Child" (Hall) **70**:31
"The Child" (Merwin) **45**:25
"Child" (Montague) **106**:288
"Child" (Plath) **37**:202, 258
"Child" (Sandburg) **2**:329
"The Child" (Wright) **14**:352
"The Child Alone" (Mistral)
See "El niño solo"
"Child and Wattle Tree" (Wright) **14**:352
"A Child Asleep" (de la Mare) **77**:94
"The Child Bearers" (Sexton) **79**:233
"Child Beater" (Ai) **72**:28-29
"Child, Child" (Teasdale) **31**:388
"The Child Dying" (Muir) **49**:299
"Child Harold" (Clare) **23**:25-6, 46
Child Harold's Pilgrimage: A Romaunt (Byron)
See *Childe Harold's Pilgrimage*
Child Harold's Pilgrimage. Canto the Fourth (Byron)
See *Childe Harold's Pilgrimage*
Child Harold's Pilgrimage. Canto the Third (Byron)
See *Childe Harold's Pilgrimage*
Childe Harold's Pilgrimage (Byron) **95**:1-68
"A Child Ill" (Betjeman) **75**:30
"A Child in the Ghetto Surrounded by Letters" (Shvarts)
See "Ditia v getto v okruzhenii bukv"
"Child Margaret" (Sandburg) **41**:296
"Child Moon" (Sandburg) **41**:334
"The Child Next Door" (Warren) **37**:297, 299
"Child of Europe" (Milosz) **8**:191-92
"Child of Our Time" (Boland) **58**:42
"Child of the Romans" (Sandburg) **41**:234, 272, 334
"Child of the Sixtieth Century" (Viereck) **27**:259, 280
"The Child on the Cliffs" (Thomas) **53**:271, 295
"Child Poems" (H. D.) **5**:305
"A Child To Be Born" (Alurista) **34**:24, 25, 39, 40
"The Child Who Is Silent" (Shapiro) **25**:303
"The Child Who Saw Midas" (Sitwell) **3**:308

"Child Wife" (Verlaine) **32**:396, 399, 411
"The Child World" (Riley)
See *A Child-World*
Childe Harold (Byron)
See *Childe Harold's Pilgrimage: A Romaunt*
Childe Harold's Pilgrimage: A Romaunt (Byron) **16**:69, 72-7, 81-90, 107, 111
"Childe Horvald to the Dark Tower Came" (Ciardi) **69**:33, 35
"A Childe My Choyce" (Southwell) **83**:257, 276, 286
"Childe Roland to the Dark" (Browning) **61**:88
"Childe Roland to the Dark Tower Came" (Browning) **2**:64, 85-6, 88
"Childe Rolandine" (Smith) **12**:302, 350, 354
"Childe-hood" (Vaughan) **81**:273, 306, 340, 368
"Childhood" (Muir) **49**:228, 238, 247, 270, 273, 287
"Childhood" (Trakl) **20**:226
"Childhood" (Walker) **20**:276-77
"Childhood among the Ferns" (Hardy) **8**:125-26; **92**:208
"The Childhood of Jesus" (Pinsky) **27**:157
"The Childhood of Parmenides" (Simic) **69**:339
"A Childish Prank" (Hughes) **7**:123, 143, 161; **89**:141
"Childish Recollections" (Byron) **95**:22-23
"Childless Father" (Wordsworth) **4**:374, 428
"Childlessness" (Merrill) **28**:221, 244, 249
"Childlessness" (Montague) **106**:288
Child-Life: A Collection of Poems (Whittier) **93**:216
"The Children" (Sexton) **79**:212, 237-38
"Children Coming Home from School" (Glück) **16**:159
"the children grow" (Alurista)
See "los niños crecen"
"Children Killed in War" (Enright) **93**:35
"Children of Adam" (Whitman) **91**:259
"Children of Darkness" (Graves) **6**:137
"Children of Darkness" (Wilbur) **51**:246, 284
"Children of Our Age" (Szymborska) **44**:275, 295
"Children of the Mississippi" (Brown) **55**:70-71, 83, 114, 151-52, 176
"Children of the Night" (Longfellow) **30**:63
"The Children of the Night" (Robinson) **1**:459, 467, 486
The Children of the Night (Robinson) **1**:459, 462-63, 466, 474
"The Children of the Poor" (Brooks) **7**:55, 62, 75, 78
"Children Selecting Books in a Library" (Jarrell) **41**:159, 179-80, 194
"Children's Children" (Brown) **55**:76, 83, 102, 152
"Children's Games" (MacNeice) **61**:177
"The Children's Hour" (Longfellow) **30**:37, 46-7
"Children's Rhymes" (Hughes) **53**:150
"The Children's Song" (Kipling) **3**:171
"A Child's Excuse" (Howe) **81**:24
"A Child's Garden" (Hall) **70**:30
A Child's Garden of Verses (Stevenson) **84**:298-300, 302, 312-18, 325, 327-28, 338-48
A Child's Garland of Verses (Stevenson)
See *A Child's Garden of Verses*
"The Child's Grave" (Blunden) **66**:7, 9
"A Child's Grave at Florence" (Barrett Browning) **6**:6
"Child's Park" (Hughes) **89**:162
"Child's Play" (Stevenson) **84**:346
"The Child's Purchase" (Patmore) **59**:212, 223, 265
"Child's Talk in April" (Rossetti) **7**:274
"Child's Terror" (MacNeice) **61**:172
A Child-World (Riley) **48**:289, 300
"chile" (Bissett) **14**:24
"A Chile" (Guillén) **23**:127
"Chillianwallah" (Meredith) **60**:325
"Chills" (Akhmadulina) **43**:18
Chills and Fever (Ransom) **61**:267, 269, 280, 305-6, 322, 324
Chills and Other Poems (Akhmadulina) **43**:11
Chills: Selected Works (Akhmadulina)
See *Oznob. Izbrannye proizvedeniia*
"Chilterns" (Brooke) **24**:56, 67
"Chimaera Sleeping" (Wylie) **23**:311, 314, 322
"The Chimera" (Barker) **77**:7
The Chimeras (Nerval)
See *Les Chimères*
"La Chimère" (Gautier) **18**:141-42
Les Chimères (Nerval) **13**:172, 174, 176, 179-80, 182, 184, 187, 191-92, 194-95
"Chimes for Yahya" (Merrill) **28**:260, 263
"The Chimney Sweeper" (Blake) **12**:7, 9, 34-5; **63**:11, 13, 15, 35-36, 38, 40-42, 47, 53, 59, 68, 70, 79-80, 82, 89, 100, 106, 114, 121, 125-27, 133-34
Chimneys (Sachs)
See *O die Schornsteine*
"China" (Empson) **104**:122
"The China Cantos" (Pound) **95**:206
China Poems (Brutus) **24**:117
"A Chinaman's Chance" (Chin) **40**:4
"Chinatown" (Song) **21**:349
"The Chinese Banyan" (Meredith) **28**:171, 175, 189
Chinese Dynasty Cantos (Pound) **4**:352
The Chinese Insomniacs (Jacobsen) **62**:287, 301, 305, 308, 316-17, 320
"The Chinese Nightingale" (Lindsay) **23**:269, 272-73, 275-76, 278, 281-82, 286-87, 291-94
The Chinese Nightingale, and Other Poems (Lindsay) **23**:292
"The Chinese Restaurant in Portrush" (Mahon) **60**:192-93
"Chinese Space" (Berssenbrugge) **115**:7, 10-11, 37
Chinesisch-deutsche Jahres-und Tageszeiten (Goethe) **5**:251
"The Chipmunk" (Hughes) **89**:162
"The Chipmunk" (Melville) **82**:107
The Chipmunk (Ignatow) **34**:337
"Chiron" (Hölderlin) **4**:148, 166
Chistes parra desorientar a la policia (Parra) **39**:291-92, 313
"Chitateli gazet" (Tsvetaeva) **14**:315
Chitra (Tagore) **8**:408-09, 415, 418
"Chiunche nasce a morte arriva" (Michelangelo) **103**:202, 306
"Chlorophyll" (Hughes) **89**:235
Chō o yumemu (Hagiwara) **18**:176
"Choc Bay" (Walcott) **46**:272
"Chocorua to Its Neighbor" (Justice) **64**:282
"Chocorua to Its Neighbor" (Stevens) **6**:335
"The Choice" (Crabbe) **97**:76
"Choice" (Cunningham) **92**:135, 140, 160
"The Choice" (Hunt) **73**:154
"The Choice" (Rossetti) **44**:219-20
A Choice Collection of Original Scottish Airs for the Voice (Burns)
See *A Select Collection of Original Scottish Airs for the Voice*
A Choice of Kipling's Verse Made by T. S. Eliot with an Essay on Rudyard Kipling (Kipling) **3**:175; **91**:152
"A Choice of Weapons" (Kunitz) **19**:148
"Choices" (Sandburg) **41**:239, 350
"Choir" (Hongo) **23**:199
"The Choir" (Kinnell) **26**:261
"The Choir Invisible" (Eliot)
See "O May I Join the Choir Invisible"
"The Choise of Valentines, or the Merie Ballad of Nashe his Dildo" (Nashe) **82**:283-84, 286-87, 289, 292-96
Choix de poésies (Verlaine) **32**:359
"Choix entre deux nations" (Hugo) **17**:101
"Cholera" (Dove) **6**:108
"Choorka" (McGuckian) **27**:110
"Choose" (Sandburg) **41**:244, 348
"Choose Something like a Star" (Frost) **71**:51
"The Choosers" (Smith) **12**:327
"Chor der Bäume" (Sachs) **78**:168
"Chor der Geretteten" (Sachs) **78**:192-93, 200, 203, 227, 232
"Chor der Sterne" (Sachs) **78**:113, 189
"Chor der Toten" (Sachs) **78**:113, 126, 187, 199
"Chor der Tröster" (Sachs) **78**:200
"Chor der Ungeborenen" (Sachs) **78**:113
"Chor der verlassenen Dinge" (Sachs) **78**:113, 168, 189
"Chor der Waisen" (Sachs) **78**:113, 196, 207
"Chorai, Ninfas, os fados poderosas" (Camões) **31**:25
"Choral Symphony" (Lanier) **50**:77
"The Choral Union" (Sassoon) **12**:242
"Chorale" (Hope) **56**:269-70
"The Chord" (Cernuda)
See "El acorde"
"Chord" (Hughes) **53**:160
Chord of Light (Herbert)
See *Struna swiatła*
"Chords" (Duncan) **75**:216
"Chöre nach Mitternacht" (Sachs) **78**:111, 113, 201, 207
"Choriambics" (Brooke) **24**:62
"Choriambics II" (Brooke) **24**:57, 60
"Choros Sequence from Morpheus" (H. D.) **5**:304
"Chorus" (Lorde) **12**:159
"Chorus" (Tennyson) **101**:245
"Chorus for One Voice" (Simic) **69**:312
"Chorus of Abandoned Things" (Sachs)
See "Chor der verlassenen Dinge"
"Chorus of Clouds" (Sachs) **78**:113
"Chorus of Comforters" (Sachs)
See "Chor der Tröster"
"A Chorus of Ghosts" (Bryant) **20**:16
"Chorus of Invisible Things" (Sachs) **78**:113
"Chorus of Orphans" (Sachs)
See "Chor der Waisen"
"Chorus of Shades" (Sachs) **78**:113
"Chorus of Stones" (Sachs) **78**:113, 199
"Chorus of the Dead" (Sachs)
See "Chor der Toten"
Chorus of the Newly Dead (Muir) **49**:238-39, 242, 244, 276
"Chorus of the Orphans" (Sachs)
See "Chor der Waisen"
"Chorus of the Rescued" (Sachs)
See "Chor der Geretteten"
"Chorus of the Saved" (Sachs) **78**:113
"Chorus of the Stars" (Sachs)
See "Chor der Sterne"
"Chorus of the Unborn" (Sachs)
See "Chor der Ungeborenen"
"Chorus of the Years" (Hardy) **92**:216, 219
"Chorus of Things Left Behind" (Sachs)
See "Chor der verlassenen Dinge"
"Chorus of Trees" (Sachs) **78**:113
"Chorus of Wanderers" (Sachs) **78**:113
"Choruses After Midnight" (Sachs)
See "Chöre nach Mitternacht"
"Choruses from the Rock" (Eliot) **31**:121
"The Chosen" (Jacobsen) **62**:320, 323
Chosen Defects (Neruda)
See *Defectos escogidos: 2000*
"A Chosen Light" (Montague) **106**:295
A Chosen Light (Montague) **106**:215, 218, 235, 243, 276-78, 289, 291, 293, 296-98, 313, 317, 327
Chosen Poems: Old and New (Lorde) **12**:142, 146, 148, 154, 157
"Choses Passagères à John Ashbery" (O'Hara) **45**:230-32, 235-36
"Le Chretien Mourant" (Lamartine) **16**:277
"Chrismus on the Plantation" (Dunbar) **5**:133-34
"Chrissie" (Ní Chuilleanáin) **34**:352
"Le Christ aux Oliviers" (Nerval) **13**:173, 177, 181, 198
"Christ Church Meadows, Oxford" (Hall) **70**:31
"Christ for Sale" (Lowell) **3**:203

"Christ Has Arisen" (Pushkin)
See "Khristos Voskres"
"Christ in Alabama" (Hughes) **1**:264; **53**:110, 143, 148-50
"Christ in Flanders" (Lowell) **3**:203
"Christ in the Universe" (Meynell) **112**:166
Christ is Arisen (Bely)
See *Hristos voskres*
Christ is Risen (Bely)
See *Hristos voskres*
"Christ of Pershing Square" (Stryk) **27**:190, 203
"Christ of the Sparrows Help Me!" (Dorn) **115**:122
"Christ Recrucified" (Cullen) **20**:72
"Christabel" (Coleridge) **11**:41-2, 51-3, 84-5, 90-1, 104, 110; **39**:120-22, 169, 176, 180, 182, 193, 224-25; **67**:276, 280, 288, 294; **100**:19, 22-23, 25-26, 33, 36-37, 58, 76, 114, 124
"Christendom" (Traherne) **70**:326
"A Christian Country" (Hughes) **53**:110
"Christian Forbearance" (Blake) **63**:29, 109
"The Christian Slave!" (Whittier) **93**:239, 312, 314-17
"The Christian Statesman" (Masters) **1**:344
"Christiane R." (Goethe) **5**:246
"Le Christianisme" (Owen) **19**:336, 341; **102**:207
"The Christians Reply" (Davenant) **99**:172, 176, 179-80
"Christianus Perfectus" (Johnson) **81**:117
"Christina" (MacNeice) **61**:173
"Christmas" (Betjeman) **75**:96, 98
"The Christmas" (Muir) **49**:290
"Christmas Abrupted" (Kennedy) **93**:151
"Christmas at Black Rock" (Lowell) **3**:201
"A Christmas Ballad" (Brodsky) **9**:2, 4
"Christmas Bells" (Longfellow) **30**:47
"The Christmas Cactus" (Clampitt) **19**:87
"A Christmas Card" (Merton) **10**:340
"A Christmas Card" (Montague) **106**:312, 356
"The Christmas Card" (Service) **70**:151
"Christmas Card *for Barry & Carla*" (Berrigan) **103**:28
"A Christmas Card of Halley's Comet" (Nemerov) **24**:289
"A Christmas Childhood" (Kavanagh) **33**:75, 81, 93, 102, 118, 133, 145-6, 151-53, 157; **105**:93, 99, 150
"A Christmas Colloquy" (Ransom) **61**:294
"Christmas Comes" (Birney) **52**:8
"Christmas Comes to Moccasin Flat" (Welch) **62**:340, 355, 370, 372, 374
"Christmas Eve" (Ammons) **16**:58, 60, 65
"Christmas Eve" (Ciardi) **69**:8, 12
"Christmas Eve" (Sexton) **2**:363
"Christmas Eve at Sea" (Masefield) **78**:6
"Christmas Eve at St. Kavin's" (Carman) **34**:225
"Christmas Eve: Australia" (Shapiro) **25**:279, 286, 296, 300
"Christmas Eve in Whitneyville" (Hall) **70**:18, 32
"Christmas Eve—Dublin, 1959" (Clarke) **112**:57
"Christmas Eve Remembered" (Kavanagh) **33**:151, 161
"Christmas Eve under Hooker's Statue" (Lowell) **3**:200, 203
"Christmas Eve—Market Square" (Page) **12**:169
"A Christmas Ghost-Story" (Hardy) **92**:269
"A Christmas Greeting" (Wright) **36**:328-29, 341, 344, 399
"Christmas in India" (Kipling) **3**:186
"Christmas in Simla" (Kipling) **3**:182
"Christmas Is Coming" (Hecht) **70**:69
"Christmas Light" (Sarton) **39**:360, 368
"Christmas Morning" (Montague) **106**:256-59, 261
"The Christmas Mummers" (Kavanagh) **33**:62, 86, 118; **105**:143, 173
"Christmas Night" (Meynell) **112**:299
"Christmas, 1971" (Heaney) **100**:335
"Christmas on Earth" (Chappell) **105**:25
"Christmas on the Hudson" (García Lorca)
See "Navidad en el Hudson"
"Christmas on the Plantation" (Dunbar)
See "Chrismus on the Plantation"
"Christmas Pines" (Mistral)
See "Pinos de Navidad"
"Christmas Poem, 1965" (Ondaatje) **28**:292
"Christmas Poem for Nancy" (Schwartz) **8**:316
"The Christmas Roses" (Jarrell) **41**:210, 214
"Christmas Shopping" (MacNeice) **61**:133-34, 138
"A Christmas Song for the Three Gaids" (Chesterton) **28**:125
"Christmas Star" (Mistral)
See "Estrella de Navidad"
"Christmas Tree" (Shapiro) **25**:269, 286
"Christmas Tree—Market Square" (Page) **12**:169
"Christmas-Day" (Traherne) **70**:302
Christmas-Eve (Browning) **2**:31-2, 44, 70-1
Christmas-Eve and Easter Day (Browning) **2**:33, 36, 70, 95
"Christmastide" (Hardy) **92**:208
"Christs bloody sweat" (Southwell) **83**:277, 284-87, 295-96
"Christs Incarnation" (Herrick) **9**:119
"Christs Nativity" (Vaughan) **81**:295, 299-300
"Christs Reply" (Taylor) **63**:280, 300
"Christ's Return out of Egypt" (Southwell) **83**:283
"Christs sleeping friends" (Southwell) **83**:284-85, 296
"Christ's Twin" (Erdrich) **52**:191
"Christs Victory" (Crashaw) **84**:71
Christus: A Mystery (Longfellow) **30**:21, 23, 39, 65-7
"Chronicle" (Berssenbrugge) **115**:37, 46
"The Chronicle" (Cowley) **90**:13, 15, 18, 21
Chronophagia (Cassian) **17**:6, 13
"Chronology" (Berssenbrugge) **115**:3
"Chrysallis" (Montale) **13**:151
"Chrysanthemums" (Kenyon) **57**:11, 24, 35
"Chrysaor" (Longfellow) **30**:27
"Chtonian Revelation: A Myth" (Warren) **37**:326
"Chu Ming-How" (Stryk) **27**:198
"Chudishche" (Shvarts) **50**:135-36
"Chüeh-chü" (Tu Fu) **9**:323
"El Chulo" (Guillén) **23**:101
"Chumban" (Tagore) **8**:407
"The Church" (Herbert) **4**:103, 113
"The Church and the Hotel" (Masters) **1**:343
"The Church at Auvers" (Thomas) **99**:305
"Church Building" (Harper) **21**:198, 200, 213
"Church Fair" (Kenyon) **57**:40
"The Church Floore" (Herbert) **4**:109, 119
"Church Going" (Larkin) **21**:228, 230, 236-37, 247, 255, 259
"The Church Militant" (Herbert) **4**:100, 130
"Church Monuments" (Herbert) **4**:100, 119
"Church Music" (Herbert) **4**:100, 131
"The Church of Brou" (Arnold) **5**:6, 9, 12, 50
"Church of England Thoughts" (Betjeman) **75**:94
"The Church of Polenta" (Carducci)
See "La chiesa di Polenta"
"The Church Porch" (Herbert) **4**:100-01, 103, 107, 126
"Church Service" (Vaughan) **81**:271
"The Church-Bell" (Wylie) **23**:328
"Churches" (Traherne) **70**:198, 244
"Church-Going" (Heaney) **18**:223
"Church-lock and Key" (Herbert) **4**:127
"Churchyard" (Gray)
See "Elegy Written in a Country Churchyard"
"Church-yard" (Gray)
See "Elegy Written in a Country Churchyard"
"Church-yard at Middleton in Sussex" (Smith)
See "Sonnet 44"
"Churn Milk Joan" (Hughes) **89**:123
"Churning Day" (Heaney) **18**:186
"The Chute" (Olds) **22**:319-22
La chute d'un ange (Lamartine) **16**:263, 265, 269-70, 285-87, 293-94, 296-97
"Chuva Oblíqua" (Pessoa) **20**:151, 165
"Chuy" (Soto) **28**:372, 382
Chyotki (Akhmatova) **2**:3, 11, 14, 17
"Ciant da li ciampanis" (Pasolini) **17**:256, 265
"Ciants di muart" (Pasolini) **17**:256
"Cicadas" (Mueller) **33**:180
"Cicadas" (Wilbur) **51**:188
"The Cicadas" (Wright) **14**:346
"Cicadas" (Zagajewski) **27**:397
"El ciego" (Borges) **32**:90
"Ciel brouillé" (Baudelaire) **1**:61, 66; **106**:103-4
"Le ciel est, par-dessus le toit" (Verlaine) **32**:362-63, 379-80
"El cielo" (Storni) **33**:292, 294-95
"Cielo de tercera" (Fuertes) **27**:31
"Los cielos" (Aleixandre) **15**:19-20
"Cierro los ojos" (Guillén) **35**:196, 198
"La cierva blanca" (Borges) **32**:90
"La cifra" (Borges) **32**:52, 56, 86
La cifra (Borges) **22**:95, 97, 99; **32**:91
"Un cigare allume que Fume" (Apollinaire)
See "Paysage"
"La Cigarette" (Ponge) **107**:182
"Cigarettes and Whiskey and Wild, Wild Women" (Sexton) **79**:242
"Cigarra en noche de luna" (Storni) **33**:293
"Cigola la carrucola del pozzo" (Montale) **13**:164
"Cima de la delicia" (Guillén) **35**:153
"Le cimetière marin" (Bishop) **3**:46
"Le cimetière marin" (Valéry) **9**:348, 351-52, 355, 358, 361, 363-80, 382, 384, 387, 389-93, 395-96, 398
"Cincinnati" (Yamada) **44**:330-32, 342-43, 347, 351
"Cincophrenicpoet" (Kaufman) **74**:212, 240
"Cinderella" (Jarrell) **41**:171
"Cinderella" (Sexton) **79**:205, 250
"Cinema of a Man" (MacLeish) **47**:126, 128, 137, 156
"Cino" (Pound) **95**:122
"Cinq septembre" (Ponge) **107**:73
"The cipher" (Borges)
See "La cifra"
The Cipher (Borges)
See *La cifra*
The Circassian (Lermontov)
See "Cherkesy"
The Circassian Boy (Lermontov)
See *Mtsyri*
"Circe" (Heaney) **100**:264
"Circe" (Hope) **56**:298-99
"Circe's Power" (Glück) **16**:171
"The Circle" (Creeley) **73**:12
"Circle and Square" (Muir) **49**:300
The Circle Game (Atwood) **8**:3, 12, 15, 18, 26-8
"Circle of Breath" (Stafford) **71**:377
"Circle of Loda" (Peacock) **87**:308
"The Circle on the Grass" (Kenyon) **57**:19
"Circles" (Hecht) **70**:108
"Circles" (Thomas) **99**:272-73
"Circles in th Sun" (Bissett) **14**:8, 19, 33
Circles on the Water (Piercy) **29**:302, 307, 313
"Circonspection" (Verlaine) **32**:354
"The Circuit of Apollo" (Finch) **21**:162, 168
"Circuit total par la lune et par la couleur" (Tzara) **27**:224
"A Circular Play. A Play in Circles" (Stein) **18**:347
"The Circular Ruins" (Borges)
See "Las ruinas circulares"

"The Circulation" (Traherne) **70**:191-92, 238, 273-75, 277, 302, 316-17, 331, 724
"Circulation of the Song" (Duncan) **2**:127
"Circulations of the Song" (Duncan) **75**:147, 192
"Círculos sin centro" (Storni) **33**:239, 269
"Circumjack Cencrastus" (MacDiarmid) **9**:157
"Circumstance" (Lowell) **13**:94
"The Circus" (Koch) **80**:303, 323
"Circus Animals" (Szymborska) **44**:312
"The Circus Animals' Desertion" (Hardy) **92**:257
"The Circus Animals' Desertion" (Yeats) **20**:307, 311, 313, 327, 332, 336; **51**:111, 141
Circus On (Cage) **58**:200
"Cirque d'hiver" (Bishop) **3**:37; **34**:52, 70
"Les Ciseaux et leur père" (Éluard) **38**:90-91
"El cisne" (Darío) **15**:113
"Los cisnes" (Darío) **15**:115
"Los Cisnes" (Storni) **33**:272
The Cistern (Seferis)
See *I Sterna*
"Citadel" (Brathwaite) **56**:93
"The Cited" (García Lorca)
See "Romance del emplazado"
"Citeres" (Guillén) **35**:202
"Cities and Thrones and Powers" (Kipling) **3**:183
Cities Burning (Randall) **86**:288, 308, 333-34, 339
"Citizen Cain" (Baraka) **4**:17, 24; **113**:13
"Citizen Kane" (Alexie) **53**:14
"A Citrine Glimpse" (Hughes) **89**:129
"Citronia" (Heine) **25**:160, 171-80
"Città in campagna" (Pavese) **13**:227
"Una città lontana" (Quasimodo) **47**:283
"City" (Betjeman) **75**:94
"The City" (Blok) **21**:24
"The City" (Cavafy) **36**:3, 13-14, 59, 73, 78
"City" (Ciardi) **69**:25
"City" (Merwin) **45**:54
"The City" (Nash) **21**:272
"The City" (Pasternak)
See "Gorod"
"The City: A Cycle" (Stryk) **27**:216
"The City Asleep" (Wright) **14**:362
"A City Child's Day" (Corso) **33**:11; **108**:7
"City Churchyard" (Kennedy) **93**:150
"A City Dead House" (Whitman) **3**:379; **91**:344-45
The City in Tears (Seifert)
See *Město v slzách*
"City in the Country" (Pavese)
See "Città in campagna"
"The City in the Sea" (Poe) **1**:426, 431, 434, 438, 443-45; **54**:278
"The City in Which I Love You" (Lee) **24**:241
The City in Which I Love You (Lee) **24**:240, 242-44
"City Johannesburg" (Serote) **113**:283, 294-95
"The City Limits" (Ammons) **16**:11, 23, 37, 46
"City Midnight Junk Strains for Frank O'Hara" (Ginsberg) **4**:47
"The City of Brass" (Kipling) **91**:111, 115
"City of Coughing and Dead Radiators" (Espada) **74**:133, 137, 150
City of Coughing and Dead Radiators (Espada) **74**:132-33, 137-39, 144-45, 147, 149-50, 152, 154-55, 169
"The City of Evenings" (Wright) **36**:310
"City of Monuments" (Rukeyser) **12**:230
"City of Shadows" (Boland) **58**:62
"The City of the Dead" (Gibran) **9**:73
"The City of the Moon" (Rexroth) **95**:281
"City of the Wind" (Stryk) **27**:191
"The City Planners" (Atwood) **8**:13
"City Psalm" (Rukeyser) **12**:221
"City Trees" (Millay) **6**:207
"City Walk-Up, Winter 1969" (Forché) **10**:141, 144, 147, 157-58
"City Winter" (Mickiewicz)
See "Zima miejska"
A City Winter (O'Hara) **45**:116
"City without a Name" (Milosz) **8**:194-95
"City without Walls" (Auden) **1**:20; **92**:66, 97
City without Walls and Many Other Poems (Auden) **92**:70
"The City-Mouse and the Country-Mouse" (Wyatt) **27**:331
"A City's Death by Fire" (Walcott) **46**:274
"The City's Love" (McKay) **2**:211
"Ciudad" (Borges) **22**:94
"Ciudad de los estíos" (Guillén) **35**:153
"Ciudad sin sueño" (García Lorca) **3**:139-40
"Ciudad viva, ciudad muerta" (Aleixandre) **15**:35
"Ciudades" (Cardenal)
See "Las ciudades perdidas"
"Las ciudades perdidas" (Cardenal) **22**:126-28, 132
"Civil Rights" (Lanier) **50**:92, 118-19
"Civil Rights Poem" (Baraka) **4**:11, 19; **113**:76
"The Civil War" (Sexton) **79**:216, 237
The Civil War (Cowley) **90**:63-78, 92-93, 95, 99, 113, 129, 153, 160-62, 165, 189, 196
"Civil Wars" (Montague) **106**:326
"Civilization and Its Discontents" (Ashbery) **26**:108, 113
"De Civitate Hominum" (Melville) **82**:3, 8, 27, 29, 36, 38, 59
"Clad All in Brown" (Swift) **9**:256-57
"Clad All in White" (Cowley) **90**:13-14
Clad in Light (Seifert)
See *Světlem oděná*
"The Claim" (Barrett Browning) **6**:14
"Clair de lune" (Apollinaire) **7**:45-6
"Clair de Lune" (Hecht) **70**:78
"Clair de lune" (Verlaine) **2**:413, 420, 429; **32**:346, 348-51, 353, 364, 370-71, 390
Claire de terre (Breton) **15**:51-52
"El Clamor" (Storni) **33**:253
Clamor (Guillén) **35**:140, 157, 170, 185, 187, 189, 195, 197, 202, 225, 228, 229, 234, 239, 241
"Clamped Almas" (Alurista) **34**:47
"The Clan of No Name" (Crane) **80**:82
"Clancy of the Mounted Police" (Service) **70**:115
Clandestine Poems (Dalton) **36**:135-36
"Clara noticia" (Guillén) **35**:202
Clarel (Melville)
See *Clarel: A Poem and Pilgrimage in the Holy Land*
Clarel: A Poem and Pilgrimage in the Holy Land (Melville) **82**:67-71, 73, 76, 78, 81, 85-86, 90, 94-96, 100, 102-3, 112-15, 117-22, 126, 139, 141-42, 145-47, 152-54, 156, 158, 164, 168, 171-73, 182, 198-99, 205, 211, 219-22, 224, 230-31, 233-40, 242, 244-47, 249, 252, 255-63
"Clarence" (Silverstein) **49**:333, 339
"Clarence Fawcett" (Masters) **36**:230
"Clarence Mangan" (Kinsella) **69**:66, 121-22
"Claribel" (Holmes) **71**:67
"Claribel" (Tennyson) **6**:358-60, 365
"Claribel A Melody" (McGuckian) **27**:83
"Clark Street Bridge" (Sandburg) **41**:273
"Clash" (Stafford) **71**:374
"The Clasped Skeletons" (Hardy) **92**:211
"Clasping of Hands" (Herbert) **4**:130
"Class" (Tomlinson) **17**:320
"Class Struggle" (Baraka) **4**:30, 38
"Class Struggle in Music" (Baraka) **4**:40; **113**:24-26, 60, 63
"The Class Will Come to Order" (Kunitz) **19**:150
"Classic" (Herbert)
See "Klasyk"
"Classic Ballroom Dances" (Simic) **69**:272, 305
Classic Ballroom Dances (Simic) **69**:264, 272, 276, 301-2, 305, 311-13, 334, 370
"Classical Spring" (Carducci)
See "Primavera classica"
"Classicism and Romanticism" (Carducci)
See "Classicismo e romanticismo"
"Classicismo e romanticismo" (Carducci) **46**:78, 80
"Claud Antle" (Masters) **1**:334
"Claude Glass" (Ondaatje) **28**:314
"The Claude Glass" (Szirtes) **51**:158
"Claus Von Stauffenberg" (Gunn) **26**:197
"Claver Cope" (Masefield) **78**:30
"Clavering" (Robinson) **35**:367
"The Clavichord" (Sarton) **39**:318
"El clavicordio de la abuela" (Darío) **15**:80
"Claw-Foot" (Plath) **37**:188
"Clay" (Baraka) **4**:30
"clay and morning star" (Clifton) **17**:29
Clean & Well Lit: Selected Poems 1987 to 1995 (Raworth) **107**:305, 307-9, 326, 338-39, 341-42
"Clean Gene" (Silverstein) **49**:347
"Cleaning Day" (Wright) **14**:356
"Cleaning the Candelabrum" (Sassoon) **12**:248, 259
"Cleaning the Well" (Chappell) **105**:5, 31-32, 41, 45, 60, 71
"Clean,like,iodoform,between,the,tall" (Villa) **22**:356-57
Cleanness (Anonymous) **76**:203-4, 207-9, 226, 229, 234-35
"Cleanthus Trilling" (Masters) **36**:243
"Clear and gentle stream" (Bridges) **28**:83
"Clear Autumn" (Rexroth) **20**:209
"A Clear Day and No Memories" (Stevens) **110**:230
"The Clear Vision" (Whittier) **93**:349
"Clear, with Light Variable Winds" (Lowell) **13**:94
"Clearances" (Heaney) **18**:228-29, 232, 238; **100**:231, 234, 252
"The Clearances" (Hugo) **68**:287-88
"Cleared" (Kipling) **3**:167; **91**:133
"The Clearing" (Baraka) **4**:5, 15; **113**:7
"The Clearing" (Berry) **28**:38
Clearing (Berry) **28**:7-9
"Clearing the Title" (Merrill) **28**:267, 269-70
"Clearness" (Wilbur) **51**:188-89, 193
"The Clearseeing" (Char)
See *Les Transparents*
Clear-seeing Ones (Char)
See *Les Transparents*
"The Cleaving" (Lee) **24**:241, 244, 248-49, 251-52
"Cleggan" (Hugo) **68**:288
"Cleis" (Teasdale) **31**:380
"Clemente's Bullets" (Espada) **74**:125, 160
"Cleon" (Browning) **2**:36, 82, 95
"Cleopomop y Heliodemo" (Darío) **15**:81
"La clepsidra" (Borges) **32**:90
"Clepsydra" (Ashbery) **26**:126, 157, 166
"The Clepsydras of the Unknown" (Elytis) **21**:119
"The Clergyman's Second Tale" (Clough) **103**:156
"Clerical Oppressors" (Whittier) **93**:207, 314, 336-37
"Clerk Saunders" (Housman) **43**:214
The Clerk's Journal: Being the Diary of a Queer Man (Aiken) **26**:25, 46-48, 50
"Clerk's Tale" (Chaucer) **19**:13, 29, 54-60; **58**:265, 272, 286
"The Cliff" (Lermontov) **18**:297
"Cliff Klingenhagen" (Robinson) **1**:467, 486
"Clifford Ridell" (Masters) **1**:344-46; **36**:194
"Cliffs" (Thoreau) **30**:227, 233-34, 242
"The Cliffs and Springs" (Thoreau) **30**:182, 191, 192, 194, 228-29, 242
"Cliffs to the Eastward" (Smith) **104**:236
"The Cliff-Top" (Bridges) **28**:67
"Clifton" (Chatterton) **104**:7-8
"The Climate of Thought" (Graves) **6**:139, 143
"Climb" (Kenyon) **57**:45

"Climbers" (Birney) **52**:34, 58
"Climbing a Mountain" (Hagiwara) **18**:177
"Climbing Alone" (Wagoner) **33**:352
"Climbing Alone All Day" (Rexroth) **20**:193
"Climbing Milestone Mountain, August 22, 1937" (Rexroth) **20**:203; **95**:259, 270, 290, 309-10, 320
"Climbing Pien-chüeh Temple" (Wang Wei) **18**:371
"Climbing T'ai-po's Peak" (Li Po) **29**:172
"Climbing the Streets of Worcester, Mass." (Harjo) **27**:66
"Climbing to the Monastery of Perception" (Wang Wei) **18**:384
"Clin d'oeil" (Péret) **33**:206-07, 214
"The Clinging Vine" (Robinson) **1**:468
"The Clipped Stater" (Graves) **6**:128, 137
"Clips" (Brathwaite) **56**:71
"Cliquante ans" (Béranger) **112**:19
"C.L.M." (Masefield) **78**:8, 89, 96
"A Cloak" (Levertov) **11**:176, 194
"La cloche fêlée" (Baudelaire) **1**:65
"Cloche fêlée" (Péret) **33**:207
Les cloches sur le coeur (Char) **56**:114, 120, 168
"The Clock" (Abse) **41**:3
"Clock" (Brathwaite) **56**:55
"The Clock" (Dickinson) **1**:108
"The Clock" (Jacobsen) **62**:322
"A Clock in the Square" (Rich) **5**:352
"The Clock of Tomorrow" (Apollinaire)
See "L'lorloge de demain"
"A Clock stopped, not the mantel's" (Dickinson)
See "The Clock"
"The Clock-Keeper" (Hall) **70**:31
"The Clod and the Pebble" (Blake) **12**:7; **63**:68, 106
"Cloe Jealous" (Prior) **102**:316
"Clonar and Tlamin" (Peacock) **87**:325, 347
"Cloony the Clown" (Silverstein) **49**:334
"Clorinda and Damon" (Marvell) **10**:268, 271
"Close by Shelley's Grave" (Carducci)
See "Presso l'Urna di Percy Bysshe Shelley"
"Close Call" (Kennedy) **93**:153
The Close Chaplet (Jackson) **44**:51, 61-2, 104
"Closed for Good" (Frost) **1**:213
"The Close of Summer" (Smith) **104**:178
"Close-Up" (Ammons) **16**:24
"The Closing Album" (MacNeice) **61**:118, 181
Clothed in Light (Seifert)
See *Světlem oděná*
"The Clothes" (Serote) **113**:292
"Clothes" (Sexton) **2**:367; **79**:315
"Clothes" (Szymborska) **44**:283
"The Clothes Pin" (Kenyon) **57**:42
"The Clothes Shrine" (Heaney) **100**:242
"The clothesline post is set" (Niedecker) **42**:150, 169
"The Cloud" (Muir) **49**:218, 294-95
"The Cloud" (Shelley) **14**:167, 171, 196, 207, 212; **67**:180
"Cloud" (Toomer) **7**:338
"The Cloud" (Walcott) **46**:236, 240, 290
"Cloud and Flame" (Berryman) **64**:90
"Cloud and Wind" (Rossetti) **44**:169
"Cloud Shadows" (Updike) **90**:352
Cloud, Stone, Sun, and Vine (Sarton) **39**:321, 326, 333-34, 338, 344
"Cloud-Catch" (Hongo) **23**:204
The Cloud-Messenger (Kālidāsa)
See *Meghadūta*
"Clouds" (Ashbery) **26**:124
"Clouds" (Brooke) **24**:57-8, 73, 85
"Clouds" (Erdrich) **52**:176
"Clouds" (Jacobsen) **62**:309
"Clouds" (Levine) **22**:214, 219, 222
"Clouds" (Tomlinson) **17**:312
The Clouds (Cernuda)
See *Las nubes*
The Clouds (Williams) **7**:370; **109**:328
"Clover" (Darío)
See "Trébol"
"Clover" (Lanier) **50**:54-55, 77
"The Clover" (Riley) **48**:328
"Clover-4" (Guillén) **35**:218
"Clover-7" (Guillén) **35**:218, 219
"Clover-8" (Guillén) **35**:218
"Clown" (Corso) **33**:25, 46-7; **108**:17, 21-22
"The Clown Chastized" (Mallarmé)
See "Le pitre châtié"
Clown War 22 (Berrigan) **103**:35
Clown's Houses (Sitwell) **3**:290, 294, 301-02
"The Club" (Yamada) **44**:349-50
"Club 26" (Niedecker) **42**:182
The Club of Queer Trades (Chesterton) **28**:97
Cluster of Songs (Tagore)
See *Gitāli*
"A Clymene" (Verlaine) **32**:351, 384, 392
"Co mysli Pan Cogito o piekle" (Herbert) **50**:39
"Co robia nasi unmarli" (Herbert) **50**:6-7
"Coal" (Lorde) **12**:153
Coal (Lorde) **12**:142, 148
"The Coal Picker" (Lowell) **13**:84
"The Coast" (Akhmadulina) **43**:56
"The Coast" (Hass) **16**:196
"The Coast Guard's Cottage" (Wylie) **23**:324
"Coast of Trees" (Ammons) **16**:45, 62
A Coast of Trees (Ammons) **16**:31, 45, 62
"The Coasts of Cerigo" (Hope) **56**:284, 288, 299
"The Coastwise Lights" (Kipling) **3**:162
"A Coat" (Yeats) **20**:320; **51**:81
A Coat for a Monkey (Matsuo Basho)
See *Sarumino*
"The Coats" (Gallagher) **9**:60
"Coats" (Kenyon) **57**:8, 20
"Cobbler Keezar's Vision" (Whittier) **93**:175, 252
"The Cobbler of Hagenau" (Longfellow) **30**:43
"Cobwebs" (Rossetti) **7**:278
"Cobwebs Are Hanging from the Mind" (Cernuda) **62**:169
"Coca-Cola and Coco Frio" (Espada) **74**:132, 139, 152
"Cocaine Lil" (Dorn) **115**:180
"Cocher ivre" (Rimbaud) **57**:253
"Cochin China" (de la Mare) **77**:114
"Cock and Jewel" (Henryson)
See "The Cock and the Jasp"
"The Cock and the Fox" (Chaucer)
See "Nun's Priest's Tale"
"The Cock and the Fox" (Henryson) **65**:18, 27, 54, 61, 81-82
"The Cock and the Jasp" (Henryson) **65**:3, 14, 23-27, 30-31, 35, 44-47, 54-55, 61, 80-81
"Cock Robin's Escape from the Alizarin of Evening" (Snodgrass) **74**:331
"Cock Robin's Roost Protects W. D. From Mr. Evil" (Snodgrass) **74**:327
"Cock-a-Doodle-Doo!" (Melville) **82**:147
"Cock-crowing" (Vaughan) **81**:321, 328, 349, 369
"Cock-Crows" (Hughes) **89**:122
"The Cocked Hat" (Masters) **1**:325-26, 328-29, 342; **36**:175
"Cockerel" (Hagiwara) **18**:173
"The Cockfighter's Daughter" (Ai) **72**:16
"The Cockroach" (Alurista)
See "La Cucaracha"
"Cockroaches of Liberation" (Espada) **74**:154
"The Cocks" (Pasternak) **6**:253
"The Cocks" (Yevtushenko) **40**:343
"Cocks and Mares" (Stone) **53**:228, 254
"Cocoa Morning" (Kaufman) **74**:243
"Coconut Palm" (Tagore)
See "Narikel"
"Cocotte" (Gozzano) **10**:178
"Coda" (Ekeloef) **23**:76, 86
"Coda" (Thomas) **99**:274
"The Code" (Frost) **1**:195, 208, 226
"Code Book Lost" (Warren) **37**:312, 365
A Code of Manners in the Forest (Zanzotto)
See *Il galateo in bosco*
"A Code of Morals" (Kipling) **3**:190
"Codicil" (Rexroth) **95**:250, 258, 260, 274
"Codicil" (Stone) **53**:229
"Codicil" (Walcott) **46**:283
"Codicillo" (Zanzotto) **65**:269
"Codziennosc duszy" (Herbert) **50**:39
"Coeur, couronne et miroir" (Apollinaire) **7**:32-6
"Le coeur du pître" (Rimbaud) **57**:253, 278
"Le coeur, l'eau non troublée" (Bonnefoy) **58**:118
Un coeur sous une soutane (Rimbaud) **57**:251
"La coeur volé" (Rimbaud) **3**:270
"Coffee" (Cunningham) **92**:170, 175, 182, 190
"Coffee and Sweet Rolls" (Stone) **53**:221
"The Coffee Imp" (Akhmadulina)
See "Kofejnyj certik"
"Coffin" (Ignatow) **34**:293
"Cogióme sin prevención" (Juana Inés de la Cruz) **24**:234
"Cogitavi vias meas" (Hardy) **92**:208
"Cohorte" (Perse) **23**:254-57
"A Coin" (Sandburg) **41**:314
"The Coin" (Teasdale) **31**:350
"The Coiner" (Kipling) **91**:126-27, 137
"Coins" (Cavafy) **36**:39
Coins and Coffins (Wakoski) **15**:338, 344, 356, 369
"Cold" (Abse) **41**:29
"Cold" (Cassian) **17**:12, 15
"The Cold" (Winters) **82**:321
"The Cold Before the Moonrise" (Merwin) **45**:20
"Cold Colloquy" (Warren) **37**:331, 333
"The Cold Cotswolds" (Masefield) **78**:55
The Cold Cotswolds (Masefield) **78**:73
"The Cold Divinities" (Wright) **36**:299, 360
"A Cold Front" (Williams) **109**:260
"Cold in the Earth" (Brontë)
See "Remembrance"
"Cold Iron" (Kipling) **3**:171
The Cold of Poetry (Hejinian) **108**:288, 290
"Cold Poem" (Oliver) **75**:287
"The Cold Room" (Winters) **82**:316
"A Cold Spring" (Bishop) **34**:61, 120
A Cold Spring (Bishop) **34**:52, 174, 189
"Cold Spring in North Salem" (Very) **86**:164
"Cold Term" (Baraka) **113**:15
"Cold-Blooded Creatures" (Wylie) **23**:314
"The Colder the Air" (Bishop) **34**:54-55
"La colère de Samson" (Vigny) **26**:366, 368, 371, 380-81, 391, 401, 412, 416
"Coleridge" (McGuckian) **27**:101
"Coleridge" (Thomas) **99**:245
Coleridge: Poetical Works (Coleridge) **100**:80
Coleridge's Verse: A Selection (Coleridge) **100**:19
"Colesberg" (Brutus) **24**:105
"Colibrí" (Espada) **74**:124, 129, 162
"Colin Clout" (Spenser)
See *Colin Clouts Come Home Againe*
Colin Clout (Skelton)
See *Collyn Cloute*
Colin Clouts Come Home Againe (Spenser) **8**:336, 367, 387, 396; **42**:248-49, 266
"The Coliseum" (Poe) **1**:439; **54**:264
"Collage" (Stone) **53**:228
"The Collapse of Zen" (Cohen) **109**:97-98
"The Collar" (Gunn) **26**:185
"The Collar" (Herbert) **4**:102-03, 112-13, 130-31
"The Collar" (Herrick) **9**:141
"A Colleague" (Hacker) **47**:120
"Collected" (Meynell) **112**:247
Collected Earlier Poems (Hecht) **70**:77-78, 80-88, 92, 105, 107-8
Collected Earlier Poems (Williams) **7**:367-69, 374-75, 378, 382, 387-88, 392-94, 406-07, 409; **109**:193, 208, 286-87, 291-92

Collected Early Poems of Ezra Pound (Pound) **4**:355; **95**:90, 115-16, 118-19, 121-22
The Collected Greed, Parts 1-13 (Wakoski) **15**:356
Collected Later Poems (Hecht) **70**:105-6, 108
Collected Later Poems (Williams) **7**:370, 375; **109**:195, 197
The Collected Longer Poems of Kenneth Rexroth (Rexroth) **20**:197, 202, 204, 209-10, 214; **95**:255, 258, 260-61, 264-65, 268-69, 271-72, 275-81, 323, 326-28
Collected Lyrics (Millay) **6**:227
Collected Poems (Aiken) **26**:21, 24, 43-5
Collected Poems (Auden) **92**:3, 6-9, 20, 22-28, 35, 51, 58, 74, 113
Collected Poems (Betjeman) **75**:22-24, 26, 29, 40, 42-43, 63-64, 66, 69, 72, 75-79, 81-82, 107-8
Collected Poems (Birney)
See *The Collected Poems of Earle Birney*
The Collected Poems (Bishop) **34**:63-70, 86-87, 89-91
Collected Poems (Boland) **58**:66, 100
Collected Poems (Bridges) **28**:74, 77-8
Collected Poems (Camões) **31**:32
The Collected Poems (Chesterton) **28**:99, 109
Collected Poems (Clarke) **112**:27, 30, 34, 61-62, 64-65, 73-76, 78, 88-89, 115-18, 125
Collected Poems (Cohen) **109**:48, 53
Collected Poems (Creeley) **73**:60-61, 63, 106
Collected Poems (Cummings) **5**:82-4, 87, 107, 111
Collected Poems (Curnow) **48**:14
Collected Poems (Das) **43**:80, 93
Collected Poems (Empson) **104**:89-91, 94, 112, 125-27, 132-33, 135, 144
Collected Poems (Frost) **1**:203
Collected Poems (Graves) **6**:153, 165, 171
Collected Poems (Hardy) **8**:89, 95-6, 98, 101, 118, 124; **92**:198, 225, 328
Collected Poems (Hecht) **70**:93
Collected Poems (Hughes) **89**:187, 206, 217, 222-25, 228-36
Collected Poems (Hugo) **68**:289, 292
Collected Poems (Jackson)
See *The Poems of Laura Riding: A New Edition of the 1938 Collection*
Collected Poems (Jarrell) **41**:144, 148, 210
Collected Poems (Kavanagh) **33**:65, 68, 73, 77, 79, 82, 85, 87, 89, 98-9, 101-4, 113-122, 128-32, 136, 164-6, 169; **105**:97-98, 108, 111-12, 136
Collected Poems (Kinsella)
See *Thomas Kinsella: Collected Poems 1956-1994*
Collected Poems (de la Mare) **77**:73, 88, 92-93
Collected Poems (Larkin) **21**:256, 258
Collected Poems (Lindsay) **23**:265, 280-82, 285-86, 288, 292, 294
Collected Poems (MacDiarmid) **9**:186
Collected Poems (MacNeice) **61**:106, 139, 141, 143-46, 166, 168-71, 173, 181, 185-86
Collected Poems (Mahon) **60**:231, 235
Collected Poems (Melville) **82**:4
Collected Poems (Mew) **107**:7, 9, 16, 57
Collected Poems (Meynell) **112**:164, 219, 303
Collected Poems (Millay) **6**:227; **61**:223, 225, 242-45
Collected Poems (Milosz)
See *Czeslaw Milosz: The Collected Poems, 1931-1987*
The Collected Poems (Montague) **106**:219, 306, 308-10, 312-17, 324, 326, 351
Collected Poems (Moore) **4**:235-36, 238, 247, 254, 271; **49**:89, 113-14, 125, 136
Collected Poems (Muir) **49**:195, 206, 208, 211, 217, 226-27, 230-35, 237-44, 253-58, 262, 269-70, 276-80, 287
Collected Poems (Olson) **19**:316
Collected Poems (Oppen) **35**:285, 286, 287, 300, 304, 3311, 320, 321, 322-25, 332, 333, 335, 336, 337, 339, 340, 341, 354
Collected Poems (Patmore) **59**:271
Collected Poems (Pinsky) **27**:168
The Collected Poems (Plath) **1**:406; **37**:196, 209, 214, 216-20, 227, 237-41, 243, 247, 260-65
Collected Poems (Raworth) **107**:316-17, 323, 325, 338, 342
Collected Poems (Robinson) **1**:467, 469, 480
Collected Poems (Sandburg) **41**:354, 357
Collected Poems (Schuyler) **88**:186-90, 193-94, 198-201, 203, 205-7, 212-13, 215-17
Collected Poems (Sitwell) **3**:299, 301, 303-05, 308, 318-21, 325
Collected Poems (Stevens) **6**:306
Collected Poems (Stevenson)
See *Robert Louis Stevenson: Collected Poems*
Collected Poems (Stryk) **27**:207, 209-10, 212-16
Collected Poems (Thomas) **53**:282, 300-303, 305
Collected Poems (Thomas) **52**:210, 217, 222, 226-27, 230-36, 239, 253, 256, 258, 263, 277, 303-4, 308, 310-11, 320, 330
Collected Poems (Tomlinson) **17**:342, 351, 355, 361
Collected Poems (Winters) **82**:337-38, 343
Collected Poems (Wright) **36**:296, 301, 304-5, 308, 316-22, 346, 350, 366, 368, 371, 384-87
The Collected Poems (Yeats) **20**:307, 336-37; **51**:108, 119, 149
The Collected Poems (Yevtushenko) **40**:365, 368
Collected Poems: Ancient Lights (Clarke)
See *Ancient Lights*
Collected Poems 1934 (Williams) **7**:360, 372, 402
Collected Poems, 1938 (Graves) **6**:166
Collected Poems, 1955 (Graves) **6**:138, 140-43, 145
Collected Poems 1987 (Enright) **93**:18-30
Collected Poems 1902-1919 (de la Mare) **77**:129
Collected Poems, 1909-1935 (Eliot) **5**:173, 176, 179, 211
Collected Poems, 1912-1944 (H. D.) **5**:297, 305
Collected Poems, 1917-1952 (MacLeish) **47**:164, 182-83, 192
Collected Poems, 1919-1976 (Tate) **50**:304-5, 307, 334
Collected Poems, 1921-1931 (Williams) **109**:290-91
Collected Poems, 1923-1953 (Bogan) **12**:93, 95-6, 120, 125
Collected Poems, 1924-1946 (Seferis) **66**:92
Collected Poems, 1924-1955 (Seferis) **66**:115, 122
Collected Poems, 1928-1953 (Spender) **71**:224, 227
Collected Poems, 1928-1985 (Spender) **71**:135, 146, 169, 179-81, 189-91, 216, 246
Collected Poems, 1929-1933 (Day Lewis) **11**:123
Collected Poems, 1930-1955 (Barker) **77**:3-4, 7, 14, 20, 28-32, 38
Collected Poems, 1930-1960 (Eberhart) **76**:11, 15-16, 27, 29, 31, 33, 35, 45-46, 48, 53, 57
Collected Poems, 1930-1970 (Hope) **56**:278-82, 301-4, 306-7
Collected Poems, 1930-1973 (Sarton) **39**:334, 344, 354, 359, 364-67
Collected Poems, 1930-1976 (Eberhart) **76**:62-66
Collected Poems 1936-1976 (Francis) **34**:244-45, 247, 251-52, 258
Collected Poems, 1937-1971 (Berryman) **64**:168
Collected Poems, 1940-1978 (Shapiro) **25**:313, 315
Collected Poems: 1945-1946 (Spicer) **78**:302
Collected Poems, 1945-1990 (Thomas) **99**:277-81, 283, 304, 308-12, 317, 358
Collected Poems, 1947-1980 (Ginsberg) **4**:71-2, 76-9, 83-4, 86, 89; **47**:35
Collected Poems, 1948-1976 (Abse) **41**:18, 20-3, 25, 27, 31, 33
Collected Poems, 1948-1984 (Walcott) **46**:259
Collected Poems, 1950-1970 (Davie) **29**:101, 111, 122
Collected Poems, 1951-1971 (Ammons) **16**:10, 20, 27, 40, 46, 54, 61
The Collected Poems, 1952-1990 (Yevtushenko) **40**:370
Collected Poems: 1956-1974 (Dorn) **115**:51, 53-54, 56-57, 79-81, 83-84, 89, 91-92, 101-10, 113-14, 119-23, 125-27, 135, 137-38, 155, 159, 192, 216, 219-21, 228
Collected Poems: 1956-1976 (Wagoner) **33**:334, 344, 347, 352, 354, 366, 369-72
Collected Poems, 1957-1982 (Berry) **28**:25-29, 32, 37-39, 43-4
The Collected Poems and Epigrams of J. V. Cunningham (Cunningham) **92**:146-47, 149-51, 161, 164-65, 170
Collected Poems and Plays (Masefield) **78**:51
Collected Poems and Prose (Mew)
See *Charlotte Mew: Collected Poems and Prose*
Collected Poems I (Spark) **72**:213, 215, 217-18, 226, 228-29, 256
The Collected Poems of A. E. Housman (Housman) **2**:175-76, 180; **43**:228, 259, 261
The Collected Poems of Archibald MacLeish (MacLeish) **47**:200-201, 203
The Collected Poems of Austin Clarke (Clarke) **112**:47, 74
The Collected Poems of Christopher Smart (Smart) **13**:347
The Collected Poems of C. P. Cavafy (Cavafy) **36**:117
The Collected Poems of D. H. Lawrence (Lawrence) **54**:162, 173, 179, 184, 186, 207, 228, 231-34, 239
The Collected Poems of Earle Birney (Birney) **52**:26-27, 44, 51, 58-59, 62, 78, 94-95
Collected Poems of Elinor Wylie (Wylie) **23**:304, 306, 312, 314, 330-31
The Collected Poems of Frank O'Hara (O'Hara) **45**:113, 119-20, 127, 132-34, 136-51, 153-57, 159-66, 171-73, 175-80, 184-85, 187, 189-93, 196, 198-202, 221-29, 231, 234, 237-39, 241-45
Collected Poems of George Seferis (Seferis) **66**:218-23
Collected Poems of H. D. (H. D.) **5**:268, 270, 276
The Collected Poems of Hart Crane (Crane) **3**:89-90
The Collected Poems of Henry Thoreau (Thoreau) **30**:182, 185, 187, 189-90, 232, 237, 256, 209-70, 272-76, 281
The Collected Poems of Howard Nemerov (Nemerov) **24**:298-99, 301
The Collected Poems of Jean Toomer (Toomer) **7**:340-41
The Collected Poems of Keith Douglas (Douglas) **106**:196, 200, 208
The Collected Poems of Kenneth Koch (Koch) **80**:318, 341
The Collected Poems of Langston Hughes (Hughes) **53**:112, 115-16, 142, 158, 167-68, 182-83, 200, 202, 205-6
The Collected Poems of Muriel Rukeyser (Rukeyser) **12**:224, 226, 235
The Collected Poems of Octavio Paz, 1957-1987 (Paz) **1**:374-76; **48**:187, 191, 248-51
The Collected Poems of Robert Frost (Frost)
See *Collected Poems*
The Collected Poems of Robert Penn Warren (Warren) **37**:382-83

Collected Poems of Robert Service (Service) **70**:129-33
The Collected Poems of Rupert Brooke (Brooke) **24**:52, 54, 61, 71
The Collected Poems of Sara Teasdale (Teasdale) **31**:327, 339, 342, 362
The Collected Poems of Sterling A. Brown (Brown) **55**:79, 87, 89-90, 93-94, 101-5, 111-12, 140, 142-43, 157, 167
The Collected Poems of Stevie Smith (Smith) **12**:307, 309, 313-17, 320, 327, 346-47, 350, 352
The Collected Poems of Ted Berrigan (Berrigan) **103**:31, 38-42, 45
The Collected Poems of Theodore Roethke (Roethke) **15**:281, 283-84, 288
The Collected Poems of Thomas MacGreevy: An Annotated Edition (Melville) **82**:24, 32, 35-36, 38-40, 45, 47, 50
The Collected Poems of Thomas Merton (Merton) **10**:336-337, 345, 348, 351
The Collected Poems of Wallace Stevens (Stevens) **6**:304; **110**:85-86, 91-97, 101-4, 106-9, 126, 146, 153-55, 157-60, 162-64, 167-68, 173-74, 176, 198, 200-204, 225, 227, 229-32, 234, 236
The Collected Poems of Wilfred Owen (Owen) **19**:351
The Collected Poems of William Carlos Williams (Williams) **109**:193, 195, 197, 207-8, 234-37, 239-41, 266, 271, 284-86, 290-92, 294-95, 297-98, 314, 316, 321, 323-25
The Collected Poems of Yvor Winters (Winters) **82**:312-26, 333-39, 342-45, 348
Collected Poetry Notebook (Césaire) **25**:48-9
The Collected Poetry of W. H. Auden (Auden) **92**:14
Collected Rhymes and Verse (de la Mare) **77**:92-93, 95, 110
Collected Shorter Poems (Eliot) **90**:207
Collected Shorter Poems, 1927-1957 (Auden) **1**:30
Collected Shorter Poems, 1930-1950 (Auden) **1**:30
Collected Shorter Poems, 1946-1991 (Carruth) **10**:89, 91
The Collected Shorter Poems of Kenneth Rexroth (Rexroth) **20**:197-98, 202, 204-05; **95**:249-50, 252-59, 261, 264, 268-74, 305-6, 321, 324-28
Collected Sonnets (Millay) **6**:227
Collected Verse (Smith) **70**:138, 140, 160
Collected Works (Akhmatova) **2**:19
Collected Works (Rossetti) **44**:176, 214, 219, 221, 227
Collected Works (Wilde) **111**:286
Collected Works of Aphra Behn (Behn)
  See *The Works of Aphra Behn*
The Collected Works of Billy the Kid: Left Handed Poems (Ondaatje) **28**:298, 304, 314-16, 327, 338-39
The Collected Works of Edgar Allan Poe (Poe) **54**:300, 305
The Collected Works of Rudyard Kipling (Kipling) **91**:111
The Collected Works of Shams (Rumi)
  See *Divan-i Shams-i Tabrizi*
Collected Works of William Morris (Morris) **55**:306-7, 309, 325
"Collected Writings" (Borges) **32**:52
Collected Writings (Rossetti) **44**:255-56
Collection for a Myriad Ages (Yakamochi)
  See *Man'yōshū*
Collection for Ten Thousand Ages (Yakamochi)
  See *Man'yōshū*
A Collection of Celebrated Love Poems (Hagiwara)
  See *Ren'aimeikashū*
Collection of Early and Modern Japanese Poetry (Tsurayuki)
  See *Kokinshu*
Collection of Myriad Leaves (Yakamochi)
  See *Man'yōshū*
Collection of One Thousand Leaves (Yakamochi)
  See *Man'yōshū*
Collection of Short Songs on Innocent Love (Hagiwara)
  See *Junjo shokyoku shu*
A Collection of the Most Esteemed Pieces of Poetry That Have Appeared for Several Years (Goldsmith) **77**:219
"Collective Dawns" (Ashbery) **26**:144, 153
"College Breakfast Party" (Eliot) **20**:125
"The College Colonel" (Melville) **82**:84, 92, 133, 194, 273
"The College Garden" (Bridges) **28**:79-80
"The Collier's Wife" (Lawrence) **54**:187, 221
"Les collines" (Apollinaire) **7**:12
"Colloque sentimental" (Verlaine) **32**:350, 352, 371, 390, 393, 396
"Colloqui con gli alberi" (Carducci) **46**:51
"The Colloquies" (Gozzano) **10**:175, 180
The Colloquies (Gozzano)
  See *I Colloqui*
"Colloquy" (Brown) **55**:114, 168-69
"Colloquy" (Jacobsen) **62**:320
"Colloquy at Peniel" (Merwin) **45**:24
"Colloquy in Black Rock" (Lowell) **3**:201, 216-17, 227
"Colloquy of the Centaurs" (Darío)
  See "Coloquio de los centauros"
Collyn Clout (Skelton)
  See *Collyn Cloute*
Collyn Cloute (Skelton) **25**:329-30, 336, 337, 341-42, 348, 356, 374
"Colna-dona" (Macpherson) **97**:174, 182, 232-33
"La colombe poisnardée et le jet d'eau" (Apollinaire) **7**:18, 20-22
"A Colombia" (Guillén) **23**:127
"Colombine" (Verlaine) **32**:351, 364, 390, 393
"The Colonel" (Forché) **10**:136, 138, 140, 145, 153, 167, 169
"Colonel Fantock" (Sitwell) **3**:293, 301, 325
"La Colonia a medianoche" (Storni) **33**:261, 295-96
"Colonial Outlook" (Curnow) **48**:26
"The Colonists" (Boland) **58**:62
"Colony" (Boland) **58**:40, 50-51, 61-62
"A Colophon" (Carman) **34**:208
"Coloquio de los centauros" (Darío) **15**:88, 92, 96, 112, 114
Color (Cullen) **20**:52-54, 56-58, 62, 66-67, 72, 77, 79, 81-83, 85-86
"The Color Sergeant" (Johnson) **24**:142
"Colorado Blvd." (Cervantes) **35**:134
"The Colored Band" (Dunbar) **5**:134, 147
"The Colored Soldier" (Hughes) **53**:114
"The Colored Soldiers" (Dunbar) **5**:129-31, 133-34, 140
"Colors" (Cullen) **20**:65
"The Colors of a Bird" (Hugo) **68**:236
"The Colors of Night" (Momaday) **25**:199, 202-203, 217-18
"Coloss. 3.3" (Herbert) **4**:130
"Colossus" (Plath) **37**:177, 185-87, 214, 216-21, 243-44, 246
The Colossus, and Other Poems (Plath) **1**:380-81, 84, 388-89, 391, 394, 396, 404, 407, 410, 414; **37**:175-90, 196
"Colour" (Thumboo) **30**:300
"The Colour Shop" (McGuckian) **27**:106
"A Coloured Print by Shokei" (Lowell) **13**:61
"A Coltrane Poem" (Sanchez) **9**:225
"The Colubriad" (Cowper) **40**:125
"Colui che fece" (Michelangelo) **103**:260-61
"Columbia" (Reed) **68**:332
"Columbia U Poesy Reading—1975" (Corso) **33**:44, 50; **108**:3, 20, 24, 33, 35
"Columbian Ode" (Dunbar) **5**:128
"The Columbine" (Very) **86**:41, 79-80, 90, 134, 151, 161
"Columbus, Ohio" (Stone) **53**:223
"Columns and Caryatids" (Kizer) **66**:75
"The Columns of the Parthenon" (Hall) **70**:30
Colyn (Skelton)
  See *Collyn Cloute*
Colyn Cloute (Skelton)
  See *Collyn Cloute*
"Comala" (Macpherson) **97**:176, 230, 318-19
"The Combat" (Muir) **49**:212, 215, 224-26, 228, 234, 284-85
"The Combat" (Thomas) **99**:262, 266
"Combat Cultural" (Moore) **4**:259; **49**:143
"Le combat inégal" (Jaccottet) **98**:174
"Combat Pay for Jodie" (Komunyakaa) **51**:9
"Combat Pay for Jody" (Komunyakaa)
  See "Combat Pay for Jodie"
"The Combe" (Thomas) **53**:278, 308, 332
"Come!" (Ignatow) **34**:323
"Come" (Kaufman) **74**:254
"Come" (Smith) **12**:316
Come and Hope with Me (Serote) **113**:286-87, 297, 299
"Come Back" (Cavafy) **36**:74
"Come before His Countenance with a Joyful Leaping" (Wagoner) **33**:330
"Come Break with Time" (Bogan) **12**:87, 101, 105-06, 122
"Come chearfull day" (Campion) **87**:12, 25, 55, 66
"Come, Come Now" (Aleixandre) **15**:15
"Come, come, what do I here" (Vaughan) **81**:272
"Come Dance with Kitty Stobling" (Kavanagh) **33**:76, 96, 104, 115; **105**:96, 111, 150
Come Dance with Kitty Stobling, and Other Poems (Kavanagh) **33**:62-4, 68, 72-3, 79, 81, 95-6, 103, 146-7; **105**:90, 95, 100, 112
"Come Death (1)" (Smith) **12**:315
"Come Death (2)" (Smith) **12**:314, 317, 319
"come down my cheek raza roja" (Alurista) **34**:23, 24, 29
"Come Down, O Maid" (Tennyson) **101**:152-53
"Come Forth" (Wright) **36**:343
"Come Hither" (Mueller) **33**:180
Come Hither! (de la Mare) **77**:92
"Come In" (Frost) **1**:197, 213, 230; **39**:234, 237, 239-40, 246, 253
"Come, Let Us Praise the Gasworks!" (Spender) **71**:215
"Come let us sound" (Campion) **87**:32, 54, 63-65, 103, 108, 111
"Come, Look Quietly" (Wright) **36**:378
"Come, O King of the Lacedaemonians" (Cavafy) **36**:4, 58
"Come on, Come back" (Smith) **12**:295
Come Out into the Sun (Francis) **34**:243, 245, 248
"Come Republic" (Masters) **1**:329, 343; **36**:177
"Come se Quando" (Bridges) **28**:76-9
"Come Thunder" (Okigbo) **7**:235
"Come to Sunny S" (Enright) **93**:21
"Come to the Bower" (Heaney) **18**:197; **100**:214, 219, 224, 308-9
"Come to the Stone . . ." (Jarrell) **41**:195, 198
"Come ultime cene" (Zanzotto) **65**:301
"Come unto Me" (Very) **86**:120
"Come with Me" (Bly) **39**:42, 91
"Come, Words, Away" (Jackson) **44**:107
"Come you pretty false-ey'd wanton" (Campion) **87**:57
"The Comedian as the Letter C" (Stevens) **6**:293, 295-96, 304, 306, 310, 330, 335; **110**:93, 145, 147, 158, 192, 239
"Comedian Body" (Francis) **34**:247
La comédie de la mort (Gautier) **18**:131-32, 134-35, 141, 143-6, 155, 159, 163
"Comédie de la soif" (Rimbaud) **57**:177, 245, 253
Comedy (Dante)
  See *La divina commedia*
"Comedy of Thirst" (Rimbaud)
  See "Comédie de la soif"

"Comes to Rest" (Cavafy) **36**:81, 109
"Com'esser, donna, può quel c'alcun vede" (Michelangelo) **103**:344-45
"The Comet" (Aleixandre) **15**:5
"Comet" (Holmes) **71**:68
"The Comet at Yell'ham" (Hardy) **8**:89
"Comfort" (Barrett Browning) **6**:21
"Comfort" (Very) **86**:136
"Comfort in Self-Despite" (Muir) **49**:245, 250-51
"The Comfort of Rooms" (Szirtes) **51**:167
"The Comic Annual" (Hood) **93**:46
"Comic Melodies" (Hood) **93**:46
"Coming" (Larkin) **21**:238, 244
"The Coming" (Very) **86**:136
"Coming and Going" (Paz) **48**:274
"Coming Awake" (Lawrence) **54**:169
"Coming Back to America" (Dickey) **40**:158, 254
"Coming Close" (Levine) **22**:220
"Coming Down" (Cruz) **37**:10
"Coming Down through Somerset" (Hughes) **7**:166; **89**:126
"The Coming Era" (Holmes) **71**:68, 117
"Coming Events" (Montague) **106**:277
"The Coming Fall" (Levertov) **11**:185
The Coming Forth by Day of Osiris Jones (Aiken) **26**:8, 11, 57
"Coming Home" (Gallagher) **9**:36
"Coming Home from the Post Office" (Levine) **22**:221, 228
"Coming Home on the 5:22" (Ciardi) **69**:14, 53
"Coming in for Supper" (Bly) **39**:44
"Coming of Age in Michigan" (Levine) **22**:220, 228
"The Coming of Arthur" (Tennyson) **101**:198, 203, 291
"The Coming of Kali" (Clifton) **17**:24
"The Coming of Miss McLean" (Service) **70**:152
"The Coming of the End (Moments of Vision)" (Hardy) **8**:92
"The Coming of War" (MacNeice) **61**:138
"The Coming of Wisdom with Time" (Yeats) **20**:338
"The Coming Storm" (Melville) **82**:134-35, 192
Coming through Slaughter (Ondaatje) **28**:298
"Commander Lowell 1887-1950" (Lowell) **3**:219, 235
"Commandments" (Lawrence) **54**:249
Comme deux gouttes d'eau (Éluard) **38**:62, 73
"Comme Dieu Dispense de Graces" (Stevens) **6**:294
"Comme on voit sur la branche" (Ronsard) **11**:218, 234, 236, 240
"Comme un beau pré despouillè de ses fleurs" (Ronsard) **11**:250
"Comme une belle fleur assise entre les fleurs" (Ronsard) **105**:201
Commedia (Dante)
See *La divina commedia*
"The Commemoration" (Muir) **49**:297
"The Commemorative Mound of the Decorated Tree" (Ishikawa)
See "Nishikigizuka"
"Commemorative of a Naval Victory" (Melville) **82**:84, 93
"Commendation" (Raleigh)
See "Walter Rawley of the Middle Temple, in Commendation of the Steele Glasse"
"Comment" (Wickham) **110**:263
"Comment against the Lamp" (Hughes) **1**:266
"Comment on War" (Hughes) **53**:112
Comment une Figue de paroles et pourquoi (Ponge) **107**:114, 116-17, 124, 144, 148, 191, 197
Commentaries of Heaven (Traherne) **70**:307-9, 320-23, 334-35
"Commentary" (Auden) **92**:102-3
"Commentary" (Berssenbrugge) **115**:38
"Commentary" (Milosz) **8**:212-13
"Comments" (Seferis) **66**:119, 122-23, 126, 170
"Comments of Kate the Cook" (Wickham) **110**:271
"Commiato" (Ungaretti) **57**:346
"A Commination" (Hope) **56**:266, 269
"A Commitment" (Eberhart) **76**:22
"Commodore Barry" (Davie) **29**:106, 109-10
"Common Beauty" (Kavanagh) **33**:140
"The Common Grave" (Dickey) **40**:196
"A Common Ground" (Levertov) **11**:169
"The Common Life" (Stevens) **110**:95
"The common living dirt" (Piercy) **29**:315, 317-19
"The Common Lot" (Dorn) **115**:125
"The Commonweal" (Swinburne) **24**:312
"A Communal Feud" (Carducci)
See "Faida di Commune"
Commune présence (Char) **56**:111, 114-17, 128, 189
"Communication I" (Angelou) **32**:28
"Communication II" (Angelou) **32**:28
"Communication in White" (Madhubuti) **5**:340
"Communion" (Erdrich) **52**:191
"Communion" (Herbert) **4**:100
"Communion" (Ignatow) **34**:311
"Communion" (Winters) **82**:345
"Communique" (Komunyakaa) **51**:41
"Communism or capitalism" (Niedecker) **42**:149
"Communist" (Berryman) **64**:84
"A Communist to Others" (Auden) **1**:15
"Communitie" (Donne) **43**:132, 153-57
"Community" (Piercy) **29**:308, 311
"The Commuted Sentence" (Smith) **12**:327
Cómo atar (Fuertes) **27**:27, 30
Cómo atar los bigotes al tigre (Fuertes) **27**:17-8, 25-7, 31, 49
"Como del cielo llovido" (Guillén) **23**:126
"Como el viento" (Cernuda) **62**:230, 235
"Como en la noche mortal'" (Guillén) **34**:228
"Como la piel" (Cernuda) **62**:234
"Como les iba diciendo" (Parra) **39**:281
"Cómo llovía, suaviño" (Castro) **41**:110-11
"Como lo siento" (Cervantes) **35**:113
Como quien espera el alba (Cernuda) **62**:172, 174, 177-79, 184, 193, 195-97, 201-2, 214, 224, 248, 250, 258
"Como quisimos" (Guillén) **23**:126
"The Compact: At Volterra" (Tomlinson) **17**:350
"La compagne du vannier" (Char) **56**:155, 188
Les compagnons dans le jardin (Char) **56**:107, 109, 120-22
"The Companion of a Mile" (Noyes) **27**:134
"Companionable Ills" (Plath) **37**:190
"The Companions" (Nemerov) **24**:263
"Companions in Hades" (Seferis) **66**:120-21, 184
"Company" (Dove) **6**:111, 119
"Company" (Smith) **12**:325
"The Company of Lovers" (Wright) **14**:336, 340, 351, 371
"A Comparative Peace" (Brutus) **24**:116
"Comparatives" (Momaday) **25**:191, 193-194
"The Comparison" (Donne)
See "Elegie VIII: The Comparison"
"Comparison" (Dunbar) **5**:125
"The Comparison" (Peacock) **87**:321
"Compás de Expera'" (Guillén) **35**:228
"Compass" (Borges) **22**:74
The Compass Flower (Merwin) **45**:52, 55, 58-9, 63, 70-2, 81, 84, 86-8, 92, 95
"Compensation" (Dunbar) **5**:121
"Compensation" (Teasdale) **31**:359
"The Complaint" (Behn) **88**:148
"The Complaint" (Cowley) **90**:180-81
"The Complaint" (Very) **86**:136
"Complaint" (Wilbur) **51**:231, 247, 312
"The Complaint" (Wordsworth)
See "The Complaint of the Forsaken Indian Woman"
Complaint (Southwell)
See *Saint Peters Complaint, with Other Poems*
"The Complaint of a Forsaken Indian Woman" (Wordsworth)
See "The Complaint of the Forsaken Indian Woman"
"Complaint of Body, the Ass, against His Rider, the Soul" (Benét) **64**:15
"Complaint of the Amorous Lizard" (Char)
See "Complainte du lézard amoureux"
"Complaint of the Dying Peasantry" (Muir) **49**:211, 299
"The Complaint of the Forsaken Indian Woman" (Wordsworth) **4**:347, 427-28; **67**:277, 282, 300, 304, 311-12, 370
"Complaint of the Poor Knight Errant" (Laforgue)
See "Complainte du pauvre chevalier-errant"
"Complainte à Notre-Dame des soirs" (Laforgue) **14**:94
"Complainte de cette bonne lune" (Laforgue) **14**:93
Complainte de la bonne défunte (Laforgue) **14**:81, 98
"Complainte de la fin des journées" (Laforgue) **14**:98
"Complainte de la lune en province" (Laforgue) **14**:98
"Complainte de l'ange incurable" (Laforgue) **14**:85, 89-90, 98
"Complainte de l'automne monotone" (Laforgue) **14**:80
"Complainte de l'époux outragé" (Laforgue) **14**:81, 93
"Complainte de Lord Pierrot" (Laforgue) **14**:81, 93, 98
"Complainte de l'organiste de Nice" (Laforgue) **14**:93
"Complainte de l'orgue de barbarie" (Laforgue) **14**:95
"Complainte des blackboulés" (Laforgue) **14**:81, 96
"Complainte des complaintes" (Laforgue) **14**:95
"Complainte des consolations" (Laforgue) **14**:81
"Complainte des débats mélancoliques et littéraires" (Laforgue) **14**:64, 97
"Complainte des formalités nuptiales" (Laforgue) **14**:81, 96
"Complainte des grands pins dans une ville abandonée" (Laforgue) **14**:81, 96
"Complainte des pianos qu'on entend dans les quertiersaisés" (Laforgue) **14**:81, 93-5
"Complainte des printemps" (Laforgue) **14**:81, 98
"Complainte des voix sous le figuier bouddhique" (Laforgue) **14**:96
"Complainte du fœtus de Poète" (Laforgue) **14**:93, 96, 98
"Complainte du lézard amoureux" (Char) **56**:167, 182
"Complainte du pauvre chevalier-errant" (Laforgue) **14**:64, 98
"Complainte du pauvre corps humain" (Laforgue) **14**:81
"Complainte du pauvre jeune homme" (Laforgue) **14**:81, 93
"Complainte du Roi de Thulé" (Laforgue) **14**:81, 86, 89, 93, 98
"Complainte du sage de Paris" (Laforgue) **14**:95
"Complainte d'un certain dimanche" (Laforgue) **14**:96-8
"Complainte d'une convalescence en mai" (Laforgue) **14**:96, 98
"Complainte propitiatoire à l'inconscient" (Laforgue) **14**:66, 94-5
"Complainte sous le figuier boudhique" (Laforgue) **14**:81
"Complainte sur certains ennuis" (Laforgue) **14**:94, 97
"Complainte sur certains temps déplacés" (Laforgue) **14**:94
"Complainte-épitaphe" (Laforgue) **14**:95

"Complainte-Placet de Faust fils" (Laforgue) **14**:95, 98
Les complaintes (Laforgue) **14**:57, 64, 66, 68-9, 70-2, 80-1, 92, 94-5, 97-8
"Complaintes des pubertés difficiles" (Laforgue) **14**:80, 98
Complaints: Containing Sundrie Small Poemes of the Worlds Vanitie (Spenser) **8**:366
"The Complement" (Carew) **29**:32
The Complete Collected Poems, 1906-1938 (Williams) **109**:283, 286-87, 291-92
The Complete Collected Poems of William Carlos Williams, 1906-1938 (Williams) **7**:348, 355
Complete English Poems (Johnson) **81**:205
The Complete Nonsense of Edward Lear (Lear) **65**:166, 169
Complete Poems (Cunningham)
See *The Poems of J. V. Cunningham*
The Complete Poems (Dickinson) **1**:102
Complete Poems (Jarrell) **41**:164-70, 178, 180, 184-86, 189, 191, 194-97, 207
Complete Poems (Rexroth) **95**:331
Complete Poems (Sandburg) **2**:322-24, 328-29, 331, 333, 340; **41**:279, 282-83, 287, 300-01, 303-4, 306, 314, 322, 359
The Complete Poems (Sexton) **79**:211, 226-32, 242, 245-46, 252-53, 257, 261
Complete Poems (Sidney) **32**:288
The Complete Poems (Thoreau) **30**:256
The Complete Poems and Fragments (Owen) **102**:149, 210-11, 213, 225, 238-39
The Complete Poems, 1927-1979 (Bishop) **3**:50, 66; **34**:94, 123-27, 130-31, 137-40, 145-47, 159, 155, 158, 170, 174-76
The Complete Poems and Plays, 1909-1950 (Eliot) **90**:217, 219-22, 225-26, 314-15, 317-21, 325, 327-29, 335-37
The Complete Poems and Selected Letters and Prose of Hart Crane (Crane) **99**:55-56, 85, 94
The Complete Poems of C.P. Cavafy (Cavafy) **36**:117
The Complete Poems of D. H. Lawrence (Lawrence) **54**:204-8, 220-27, 239-40, 243-45, 249-50
The Complete Poems of Edwin Muir (Muir) **49**:291
The Complete Poems of Frances Ellen Watkins Harper (Harper) **21**:197
The Complete Poems of Hart Crane: The Centennial Edition (Crane) **99**:84-85, 87-91, 94, 99, 102, 109
The Complete Poems of John Wilmot, Earl of Rochester (Wilmot) **66**:265
The Complete Poems of Keith Douglas (Douglas) **106**:196, 199, 206
The Complete Poems of Marianne Moore (Moore) **4**:251, 254, 256, 270; **49**:122, 144, 149-50, 184-85, 188
The Complete Poems of Patrick Kavanagh (Kavanagh) **105**:140, 143-45, 172-77
The Complete Poem's of Paul Laurence Dunbar (Dunbar) **5**:120, 136
Complete Poems of Robert Frost (Frost) **39**:233
The Complete Poems of Robert Louis Stevenson (Stevenson) **84**:334
The Complete Poems of Thomas Hardy (Hardy) **92**:199-200, 264, 266-77, 304-5, 309, 317, 322, 325, 358-59, 361-63, 365-66
Complete Poems of Walter de la Mare (de la Mare) **77**:109, 116, 120, 148-49
The Complete Poetical Works (Byron)
See *Lord Byron: The Complete Poetical Works*
The Complete Poetical Works (Lowell) **13**:95
The Complete Poetical Works of Percy Bysshe Shelley (Shelley) **67**:183
Complete Poetical Works of Samuel Taylor Coleridge (Coleridge) **11**:44, 71; **39**:215-16
The Complete Poetry and Prose of William Blake (Blake) **63**:82, 84
"The Complete Prelude" (Berrigan) **103**:34
Complete Verse (Belloc) **24**:23, 36, 39
Complete Works (Aleixandre)
See *Obras completas*
Complete Works (Auden) **92**:52
Complete Works (Borges)
See *Obras completas*
Complete Works (Mandelstam) **14**:106
Complete Works: From This Condensery (Niedecker)
See *From This Condensery: The Complete Writings of Lorine Niedecker*
The Complete Works of Edgar Allan Poe (Poe) **54**:302, 331, 337
"The Complete Works of Francois Villon" (Villon) **13**:413
The Complete Works of Geoffrey Chaucer (Chaucer) **58**:303
The Complete Works of Lewis Carroll (Carroll) **74**:26-27
Complete Works of Philip Sidney (Sidney) **32**:235, 244-47, 249-50, 256, 257-58, 260, 268
The Complete Works of Thomas Chatterton (Chatterton) **104**:30, 37-38, 51-58, 66
"The Complex" (Ignatow) **34**:286
"Compleynt to the Muse" (Berrigan) **103**:36
"Complicate" (Kunitz) **19**:156
"Complicity" (Gallagher) **9**:37
"Compline" (Auden) **92**:43
"Compline" (Berryman) **64**:118, 120
"Composed at a Time When I Was in Love, as I Saw the Burnt-over Fields Along the Road During a Trip" (Tsurayuki)
See *Kokinshu "791"*
"Composed at Clevedon, Somersetshire" (Coleridge) **100**:21, 24
"Composed, Composed" (Stafford) **71**:283
"Composed during a Walk on the Downs, in November 1787" (Smith) **104**:164, 320
"Composed on Jade Maiden Spring in Ying Cheng, Anzhou" (Li Po) **29**:179, 182
"Composed on the Cold Food Day" (Wang Wei) **18**:362
"Composed When I Heard a Wood-Thrush Sing" (Tsurayuki)
See *Kokinshu "160"*
"Composed When I Visited a Mountain Temple" (Tsurayuki)
See *Kokinshu "117"*
"Composed When I Was Weak With Illness" (Tsurayuki)
See *Kokinshu "861"*
"Composición escrita en un ejemplar de la gesta de Beowulf" (Borges) **32**:63, 94, 105-06, 133
"Composition" (Das) **43**:77-80, 85
"Composition as Process—I. Changes" (Cage) **58**:205
"Composition in Bhairavi" (Tagore)
See "Bhairavi gan"
"Composition in Retrospect" (Cage) **58**:200, 206, 208
"The Composition of the Cell" (Hejinian) **108**:290
"Comprehending" (Ortiz) **17**:246
"Comptine" (Césaire) **25**:31
"Compulsory Chapel" (Walker) **30**:347
"Comrades Four" (McKay) **2**:225
Comus: A Maske (Milton) **29**:200, 212, 221, 226, 228, 243, 252, 272
"Con Bacach O'Neill, 1542" (Montague) **106**:342
"Con la Carta de la Habana" (Guillén) **23**:126
Con las horas contadas (Cernuda) **62**:172-73, 179, 204, 215, 224, 257
"The Concealment: Ishi, the Last Wild Indian" (Stafford) **71**:265, 280, 292, 326
"Conceit begotten by the eyes" (Raleigh) **31**:212, 214
"Conceit of Master Gysbrecht" (Browning) **2**:38
"Conceive a Man, Should He Have Anything" (Cummings) **5**:106
"Conceptio B. Virginis sub porta aurea" (Southwell)
See "The Virgin Mary's Conception"
"Conception" (Southwell)
See "The Virgin Mary's Conception"
"Concerning Geoffray Teste Noire" (Morris) **55**:299, 301-02
"Concerning Some Recent Criticism of His Work" (Doty) **53**:61
"Concerning the Conversation of Mr H—" (Wickham) **110**:264
"Concerning the Right to Life" (Graham) **59**:159
"The Concert" (Millay) **6**:215
"The Concert" (Yevtushenko) **40**:340
"Concert at the Railroad Station" (Mandelstam)
See "Koncert na vokzale"
"Concert in the garden" (Paz)
See "Concierto en el jardin"
"The Concert of Hyacinths" (Elytis) **21**:119
Concert on the Island (Seifert)
See *Koncert na ostrově*
"Concerto to a Runaway" (Bissett) **14**:9
"Conch" (Herbert)
See "Muszla"
"Conch-Shell" (Wright) **14**:364
"El concierto" (Guillén) **35**:185
"Concierto en el jardin" (Paz) **48**:207
Le concile féerique (Laforgue) **14**:72, 81, 96
"Conciliator, Who Had Never Believed" (Hölderlin) **4**:178
"Conclusion" (Sassoon) **12**:258
"Conclusioni provvisorie" (Montale) **13**:131
"Concobar" (Clarke) **112**:29, 43, 89
"Concord" (Swinburne) **24**:324, 326
"Concord Hymn" (Emerson) **18**:111
"Concord Hymn" (Spicer) **78**:294
"Concord Ode" (Emerson) **18**:84, 88
"Concord River" (Rich) **5**:354
"Concourse" (Corso) **108**:15
"Concurrence" (Hughes) **89**:211
"The Condemned" (Page) **12**:174-75
"La condena" (Mistral) **32**:176
Condensery (Niedecker)
See *From This Condensery: The Complete Writings of Lorine Niedecker*
"La condition botanique" (Hecht) **70**:82, 91
"Condotto da molt'anni all'ultime'ore'" (Michelangelo) **103**:306
"Conduct and Work" (Hall) **70**:30
"The Conductor" (Thomas) **99**:236
"Coney Island" (Corso) **108**:38
A Coney Island of the Mind (Ferlinghetti) **1**:164-65, 167-77, 184, 187
"A Confederate Veteran Tries to Explain the Event" (Warren) **37**:341
"A Conference of the Powers" (Kipling) **3**:160
Confessio Amantis (Gower) **59**:3-7, 9, 11-13, 15, 17, 20-22, 25-31, 39, 41-48, 54-59, 61-63, 65-70, 72, 76-80, 82-84, 87-89, 94-100, 103, 106-07, 109-11, 113-14, 116-19
"Confession" (Baudelaire) **1**:61
"confession" (Clifton) **17**:37
"Confession" (Glück) **16**:160
"Confession" (Heaney) **18**:243
"The Confession" (Lermontov)
See "Ispoved"
"A Confession" (Milosz) **8**:197
Confession Amantis (Gower)
See *Confessio Amantis*
"The Confession of Queen Gormlai" (Clarke) **112**:29, 34, 90-91
"Confession of the Tenant in Apartment #2" (Espada) **74**:116
"A Confession to a Friend in Trouble" (Hardy) **92**:241
"Confession to J. Edgar Hoover" (Wright) **36**:342

"Confession to Settle a Curse" (Waldrop) **109**:167
"The Confessional" (Browning) **2**:30; **61**:88
"Confessional" (Chesterton) **28**:95
"Confessions" (Barrett Browning) **6**:32
"The Confessions of a Bachelor" (Whittier) **93**:200
"Confessions of a Second-Rate, Sensitive Mind" (Tennyson) **6**:347
"The Confessions of Count Mowgli de Sade" (Nash) **21**:267
"Confessions of the Life Artist" (Gunn) **26**:207, 211, 226
"The Confidant" (Crabbe) **97**:95
"The Confidantes" (Kumin) **15**:215
"The Confidant's Alley" (Char) **56**:162
"Confidential Instructions" (Kunitz) **19**:148
"Configurations" (Ammons) **16**:23
Configurations (Paz) **1**:355
"Confined Love" (Donne) **43**:166, 168-70
"Confinement" (McGuckian) **27**:101
"Confirmation" (Baraka) **113**:16
"Confirmation" (Erdrich) **52**:191
"The Confirmation" (Muir) **49**:232, 289
"The Confirmation" (Shapiro) **25**:286, 300
"Confiteor" (Trakl) **20**:263-64, 269
"Le *Confiteor* de l'artist" (Baudelaire) **106**:88
"The Conflict" (Day Lewis) **11**:126, 150
"The Conflict of Convictions" (Melville) **82**:83, 91, 130-31, 134, 190-91, 205, 207, 209-10
"Conflicting Occupation" (Wickham) **110**:266
"Conformity" (Kennedy) **93**:145
"Confusion" (Rexroth) **95**:257
"Confusion of the Senses" (Rexroth) **20**:221
"Congé au vent" (Char) **56**:150, 182
"Congedo" (Carducci) **46**:65, 74, 81
"Congo" (Lindsay) **23**:264, 266, 268, 270, 272-73, 275-76, 278, 282-84, 286-87, 289, 294, 297
The Congo and Other Poems (Lindsay) **23**:267-68, 295
"The Congo Love Song" (Johnson) **24**:151
"A Congratulatory Poem to Her Most Sacred Majesty on the Universal Hopes of All Loyal Persons for a Prince of Wales" (Behn) **13**:32; **88**:22, 101-02
A Congratulatory Poem to . . . Queen Mary upon Her Arrival in England (Behn) **13**:9
"A Congregation" (Duncan) **75**:175
"Congress of the Insomniacs" (Simic) **69**:366-67
"Conjectural Poem" (Borges)
See "Poema conjetural"
"Conjecture" (Hardy) **92**:295
Los conjurados (Borges) **22**:95, 99; **32**:86, 91, 111
"Conjuration" (Wilbur) **51**:187-88, 193
Conjurations (Werfel)
See *Beschwörungen*
Conjure: Selected Poems, 1963-1970 (Reed) **68**:323-26, 329-33, 335, 340, 347-49
"Conjuries That Endure" (Moore) **49**:161
"Conjuring in Heaven" (Hughes) **7**:159
"Conjuring Monkey" (Baraka) **113**:63
"Conlath and Cuthona" (Macpherson) **97**:230
Connecting the Dots (Kumin) **15**:224
"Connections" (Stafford) **71**:275, 277-78, 280, 296-98
"Connections" (Wright) **14**:376-77
"Conneries" (Rimbaud) **57**:252
"The Connoisseuse of Slugs" (Olds) **22**:312
"Connubii Flores, or the Well-Wishes at Weddings" (Herrick) **9**:86, 112
"The Conquererors" (Dunbar) **5**:131
"Conqueror" (Brathwaite) **56**:60
"The Conqueror Worm" (Poe) **1**:437, 443; **54**:272
"The Conqueror's Song" (Duncan) **75**:122
"Conquest" (Williams) **109**:239
"Conquête de l'aube" (Césaire) **25**:10
"Conquistador" (Hope) **56**:266, 276, 286, 293, 302
Conquistador (MacLeish) **47**:127-28, 130, 133, 137-40, 150, 152, 156, 158, 163, 188-90, 194-95, 197-204, 211, 213-14, 239, 253-54
"Conrad in Twilight" (Ransom) **61**:275
"Conrad Kain" (Birney) **52**:58
Conrad Wallenrod (Mickiewicz)
See *Konrad Wallenrod*
"A Conrado Benítez" (Guillén) **23**:128
"The Cons cientious Objector" (Shapiro) **25**:297
"Consalvo" (Leopardi) **37**:79
"Conscience" (Herbert) **4**:109, 129
"La Conscience" (Hugo) **17**:65, 85
"Conscience and Remorse" (Dunbar) **5**:115, 125
"The Conscience of a Conservative" (Raworth) **107**:285
"Les consciences atténuantes" (Tzara) **27**:235
"Conscious" (Owen) **19**:347, 361-63; **102**:157, 230-31
"Consciousness" (Milosz)
See "Świadomość"
"Conscript" (Larkin) **21**:225
"The Conscript" (MacNeice) **61**:141
"Conscription Camp" (Shapiro) **25**:313, 324-25
"Conscripts" (Sassoon) **12**:242, 280
"The Consecrating Mother" (Sexton) **2**:374; **79**:233, 241, 245
"A Consecration" (Masefield) **78**:68, 75, 94
"The Consecration of Henry V" (Carducci)
See "La Sacra di Enrico Quinto"
"Conseil d'ami" (Valéry) **9**:391
"Conseil de la sentinelle" (Char) **56**:172
"Consequences" (Meredith) **28**:213
"Conserving the Magnitude of Uselessness" (Ammons) **16**:54
"Consider Me" (Hughes) **53**:122
"Considerations" (Sarton) **39**:321
"Considerations on Part of the Eighty-Eighth Psalme" (Prior) **102**:330
considering how exaggerated music is (Scalapino) **114**:275, 283, 289
"Considering the Snail" (Gunn) **26**:201, 207-208, 210, 213
"Consolatio Nova" (Cunningham) **92**:163
"Consolation" (Collins) **68**:219
"Consolation" (Ignatow) **34**:281-82
"Consolation" (McKay) **2**:225
"Consolation" (Wickham) **110**:310
Les consolations (Sainte-Beuve) **110**:3, 9, 13, 17-20, 41, 43, 46, 48, 51, 53-55, 57-58, 63, 69
"Consolations" (Stafford) **71**:371
"Consolations of Philosophy" (Mahon) **60**:134, 140
"Consolatory Verses for the Middle Years" (Barker) **77**:18
"The Consonance" (Cernuda) **62**:182
"Consorting with Angels" (Sexton) **2**:363; **79**:233-34, 281, 315-16
"The Conspiracy" (Creeley) **73**:7
"Conspiracy" (Spicer) **78**:261, 271, 305
The Conspirators (Borges)
See *Los conjurados*
Constab Ballads (McKay) **2**:208, 210, 216, 221-22, 225-27
"The Constabiliad" (Chatterton) **104**:72
"A Constable Calls" (Heaney) **100**:225, 267, 297
"Constance" (Gower) **59**:48, 68-70, 107-8
Constance (Kenyon) **57**:6, 11, 19-20, 23-24, 35, 37-38, 40, 45-46
"Constance Hately" (Masters) **36**:218
"Constancie" (Herbert) **4**:109
"The Constant" (Ammons) **16**:6
"The Constant" (Cowley) **90**:116
"Constant" (MacNeice) **61**:178
"Constant April" (Spender) **71**:217
"Constantly Risking Absurdity" (Ferlinghetti) **1**:182
"The Constellation" (Barker) **77**:7
"Constellation" (Stryk) **27**:208, 212
Constellations (Breton) **15**:48-9, 55, 59-60, 62
"Construction" (Shapiro) **25**:295
"Constructions" (Loy) **16**:316
"Construyendo una Balsa" (Alurista) **34**:16, 24, 29, 47
"The Consuliad" (Chatterton)
See "The Constabiliad"
"Consultorio sentimental" (Parra) **39**:277
"La consumación" (Mistral) **32**:191
"Consumer's Report" (Kennedy) **93**:130
"The Consumptive" (Hughes) **53**:115
"A Contact" (MacNeice) **61**:127
"Conte" (Rimbaud) **3**:261-63; **57**:174, 245, 247, 254, 271, 275
"Conte Colibri" (Césaire) **25**:44-5
"Contemplando Florencia" (Guillén) **35**:227
"Contemplation" (Traherne) **70**:171
"Contemplation Basket" (Sandburg) **41**:323
"Contemplation of Beauty" (Carducci)
See "Contemplazione della bellezza'"
"Contemplations" (Bradstreet) **10**:7-8, 19-21, 27-30, 35, 42, 65
Les contemplations (Hugo) **17**:50, 53-54, 64, 66-67, 74, 78, 80-84, 86-87, 89-92, 95
The Contemplative Quarry (Wickham) **110**:259-60, 275, 295, 297, 309
"Contemplazione della bellezza'" (Carducci) **46**:75
"A Contemporary" (Cernuda) **62**:172
"The Contender" (Hughes) **7**:155; **89**:216
"Content and rich" (Southwell) **83**:280, 323
"Content, to my dearest Lucasia" (Philips) **40**:297
"The Contention" (Sassoon) **12**:259
"Contentment" (Holmes) **71**:68, 83
"Contest of the Bards" (Ginsberg) **4**:58-9
"The Continent" (Duncan) **2**:109-13; **75**:245
"The Continental Can Company at Six O'Clock" (Wright) **36**:391
"Continent's End" (Jeffers) **17**:131
"Contingency" (Ammons) **16**:6
Continual Dew: A Little Book of Bourgeois Verse (Betjeman) **75**:6, 57, 60, 68-69, 76, 107
Continuation des amours (Ronsard) **11**:220, 230; **105**:198, 272
The Continuous Life (Strand) **63**:197-98
"Continuum" (Levertov) **11**:207-09
Continuum: New and Later Poems, 1972-1988 (Curnow) **48**:32-35, 37-40
"Contra el verso retórico" (Martí) **76**:106
Contra Mortem (Carruth) **10**:71, 83
"A Contract" (Lermontov) **18**:303-4
"The Contract" (Patmore) **59**:207, 223, 259, 264, 267-68, 276
"Contralto" (Gautier) **18**:157
"The Contraption" (Swenson) **14**:250
"Contrapunto final" (Guillén) **35**:188
"The Contrariness of the Mad Farmer" (Berry) **28**:20
"The Contrary Poet" (Jarrell) **41**:139
"The Contrast" (Harper) **21**:207, 216
"Contravening" (Char)
See "Obéissez à vos porcs qui existent . . ."
"Contre les bûcherons de la forêt de Gastine" (Ronsard) **11**:236-37, 242
"Contre une maison sèche" (Char) **56**:154
"Le Contrediz de Franc Gontier" (Villon) **13**:415
"Contrevenir" (Char)
See "Obéissez à vos porcs qui existent . . ."
"The Contrite Heart" (Cowper) **40**:53-4
"Control" (Sarton) **39**:368
"Control Burn" (Snyder) **21**:292
"Contusion" (Plath) **1**:391, 394
"A Conundrum" (Carman) **34**:208
"The Conundrum of the Workshop" (Kipling) **3**:167
"The Convalescent" (Gozzano) **10**:177
"The Convalescent" (Service) **70**:130
"Convalescenza" (Quasimodo) **47**:271
"The Convent Threshold" (Rossetti) **7**:267, 281-2, 291, 295-6, 298
"Conventionality" (Kipling) **3**:190

"The Convergence of the Twain" (Hardy) **8**:116; **92**:230
"Convergences" (Warren) **37**:326, 336, 350
"Conversacíon" (Cardenal) **22**:117
"Conversación galante" (Parra) **39**:286
"Conversation" (Ai) **72**:23
"Conversation" (Berryman) **64**:83
"Conversation" (Bishop) **34**:89
"Conversation" (Cowper) **40**:43, 45, 48, 50, 71
"Conversation" (Curnow) **48**:57, 61
"Conversation" (Giovanni) **19**:118
"The Conversation" (Masters) **1**:326
"Conversation" (Mickiewicz)
See "Rozmowa"
"The Conversation. A Tale" (Prior) **102**:313, 319
"A Conversation at Dawn" (Hardy) **92**:286
Conversation at Midnight (Millay) **6**:220, 223, 244
"Conversation in Moscow" (Levertov) **11**:197
"Conversation in the Park" (Hacker) **47**:86, 95
"The Conversation of Prayer" (Thomas) **2**:390; **52**:263
"Conversation with a Fireman from Brooklyn" (Gallagher) **9**:44, 60
"Conversation with a Stone" (Szymborska) **44**:299, 314
"Conversation with an American Writer" (Yevtushenko) **40**:343, 345
"Conversation with Calliope" (Hope) **56**:274, 294-95
"Conversation With Death" (Seifert) **47**:334
"Conversation With Landor" (Hope) **56**:292
"A Conversation with Leonardo" (Ciardi) **69**:25
"Conversation With My Friend Kwang Min Ah Loong Kwang of Outram Park" (Thumboo) **30**:333
"Conversation with my Inspiration" (Tsvetaeva)
See "Razgovor s geniem"
"Conversation with the Devil" (Jarrell) **41**:177, 195, 199
Conversations Introducing Poetry, Chiefly on Subjects of Natural History, for the Use of Children and Young Persons (Smith) **104**:151, 154-56, 165, 177-78, 225, 271, 338, 340, 342-43, 345-48, 353
"Conversations with Jeanne" (Milosz) **8**:213
"Conversations with Trees" (Carducci)
See "Colloqui con gli alberi"
"Conversing with Paradise" (Nemerov) **24**:285
"Conversion" (Toomer) **7**:320, 334
"The Conversion of St. Paul" (Betjeman) **75**:97-98
"The Convert" (Crabbe) **97**:111-12
"The Convert" (Shapiro) **25**:286, 296, 298
"Convict" (Brown) **55**:144, 155, 2110
"The Convict" (Wordsworth) **4**:373; **67**:278, 295, 337, 347, 370
"Convicts" (Das) **43**:85
Convivio (Dante) **108**:82-84, 94-95, 99, 101-3, 105-8, 114-15, 133
"Convivio!" (Williams) **7**:361
Convivio (Dante) **21**:48-53, 66, 73-4, 83, 87-92
Le Convoi de Manuel (Béranger) **112**:9
"Convoy" (MacNeice) **61**:140
"Cook County" (MacLeish) **47**:213
"Cooking" (Stein) **18**:322-326
"A Cooking Egg" (Eliot) **5**:184
"The Cookout" (Ignatow) **34**:318
"Cook's Mountains" (Page) **12**:183, 190
"Cool Dark Ode" (Justice) **64**:291
"A Cool Head in an Emergency" (Curnow) **48**:18
"Cool Liquid Comes" (Dorn) **115**:86, 132, 176-77
"Cool Park, 1929" (Yeats)
See "Coole Park, 1929"
"Cool Tombs" (Sandburg) **41**:235, 240, 245, 250, 253, 266-67, 272, 276-77, 297, 313, 339
"Cool Water under Bridges" (Kavanagh) **105**:176
"The Cool Web" (Graves) **6**:172
"Coole Park, 1929" (Yeats) **20**:322
"Coole Park and Abbey Theatre 1951" (Montague) **106**:306
Coon Dog Wess (Riley) **48**:306
"Coon Song" (Ammons) **16**:19, 41, 44, 46
"Cooney Potter" (Masters) **36**:170
"Coopérants du contingent" (Senghor) **25**:255
"Cootchie" (Bishop) **34**:69, 137-38, 189
"La copa" (Storni) **33**:254
"La copa envenenada" (Martí) **76**:105
Copacetic (Komunyakaa) **51**:15, 30, 33-34, 36
"Copacetic Mingus" (Komunyakaa) **51**:15, 31, 33
"Coplas" (Mistral) **32**:153, 176, 178
"Coplas americans" (Guillén) **23**:126
"Cop-Out Session" (Knight) **14**:46, 52
"Copper Red and the Seven Dachsies" (Cassian) **17**:3
Copper Sun (Cullen) **20**:56-59, 61-62, 64-65, 75, 77, 85-86
"cops" (Baraka) **4**:12
"The Copulating Gods" (Kizer) **66**:75-77, 79-80
The Copy of a Letter, Lately Written in Meter, by a Young Gentlewoman: To Her Unconstant Lover (Whitney) **116**:250-51, 256-61, 264-65, 268-69, 271-72, 276-77, 281, 288, 291, 308, 310
"Coq au vin" (Ciardi) **69**:11
"A Coquette Conquered" (Dunbar) **5**:122
"Coquette et Froide" (Howe) **81**:47
"Coquette et Tendre" (Howe) **81**:47
"Coquetterie posthume" (Gautier) **18**:125, 157-60, 163
"Les coquillages" (Verlaine) **32**:349, 391
"Le cor" (Vigny) **26**:369, 402-403, 410
"Cor Mio" (Rossetti) **7**:278
"Cora of Pigeon Run" (Wagoner) **33**:367
"Corail" (Char) **56**:171
"Coral" (Char)
See "Corail"
"Coral Atoll" (Randall) **86**:290, 334
El corazón amarillo (Neruda) **4**:287, 289
El corazón con que vivo (Guillén) **23**:133
"El corazón de Pedro de Valdivia" (Neruda) **4**:293
"Corazón Lapida" (Alurista) **34**:47
"El corazón magellanico" (Neruda) **4**:281
"Les Corbeaux" (Rimbaud) **57**:244, 253
"The Cord" (Stone) **53**:221, 254
"Cordillera" (Espada) **74**:128, 139-41
"Cordura" (Cernuda) **62**:213, 215
"Cori descrittivi di stati d'animo di Didone" (Ungaretti) **57**:339
"Corinna, Pride of Drury-Lane" (Swift) **9**:283-84
"Corinna's Going a-Maying" (Herrick) **9**:99-101, 104-05, 116, 120, 122-23, 125, 132, 137, 142, 145
"Coriolanus and His Mother" (Schwartz) **8**:282-83, 290-91, 297-98, 301, 308-09, 312
Cork (Ní Chuilleanáin) **34**:381-82
Les Cormorans (Jaccottet) **98**:191
"A Cormorant" (Hughes) **89**:133
"Corn" (Lanier) **50**:55, 61, 66, 69-71, 74, 85, 90-91, 98, 106-8
Corn Law Rhymes. The Ranter, Written and Published by Order of the Sheffield Mechanics' Anti-Bread Tax Society (Elliott) **96**:156, 158, 161-62, 166-70, 173, 180-83, 187
"The Corner" (de la Mare) **77**:113
"The Corner of My Community" (Paredes)
See "Esquinita de mi pueblo"
"The Corner of Night and Morning" (Lowell) **13**:64
"The Corner of the Eye" (Warren) **37**:326
"Corner seat" (MacNeice) **61**:160
"Cornet Solo" (Day Lewis) **11**:145
Cornhuskers (Sandburg) **2**:302, 304, 307, 309, 313-14, 316, 323, 338-39; **41**:239-40, 242-43, 244, 248, 250, 256, 266-67, 269-70, 274, 277, 282, 296-97, 313, 318, 325-29, 339, 351, 357
"Cornish Heroic Song for Valda Trevlyn" (MacDiarmid) **9**:180, 183
"Corno Inglese" (Montale) **13**:105
"A Corn-Song" (Dunbar) **5**:122
"The Cornucopia" (Barker) **77**:7
"Corollary" (Chappell) **105**:52
"Corona" (Hacker) **47**:107
La Corona (Donne) **1**:136-39, 145, 147; **43**:112-15
"A Coronal" (Williams) **7**:345, 362
"Coronation Soliloquy" (Hunt) **73**:152
"The Coronet" (Marvell) **10**:267, 271, 274, 277, 293, 313-14; **86**:257
A Coronet for His Mistresse Philosophie (Chapman)
See *Ovids Banquet of Sense. A Coronet for His Mistresse Philosophie, and His Amorous Zodiacke. With a Translation of a Latine Coppie, Written by a Fryer, Anno Dom. 1400*
"Corot" (Lawrence) **54**:228
"The Corporal" (Gunn) **26**:224
"Corporal Punishment" (Clarke) **112**:122
Corps perdu (Césaire) **25**:30-2, 35, 44
Corpse and Mirror (Yau) **61**:329
"The Corpse of a Cat" (Hagiwara)
See "Neko no shigai"
"Corpse Song" (Atwood) **8**:23, 25
"Correct Usages" (Dorn) **115**:133
"Correction: Eve Delved and Adam Span" (Nash) **21**:273
"Correspondances" (Baudelaire) **1**:55, 65, 69-70; **106**:32-33, 35-36, 86-87, 114-15, 117, 124, 134-35, 137, 144, 160
"Correspondances" (Char) **56**:201
"Correspondence" (Howe) **81**:30
"Correspondence" (Thomas) **99**:274
"Correspondences" (Rukeyser) **12**:226, 233
"La Corrida" (Hayden) **6**:194
"El Corrido de Gregorio Cortez" (Paredes) **83**:11, 16-18
"The Corridor" (Gunn) **26**:193
"Corridors" (Das) **43**:85, 91
"El corro luminoso" (Mistral) **32**:175
"Cors de chasse" (Apollinaire) **7**:42
The Corsair (Byron) **16**:91-5, 109; **95**:55
The Corsair (Lermontov) **18**:299
"Corsica" (Cruz) **37**:15
"Corson's Inlet" (Ammons) **16**:21, 23, 29, 35-7, 54
Corson's Inlet (Ammons) **16**:4-5, 20, 28
"The Cortege" (Gibran) **9**:73
"Cortege" (Verlaine) **32**:349, 391
"Cortège for Rosenbloom" (Stevens) **6**:293
Cortege of Orpheus (Apollinaire)
See *Le bestiaire; ou, Cortège d'Orphée*
"Cory" (Robinson)
See "Richard Cory"
"Corydon. Phillario. Or, Mira's Picture. A Pastoral" (Leapor)
See "Mira's Picture"
"Cosas" (Borges) **32**:89
"Così siamo" (Zanzotto) **65**:265
Cosmic Carols (Service) **70**:140, 144
"Cosmic Comics" (Nemerov) **24**:301
"The Cosmology of Finding Your Place" (Dorn) **115**:57, 109
"The Cossack" (Pushkin) **10**:407
"Cossack Cradlesong" (Lermontov) **18**:268, 278, 281, 304
"The Cost" (Hecht) **70**:78, 97-98
"The Cost of Pleasure" (Bryant) **20**:46
"Costa Magic" (Loy) **16**:313
"The Costa San Giorgio" (Loy) **16**:313, 318-20, 322, 327
"Costei pur si delibra" (Michelangelo) **103**:193, 199

"Costly Speech" (Hughes) **89**:274
"The Cottage Dweller" (Tagore)
See "Kutir-vasi"
"The Cottage Hospital" (Betjeman) **75**:11, 31, 77
"Cottage Street, 1953" (Wilbur) **51**:245-46, 250-51, 265, 281, 289-90
"The Cottar's Saturday Night" (Burns) **6**:50, 57, 74, 79, 96
"The Cotter's Saturday Night" (Burns) **114**:18-19, 27-28, 67, 75, 80, 98, 166
Cotton Candy on a Rainy Day (Giovanni) **19**:114, 116-18, 123, 125, 128, 130, 134, 137, 142-43
"Cotton Song" (Toomer) **7**:319, 321
"Cottonmouth Country" (Glück) **16**:139
"Le coucher du soleil romantique" (Baudelaire) **106**:49
"Cougar Meat" (Gallagher) **9**:59, 62
"Could Have" (Szymborska)
See "Wszelki wypadek"
Could Have (Szymborska)
See *Wszelki wypadek*
"Could Man Be Drunk for Ever" (Housman) **2**:195
"Could my heart more tongues imploy" (Campion) **87**:58, 70
A Couleii Plantarum (Cowley)
See *Plantarum*
"Councell to a Bachelor" (Moore) **49**:109
"The Council Reports in 8 Fragments" (Corso) **108**:12
"Councourse Didils" (Corso) **108**:13
"The Counsel" (Behn) **88**:149
"counsel at the highest level" (Enzensberger) **28**:143
"Count Gismond" (Browning) **61**:88; **97**:31, 35, 37-38
Count Nulin (Pushkin)
See *Graf Nulin*
"Count the Roses" (Oliver) **75**:343
"Counter Serenade" (Viereck) **27**:263
"Counter-Attack" (Sassoon) **12**:256-57, 264-65, 277-78
Counter-Attack and Other Poems (Sassoon) **12**:242, 250, 253, 257-58, 260, 263-64, 266-69, 272, 276-77
"A Counterpoint" (Aiken) **26**:4
"Counterpoint" (Darwish) **86**:34
Counterpoint (Thomas) **99**:322-24, 327, 339
"Counter-Walk, Reversals" (Viereck) **27**:277
"The Countess" (Whittier) **93**:175, 247, 267
The Countess Cathleen (Yeats) **20**:298, 302-3, 353; **51**:72, 75
"Countess Erica Blaise: Chorus" (Kaufman) **74**:174, 259
The Countess from Minneapolis (Guest) **55**:217, 219-20
The Countess of Pembroke's Arcadia (Sidney) **32**:218-20, 225-31, 233-34, 236-37, 239-45, 248-49, 252-53, 255-56, 258-61, 264-69, 272-73, 277, 290, 320, 323-24
The Countesse of Mountgomeries Urania (Wroth) **38**:242-47, 249-51, 254-56, 258-59, 262-68, 272, 274-76, 278-82, 285-93, 296, 298, 304, 307, 309, 311, 314, 316-25, 328-29, 331, 333-34
Counting Backward (Cassian) **17**:6
"Counting Clouds" (Welch) **62**:338
"The Counting Houses" (Merwin) **45**:37
"Counting Small-Boned Bodies" (Bly) **39**:21, 50, 91, 94
"Counting the Beats" (Graves) **6**:136-37, 155
"Countrey Iigge" (Deloney) **79**:56
"Country" (Cernuda) **62**:173
"The Country" (Collins) **68**:210
"Country and Western" (Hacker) **47**:87-88, 113
"Country & Western II" (Hacker) **47**:88
The Country between Us (Forché) **10**:136-38, 140, 143-46, 148, 150-53, 155, 157-59, 161, 165-66, 169
"A Country Burial" (Dickinson) **1**:79
"The Country Clergy" (Thomas) **99**:233, 245
"Country Cures" (Thomas) **99**:240
"The Country Fiddler" (Montague) **106**:291, 316, 328
"A Country Girl" (McKay) **2**:224
"A Country House" (Sarton) **39**:345
"A Country Life" (Jarrell) **41**:137, 139, 153-54, 168, 175
"Country Life" (Philips) **40**:269
"A Country Life: To His Brother, Master Thomas Herrick" (Herrick) **9**:86, 110-13, 115
"The Country Life, to the Honoured Master Endimion Porter, Groome of the Bed-Chamber to His Majesty" (Herrick) **9**:101, 139, 144
"Country Lover" (Angelou) **32**:15
"Country Lunch" (Simic) **69**:280
The Country Muse Revived (Vaughan)
See *Thalia Rediviva: The Pass-Times and Diversions of a Countrey-Muse, in Choice Poems on Several Occasions. With Some Learned Remains of the Eminent Eugenius Philalethes. Never Made Publick Till Now*
The Country of a Thousand Years of Peace and Other Poems (Merrill) **28**:220, 225, 228-29, 231, 234, 238-42, 244, 246-47, 259
"Country of Marriage" (Berry) **28**:11-13, 44
The Country of Marriage (Berry) **28**:7, 13
The Country of Two Mists (Clarke) **112**:29
"Country Places" (Hope) **56**:277
The Country Scene (Masefield) **78**:56, 97, 99-100
"Country School" (Curnow) **48**:29
Country Sentiment (Graves) **6**:127, 129, 132
"The Country Squire and the Mandrake" (Smart) **13**:348
"Country Stars" (Meredith) **28**:180, 192
"Country Town" (Wright) **14**:350
"A Country Walk" (Kinsella) **69**:69-70, 76, 80, 84, 86-87, 89, 95
"The Country Was" (Jarrell) **41**:184
"The Country Whore" (Pavese)
See "La puttana contadina"
"The Countryless: Refugees of Science" (Winters) **82**:338, 340
"The Countryman" (Stevens) **110**:163
"The Countryman's Return" (Thomas) **52**:263
"The Countryside" (Pushkin)
See "Derevnya"
"County" (Betjeman) **75**:33
"The County Ball" (Patmore) **59**:230-31, 233, 260
"County Ward" (Soto) **28**:370, 376-77
"Le Coup de couteau du soleil dans le dos des villes surprises" (Césaire) **25**:30
Un coup de dés jamais n'abolira le hasard (Mallarmé) **4**:192, 199, 202-03, 208-09, 217-18; **102**:12, 40-41, 45, 51, 62-63, 71-72, 87-89, 91-92, 98, 101, 124, 135
"Coup d'evential..." (Apollinaire) **7**:34-5
"The Couple" (Cassian) **17**:11
"Courage" (Akhmatova)
See "Muzhestvo"
"Courage" (Randall) **86**:339-40
"Courage Means Running" (Empson) **104**:85, 117
"The Courage of Shutting Up" (Plath) **37**:255
"La courbe de tes yeux" (Éluard) **38**:71, 101, 104-7
"The Couriers" (Plath) **37**:258
"Courmayeur" (Carducci) **46**:49
Cours naturel (Éluard) **38**:68
"The Course of a Particular" (Stevens) **110**:205
"The Course of True Love" (Patmore) **59**:230, 233
Court Poems (Montagu) **16**:338
"A Courtesy" (Wylie) **23**:322
"The Courtin'" (Holmes) **71**:85
"The Courts" (Meynell) **112**:154, 232, 303
"Courtship" (Dove) **6**:112
The Courtship of Miles Standish (Longfellow) **30**:16, 21, 24-5, 35, 39, 44, 59, 61, 65, 74, 79-82, 84-8, 99
"The Courtship of the Yonghy Bonghy Bo" (Lear) **65**:149, 155-56, 165
"Courtyard in Winter" (Montague) **106**:280
"A Courtyard Thaw" (Wilbur) **51**:187, 208, 220
"Courtyards in Delft" (Mahon) **60**:146, 148, 156, 161, 175-76, 190-92, 200-202, 211, 213, 219-20
Courtyards in Delft (Mahon) **60**:148, 161
"Cousin Kate" (Rossetti) **7**:270, 276, 280, 289, 291
"Cousin Sidney" (Abse) **41**:22
"Couteaux midi" (Césaire) **25**:37
"The Cove" (Clampitt) **19**:83
"The Covenant" (Muir) **49**:245-46, 249-50, 292
"Covenant" (Thomas) **99**:292
Covent Garden Drolery (Behn) **88**:69-71, 75, 106, 163
"Cover Her Face" (Kinsella) **69**:83, 103
"Cover Me Over" (Eberhart) **76**:49
"Covered Bridge" (Warren) **37**:376
"Covering the Massacre" (Kennedy) **93**:153
"Coversation" (Tagore)
See "Sambhashan"
"The Cow" (Nash) **21**:278
"The Cow" (Stevenson) **84**:316, 343
"The Cow in Apple Time" (Frost) **1**:195, 197
The Cow Jumped over the Moon (Birney) **52**:97
"The Coward" (Spender) **71**:138, 147, 202-3, 226
"Cowley Rider" (Masters) **1**:334
"Cowper's Grave" (Barrett Browning) **6**:6, 21
"Cows: A Vision" (Gallagher) **9**:36
"The Cows at Night" (Carruth) **10**:85
"The Coy Mistress" (Marvell)
See "To His Coy Mistress"
"The Coy-Dogs" (Jacobsen) **62**:333
"The Coyote in the Zoo" (Stafford) **71**:334
"Crab" (Brathwaite) **56**:61
"Crab Orchard Sanctuary: Late October" (Kinsella) **69**:72
"Crab-Angel" (Loy) **16**:307
"The Crack" (Levertov) **11**:159
"The Cracked Bell" (Baudelaire)
See "La cloche fêlée"
"cracked walls" (Alurista)
See "grietas paredes"
"The Crack-up of American Optimism" (Viereck) **27**:284
"Cradle" (Whitman)
See "Out of the Cradle Endlessly Rocking"
"A Cradle Song" (Blake) **12**:7, 10, 33; **63**:9-10, 25, 30, 33-34, 68, 90, 92, 102, 112, 120, 128
"A Cradle Song" (Yeats) **20**:337
"Cradle Song at Twilight" (Meynell) **112**:183, 185-86, 222, 299
"Cradle Song for Eleanor" (MacNeice) **61**:139, 160
"Cradle Song for Miriam" (MacNeice) **61**:128
"Craft" (Ciardi) **69**:53
Craft (Tsvetaeva)
See *Remeslo*
"A Craftsman of Bowls" (Cavafy)
See "A Craftsman of Wine Bowls"
"A Craftsman of Wine Bowls" (Cavafy) **36**:34, 106
Craftsmanship (Tsvetaeva)
See *Remeslo*
"Crag Jack's Apostasy" (Hughes) **7**:147; **89**:140
"Craigvara House" (Mahon) **60**:193
"Cramped in That Funnelled Hole" (Owen) **19**:336; **102**:225
Cranial Guitar (Kaufman) **74**:236, 238-39, 249-50, 252-54
"Crannog" (Montague) **106**:320, 328
"Cranston Near the City Line" (Berrigan) **103**:3, 35-36, 38
"Crash at Leithfield" (Curnow) **48**:29
"Crass Times" (Viereck) **27**:278, 281

"Crass Times Redeemed by Dignity of Souls" (Viereck) **27**:258-60, 273
"The Crate" (Ponge)
See "Le cageot"
"La cravate et la montre" (Apollinaire) **7**:32, 34-5
"Craving for Spring" (Lawrence) **54**:214
"Crazy About Her Shrimp" (Simic) **69**:338
"Crazy Carlson's Meadow" (Bly) **39**:67, 100
"Crazy Dream" (Silverstein) **49**:342
"Crazy Horse names his daughter" (Clifton) **17**:25
"Crazy Jane" (Day Lewis) **11**:151
"Crazy Jane and Jack the Journeyman" (Yeats) **20**:328
"Crazy Jane Talks with the Bishop" (Yeats) **20**:327-28
"A Crazy Spiritual" (Ginsberg) **4**:79
"Crazy Weather" (Ashbery) **26**:153
"The Created" (Very) **86**:135
"Created and Abandoned" (Spark) **72**:255, 264
"Creating the World" (Milosz) **8**:214
"creation" (Clifton) **17**:37
"The Creation" (Gibran) **9**:73
"The Creation" (Johnson) **24**:128-29, 133, 139, 143-44, 149, 152-53, 156, 164, 166-69
Creation (Noyes) **27**:138
"The Creation" (Very) **86**:138
"The Creation, according to Coyote" (Ortiz) **17**:231
"Creation Morning" (Kennedy) **93**:142, 149
"Creation Myth" (Berry) **28**:9
"Creation of Anguish" (Nemerov) **24**:261, 285
"Creation-Annihilation" (Wright) **14**:375
The Creative Writer (Birney) **52**:19, 47, 76, 78, 80, 82
"creative writing class" (Bukowski) **18**:19
"The Creator" (Douglas) **106**:186
"Creature" (Berrigan) **103**:26
"Creatures" (Jacobsen) **62**:309
"Creatures" (Kumin) **15**:182
"Creatures in the Dawn" (Aleixandre)
See "Criaturas de la Aurora"
"Crecen altas las flores" (Guillén) **23**:126
"Credat Judaeus" (Kipling) **3**:194
"Credences of Summer" (Ashbery) **26**:153
"Credences of Summer" (Stevens) **6**:306, 335, 338; **110**:173, 190, 193-94, 216, 227-29
"The Creditor" (MacNeice) **61**:132
"Credo" (Jeffers) **17**:117, 129
"Credo" (Kumin) **15**:213, 215-16, 224
"Credo" (Mistral) **32**:174
"Credo" (Robinson) **1**:485-86
"Credo" (Snodgrass) **74**:328
"Credo" (Stryk) **27**:198
"Credo Adoration" (Wagoner) **33**:372
"Credo in Intellectum Videntem" (Tate) **50**:256
"Credo in unam" (Rimbaud) **57**:255
"Creed" (Mistral)
See "Credo"
"Creed" (Spencer) **77**:328, 330, 332, 334, 341, 343
"Creeley" (Birney) **52**:29
"Cremation" (Thumboo) **30**:321-22
"The Cremation of Sam McGee" (Service) **70**:116, 124-26, 152, 158, 160-61, 164-65
"The Cremona Violin" (Lowell) **13**:60, 77, 96
"Crêpe de Chine" (Doty) **53**:72
"Crepuscolo di sabbiatori" (Pavese) **13**:226
Crepúsculario (Neruda) **4**:276, 278
"Crépuscule" (Apollinaire) **7**:40
"Le Crépuscule" (Baudelaire) **106**:88-89
"Crépuscule" (Hugo) **17**:67, 81-82
"Le crépuscule du soir" (Baudelaire) **1**:58-9
"Crepuscule with Nellie" (Simic) **69**:278
"The Crescent Moon" (Yakamochi) **48**:105
"Crescent Moon like a Canoe" (Piercy) **29**:323
Cresseid (Henryson)
See *The Testament of Cresseid*
"Crest and Gulf" (Patmore) **59**:262
Le Creux de la vallée (Sainte-Beuve) **110**:38-39
"The Crevasse" (Tsvetaeva)
See "Rasshchelina"
"Crevasses" (Césaire) **25**:33
"Crèvecoeur" (Niedecker) **42**:95, 100, 104, 109
"La Crevette dans tous ses états" (Ponge) **107**:129, 161
"La Crevette exagérée" (Ponge) **107**:73-74
"The Crew of the Chelyuskin" (Tsvetaeva)
See "Chelyuskintsy"
"Le cri de l'âme" (Lamartine) **16**:266
"Criaturas de la Aurora" (Aleixandre) **15**:6, 15, 38
The Cricket (Tuckerman)
See *Frederick Goddard Tuckerman: The Cricket, Printed from His Notebooks with Permission of His Granddaughter Margaret Tuckerman Clark*
"Cricket Master" (Betjeman) **75**:25, 58
"The Crime" (Corso) **108**:21
"Crime" (Warren) **37**:284, 288-89, 323, 332-33
"Crime of Love" (Verlaine)
See *Crimen Amoris*
Crimean Sonnets (Mickiewicz)
See *Sonety Krymskie*
Crimen Amoris (Verlaine) **32**:369, 370-71, 396
The Criminal (Lermontov) **18**:299
"The Crimson Cyclamen" (Williams) **7**:350, 354
"Criollo You Lived Prohibition" (Alurista) **34**:28
"The Cripple" (Ai) **72**:29
"Cripple" (Sandburg) **41**:243
"Cripples and Other Stories" (Sexton) **2**:363, 365; **79**:204
"Crise de vers" (Mallarmé) **102**:21, 27, 33, 81, 83, 108, 115, 128
"The Crisis" (Creeley) **73**:5, 7
"The Crisis" (Wagoner) **33**:369
"The Crisis" (Whittier) **93**:209
"Crispus Attucks McKoy" (Brown) **55**:82-83, 120, 122
"Le Cristal automatique" (Césaire) **25**:20
"Cristal et fumée" (Jaccottet) **98**:201
Cristal et fumée (Jaccottet) **98**:201
"The Critiad" (Winters) **82**:345
"The Critic" (O'Hara) **45**:224
"The Critic and the Writer of Fables" (Finch) **21**:163
A Critical Fable (Lowell) **13**:65, 74-6
"Critical Observations" (MacLeish) **47**:145, 164
"Critics and Connoisseurs" (Moore) **4**:232, 257, 270; **49**:98, 112-13, 116, 127
"Critics on the Lawn" (MacLeish) **47**:197
"Critique de la poésie" (Éluard) **38**:68
"De Critters' Dance" (Dunbar) **5**:145
"Crocidiles" (Reed) **68**:330
"La Crocifissione" (Pasolini) **17**:265
"The Crocodile" (Carroll) **74**:29
"Croesus" (Char) **56**:129
"Croesus in Autumn" (Warren) **37**:319, 331, 333
"Croft" (Smith) **12**:333
"A la croix" (Lamartine) **16**:284
"Croma" (Macpherson) **97**:248, 319
"Crón Tráth na nDéithe" (Melville) **82**:9, 12, 29, 37, 44
"Crone Rhapsody" (Koch) **80**:301
Cronica tripertita (Gower) **59**:25-26, 32-33, 113
"The Crooked Stick" (Wylie) **23**:301
"Croon" (Hughes) **53**:161
"Crootey Songo" (Kaufman) **74**:212, 216, 246-47
"Croquis parisien" (Verlaine) **32**:375-76, 387-88
"Cross" (Hughes) **1**:235, 243, 263-64; **53**:85, 126, 143
"The Cross" (Tate) **50**:231, 243, 255, 257, 306
"The Cross of Snow" (Longfellow) **30**:21, 27, 51
"The Cross Spider" (Swenson) **14**:273
"Cross Ties" (Kennedy) **93**:138-41, 143, 147, 149
Cross Ties (Kennedy) **93**:143-44, 147-50, 152
"The Crosse" (Donne) **1**:136; **43**:155
"The Crosse" (Herbert) **4**:111
"The Crossed Apple" (Bogan) **12**:101, 110-11
"Crosses of Harmony and Disharmony" (Duncan) **75**:124
"Crossing" (Brown) **55**:176
"Crossing" (MacLeish) **47**:164, 214
"Crossing Aguadilla" (Tomlinson) **17**:361
"Crossing alone the nighted ferry" (Housman) **43**:245
"Crossing Brooklyn Ferry" (Sexton) **2**:361
"Crossing Brooklyn Ferry" (Tomlinson) **17**:337
"Crossing Brooklyn Ferry" (Whitman) **3**:377, 379, 391-93, 399-400, 410, 415; **91**:207
"The Crossing of the Removed" (Merwin) **45**:46
"Crossing Our Campground" (Stafford) **71**:375
"Crossing Over" (Meredith) **28**:200
"Crossing the Atlantic" (Sexton) **2**:363
"Crossing the Bar" (Tennyson) **6**:359
"Crossing the Desert" (Stafford) **71**:317, 336
"Crossing the Frontier" (Hope) **56**:278, 285-86
"Crossing the River" (Brathwaite) **56**:7, 85
"Crossing the Swamp" (Oliver) **75**:288
"Crossing the Tropics" (Melville) **82**:142
"Crossing the Tuscan Maremma" (Carducci)
See "Traversando la Maremma Toscana"
Crossing the Water: Transitional Poems (Plath) **1**:391, 394, 396, 404; **37**:190-91
"Crossing the Yellow River to Ch'ing-ho" (Wang Wei) **18**:362, 366-68, 373
"Crossings" (Hogan) **35**:259, 277
"Crossroads" (Gunn) **26**:214
"The Cross-Roads" (Lowell) **13**:60, 76-7
"Crotchets" (Nemerov) **24**:290
"Le Crotin" (Ponge) **107**:102
"Crow" (Cervantes) **35**:105
"The Crow" (Creeley) **73**:7
"Crow" (Oliver) **75**:334
Crow (Hughes)
See *Crow: From the Life and Songs of the Crow*
"Crow Alights" (Hughes) **7**:130; **89**:155
"Crow and Mama" (Hughes) **7**:132; **89**:141
"Crow and the Birds" (Hughes) **7**:159
The Crow and the Heart (Carruth) **10**:70, 78, 89
"Crow and the Sea" (Hughes) **7**:144
"Crow Blacker Than Ever" (Hughes) **7**:138
"Crow Communes" (Hughes) **7**:143
Crow: From the Life and Songs of the Crow (Hughes) **7**:129-30, 133, 137-43, 145, 152-53, 155-61, 163, 168-71; **89**:101, 114-15, 119, 121, 131, 134, 137-38, 140-42, 144-45, 150, 155, 157, 159-61, 188, 193-94, 199, 216, 228, 232-34
"Crow Frowns" (Hughes) **7**:159
"Crow Goes Hunting" (Hughes) **7**:142, 160-61
"Crow Hill" (Hughes) **7**:131, 150; **89**:150-51
"Crow Hill" (O'Hara) **45**:142
"Crow Jane in High Society" (Baraka) **4**:16
"Crow Jane in High Society" (Baraka) **113**:11
"Crow Jane" sequence (Baraka) **113**:47-48, 52, 63
"Crow Jane's Manner" (Baraka) **113**:11, 49
"Crow on a Withered Branch" (Matsuo Basho) **3**:32
"Crow on the Beach" (Hughes) **7**:138, 144
"Crow Sickened" (Hughes) **7**:138
"Crow Song" (Atwood) **8**:25
"The Crowd" (Masefield) **78**:90
crowd and not evening or light (Scalapino) **114**:275, 283, 288, 319
"The Crowded Countries of the Bomb" (Oppen) **35**:293, 298
"The Crowded Street" (Bryant) **20**:5, 36
"A Crowded Trolley Car" (Wylie) **23**:309, 328, 332
"Crowdieknowe" (MacDiarmid) **9**:156
"Crowds" (Baudelaire)
See "Les foules"

"The Crowds for Communion" (Montague) **106**:257-59, 261
"Crowing-Hen Blues" (Hughes) **1**:256
"The Crown of Bays" (Smith) **12**:319
"The Crown of Gold" (Smith) **12**:295, 315
"Crown of Thorns" (Celan)
See "Dornenkranz"
"Crowned Out" (Celan) **10**:113
Crowned with Dreams (Rilke) **2**:280
"Crowns and Garlands" (Hughes) **1**:252; **53**:115
"Crows" (Rimbaud)
See "Les Corbeaux"
"Crow's Account of St. George" (Hughes) **7**:161, 171; **89**:141
"Crow's Account of the Battle" (Hughes) **7**:133, 144, 152
"Crow's Battle Fury" (Hughes) **7**:143
"Crow's Elephant Totem Song" (Hughes) **7**:138, 144
"Crow's First Lesson" (Hughes) **89**:141, 199
"The Crows kep' flyin' up, boys" (Gilmore) **87**:294-98
"Crow's Last Stand" (Hughes) **7**:123, 144
"Crow's Nerve Fails" (Hughes) **7**:144
"Crow's Nests" (Wilbur) **51**:335
"Crows on the North Slope" (Merwin) **45**:20
"Crow's Playmates" (Hughes) **7**:144
"Crow's Song about England" (Hughes) **89**:142-44
"Crow's Theology" (Hughes) **7**:159, 161
"Crow's Undersong" (Hughes) **7**:167; **89**:142, 144, 150
"Crow's Vanity" (Hughes) **7**:144
"Croydon" (Betjeman) **75**:106
"La Cruche" (Ponge) **107**:104, 184
"Crucibles of Love" (Graves) **6**:172
"Le crucifix" (Lamartine) **16**:278
Crucifix in a Deathhand: New Poems, 1963-1965 (Bukowski) **18**:21
"The Crucifix in the Filing Cabinet" (Shapiro) **25**:286, 290, 300
"Crucifixion" (Akhmatova)
See "Raspiatie"
"The Crucifixion" (Akhmatova)
See "Raspiatie"
"Crucifixión" (García Lorca) **3**:140
"The Crucifixion" (Johnson) **24**:128, 144, 156, 165, 169
"Crucifixion on Thursday" (Wright) **36**:335, 337
"The Cruel Falcon" (Jeffers) **17**:117, 120
"The Cruel Lover" (Wickham) **110**:268
"The Cruell Maid" (Herrick) **9**:101
Cruelty (Ai) **72**:3, 5-6, 9, 21, 28
"Cruelty and Love" (Lawrence) **54**:236-37
"The Cruise" (Merrill) **28**:239, 241
"Cruisers" (Kipling) **91**:86
"Cruising 99" (Hongo) **23**:196-98
"Crumble-Hall" (Leapor) **85**:201-2, 204, 215-17, 222, 224-29, 238, 241, 251, 268-69, 277, 285, 287-89
"Crumbs or the Loaf" (Jeffers) **17**:130
"Crusade" (Warren) **37**:318
"Crusades of Silence" (Césaire) **25**:18
Crusoé (Perse) **23**:231
"Crusoe in England" (Bishop) **3**:48, 63-4, 66-7, 70; **34**:54, 74, 80, 82, 97, 104, 121, 146
"Crusoe's Island" (Walcott) **46**:231, 274, 280, 283-84
"Crusoe's Journal" (Walcott) **46**:231, 238, 274, 280, 283-84
"La cruz" (Parra) **39**:288
"The Cry" (Levertov) **11**:198
"The Cry" (Masters) **1**:326
"The Cry" (Thomas) **99**:234
"Cry Ararat!" (Page) **12**:168, 190, 198
Cry Ararat! Poems New and Selected (Page) **12**:167, 179, 184, 190, 197
"Cry Faugh" (Graves) **6**:135
"The Cry of Midnight" (Patmore) **59**:277
"The Cry of the Children" (Barrett Browning) **6**:6, 17, 21, 27, 30, 42
"The Cry of the Human" (Barrett Browning) **6**:7, 21
"Cry to Rome: From the Chrysler Building Tower" (García Lorca) **3**:141
"Crying" (Kinnell) **26**:260
"Cryptic Version of Ecstasy" (Bell) **79**:35
"The Crystal" (Aiken) **26**:29-30, 45
"The Crystal" (Barker) **77**:5, 44
"The Crystal" (Lanier) **50**:51
"The Crystal Cabinet" (Blake) **12**:36
"Crystal Gazer" (Plath) **37**:208
"The Crystal Gazer" (Teasdale) **31**:323, 371-72, 379, 389
"The Crystal Lithium" (Schuyler) **88**:186, 189, 192, 198, 201, 225
The Crystal Lithium (Schuyler) **88**:189, 194, 201
"The Crystal Sun" (Winters) **82**:312-15, 335-37, 339
"Crystals Like Blood" (MacDiarmid) **9**:187
Cuaderno San Martín (Borges) **22**:71, 73, 93-4; **32**:38, 84, 95, 109
"Cuadros y angulos" (Storni) **33**:247, 250, 275
"a cualquier hora" (Alurista) **34**:33
"Cualquier tiempo pasado fue peor" (Guillén) **23**:126
"Cuando entre la sombra oscura" (Bécquer)
See "Rima 28"
"Cuando la cucaracha camine" (Alurista) **34**:24
"Las cuatro calles" (Guillén) **35**:157, 188
"Los cuatro ciclos" (Borges) **32**:65
"Cuba, 1962" (Ai) **72**:4, 6
"La Cucaracha" (Alurista) **34**:10, 46
"Cucarachas in paradise" (Birney) **52**:37
"Cuchualain" (Day Lewis) **11**:151
"The Cuckold's Song" (Cohen) **109**:4, 18
"Cuckoo" (Wagoner) **33**:356
"Cuckoo Song" (H. D.) **5**:267
"The Cuckoo-clock" (Wordsworth) **67**:328
"The Cuckoo's Path" (Cernuda)
See "Vereda del cuco"
"Cudjoe Fresh from de Lecture" (McKay) **2**:224, 226
La cueca larga (Parra) **39**:260, 270, 272, 277, 279, 286-87, 292, 300, 303
La cueca larga y otros poemas (Parra)
See *La cueca larga*
"La cuenta-mundo" (Mistral) **32**:161, 166
"Cuento de dos jardines" (Paz) **1**:361, 363; **48**:191, 207-8, 210, 264
"Cuerpo en pena" (Cernuda) **62**:230
"The Cuirassiers of the Frontier" (Graves) **6**:133
Cuisine Bourgeoise (Stevens) **110**:149-50, 153
"The Culprit" (Housman) **2**:162, 164, 169, 179, 186
"The Cultivated Rose" (Owen) **102**:152
"The Cultivation of Philosophy" (Herbert)
See "Uprawa filozofii"
"Cultural Directives" (Szirtes) **51**:163
"Cultural Exchange" (Hughes) **1**:250, 252
"Cultural Exchange" (Kenyon) **57**:45
"Cultural Exchanges" (Hacker) **47**:113
"Cultural Freedom" (Enright) **93**:21
"Culture and Anarchy" (Rich) **5**:386
"The Culture-Hug Blues" (Viereck) **27**:279
"cum cum cum cumly witchcraft i know you care" (Bissett) **14**:34
"Cum Ratione Insanire" (Cowper) **40**:102-3
"The Cumberland" (Melville) **82**:204, 270
"La cumbre" (Guillén) **35**:188
Cuna, rosas, balcón (Guillén) **35**:159
"The Cup" (Wright) **14**:347
Cup of Blizzards (Bely)
See *Kubok metelej: Chetviortiia simfoniia*
"Cup of Jamshid" (Hafiz) **116**:15
"The Cup of Paint" (Lindsay) **23**:286
The Cup of Snowstorms (Bely)
See *Kubok metelej: Chetviortiia simfoniia*
"Cupid and Ganymede" (Prior) **102**:313
"Cupid and Psyche" (Elytis) **21**:135
"Cupid and Psyche" (Morris) **55**:306
"Cur secessisti?" (Char) **56**:151
"Curacao" (Birney) **52**:22
"Curatia Dionisia" (Herbert) **50**:9
"The Cure" (Graves) **6**:155
"The Cure" (Thomas) **99**:235
"A Cure at Porlock" (Clampitt) **19**:87
"A Cure of Souls" (Levertov) **11**:171
"Curettage" (Benn) **35**:4, 8
"A Curfew" (Clampitt) **19**:91
"Curfew" (Yamada) **44**:341
"A Curious Man's Dream" (Baudelaire)
See "Le rêve d'un curieux"
Curious Poems on Several Occasions (Duck)
See *Poems on Several Subjects*
"Curl Up and Diet" (Nash) **21**:265
"Curlews Lift" (Hughes) **89**:121
"Curly Ivy" (Stern) **115**:249
"Currency" (Koch) **80**:326-27, 340
"The Current" (Berry) **28**:14-15
"The Current" (Merwin) **45**:34, 48, 86, 100
"The Current" (Montague) **106**:328
"The Currents" (Duncan) **75**:216-17
"Curriculum Vitae" (Mueller) **33**:195
"The Curse" (Berryman) **64**:83
"The Curse" (Clarke) **112**:83
"The Curse" (Millay) **6**:211
"A Curse" (Snodgrass) **74**:332
"A Curse against Elegies" (Sexton) **2**:351
"A Curse for a Nation" (Barrett Browning) **6**:27
"The Curse of Cromwell" (Yeats) **20**:326
The Curse of Kehama (Southey) **111**:177, 199, 202, 214, 219-20, 225, 254, 276, 279
"The Curse of the Charter-Breakers" (Whittier) **93**:336
"The Curse of the Wandering Foot" (Riley) **48**:303
"Curtain" (Dunbar) **5**:119
"The Curtain" (Wright) **14**:355
"Curtains" (Cisneros) **52**:157, 160
"Curtains" (Stone) **53**:230, 238, 251
"The Curve" (Levertov) **11**:176
"The curve of your eyes" (Éluard)
See "La courbe de tes yeux"
"Cushenden" (MacNeice) **61**:108
"Cusín and Tata" (Espada) **74**:124-25
"The Custard Sellers" (Schuyler) **88**:200
"Custer Speaks" (Alexie) **53**:4
"Custodian" (Kumin) **15**:223
The Customs House and Other Verses (Montale)
See *La casa dei doganieri e altri versi*
"The Customs-Officer's House" (Montale)
See "La casa dei doganieri"
"Cut" (Plath) **1**:385, 392; **37**:232, 257
"A Cutlet" (Stein) **18**:349
"Cutting Down a Tree" (Wagoner) **33**:352
"The Cutting Edge" (Levine) **22**:215
"Cutting the Grapes Free" (Piercy) **29**:312
"Cuttings" (Roethke) **15**:291, 296-98, 312
"Cuttings (Later)" (Roethke) **15**:260, 297-98, 302, 312, 314
Cuttlefish Bones (Montale)
See *Ossi di seppia*
"Cutty Sark" (Crane) **3**:84, 90, 106
"Cutworm" (Wagoner) **33**:356
"Cuzoe remeslo" (Akhmadulina) **43**:3, 65
"Cybernetics" (Nemerov) **24**:261, 282-83, 301
"The Cycads" (Wright) **14**:346
"The Cyclads" (Aiken) **26**:36
"The Cyclamen" (Amichai) **38**:15
The Cycle (Dorn) **115**:87, 94, 96-98, 153, 157, 167-68, 207
"The Cycle" (Dorn) **115**:76, 115, 132, 174-75, 177-78, 191-92
"The Cycle" (Jeffers) **17**:141
"The Cycle" (Roethke) **15**:265
"Cycle of Six Lyrics" (Barker) **77**:14
"The Cyclical Night" (Borges)
See "La noche cíclica"
"Cyclops" (Shelley) **14**:227
"Le Cye" (Scève) **111**:5
"Le cygne" (Baudelaire) **1**:45, 66, 71; **106**:13-15, 17, 19, 81, 101, 124, 136-38, 149

"Cyngor y Biogen" (Dafydd ap Gwilym) **56**:210
"Cynthia" (Shvarts) **50**:141, 160
Cynthia (Raleigh)
See *The Ocean to Cynthia*
"Cyparissus" (Duncan) **2**:103
"Cypress Avenue" (Davie) **29**:110
"The Cypress Tree of Ceylon" (Whittier) **93**:222, 239
"Cypresses" (Francis) **34**:265
Cyprus, to which Apollo Assigned Me . . . (Seferis)
See *Kypron, hou m'ethespisen . . .*
"Cyrano en España" (Darío) **15**:80
"Cyrano in Spain" (Darío)
See "Cyrano en España"
"Cyrchu Lleian" (Dafydd ap Gwilym) **56**:210-11
"Cystudd Cariad" (Dafydd ap Gwilym) **56**:247
"Cythere" (Verlaine) **32**:350
"Czaty" (Mickiewicz) **38**:212
"Czatyr Dagh" (Mickiewicz)
See "Czatyrdah"
"Czatyrdah" (Mickiewicz) **38**:221-23
Czeslaw Milosz: The Collected Poems, 1931-1987 (Milosz) **8**:190-91, 197-98, 202, 206-07, 213-15
"Czwarta nad ranem" (Szymborska) **44**:289
"D. R." (Zukofsky) **11**:351, 396
"D. Scarlatti" (Corso) **33**:41
"da Dittico e fistole" (Zanzotto) **65**:297, 299
"Da Ghène" (Zanzotto) **65**:302
"Da, ia lezhu v zemle . . ." (Mandelstam) **14**:151
"Da terra" (Castro) **41**:88
"Da una torre" (Montale) **13**:113
"Da un'altezza nuova" (Zanzotto) **65**:265, 275
"Dacnyj roman" (Akhmadulina) **43**:66
"Dada Zodji" (Baraka) **113**:17
"Daddy" (Plath) **1**:382-83, 386-87, 392-93, 395-97, 400-02, 406-07, 414; **37**:196-98, 200, 212, 216, 219-22, 227-29, 232-35, 243-44, 246-47, 255-56, 260, 268
"The Daddy Long-Legs and the Fly" (Lear) **65**:147, 149, 153, 156, 160
"'Daddy' Warbucks" (Sexton) **79**:241
"Daedalus" (Barker) **77**:5-6, 8, 28, 35, 38, 44
"Daedalus" (Sikelianos) **29**:365-66, 368, 370-71
"The Daemon" (Bogan) **12**:100, 110
The Daemon of the World (Shelley) **14**:185; **67**:184-85
The Daffodil Fields (Masefield) **78**:22, 30, 51, 54, 56, 58, 60, 63, 91
The Daffodil Murderer (Sassoon) **12**:252, 270, 274-77
"Daffodildo" (Swenson) **14**:277, 287
"Daffodils" (Hughes) **89**:162, 181, 191
"Daffy Duck in Hollywood" (Ashbery) **26**:153
"The dagger" (Borges)
See "El puñal"
"Dagrau Serch" (Dafydd ap Gwilym) **56**:245-46
"Daguerreotype Taken in Old Age" (Atwood) **8**:39
"Un dahlia" (Verlaine) **2**:431
"The Dahlia Gardens" (Clampitt) **19**:82, 90-1
"Dahomey" (Lorde) **12**:160
"Daily Commerce" (Cohen) **109**:70
"Daily Express" (Betjeman) **75**:69
"The Daily Globe" (Nemerov) **24**:278
The Daily Holidays (Cassian) **17**:6
"Daily News Report" (Randall) **86**:335
"Les daimons" (Ronsard) **11**:225, 279, 281-82
"The Daimyo's Pond" (Blunden) **66**:17-18
"The Dainty Monsters" (Ondaatje) **28**:292-93
The Dainty Monsters (Ondaatje) **28**:291-92, 294, 298-99, 318, 327, 331-32, 335
"The Dairyman's Child" (Melville) **82**:107, 152
"Daisies" (Carman) **34**:207
"Daisies Are Broken" (Williams) **7**:406
"Daisy" (Meynell)
See "To a Daisy"
"The Daisy" (Tennyson) **6**:357, 360; **101**:122, 125, 247
"Daisy Fraser" (Masters) **1**:334; **36**:182, 227
"Daisy-Cutter" (McGuckian) **27**:76, 103
"Daisy's Song" (Keats) **1**:311
"Dakar" (Borges) **32**:38
"Dakar Doldrums" (Ginsberg) **4**:72
"Dal ciel discese, e col mortal suo, poi" (Michelangelo) **103**:220, 318
"Dal cielo" (Zanzotto) **65**:273
"The Dale" (Lamartine)
See "Le vallon"
"Dalhousie Farm" (Meredith) **28**:181
"Dalla Sua Pace" (Hope) **56**:287
"Dalle rive del Balaton" (Quasimodo) **47**:289
"The Dalliance of the Eagles" (Whitman) **3**:397; **91**:207-8
"The Dam" (Rukeyser) **12**:210
Dam 'ah wabitisāmah (Gibran) **9**:73, 75, 77-8, 81
"Dam Neck, Virginia" (Eberhart) **76**:24, 58
"Damascus Blade" (Tolson) **88**:344
"Damastes (Also Known as Procrustes) Speaks" (Herbert)
See "Damastes z przydomkiem Prokustes mówi"
"Damastes z przydomkiem Prokustes mówi" (Herbert) **50**:16, 44
"Dame Myra Hess playing to the troops" (Masefield) **78**:89
"The Dame of Athelhall" (Hardy) **92**:219
"Dämmerung" (Celan) **10**:124-25
"Dämmerung" (Stramm) **50**:174-75, 194, 199, 209
"The Damnation of Byron" (Hope) **56**:266, 268, 289, 301, 303
The Damnation of Vancouver (Birney) **52**:21-22
"Damned" (Berryman) **64**:93, 95
Damned Album (Rimbaud)
See *Album zutique*
"Damned Women" (Baudelaire)
See "Femmes damnées"
"Damon and Strephon. A Pastoral Complaint" (Leapor) **85**:248
"Damon Being Asked a Reason for Loveing" (Behn) **13**:18
"Damon the Mower" (Marvell) **10**:266, 293, 295-97, 315
"The Dampe" (Donne) **1**:130
"Damson" (Heaney) **100**:305
"Dan y Bargod" (Dafydd ap Gwilym) **56**:225, 227-31, 233
"The Dance" (Baraka) **4**:16; **113**:10, 140
"Dance" (Cassian) **17**:13
"The Dance" (Crane) **3**:84, 86, 88, 90
"The Dance" (Curnow) **48**:29
"The Dance" (Larkin) **21**:259
"The Dance" (Patmore) **59**:233
"Dance" (Pavese)
See "Balletto"
"The Dance" (Roethke) **15**:266-67, 269, 273, 279
"The Dance" (Williams) **109**:300-301, 303-4
"The Dance at the Phoenix" (Hardy) **8**:99
"Dance in the Quenis Chalmer" (Dunbar) **67**:39, 82
"Dance: Nicaragua" (Jordan) **38**:127
"The Dance of Death" (Blok)
See "Danse macabre"
"Dance of Death" (García Lorca)
See "Danza de la muerte"
The Dance of Death (Auden) **1**:8
"The Dance of the Eunuchs" (Das) **43**:72
"Dance of the Girls' Chemises" (Seifert) **47**:324
"Dance of the Hanged" (Rimbaud)
See "Bal des pendus"
"Dance of the Macabre Mice" (Stevens) **6**:296
"Dance of the Sevin Deidly Synnis" (Dunbar) **67**:15, 17-18, 76-79, 81-82
"The Dance of the Solids" (Updike) **90**:355-56
"Dance on, dance on" (Clough) **103**:155
"Dance Suite, Inter Alia" (Snodgrass) **74**:330, 333, 335
"Dance the Orange" (Hayden) **6**:196
"The Dancer" (H. D.) **5**:305
"The Dancer" (Sachs)
See "Die Tänzerin"
"A Dancer's Life" (Justice) **64**:267
"The Dancers of the Field" (Carman) **34**:209
"Dances of Death" (Blok)
See "Danse macabre"
"Dancin' in the Rain" (Silverstein) **49**:342
"The Dancing" (Stern) **115**:293
"The Dancing Ape" (Spicer) **78**:302
The Dancing Bears (Merwin) **45**:3, 5-6, 8-11, 21, 24, 29, 90-92
Dancing David (Shvarts)
See *Tantsuiushchii David*
"Dancing Man" (Welch) **62**:346
"Dancing on the Grave of a Son of a Bitch" (Wakoski) **15**:346
Dancing on the Grave of a Son of a Bitch (Wakoski) **15**:336, 348, 365
"Dancing Pants" (Silverstein) **49**:347
"Danger" (Corso) **33**:26
"The Danger of Writing Defiant Verse" (Parker) **28**:350, 363
"A Dangerous Land" (Amichai) **38**:32-33
"Dangerous Thoughts" (Cavafy) **36**:79
"The Dangerous Year" (Berryman) **64**:84-85
"Dangers" (Cavafy) **36**:50
Dangers (McHugh) **61**:190, 196, 205
Dangling in the Tournefortia (Bukowski) **18**:15
"Daniel Bartoli" (Browning) **2**:84
"Daniel Grose" (Ní Chuilleanáin) **34**:369, 371
"The Daniel Jazz" (Lindsay) **23**:264, 270, 286
"Daniel Neall" (Whittier) **93**:314
"Die Dänin" (Benn) **35**:72
"A Danish Refuge" (Mahon) **60**:177
"Danny Deever" (Kipling) **3**:170-71, 179, 188-89, 191; **91**:97, 148-49, 152
"Dans la brume" (Éluard) **38**:71
"Dans la danse" (Éluard) **38**:70
"Dans la grotte" (Verlaine) **32**:349, 351, 391, 393
"Dans la marche" (Char) **56**:202
Dans la pluie giboyeuse (Char) **56**:138
"Dans le cylindre des tribulations" (Éluard) **38**:70
Dans le leurre du seuil (Bonnefoy) **58**:110, 113-14, 123, 137-40, 145, 150, 156-58, 161-62, 165-66, 168-70
"Dans le restaurant" (Eliot) **5**:185
"Dans ma péniche" (Cernuda) **62**:200
"Dans un tourbillion de neige" (Jaccottet) **98**:174
"Dansa di Narcís" (Pasolini) **17**:281
"Danse Africaine" (Hughes) **53**:83, 143
"Danse macabre" (Blok) **21**:6, 14, 20; **106**:6
"Danse russe" (Williams) **7**:353, 367, 408; **109**:264
"Dante" (Carducci) **46**:52, 76
"Dante at Verona" (Rossetti) **44**:167, 202
Dante at Verona and Other Poems (Rossetti) **44**:184-86, 200
"Dante Etudes" (Duncan) **75**:205, 232, 261
"Dante Études, Book Two" (Duncan) **2**:114-16, 127
Dante's Purgatory (Dante)
See *La divina commedia*
"Danza de la muerte" (García Lorca) **3**:121
"La danza del espiritu" (Cardenal) **22**:131
"Danza irregular" (Storni) **33**:283
"danza leonina" (Alurista) **34**:46
"Danzón porteño" (Storni) **33**:262, 296
"Daphnaida" (Spenser) **8**:365, 367
"Daphne" (Carman) **34**:208-09
"Daphne" (Meredith) **60**:244
"Daphne and Apollo" (Prior) **102**:313, 317
"Daphne Heard with Horror the Addresses of the God" (Boland) **58**:14, 33-35, 58, 88
"Daphne with Her Thighs in Bark" (Boland) **58**:14, 19, 45
"Daphnis. An Elegiac Eclogue" (Vaughan) **81**:363, 366
"Daphnis and Chloe" (Marvell) **10**:265, 271, 291-92, 301; **86**:241, 245, 262

"Daphnis et Thyrsis" (Ronsard) **105**:272
Dare e avere (Quasimodo) **47**:289
"Dareios" (Cavafy)
See "Darius"
"Darest Thou Now O Soul" (Whitman) **3**:378
"Darien" (Graves) **6**:137, 144, 168
"Dariu tebe siiu tetrad" (Akhmadulina) **43**:40
"Darius" (Cavafy) **36**:35, 43-49, 91, 93
"Darius" (Gower) **59**:58
"The Dark" (Stone) **53**:240-41, 255, 259
"The Dark and the Fair" (Kunitz) **19**:162, 169
"Dark August" (Walcott) **46**:236
"Dark Blood" (Walker) **20**:273, 282
"A Dark Brown Dog" (Crane) **80**:76
"Dark Ceiling" (Dorn) **115**:122, 156
"The Dark Château" (de la Mare) **77**:63, 71, 116
"A Dark Christmas Song" (Shvarts) **50**:134
"The Dark Cup" (Teasdale) **31**:358, 360
"Dark Dreadful Death" (Barker) **77**:4
"Dark Eye in September" (Celan) **10**:112
"Dark Farmhouses" (Simic) **69**:318
"The Dark Forest" (Thomas) **53**:297
"Dark Gift" (Wright) **14**:338, 353, 356
"Dark Girl's Rhyme" (Parker) **28**:356
Dark Harbor: A Poem (Strand) **63**:189, 193-94, 197-99
"The Dark Hills" (Robinson) **1**:468
Dark Horses: New Poems (Kennedy) **93**:133, 146, 150-52
The Dark Houses (Hall) **70**:26, 30-31, 34
"Dark Ireland" (Kavanagh) **33**:100; **105**:150
"Dark Night of the Soul" (Warren) **37**:348, 350
A Dark Octave (Waldrop) **109**:167
"Dark of the Moon" (Brown) **55**:73, 159
Dark of the Moon (Teasdale) **31**:327, 330, 333, 335, 338, 341, 347, 349, 370-72, 379-80, 389
The Dark One (Tagore)
See *Shyamali*
"The Dark Ones" (Wright) **14**:373
"Dark Prophecy: I Sing of Shine" (Knight) **14**:39
"Dark Rooms" (Montague) **106**:328
"Dark Satanic Mills" (Lawrence) **54**:249
"Dark Song" (Ammons) **16**:4
"Dark Song" (Sitwell) **3**:291
"Dark Spring" (Winters) **82**:314
Dark Summer (Bogan) **12**:87, 89, 105-06, 120-23
"Dark Symphony" (Tolson) **88**:329-30, 336-38, 343
"Dark thoughts are my companions" (Cunningham) **92**:149
"Dark Waters of the Beginning" (Okigbo) **7**:231
"The Dark Well" (Thomas) **99**:235
"Dark Wild Honey" (Swenson) **14**:276
Dark World (Carruth) **10**:71, 91
"Dark Youth of the U.S.A." (Hughes) **53**:114
Darkening Star (Sachs)
See *Sternverdunkelung*
Darker: Poems (Strand) **63**:139, 141-42, 145, 152, 159-60, 166, 169, 173-77, 191, 198
"Darkling Summer, Ominous Dusk, Rumorous Rain" (Schwartz) **8**:319
"The Darkling Thrush" (Hardy) **8**:98, 105-6, 121, 131; **92**:197, 228, 261, 319, 326
"Darkness" (Aleixandre) **15**:5
"Darkness" (Byron) **16**:86, 89
"Darkness" (Hughes) **89**:197
"Darkness and Light" (Spender) **71**:165-66, 187, 209-10, 229
"The Darkness and the Light Are Both Alike to Thee" (Hecht) **70**:108
The Darkness Around Us Is Deep (Stafford) **71**:364
"Darkness Chex George Whitman" (Ferlinghetti) **1**:183
"Darkness of Death" (Pasternak) **6**:253
"Darkwalking Endlessly" (Kaufman) **74**:181
"Darling! Because My Blood Can Sing" (Cummings) **5**:108
"Darling Daughters" (Smith) **12**:326
"Darling, It's Frightening! When a Poet Loves ..." (Pasternak) **6**:251
"Darling Room" (Tennyson) **6**:353
"Dar-thula" (Macpherson) **97**:181, 230, 246, 250, 264, 308
"Darwin" (Niedecker) **42**:95, 100, 104, 109
"Darwin in 1881" (Schnackenberg) **45**:329-30, 336, 338
"Dary Tereka" (Lermontov) **18**:268, 281, 290, 295
"Dash" (Spicer) **78**:294
"Dat Dirty Rum" (McKay) **2**:222
"Dat ol' Mare o' Mine" (Dunbar) **5**:134
"Date a volar" (Storni) **33**:251
"Date Lilia" (Hugo) **17**:94
"Dates" (Ondaatje) **28**:327, 331
"Dates: Penkhull New Road" (Tomlinson) **17**:347, 352
"Dative Haruspices" (Rexroth) **20**:215
Dauber (Masefield) **78**:6, 16, 21-22, 26, 32, 38, 51, 56, 58, 60, 63, 89, 92, 105-6
"Daughter" (Berssenbrugge) **115**:29-31
"Daughter" (Dickey) **40**:256
"A Daughter I" (Levertov) **11**:209
"A Daughter II" (Levertov) **11**:209
"Daughter Moon" (Wakoski) **15**:366
"The daughter of Menkera" (Cavafy) **36**:53
"The Daughter of the Forest" (Gibran)
See "Amām 'arsh al-jamāl"
"Daughter of the Horse-Leech" (Wickham) **110**:271
"A Daughter Returns" (Hardy) **92**:246
"Daughter to Archeologist" (Jacobsen) **62**:320
Daughters, I Love You (Hogan) **35**:247, 252
"Daughters of Colony" (Boland) **58**:40, 62
Daughters of Dawn (Carman) **34**:205, 212
Daughters of Fire (Nerval)
See *Les filles du feu*
"D'autres amants ont eu, dans leur marche amoureuse" (Sainte-Beuve) **110**:49
"Davanti ad una Cattedrale" (Carducci) **46**:23, 60
"Davanti al simulacro d'Illaria del Carretto" (Quasimodo) **47**:280
"Davanti il castel vecchio di Verona" (Carducci) **46**:52
"Davanti San Guido" (Carducci) **46**:50, 57-58, 65, 79-80
"David" (Birney) **52**:3-5, 7-8, 11, 21, 25, 27, 31, 34-35, 44-47, 58, 62, 65-66, 79, 102-3
"David" (Pasolini) **17**:252, 281
"David and Bathsheba in the Public Garden" (Lowell) **3**:205-06, 215
David and Goliah (Drayton) **98**:46-47, 49
David and Other Poems (Birney) **52**:3-4, 6, 11, 26, 43, 45, 58
David Archer (Barker)
See *In Memory of David Archer*
Davideis (Cowley) **90**:8-9, 19-23, 38-41, 45, 55, 61, 70, 73-75, 82, 84-87, 89-90, 98, 114, 118, 127-32, 152-53, 156, 158-61, 164-65, 169-76, 179, 188-94, 196-97
"David's Lamentation for Saul and Jonathan" (Bradstreet) **10**:6
"David's Night at Veliès" (Merrill) **28**:220
"David's Peccavi" (Southwell) **83**:240
"Davis Matlock" (Masters) **36**:184
"Davy Jones' Door-Bell" (Lindsay) **23**:264
"Dawlish Fair" (Keats) **1**:311
"Dawn" (Akhmadulina) **43**:55
"Dawn" (Borges)
See "Amanecer"
"Dawn" (Brathwaite) **56**:100
"Dawn" (Brooke) **24**:53, 64, 82
"Dawn" (Dunbar) **5**:125, 128
"Dawn" (García Lorca)
See "La aurora"
"Dawn" (Heaney) **100**:206
"Dawn" (Herbert)
See "Swit"
"Dawn" (de la Mare) **77**:94
"Dawn" (Paz) **48**:180, 274
"Dawn" (Rimbaud)
See "Aube"
"Dawn" (Teasdale) **31**:331
"Dawn" (Thumboo) **30**:301
"Dawn Adventure" (Lowell) **13**:63
"Dawn after Storm" (Zukofsky) **11**:368
"Dawn Bombardment" (Graves) **6**:144
The Dawn Breakers: Les Matinaux (Char)
See *Les matinaux*
"Dawn Chorus" (Mahon) **60**:148
"Dawn Eyed Cosmos" (Alurista) **34**:42
"Dawn near an Old Battlefield, in a Time of Peace" (Wright) **36**:378
"The Dawn of the Tired Man" (Guillén) **35**:217, 218
"Dawn on the Warm Springs Reservation" (Stafford) **71**:340
"The Dawn Wind" (Kipling) **3**:183
"Dawn Wind Unlocks the River Sky" (Chappell) **105**:26, 43-44
"Dawnbreaker" (Hayden) **6**:198
"The Dawning" (Herbert) **4**:102
"The Dawning" (Vaughan) **81**:306, 313
Dawn's Eye (Alurista) **34**:15-16, 21-22, 26-29, 31
"Dawn's Rose" (Hughes) **7**:138, 144, 159
"Day" (Ammons) **16**:12
"The Day" (Muir) **49**:245-46, 248, 290
"The Day After" (Soto) **28**:302
"Day after Chasing Porcupines" (Welch) **62**:374
Day after Day (Quasimodo)
See *Giorno dopo giorno*
"Day after Halloween" (Silverstein) **49**:334
"The Day after To-Morrow" (Patmore) **59**:208
"Day and Night" (Montale)
See "Giorno e notte"
"Day and Night" (Muir) **49**:217
"The Day before the Last Day" (Muir) **49**:257
"The Day Before the St. Petersburg Flood of 1824" (Mickiewicz)
See "The Day Preceding the St. Petersburg Flood of 1824"
"The Day Before the Trial" (Swinburne) **24**:355
A Day Book (Creeley) **73**:14, 20-23, 35, 39, 58, 62, 79, 91, 93, 104
Day by Day (Lowell) **3**:231-32
"The Day Calling Us to a New Life" (Very) **86**:112
"The Day Dream" (Coleridge) **11**:91, 106
"The Day-Dream" (Tennyson) **101**:245
"The Day I Was Older" (Hall) **70**:17, 34
"A Day in an Undisciplined Garden" (Enright) **93**:9
"The Day Is a Poem" (Jeffers) **17**:141
"The Day is Done" (Dunbar) **5**:126
"The Day is Done" (Longfellow) **30**:27, 46, 52, 103, 109
"The Day Is Gone" (Keats) **1**:279
"The Day Lady Died" (O'Hara) **45**:125, 131, 137, 154, 177, 184-86, 216, 243
"TH DAY MAY CUM" (Bissett) **14**:34
"The Day Millicent Found the World" (Stafford) **71**:370
"Day My Dream" (Ignatow) **34**:278, 314-15
"The Day of Battle" (Housman) **2**:160
"The Day of Judgement" (Swift) **9**:259, 265, 281, 295
"The Day of Judgement" (Vaughan) **81**:296, 313, 369
The Day of Judgement (Werfel)
See *Der Gerichtstag*
"Day of Kings" (Hugo) **17**:58
"Day of Renewal" (MacNeice) **61**:110
"A Day of Sunshine" (Longfellow) **30**:109
"Day of the Daughter of Hades" (Meredith) **60**:246-47, 250, 259, 284, 330-32
"The Day of the Eclipse" (Merrill) **28**:239, 243
"Day of the Refugios" (Ríos) **57**:319, 322
"A Day on the Big Branch" (Nemerov) **24**:257, 261
"Day or Night" (Rossetti) **7**:276

"The Day Preceding the St. Petersburg Flood of 1824" (Mickiewicz) **38**:168
"Day Six O'Hare Telephone" (Merton) **10**:336
"Day That I Have Loved" (Brooke) **24**:58, 62, 76
"The Day the Children Took Over" (Welch) **62**:340, 346, 370, 374
"The Day the First Snow Fell" (Brathwaite) **56**:65
"The Day the Mountains Move" (Yosano)
See "Yama no ugoku hi"
"The Day They Eulogized Mahalia" (Lorde) **12**:156
"The Day to the Night" (Meynell) **112**:158, 192
"Day Trip to Donegal" (Mahon) **60**:182, 184
"The day was five-headed" (Mandelstam)
See "Den' stoial na piati golovakh"
"A Day With Her" (McGuckian) **27**:76, 102
"The Day You Were Born" (Song) **21**:344
Dayarikkurippukal (Das) **43**:84
"Daybreak" (Borges)
See "Amanecer"
"Daybreak" (Hagiwara) **18**:178
"Daybreak" (Hughes) **1**:255
"Daybreak" (Kinnell) **26**:260-61
"Daybreak" (Longfellow) **30**:46-7
"Daybreak" (Merwin) **45**:9, 26
"Daybreak" (Soto) **28**:377-78
"Daybreak" (Spender) **71**:158
"Daybreak in Alabama" (Hughes) **53**:109, 150-53
"The Day-Dream" (Rossetti) **44**:172
"A Daydream in Summer" (Clare) **23**:25
"Daylight and Moonlight" (Longfellow) **30**:33, 41
"Daylight Savings" (Parker) **28**:362
"Daylilies on the Hill" (Hall) **70**:43
"Days" (Emerson) **18**:76, 82, 84, 88-91, 96, 102
"The Days" (Hall) **70**:24, 27, 31
"Days" (Larkin) **21**:235, 246
Days and Nights (Brathwaite) **56**:88-89
Days and Nights (Koch) **80**:341
"Day's Ending" (Teasdale) **31**:328, 333, 371, 380
"The Days Gone By" (Whittier) **93**:201
"Days of '49" (Dylan) **37**:60
"Days of 1896" (Cavafy) **36**:75-6, 78
"Days of 1903" (Cavafy) **36**:74
"Days of 1908" (Cavafy) **36**:80
"Days of 1909, '10, and '11" (Cavafy) **36**:80, 86
"Days of 1935" (Merrill) **28**:235, 256
"Days of 1941 and '44" (Merrill) **28**:270
"Days of 1944: Three Friends" (Hacker) **47**:87
"Days of 1964" (Merrill) **28**:220-21, 250-51
"Days of 1971" (Merrill) **28**:230, 235, 258
"Days of 1992" (Hacker) **47**:107
"Days of April '43" (Seferis) **66**:179, 210
"Days of June '41" (Seferis) **66**:178
"The Days of Nietzsche" (Stern) **115**:248
"The Day's Ration" (Emerson) **18**:88
"Day's run" (Borges)
See "Singladura"
The Days Run Away Like Wild Horses over the Hills (Bukowski) **18**:14, 19
"Daystar" (Dove) **6**:111
"De Ægypto" (Pound) **95**:159
"De Guiana, carmen Epicum" (Chapman) **96**:96, 99-101, 138, 141
"De la modification des choses par la parole" (Ponge) **107**:236-40
De la nature morte et de Chardin (Ponge) **107**:135, 164, 167-68, 182
"Las de l'amer repos" (Mallarmé) **4**:203; **102**:95, 100
De monarchia (Dante) **108**:103, 107
"De profondis clamavi" (Baudelaire) **106**:126
De vulgari eloquentia (Dante) **108**:193
"Dea Roma" (Lowell) **3**:199-200
"Deacon Taylor" (Masters) **1**:323
"The Deacon's Masterpiece; or, The Wonderful 'One-Hoss' Shay" (Holmes) **71**:66, 68, 74, 85, 88, 92, 94, 103, 108-9, 118, 121, 127
"The Dead" (Brooke) **24**:63, 74
"The Dead" (Day Lewis) **11**:147
"The Dead" (Herbert)
See "Umarli"
"The Dead" (Montale)
See "I morti"
"The Dead" (Very) **86**:88, 118, 135, 140, 151
The Dead and the Living (Olds) **22**:309-10, 314-16, 318-19, 321-22, 324, 326, 328, 338-39
"The Dead and the Living One" (Hardy) **92**:269
"Dead Are My People" (Gibran) **9**:73
"The Dead at Quang Tri" (Komunyakaa) **51**:37
"The Dead-Beat" (Owen) **19**:347; **102**:142, 145, 167, 181, 230, 232, 243
"Dead before Death" (Rossetti) **7**:288
"The Dead Beggar" (Smith) **104**:207, 325
"Dead Boy" (Ransom) **61**:269, 297, 310, 315-16
"The Dead by the Side of the Road" (Snyder) **21**:292-93
"A Dead Child Speaks" (Sachs) **78**:226, 231
"The Dead Christ" (Howe) **81**:21, 27
"Dead Farms, Dead Leaves" (Hughes) **89**:121, 151
"The Dead Feast of the Kol-Folk" (Whittier) **93**:221
"The Dead Fox Hunter" (Graves) **6**:166
The Dead Friend (Southey) **111**:244
"Dead Gallop" (Neruda)
See "Galope muerto"
"Dead Hand" (Merwin) **45**:8
"A Dead Harvest" (Meynell) **112**:247, 260
"The Dead Heart" (Sexton) **79**:254
"Dead Horse in Field" (Warren) **37**:341
"The Dead in Melanesia" (Jarrell) **41**:174
"Dead is the roote" (Raleigh) **31**:283
"The Dead King" (Kipling) **3**:182
The Dead Kingdom (Montague) **106**:270, 272, 277, 280-82, 286, 288-89, 292, 294, 299, 306-9, 312, 315, 317, 319-20, 322, 326, 346, 351, 353, 356
"The Dead Lady Canonized" (Baraka) **113**:11, 47, 49-50
"Dead Language" (Patmore) **59**:222
The Dead Lecturer (Baraka) **4**:5-6, 16-17, 23, 31, 37; **113**:7-10, 12-14, 27, 40-41, 47, 49, 55, 67, 77, 92, 96, 99, 127, 133, 139, 141, 147-48, 150-51
"The Dead Man Walking" (Hardy) **92**:257
"The Dead: Mazda Wake" (Winters) **82**:318
"Dead Men" (Douglas) **106**:203-4
"Dead Men's Love" (Brooke) **24**:53, 56
"Dead Musicians" (Sassoon) **12**:267
"Dead of Night" (Mahon) **60**:211
"The Dead of Ninety-Two" (Rimbaud)
See "Morts de quatre-vingt-douze et de quatre-vingt-treize"
"The Dead Pan" (Barrett Browning) **6**:7, 19
The Dead Priestess Speaks (H. D.) **5**:305
"The Dead Princess and the Seven Heroes" (Pushkin)
See "Skazka o Mertvoy Tsarevne"
"The Dead Prophet" (Tennyson) **101**:199
"The Dead Quire" (Hardy) **92**:211, 271-72, 277
"The Dead Shall Be Raised Incorruptible" (Kinnell) **26**:245, 251, 254, 267
"The Dead Ship of Harpswell" (Whittier) **93**:176
"Dead Soldiers" (Chappell) **105**:3, 58, 70
"Dead Tree" (Mistral)
See "Arbol muerto"
"The Dead II" (Brooke) **24**:59, 88
"The Dead Wingman" (Jarrell) **41**:171
"Dead Worthies" (Thomas) **99**:310
"The Deadly Eyes Are Stars" (Baraka) **113**:75
"Deaf Donald" (Silverstein) **49**:327
"Deaf Poem" (Gallagher) **9**:62
"Deaf School" (Hughes) **89**:129, 216-17
"Deaf-Mutes at the Ballgame" (Jacobsen) **62**:300, 313
"The Dean" (Patmore) **59**:229-30
"Dean Dixon, Welcome Home" (Stryk) **27**:204
"The Dean of St. Patrick's to Thomas Sheridan" (Swift) **9**:295
"The Dean to Himself on St. Cecilia's Day" (Swift) **9**:295
The Dean's Provocation for Writing the "Lady's Dressing Room" (Montagu) **16**:345
"The Dean's Reasons For Not Building at Drapier's Hill" (Swift) **9**:295
"Dear Child of God" (Smith) **12**:335
"Dear Female Heart" (Smith) **12**:295
"Dear Folks" (Kavanagh) **33**:64; **105**:96-97, 121
"Dear Joe" (Schuyler) **88**:176
"Dear John Wayne" (Erdrich) **52**:173
"Dear Judas" (Jeffers) **17**:109-10, 144
Dear Judas and Other Poems (Jeffers) **17**:109, 124, 135
"Dear Landlord" (Dylan) **37**:56
"Dear Little Sirmio" (Smith) **12**:331
Dear Lovely Death (Hughes) **53**:112, 115
"Dear Mr. President" (Hughes) **53**:115
"Dear Muse" (Smith) **12**:335
"Dear Patron of My Virgin Muse" (Burns) **6**:84
"Dear Paul:" (Niedecker) **42**:95
"Dear Possible" (Jackson) **44**:29
"Dear Reader" (Collins) **68**:218
"Dear Robert" (Ignatow) **34**:345
"Dear Strager Extant in Memory by the Blue Juaniata" (Kinnell) **26**:250, 267
"Dear Toni" (Lorde) **12**:157
"Dear Villon, Dear Milarepa" (Corso) **33**:34
"Death" (Baudelaire) **106**:34
"Death" (Corso) **33**:35, 47; **108**:16-18, 33
"Death" (Herbert) **4**:113
"Death" (Lermontov)
See "Smert"
"Death" (Macpherson) **97**:251
"Death" (O'Hara) **45**:229
"Death" (Olds) **22**:325
"Death" (Shelley) **14**:166
"Death" (Stevenson) **84**:306
"Death" (Vaughan) **81**:296
"Death and Birth" (Swinburne) **24**:324
"Death and Co." (Plath) **1**:397; **37**:213, 230, 233, 258
"Death and Daphne" (Swift) **9**:260
"Death and Doctor Hornbook" (Burns) **6**:56, 88; **114**:6, 8-9, 42, 118
"The Death and Dying Words of Poor Mailie, the Author's Only Pet Yowe, an Unco Mournfu' Tale" (Burns) **6**:52, 61, 63-4; **114**:87, 102, 155
"Death and Engines" (Ní Chuilleanáin) **34**:353, 361-62
"The Death and Last Confession of Wandering Peter" (Belloc) **24**:5
"Death and Love" (Barrett Browning) **6**:16
"Death and Morality" (Olds) **22**:323, 342
"Death and Murder" (Olds) **22**:326
"The Death and Resurrection of the Birds" (Wagoner) **33**:333
Death and Taxes (Parker) **28**:349-51, 363-65
"Death and the Compass" (Borges)
See "La muerte y la brújula"
"Death and the Maiden" (Nemerov) **24**:259, 268, 270-71
"Death and the Maiden" (Wylie) **23**:317
"Death and the Sun" (Mahon) **60**:176, 195, 210, 214
"Death As Death" (Jackson) **44**:8
"The Death Baby" (Sexton) **2**:373; **79**:193, 195-97, 200, 210
"Death Ballad" (Berryman) **64**:94
"Death by Water" (Cavafy) **36**:8
"Death Carol" (Whitman) **3**:378
"Death Chant" (Hughes) **53**:119
"Death Comes at Puberty" (Corso) **108**:7

"Death, corollary to Life" (Villa) **22**:354
"The Death Dance" (Madhubuti) **5**:339
"Death, from a Distance" (Wilbur) **51**:273
"Death Fugue" (Celan)
See "Todesfuge"
"Death, Great Smoothener" (Swenson) **14**:250, 286
"Death in Harlem" (Hughes) **53**:101, 114
"Death in Ilium" (Kinsella) **69**:97
"Death in Leamington" (Betjeman) **75**:7, 20, 22, 29, 59, 76-78
"Death in Mexico" (Levertov) **11**:205-06, 209
"Death in Moonlight" (Kunitz) **19**:155
"A Death in the Desert" (Browning) **2**:36, 45, 72-73, 95
"A Death in the Desert" (Tolson) **17**:328
Death in This Garden (Bunuel)
See *La mort en ce jardin*
"Death in Yorkville" (Hughes) **53**:111
"Death Invited" (Swenson) **14**:266, 286
"Death Is a Woman" (Harjo) **27**:68, 70, 72-3
"Death Is Not as Natural as You Fags Seem to Think" (Baraka) **113**:14
Death Is Still Celebrating Life (Sachs)
See *Noch feiert Todd das Leben*
"Death Is the Beginning of a New Form" (Baraka) **113**:18
"Death Is the Mother of Beauty" (Stevens) **110**:229
"The Death King" (Sexton) **79**:200
Death Mask and Clover (Storni)
See *Mascarilla y trébol*
Death meditated (Ungaretti)
See *La morte meditata*
The Death Notebooks (Sexton) **2**:360-61, 367-68, 370-72; **79**:190, 192-93, 195-97, 199-201, 209-11, 213-14, 216-19, 225, 231-32, 234, 237-39, 242, 244, 251, 284, 333, 340
"Death of a Bomber" (Ciardi) **69**:26
"Death of a Cat" (MacNeice) **61**:128
"Death of a Ceiling" (McGuckian) **27**:90
"The Death of a Cranefly" (Wagoner) **33**:357
"Death of a Critic" (Bell) **79**:3-4
"Death of a Favorite Bird" (Merwin) **45**:9
"Death of a Favorite Cat" (Gray)
See "Ode on the Death of a Favourite Cat, Drowned in a Tub of Gold Fishes"
"Death of a Frog" (Hagiwara)
See "Kaeru no shi"
"The Death of A. G. A." (Brontë) **8**:65, 74
"Death of a Ladies' Man" (Cohen) **109**:70
Death of a Ladies' Man (Cohen) **109**:35, 71-72
"Death of a Lady's Man" (Cohen) **109**:23, 26, 33, 40, 68, 70
Death of a Lady's Man (Cohen) **109**:17, 19, 22-27, 29-30, 34-35, 66-72, 111-12
"Death of a Lawn Mower" (Ignatow) **34**:343
"Death of a Naturalist" (Heaney) **18**:200, 207, 247-48, 252; **100**:263
Death of a Naturalist (Heaney) **18**:186, 189-90, 192, 194, 199-201, 205-8, 215, 220, 238, 247, 255; **100**:194, 219-21, 231-32, 263-64, 291-92, 297, 325, 334, 344, 349, 351
"Death of a Poet" (Thomas) **99**:234
"Death of a Queen" (Kinsella) **69**:116-17
"Death of a Student" (Shapiro) **25**:309, 316
"The Death of a Toad" (Wilbur) **51**:186, 214, 266, 297, 299
"Death of a Young Son by Drowning" (Atwood) **8**:38-9
"Death of an Actress" (MacNeice) **61**:139
"Death of an Alcoholic" (Hagiwara) **18**:167, 178
"Death of an Old Lady" (MacNeice) **61**:111
"Death of Antoñito the Camborio" (García Lorca)
See "Muerte de Antoñito el Camborio"
"The Death of Artists" (Baudelaire)
See "La mort des artistes"
"The Death of Aunt Alice" (Abse) **41**:10
"Death of Autumn" (Millay) **6**:236
The Death of Blanche the Duchess (Chaucer)
See *Book of the Duchess*
"The Death of Channing" (Bryant) **20**:46
The Death of Cock Robin (Snodgrass) **74**:323-26, 328
"The Death of Crazy Horse" (Clifton) **17**:25
The Death of Cuchullin (Clarke) **112**:43-44
"The Death of Cuthullin" (Macpherson) **97**:230-31
"Death of Deaths" (Stramm)
See "Urtod"
"Death of Emma Goldman" (Shapiro) **25**:311, 324
"The Death of Francisco Pizarro" (Ai) **72**:23
"The Death of Fred Clifton" (Clifton) **17**:25, 27
"The Death of God" (Montale)
See "La morte di Dio"
"Death of Little Boys" (Tate) **50**:228, 236, 246-48, 280, 296, 305, 311, 325
"The Death of Lovers" (Baudelaire)
See "La mort des amants"
"The Death of Manolete" (Barker) **77**:19
"The Death of Marilyn Monroe" (Mahon) **60**:181
"The Death of Mr. Mounsel" (Smith) **12**:323
"The death of my poor father" (Niedecker) **42**:138
"The Death of Nicou" (Chatterton) **104**:68, 74
"The Death of Nick Charles" (Baraka) **113**:4, 7
"The Death of Oenone" (Tennyson) **6**:360; **101**:120, 124-28
The Death of Oenone, Akbar's Dream, and Other Poems (Tennyson) **101**:119, 124
"The Death of Oscar" (Macpherson) **97**:196, 209
"The Death of Our Lady" (Southwell) **83**:282, 284
"The Death of Pan" (Barrett Browning)
See "The Dead Pan"
"The Death of Potchikoo" (Erdrich) **52**:193
"The Death of Professor Backwards" (Kennedy) **93**:130
"The Death of Reason" (Boland) **58**:18, 60
"The Death of Richard Wagner" (Swinburne) **24**:323, 329
"The Death of See" (Williams) **109**:195
"The Death of Smet-Smet" (Brooke) **24**:56, 66
"Death of Socrates" (Lamartine)
See *La morte de Socrate*
"The Death of St. Narcissus" (Eliot) **90**:221, 286, 301
"Death of the American Indian's God" (Corso) **33**:49
"The Death of the Ball Turret Gunner" (Jarrell) **41**:145, 168, 173, 178-79, 182, 187, 189, 203, 205, 218
"The Death of the Baron" (Lawrence) **54**:229-30
"The Death of the Beloved" (Rilke) **2**:272-73
"The Death of the Bird" (Hope) **56**:266, 272
"The death of the Emperor Tacitus" (Cavafy) **36**:53, 57
"The Death of the Fathers" (Sexton) **2**:356, 365-67; **79**:207
"The Death of the Firstborn" (Dunbar) **5**:140
"The Death of the Flowers" (Bryant) **20**:9, 12
"The Death of the Hat" (Collins) **68**:210
"The Death of the Hired Man" (Frost) **1**:195, 197, 209, 216, 221, 226, 228-29; **39**:246, 253
"Death of the Hungarian hot pepper bush" (Piercy) **29**:315
"Death of the Kapowsin Tavern" (Hugo) **68**:236, 252, 284, 287
Death of the Kapowsin Tavern (Hugo) **68**:235, 237, 258-59, 265, 271, 281-82, 287
"Death of the Lord Protector" (Marvell)
See "Poem upon the Death of O. C."
"Death of the Poet" (Lermontov)
See "Smert' poeta"
"Death of the Poet" (Pasternak) **6**:268
"The Death of the Princess" (Senghor) **25**:232
"The Death of the Public Servant" (Kizer) **66**:67
"The Death of the Sheriff" (Lowell) **3**:200, 206
"The Death of the Slave Lewis" (Howe) **81**:30
"The Death of the Wolf" (Vigny)
See "La mort du loup"
"The Death of Yeats" (Barker) **77**:47-48
"A Death on Easter Day" (Swinburne) **24**:319
"Death Piece" (Roethke) **15**:272
"The Death Room" (Graves) **6**:142, 144
"Death Shall Have No Dominion" (Thomas)
See "And Death Shall Have No Dominion"
"Death Snips Proud Men" (Sandburg) **41**:313
"Death Song" (Wagoner) **33**:344
"A Death Song for Alfred Linnell" (Morris) **55**:340
"A Death Sonnet for Custer" (Whitman) **91**:278
"Death, That Struck when I Was Most Confiding" (Brontë) **8**:65
"Death the Barber" (Williams) **7**:388
"Death the Carnival Barker" (Hecht) **70**:94
"Death the Copperplate Printer" (Hecht) **70**:93
"Death the Film Director" (Hecht) **70**:92, 94
"Death the Hypocrite" (Hecht) **70**:92
"Death the Inquisitor" (Hecht) **70**:93, 100-101
"Death the Judge" (Hecht) **70**:92
"Death the Mexican Revolutionary" (Hecht) **70**:92
"Death the Oxford Don" (Hecht) **70**:92
"Death the Poet" (Hecht) **70**:95
"Death the Scholar" (Hecht) **70**:92
"Death the Whore" (Hecht) **70**:94, 108
"Death to a Star" (Raworth) **107**:302
"Death to This Book" (Cohen) **109**:24, 71
"Death to Van Gogh's Ear!" (Ginsberg) **4**:63, 74-5
"Death While Journeying" (Dorn) **115**:80-81, 121
"The Death-Bed" (Hood) **93**:62, 81, 121-22
"A Death-Day Recalled" (Hardy) **8**:136
"Death-in-Love" (Rossetti) **44**:204
"Deaths" (Swenson) **14**:286
"Deaths and Entrances" (Thomas) **2**:380-82, 388, 390
Deaths and Entrances (Thomas) **52**:219, 239, 252, 286
"Death's Echo" (Auden) **92**:86
"Death's Lecture at the Funeral of a Young Gentleman" (Crashaw) **84**:47, 69
"The Deaths of the Other Children" (Atwood) **8**:39
"The Deaths of Uncles" (Kumin) **15**:202
"Death's Ramble" (Hood) **93**:44, 52, 80
Le debat de deux amans (Christine de Pizan) **68**:3, 22-23, 98-99, 139, 142, 144-45, 148-53, 172
"Debat du cuer et du corps de Villon" (Villon) **13**:394, 396
"The Debate" (Ignatow) **34**:282
"The Debate" (Lermontov) **18**:295, 297
The Debate of Two Lovers (Christine de Pizan)
See *Le debat de deux amans*
"Debate with the Rabbi" (Nemerov) **24**:277
"La débauche" (Gautier) **18**:164
Debits and Credits (Kipling) **91**:137
"Deborah as Scion" (Dickey) **40**:211-12, 238
"Deborah Burning a Doll Made of House-Wood" (Dickey) **40**:211-12, 236
"Deborah in Ancient Lingerie, in Thin Oak over Creek" (Dickey) **40**:237
"Deborah in Mountain Sound: Bell, Glacier, Rose" (Dickey) **40**:228
"Deborah, Moon, Mirror, Right Hand Rising" (Dickey) **40**:211-12, 236
"Dèbris" (Césaire) **25**:8-9
"Debris" (Whitman) **91**:319-20
"Debris of Life and Mind" (Stevens) **110**:96
"The Debt" (Dunbar) **5**:120, 125
"A Debt" (Merwin) **45**:20
"Debt" (Oppen) **35**:315
"Debt" (Teasdale) **31**:325, 352
"Debtor" (Teasdale) **31**:360

Début et fin de la neige (Bonnefoy) **58**:150-51, 154
"Dec. 28, 1974" (Schuyler) **88**:187-88, 200
"A Decade" (Lowell) **13**:97
"The Decadence" (Pound) **95**:100
"Decalogue of the Artist" (Mistral) **32**:144
"Decay" (Herbert) **4**:102
"The Decay of Vanity" (Hughes) **7**:113
"Decease, Release: Dum Morior Orior" (Southwell) **83**:252, 278, 286
"December" (Akhmadulina) **43**:3
"December" (Belloc) **24**:29
"December" (Schuyler) **88**:189
"December" (Simic) **69**:283-84
"December 1" (Milosz) **8**:215
"December 4th" (Sexton) **2**:372
"December 9th" (Sexton) **2**:352-53
"December 10th" (Sexton) **2**:364
"December 12th" (Sexton) **2**:352-53
"December 14th" (Sexton) **2**:353
"December 16th" (Sexton) **2**:352-53
"December 18th" (Sexton) **2**:352
"December 24th, Paris—Notre Dame" (Cisneros) **52**:161
"December, 1903" (Cavafy) **36**:42, 107
"December 1920" (Seifert) **47**:331
"December Among the Vanished" (Merwin) **45**:20, 23
"December Eclogue" (Winters) **82**:313, 337
"December Night" (Lawrence) **54**:169
"December Night" (Merwin) **45**:20, 34
Decennalia (Carducci) **46**:4-5, 47
"Deceptions" (Hughes) **89**:125
"Deceptions" (Larkin) **21**:237
"Dechtire" (Melville) **82**:38
"Decidme anoche" (Cernuda) **62**:201, 247, 249, 252-53
"Deciduous Branch" (Kunitz) **19**:147
"The Deciduous Trees" (Meredith) **28**:190
"Decision to Forget" (Seferis) **66**:165, 171-72, 220
"The deck that pouts" (Piercy) **29**:314
Declaration (Wyatt) **27**:369
"Déclaration foraine" (Mallarmé) **102**:116
"Declaration of Independence" (Parra)
See "Acta de independecia"
"Declarations" (Hughes) **53**:101
"Déclarer son nom" (Char) **56**:111, 179
"Declaring One's Name" (Char)
See "Déclarer son nom"
"Decline" (Trakl)
See "Untergang"
"Declining hours I, II, III" (Zanzotto)
See "Ore calanti I, II, III"
"Declivio su Lorna" (Zanzotto) **65**:274
"De-Composition" (Birney) **52**:85
"The Deconstruction of Emily Dickinson" (Kinnell) **26**:294
"Decorum and Terror Homage to Goethe and Hart Crane" (Viereck) **27**:279
"Dedans des Pres je vis une Dryade" (Ronsard) **105**:197, 280
"Dedham, vu de Langham" (Bonnefoy) **58**:141
"Dedica" (Pasolini) **17**:281
"Dedication" (Akhmatova)
See "Posvyashchenie"
"Dedication" (Arnim)
See "Zueignung"
"Dedication" (Char) **56**:159-60, 162
"Dedication" (Curnow) **48**:27
"The Dedication" (Herbert) **4**:125
"Dedication" (Kinsella) **69**:137-38
"A Dedication" (Merrill) **28**:240
"Dedication" (Milosz) **8**:193
"The Dedication" (Vaughan) **81**:319
"Dedication" (Wylie) **23**:303
Dedication (Ekeloef) **23**:75-6
"Dedication for a Plot of Ground" (Williams) **7**:362, 394
"Dedication in Time" (Schwartz)
See "Time's Dedication"
"Dedication of the Cook" (Wickham) **110**:270, 304
"A Dedication of Three Hats" (Gray) **6**:166
"Dedication to Gavin Hamilton" (Burns) **114**:60, 147
"Dedication to Hunger" (Glück) **16**:151, 154-55
"Dedication: To William Morris" (Swinburne) **24**:313
"Dedications" (Rich) **5**:401
Dedications and Other Darkhorses (Komunyakaa) **51**:6, 29, 33, 52
"Dedicatory Epistle" (Swinburne) **24**:351
"Dedicatory Ode" (Belloc) **24**:3, 6, 8, 11
"Dedicatory Poem" (Meredith) **28**:187
"Dedicatory Poem to Collected Poems, 1925-1948, To Hedli" (MacNeice) **61**:140, 146-47
"The Deeds of Jason" (Morris) **55**:305
"Deem as ye list upon good cause" (Wyatt) **27**:354
"The Deep" (Winters) **82**:315, 317, 323, 325
"A Deep Breath at Dawn" (Hecht) **70**:97-98
"A deep gentle garden falling to the Oka" (Akhmadulina)
See "Glubokij neznyj sad, vpadajuscij v Oku"
"Deep in the Night" (Teasdale) **31**:336
"Deep Light" (Stafford) **71**:373
"The Deep Sea Cables" (Kipling) **3**:162; **91**:85
Deep Song (García Lorca)
See *Poema del cante jondo*
"Deep Woods" (Nemerov) **24**:288
"The Deeper Friendship" (Blunden) **66**:29, 32
"Deeper Than Love" (Lawrence) **54**:186
"Deeply Morbid" (Smith) **12**:329, 346
"Deep-sea Fishing" (MacDiarmid) **9**:167
"Deer among Cattle" (Dickey) **40**:158
"Deer Dancer" (Harjo) **27**:71
"Deer Enclosure" (Wang Wei)
See "Deer Park"
"Deer Park" (Wang Wei) **18**:383, 385-86, 391, 393
"Deer Season" (Kenyon) **57**:4, 39
"Deer Stolen" (Stafford) **71**:297
"Deer Walled" (Wang Wei)
See "Deer Park"
"The Deer's Eye the Hunter's Nose" (Dorn) **115**:106
"Deerslayer's Campfire Talk" (Stafford) **71**:283
"The Defeat" (Mistral)
See "La derrota"
"The Defeated" (Kavanagh) **33**:86, 103, 118, 121; **105**:110, 120, 143
"Defeated Saviour" (Wright) **36**:290-91
"A Defective Santa Claus" (Riley) **48**:301
Defectos escogidos: 2000 (Neruda) **4**:287
Defence (Wyatt) **27**:369-70
"The Defence of Guenevere" (Morris) **55**:238, 247, 257, 263-65, 267, 269, 300-302, 318-19, 348
The Defence of Guenevere, and Other Poems (Morris) **55**:239-40, 247, 251-52, 258, 266-67, 278-79, 284, 298-99, 301-2, 308-9, 322-23, 328-29, 344, 346, 348-49
"Defending My Tongue" (Clifton) **17**:28
Defenestration of Prague (Howe) **54**:39-42, 59, 61-65
"Defensa de Violeta Parra" (Parra) **39**:285
"Defensa del árbol" (Parra) **39**:304
"Defense of the Tree" (Parra)
See "Defensa del árbol"
Defensive Rapture (Guest) **55**:183, 204
"Deferred" (Hughes) **53**:123, 193
"Definition" (Chappell) **105**:52
"Definition" (Wickham) **110**:270, 311
"definition for blk / children" (Sanchez) **9**:224, 232
"Definition in the Face of Unnamed Fury" (Dove) **6**:111
"Definition of Blue" (Ashbery) **26**:119, 123
"Definition of Creativity" (Pasternak) **6**:271
"The Definition of Love" (Marvell) **10**:264, 266, 271, 274, 277, 291, 294, 299-303, 312, 316, 319; **86**:178, 191, 222, 245, 263
"Definition of Love" (Sarton) **39**:322
"The Definition of Love" (Warren) **37**:288
"The Definition of Poetry" (Pasternak)
See "Opredelenyie poezii"
"The Definition of the Creative Power" (Pasternak) **6**:254
"Definitions of Old Age" (MacLeish) **47**:206
"Degas 'Absinthe'" (Thomas) **99**:306-7
"Degas 'Mademoiselle Dihau at the Piano'" (Thomas) **99**:306
"Degas 'Musicians in the Orchestra'" (Thomas) **99**:307, 310
"Degas 'Portrait of a Young Woman'" (Thomas) **99**:305-6
"Degas 'Women Ironing'" (Thomas) **99**:305
"Degas's Laundresses" (Boland) **58**:45
"Degrees of Gray in Philipsburg" (Hugo) **68**:238, 255, 264, 267, 270, 274, 285, 287-88, 290
"Deh fammiti vedere in ogni loco!" (Michelangelo) **103**:289, 307
"Deher milan" (Tagore) **8**:407
"Dehorning" (Hughes) **7**:166; **89**:125
Dehors la nuit est gouvernée (Char) **56**:159, 162, 185-86, 189
"Deianira, Hercules, and Nessus" (Gower)
See "Tale of Deianira, Hercules, and Nessus"
"Dein Leib im Rauch durch die Luft" (Sachs) **78**:113
"Dein Name ist dir verlorengegangen" (Sachs) **78**:165
"Dein Schimmer" (Celan) **10**:124-25
"Deir El Bahari: Queen Hatsheput's Temple" (Enright) **93**:32
"Deities" (Montague) **106**:271
"The Deity" (Whittier) **93**:194
"Déjame esta voz" (Cernuda) **62**:235
"Dejaneira" (Arnold) **5**:8
"Dejection" (Muir) **49**:205, 250
"Dejection" (Shelley)
See "Dejection: An Ode"
"Dejection: An Ode" (Coleridge) **11**:41, 52-3, 58, 69-73, 90-2, 105-09; **39**:162-63, 166-67, 176, 179-80; **67**:286
"Dejection: An Ode" (Hardy) **92**:257
"Dejection: An Ode" (Shelley) **14**:168
Dejection: An Ode (Coleridge) **100**:19, 22-26, 104
"Dekabr" (Akhmadulina) **43**:17
"Del infierno y del cielo" (Borges) **32**:85-6, 139
"Delay Has Danger" (Crabbe) **97**:106, 114-16
"Delayed by Mongol Forces at National Airport" (Chappell) **105**:37
"Delfica" (Nerval) **13**:181, 194
"Delgusa Gardens" (Stryk) **27**:192
"Delhi 1984" (Das) **43**:83
"Delia Rexroth" (Rexroth) **95**:272
"Delicate Criss-Crossing Beetle Trails Left in the Sand" (Snyder) **21**:300
"Delicia" (Paz) **48**:184
"Deliciae Sapientiae de Amore" (Patmore) **59**:223, 276
Délie, Object de plus haulte vertu (Scève) **111**:2-5, 7, 9-11, 14-25, 27-29, 31-38, 46-47, 49-53, 55-56, 60, 69-76, 84-85, 88, 92, 96, 100-106, 108-9, 111-12, 115-20, 123-28, 130-35, 138-41, 143, 145-46, 149, 151, 153, 164
"Delight" (Paz)
See "Delicia"
"Delight in Disorder" (Herrick) **9**:111-12, 115-16, 132, 135
"Delight in Disorder" (Patmore) **59**:232
"Delight in Water" (Masefield) **78**:30
"The Delight Song of Tsoai-talee" (Momaday) **25**:189, 196, 204, 213, 220

Delights of the Muses (Crashaw)
See *Steps to the Temple. Sacred Poems With Other Delights of the Muses*
"The Delinquent" (Dunbar) **5**:119
"Délires" (Rimbaud) **57**:243, 249, 252, 254, 279
"Délires I" (Rimbaud) **57**:191, 199, 229
"Délires II" (Rimbaud) **57**:174, 191, 199
"The Delirium Waltz" (Strand) **63**:188, 199
"Deliverance" (Graves) **6**:157
"The Deliverance" (Harper) **21**:192, 199-201, 211
"Deliverance From a Fit of Fainting" (Bradstreet) **10**:26, 61-62
"Delivers" (Hughes) **89**:147
"The Dell of E—" (Tennyson) **101**:250
"Della primavera trasportata al morale" (Williams) **7**:408; **109**:193, 283
"Delphi" (H. D.) **5**:305
"The Delphic Oracle upon Plotinus" (Yeats) **20**:312, 329, 334
"Delphic Song" (Sikelianos) **29**:367
"Delphine et Hippolyte" (Baudelaire)
See "Femmes damnées"
"Delta" (Montale) **13**:134, 164
"Delta" (Tolson) **88**:236, 269, 306, 328, 331
"Delta" (Walker) **20**:272-73, 275, 278, 281-83
"The Deluge" (Vigny)
See "Le déluge"
"Le déluge" (Vigny) **26**:367, 380-81, 391, 398, 401-402, 411
"Delusion?-No!" (Warren) **37**:379
Delusions, Etc. of John Berryman (Berryman) **64**:77-78, 81, 95, 97-98, 118-20, 163, 170-71
"Dem aufgehenden Vollmonde" (Goethe) **5**:249
"Demain" (Brossard) **80**:25
"Demain dès l'aube" (Hugo) **17**:64
"Démarrage" (Tzara) **27**:229-31
The Demesne of the Swans (Tsvetaeva)
See *Lebediny stan*
Demeter, and Other Poems (Tennyson) **101**:119
"Demeter and Persephone" (Tennyson) **101**:119-20, 122-25, 127-28
"Demetrius Soter" (Cavafy) **36**:20
"Demi-Exile. Howth" (Davie) **29**:107, 109, 119
"Demiurge" (Lawrence) **54**:199, 250
"The Demiurge's Laugh" (Frost) **1**:213; **39**:231
"Demobilization" (Shapiro) **25**:273, 296
"Democracy" (Cohen) **109**:63
"Democracy" (Hughes) **1**:241, 252, 258; **53**:153
"Democracy" (Rimbaud)
See "Démocratie"
"The Democratic Order" (Walker) **30**:350
"Démocratie" (Rimbaud) **57**:182-83, 199, 246
"Democritus and Heraclitus" (Prior) **102**:306
"Demolition" (Doty) **53**:45-46
"Demolition," (Kaufman) **74**:254
"The Demon" (Pushkin) **10**:406, 412-13, 418
The Demon (Lermontov) **18**:271-72, 274, 279, 282-83, 297-98, 302
"Demon and Beast" (Yeats) **51**:76, 110
"Le démon de l'analogie" (Mallarmé) **102**:37-38, 41, 43-47, 108
"The Demon Lover" (Rich) **5**:392
"The Demon of Fornication" (Seferis) **66**:212
"Demon Time" (Muir) **49**:296
"Demonology" (Ronsard)
See "Les daimons"
"The Demon-Ship" (Hood) **93**:44, 52, 73, 80
"A Demonstration" (Patmore) **59**:234
"The Demonstration" (Traherne) **70**:192, 264, 274-75, 317
"Demos and Dionysus" (Robinson) **1**:470, 487; **35**:368
"An den Mond" (Goethe) **5**:246-47
"Den' stoial na piati golovakh" (Mandelstam) **14**:152
"Den' 12 marta" (Akhmadulina) **43**:19, 40
"Dend' aquí vexo un camiño" (Castro) **41**:92, 101
"Denial" (Herbert)
See "Deniall"
"Denial" (Seferis) **66**:117-18, 120
"Deniall" (Herbert) **4**:114, 119-20
"Denise Levertov from Butte" (Hugo) **68**:257
"Denouement" (Stone) **53**:228
"Une dentelle s'abolit" (Mallarmé) **102**:27-28, 30-31, 33, 98, 101-2
"Denver Doldrum" (Ginsberg) **4**:74
"Deo Gratias" (Montague) **106**:314
"The Deodand" (Hecht) **70**:66-69, 71, 86, 94
"Deola Thinking" (Pavese) **13**:205
"Deola's Return" (Pavese)
See "Ritorno di Deola"
"Départ" (Gautier) **18**:155
"Départ" (Rimbaud) **57**:194, 224-25, 230, 236, 239, 248
"Department of Public Monuments" (Simic) **69**:287, 319
Departmental Ditties (Kipling) **3**:155-56, 159, 165, 182, 190-91; **91**:132
"Departure" (Carducci)
See "Dipartita"
"Departure" (Forché) **10**:137, 144, 156, 169
"Departure" (Glück) **16**:142, 149-50, 172
"Departure" (Kinsella) **69**:130
"Departure" (Lawrence) **54**:197, 201
"Departure" (Millay) **6**:211
"The Departure" (Olds) **22**:310, 312, 321-22
"Departure" (Patmore) **59**:209, 222
"Departure" (Plath) **1**:388, 407-08; **37**:184
"Departure" (Rimbaud)
See "Départ"
"The Departure" (Tennyson) **101**:245
"Departure" (Tomlinson) **17**:336, 346
"Departure" (Warren) **37**:312
"Departure for Vaud" (Zanzotto)
See "Partenza per il Vaud"
"The Departure from Hydra" (Koch) **80**:300
"Departure in the Dark" (Day Lewis) **11**:145
"The Departure of Summer" (Hood) **93**:66, 117
"Departure Platforms" (Kinsella) **69**:79, 133, 135
"The Departure Song of the Divine Strings" (Li Ho) **13**:52
Departures (Justice) **64**:252, 254-55, 257, 261-62, 272, 275-76, 280, 288-90
"Departure's Girl-Friend" (Merwin) **45**:8
Dependencies (Mueller) **33**:178-80
Depends: A Poet's Notebook (Montale)
See *Quaderno de quattro anni*
"Depopulation of the Hills" (Thomas) **99**:269
"Deposition from love" (Carew) **29**:3-4, 46
"Depressed by a Book of Bad Poetry, I Walk Toward an Unused Pasture and Invite the Insects to Join Me" (Wright) **36**:296, 326, 340-41, 350
"Depression" (Bly) **39**:7, 10, 79-80, 89-90
"Depression Before Spring" (Stevens) **6**:313
"Depression in Winter" (Kenyon) **57**:3, 43
"Depression Years" (Niedecker) **42**:104, 131
"Dept. of Philosophy" (Enzensberger) **28**:151
"Depth of Love" (Graves) **6**:172
"The Depths" (Apollinaire)
See "Loin du pigeonnier"
"DeQuincey At Grasmere" (Mahon) **60**:140, 181, 184, 215
"Deranged Gutbucket Pigtongue Clapper Heart" (Baraka) **113**:78
"The Derelict" (Ignatow) **34**:292, 305
"The Derelict" (Kipling) **3**:183; **91**:86, 153
"Derevnya" (Pushkin) **10**:421
"Derev'ya" (Tsvetaeva) **14**:317
Derivations: Selected Poems, 1950-1956 (Duncan) **2**:105-6; **75**:166, 176, 181-82, 228-29
"Le dernier chant de pèlerinage de Childe Harold" (Lamartine) **16**:268, 279, 292
"Dernier jour du monde" (Hugo) **17**:87, 89
"Dernier malheur dernière chance" (Péret) **33**:203, 231
"Un dernier rêve" (Sainte-Beuve) **110**:56
Dernier Vœu (Sainte-Beuve) **110**:39
"Dernière Levée" (Breton) **15**:50
"Dernièrement" (Péret) **33**:231
Dernières Poésies (Gautier) **18**:143
"Derniers gestes" (Bonnefoy) **58**:172, 176
Derniers vers (Rimbaud) **3**:285; **57**:175, 202, 208, 216, 250, 252, 260
Les derniers vers de Jules Laforgue (Laforgue) **14**:56-7, 59-62, 68-77, 80-3, 88, 93, 95-7
Les derniers vers de Pierre de Ronsard, gentilhomne vandomois (Ronsard) **11**:244, 269, 274; **105**:201
De derrière les fagots (Péret) **33**:202, 204, 220-21, 230
"La derrota" (Mistral) **32**:181, 191
"Derry Morning" (Mahon) **60**:146, 148, 150, 196, 232
"Des Beautés qui'il voudroit en s'amie" (Ronsard) **11**:247
"Des cris étouffés" (Péret) **33**:209, 213
"Des éventails brisés" (Éluard) **38**:91
"Des Faux" (Apollinaire) **7**:46
"Des imagistes" (Williams) **7**:345
"Des raisons d'écrire" (Ponge) **107**:139
"Desajuste en el desgaste" (Fuertes) **27**:27
"La desásída" (Mistral) **32**:189
"descarga en cueros" (Cruz) **37**:12
"Descartes" (Borges) **32**:58
"Descartes and the Stove" (Tomlinson) **17**:319
"The Descendants" (Das) **43**:73, 85
The Descendants (Das) **43**:74, 80, 85-87, 90, 93
"Descending Figure" (Glück) **16**:151
Descending Figure (Glück) **16**:130-34, 144, 147, 150-51, 153-56, 159, 170
"The Descent" (Brooke) **24**:77
"The Descent" (Kinnell) **26**:236, 252, 280
"The Descent" (Williams) **7**:403
"The Descent from the Cross" (Rossetti) **7**:264, 285
"Descent of Dorelia" (Wickham) **110**:254, 270
"The Descent of Odin, an Ode" (Gray) **2**:146, 148-49, 152
"The Descent of Winter" (Williams) **109**:273, 276
The Descent of Winter (Williams) **7**:349, 352-53, 368, 400, 402; **109**:283-84
"A Descent through the Carpet" (Atwood) **8**:12, 19
"Description" (Doty) **53**:66
"Description" (Graham) **59**:130, 171-72
"Description" (Silverstein) **49**:340
"A Description of a City Shower" (Swift) **9**:252, 265, 275-79
"A Description of a Journey" (Duck) **89**:10-12, 28, 37, 60-63, 67, 73-74, 77
"Description of a Masque" (Ashbery) **26**:170
"Description of a Pain in the Solar Plexus" (Akhmadulina) **43**:8
"The Description of Cooke-ham" (Lanyer) **60**:2, 9, 11, 15, 17, 20, 22, 33, 36, 40, 43-44, 48, 81, 88-90, 99, 101-3, 110-12, 114-15
"The Description of Elizium" (Drayton) **98**:18
"Description of Hampstead" (Hunt) **73**:150
"A Description of Some Confederate Soldiers" (Jarrell) **41**:127, 183
"Description of the Author's Bed-Chamber" (Goldsmith) **77**:215, 252
"A Description of the Fifteenth of November: A Portrait of T. S. Eliot" (Stein) **18**:341
"A Description of the King" (Herbert) **50**:31-32
"Description of the Morning" (Swift) **9**:265
"Description without Place" (Stevens) **6**:338; **110**:84, 121-22, 124-25, 163-64, 173, 176, 202
Descriptive Sketches (Wordsworth) **4**:372; **67**:269-70, 277, 280
"Desde los cuatro puntos cardinales" (Castro) **41**:118
"El Desdichado" (Nerval) **13**:174-75, 178-80, 184-87, 195
"Desecration of the Gravestone of Rose P.

(1897-1924)" (Pinsky) **27**:175
Le desert (Lamartine) **16**:276, 282, 284, 286
"Desert Flowers" (Douglas) **106**:203, 205
"The Desert Music" (Williams) **7**:374; **109**:274, 276
The Desert Music, and Other Poems (Williams) **7**:371, 402-03; **109**:199, 202-3, 261, 263, 274
"Desert Places" (Frost) **1**:213, 229; **39**:233, 246, 253
"Desert Pools" (Teasdale) **31**:364
Desert Run (Yamada) **44**:323, 328-29, 344, 346, 348-49, 351
"Desert Storm" (Yamada) **44**:340, 346
"The Desert-Born" (Hood) **93**:105
"The Deserted House" (Reese) **29**:338, 345, 352
"The Deserted House" (Tennyson) **6**:358
"The Deserted Inn" (Carman) **34**:208
"The Deserted Plantation" (Dunbar) **5**:117, 123
The Deserted Village (Goldsmith) **77**:153, 158, 160, 162-63, 165, 171-73, 175, 178-81, 184, 188-92, 194-95, 197, 203, 205, 208-10, 212-15, 218, 221-22, 228-32, 236-40, 243, 247, 250-56, 259-70, 272-75, 278-81, 283, 286, 288-89, 291-94, 298-305, 310-19
"The Deserter" (Ai) **72**:29-31
"The Deserter" (Smith) **12**:300, 330-31, 333
"Desertion" (Brooke) **24**:57, 63
"Les déserts de l'amour" (Rimbaud) **57**:173-75, 177, 191, 243
"Deserts of Love" (Rimbaud)
See "Les déserts de l'amour"
"Le Désespéranto" (Tzara) **27**:234
"Le désespoir" (Lamartine) **16**:279, 282-83, 290-91, 293
"Desfina" (Heaney) **100**:240
"Design" (Frost) **1**:227-28; **39**:253
"The Design" (Traherne) **70**:273, 312, 316
The Design on the Oriole (Stafford) **71**:334-35
"The Designe" (Traherne)
See "The Design"
Designs by Mr. R. Bentley for Six Poems by Mr. T. Gray (Dodsley) **80**:123-24, 131, 165
"Désir" (Apollinaire) **7**:3
"Desir" (Lamartine) **16**:281
"Le Désir de la Gloire" (Hugo) **17**:88
"Desire" (Hughes) **1**:240
"Desire" (Toomer) **7**:338
"Desire" (Traherne) **70**:175, 194-95, 256, 275-76, 318
Desire (Dylan) **37**:64
"Desire for Spring" (Koch) **80**:342
"Desire Is a World by Night" (Berryman) **64**:88
"Desires for God's Presence" (Very) **86**:166
"Desires of Men and Women" (Berryman) **64**:82
"Desk" (Tsvetaeva)
See "Stol"
"Desnudo" (Guillén) **35**:156
"A Desoignated National Park" (Ortiz) **17**:227
"Desolación" (Mistral) **32**:203-05
Desolación (Mistral) **32**:147, 149-59, 161, 164, 170, 173, 175, 178-81, 183, 187, 190-91, 194, 200, 203
Desolación de la quimera (Cernuda) **62**:173, 215, 223, 265
Desolation (Mistral)
See *Desolación*
Desolation Is a Delicate Thing (Wylie) **23**:322
"Desolation Row" (Dylan) **37**:46-9, 51, 54-5, 60
"Despair" (Baudelaire)
See "Spleen"
"Despair" (Berryman) **64**:94, 171
"Despair" (Lamartine)
See "Le désespoir"
"Despair" (Sexton) **79**:241
"Despair" (Werfel)
See "Verzweiflung"
Despair (Mistral)
See *Desolación*
"Despair in Being Tedious" (Duncan) **75**:179
"Una despedida" (Borges) **22**:94; **32**:38
"Despedida" (Cernuda) **62**:265, 270
"Desperata" (Carducci) **46**:50
"A Desperate Vitality" (Pasolini)
See "Una Disperata Vitalita"
"Despite and Still" (Graves) **6**:154
"Despondency, an Ode" (Burns) **6**:71
"La desserte du sang bleu" (Ponge) **107**:130
Les Destinees (Vigny)
See *Les destinées: Poèmes philosophiques*
Les destinées: Poèmes philosophiques (Vigny) **26**:366-69, 371-72, 391-92, 394, 397, 401-4, 412-13
"Destinie" (Cowley) **90**:104-5, 180, 182
The Destinies: Philosophical Poems (Vigny)
See *Les destinées: Poèmes philosophiques*
"Destino de la carne" (Aleixandre) **15**:38
"Destino del poeta" (Paz) **1**:358
"Destiny" (Arnold) **5**:43, 50
"Destiny" (Corso) **33**:50
Destiny (Hagiwara)
See *Shukumei*
"The Destiny of Nations" (Coleridge) **11**:49, 63-4, 80; **39**:167; **100**:11, 13, 23, 34, 86, 100, 102, 107
Deštník z Piccadilly (Seifert) **47**:317-21, 329, 336
"The Destroyer" (Graves) **6**:166
"Destroyers" (Kipling) **3**:183; **91**:66, 86
La destrucción o el amor (Aleixandre) **15**:14-16, 18, 21-6, 31-4, 39-40, 42
"La destruction" (Baudelaire) **1**:63, 71; **106**:24, 29-30, 92, 95, 97-98, 128
"The Destruction of Long Branch" (Pinsky) **27**:161, 163-5
Destruction or Love (Aleixandre)
See *La destrucción o el amor*
"Destructive Force" (Stevens) **110**:200
"Desvelada" (Mistral) **32**:152, 176
"Deszcz" (Herbert) **50**:8
"Detail" (Williams) **7**:369
Detail and Parody for the Poem Paterson (Williams) **109**:337
"Details for Paterson" (Williams) **109**:337
"The Detective" (Plath) **37**:232
"Detente, sombra de mi bien esquivo" (Juana Inés de la Cruz) **24**:180, 184, 187, 238
"Detraction Execrated" (Suckling) **30**:130
"Detroit Conference of Unity and Art" (Giovanni) **19**:115
"Detskii sad cherez 30 let" (Shvarts) **50**:149-55, 160
"Deus Amanz" (Marie de France)
See "Les Dous Amanz"
"Deutsch Durch Freud" (Jarrell) **41**:158-59, 194-95
"Der Deutsche dankt" (Goethe) **5**:248
"Deutsches Requiem" (Borges) **32**:115
Deutschland: Ein Wintermärchen (Heine) **25**:132-38, 152, 179
Deux Amans (Christine de Pizan)
See *Le debat de deux amans*
"Deux Barques" (Bonnefoy) **58**:168
"Les deux bonnes soeurs" (Baudelaire) **106**:24, 26-27
"Deux poèmes" (Char) **56**:120
Deuxième édition du cinquiesme livre des odes (Ronsard) **11**:246
"Devancier" (Char) **56**:118
Devastation (Mistral)
See *Tala*
"Developers at Crystal River" (Merrill) **28**:261
"Development" (Browning) **2**:96
"The Deviation" (Glück) **16**:135-36
The Devil and Billy Markham (Silverstein) **49**:314-16, 318
"The Devil and the Lady" (Tennyson) **6**:372, 408-09
"The Devil at Berry Pomeroy" (Graves) **6**:142, 144
"Devil on Ice" (Davie) **29**:114-15
"Devils" (Douglas) **106**:186
"The Devils" (Pushkin)
See "Besy"
"The Devil's Advice to Story Tellers" (Graves) **6**:143
"The Devon Maid" (Keats) **1**:311
"A Devonshire Folk Song" (Noyes) **27**:136
"Devonshire Street, W. 1" (Betjeman) **75**:26
"Dévotion" (Rimbaud) **57**:228, 230, 251, 271, 275, 282-84
"Devotion: That It Flow; That There Be Concentration" (Gallagher) **9**:45, 59
"Devotion to Duty" (Sassoon) **12**:257-58
The Devotional Poems of Mirabai (Mirabai) **48**:153-56
"Devotions" (Wright) **36**:337
"Devotions of a Painter" (Hecht) **70**:101
Devotions on Emergent Occasions (Donne) **43**:133, 151
"Devyatsat pyaty god" (Pasternak) **6**:265, 272
"Dew" (Teasdale) **31**:357
"Dezember" (Trakl) **20**:265
Dhakirah lil-nisyan: al-zaman, Bayrout, al-makan, ab 1982 (Darwish) **86**:3, 17
"Dharma" (Collins) **68**:205
"Dharma prachar" (Tagore) **8**:407
"Di morte certo, ma non già dell'ora" (Michelangelo) **103**:274
"Diabetes" (Dickey) **40**:191, 199, 219
"A Diagram of Life" (Swenson) **14**:262
"Diagrams" (Gunn) **26**:195-196, 198
"The Dial Tone" (Nemerov) **24**:262
"Dialectic" (Cassian) **17**:13
"Dialectic" (Thomas) **99**:266
"Dialogo" (Quasimodo) **47**:284, 289
Diálogos del conocimiento (Aleixandre) **15**:6-7, 12-13, 16-17, 39
"A Dialogue" (Herbert) **4**:130
"A Dialogue" (Ignatow) **34**:207, 340
"Dialogue" (Muir) **49**:299
"Dialogue" (Sarton) **39**:325, 338
"A Dialogue" (Swinburne) **24**:323
"Dialogue" (Thomas) **99**:257, 261
"Dialogue" (Wright) **14**:343
"Dialogue Between Ghost and Priest" (Plath) **37**:200
"Dialogue between Mr. John Lock and Seigneur de Montaigne" (Prior) **102**:286, 288
"A Dialogue between Old England and New" (Bradstreet) **10**:5, 17, 21, 33
"A Dialogue between Strephon and Daphne" (Wilmot) **66**:329, 347
"A Dialogue between the Resolved Soul, and Created Pleasure" (Marvell) **10**:265, 271, 274, 277, 290-91, 294, 314; **86**:190, 195, 257
"A Dialogue between the Soul and Body" (Marvell) **10**:265, 271, 274, 290, 313, 316; **86**:183, 190, 237
"A Dialogue between the Two Horses" (Marvell) **10**:276
"A Dialogue between Thyrsis and Dorinda" (Marvell) **10**:271, 314
"A Dialogue for an Entertainment at Court" (Behn) **88**:150-51
"Dialogue of Island and Time" (Curnow) **48**:11, 29
"Dialogue of Outer Space" (Ciardi) **69**:49
"A Dialogue of Self and Soul" (Yeats) **20**:313, 315-16, 327, 333, 337; **51**:104, 111, 152
"A Dialogue of Watching" (Rexroth) **20**:218; **95**:260
"A Dialogue on Poverty" (Yakamochi)
See "Bingu mondo no uta"
"Dialogue on Women's Rights" (Harper) **21**:198
"Dialogue Over a Ouija Board: A Verse Dialogue" (Plath) **37**:209, 211-12, 236

"Dialogue with Four Rocks" (Curnow) **48**:20, 38-39, 65-67
"Dialogue—2 Dollmakers" (Corso) **33**:23
Dialogues (Prior) **102**:285-89, 294-96, 300
Dialogues, Etc. (Barker) **77**:40
Dialogues of Knowledge (Aleixandre)
See *Diálogos del conocimiento*
"Dialogues of the Dogs" (Burns)
See "The Twa Dogs"
"Diamant du coeur" (Gautier) **18**:130, 157
"Diamantina" (Montale) **13**:138
"A Diamond" (Spicer) **78**:253
The Diamond Cutters, and Other Poems (Rich) **5**:350, 352-54, 358, 362-63, 368-69, 388, 392
"The Diamond Merchant" (Wakoski) **15**:348
The Diamond Merchant (Wakoski) **15**:325
"Diaper" (Birney) **52**:21-22
"Diaries" (Cage) **58**:182-83
Diario del '71 (Montale) **13**:138, 144, 158
Diario del '71 e del '72 (Montale) **13**:138-39, 152, 160, 168
Diario del '72 (Montale) **13**:138, 144
El diario que a diario (Guillén) **23**:111, 133
"Diarmuid of the Beautiful Hands" (Melville) **82**:47-48
Diaro de un poeta recien casado (Jiménez) **7**:197, 201-02, 208, 212, 214
"Diary" (Stern) **115**:276-77
Diary: How to Improve the World (You Will Only Make Matters Worse) Continued, Part 3 (Cage) **58**:195, 201-2
"Diary of a Change" (Rukeyser) **12**:218
"Diary of a Naturalist" (Milosz) **8**:206
Diary of a Newly-Wed Poet (Jiménez)
See *Diaro de un poeta recien casado*
"The Diary of a Nobody" (Betjeman) **75**:77
Diary of '71 and '72 (Montale)
See *Diario del '71 e del '72*
"Diaspora" (Auden) **92**:115
"Diaspora" (Lorde) **12**:138, 140
"Il diaul cu la mari" (Pasolini) **17**:253
"Dibujos animados" (Storni) **33**:262, 294
"Dice mía" (Darío) **15**:113
"Dices que no te acuerdas, Clori, y mientes" (Juana Inés de la Cruz) **24**:234
"La dicha" (Borges) **22**:95, 99
"Der Dichter" (Werfel) **101**:322, 325
"Dichterberuf" (Hölderlin) **4**:169
"Dichtung" (Baraka) **4**:17
"Dichtung und Wahrheit" (Curnow) **48**:13, 16-17
"Dichtung und Wahrheit" (Hecht) **70**:65, 67, 86-87
Dichtungen (Char) **56**:111
"Dick, a Maggot" (Swift) **9**:296
"Dick King" (Kinsella) **69**:95, 121, 137
"Dick Sapper" (Masters) **36**:211
"Dick Straightup" (Hughes) **89**:189
"Der dicke Mann im Spiegel" (Werfel) **101**:345
"The Dictators" (Neruda) **4**:282
"The Dictatorship of the Proletariat" (Baraka) **4**:38-9; **113**:24, 36
"Dictée en présence du glacier du Rhône" (Hugo) **17**:91
"Diction" (Creeley) **73**:89
"The Dictionaries" (Soto) **28**:399
"The Dictionary of the Wolf" (Tolson) **88**:349-50
Did Adam Name the Vinegarroon? (Kennedy) **93**:146
"Did Tosti Raise His Bowler Hat?" (Melville) **82**:38
"Did you know that hair is flying around" (Ignatow) **34**:325
"Didactic Piece" (Bogan) **12**:122
"Dido" (O'Hara) **45**:155
"Dido's Farewell to Aeneas" (Smith) **12**:331
"An die Hofnung" (Hölderlin) **4**:148
"An die jungen Dichter" (Hölderlin) **4**:165
"An die Natur" (Hölderlin) **4**:142
"An die Verstummten" (Trakl) **20**:232, 236
"Died of Starvation" (Harper) **21**:191, 203, 210, 216
"Died of Wounds" (Sassoon) **12**:262
Dien cai dau (Komunyakaa) **51**:3, 6, 8-10, 15, 20, 33, 36-37, 39, 42, 52, 54, 56-57, 61, 63
"Un diente" (Storni) **33**:240, 262, 284
"Dies Irae" (Lawrence) **54**:249
"Dies Iræ, dies illa" (Crashaw) **84**:9, 15, 18-19, 156
"Dies irie sic" (Brathwaite) **56**:93
"Diese Jahrtausende" (Sachs) **78**:165
"Dietro il paesaggio" (Zanzotto) **65**:293
Dietro il paesaggio (Zanzotto) **65**:262-65, 273, 287-91, 293-94, 317-19, 321, 331, 338
"Dieu" (Lamartine) **16**:265-66, 272, 274, 277, 285, 290-91
Dieu (Hugo) **17**:65-66, 73-74, 81, 84, 86, 91
"Difference" (Benét) **64**:22
"Difference" (Doty) **176**:19, 48
"A Difference of Zoos" (Corso) **108**:7, 40
"The Differences" (Gunn) **26**:224
Differences for Four Hands (Waldrop) **109**:137, 178
"Differences from Yesterday" (Schuyler) **88**:187
"A Different Image" (Randall) **86**:343
"Different Living" (Spender) **71**:180
"The Difficult Land" (Muir) **49**:230, 280, 299
"Difficult Scene" (Sarton) **39**:321
"Difficulties Arising from the Uncharitable Carriages of Christians" (Taylor) **63**:217, 281, 284, 288
"Difficulties Arising from the Uncharitable Carriages of *Saints* " (Taylor) **63**:289
"Diffrazioni, eritemi" (Zanzotto) **65**:285
"Diffugere Nives" (Noyes) **27**:136
"Dig and Be Dug" (Hughes) **53**:190-91
"Digging" (Heaney) **18**:200, 206-8, 216, 243; **100**:195, 205, 215, 271, 297, 320, 324, 326, 329-30, 355
"Digging for China" (Wilbur) **51**:188, 198, 203, 267
"Digging I" (Thomas) **53**:295, 325-26, 328
"The Digging Skeleton" (Heaney) **100**:215
"The Dignities" (Duncan) **75**:250
"Dignity of Soul" (Viereck) **27**:281
"Digo que yo no soy un hombre puro" (Guillén) **23**:123-24
"A Digression" (Wilbur) **51**:334-35
The Digression (Mickiewicz) **38**:168-69
"Digression on Number 1, 1948" (O'Hara) **45**:241
"Digue Dondaine, Digue Dondon" (Winters) **82**:313
Dikopis' poslednego vremeni (Shvarts) **50**:162-63
"Diktaren om dikten" (Ekeloef) **23**:90
"Dilemma" (Ignatow) **34**:275, 323
"The Dilemma" (Muir) **49**:229, 241
"Dilemma" (Parker) **28**:362
"The Dilemma" (Randall) **86**:324-25, 327
"The Dilemma of Iphis" (Clarke) **112**:133
"Dili" (Pasolini) **17**:251
"Diligence Is to Magic As Progress Is to Flight" (Moore) **49**:113, 134, 161
"El dilitada guerra" (Neruda) **4**:295
"Dillinger" (Spicer) **78**:286
"Dilton Marsh Halt" (Betjeman) **75**:32
"Dimanche, ou l'artiste" (Ponge) **107**:72
"Dimanches" (Laforgue) **14**:72-3, 76, 78
"Dime" (Hughes) **53**:123
"Dime vencedor rapaz" (Juana Inés de la Cruz) **24**:234
"Dimensions" (Banks) **44**:44, 71, 78-9, 87
"Dimisión de Sancho" (Guillén) **35**:234, 239
"Dimmi di gratia, Amor, se gli ochi mei" (Michelangelo) **103**:177
"Dinanzi alle terme di Caracalla" (Carducci) **46**:39, 52, 82-83, 86-88
Dining (Nash) **21**:269
"Dining Out with Doug and Frank" (Schuyler) **88**:186-87, 205, 225
"Dining-Room Tea" (Brooke) **24**:77-8, 82, 88
"The Dinner" (Hope) **56**:304
"Dinner at George & Katie Schneerman's" (Berrigan) **103**:8
"Dinner Guest: Me" (Hughes) **1**:252; **53**:115, 146
"Dinner Party" (Kenyon) **57**:6
"The Dinner Party" (Lowell) **13**:79
"Dinosaur Love" (Berrigan) **103**:28
"Il Dio-Caprone" (Pavese) **13**:204, 207
"Diogenes" (Moore) **49**:116
"Dionysus" (Elytis) **21**:119
"Dionysus Encradled" (Sikelianos) **29**:368
"Dionysus' Escort" (Cavafy) **36**:46, 49
"Dionysus in Doubt" (Robinson) **1**:470
Dionysus in Doubt (Robinson) **1**:470
"Dionysus in Old Age" (Viereck) **27**:295
"Diorama" (Komunyakaa) **51**:63
Dios deseado y deseante: Animal de fondo con numerosos poemas ineditos (Jiménez) **7**:197, 207
"¡Dios las maldiga!" (Martí) **76**:107
"Dios llama al fontanero" (Fuertes) **27**:28
"Dios lo quiere" (Mistral) **32**:151, 176
"Dios-fuerza" (Storni) **33**:262, 294-95
"Dipartita" (Carducci) **46**:50
"Diplomacy: The Father" (Snodgrass) **74**:289
"The Dipper" (Oliver) **75**:334
"Dipper" (Wagoner) **33**:356
"Dipperful" (Chappell) **105**:20, 39
Dipsychus (Clough) **103**:51, 54, 57-59, 67, 69-71, 74-75, 79, 93-94, 96-97, 103, 105-9, 111, 116, 122, 139-40, 155, 161-67
"Diptych with Votive Tablet" (Paz)
See "Preparatory Exercise (Dyptych with Votive Tablet)"
"Diré como nacisteis" (Cernuda) **62**:200, 236-37
"Direct Interpretation" (Wickham) **110**:265
Directed by Desire: The Collected Poems of June Jordan (Jordan) **38**:120-21
"Directions to the Nomad" (Welch) **62**:339, 371
Directionscore: Selected and New Poems (Madhubuti) **5**:330, 336, 346
"The Directive" (Duncan) **75**:262
"Directive" (Frost) **1**:213, 227; **39**:253; **71**:50
"Director of Alienation" (Ferlinghetti) **1**:187
"Director of Photography: Voiceover" (Carson) **64**:222
"Dirge" (Dylan) **37**:54-5
"Dirge" (Emerson) **18**:69, 102
"Dirge" (Smith) **12**:292, 344
"A Dirge" (Tennyson) **6**:359
"Dirge for a Righteous Kitten" (Lindsay) **23**:281
"Dirge for a Town in France" (Merton) **10**:350
"Dirge for an Infant" (Hunt) **73**:138
"Dirge for the New Sunrise (August 6, 1945)" (Sitwell) **3**:327
"Dirge in Cymbeline" (Collins) **72**:56, 58, 62, 117
"Dirge in the Woods" (Meredith) **60**:258, 289, 299, 327, 333-34
"Dirge of the Mad Priest" (Montague) **106**:275
"A Dirge upon the Death of the Right Valiant Lord, Bernard Stuart" (Herrick) **9**:131
"Der Dirigent" (Werfel) **101**:312
"Dirt and Not Copper" (Stein) **18**:319, 328
"Dirty Ears" (Corso) **33**:23
"Dirty English Potatoes" (Kennedy) **93**:149
"The Dirty Hand" (Strand) **63**:180-82
"The Dirty Word" (Shapiro) **25**:299
"Dîs Aliter Visum" (Browning) **2**:68
"Disabled" (Owen) **19**:336, 354, 357; **102**:149, 167, 169-71, 173, 185, 203, 214, 231, 263
Disabled and Other Poems (Owen) **102**:147, 222
"The Disabled Debauchee" (Wilmot) **66**:266, 268, 272, 276, 308-10, 321, 329, 339, 368-69
"Disappearing" (Carver) **54**:13
"The Disappearing Island" (Heaney) **18**:232
"Disappointed" (Enzensberger) **28**:167

"The Disappointment" (Behn) **13**:7, 10-11, 13-14, 16, 25-6, 28; **88**:4, 7-8, 10, 16, 18, 31, 54, 56-60, 85-87, 92-93, 138, 149, 152-53
"The Disappointment" (Leapor) **85**:285
"Disarmament" (Whittier) **93**:189
"A Disaster" (Hughes) **7**:142, 160-61
"Disaster" (Valéry)
See "Sinistre"
"Disasters" (Oppen) **35**:300, 302
"The Discharge" (Herbert) **4**:109, 113, 120, 129
"The Disciple" (Berryman) **64**:87, 90
"The Disciple" (Very) **86**:43, 113
"Disciplina antica" (Pavese) **13**:226
"Discipline" (Herbert)
See "Throw Away Thy Rod"
"Discipline" (Lawrence) **54**:179
The Discipline of the Harp (Cassian) **17**:6
"Disclaimer of the Person" (Jackson) **44**:44, 71, 78-9, 87
"The Disclosure" (Levertov) **11**:169
The Disconsolate Chimera (Cernuda)
See *Desolación de la quimera*
"Discontents in Devon" (Herrick) **9**:108
"Discord" (Corso) **108**:30
"Discord" (Swinburne) **24**:324
"Discord in Childhood" (Lawrence) **54**:234-36
"La Discorde en ménage" (Éluard) **38**:91
Discorsi storici e letterari (Carducci) **46**:55
"Discotheque" (Merrill) **28**:254
"Discouragement" (Hardy) **92**:241, 245
Discours (Ronsard)
See *Discours des misères de ce temps*
Discours à Jean Morel (Ronsard) **105**:285
"Discours à Pierre Lescot" (Ronsard) **11**:266
"Discours au Roy" (Ronsard) **11**:244, 284, 291
"Discours de misères de ce temps" (Ronsard) **11**:248
Discours des misères de ce temps (Ronsard) **11**:224, 250; **105**:273-75, 333
"Discours en forme d'élégie" (Ronsard) **11**:248
"A Discourse between England's Ill Genius and His Companion" (Barker) **91**:48
"The Discourse of the Good Thief" (Parra) **39**:310
A Discourse of the Present Troobles in Fraune, and Miseries of This Time, Compyled by Peter Ronsard Gentilman of Vandome, and Dedicated unto the Quene Mother (Ronsard)
See *See Discours des miseres de ce temps, a la Royne mere du Roy*
The Discourses of Rumi (Rumi)
See *Fihi ma fihi*
"Discovered in Mid-Ocean" (Spender) **71**:133, 179, 216
"The Discoverer of the North Cape" (Longfellow) **30**:40
"Discovering Michael as the King of Spain" (Wakoski) **15**:329
"The Discovery" (Cowley) **90**:112-13, 116-17, 119
"Discovery" (Curnow) **48**:4
"The Discovery" (Hardy) **8**:101
"The Discovery of the Madeiras" (Frost) **1**:196, 206
"The Discovery of the Pacific" (Gunn) **26**:207-08
Discrepancies and Apparitions (Wakoski) **15**:323-24
"Discrete Series" (Oppen) **35**:327-28
Discrete Series (Oppen) **35**:282, 283, 288, 295-96, 300-01, 309, 319-20, 324-30, 332, 340-43, 345
"Discretions of Alcibiades" (Pinsky) **27**:162
"Discursos" (Parra) **39**:261, 273
Discusión (Borges) **32**:38
Discussions (Borges)
See *Discusión*
"Disdaine Returned" (Carew) **29**:32-34
"Disembarking at Quebec" (Atwood) **8**:36, 40
"Disenchantment a Tone Poem" (Aiken) **26**:7, 29
"Disguised as Cock Robin, W. D. Escapes" (Snodgrass) **74**:327
"A Dish of Peaches in Russia" (Stevens) **110**:202
"The Dishonest Mailmen" (Creeley) **73**:9, 28
"Disillusionment" (Hughes) **1**:246
"The Disinherited" (Nerval)
See "El Desdichado"
"The Dismal Chimes of Bells" (Lermontov) **18**:302
Dismantling the Silence (Simic) **69**:262, 264, 272, 274, 299, 311-12, 315, 335, 370
"Dismissal" (Dorn) **115**:234
"The Dismissal of Tyng" (Harper) **21**:190, 218
"The Disoblig'd Love" (Behn) **13**:20
"The Disorder" (Chin) **40**:27
"Disorder Overtakes Us All Day Long" (Schwartz) **8**:285
"Una Disperata Vitalita" (Pasolini) **17**:257-58, 286, 288-89
"Dispersal" (Sassoon) **12**:259
"Dispersiones, alianzas" (Paz) **48**:209
"Dispersions, alliances" (Paz)
See "Dispersiones, alianzas"
"Displaced People" (Pavese) **13**:218
"Displaced Person Looks at a Cage-Bird" (Enright) **93**:15, 18
"The Displeasure of the Seleucid" (Cavafy) **36**:3
"Disposal" (Snodgrass) **74**:290
"The Dispossessed" (Berryman) **64**:89-90, 161
The Dispossessed (Berryman) **64**:69-70, 77, 79, 81, 85, 88-90, 117, 154, 168, 182, 189
"Disputation" (Heine) **25**:170
"Dispute" (Stramm)
See "Zwist"
"The Disquieted Muses" (Plath)
See "The Disquieting Muses"
"The Disquieting Muses" (Plath) **1**:388, 407; **37**:181-82, 185, 254
"Disquisition" (Davenant)
See "The Philosophers Disquisition to the Dying Christian"
"Dissatisfaction" (Traherne) **70**:244, 302, 330
"Dissatisfaction with Metaphysics" (Empson) **104**:122
"Dissect This Silence" (Kunitz) **19**:148
"The Dissecting Table" (Szirtes) **51**:157
"The Dissembler" (Cowley) **90**:13-14, 34, 116
Dissentient Voice (Davie)
See *Dissentient Voice: The Ward-Phillips Lectures for 1980 with Some Related Pieces*
Dissentient Voice: The Ward-Phillips Lectures for 1980 with Some Related Pieces (Davie) **29**:93, 112-15
"The Dissolution" (Donne) **1**:154
"Distance" (Creeley) **73**:45-46
"Distance" (Jacobsen) **62**:318
"Distance" (Kumin) **15**:223-24
"Distance" (Milosz)
See "Odlegtose"
"Distance" (Parker) **28**:364
"The Distance Between: Picnic of Old Friends" (Warren) **37**:377
"Les Distances" (Jaccottet) **98**:174, 186
"The Distances" (Merwin) **45**:48
"Distances" (Okigbo) **7**:228, 234-35, 240-41, 243-47, 251, 253, 255
"Distancia" (Borges) **22**:92
Distant Byways (Matsuo Basho)
See *Oku no hosomichi*
"The Distant Winter" (Levine) **22**:212, 216
"Distanza" (Zanzotto) **65**:274
"Distinctions" (Tomlinson) **17**:314, 328
"Distraction" (Douglas) **106**:196
"Distraction and Definition" (Curnow) **48**:58
"El distraído" (Guillén) **35**:187
"Distress Sale" (Carver) **54**:29
"The Distressed Damsel" (Smart) **13**:348
"A Distressed Player" (Smith)
See "Written for the Benefit of a Distressed Player, Detained at Brighthelmstone for Debt, November 1792"
"District and Circle" (Heaney) **100**:330
District and Circle (Heaney) **100**:330-31, 333
"A District in the City" (Hugo) **68**:234
"The disturbance" (Piercy) **29**:314
"A Disused Shed in Co. Wexford" (Mahon) **60**:136-37, 140, 149, 151, 155-56, 158, 161, 169-71, 183, 202, 205, 211, 215, 220, 237
"Dit de la force d l'amour" (Éluard) **38**:78
Le dit de la pastoure (Christine de Pizan) **68**:3, 9, 21, 25-26, 142-43
Le dit de la rose (Christine de Pizan) **68**:3, 6, 39-40, 42-45, 87, 142-43
Le Dit de Poissy (Christine de Pizan) **68**:3, 23-24, 28-29, 31-33, 98-99, 139, 142-50, 172
"Dit d'errance" (Césaire) **25**:31, 38, 44
"Dithyrambes" (Ronsard) **11**:230-32; **105**:272, 274, 331
"Ditia v getto v okruzhenii bukv" (Shvarts) **50**:162-63
Le Ditié de Jehanne d'Arc (Christine de Pizan) **68**:61, 138, 175, 192
Le dittie sur Jeanne d'Arc (Christine de Pizan)
See *Le Ditié de Jehanne d'Arc*
"Ditty" (Hardy) **8**:90
"Ditty" (Simic) **69**:302
"Ditty" (Tate) **50**:231, 246, 283, 285
"Ditty of Aristippus" (Melville) **82**:114
"Diuturna enfermedad de la Esperanza" (Juana Inés de la Cruz) **24**:225
"La Diva" (Gautier) **18**:135-140
"Divagación" (Darío) **15**:96, 103-05, 119-20
Divagations (Mallarmé) **4**:202, 210; **102**:66, 83, 135
Divan (Hafiz) **116**:3-6, 14-15, 22-23, 30-31, 36-37, 42
Divan-i Shams-i Tabrizi (Rumi) **45**:274-76, 281-91, 313, 320-21, 323-24
"The Diver" (Hayden) **6**:187, 193, 198
"The Diverse Causes" (Ondaatje) **28**:292
Diversifications (Ammons) **16**:24, 61
A Diversity of Creatures (Kipling) **91**:133
"Divertidas estancias a don Juan" (Storni) **33**:280, 305
"The Diverting History of John Gilpin" (Cowper) **40**:48
La divina commedia (Dante) **21**:48-57, 59, 63, 65-6, 69, 73-7, 80-5, 87-8, 90-3, 95, 97-9, 102, 104-05, 108-11; **108**:60-240
"Divina psiquis" (Darío) **15**:101
Divine and Morall Songs (Campion)
See *The First Booke of Ayres*
Divine Comedies: Poems (Merrill) **28**:220-21, 224-25, 227-32, 246, 260, 263, 272, 281
Divine Comedy (Dante)
See *La divina commedia*
The Divine Comedy: Hell, Purgatory, Heaven (Dante)
See *La divina commedia*
The Divine Comedy of Dante Alighieri (Dante)
See *La divina commedia*
The Divine Comedy of Dante Alighieri: Purgatorio (Dante)
See *La divina commedia*
"The Divine Image" (Blake) **12**:5, 7, 33; **63**:10, 14, 33, 49, 68, 81-84, 100, 109, 119, 121, 125, 127-29
"A Divine Mistris" (Carew) **29**:9
The Divine Pilgrim (Aiken) **26**:10, 22, 47, 53
The Divine Poem of Musaeus (Chapman) **96**:35, 85
Divine Poems (Donne) **1**:158
Divine Poems (Waller) **72**:360, 362
"The Divine Privilege" (Meynell) **112**:165, 177
"Divine Psyche" (Darío)
See "Divina psiquis"
"Divine Reflections" (Traherne) **70**:183
The Divine Tragedy (Longfellow) **30**:23, 39, 59, 65, 67
"The Diviner" (Heaney) **18**:200; **100**:195, 334, 349

"Diving Board" (Silverstein) **49**:343
"Diving into the Wreck" (Rich) **5**:371, 374, 376, 394-95
Diving into the Wreck: Poems, 1971-1972 (Rich) **5**:360, 362, 365, 367-68, 370-72, 384, 388-90, 393
"Divinità in incognito" (Montale) **13**:133
"Divinitie" (Herbert) **4**:108, 130
"Divinity" (Kinnell) **26**:286
"Division" (Bogan) **12**:98, 106, 121
"The Division" (Hardy) **8**:93
"Division" (Montague) **106**:296
"The Division of Parts" (Sexton) **2**:351, 359-60, 367; **79**:187, 214
"Divisions upon a Ground" (Hecht) **70**:91
"Divorce" (Mueller) **33**:175
"Divorce" (Sexton) **79**:241
"Divorce" (Wickham) **110**:270-71, 276, 308
"A Divorce of Lovers" (Sarton) **39**:333, 338, 345, 354, 365
"The Divorce Papers" (Sexton) **2**:356, 367
"Divorce, Thy Name Is Woman" (Sexton) **2**:359; **79**:208, 241
"Divorcing" (Levertov) **11**:197
Dīwān (Ekeloef)
See *Dīwān över fursten av Emigón*
Diwan (Rumi)
See *Divan-i Shams-i Tabrizi*
Dīwān över fursten av Emigón (Ekeloef) **23**:63-5, 67-71, 77-8, 85
Diwan-i shams-i tabrizi (Rumi)
See *Divan-i Shams-i Tabrizi*
"Dixon" (Hugo) **68**:251
"Les djinns" (Hugo) **17**:63, 70, 76
Dlatego zyjemy (Szymborska) **44**:268, 281, 318
"D N A" (Berrigan) **103**:36
"Do." (Cummings) **5**:106
"Do" (Tolson) **88**:255, 330-31
"Do Apollina" (Herbert) **50**:7
"Do Ateny" (Herbert) **50**:7
"¡Do íntimo!" (Castro) **41**:88
"Do Jōzefa Sadzika" (Milosz) **8**:190
"Do Marka Aurelego" (Herbert) **50**:7
"Do not compare: the living are incomparable" (Mandelstam)
See "Ne sravnivai: zhivushchii nesravnim"
"Do Not Embrace Your Mind's New Negro Friend" (Meredith) **28**:187
"Do Not Forget the Heathen" (Stevenson) **84**:342
"Do Not Go Gentle into That Good Night" (Thomas) **52**:218, 239, 276, 312-15, 325-29
"Do Not Touch" (Pasternak) **6**:260
"Do Not Touch the Exhibits" (Curnow) **48**:36, 51-52, 59-62
"Do Not Weep, Maiden, for War Is Kind" (Crane)
See "War Is Kind"
"Do przyjaciól Moskali" (Mickiewicz) **38**:169
"Do Take Muriel Out" (Smith) **12**:331, 337
"Do the Others Speak of Me Mockingly, Maliciously?" (Schwartz) **8**:306
"Do You Reckon?" (Hughes) **53**:115
"Do You Remember, Springfield?" (Benét) **64**:13-14
"Do You Think..." (Creeley) **73**:87
"Doc Hill" (Masters) **1**:327; **36**:164, 172, 183, 202
"Dock Rats" (Moore) **4**:251; **49**:101
"Docker" (Heaney) **18**:200; **100**:199
"Dockery and Son" (Larkin) **21**:228-31, 233, 236-37, 241
"Docking at Palermo" (Hugo) **68**:270
"The doctor" (Abse) **41**:21
"The Doctor" (Smith) **12**:330
"The Doctor and the Devils" (Thomas) **52**:252
"Doctor Doctor" (Enright) **93**:20-21
Doctor Drink: Poems (Cunningham) **92**:137, 175
"Doctor Mohawk" (Lindsay) **23**:285, 287
"The Doctor of the Heart" (Sexton) **2**:365
Doctor Spock's Monologue (Yevtushenko) **40**:357
"Doctrinal Point" (Empson) **104**:119, 121
"A Document" (Wright) **14**:356, 362
"Documentary" (Simic) **69**:308
"A Documentary from America" (Stafford) **71**:295, 299
"Dodger Point Lookout" (Snyder) **21**:300
"Dodwells Road" (Wilbur) **51**:215-16
"Does Haughty Gaul" (Burns) **114**:55
"Does It Matter?" (Sassoon) **12**:267-68, 285
"Does the Road Wind Up-Hill all the Way?" (Rossetti) **7**:293
Does the Secret Mind Whisper? (Kaufman) **74**:194, 199, 212, 252
"Dog" (Ferlinghetti) **1**:184
"Dog" (Ransom) **61**:314-15
"The Dog" (Werfel)
See "Der Hund"
"The Dog and the Water-Lily: No Fable" (Cowper) **40**:125, 127
"Dog Dreaming" (Merwin) **45**:23
"Dog Lake with Paula" (Hugo) **68**:261
"The Dog Muses" (Hardy)
See "Why She Moved House"
"A Dog Named Ego, the Snowflakes as Kisses" (Schwartz) **8**:307, 314
"De Dog Rose" (McKay) **2**:223
"A Dog Sleeping on My Feet" (Dickey) **40**:178, 181-82, 231, 257
"The Dog-Days" (Cunningham) **92**:133, 135, 162, 166
"Dog-Days" (Lowell) **13**:64
"Dogfish" (Oliver) **75**:296
"Dog-God Fights the Dollars" (Sexton) **79**:288-89
"Dog-God's Wife Adopts a Monkey" (Sexton) **79**:288-89
"Dogon Eclipse" (Mackey) **49**:5-6
"Dogovor" (Lermontov) **18**:303-4
"The Dogs" (Hunt) **73**:152
"The Dogs are Eating Your Mother" (Hughes) **89**:162, 177, 273, 275
"Dogs Are Shakespearean, Children Are Strangers" (Schwartz) **8**:306, 312
"A Dog's Best Friend Is His Illiteracy" (Nash) **21**:273
"A Dog's Life" (MacDiarmid) **9**:155
"Dog-Tired" (Lawrence) **54**:206
"A Doing Nothing Poem" (Bly) **39**:70
"Dolce Ossessione" (Viereck) **27**:259
"Le dolci rime d'amor ch'io solia" (Dante) **21**:88
"The Doll" (Berssenbrugge) **115**:29, 31-32
"The Doll" (Lowell) **13**:84-5
"The Doll" (Wylie) **23**:321
"Doll Poem" (Corso) **33**:25, 41
"The Dolls" (Yeats) **20**:336, 340
"A Doll's 'Arabian Nights'" (Lindsay) **23**:264, 277
"The Dolls Museum in Dublin" (Boland) **58**:18-19, 61, 96-98
"Dolly's Mistake" (Clare) **23**:40
"Dolor" (Storni) **33**:246
"Dolores" (Swinburne) **24**:308-09, 360, 362-63
"Dolorida" (Vigny) **26**:401, 411
"Dolorous Echo" (Kaufman) **74**:216
The Dolphin (Lowell) **3**:224, 229-30, 232-33, 239-41
"The Dolphins and the Lovers" (Morris) **55**:306
Dom tvorchestva (Akhmadulina) **43**:7-8
A Dome of Many-Coloured Glass (Lowell) **13**:60, 69
"The Dome of Sunday" (Shapiro) **25**:279-80, 283, 286, 295, 305, 308, 310, 315-17, 324-25
"La Domenica Uliva" (Pasolini) **17**:256
The Domesday Book (Masters) **1**:330-33, 335-36, 339; **36**:194-95
"Domestic Economy" (Wickham) **110**:269
"A Domestic Faust" (Szirtes) **51**:169
"Domestic Interior" (Boland) **58**:45-46, 51-52, 54-56, 61
"A Domestic Poem" (Barker) **77**:20
"Domestic Poem for a Summer Afternoon" (Page) **12**:181
Domestic Scenes (Duncan) **75**:126, 129, 175
"The Domestic Science of Sunday Dinner" (Goodison) **36**:158
"Domestic Song" (Ignatow) **34**:323
"Domicilium" (Hardy) **92**:197-201, 241, 319
Domik v Kolomne (Pushkin) **10**:366, 381-86, 391, 400
"Domiki staroi Moskvy" (Tsvetaeva) **14**:318
"The Dominant Thought" (Leopardi)
See "Il Pensiero Dominante"
"Domination of Black" (Justice) **64**:282
"Domination of Black" (Stevens) **6**:293-94
"Dominique aujourd'hui présente" (Éluard) **38**:78
"Le Dompteur de lions se souvient" (Tzara) **27**:224
"Don du poème" (Mallarmé) **4**:196; **102**:72, 94, 101
"Don is a Battell" (Dunbar) **67**:7
"Don José" (Quintana) **36**:255
"Don Juan" (Clare) **23**:26
Don Juan (Byron) **16**:77-88, 90-2, 95-102, 106-08, 110-13, 115-17, 120; **95**:14, 24, 26, 35, 37-38, 51
"Don Juan aux enfers" (Baudelaire) **1**:47
"Don Juan gesellte sich zu uns" (Benn) **35**:48
"Don Juan in Hades" (Baudelaire)
See "Don Juan aux enfers"
"Don Juan's Farewell" (Montague) **106**:311
"Don Julian II" (Quintana) **36**:275
"Donatello's Statue of Saint George" (Carducci)
See "San Giorgio di Donatello"
"La doncella y la muerte" (Parra) **39**:287
Donde habite el olvido (Cernuda) **62**:171, 199-201, 203-4, 213, 221, 254
"Done Into Verse" (Belloc) **24**:43-4
"Donegal Triptych" (MacNeice) **61**:112, 119-20
"Donelson" (Melville) **82**:84, 93, 191, 204
"Dong, Sounds the Brass in the East" (Thoreau) **30**:182, 193, 202, 220
The Dong with a Luminous Nose (Lear) **65**:144, 149-50, 154-56, 160, 199
"The Donkey" (Chesterton) **28**:101
"The Donkey" (Smith) **12**:318
"Donna Clara" (Heine) **25**:145
"Donna me prega" (Cavalcanti) **114**:200-202, 204-6, 208-10, 215, 255
"Donne che avete intelletto d'amore" (Dante) **21**:73, 86
"Donne perdute" (Pavese) **13**:225
"Donner à voir" (Éluard) **38**:102
Donner à voir (Éluard) **38**:100, 107
"Donnerbach mühle" (Char) **56**:190-91, 193-95, 200
"Donneycarney" (Joyce)
See "XXXI"
"Don't Apologize for What You Did" (Darwish)
See "La Ta'adir Amma Fa'alt"
"Don't Be Cross Amanda" (Nash) **21**:271
Don't Cry, Scream (Madhubuti) **5**:324-25, 328, 336, 338, 340-46
"Don't Go Home with Your Hard-On" (Cohen) **109**:69
Don't Go Out of the Door (Li Ho) **13**:42
"Don't Grow Old" (Ginsberg) **4**:84
"Don't Laugh at my Prophetic Anguish" (Lermontov) **18**:281
"Don't Look Now But Mary Is Everbody" (Viereck) **27**:258, 274, 278
"Don't shoot the rail!" (Niedecker) **42**:150
"Don't Shoot the Warthog" (Corso) **33**:40, 43
"Don't Trust Yourself" (Lermontov) **18**:281
"Don't Wanna Be" (Sanchez) **9**:229
"Don't Worry, Son, You're in the Care of Mental Health Professionals" (Espada)

74:138
"Don't write about the storm" (Akhmadulina)
See "Ne pisat' o groze"
"Doom" (Darío)
See "Lo fatal"
"Doom Is the House without the Door" (Dickinson) **1**:111
"The Doom of King Acrisius" (Morris) **55**:242, 329
"Doomsday" (Borges) **32**:91
"Dooms-day" (Herbert) **4**:131
"The Door" (Creeley) **73**:31-32, 46
"A Door" (Merwin) **45**:72, 74-5, 77-9
The Door in the Wall (Tomlinson) **17**:360-61
Door into the Dark (Heaney) **18**:191, 194-95, 199-201, 203, 205-6, 209, 215, 220, 225-26, 238; **100**:193-94, 214, 219-20, 231, 243, 263, 349
"Door to the River" (Doty) **53**:61
"Doors" (Wagoner) **33**:335
"Doors, Doors, Doors" (Sexton) **2**:349; **79**:204
"Dopa una fuga" (Montale) **13**:134
"Dope" (Baraka) **4**:40; **113**:26
"Dopo Aspromonte" (Carducci) **46**:5, 51
"Doppel-Konzert" (Benn) **35**:26
"Dora" (Tennyson) **6**:360
"Dora Maar" (Guest) **55**:185
"Dora Markus" (Montale) **13**:106, 113-14, 119
"Dora Williams" (Masters) **1**:347
"Dorchester Giant" (Holmes) **71**:68
"Dorinda at her Glass" (Leapor) **85**:261, 293
"Dorking" (de la Mare) **77**:114
"Dormant Windows and Door onto the Roof" (Char) **56**:146
"Le dormeur du val" (Rimbaud) **57**:190-91, 203
"La dormeuse" (Valéry) **9**:365-66, 374, 387, 392-93, 396
Dormir, dormir dans les pierres (Péret) **33**:204, 224, 230-31
"Dormit Flumen" (Birney) **52**:27
"Dornenkranz" (Celan) **10**:128-30
"Dorothée" (Baudelaire)
See "La belle Dorothée"
"Dorothy Q., a family Portrait" (Holmes) **71**:68, 72, 93
"Dorset" (Betjeman) **75**:69
"The Dorsetshire Labourer" (Hardy) **92**:248
"Dort und Hier" (Werfel) **101**:315
"Las dos cartas" (Guillén) **23**:126
"Dos cuerpos" (Paz) **48**:199-200
"Las dos (juguete romántico)" (Bécquer) **113**:262
"Dos niños" (Guillén) **23**:139
"Dos patrias" (Martí) **76**:96-97
"Dos peras" (Guillén) **35**:204
"Dos versiones de 'Ritter, Tod und Teufel'" (Borges) **32**:89
"Dos vidas" (Aleixandre) **15**:7
"Dostoievski y la hermosura física" (Cernuda) **62**:270
"Dot de Maubergeonne" (Char) **56**:151
"Dot Leedle Boy" (Riley) **48**:334
"Dotage" (Herbert) **4**:130
"Dotterel" (Wright) **14**:348
"Les Douaniers" (Rimbaud) **57**:203, 205
"Double Absence" (Muir) **49**:299
The Double Axe and Other Poems (Jeffers) **17**:123-24, 130, 136, 146-47
"The Double Chamber" (Baudelaire)
See "La chambre double"
"The Double Dream of Spring" (Ashbery) **26**:115
The Double Dream of Spring (Ashbery) **26**:115, 118-119, 124-125, 128, 130, 138, 144, 148-149, 153-154, 169
"Double Feature" (Hayden) **6**:194-95
"The Double Hellas" (Rexroth) **95**:276
"The Double Image" (Sexton) **2**:350, 355-56, 359, 361-63, 372; **79**:187, 189-90, 226, 247, 258, 271, 280-81, 296-98, 300-303
"Double Image" (Wright) **14**:348
The Double Image (Levertov) **11**:163-64
"The Double Looking Glass" (Hope) **56**:284, 286-87, 306
The Double Man (Auden) **92**:104
"Double Monologue" (Rich) **5**:374
"Double Negative" (Nemerov) **24**:289
"Double Ode" (Rukeyser) **12**:225
Double Persephone (Atwood) **8**:21
"The Double Shame" (Spender) **71**:148
"Double Sonnet" (Hecht) **70**:77-78, 89, 91
"The Double Standard" (Harper) **21**:187, 191, 207
"The Double Transformation: a Tale" (Goldsmith) **77**:215
The Double Tree: Selected Poems, 1942-1976 (Wright) **14**:366
"The Double Voice" (Atwood) **8**:16, 32
"Doubled Mirrors" (Rexroth) **20**:217; **95**:260, 294
"The Double-Headed Snake of Newbury" (Whittier) **93**:173, 227, 239, 251, 346
"Doubleness in Time" (Warren) **37**:376-77
"Double-Nine Festival" (Li Po) **29**:183
"The Doubt of Truth" (Corso) **33**:36
"Doubt on the Great Divide" (Stafford) **71**:361
"The Doubtful Passage" (Cardenal)
See "El estrecho dudoso"
"Doubts" (Brooke) **24**:57, 85
"Doubts" (Teasdale) **31**:356
"Doulce chose est que mariage" (Christine de Pizan) **68**:37
"Les Dous Amanz" (Marie de France) **22**:258, 269, 271-73, 275
Douve (Bonnefoy)
See *Du mouvement et de l'immobilité de Douve*
"A Dove" (Hughes) **89**:147
"The Dove" (Prior) **102**:314
"The Dove Breeder" (Hughes) **7**:116
"The Dove in Spring" (Stevens) **6**:313
"Dove la luce" (Ungaretti) **57**:349
The Dove of Popular Flight—Elegies (Guillén)
See *La paloma de vuelo popular: Elegiás*
"Dove or Swan" (Yeats) **51**:86-87
"Dover" (Auden) **1**:16
"Dover Beach" (Arnold) **5**:8, 13, 16-18, 35, 38, 47, 49, 53, 58, 64-5
"Dover Beach—A Note to That Poem" (MacLeish) **47**:157-58
"Dover: Believing in Kings" (Dickey) **40**:176, 178-79, 183
"The Dover Bitch" (Hecht) **70**:60-62, 80, 92
"Dov'era il tennis" (Montale) **13**:160
"Doverrit with Dreme" (Dunbar) **67**:6, 14
"Doves" (Duncan) **75**:245
"The Doves and the Crows" (Hood) **93**:99-100
"The Doves of Mérida" (Wagoner) **33**:349
"Dow Kritt" (Masters) **36**:218
"Dowager" (Montague) **106**:246
"Down" (Graves) **6**:142, 144
"Down and Out" (Hughes) **53**:113, 137
"Down & Back" (Berryman) **64**:101-2
"Down at the bottom of things" (Piercy) **29**:314
"Down in Dallas" (Kennedy) **93**:138
"Down There" (Cisneros) **52**:146
"Down to the Capital" (Riley) **48**:288, 302, 352
"Down, Wanton, Down!" (Graves) **6**:151, 153, 165
"Down Where I Am" (Hughes) **53**:109
Down-Adown-Derry (de la Mare) **77**:58
"Down-Hall: A Ballad" (Prior) **102**:313, 316
"The Downland" (Masefield) **78**:44, 55
"The Downs" (Bridges) **28**:67, 83
"Downstream" (Carver) **54**:18
"Downstream" (Kinsella) **69**:69-70, 80, 85-87, 90, 101, 104
Downstream (Kinsella) **69**:66, 80, 82-83, 85, 95-96, 103-4, 121-22, 137
"Downstream II" (Kinsella) **69**:104
"The Dowser" (MacNeice) **61**:139
"Dowson and Company" (Mahon) **60**:133
"Dozing on the Lawn" (MacLeish) **47**:206
"Dr. Johnson on the Hebrides" (Heaney) **100**:264
"Dr. P.h.D. Dark, Hypnotist" (Snodgrass) **74**:324, 334
"Dr. Swift to Mr. Pope while He Was Writing the Dunciad" (Swift) **9**:295
"The Draft Horse" (Frost) **1**:213; **39**:241; **71**:43
A Draft of Eleven New Cantos (XXXI-XLI) (Pound) **4**:321-22, 353, 357-58; **95**:204
A Draft of Shadows (Paz)
See *Pasado en claro*
A Draft of XVI Cantos (Pound) **95**:102
Drafts (Eliot)
See *T. S. Eliot, The Waste Land: A Facsimile and Transcript of the Original Drafts Including the Annotations of Ezra Pound*
Drafts and Fragments of Cantos CX to CXVII (Pound) **4**:352-54; **95**:192
"Dragon" (Ondaatje) **28**:298
"The Dragon and the Undying" (Sassoon) **12**:278
"The Dragon and the Unicorn" (Rexroth) **20**:204, 221
The Dragon and the Unicorn (Rexroth) **20**:181-82, 184, 192, 205, 208, 210, 212-14; **95**:249, 254, 257-59, 261-64, 272, 274-75, 278-81, 294-302, 311, 323, 326, 338-40
"Dragon Music" (Hope) **56**:285
"The Dragonfly" (Bogan) **12**:107-08
"Dragon's Blood" (Reed) **68**:332-33
Dragon's Blood (Yau) **61**:348
Drake (Noyes) **27**:114-15, 119, 123, 125, 127, 134
"Drama" (Das) **43**:85
"Drama for Winter Night (Fifth Avenue)" (Hughes) **53**:115
"A Drama of Exile" (Barrett Browning) **6**:6, 20-21, 26, 31, 34, 46; **62**:35, 38, 112
Dramatic Lyrics (Browning) **2**:26, 35, 66, 94; **61**:87
"Dramatic Poem: Voice of Silence" (Ishikawa)
See "Gekishi: Chimmoku no koe"
Dramatic Romances and Lyrics (Browning) **2**:94; **61**:87
Dramatis Personae (Browning) **2**:34, 45, 94-5; **61**:16, 57, 87
Dramatis Personae (Yeats) **20**:328
"The Draped Mirrors" (Borges) **32**:66
Drat These Brats (Kennedy) **93**:134
"Drawer" (Herbert) **50**:4
"Drawing" (Oppen) **35**:288, 294
"Drawing from the Past" (Kenyon) **57**:41
"Drawing Lessons" (Nemerov) **24**:302-03
Drawing-Room Verses (Parra)
See *Versos de salón*
Drawn by Stones, by Earth, by Things That Have Been in Fire: Poems (Bell) **79**:33
"The Drawn-Out War" (Neruda)
See "El dilitada guerra"
"Dread Song" (Walcott) **46**:291
"The Dream" (Barrett Browning) **6**:19
"The Dream" (Behn) **88**:30, 149, 152
"The Dream" (Berry) **28**:38
"A Dream" (Blake) **12**:7, 33-4; **63**:7, 9, 76, 82-83, 100
"The Dream" (Bogan) **12**:111
"The Dream" (Borges) **32**:60
"A Dream" (Bryant) **20**:15
"A Dream" (Burns) **6**:89; **114**:22-23, 45, 53-54, 135, 137-38, 144-47
"The Dream" (Byron) **16**:73, 76
"The Dream" (Creeley) **73**:10, 46
"Dream" (Dunbar) **67**:17-19
"Dream" (Heaney) **18**:201
"The Dream" (Hope) **56**:266, 268
"The Dream" (Ignatow) **34**:290, 317
"A Dream" (Jarrell) **41**:168
"Dream" (Juana Inés de la Cruz)
See *El Sueño*
"The Dream" (Kinsella) **69**:143, 145
"The Dream" (Leopardi)
See "Il Sogno"

"The Dream" (Mickiewicz)
See "Sen"
"Dream" (Riley) **48**:315
"The Dream" (Roethke) **15**:288-89
"The Dream" (Sassoon) **12**:267
"A Dream" (Schnackenberg) **45**:329-30
"Dream" (Southey) **111**:256
"The Dream" (Stryk) **27**:204
"A Dream" (Swenson) **14**:288
"Dream" (Tagore)
See "Svapna"
"Dream" (Wright) **14**:367, 373
A Dream (Keats) **96**:348
The Dream (Masefield) **78**:51, 73
"The Dream, 1863" (Hayden) **6**:180, 188
"Dream and Madness" (Trakl)
See "Traum und Umnachtung"
"Dream Avenue" (Simic) **69**:337
"Dream Boogie" (Hughes) **1**:266; **53**:123, 159, 190, 197, 206
"Dream Boogie: Variation" (Hughes) **53**:92
"A Dream Deferred" (Hughes) **1**:266; **53**:150-51
"Dream Drumming" (Rukeyser) **12**:222
"The Dream Flood" (Dickey) **40**:180-81
"A Dream in Three Colours" (McGuckian) **27**:90
"The Dream Language of Fergus" (McGuckian) **27**:83, 88-90
"A Dream Lies Dead" (Parker) **28**:363
The Dream of a Common Language: Poems, 1974-1977 (Rich) **5**:373-76, 378, 384, 389
"Dream of a Large Lady" (Kizer) **66**:64
"The Dream of Angling the Dream of Cool Rain" (Wakoski) **15**:365
"Dream of Berlin" (O'Hara) **45**:163
"A Dream of Burial" (Wright) **36**:313
"A Dream of Comparison" (Smith) **12**:330, 332-33, 345, 352
"Dream of Constantine" (Schnackenberg) **45**:333
The Dream of Eugene Aram (Hood) **93**:46, 60, 62, 64, 81, 83, 89, 118
"A Dream of Fair Women" (Tennyson) **6**:353, 359-60; **101**:139, 144, 237
"A Dream of Games" (Jacobsen) **62**:302-3
"A Dream of John Brown: On His Return Trip Home" (Spencer) **77**:338-39
"A Dream of July" (Montague) **106**:311
"The Dream of Knowledge" (Schwartz) **8**:297, 311
"Dream of Light in the Shade" (Stone) **53**:228
"A Dream of Nourishment" (Smith) **12**:326
"The Dream of Now" (Stafford) **71**:369
"The Dream of Private Clitus" (Jones) **116**:112, 114, 159, 214, 216, 224
"A Dream of Small Children" (Song) **21**:341, 343
"Dream of Summer" (Carducci)
See "Sogno d'estate"
"Dream of the City Shopwoman" (Hardy) **92**:241, 246
"Dream of the Future" (Jeffers) **17**:141
"The Dream of the Unified Field" (Graham) **59**:137, 151, 159-61, 168, 185
The Dream of the Unified Field: Selected Poems 1974-1994 (Graham) **59**:146, 151, 160, 169, 181-83
"A Dream of What I Missing" (Bly) **39**:42
"A Dream of Whitman Paraphrased, Recognized and Made More Vivid by Renoir" (Schwartz) **8**:318
"Dream of Wild Birds" (Stone) **53**:229
"Dream of Youth" (Tagore)
See "Yauvan-svapna"
"A Dream or No" (Hardy) **8**:135
"A Dream Pang" (Frost) **39**:230-31, 237, 246
"The Dream Question" (Hardy) **92**:217
"A Dream (Real)" (Ekeloef) **23**:80
"A Dream Sestina" (Justice) **64**:253
"Dream Song 1" (Berryman) **64**:80, 143, 165
"Dream Song 2" (Berryman) **64**:138-39, 141-43, 192
"Dream Song 3" (Berryman) **64**:157
"Dream Song 4" (Berryman) **64**:141, 143
"Dream Song 5" (Berryman) **64**:141
"Dream Song 6" (Berryman) **64**:141
"Dream Song 7" (Berryman) **64**:141
"Dream Song 8" (Berryman) **64**:78
"Dream Song 9" (Berryman) **64**:79, 141
"Dream Song 10" (Berryman) **64**:143
"Dream Song 11" (Berryman) **64**:141
"Dream Song 13" (Berryman) **64**:148
"Dream Song 14" (Berryman) **64**:149
"Dream Song 15" (Berryman) **64**:186
"Dream Song 16" (Berryman) **64**:79
"Dream Song 20" (Berryman) **64**:141
"Dream Song 22" (Berryman) **64**:159
"Dream Song 26" (Berryman) **64**:147
"Dream Song 29" (Berryman) **64**:79, 81, 141
"Dream Song 35" (Berryman) **64**:182-83
"Dream Song 36" (Berryman) **64**:143, 163
"Dream Song 37" (Berryman) **64**:141, 183
"Dream Song 40" (Berryman) **64**:141
"Dream Song 42" (Berryman) **64**:144
"Dream Song 49" (Berryman) **64**:152
"Dream Song 51" (Berryman) **64**:140
"Dream Song 54" (Berryman) **64**:142
"Dream Song 56" (Berryman) **64**:116
"Dream Song 57" (Berryman) **64**:143
"Dream Song 60" (Berryman) **64**:140-41
"Dream Song 68" (Berryman) **64**:141
"Dream Song 74" (Berryman) **64**:150
"Dream Song 75" (Berryman) **64**:165
"Dream Song 77" (Berryman) **64**:79, 130-31, 151
"Dream Song 80" (Berryman) **64**:164
"Dream Song 82" (Berryman) **64**:164
"Dream Song 84" (Berryman) **64**:142
"Dream Song 90" (Berryman) **64**:78
"Dream Song 94" (Berryman) **64**:159
"Dream Song 96" (Berryman) **64**:142
"Dream Song 114" (Berryman) **64**:141
"Dream Song 124" (Berryman) **64**:80
"Dream Song 126" (Berryman) **64**:141
"Dream Song 153" (Berryman) **64**:151
"Dream Song 157" (Berryman) **64**:115
"Dream Song 170" (Berryman) **64**:152
"Dream Song 172" (Berryman) **64**:164
"Dream Song 185" (Berryman) **64**:142
"Dream Song 187" (Berryman) **64**:164
"Dream Song 198" (Berryman) **64**:183-84
"Dream Song 199" (Berryman) **64**:142
"Dream Song 220" (Berryman) **64**:141
"Dream Song 232" (Berryman) **64**:142
"Dream Song 242" (Berryman) **64**:80, 159
"Dream Song 260" (Berryman) **64**:150
"Dream Song 273" (Berryman) **64**:142
"Dream Song 281" (Berryman) **64**:182
"Dream Song 283" (Berryman) **64**:182
"Dream Song 291" (Berryman) **64**:186
"Dream Song 294" (Berryman) **64**:157
"Dream Song 297" (Berryman) **64**:152
"Dream Song 301" (Berryman) **64**:152
"Dream Song 302" (Berryman) **64**:186
"Dream Song 303" (Berryman) **64**:161
"Dream Song 309" (Berryman) **64**:117
"Dream Song 311" (Berryman) **64**:117, 149
"Dream Song 312" (Berryman) **64**:117, 182-83, 185
"Dream Song 313" (Berryman) **64**:117
"Dream Song 314" (Berryman) **64**:117
"Dream Song 315" (Berryman) **64**:184, 187
"Dream Song 317" (Berryman) **64**:152
"Dream Song 321" (Berryman) **64**:117
"Dream Song 324" (Berryman) **64**:116-17
"Dream Song 325" (Berryman) **64**:77, 152
"Dream Song 331" (Berryman) **64**:185
"Dream Song 334" (Berryman) **64**:184
"Dream Song 336" (Berryman) **64**:89
"Dream Song 339" (Berryman) **64**:144
"Dream Song 355" (Berryman) **64**:143
"Dream Song 361" (Berryman) **64**:187
"Dream Song 366" (Berryman) **64**:80, 118, 142
"Dream Song 372" (Berryman) **64**:186
"Dream Song 382" (Berryman) **64**:165
"Dream Song 384" (Berryman) **64**:183
"Dream Song 385" (Berryman) **64**:122, 131
The Dream Songs (Berryman) **64**:68-69, 71-74, 76-78, 80, 88, 90, 92-93, 97-99, 101, 110, 112, 115-18, 121-34, 138-44, 147-48, 150-54, 156, 158-62, 165, 168-71, 181, 183-84, 186-90, 192
"Dream Variations" (Hughes) **1**:248; **53**:84
"Dream Vision" (Cunningham) **92**:165
"A Dream within a Dream" (Poe) **1**:434
Dream Work (Oliver) **75**:284-85, 287, 289, 292-94, 296, 299-300, 302, 305
"Dream—August 1979" (Goodison) **36**:148
"Dream-City of an Emigrant" (Werfel)
See "Traumstadt eines Emigranten"
"Dreamdust" (Hughes) **1**:241
"The Dreame" (Donne) **1**:147, 152; **43**:130, 133, 186-88
"The Dreame" (Herrick) **9**:109
"A Dreamed Realization" (Corso) **33**:48; **108**:18, 40
"The Dreamer" (de la Mare) **77**:94
"The Dreamer" (Pushkin) **10**:407
"The Dreamer" (Tennyson) **6**:372
"Dreamers" (Sassoon) **12**:284, 286
"The Dreamer's Song" (Ortiz) **17**:245
"The Dream-Follower" (Hardy) **8**:108
"Dreaming in the Shanghai Restaurant" (Enright) **93**:21
Dreaming of Butterflies (Hagiwara)
See *Chō o yumemu*
"Dreaming of Hair" (Lee) **24**:242, 247
"The Dreaming Saw" (Char)
See "La Scie rêveuse"
"Dreaming Winter" (Welch) **62**:339, 345
"Dream-Land" (Poe) **1**:433-34, 436, 438; **54**:308
"Dreamland" (Rossetti) **44**:259
"Dreams" (Giovanni) **19**:110
"Dreams" (Jarrell) **41**:168
"Dreams" (Oliver) **75**:285
"Dreams" (Poe) **1**:436
"Dreams" (Schuyler) **88**:189
"Dreams" (Sexton) **79**:193
"Dreams" (Traherne) **70**:269, 288
"Dreams about Clothes" (Merrill) **28**:254
"Dreams in War Time" (Lowell) **13**:84
"Dreams of a Summer Night" (Barker) **77**:40
Dreams of Georgia (Akhmadulina)
See *Sny o Gruzii*
"The Dreams of My Heart" (Teasdale) **31**:59
"Dreams of Suicide," (Meredith) **28**:199, 205
"Dreams of Water" (Justice) **64**:275
"Dreams Old and Nascent: Old" (Lawrence) **54**:175
"Dreams To Have" (Stafford) **71**:289
"Dreamtigers" (Borges)
See "El hacedor"
Dreamtigers (Borges)
See *El hacedor*
"The Dreamt-Of Place" (Muir) **49**:231, 243, 265
"Drear Nighted December" (Keats)
See "In Drear Nighted December"
"Dregy" (Dunbar) **67**:59-65
Drei alte Männer (Benn) **35**:33, 34
"Drei Blicke in einen Opal" (Trakl) **20**:261-62
Dresden Forefathers' Eve Wilno Forefathers' Eve (Mickiewicz)
See *Dziady III*
"Dressed All in Pink" (Randall) **86**:286, 288
Dressed in Light (Seifert)
See *Světlem oděná*
"Dressing" (Vaughan) **81**:263, 297, 368
"Dressing to Wait a Table" (McKay) **2**:205
"Drewniana kostka" (Herbert) **50**:4-7, 17
"Dried Marjoram" (Lowell) **13**:61
"The Drifter off Tarentum" (Kipling) **3**:183
"The Drifter's Escape" (Dylan) **37**:49
"Drifting" (Crabbe) **97**:76
"Drifting" (Dickey) **40**:231

Drifting into War (Bissett) **14**:10, 33
Driftlake: A Lieder Cycle (Chappell) **105**:37
"Driftwood" (Teasdale) **31**:359
"Driftwood" (Wilbur) **51**:187, 192, 229
"A Driftwood Altar" (Ashbery) **26**:163
"Driftword" (Brathwaite) **56**:70, 90, 97
"Drink, Eat, Sleep" (Kenyon) **57**:3
"A Drink of Water" (Heaney) **100**:318, 343
"Drink to Me Only with Thine Eyes" (Jonson)
See "Song to Celia"
"Drinker" (Char)
See "Buveuse"
"The Drinker" (Lowell) **3**:212
"Drinking Alone by Moonlight" (Li Po) **29**:188
"Drinking From a Helmet" (Dickey) **40**:155-56, 159-60, 190, 192, 208-9, 231
"Drinking Song" (Hardy) **92**:220
"The Drive Home" (Merwin) **45**:92
"Driven on Strike" (Gilmore) **87**:300
"The Driver" (Dickey) **40**:257-58
"Drivers of Diaper-Service Trucks Are Sad" (Kennedy) **93**:143
"Driving Gloves" (Wakoski) **15**:347
"Driving Home the Cows" (Reese) **29**:330
"Driving Montana" (Hugo) **68**:303
"Driving My Parents Home at Christmas" (Bly) **39**:86
"Driving South" (Montague) **106**:245, 249, 251, 253, 340
"Driving through Ohio" (Bly) **39**:6
"Driving through the Wind River Reservation: A Poem of Black Bear" (Oliver) **75**:300-301
"Driving to Town Late to Mail a Letter" (Bly) **39**:23
"Driving toward the Lac Qui Parle River" (Bly) **39**:73, 83
"Droga nad przepascic w Czufut-Kale" (Mickiewicz) **38**:222-23
"Drohungen" (Benn) **35**:47
"Droll Husband" (Ignatow) **34**:202
"A Drop of Gin" (Hood) **93**:84, 101-2
"Dropping Eyelids Among the Aerial Ash" (Ammons) **16**:39
"Drought" (Alexie) **53**:4
"Drought" (Brathwaite) **56**:61
"Drought" (Wright) **14**:353
"Drought Year" (Wright) **14**:366
"The Drowned" (Spender) **71**:147
"The Drowned Child" (Glück) **16**:129-30, 150
"The Drowned Girl" (Szirtes) **51**:178
"Drowning" (Thomas) **99**:270
"The Drowning Poet" (Merrill) **28**:225
"Drowning With Others" (Dickey) **40**:179-80, 206
Drowning with Others (Dickey) **40**:158, 175-77, 180, 182, 190, 204, 206-7, 211-12, 225, 230-32, 257, 261-62
"Drozhzhi mira dorogie" (Mandelstam) **14**:153
The Drug Shop, or Endymion in Edmonstoun (Benét) **64**:18
"Drug Store" (Shapiro) **25**:268, 295, 319, 322
"Drugged" (de la Mare) **77**:77
"Drugoe" (Akhmadulina) **43**:7, 65
"Drugs" (Spicer) **78**:294
"Drugs and the Market" (Dorn) **115**:160
"Drugs in the Forehead" (Espada) **74**:121
"Druid Stones at Kensaleyre" (Hugo) **68**:294
"Druidic Rimes" (Nemerov) **24**:301
"The Druid's Prophecies" (Tennyson) **101**:193
"Drum" (Brathwaite) **56**:75
"A Drumlin Woodchuck" (Frost) **1**:213; **39**:233, 246-47
"Drummer Hodge" (Hardy) **8**:121
"Drumnotes" (Sandburg) **41**:241
"Drums" (Okigbo) **7**:234
"Drum-Taps" (Whitman) **91**:207
Drum-Taps (Whitman) **3**:389, 414, 418; **91**:214, 278
"Drunk Coachman" (Rimbaud)
See "Cocher ivre"
The Drunk in the Furnace (Merwin) **45**:3, 5, 7-9, 18, 24, 27-8, 31, 52, 70-1, 74
A Drunk Man Looks at the Thistle (MacDiarmid) **9**:151-52, 158, 167-70, 173, 175, 181, 186, 189-93
"The Drunkard" (Sitwell) **3**:299
"The Drunkard to His Bottle" (Whittier) **93**:200
"The Drunkards and the Tavern" (Rumi) **45**:278
"The Drunkard's Child" (Harper) **21**:191, 210, 216
"The Drunkard's Funeral" (Lindsay) **23**:269, 283-84
"The Drunkards in the Street" (Lindsay) **23**:284
"Drunken Americans" (Ashbery) **26**:167
"The Drunken Boat" (Rimbaud)
See "Le bateau ivre"
"The Drunken Fisherman" (Lowell) **3**:199-200, 202, 204, 212
"The Drunken Minstrel Rags His Bluegrass Lute" (Snodgrass) **74**:329, 334
"Drunks" (Berryman) **64**:100
"Dry Hill" (Mahon) **60**:142
"Dry Loaf" (Stevens) **110**:201
"The Dry Salvages" (Eliot) **5**:164-65, 167-69, 180-81, 183, 186, 210
The Dry Salvages (Eliot) **90**:328
"The Dry Stone Mason" (Merwin) **45**:23
Dry Sun, Dry Wind (Wagoner) **33**:324-25, 364-70, 373
"Dryads" (Sassoon) **12**:240, 275
Du (Stramm) **50**:189-90, 195, 198, 200-202, 204, 206, 208, 214
"Du Bay" (Niedecker) **42**:98, 151
"Du coton dans les oreilles" (Apollinaire) **7**:22
"Du haut de la muraille de Paris" (Hugo) **17**:100
"Du liegst" (Celan) **10**:98
Du mouvement et de l'immobilité de Douve (Bonnefoy) **58**:108-9, 120, 123-24, 127, 130-35, 147, 150, 161, 171, 173, 176
"Du sei wei du" (Celan) **10**:100-01
"Dualidá en una despedida" (Borges) **32**:57, 83
"Dualism" (Reed) **68**:339
"Dualities" (Abse) **41**:13
"Duality" (Abse) **41**:6, 9
"Duality on Saying Farewell" (Borges)
See "Dualidá en una despedida"
"Dublin" (MacNeice) **61**:109, 118
"Dublin Georgian" (Davie) **29**:110, 120-1
"Dublinesque" (Larkin) **21**:237, 244
"Dubrovnik October 14, 1980, 10:45 p. m." (Ginsberg) **4**:62
Duc des vrais amans (Christine de Pizan)
See *Le livre du duc des vrais amans*
"The Duchess Potatoes" (Wakoski) **15**:330
"The Duck and the Kangaroo" (Lear) **65**:147-49, 153
"Duck Blind" (Hass) **16**:217
"A Duck for Dinner" (Stevens) **6**:322
"The Duckpond" (Stryk) **27**:188, 195-97, 202-03, 206
Ducks (Bly) **39**:71
"Due donne in cima de la mente mia" (Dante) **21**:74
"Due nel crepuscolo" (Montale) **13**:107, 150
"Due sigarette" (Pavese) **13**:225-28
"Le due Torri" (Carducci) **46**:52
"Dueil angoissieux, rage demesuree" (Christine de Pizan) **68**:19
"The Duel" (Cowley) **90**:15
"Duel" (Hagiwara) **18**:167
"A Duel" (Morris) **55**:238
"Duet for a Chair and a Table" (Spicer) **78**:271, 305
"Duet, with Muffled Brake Drums" (Updike) **90**:348, 352
"Du-Gedichte" (Stramm) **50**:198
"The Dug-Out" (Sassoon) **12**:281, 283
Duineser Elegien (Rilke) **2**:268-69, 279-82, 285-87, 294-95
Duino Elegies (Rilke)
See *Duineser Elegien*
Duino Elegies/Elegies (Rilke)
See *Duineser Elegien*
"Duke Mantee" (Baraka) **113**:6
Duke of Albany (Skelton) **25**:330
"Duke: Playing Piano at 70" (Brathwaite) **56**:55, 61
El dulce daño (Storni) **33**:235-36, 240-41, 246-48, 250, 274-77, 283, 287, 297, 307
"Dulce et decorum est" (Owen) **19**:347, 353, 357, 359-61, 364-65, 370-71; **102**:142, 145-46, 167, 171-72, 203, 210, 213, 219-21, 226, 228, 230, 242, 246, 248-50, 255-56, 259, 265-66, 275-76
"Dulce Ridentem" (Benét) **64**:22
"Dulcia Linquimus Arva" (Borges) **22**:79; **32**:84
"The Dull Relief of General Pain—Oxycontin, Roxicodone and Codeine in General" (Dorn) **115**:232
"Dull Water Spirit and Protean God" (Thoreau) **30**:216
"Dully Gumption's Addendum" (Hughes) **7**:120
"Dulnesse" (Herbert) **4**:112
"Dulzura" (Mistral) **32**:179
"La dulzura del ángelus" (Darío) **15**:81, 96
Dum Morior Orior (Southwell)
See "Decease, Release: Dum Morior Orior"
"Duma" (Lermontov) **18**:268-69, 279, 281, 283, 297, 304
"La dumaiu: kak ia byla glupa" (Akhmadulina) **43**:7
"The Dumb Orators" (Crabbe) **97**:86, 95-96, 104, 106
"Dumbbell Rhymes" (Snodgrass) **74**:329, 331
"Dumbshow" (Montague) **106**:329
"The Dumfries Volunteers" (Burns) **114**:97, 143, 190
"Dumnesse" (Traherne) **70**:170, 173, 190, 256, 268, 315
"The Dump" (Hall) **70**:8
"The Dump" (Shvarts)
See "Svalka"
"Dunbar" (Spencer) **77**:341
"Duncan" (Gunn) **26**:228
"Duncan Gray" (Burns) **6**:57, 59, 100
The Dunciad (Pope) **26**:304-305, 314-17, 319, 321-22, 326-27, 334, 338-40, 357-61
Dunciad in Four Books (Pope) **26**:358-59
Dunciad Minimus (Hope)
See *Dunciad Minor: An Heroick Poem*
Dunciad Minor: An Heroick Poem (Hope) **56**:302
Dunciad Variorum (Pope) **26**:356-61
"Dunction Hill" (Belloc) **24**:10, 49
"Dunedin" (Curnow) **48**:12
"The Dungeon" (Coleridge) **67**:278, 280, 295, 337
"The Dungeon" (Wordsworth) **4**:373
"Dunkler Sommer" (Benn) **35**:67, 68
"Duns Scotus" (Lowell) **3**:201
"Duns Scotus's Oxford" (Hopkins) **15**:144
"Dünya Guzeli" (Cavafy) **36**:52
The Duplications (Koch) **80**:312, 333
"Dura Mater" (Kinsella) **69**:129, 141
A Durable Fire (Sarton) **39**:340, 342-43
"Duranta asha" (Tagore) **8**:407
"Duration" (Paz) **1**:355
"Duration of Water" (Berssenbrugge) **115**:11
Durch die Stunde (Benn) **35**:6
"Durch jede Stunde" (Benn) **35**:9
"Durchs Erlenholz kam sie entlang gestrichen" (Benn) **35**:45, 50
"Durham in March" (Tomlinson) **17**:361
"During a Solar Eclipse" (Nemerov) **24**:288
"During a Transatlantic Call" (Lowell) **3**:241
"During Fever" (Lowell) **3**:206, 220, 243, 245
"During the Eichmann Trial" (Levertov) **11**:169, 193
"During the Passaic Strike of 1926" (Zukofsky) **11**:351, 396
"During Wind and Rain" (Hardy) **8**:88, 113; **92**:197-98, 200-201
"Durwood Collins" (Hughes) **53**:115

"Dusha" (Pasternak) **6**:267, 285
"Dusha moja mrachna" (Lermontov) **18**:302
"Dusk" (Spender) **71**:188
"Dusk in Winter" (Merwin) **45**:20, 23
"The Dusk of Horses" (Dickey) **40**:190
"Dusk on English Bay" (Birney) **52**:4, 39
"Dusk on the Bay" (Birney) **52**:5-6, 8, 24
"The Dust" (Brathwaite) **56**:69, 76, 84, 95, 100
"Dust" (Brooke) **24**:57
"Dust" (Dickey) **40**:160
"Dust" (Hughes) **89**:211
"The Dust" (Reese) **29**:330, 333
"Dust" (Wright) **14**:379
"Dust Bowl" (Hughes) **1**:240
"Dust in the Eyes" (Frost) **1**:195
"The Dust Made Flesh" (Spender) **71**:179-80, 191, 216-17
"Dust of Snow" (Frost) **1**:195, 218
"Dust to Dust" (Masefield) **78**:48
"Dusting" (Dove) **6**:111, 113
"The Dust-Layers" (Melville) **82**:109
"The Dustman" (Carman) **34**:200, 213
"Dusty Braces" (Snyder) **21**:293
"Dusza Pana Cogito" (Herbert) **50**:39, 41
"A Dutch Christmas" (Melville) **82**:154
"A Dutch Courtyard" (Wilbur) **51**:188, 192-93, 296, 325
"Dutch Graves in Bucks County" (Stevens) **6**:302; **110**:122
"The Dutch in the Medway" (Kipling) **91**:110
"Dutch Interiors" (Kenyon) **57**:26, 38-39, 46
"Dutch Painters" (Zagajewski) **27**:403
"A Dutch Picture" (Longfellow) **30**:71
"Duwamish" (Hugo) **68**:238, 258-59, 263, 265, 274, 287
"Duwamish Head" (Hugo) **68**:235-36, 258-59, 270
"Dva brata" (Lermontov) **18**:299
"Dva sokola" (Lermontov) **18**:288
Dvenadsat (Blok) **21**:8-12, 16-17, 21-2, 26-9, 31, 33-9, 41-3
"Dvukh stanov ne beots, a— esli gost sluchainyi" (Tsvetaeva) **14**:325
"The Dwarf" (Stevens) **110**:222
Dwarf Bamboo (Chin) **40**:3, 8, 27-8
"The Dwelling-Place" (de la Mare) **77**:71, 116
"Dwie krople" (Herbert) **50**:8
"Dwie malpy Bruegla" (Szymborska) **44**:281, 286, 311-13
"D-Y Bar" (Welch) **62**:370
"Dyâli" (Césaire) **25**:40
"Dyddgu" (Dafydd ap Gwilym) **56**:247
"The Dying" (Chappell) **105**:65
"A Dying Art" (Mahon) **60**:132
"Dying Away" (Meredith) **28**:200
"The Dying Bondman" (Harper) **21**:187, 207
"The Dying Christian" (Harper) **21**:208, 215-16
"The Dying Girl to Her Mother" (Dobell) **100**:166
"The Dying Goddess" (Kizer) **66**:75
"Dying in the Forest" (Werfel)
See "Sterben im Walde"
"The Dying Mother" (Harper) **21**:197
"The Dying Queen" (Harper) **21**:198
"The Dying Swan" (Tennyson) **6**:359, 389-91
"The Dykes" (Kipling) **3**:182; **91**:71-73, 154
"Dynamik" (Benn) **35**:69
"Dynamiter" (Sandburg) **41**:234, 273, 347, 349, 351, 365
The Dynasts (Hardy) **92**:209, 215-21, 223, 225, 236, 246, 262-63, 269, 292
The Dynasts: A Drama of the Napoleonic Wars (Hardy) **8**:79-81, 85-7, 95-6, 104, 108, 111, 121-22
The Dynasty of Raghu (Kālidāsa)
See *Raghuvamśa*
"Dyne" (Char) **56**:155
"Dytiscus" (MacDiarmid) **9**:157, 183
"Dyvers Dothe Use" (Wyatt) **27**:316
"Dyvers Thy Death" (Surrey) **59**:327
"Dzhulio" (Lermontov) **18**:300
Dziady III (Mickiewicz) **38**:153-54, 157, 159, 161, 164-65, 167-69, 184, 190-92, 218-19, 229, 231
"D-Zug" (Benn) **35**:35, 46, 47, 54, 77
"E. & O. E." (Tolson) **88**:244, 255, 273, 279, 282-83, 293, 295-98, 303, 314, 334, 338
"E. C. Culbertson" (Masters) **36**:230, 232
"E la madre-norma" (Zanzotto) **65**:320
"E. P. Ode Pour L'Election de son Sepulchre" (Pound) **4**:319
"E pò, muci" (Zanzotto) **65**:269
"E Questo il nido in che la mia Fenice?" (Hope) **56**:281
"Each and All" (Emerson) **18**:84, 94-96, 98-101, 107
"Each Bird Walking" (Gallagher) **9**:44
"Each Day of Summer" (Swenson) **14**:276
"Each in His Season" (Snodgrass) **74**:330
Each in His Season (Snodgrass) **74**:329-31, 335
"Each One, Pull One" (Walker) **30**:344
Each Other (Werfel)
See *Einander*
"Each Small Gleam Was a Voice" (Crane) **80**:52, 70
"Each Stone" (Ignatow) **34**:325
"Eagle" (Kunitz) **19**:147
"The Eagle" (Tate) **50**:231, 256
"The Eagle" (Tennyson) **101**:237
"The Eagle and the Mole" (Wylie) **23**:301, 309, 322, 327, 334
"Eagle Confin'd in a College Court" (Smart) **13**:341
"Eagle Descending" (Warren) **37**:357
Eagle or Sun? (Paz)
See *Águila o sol?*
"Eagle Poem" (Harjo) **27**:67
"The Eagle That Is Forgotten" (Lindsay) **23**:277, 288, 294, 296
"The Eagle-Feather Fan" (Momaday) **25**:217
"Eagles" (Dickey) **40**:248
The Eagle's Mile (Dickey) **40**:230, 239, 259
"ΕΠΙΝΙΚΙΟΝ" (Cowper) **40**:103
"Ear Muff Tree Ripening" (Birney) **52**:28
"Earliest Memory" (Corso) **33**:44
"The Early Anthropologists" (Mahon) **60**:193
"Early Bright" (Hughes) **53**:191-92
"Early Chronology" (Sassoon) **12**:245
"Early Days of the Construction of Our Library" (Williams) **109**:196
"An Early Dutch Scene" (Corso) **108**:8
"Early Evening Quarrel" (Hughes) **1**:247; **53**:119
"Early January" (Merwin) **45**:20
"Early Losses: A Requiem" (Walker) **30**:354
"Early Loves" (Kaufman) **74**:235
"Early Lynching" (Sandburg) **2**:330
"Early March" (Sassoon) **12**:254, 259
"An Early Martyr" (Williams) **7**:353, 368; **109**:195
An Early Martyr, and Other Poems (Williams) **7**:350, 399, 402; **109**:282-88
"Early Mondrian" (O'Hara) **45**:125
"The Early Morning" (Belloc) **24**:5, 34
"The Early Morning" (Corso) **108**:39
"Early Morning: Cape Cod" (Swenson) **14**:276
"The Early Morning Light" (Schwartz) **8**:294
"Early Morning Writings" (Corso) **33**:24
The Early Motion (Dickey) **40**:208-9
"The Early Ones" (Stafford) **71**:42
"Early Poems" (Justice) **64**:249, 272
Early Poems (Clarke) **112**:34, 189
Early Poems (Crane) **3**:90-1
Early Poems (Noyes) **27**:138
Early Poems, 1935-1955 (Paz) **1**:373, 375; **48**:191, 198, 200, 251
The Early Poems of Yvor Winters (Winters) **82**:312, 335
"The Early Purges" (Heaney) **100**:326
"Early Reading" (Masefield) **78**:45
"Early Recollections" (Ní Chuilleanáin) **34**:350, 352
"Early Spring" (Werfel) **101**:344
"An Early Start" (Clarke) **112**:54, 68
"An Early Unconverted Saint" (Thoreau) **30**:202
Early Verse of Rudyard Kipling, 1877-99: Unpublished, Uncollected, and Rarely Collected Poems (Kipling) **3**:193
Early Writing: 1946-1950 (O'Hara) **45**:127, 130, 153, 155, 222, 224-25
"Earnest Cry and Prayer" (Burns) **114**:53
"The Earrings" (Montale)
See "Gli orecchini"
"Ears in the Turrets Hear" (Thomas) **2**:379
"Earth" (Bryant) **20**:4, 17, 19, 35, 47
"The Earth" (Noyes) **27**:129
"The Earth" (Sexton) **2**:372, 374
"The Earth" (Stafford) **71**:278, 284, 296
"Earth" (Thomas) **99**:236, 295
"Earth" (Toomer) **7**:333
"The Earth" (Very) **86**:45
"Earth Again" (Milosz) **8**:209
"Earth and a Wedded Woman" (Meredith) **60**:249
"Earth and Fire" (Berry) **28**:11
"Earth and I Give You Turquoise" (Momaday) **25**:188, 193, 207
"Earth and Its Atmosphere" (Niedecker) **42**:94
"Earth and Man" (Meredith) **60**:256, 279, 290, 296-98, 331, 339
The Earth Compels (MacNeice) **61**:136-37, 181
Earth Deities, and Other Rhythmic Masques (Carman) **34**:205, 212
"The Earth Drum" (Dickey) **40**:224, 227
"Earth Dweller" (Stafford) **71**:269, 278
"Earth, earth, you feed on people" (Shvarts) **50**:142
"Earth Emergent Drifts the Fire River" (Chappell) **105**:26, 35, 43, 62
"The Earth Falls Down" (Sexton) **79**:238
The Earth Gods (Gibran) **9**:71, 75, 80
"Earth has Shrunk in the Wash" (Empson) **104**:91, 122
"The Earth in Snow" (Blok) **21**:4-5
"The Earth is Called Juan" (Neruda)
See "La tierra se llama Juan"
"The Earth Is Closing on Us" (Darwish) **86**:28
"The Earth Lantern" (Bissett) **14**:7
"Earth Psalm" (Levertov) **11**:170
"Earth Songs" (Spencer) **77**:326
Earth Took from Earth (Graham) **59**:184
"Earth Triumphant" (Aiken) **26**:7
Earth Triumphant (Aiken) **26**:21, 50
"An Earth upon Heaven" (Hunt) **73**:134
"Earth Walk" (Meredith) **28**:214
Earth Walk: New and Selected Poems (Meredith) **28**:178, 180-81, 194-95, 207, 210, 213-15
"Earth Your Dancing Place" (Swenson) **14**:283
"The Earthenware Head" (Hughes) **89**:162, 261
Earthlight (Breton) **15**:73-4
"Earthly Anecdote" (Stevens) **110**:146-47, 153, 235
"Earthly Creatures" (Wylie) **23**:311
"Earthly Message" (Mistral)
See "Recado terrestre"
The Earthly Paradise (Morris) **55**:242, 245, 247-54, 257-60, 262, 268, 273-75, 277, 285-87, 289, 291-94, 296-97, 304-9, 311, 314-17, 323, 325, 328-32, 336, 340-41
Earth-moon (Hughes) **89**:193
"Earth-Numb" (Hughes) **89**:128, 151-52
Earth-numb (Hughes) **89**:156
The Earth-Owl and Other Moon-People (Hughes) **7**:120
"Earthquake" (Stone) **53**:247, 257-58
"Earth's Answer" (Blake) **12**:7, 35, 44; **63**:17, 23, 88, 90, 95, 104-5
"Earth's Bubbles" (Blok) **21**:14, 24, 31
"Earth's Children Cleave to Earth" (Bryant) **20**:16
"Earth's Lyric" (Carman) **34**:207
"Earth's Winter Song" (Duncan) **75**:132
"Earthsleep" (Chappell) **105**:60, 72

Earthsleep (Chappell) **105**:5, 25, 28-30, 34-35, 40, 44-47, 53, 67-68, 70-72, 74-75
"Earth-Song" (Emerson) **18**:79, 88
"Earthy Anecdote" (Stevens) **6**:294
"Earwigs" (Carver) **54**:14
"Ease" (Traherne) **70**:272, 315-16
"East Bronx" (Ignatow) **34**:306
"East Coker" (Eliot) **5**:164, 167-69, 171, 179-82, 198, 210
"East Coker" (Masefield) **78**:84
"East Coker" (Roethke) **15**:279
East Coker (Eliot) **90**:216
"East Fifth St. (N.Y.)" (Kaufman) **74**:194
"East of Suez" (Kipling) **3**:179
"East of the Sun and West of the Moon" (Merwin) **45**:6, 29
"East of the Sun West of the Moon" (Wakoski) **15**:348
"East River" (Swenson) **14**:254
East Slope (Paz)
See *Ladera este*
"The East that is Now Pale, the East that is Now Silent" (Bely)
See "Vostok pobledneuskii, vostok onemesvshii"
"East, West, North, and South of a Man" (Lowell) **13**:87
East Wind (Lowell) **13**:76, 84-5
"An East Window on Elizabeth Street" (Schuyler) **88**:216
"Eastbourne" (Montale) **13**:106, 109, 120-21, 128-29, 148, 152
"An East-End Coffee-Stall" (Noyes) **27**:140
"An East-End Curate" (Hardy) **8**:101
"Easter" (Herbert) **4**:100, 120
"Easter" (Kinnell) **26**:238, 279
"Easter" (O'Hara) **45**:130, 135, 137, 148, 191, 242
"Easter" (Studwell)
See "Easter: Wahiawa, 1959"
Easter Day (Browning) **2**:32, 45, 71-2, 75
"Easter Day" (Clough) **103**:54, 67, 71, 74-75, 94, 107, 115-16, 137, 155, 167
"Easter Day" (Crashaw) **84**:35
"Easter Eve 1945" (Rukeyser) **12**:225
"Easter Greeting" (Niedecker) **42**:109
"Easter Hymn" (Hope) **56**:266, 285
"Easter Hymn" (Housman) **2**:184; **43**:257
"Easter Monday" (Spender) **71**:152, 207, 224
"Easter Moon and Owl" (Wright) **14**:373, 375
"Easter Morning" (Ammons) **16**:30-2, 46, 63-4
"Easter Morning" (Sarton) **39**:342
"Easter Night" (Meynell) **112**:175, 177
"Easter, 1916" (Walcott) **46**:307
"Easter 1916" (Yeats) **20**:311, 313-14, 323, 325, 327, 349
"Easter, 1968" (Sarton) **39**:328
"Easter of the Greeks" (Sikelianos) **29**:366-67
"Easter: Wahiawa, 1959" (Song) **21**:331, 335, 338, 340, 342-43, 350
"Easter Wings" (Herbert) **4**:114, 120, 130
Eastern Lyrics (Hugo)
See *Les orientales*
Eastern Slope (Paz)
See *Ladera este*
"Eastern Tempest" (Blunden) **66**:24, 26, 28
"Eastern War Time" (Rich) **5**:398
Easters (Zanzotto)
See *Pasque*
"Eastport to Block Island" (Rich) **5**:352
"Easy Comedy" (Meredith) **60**:292
"Easy Lessons in Geophagy" (Rexroth) **95**:271
Eat Crow (Hughes) **89**:99
"Eating Fire" (Atwood) **8**:27-8
"Eating Out the Angel of Death" (Simic) **69**:263
"Eating Poetry" (Strand) **63**:161
"Eating the Cookies" (Kenyon) **57**:19, 38
"Eating the Dead" (Brathwaite) **56**:11-12, 74, 87, 100
Eating the Honey of Words: New and Selected Poems (Bly) **39**:115, 117
"Eating the Pig" (Hall) **70**:9, 27, 32-33, 39
"L'Eau des larnes" (Ponge) **107**:143
"Eaux-meres" (Char) **56**:184
"The Eavesdropper" (Carman) **34**:203-04, 210-11, 216
"Eavesdropper" (Plath) **37**:258
"Ebar phirao more" (Tagore) **8**:409
"Ébauche d'un serpent" (Valéry) **9**:352-53, 365-67, 371, 374, 384, 387, 390, 394-99
Ebb and Flow (Ishikawa) **10**:212-13, 215
"The Ebb Begins from Dream" (Birney) **52**:21, 36, 92
"éboulis" (Césaire) **25**:45
L'Ecarlate (Char) **56**:111, 115-16
"Ecce homo" (Berryman) **64**:97
"Ecce homo" (Corso) **33**:26, 41, 47; **108**:16
"Ecce Puer" (Joyce) **22**:140-41, 147-48, 151-52
"Eccho" (Cowley) **90**:115
"The Ecchoing Green" (Blake) **63**:6, 68, 100, 121-22
"The Ecclesiast" (Ashbery) **26**:114
"Ecclesiastes" (Mahon) **60**:182, 216-17, 229
"Ecclesiastes 1:9" (Borges)
See "Eclesiastés 1.9"
Ecclesiastical Sketches (Wordsworth) **4**:399
Ecclesiastical Sonnets (Wordsworth)
See *Ecclesiastical Sketches*
"Echo" (Lorde) **12**:155
"Echo" (Rossetti) **7**:280-81
"Echo" (Tagore)
See "Pratidhyani"
L'Echo bouge beau (Brossard) **80**:5
The Echo Moves Beautiful (Brossard)
See *L'Echo bouge beau*
"Echoes" (Carroll) **18**:46
"Echoes" (Creeley) **73**:96
"Echoes" (Jackson) **44**:7
"Echoes" (Thomas) **99**:288-89, 292-93
Echoes (Creeley) **73**:95, 97, 109, 118
"Echoes and Shadows" (Stone) **53**:244, 257, 259
Echoes from Vagabondia (Carman) **34**:205, 208, 228-29
The Echoes Return Slow (Thomas) **99**:263-67, 278-82, 309, 311-12, 322, 326-27, 332, 336-37, 352, 354
"The Echoing Green" (Blake) **12**:7
"L'eclair" (Rimbaud) **57**:191, 195, 243
"L'Eclairage du pénitencier" (Char) **56**:134, 151
"L'eclatante victoire de Saarebrück" (Rimbaud) **3**:283; **57**:203, 205, 253
"Eclesiastés 1.9" (Borges) **32**:91
"El eclipse" (Jiménez) **7**:200
Eclipse (Hogan) **35**:247, 255
Eclipse of Stars (Sachs)
See *Sternverdunkelung*
Eclipse of the Stars (Sachs)
See *Sternverdunkelung*
"Ecloga I" (Zanzotto) **65**:265
"Ecloga IX" (Zanzotto) **65**:270
"Ecloga VII" (Zanzotto) **65**:265
"Ecloghe IX" (Zanzotto) **65**:266
"Ecloghe VIII" (Zanzotto) **65**:266
"Eclogue" (Oppen) **35**:308
"Eclogue" (Ronsard) **11**:262
"Eclogue" (Stevens) **6**:333
"Eclogue 4" (Vergil) **12**:363, 370, 372, 382-85, 392
"Eclogue 6" (Vergil) **12**:365, 371
"Eclogue 10" (Vergil) **12**:370-71
"Eclogue between the Motherless" (MacNeice) **61**:135, 137
"Eclogue by a Five-barred Gate" (MacNeice) **61**:127
Eclogue, Elegy, Ode (Cernuda)
See *Égloga, elegía, oda*
"An Eclogue for Christmas" (MacNeice) **61**:124-25, 129
"Eclogue from Iceland" (MacNeice) **61**:107, 133
"Eclogue I: The Months" (Bridges) **28**:67, 84
"Eclogue II" (Bridges) **28**:87-8
"Eclogue IV" (Collins) **72**:57, 59
"Eclogue IV: Winter" (Brodsky) **9**:22, 28-9
"Eclogue of the Liberal and the Poet" (Tate) **50**:252, 257
"An Eclogue, or Pastorall between Endymion Porter and Lycidas Herrick" (Herrick) **9**:86
"Eclogue V: Summer" (Brodsky) **9**:21, 28
"Eclogues" (Herrick) **9**:89
Eclogues (Collins) **72**:78
Eclogues (Petrarch) **8**:246
Eclogues (Vergil)
See *The Eclogues of Virgil*
The Eclogues of Virgil (Vergil) **12**:365, 370-72, 375, 383, 388
"Eclore en hiver" (Char) **56**:141, 156
"Ecologue" (Ginsberg) **4**:54, 82, 85, 89
"Economia de Tahuantinsuyo" (Cardenal) **22**:127-28, 132
"Economic Man" (Nemerov) **24**:289
"Economics and Exodus" (Walcott) **46**:279
"Economy" (Merwin) **45**:8
"The Economy of Tahuantinsuyo" (Cardenal)
See "Economia de Tahuantinsuyo"
Ecopoemas (Parra) **39**:312
Ecopoems (Parra)
See *Ecopoemas*
"Ecoutez la chanson bien douce" (Verlaine) **2**:416
"Écrit sur la Porte" (Perse) **23**:231
"Les Écrits s'en vont" (Breton) **15**:51
"Ecstasy" (Bell) **79**:35
"The Ecstasy" (Carruth) **10**:71
"The Ecstasy" (Cernuda)
See "El éxtasis"
"The Ecstasy" (Donne)
See "The Exstasie"
"Ecstatsy" (Mistral)
See "Extasis"
"The Ed Meese Scrolls" (Dorn) **115**:162-63
"Eddi's Service" (Kipling) **3**:183
"An Eddy" (Carew) **29**:10, 48
"Eden" (Dickey) **40**:225
"Eden" (Tomlinson) **17**:342, 354
"Eden" (Traherne) **70**:185-86, 194, 204, 221, 228, 246, 266-67, 273, 275, 288, 314
"Eden" (Walcott) **46**:278
"Eden" (Wright) **14**:336, 341
"Eden Bower" (Rossetti) **44**:166-67
"Eden Retold" (Shapiro) **25**:290
"Eden Were Elysium" (Corso) **33**:49; **108**:6
"The Edge" (Char)
See "Seuil"
"The Edge" (Glück) **16**:125, 153
"Edge" (Montague) **106**:247, 288
"Edge" (Plath) **1**:391, 393, 397; **37**:232, 258, 267-69
"The Edge" (Stryk) **27**:198, 203
The Edge of Being (Spender) **71**:139, 146, 170, 188-90, 216
"Edge of Love" (Aleixandre)
See "Filo del amor"
"The Edge of the World" (Silverstein) **49**:312
"Edgehill Fight" (Kipling) **3**:183
"Edible Aid" (Enright) **93**:18
Edifico Sayonara (Yau) **61**:334, 348
"Edina, Scotia's Darling Seat!" (Burns) **6**:74; **114**:4, 42
"Edinburgh Villanelle" (Spark) **72**:226, 256
"Edinstvennye dni" (Pasternak) **6**:286
"Editor Whedon" (Masters) **36**:182, 230, 232, 240
"Editorial Impressions" (Sassoon) **12**:268
"Edmondson, VC" (Gilmore) **87**:303
"Edmonton, Thy Cemetery" (Smith) **12**:293, 300
"Edmund to Gloucester" (Snodgrass) **74**:291
"Education" (Madhubuti) **5**:338
"Education a Failure" (Williams) **7**:370
"Education and Government" (Gray)
See "Essay on the Alliance of Education and Government"
"Education by Poetry" (Frost) **39**:241, 253

"An Education in the Eighties" (Stone) **53**:248-49, 257
"Edvard Munch" (Mahon)
See "The Studio"
"Edward Gray" (Tennyson) **6**:358
"Edward III" (Blake)
See "King Edward the Third"
"Edward Shore" (Crabbe) **97**:95, 97, 112, 120
Edwin and Angelina (Goldsmith) **77**:184, 186, 219-20, 222
"Edwin Morris" (Tennyson) **101**:161
"The Eel" (Montale)
See "L'anguilla"
"Eel" (Rukeyser) **12**:211
"The Eemis Stane" (MacDiarmid) **9**:158, 187
"eet me alive" (Bissett) **14**:34
"Efectos del bautismo" (Paz) **48**:210
"Effacement du Peuplier" (Char) **56**:183
"Effacing of the Poplar" (Char)
See "Effacement du Peuplier"
"Les effarés" (Rimbaud) **57**:184, 196, 202-3, 205, 244, 249, 253
"The Effect" (Sassoon) **12**:285
"The effects of baptism" (Paz)
See "Efectos del bautismo"
"The Effects of Mans Apostasy" (Taylor) **63**:264
"The Effectual Marriage" (Loy) **16**:333
"Effet de nuit" (Verlaine) **32**:387
"Effie" (Brown) **55**:110
"Effigy of a Nun" (Teasdale) **31**:371, 389
"Effilage du sac de jute" (Char) **56**:147
"Effort at Speech" (Meredith) **28**:214
Effort at Speech: New and Selected Poems (Meredith) **28**:216-17
"Efforts of Affection" (Moore) **49**:102, 126-27
L'Effraie et autres poésies (Jaccottet) **98**:148-49, 171-75, 182, 195
"Effusion XXXV" (Coleridge) **100**:20-21, 24
Efterlämnade dikter (Ekeloef) **23**:78
"L'égalité des sexes" (Éluard) **38**:66
The Egerton Ms (Wyatt) **27**:360
"The Egg" (Glück) **16**:125, 138-39
"The Egg and the Machine" (Frost) **1**:203
"Egg-Head" (Hughes) **7**:116, 118, 135, 140, 161; **89**:149
"Eggs" (Hagiwara) **18**:168
"Eggs" (Olds) **22**:311, 338
"Eggs and Nestlings" (Wright) **14**:348
"Egle" (Carducci) **46**:49, 87
"Egloga" (Cernuda) **62**:202, 249-51
Égloga, elegía, oda (Cernuda) **62**:170, 202, 249-50
Eglogs (Drayton)
See *Idea. The Shepheards Garland, Fashioned in Nine Eglogs. Rowlands Sacrifice to the Nine Muses*
"Ego" (Shapiro) **25**:320
"Ego Tripping" (Giovanni) **19**:118, 123, 141
"The Egoist" (Neruda)
See "El egoísta"
"The Egoist" (Wickham) **110**:263-64
"El egoísta" (Neruda) **4**:290
Egorushka (Tsvetaeva) **14**:326-27
Ego-Tripping and Other Poems for Young People (Giovanni) **19**:123, 136
"Egy ev" (Illyés) **16**:239
"The Egyptian Cat" (Enright) **93**:32
"An Egyptian Pulled Glass Bottle in the Shape of a Fish" (Moore) **49**:89, 101
"Ehcu Fugaces" (Belloc) **24**:10
"Eheu! Fugaces, Posthume, Posthume, Labuntur Ani" (Very) **86**:58
"ehre sei der sellerie" (Enzensberger) **28**:140
"The Eichmann Trial" (Levertov)
See "During the Eichmann Trial"
"Eidolon" (Warren) **37**:280, 282-84, 288, 331
"VIII" (Joyce) **22**:144-45, 153, 167, 170, 173
"8 Ahau" (Cardenal)
See "Katun 8 Ahau"
"Eight Balloons" (Silverstein) **49**:331
Eight Days (Seifert)
See *Osm dnů*
"Eight Drinking Immortals" (Tu Fu) **9**:330
"8e vision" (Lamartine) **16**:265
"Eight for Ornette's Music" (Rexroth) **95**:253, 274
"Eight Hundred A.D. On the Ward" (Espada) **74**:120
"Eight Laments" (Tu Fu) **9**:333-38, 341-42
"Eight Little Dogs" (Mistral)
See "Ocho Perritos"
"Eight Observations on the Nature of Eternity" (Tomlinson) **17**:328
"Eight O'Clock" (Housman) **2**:162, 164, 169, 182; **43**:254
"Eight O'Clock" (Teasdale) **31**:359
"Eight Riddles from Symphosius" (Wilbur) **51**:273, 301
"824. Der Frauen Liebe und Leben" (Benn) **35**:46
"Eight Years After" (Davie) **29**:108
"Eight years after Viet Nam" (Quintana) **36**:257
"XVIII" (Joyce) **22**:145, 165, 167, 169
"1886" (Benn) **35**:71
"18 Nov 71" (Brutus) **24**:123
18 Poems (Thomas) **2**:378, 382, 384; **52**:245, 252, 271, 311
"18 Rugby Street" (Hughes) **89**:162, 177-78, 270
"Eighteen West Eleventh Street" (Merrill) **28**:222, 244, 258
"1887" (Housman) **2**:192, 194
"1805" (Graves) **6**:152
"Eighteenth Century Harp Songs" (Clarke) **112**:124
"Eighth Air Force" (Jarrell) **41**:138, 171, 173-74, 177, 189, 204-5
"The Eighth Crusade" (Masters) **1**:330
"Eighth Duino Elegy" (Rilke)
See "Eighth Elegy"
"Eighth Elegy" (Rilke) **2**:291, 293
Eighth Isthmian (Pindar)
See *Isthmian 8*
"Eighth Nymphal" (Drayton) **98**:51
Eighth Olympian (Pindar)
See *Olympian 8*
"Eighth Psalm" (Sexton) **79**:220, 222, 232, 336
Eighth Pythian (Pindar)
See *Pythian 8*
80 Flowers (Zukofsky) **11**:392
Eighty-Five Poems (MacNeice) **61**:141
"84th Street, Edmonton" (Atwood) **8**:9
89 Clouds (Strand) **63**:199
"Eikon Basilike" (Howe) **54**:134-35
Einander (Werfel) **101**:300, 314, 318, 336, 347-48, 356-59
"Einsamer nie—" (Benn) **35**:8, 20
Einstein (MacLeish) **47**:125, 127, 130, 136, 154, 183, 185-87, 191-92, 194-95, 215-17, 220-22, 239
"Einstein Freud & Jack" (Nemerov) **24**:302
"The Einstein Intersection" (Berrigan) **103**:25
"Einzelheiten" (Benn) **35**:8
"Der Einzige" (Hölderlin) **4**:150, 156, 166
"Eire" (Clarke) **112**:139
"Eisenhower's Visit to Franco, 1959" (Wright) **36**:284, 358
*Eistre au Dieu d****ours* (Christine de Pizan) **68**:85
"Ejercicios respiratorios" (Parra) **39**:272
Ejercicios respiratorios (Parra) **39**:278
"Ejercicios retóricos" (Parra) **39**:268
"Ekloga 4-aya: Zimnyaya" (Brodsky)
See "Eclogue IV: Winter"
"The Elderly Nun" (Shvarts)
See "Staritsa"
"Elders" (Hecht) **70**:108
"The Elders at their services" (Cunningham) **92**:137
"Eldorado" (Poe) **1**:433, 439
Eleanor Rumming (Skelton)
See *The Tunnynge of Elynour Rummynge*
"Eleanore" (Tennyson) **6**:350
"Eleanor's Letters" (Hall) **70**:26, 33
"Elected Silence" (Sassoon) **12**:258
"Elections" (Melville) **82**:48-49
"The Elections to the Hebdomadal Council" (Carroll) **74**:72, 104
"Electra en la niebla" (Mistral) **32**:208-10
"Electra on Azalea Path" (Plath) **1**:410-11; **37**:214-15, 217, 219-20, 243-44, 246, 248-50
"Electra-Orestes" (H. D.) **5**:305
"Electric Drills" (Yau) **61**:329, 337, 340-41, 343, 345
"Electric Elegy" (Zagajewski) **27**:389
"Electric Iron" (Duncan) **75**:175
"Electric Light" (Heaney) **100**:241
Electric Light (Heaney) **100**:237-43, 273, 321, 324-30
"The Electric Tram" (Noyes) **27**:122
"Electrical Storm" (Hayden) **6**:186, 194-95
Elefantina's Dream (Kennedy) **93**:135
"Elegía" (Borges) **22**:95; **32**:58, 90
"Elegía" (Zanzotto) **65**:290, 292-93
Elegía (Neruda) **4**:287
Elegía a Jacques Roumain (Guillén) **23**:133
"Elegía a Jesús Menéndez" (Guillén) **23**:100-101, 125
"Elegía a un joven muerto en el frente" (Paz) **1**:352; **48**:179
"Elegía anticipada" (Cernuda) **62**:179, 265-67, 269-70
"Elegia del Monte Spluga" (Carducci) **46**:51, 89
Elegia e altri versi (Zanzotto) **65**:262, 265, 274, 287-91, 293-95
"L'elegia in petèl" (Zanzotto) **65**:268-69, 277, 279, 311, 315-16, 327
"Elegía moderna del motivo cursi" (Guillén) **23**:109-10, 128
Elegia na odejscie (Herbert) **50**:36, 40-41
"Elegia pasquale" (Zanzotto) **65**:291, 294
"Elegiac Calculation" (Szymborska)
See "Rachunek Elegijny"
"Elegiac Calculations" (Szymborska)
See "Rachunek Elegijny"
"Elegiac Feelings American" (Corso) **33**:19, 36, 54; **108**:10
Elegiac Feelings American (Corso) **33**:18, 35-7, 44, 49, 50; **108**:3, 9, 13, 15, 20, 29, 33, 43-44
"An Elegiac Fragment" (Duncan) **2**:101
"Elegiac Lament" (Stampa) **43**:296
"Elegiac Poem" (Yakamochi)
See "Bankashi"
"An Elegiac Poem on the Death of George Whitefield" (Wheatley) **3**:336, 340, 343, 348
Elegiac Sonnets, and Other Essays (Smith) **104**:160-62, 165, 167-68, 170, 177, 179, 186-89, 194, 196-97, 203, 205-10, 212-13, 230, 232-34, 243, 246, 248-49, 251, 254, 267, 270-71, 273-76, 279-87, 289, 293, 295, 301, 304-5, 307, 309, 318, 320-23, 325-26, 330-31, 338-40, 344, 353
Elegiac Sonnets, and Other Poems (Smith)
See *Elegiac Sonnets, and Other Essays*
"Elegiac Stanzas" (Barker) **77**:4
"Elegiac Stanzas" (Wordsworth) **4**:406-07
"Elegiac Verse vi" (Longfellow) **30**:41
"Elegiac Verses" (Longfellow) **30**:41
"Elegíade los portones" (Borges) **32**:84
Elegiarum liber (Campion) **87**:96
"El elegido" (Cernuda) **62**:219
"An Elegie" (Campion) **87**:48-50, 68
"Élégie" (Gautier) **18**:135
"Elegie" (Goethe) **5**:248, 251
"Elegie IV: The Perfume" (Donne) **1**:130
"Elegie VIII: The Comparison" (Donne) **1**:124
"Elegie XI: The Bracelet" (Donne) **1**:122
"Elegie XII: His parting from her" (Donne) **1**:130
"Elegie XVI: On his mistris" (Donne) **1**:130
"Elegie XIX" (Donne) **43**:173

"Elégie XXIIII" (Ronsard) **11**:228; **105**:249, 251, 254-55, 257, 259, 264-65, 267-68
"Elegie à Cassandre" (Ronsard) **11**:246, 248; **105**:215-17
"L'Elégie à Guillaume des Autels sur le Tumulte d'Amboise" (Ronsard) **11**:248; **105**:275
"Elegie à Hélène" (Ronsard) **11**:229
"l'elegie à J. Hurault, sieur de la pitardière" (Ronsard) **11**:249
"Elegie á Janet, peintre du Roi" (Ronsard) **11**:243, 247
"L'elégie à Lovs de Masures" (Ronsard) **11**:248
"Elégie à Marie Stuart" (Ronsard) **11**:224, 237
"Elegie à M. A. De Muret" (Ronsard) **11**:246, 248
"Elegie à son livre" (Ronsard) **11**:248
"Elegie au Seigneur Baillon, trésorier de l'Epargne du Roi" (Ronsard) **11**:249
"Elegie au Seigneur L'Huillier" (Ronsard) **11**:242
"Elégie Au Sieur Barthelemi Del-Bene" (Ronsard) **105**:221
"Elégie contre les bûcherons de la forêt de Gâtine" (Ronsard)
See *See "Elégie XXIIII"*
"Elégie de minuit" (Senghor) **25**:255
"Elégie des circoncis" (Senghor) **25**:255
"Elégie des eaux" (Senghor) **25**:255, 258
"Elégie des Saudades" (Senghor) **25**:233
"Elegie du printemps" (Ronsard) **11**:242, 250
"Elegie du Verre à Jan Brinon" (Ronsard) **11**:247
"Elegie en forme d'épitaphe d'Antoine Chateignier" (Ronsard) **11**:246, 248
"An Elegie on the death of Mr. R. Hall" (Vaughan) **81**:364
"An Elegie on the death of Mr. R. W." (Vaughan) **81**:258, 336
"An Elegie on the La: Pen: sent to my Mistresse out of France" (Carew) **29**:61-62, 71-73
"Elegie on the Lady Jane Pawlet, Marchion: of Winton" (Jonson) **17**:206
"Elégie ou Amour Oyseau" (Ronsard) **105**:221
"Elégie pour Georges Pompidou" (Senghor) **25**:254-55, 257-59
"Elégie pour Jean-Marie" (Senghor) **25**:255-56, 259
"Elégie pour Martin Luther King" (Senghor) **25**:258
"An Elegie upon that Honourable and renowned Knight Sir Philip Sidney, who was untimely slaine at the Seige of Zutphen, Anno, 1586" (Bradstreet) **10**:31, 48, 54
"An Elegie upon the Death of the Deane of Pauls, Dr. John Donne" (Carew) **29**:17, 22, 63, 75
"Elegie upon the untimely death of the incomparable Prince Henry" (Donne) **1**:122
"Elegier I" (Ekeloef) **23**:76
"The Elegies" (Borges) **32**:94
"Elegies" (Sainte-Beuve) **110**:38
"Elegies" (Spicer) **78**:250
"Elegies" (Stafford) **71**:371
Elegies (Donne) **1**:129-30, 147; **43**:112, 166, 170, 187, 191, 200
Elegies (Drayton) **98**:77-79
Elegies (Jiménez)
See *Elejías*
Elegies (Ovid)
See *Tristia*
Elegies (Rilke)
See *Duineser Elegien*
Elegies (Rukeyser) **12**:207, 211-13
"Elegies And Epistles" (Wylie) **23**:311
"Elegies for Paradise Valley" (Hayden) **6**:191-92, 194-95
Elégies majeures (Senghor) **25**:254-56, 258
Elegies of Gloom (Ovid)
See *Tristia*
The Elegies of Jutting Rock (Elytis)
See *Ta eleýa tis Oxópetras*
"Elegies on the Cardinal Points" (Shvarts) **50**:139
"Èlegiia na rentgenovskii snimok moego cherepa" (Shvarts) **50**:132, 140, 145, 147, 160
"Elegija" (Pushkin) **10**:413-14
"Elegy" (Angelou) **32**:28
"Elegy" (Berry) **28**:14-17, 19, 31
"Elegy" (Borges)
See "Elegía"
"Elegy" (Ciardi) **69**:37
"Elegy" (Cohen) **109**:3, 14, 48
"Elegy" (Ekeloef)
See *En Mölna-elegi*
"Elegy" (Eliot) **90**:301
"Elegy" (Hacker) **47**:79
"Elegy" (Heaney) **18**:241-43; **100**:274, 281, 288
"The Elegy" (Hope) **56**:304, 306
"Elegy" (Jonson) **17**:175
"Elegy" (Marvell)
See "Poem upon the Death of O. C."
"Elegy" (Pushkin)
See "Elegija"
"Elegy" (Roethke) **15**:267
"Elegy" (Stafford) **71**:262, 280, 287, 291, 369
"Elegy" (Thomas) **52**:277, 327
"Elegy" (Thoreau) **30**:168, 278-81, 293
"Elegy" (Walcott) **46**:228-30, 273, 275-76, 285-86
"Elegy" (Walker) **20**:278-79
"Elegy" (Zagajewski) **27**:396
"Elegy" (Zanzotto)
See "Elegia"
Elegy (Neruda)
See *Elegía*
Elegy and Other Verses (Zanzotto)
See *Elegia e altri versi*
"Elegy Anticipating Death" (Barker) **77**:4
"Elegy before Death: At Settignano" (Day Lewis) **11**:151
"Elegy fo Chloe Nguyen" (Chin) **40**:9
"Elegy for a Cricket" (Cunningham) **92**:165-66, 175
"Elegy for a Dead Soldier" (Shapiro) **25**:263, 269, 277, 279-80, 288-89, 295, 310, 316
"Elegy for a Firtree" (Wagoner) **33**:357
"Elegy for a friend killed in the civil war" (Paz)
See "Elegía a un joven muerto en el frente"
"Elegy for a Long-haired Student" (Stryk) **27**:203
"Elegy for a Nature Poet" (Nemerov) **24**:293
"Elegy for a Still-Born Child" (Heaney) **100**:233
"Elegy for a Woman Who Remembered Everything" (Wagoner) **33**:348
"Elegy for a Youth Changed to a Swan" (Boland) **58**:37
"Elegy for Alto" (Okigbo) **7**:231, 235, 244
"An Elegy for D. H. Lawrence" (Williams) **7**:350, 354-55; **109**:195, 286
An Elegy for Departure (Herbert)
See *Elegia na odejscie*
"Elegy for Eugenesis" (Tate) **50**:319
"Elegy for Father Stephen" (Merton) **10**:344
"An Elegy for Five Old Ladies" (Merton) **10**:333, 343
"Elegy for Georges Pompidon" (Senghor)
See "Elégie pour Georges Pompidou"
"Elegy for Jane" (Roethke) **15**:309
"Elegy for Jean-Marie" (Senghor)
See "Elégie pour Jean-Marie"
"Elegy for John Donne" (Brodsky)
See "The Great Elegy for John Donne"
"Elegy for Margaret" (Spender) **71**:146-47, 162-63, 187-88, 190
"Elegy for Martin Luther King" (Senghor)
See "Elégie pour Martin Luther King"
"Elegy for Minor Poets" (MacNeice) **61**:115
"Elegy for My Father" (Strand) **63**:143, 163-65, 173, 198
"Elegy for N. N." (Milosz) **8**:186, 207
"Elegy: For Robert Lowell" (Brodsky) **9**:7, 8
"Elegy for Slit-Drum" (Okigbo) **7**:233, 235, 244
Elegy for the Departure (Herbert)
See *Elegia na odejscie*
"Elegy for the Monastery Barn" (Merton) **10**:331, 342, 349
"An Elegy for the Poet Morgan Blum" (Wright) **36**:335, 341-42
"Elegy for Thelonious" (Komunyakaa) **51**:33
"An Elegy for W.C.W., the lovely man" (Berryman)
See "Dream Song 324"
"Elegy for Wesley Wells" (Hall) **70**:6, 15, 17, 30
"Elegy for Y. Z." (Milosz) **8**:174, 198, 203
"Elegy I" (Ciardi) **69**:35
"Elegy II" (Barker) **77**:34
"Elegy II" (Ciardi) **69**:35
"Elegy III, Cavalcante" (Ciardi) **69**:35
"Elegy in a Cube" (Ciardi) **69**:34
"Elegy in a Firelit Room" (Wright) **36**:279, 373
"Elegy in a Kensington Churchyard" (Spark) **72**:246
"Elegy in a Spider's Web" (Jackson) **44**:5, 103
"Elegy in April and September" (Owen) **102**:212
Elegy in April and September (Owen) **19**:366
"The Elegy in Petèl" (Zanzotto)
See "L'elegia in petèl"
"Elegy: Jefferson Davis, 1818-1889" (Tate) **50**:306
"Elegy Just in Case" (Ciardi) **69**:5, 11, 27, 50, 55, 57
"Elegy of Fortinbras" (Herbert)
See "Tren Fortynbrasa"
"Elegy of the Circumcised" (Senghor)
See "Elégie des circoncis"
"An Elegy of the Impossible Memory" (Borges) **32**:58
"Elegy of the Waters" (Senghor)
See "Elégie des eaux"
"Elegy of the Wind" (Okigbo) **7**:235
"Elegy: On a Lady Whom Grief for the Death of Her Betrothed Killed" (Bridges) **28**:87
"Elegy on an X-Ray of My Skull" (Shvarts)
See "Èlegiia na rentgenovskii snimok moego cherepa"
"Elegy on Captain Matthew Henderson" (Burns) **114**:120
Elegy on Dead Fashion (Sitwell) **3**:295, 300, 304
"Elegy on my Father" (Curnow) **48**:4, 44-46, 51
"Elegy on Poor Mailie" (Burns)
See "The Death and Dying Words of Poor Mailie, the Author's Only Pet Yowe, an Unco Mournfu' Tale"
"An Elegy on That Glory of Her Sex, Mrs. Mary Blaize" (Goldsmith) **77**:188, 214
"Elegy on the Death of a Mad Dog" (Goldsmith) **77**:214
"Elegy on the Death of King James" (Finch) **21**:169
"Elegy on the Death of Michael Roberts" (Barker) **77**:12
"Elegy on the Death of Robert Ruisseaux" (Burns) **6**:67
"Elegy on the Death of the Right Honourable ***" (Goldsmith) **77**:214
"Elegy on the Dust" (Gunn) **26**:190-191, 193, 203
"Elegy on the Ruins of Pickworth Rutlandshire Hastily composed and written with a Pencil on the Spot'" (Clare) **23**:12
"Elegy: The Summer-House on the Mound" (Bridges) **28**:80, 84

"Elegy to a young man killed on the front" (Paz)
See "Elegía a un joven muerto en el frente"
"Elegy to gates" (Borges)
See "Elegíade los portones"
"Elegy to Mount Spluga" (Carducci)
See "Elegia del Monte Spluga"
"Elegy to the Memory of an Unfortunate Lady" (Jonson) **17**:206
"Elegy to the Memory of an Unfortunate Lady" (Pope) **26**:314, 319, 324
"Elegy upon Anacreon, Who was Choked by a Grape-Stone" (Cowley) **90**:15
"Elegy Written in a Country Churchyard" (Gray) **2**:134-37, 139-43, 145, 148, 151-52, 155; **80**:117-287
"Elegy Written in a Suburban Churchyard" (Wagoner) **33**:355
"Elegy written in Poet's Corner, Westminster Abbey" (Hunt) **73**:134
"Elegy Written on a Frontporch" (Shapiro) **25**:295
"Elegy XLII" (Jonson)
See *The Under-Wood XLII*
Elejías (Jiménez) **7**:184
"Element" (Page) **12**:168, 170
"Elemental" (Ai) **72**:33
"Elemental Metamorphosis" (Kunitz) **19**:155
The Elemental Odes (Neruda)
See *Odas elementales*
"Elementary" (Spark) **72**:229
Elementary Odes (Neruda)
See *Odas elementales*
"The Elementary Scene" (Jarrell) **41**:153, 169
"An Elementary School Classroom in a Slum" (Spender) **71**:154, 186, 191, 224
"Elements" (Bradstreet)
See "The Four Elements"
"The Elements" (Bradstreet)
See "The Four Elements"
"The Elements" (Emerson) **18**:77
"The Elements" (Yau) **61**:335
"Elements And Angels" (Wylie) **23**:311
The Elements of San Joaquin (Soto) **28**:369, 371, 373, 376, 383-85
"The Elements of the Poem" (Char) **56**:144-45
"Elena Ceauçescu's Bed" (Snodgrass) **74**:332
"Eleonora Duse" (Lowell) **13**:91
"Elephant" (Goodison) **36**:155
"Elephants" (Moore) **4**:235, 260; **49**:94, 106, 108, 117, 119, 130
"Eleutheria" (Wright) **36**:289
"Elevated" (McHugh) **61**:191
"Élévation" (Baudelaire) **1**:46, 70; **106**:6, 59, 71, 104, 125, 134, 165
"Elevator Boy" (Hughes) **1**:263; **53**:181
"XI" (Joyce) **22**:136, 138, 145, 164, 169-70
"Eleven" (MacLeish) **47**:145, 164-65, 197, 212-13
"Eleven Addresses to the Lord" (Berryman) **64**:95, 100, 103, 118-19, 171
Eleven New Cantos (Pound)
See *A Draft of Eleven New Cantos*
"Eleven O'Clock at Night" (Bly) **39**:99
"11 Outlined Epitaphs" (Dylan) **37**:54, 68
Eleven Planets (Darwish)
See *Ahada 'Ashara Kawkaban*
"Eleven Planets in the Last Andalusian Sky" (Darwish) **86**:29
Eleven Poems (Blunden) **66**:6
Eleven Poems on the Same Theme (Warren) **37**:286, 288, 322-24, 332, 380
11 rue Daguerre (Montague) **106**:295-99, 313
"Eleven Times a Poem" (Corso) **33**:18, 24
Eleven Untitled Poems (Stafford) **71**:318
"11/8" (Williams) **7**:368
"The 11th: and Last Booke of the Ocean to Scinthia" (Raleigh) **31**:228, 300-06
"Eleventh Century Doors" (Kumin) **15**:180
"11th Floor, West 4th Street" (Swenson) **14**:261
Eleventh Nemean (Pindar)
See *Nemean 11*
Eleventh Olympian (Pindar)
See *Olympian 11*
Eleventh Pythian (Pindar)
See *Pythian 11*
"El-Hajj Malik El-Shabazz" (Hayden) **6**:176, 180-81, 187, 196
"Elidore" (Tuckerman) **85**:303, 319
"Eliduc" (Marie de France) **22**:239, 245, 248, 258, 265, 268-75, 278, 281-82, 294
"Elijah Browning" (Masters) **36**:191
"Elinda's Glove" (Lovelace) **69**:189, 194, 224
"Elinor Cobham to Duke Humphrey" (Drayton) **98**:66
Elinor Rumming (Skelton)
See *The Tunnynge of Elynour Rummynge*
"Elinoure and Juga" (Chatterton) **104**:11
"Élisabeth petite fille" (Char) **56**:120
"Eliseo" (Pound) **95**:235-37, 239-40
"Elite Profession" (Yakamochi) **48**:100
"The Elixir" (Herbert) **4**:134
"Eliza Harris" (Harper) **21**:190, 192, 194, 201, 204-05, 215
"Elizabeth" (Ondaatje) **28**:292
"Elizabeth" (Poe) **1**:446
"Elizabeth Gone" (Sexton) **2**:359
Elk Heads on the Wall (Ríos) **57**:312
"The Elk Song" (Hogan) **35**:257
"Ella Mason and Her Eleven Cats" (Plath) **37**:253
"Elle me dit un jour ou m'écrivit peut-être" (Sainte-Beuve) **110**:49
"Ellen Hanging Clothes" (Reese) **29**:330, 348
"Ellen Irwin" (Wordsworth)
See "Ellen Irwin, or the Braes of Kirtle"
"Ellen Irwin, or the Braes of Kirtle" (Wordsworth) **67**:327-28, 345
"Ellen Orford" (Crabbe) **97**:129
"Elliott" (Whittier) **93**:167
"Elliott Hawkins" (Masters) **36**:230
"Ellsmereland" (Birney) **52**:79
"Elm" (Plath) **1**:390, 394
"Elm" (Stryk) **27**:212
"The Elm Tree" (Hood) **93**:44, 83, 99-100, 105, 117
"Elmet" (Hughes) **89**:122-23
Elmet (Hughes)
See *Remains of Elmet: A Pennine Sequence*
"Elms" (Glück) **16**:152
"Eloa" (Vigny)
See "Eloa ou la soeur des anges"
"Eloa ou la soeur des anges" (Vigny) **26**:391, 398, 411
Eloge d'une Soupçonnée (Char) **56**:163, 184-85, 189-90, 194
Éloges (Perse) **23**:209-11, 217, 222, 229-32, 234, 237, 241-43, 254
"Elogio de la seguidilla" (Darío) **15**:114
"Elogio de la sombra" (Borges) **32**:62, 140
Elogio de la sombra (Borges) **22**:71, 75-6; **32**:38, 41, 57, 59, 61, 66, 86, 88-9, 111, 116
"Elohim merakhem 'al yaldei hagan" (Amichai) **38**:5, 12, 14, 53
"Eloisa to Abelard" (Pope) **26**:304, 318-19, 326, 339
"Eloquence d'Orion" (Char) **56**:145
Eloquence in the Vernacular Tongue (Dante)
See *De vulgari eloquentia*
Elpenor (MacLeish) **47**:254
"Elsa Wertman" (Masters) **36**:171
"Elsewhere" (Sassoon) **12**:252
"Elsewhere" (Schuyler) **88**:206
"A Elvire" (Lamartine) **16**:290
"Elvis Presley" (Gunn) **26**:219
Elympics (Kennedy) **93**:135
Elynour Rummyng (Skelton)
See *The Tunnynge of Elynour Rummynge*
"Elysian Fields" (Hacker) **47**:103, 107
"Elysium" (Pound)
See "Eliseo"
"Em quanto quis Fortuna que tivesse" (Camões) **31**:24
"Email is MEmail" (Dorn) **115**:232
"The Emancipators" (Jarrell) **41**:143, 179
Emaux et camées (Gautier) **18**:127-28, 130, 138, 146, 154, 156, 158-59, 161, 164
"Embankment at Night, Before the War: Outcasts" (Lawrence) **54**:221-22
"Embarking on the Study of Anglo-Saxon Grammar" (Borges) **32**:94
Embassy Poetry Reading (Hacker) **47**:113
"Emblems" (Tate) **50**:230-31, 255
Emblems of a Season of Fury (Merton) **10**:334, 343, 349-51
"Emblems of Conduct" (Crane) **3**:82; **99**:11, 14, 17
"The Embrace" (Glück) **16**:156
"Embro Hie Kirk" (Stevenson) **84**:329-30
"Emerald" (Doty) **53**:60-61
"The Emerald" (Merrill) **28**:222, 244, 257
Emerald Ice: Selected Poems 1962-1987 (Wakoski) **15**:370, 372
"The Emerald Isle" (Whittier) **93**:194
"Emergency Clinic" (Ignatow) **34**:286, 318
"Emergency Haying" (Carruth) **10**:91
"The Emergency Maker" (Wagoner) **33**:327
Emergency Poems (Parra) **39**:263, 270, 279, 287, 292, 306, 308-12
"TH EMERGENCY WARD" (Bissett) **14**:10-11, 17, 34
"Emerging" (Thomas) **99**:255, 261, 263, 358
"Emerson" (Borges) **32**:45, 113-14, 116
"Emigrada judía" (Mistral) **32**:186
"L'emigrant de Landor Road" (Apollinaire) **7**:42, 47
"Emigranten" (Ekeloef) **23**:61
"The Emigrants" (Brathwaite) **56**:28, 99
"Emigrants" (Montague) **106**:261
The Emigrants: A Poem, in Two Books (Smith) **104**:167, 180, 197, 201-3, 211-13, 219-22, 224-30, 232-35, 237-41, 293-99, 301, 305-6, 309, 322, 324-26
"Emilie vor ihrem Brauttag" (Hölderlin) **4**:141
"Emily Before Her Wedding" (Hölderlin)
See "Emilie vor ihrem Brauttag"
"Emily Brontë" (Bridges) **28**:88
"Emily Bronte" (Hughes) **89**:123
"Emily Brosseau" (Masters) **1**:333
"Emily Dickinson" (Tate) **50**:308
"Emily Dickinson in Southern California" (Kennedy) **93**:143
Emily Dickinson in Southern California (Kennedy) **93**:143
"Emily Hardcastle, Spinster" (Ransom) **61**:271, 274, 301, 303, 306
"Emily Sparks" (Masters) **1**:327, 347; **36**:169, 172, 183
"Emily, This Place, and You" (Stafford) **71**:374
"Emma and Eginhard" (Longfellow) **30**:63
Empathy (Berssenbrugge) **115**:7-13, 15, 18-19, 21, 23, 28, 36-41, 47
"Empathy" (Berssenbrugge) **115**:12, 24, 41
"Empathy Again" (Stone) **53**:258
"Empathy and New Year" (Schuyler) **88**:179
"Empedocles" (Meredith) **60**:250, 295
Empedocles (Hölderlin)
See *Empedokles*
"Empedocles on Etna" (Arnold) **5**:5, 9-10, 12, 23, 35-6, 42-3, 45, 50-1, 56-7
Empedocles on Etna, and Other Poems (Arnold) **5**:2, 25, 30, 35, 42, 50, 55, 57
"Empedoklean Reveries" (Duncan) **75**:156
Empedokles (Hölderlin) **4**:146
"Empeoro y mejoro" (Fuertes) **27**:15
"The Emperor" (Simic) **69**:305
"The Emperor of Ice-Cream" (Stevens) **6**:293, 296; **110**:91, 173
"The Emperor's Dream" (Herbert) **50**:4, 31
"The Emperor's Entry into Rome" (Gower) **59**:58
"The Emperor's New Sonnet" (Villa) **22**:351
"Emperors of the Island" (Abse) **41**:6
"An Emphasis Falls on Reality" (Guest) **55**:196, 198
"Empire" (Graham) **59**:186

"The Empire" (Tennyson) **101**:269
"Empire Builders" (MacLeish) **47**:146, 189
Empire Burlesque (Dylan) **37**:59
"Empire of Dreams" (Simic) **69**:295, 313, 334-35
"Employment I" (Herbert) **4**:100, 111
"Employment II" (Herbert) **4**:111, 131
"Employments" (Herbert) **4**:100
"Emplumada" (Cervantes) **35**:104, 107, 113, 114, 115, 119, 121, 134
Emplumada (Cervantes) **35**:103, 104, 105, 106, 107, 108, 109, 110, 112, 113, 115, 119, 120, 121, 123, 127, 128, 129, 130, 132, 133, 134, 135
"Emporium" (Shapiro) **25**:295
Empty Chestnuts (Matsuo Basho)
See *Minashi Guri*
"The Empty Church" (Thomas) **99**:350, 357
"Empty Drawing Room" (Borges)
See "Sala vacía"
"The Empty Hills" (Winters) **82**:344
"The Empty House" (Spender) **71**:139
"Empty Mirror" (Rexroth) **95**:260, 273
Empty Mirror (Ginsberg) **4**:48, 73, 80, 91; **47**:31, 46
"An Empty Place" (Bly) **39**:87
"The Empty Purse" (Meredith) **60**:254, 256, 259, 328, 335
"Empty talk" (Borges)
See "Vanilocuencia"
"An Empty Threat" (Frost) **39**:246
"Empty White Blotch on Map of Universe: A Possible View" (Warren) **37**:383
"Empty Words" (Cage) **58**:183
Empty Words: Writings, '73-'78 (Cage) **58**:183, 185-88, 191-92, 195-99, 203, 205, 207, 212, 220
"En avant" (Péret) **33**:230
"En bateau" (Verlaine) **2**:431; **32**:350, 389-91
"En ces heures souvent que le plaisir abrège" (Sainte-Beuve) **110**:65, 68
"En dröm" (Ekeloef) **23**:57, 76
"En la Ausencia" (Fuertes) **27**:44
"En la plaza" (Aleixandre) **15**:6, 11-12, 17
"En las constelaciones" (Darío) **15**:99, 101
En las orillas del Sar (Castro) **41**:79-85, 87, 96-106, 111-14, 116, 118
En m'en revenant un soir d'été (Sainte-Beuve) **110**:39
"En medio de la multitud" (Cernuda) **62**:238, 256
En natt i Otocăc (Ekeloef) **23**:63, 69, 76
En natt på horisonten (Ekeloef) **23**:77
En natt vid horisonten (Ekeloef) **23**:62, 89
"En patinant" (Verlaine) **32**:349-50, 391
"En pocas palabras" (Fuertes) **27**:49
"En que describe racionalmente los efectos irracionales del amor" (Juana Inés de la Cruz) **24**:186
"En revenant du convoi de Gabrielle" (Sainte-Beuve) **110**:56
En självbiografi (Ekeloef) **23**:90
"En sourdine" (Verlaine) **32**:351, 354, 393
"En suma" (Guillén) **35**:229
En trente-trois morceaux (Char) **56**:142-43, 159
"En Trinacria" (Darío) **15**:107-09
"En último término" (Guillén) **35**:232
En un vasto dominio (Aleixandre) **15**:4, 7, 11-12, 17, 34, 41
"En una primavera" (Storni) **33**:278
"En vano tu canto suena" (Juana Inés de la Cruz) **24**:225
"En värld är varje människa" (Ekeloef) **23**:57
"En verklighet" (Ekeloef) **23**:76
"En vertu de l'amour" (Éluard) **38**:78
Enamels and Cameos (Gautier)
See *Emaux et camées*
"El enamorado" (Borges) **22**:95; **32**:65-6
"The Enamoured Sage" (Meredith) **60**:328
"An Encampment at Morning" (Merwin) **45**:53
"Encargo a Blanca" (Mistral) **32**:184-85, 189
"The Enchanted Island" (Noyes) **27**:121-23
"The Enchanted Knight" (Muir) **49**:204
"Enchanter's Handmaiden" (Wylie) **23**:324
"The Enchantment of the Flat Stone" (Castro)
See "O encanta da Pedra Chan"
"Enchantment through Fire" (Blok) **21**:20
Les Enclaves Gaulois (Béranger) **112**:9
"Enclosed in the deep recesses of the sea" (Johnson)
See "Ponti Profundis"
"The Enclosure" (Dickey) **40**:175, 180, 189, 224
"Enclosure" (Montague) **106**:243
"Encore eux" (Char) **56**:189
"An Encounter" (Duncan) **75**:175
"An Encounter" (Frost) **39**:232, 241
"The Encounter" (Glück) **16**:167
"Encounter" (Guillén) **35**:218
"Encounter" (Pavese) **13**:202
"Encounter" (Thomas) **99**:246
"Encounter" (Wright) **14**:374
"Encounter at a Greyhound bus station" (Abse) **41**:31
Encounter in April (Sarton) **39**:318, 320, 326, 329, 334, 345, 349-51, 353-56
"Encounter in August" (Kumin) **15**:209
"Encounter in the Cage Country" (Dickey) **40**:150, 152, 161, 168-69, 232
Encounters (Aleixandre) **15**:4
"Encoures au Lecteur" (Ronsard) **11**:249
"The Encrease" (Cowley) **90**:29
"El encuentro" (Mistral) **32**:175
"The End" (Creeley) **73**:5
"The End" (Dorn) **115**:202
"End" (Hughes) **1**:240
"The End" (Merwin) **45**:42
"The End" (Owen) **19**:334; **102**:203, 265-66
"The End" (Pasternak) **6**:268
"An End" (Rossetti) **7**:280
"The End" (Tomlinson) **17**:340
The End and the Beginning (Szymborska)
See *Koniec i poczatek*
"An End in Spring" (Merwin) **45**:9, 22, 32
The End of a Fine Epoch (Brodsky)
See *Konets prekrasnoy epokhi*
"End of a Hot Day" (Enright) **93**:11-12
"The End of a Journey" (Hope) **56**:278, 299, 303
"End of a Year" (Lowell) **3**:228
"End of Another Home Holiday" (Lawrence) **54**:187
"The End of Antony" (Cavafy) **36**:40
The End of Beauty (Graham) **59**:130-39, 142-43, 151-52, 154-59, 161, 168-69, 171, 173, 179, 184, 187-93, 195
"The End of March" (Bishop) **3**:48-9, 72; **34**:54, 131
"The End of Night" (Darwish) **86**:32
"The End of 1968" (Montale)
See "Fine del '68"
"End of Play" (Graves) **6**:137
"The End of Science Fiction" (Mueller) **33**:176
"End of Season" (Warren) **37**:284, 287, 332
"End of Summer" (Amichai) **38**:34
"End of Summer" (Kunitz) **19**:186
"End of Summer ... 1969" (Stone) **53**:218
"The End of the 22 Boock, entreatings of Sorrow" (Raleigh) **31**:246
"The End of the Boockes, of the Ocean Love to Scinthia, and the Beginninge of the 22 Boock Entreating of Sorrow" (Raleigh) **31**:240, 258, 301
"The End of the Episode" (Hardy) **8**:91; **92**:256
"End of the Man Experiment" (Stafford) **71**:330
"The End of the Owls" (Enzensberger) **28**:142, 147
"The End of the Rainbow" (Jarrell) **41**:155-58, 160, 163-64, 170-71, 215-16, 218
"The End of the Search" (Masters) **1**:344
"The End of the Weekend" (Hecht) **70**:89, 91
"The End of the World" (Glück) **16**:152
"End of the World" (Jeffers) **17**:141
"The End of the World" (MacLeish) **47**:130, 143, 158, 164, 178, 185, 196, 213
"End of the World: Weekend, near Toronto" (Atwood) **8**:13
"The End of the Year" (Duncan) **75**:175, 243
"End of the Year" (Tagore)
See "Varshashesh"
"End of the Year 1912" (Hardy) **8**:124
"The End of Your Life" (Levine) **22**:214
Endeavors of Infinite Man (Neruda)
See *Tentativa del hombre infinito*
"Endecasílabo" (Parra) **39**:272
Endimion and Phoebe. Ideas Latmus (Drayton) **98**:7, 41
"An Ending" (Kipling) **3**:194
"The Ending" (Masefield) **78**:90
"An Ending" (Mew) **107**:34-35
"Ending With a Line By Lear" (Bell) **79**:35
"Endings" (Boland) **58**:53
"Endings" (Walcott) **46**:236, 240
The Endless Cueca Dance (Parra)
See *La cueca larga*
"Endless Life" (Ferlinghetti) **1**:180, 182-83, 185
Endless Life: Selected Poems (Ferlinghetti) **1**:180, 182, 184-85
"En-Dor" (Kipling) **91**:154
Endor (Nemerov) **24**:261
Endocrinology (Berssenbrugge) **115**:8, 11, 13, 15, 39, 47
"Ends" (Frost) **1**:213
"Endurance" (Forché) **10**:141-42, 144, 147, 156
"Endymion" (Longfellow) **30**:103
"Endymion" (Nemerov) **24**:259
Endymion (Keats)
See *Endymion: A Poetic Romance*
Endymion: A Poetic Romance (Keats) **1**:275-79, 282, 288, 290-91, 308-09, 311, 313-14 **96**:193, 196, 204, 214, 220-21, 225-27, 236, 241, 245-46, 249, 257-58, 263-64, 270-76, 283-85, 291, 294, 304, 339, 342, 347-50, 353-54, 369, 373
Endymion and Phoebe (Drayton)
See *Endimion and Phoebe. Ideas Latmus*
"The Enemies" (Cavafy) **36**:94, 95-97, 99
"Enemies" (Sassoon) **12**:242
Enemies: Poems 1934-36 (Curnow) **48**:24, 26
"Enemigo" (Guillén) **35**:228
"The Enemy" (Baudelaire)
See "L'Ennemi"
"The Enemy of the Herds, the Lion" (Jacobsen) **62**:320, 322
"Energies" (Boland) **58**:53
The Energy of Slaves (Cohen) **109**:17, 19, 22, 29, 33, 71, 89, 92, 111
"Enfance" (Rimbaud) **3**:262, 265; **57**:184, 236, 238-39, 243, 249-50, 278, 294
"Enfance I" (Rimbaud) **57**:283-84
"Enfance III" (Rimbaud) **57**:227
"Enfance V" (Rimbaud) **57**:281
"L'Enfance d'Adèle" (Sainte-Beuve) **110**:47-48
"Enfans d'Adam" (Whitman)
See "Children of Adam"
"L'Enfant grect" (Hugo) **17**:75
"Enfant je m'étais dit et souvent répété" (Sainte-Beuve) **110**:65-66
"L'Enfant rêveur" (Sainte-Beuve) **110**:51
Les Enfants de la France (Béranger) **112**:9
"Les Enfants du quadrilatère" (Péret) **33**:201
"Enfermera de pulpos" (Fuertes) **27**:8, 26
"Enfidaville" (Douglas) **106**:201, 203
"Engaged" (Paz)
See "Los novios"
"The Engagement" (Swenson) **14**:265
"Engführung" (Celan) **10**:96, 99, 117
"The Engine Drain" (Smith) **12**:327
"England" (Borges) **32**:58
"England" (Davie) **29**:98-99, 103
"England" (de la Mare) **77**:142
"England" (Moore) **4**:251; **49**:95, 97, 102
"England 1830" (Clare) **23**:37
"England: An Ode" (Swinburne) **24**:312

"England Before the Storm" (Meredith) **60**:250
"England in 1819" (Shelley) **14**:210
England in Time of War (Dobell) **100**:148, 152, 160, 163, 171-72, 176, 178
"England, Its Latitude and Some of Its Conditions, the Seriousness of Ghosts" (Dorn) **115**:137
"England's Answer" (Kipling) **91**:85
"England's Day" (Dobell) **100**:141, 146
"England's Difficulty" (Heaney) **100**:286
"England's Good Genius" (Barker) **91**:50
Englands Heroicall Epistles (Drayton) **98**:3-8, 10, 24, 26, 30, 38, 41, 53, 55-57, 66, 93, 99-101, 104-7, 113, 123-24, 127
"Englisches Café" (Benn) **35**:46, 47, 67
"The English" (Hughes) **53**:115
An English Apocalypse (Szirtes) **51**:173, 175, 179
English as a Second Language (Mueller)
See *Second Language*
English Bards and Scotch Reviewers (Byron) **16**:77, 82; **95**:20, 23, 30
"The English Bull Dog, Dutch Mastiff, and Quail" (Smart) **13**:348
"English Cocker: Old and Blind" (Warren) **37**:341
"The English Flag" (Kipling) **3**:157, 161; **91**:82, 85-86, 101, 164-66
"An English Garden in Austria" (Jarrell) **41**:154, 174, 196
"The English Graves" (Chesterton) **28**:99
"English Horn" (Montale)
See "Corno Inglese"
"English Idylls" (Tennyson) **6**:409
"English Lessons" (Pasternak) **6**:251
"The English Metres" (Meynell) **112**:154, 173
"An English Padlock" (Prior) **102**:314
"English Poem" (Borges) **32**:58
English Poems (Blunden) **66**:7-8, 17, 24
"An English Revenant" (Davie) **29**:108
"English Thornton" (Masters) **36**:199
"An English Wood" (Graves) **6**:144, 166
"English Words" (Szirtes) **51**:169, 177
The English Works of George Herbert (Herbert) **4**:103
"The Englishman" (de la Mare) **77**:133
"The Englishman in Italy" (Browning) **2**:62
"The Englishman in Sorrento" (Browning) **2**:38
"Engomi" (Seferis) **66**:152, 206
"Enid and Nimüe: The True and the False" (Tennyson) **101**:202
"An Enigma" (Poe) **1**:446
"Enigma" (Prior) **102**:306
"Enigma" (Thomas) **99**:241
"Enigma for an Angel" (Brodsky) **9**:2
"Enivrez-vous" (Baudelaire) **1**:58
"The Enjoyment" (Cowley) **90**:14
"The Enkindled Spring" (Lawrence) **54**:175
"L'Ennemi" (Baudelaire) **106**:71, 135
"Ennui" (Baudelaire) **106**:138
"Ennui" (Viereck) **27**:263
"Enoch" (Very) **86**:44, 46, 88, 126, 158
"Enoch Arden" (Tennyson) **101**:134, 215, 251
Enoch Arden, and Other Poems (Tennyson) **6**:360, 365
"Enoch Dunlap" (Masters) **36**:182
"Enough" (Creeley) **73**:44, 49-50
"Enough" (Teasdale) **31**:322
"Enough" (Yamada) **44**:350, 351
"Enough: Jamestown, 1607-1957" (Moore) **4**:260; **49**:132-33, 141, 150
Enough Rope (Parker) **28**:345-48, 351, 353, 356-57, 359-61
"The Enquirie" (Traherne) **70**:191, 273, 288, 316
"The Enquiry" (Leapor) **85**:217
"The Enquiry" (Philips) **40**:296
"Enriching the Earth" (Berry) **28**:11, 43
"Enryo" (Yamada) **44**:333-34, 346
Enseignemens et Proverbes moraux (Christine de Pizan) **68**:96-97, 111
Enslaved and Other Poems (Masefield) **78**:14, 49, 51, 58, 63
"L'Entaile" (Bonnefoy) **58**:136
"Entbehren" (Howe) **81**:28
"Enter No (Silence Is the Blood Whose Flesh)" (Cummings) **5**:111
"Entering History" (Stafford) **71**:374
"Entering the Kingdom" (Oliver) **75**:293
"Entering the Kingdom of the Moray Eel" (Wright) **36**:358, 378
"Entering the Temple in Nîmes" (Wright) **36**:359
"L'enterrement" (Verlaine) **2**:431
"Entertaining the Canary" (Simic) **69**:305
"L'enthousiasme" (Lamartine) **16**:276, 290
"The Enthusiast" (Melville) **82**:76, 105, 147-48
The Enthusiastic Slinger (Neruda)
See *El hondero entusiasta, 1923-1924*
Enthussiasts' Highway (Yevtushenko) **40**:349
The Entire Son (Guillén)
See *El son entero*
"Entirely" (MacNeice) **61**:139
"Entrada a la madera" (Neruda) **4**:277, 306-07
"Entrance into Wood" (Neruda)
See "Entrada a la madera"
"Entrance Visa" (Enright) **93**:8, 18
"Entre autres" (Éluard) **38**:70
"Entre autres Ombres" (Éluard) **38**:85
Entre la piedra y la flor (Paz) **1**:369; **48**:177, 185, 229, 244
"Entre Lo Que Veo y Digo..." (Paz) **48**:189, 250-51, 273
"Entrevu en Egypte" (Jaccottet) **98**:201
Entries (Berry) **28**:30-1
"Entropy" (Mahon) **60**:134, 138
"Entry in an Album" (Lermontov) **18**:302
"Entwurf einer Hymne an die Madonna" (Hölderlin) **4**:150
"The Envelope" (Kumin) **15**:203, 207, 221-22
"The Enviable Isles" (Melville) **82**:104
"Envoi" (Boland) **58**:4, 6, 29, 35, 48
"Envoi" (Cunningham) **92**:136
"Envoi" (Ignatow) **34**:324
"Envoi" (Kennedy) **93**:149
"L'Envoi" (Melville) **82**:106
"Envoi" (Meredith) **28**:174, 187
"L'Envoi" (Morris) **55**:253
"Envoi" (Pound) **95**:122
"L'Envoi" (Tennyson) **101**:245
"Envoi" (Ungaretti)
See "Commiato"
"Envoi" (Wickham) **110**:269
"Envoi" (Wilbur) **51**:273
"Envoûtement à La Renardière" (Char) **56**:150
"Envoy" (Johnson) **24**:145
"Envoy" (Service) **70**:115, 141
"L'Envoy" (Vaughan) **81**:298, 336, 339, 351-52
"The Envoy of Mr. Cogito" (Herbert)
See "Przeslanie Pana Cogito"
"Envoy to Africa" (Hughes) **53**:115
Envoy to Bukton (Chaucer) **58**:231, 279, 369
"The Envoys" (Merrill) **28**:220
"Envy" (H. D.) **5**:305
"Envy" (Yevtushenko) **40**:344
"The Envy of Poor Lovers" (Clarke) **112**:54, 68
"The Eolian Harp" (Coleridge)
See "The Aeolian Harp"
The Eolian Harp (Coleridge) **100**:19-21, 23-24, 26, 56, 75
"L'Epars, l'indivisible" (Bonnefoy) **58**:168
"L'epaule" (Bonnefoy) **58**:118-19
Les épaves (Baudelaire) **106**:152, 174
"Ephemera" (Lowell) **13**:74
"Ephemera" (Yeats) **20**:337
"Ephemerid" (Loy) **16**:316
"Ephemeron" (Carman) **34**:209
"Ephraim" (Merrill)
See "The Book of Ephraim"
"Ephyphatha" (MacDiarmid) **9**:156
"L'épi de cristal égrène dans les herbes sa moisson transparente" (Char) **56**:156
"Epic" (Kavanagh) **33**:81, 100, 103, 142, 145-47; **105**:99, 124, 176
"The Epic" (Tennyson) **101**:121, 168, 240, 248, 265, 286
The Epic of Gilgamesh (Anonymous) **87**:131-279
An Epicede or Funerall Song: On the Death, of Henry Prince of Wales (Chapman) **96**:36-38, 59
"Epick Ode" (Davenant) **99**:177
"The Epicure" (Cowley) **90**:15
"Epidaurus" (Birney) **52**:78
"Epidermal Macabre" (Roethke) **15**:272
"Epigram" (Cowper) **40**:103
"Epigram" (Prior) **102**:306-7
"Epigram I" (Rexroth) **20**:180
"Epigram 8" (Cunningham) **92**:135, 137, 189
"Epigram 9" (Cunningham) **92**:136
"Epigram 11" (Cunningham) **92**:156
"Epigram 12" (Cunningham) **92**:136-37, 190
"Epigram 14" (Cunningham) **92**:137, 161, 191-92
"Epigram 16" (Cunningham) **92**:159
"Epigram 19" (Cunningham) **92**:137
"Epigram 20" (Cunningham) **92**:136
"Epigram 23" (Cunningham) **92**:136-37, 156
"Epigram 27" (Cunningham) **92**:137, 158
"Epigram 28" (Cunningham) **92**:146, 159, 168
"Epigram 29" (Cunningham) **92**:191
"Epigram 33" (Cunningham) **92**:167
"Epigram 35" (Cunningham) **92**:136-37
"Epigram 36" (Cunningham) **92**:159
"Epigram 37" (Cunningham) **92**:159, 191
"Epigram 42" (Cunningham) **92**:137
"Epigram 43" (Cunningham) **92**:135, 137, 139, 157-58, 187-88, 190
"Epigram 55" (Cunningham) **92**:147
"Epigram 59" (Cunningham) **92**:157
"Epigram 60" (Cunningham) **92**:158
"Epigram 62" (Cunningham) **92**:158, 169
"Epigram 88" (Cunningham) **92**:157
"Epigram 92" (Cunningham) **92**:166
"Epigram CI" (Jonson) **17**:158, 167, 173, 175, 182, 189-90, 208
"Epigram CII" (Jonson) **17**:157, 197
"Epigram CIII" (Jonson) **17**:197-98, 202
"Epigram CIV" (Jonson) **17**:202
"Epigram CVII" (Jonson) **17**:166
"Epigram CVIII" (Jonson) **17**:166
"Epigram CXVI" (Jonson) **17**:164
"Epigram CXXIV" (Jonson) **17**:193
"Epigram CXXXIII" (Jonson) **17**:189
"Epigram IV" (Jonson) **17**:156
"Epigram LIX" (Jonson) **17**:164
"Epigram LXV" (Jonson) **17**:157, 197
"Epigram LXXVI" (Jonson) **17**:159, 174, 192, 198, 200, 205, 214
"Epigram on Lady Elizabeth" (Jonson)
See "Epigram CXXIV"
"Epigram: To a Friend, and Sonne" (Jonson)
See *The Under-Wood LXIX*
"Epigram to The Judge Is Fury" (Cunningham) **92**:164
"Epigram X" (Jonson) **17**:157
"Epigram XCI" (Jonson) **17**:201
"Epigram XCIV" (Jonson) **17**:159, 202
"Epigram XIV" (Jonson) **17**:166, 174
"Epigram XLIII" (Jonson) **17**:199
"Epigram XLV" (Jonson) **17**:193
"Epigram XVIII" (Jonson) **17**:179
"Epigram XXIII" (Jonson) **17**:197
"Epigram XXXV" (Jonson) **17**:156
"Epigramas" (Guillén) **23**:121
Epigramas (Cardenal) **22**:104, 117, 124-25, 131
"Epigramas, II" (Guillén) **35**:229
Epigrammata (Martial) **10**:243
"The Epigrammatist" (Chappell) **105**:52
Epigrammaton libri (Martial)
See *Epigrammata*
Epigrammatum Sacrorum Liber (Crashaw) **84**:3, 9-10, 12, 31, 153, 164
"Epigrams" (Kennedy) **93**:150

Epigrams (Campion)
See *Thomas Campiani Epigrammatum Libri II. Umbra. Elegiarum liber unus*
Epigrams (Cardenal)
See *Epigramas*
Epigrams (Jonson) **17**:156-58, 169, 179, 196-97, 201-02, 206
Epigrams (Martial)
See *Epigrammata*
"Epigraph for a Banned Book" (Kennedy) **93**:145
"Epigraph for a Condemned Book" (Baudelaire)
See "Épigraphe pour un livre condamné"
"Épigraphe pour un livre condamné" (Baudelaire) **106**:92, 139
"Epigraphs Written on Air" (Sachs)
See "Grabschriften in die Luft geschrieben"
"Epilog" (Heine) **25**:162, 178
"Epilogos" (Duncan) **75**:127, 134-35
"Epilogue" (Akhmatova) **55**:4-6, 8, 10-11, 13, 15, 19, 43, 50, 54, 61
"Epilogue" (Behn) **88**:71
"Epilogue" (Brathwaite) **56**:67, 84
"Epilogue" (Browning) **61**:16
"Epilogue" (Carman) **34**:234
"Epilogue" (Ciardi) **69**:53
"Epilogue" (Cullen) **20**:57
"Epilogue" (Housman) **43**:219
"Epilogue" (Hughes) **53**:106
"The Epilogue" (Masters) **36**:195-96, 212, 220, 223, 243
"Epilogue" (Tennyson) **101**:264
"Epilogue" (Verlaine) **2**:432
"Epilogue (1)" (Akhmatova) **55**:27, 39, 57-58, 63
"Epilogue (2)" (Akhmatova) **55**:4, 28, 32, 39, 55-57, 60-61, 63-64
"Epilogue: Driving South" (Montague)
See "Driving South"
"Epilogue for FDR" (Ignatow) **34**:325
"Epilogue: For Howard Baker" (Winters) **82**:330, 345
"Epilogue for Jim" (Spicer) **78**:302
"The Epilogue of the Man of Law's Tale" (Chaucer) **58**:288
"Epilogue to a Human Drama" (Spender) **71**:146, 190
"Epilogue" to Gaudete (Hughes) **89**:114-15, 124, 129-30
"Epilogue to the Breakfast-Table Series" (Holmes) **71**:65, 68
"Epilogue to the Drama Founded on 'St. Roman's Welle'" (Scott) **13**:293
Epilogue to the Satires (Pope) **26**:319-20, 340
"Epilogue to the Tragedy of Jane Shore" (Finch) **21**:154
"Epilogues" (Akhmatova) **55**:6
"Epimetheus; or, The Poet's Afterthought" (Longfellow) **30**:103
Epinicia (Pindar) **19**:378
"Epiphany" (Hughes) **89**:206
"Epiphany" (Kennedy) **93**:150
"An Epiphany" (Stafford) **71**:295
"Epiphany" (Thomas) **99**:357, 359
Epipsychidion (Shelley) **14**:163, 171, 173-75, 178, 187, 189, 192-93, 196-97, 208, 233-37, 239-40; **67**:136-39, 171, 175-78, 180
"Episode" (Herbert) **50**:4
"Episode" (Valéry) **9**:391
"Episode of Hands" (Crane) **99**:73, 87-88
"Epistemology" (Wilbur) **51**:192, 211, 217
"Epistle II" (Barker) **77**:30-31, 38
Epistle III (Pope) **26**:325-26
Epistle IV (Pope) **26**:325
"Epistle" (Darío)
See "Epístola"
"Epistle" (Lee) **24**:242
"Epistle" (Spender) **71**:216
"Epistle" (Tate) **50**:256
"An Epistle answering one that asked to be Sealed of the Tribe of Ben" (Jonson)
See *The Under-Wood XLVII*
"Epistle Containing the Strange Medical Experiences of Karshish the Arab Physician" (Browning) **2**:36
"Epistle Dedicatory" (Behn) **88**:71
"An Epistle: Edward Sackville to Venetia Digby" (Hope) **56**:268-69, 273, 280
"Epistle from a Taylor to Robert Burns" (Burns) **114**:21, 89
"An Epistle from Ardelia to Mrs. Randolph in answer to her Poem upon Her Verses" (Finch) **21**:167
"Epistle from Esopus to Maria" (Burns) **114**:55
"An Epistle from Holofernes" (Hope) **56**:273, 296
"Epistle from Mrs. Yonge to Her Husband" (Montagu) **16**:346
"An Epistle from the Devil" (Crabbe) **97**:157
"An Epistle, Inviting a Friend to Supper" (Jonson)
See "Epigram CI"
"Epistle John Hamilton to Reynolds" (Keats) **1**:289, 305
"An Epistle Mendicant" (Jonson)
See *The Under-Wood LXXI*
"The Epistle of Deborah Dough" (Leapor) **85**:252, 284, 295
"Epistle of Mistres Shore" (Drayton) **98**:104
Epistle, On the Art of Poetry (Horace)
See *Ars Poetica*
"Epistle to a Friend" (Jonson)
See *The Under-Wood XXXVII*
"Epistle to a Friend, to perswade him to the Warres" (Jonson)
See *The Under-Wood XV*
"An Epistle to a Lady" (Leapor) **85**:183, 187-88, 236, 259, 284, 289
"Epistle to a Lady" (Waller) **72**:286
"An Epistle to a Lady, Who Desired the Author to Make Verses on Her, in the Heroick Style" (Swift) **9**:256, 259-60, 281
"Epistle to a Young Friend" (Burns) **6**:71, 96; **114**:67, 146
Epistle to Arbuthnot (Pope)
See *An Epistle to Dr. Arbuthnot*
"An Epistle to Artemisia. On Fame." (Leapor) **85**:183, 213-14, 234, 249, 257, 259, 267, 285, 287, 289
"Epistle to Augusta" (Byron) **16**:86
Epistle to Augustus (Pope) **26**:320-21
An Epistle to Bathurst (Pope) **26**:340
"Epistle To Be Left in the Earth" (MacLeish) **47**:127, 154-55, 188, 196
An Epistle to Burlington (Pope) **26**:353, 359
"Epistle to Davie" (Burns) **114**:41, 140, 147
"Epistle to Dr. Arbuthnot" (Pope) **26**:318, 338, 361
An Epistle to Dr. Arbuthnot (Pope) **26**:311, 320, 339-46
"Epistle to Dylan Thomas" (Barker) **77**:46
"Epistle to Elizabeth Countesse of Rutland" (Jonson)
See *The Forest XII*
"Epistle to J. Goldie, Kilmarnock" (Burns) **114**:60
"Epistle to J. Lapraik" (Burns)
See "Epistle to John Lapraik"
"Epistle to J. R******" (Burns)
See "Epistle to John Rankine, Enclosing Some Poems"
"Epistle to J[ames] S[mith]" (Burns) **114**:59
"Epistle to John Lapraik" (Burns) **114**:112-13, 138
"Epistle to John Rankine, Enclosing Some Poems" (Burns) **6**:65, 83; **114**:45
"Epistle: To Katherine, Lady Aubigny" (Jonson)
See *The Forest XIII*
"Epistle to Léon-Paul Fargue" (MacLeish) **47**:190
"An Epistle to Master John Selden" (Jonson)
See *The Under-Wood XVI*
"Epistle to Mastre Canynge on Aella" (Chatterton)
See "Letter to Mastre Canynge"
"Epistle to Prince William Henry" (Crabbe) **97**:76
"Epistle to Reynolds" (Keats) **96**:284, 310
"Epistle to Robert Graham of Fintry" (Burns) **114**:22, 42, 140
"Epistle to Sir Edward Sacvile, now Earl of Dorset" (Jonson)
See *The Under-Wood XIII*
"Epistle to the Olympians" (Nash) **21**:279-80
"Epistle to the Rev. John M'Math" (Burns) **114**:60
"Epistle to William Simpson of Ochiltree, May 1785" (Burns) **6**:69; **114**:31, 59, 60, 141
"The Epistles" (Burns) **6**:49, 66-71, 79, 81; **114**:52, 59-60
Epistles (Crabbe)
See *Poetical Epistles, with a Preface by the learned Martinus Scriblerus*
Epistles (Drayton)
See *Englands Heroicall Epistles*
Epistles (Horace) **46**:97, 99-100, 102, 104, 114, 117-19, 131, 137, 140, 142, 145-46, 152-53, 163, 173, 191, 198, 203-6, 209, 211, 214, 222
Epistles (Ovid)
See *Heroides*
Epistles, Book I (Horace) **46**:95
Epistolæ Heroidum (Ovid)
See *Heroides*
"Epístola" (Darío) **15**:89-90
"Epistola a monsenor Casaldaliga" (Cardenal) **22**:103
"An Epistolary Essay from M.G. to O.B." (Wilmot) **66**:266, 284-86
"Epistre a ses amis" (Villon) **13**:395
L'epistre au dieu d'amours (Christine de Pizan) **68**:3, 6, 22-23, 35, 39-42, 47-48, 51-55, 69, 71-72, 106-10, 119, 123
L'Epistre d'Othéa la Deesse, que Elle Envoya a Hector de Troye Quant Il Estoit en l'Age de Quinze Ans (Christine de Pizan) **68**:3, 22, 25-26, 61, 73, 77, 111-14, 119-21, 123-24, 138, 145, 171-72
"Epi-Strauss-ium" (Clough) **103**:70, 81, 112, 116
"Epitáfio de B Dias" (Pessoa) **20**:155
"Epitafio para mi tumba" (Storni) **33**:236
"Epitaph" (Blunden) **66**:27-28
"Epitaph" (Coleridge) **39**:178
"Epitaph" (Cunningham) **92**:146
"Epitaph" (Merwin) **45**:19, 93
"Epitaph" (Muir) **49**:206
"Epitaph" (Parra) **39**:300
"Epitaph" (Tsvetaeva)
See "Nadgrobie"
"Epitaph" (Williams) **7**:345
"Epitaph" (Wylie) **23**:322-23
"The Epitaph at Corinth" (Rexroth) **95**:260
"The Epitaph Ending in And" (Stafford) **71**:268, 329
"Epitaph for a Darling Lady" (Parker) **28**:346
"Epitaph for a Lady's Man" (Wagoner) **33**:351
"Epitaph for a Poet" (Cullen) **20**:60
"Epitaph for an Old Woman" (Paz) **48**:189
"Epitaph for Anton Schmidt" (Gunn) **26**:203
"Epitaph for Flann O'Brien" (Mahon) **60**:134
"Epitaph for G. K. Chesterton" (Hardy) **92**:320
"Epitaph for John McCutcheon" (MacLeish) **47**:197
"Epitaph for Liberal Poets" (MacNeice) **61**:141
"Epitaph for Many Young Men" (Barker) **77**:20
"Epitaph for My Father" (Walker) **20**:289, 293
"Epitaph for Robert Flaherty" (Mahon) **60**:138
"Epitaph for the Race of Man" (Millay) **6**:217, 230
Epitaph for the Young: A Poem in XII Cantos (Walcott) **46**:277

"Epitaph. H. S. E. Georgius Churchill" (Prior) **102**:307
"Epitaph: Hubert Hastings, Parry" (Bridges) **28**:77
"Epitaph of Antiochos, King of Commagene" (Cavafy)
See "Epitaph of Antiochos, King of Kommagini"
"Epitaph of Antiochos King of Kommagênê" (Cavafy)
See "Epitaph of Antiochos, King of Kommagini"
"Epitaph of Antiochos, King of Kommagini" (Cavafy) **36**:8, 40, 111
"Epitaph on an Army of Mercenaries" (Housman) **2**:177; **43**:245, 261
"Epitaph on an Engraver" (Thoreau) **30**:227
"Epitaph on Claudy Philips" (Johnson) **81**:212, 215, 217, 235, 239
"Epitaph on Edward Purdon" (Goldsmith) **77**:193
"Epitaph on her Son H.P. at St. Syth's Church" (Philips) **40**:296
"Epitaph on Hogarth" (Johnson) **81**:188, 216, 235
"Epitaph on Salathiel Pavy" (Jonson)
See "Epitaph on Salomon Pavy"
"Epitaph on Salomon Pavy" (Jonson) **17**:179
"Epitaph on the Lady S. Wife to Sir W.S." (Carew) **29**:62
"Epitaph on the Politician Himself" (Belloc) **24**:31, 40
"Epitaph on the Tombstone of a Child, the last of Seven that died before" (Behn) **88**:42-48, 50
"Epitaph on Thomas Clere" (Surrey) **59**:322-24
"Epitaph on True, her Majesty's Dog" (Peacock) **87**:321
"Epitaph Proposed for the Headstone of S. R. Quiett" (Kennedy) **93**:152-53
"Epitaph: Thaw" (Carson) **64**:223
"Epitaph: The Poet" (Chappell) **105**:50
"Epitaph: The Reprobate" (Chappell) **105**:50
"Epitaph to Master Vincent Corbet" (Jonson) **17**:174
"An Epitaph to Saunt'ring Jack, and Idle Joan" (Prior) **102**:294, 308, 325-26
"An Epitaph upon a Child" (Herrick) **9**:129
"An Epitaph upon a Virgin" (Herrick) **9**:131
"An Epitaph upon a Young Married Couple" (Crashaw) **84**:69
"The Epitaph upon Gilbert Glanvill Bishop of Rochester, as Written in Rochester Cathedral. Translated" (Prior) **102**:308
"Epitaph: Zion" (Carson) **64**:223, 231
"Epitaphe Villon" (Villon) **13**:390, 394, 408, 410-11, 417-18
Epitaphium Damonis (Milton) **29**:241
"Epitaphs and Epigraphs" (Barker) **77**:13
"Epitaphs of the War" (Kipling) **3**:171, 192; **91**:153
"Epitaphs Written into the Air" (Sachs)
See "Grabschriften in die Luft geschrieben"
"Epithalamie on Sir Clipseby Crew and His Lady" (Herrick)
See "A Nuptiall Song, or Epithalamie on Sir Clipseby Crew and His Lady"
"An Epithalamie to Sir Thomas Southwell and His Ladie" (Herrick) **9**:86
"Epithalamion" (Abse) **41**:14, 18
"Epithalamion" (Herrick)
See "A Nuptiall Song, or Epithalamie on Sir Clipseby Crew and His Lady"
"Epithalamion" (Hopkins) **15**:124
"Epithalamion" (Spender) **71**:160
Epithalamion (Spenser) **8**:336, 389
"Epithalamion after a War" (Ciardi) **69**:40, 52
"An Epithalamion, or mariage song on the Lady Elizabeth, and Count Palatine being married on St. Valentines day" (Donne) **1**:124
"The Epithalamium" (Housman) **2**:199; **43**:249
"Epithalamium" (Pessoa) **20**:165, 169
"Epithalamium at St. Michael's Cemetery" (Ciardi) **69**:51
"An Epitome" (Sassoon) **12**:260
"Epitome" (Spencer) **77**:330-31
"Epitre a M. de Sainte-Beuve" (Lamartine) **16**:267
"Épître à Marie d'Orléans" (Villon) **13**:399, 413
"Epîtres à la Princesse" (Senghor) **25**:255
Epode (Jonson)
See *The Forest XI*
Epodes (Horace) **46**:99, 114, 137, 149, 155, 193, 197-98, 221-22
"Eponina" (Tuckerman) **85**:309
The Epping Hunt (Hood) **93**:44, 46, 61, 89
"Epsilon" (Tolson) **88**:236-37, 267, 270, 304, 319
"Epte Wood" (Char)
See "Le bois de l'epte"
"Equal Opportunity" (Lorde) **12**:140
"The Equality of the Sexes" (Éluard)
See "L'égalité des sexes"
"Equilibrist" (Swenson) **14**:274, 283
"The Equilibrists" (Ransom) **61**:267-69, 272, 297, 299, 306, 308, 311
"Equinox" (Lorde) **12**:157
"Equitan" (Marie de France) **22**:239-41, 258, 265, 269, 271, 278, 296-98
"ER" (Banks) **44**:45
"Era in penser d'amor quand i' trovai" (Cavalcanti) **114**:224, 235-36
"Era la última noche" (Castro) **41**:84
"Era un aire suave" (Darío) **15**:79, 95, 107, 109, 118-19
"Era vicino il dí che 'l Creatore (Stampa) **43**:285
"Eran, he ran" (Alurista) **34**:22, 29
Erasmus Wilson (Riley) **48**:358
"Erasures" (Chappell) **105**:67
Erato e Apòllion (Quasimodo) **47**:277, 279, 293, 300, 302
"Ere Sleep Comes Down to Soothe the Weary Eyes" (Dunbar) **5**:121, 124
"The Eremites" (Graves) **6**:140
"Erfüllung" (Stramm) **50**:168, 189, 195, 202
"Erhört" (Stramm) **50**:176, 191-93, 209
"Erige Cor Tuum ad Me in Coelum" (H. D.) **5**:307
Eril (Perse) **23**:246
"Erinna" (Eliot) **20**:137
"Erinna to Sappho" (Wright) **36**:335
"Erinnerung" (Stramm) **50**:172, 174, 189, 198
"Erinnerung an Frankreich" (Celan) **10**:121
"Eripeteia" (Hecht) **70**:86
"Eris in Eros" (Duncan) **75**:247
"eriuuerung un die schrecken der jugend" (Enzensberger) **28**:136
"Das erkaltende Herz" (Werfel) **101**:346
Erklärung (Heine) **25**:162
"Erl-King" (Goethe)
See *Erlkönig*
Erlkönig (Goethe) **5**:239, 254, 257
"A Ermes" (Quasimodo) **47**:297
"L'ermite" (Apollinaire) **7**:46-7
"Ermunterung" (Hölderlin) **4**:148
"Eroded Hills" (Wright) **14**:353, 378
Eroding Witness (Mackey) **49**:2-5, 7, 11, 15, 17-18, 21-22, 25-26, 30-33, 35, 42-43, 51-53, 58-59, 66, 71, 77
"Eroica" (Ginsberg) **4**:62
"L'eroismo" (Montale) **13**:156
"Eros" (Bridges) **28**:74-5, 86-7
"Eros" (Komunyakaa) **51**:64
"Eros" (Oppen) **35**:309, 310-11, 314
"A Eros" (Storni) **33**:242, 257, 284, 293-94
"Eros and Psyche" (Patmore) **59**:212, 223, 265, 267
Eros and Psyche (Bridges) **28**:47, 59, 68, 86
"Eros at Temple Stream" (Levertov) **11**:169
Eros in Dogma (Barker) **77**:41
"Éros suspendu" (Char) **56**:120
"Eros Turannos" (Robinson) **1**:468, 490, 493-94, 497
"Erosion" (Graham) **59**:148-49, 179
Erosion (Graham) **59**:132-33, 135, 139-40, 142-44, 146-47, 151, 154-58, 161, 168-69, 174, 176, 178-79, 184, 187
"Erosion: Transkei" (Brutus) **24**:113
Erotic Adventures (Ovid)
See *Amores*
"The Erotic Poetry of Sir Isaac Newton" (Randall) **86**:292, 344
"Erotikos Logos" (Seferis) **66**:89, 92, 97, 110, 125, 127, 170, 182, 185
The Errancy (Graham) **59**:163-64, 168-69, 175, 180, 182, 185-88
"Errand" (Carver) **54**:18
"The Errand" (Heaney) **100**:244
"The Errand Boy I" (Ignatow) **34**:271, 273, 278, 305, 316
"The Errand Boy II" (Ignatow) **34**:273
"The Errigal Road" (Montague) **106**:246-47
"Errol Flynn—On His Death" (Corso) **33**:37
"Error and Loss" (Morris) **55**:340
"Der erste Verwundeten-Transport 1914" (Werfel) **101**:348
"Erster Frühling" (Werfel)
See "Early Spring"
"Erwache, Friederike" (Goethe) **5**:246
"Erwiderung an Alexander Lernet-Holenia" (Benn) **35**:35
"Es así" (Neruda) **4**:311
"Es ist ein Garten" (Benn) **35**:71
"Es obligatorio" (Fuertes) **27**:12
"Es olvido" (Parra) **39**:270, 285, 296
"Es War Einmal" (Smith) **12**:312
"Escaparate" (Borges) **22**:92
"The Escape" (Dickey) **40**:196, 254
"The Escape" (Levine) **22**:233
"Escape" (MacLeish) **47**:182
"The Escape" (Muir) **49**:199, 232, 251, 289
"The Escape" (Sachs) **78**:227, 233
"Escape" (Wylie) **23**:301, 309, 329
"Escape at Bedtime" (Stevenson) **84**:328
The Escape into You: A Sequence (Bell) **79**:6, 32, 38-39
"Escaped from the Archipelago" (Char)
See "Evadé d'archipel"
"Escapist—Never" (Frost) **71**:5, 9
"Escargots" (Ponge) **107**:131, 190, 200-201
"Eschatological Forebodings of Mr. Cogito" (Herbert)
See "Przeczucia eschatologiczne Pana Cogito"
"Esclava" (Storni) **33**:254, 278
"Escolares" (Guillén) **23**:127
"Un escolio" (Borges) **32**:65
"Escrito" (Fuertes) **27**:48
"Escrito en el agua" (Cernuda) **62**:218-20
"Escritura" (Paz) **48**:272
"Escultura inacabada (David-Apolo, de Miguel Ángel)" (Cernuda) **62**:200, 266-67, 269
"Esequie della guida E.R." (Carducci) **46**:88, 90
"Esistere psichicamente" (Zanzotto) **65**:278
"Eskimo and Others" (Schwerner) **42**:204
"The Eskimo National Anthem" (Stafford) **71**:283, 321
"Eso Basta" (Guillén) **35**:201
Esope (Marie de France)
See *The Fables*
Espacia (Jiménez) **7**:203, 213-14
"Espadas" (Borges) **32**:95
Espadas como labios (Aleixandre) **15**:6, 18, 21, 30-1, 39-41
España (Gautier) **18**:155
España en el corazón (Neruda)
See *España en el corazón: himno a las glorias del pueblo en la guerra (1936-1937)*
España en el corazón: himno a las glorias del pueblo en la guerra (1936-1937) (Neruda) **4**:278, 283, 287, 307-9, 311; **64**:298, 300, 305, 326-27

"Espantapájaros" (Borges) **32**:125
"Especially When the October Wind" (Thomas) **2**:384; **52**:258, 260, 264, 268
"Espejo" (Paz) **48**:176
"Los espejos" (Borges) **32**:60, 66, 77, 133
"La espera" (Borges) **32**:66
"La espera inútil" (Mistral) **32**:161
"Esperanto" (Tolson) **88**:343
"Los espinos" (Cernuda) **62**:195, 214
"Espíritu sin nombre" (Bécquer)
See "Rima 5"
"L'espoir luit comme un brin de paille dans l'étable" (Verlaine) **2**:416
The Espousals (Patmore)
See *The Angel in the House, Book II: The Espousals*
"L'Esprit" (Rimbaud) **57**:246
"L'Esprit de Géométrie et L'Esprit de Finesse" (Cunningham) **92**:182
"L'Esprit pur" (Vigny) **26**:371, 374, 392, 402-4, 413
"L'esprit saint" (Lamartine) **16**:264, 277
Espurgatoire (Marie de France)
See *L'Espurgatoire Saint Patrice*
L'Espurgatoire Saint Patrice (Marie de France) **22**:287-89, 291, 293, 300
"Esquinita de mi pueblo" (Paredes) **83**:32, 65-66
"Essai de la débilité mentale" (Éluard) **38**:96
"Essai de la manie aiguë" (Éluard) **38**:96
"An Essay at War" (Duncan) **75**:181, 228, 261
"Essay Lamenting His Own Long Illness" (Yakamochi)
See "Jin'a jiiai bun"
An Essay on Criticism (Pope) **26**:300, 302-303, 314-15, 318, 320-22, 340
"Essay on Error (2nd Draft)" (Carson) **64**:223
"An Essay on Happiness" (Leapor) **85**:186
"Essay on Man" (Ciardi) **69**:32
An Essay on Man (Pope) **26**:304, 307-308, 314, 318, 326, 328-33, 335, 338-40, 351-56, 359
"Essay on Mind" (Barrett Browning) **6**:27
An Essay on Mind, with other Poems (Barrett Browning) **6**:19-20, 26
"Essay on Poetics" (Ammons) **16**:10-11, 23, 28, 47-9
"Essay on Psychiatrists" (Pinsky) **27**:144-5, 160, 162, 173, 175-6
Essay on Rime (Shapiro) **25**:264-65, 267-68, 270, 274-79, 285, 288, 290-91, 296, 310, 319, 322-23
"Essay on Stone" (Carruth) **10**:83
"Essay on Style" (O'Hara) **45**:161
"Essay on the Alliance of Education and Government" (Gray) **2**:136; **80**:164, 182, 249
"An Essay on War" (Duncan) **2**:105
"Essay on What I think about Most" (Carson) **64**:223, 237
"An Essay on William Carlos Williams" (Cruz) **37**:20, 25
"An Essay on Woman" (Leapor) **85**:215-17, 234, 248, 252, 259, 287
Essays and Poems (Very) **86**:36, 46-49, 58-59, 84, 95, 102, 105, 110, 127-30, 137, 139, 147-49, 151, 154-62, 164-65, 168
Essays in Divinity (Donne) **43**:113, 118-22, 127
"Essays of a Song to the Muse" (Carducci)
See "Saggi di un canto alle Muse"
"Esse" (Milosz) **8**:182, 187
"Esse quid hoc dicam" (Campion) **87**:101
"Essential Beauty" (Larkin) **21**:229
The Essential Etheridge Knight (Knight) **14**:52-3
Essex Poems, 1963-1967 (Davie) **29**:113, 122-23
"Est' tajna u menja ot cudnogo cvetenija" (Akhmadulina) **43**:19, 21, 23, 46
"Está bien" (Guillén) **23**:127
"Está el bisonte imperial" (Guillén) **23**:125
"Esta Noche" (Doty) **53**:46, 52
"Esta tarde, mi bien, cuando te hablaba" (Juana Inés de la Cruz) **24**:180
"Estación del Norte" (Guillén) **35**:157
La estación violenta (Paz) **1**:353, 359-60, 362; **48**:245
"Estar del cuerpo" (Aleixandre) **15**:35
"The Estate" (Traherne) **70**:191, 253, 273, 316
"Estate di San Martino" (Pavese) **13**:244
"Estatua ecuestre" (Guillén) **35**:157, 174, 175, 176
"Una estatua en el silencio" (Neruda) **4**:289
"Estatura del vino" (Neruda) **4**:277, 301
"Este grave daño" (Storni) **33**:274
"Este libro" (Fuertes) **27**:17, 38
"Este libro" (Storni) **33**:237, 251
"Este que ves engaño colorido" (Juana Inés de la Cruz) **24**:225
Esthétique du mal (Stevens) **6**:300, 302; **110**:80, 86, 92, 122, 124, 181-83, 185-86
"Estimable Mable" (Brooks) **7**:94
Estío (Jiménez) **7**:212
"Estival" (Darío) **15**:117
"The Estranged" (Ai) **72**:29
"El estrecho dudoso" (Cardenal) **22**:119-23, 125-27
"Estrella de Navidad" (Mistral) **32**:185
"Estuary" (Merwin) **45**:54
"Estudio preliminar" (Darío) **15**:80
"Et Dona Ferentes" (Kipling) **91**:65, 88-90
"Et Le Sursaut Soudain" (Senghor) **25**:248
Et moi aussi je suis peintre (Apollinaire) **7**:34
"Et Resurrexit" (Curnow) **48**:24
"Eta" (Tolson) **88**:237, 258, 271, 304, 316-17, 324
Les états-généraux (Breton) **15**:50, 52, 62
"Etched Away" (Celan) **10**:97
"Été" (Valéry) **9**:351, 373, 392
"Été" (Verlaine) **32**:400-05
"Eternal Death" (Tagore)
See "Ananta maran"
"The Eternal Goodness" (Whittier) **93**:344
"Eternal Life" (Tagore)
See "Ananta jivan"
"Eternal Love" (Hafiz) **116**:15
Eternal Sections (Raworth) **107**:291, 302, 306-7, 310-14, 327-28, 336
"Eternal tripas" (Alurista) **34**:28, 29
Eternidades (Jiménez) **7**:187, 208, 212-13
"L'eternité" (Rimbaud) **57**:250
"Eternite de la nature, brievete de l'homme" (Lamartine) **16**:283
"Eternity" (Crane) **3**:90
"An Eternity" (Williams) **7**:394
"Eternity" (Winters) **82**:315-16, 318
Eternity (Smart)
See *On the Eternity of the Supreme Being*
"The Eternity of Nature" (Clare) **23**:3-4, 26
"Eterno" (Ungaretti) **57**:342
Eterno femminino regale (Carducci) **46**:12, 55
"Ethelinda" (Smart)
See "To Ethelinda"
"Ether Either" (Howe) **54**:119-20
"Ethiopia" (Harper) **21**:189, 202, 208, 215, 217
Éthiopiques (Senghor) **25**:231-32, 238, 241, 255
"Ethnobotany" (Snyder) **21**:297
"Les etiquettes jaunes" (O'Hara) **45**:119
"Eto ja" (Akhmadulina) **43**:39, 49-50
"L'étoile" (Wilbur) **51**:188, 192, 324-26
"L'étoile a pleuré rose" (Rimbaud) **57**:174
"Les étoiles" (Lamartine) **16**:291
"Eton" (Gray)
See "Ode on a Distant Prospect of Eton College"
"Eton College Ode" (Gray)
See "Ode on a Distant Prospect of Eton College"
"Eton Ode" (Gray)
See "Ode on a Distant Prospect of Eton College"
"Les étrennes des orphelins" (Rimbaud) **57**:196, 245, 249, 252, 299, 301
Etroits sont les vaisseaux (Perse) **23**:244-45
"Etude" (Stryk) **27**:183, 189
"Etude de mains" (Gautier) **18**:129, 158
"The Eucalypt and the National Character" (Wright) **14**:374
"L'eucalyptus" (Quasimodo) **47**:275, 301
"An euch, die das neue Haus bauen" (Sachs) **78**:199, 201
"Euclid" (Millay) **6**:211
"Euclid Avenue" (Simic) **69**:302
Eugene Aram (Hood)
See *The Dream of Eugene Aram*
"Eugene Carman" (Masters) **1**:324; **36**:230
"Eugene Delacroix Says" (Dorn) **115**:127
Eugene Onegin (Pushkin)
See *Yevgeny Onegin*
"Eugenics" (Wickham) **110**:254
"Eulalie— A Song " (Poe) **1**:441
"Eulenspiegelei" (Smith) **12**:327, 342
"Eulogy for Slick" (Knight) **14**:49
"Eulogy on Vladimír Holan" (Seifert)
See "Pocta Vladimíru Holanovi"
"Las euménidas bonaerenses" (Storni) **33**:294-95
"Eupheme" (Jonson) **17**:213
"Euphoria" (Ekeloef) **23**:76
"Euphrosyne" (Arnold) **5**:43
Eureka: A Prose Poem (Poe) **1**:422-24, 430-31, 437-38, 442-43, 450; **54**:276, 334, 336-37
"Europe" (Ashbery) **26**:113, 118, 138, 151
"Europe" (Whitman) **91**:201
Europe: A Prophecy, 1794 (Blake) **12**:13, 26, 35, 57, 61
"Europe and America" (Ignatow) **34**:274
The Europe of Trusts: Selected Poems (Howe) **54**:79, 84, 99, 102, 123, 126-27, 129-30, 134, 137, 139-40
"European Nocturne" (Birney) **52**:3
"Eurydice" (H. D.) **5**:298, 304
"Eurydice in Hell" (Spicer) **78**:299
"Eurymédon et Callirée" (Ronsard)
See *See "Les Amours d'Eurymédon et Callirée"*
"Euthanasia" (Tate) **50**:305
Euthymicæ Raptus: Or The Teares of Peace (Chapman) **96**:55, 115, 120-21, 123, 133
"Eva" (Whittier) **93**:337
"Evacuation" (Yamada) **44**:339-42, 346-47
"Evadé d'archipel" (Char) **56**:145
"Evadne" (H. D.) **5**:267
"Evalena Fayner" (Masters) **36**:212
Evangeline: A Tale of Acadie (Longfellow) **30**:16, 20-1, 24, 30, 34-5, 38-40, 44, 52-56, 59-60, 64, 66, 71, 92, 99
"Evangelist" (Davie) **29**:93-94, 108, 111-12, 114-15
"The Evangelist" (Heaney) **100**:263
"The Evangelistic Beasts" (Lawrence) **54**:193-94, 224
"Evans" (Thomas) **99**:234, 269
"Evanston 4 June 72" (Brutus) **24**:123
"Eva's Farewell" (Harper) **21**:201, 208, 218
"Evasion" (Tzara) **27**:230-31
"Eve" (Rossetti) **7**:264, 291
"Eve" (Williams) **7**:350, 354, 394-95
"Eve in Heaven" (Wylie) **23**:326
"The Eve of All Souls" (Clampitt) **19**:87
"The Eve of Creecy" (Morris) **55**:238, 299-300
"The Eve of March 30" (Akhmadulina)
See "Noch' na 30 marta"
"The Eve of St. Agnes" (Keats) **1**:279, 282, 285-6, 288, 296, 298, 307-10
The Eve of St. Agnes (Keats) **96**:208, 217, 236-38, 242-43, 246, 286, 288, 291, 299-300, 302, 340-41, 347-48, 373-74
"The Eve of St. Agnes" (Morris) **55**:247
"The Eve of St. John" (Scott) **13**:269
"Eve of St. Mark" (Keats)
See "The Eve of St. Mark"
"The Eve of St. Mark" (Keats) **1**:279, 304
The Eve of St. Mark (Keats) **96**:288, 291
"Eve Scolds" (Wright) **14**:373, 375
"Eve Sings" (Wright) **14**:373

"Eve to her Daughter" (Wright) **14**:356
"Evelyn" (Stryk) **27**:208
"Evelyn Hope" (Browning) **2**:38
"Evelyn Ray" (Lowell) **13**:66, 91
"Even" (Burns) **6**:50
Even a Fist (Amichai)
See *Gam ha'egrof haya pa'am yad ptuba ve'etsba'ot*
"Even Egrets Err" (Updike) **90**:351
"Even If All Desires Things Moments Be" (Cummings) **5**:95
Even in Quiet Places (Stafford) **71**:372-73
"The Even Sea" (Swenson) **14**:249, 263
"Even So" (Enright) **93**:33
"Even Song" (Herbert) **4**:133
"Even such is Time" (Raleigh) **31**:215-16
Even the Fist Once Was an Open Hand and Fingers (Amichai)
See *Gam ha'egrof haya pa'am yad ptuba ve'etsba'ot*
"Evening" (Carver) **54**:28
"Evening" (de la Mare) **77**:94
"Evening" (Merton) **10**:340
"Evening" (Merwin) **45**:23
"Evening" (Trakl)
See "Der Abend"
"Evening" (Wheatley)
See "An Hymn to the Evening"
Evening (Akhmatova)
See *Vecher*
Evening Album (Tsvetaeva)
See *Vecherny albom*
"Evening and Morning" (Benét) **64**:22
"Evening at a Country Inn" (Kenyon) **57**:20, 39, 42
"Evening at the old Nalapat House" (Das) **43**:80
"The Evening Bell" (Ishikawa)
See "Yube no kane"
"Evening, by a Tailor" (Holmes) **71**:68, 85
"Evening Chess" (Simic) **69**:278
"The Evening Choir" (Very) **86**:162
"Evening Dance of the Grey Flies" (Page) **12**:190
Evening Dance of the Grey Flies (Page) **12**:181, 198-99
"The evening darkens over" (Bridges) **28**:87
"An Evening Dream" (Dobell) **100**:139, 177-78
"Evening Fantasy" (Hölderlin) **4**:140
"Evening Harmony" (Baudelaire)
See "Harmonie du soir"
"Evening Hawk" (Warren) **37**:309, 331, 356, 360
"Evening Hour" (Warren) **37**:337
"Evening in Connecticut" (MacNeice) **61**:139
"Evening in France" (Sarton) **39**:332
"An Evening in Saint Peter's" (Carducci)
See "Un Sera in San Pietro"
"Evening in the Cathedral" (Cernuda) **62**:178
"Evening in the Country" (Ashbery) **26**:124, 159
"Evening in the Sanitarium" (Bogan) **12**:92, 99-101, 107, 121
"The Evening Land" (Lawrence) **54**:196
"An Evening Light" (Curnow) **48**:51
"Evening Music" (Sarton) **39**:324
"The Evening of Ants" (Soto) **28**:378-79
"The Evening of the Holiday" (Leopardi)
See "La sera del dí di festa"
"The Evening of the Second Day" (Chappell) **105**:38
"Evening of the Visitation" (Merton) **10**:339
"Evening on the Broads" (Swinburne) **24**:313, 322, 329, 343
"Evening on the Lake—(dolce)" (Spender) **71**:178, 215
"Evening Orison" (Rimbaud)
See "Oraison du soir"
"The Evening Primrose" (Parker) **28**:349, 351, 363
"Evening Ride" (Francis) **34**:251
"Evening sail to Richmond" (Wordsworth)
See "Lines Written near Richmond"
"The Evening Sea" (Ishikawa)
See "Yūbe no umi"
"Evening Shadows" (Longfellow) **30**:109
"Evening Song" (Carducci)
See "Serenata"
"Evening Song" (Hughes) **53**:160
"Evening Song" (Lanier) **50**:77; **50**:56
"Evening Song" (Toomer) **7**:320
"An Evening Song" (Werfel) **101**:347
Evening Songs (Tagore)
See *Sandhya sangit*
"Evening Star" (Bogan) **12**:98, 100
"The Evening Star" (Longfellow) **30**:27
"Evening Star" (Poe) **1**:448
"Evening Sun" (Kenyon) **57**:29
"The Evening That Love Enticed You Down into the Ballroom" (Ronsard)
See "Le soir qu'amour vous fist en la salle descendre"
An Evening Thought: Salvation by Christ with Penetential Cries (Hammon) **16**:176-79, 183-87
"Evening Twilight" (Baudelaire)
See "Le crépuscule du soir"
"An Evening Under Newly Cleared Skies" (Wang Wei) **18**:369
"Evening Voluntary" (Wordsworth) **4**:408
An Evening Walk (Wordsworth) **67**:270, 277, 280
An Evening Walk: An Epistle in Verse (Wordsworth)
See *An Evening Walk*
"Evening with Lee Shore and Cliffs" (Merwin) **45**:7, 9
"Evening—Regatta Day" (Masefield) **78**:94
"The Evenings of Certain Lives" (Benn) **35**:9
"Evensong" (Aiken) **26**:5
"The Event" (Dove) **6**:110, 112, 114
"Event" (Plath) **37**:264
"An Event" (Wilbur) **51**:189, 216, 338
"Eventails" (Mallarmé) **102**:98
Events and Wisdoms: Poems, 1957-1963 (Davie) **29**:110-11, 123, 129
"Ever mine hap is slack" (Wyatt) **27**:357
"Ever So Tragic" (Simic) **69**:287, 289
"Everlasting Flowers for a Dead Mother" (Lawrence) **54**:245
"The Everlasting Gospel" (Blake) **12**:31; **63**:49
The Everlasting Mercy (Masefield) **78**:16, 20, 26, 28-30, 35, 52, 56-59, 63, 67-68, 70, 91-93, 104
"The Everlasting Voices" (Yeats) **20**:309
"Everness" (Borges) **22**:89; **32**:60, 69, 88
"Every Beauty" (Werfel)
See "Jede Schönheit"
"Every Blessed Day" (Levine) **22**:221
"Every Lovely Limb's a Desolation" (Smith) **12**:314
Every Man in His Own Way: An Epistle to a Friend (Duck) **89**:67
"Every Soul Is a Circus" (Lindsay) **23**:274, 280
"Every Traveler Has One Vermont Poem" (Lorde) **12**:138
Everybody Knows (Cohen) **109**:80
"Everyman's Odyssey" (Hughes) **89**:139
Everyone Sang (Sassoon) **12**:280, 284, 289
"Everything and Nothing" (Borges) **32**:137
"Everything Came True" (Pasternak) **6**:266
"Everything: Eloy, Arizona, 1956" (Ai) **72**:3
"Everything Is Going to Be All Right" (Mahon) **60**:198, 238
"Eve's Apologie in defence of Women" (Lanyer) **60**:18, 20, 23, 34-35, 50, 53, 63, 67, 70, 72, 86, 96-98, 100
"Eve's Story" (Ai) **72**:12-13
"eve's version" (Clifton) **17**:29, 36
"Eve-Song" (Gilmore) **87**:302
Evgeni Onegin (Pushkin)
See *Yevgeny Onegin*
"Evidence" (Harjo) **27**:64
"The Evidence" (Traherne) **70**:303
"Evidence: From a Reporter's Notebook" (Ai) **72**:9
"Evil" (Rimbaud)
See "Le mal"
"The Evil" (Rimbaud)
See "Le mal"
"The Evil Eye" (Ciardi) **69**:11, 33, 47
"The Evil Seekers" (Sexton) **79**:215
"Evil Spring" (Akhmadulina)
See "Plokhaia vesna"
"The Evil World-Soul" (Lawrence) **54**:198
"Eviradnus" (Hugo) **17**:59, 61
"Evolution" (Alexie) **53**:30-31
"Evolution" (Swenson) **14**:247, 251, 255, 275, 283-84, 286
"Evolution from the Fish" (Bly) **39**:13
"Evolutionary Poem No. 1" (Knight) **14**:42
"Evolutionary Poem No. 2" (Knight) **14**:42
"Evolution-Sustenance-Dissolution" (Tagore)
See "Srishti-sthiti-pralaya"
"The Evolver" (Baraka) **4**:24
"Evrion's Tomb" (Cavafy) **36**:112
"evry whun at 2 oclock" (Bissett) **14**:33
"An Ew Erra" (Enright) **93**:36
"Ewigkeit" (Borges) **32**:88
"Ex ponto" (Ekeloef) **23**:76
"Ex Trivio" (Clarke) **112**:123
"Ex vermibus" (MacDiarmid) **9**:190
"Exactly what is unexact" (Villa) **22**:354
"Exageraciones divinas" (Fuertes) **27**:30
"The Exaggeration of Despair" (Alexie) **53**:34
"The Exam" (Olds) **22**:324
"The Examination" (Snodgrass) **74**:291, 313
"Examination" (Wickham) **110**:264, 293
"Examination at the Womb-Door" (Hughes) **7**:159
"Examination of the Hero in a Time of War" (Stevens) **6**:318; **110**:168, 203-4
"The Example" (Belloc) **24**:27
"Examples of Created Systems" (Meredith) **28**:200
"Ex-Basketball Player" (Updike) **90**:349-50
"Excavation of Troy" (MacLeish) **47**:191
"The Excavator" (Yevtushenko) **40**:347
"An Excelente Balade of Charitie" (Chatterton) **104**:4, 16-17, 22-23, 62, 68, 74
"Excellence" (Francis) **34**:254-55
"An Excellent Memory" (Curnow) **48**:46
"An Excellent New Ballad; or, The True English Dean to Be Hang'd for a Rape" (Swift) **9**:267
"Excelsior" (Longfellow) **30**:14, 21-3, 26-7, 34, 36, 45, 103, 107, 109-10
"Excerpt from a Letter" (Seifert)
See "Úryvek z dopisu"
"Excerpts from the Lexicon Abomunon" (Kaufman) **74**:180, 211
"The Excesses of God" (Jeffers) **17**:132
"The Exchange" (Swenson) **14**:255, 288
"An Exchange of Gifts" (Sarton) **39**:326
"Exchanges" (Dickey) **40**:223
"Exchanging Hats" (Bishop) **3**:64; **34**:106
Exclamations: Music of the Soul (Nishiwaki) **15**:237
"Exclusive Blue" (Francis) **34**:244
"The Excrement Poem" (Kumin) **15**:207
"La excursión" (Fuertes) **27**:17
The Excursion (Keats) **96**:349
Excursion (Wordsworth)
See *The Excursion, Being a Portion of "The Recluse"*
The Excursion, Being a Portion of "The Recluse" (Wordsworth) **4**:377-78, 383, 392, 397-99, 402-03, 405-09; **67**:251, 261, 310, 318
"Excuse" (Arnold)
See "Urania"
"The Excuse" (Raleigh) **31**:216, 313
"Excuse" (Walker) **30**:355
"Execration upon Vulcan" (Jonson)
See *The Under-Wood XLV*

"The Execution of Stenka Razin" (Yevtushenko) **40**:338, 347
"The Executioner" (Hughes) **89**:149
"Executive" (Betjeman) **75**:33, 39
"The Executive's Death" (Bly) **39**:49
Exegi monumentum (Horace) **46**:97
"Exequy" (Eliot) **90**:301-2
"Exercise" (Merwin) **45**:40, 83
Exercise Book (Seferis)
See *The Book of Exercises*
"Exercise on a Sphere" (Hope) **56**:277
"Exercises/Explorations" (Spender) **71**:251
"Exeter" (Betjeman) **75**:20, 69-72, 79
"Exeunt" (Wilbur) **51**:330
"The Exhibition" (Chatterton) **104**:52
"Exhibitionist" (Boland) **58**:44-45, 98
"Exhortation" (Bogan) **12**:122
"An Exhortation" (Hardy)
See "A Young Man's Exhortation"
"Exhortation" (Hölderlin)
See "Ermunterung"
Exhortation au camp du Roy pour bien combatre le iour de la bataille (Ronsard) **105**:232-34
Exhortation pour la paix (Ronsard) **105**:232-35
Exil (Perse) **23**:209, 211, 213-14, 216-18, 221-22, 231, 234, 240-42, 246, 248-50, 252, 254, 256
"Exile" (Auden) **92**:101
"The Exile" (Elliott) **96**:157, 159
"Exile?" (Enright) **93**:15
"Exile" (Hall) **70**:32
"Exile" (Hecht) **70**:98-100
"Exile" (Melville) **82**:38-39
Exile and Other Poems (Perse)
See *Exil*
"The Exiles" (Auden) **92**:61
"Exiles" (Cavafy) **36**:40
"Exiles" (Strand) **63**:157
"The Exiles" (Whittier) **93**:198, 243-44
Exiles and Marriages (Hall) **70**:15, 26, 30
"The Exile's Departure" (Whittier) **93**:193, 260
"Exiles from Their Land, History Their Domicile" (Spender) **71**:166, 182, 186, 190, 208, 224
"Exile's Letter" (Li Po) **29**:141
"Exile's Letter" (Pound) **95**:171
"Exile's Letter: After the Failed Revolution" (Chin) **40**:12, 15
"The Exiles' Line" (Kipling) **91**:82, 85
"The Exile's Return" (Lowell) **3**:200, 202, 234
"The Exile's Secret" (Holmes) **71**:94
"Existence and Presence" (Graham) **59**:169
"The Exit" (Elytis) **21**:134
"Exit Line" (Ciardi) **69**:53
"Exit Molloy" (Mahon) **60**:133
"Exit, Pursued by a Bear" (Nash) **21**:271
"Ex-Judge at the Bar" (Tolson) **88**:330, 343
"Exmoor" (Clampitt) **19**:81, 88
"Exodus" (Cohen) **109**:17, 50
"Exodus" (Oppen) **35**:285
"Exodus" (Winters) **82**:320
"The Exorcism" (Roethke) **15**:274, 278
"Exorcism" (Snodgrass) **74**:291
"The Exorcists" (Sexton) **79**:275
"Exordium" (Noyes) **27**:127
"Exotic Perfume" (Baudelaire)
See "Parfum exotique"
"The Expatriate" (Forché) **10**:138, 141, 144, 156
"The Expatriates" (Sexton) **2**:359
"Expect Nothing" (Walker) **30**:339, 353
"Expecting the Barbarians" (Cavafy) **36**:7
"An Expedient-Leonardo da Vinci's-and a Query" (Moore) **4**:242; **49**:144-45
"The Expedition of Nadir Shah into Hindostan" (Tennyson) **101**:143
"Expendable" (Hughes) **53**:116
"The expense of spirit in a waste of shame" (Shakespeare)
See "Sonnet 129"
"Experience" (Cunningham) **92**:138
"Experience" (Spender) **71**:208, 224
Experience (Blake)
See *Songs of Innocence and of Experience: Shewing the Two Contrary States of the Human Soul*
"The Experience" (Taylor) **63**:268, 270
"Experience Evoked" (Eberhart) **76**:55
"Experience Is the Angled Road" (Dickinson) **1**:111
Experimenting with an Amen (Thomas) **99**:261, 264-66, 275, 282, 318, 320, 324-25
"L'Expiation" (Hugo) **17**:79-80
"The Expiration" (Donne) **1**:130; **43**:128, 133
"Explaining a Few Things" (Neruda)
See "Explico algunas cosas"
"The Explanation" (Kipling) **3**:183
"Explanation" (Pasternak) **6**:266
"Explanation and Apology, Twenty Years After" (Carruth) **10**:78
An Explanation of America (Pinsky) **27**:143-46, 153, 155-56, 162-63, 173, 176
"Explico algunas cosas" (Neruda) **4**:297, 310-11
"Exploit of the Steam Cylinder" (Char) **56**:162
"Explorations" (MacNeice) **61**:140
"The Explorer" (Kipling) **91**:64
"The Explorers" (Atwood) **8**:13
"The Explorers" (Hope) **56**:266
"The Explorers" (Rich) **5**:362
"Explorers" (Simic) **69**:272, 325, 371
"Explosion" (Harjo) **27**:56
"Una exposición" (Guillén) **35**:216
"Expostulation" (Cowper) **40**:50, 52, 106, 116, 127
"Expostulation" (Whittier) **93**:314-15
"Expostulation and Reply" (Wordsworth) **4**:419; **67**:277, 285-86, 301, 312, 346, 365, 370
"An Expostulation with Inigo Jones" (Jonson) **17**:181-82
"Exposure" (Heaney) **18**:194, 205; **100**:195, 199, 225-26, 237, 266-68, 278
"Exposure" (Owen) **19**:327, 332, 334; **102**:142, 167, 169-72, 181, 205, 212, 225, 263, 265
Exposure in the Fields (Matsuo Basho)
See *Nozarashi kikō*
"La expresión" (Guillén) **35**:229, 230
"Express" (Sandburg) **2**:340
"The Express" (Spender) **71**:140-41, 172, 180, 218, 220, 225
"Express Your Will" (Ignatow) **34**:323-24
"Expression" (Clare) **23**:44
"Expression" (Gunn) **26**:217
"Expressions of Sea Level" (Ammons) **16**:29, 42, 46; **108**:22
Expressions of Sea Level (Ammons) **16**:4-5, 20, 27, 53
"Express-Zug" (Benn) **35**:9
"The Expulsion" (Stern) **115**:270
"Exspecto Resurrectionem" (Mew) **107**:18, 63
"The Exstasie" (Donne) **1**:126, 128, 130, 135, 147, 152; **43**:125, 132
"L'Extase" (Éluard) **38**:75, 87
"Extase" (Hugo) **17**:91
"The Extasie" (Cowley) **90**:104, 106
"The Extasie" (Traherne) **70**:189
"El éxtasis" (Cernuda) **62**:222
"Extasis" (Mistral) **32**:152, 176
"An Extasy of Joy" (Taylor) **63**:264, 280-81
"An Extempore Effusion on Being Appointed to the Excise" (Burns) **114**:33
"Extempore [on the *Loyal Natives'* Verses]" (Burns) **114**:140
"Extempore Effusion upon the Death of James Hogg" (Wordsworth) **4**:402
"Extempore Elegy" (Johnson) **81**:241, 246
"Exterior Possessions" (Char)
See "Possessions extérieures"
"An Extra Joyful Chorus for Those Who Have Read This Far" (Bly) **39**:27-8, 68
"An Extract from 'A New England Legend'" (Whittier) **93**:221
"The Extraction of Concept from Nature" (Ciardi) **69**:33
"Extracts from a Diary of Dreams" (Clarke) **112**:68, 139-40
"Extracts from Addresses to the Academy of Fine Ideas" (Stevens) **6**:314; **110**:202-3, 215, 222
Extracts from an Opera (Keats) **1**:311
"Un extraño" (Gallagher) **9**:66
"Extraño accidente" (Fuertes) **27**:14, 27
"L'Extravagant" (Char) **56**:143, 153-54, 170
"The Extravagant One" (Char)
See "L'Extravagant"
Extravagario (Neruda) **4**:290
"Extreme Unction" (Erdrich) **52**:191
"Extremes and Moderations" (Ammons) **16**:10-11, 18, 23, 28, 47-9
Exultations (Pound) **4**:317; **95**:111-12, 114-18, 120, 123
"Exvoto pour un naufrage" (Césaire) **25**:32
"Eyasion" (Tzara) **27**:230
"The Eye" (Creeley) **73**:7
"Eye" (Storni)
See "Ojo"
"The Eye" (Tate) **50**:275, 290-91, 293
"The Eye" (Wilbur) **51**:236, 278-80, 287, 314
"The Eye and Ear" (Very) **86**:115
"Eye and Tooth" (Lowell) **3**:215
"The Eye is More or Less Satisfied with Seeing" (Curnow) **48**:10, 24
"Eye of God" (Duncan) **75**:115, 118, 132
"The Eye of the Storm" (Wagoner) **33**:370
"Eyeball Television" (Komunyakaa) **51**:41
"The Eye-Beaters" (Dickey) **40**:164, 166, 177-78, 181, 183, 188-90, 196, 199-200, 202-3, 220-21, 242-43, 248, 256-57
The Eye-Beaters, Blood, Victory, Madness, Buckhead, and Mercy (Dickey) **40**:165-66, 187-88, 194, 199-200, 202, 219-20, 229, 239, 242-48
"The Eyeglasses" (Williams) **7**:381-83
"The Eye-Mote" (Plath) **1**:389; **37**:177-78, 180, 182
"Eyes" (Amichai) **38**:36-7
"Eyes" (Corso) **33**:16, 50
"Eyes" (Seifert)
See "Ŏi"
"Eyes and Tears" (Marvell) **10**:270-71; **86**:269
Eyes at the Back of Our Heads (Levertov)
See *With Eyes at the Back of Our Heads*
"Eyes at the Window" (Schuyler) **88**:179
"Eyes Fastened with Pins" (Simic) **69**:317
"The Eyes of Children at the Brink of the Sea's Grasp" (Jacobsen) **62**:315
"Eyes of Summer" (Merwin) **45**:33
"The Eyes of the Poor" (Baudelaire)
See "Les yeux des pauvres"
"Eyes of Water" (Cernuda)
See "Ojos de agua"
Eyeshot (McHugh) **61**:207
"Ezekiel Saw the Wheel" (Montale) **13**:109, 129, 165
"Ezerskij" (Pushkin) **10**:391, 394
"Ezra Pound" (Clarke) **112**:91
"F and H" (Crane)
See "For the Marriage of Faustus and Helen"
"F O Matthiessen An Anniversary" (Shapiro) **25**:320, 322, 324
"Fa" (Tolson) **88**:331
"Fabergé" (Schuyler) **88**:204
Fabilles (Henryson)
See *The Morall Fabillis of Esope the Phrygian*
Fabillis (Henryson)
See *The Morall Fabillis of Esope the Phrygian*
"Fable" (Cassian) **17**:13
"A Fable" (Cowper) **40**:124
"Fable" (Emerson) **18**:103-4
"A Fable" (Glück) **16**:161
"A Fable" (Hughes) **89**:101
"Fable" (Merwin) **45**:6, 9
"Fable" (Ponge) **107**:89-90, 92-93, 96, 173-75

"Fable" (Thomas) **99**:266
"The Fable" (Winters) **82**:338, 342, 346-47
"Fable" (Wylie) **23**:310, 316, 319
"Fable of the Cock and the Fox" (Chaucer)
See "Nun's Priest's Tale"
"The Fable of the Fragile Butterfly" (Wakoski) **15**:333
"Fable of two gardens" (Paz)
See "Cuento de dos jardines"
Fables (Henryson)
See *The Morall Fabillis of Esope the Phrygian*
The Fables (Marie de France) **22**:287-88
Fables (Smart) **13**:341
"Fables about Error" (Meredith) **28**:175, 194, 213, 215
The Fables of La Fontaine (Moore) **49**:125, 136
"Fables of the Moscow Subway" (Nemerov) **24**:268
"Fabrications" (Wilbur) **51**:332
La Fabrique du pré (Ponge) **107**:115-17, 120, 144, 190, 197, 201, 206, 238, 264-67
"The Fabulists, 1914-1918" (Kipling) **3**:172
"Fabulous Ballard" (Wylie) **23**:321
Façade (Sitwell) **3**:294, 303, 306, 319, 322, 325, 328
"The Face" (Jarrell) **41**:190, 200, 214
"The Face" (Levine) **22**:224
"A Face" (Moore) **49**:126-27, 129
"The Face" (Muir) **49**:296
"The Face" (Thomas) **99**:245
"Face" (Toomer) **7**:310, 333
The Face against the Glass (Francis) **34**:245, 264
"Face and Image" (Tomlinson) **17**:348
"The Face and the Wind" (Paz) **48**:272-73
"Face behind the Pane (An Old Man's Gaze)" (Aleixandre)
See "Rostro tras el cristal (Mirada del viejo)"
"The Face in the Stream" (Carman) **34**:212
"Face Lift" (Plath) **1**:394; **37**:254
"The Face of War" (Hughes) **53**:111
"Face to Face" (Chappell) **105**:66
"Face Your Fears Carnal" (Alurista) **34**:25, 42
"Face-Lift" (Mueller) **33**:191
"Faces" (Randall) **86**:289
"The Faces" (Stryk) **27**:202
"Faces" (Teasdale) **31**:360
"Faces" (Whitman) **3**:397; **91**:230
"Faces from a Bestiary" (Kennedy) **93**:148
"Faces in the Fire" (Carroll) **74**:65
"Facile est bien" (Éluard) **38**:84
"La Facilité en personne" (Éluard) **38**:86
"Facility" (Service) **70**:129
"Facing" (Swenson) **14**:284, 286
"Facing Africa" (Dickey) **40**:150, 176, 178
"Facing It" (Komunyakaa) **51**:9, 42, 54, 57
"Facing the Oxford" (Guillén)
See "Frente al Oxford"
Facing the Tree (Ignatow) **34**:306-10, 322-24
"Facing the Way" (Walker) **30**:354-55
"Facing Wine with Memories of Lord Ho; Introduction and Two Poems" (Li Po) **29**:146, 187
"Fackelzug" (Celan) **10**:127
Facsimile (Eliot)
See *T. S. Eliot, The Waste Land: A Facsimile and Transcript of the Original Drafts Including the Annotations of Ezra Pound*
"Fact" (Hughes) **53**:160
The Fact of a Doorframe: Poems Selected and New, 1950-1984 (Rich) **5**:388-89
"The Fact of their Two Bodies" (Ríos) **57**:325
"Facteur Cheval" (Breton) **15**:50
"Faction du muet" (Char) **56**:118, 141, 198
"Factory" (Simic) **69**:302, 305
"Factory Windows Are Always Broken" (Lindsay) **23**:268, 273, 276
"Facts" (Levine) **22**:221
"Facts" (Snyder) **21**:295-97
"Facts" (Waldrop) **109**:124
"The Facts and Issues" (Berryman) **64**:120
"The Facts of Life" (Mahon) **60**:197
"Fadaises" (Verlaine) **32**:386
"Faded Leaves" (Arnold) **5**:13
Fadensonnen (Celan) **10**:96, 98
"A Fading of the Sun" (Stevens) **110**:181
The Faerie Queene (Spenser)
See *The Faerie Queene, Disposed into Twelve Bookes Fashioning XII Morall Vertues*
The Faerie Queene, Disposed into Twelve Bookes Fashioning XII Morall Vertues (Spenser) **8**:323-25, 327-28, 330, 332-34, 337, 339, 341-47, 349-50, 354, 360-61, 363, 365, 369, 371-72, 374-78, 380-82, 384-85, 388-93, 395-97; **42**:211-370
"Fafaia" (Brooke) **24**:62
"Fafnir and the Knights" (Smith) **12**:302, 329
"Le fagot harmonieux" (Éluard) **38**:91
Fahrt ins Staublose (Sachs) **78**:111-12, 114, 120-22, 125-27, 130-31, 156, 168, 170, 176-77, 207-8, 210
"Faida di Commune" (Carducci) **46**:53
"The Failed Spirit" (Smith) **12**:333
"Failure" (Brooke) **24**:75
"A Failure" (Day Lewis) **11**:147
"The Failure of a Secular Life" (Cohen) **109**:89
"The Failure of Buffalo to Levitate" (Hass) **16**:195
"Faim" (Rimbaud) **3**:271, 282
"Faim rouge" (Char) **56**:150
"Faina" (Blok) **21**:20
Faina (Blok) **21**:24
"Faine would I wed a faire yong man that day and night could please mee" (Campion) **87**:72, 91
"Fair Chloris in a pigsty lay" (Wilmot)
See "Song to Chloris"
"Fair Choice" (Hughes) **7**:135
"Fair Clarinda" (Behn)
See "To the Fair Clarinda Who Made Love to Me, Imagin'd More than Woman"
"Fair Daffodils" (Herrick)
See "To Daffadills"
"Fair Day" (Thomas) **99**:258
"Fair Elenor" (Blake) **12**:31
"'Fair Helena' by Rackham" (Pound) **95**:117
"The Fair in the Woods" (Gunn) **26**:219
"Fair Ines" (Hood) **93**:58, 79, 117
"Fair Margaret's Bridal Eve" (Meredith) **60**:251
"Fair nymph, remember all your scorn" (Behn) **88**:111
"The Fair One in My Mind" (Tagore)
See "Manas-sundari"
"Fair Quakeress" (Whittier) **93**:262
Fair Realism (Guest) **55**:185, 189, 198
"Fair Recluse" (Smart) **13**:341
"The Fair Singer" (Marvell) **10**:270-71, 294, 300
"Fair Weather" (Parker) **28**:348
"The Faire Begger" (Lovelace) **69**:227-28
"Faire des pieds et des mains" (Péret) **33**:230
"Faire du chemin avec . . ." (Char) **56**:146, 199
"Faire, great, and good" (Donne) **43**:105
"Faire Rocks, Goodly River" (Sidney) **32**:235
"Faire seeke not to be feared" (Sidney) **32**:235
"A Fairer Hope, A Brighter Morn" (Harper) **21**:190
"The Fairest One of All" (Kumin) **15**:201, 222
"Fairfield" (Hugo) **68**:267, 294
"The Fairie Temple: or, Oberons Chappell. Dedicated to Mr. John Merrifield, Counsellor at Law" (Herrick) **9**:86
"The Fairies" (Enright) **93**:4
Fairies and Fusiliers (Graves) **6**:165
"The Fairy" (Blake) **12**:34
"The Fairy Goldsmith" (Wylie) **23**:301, 318-21, 325-26, 329-30, 332
"Fairy Land" (Poe) **1**:440
"Fairy Legends" (Collins) **72**:107
"A Fairy Tale" (Lowell) **13**:96
"Fairy Tales" (Pushkin)
See "Skazki"
Fairy Tales (Pushkin)
See *Skazki*
"Fairytale" (Wright) **14**:338
"A Fairytale about the Rain" (Akhmadulina)
See "Skazka o dozhde"
"A Fairy-Tale for Children" (Lermontov)
See *Skazka dlya detey*
A Fairytale for Children (Lermontov)
See *Skazka dlya detey*
"Faith" (Herbert) **4**:100, 119
"Faith" (Lamartine)
See "La foi"
"The Faith" (Nemerov) **24**:287
"Faith and Doubt" (Suckling) **30**:156
"Faith and Works" (Spark) **72**:220
"Faith Healer" (Komunyakaa) **51**:34
"Faith Healing" (Larkin) **21**:229-30, 258
"Faith, Hope, and Poetry" (Heaney) **100**:226
Faith in Life (Guillén)
See *Cántico*
"A Faith on Trial" (Meredith) **60**:256, 258, 262, 284, 287, 289, 299, 327, 333-34
"Faith Upon the Waters" (Jackson) **44**:28, 61
"The Faithful" (Enright) **93**:26
"The Faithful" (Jacobsen) **62**:312
Faithful for Ever (Patmore) **59**:221, 243-44
"The Faithful Friend" (Cowper) **40**:126
"The Faithful Mother" (Wickham) **110**:308
"Faithful Sleep Grants Us" (Cernuda) **62**:170
"Faithfully Tinyig at Twilight Voice" (Cummings) **5**:110
"Faithless" (Stramm)
See "Untreu"
"The Faithless Bride" (García Lorca)
See "La casada infiel"
"Faithless Nelly Gray" (Hood) **93**:44, 47, 72, 121
"Faithless Sally Brown" (Hood) **93**:44, 51-52, 62, 72, 122
"The Faithless Wife" (García Lorca)
See "La casada infiel"
"Fakes" (Apollinaire)
See "Des Faux"
"The Falcon" (Lovelace) **69**:187, 229, 238, 244-45, 250, 252, 254
"The Falcon" (Patmore) **59**:218, 240, 243
"The Falcon" (Wylie) **23**:328
"Falcon City" (Tsvetaeva)
See "Sokolinya slobodka"
"The Falcon of Ser Federigo" (Longfellow) **30**:62
"The Falcon Woman" (Graves) **6**:156, 172
"The Fall" (Ammons) **16**:42
"Fall" (Bly) **39**:7, 71
"Fall" (Darío)
See "Autumnal"
"Fall" (Keats)
See *The Fall of Hyperion: A Dream*
"The Fall" (Muir) **49**:240, 270, 278
"Fall" (Neruda)
See "Otoño"
"Fall" (Niedecker) **42**:100
"The Fall" (Sarton) **39**:342
"The Fall" (Spark) **72**:217, 228-29
"The Fall" (Waller) **72**:332, 371
"The Fall" (Wilmot) **66**:267, 309, 329, 339-44
The Fall (Keats)
See *The Fall of Hyperion: A Dream*
"Fall 1961" (Lowell) **3**:215
"Fall and Spring" (Soto) **28**:399, 403
"fall by Fury" (Birney) **52**:59
"Fall Comes in Back-Country Vermont" (Warren) **37**:345
"Fall Festival" (Hölderlin) **4**:141
"Fall in Connecticut" (Amichai) **38**:22
"Fall Journey" (Stafford) **71**:280, 291
"Fall, Leaves, Fall" (Brontë) **8**:68-9
"Fall of a City" (Spender) **71**:202, 204, 227

The Fall of America: Poems of These States 1965-1971 (Ginsberg) **4**:53-7, 59, 63-4, 66-7, 81
The Fall of an Angel (Lamartine)
See *La chute d'un ange*
"Fall of Europe" (Mistral)
See "Caída de Europa"
The Fall of Hyperion: A Dream (Keats) **1**:287; **96**:198-200, 213-17, 242, 247, 268, 282, 288-89, 300, 309, 349
"The Fall of Jerusalem" (Tennyson) **101**:193
"The Fall of Night" (Merton) **10**:340
"The Fall of Richmond" (Melville) **82**:92, 134, 207, 270
"The Fall of Rome" (Auden) **1**:23
"The Fall of Rome" (Carson)
See "The Fall of Rome: A Traveller's Guide"
"The Fall of Rome: A Traveller's Guide" (Carson) **64**:200, 229
The Fall of the City (MacLeish) **47**:139-40, 148, 151-52, 159, 161-63, 242, 247, 256
"The Fall of the Leaf" (Thoreau) **30**:215, 281-82, 287, 295
"The Fall of the Muse" (Mueller) **33**:182
"The Fall of Zalona" (Brontë) **8**:59
"Fall, Sierra Nevada" (Rexroth) **20**:205-06; **95**:287-88
"Fall Song" (Kennedy) **93**:145
"Fall Time" (Sandburg) **2**:316; **41**:313
"The Fallen" (Hogan) **35**:259
"The Fallen" (Wagoner) **33**:327
"The Fallen Angels" (Sexton) **2**:373; **79**:217
"Fallen Leaves" (Illyés) **16**:243
"Fallen Leaves" (Sandburg) **41**:360
"Fallen Majesty" (Yeats) **20**:330
"Fallen Moon" (Aleixandre) **15**:18, 20, 22
"The Fallen Tower of Siloam" (Graves) **6**:137, 143
"The Fallen Tree" (Bly) **39**:53
"Fallen Tree in a Churchyard" (Ní Chuilleanáin) **34**:350
"Fallen Women" (Pavese)
See "Donne perdute"
"Fallgrief's Girlfriends" (Hughes) **89**:139, 211
"Falling" (Dickey) **40**:152-54, 158, 160, 167-68, 176, 195, 199, 201, 208-9, 224, 232, 241, 256, 258, 263
"Falling Asleep by Firelight" (Meredith) **28**:171
"Falling Asleep over the 'Aeneid'" (Lowell) **3**:205
"The Falling Dolls" (Sexton) **79**:214
"Falling into Holes in Our Sentences" (Bly) **39**:41, 43
"Falling Leaves and Early Snow" (Rexroth) **20**:207; **95**:259
Falling, May Day Sermon, and Other Poems (Dickey) **40**:160, 192, 194, 197, 229, 232
"The Falling of the Leaves" (Yeats) **20**:344
The Falling Star's Path (Yosano) **11**:301
Falling Up (Silverstein) **49**:319, 340-43, 345-48
"The Fallow Dear at the Lonely House" (Hardy) **92**:361-63, 367
"The Fallow Deer at the Lonely House" (Hardy) **8**:124
"The Falls" (Kinnell) **26**:257
"Falls Country" (Wright) **14**:378
"The Falls of Love" (Moss) **28**:137, 140, 144
The False and True Green (Quasimodo)
See *Il falso e vero verde*
False Creek Mouth (Birney) **52**:67
"The False Heart" (Belloc) **24**:31
False Justice (Hagiwara)
See *Kyomō no seigi*
"False Nightmare" (Tate) **50**:253, 256, 274
"False Prophet" (Wylie) **23**:310, 324
"False Security" (Betjeman) **75**:104
"A False Spring" (Boland) **58**:56-57, 60
"A False Step" (Barrett Browning) **6**:23
"False Youth, Autumn, Clothes of the Age" (Dickey) **40**:223, 230, 232
"False Youth II" (Dickey) **40**:152
"False Youth: Two Seasons" (Dickey) **40**:260
"Falsetto" (Montale) **13**:115-16
"Falso Brilhante" (Mackey) **49**:5-6
Il falso e vero verde (Quasimodo) **47**:286-87
Fama y obras pósthumas (Juana Inés de la Cruz) **24**:227-29, 231
"Fame" (Borges) **32**:58-9
"Fame" (Mew) **107**:35, 58
"La familia" (Cernuda) **62**:172, 178-79, 214, 258
"Familiar Letter to Siegfried Sassoon" (Graves) **6**:131
"Familiarity" (Blunden) **66**:29
"Families and Friends" (Mueller) **33**:193
"La Famille du Sage" (Ponge) **107**:142
"Family" (Brooks) **7**:93
"The Family" (Cernuda)
See "La familia"
"The Family" (Creeley) **73**:115
"Family Affairs" (Angelou) **32**:7
"Family Album" (Szymborska)
See "Album Rodzinny"
"Family Group" (MacLeish) **47**:205, 215
"The Family in Spring" (Soto) **28**:400
"The Family Name" (Guillén)
See "El apellido"
"Family Of" (Walker) **30**:347
Family Pictures (Brooks) **7**:63-4, 66, 83, 91, 94-5
"Familiar Poem" (Chappell) **105**:34-35, 67
"Family Portraits" (Hardy) **92**:317
"Family Reunion" (Erdrich) **52**:176, 185
Family Reunion (Nash) **21**:267-68
"A Family Turn" (Stafford) **71**:302
"The Famine" (Longfellow) **30**:28
"The Famine Road" (Boland) **58**:37, 42
"Famous Blue Raincoat" (Cohen) **109**:70
"Famous Poet" (Hughes) **7**:114, 139; **89**:186
The Famous Tragedy of the Queen of Cornwall (Hardy) **8**:95
"Famyliar and friendly Epistles" (Whitney) **116**:265, 311
"The Fan" (Montale)
See "Il ventaglio"
"Fan Poems" (Guest) **55**:213
"A Fancy" (Carew) **29**:70-72, 74-76
"Fancy" (Cunningham) **92**:135
"Fancy" (Smith)
See "Sonnet 47"
"Fancy Concert" (Hunt) **73**:138
"Fancy Etchings" (Harper) **21**:193, 197
"Fancy's Knell" (Housman) **43**:251
"Fanfara" (Montale) **13**:134
"Fanfare, Coda and Finale" (Walker) **20**:294
The Fanfarlo and Other Verse (Spark) **72**:219, 223, 246
"Fanny" (Kizer) **66**:69
"Fanny Kemble's Child" (Howe) **81**:49
"Fanscombe Barn" (Finch) **21**:143
"Fantaisie à sa dame" (Ronsard) **105**:219, 221
"Fantaisies d'hiver" (Gautier) **18**:129
"Fantasia" (Carducci) **46**:41-42, 64, 86-87
"Fantasia" (Holmes) **71**:67, 92
"Fantasia on 'The Nut-Brown Maid'" (Ashbery) **26**:134, 140, 156, 162
"Los fantasmas del deseo" (Cernuda) **62**:197, 221
"A Fantasy" (Glück) **16**:158, 163
"Fantasy" (O'Hara) **45**:171, 173-74
"Fantasy in Purple" (Hughes) **53**:122
"Fantoches" (Verlaine) **2**:430; **32**:350, 390-91
"Un fantôme" (Baudelaire) **1**:64; **106**:103-4, 130, 153
"Fantômes" (Césaire) **25**:10
"Far Away" (Guillén)
See "Allá lejos"
"Far Away and Long Ago" (Stevens) **6**:293
"A Far Cry from Africa" (Walcott) **46**:234, 236, 285, 307, 312, 322
"Far East" (Blunden) **66**:24, 26
"The Far Field" (Roethke) **15**:280, 310, 317
The Far Field (Roethke) **15**:271, 282-83, 303, 309, 311
Far Horizons (Carman) **34**:205, 211
"Far in a Western Brookland" (Housman) **2**:180; **43**:245
"Far Known to Sea and Shore" (Housman) **2**:179
"Far Niente" (Gautier) **18**:172
"Far Off" (Jiménez)
See "A lo lejos"
"Far Off-Shore" (Melville) **82**:73, 86
"Far Rockaway" (Schwartz) **8**:291, 302-03, 305
"Far West" (Snyder) **21**:300
"Far West Once" (Warren) **37**:376
"La farandola dei fanciulli" (Montale) **13**:116
"Fare Thee Well" (Byron) **95**:5, 8, 10
"Fare Well" (Berryman) **64**:88-89
"Fare Well" (de la Mare) **77**:106, 134, 142-43
"Farewel Love and all thy lawes for ever" (Wyatt) **27**:304, 317-18, 340-41
"Farewell" (Amichai) **38**:12
"Farewell" (Carducci) **46**:7, 49
"Farewell" (Dobell) **100**:139
"The Farewell" (Hope) **56**:305
"Farewell" (Kinnell) **26**:287
"Farewell" (Kipling) **3**:189
"The Farewell" (Lamartine)
See "L'adieu"
"Farewell" (Lermontov) **18**:301
"A Farewell" (Owen) **19**:336
"A Farewell" (Patmore) **59**:209
"Farewell" (Smith) **12**:301, 339
"The Farewell" (Spender) **71**:216
"Farewell" (Tagore)
See "Viday"
"A Farewell" (Tennyson) **101**:250
"Farewell" (Thoreau) **30**:181
"Farewell" (Wang Wei) **18**:387
"The Farewell" (Whittier) **93**:183, 343
"Farewell Angelina" (Dylan) **37**:58-59, 65
"Farewell Falce Love" (Raleigh)
See "Farewell to False Love"
"Farewell in the Mountains" (Wang Wei) **18**:387
"Farewell Life" (Hood) **93**:81
"Farewell Love, and all thy laws for ever!" (Wyatt)
See "Farewel Love and all thy lawes for ever"
"A Farewell Picture" (Stafford) **71**:299
"Farewell Rehearsed" (Tate) **50**:307
Farewell, Spring! (Seifert)
See *Jaro sbohem*
"The Farewell Stairway" (Guest) **55**:185, 188-90
"Farewell Sweet Dust" (Wylie) **23**:322
"A Farewell to Alexandria" (Brontë) **8**:73
"A Farewell to America" (Wheatley)
See "To the Empire of America Beneath the Western Hemisphere. Farewell to America"
"Farewell to Arcady" (Dunbar) **5**:140
"Farewell to Barn and Stack and Tree" (Housman) **2**:161
"A Farewell to Celadon, on His Going to Ireland" (Behn) **13**:8
"A Farewell to Celladon" (Behn) **88**:136, 147-48, 151, 153
"A Farewell to False Love" (Raleigh)
See "Farewell to False Love"
"Farewell to False Love" (Raleigh) **31**:201, 282-85, 295, 297, 304-05, 312-13
"Farewell to Florida" (Stevens) **6**:297, 305; **110**:91-93, 95, 147
"Farewell to Heaven" (Tagore)
See "Svarga ha'ite biday"
"Farewell to love" (Donne) **1**:147; **43**:172-75
"Farewell to Love" (Suckling) **30**:118, 125, 141, 145
"Farewell to Matilda" (Peacock) **87**:321
"Farewell to Meirion" (Peacock) **87**:328-29
"Farewell to Nancy" (Burns) **6**:58
"Farewell to Poetry" (Herrick) **9**:95, 102, 136

"A Farewell to Poetry, with a Long Digression on Anatomy" (Barker) **91**:42
"The Farewell to the Brethren of St. James' Lodge, Tarbolton" (Burns) **114**:59, 87
"Farewell to the Court" (Raleigh) **31**:211, 243, 249-51, 259, 266, 279, 313
"Farewell to the Farm" (Stevenson) **84**:315
"A Farewell to the Reader" (Whitney) **116**:272, 311
"Farewell to the Vertuous Gentle-woman" (Jonson)
See "To the World. A Farwell for a Gentle-woman, Vertuous and Nobel"
"Farewell to Van Gogh" (Tomlinson) **17**:301, 314
"Farewell without a Guitar" (Stevens) **110**:92
La farfalla di Dinard (Montale) **13**:161
Le farfalle (Gozzano) **10**:177-78, 184
"The Faring" (Tomlinson) **17**:349
"The Faring" (Warren) **37**:302
"Farish Street" (Walker)
See *My Farish Street Green*
Färjesång (Ekeloef) **23**:57, 62, 76
"The Farm" (Chappell) **105**:65-66
"The Farm" (Creeley) **73**:46
"The Farm" (MacLeish) **47**:130, 145
"Farm Child" (Thomas) **99**:244
"The Farm Child's Lullaby" (Dunbar) **5**:138
"The Farm on the Great Plains" (Stafford) **71**:257-58, 276, 287, 289, 295, 299, 302, 374
"Farmer" (Stryk) **27**:203, 210
"The Farmer" (Williams) **7**:384; **109**:192, 207, 283
"The Farmer's Bride" (Mew) **107**:4, 9, 29-32, 34-35, 38, 50, 56
The Farmer's Bride (Mew) **107**:4, 6, 29, 31-33, 35-37, 39, 47, 49-50, 57, 59-60, 63
"Farmer's Death" (MacDiarmid) **9**:187, 191
"The Farmer's Wife" (Sexton) **2**:350
"The Farmer's Wife" (Tomlinson) **17**:311, 349, 358
Farming: A Handbook (Berry) **28**:5-7, 11-12, 35-6, 43
"Farming Peter" (Thomas) **99**:274, 310
Farm-Rhymes (Riley)
See *Riley Farm-Rhymes*
Farmstead of Time (Celan)
See *Zeitgehöft*
"Faro en la noche" (Storni) **33**:247, 268
"Farre off" (Ondaatje) **28**:336
"Farrelly's Half-barrel of Stout" (Kavanagh) **33**:91, 96
"Farwell Frost, or Welcome the Spring" (Herrick) **9**:109
Farys (Mickiewicz) **38**:158-167
"Fascist Festival" (Niedecker) **42**:95
"Fase d'oriente" (Ungaretti) **57**:342
"Fashionable Eclogue" (Holmes) **71**:67, 71
"Fast as You Can Count to Ten" (Ciardi) **69**:14
"Fast Rode the Knight" (Crane) **80**:40, 52, 76
"Fast-Anchor'd Eternal O Love!" (Whitman) **3**:396
"Fasternis Evin in Hell" (Dunbar) **67**:84, 86, 128
Fasti (Ovid) **2**:238, 241, 243-45, 253-55, 260-61
De Fastis (Ovid)
See *Fasti*
"Fat" (Kenyon) **57**:12
"Fat Cats in Egypt" (Kennedy) **93**:153
"Fat Lip" (Guillén)
See "Negro bembón"
"The Fat Man in the Mirror" (Lowell) **3**:205
"The Fat Man in the Mirror" (Werfel)
See "Der dicke Mann im Spiegel"
"Fat William and the Trains" (Sitwell) **3**:301
"Fata Morgana" (Longfellow) **30**:103
"Fata Morgana" (Rossetti) **7**:280
Fata Morgana (Breton) **15**:51-2, 55, 62
"Lo fatal" (Darío) **15**:96
"Fatal Interview" (Wylie) **23**:305
Fatal Interview (Millay) **6**:213, 215-16, 218, 224, 230, 235, 239, 241, 243
"Fatal Sisters" (Gray) **2**:135
"Fate" (Ai) **72**:11, 13
"Fate" (Olds) **22**:311, 322
Fate: New Poems (Ai) **72**:9-10, 13-17
The Fate of the Jury: An Epilogue to Domesday Book (Masters) **36**:194-95
"Fate Playing" (Hughes) **89**:162, 180
"The Fates" (Owen) **19**:342
"The Fates" (Spender) **71**:145, 149, 188
"Father" (Bell) **79**:3
"The Father" (Chappell) **105**:65-66
"Father" (Herbert)
See "Mój ojciec"
"Father" (Quintana) **36**:275, 275
The Father (Olds) **22**:319-21, 323-24, 326, 330, 332-34, 338, 340-42
"Father and Daughter" (Eberhart) **76**:44
"Father and Daughter" (Sanchez) **9**:220-21, 229
"Father and Daughter" (Song) **21**:337
"Father and Farther" (Alexie) **53**:15
"Father and Son" (Eberhart) **76**:44
"Father and Son" (Ignatow) **34**:323
"Father and Son" (Kenyon) **57**:5
"Father and Son" (Kunitz) **19**:152, 154, 165, 175, 177-79
"Father and Son" (Schwartz) **8**:301-03, 305, 314
"Father and Son" (Stafford) **71**:280
"Father and Son" (Werfel)
See "Vater und Sohn"
"Father Ch., Many Years Later" (Milosz) **8**:181, 202, 205
"Father Explains" (Milosz) **8**:207
"Father Father Abraham" (Johnson) **24**:160
"A Father for a Fool" (Smith) **12**:333
"Father Guzman" (Stern) **115**:263
"Father Mat" (Kavanagh) **33**:61, 74-5, 99, 127, 130-1, 138; **105**:92-93
"Father Missouri" (Brown) **55**:71
"The Father of My Country" (Wakoski) **15**:324, 345, 354, 358
The Father of the Predicaments (McHugh) **61**:202-3, 206
"A Father of Women" (Meynell) **112**:161, 171, 174-78, 222, 231
A Father of Women, and Other Poems (Meynell) **112**:159, 165, 168, 171, 174-75, 178
"Father, on His Unsonment" (Villa) **22**:349
"A Father out Walking on the Lawn" (Dove) **6**:109
"Father Smith" (Ciardi) **69**:25
"Father William" (Carroll) **74**:29
"Fatherhood" (Pavese) **13**:203
"The Fathers" (Muir) **49**:233, 245, 248-49
"The Fathers" (Sassoon) **12**:168, 282
"Father's Bedroom" (Lowell) **3**:219-20
"Father's Song" (Kumin) **15**:201
"Father's Voice" (Stafford) **71**:280, 291
"Fatigue" (Belloc) **24**:49
"Fatigue" (Lowell) **13**:60
The Fatigue (Jones) **116**:61, 115, 118, 159-60, 198, 224
"Fatima" (Tennyson) **101**:139, 143, 244
"The Fault" (Montague) **106**:245, 251, 264, 278, 325, 340
A Faulx contente (Char) **56**:144, 187
"The Faun" (Carman) **34**:199
"The Faun" (Plath) **1**:388; **37**:182
"The Faun Sees" (Zukofsky) **11**:368
Faune (Mallarmé)
See *L'après-midi d'un faune*
"Le Faune" (Verlaine) **32**:350, 391
"The Fauré Ballade" (Schuyler) **88**:200
"La fausse morte" (Valéry) **9**:393, 396
"Faust" (Ashbery) **26**:118
A Faust Book (Enright) **93**:22, 27-28, 36
"Faustina; or, Rock Roses" (Bishop) **3**:60; **34**:87, 138, 189
"Faustus and Helen" (Crane)
See "For the Marriage of Faustus and Helen"
"Faustus and Helen (II)" (Crane) **3**:79, 80, 96, 98, 100
"Faustus and I" (Sexton) **2**:367, 373
Faute de sommeil, l'écorce . . . (Char)
See *La nuit talismanique*
"La Faux relevée" (Char) **56**:120, 144
"Favor of Alexander Balas" (Cavafy) **36**:75
"Favrile" (Doty) **53**:61
"The Fawn" (Millay) **6**:214
"Faynting I folowe" (Wyatt) **27**:343
"F.B.I. Memo" (Randall) **86**:329, 336
"Fe Me Sal" (McKay) **2**:225
"The Fear" (Frost) **39**:247
"Fear" (Merwin) **45**:84
"Fear" (Silverstein) **49**:334
"Fear and Fame" (Levine) **22**:228
"Fear and Trembling" (Warren) **37**:326, 380
"Fear Is Hope" (Moore) **49**:113, 149
"Fear Is What Quickens Me" (Wright) **36**:332
"The Fear of Beasts" (Meredith) **28**:171
"The Fear of Bo-talee" (Momaday) **25**:189, 212-13
"Fear of Death Awakens Me" (Kenyon) **57**:35, 45
"The Fear of Death Disturbs Me" (Meredith) **28**:181
"The Fearful" (Plath) **37**:269
"Fearless" (Tagore)
See "Nirbhay"
"Fears" (Yevtushenko) **40**:350
"Fears and Scruples" (Browning) **2**:59
Fears in Solitude, Written in 1798 during the alarm of an invasion. To Which Are Added, France, an Ode; and Frost at Midnight (Coleridge) **11**:100; **39**:177; **100**:21, 23
"The Feast" (Wagoner) **33**:358, 370
"The Feast of Famine" (Stevenson) **84**:332
"The Feast of Stephen" (Hecht) **70**:68, 85, 107-8
The Feast of the Assumption 1676 (Juana Inés de la Cruz) **24**:177
The Feast of the Poets (Hunt) **73**:135, 137, 148, 151-52, 169, 195, 202, 208, 212
"A Feather for Voltaire" (Graham) **59**:132, 175
"Feathers from the Hill" (Merwin) **45**:61
"A Feaver" (Donne) **1**:126, 130, 153
"February" (Chappell) **105**:33, 65
"February" (Hughes) **7**:147
"February" (Kumin) **15**:222
"February" (Merwin) **45**:33
"February" (Meynell) **112**:158
"February" (Schuyler) **88**:181, 193
"February" (Teasdale) **31**:364
"February 6, 1960" (Sexton) **79**:196
"february 11, 1990" (Clifton) **17**:30
"February 13, 1975" (Schuyler) **88**:200, 205
"February 17th" (Hughes) **89**:114, 151, 157, 207-8
"February 17th" (Sexton) **79**:244
"February 20th" (Sexton) **79**:284
"February Afternoon" (Thomas) **53**:294, 321, 325
"February Air" (Berrigan) **103**:5, 37
"February Full Moon" (Akhmadulina)
See "Fevral'skoe polnolunie"
"February Evening in New York" (Levertov) **11**:167
February in Sydney (Komunyakaa) **51**:33-34
"February Midnight" (Jacobsen) **62**:331
"A February Night" (Masefield) **78**:100
"February Seventeenth" (Hughes) **7**:162, 165
"February Twilight" (Teasdale) **31**:334
"The Feckless Dinner Party" (de la Mare) **77**:90
"The Fed" (Blok) **21**:11
"Federico's Ghost" (Espada) **74**:125, 130, 142-43

"Feed Still Thyself Thou Fondling With Belief" (Raleigh)
See "Feede Still Thy Selfe, Thou Fondling With Belief!"
"feed th prisoners now baby" (Bissett) **14**:32
"Feede Still Thy Selfe, Thou Fondling With Belief!" (Raleigh) **31**:201, 212, 219
"The Feeders" (Davie) **29**:110
"Feeding Out Wintery Cattle at Twilight" (Hughes) **7**:166
"Feel Me" (Swenson) **14**:267, 270, 288
"Feeling and Form" (Hacker) **47**:104
"Feeling and Precision" (Moore) **4**:251
A Feeling for Leaving (Berrigan) **103**:31, 35
"Feeling Fucked Up" (Knight) **14**:43, 46
"The Feelings" (Olds) **22**:326
"Feelings on Getting Older" (Corso) **33**:43; **108**:4, 20
"Feet in Winter, Head in the Sun" (Bell) **79**:22
"The Feet of the Young Men" (Kipling) **91**:64
Fekete feher (Illyés) **16**:232
"Feliciano me adora y le aborrezco" (Juana Inés de la Cruz) **24**:183
"Felicity" (Traherne) **70**:244, 302, 314
"Felix Randal" (Hopkins) **15**:170
"Fellatio" (Updike) **90**:357
Felling (Mistral)
See *Tala*
"The Felloe'd Year" (Graves) **6**:137
"A Fellow Being" (Curnow) **48**:19, 60, 62
"Fellow Citizens" (Sandburg) **41**:233, 239, 296, 365
"Fellow Creatures" (Nash) **21**:265
"The Fellow Pilgrim" (Howe) **81**:23, 25, 47
"The Female Exile" (Smith) **104**:212, 325-26
Female Lovers (Brossard)
See *Amantes*
"The Female Vagrant" (Wordsworth) **4**:373, 419; **67**:276-78, 282-84, 295, 304, 331, 337, 345-46, 366-70
"Femenina" (Storni) **33**:306
"Feminist Manifesto" (Loy) **16**:329, 332, 334
"Femme a la blonde aisselle coiffant sa chevelure a la lueur des etioles" (Breton) **15**:48
"La Femme adultere" (Vigny) **26**:381, 410-11
"Femme dans la nuit" (Breton) **15**:48
"Femme et chatte" (Verlaine) **2**:431
"Femme et oiseau" (Breton) **15**:48, 55-6, 58-60
"Femme noire" (Senghor) **25**:224, 239
"Femmes au bord d'un lac a la surface irisee par le passage d'un cygne" (Breton) **15**:49
"Femmes damnées" (Baudelaire) **1**:62; **106**:23-26
"Femmes sur la plage" (Breton) **15**:48
"Fenaison" (Char) **56**:152, 156
"The Fence" (Erdrich) **52**:187
"A Fence" (Sandburg) **41**:236, 239, 252, 316
"Fence Posts" (Snyder) **21**:307
"Fence Wire" (Dickey) **40**:191, 257
"La fenêtre" (Ponge) **107**:73, 195
"Les fenêtres" (Apollinaire) **7**:18, 36, 44
"Les fenêtres" (Baudelaire) **1**:59; **106**:90
"Les fenêtres" (Mallarmé) **4**:208; **102**:100-01, 109
Fenêtres dormantes et porte sur le toit (Char) **56**:146, 177, 185-89, 199
"The Fenyeit Freir" (Dunbar) **67**:117, 128
"Lo feo" (Mistral) **32**:145
"Feodosija" (Mandelstam) **14**:113
"Fergus and the Druid" (Yeats) **51**:72, 148
"Feria sexta in Parasceve" (Zanzotto) **65**:269
"Feria sexta in Parasceve (Variante)" (Zanzotto) **65**:269
Ferishtah's Fancies (Browning) **2**:59
"Ferlinghetti" (Spicer) **78**:283, 294, 331
"A fermosura desta fresca serra" (Camões) **31**:25
"Fern" (Hughes) **7**:121; **89**:216
"Fern Beds in Hampshire County" (Wilbur) **51**:248
"Fern Hill" (Montague) **106**:243
"Fern Hill" (Thomas) **2**:382, 385, 392, 396-99, 405; **52**:219, 247-48, 252, 256, 262, 270, 273-75, 277, 281, 283, 285-86, 314-15, 321-22, 330-31
"Fernão de Magalhães" (Pessoa) **20**:155
"Fern-Beds in Hampshire Country" (Wilbur)
See "Fern Beds in Hampshire County"
"Ferns" (Das) **43**:86
"Ferns" (Stafford) **71**:315, 332
Ferrements (Césaire) **25**:13, 23, 32, 44
"The Ferry" (Akhmadulina)
See "Parom"
Ferrying Across (Tagore)
See *Kheya*
"Les Fers" (Ronsard) **105**:273
Fervor de Buenos Aires (Borges) **22**:68-9, 71-2, 79, 93-4; **32**:37-9, 52-3, 60, 80-3, 95, 102-03, 109, 120-22, 125, 127, 131, 133, 139
Fervor of Buenos Aires (Borges)
See *Fervor de Buenos Aires*
"Fessler's Bees" (Riley) **48**:288
"Ein feste Burg ist unser Gott" (Whittier) **93**:213, 343, 347
"A Festival" (Moore) **49**:142
"Festival of Spring" (Tagore)
See "Vasanter Kusumer mela"
"The Festivals" (Duncan) **75**:176
"Festividad" (Guillén) **35**:155, 157
Festus (Aiken) **26**:7, 29
"Fetchin' Water" (McKay) **2**:216, 223
"Fetching a Nun" (Dafydd ap Gwilym)
See "Cyrchu Lleian"
"The Fête" (Mew) **107**:7, 30, 38-39, 57-58
Fête de la patience (Rimbaud) **57**:252-53
"Fête des arbres et du chasseur" (Char) **56**:170, 173
"Fête d'hiver" (Rimbaud) **57**:236, 240, 273
"Fêtes de la faim" (Rimbaud) **3**:259; **57**:245
Fêtes galantes (Verlaine) **2**:413-15, 424-25, 430-32; **32**:342, 346-53, 359, 364, 366, 368, 370-71, 384, 389-90, 392-95, 399
"Le Feu" (Ponge) **107**:185
Feu central (Péret) **33**:231
"Un feu va devant nous" (Bonnefoy) **58**:119
"Feuer-Nacht" (Bogan) **12**:94, 121
"Feuertaufe" (Stramm) **50**:170, 220-21
"Le Feuillage éclairé" (Bonnefoy) **58**:125
Les feuilles d'automne (Hugo) **17**:42-45, 52, 63, 66, 68, 90-93
Feuillets d'Hypnos (Char) **56**:106-7, 109-10, 112, 131-32, 160, 169, 175, 181, 185, 189-91, 196
"Les Feux" (Ronsard) **105**:273
"Fever" (Akhmadulina) **43**:9
"Fever" (Brathwaite) **56**:51
"A Fever" (Donne)
See "A Feaver"
"Fever" (Gunn) **26**:220
"The Fever" (Hughes) **89**:191, 246
"A Fever" (Merrill) **28**:221
"Fever 103°" (Plath) **1**:382, 386, 393; **37**:232-33, 240, 256
"Fever Ship" (Masefield) **78**:68, 95
"Fever-Chills" (Masefield) **78**:95
"Feverscape: The Silver Planet" (Chappell) **105**:26, 43, 60
"Fevral'skoe polnolunie" (Akhmadulina) **43**:11, 36, 40, 42, 45
"A Few Coins" (Soto) **28**:371
"A Few Days" (Schuyler) **88**:177, 179, 181-82, 192, 198, 200-201, 204
A Few Days (Schuyler) **88**:174-77, 183, 189, 193, 201, 216
A Few Figs from Thistles (Millay) **6**:207-8, 211-12, 227, 230, 233-35, 237, 239
A Few Late Chrysanthemums (Betjeman) **75**:11, 63-64, 81
"Fiammetta Breaks Her Peace" (Dove) **6**:109
"Les fiançailles" (Apollinaire) **7**:43-4, 46, 48
"Fibrous Ruin" (Jordan) **38**:119
"Ficha Ingreso Hospital General" (Fuertes) **27**:3
"The Fiction Writer" (Jacobsen) **62**:301
"The Fiddle" (Riley) **48**:282
"The Fiddler Crab" (Jacobsen) **62**:327
"Fiddler Jones" (Masters) **1**:333
"Fidel in Ohio" (Espada) **74**:147
"Fidelia and Her Friend: the Third Dialogue" (Barker) **91**:50
"Fidelia arguing with her self on the difficulty of finding the true Religion" (Barker) **91**:50
"Fidelia having seen the Convent at St. James's" (Barker) **91**:50
"Fidelia" Poems (Barker) **91**:32
"Fidelity" (Hughes) **89**:251
"Fidelity" (Lawrence) **54**:185, 218
"Fidelity" (Wordsworth) **4**:383
"Field" (Abse) **41**:3
"Field" (Soto) **28**:375, 377-78, 384-85
"Field" (Stafford) **71**:278
Field (Duncan)
See *The Opening of the Field*
"Field and Forest" (Jarrell) **41**:153-54
"Field Bath" (Mahon) **60**:141
Field Guide (Hass) **16**:194-95, 197, 199-201, 209, 212, 214, 216, 222, 228
"A Field Hospital" (Jarrell) **41**:147, 168
"The Field of Battle" (Southey) **111**:254
"A Field of Light" (Roethke) **15**:248, 254, 304, 307
"The Field of the Potter" (Muir) **49**:239
"The Field Pansy" (Clampitt) **19**:94, 96
"Field Report" (Corso) **33**:44; **108**:23, 25
"Field Work" (Heaney) **18**:245
Field Work (Heaney) **18**:197-99, 211-12, 215, 238-40, 242, 245-47, 255-57; **100**:205-6, 231, 233, 236-37, 239-40, 243, 273-75, 278, 281, 284, 287, 297, 299, 313, 321, 324, 337, 343, 352
"Fieldpath" (Stafford) **71**:279
Fields of Grace (Eberhart) **76**:53
"The Fields of Melancholy and Chearfulness" (Leapor) **85**:249
Fields of Wonder (Hughes) **1**:240-44, 247, 268; **53**:149
"The Fiend" (Dickey) **40**:151, 153, 158, 172, 189, 196, 213, 215-16, 226-27, 241, 256, 259, 263
"Fiend, Dragon, Mermaid" (Graves) **6**:142, 145
"Fierce Hope" (Tagore)
See "Duranta asha"
"Fiesole" (Carducci) **46**:49, 76, 81, 84, 88
"Fiesta" (Pasolini) **17**:253
"Fiesta" (Storni) **33**:281
"Fiez-vous donc à moi . . ." (Rimbaud) **57**:248
Fifine at the Fair (Browning) **2**:42-4, 50, 72, 75, 80, 82, 96; **61**:32
"XV" (Joyce) **22**:138, 145, 170
Fifteen Dead (Kinsella) **69**:103, 134
Fifteen False Propositions about God (Spicer) **78**:241, 273, 275, 279, 305-6
Fifteen Poems (Spicer) **78**:341
"Fifteen to Eighteen" (Hacker) **47**:82
"Fifteen Years After" (Thumboo) **30**:300, 329, 332
"The Fifteenth Amendment" (Harper) **21**:197
"Fifteenth Farewell" (Bogan) **12**:86
Fifth Decad of Cantos (Pound) **4**:324
"Fifth Grade Autobiography" (Dove) **6**:120
Fifth Nemean (Pindar)
See *Nemean 5*
"Fifth Psalm" (Sexton) **79**:220
"Fifth Sunday After Easter" (Kinsella) **69**:80
"50" (Rexroth) **95**:349
"Fifty Faggots" (Thomas) **53**:328, 346, 349-50
"50-50" (Hughes) **1**:247
"55 Eltisley" (Hughes) **89**:190
55 Poems (Zukofsky) **11**:341
"Fifty for Richard Nonas" (Yau) **61**:337
"Fifty Males Sitting Together" (Bly) **39**:103
"The 59th Bear" (Hughes) **89**:162
Fifty Poems (Cummings) **5**:84, 107-08
50 Poems (Cummings)
See *Fifty Poems*

Fifty Poems (Dafydd ap Gwilym) **56**:221
"52 Oswald Street" (Kinnell) **26**:258
"Fifty Years" (Johnson) **24**:127, 131, 143, 145-47, 154, 157-60
Fifty Years, and Other Poems (Johnson) **24**:127, 131, 141-49, 152-55, 157, 159, 162, 166
"Fight" (Bukowski) **18**:15
"Fight" (Sandburg) **41**:238
Fight Back: For the Sake of the People, for the Sake of the Land (Ortiz) **17**:222-223, 233, 239, 244
"Fight Him Fair Nigger" (Knight) **14**:49
"The Fight on the Beach" (Masefield) **78**:47, 92
"The Fight on the Wall" (Masefield) **78**:47, 92
"Fight to a Finish" (Sassoon) **12**:267
"'Fighting Mac.' A Life Tragedy" (Service) **70**:153
"Fighting South of the Ramparts" (Li Po) **29**:139
Fighting Terms: A Selection (Gunn) **26**:181, 183, 188, 197, 199-200, 205-206, 210-12, 215-19, 229
"La figlia che piange" (Eliot) **5**:153, 184; **31**:92; **90**:212
"La figue" (Ponge) **107**:169, 192, 194
"La figue l'oeillet et la pipe a opium" (Apollinaire) **7**:32
"Una figura della donna mia" (Cavalcanti) **114**:223-25
"Figure" (Jacobsen) **62**:325
"The Figure" (Thomas) **99**:269
"Figure for a Landscape" (Mueller) **33**:180
"Figure from Polities" (Meredith) **28**:187
"The Figure I Drawn in Wire" (Ciardi) **69**:33
"The Figure in the Scene" (Hardy) **8**:137; **92**:257
"Figure of Eight" (MacNeice) **61**:127
"FIGURE SKATER" (Birney) **52**:29, 76, 81-82
"The Figured Wheel" (Pinsky) **27**:163, 165, 173-6
The Figured Wheel (Pinsky)
See *The Figured Wheel: New and Collected Poems, 1966-1996*
The Figured Wheel: New and Collected Poems, 1966-1996 (Pinsky) **27**:175
"The Figurehead" (Shapiro) **25**:316, 325
"Figures" (Hayden) **6**:196
The Figures of Human (Ignatow)
See *Figures of the Human*
"Figures of Speech" (Duncan) **75**:176
"Figures of the Human" (Ignatow) **34**:277
Figures of the Human (Ignatow) **34**:274, 276-77, 281-82, 312
Figures of Thought: Speculations on the Meaning of Poetry and Other Essays (Nemerov) **24**:299, 303
"Figurine" (Hughes) **1**:245
Fihi ma fihi (Rumi) **45**:259, 261-62, 273-78, 320
"La fileuse" (Valéry) **9**:391
"Los filibusteros" (Cardenal) **22**:110
"Fill for me a brimming bowl" (Keats) **96**:255, 257, 339, 348
"La Fille de Jephte" (Vigny) **26**:401, 410
Les filles du feu (Nerval) **13**:176-78, 192, 195
"Filling Out a Blank" (Wagoner) **33**:327
"Filling Station" (Bishop) **34**:118, 149
"Filling the Boxes of Joseph Cornell" (Wakoski) **15**:324
"The Film of God" (Thomas) **99**:359
"Film Script" (Mueller) **33**:193
"Filo del amor" (Aleixandre) **15**:19, 23
Filò: per il Casanova di Fellini (Zanzotto) **65**:263, 268-69, 279, 321, 326, 328, 333-34, 338
"Fin de Fête" (Mew) **107**:57, 59
"La fin de la journée" (Baudelaire) **1**:54; **106**:22
"La fin de l'automne" (Ponge) **107**:133
La fin de Satan (Hugo) **17**:65, 74, 81, 84, 88, 91
"Fin d'hiver" (Jaccottet) **98**:147
Final (Guillén) **35**:185, 213-14, 225-26, 227, 229, 230, 232, 234
"Final Call" (Hughes) **1**:252
"Final Curve" (Hughes) **53**:125
"Final Examination" (Cohen) **109**:26, 72
"Final Face" (Aleixandre) **15**:4
"Final Fire" (Aleixandre) **15**:18-19
"Final Shadow" (Aleixandre) **15**:16
"The Final Slope" (Stryk) **27**:203
"Final Soliloquy of the Interior Paramour" (Stevens) **110**:91, 95-97, 215, 226-27
"the final solution" (Sanchez) **9**:224
"A Final Sonnet" (Berrigan) **103**:5, 7, 14-16
"Finale" (Guillén) **35**:214
"Finale" (Hughes) **89**:198, 200
"Finale" (Longfellow) **30**:66
"Finale" (Mallarmé) **102**:19-20
"Finale" (Wagoner) **33**:365
"Finally" (Jacobsen) **62**:305
"Finally" (Merwin) **45**:24, 101
"A Finch Sitting Out a Windstorm" (Wright) **36**:393
"Finding" (Brooke) **24**:57-8
"Finding a Long Gray Hair" (Kenyon) **57**:23, 36-37, 43
"Finding a Teacher" (Merwin) **45**:92, 98
"Finding an Ant Mansion" (Bly)
See "Finding an Old Ant Mansion"
"Finding an Old Ant Mansion" (Bly) **39**:67, 99
"The Finding of Reasons" (Merwin) **45**:49
"The Finding of the Moon" (Wright) **14**:356
"Finding the Father" (Bly) **39**:44, 100
Finding the Islands (Merwin) **45**:72
"Finding the One Brief Note" (Kumin) **15**:215
"Finding the Right Direction" (Wagoner) **33**:352
Findings (Berry) **28**:5
"Fine Arts" (Birney) **52**:29
Fine Clothes to the Jew (Hughes) **1**:237-38, 244, 246, 254-55, 258, 260, 262-63, 268-71; **53**:79, 86, 106, 135-36, 138, 140, 164, 170, 181-83, 199
"Fine del '68" (Montale) **13**:134
"La fine dell'infanzia" (Montale) **13**:115-16
Fingal. An Ancient Epic Poem, in six books; together with several other Poems, composed by Ossian, the son of Fingal; translated from the Galic language, by James Macpherson (Macpherson) **97**:172, 175, 177, 182, 187-88, 194, 196, 202-3, 207-9, 216, 218-19, 223-24, 226-33, 236, 245, 248-49, 253-54, 263-67, 279, 281, 290, 292-93, 297, 305-15, 319, 330, 334, 343-51
The Finger (Creeley) **73**:91
"A Finger to the Lips" (Akhmadulina)
See "Palec na gubax"
"Fingerprints" (Cohen) **109**:68
"Finis" (Montale) **13**:139
"Finis Poloniae" (Benn) **35**:66
"Finisterne" (Montale) **13**:156, 165-66
"Finisterre" (Warren) **37**:380
Finisterre (Montale) **13**:103, 106, 127-30
"Finn and the Chess-Men" (Masefield) **78**:41
"Finnish Champion" (Mistral)
See "Campeón Finlandés"
"Fins" (Sandburg) **2**:307
"Fiolfar" (Peacock) **87**:325, 347
"The Fire" (Atwood) **8**:39
"The Fire" (Belloc) **24**:32
"The Fire" (Brodsky) **9**:2
"The Fire" (Duncan) **2**:116; **75**:232, 250, 253-55, 258
"The Fire" (Glück) **16**:127
"Fire" (Hughes) **53**:117, 119
"Fire" (Toomer) **7**:333
"Fire" (Zagajewski) **27**:380
"Fire and Earth" (Alurista) **34**:22
"Fire and Ice" (Frost) **1**:194, 197
"Fire and Sleet and Candlelight" (Wylie) **23**:301, 307
"Fire at Murdering Hut" (Wright) **14**:339
"Fire by the River" (Wagoner) **33**:333
"Fire Island" (Swenson) **14**:271, 285-86
"Fire Now Wakening on the River" (Chappell) **105**:5, 26, 43
"The Fire of Despair Has Been Our Saviour" (Bly) **39**:84
"The Fire of Drift-Wood" (Longfellow) **30**:36, 42
"Fire on the Hills" (Jeffers) **17**:117, 127
"Fire Poem" (Merrill) **28**:241-42
"Fire Practice" (McKay) **2**:225
"Fire Report—No Alarm" (Corso) **108**:47
The Fire Screen (Merrill) **28**:220-21, 228, 230-31, 258, 264, 281
Fire Sequence (Winters) **82**:312, 314, 316-17, 320, 324-25, 336
"Fire Song" (Ekeloef) **23**:51
"Fire Station" (Bukowski) **18**:16
"'Fire Stop Thief Help Murder Save the World'" (Cummings) **5**:107
"Fire Storm" (Alexie) **53**:54
"A Fire Truck" (Wilbur) **51**:218, 301
"The Firebombers" (Sexton) **2**:365
"The Firebombing" (Dickey) **40**:151, 154-55, 157-58, 175, 184, 193-94, 209, 212-15, 231-32, 241, 246, 252-53, 255, 259
"The Fireborn Are at Home in Fire" (Sandburg) **41**:301
"Fired" (Hughes) **1**:247
"The Fired Pot" (Wickham) **110**:269, 308
"Fireflies" (Swenson) **14**:250
"Fireletter" (Chappell) **105**:62
"Fireman's Lift" (Ní Chuilleanáin) **34**:361, 368-69
"The Firemen's Ball" (Lindsay) **23**:265, 268, 281
"Firenze" (Ferlinghetti) **1**:183
Fires: Essays, Poems, Stories, 1966-1982 (Carver) **54**:3, 7, 20, 31
The Fires of Baal (Clarke) **112**:27-28, 33, 40, 42-43, 72, 74, 78, 89
"Fireside" (Heaney) **100**:206
"Firewall" (Raworth) **107**:336
"Firewarden on Kearsage" (Francis) **34**:244
"Firewater" (Chappell) **105**:35, 40-41, 57, 62, 69
"Firewood" (Chappell) **105**:23-25, 28, 30, 40-41, 44, 59, 72-74
"Fireworks" (Shapiro) **25**:269
Fir-Flower Tablets (Lowell) **13**:64, 74, 93
"The Firing Squad is Singing in Chile" (Espada) **74**:154
"The 1st" (Clifton) **17**:17
"First" (Kipling) **3**:160
"First, a poem must be magical" (Villa) **22**:352
First Alluvia (Char)
See *Premières alluvions*
"The First American" (Toomer) **7**:337
First and Last Loves (Betjeman) **75**:15, 51-52, 81
"The First and Last Night of Love" (Cassian) **17**:4, 6
First and Last Words (Chappell) **105**:16, 19-20, 22, 38-39, 47, 65
The First and Second Anniversaries (Donne)
See *The Anniversaries*
The First Anniversarie. An Anatomie of the World. Wherein By Occasion of the untimely death of Mistris Elizabeth Drury, the frailtie and decay of this whole World is represented (Donne) **1**:122, 145-50, 152, 155-57; **43**:132-33
"The First Anniversary of the Government Under His Highness the Lord Protector" (Marvell)
See "The First Anniversary of the Government under O. C."
"The First Anniversary of the Government under O. C." (Marvell) **10**:270-71, 290, 294, 305, 312, 318
"The First Autumn" (Sarton) **39**:345
First Awakenings: The Early Poems of Laura Riding (Jackson) **44**:66, 68
First Book (Blok) **21**:2

The First Book of Urizen (Blake)
See *The Book of Urizen*
The First Booke of Ayres (Campion) **87**:7, 12, 25-26, 42, 51, 54, 56-57, 65-69, 97-98, 101-3
"First Calf" (Heaney) **18**:203; **100**:203, 205
"First Carolina Said Song" (Ammons) **16**:5
"The First Celestial Adventure of M Antipyrine" (Tzara) **27**:249
The First Cities (Lorde) **12**:137
"First Communion" (Kinnell) **26**:239
"First Communions" (Rimbaud)
See "Les premières communions"
"First Confession" (Kennedy) **93**:141, 147-48
"First Dances" (O'Hara) **45**:114
"First Day of the Future" (Kinnell) **26**:277
"The First Days" (Wright) **36**:314, 378
"First Death" (Enright) **93**:11-13, 32
"First Death" (Justice) **64**:272-73, 279
"First Death in Nova Scotia" (Bishop) **34**:82
"First Debate between the Body and the Soul" (Eliot) **90**:300
The First Decade: Selected Poems (Duncan) **2**:105-6
The First Decade: Selected Poems, 1940-1950 (Duncan) **75**:174-75, 180, 243
"First Dream" (Juana Inés de la Cruz)
See *El Sueño*
First Dream (Juana Inés de la Cruz)
See *El Sueño*
"First Early Mornings Together" (Pinsky) **27**:144
"First Eclogue" (Chatterton) **104**:8
"The First Eight Days of the Beard" (Kenyon) **57**:46
"First Elegy" (Rilke) **2**:281, 286
"First Elegy" (Rukeyser) **12**:219
"First Encounter" (Quintana) **36**:272
The First Encounter (Bely)
See *Pervoe svidanie*
"First Epistle of the First Book of Horace" (Pope)
See *Satires and Epistles of Horace, Imitated*
"First Fig" (Millay) **6**:227
"First Fight. Then Fiddle" (Brooks) **7**:75
"First Find" (Corso) **108**:11
The First Four Books of Poetry (Merwin) **45**:52
"First Frost" (Simic) **69**:365
"First Georgic" (Vergil) **12**:364
"The First Gloss" (Heaney) **18**:216
"First Goodbye" (Glück) **16**:165-67
The First Half of "A"-9 (Zukofsky) **11**:339, 396-97
"First Hymn to Lenin" (MacDiarmid) **9**:177-78, 182
First Hymn to Lenin, and Other Poems (MacDiarmid) **9**:158, 162, 171, 177, 196
"A 'First Impression' (Tokyo)" (Blunden) **66**:7-9, 17-18
"First Inclined to Take What It Is Told" (Brooks) **7**:74
First Indian on the Moon (Alexie) **53**:5-11, 30-31, 34, 40
"First Known When Lost" (Thomas) **53**:328
"The First Law of Motion" (Wagoner) **33**:334
"The First Leaf" (Snodgrass) **74**:292
"First Lesson about Man" (Merton) **10**:344-45
"First Letters from a Steamer" (McGuckian) **27**:82
"First Light" (Kinsella) **69**:118
First Light (Wagoner) **33**:359, 361-62, 364
"First Love" (Leopardi)
See "Il Primo Amore"
"The First Man" (Gunn) **26**:191
"First Meditation" (Roethke) **15**:272, 274, 279
The First Meetings (Bely)
See *Pervoe svidanie*
"First Memory" (Glück) **16**:157
First Mill (Char)
See *Moulin premier*
"First, Mills" (Hughes) **7**:149
"First Moment of Autumn Recognized" (Warren) **37**:379
The First Morning (Viereck) **27**:264-65
First Morning (Viereck) **27**:280-81, 283
First Nemean (Pindar)
See *Nemean 1*
"First News from Villafranca" (Barrett Browning) **6**:23-4
"First Night" (Olds) **22**:309
"The First Noni Daylight" (Harjo) **27**:64
"First Objectives" (MacDiarmid) **9**:154
"The First of All My Dreams Was of" (Cummings) **5**:109
"The First of January" (Lermontov) **18**:201
"The First of May" (Guest) **55**:218
First Olympian (Pindar)
See *Olympian 1*
"A First on TV" (Ignatow) **34**:310, 318
"First Page" (Stein) **18**:313
"The First Part" (Page) **12**:190
"First Poem" (Duncan) **75**:265
First Poems (Cernuda)
See *Primeras poesías*
First Poems (Merrill) **28**:224, 228-9, 233-4, 238-40, 243-4, 262, 281
First Poems (Muir) **49**:211, 227-29, 235, 237-39, 270, 277, 286-88
First Poems, 1946-1954 (Kinnell) **26**:279
"First Praise" (Williams) **7**:405
"First Psalm" (Sexton) **79**:220
First Pythian (Pindar)
See *Pythian 1*
"The First Rain" (Sikelianos) **29**:367, 373
First Satire of the Second Book of Horace Imitated (Pope)
See *Satires and Epistles of Horace, Imitated*
"The First, Second, Third and Fourth Circles" (Szirtes) **51**:172, 177
"1st September 1939" (Raworth) **107**:335
"The First Shall Be Last" (Very) **86**:140
"First Sight of Her and After" (Hardy) **92**:370
"First Snow" (Sarton) **39**:318-19
"The First Snow in Alsace" (Wilbur) **51**:187, 192, 266-67, 295, 315-19, 321
"First Snow in Lake County" (Mueller) **33**:180
"First Song" (Akhmatova)
See "Pervaya pesenka"
"First Song" (Kinnell) **26**:253, 257
First Song (Kinnell) **26**:236-38, 253, 262
"First South and Cambridge" (Hugo) **68**:234
"The First Step" (Cavafy) **36**:28, 100, 108
"The First Step" (Koch) **80**:302, 309
the first sufi line (Bissett) **14**:17
"First Summer After a War" (Ciardi) **69**:5, 26, 28
"The First Sunday in Lent" (Lowell) **3**:206
The First Symphony (Bely)
See *Severnaia simfoniia: Pervia geroicheskaia*
"First the fish must be caught . . ." (Carroll) **74**:29
"The First Time" (Shapiro) **25**:283, 300, 302, 320
"The First Time" (Warren) **37**:367, 376
"The First Transport of Wounded 1914" (Werfel)
See "Der erste Verwundeten-Transport 1914"
"The First Vision of Helen" (Benét) **64**:49
First Voronezh Notebook (Mandelstam) **14**:149, 152, 154
First We Take Manhattan (Cohen) **109**:78
"First We Take Manhattan" (Cohen) **109**:32, 82
"First Woman" (Jacobsen) **62**:320, 323, 325
"The First Word" (Wagoner) **33**:370
"The First-Born" (Hope) **56**:277
Firstborn (Glück) **16**:124-25, 127, 130-32, 134, 138-40, 143-44, 147-49, 151, 153
"Der Fischer" (Goethe) **5**:239
"The Fish" (Bishop) **3**:37, 39, 42-3, 50-2, 54, 60, 66, 69, 75; **34**:53, 78, 90, 116, 187, 189
"The Fish" (Brooke) **24**:58, 63, 65, 87
"Fish" (Lawrence) **54**:189, 191, 224, 232-33
"The Fish" (Moore) **4**:236, 243, 252, 257; **49**:89-90, 98-99, 101, 155
"The Fish" (Oliver) **75**:286, 302
"Fish" (Stryk) **27**:209
"The Fish Counter at Bonneville" (Stafford) **71**:293, 326
"Fish Crier" (Sandburg) **2**:332, 338; **41**:234, 239, 267, 269, 287, 320, 365
"Fish Monger" (Sandburg)
See "Fish Crier"
"A Fish: On Beauty" (Bell) **79**:14
"Fish Peddler and Cobbler" (Rexroth) **95**:254, 259, 274, 289-90, 312-14
Fish Souls (Berssenbrugge) **115**:7
"The Fish that Walked" (Sexton) **2**:370, 373; **79**:216
"The Fish, the Man, and the Spirit" (Hunt) **73**:155
"Fisherman" (Kinnell) **26**:260
"The Fisherman" (Yeats) **20**:324-25
"The Fisherman and the Fish" (Pushkin)
See "Skazka o Rybake i Rybke"
The Fisherman's Art (Ovid)
See *Halieutica*
"The Fisherman's Wife" (Wagoner) **33**:348
"The Fishermen" (Whittier) **93**:172
"The Fisher's Son" (Thoreau) **30**:217, 233, 284, 293
"The Fisherwoman" (Ignatow) **34**:315-16
"Fishing" (Hogan) **35**:271
"Fishing" (Thomas) **99**:273, 356
"Fishing at Dawn" (Hughes) **7**:120
"Fishing for Eel Totems" (Atwood) **8**:12
"Fishing the White Water" (Lorde) **12**:137
"Fishing with My Daughter in Miller's Meadow" (Stryk) **27**:204, 208, 214
"Fishnet" (Lowell) **3**:229
"Fission" (Graham) **59**:135, 143-45, 156
"Fist" (Levine) **22**:214, 223, 227
"The Fist" (Walcott) **46**:236, 279
The Fist Too Was Once the Palm of an Open Hand and Fingers (Amichai)
See *Gam ha'egrof haya pa'am yad ptuba ve'etsba'ot*
"A Fit against the Country" (Wright) **36**:336, 339, 343, 360
"Fit of Fainting" (Bradstreet)
See "Deliverance From a Fit of Fainting"
"A Fit of Rime Against Rime" (Jonson)
See *The Under-Wood XXXI*
"The Fitting" (Millay) **6**:230, 239
"The Fitting of the Mask" (Kunitz) **19**:154
"V" (Joyce) **22**:138, 162, 167
"Five Accounts of a Monogamous Man" (Meredith) **28**:171, 175, 193-94, 213
"Five Aspects of Fear" (Levertov) **11**:164
"The Five Carlins" (Burns) **114**:89
"The Five Day Rain" (Levertov) **11**:169
"The Five Faces of Pity" (Barker) **77**:11, 14
"Five Flights Up" (Bishop) **3**:48-9, 72; **34**:82, 149
"Five Grotesque Pieces" (Stevens) **110**:95
"500 American Postcards" (Berrigan) **103**:42
Five Indiscretions (Ríos) **57**:323, 325
"5. Jahrhundert" (Benn)
See "V. Jahrhundert"
"5 Jan 72" (Brutus) **24**:124
"Five Men" (Herbert) **50**:4, 25, 33-35
Five Men and Pompey (Benét) **64**:5, 18, 50
Five Men and Pompey: A Series of Dramatic Portraits (Benét)
See *Five Men and Pompey*
The Five Nations (Kipling) **3**:192; **91**:61-67, 72-74, 140-43, 171-76
"Five O'Clock Shadow" (Betjeman) **75**:13
"Five Poems about Poetry" (Oppen) **35**:299, 336
"Five Poems by Mr. S. Thalassinos" (Seferis) **66**:163, 184
"Five Senses" (Wright) **14**:348, 363

Five Senses: Selected Poems (Wright) **14**:348, 354, 361, 371
"Five Songs" (Rilke)
See "Fünf Gesänge"
"Five Stories and a Sequel" (Holmes) **71**:9494
"Five Things" (Goethe) **5**:228
Five Variations on a Theme (Sitwell) **3**:304
"Five Vignettes" (Toomer) **7**:332
"Five Walks on the Edge" (Viereck) **27**:277
"Five Words for Joe Dunn on His Twenty-Second Birthday" (Spicer) **78**:302
"Five-and-Dime, Late Thirties" (Kennedy) **93**:152
"Five-Finger Exercises" (Eliot) **5**:185
"Le flacon" (Baudelaire) **1**:45; **106**:6, 115, 122
"The Flag of England" (Kipling) **91**:64
"Flagellant's Song" (Kennedy) **93**:144
Flagons and Apples (Jeffers) **17**:133, 138
"Flags" (Owen) **102**:205
"Le flambeau vivant" (Baudelaire) **1**:56, 61
"Les Flambeaux" (Bonnefoy) **58**:153
"The Flame" (Pound) **95**:121
Flame and Shadow (Teasdale) **31**:322-25, 327, 330, 333, 338, 340, 347, 351, 355, 357-58, 360, 370-71, 379, 388
"The Flame Tree" (Wright) **14**:347
"Flame-Heart" (McKay) **2**:216, 228
"The Flaming Heart" (Crashaw) **84**:19, 32-33, 53, 55-56, 60-67, 69, 108-9, 115, 120-23, 125, 129-30
"Flammonde" (Robinson) **1**:462, 468, 476; **35**:363
"Flanders" (Hughes) **89**:102
"Flanders Now" (Blunden) **66**:40
"The Flash" (Dickey) **40**:152, 160
"Flash" (Stone) **53**:220
"Flash Flood" (Snodgrass) **74**:291
"Flashes and Dedications" (Montale)
See "Flashes e dediche"
"Flashes e dediche" (Montale) **13**:106, 166-67
"Flat Lands" (Sandburg) **41**:328
"A Flat One" (Snodgrass) **74**:293
"Flat-Foot Drill" (McKay) **2**:225
"Flatland" (Hope) **56**:275
"Flatted Fifth" (Hughes) **1**:267; **53**:92, 114, 191
"Flaubert in Egypt" (Warren) **37**:306, 340
"The Flaw" (Lowell) **3**:226-28
"The Flaw in Paganism" (Parker) **28**:351, 363
"A Flayed Crow in the Hall of Judgement" (Hughes) **7**:165
The Fle From Me (Wyatt)
See "They fle from me"
"The Flea" (Donne) **1**:134, 152
"Flèche D'or" (Merrill) **28**:254
"Fleckno" (Marvell) **10**:271, 294
"Flee on Your Donkey" (Sexton) **2**:351, 363-64; **79**:187
"Flee to the Mountains" (Very) **86**:120
"Fleeing from Eternity" (Hughes) **89**:142-43
"The Fleet" (Tennyson) **101**:269
The Fleeting and Other Poems (de la Mare) **77**:94
Fleeting Moments (Tagore)
See *Kshanikā*
Fleeting Thoughts (Tagore)
See *Kshanikā*
"Fleeting Words" (Darwish)
See "Pass through Fleeting Words"
"Fleisch" (Benn) **35**:49, 50
Fleisch (Benn) **35**:3, 29, 30, 31, 50, 77
"Fleming Helphenstine" (Robinson) **1**:466
"Flemish Rain" (Szirtes) **51**:171
"Flesh" (Wright) **14**:347
"The Flesh and the Spirit" (Bradstreet) **10**:7-8, 13, 21, 29-30, 38
"Fletcher McGee" (Masters) **1**:345; **36**:190, 221
"Fletcher Oak" (Oliver) **75**:313
"Fletches" (Brathwaite) **56**:91
"La Fleur qui fait le printemps" (Gautier) **18**:128-29
"Fleurette" (Service) **70**:130
"Fleurs" (Rimbaud) **57**:175, 234, 236, 250, 254, 284
"Fleurs couleur bleue" (Jaccottet) **98**:168
Les fleurs du mal (Baudelaire) **1**:44-51, 53-8, 60, 62-5, 67-71; **106**:1-179
"Flexibilité de l'oubli" (Char) **56**:127
"Flexibility of Forgetfulness" (Char)
See "Flexibilité de l'oubli"
"Flies" (Hall) **70**:16, 28, 34
"Flies Enter through a Closed Mouth" (Neruda)
See "Por boca cerrada entran moscas"
"Flight" (Brooke) **24**:56
"Flight" (Corso) **108**:8
"Flight" (Hughes) **53**:198-99, 201, 206
"The Flight" (Mickiewicz)
See "Ucieczka"
"The Flight" (Mistral)
See "La fuga"
"The Flight" (Randall) **86**:340
"The Flight" (Roethke) **15**:302
"Flight" (Seferis) **66**:125
"Flight" (Sexton) **2**:347, 361
"The Flight" (Teasdale) **31**:322, 325
"The Flight" (Very) **86**:136
The Flight (Das)
See *Palayanam*
Flight among the Tombs (Hecht) **70**:92, 94, 100, 108
Flight and Metamorphosis (Sachs)
See *Flucht und Verwandlung*
"Flight into Egypt" (Auden) **1**:38
"The Flight into Egypt" (Merton) **10**:330
"The Flight into Egypt" (Southwell) **83**:283
A Flight of Cranes (Tagore)
See *Balākā*
A Flight of Swans (Tagore)
See *Balākā*
"The Flight of the Duchess" (Browning) **97**:31, 33
"The Flight of the Earls" (Montague) **106**:310, 328
"Flight of the Heart" (MacNeice) **61**:139
"The Flight Path" (Heaney) **100**:240, 275, 278-79, 339
Flight to Africa (Clarke) **112**:62, 67, 80-81, 92
"Flight to Africa" (Clarke) **112**:63
"Flight to the City" (Williams) **7**:385, 387-88
"Flighting for Duck" (Empson) **104**:94
"Flippancies" (Wilbur) **51**:301
"Flippancies 1: The Star System" (Wilbur) **51**:285
"Flippancies 2: What's Good for the Soul is Good for Sales" (Wilbur) **51**:285
"The Flitting" (McGuckian) **27**:78, 97
"Floating" (Rexroth) **20**:216; **95**:260, 271
"Floating of the River of Han" (Wang Wei) **18**:362
"The Flock at Dawn" (Clarke) **112**:57
"The Flood" (Bishop) **34**:94
"The Flood" (Erdrich) **52**:186
"The Flood" (Tomlinson) **17**:333
"The Flood" (Wright) **14**:337-38
The Flood (Tomlinson) **17**:332, 336, 349, 354
"The Flood of Years" (Bryant) **20**:10, 16-18
"Flooded Meadows" (Gunn) **26**:219
"Flooding" (Celan) **10**:105
La flor (Castro) **41**:93-4, 97, 103
"Flora" (Morris) **55**:323, 325
"Flora" (Smith) **104**:152, 156-57, 178, 345, 347
"The Floral Apron" (Chin) **40**:29
"Floramelia" (Leapor) **85**:248, 286
"Florence" (Lowell) **3**:213, 236
"Florence Nightingale and Her Praisers" (Howe) **81**:49
Flores del destierro (Martí) **76**:106, 132
Floricanto en Aztlán (Alurista) **34**:3-5, 14-17, 21, 26, 31-36, 38-41, 45-48
"Florida" (Bishop) **3**:37; **34**:79, 116, 130
"La florida" (Guillén) **35**:153, 155, 156
"A Florida Sunday" (Lanier) **50**:56
"Flotsam" (de la Mare) **77**:64, 77
"Flounders" (Hughes) **89**:162, 177, 191, 262
Flow Chart (Ashbery) **26**:164
"Flow Gently Sweet Afton" (Burns)
See "Sweet Afton"
"The Flower" (Creeley) **73**:89-90
"The Flower" (Herbert) **4**:104, 109, 113, 118, 127, 131-32
"The Flower and the Rock" (Page) **12**:178
Flower, Fist, and Bestial Wail (Bukowski) **18**:3, 5
Flower Herding on Mount Monadnock (Kinnell) **26**:236, 257, 290
"Flower in the Crannied Wall" (Tennyson) **6**:358
Flower Into Animal (Spark) **72**:256
"The Flower Master" (McGuckian) **27**:78
The Flower Master (McGuckian) **27**:77-80, 84-85, 95-97, 101, 104
"Flower of Five Blossoms" (Kinnell) **26**:286
"The Flower of Old Japan" (Noyes) **27**:116-17, 139
The Flower of Old Japan (Noyes) **27**:116, 139
"A Flower Passage" (Wright) **36**:364, 400
"Flower Poem" (Hope) **56**:285, 298-99
"The Flower Sutra" (Rexroth) **95**:282
Flower Wreath Hill (Rexroth)
See *On Flower Wreath Hill*
"Flowered Sitting Room" (McGuckian) **27**:105
"The Flower-Fed Buffaloes" (Lindsay) **23**:279
"A Flowering Absence" (Montague) **106**:292, 294, 312, 319, 326, 329
"The Flowering of the Rod" (H. D.) **5**:271-72, 274-75, 293, 296, 306, 309, 314-16
"Flowering Plum" (Glück) **16**:128, 154
"The Flowering Tree" (Bridges) **28**:77, 80
"Flowers" (Akhmadulina)
See "Tsvety"
"Flowers" (Brathwaite) **56**:61
"The Flowers" (Kipling) **3**:161, 167
"The Flowers" (Masefield) **78**:30
"Flowers" (Rimbaud)
See "Fleurs"
Flowers and Insects: Some Birds and a Pair of Spiders (Hughes) **89**:232
"Flowers and Men" (Lawrence) **54**:179
"Flowers by the Sea" (Williams) **109**:284
Flowers for Hitler (Cohen) **109**:7-8, 12-15, 17-18, 20, 29, 31, 43, 57-59, 73, 75-77, 82-83, 87-89, 92, 113
"flowers in the lake" (Alurista) **34**:34
"Flowers in Winter" (Whittier) **93**:172
The Flowers of Evil (Baudelaire)
See *Les fleurs du mal*
"The Flowing of the Sangarios" (Masefield) **78**:99
"Fluch" (Stramm) **50**:189
Flucht und Verwandlung (Sachs) **78**:111, 155, 157, 161, 164, 168, 170-72, 175, 218-19, 225
"The Flume" (Bogan) **12**:95, 121
"Flumen Tenebarum" (Wilbur) **51**:186
"La flûte" (Vigny) **26**:367, 392, 403, 413
"Flute Notes from a Reedy Pond" (Plath) **1**:389
"Flute of Spring" (Carman) **34**:208
"A Flute Overhead" (Rexroth) **95**:255
"A Flute Overheard" (Rexroth) **20**:195
"Flute Song" (Paredes) **83**:12, 38
"Flute-Maker, with an Accompaniment" (Browning) **2**:88
"Flutender" (Celan) **10**:105
"Flux" (Eberhart) **76**:29, 51
"Flux" (Sandburg) **41**:313
"FLux et reflux" (Hugo) **17**:100
"The Fly" (Blake) **12**:7, 34; **63**:42, 54, 68, 106-07
"The Fly" (Brodsky) **9**:29
"The Fly" (Cohen) **109**:3
"The Fly" (Kinnell) **26**:255
"Fly" (Merwin) **45**:20
"The Fly" (Shapiro) **25**:269, 324, 326
"The Fly" (Wilbur) **51**:191

"A Fly about a Glass of Burnt Claret" (Lovelace) **69**:179, 185, 198, 229, 250
"A Fly Caught in a Cobweb" (Lovelace) **69**:168, 171, 185, 187, 197, 229, 240-46, 250, 253, 256
"A Fly that flew into my Mistress her Eye" (Carew) **29**:87
"Flying Above California" (Gunn) **26**:201, 219
"Flying Crooked" (Graves) **6**:149, 151
"The Flying Eagles of Troop" (Wright) **36**:363, 372, 392
"Flying Fish" (Sandburg) **41**:263
"Flying Home" (Kinnell) **26**:259, 261
"Flying Home from Utah" (Swenson) **14**:261
"The Flying Islands of the Night, a fantastic drama in verse" (Riley) **48**:289
"Flying out of It" (Ferlinghetti) **1**:175
"Flying to Byzantium" (Merrill) **28**:221
"Flying Underground" (Giovanni) **19**:143
"Flyting" (Dunbar) **67**:4, 6, 44, 86, 103, 105, 111-12, 114, 116-20, 122-24, 128
"Foam" (Enzensberger) **28**:146-48, 156
"La Foce" (MacLeish) **47**:197
"Fodder" (Heaney) **100**:193, 334, 336
"The Foe" (Very) **86**:136
"The Foes of Mankind" (Crabbe) **97**:157
"Fog" (Berssenbrugge) **115**:13, 26-27, 38, 41
"Fog" (Cassian) **17**:6
"Fog" (Doty) **53**:46, 64, 71-74
"Fog" (Merwin) **45**:7
"Fog" (Sandburg) **2**:301, 303; **41**:228, 234, 239, 250, 276, 281, 298, 348, 358
"Fog" (Seferis) **66**:121, 123-24, 143-44, 170, 180-81
"Fog" (Soto) **28**:377, 384
"Fog" (Thoreau) **30**:190, 194, 207, 216, 235, 257
"Fog" (Warren) **37**:303, 380
"Fog Argument" (Doty) **53**:51, 54
"Fog Envelops the Animals" (Dickey) **40**:176, 183-85, 189-90
"Fog Suite" (Doty) **53**:60
"The Foggy, Foggy Blue" (Schwartz) **8**:317
"Fog-Horn" (Merwin) **45**:7
"Fogs and Fires" (Sandburg) **41**:237
"La foi" (Lamartine) **16**:277, 291
"The Foilage Lit" (Bonnefoy)
See "Le Feuillage éclairé"
"Folastrie 1" (Ronsard) **105**:327
"Folastrie 2" (Ronsard) **105**:282-83, 327
"Folastrie 3" (Ronsard) **105**:272, 282, 328-29
"Folastrie 4" (Ronsard) **105**:281-82, 329-30
"Folastrie 5" (Ronsard) **105**:282, 329
"Folastrie 6" (Ronsard) **105**:330
"Folastrie 8" (Ronsard) **105**:190, 330
Folastries (Ronsard)
See *See Le livret de folastries à Janot Parisien*
"The Fold" (Meynell) **112**:191, 193, 299
"Foldath" (Peacock) **87**:325, 347
The Folding Cliffs (Merwin) **45**:102-9
Foliage (Hunt) **73**:136, 145, 162, 196, 211-12, 218, 231
"Folie de Minuit" (Lowell) **13**:90-1
"Folk" (Cohen) **109**:89, 91
"A Folk Singer of the Thirties" (Dickey) **40**:256
"Folk Song" (Cohen) **109**:50
"Folk Song" (Parker) **28**:355
"Folk Song" (Stafford) **71**:290
"Folk Tune" (Wilbur) **51**:217
"The Folk-Mote by the River" (Morris) **55**:340
"The Folks Inside" (Silverstein) **49**:341
"Folktale" (Hughes) **89**:190
"Folkways" (Brathwaite) **56**:75, 83, 99
Follas novas (Castro) **41**;79, 87-91, 93, 95-8, 100-2, 105-6, 111-16
"Follas novas IV" (Castro) **41**:89
"Follas novas VI" (Castro) **41**:91
"Follies" (Sandburg) **2**:303
"Follow that Stagecoach" (Wakoski) **15**:323
"Follow thy fair sun" (Campion)
See "Followe thy faire sunne"
"Follow Your Saint" (Campion) **87**:8, 39-42, 44-45, 64, 67, 97-99
"Followe thy faire sunne" (Campion) **87**:23, 36, 64, 97-98
"Follower" (Heaney) **18**:200; **100**:205, 328-29
"Following" (Ní Chuilleanáin) **34**:373
"Following the Markings of Dag Hammarskjöld: A Gathering of Poems in the Spirit of His Life and Writings" (Stafford) **71**:321
"Following the Recipe of Ancient Greco-Syrian Magicians" (Cavafy) **36**:63, 86, 112
"Following the 27th Day of February" (Akhmadulina)
See "Vosled 27 dnju fevralja"
"Following the 27th Day of March" (Akhmadulina)
See "Vosled 27 dnju marta"
"Folly" (MacDiarmid) **9**:153
"The Folly of Being Comforted" (Yeats) **20**:356
"Fonction du poète" (Hugo) **17**:77, 97
"Ae Fond Kiss" (Burns) **114**:120, 168
"Fond Memory" (Boland) **58**:3, 19
"La Fontaine de sang" (Baudelaire) **106**:24, 26
"Fontainebleau" (Teasdale) **31**:339
"Fontana di aga del me pais" (Pasolini) **17**:259
"Food" (Corso) **33**:47; **108**:21, 24, 31
"Food" (Jacobsen) **62**:319
"Food" (Sexton) **79**:240
"The Food Chain" (Kumin) **15**:208
"Food for Fire, Food for Thought" (Duncan) **2**:120-21; **75**:188
"Food of Love" (Kizer) **66**:79-80
"The Fool" (Service) **70**:119
"A Fool, A Foul Thing, A Distressful Lunatic" (Moore) **49**:121
"The Fool by the Roadside" (Yeats) **51**:108
"Fool Errant" (Lowell) **13**:83
"Fool o' the Moon" (Lowell) **13**:67, 83, 86
Fool Youngens (Riley) **48**:292
"Fooling God" (Erdrich) **52**:186, 191
"Foolish About Windows" (Sandburg) **41**:287
"The Foolish Heart" (Cullen) **20**:59
"Foolish Men" (Juana Inés de la Cruz)
See "Hombres necios que acusáis"
"Foolish Pride" (Castro)
See "Sobrera"
"The Fools' Paradise" (Morris) **55**:306
"The Fool's Song" (de la Mare) **77**:58
"Foot of Pride" (Dylan) **37**:59
"Football at Slack" (Hughes) **89**:122
"The football sprang and fell" (Housman) **43**:259
"A Footnote (from Marx's Chapter on the Working Day)" (Spender) **71**:224
"Footnote on Monasticism: Dingle Peninsula" (Montague) **106**:275
"Footnote to Howl" (Ginsberg) **4**:65, 68, 70; **47**:9-11, 34, 36-37, 44-45, 47, 61
Footprints (Levertov) **11**:189
"The footsteps" (Cavafy) **36**:57
"The Footsteps of Angels" (Longfellow) **30**:45, 96, 109
"The Foot-Washing" (Ammons) **16**:58
"For—" (Corso) **33**:49; **108**:5
"For" (Zukofsky) **11**:349
"For a better love/sex" (Dalton)
See "Para un mejor amor"
"For a Birthday" (Gunn) **26**:206
"For a College Yearbook" (Cunningham) **92**:139, 170
"For a Dead Citizen" (Tate) **50**:228, 306
"For a Dead Lady" (Robinson) **1**:461, 490, 492-93
"For a Dead Vole" (Smith) **12**:317
"For a Fatherless Son" (Plath) **1**:397; **37**:254, 260
"For a few Hopi Ancestors" (Rose) **13**:233
"For a Fiftieth Anniversary" (Hacker) **47**:107
"For a Friend" (Ignatow) **34**:313
"For a Good Dog" (Nash) **21**:268
"For a Grave at Komarovo" (Hope) **56**:282
"For a Lady Who Must Write Verse" (Parker) **28**:363
"For a Lamb" (Eberhart) **76**:14, 34, 38-39, 53, 60-61
"For a Lost Child" (Stafford) **71**:371
"For a Lovely Lady" (Cullen) **20**:52, 55
"For a Marriage" (Bogan) **12**:94
"For a Masseuse and Prostitute" (Rexroth) **95**:272, 333
"For a Muse Meant" (Duncan) **2**:105
"For a Pastoral Family" (Wright) **14**:375, 378
"For a Photograph of My Mother at the Beach" (Stone) **53**:227
"For a Picture of St. Dorothea" (Hopkins) **15**:144, 159-62
"For a Poet" (Cullen) **20**:85
"For a Russian Poet" (Rich) **5**:383
"For a Sad Lady" (Parker) **28**:360
"For a Self-Possessed Friend" (Warren) **37**:331
"For a street in the West" (Borges)
See "Para una calle del Oeste"
"For a' that" (Scott) **13**:293
"For A' That and A' That" (Burns)
See "Is There for Honest Poverty"
"For A' That and A' That'" (Burns)
"For a Woman Who Dreamed All the Horses were Dying" (Wagoner) **33**:349
"For a Woman Who Phoned Poetry Northwest Thinking It Was Poultry Northwest" (Wagoner) **33**:373
"For a Young Artist" (Hayden) **6**:187, 189-90, 196, 198
"For All Blasphemers" (Benét) **64**:8, 21
"For All We Have and Are" (Kipling) **91**:107
"For All Who Ever sent Lace Valentines" (Lindsay) **23**:265
"For All You Know" (Cervantes) **35**:113
"For Alva Benson and For Those Who Have Learned to Speak" (Harjo) **27**:55, 64
"For Ammonis, Who Died at 29, in A.D. 610" (Cavafy) **36**:8, 111
"For an Assyrian Frieze" (Viereck) **27**:260, 280
"For an Emigrant" (Jarrell) **41**:168, 184, 213
"For an Irish Book, 1929" (Melville) **82**:10, 34, 49-50
"For Andy Goodman—Michael Schwerner—and James Chaney (Three Civil Rights Workers Murdered in Mississippi on June 21, 1964)" (Walker) **20**:277-78, 287
"For Ann Scott-Moncrieff (1914-1943)" (Muir) **49**:232, 245
"For Anna Mae Pictou Aquash, Whose Spirit Is Present Here and in the Dappled Stars (For We Remember the Story and Tell It Again So that We May All Live)" (Harjo) **27**:71
"For Anne at Passover" (Kumin) **15**:180
"For Annie" (Poe) **1**:425, 434, 437, 444-45, 447
"For Anton Dolin in Carnival" (Wickham) **110**:267
"For Any Member of the Security Police" (Jacobsen) **62**:320
"For Anyone Dressed in Marble" (Cohen) **109**:8
"For Billy Holt" (Hughes) **89**:120, 150
"For Black People" (Madhubuti) **5**:327, 345
"For Black Poets Who Think of Suicide" (Knight) **14**:42
"For C." (Wilbur) **51**:332, 335
"For Chekhov" (Hass) **16**:199, 214
"For Children, If They'll Take 'Em" (Kennedy) **93**:147
"For City Spring" (Benét) **64**:8
"For Clarice" (Brooks) **7**:56
"For Crow Jane" (Baraka) **113**:10-11, 48, 63
"For Danton" (Tomlinson) **17**:345-46, 350
"For Dave: 1976" (Jordan) **38**:122
"For Deliverance from a Fever" (Bradstreet) **10**:36, 60
"For Don Drummond" (Goodison) **36**:154

"For E. J. P." (Cohen) **109**:112
"For Each of You" (Lorde) **12**:154, 157
"For Edward Long" (Cervantes) **35**:107, 113, 117
"For Eleanor and Bill Monahan" (Williams) **7**:392-93; **109**:261
"For Eleanor Boylan Talking with God" (Sexton) **2**:371
"For Eli Jacobsen" (Rexroth) **20**:181
"For Eli Jacobson" (Rexroth) **95**:250, 260, 314-17, 349
"For Ellen" (Wilbur) **51**:223
"For Eric Dolphy" (Knight) **14**:39
For Farish Street (Walker)
See *My Farish Street Green*
"For Freckle-Faced Gerald" (Knight) **14**:41-2
"For George Lamming" (Birney) **52**:15, 102
"For George Santayana" (Lowell) **3**:219
"For God While Sleeping" (Sexton) **2**:351, 360-61, 371
"For Godsake hold your tongue, and let me love" (Donne)
See "The Canonization"
"For Guillaume Apollinaire" (Meredith) **28**:194, 208
"For Gwendolyn Brooks" (Giovanni) **19**:113
"For Gwendolyn Brooks, Teacher" (Randall) **86**:291, 301, 337, 343
"For Harvey" (Spicer) **78**:268
"For Helen" (Stryk) **27**:203
"For Hettie in Her Fifth Month" (Baraka) **4**:15
"For His Father" (Meredith) **28**:180, 191, 194
"For His Own Epitaph" (Prior) **102**:308
"For Homer" (Corso) **108**:35
"For Hope" (Cowley) **90**:6, 14
"For Howard Baker" (Winters)
See "Epilogue: For Howard Baker"
"For I Have Done a Good and Kindly Deed" (Werfel)
See "Ich habe eine gute Tat getan"
"For initiation of 7 = 4" (Yeats) **51**:77
For Instance (Ciardi) **69**:56
"For Jack Spicer, until His Return" (Duncan) **75**:129
"For Jane Myers" (Glück) **16**:128
"For Jessica, My Daughter" (Strand) **63**:182
"For Jim, Easter Eve" (Spencer) **77**:341, 343
"For Joe" (Spicer) **78**:362-64
"For Joel" (Creeley) **73**:49
"For John Clare" (Ashbery) **26**:125
"For John Keats" (Graham) **59**:179
"For John, Who Begs Me Not to Enquire Further" (Sexton) **2**:347, 350, 357; **79**:189-90, 202, 247, 274-75, 281, 286, 296, 298-99, 301-5
"For Johnny Pole on the Forgotten Beach" (Sexton) **2**:349-50, 353
"For Julia in Nebraska" (Rich) **5**:385
"For K. J., Leaving and Coming Back" (Hacker) **47**:87
"For K. R. Who Killed Himself in Charles Street Jail" (Corso) **108**:17
"For Keats and Mozart" (Sarton) **39**:319, 354-56, 358
"For Koras and Balafong" (Senghor) **25**:231
"For Lil' Bit" (Jordan) **38**:127
For Lizzie and Harriet (Lowell) **3**:224, 226
"For Lori, This Christmas I Want to Thank You in This Way" (Tapahonso) **65**:249
"For Love" (Creeley) **73**:10, 33
For Love: Poems, 1950-1960 (Creeley) **73**:3-4, 6-8, 11-12, 17, 26-27, 29-30, 33-34, 36, 38-42, 49, 103, 106, 109, 115, 121
"For Luke O'Connor" (Masefield) **78**:89
"For M." (Zagajewski) **27**:396
"For Malcolm, a Year After" (Knight) **14**:38
"For Marianne Moore" (Ignatow) **34**:306
"For marilyn m" (Bukowski) **18**:22
"For Mark Rothko" (Graham) **59**:170, 177
"For Marthe" (Rexroth) **95**:258
"For Memory" (Rich) **5**:395
"For Miles" (Corso) **33**:14, 43
"For Miriam" (Tomlinson) **17**:336-37, 349
"For Monet" (Sarton) **39**:362
"For Mr. Death Who Stands with His Door Open" (Sexton) **2**:367, 372; **79**:199-200, 231
"For My Brother" (Song) **21**:331, 341
"For My Brother Hanson" (Merwin) **45**:24, 85
"For My Brother Reported Missing in Action, 1943" (Merton) **10**:331-32, 342, 349
"For My Contemporaries" (Cunningham) **92**:174-75, 182
"For My Daughter" (Ignatow)
See "For My Daughter in Reply to a Question"
"For My Daughter in Reply to a Question" (Ignatow) **14**:348, 355, 362; **34**:293, 305
"For My Lady" (Sanchez) **9**:209, 225
"For My Lover, Returning to His Wife" (Sexton) **2**:353, 372
"For my Mother: Genevieve Jules Creeley April 8 1887-Oct 7 1972" (Creeley) **73**:55
"For My Mother (May I Inherit Half Her Strength)" (Goodison) **36**:141, 154
"For My Mothers" (Glück) **16**:132, 138, 149; **160**:4-5, 45
"For My Own Monument" (Prior) **102**:294, 308
"For My People" (Walker) **20**:272, 274, 280-81, 283, 285, 289, 294
For My People (Walker) **20**:274-76, 281-83, 285-86, 289, 292-93
"For My Sister Molly Who in the Fifties" (Walker) **30**:339, 365
"For My Son on the Highways of His Mind" (Kumin) **15**:192, 201
"For New England" (Wright) **14**:340, 362
"For Nineteenth-Century Burials" (Betjeman) **75**:107
"For Nobody Else" (Ignatow) **34**:327
"For Now" (Merwin) **45**:14, 24
"For One Available Rose" (Seferis) **66**:125
"For One Moment" (Ignatow) **34**:272, 277
"For One Must Want / To Shut the Other's Gaze" (Graham) **59**:188
"for our mothers who gave us birth" (Sanchez)
See "Kwa Mamu Zetu Waliotuzaa (for our mothers who gave us birth)"
"For Patt, Whispering to a Burro" (Wagoner) **33**:348
"For Paul" (Niedecker) **42**:95, 99, 102, 123-24, 150, 172
"For Paul Dorn" (Raworth) **107**:274
"For Paul, Group Eight" (Niedecker) **42**:123-25
"For Peter Wee" (Thumboo) **30**:313-14, 329
"For Pharish Pinckney, Bindle Stiff During the Depression" (Randall) **86**:289, 343, 347
"For Poems for The St. Louis Sporting News" (Spicer) **78**:246
"For Precision" (Wright) **14**:342-43, 347
"For Proserpine" (Kunitz) **19**:175
"For Proust" (Merrill) **28**:248
"For R. C. B." (Parker) **28**:362
"For Rhoda" (Schwartz) **8**:282
"For Robert" (Spicer) **78**:292
"For Robert Frost" (Kinnell) **26**:284
"For Rosa Parks" (Goodison) **36**:141, 154
"For Rose" (Ignatow) **34**:345
"For Sale" (Lowell) **3**:219-20
"For Sale" (Silverstein) **49**:339
"For Saundra" (Giovanni) **19**:114-15, 139
"For Semra, with Martial Vigor" (Carver) **54**:6
"For Shoshana-Pat Swinton" (Piercy) **29**:300, 303
"For Sidney Bechet" (Larkin) **21**:227
"For Signs" (Gunn) **26**:204, 214
"For Steve" (Birney) **52**:4, 8, 39-40
"For the Altarpiece of the Roseau Valley Church, Saint Lucia" (Walcott) **46**:238, 240, 278, 280
"For the Anniversary of My Death" (Merwin) **45**:26, 31
"For the Asians Dying" (Merwin)
See "The Asians Dying"
"For the Bed at Kelmscott" (Morris) **55**:329
"For the Better" (Finch) **21**:181
"for the blind" (Clifton) **17**:26
"For the Boy Who Was Dodger Point Lookout Fifteen Years Ago" (Snyder) **21**:288
"For the Children" (Snyder) **21**:298
"For the Chinese New Year and for Bill Berkson" (O'Hara) **45**:133
"For the Commander of The Eliza" (Heaney) **18**:186-87, 200, 207
"For the Commemoration Services" (Holmes) **71**:94
"For the Conjunction of Two Planets" (Rich) **5**:360
"For the Death of Lombardi" (Dickey) **40**:223, 229, 253
"For the Duration" (Hughes) **89**:217
"For the Far-Out Experimental Writer" (Cruz) **37**:18-19
"For the Felling of a Tree in Harvard Yard" (Rich) **5**:359
"For the Furies" (Piercy) **29**:314
"For the Ghost of Robert Frost" (Francis) **34**:259, 265
"For the Grave of Daniel Boone" (Stafford) **71**:299
For the Guitar (Borges)
See *Para las seis cuerdas*
"For the Heroes Are Dipped in Scarlet" (Lawrence) **54**:198-201
"For the Hillmother" (Montague) **106**:286
"For the Kent State Martyrs" (Brutus) **24**:119
"For the Lady, Olivia Porter" (Davenant) **99**:177
"For the Last Wolverine" (Dickey) **40**:176, 197, 253, 257
"For the Marriage of Faustus and Helen" (Crane) **3**:81, 83, 90, 92, 95, 97; **99**:8, 10-14, 16-17, 19-23, 27, 34, 40-43, 46, 48-50, 68, 73, 79-81, 85, 89, 100-101
"For the Mother" (Montague) **106**:271
"For the New Railway Station in Rome" (Wilbur) **51**:219
"For the New Union Dead in Alabama" (Dorn) **115**:54, 127, 156
"For the Nightly Ascent of the Hunter Orion Over a Forest Clearing" (Dickey) **40**:184-85
"For the One Who Would Not Take His Life in His Hands" (Schwartz) **8**:313
"For the One Who Would Take Man's Life In His Hands" (Schwartz) **8**:301, 313
"For the Prisoners in South Africa" (Brutus) **24**:111
"For the Proclamation of the Kingdom of Italy" (Carducci)
See "Per la Proclamazione del Regno d'Italia"
"For the Quaternary Age" (Wright) **14**:373
"For the Record" (Lorde) **12**:140
For the renewing of his vows at Christmas-time (Southwell) **83**:231
"For the Restoration of My Dear Husband from a Burning Ague" (Bradstreet) **10**:26, 62
"For the Revolutionary Outburst by Black People" (Baraka) **4**:39; **113**:25
"For the Shop" (Cavafy) **36**:105-106
For the six strings (Borges)
See *Para las seis cuerdas*
"For the Stranger" (Forché) **10**:144, 157, 168
"For the Student Strikers" (Wilbur) **51**:283, 301
For the Time Being (Auden) **1**:17, 23, 34, 36-7; **92**:95, 119, 123, 129
"For the Union Dead" (Lowell) **3**:211-14, 223-24, 226, 232
For the Union Dead (Lowell) **3**:211-14, 223-24, 226, 232
For the Unlost (Jacobsen) **62**:320
"For the Warming of an Artist's Studio" (Wagoner) **33**:330
"For the Word is Flesh" (Kunitz) **19**:147, 152
"For the Year of the Insane" (Sexton) **2**:363

"For Those" (Corso)
"For Those Sisters & Brothers in Gallup" (Ortiz) **17**:232
"For Those Who Are as Right as Any" (Benét) **64**:14
"For Though the Caves Were Rabitted" (Thoreau) **30**:182, 237
"For Tom Postell, Dead Black Poet" (Baraka) **4**:10-11, 19; **113**:75
"For Two Girls Setting Out in Life" (Viereck) **27**:262
"For Two Lovers in the Year 2075 in the Canadian Woods" (Meredith) **28**:199
"For Unborn Malcolms" (Sanchez) **9**:218-19, 224, 233
"For Virginia Chavez" (Cervantes) **35**:107, 108, 113, 120, 121, 134
"For Vivian" (Randall) **86**:290
"For W. C. W." (Creeley) **73**:51-52, 110-13
"For Walter and Lilian Lowenfels" (Piercy) **29**:303
"For Whittier's Seventieth Birthday" (Holmes) **71**:68, 93
"For Wilf and His House" (Cohen) **109**:17, 48
"For Wilfred Owen" (Jacobsen) **62**:307
"For You" (Berrigan) **103**:6
For You: Poems (Carruth) **10**:83
"For Your Fear" (Ignatow) **34**:320-21
"Forage Sestina" (Hacker) **47**:79
Forbidden Entries (Yau) **61**:334-36, 348, 357-58
Forbidden Pleasures (Cernuda)
See *Los placeres prohibidos*
"Force" (Walcott) **46**:240, 279
"Force clémente" (Char) **56**:155-56
"La Force de l'habitude" (Éluard) **38**:96
Force of Light (Celan)
See *Lichtzwang*
"The Force That through the Green Fuse Drives the Flower" (Thomas) **2**:384-84; **52**:227, 232, 256, 263, 267-68, 310, 314, 330-31, 336
"The Forces of Love Reassemble W. D.: Instructions" (Snodgrass) **74**:331
"Forces, the Will, & the Weather" (Stevens) **110**:137, 139, 141-42, 149, 202
"Forcing House" (Roethke) **15**:295
"Ford Madox Ford" (Lowell) **3**:219
"Ford Manor" (Mahon) **60**:139, 143
"Forebears" (Pavese)
See "Antenati"
"Foreboding" (Carver) **54**:18
"Foreclosure" (Brown) **55**:151-52
"Foreclosure" (Niedecker) **42**:101
Forefathers' Eve (Mickiewicz)
See *Dziady III*
"Foreign Children" (Stevenson) **84**:299, 341-44, 348
"Foreign Flower" (Tagore)
See "Videshi phul"
"Foreign Lands" (Stevenson) **84**:314-15, 344
"Foreign Verse" (Seferis)
See "Reflections on a Foreign Line of Verse"
"Foreigner" (Page) **12**:170
"The Foreigner at Home" (Stevenson) **84**:348
The Forerunner (Gibran) **9**:69, 71, 75, 79
"Forerunners" (Emerson) **18**:79, 84
"Foreshadowing" (Wagoner) **33**:367
The Forest I (Jonson) **17**:180, 194
The Forest II (Jonson) **17**:158-9, 161, 163, 165, 169, 182, 189, 202-06, 209, 214
The Forest III (Jonson) **17**:158-59, 161, 163, 192, 210
"The Forest" (Simic) **69**:269, 272
"Forest" (Swenson) **14**:268
"The Forest" (Wright) **14**:348, 361
The Forest (Jonson) **17**:158-59, 169, 180, 194
"The Forest Hymn" (Bryant) **20**:3, 14, 18, 23, 29, 33
"Forest Fire" (Das) **43**:85
Forest Leaves (Harper) **21**:185
Forest Moon (Paz)
See *Luna silvestre*
"The Forest of Wild Thyme" (Noyes) **27**:116
The Forest of Wild Thyme (Noyes) **27**:139
"Forest Path" (Ishikawa)
See "Mori no michi"
"The Forest Path" (Wright) **14**:339
"The Forest Road" (Mew) **107**:35-36, 58, 61, 63
The Forest VII (Jonson) **17**:176
"Forest Worship" (Elliott) **96**:165
The Forest XI (Jonson) **17**:159, 172
The Forest XII (Jonson) **17**:158, 160, 214, 217
The Forest XIII (Jonson) **17**:158, 160, 163, 192
The Forest XV (Jonson) **17**:162, 171-72
"Forests" (de la Mare) **77**:148
The Forests of Lithuania (Davie) **29**:95-96, 109
"Forêt dans la Hache" (Breton) **15**:52
"La foret merveilleuse ou je vis donne un bal" (Apollinaire) **7**:3
"Forever Beyond the Limits of the World" (Sachs)
See "Immer hinter den Rändern der Welt"
"Forever in My Dream & in My Morning Thought" (Thoreau) **30**:192
"Forever Mountain" (Chappell) **105**:26
"The Forge" (Heaney) **18**:200, 221, 223
"The Forger" (Mahon) **60**:169, 199
"Le forgeron" (Rimbaud) **3**:277, 283, 285; **57**:184, 202, 244, 248, 251, 257, 290-91
"Forget" (Lawrence) **54**:250
"Forget not Yet" (Wyatt) **27**:315, 324, 357
Forget Me Not (Clarke) **112**:45, 68
"Forget Me Not" (Clarke) **112**:93
"For-Get-Me-Not" (Stein) **18**:313
"The Forging" (Borges)
See "Forjadura"
"Forgive Me My Sisters" (Sachs)
See "Verzeiht ihr meine Schwestern"
"Forgiveness" (Cunningham) **92**:136
"forgiving my father" (Clifton) **17**:18
"Forgotten Arietta" (Verlaine)
See "Ariettes oubliées"
"Forgotten Girlhood" (Jackson) **44**:106
"Forgotten Girlhood: in Laddery Street: All the Way Back" (Jackson) **44**:107
"Forgotten Girlhood: in Laddery Street: Herself" (Jackson) **44**:94
"A Forgotten Miniature" (Hardy) **8**:137-38
"The Forgotten Pram" (Shvarts) **50**:143
"Forgotten Song" (Ashbery) **26**:162
"Forgotten the Red Leaves" (Douglas) **106**:186
"Forjadura" (Borges) **22**:72
"Fork" (Simic) **69**:264, 314
"Forks with Points Up" (Ignatow) **34**:313
"The Forlorn Sea" (Smith) **12**:326
"Die Form" (Benn) **35**:63
A Form of Women (Creeley) **73**:3, 27
"Form without Love" (Aleixandre) **15**:18-19, 22-3
"Forma en torno" (Guillén) **35**:228
"Formal" (Raworth) **107**:324
Formal Division (Char)
See *Partage formel*
"Formal Feeling" (Boland) **58**:41
"Formalist" (Wickham) **110**:293
"The Formation of a Separatist, I" (Howe) **54**:59
Formations (Cage) **58**:221, 224
"Former Life" (Baudelaire)
See "La Vie antérieure"
"Formerly a Slave" (Melville) **82**:104
Formerly and Not So Long Ago (Verlaine)
See *Jadis et naguère*
"Forming Child" (Ortiz) **17**:225, 231
Forms of Exile (Montague) **106**:270, 275, 284, 306, 312, 315, 325, 330-31, 334
"Forms of Love" (Oppen) **35**:299, 304
"Forms of the Earth at Abiquiu" (Momaday) **25**:201-203
"Formula" (Hughes) **53**:169-71
"The Forsaken" (Lowell) **13**:62
"A Forsaken Garden" (Swinburne) **24**:324, 338, 344
"A Forsaken Lady" (Lovelace) **69**:178
"The Forsaken Merman" (Arnold) **5**:5-8, 12-13, 17-18, 34-5, 38-9, 42, 49
"The Forsaken One" (Mistral)
See "La desásída"
Forslin (Aiken) **26**:6-7, 27
"Fort Benton" (Hugo) **68**:267
"Fort Casey, without Guns" (Hugo) **68**:270
"Fort Kurt Porjescz, Missing in Action, 1 April 1945" (Ciardi) **69**:26
"Forth went the candid man" (Crane) **80**:52
"Forties Flick" (Ashbery) **26**:149
"Fortiés tu Ai-Yiánni" (Seferis) **66**:196
"The Fortress" (Sexton) **2**:362; **79**:226-28, 231, 257-58, 260-62, 264, 266-67
The Fortunate Traveller (Walcott) **46**:247-48, 259, 322-23
"Fortunatus Nimium" (Bridges) **28**:73, 75, 89-90
"Fortune..." (Ferlinghetti) **1**:183
Fortune Hath Taken Thee Away My Love (Raleigh)
See "Fortune hathe taken away my love"
"Fortune hathe taken away my love" (Raleigh) **31**:245, 280, 304, 313
"Fortune, Nature, Love" (Sidney) **32**:235, 241
"Fortune's Falsehood" (Southwell) **83**:281
Fortune's Mutation (Christine de Pizan)
See *Le livre de la mutacion de fortune*
"The Fortunes of Gyges" (Morris) **55**:306
"Fortune-telling" (Herbert) **50**:19
"Fortune-Telling" (Tsvetaeva)
See "Gadan'e"
"44th Birthday Evening, at Harris's" (Berrigan) **103**:36
"Forty Singing Seamen" (Noyes) **27**:133
Forty Singing Seamen and Other Poems (Noyes) **27**:133
"Forty Years" (Oliver) **75**:329
"45' for a Speaker" (Cage) **58**:201
45 Mercy Street (Sexton) **2**:356, 359, 367, 374; **79**:198, 210, 214-15, 219, 225, 233-34, 238-42, 244-45, 251
"45 Mercy Street" (Sexton) **79**:239-40, 242
"XLI et dernière" (Sainte-Beuve) **110**:45
XLI Poems (Cummings) **5**:104
"Forty-Three-Year-Old Woman, Masturbating" (Ai) **72**:29
"Forward! Forward!" (Carducci)
See "Avanti! Avanti!"
"Forward Observers" (Stryk) **27**:203
"La forza d'un bel viso a che mi sprona?" (Michelangelo) **103**:307
Fosfeni (Zanzotto) **65**:273, 277-78, 289, 296-97, 301-3
"Fossile sanguinaire" (Char) **56**:154
"Fosterage" (Heaney) **100**:225, 266-72, 351
"The Fostering of Aslaug" (Morris) **55**:307, 329
"Fosterling" (Heaney) **18**:259; **100**:268
"The Foster-Mother's Tale" (Coleridge) **67**:280, 295, 338-39, 365
"Le Fou" (Creeley) **73**:39-40, 101
Le Fou (Creeley) **73**:3
"Les foules" (Baudelaire) **1**:59; **106**:89
"Found" (Rossetti) **44**:172
"Found in a Storm" (Stafford) **71**:299
Found Objects (Zukofsky) **11**:346
"found paean to vancouver by rudyard kipling (1890)" (Birney) **52**:43
"The Foundation" (Yamada) **44**:326
"Founders Day. A Secular Ode on the Ninth Jubilee of Eton College" (Bridges) **28**:67, 71
"Founding Fathers, Nineteenth-Century Style, Southeast U.S.A." (Warren) **37**:340
"The Fountain" (Bryant) **20**:4, 43, 47
"The Fountain" (Wordsworth) **4**:374, 399; **67**:287, 328
"A Fountain, a Bottle, a Donkey's Ears, and Some Books" (Frost) **1**:194

"The Fountain of Ammannati" (Stryk) **27**:183-84, 192
The Fountain of Bahchisard (Pushkin)
See *Bakhchisaraiski Fontan*
"Fountain Piece" (Swenson) **14**:263-64
"The Fountains of Aix" (Swenson) **14**:250, 255, 285-86
"Four" (Creeley) **73**:115
"IV" (Joyce) **22**:145, 163, 166, 168, 173
"The Four" (Lawrence) **54**:250
"Four Ages" (Char) **56**:162
"The Four Ages" (Nemerov) **24**:293-24, 297
"The Four Ages of Man" (Bradstreet) **10**:4, 17, 30, 45
"Four a.m." (Szymborska)
See "Czwarta nad ranem"
"Four Auguries" (Atwood) **8**:27-8
Four Books of Odes (Ronsard)
See *See Les quatre premiers livres des odes de Pierre de Ronsard, ensemble son bocage*
"The Four Brothers" (Sandburg) **2**:302; **41**:240, 270, 297
"Four Canzones" (Okigbo) **7**:247-48
Four Canzones (Okigbo)
See "Four Canzones"
"The Four Cycles" (Borges)
See "Los cuatro ciclos"
"Four Dancers at an Irish Wedding" (Gallagher) **9**:37
"4 daughters" (Clifton) **17**:25
"Four Dheetziyama Poems" (Ortiz) **17**:225
"4e époque" (Lamartine) **16**:264
"The Four Elements" (Bradstreet) **10**:11, 17, 41
"Four Evasions" (Atwood) **8**:24, 27-8
"Four Eyes" (Ondaatje) **28**:292, 329, 331
"Four feet between" (Birney) **52**:34, 37, 47, 79, 97
"Four for Sir John Davies" (Roethke) **15**:263, 273-74, 286
Four for Traine (Mackey) **49**:17
"The Four Freedoms" (Paredes) **83**:29
"The Four Gospels" (Goethe) **5**:229
"Four in a Family" (Rukeyser) **12**:223
"Four in the Morning" (Szymborska)
See "Czwarta nad ranem"
"Four Kantian Lyrics" (Tomlinson) **17**:311, 342
"Four Lakes' Days" (Eberhart) **76**:9, 13, 15, 35
"Four Last Things" (Vaughan) **81**:351
"Four Legs, Three Legs, Two Legs" (Empson) **104**:91, 119
"Four Little Elegies" (O'Hara) **45**:171-73
"Four March Watercolours" (Hughes) **89**:135
"Four Men" (Francis) **34**:245
The Four Men (Brooke) **24**:89
"The Four Monarchies" (Bradstreet) **10**:4-5, 17-18, 20-1, 27, 31, 33-4, 40, 46-7
"Four Notions of Love and Marriage" (Momaday) **25**:189
"Four O'Clock Summer Street" (McGuckian) **27**:82, 90
"4 Other Countries" (Zukofsky) **11**:348
"Four Poems" (Bishop) **34**:89
"Four Poems" (Schuyler) **88**:199
"Four Poems for Ramparts" (Spicer) **78**:245
"Four Poems from New Zealand" (Wright) **14**:377
"Four Portraits of Fire" (Cervantes) **35**:104, 117
"Four Preludes on Playthings of the Wind" (Sandburg) **2**:316, 340; **41**:270-72, 274, 276, 298, 314
The Four Quartets (Eliot) **5**:162-65, 174, 178-80, 182, 186, 196, 198, 200, 205-06, 208, 210-11; **31**:117, 119, 124, 133, 138, 169; **90**:255, 304, 312
"Four Sad Poems on the Delaware" (Stern) **115**:253
"The Four Seasons of the Year" (Bradstreet) **10**:17, 44
"Four Sides to a House" (Lowell) **13**:61
"Four Sonnets" (Nemerov) **24**:256
"The Four Sorrows" (Marie de France)
See "Le Chaitivel"
"Four Tales Told by an Idiot" (Hughes) **89**:128
"4/25/89 late" (Clifton) **17**:30
"Four Villonesques on Desire" (Szirtes) **51**:172
"Four Walks in the Country near Saint Brieuc" (Mahon) **60**:133, 138
"Four Ways of Knowledge" (Bly) **39**:67
"Four Winds" (MacNeice) **61**:113
"Four Winds" (Teasdale) **31**:365
Four Year Old Girl (Berssenbrugge) **115**:2, 8, 11, 15-18, 28, 31, 34, 39-40, 47
"Four Year Old Girl" (Berssenbrugge) **115**:17, 29-34
"Four Years Later" (Creeley) **73**:79
The Four Years' Notebook (Montale)
See *Quaderno de quattro anni*
The Four Zoas: The Torments of Love and Jealousy in the Death and Judgement of Albion the Ancient Man (Blake) **12**:13-21, 25-9, 32, 35-8, 41, 47, 49-50, 60-4, 73; **63**:18
"La Fourmi" (Péret) **33**:210
"Fourteen" (Hacker) **47**:80
"XIV" (Joyce) **22**:138, 145, 160, 163-66, 168-70
"14 de julio" (Cisneros) **52**:152
"14 Dec." (Ammons) **16**:22
Fourteen Men: Verses (Gilmore) **87**:282-84, 300-301, 303
Fourteen Poems by O. V. de L. Milosz (Rexroth) **95**:251
Fourteenth Olympian (Pindar)
See *Olympian 14*
The Fourth Booke of Ayres (Campion) **87**:25, 32-33, 47, 59, 69-72, 97, 103
"Fourth Eclogues" (Sidney) **32**:301
"Fourth Georgic" (Vergil) **12**:365, 371
"Fourth Meditation" (Roethke) **15**:272, 278
"Fourth Mesostic" (Cage) **58**:214
"The Fourth Month of the Landscape Architect" (Rich) **5**:384
Fourth Nemean (Pindar)
See *Nemean 4*
"Fourth of July" (Hughes) **7**:119; **89**:101
"Fourth of July" (Snodgrass) **74**:290
"The Fourth of July" (Wilbur) **51**:234-36, 238, 281-82
"Fourth of July in Maine" (Lowell) **3**:226
"Fourth Poem from Nicaragua Libre: Report from the Frontier" (Jordan) **38**:131
"Fourth Psalm" (Sexton) **79**:220
Fourth Pythian (Pindar)
See *Pythian 4*
Fourth Quarter and Other Poems (Wright) **14**:372-75
Fourth Satire of Donne (Pope)
See *Satires of Dr. Donne Versified*
The Fourth Symphony (Bely)
See *Kubok metelej: Chetviortiia simfoniia*
"Fourth Time Around" (Dylan) **37**:51
Fowre Hymnes (Spenser) **8**:331-32, 334, 337, 390
"The Fox" (Tomlinson) **17**:327
"Fox" (Wright) **14**:376
"The Fox and the Wolf" (Henryson) **65**:5, 28, 54, 79, 81-82
"Fox Hunting" (Masefield) **78**:52
"The Fox, the Wolf, and the Cadger" (Henryson) **65**:5, 18, 54, 64
"The Fox, the Wolf, and the Husbandman" (Henryson) **65**:7, 18, 27, 54-55, 64, 110
"Fox Trot" (Sitwell) **3**:297, 303
"Foxes' Moon" (Tomlinson) **17**:343
"Foxhunt" (Hughes) **7**:166
"Fra Lippo Lippi" (Browning) **2**:37, 88, 95; **61**:5, 92; **97**:11, 37, 46
Fra Rupert (Landor) **5**:95
"Frage" (Stramm) **50**:170, 188, 208-9
"Fragility" (Kinsella) **69**:109
"Fragment" (Ashbery) **26**:118, 125, 135, 144, 156-157
"Fragment" (Borges)
See "Fragmento"
"A Fragment" (Bryant)
See "Inscription for the Entrance into a Wood"
"A Fragment" (Burns) **114**:94, 135
"Fragment" (Creeley) **73**:96
"Fragment" (Finch) **21**:140, 172
"Fragment" (Johnson) **24**:142, 148
A Fragment (Keats)
See *Hyperion*
"Fragment: As Bronze may be much Beautified" (Owen) **19**:352
"Fragment from Correspondence" (Nemerov) **24**:298
"Fragment: I saw his Round Mouth's Crimson" (Owen) **19**:352
"Fragment of a Gothic Tale" (Wordsworth) **67**:354
"Fragment of a Meditation" (Tate) **50**:231, 243, 249, 317
Fragment of a Series of Elegies (Southwell) **83**:230
"Fragment of an Agon" (Eliot) **90**:208
"Fragment of an 'Antigone'" (Arnold) **5**:48-9
"Fragment of New York, 1929" (Eberhart) **76**:8, 42
"Fragment Thirty-Six" (H. D.) **5**:268, 270
"Fragment: To a Mirror" (Justice) **64**:272
"Fragment: Welcome joy, and welcome sorrow" (Keats)
See "Welcome joy, and welcome sorrow"
Fragmenta Aurea (Suckling) **30**:117, 120, 125, 149, 155, 158
"Fragmente" (Benn) **35**:34, 36
"Fragmento" (Borges) **32**:87, 94-5
"Fragments" (Masefield) **78**:91
"Fragments" (Yeats) **51**:108
Fragments Descriptive of the Miseries of War (Smith) **104**:219
"Fragments du narcisse" (Valéry) **9**:348, 365-66, 372, 393, 395-96
"Fragments from a Parable (of the 1950's)" (Jordan) **38**:120-23, 144
"Fragments from a Poem to be entitled 'The Sentimental Exile'" (Brooke) **24**:68, 80, 89
"Fragments from an Apocryphal Gosepel" (Borges) **32**:140
"Fragments from Italy" (Ciardi) **69**:8, 11
"Fragments from the Deluge" (Okigbo) **7**:231, 246, 255
"Fragments of a Lost Gnostic Poem" (Melville) **82**:74-75, 151, 200
"Fragments of an Albigensian Rime" (Duncan) **75**:232
Fragments of Ancient Poetry, collected in the Highlands of Scotland, and translated from the Galic or Erse Language (Macpherson) **97**:172, 192-94, 196-97, 199, 209-10, 212, 217-18, 221-25, 227-29, 231, 236-37, 239, 245, 249, 252, 279-82, 298, 305-17, 330, 334-35, 343-45, 347-51
"Fragmentum Umbrae" (Campion) **87**:4
"Fragoletta" (Swinburne) **24**:361-62
"Frailtie" (Herbert) **4**:135
"The Frailty" (Cowley) **90**:29
"Frailty" (Herbert)
See "Frailtie"
"Le Fraisne" (Marie de France) **22**:241, 248, 258, 269, 271-72, 275, 277-78, 282
"La Fraisne" (Pound) **95**:122
"Frame" (Rich) **5**:396
"Frame Structures" (Howe) **54**:108
Frame Structures: Early Poems, 1974-1979 (Howe) **54**:107-9, 124, 128, 130, 133-34, 140
"A Framed Photograph" (Curnow) **48**:42, 47-49
Frameless Windows, Squares of Light (Song) **21**:334, 344, 345-46
Framework (Parra)
See *Obra gruesa*

"Framing" (Graham) **59**:174
"Frammento" (Leopardi) **37**:81
"Frammento alla morte" (Pasolini) **17**:295
"France" (Sassoon) **12**:276, 278
"France 1870" (Meredith) **60**:250, 260
"France: An Ode" (Coleridge)
See "Ode to France"
"Francesco Petrarca" (Carducci) **46**:50
La Franciade (Ronsard)
See *Les quatre premiers livres de la Franciade*
"Francie's Fingers" (Wylie) **23**:324
"Francina" (Brathwaite) **56**:68, 76, 95
"Francine's Room" (Erdrich) **52**:178
"Francis Furini" (Browning) **2**:72, 75, 84-5
"Franciscæ meæ laudes" (Baudelaire) **106**:103, 126
"Francisco, I'll Bring You Red Carnations" (Levine) **22**:225
"La frangia dei capelli" (Montale) **13**:111, 128
"Frank and Billy" (Colwin) **39**:270, 279, 292, 300, 302, 312
"The Frank Courtship" (Crabbe) **97**:95, 102, 104, 147-48
"Frank O'Hara" (Berrigan) **103**:4, 30, 34, 40
"Frankie and Johnny" (Brown) **55**:71, 74, 102-4, 154-55
"Franklin's Prologue" (Chaucer) **58**:234
"Franklin's Tale" (Chaucer) **19**:11-13, 15, 17, 27, 33, 47, 53, 61; **58**:234, 249-50, 351
"Franz Schubert A Press Conference" (Zagajewski) **27**:382, 385, 401
"Frase" (Storni) **33**:268
"Frases" (Parra) **39**:273
"Frater Ave atque Vale" (Tennyson) **101**:236
"Fraud" (Blok) **21**:37
"Fraulein Reads Instructive Rhymes" (Kumin) **15**:180
"Frayed" (Birney) **52**:16
"Fraying the Jute Sack" (Char)
See "Effilage du sac de jute"
"Freaks" (Alexie) **53**:31
"The Freaks" (Das) **43**:85
"Frederick Douglass" (Dunbar) **5**:131, 134, 143
"Frederick Douglass" (Hayden) **6**:176, 183, 188, 196, 199
"Frederick Douglass and the Slave Breaker" (Randall) **86**:334, 341, 343
"Frederick Douglass: 1817-1895" (Hughes) **53**:150
Frederick Goddard Tuckerman: The Cricket, Printed from His Notebooks with Permission of His Granddaughter Margaret Tuckerman Clark (Tuckerman) **85**:310, 316, 318, 321-22, 324, 326, 331, 333, 335-39, 341-42
"Fredericksted Dusk" (Walcott) **46**:278
"Frederiksted Nights" (Walcott) **46**:236, 278
"Free" (McKay) **2**:225
"The Free" (Merwin) **45**:42
"Free Fantasia: Tiger Flowers" (Hayden) **6**:194-95
"Free Flight" (Jordan) **38**:124
"Free Labor" (Harper) **21**:217-18
"Free Rhythms" (Wickham) **110**:264
"Free Spirit" (Cruz) **37**:13
"Free the Goldfish" (Simic) **69**:305
"Free Thoughts" (Blok) **21**:31
"Free Will" (Meynell) **112**:178
"The Freebooters" (Cardenal)
See "Los filibusteros"
"Freedman" (Heaney) **18**:205; **100**:224
"Freedom" (Hughes) **1**:252; **53**:153
"Freedom" (Kavanagh) **33**:115
Freedom Lament and Song (Serote) **113**:287-88
"Freedom New Hampshire" (Kinnell) **26**:236, 238, 242, 284, 289
"Freedom of Speech" (Hughes) **89**:162, 245, 274
Freedom on Oath (Paz)
See *Libertad bajo palabra*
Freedom on Parole (Paz)
See *Libertad bajo palabra*
"Freedom Train" (Hughes) **1**:244; **53**:109, 193
Freedom under Parole (Paz)
See *Libertad bajo palabra*
Freedom under Word (Paz)
See *Libertad bajo palabra*
"Freedom's Plow" (Hughes) **1**:250, 258; **53**:116, 145
The Freeing of the Dust (Levertov) **11**:197-98, 213
"Freeing the Boat" (Tu Fu) **9**:320
Freely Espousing: Poems (Schuyler) **88**:179-82, 189, 193, 197, 201-2, 221
"Freeway 280" (Cervantes) **35**:112, 113, 121, 131
"Freezing" (Meredith) **28**:177
"La frégate 'La Sérieuse'" (Vigny) **26**:411
"The French Child's Sunday" (Corso) **33**:25
French Leave: Translations (Kennedy) **93**:145-47, 150
"The French Master" (Abse) **41**:3, 9
"The French People to Armand Carrell" (Dobell) **100**:166
"French Pioneers" (Benét) **64**:53-54
"A French Poem" (Merton) **10**:337
"French Poems" (Ashbery) **26**:118
The French Revolution (Blake) **12**:13, 25, 63; **63**:134
"A French Rooster" (Stein) **18**:313
"Frente al Oxford" (Guillén) **23**:126
"Frenzy" (Sexton) **2**:368; **79**:211, 222, 237
"Frenzy in the Wake" (Melville) **82**:134, 275-76
"The Frenzy of Suibhne" (Clarke) **112**:86
"Fréquence" (Char) **56**:145, 153
Frequencies (Thomas) **99**:259, 261-64, 266-67, 270, 273-74, 282, 284, 315, 319, 337-39, 350, 353, 355-60
Les Frères de mémoire (Char) **56**:115-16
"Frères humains qui apres nous vivez" (Villon)
See "Epitaphe Villon"
"Fresca rosa novella" (Cavalcanti) **114**:228
Frescoes for Mr. Rockefeller's City (MacLeish) **47**:130, 134-35, 138-40, 143, 146-47, 151, 189-90, 240, 254-55
"Fresh Air" (Koch) **80**:292-93, 313-14, 320
Fresh Brats (Kennedy) **93**:134
"Fresh Stain" (Gallagher) **9**:62, 64
"The Fresh Start" (Wickham) **110**:303
"Freshman Blues" (Berryman) **64**:79
"Freshness" (Yevtushenko) **40**:343
Fresko-Sonett (Heine) **25**:160
"Fresne" (Marie de France)
See "Le Fraisne"
"Freudenhaus" (Stramm) **50**:170-71, 175, 189, 198, 204, 209
"F. R. Higgins" (Clarke) **112**:93
"The Friar's Prologue" (Chaucer) **58**:291, 320
"Friar's Tale" (Chaucer) **19**:11, 13-14
"Friday, the 13th" (Spicer) **78**:256, 304
"Friday the Thirteenth" (Ginsberg) **4**:75
"Friday: The Toilette: Lydia" (Montagu) **16**:338, 347-49
"A Friend" (Philips) **40**:274, 298
"The Friend" (Piercy) **29**:308-09
"The Friend" (Smith) **12**:318
"A Friend" (Snodgrass) **74**:293
"The Friend" (Thoreau) **30**:227
"Friend Master T. L." (Whitney) **116**:312
"The Friend of Grandmother Speranza" (Gozzano)
See "L'amica di nonna speranza"
"The Friend of the Fourth Decade" (Merrill) **28**:220-21, 269
"Friend Who Has Been Reading Jacques Lacan" (Hass) **16**:199
"The Friend Who Is Sleeping" (Pavese)
See "Adventures"
"Friendless" (Berryman) **64**:100-101, 103
"Friendly Epistle to Mrs. Fry" (Hood) **93**:116
"Friends" (Ashbery) **26**:145
"The Friends" (Patmore) **59**:204, 230
"Friends" (Sexton) **2**:365
"Friends Beyond" (Hardy) **92**:359
"Friends, When I loved" (Cavafy) **36**:52
"Friendship" (Cowper) **40**:44
"Friendship" (Stryk) **27**:204, 208
"Friendship" (Thoreau) **30**:273, 285, 293
"Friendship Between Ephelia and Ardelia" (Finch) **21**:164
"Friendship Heights" (Curnow) **48**:42
"Friendship in Embleme or the Seal To My Dearest Lucasia" (Philips) **40**:281, 296, 313, 320, 322-24
"Friendship's Garland" (Heaney) **100**:267, 270-71
"Friendship's Mystery. To My Dearest Lucasia" (Philips) **40**:296, 298, 318
"Friendship's Steadfastness" (Thoreau) **30**:265
"The Frigate Pelican" (Moore) **49**:98-99, 134
"Fright" (Storni)
See "Miedo"
"The Frightened Man" (Bogan) **12**:86
"Frightening Toys" (Simic) **69**:300
The Frightening World (Blok) **21**:25
"Frilot Cove" (Brown) **55**:114
"Frimaire" (Lowell) **13**:97
"Fríos" (Storni) **33**:246
"Friso" (Darío) **15**:112
"Frisson" (Gautier) **18**:164
Frissons Apparents (Raworth)
See *Visible Shivers*
"Fritz" (Stern) **115**:289
"A Frivolous Conversation" (Milosz) **8**:194
"Frog" (Spicer) **78**:252, 304
"Frog Autumn" (Plath) **1**:388
"The Frog Prince" (Smith) **12**:305, 323, 341
"The Frog, That Naked Creature" (Sarton) **39**:325, 334
"Froid jaune" (Tzara) **27**:227
"A Frolick" (Herrick) **9**:103
"From a Child" (Waller) **72**:373
"From a Daybook" (Swenson) **14**:273
"From a Diary of Dreams" (Clarke)
See "Extracts from a Diary of Dreams"
"From a Dream" (Ignatow) **34**:291-92, 341
"From a Dream of a Hell" (Werfel)
See "Aus dem Traum einer Hölle"
"From a Litany" (Strand) **63**:152, 198
"From a New Height" (Zanzotto) **65**:275-76
"From a Notebook" (Merrill) **28**:248
"From a Notebook, October '68—May '69" (Levertov) **11**:176, 180, 195
"From a Phrase of Simone Weil's and Some Words of Hegel's" (Oppen) **35**:335
"From a Railway Carriage" (Stevenson) **84**:315
"From a Stormy Night" (Rilke)
See "Aus einer Sturmnacht"
"From a Suburban Window" (Abse) **41**:9
"From a Survivor" (Rich) **5**:360
"From a Tower" (Montale)
See "Da una torre"
"From a Train Window" (Millay) **6**:214
"From a Train-Window" (Sarton) **39**:320
"From All Our Journeys" (Sarton) **39**:332, 337
"From Amsterdam" (Alurista) **34**:21, 23
"From an Almanac" (Baraka) **113**:5-7
"From an Island You Cannot Name" (Espada) **74**:123
"From an Old House in America" (Rich) **5**:373-74, 394
"From Ancient Fangs" (Viereck) **27**:263
"From Another Sore Fit" (Bradstreet) **10**:61-2
"From Brecht's A Short Organum for the Theatre" (Graham) **59**:137-38
"From Dawn to Noon" (Rossetti) **44**:169
"From Disaster" (Oppen) **35**:290, 297
"From Eastern Oregon" (Stafford) **71**:276, 298
"From Far Dakota's Cañons" (Whitman) **91**:278
"From far, from eve and morning" (Housman) **43**:245
From Feathers to Iron (Day Lewis) **11**:123-24, 128-30, 135, 138-39, 142, 148-52
"From Fortune's Reach" (Southwell) **83**:281

From Gloucester Out (Dorn) **115**:126, 135, 154
"From Gloucester Out" (Dorn) **115**:57
"From Grants to Gallup, New Mexico" (Ortiz) **17**:233
"From Her Boy" (Stevenson) **84**:347
"From Her in the Country" (Hardy) **92**:241, 246
"From here I see a road" (Castro)
See "Dend' aquí vexo un camiño"
"From Here to There" (Wagoner) **33**:337, 340, 345, 363
"From House to Home" (Rossetti) **7**:260-1, 276, 282, 284, 290
"From Little Acorns" (Enright) **93**:36
"From love's first fever to her plague" (Thomas) **52**:247, 334-35
From Man (Amichai)
See *Me'adam*
"From Memory" (Forché) **10**:135
"From Memory" (Zagajewski) **27**:396
"From Morpheus" (H. D.) **5**:270
"From My Diary, July, 1914" (Owen) **19**:338, 343, 346; **102**:184, 203, 225-26
"From My Journal" (Kinsella) **69**:129
"From My Notes for a Series of Lectures on Murder" (Smith) **12**:343
"From My Own Tomb-Stone" (Prior)
See "For My Own Monument"
"From Mythology" (Herbert) **50**:34
"From Newport to Rome" (Howe) **81**:21, 26
"From Orient Point" (Hacker) **47**:87
"From Pent-Up Aching Rivers" (Whitman) **91**:259
"From Perugia" (Whittier) **93**:269
"From Petrarch" (Smith)
See "Sonnet 13"
"From Room to Room" (Kenyon) **57**:26
From Room to Room (Kenyon) **57**:2, 4, 6, 19, 22-23, 26, 36, 39, 45
From Sand Creek (Ortiz)
See *From Sand Creek: Rising in This Heart Which Is Our America*
From Sand Creek: Rising in This Heart Which Is Our America (Ortiz) **17**:222, 230, 234, 239-240
"From Sea to Shining Sea" (Jordan) **38**:123
From Snow and Rock, from Chaos: Poems, 1965-1972 (Carruth) **10**:71, 91
"From something, nothing" (Piercy) **29**:315
"From Superstition" (Pasternak) **6**:260
"From the Anthill" (Shvarts) **50**:159
"From the Book of Local Miracles, Largely Unrecorded" (Goodison) **36**:154
From the Book of Myths (Carman) **34**:205, 208, 222
"From: The Book of the Dead Man" (Bell) **79**:41
From the Book of the Myths (Carman)
See *From the Book of Myths*
From the Book of the Valentines (Carman)
See *From the Book of Valentines*
From the Book of Valentines (Carman) **34**:205, 210, 226
From the Cables of Genocide: Poems on Love and Hunger (Cervantes) **35**:121, 132, 134, 135
"From the Cave" (Lorde) **12**:143
"From the Childhood of Jesus" (Pinsky) **27**:164, 175
"From the Coptic" (Smith) **12**:313-14
"From the Corpse Woodpiles, from the Ashes" (Hayden) **6**:194-95, 198
"From the Crest" (Berry) **28**:43
"From the Cupola" (Merrill) **28**:222-3, 226, 228, 234-5, 250, 257, 270
From the Cutting Room Floor (Merrill) **28**:269
"From the Dark Tower" (Cullen) **20**:57-58, 63, 70, 76
"From the Dressing Room" (McGuckian) **27**:98
"From the East of Life Joybeams Did Strike" (Tennyson) **101**:245
"From the Eleventh Finger" (Wakoski) **15**:350
"From the End" (Herbert)
See "Od konca"
"From 'The Enshrinement of the Ideal,' Part iv" (Spender) **71**:216
From the First Nine (Merrill) **28**:263
"From the First Underworld" (McGuckian) **27**:105
"From the Flats" (Lanier) **50**:56
"From the four points of the compass" (Castro)
See "Desde los cuatro puntos cardinales"
"From the Frontier of Writing" (Heaney) **18**:231-32
"From the Garden" (Sexton) **2**:351
"From the Gradual Grass" (Stafford) **71**:268, 287
From the Green Book of Bards (Carman) **34**:205, 209-10, 223
From the Green Book of the Bards (Carman)
See *From the Green Book of Bards*
"From the Hazel Bough" (Birney) **52**:8, 25, 85, 90-93
"From the Heart" (Castro)
See "¡Do íntimo!"
"From the House Journals" (Berrigan) **103**:34
"From the House of Yemanjá" (Lorde) **12**:151
"From the Land" (Castro)
See "Da terra"
"From the Lives of Things" (Zagajewski) **27**:389
"From the Lookout Rock" (Wilbur) **51**:291-92
"From the Mabinogion" (Duncan) **75**:198
"From the Motorway" (Tomlinson) **17**:354-55
"From the New World" (Graham) **59**:135, 156, 160
"From the Painting Back from Marketby Chardin" (Boland) **58**:46
"From the Paris Commune to the Kronstadt Rebellion" (Rexroth) **95**:270, 305, 307, 309, 332
"From the Reformation Journal" (Graham) **59**:189
"From the Rising of the Sun" (Milosz)
See "Gdzie wschodzi slonce i kêdy zapada"
From the Rising of the Sun (Milosz)
See *Gdzie wschodzi slonce i kêdy zapada*
"From the Same" (Belloc) **24**:32
"From The School Anthology: Albert Frolov" (Brodsky) **9**:4
"From the Sea" (Teasdale) **31**:322, 379
"From the Seacoast" (Tsvetaeva)
See "S morya"
"From the Shore" (Sandburg) **41**:364
From the Sick-Bed (Tagore)
See *Rogsajyae*
"From 'The Snow Lamp'" (Hayden) **6**:194-95
"From the Surface" (Pinsky) **27**:145
"From the Top of the Stairs" (Herbert) **50**:14, 43
"From the Top of the Stairs" (Zagajewski) **27**:382
"From the Wave" (Gunn) **26**:196-197, 204, 215
"From the Wellington Museum" (Wright) **14**:377
"From the White Place" (Song) **21**:331, 340
"From the Woolworth Tower" (Teasdale) **31**:331, 335
"From This Condensery" (Niedecker) **42**:103
From This Condensery: The Complete Writings of Lorine Niedecker (Niedecker) **42**:96-7, 102-3, 110, 118-25, 127, 135-41, 143-44, 148-52, 155, 167
From Threshold to Threshold (Celan)
See *Von Schwelle zu Schwelle*
"From thy far sources" (Clough) **103**:52
"From Time" (Dickey) **40**:236
From Time to Time (Ciardi) **69**:25, 31-35, 40, 55
"From Tuscan cam my ladies worthi race" (Surrey) **59**:315, 322
"From Virgil" (Oppen) **35**:314
"From What Country Are You?" (Cernuda)
See "De qué país eres tú?"
From Where the Sun Rises to Where It Sets (Milosz)
See *Gdzie wschodzi slonce i kêdy zapada*
"From Where We Sit: Corpus Christi" (Cervantes) **35**:113, 117
"Frondes Agrestes" (Tomlinson) **17**:315, 359
"A Front" (Jarrell) **41**:147, 149-50, 152, 173, 177, 189, 201
"Front de la rose" (Char) **56**:156
"Front Door Soliloquy" (Graves) **6**:143
"Front Lines" (Snyder) **21**:297, 319
The Front Matter: Dead Souls (Scalapino) **114**:284, 287-88, 297-301, 305, 319, 339
"Front the Ages with a Smile" (Masters) **1**:335
"The Frontier" (Masefield) **78**:44
"The Frontier" (Wright) **36**:398
"Frontispiece" (Komunyakaa) **51**:55
"Frontispiece" (Swenson) **14**:249, 253
"Die Frösche von Bikini" (Enzensberger) **28**:150
"Frost" (Thomas) **99**:241
"Frost at Midnight" (Coleridge) **11**:51, 53, 57-8, 84, 89, 97, 100, 102-04; **39**:169, 221; **67**:281; **100**:19-21, 25-26, 34
"Frost at Midnight" (Southey) **111**:193
Frost: Collected Poems, Prose, and Plays (Frost) **39**:256
"Frost Flowers" (Lawrence) **54**:185, 187
"The Frost of Death Was on the Pane" (Dickinson) **1**:104
"The Frost Spirit" (Whittier) **93**:270
"Frost-Bamboo Ranges" (Wang Wei) **18**:362
"Frostfeuer" (Stramm) **50**:202
"A Frosty Night" (Graves) **6**:141
"Froth" (Eberhart) **76**:54
"The Frowardness of the Elect in the Work of Conversion" (Taylor) **63**:212
"The Frozen City" (Nemerov) **24**:255
"The Frozen Greenhouse" (Hardy) **8**:92
"The Frozen Sea" (Merwin) **45**:7
Das Frühwerk (Celan) **10**:121
"Fruit" (Francis) **34**:244
"Fruit" (Mistral)
See "Fruta"
"Fruit" (Zagajewski) **27**:394
"Fruit from Travel Long Ago" (Melville) **82**:97
"The Fruit Gift" (Whittier) **93**:230, 239
"Fruit of the Flower" (Cullen) **20**:52-53, 86
"Fruit on a Straight-Sided Tray" (Boland) **58**:53, 58
"The Fruit Shop" (Lowell) **13**:78
"Fruitlands" (Toomer) **7**:323
"The Fruits of the Season" (Wright) **36**:311
"Frustration" (Parker) **28**:362
"Fruta" (Mistral) **32**:194-95
"fruto de bronce" (Alurista) **34**:37
"Fuerza blanca" (Storni) **33**:248
"Fuerzas" (Storni) **33**:294, 301
"La fuga" (Mistral) **32**:161, 181, 208, 210
"Fuga" (Pasolini) **17**:264
"La Fugitif" (Éluard) **38**:90-93
"The Fugitive" (Éluard)
See "La Fugitif"
"The Fugitive" (Lermontov) **18**:282
"The Fugitive" (Meynell) **112**:219-20
"The Fugitive" (Stryk) **27**:198
Fugitive (Tagore)
See *Palātakā*
Fugitive Pieces (Byron) **16**:86; **95**:21, 23, 29-30, 33
"The Fugitive's Wife" (Harper) **21**:206
"El fugitivo" (Neruda) **4**:292
"Fugue for Ann Griffiths" (Thomas) **99**:254, 276, 311, 313
"A Fugue of Wings" (Sarton) **39**:342
The Führer Bunker (Snodgrass) **74**:315-23, 325
"Fuisse" (Zanzotto) **65**:263
"Fuite d'Enfance" (Smith) **12**:325, 344
"Fukú!" (Yevtushenko) **40**:357-58
Fukú (Yevtushenko) **40**:358
"Fulbright Scholars" (Hughes) **89**:235, 270
"Fulfilment" (Pasternak) **6**:267

"Full Circle" (de la Mare) **77**:113
"Full Circle" (Viereck) **27**:267-68
"Full Fathom Five" (Plath) **1**:388-89; **37**:179, 181-82, 214, 216-21, 241, 243-45, 254
"Full Moon" (Graves) **6**:136, 151
"Full Moon" (Hayden) **6**:187, 194-95
"Full Moon" (Rexroth) **95**:322
"Full Moon" (Wylie) **23**:322
"Full Moon and Little Frieda" (Hughes) **7**:137, 142, 168; **89**:99, 110-11
"Full Moon New Guinea" (Shapiro) **25**:325
"The Full of Joy Do Not Know; They Need Not" (Eberhart) **76**:68, 73
"Full Well Yt Maye be Sene" (Wyatt) **27**:316
"Fullness" (Traherne) **70**:190, 271-72, 302, 313, 315, 332-33
"Fullnesse" (Traherne)
See "Fullness"
"Fulness" (Traherne)
See "Fullness"
"Fumatori di carta" (Pavese) **13**:225, 227
"Fundamental Disagreement with Two Contemporaries" (Rexroth) **20**:196
"The Funeral" (Brooks) **7**:53, 87
"The Funeral" (de la Mare) **77**:105, 129, 149
"Funeral Address" (Parra) **39**:278
"Funeral Anthem" (Hunt) **73**:134
"The Funeral Bell" (Thoreau) **30**:193
"Funeral Blues" (Auden) **92**:51
"Funeral Hymn" (Elliott) **96**:164
"The Funeral of Bobo" (Brodsky) **9**:8
"The Funeral of Sarpedon" (Cavafy) **36**:53, 108
"The Funeral of Youth" (Brooke) **24**:53, 78
"Funeral Rites" (Heaney) **18**:203-4, 210-11; **100**:223, 233
"A Funeral Toast" (Carducci)
See "Brindisi funebre"
"Funeral Tree of the Sokokis" (Whittier) **93**:172
"The Funerall" (Donne) **1**:130
"A Funerall Elegie" (Donne) **1**:146-47, 154-58; **24**:151, 184-85, 188
"The Funerall Rites of the Rose" (Herrick) **9**:126
"Funere mersit acerbo" (Carducci) **46**:38, 51, 76, 78
"Funes" (Borges)
See "Funes el memorioso"
"Funes el memorioso" (Borges) **32**:83
"Funes, His Memory" (Borges)
See "Funes el memorioso"
"Funes, the Memorious" (Borges)
See "Funes el memorioso"
"Funes the Memorious" (Borges)
See "Funes el memorioso"
"Fünf Gesänge" (Rilke) **2**:265-69, 273
"Fünf Gesänge August, 1914" (Rilke)
See "Fünf Gesänge"
"Funk" (Service) **70**:130
Funk Lore (Baraka) **113**:114
"Funland: A Poem in Nine Parts" (Abse) **41**:10, 16-17, 19-20, 22-3, 26, 28, 30-2
Funland and Other Poems (Abse) **41**:10, 12, 15-16, 28
"Funnel" (Sexton) **2**:345, 350; **79**:211
"Funny Stanzas to Don Juan" (Storni)
See "Divertidas estancias a don Juan"
"Für die Mouche" (Heine) **25**:148
Fureur et mystère (Char) **56**:112, 115, 131-32, 134-35, 141, 143, 145, 149-57, 161, 167, 177, 185-86, 188, 190, 200
"Furi alla Certosa di Bologna" (Carducci) **46**:52, 59
Die Furie des Verschwindens (Enzensberger) **28**:150, 159, 161, 163
"The Furies" (Masters) **1**:329, 343; **36**:176
"The Furies" (Sarton) **39**:342
"The Furies" (Sexton) **2**:367; **79**:239, 253
Furioso (Ariosto)
See *Orlando furioso di Ludovico Ariosto de Ferrara*
"Furious Versions" (Lee) **24**:240, 243, 248, 251
"The Furious Voyage" (Graves) **6**:130, 143
"Furniture Mover" (Simic) **69**:272
"The Furniture of a Woman's Mind" (Swift) **9**:295
Furor and Mystery (Char)
See *Fureur et mystère*
"Fürstin" (Goethe) **5**:249
"Further Arrivals" (Atwood) **8**:36, 39
"Further Instructions" (Pound) **95**:161
"Further Notes (taken from 'Abomunimus und Religion')" (Kaufman) **74**:211
A Further Range (Frost) **1**:195-97, 202; **39**:232-33
"Furthermore" (Howe) **81**:49
"The Fury of Abandonment" (Sexton) **79**:214
"The Fury of Aerial Bombardament" (Eberhart) **76**:8, 16, 19, 21, 24, 26, 42-43, 51, 58-59, 62, 66-67
"The Fury of Cocks" (Sexton) **79**:218
"The Fury of Flowers and Worms" (Sexton) **79**:215
"The Fury of Overshoes" (Sexton) **79**:213
"Fury Of Rain" (Harjo) **27**:66
"The Fury of Sundays" (Sexton) **2**:367, 373
"The Fury of Sunrises" (Sexton) **79**:201, 238, 243
"The Fury of the Cocks" (Sexton) **2**:371
"Fuscello teso" (Montale) **13**:134
"Les fusillés" (Hugo) **17**:101
"Futility" (Owen) **19**:330, 342, 347, 359, 365-68; **102**:143, 161, 167, 170-71, 264-65
"The Future" (Arnold) **5**:18, 43-5
"The Future" (Cohen) **109**:61, 63-64
"The Future" (Ignatow) **34**:306
The Future (Cohen) **109**:35, 62, 78, 98, 103
"Future and Past" (Barrett Browning) **6**:16
"Future Conditional" (Hacker) **47**:99
"The Future Life" (Bryant) **20**:4, 9
"Future Poetry" (Meynell) **112**:156
"Future Present" (Shapiro) **25**:324
"Future Religion" (Lawrence) **54**:197-98, 201, 203
"Futures" (Alexie) **53**:30
"Futuro" (Guillén) **23**:99
"Futuro" (Mistral) **32**:174
"Fuzzy-Wuzzy" (Kipling) **3**:156, 158, 167, 186-87
"G. W." (Whitney)
See "To her Brother. G. W."
"Gadan'e" (Tsvetaeva) **14**:312-14
"Gaiety" (Sitwell) **3**:294
"Gairmscoile" (MacDiarmid) **9**:188-89, 193
"Gakusei" (Ishikawa) **10**:215
"Le Galant Tireur" (Baudelaire) **106**:90
"Galatea Encore" (Brodsky) **9**:25, 27
"Galaxies are simpler" (Jacobsen) **62**:317
"Galerías Preciadas" (Fuertes) **27**:13-4
"Le galet" (Ponge) **107**:133, 135, 222-24
Galician Songs (Castro)
See *Cantares gallegos*
"Galla Placidia" (Ekeloef) **23**:60
Gallant Festivals (Verlaine)
See *Fêtes galantes*
"Galleria Umberto I" (Hugo) **68**:285
"The Gallery" (Marvell) **10**:271, 300
A Gallery of Harlem Portraits (Tolson) **88**:234, 248-58, 261, 264, 267, 274, 278, 281, 305, 336-37, 343, 345
"The Galley" (Kipling) **3**:182
"The Galley-Slave" (Kipling) **3**:157
Gallician songs (Castro)
See *Cantares gallegos*
"Una gallina" (Storni) **33**:296
"Gallo cedrone" (Montale) **13**:108, 111
"The Galloping Cat" (Smith) **12**:311
"Galloping Horses" (Bly) **39**:38, 42
"The Gallows" (Thomas) **53**:278, 295, 317
"The Gallows" (Whittier) **93**:356-57, 359
Galoots (Sandburg) **41**:251
"Galope muerto" (Neruda) **64**:337
"Galw ar Ddwynwen" (Dafydd ap Gwilym) **56**:211
"Galway Bay" (Barker) **77**:13
Gam ha'egrof haya pa'am yad ptuba ve'etsba'ot (Amichai) **38**:32
"The Gambler: A Ballet with Words" (Kavanagh) **33**:79
"Gambling in Stateline, Nevada" (Wright) **36**:341, 366
"The Game" (Abse) **41**:7
"The Game" (Corso) **108**:16
"The Game" (Glück) **16**:124
"Game after Supper" (Atwood) **8**:3
"The Game and the Poets" (Benét) **64**:52
"A Game at Salzburg" (Jarrell) **41**:139, 153, 173, 177, 185, 196, 208, 216
"The Game Between the Jews and the Indians Is Tied Going into the Bottom of the Ninth Inning" (Alexie) **53**:41
"Game Mistress" (Cassian) **17**:11
"A Game of Fives" (Carroll) **74**:8
"A Game of Monopoly in Chavannes" (Kumin) **15**:211
"A Game of Scrabble" (Jacobsen) **62**:302
"Gamecock" (Dickey) **40**:258
"Games" (Randall) **86**:291
"Games Two" (Wilbur) **51**:282
"Gamma" (Tolson) **88**:236, 269, 324-25
"Gammes de l'accordeur" (Char) **56**:187
"Gangrene" (Levine) **22**:212
"The Gangster's Death" (Reed) **68**:323, 325, 329, 332
"Ganymed" (Goethe) **5**:247, 254
"Ganymede" (Hölderlin) **4**:148, 166
"The Gap" (Thomas) **99**:261-62, 356
"The Gap" (Tomlinson) **17**:347
"A Garage in Co. Cork" (Mahon) **60**:146, 151, 189, 211
"Garage Sale" (Shapiro) **25**:322
"Garbo at the Gaumont" (McGuckian) **27**:107, 109-111
"The Garden" (Akhmadulina)
See "Sad"
"Garden" (Cernuda)
See "Jardín"
"The Garden" (Chappell) **105**:39
"The Garden" (Cowper) **40**:45, 48-52, 110, 123, 141-42
"The Garden" (Glück) **16**:130, 150-51, 168
"Garden" (Goodison)
See "Garden of the Women Once Fallen"
"Garden" (H. D.) **5**:275, 303
"The Garden" (Hall) **70**:9
"The Garden" (Marvell) **10**:266, 268, 271-73, 277, 283-85, 287-92, 294, 297, 311, 313-14, 318; **86**:178, 183, 190, 196, 204, 237
"The Garden" (Meynell) **112**:162, 190, 230
"The Garden" (Montale)
See "L'orto"
"The Garden" (Very) **86**:43, 151
The Garden (Glück) **16**:129
"Garden Abstract" (Crane) **3**:81
"Garden by Moonlight" (Lowell) **13**:64, 98
"Garden City" (Stafford) **71**:265
"Garden Fancies" (Browning) **61**:88
"The Garden in September" (Bridges) **28**:67, 83
"Garden Incident" (Spencer) **77**:330
The Garden: New and Selected Poetry and Prose (Akhmadulina)
See *Sad. Novye stikhi*
"The Garden of Boccaccio's" (Coleridge) **11**:104-09
"the garden of delight" (Clifton) **17**:36
"The Garden of Earthly Delights" (Milosz) **8**:181, 209
"The Garden of Epicurus" (Meredith) **60**:257
"The Garden of Gethsemane" (Pasternak) **6**:285
"Garden of Love" (Blake) **12**:7, 33; **63**:29-30, 92, 108, 134
"The Garden of Metrodorus" (Melville) **82**:75
"Garden of Nightingales" (Blok)
See "The Nightingale Garden"
"The Garden of Proserpine" (Swinburne) **24**:345

The Garden of the Prophet (Gibran) **9**:75
"The Garden of the White Rose" (Dorn) **115**:231, 233-34
"Garden of the Women Once Fallen" (Goodison) **36**:142, 154
"The Garden: On prospect of a fine day in early autumn" (Warren) **37**:283-84, 286, 288, 321-22, 331
"The Garden Party" (Belloc) **24**:27
"The Garden Party" (Davie) **29**:93
"The Garden Seat" (Hardy) **8**:100
"The Garden Sees" (Elytis) **21**:132
"The Garden Wall" (Levertov) **11**:169
"Garden Waters" (Warren) **37**:333
"Gardener" (Graves) **6**:151
"Gardener" (Silverstein) **49**:342, 347
"The Gardener" (Stevenson) **84**:299
Gardeners and Astronomers (Sitwell) **3**:321
"The Gardener's Daughter" (Tennyson) **6**:354; **101**:161
"The Gardens" (Oliver) **75**:286
"The Gardens of the Villa d'Este" (Hecht) **70**:82-83, 91, 97
"La gare" (Ponge) **107**:73, 132
"Gare" (Tzara) **27**:223-24
"Gare au bord de la mer" (Laforgue) **14**:76
"Gareth and Lynette" (Tennyson) **101**:198, 228, 230-32
"Gargoyle" (Sandburg) **41**:251, 270, 313
"The Garland" (Prior) **102**:317
Garland (Skelton)
See *The Garlande of Laurell*
"Garland for You" (Warren) **37**:332
The Garland of Good Will (Deloney) **79**:59
The Garland of Laurel (Skelton)
See *The Garlande of Laurell*
Garland of Laurell (Skelton)
See *The Garlande of Laurell*
Garland of Songs (Tagore)
See *Gitimālya*
Garlande (Skelton)
See *The Garlande of Laurell*
The Garlande of Laurell (Skelton) **25**:350-51, 353, 356, 369-75
"The Garrison of Cape Ann" (Whittier) **93**:247, 270, 344, 347
"Gas or Novacaine" (Rexroth) **95**:271
"Gaslight" (Raworth) **107**:332
Gasoline (Corso) **33**:5, 8, 13-15, 22, 35-6, 38-43, 45-48, 54; **108**:3, 32, 34-35
Gasoline/Vestal Lady (Corso) **108**:15-17, 19, 21-22, 24
"Gaspar Becerra" (Longfellow) **30**:88
"Gate" (Ai) **72**:12
"The Gate" (Muir) **49**:197, 249
"The Gate at the Center" (Olson) **19**:283
"The Gate in His Head" (Ondaatje) **28**:294, 296, 322, 327, 334
"The Gatekeeper" (Hughes) **89**:197, 199
"The Gates" (Rukeyser) **12**:224
The Gates (Rukeyser) **12**:220, 222, 225
The Gates of Paradise (Blake) **12**:46
"The Gates of the Arsenal" (Milosz) **8**:191
The Gates of Wrath: Rhymed Poems, 1948-1952 (Ginsberg) **4**:55-7, 63, 79, 91
"The Gateway" (Hope) **56**:279-80
"The Gateway" (Wright) **14**:338, 346
The Gateway (Wright) **14**:334, 336-38, 341, 345-46, 349, 354, 374
"Gather Ye Rosebuds while Ye May" (Herrick)
See "To the Virgins, to Make Much of Time"
"A Gathered Church" (Davie)
See *A Gathered Church: The Literature of the English Dissenting Interest, 1700-1930*
A Gathered Church: The Literature of the English Dissenting Interest, 1700-1930 (Davie) **29**:101, 112-13
"Gathering Apricots" (Milosz) **8**:212, 215
"Gathering Leaves" (Frost) **1**:218
The Gathering Storm (Empson) **104**:89-91, 97, 117, 126
Gathering the Tribes (Forché) **10**:132-35, 137, 141-43, 145, 148, 152, 156, 158, 165-66, 168-69
"GATSBY'S THEORY OF AESTHETICS" (Baraka) **4**:19, 24; **113**:152
"Le Gaucher" (Char) **56**:151
Gaudete (Hughes) **7**:154-58, 161-65, 171; **89**:101, 114-15, 119, 121, 124, 129-30, 137-38, 144-45, 151, 158-59, 194, 233-34
Gaudier-Brzeska: A Memoir, Including the Published Writings of the Sculptor and a Selection from His Letters (Pound) **95**:90
"Gauge" (Hughes) **53**:191
"Gauguin" (Walcott) **46**:242
"The Gaurus" (Gray) **80**:137, 250
Gautama the Enlightened and Other Verse (Masefield) **78**:91
"A gave in the West" (Davie) **29**:110
The Gavriiliada (Pushkin)
See *Gavriiliada*
Gavriiliada (Pushkin) **10**:364, 410-12
Gawain (Anonymous)
See *Sir Gawain and the Green Knight*
"Gay Chaps at the Bar" (Brooks) **7**:70, 73, 89
"Gay Cities" (Kavanagh) **105**:163
"The Gazers" (Cowley) **90**:114
"Gazing Intently at the Peaches and Plums in My Spring Garden" (Yakamochi) **48**:106
"Gazing on the Great Peak" (Tu Fu) **9**:329
"Gazing on the Peak" (Tu Fu) **9**:328
"Gde, vysokaya, tvoy tsyganyonok" (Akhmatova) **2**:12
"Gdzie wschodzi slonce i kêdy zapada" (Milosz) **8**:203-05
Gdzie wschodzi slonce i kêdy zapada (Milosz) **8**:174-75, 178, 186, 188, 195-97, 206-07
"Le Géante" (Baudelaire) **106**:126, 128
"Le géant blanc lépreux du paysage" (Tzara) **27**:226-28
"Gebet um Reinheit" (Werfel) **101**:349
"Gebete für den toten Bräutigam" (Sachs) **78**:111, 113, 132, 168, 191
"geburtsanzeige" (Enzensberger) **28**:135
"Der Geburtstag" (Benn) **35**:8
"Geddondillo" (Nash) **21**:269
Gedichte (Trakl) **20**:245, 250
Gedichte (Werfel) **101**:319, 344-50, 360
Gedichte aus den Jahren 1908-1945 (Werfel) **101**:349-50, 360-61
Gedichte aus dreßig Jahren (Werfel) **101**:344, 350, 360
Gedichte, 1853 und 1854 (Heine) **25**:146, 161, 178
Gedichte 1938-1944 (Celan) **10**:121-24, 129
Gedichte: 1955-1970 (Enzensberger) **28**:159
"The Geese" (Graham) **59**:185
"The Geese" (Sarton) **39**:361
"Geese Gone Beyond" (Snyder) **21**:308
"Gefallen" (Stramm) **50**:202, 218
"Geffreidos" (Davenant)
See "Jeffereidos"
"gegen die lämmer" (Enzensberger) **28**:135
"Gegen-Strophen" (Rilke) **2**:295
"Gehazi" (Kipling) **3**:171, 182
"Geheimnis brach aus dem Geheimnis: Sohar: Schöpfungskapitel" (Sachs) **78**:121
Gehirne (Benn) **35**:3
"Der Geist" (Werfel) **101**:346
"Gekishi: Chimmoku no koe" (Ishikawa) **10**:213
"Gemini" (Wilbur) **51**:301
"Gen. Rodimestev's Story (Stalingrad)" (Niedecker) **42**:151
"The Genealogy of My Hero" (Pushkin)
See "Rodoslovnaya Moego Geroya"
"The General" (Sassoon) **12**:268
"General Bloodstock's Lament for England" (Graves) **6**:143
"A General Communion" (Meynell) **112**:221
"The General Elliot" (Graves) **6**:150
"General Joubert" (Kipling) **91**:144
"General Martínez" (Dalton) **36**:127
"General Prologue" (Chaucer) **19**:13, 15, 23-5, 34-6, 43-5, 50-2, 54, 60; **58**:231-2, 242, 247, 264-5, 272, 288, 342
"The General Prologue to The Canterbury Tales" (Chaucer)
See "General Prologue"
"The General Public" (Benét) **64**:21, 49, 51-52, 55
"General Quiroga Rides to His Death in a Carriage" (Borges)
See "El General Quiroga va en coche al muere"
"El General Quiroga va en coche al muere" (Borges) **32**:84
General Song (Neruda)
See *Canto general de Chile*
"General William Booth Enters into Heaven" (Lindsay) **23**:267, 276-78, 289, 294, 297
General William Booth Enters into Heaven, and Other Poems (Lindsay) **23**:264, 278, 282-83, 292
"The Generals" (Ferlinghetti) **1**:183
"Generals" (Silverstein) **49**:313, 347
"Generation" (Clifton) **17**:26
"Generation" (Page) **12**:177
"Generation III" (Lorde) **12**:143
Generation Risen (Masefield) **78**:81, 89, 100
Generations: A Memoir (Clifton) **17**:23, 25-27, 32
"The Generations of Men" (Frost) **1**:193
"Una generazione" (Pavese) **13**:213
"The Generous Enemy" (Borges) **32**:95
"Genesis" (Knight) **14**:52
"Genesis" (MacNeice) **61**:125
"Genesis" (Roethke) **15**:291-96
"Genesis" (Shapiro) **25**:284
"Genesis" (Winters) **82**:320
Genesis: Book One (Schwartz) **8**:283-84, 301, 304, 308-10
"Genesis of After the Cries of the Birds" (Ferlinghetti) **1**:186
"Genetic Expedition" (Dove) **6**:122
"Geneva Restored" (Tomlinson) **17**:311, 359
"Genevieve" (Lorde)
See "Memorial II"
"Genevieve and Alexandra" (Robinson) **1**:470
"Genghis Chan: Private Eye I" (Yau) **61**:350
"Genghis Chan: Private Eye III" (Yau) **61**:353
"Genghis Chan: Private Eye IV" (Yau) **61**:351
"Genghis Chan: Private Eye VI" (Yau) **61**:352
"Genghis Chan: Private Eye VII" (Yau) **61**:353
"Genghis Chan: Private Eye VIII" (Yau) **61**:352-53
"Genghis Chan: Private Eye XIX" (Yau) **61**:354
"Genghis Chan: Private Eye XXII" (Yau) **61**:353
"Genghis Chan: Private Eye XXIV" (Yau) **61**:355
"Genghis Chan: Private Eye XXIX" (Yau) **61**:357
"Genghis Chan: Private Eye XXV" (Yau) **61**:336
"Genghis Chan: Private Eye XXX" (Yau) **61**:357
"Génie" (Rimbaud) **3**:261-62; **57**:171, 173-75, 194, 251, 265, 282
"Le génie dans l'obsurité" (Lamartine) **16**:290
"The Genie in the Bottle" (Wilbur) **51**:205
"Genie's Prayer under the Kitchen Sink" (Dove) **6**:123
"The Genius" (Cohen) **109**:4, 56-58
"The Genius" (MacLeish) **47**:192
"Genius" (Rimbaud)
See "Génie"
The Genius of the Thames: A Lyric Poem, in Two Parts (Peacock) **87**:307, 309-12, 316-19, 322-23, 325-31, 337, 341-44, 346-49
"Gente che non capisce" (Pavese) **13**:218, 227
"Gentle Armour" (Hunt) **73**:137, 150
"Gentle Lady" (Joyce)
See "XXVIII"
"Gentle Reader" (Jacobsen) **62**:277, 301, 324

"Gentle Shepherd!" (Collins) **72**:42
"The Gentle Weight Lifter" (Ignatow) **34**:286, 316
The Gentle Weight Lifter (Ignatow) **34**:271, 274-76, 279-80, 311, 314, 325
"The Gentleman Farmer" (Crabbe) **97**:95-97, 102, 104
"The Gentleman from Shallot" (Bishop)
See "The Gentleman of Shallot"
"The Gentleman of Shallot" (Bishop) **3**:37; **34**:52, 189
"Gentleman-Rankers" (Kipling) **3**:161
"A Gentleman's Bedroom" (Ní Chuilleanáin) **34**:349, 353
"Gentlemen, I Address You Publicly" (Rexroth) **20**:184; **95**:270
"The Gentlest Lady" (Parker) **28**:362
"Geographers" (Shapiro) **25**:270
"The Geographic Center" (Kumin) **15**:215-16
Geography (Dorn) **115**:78, 104, 119, 122, 126-28, 135-37, 140, 154-57, 219-20, 228, 237
Geography III (Bishop) **3**:48-9, 63, 66, 69, 73, 75; **34**:54, 59, 94-97, 111, 139, 146, 158, 174, 176, 188, 193
The Geography of Lograire (Merton) **10**:334-35, 338, 348, 351
"Geography of the Trinity Corona" (Cruz) **37**:10
"Geometric Poem" (Corso) **33**:18, 24-5, 49; **108**:11-13, 20
"Geometry" (Ransom) **61**:267, 293-94
"George" (Randall) **86**:285, 288-89, 302, 305, 343, 346
"George Gray" (Masters) **36**:170
"George Jackson" (Dylan) **37**:62
"George Meredith, 1828-1909" (Hardy) **92**:255, 326
"George Moore" (Moore) **49**:113-14
"George Trimble" (Masters) **36**:182
"George Washington and the Invention of Dynamite" (Wakoski) **15**:358
"George Washington and the Loss of His Teeth" (Wakoski) **15**:357
The George Washington Poems (Wakoski) **15**:324, 357-58
"George Washington: the Whole Man" (Wakoski) **15**:359
"Georgeline" (Rose) **13**:236
"Georges Braque" (Éluard) **38**:71
"Georgia Dusk" (Toomer) **7**:310, 319-20, 334
"Georgians" (Muir) **49**:228
"Geórgicas" (Guillén) **35**:229
Georgics (Vergil) **12**:358-61, 364-66, 370-71, 373-77, 383, 385-86, 391-92
"Georgie Grimes" (Brown) **55**:154
"Geraldine" (Brontë) **8**:67, 73-4
"Geranium" (Dorn) **115**:125
"Geraniums" (Hogan) **35**:257
"Gerard Manley Hopkins" (Clarke) **112**:91, 93, 122
"Geriatric" (Thomas) **99**:324
Der Gerichtstag (Werfel) **101**:300-301, 308, 318-19, 321, 324, 326, 348-49, 358-61
"The German Girls! The German Girls!" (MacLeish) **47**:149, 190, 255
"Germanien" (Hölderlin) **4**:149
Germany: A Winter's Tale (Heine)
See *Deutschland: Ein Wintermärchen*
"Gerontion" (Day Lewis) **11**:151
"Gerontion" (Eliot) **5**:160-62, 165, 171, 173, 183-85, 189, 195-97, 204, 209
"Gerontion" (Tate) **50**:285
Gerontofagia pero (Dalton) **36**:129
"Gerry's Jazz" (Komunyakaa) **51**:34
"Gertha's Lovers" (Morris) **55**:331
Gesammelte Gedichte (Benn) **35**:8
Gesammelte Werke (Celan) **10**:100-01, 124
Gesammelte Werke: Das lyrische Werk (Werfel) **101**:345-49
"Gesang der Geister über den Wassern" (Goethe) **5**:239
"Gesang der Memnonssäule" (Werfel) **101**:322
"Gesang des Abgeschiedenen" (Trakl) **20**:240-41
"Gesänge" (Benn) **35**:45, 47, 72
"Gesänge I" (Benn) **35**:26, 31
"Gesänge II" (Benn) **35**:31
"Gesta maximalista" (Borges) **22**:92
"Gestalt at Sixty" (Sarton) **39**:340
"The Gesture" (Oppen) **35**:299
"A Gesture by a Lady with an Assumed Name" (Wright) **36**:335
"A Gesture Toward an Unfound Renaissance" (Stafford) **71**:379
Gesualdo (Hejinian) **108**:267
"Get hence foule Griefe, the canker of the minde" (Sidney) **32**:250
"Get the Gasworks" (Ignatow) **34**:341
"Gethsemane" (Kipling) **3**:171
"Gethsemani" (Lamartine) **16**:297
Gethsemani, Ky. (Cardenal) **22**:103, 125-26
"Getting Down to Get Over" (Jordan) **38**:124
"Getting in the Wood" (Snyder) **21**:300, 302
"Getting There" (Plath) **1**:412; **37**:202, 241, 258
"Getting There" (Wagoner) **33**:352, 362-63
"Getting Things Straight" (Welch) **62**:337-38, 346, 361
"Getting Throught" (Merrill) **28**:248
"Getting to the Heart of the Poem" (Corso) **108**:3
"Getting to the Poem" (Corso) **33**:35-6
"Getting Up Early" (Bly) **39**:76
"Gettysburg: July 1, 1863" (Kenyon) **57**:12, 20, 44
"Gettysburg. The Check" (Melville) **82**:133
"Geue place ye louers" (Surrey) **59**:306-9, 330
"gewimmer und firmament" (Enzensberger) **28**:136
"Gewisse Lebensabende" (Benn) **35**:9
"Gewitter" (Stramm) **50**:172
"Das Gewitter" (Trakl) **20**:237-38, 251, 257
"The Geysers" (Gunn) **26**:198, 204, 208, 220
"Ghazal at Full Moon" (Jordan) **38**:145
"Ghede Poem" (Mackey) **49**:3
"Ghetto" (Borges)
See "Judería"
"Ghetto Girls" (Randall) **86**:334
"A Ghost" (Baudelaire)
See "Un fantôme"
"The Ghost" (de la Mare) **77**:148
"Ghost" (Lowell) **3**:203
"The Ghost" (Teasdale) **31**:356
"A Ghost, A Real Ghost" (Jarrell) **41**:153, 158, 169
"Ghost Crabs" (Hughes) **7**:137, 158-59; **89**:103, 149
"The Ghost Hammer" (Pinsky) **27**:158
"Ghost House" (Frost) **39**:246
"The Ghost in the Trunk of the Car" (Espada) **74**:158
"A Ghost May Come" (Ginsberg) **4**:74
"Ghost of a Chance" (Rich) **5**:363, 370
"The Ghost of the Past" (Hardy) **92**:295-96, 374
"The Ghost Ship" (Strand) **63**:153
"Ghosts" (Oliver) **75**:285, 287, 299-300
"Ghosts" (Sexton) **2**:350
"Ghosts, Angels, Unicorns" (Abse) **41**:22
"Ghosts as Cocoons" (Stevens) **6**:297
"Ghosts at Garnet" (Hugo) **68**:287
"Ghosts in a Field of Mint" (Hugo) **68**:253
"The Ghost's Leave-taking" (Plath) **1**:381, 388; **37**:182
"Ghosts of 1619" (Hughes) **53**:152
"Ghosts of a Lunatic Asylum" (Benét) **64**:23
"The Ghosts of the Buffaloes" (Lindsay) **23**:275, 279, 287
"The Ghost's Petition" (Rossetti) **7**:273
"Già la pioggia è con noi" (Quasimodo) **47**:281
"Giacometti" (Wilbur) **51**:186
Giambi ed epodi (Carducci) **46**:8, 13, 37, 47, 50, 73, 80, 89
"The Giant Puffball" (Blunden) **66**:4
"Giant Toad" (Bishop) **3**:65
"Giant Turtle" (Corso) **33**:48
"The Giant's Wife" (Carducci)
See "La Moglie del Gigante"
"The Giaour" (Elliott) **96**:157, 183
The Giaour (Byron)
See *The Giaour: A Fragment of a Turkish Tale*
The Giaour: A Fragment of a Turkish Tale (Byron) **16**:91-92; **95**:55, 57
"The Giaour and the Pacha" (Wilbur) **51**:186-88, 192, 327
"The Gibber" (Roethke) **15**:262
"Gibraltar" (Hughes) **89**:189
"Gibson" (Baraka) **4**:30
"Gic to Har" (Rexroth) **20**:193
"Gidget Agonistes" (Ashbery) **26**:137
"The Gift" (Bukowski) **18**:5
"Gift" (Cohen) **109**:53
"The Gift" (Carver) **54**:23
"The Gift" (Glück) **16**:151
"The Gift" (H. D.) **5**:266, 270, 303
"The Gift" (Lee) **24**:240
"Gift" (Milosz) **8**:209
"Gift" (Tagore)
See "Upahar"
"The Gift" (Teasdale) **31**:344
"The Gift" (Williams) **7**:371
"Gift for a Believer" (Levine) **22**:223, 225
"The Gift of a Satin Brocade" (Tu Fu) **9**:318
"The Gift of Fire" (Mueller) **33**:174
"The Gift of God" (Robinson) **1**:462, 467-68
"The Gift of Harun Al-Rashid" (Yeats) **20**:319; **51**:72
"The Gift of the Sea" (Kipling) **3**:183
"The Gift Outright" (Frost) **1**:212-13, 224
"Gift Poem" (Rukeyser) **12**:231
"Gift to a Jade" (Wickham) **110**:275, 277, 299
"The Gift to Be Simple" (Chappell) **105**:20
Gifts at Meeting (Wylie) **23**:320
"Gifts of Rain" (Heaney) **18**:201, 210; **100**:194-95, 233, 269, 295, 337
"The Gifts of the Terek" (Lermontov)
See "Dary Tereka"
"Gigolo" (Plath) **37**:258
"Gigot Sleeves" (McGuckian) **27**:107-109
"Gil angeli elettial gran bene infinito" (Michelangelo) **103**:186
"A Gilded Lapse of Time" (Schnackenberg) **45**:331-33, 341
A Gilded Lapse of Time: Poems (Schnackenberg) **45**:331, 333-34, 339, 342-43, 345-50
"The Gilded Man" (Ai) **72**:3, 5
Gilgamesh (Anonymous)
See *The Epic of Gilgamesh*
Gilgamesh Epic (Anonymous)
See *The Epic of Gilgamesh*
Gilgamish (Anonymous)
See *The Epic of Gilgamesh*
"Gilles" (Spender) **71**:178
"The Gilliflower of Gold" (Morris) **55**:299, 301
"Gin" (Levine) **22**:220
"La ginestra" (Leopardi) **37**:79-80, 92-93, 98, 102-3, 107, 109, 111-12, 118, 124-25, 132-33, 156-60
"Ginga no jo" (Matsuo Basho) **3**:13
"Gino" (Das) **43**:73, 87-88
"Ginsberg (for Allen)" (Kaufman) **74**:195
"Ginza Samba" (Pinsky) **27**:175
"Giorgio de Chirico" (Éluard) **38**:69-70, 103-5
"Giorgionismo" (Melville) **82**:38
Giorno dopo giorno (Quasimodo) **47**:266, 281-85
"Giorno e notte" (Montale) **13**:111
"Una giovane donna di Tolosa" (Cavalcanti) **114**:223, 238
"Giovanni and the Indians" (Page) **12**:168
"Giovanni Franchi" (Loy) **16**:333
"Giovanni's Rape of the Sabine Women at Wildenstein's" (Oppen) **35**:311, 312
"The Gipsies" (Mahon) **60**:134, 209

Gipsies (Pushkin)
See *Tsygany*
"Gipsies in the Snow" (Masefield) **78**:99
"Gipsies Revisited" (Mahon) **60**:134
Gipsy Ballads (Lorca)
See *Primer romancero gitano*
"A Girl" (Wright) **36**:396
"A Girl and a Bird" (Dafydd ap Gwilym)
See "Merch ac Aderyn"
"Girl Beatnik" (Yevtushenko) **40**:345
"Girl Child" (Benét) **64**:8, 14
"Girl Drowned in a Well" (García Lorca) **3**:139
"The Girl Engaged to the Boy Who Died" (Stafford) **71**:289
"A Girl in a Library" (Jarrell) **41**:140, 158-59, 171, 185, 189-91, 210-11, 216-17
"A Girl in a Window" (Wright) **36**:315, 336
"Girl in a Yellow Dress" (Thomas) **99**:305-6
A Girl in Winter (Larkin) **21**:225, 232
"The girl of live marble" (Gunn) **26**:212
"The girl outside your window . . ." (Snodgrass) **74**:334
"Girl Powdering Her Neck" (Song) **21**:347
"A Girl Sewing" (Szirtes) **51**:158
"The Girl the North Wind Brought" (Elytis) **21**:123
"The Girl Toy" (Cohen) **109**:4
"A Girl Walking into a Shadow" (Wright) **36**:396
"The Girl Who Died No. 1" (Walker) **30**:339
"The Girl Who Died No. 2" (Walker) **30**:339, 365
"The Girl Who Loves to Shoot" (Smith) **12**:326
"Girls Bathing, Galway, 1965" (Heaney) **18**:224
"Girls in the Plural" (McGuckian) **27**:92-94
"Girls in their Season" (Mahon) **60**:138
"A Girl's Mood" (Reese) **29**:331
"The Girls of Llanbadarn" (Dafydd ap Gwilym)
See "Merched Llanbadarn"
"Girls on the Bridge" (Mahon) **60**:148, 201-2
"The Girls on the Pier" (Mahon) **60**:200
"Girl's Song" (Bogan) **12**:90, 100
"Girls Working in Banks" (Shapiro) **25**:306, 322
"Gislebertus' Eve" (Berryman) **64**:96
"Git Dough" (Guillén)
See "Búscate plata"
Gitāli (Tagore) **8**:413, 427
"Gitanes" (Raworth) **107**:275
Gitanjali (Tagore) **8**:402, 412-14, 416, 418
Gitimālya (Tagore) **8**:413
"Giunto è già 'l corso della vita mia" (Michelangelo) **103**:275, 283, 306
"Giuseppe Caponsacchi" (Browning) **2**:41
"La giustizia pia del lavoro" (Carducci) **46**:65
"Give All to Love" (Emerson) **18**:85, 88, 113
"Give and Take" (Meredith) **28**:199
"Give me your patience, sister, while I frame" (Keats) **96**:206
"Give Way, Ye Gates" (Roethke) **15**:252, 261, 298-99, 301-02
Give Your Heart to the Hawks and Other Poems (Jeffers) **17**:135, 142-43, 147
"A Given Grace" (Tomlinson) **17**:309, 316, 335
"The Given Love" (Cowley) **90**:12-13, 35, 114
"Given to Li Po" (Tu Fu) **9**:330
"The Giver" (Teasdale) **31**:388
"Giving Myself Up" (Strand) **63**:150, 173-75, 198
The Giving Tree (Silverstein) **49**:305, 320-21, 346, 348-49
The Giving Tree and Other Shel Silverstein Songs (Silverstein) **49**:319
"Givings" (Ammons) **16**:63
"Gladiolus" (McGuckian) **27**:96
"Gladly Still" (Borges)
See "Jactancia de quietud"
"The Gladness of Nature" (Bryant) **20**:40
"Gladness of the Best" (Hecht) **70**:63-65, 108
"Gladstone Street" (Tomlinson) **17**:319
"The Glance" (Herbert) **4**:132
"A Glance from the Bridge" (Wilbur) **51**:209
"Glances" (Stafford) **71**:261
"Glanmore Eclogue" (Heaney) **100**:239, 328-30
"Glanmore Sonnets" (Heaney) **18**:198; **100**:231, 235, 239, 261, 287
"Glanmore Sonnets IV" (Heaney) **18**:238
"Glass" (Das) **43**:89
"Glass" (Francis) **34**:248
"The Glass" (Mistral)
See "El vaso"
"The Glass" (Olds) **22**:323, 332
"Glass" (Wakoski) **15**:325
"The Glass Air" (Page) **12**:178
The Glass Air (Page) **12**:189-90
"The Glass Essay" (Carson) **64**:199, 201, 204, 207, 209, 213, 217, 220, 231
A Glass Face in the Rain (Stafford) **71**:324, 329, 333, 343, 349, 352, 371, 376, 378
"Glass Falling" (MacNeice) **61**:133
"A Glass House" (Ní Chuilleanáin) **34**:382
Glass, Irony and God (Carson) **64**:199-200, 202, 204-5, 207, 210, 216-17, 221, 223, 225, 228-29, 231, 233-35
"The Glass King" (Boland) **58**:7
"A Glass of Water" (Sarton) **39**:339
"The Glass of Water" (Stevens) **110**:191, 201
"Glazed Glitter" (Stein) **18**:322
"The Gleaners" (Merwin) **45**:8
"Gleaning" (Jarrell) **41**:180, 210
Glen Apacheria (Dorn)
See *Recollections of Gran Apacheria*
"Gleneden's Dream" (Brontë) **8**:67
"Glengormley" (Mahon) **60**:132, 165, 181, 185, 191-92, 234
"Glimpse" (Hughes) **7**:153; **89**:142, 150
"Glimpse Between Buildings" (Stafford) **71**:284
"The Glimpse of the Coming Day" (Morris) **55**:339
"Glimpse of the Ice" (Merwin) **45**:20, 28
"Glimpses in the Woods" (Stafford) **71**:299
"The Global Lobal Blues" (Viereck) **27**:279
"Global Village" (Mahon) **60**:229
"The Globe in North Carolina" (Mahon) **60**:147-48, 151, 156, 172-74, 190, 194, 196-97, 215
"Globe of Gneiss" (Warren) **37**:314-15, 317
"La gloire" (Lamartine) **16**:276, 298
"Gloire de Dijon" (Lawrence) **54**:189, 191
"Gloria" (Francis) **34**:244
"Gloria de Carlos V" (Melville) **82**:5-6, 28, 36, 38
"The Glorious Epiphany" (Crashaw)
See "To the Glorious Epiphany"
"A Glorious Twilight" (Chappell) **105**:51
"The Glory" (Ciardi) **69**:54
"The Glory" (Thomas) **53**:275, 281-82
"The Glory Is fallen Out of" (Cummings) **5**:105
"The Glory of and Grace in the Church Set Out" (Taylor) **63**:284, 301
"The Glory of Ptolemies" (Cavafy) **36**:73, 75
"The Glory of the Day Was in Her Face" (Johnson) **24**:154
The Glory of the Nightingales (Robinson) **1**:472-73, 475, 479, 483
"Glory of Women" (Sassoon) **12**:267
"Glossary" (Brathwaite) **56**:86
Glossolalia Poéma o zvuke (Bely) **11**:9, 11
"Glove" (Abse) **41**:9
"The Glove" (Browning) **2**:29, 38
"The Glove and the Lions" (Hunt) **73**:162
"Glowing Enigmas" (Sachs)
See *Glühende Rätsel*
Glowing Enigmas (Sachs)
See *Glühende Rätsel*
"Glowing Riddles" (Sachs)
See *Glühende Rätsel*
Glowing Riddles (Sachs)
See *Glühende Rätsel*
"Glubokij neznyj sad, vpadajuscij v Oku" (Akhmadulina) **43**:18
"Glubokim golosom proroka" (Akhmadulina) **43**:3
"Glück der Entfernung" (Goethe) **5**:246
Glühende Rätsel (Sachs) **78**:110-11, 114, 161, 165, 170-74, 176-77, 211
"The Glutton" (Graves) **6**:150
"The Glutton" (Very) **86**:96
"Gnat-Psalm" (Hughes) **7**:136-37, 159; **89**:110-11, 157
"Gnessuluogo" (Zanzotto) **65**:277
"The Gnome, the Gnat, and the Gnu" (Silverstein) **49**:342
Gnomes and Occasions (Nemerov) **24**:284-86, 288
"Gnomic Verses" (Creeley) **73**:96
"The Gnomies" (de la Mare) **77**:129
"Gnothi Seauton" (Emerson) **18**:97
"Go" (Ai) **72**:10, 12, 19
"Go and Look for Bread" (Guillén)
See "Búscate plata"
"Go away!" (Hugo) **68**:267
"Go burning sighs" (Wyatt)
See "Goo burnyng sighes"
"Go by Brooks" (Cohen) **109**:18
"Go Down Death" (Johnson) **24**:128-29, 139, 144, 156, 164-65, 167, 169
"Go, Fetch to Me a Pint o' Wine" (Burns) **6**:76
"Go Fishing" (Hughes) **89**:133
"Go Get Money" (Guillén)
See "Búscate plata"
Go Go (Williams) **109**:267
"Go Home, The Act Is Over" (Abse) **41**:4
"Go it, Granny - Go it, Hog!" (Warren) **37**:346
"Go, Lovely Rose!" (Waller) **72**:271, 297, 336-37, 350, 360, 371, 376
"Go Slow" (Hughes) **53**:151-52
"Go to the Shine That's on a Tree" (Eberhart) **76**:34, 49, 68-69
"The Goal of Intellectual Man" (Eberhart) **76**:7, 24, 38, 51, 57
"Go-and-Get-the-Enemy-Blues" (Hughes) **53**:145
"Goat Ode in Mid-Dive" (Viereck) **27**:295
"The Goat of Slieve Donard" (Kavanagh) **33**:99, 103
"The Goatherds" (Winters) **82**:313, 317
"Goats and Monkeys" (Walcott) **46**:229-30, 283
"Goat's Leaf" (Marie de France)
See "Chevrefoil"
"Gobernador" (Guillén) **23**:127
The Goblet of Blizzards (Bely)
See *Kubok metelej: Chetviortiia simfoniia*
"The Goblet of Life" (Longfellow) **30**:13, 26, 37, 103
"Goblin Market" (Rossetti) **7**:259, 261, 266, 268, 272-3, 279-80, 282, 288-94, 298-304
Goblin Market, and Other Poems (Rossetti) **7**:259, 261, 279, 296-7
"Goblin Revel" (Sassoon) **12**:240
"The God" (Hughes) **89**:182
"God" (Swenson) **14**:281, 281, 286
The God (H. D.) **5**:303
"The God Abandons Antony" (Cavafy) **36**:7, 8, 20, 28, 40, 74, 76
"God and Devil" (Smith) **12**:331
"A God Came to a Man" (Crane) **80**:81
"God Curse Women" (Martí)
See "¡Dios las maldiga!"
God Desired and Desiring (Jiménez)
See *Dios deseado y deseante: Animal de fondo con numerosos poemas ineditos*
"God Fashioned the Ship of the World" (Crane) **80**:80, 98
"The God Forsakes Anthony" (Cavafy)
See "The God Abandons Antony"
"God Forsakes Antony" (Cavafy)
See "The God Abandons Antony"
"God Has Mercy on Kindergarten Children" (Amichai)
See "Elohim merakhem 'al yaldei hagan"
"God Has Pity on the Kindergarten Children" (Amichai)
See "Elohim merakhem 'al yaldei hagan"

"God Help the Wolf After Whom the Dogs Do Not Bark" (Hughes) **89**:273
"God in Woman" (Kavanagh) **33**:63, 137
"God Is a Distant, Stately Lover" (Dickinson) **1**:93
"God Is a Masturbator" (Corso) **108**:43
"God Is Love" (Prior) **102**:331
"God Lay Dead in Heaven" (Crane) **80**:80
"God Not Afar Off" (Very) **86**:166
"The God of Broken Things" (Komunyakaa) **51**:65
"The God of Flowers" (Levertov) **11**:198
"The God of the Poor" (Morris) **55**:340
"The God of Youth" (Hölderlin)
See "Der Gott der Jugend"
"God Pities the Kindergarten Children" (Amichai)
See "Elohim merakhem 'al yaldei hagan"
"God Said" (Ignatow) **34**:274
"God? She's Black" (Corso) **33**:49; **108**:7, 54
"God slain by Troops" (Niedecker) **42**:149
"God Speaks" (Smith) **12**:335
"God the Drinker" (Smith) **12**:326-27
"God the Eater" (Smith) **12**:326, 333
"God the Father in the Evening" (Werfel)
See "Gotvater am Abend"
"God to Hungry Child" (Hughes) **53**:116
"God Wills It" (Mistral)
See "Dios lo quiere"
"God Works in a Mysterious Way" (Brooks) **7**:74
Godbey (Masters) **1**:339
"God-closed Age" (Corso) **33**:49
"The Goddess" (Levertov) **11**:159, 168
"Goddess in the Wood" (Brooke) **24**:57
"Goddwyn" (Chatterton) **104**:3
Godel's Proof, New Poems 1965 (Rexroth) **20**:196; **95**:252, 255, 257, 268-69, 274, 326
"Godfather Death" (Sexton) **79**:191
"God-Forgotten" (Hardy) **8**:104, 121; **92**:262
"The Godhead as Lynx" (Sarton) **39**:342, 365, 367
"Godiva" (Hunt) **73**:162
"The Godmonger" (Sexton) **79**:214, 237
"GoDo" (Birney) **52**:83
"Godolphin Horne Who Was Cursed with the Sin of Pride and Became a Boot-Black" (Belloc) **24**:26
"Godred Crovan" (Chatterton) **104**:72
"Gods" (Cullen) **20**:53
"The Gods" (Merwin) **45**:21-2, 28, 49
"Gods" (Sexton) **2**:373; **79**:213
"God's Acre" (Longfellow) **30**:64
"Gods and Men" (Clarke) **112**:29
"The Gods Are Here" (Toomer) **7**:336
"God's Backside" (Sexton) **79**:211
"God's Beloveds Remain True" (Carson) **64**:233
"Gods Can Die" (Thumboo) **30**:300, 301, 322, 323, 329
Gods Can Die (Thumboo) **30**:299, 300, 303, 322, 328
"Gods Change, Prayers Are Here to Stay" (Amichai) **38**:48-51, 55-56
"God's Denunciations Against Pharoah Hophra" (Tennyson) **101**:193
Gods Determinations Touching His Elect: And the Elects Combat in Their Conversion, and Coming Up to God in Christ: Together with the Comfortable Effects Thereof (Taylor) **63**:203, 206, 210-11, 213-15, 217-18, 228, 231, 237-42, 264, 276-78, 280-85, 287-93, 295-98, 300-302, 315, 317-18, 321, 323, 347, 353
"God's Education" (Hardy) **8**:121; **92**:290
"God's Fatherly Care" (Very) **86**:166
"God's Funeral" (Hardy) **8**:131; **92**:290
"God's Host" (Very) **86**:165
"God's Providence" (Herrick) **9**:91
"Gods Selecting Love in the Decree" (Taylor) **63**:212, 279
"God's Skallywags" (Service) **70**:141
"God's Spies" (Howe) **54**:129
"God's Story" (Thomas) **99**:257, 261
God's Trombones: Seven Negro Sermons in Verse (Johnson) **24**:128-29, 132-33, 141, 143-44, 149, 152-56, 159, 161, 164-70
"God's Wheel" (Silverstein) **49**:328
"God's World" (Millay) **6**:205, 215; **61**:213, 222
"God's World" (Pasternak) **6**:268-69
"Godspeed" (Whittier) **93**:218
"God-Spell" (Duncan) **75**:121
"Goe, and catche a falling starre" (Donne)
See "Song. 'Goe, and catche a falling starre'"
"Goebbels Abandons His Novel and Joins the Party" (Cohen) **109**:89
Goethe's Roman Elegies (Goethe)
See *Römische Elegien*
Goethe's Works (Goethe) **5**:223
"Gofyn Cymod" (Dafydd ap Gwilym) **56**:246
"Gog" (Hughes) **7**:126, 139; **89**:101, 112, 137, 140-41
"The Go-goat" (Pavese)
See "Il Dio-Caprone"
"Goin' to Acapulco" (Dylan) **37**:59
"The Going" (Hardy) **8**:91, 113, 118, 133-35; **92**:318, 325, 329
"Going" (Larkin) **21**:227, 242
"Going Away" (Hagiwara)
See "Ryojō"
"Going Away" (Kenyon) **57**:15
"Going Away from the River" (Hacker) **47**:88
"Going Back to Oxford" (Ní Chuilleanáin) **34**:349, 351
"Going Back to the River" (Hacker) **47**:88
"Going Down" (Ignatow) **34**:342
Going for the Rain (Ortiz) **17**:222, 226-227, 231-232, 238, 244
"Going for Water" (Frost) **39**:230
"Going from the Capital to Feng-hsien, Singing My Feelings" (Tu Fu) **9**:332
"Going, Going, Gone" (Dylan) **37**:63-5
"Going Home" (Dickey) **40**:200
"Going Home" (Mahon) **60**:140, 184, 231-32
"Going Home" (Service) **70**:119
"Going Home" (Szymborska)
See "Powroty"
"Going On" (Stafford) **71**:371
"Going Out to Check the Ewes" (Bly) **39**:42-43
Going Places (Stafford) **71**:315, 318, 336, 342
"Going the Rounds: A Sort of Love Poem" (Hecht) **70**:88
"Going To and Fro" (Lowell) **3**:215
"Going to Church" (Patmore) **59**:233
"Going to Horse Flats" (Jeffers) **17**:141
"Going to Pieces" (Wagoner) **33**:333
"Going to Remake This World" (Welch) **62**:338, 346, 348, 370, 373-74
"Going to School" (Shapiro) **25**:291, 320, 326
"Going to the Bakery" (Bishop) **34**:116, 139, 141
"Going to the Warres" (Lovelace)
See "To Lucasta: Going to the Warres"
"Going to Walden" (Oliver) **75**:323
Going to War with All My Relations: New and Selected Poems (Rose) **13**:242
Going Up to Sotheby's (Spark) **72**:245-47, 255
"going uptown to visit miriam" (Cruz) **37**:22
"Gold" (Cowley) **90**:15
"Gold and Black" (Ondaatje) **28**:328
The Gold Cell (Olds) **22**:314-16, 318-21, 324, 326, 328
"Gold Coast Customs" (Sitwell) **3**:300, 305-06, 308-09, 314, 316, 319-20, 325-26
"Gold Flower" (Stern) **115**:249
"Gold Hair" (Browning) **2**:95
"The Gold Hesperidee" (Frost) **39**:235; **71**:22-23
Gold in Azure (Bely)
See *Zoloto v lazuri*
"The Gold Key" (Sexton) **2**:364; **79**:321-22
"The Gold Lily" (Glück) **16**:170
"The Gold Man on the Beckler" (Hugo) **68**:256
"The Gold of the Tigers" (Borges) **32**:66, 140
The Gold of the Tigers: Selected Later Poems (Borges)
See *El oro de los tigres*
"Gold on Oak Leaves" (Oppen) **35**:301
"A Gold Ring from the Tomb of Isopata" (Hope) **56**:292
"The Golden Age" (Behn) **13**:8, 22, 26, 32-34, 39; **88**:32, 86, 145, 147-53, 160-62, 165
"Golden Age" (Rimbaud)
See "Age d'or"
"The Golden Boat" (Tagore)
See "Sonar tari"
The Golden Boat (Tagore)
See *Sonar tari*
"The Golden Bough" (Mahon) **60**:151, 169, 195
"Golden Bough" (Wylie) **23**:314
"The Golden Boy" (Hughes) **89**:125
"Golden Brown Blues" (Hughes) **53**:136
The Golden Chains (Barker) **77**:23, 33, 40, 49
"The Golden Cockerel" (Reisman)
See "Skazka o Zolotom Petushke"
"TH GOLDEN DAWN" (Bissett) **14**:24, 32
"The Golden Echo" (Hopkins) **15**:125, 152
"The golden gates of sleep unbar" (Shelley) **14**:177
"Golden Hair" (Owen) **19**:338
The Golden Hynde and Other Poems (Noyes) **27**:117
The Golden Legend (Longfellow) **30**:16-18, 23-5, 35, 38-9, 56, 65, 73, 75
"Golden Milestone" (Longfellow) **30**:27, 42
"The Golden Net" (Blake) **12**:36
Golden Sardine (Kaufman) **74**:179, 181-82, 184-85, 194-95, 212-13, 216, 234-35, 238, 241, 250, 253, 268-69, 271, 275-76
"Golden Section" (Rexroth) **95**:273
"Golden Silences" (Rossetti) **7**:271
"The Golden Stool" (Brathwaite) **56**:86
"The Golden Supper" (Tennyson) **6**:374
"The Golden Targe" (Dunbar) **67**:34, 38, 42, 46, 54-58, 91-96, 101, 109, 120, 126
"The Golden Tortoise" (Darío)
See "La tortuga de oro..."
The Golden Treasury of Magazine Verse (Braithwaite) **52**:106-7
"Golden Venetian Light" (Olson) **19**:305
"The Golden Whales of California" (Lindsay) **23**:264, 269, 274, 288
"Golden Wings" (Morris) **55**:238, 267, 279, 282, 300-302
The Golden Year (Riley) **48**:327
"The Golden Year" (Tennyson) **101**:241
"Golders Green" (Melville) **82**:38
"Goldfish" (Bukowski) **18**:5
"Goldilocks and Goldilocks" (Morris) **55**:340
"goldner schnittmusterbogen zur poetischen wiederaufrüstung" (Enzensberger) **28**:136-37, 141
"The Goldsmith" (Sassoon) **12**:257
"The Golem" (Borges) **32**:60, 63
"Le golfe de Baïa" (Lamartine) **16**:277, 290, 302
"Le golfe de Genes" (Lamartine) **16**:266
"Golgotha" (Kennedy) **93**:132, 142
"Golgotha" (Sassoon) **12**:261-62
"Goliath of Gath. 1 Sam. Chap. XVII" (Wheatley) **3**:354-55, 357-61
"Golliardic Song" (Hecht) **70**:108
"Golos proshlogo" (Bely) **11**:24
"El golpe" (Neruda) **4**:288
Gondibert: An Heroic Poem (Davenant) **99**:157-62, 167-73, 175-77, 179, 183-87, 194, 202-4, 206-7, 209-11, 219, 226
"Gone" (Heaney) **18**:201
"Gone" (Montague) **106**:292
"Gone" (Sandburg) **2**:303, 316; **41**:242, 312, 318, 336
"Gone?" (Thomas) **99**:270, 312, 357
"Gone, Gone Again" (Thomas)
See "Blenheim Oranges"
"Gone, Gone, Gone" (Bly) **39**:72-72

"Gone the Last Danger on Earth" (Corso) **33**:49; **108**:6
"Goner's Boner" (McHugh) **61**:208
"The Gong-gong" (Brathwaite) **56**:6
"Góngora" (Cernuda) **62**:175
"Goo burnyng sighes" (Wyatt) **27**:352
"Good Advice" (Stone) **53**:256-57
"Good and Bad Children" (Stevenson) **84**:344
"A Good Boy" (Stevenson) **84**:343-44
"Good By Ladies" (Kavanagh) **105**:164
"A Good Day for Seeing Your Limitations" (Hugo) **68**:260
"The Good Fight" (Cohen) **109**:27
The Good Fight (Kinsella) **69**:141
"Good Frend" (H. D.) **5**:297, 302
"Good Friday" (Clampitt) **19**:81, 88
"Good Friday" (Donne)
See "Goodfriday 1613: Riding Westward"
"Good Friday" (Herbert) **4**:120
"Good Friday" (Rossetti) **7**:268, 283
"Good Friday" (Snodgrass) **74**:284
"Good Friday and Easter Morning" (Ammons) **16**:63
Good Friday and Other Poems (Masefield) **78**:44, 55, 63, 92
"Good Friday on the Bus" (Stone) **53**:223
"Good Friday: Rex Tragicus, or Christ Going to His Crosse" (Herrick) **9**:109, 121
"Good Friday, Riding Westward" (Ní Chuilleanáin) **34**:363
Good Intentions (Nash) **21**:266
A Good Journey (Ortiz) **17**:224-27, 229-30, 232-33, 240, 244
"A Good Knight in Prison" (Morris) **55**:299, 301-2
"Good ladies, you that have your pleasure in exyle" (Surrey) **59**:297, 306-7, 310, 352
"The Good Life" (Hughes) **7**:119
Good Luck in Cracked Italian (Hugo) **68**:237, 249, 265-66, 271, 273, 281, 283, 291
"A Good Man" (Riley) **48**:301
"The Good Man" (Werfel)
See "Der gute Mensch"
"Good Man, Bad Woman" (Stevens) **110**:91, 97
"A Good Man in a Bad Time" (MacLeish) **47**:206
"The Good Man in Hell" (Muir) **49**:197, 202
"A Good Memory" (Komunyakaa) **51**:36
"Good men, shew, if you can tell" (Campion) **87**:57, 67, 89-90
"Good Morning" (Hughes) **53**:193
"Good Morning, America" (Sandburg) **2**:330; **41**:288-89, 339, 341, 346
Good Morning, America (Sandburg) **2**:318-19, 321, 323; **41**:271, 274-75, 277, 284, 302, 319, 325, 330
"Good Morning Revolution" (Hughes) **1**:268; **53**:144
Good Morning, Revolution: Uncollected Social Protest Writings (Hughes) **53**:110-13
Good News About the Earth (Clifton) **17**:16, 22-24, 26, 35
"A Good Night" (Montague) **106**:245, 340
"Good Night" (Williams) **7**:348
"The Good, Old-Fashioned People" (Riley) **48**:300, 353
"The Good Part" (Longfellow) **30**:48
"A Good Play" (Stevenson) **84**:313, 317, 346, 348
"The Good Servant" (Wilbur) **51**:188
"Good Ships" (Ransom) **61**:301, 309, 311
The Good Song (Verlaine)
See *La bonne chanson*
"A Good Time Going" (Holmes) **71**:68
A Good Time Was Had by All (Smith) **12**:292, 314-15, 317, 325
Good Times: Poems (Clifton) **17**:16-17, 20-21, 23-24, 26, 31, 35
"The Good Town" (Muir) **49**:197, 205, 229, 256, 258, 265, 277, 282-83, 299
Good Woman: Poems and a Memoir, 1969-1980 (Clifton) **17**:25-26, 38
"Good-By, Jim" (Riley) **48**:290
"Goodbye!" (Baraka) **4**:11
"Goodbye" (Betjeman) **75**:13, 96
"Good-bye" (Emerson) **18**:74
"Goodbye" (Kinnell) **26**:292
"Goodbye Christ" (Hughes) **1**:268; **53**:144
"Goodbye, Morbid Bear" (Stern) **115**:259
Goodbye Spring (Seifert)
See *Jaro sbohem*
"Goodbye to Great Spruce Head Island" (O'Hara) **45**:163
"Goodbye to Illinois" (Dorn) **115**:120
"Goodbye to London" (MacNeice) **61**:177
"Goodbye to Serpents" (Dickey) **40**:192
"Good-bye to the Mezzogiorno" (Auden) **1**:17
"Goodbye to the Poetry of Calcium" (Wright) **36**:304, 340, 371
"Goodbye, Unwashed Russia" (Lermontov) **18**:281
"Goodfriday 1613: Riding Westward" (Donne) **1**:139, 158-59; **43**:118, 121-22, 133, 148-49, 178-79
"Goodman Jacksin and the Angel" (Barker) **77**:16, 18, 39
"Goo-dmore-ning(en" (Cummings) **5**:107
"Goodmorning with Light" (Ciardi) **69**:11
"The Good-Morrow" (Amichai) **38**:43
"The good-morrow" (Donne) **1**:125, 130-34, 147, 152-54; **43**:128, 133
"Goodness" (Traherne) **70**:194, 196-97, 275, 277-78, 289, 312, 317-18
"Goodnesse" (Traherne)
See "Goodness"
"Good-Night" (Heaney) **100**:206
"Goodnight" (Lee) **24**:241
"The Goodnight" (Ondaatje) **28**:318
"Goodnight Laides, Goodnight Sweet Ladies" (Walcott) **46**:230
Goodnight Willie Lee, I'll See You in the Morning (Walker) **30**:346, 348-50, 353-55
"Goody Blake and Harry Gill" (Wordsworth) **4**:381, 414; **67**:276-78, 282, 286, 295-96, 299, 312, 328, 330, 337, 339-40, 345-46, 358-59, 362, 367-68
"Gook Nigger" (Quintana) **36**:275
"Gooks" (Quintana) **36**:272
"The Goose" (Stryk) **27**:203
"Goose Fair" (Lawrence) **54**:240
"The Goose Fish" (Nemerov) **24**:261, 289-90
"Goose Pond" (Kunitz) **19**:178
"The Goose Shed" (Dafydd ap Gwilym)
See "Y Cwt Gwyddau"
"Gooseberry Fool" (Clampitt) **19**:86
"Góra Kikineis" (Mickiewicz) **38**:222-23
"Gorbunov and Gorchakov" (Brodsky) **9**:4-6, 10-12, 26-7
"The Gorge" (Stryk) **27**:189, 203
"Gorilla" (Silverstein) **49**:305
"Gorod" (Pasternak) **6**:264
"Gorodok" (Pushkin) **10**:410
"Gospel" (Dove) **6**:117
"Gospel" (Simic) **69**:297
"The Gossamers" (Tomlinson) **17**:310, 312
"Gost" (Lermontov) **18**:288
"Got To Be on Time" (Alurista) **34**:31, 42
"Gothic Letter on a Hot Night" (Atwood) **8**:24
"Der Gott der Jugend" (Hölderlin) **4**:142
"Gott im Mittelalter" (Rilke) **2**:275
"Die Götter Griechenlands" (Heine) **25**:145
Götterdämmerung (Heine) **25**:145
"Das Göttliche" (Goethe) **5**:239
"Gotvater am Abend" (Werfel) **101**:316
"Le Gouffre" (Baudelaire) **106**:127
"The Gourd Dancer" (Momaday) **25**:198-99, 214-16, 221
The Gourd Dancer (Momaday) **25**:193-97, 200-202, 205, 212, 216, 219-20
"Le goût du néant" (Baudelaire) **1**:68; **106**:127
"Government" (Sandburg) **41**:348
"Gow's Watch" (Kipling) **3**:181
"GP" (Enright) **93**:32
"Gra Pana Cogito" (Herbert) **50**:25, 38, 41
"Grabaciones" (Cardenal) **22**:131-32
"Grabschrift" (Sachs) **78**:159
"Grabschriften in die Luft geschrieben" (Sachs) **78**:111, 113, 168, 190, 193, 199, 201
"Grace" (Emerson) **18**:98
"Grace" (Herbert) **4**:111, 129
"Grace" (Jackson) **44**:5
"Grace" (Mistral)
See "La gracia"
"Grace" (Ransom) **61**:294
"Grace" (Wilbur) **51**:187, 193, 209
"Grace Abounding" (Ammons) **16**:63
"Grace before Meat" (Chappell) **105**:51
Grace before Ploughing (Masefield) **78**:44-45, 49
"Grace before Sleep" (Teasdale) **31**:341
Grace Notes (Dove) **6**:120-22
"The Grace of Time" (Guillén) **35**:218
"Graceland" (Sandburg) **41**:226, 239
"Grace's House" (Merton) **10**:340-41, 350, 353
"La gracia" (Mistral) **32**:181
Gracias Haus (Merton) **10**:341
"Grackles, Goodbye" (Warren) **37**:346
"Gradual" (Thomas) **99**:299
Graf Nulin (Pushkin) **10**:366, 386, 390, 400-01
"Graffiti from the Gare Saint-Manqué" (Hacker) **47**:81
"Grafo-mundo" (Cruz) **37**:31, 35-36
"A Grafted Tongue" (Montague) **106**:251, 310, 316, 329
"Grafton Street Admiration" (Kavanagh) **105**:164
A Grain of Mustard Seed (Sarton) **39**:328-29, 339-40, 342, 365-66
"La Graine" (Perse) **23**:228
"Grainne's Sleep Song" (McGuckian) **27**:82
Grains et issues (Tzara) **27**:241-42, 251-52
"Grammar and Goodness" (Hughes) **53**:97
"The Grammarian's Funeral" (Browning) **2**:37, 51
"La gran aventura" (Guillén) **35**:202
"Gran silencio" (Guillén) **35**:155
El gran zoo (Guillén) **23**:100
"Granaten" (Stramm) **50**:188, 205, 222
"Granatfeuer" (Stramm) **50**:222
"Grand Canyon" (Hughes) **89**:162
"The Grand Canyon" (Merrill) **28**:247, 272
"Grand complainte de la ville de Paris" (Laforgue) **14**:97
"Grand Galop" (Ashbery) **26**:126, 143
Le grand jeu (Péret) **33**:201-03, 207, 212, 215-18, 220, 223-24, 230
"Le grand jour" (Éluard) **38**:71
"Grand Marshal Kao's Dapple" (Tu Fu) **9**:330
"Le Grand Midi" (Césaire) **25**:29-30
Le Grand Recueil (Ponge) **107**:71, 74, 78, 90, 95, 98, 100-101, 104, 114, 116-20, 124, 127-40, 142-44, 147-48, 157, 161-64, 167, 173, 175, 182, 184, 186, 192-95, 198-200, 207-10, 220-21, 224-25, 227, 236, 238, 240, 263
"The Grand Question Debated" (Swift) **9**:260
"Grand River Marshes" (Masters) **1**:330, 333
Le Grand Testament (Villon)
See *Le Testament*
"The Grand View" (Abse) **41**:3, 14, 25
"Une grande dame" (Verlaine) **2**:430-31
"La grande maison inhabitable" (Éluard) **38**:69, 84
"La grande neige" (Bonnefoy) **58**:153
"Grandes conspiraces" (Éluard) **38**:71
"The Grandfather" (Guillén)
See "El abuèlo"
"Grandfather" (Mahon) **60**:132
"Grandfather Arthur Winslow" (Lowell) **3**:200
"Grandfather at the Rest Home" (Welch) **62**:343
"Grandfather in the Old Men's Home" (Merwin) **45**:18
"Grandfather, Your Wound" (Sexton) **79**:210-11
"Grandma We Are Poets" (Clifton) **17**:29-30

"Grandma's Man" (Welch) **62**:345, 347, 370, 374
"Grandmother Dying" (Merwin) **45**:8
"Grandmother in the Garden" (Glück) **16**:124
"Grandmother Speranza's Friend" (Gozzano)
See "L'amica di nonna speranza"
"Grandmother Watching at Her Window" (Merwin) **45**:8
"Grandmother's Clavichord" (Darío)
See "El clavicordio de la abuela"
"Grandmother's Father" (Quintana) **36**:275
"Grandmother's Story of Bunker-Hill Battle, as she saw it from the Belfry" (Holmes) **71**:68, 73, 93
"Grandparents" (Lowell) **3**:217-20
"Grand-Pré" (Carman)
See "Low Tide on Grand Pré"
"Les Grands Mutiles" (Service) **70**:132
"Granite and Steel" (Moore) **4**:259, 261; **49**:144
The Granite Pail: The Selected Poems of Lorine Niedecker (Niedecker) **42**:103-7, 109-10, 155, 165, 170, 173-74, 176, 178
"Granny" (Riley) **48**:340
"Granted This World" (Sarton) **39**:320, 322
Granth (Kabīr)
See *The Adi Granth*
"Grant's Tomb Revisited" (Shapiro) **25**:322
"Granville Calhoun" (Masters) **36**:229
"Grape Sherbet" (Dove) **6**:106, 109
"The Grapes" (Hecht) **70**:81, 86
"Grapes: Still-Life" (Spencer) **77**:326, 331
"The Graph" (Ciardi) **69**:55
"Graph for Action" (Williams) **7**:369
"Graphemics #5" (Spicer) **78**:343
"Grappa in September" (Pavese) **13**:218
"Grappling in the Central Blue" (Kumin) **15**:209-10
"Grass" (Bly) **39**:69
"Grass" (Sandburg) **41**:240, 266-67, 270, 288, 297, 328
"Grass from the Battle-field" (Dobell) **100**:139
"Grasse: The Olive Trees" (Wilbur) **51**:206-7, 293
"The Grasse-hopper" (Lovelace) **69**:156, 159, 167, 169, 171-76, 180-81, 183, 198-202, 237-38, 249-53, 256
"Grasses" (Gunn) **26**:219
"Grasshopper" (Kennedy) **93**:146
"A Grasshopper" (Wilbur) **51**:190, 301
The Grasshopper (Cowley) **90**:59
"Grasshopper and the Cricket" (Hunt) **73**:154-55
"Gratiana dauncing and singing" (Lovelace) **69**:192, 225, 228, 232, 235-36
"Gratitude" (Lermontov) **18**:281
"Gratitude" (Smart) **13**:361
"Gratitude, a Pastoral" (Duck) **89**:4
"The Grauballe Man" (Heaney) **18**:210-11; **100**:216-19, 223, 282-83, 285, 309
"A Grave" (Moore) **4**:243, 251; **49**:89, 94, 98, 101, 150-51, 153-55
"The Grave" (Winters) **82**:346, 348-49
"A Grave Illness" (Page) **12**:199
"The Grave of Manuel" (Béranger) **112**:14
"The Grave of the Countess Potocka" (Mickiewicz)
See "Grób Potockiej"
"Grave Piece" (Eberhart) **76**:40
"The Grave that Time Dug" (Spark) **72**:220
"A Grave Unvisited" (Thomas) **99**:310, 321
"The Gravedigger" (Carman) **34**:213
"The Gravel Walks" (Heaney) **100**:321
"Gravelly Run" (Ammons) **16**:29
The Graver and the Pen (Stevenson) **84**:302
"Graves" (Sandburg) **2**:303; **41**:338
"Graves Are Made to Waltz On" (Viereck) **27**:258
"Graves at Mukilteo" (Hugo) **68**:235, 238
"Graves in Queens" (Hugo) **68**:255
"Graves of the Harem" (Mickiewicz)
See "Mogiły haremu"
"The Grave-Tree" (Carman) **34**:211, 220-21
"A Graveyard" (Moore) **49**:150, 152
"The Graveyard" (Very) **86**:140
"Graveyard at Bolinas" (Hass) **16**:196, 209
"The Graveyard by the Sea" (Valéry)
See "Le cimetière marin"
"A Graveyard in Queens" (Montague) **106**:271
"A Graveyard in the Middle of the Sea" (Moore) **49**:150-51
Gravities (Waldrop)
See *Reluctant Gravities*
"Gravy" (Carver) **54**:17, 19
"Gray" (Cavafy) **36**:74
"Gray" (Walker) **30**:343
"Gray Dogs" (Ríos) **57**:328
"Gray Eyes" (Gallagher) **9**:51
"Gray Fox in a Roadside Zoo" (Wagoner) **33**:374
"A Gray Thought" (Schuyler) **88**:185
"the gray woods exploding" (Birney) **52**:34-36
"Grażyna" (Mickiewicz) **38**:164, 166, 219
"The Great Adventure of Max Breuck" (Lowell) **13**:60, 96
"Great American Waterfront Poem" (Ferlinghetti) **1**:188
"Great Are the Myths" (Whitman) **91**:231, 319
"The Great Blue Heron" (Kizer) **66**:63
"The Great Bones of Claverack" (Taylor) **63**:321-22
"Great Canzon" (Rexroth) **20**:190; **95**:250, 260, 273
"The Great Carbuncle" (Plath) **37**:237-38, 241
"Great Chain of Being" (Kennedy) **93**:144
"The Great Chinese Dragon" (Ferlinghetti) **1**:176
"The Great Cloak" (Montague) **106**:237, 287
The Great Cloak (Montague) **106**:237, 240, 242-43, 247, 280, 287-90, 298-99, 306-7, 309, 311-12, 315, 317, 327
"Great Day in the Cows' House" (Hall) **70**:15, 18, 34, 36
"Great Dog Poem No. 2" (Strand) **63**:183, 186
"The Great Elegy for John Donne" (Brodsky) **9**:2, 4, 10, 26
"The Great Explosion" (Jeffers) **17**:130
"The Great Figure" (Williams) **7**:399, 401, 410
"The Great Fillmore Street Buffalo Drive" (Momaday) **25**:221
"Great Friend" (Thoreau) **30**:192
"The Great Genius" (Berrigan) **103**:45
"The Great Homecoming" (Sikelianos) **29**:373
"Great House" (Walcott)
See "Ruins of a Great House"
"The Great Hunger" (Kavanagh) **33**:61, 65-7, 71, 84, 92, 95-7, 124, 134-36, 140-4, 163-6; **105**:90-93, 98-100, 154-55, 162-63, 172
The Great Hunger (Kavanagh) **33**:58-9, 64, 70-2, 74-5, 77-81, 84-5, 87, 98, 100-105, 113-5, 117, 123-4, 126-131, 141, 146-7, 149, 154-6, 158-9, 161-2, 167, 169-71; **105**:102-3, 109, 114, 122-34, 136-37, 144-45, 158-61, 168, 171-79
"The Great Hunt" (Sandburg) **2**:300, 316; **41**:225
"Great Infirmities" (Simic) **69**:276
"The Great Lament of My Obscurity One" (Tzara) **27**:249
"The Great Lover" (Brooke) **24**:53, 56-7, 59, 65, 78, 87-8
"The great Macedon" (Surrey) **59**:303
"Great Measures" (Hogan) **35**:277-78
"The Great Mother" (Snyder) **21**:297
"The Great Nebula of Andromeda" (Rexroth) **20**:190
"A Great Number" (Szymborska)
See "Wielka liczba"
A Great Number (Szymborska)
See *Wielka liczba*
"The Great Palace of Versailles" (Dove) **6**:111
"Great Performances" (Mueller) **33**:192
"The Great Plain of India Seen from the Air" (Sarton) **39**:327, 340
"The Great Poet Returns" (Strand) **63**:197
"Great Praises" (Eberhart) **76**:50, 59
Great Praises (Eberhart) **76**:9, 13, 30-31, 48
"A Great Procession of Priests and Laymen" (Cavafy) **36**:36, 63
"The Great Pyramid" (Melville) **82**:97-98, 150-51
"Great Snoring and Norwich" (Sitwell) **3**:301
"The Great Society" (Bly) **39**:9
"The Great Society, Mark X" (Nemerov) **24**:280
"Great Spirits Now on Earth Are Sojourning" (Keats) **96**:199
"The Great Sunset" (Jeffers) **17**:130
"Great Things" (Hardy) **8**:112; **92**:214
Great Tranquillity: Questions and Answers (Amichai)
See *Shalvah gedolah: She'elot utshuvot*
"The Great Transparencies" (Sarton) **39**:340
"Great Unaffected Vampires and the Moon" (Smith) **12**:330-31
The Great Valley (Masters) **1**:329, 332, 342-43; **36**:176, 183
"Great Weaver" (Carman) **34**:212
The Great Whirl of Exile (Quintana) **36**:275-76
"Greater Love" (Owen) **19**:327, 332, 335, 337, 344, 347, 353-54, 358-59; **102**:150, 168-69, 171-72, 209, 225-26, 239-40
Greater Testament (Villon)
See *Le Testament*
"The Greater Whiteness" (Swenson) **14**:264
"Grecian Urn" (Keats)
See "Ode on a Grecian Urn"
"El Greco: Espolio" (Birney) **52**:11, 41, 44
"Greece" (Corso) **33**:6, 36, 49; **108**:17-18, 22
"Greece" (Thoreau) **30**:251
Greed (Ai) **72**:9, 21
Greed (Wakoski) **15**:325, 331, 351-52, 355-56, 372
Greed, Parts 1 & 2 (Wakoski) **15**:324
Greed, Parts 8, 9, 11 (Wakoski) **15**:345-46
Greed, Parts 5-7 (Wakoski) **15**:347
"The Greed to Be Fulfilled" (Wakoski) **15**:357
"Greek Anthology" (MacLeish) **47**:196
"Greek Architecture" (Melville) **82**:74
"Greek Masonry" (Melville) **82**:74
"The Greek Revolution" (Carducci)
See "Per la Rivoluzione di Grecia"
"The Greek Women" (Merton) **10**:349
"The Greeks Are Coming!" (Lawrence) **54**:197-98, 201, 203, 227
"Green" (Lawrence) **54**:178
"Green" (Verlaine) **2**:415; **32**:399
"Green: An Epistle" (Hecht) **70**:65, 71-75, 91, 109
Green and Black: Selected Writings (Scalapino) **114**:283, 320
"Green and Red, Verde y Rojo" (Espada) **74**:122
"Green Apples" (Randall) **86**:341
"Green Apples" (Stone) **53**:228
The Green Book of the Bards (Carman)
See *From the Green Book of Bards*
"Green Categories" (Thomas) **99**:233, 242, 269
"Green Flows the River of Lethe-O" (Sitwell) **3**:309
"Green, Green Rocky Road" (Kaufman) **74**:205
"Green Grow the Rashes O" (Burns) **6**:67, 74; **114**:37
The Green Helmet (Yeats) **20**:328; **51**:71
"Green Lantern's Solo" (Baraka) **4**:16; **113**:14, 41, 127, 140, 148
"Green Linnaeus" (Zagajewski) **27**:394
"The Green Man" (Olson) **19**:283
"The Green Man: For the Boston Strangler" (Atwood) **8**:7
"Green Memory" (Hughes) **1**:267
"The Green Menagerie" (Viereck) **27**:296
"A Green Mother" (Hughes) **89**:150
Green Night of Labyrinth Park (Brossard)
See *La Nuit verte du Parc Labyrinthe*
Green Notebook (Jaccottet)
See *Cahier de verdure*
"The Green Parrakeet" (Lowell) **13**:88

"Green Red Brown and White" (Swenson) **14**:261
"Green River" (Bryant) **20**:14, 16, 19, 34, 42
"Green Roads" (Thomas) **53**:297, 329
"The Green Shelf" (Hall) **70**:32
"Green Song" (Sarton) **39**:324
"Green Song" (Sitwell) **3**:312, 317
Green Song and Other Poems (Sitwell) **3**:308, 320
"Green Stream" (Wang Wei) **18**:378
The Green Wall (Wright) **36**:278, 291-94, 296, 299, 301-3, 314-15, 318, 335-38, 340, 343, 348-49, 35 7, 359, 361-62, 371, 373, 387, 389-90, 395, 398-99
The Green Wave (Rukeyser) **12**:204-05, 209, 213
"Green Ways" (Kunitz) **19**:162
"The Green Well" (Kumin) **15**:215
Green with Beasts (Merwin) **45**:3, 5-7, 9-11, 18, 21, 23-4, 28-9, 32, 53
"The Green Wolf" (Hughes) **89**:99, 106
"Green Wood" (Pavese) **13**:218
"Greenaway" (Betjeman) **75**:26, 79
"The Greenest Continent" (Stevens) **6**:317-19; **110**:137
"The Greenhouse" (Merrill) **28**:243-44
"Greenwich Avenue" (Schuyler) **88**:192
"Greenwich Village" (Corso) **108**:16
"Greenwich Village Suicide" (Corso) **33**:46
"The Greeting" (Tomlinson) **17**:354
"A Greeting" (Whittier) **93**:338
"A greeting to L. F." (Paz)
See "Saludo a León Felipe"
"Greetings for His Own Birthday" (Ungaretti)
See "Auguri per Proprio Compleanno"
"Greetings to the Eagle" (Darío)
See "Salutación al águila"
"Greetings to the Optimist" (Darío)
See "Salutación del optimista"
"Grège" (Char) **56**:155
"Gregorias" (Walcott) **46**:322
"Les grenades" (Valéry) **9**:387-90, 394, 396
"Grenades Are Not Free" (Sanchez) **9**:235
"Die Grenadiere" (Heine) **25**:140
"Le Grenier" (Béranger) **112**:21
"Grenouille" (Guillén) **23**:111
"La grenouille" (Ponge) **107**:131
"Grenzen der Menschheit" (Goethe) **5**:239
"Los Grernios en el frente" (Neruda) **4**:309
"Gretel in Darkness" (Glück) **16**:125, 140, 143-44, 149
"Gretna Green" (Crabbe) **97**:114, 116
"Grey" (Tapahonso) **65**:224
"The Grey Heron" (Kinnell) **26**:259
"Grey Liffey" (Kavanagh) **105**:175-76
"The Grey Monk" (Blake) **12**:35-7, 70
"The Grey Ones" (MacNeice) **61**:178
"Grey Sparrow" (Levertov) **11**:160
"Greyday" (Angelou) **32**:30
"Greyness is All" (MacNeice) **61**:178
"Greystone Cottage" (Hugo) **68**:294
The Grid of Language (Celan)
See *Sprachgitter*
Un grido e paesaggi (Ungaretti) **57**:339
"Grief" (Barrett Browning) **6**:41
"Grief" (Hughes) **89**:182
Grief (Ungaretti)
See *Il dolore*
"A Grief Ago" (Thomas) **2**:405; **52**:226, 262, 335
"Grief for Dead Soldiers" (Hughes) **7**:114-15
"The Grief of Men" (Bly) **39**:100-01
"Grief Thief of Time" (Thomas) **2**:405; **52**:321
"grietas paredes" (Alurista) **34**:33
"Grifel' naja oda" (Mandelstam) **14**:121-22, 129, 148
"Griffey the Cooper" (Masters) **36**:183, 221
"Griffin of the Night" (Ondaatje) **28**:329
"Griggby's Station" (Riley) **48**:292, 315
"La Grille" (Char)
See "Je ne suis pas seul . . ."
"The Grindstone" (Frost) **1**:197; **39**:235
"La Grisette" (Holmes) **71**:83
"Grito for Nicaragua" (Espada) **74**:15, 155
"Grób Potockiej" (Mickiewicz) **38**:149, 222
"The grocer Hudson Kearley, he" (Belloc) **24**:41
"Grodek" (Trakl) **20**:226, 229, 236-38, 244, 250-51, 253, 255-58, 260
"The Groom's Still Waiting at the Altar" (Dylan) **37**:65
"Groping" (Thomas) **99**:274, 337
"The Grosbeaks" (Winters) **82**:319
"Grosse Fuge" (Doty) **53**:54
"La Grosse Margot" (Villon)
See "Ballade de la Grosse Margot"
"Grosses Geburtstagsblaublau mit Reimzeug und Assonanz" (Celan) **10**:124
"Grotesques" (Graves) **6**:142, 144
"Grotesques" (Verlaine) **32**:387
"The Ground Is the Only Figure" (Waldrop) **109**:185
"The Ground Mist" (Levertov) **11**:160
"A Ground Vine" (Melville) **82**:77
Ground Work: Before the War (Duncan) **2**:114-17, 119, 125; **75**:145-47, 156-59, 161-62, 171-72, 179, 188, 190-92, 204-6, 232-33, 260
Ground Work II: In the Dark (Duncan) **2**:119, 127; **75**:190, 205, 208, 232-33, 250, 258-59
"Ground Zero" (Stafford) **71**:329
"The Groundhog" (Eberhart) **76**:3-4, 14, 17, 28-29, 34, 38-40, 50, 56, 58-59, 64-65, 67-68, 72-73
"The Grove" (Muir) **49**:231
"Groves of Academe" (Hacker) **47**:103
"Growing" (Rexroth) **95**:328
"Growing Dark" (Schuyler) **88**:188-89, 191, 204
"Growing in Spirit" (Cavafy) **36**:94, 99-100
"Growing Into Love" (Kennedy) **93**:138
Growing into Love (Kennedy) **93**:138-43, 148, 152
"Growing Old" (Arnold) **5**:13, 19, 23
"Growing Pains" (Corso) **108**:8
"Grown-up" (Millay) **6**:234-5
"Growth" (Jackson) **44**:96
"Growth" (Levine) **22**:220, 228
"The Growth of 'Lorraine'" (Robinson) **1**:461; **35**:368
The Growth of Love (Bridges) **28**:49, 68, 71, 86-8
the gRReat adventure? (Hejinian) **108**:288
"Grub First, Then Ethics" (Auden) **1**:24
"Guadalcanal" (Randall) **86**:289
"Guadeloupe, W.I." (Guillén) **23**:99
"Guadelupe" (Birney) **52**:18
The Guard (Hejinian) **108**:304, 311-14
"Guardia roja" (Borges) **32**:122
"The Guardian" (Strand) **63**:156, 175-77
"The Guardian Angel" (Browning) **2**:73
"The Guardian Angel of the Little Utopia" (Graham) **59**:166-67, 182
"The Guardian Angel of the Swarm" (Graham) **59**:167
The Guardian of the Flock (Pessoa) **20**:167-68
"The Guardians" (Merwin) **45**:53, 84
"The Guard's advice" (Char)
See "Conseil de la sentinelle"
"Guata, Manetto" (Cavalcanti) **114**:228
"Gubbinal" (Stevens) **110**:141
"Gudalajara Hospital" (Ai) **72**:7
"Gude Counsale" (Dunbar) **67**:25
"The Guelder Roses" (Lawrence) **54**:227-31, 234, 236
"Guendolen" (Morris) **55**:238
"Guenevere" (Teasdale) **31**:329, 344, 349
"La Guêpe" (Ponge) **107**:73, 109
"A Guerilla Handbook" (Baraka) **4**:16; **113**:9
"Guernica" (Thomas) **99**:336, 339
"Guerre" (Breton) **15**:62
"Guerre" (Rimbaud) **3**:264; **57**:249
"The Guess" (Muir) **49**:195, 289
"Guess Who" (Chappell) **105**:67
"A Guest Arrives" (Tu Fu) **9**:323
"Guest Room" (Oppen) **35**:312, 342
"Guía comercial" (Fuertes) **27**:12
"El guía de la abadía" (Fuertes) **27**:30
"A guichard" (Lamartine) **16**:286
"Guide" (Ammons) **16**:20, 34, 57
"The Guide" (Hughes) **89**:195
"A Guide to Dungeness Spit" (Wagoner) **33**:327-28, 344
Guide to Kulchur (Pound) **4**:354, 359; **95**:108
"A Guide to Poetry" (Ciardi) **69**:4, 32
"A Guide to the Field" (Wagoner) **33**:364
Guide to the Ruins (Nemerov) **24**:255, 260, 264
Guide to the Underworld (Ekeloef) **23**:85
"A Guided Tour through the Zoo" (Ignatow) **34**:305
"The Guiding Sound" (Akhmadulina)
See "Zvuk ukazuiushchii"
"Guigemar" (Marie de France)
See "Lay of Guigemar"
"Guignol" (Service) **70**:144
"Le Guignon" (Baudelaire) **106**:71
"Guildeluec and Gualadun" (Marie de France)
See "Eliduc"
Guillén Man-making Words (Guillén) **23**:102, 104, 120
"A Guiltless Lady Imprisoned" (Lovelace) **69**:181, 183, 228-29
"The Guilty Man" (Kunitz) **19**:160
"Guilty on Both Counts" (Yamada) **44**:346
"Guinea Woman" (Goodison) **36**:141, 154
"Guinevere" (Tennyson) **101**:195, 204, 206, 208-9, 288
"Guinness" (Hughes) **7**:123
"Guinness Was Bad for Me" (Clarke) **112**:122
"A Guiseppe Garibaldi" (Carducci) **46**:52
"Guiseppe Mazzini" (Carducci) **46**:72
"Guitar or Moon" (Aleixandre)
See "Guitarra o luna"
"Guitare" (Laforgue) **14**:80
"Guitarists" (Paredes)
See "Guitarreros"
"Guitarra o luna" (Aleixandre) **15**:20
"Guitarras y mujeres" (Paredes) **83**:63
"Guitarreros" (Paredes) **83**:7-8, 12, 39, 57, 59, 62-64, 66
"Guitars and Women" (Paredes)
See "Guitarras y mujeres"
"The Gulf" (Levertov) **11**:194
"The Gulf" (Walcott) **46**:230, 322
The Gulf, and Other Poems (Walcott) **46**:229-30, 233-39, 248, 259, 275, 285-87, 321-23
"Gulf of Georgia" (Birney) **52**:4, 8
"The Gulkana" (Hughes) **89**:135, 217
"Gull" (Sexton) **79**:240
"Gulls" (Hayden) **6**:185, 193-94
"Gulls" (Williams) **7**:378
"Gulls in the Park" (Cernuda) **62**:169, 172
"The Gulls upon the Saltings" (Masefield) **78**:97
"Gum" (Toomer) **7**:333
"Gumber" (Belloc) **24**:10
"Gum-Trees Stripping" (Wright) **14**:341-42, 347
"The Gun" (Shapiro) **25**:269, 295, 297, 312
"The Gun of Billy the Kid" (Stafford) **71**:258
"Gunga Din" (Kipling) **3**:157-58, 179, 187-89, 191
"The Gunman and the Debutante" (Parker) **28**:354
"Gunnar Thorgilsson" (Borges) **32**:63, 65
"Gunnar's Howe Above the House at Lithend" (Morris) **55**:340
"Guns as Keys: And the Great Gate Swings" (Lowell) **13**:60, 64, 72, 81-2
Gunslinger (Dorn) **115**:51-55, 57-58, 66-67, 85, 112-17, 143-45, 148-50, 153-57, 164, 166, 169-72, 174-80, 182-83, 187-95, 202, 204-6, 209, 211, 213, 216, 218, 220-21, 227, 231, 236-37, 240
Guru Granth (Kabīr)
See *The Adi Granth*
"Der gute Mensch" (Werfel) **101**:347
"The Gutteral Muse" (Heaney) **100**:321

"The Guttural Muse" (Heaney) **18**:198, 217
"Guy" (Emerson) **18**:111
"Guyana" (Walcott) **46**:237, 325
"Guyana Lovesong" (Goodison) **36**:154
Gwaith Dafydd ap Gwilym (Dafydd ap Gwilym) **56**:207-12, 241, 245-47, 249, 254-55
"Gwin, King of Norway" (Blake) **12**:60
"Le gymnaste" (Ponge) **107**:129, 137, 142, 190, 254
Gymnopaidia (Seferis) **66**:90, 92, 94, 105, 147-49
"The Gymnosophist" (Ekeloef) **23**:63, 86
"Gypsies" (Clare) **23**:15
The Gypsies (Pushkin)
See *Tsygany*
"The Gypsy" (Thomas) **53**:300
Gypsy Balladeer (García Lorca)
See *Primer romancero gitano*
Gypsy Ballads (García Lorca)
See *Primer romancero gitano*
The Gypsy Ballads (García Lorca)
See *Primer romancero gitano*
"Gypsy Man" (Hughes) **1**:270
"The Gypsy Nun" (García Lorca)
See "La monja gitana"
"Gypsy Verses" (Shvarts)
See "Tsyganskie stikhi"
"The Gyres" (Yeats) **20**:314, 333; **51**:112
"Gyrtt in my giltlesse gowne" (Surrey) **59**:315
"H" (Rimbaud) **3**:261; **57**:254, 271, 282
"H. O." (Borges) **22**:80-1, 95
"Los H. P. (Hijos Pródigos)" (Dalton) **36**:128-29, 131-33
"H. Scriptures" (Vaughan) **81**:337, 343
"The H. Scriptures II" (Herbert)
See "Holy Scriptures 2"
"Ha chi je na I Am Coming" (Forché) **10**:134
"Ha'ani lo ma'amin sheli" (Amichai) **38**:9
"Habberton's Plow" (Benét) **64**:19
"Habit" (Stone) **53**:229, 238
"The Habit of Perfection" (Hopkins) **15**:136
"A Habitable Grief" (Boland) **58**:62
"Habitación de al lado" (Cernuda) **62**:230
El habitante y su esperenza (Neruda) **4**:276, 281
"Habitat" (Stone) **53**:228
"Habits" (Giovanni) **19**:118
"L'habitude" (Éluard) **38**:69
"Habla un busto de Jano" (Borges) **32**:90
"Hablando al Padre" (Mistral) **32**:155
"Hablo de la ciudad" (Paz) **48**:188-89
"Hace falta saber" (Cernuda) **62**:240
"Hace frio" (Parra) **39**:272
"El hacedor" (Borges) **22**:76, 95; **32**:58
El hacedor (Borges) **22**:71; **32**:46, 59-62, 66, 86, 91, 94, 111, 132-33, 139
"Hacia el nombre" (Guillén) **35**:210-11
"Hacia el poema" (Guillén) **35**:195, 196, 197, 198, 211, 229
Hacia el sueño (Guillén) **35**:156
"Hacia la esclava Quisqueya" (Guillén) **23**:125
"Hacia la poesía" (Guillén) **35**:229
"Hacia la tierra" (Cernuda) **62**:179, 250-51
"The Hacked Priest" (Shvarts)
See "Zarublennyi sviashchennik"
"The Hacker Schoolhouse" (Very) **86**:54
"Had I man's fair form" (Keats) **96**:346
"Had I not this life decreed" (Villa) **22**:354
"Haecceity" (Cunningham) **92**:174, 177, 181
"Hafen" (Celan) **10**:105
"Haffār al-qubūr" (Gibran) **9**:79
"The Hag Is Astride" (Herrick) **9**:86
"The Hag of Beare" (Montague)
See "The Sean Bhean Vocht"
"A Hagging Match" (Heaney) **100**:331
"The Haggis of Private McPhee" (Service) **70**:120-21, 123, 130
"Hagia Sophia" (Merton) **10**:334
"The Haglets" (Melville) **82**:73, 86, 97, 142, 163-64
"Hago versos, señores" (Fuertes) **27**:49
"Haidekampf" (Stramm) **50**:175, 188
"Haiku" (Sanchez) **9**:230
"Haiku for a Young Waitress" (Birney) **52**:22
"Hail in Kharkov" (Yevtushenko) **40**:345
"Hail Mary" (Stafford) **71**:257, 288
"Hail, Star of Science!" (Whittier) **93**:196
"Hailstones" (Heaney) **18**:237; **100**:234, 251
Haine du peu d'amour (Char) **56**:115
"Hair" (Baudelaire)
See "La Chevelure"
"Hair" (Bly) **39**:16, 18, 28, 68
"Hair" (Corso) **33**:15, 34, 43, 47; **108**:31
"The Hair" (Herbert) **50**:4
"Hair" (Ní Chuilleanáin) **34**:364
"hair lightener" (Niedecker) **42**:127
"Haircut" (Shapiro) **25**:288, 318, 322
"Hairy" (Swenson) **14**:253
"Halahal" (Tagore) **8**:405
Halat hisar (Darwish) **86**:28, 30, 32-33
"Halcyon" (H. D.) **5**:304
"Hale, sterne superne! Hale, in eterne" (Dunbar) **67**:21
"Haleakala Crater, Maui" (Bell) **79**:25
"Half and Hour" (Cavafy) **36**:39, 41, 42, 107
"Half Measure" (Yevtushenko) **40**:366
"The Half of Life Gone" (Morris) **55**:338, 340
Half Sun Half Sleep (Swenson) **14**:260, 285
"Half-Ballad of Waterval" (Kipling) **91**:173
The Halfbreed Chronicles and Other Poems (Rose) **13**:235-36, 239-40
"Half-Caste Girl" (Wright) **14**:351
"Half-Deity" (Moore) **49**:99, 101
"Half-dream" (Wright) **14**:373
"The Half-moon Westers Low, My Love" (Housman) **2**:183
"Hälfte des Lebens" (Hölderlin) **4**:143, 148, 167
"Halfway" (Ammons) **16**:6
Halfway (Kumin) **15**:179, 192, 198
Halfway to Silence (Sarton) **39**:347, 360-62, 367-68
Halieticon/On Fishing (Ovid)
See *Halieutica*
Halieutica (Ovid) **2**:232, 242, 253
"The Hall and the Wood" (Morris) **55**:340
"The Hall of Judgment" (Hughes) **89**:195, 197
"The Hall of Mirrors" (Snodgrass) **74**:324
"Hall Sands" (Masefield) **78**:96
"Hallelujah:A Sestina" (Francis) **34**:255
Halleyová kometa (Seifert) **47**:317, 327-28, 335
"Halley's Comet" (Rexroth) **95**:349
Halley's Comet (Seifert)
See *Halleyová kometa*
"Hallowe'en" (Aiken) **26**:30, 41, 45, 53
"Hallowe'en" (Burns) **6**:50, 55, 57, 77, 91; **114**:60, 90
"Halloween" (Corso) **108**:7
"Halloween" (Hecht) **70**:69
"Halloween Poem" (Cohen) **109**:13, 47
"Hallowind" (Chappell) **105**:5, 16, 18, 36, 39, 44, 71, 75
"Halls" (Abse) **41**:28
"Halmaherra" (Randall) **86**:289
"Halsted Street Car" (Sandburg) **41**:239, 273, 287, 337, 340, 349
"A Halt in the Desert" (Brodsky)
See "Ostanovka v pustyne"
"Haman" (Hecht) **70**:108
"Hamatreya" (Emerson) **18**:79, 102-4, 111
"The Hambone and the Heart" (Sitwell) **3**:295
"The Ham-Bone of a Saint" (Shapiro) **25**:300
"El hambre" (Guillén) **23**:116
"Hame" (MacDiarmid) **9**:192
"Hamilton Greene" (Masters) **36**:171
"Hamlen Brook" (Wilbur) **51**:249-50, 311
The Hamlet of A. MacLeish (MacLeish) **47**:125, 128-29, 136-37, 140, 143-44, 147, 150, 153, 158, 178, 187-88, 190-91, 197, 213, 222-27, 253
The Hammer with No Master (Char)
See *Le marteau sans maître*
"The Hammers" (Lowell) **13**:60, 78
"Hammock" (Silverstein) **49**:334
"Hampstead" (Seferis) **66**:143, 151, 163, 170, 182, 184-85
"Hampstead Autumn" (Spender) **71**:225, 251
"Han venido" (Storni) **33**:245, 278
"Ha'nacker Mill" (Belloc) **24**:8, 22
"HAND" (Bissett) **14**:32
"The Hand" (Douglas) **106**:186
"The Hand" (Thomas) **99**:257, 261-62, 294
"The Hand and the Foot" (Very) **86**:113, 136
"The Hand at Callow Hill Farm" (Tomlinson) **17**:311
"Hand Crocheted Rug" (Niedecker) **42**:119-20, 123
"Hand Games" (Piercy) **29**:311
"The Hand of God in the World" (Amichai)
See "Yad elohim ba'olam"
"A Hand of Snapshots" (MacNeice) **61**:111, 120-21
"The Hand That Signed the Paper" (Thomas) **2**:388; **52**:263
"A Handbook of Surfing" (Guest) **55**:219
"Handed Down" (Clampitt) **19**:102
A Handful of Lavender (Reese) **29**:330, 332, 335-3336, 339, 345-346, 351
A Handful of Sand (Ishikawa)
See *Ichiaku no suna*
"Handfuls" (Sandburg) **41**:227, 236, 269-70, 296
"The Handicapped at Risen Hotel" (Wakoski) **15**:369
"The Handing Down" (Berry) **28**:38
"Handprints" (Rose) **13**:238
"Handrolled Cigarettes" (Yevtushenko) **40**:369
"Hands" (Benét) **64**:21, 23
"Hands" (Birney) **52**:5-6, 8, 37, 39, 46, 66
"Hands" (Justice) **64**:270
"Hands" (Levertov) **11**:159
"Hands All Round" (Tennyson) **101**:194, 269
The Hands of Day (Neruda)
See *Las manos del día*
"The Hands of God" (Lawrence) **54**:193, 197, 250
"The Hands of the Betrothed" (Lawrence) **54**:189
The Hands of Venus (Seifert)
See *Ruce Venušiny*
"Hands, on a Trip to Wisconsin" (Meredith) **28**:175
Hands Up! (Dorn) **115**:122, 125-26, 135, 154-55, 219
"Hands Up" (Dorn) **115**:125
"Hands Without Irons Become Dragonflies" (Espada) **74**:145-46
Handshakes (Illyés)
See *Kezfogasok*
"Handsome Harry" (Howe) **81**:23, 47
"Handsome Nell" (Burns) **114**:41
"A Handy Bait In Pellet Form" (Curnow)
See "A Balanced Bait in Handy Pellet Form"
"Hang up your weaponed wit" (Cunningham) **92**:137
"The Hanged Man" (Rexroth) **95**:255
"Hanging in Heaven" (Hagiwara)
See "Tenjō Ishi"
"The Hanging Man" (Plath) **37**:208
"Hanging of the Crane" (Longfellow) **30**:30, 49, 103
"Hanging Pictures in Granny's Room" (Kenyon) **57**:23
"Hangman" (Ai) **72**:3, 29
"The Hangman at Home" (Sandburg) **41**:254, 277
"Hangman's Oak" (Millay) **6**:217
"Hangover Mass" (Kennedy) **93**:148
Hangover Mass (Kennedy) **93**:147-48
"Hangover Square" (Mahon) **60**:236
"Hanmer" (Collins) **72**:100
"Hannibal and Napoleon" (Bishop) **34**:87
"Hanoi Hannah" (Komunyakaa) **51**:8, 28, 33, 40, 60-61, 64

"Hans Carvel" (Prior) **102**:314-15
"Hansel and Gretel" (Sexton) **2**:364, 368; **79**:330
"Hap" (Hardy) **92**:224, 241, 244, 319, 342
"Hapax" (Rexroth) **20**:217, 220
"Happening on a German Train" (Corso) **108**:8
"Happier Dead" (Baudelaire)
See "Le mort joyeux"
"The Happiest Day..." (Poe) **1**:432
"Happiness" (Borges)
See "La dicha"
"Happiness" (Ciardi) **69**:54
"Happiness" (Glück) **16**:131, 144, 151
"Happiness" (Kenyon) **57**:18, 20, 25, 43, 46
"Happiness" (Owen) **19**:355
"Happiness" (Philips) **40**:271
"Happiness" (Sandburg) **2**:308, 332, 334; **41**:296, 365
"Happiness, a Poem" (Chatterton) **104**:51
"Happiness in Herat" (Paz) **1**:361
"Happiness of Solitude" (Cernuda)
See "Alegría de la soledad"
Happy Birthday (Corso)
See *The Happy Birthday of Death*
The Happy Birthday of Death (Corso) **33**:8, 15, 34-7, 43, 45-8; **108**:3, 15-19, 21-26, 30-34, 40
"A Happy Calf" (Hughes) **89**:125
"The Happy Journalist" (Belloc) **24**:29
The Happy Man (Hall) **70**:14-17, 19, 29, 34-35
"The Happy Marriage" (MacLeish) **47**:183, 190, 209-10
The Happy Marriage, and Other Poems (MacLeish) **47**:125, 127, 131-32, 150, 183, 207, 222
"Happy New Year" (Enright) **93**:5, 19
"Happy New Year" (Niedecker) **42**:96
"Happy Warrior" (Wordsworth) **4**:391
"Harbor" (Celan) **10**:105
"The Harbor" (Sandburg) **41**:239, 267, 327, 329, 336-37, 349-50, 364
"The Harbor at Seattle" (Hass) **16**:217, 226
"Harbor Dawn" (Crane) **3**:88-9
"The Harbour" (Belloc) **24**:29
"Harbour" (Brathwaite) **56**:61, 89
"Harbour" (Thomas) **99**:272
"The Harbour" (Walcott) **46**:272, 274
"Hard Daddy" (Hughes) **1**:270; **53**:82, 140
"A Hard Death" (Sarton) **39**:328-29
Hard Facts (Baraka) **113**:24-25, 42-43, 126
Hard Facts: Excerpts (Baraka) **4**:29, 36-9
"Hard Fist" (Ammons) **16**:44
The Hard Hours (Hecht) **70**:73, 77-78, 80-89, 91-93, 108
Hard Labor (Pavese)
See *Lavorare stanca*
A Hard Land (Illyés)
See *Nehez fold*
"Hard Lard" (Ammons) **16**:43
"Hard Lines" (Zukofsky) **11**:351
Hard Lines (Nash) **21**:263
Hard Loving (Piercy) **29**:308-09, 311
"Hard Luck" (Hughes) **1**:255, 269
"Hard Roads in Shu" (Li Po) **29**:144
"Hard Rock Returns to Prison" (Knight) **14**:42, 52
"Hard Time Blues" (Hughes) **53**:81
"Hard Times" (Ashbery) **26**:154
"Hard Times" (McKay) **2**:209
"The Hard Times in Elfland" (Lanier) **50**:107-8
"Hard Times Redeemed by Soft Discarded Values" (Viereck) **27**:258-59
"Hard to Take" (Tapahonso) **65**:259
"Hard Weather" (Meredith) **60**:298
"Hardcastle Crags" (Hughes) **7**:149
"Hardcastle Crags" (Plath) **1**:388; **37**:180, 182-83, 208
"Hardening into Print" (Eberhart) **76**:70-71
"Hardships of Travel" (Li Po) **29**:141
"Hare" (Kennedy) **93**:146
"Hare Drummer" (Masters) **36**:183
"The Harem at Erechtheion" (Ekeloef) **23**:66
"Harem Trousers" (McGuckian) **27**:90
"Harem's Graves" (Mickiewicz)
See "Mogiły haremu"
"Hark" (de la Mare) **77**:111
"Hark, all you ladies that do sleep" (Campion) **87**:4, 7, 12, 63-64
"Harlem" (Hughes) **53**:173
"Harlem" (Tolson) **88**:250-52
"Harlem Dance Hall" (Hughes) **1**:247
"The Harlem Dancer" (McKay) **2**:213-14
Harlem Gallery: Book One, The Curator (Tolson) **88**:233-35, 237, 242-46, 248, 254-64, 266-67, 270, 278, 287-98, 302-20, 323-26, 328-29, 331-34, 337, 340, 342-45, 353, 362, 364
"Harlem Hopscotch" (Angelou) **32**:29
"Harlem Montana: Just Off the Reservation" (Welch) **62**:339, 347, 357, 370, 372-73
"Harlem Night Club" (Hughes) **53**:82
Harlem Portraits (Tolson)
See *A Gallery of Harlem Portraits*
"Harlem Shadows" (McKay) **2**:213
Harlem Shadows (McKay) **2**:213-14, 227
"Harlem Sweeties" (Hughes) **1**:247
Harlem Vignettes (Tolson) **88**:242-44, 257, 277-78, 280-81, 293-94, 303, 305, 311, 316-18, 320, 333
"Harlem Wine" (Cullen) **20**:63
"The Harlequin of Dreams" (Lanier) **50**:56
"The Harm of Living" (Montale)
See "Il male di vivere"
"Harmless" (Hecht) **70**:85
"Harmonie du soir" (Baudelaire) **1**:46, 68-9, 71; **106**:86, 88, 102, 104, 130, 134-36
Les harmonies (Lamartine) **16**:262-67
Harmonies poétiques et religieuses (Lamartine) **16**:279-82, 285-86, 292-93
Harmonies religieuses (Lamartine) **16**:257-62
"Harmonium" (Sandburg) **41**:271
Harmonium (Stevens) **6**:292, 294-95, 297-98, 300-01, 305, 309-11, 313-15, 329-30, 332-33, 336-37; **110**:93, 95, 132, 138, 140-43, 146, 174, 193, 235, 242
"Harmony at the Fair Grounds" (Yamada) **44**:341, 347
"Harmony with Nature" (Very)
See "Man in Harmony with Nature"
Harold (Byron)
See *Childe Harold's Pilgrimage*
Harold the Dauntles (Scott) **13**:269, 281, 312
Harold's Leap (Smith) **12**:335
"Harom oreg" (Illyés) **16**:239
"The Harp" (Cernuda)
See "El arpa"
"The Harp and the King" (Wright) **14**:343, 347
"Harp, Harp the Voice of Cymry" (Tennyson) **101**:195
"The Harp Song of the Dane Women" (Kipling) **3**:171, 183
"The Harper's Song" (Masefield) **78**:69
"Harpo" (Corso) **108**:51
Harps and Violins (Blok) **21**:25-6
"The Harps of Heaven" (Dobell) **100**:183, 187, 189
"Harpsichord & Salt Fish" (Niedecker) **42**:94, 97, 102
Harpsichord & Salt Fish (Niedecker) **42**:100
"The Harp-Weaver" (Millay)
See "The Ballad of the Harp-Weaver"
The Harp-Weaver, and Other Poems (Millay) **6**:211, 214-15, 224-25, 228, 230-31, 242
"Harriet Beecher Stowe" (Dunbar) **5**:128
"Harriet Tubman" (Walker) **20**:289
"Harriet's Donkey" (Lowell) **3**:241
"Harrison Street Court" (Sandburg) **41**:336
"The Harrowing of Hell" (Rilke) **2**:275
"Harrow-on-the-Hill" (Betjeman) **75**:12
"Harry Carey Goodhue" (Masters) **36**:218, 228-29
"Harry Gill" (Wordsworth)
See "Goody Blake and Harry Gill"
"Harry Ploughman" (Hopkins) **15**:134, 160
"Harry Semen" (MacDiarmid) **9**:180, 196-97
"Harry Wilmans" (Masters) **36**:182
"Hart-Leap Well" (Wordsworth)
See "Hartleap Well"
"Hartleap Well" (Wordsworth) **4**:404, 414, 427-28; **67**:327, 331
"Harvest" (Levine) **22**:218
"Harvest" (McGuckian) **27**:100
"Harvest" (Sitwell) **3**:311
"Harvest" (Soto) **28**:377
"The Harvest" (Walcott) **46**:236
"The Harvest Bow" (Heaney) **18**:243; **100**:333
"Harvest Festival" (Tomlinson) **17**:328
"The Harvest Knot" (Heaney)
See "The Harvest Bow"
"The Harvest Moon" (Longfellow) **30**:42
"Harvest Song" (Toomer) **7**:311, 317, 320, 333, 335
"The Harvesting" (Hughes) **89**:107
"The Harvest-Supper" (Hardy) **92**:264
"Harwood Alley Song" (Kaufman) **74**:253
"Harzreise im Winter" (Goethe) **5**:247
"Has She Forgotten?" (Riley) **48**:323
"Has Your Soul Sipped" (Owen) **19**:346, 352; **102**:150
"The Has-Been" (Sandburg) **41**:314
"The Haschish" (Whittier) **93**:319, 344
"Hassan; or, The Camel-Driver" (Collins) **72**:80
"Hassan's Journey into the World" (Thomas) **2**:402
"Hast My Nannette" (Prior) **102**:309
"Hastings" (Chatterton)
See "The Battle of Hastings"
"Hastings Street Girls" (Randall) **86**:334, 348
"Hastynges" (Chatterton)
See "The Battle of Hastings"
"Hat" (Silverstein) **49**:311
"Hate Blows a Bubble of Despair into" (Cummings) **5**:107
"Hate whome ye list" (Wyatt) **27**:325
"Hate-bridled Fishermen" (Walcott) **46**:272
"Hatem—, i.e. Goethe" (Goethe) **5**:228
"Hatred" (O'Hara) **45**:223
"Hatred" (Szymborska)
See "Nienawisc"
"Hatred of Men with Black Hair" (Bly) **39**:12, 50
The Haunch of Venison, a Poetical Epistle to Lord Clare (Goldsmith) **77**:191-92, 221, 223-24
"Haunted" (de la Mare) **77**:80
"Haunted" (Sassoon) **12**:240
"The Haunted Chamber" (Longfellow) **30**:103
"Haunted Country" (Jeffers) **17**:117
"Haunted Gate" (Masefield) **78**:44
"Haunted House" (Graves) **6**:142
"A Haunted House" (Swenson) **14**:248
The Haunted House (Hood) **93**:44, 62, 81, 85-86, 105, 107, 117, 119
"Haunted Houses" (Longfellow) **30**:27
"Haunted in Old Japan" (Noyes) **27**:127
"The Haunted Oak" (Dunbar) **5**:131
"The Haunted Palace" (Poe) **1**:424, 437-38, 443
"The Haunter" (Hardy) **8**:93, 118, 135, 138; **92**:259, 262
"Hauntings" (Brooke) **24**:57, 85
"Haunts" (Sandburg) **41**:241, 270
"Der Hausierer" (Sachs) **78**:188
"Havana Dreams" (Hughes) **53**:122
"Havana Rose" (Crane) **3**:90
Have Come, Am Here (Villa) **22**:346-47, 351
"Have Fun" (Silverstein) **49**:335
"Have Me" (Sandburg) **41**:313
"Have Mercy upon Me My Soul" (Gibran) **9**:73
"Have Travelled that Vernal Avenue" (Barker) **77**:6
"Have You Ever Eaten Stars?" (Warren) **37**:383
"Have You Heard This One?" (Stafford) **71**:294
"Haverhill" (Whittier) **93**:223
"Having a Coke with You" (O'Hara) **45**:118, 132

"Having Been Asked 'What Is a Man?' I Answer" (Levine) **22**:220
"Having Confessed" (Kavanagh) **33**:88, 119
"Having It Out With Melancholy" (Kenyon) **57**:11, 14-15, 19, 24, 27-28, 36, 40, 46
"Having Kittens About Having Babies" (Hacker) **47**:84, 100
"Having Lost My Sons, I Confront the Wreckage of the Moon: Christmas, 1960" (Wright) **36**:287, 340
"Having No Ear" (Davie) **29**:114-15
"The Haw Lantern" (Heaney) **18**:230, 233
The Haw Lantern (Heaney) **18**:226-28, 230, 232-33, 237; **100**:221, 234, 237, 251-52
"Hawk" (Walcott) **46**:286
"The Hawk in the Rain" (Hughes) **7**:117-18, 121, 129, 165
The Hawk in the Rain (Hughes) **7**:112-13, 115-20, 123, 131, 135-36, 139-41, 150, 162-63, 165-66; **89**:101, 132, 137-40, 145, 149-50, 156, 169, 186, 206, 209-11, 216, 221, 225
"Hawk Lawler: Chorus" (Kaufman) **74**:274
"Hawk Roosting" (Hughes) **7**:113, 125, 140-41, 151, 164, 169; **89**:149-50, 155-56, 164-65, 207, 223
"The Hawks" (Montale) **13**:149
"Hawks" (Tomlinson) **17**:347
"The Hawk's Cry in Autumn" (Brodsky) **9**:27
"Hawkshead and Dachau in a Christmas Glass" (Davie) **29**:108
"Haworth Parsonage" (Hughes) **89**:123
"The Hawthorn Hath a Deathly Smell" (de la Mare) **77**:60
"The Hawthorn Hedge" (Wright) **14**:336, 340
"Hawthorn Tide" (Swinburne) **24**:313, 317-18
"The Hawthorn Tree" (Glück) **16**:171
"Hawthorne" (Lowell) **3**:212, 216
"The Hawthorns" (Cernuda) **62**:172
"Hawthorns" (Heaney) **100**:334-35
"Hay" (Tomlinson) **17**:347, 354
"Hay cortesías que merecen palos" (Parra) **39**:273
"Hay Fever" (Hope) **56**:277-78
"Hay un día feliz" (Parra) **39**:299, 303
"Hayāt al-hubb" (Gibran) **9**:78
"Haycutters" (Stafford) **71**:375
"The Hayloft" (Stevenson) **84**:346-47
"Haymaking" (Thomas) **53**:267, 325, 327-29, 349
"The Haystack in the Floods" (Morris) **55**:238, 248, 252, 258, 301, 303
"The Hayswater Boat" (Arnold) **5**:50
Hazard, the Painter (Meredith) **28**:179, 195-99, 206-07, 214, 216
"Hazard's Optimism" (Meredith) **28**:202, 215
"Haze" (Schuyler) **88**:182
"Haze" (Thoreau) **30**:190, 294
"The Hazel Grove" (Pasternak) **6**:252
"The Hazel Leaf" (Warren) **37**:330
Ha-Zeman (Amichai) **38**:2, 18-19, 23
Hazman (Amichai) **38**:31
"He" (Borges) **32**:60
"He" (Ferlinghetti) **1**:174-76
"He" (Thomas) **99**:238, 317
"He Abjures Love" (Hardy) **8**:90; **92**:242, 245, 249
"He Acts" (Zagajewski) **27**:385
"He and I" (Rossetti) **44**:204, 253-56, 259
"He agrees with Henry Ford" (Thomas) **99**:249
"He and She" (Thomas) **99**:312
"He Asked about the Quality" (Cavafy) **36**:68, 74, 81
"He Came to Read" (Cavafy) **36**:76, 77-78
"He Comes Among" (Barker) **77**:44-45
"He Cracked a Word" (Curnow) **48**:13
"He 'Digesteth Harde Yron'" (Moore) **49**:161
"He Doesn't Know It" (Aleixandre) **15**:4
"He Follows Himself" (Hardy) **92**:375
"He Has a Good Time There" (Duncan) **2**:101
"He hath put all things under his feet" (Bryant) **20**:7
"He Heard the Newsboys Shouting 'Europe! Europe!'" (Schwartz) **8**:293
"He Held Radical Light" (Ammons) **16**:34
"He Himself" (Cavafy) **36**:49
"He Inadvertently Cures His Love-Pains" (Hardy) **92**:236-37
"He Is Last Seen" (Atwood) **8**:10
"He is Na Dog" (Dunbar) **67**:4, 8
"He is not ded" (Wyatt)
See "He is not ded that sometyme hath a fall"
"He is not ded that sometyme hath a fall" (Wyatt) **27**:337-338, 340, 343
"He is sometimes contrary" (Thomas) **99**:249
"He lived—childhood summers" (Niedecker) **42**:141
"He Loves and he Rides Away" (Dobell) **100**:139
"He Resigns" (Berryman) **64**:97
"He Revisits His First School" (Hardy) **8**:102
"He Said Come" (Walker) **30**:339
"He Sees Through Stone" (Knight) **14**:43
"He Swears" (Cavafy) **36**:73
"He that hes gold and grit riches" (Dunbar) **67**:13
"He that loves a rosy cheek" (Carew)
See "Disdaine Returned"
"He venido para ver" (Cernuda) **62**:236-37
"He Was a Man" (Brown) **55**:120
"He who finds a horseshoe" (Mandelstam)
See "Nashedshij podkovu"
"He who found a Horseshoe" (Mandelstam)
See "Nashedshij podkovu"
"He Will Not Leave a Note" (Ríos) **57**:326
"The Head above the Fog" (Hardy) **8**:97
"Head against White" (Atwood) **8**:27
"Head and Bottle" (Thomas) **53**:300
Head and Heart (Guillén)
See *Cerebro y corazón*
"Head of a Woman" (McGuckian) **27**:101
"Head of Hair" (Paz)
See "Cabellera"
"The Head-Aim" (Dickey) **40**:158
"The Headless Moon" (Shvarts)
See "Luna bez golovy"
"Headline" (Thomas) **99**:273
"Headphone Harold" (Silverstein) **49**:340, 347
The Heads of the Town up to the Aether (Spicer) **78**:241, 262, 267, 269, 273, 275-76, 278-79, 281, 283-89, 291, 294-96, 299, 308-11, 328, 339, 354, 362-63
"Headwaters" (Momaday) **25**:197
"Healing Animal" (Harjo) **27**:70
Healing Earthquakes (Baca) **41**:74-7
"The Healing of Mis" (Clarke) **112**:127, 129
"The Health of Captains" (Ciardi) **69**:12, 36
"The Health-Food Diner" (Angelou) **32**:27, 29
"Hear Me" (Levine) **22**:223
"Heard Under a Tin Sign at the Beach" (Stafford) **71**:340
"Hearing" (Berssenbrugge) **115**:5-6
"Hearing Inside Out" (Cruz) **37**:35
"Hearing the Song" (Stafford) **71**:334
"Hearn in Matsue" (Stryk) **27**:187, 208
"Hearsay" (Komunyakaa) **51**:65
Hearse (Hughes) **53**:115
"The Heart" (Trakl)
See "Das Herz"
"The Heart" (Very) **86**:91
"Heart and Mind" (Sitwell) **3**:312, 323
"The Heart and the Lyre" (Bogan) **12**:126
A Heart Beneath a Cassock (Rimbaud)
See *Un coeur sous une soutane*
"Heart, Crown and Mirror" (Apollinaire)
See "Coeur, couronne et miroir"
"The Heart Growing Cold" (Werfel)
See "Das erkaltende Herz"
"Heart o' the North" (Service) **70**:148
"The Heart of a Constab" (McKay) **2**:216, 225-26
"Heart of Autumn" (Warren) **37**:313, 334, 338, 349, 358-60, 366
"The Heart of Harlem" (Hughes) **53**:116
"Heart of Hunger" (Espada) **74**:128
"The Heart of Pedro de Valdivia" (Neruda)
See "El corazón de Pedro de Valdivia"
"The Heart of Something" (Ciardi) **69**:34
"The Heart of Sourdough" (Service) **70**:114-15
"Heart Stirrings" (McKay) **2**:223
"Heartbeat" (Harjo) **27**:56
"Heartease" (Goodison) **36**:140
Heartease (Goodison) **36**:140-41, 143, 147-48, 151, 153, 158
"Heartease I" (Goodison) **36**:151, 154
"Heartease II" (Goodison) **36**:154
"Heartease III" (Goodison) **36**:152, 154
"Heartease New England 1987" (Goodison) **36**:153
"The Hearth" (Cohen) **109**:8
"The Hearth" (Thomas) **99**:296
"Hearthside Story" (Kennedy) **93**:138
"Heartland" (Hogan) **35**:256
"Heartless Rhoda" (McKay) **2**:221
"Hearts" (Berrigan) **103**:4-5, 7
"The Hearts" (Pinsky) **27**:157-8, 161, 164-5, 170
"Hearts' and Flowers'" (MacLeish) **47**:185
"The Heart's Astronomy" (Howe) **81**:24-25
The Heart's Garden/The Garden's Heart (Rexroth) **20**:204, 209-10, 213-14; **95**:255, 260-65, 268, 275, 280-82, 334, 340
"The Heart's Graveyard Shift" (Komunyakaa) **51**:36
The Heart's Journey (Sassoon) **12**:258, 271, 289
"Heart's Needle" (Snodgrass) **74**:282-83, 286, 291-92, 296, 301, 305, 308, 312, 314
Heart's Needle (Cunningham) **92**:157
Heart's Needle (Snodgrass) **74**:281, 283-84, 289-92, 295-96, 298-99, 305, 310, 312-13, 315, 320, 323, 326, 923
"Hearts Together" (Betjeman) **75**:36
"Heat" (H. D.)
See "Garden"
"Heat" (Reese) **29**:336
The Heat Bird (Berssenbrugge) **115**:9-11, 28
"Heat makes th heart's window for Martina" (Bissett) **14**:32
"The Heat Rises in Gusts" (Stern) **115**:259
"The Heated Minutes" (MacNeice) **61**:137
"The Heath" (Cernuda)
See "El brezal"
"Heather Bell Chorus" (Kaufman) **74**:241, 243
"Heatwave" (Hughes) **7**:120
"L'héautontimorouménos" (Baudelaire) **1**:63; **106**:10, 126, 154, 168
"L'Héautontimorouménos" (Char) **56**:197-98
"Heave" (Corso) **108**:17
"Heaven" (Brooke) **24**:56, 64, 73, 78
"Heaven" (Herbert) **4**:102, 114, 130
"Heaven" (Tagore)
See "Svarga"
"Heaven Alive" (García Lorca) **3**:141
Heaven and Earth (Byron) **16**:88-89, 102-06, 109
"Heaven Is but the Hour" (Masters) **1**:344
"The Heaven of Animals" (Dickey) **40**:161, 163, 168, 183, 190, 207, 230
"Heavenly City, Earthly City" (Duncan) **2**:105
Heavenly City, Earthly City (Duncan) **2**:100, 126; **75**:128-29, 139, 157, 173, 175, 181, 225, 252, 261
"The Heavenly Feast" (Schnackenberg) **45**:337
Heavens and Earth: A Book of Poems (Benét) **64**:19
"Heavensgate" (Okigbo) **7**:250-51
Heavensgate (Okigbo) **7**:221-25, 228, 231-32, 236, 240, 242, 245, 247-48
"The Heaviness of Clay" (Seifert) **47**:328
"The Heavy Bear Who Goes with Me" (Schwartz) **8**:290-91, 297, 306-09, 311, 313-14
"Heavy Water Blues" (Kaufman) **74**:208
"die hebammen" (Enzensberger) **28**:140
"Heber" (Smith) **12**:327, 354

"Hebräische Melodien" (Heine) **25**:170, 175
"Hebrew Melodies" (Heine)
See "Hebräische Melodien"
"Hebrews 12" (Thomas) **99**:324-25
"The Hebrides" (MacNeice) **61**:122, 134, 137
"Heccar and Gaira" (Chatterton) **104**:73
"Hector in the Garden" (Barrett Browning) **6**:16
"Hector Kane" (Robinson) **1**:476
"Hedge Island, a Retrospect and a Prophecy" (Lowell) **13**:72, 82
"A Hedge of Rubber Trees" (Clampitt) **19**:98
"The Hedgeapple" (Bell) **79**:26
"The Hedgehog" (Clare) **23**:7
"Hedgerows" (Tomlinson) **17**:354
"Hedge-School" (Heaney) **100**:241
"He-goat God" (Pavese)
See "Il Dio-Caprone"
"Heidenröslein" (Goethe) **5**:254
"Height" (Ammons) **16**:6
"The Height of the Ridiculous" (Holmes) **71**:68, 82, 88, 123
The Heights of Macchu Picchu (Neruda)
See *Alturas de Macchu Picchu*
"Heil Heilige Nacht!" (Nash) **21**:266
"The Heiligenstadt Testament" (Shapiro) **25**:307
"Heimkehr" (Heine) **25**:130-37, 139, 141-42, 144-45, 158, 161, 163-64
Die Heimkehr (Heine) **25**:161
"Die Heimkehr No 20" (Heine) **25**:144
"Die Heimkehr No 25" (Heine) **25**:144
"Heimkunft" (Hölderlin) **4**:141, 146
"Heimlichkeit" (Stramm) **50**:189, 191, 201
"Heine La Salle" (Masters) **1**:334
"Heine's Grave" (Arnold) **5**:34, 52, 63-4
Heinrich Heine's Book of Songs (Heine)
See *Buch der Lieder*
"Heinrich Mann zum sechzigsten Geburtstag" (Benn) **35**:34
"Heiress and Architect" (Hardy) **92**:241, 246, 248
"The Heirs of Stalin" (Yevtushenko)
See "Stalin's Heirs"
Hélé ena (Vigny) **26**:367
"Helen" (Elytis) **21**:131
"Helen" (H. D.) **5**:268, 300
"Helen" (Parker) **28**:362
"Helen" (Seferis) **66**:99, 171, 194, 211
Helen in Egypt (H. D.) **5**:276-84, 292-93, 297-301
"Helen of Troy" (Masters) **1**:325, 328, 342; **36**:175
"Helen of Troy" (Teasdale) **31**:345
Helen of Troy, and Other Poems (Teasdale) **31**:321, 324, 329, 331, 340, 345, 362, 370, 378-79
"Hélène" (Valéry) **9**:380
"Hélène, la reine triste" (Valéry) **9**:380, 391
"Helen's Rape" (Gunn) **26**:182-183
"Helián" (Trakl) **20**:239-40, 253, 259
"Helicon" (Heaney) **18**:207
"Heliodora" (H. D.) **5**:270
Heliodora, and Other Poems (H. D.) **5**:267-68, 304-05
"Helios and Athene" (H. D.) **5**:290-92, 305
"Hell" (Graves) **6**:151
Hell (Dante)
See *Inferno*
"The Hell Cantos" (Pound) **4**:328, 357, 360; **95**:153
"Hell Fire Club" (Montague) **106**:246
"Hell Gate" (Housman) **2**:162, 165, 167, 199; **43**:210, 250-51
"The Hell Poem" (Berryman) **64**:93-94
Hellas (Shelley) **14**:171, 175, 188-9, 195, 197, 241; **67**:148-49
"Hellenistics" (Jeffers) **17**:117
"Hello" (Corso) **33**:6; **108**:17
"Hello" (Creeley) **73**:36, 48, 89
"Hello, drug addict" (Ignatow) **34**:323, 325, 341
Hello: Journal, February 29-May 3, 1976 (Creeley) **73**:16, 59, 92-93
Hello, La Jolla (Dorn) **115**:104, 109-10, 120, 133-34, 157, 160-61, 222-23, 230
"Hello Mudda, Hello Fadda" (Silverstein) **49**:346
"The Helmet" (Levine) **22**:223
Helmet of Clay (Seifert)
See *Přilba hlíny*
"The Helmet of Goliath" (Duncan) **75**:227-28
"Helmeted Boy" (Randall) **86**:290
A Helmetful of Earth (Seifert)
See *Přilba hlíny*
Helmets (Dickey) **40**:158, 160, 187, 190-92, 208, 212, 231-32, 257, 261-62
"Heloise" (Berrigan) **103**:4
"The Helmsman: An Ode" (Cunningham) **92**:135, 158, 166, 168, 175, 189-90
"Helpstone" (Clare) **23**:11, 39
"Helter Skelter; or, The Hue and Cry after the Attorneys Going to Ride the Circuit" (Swift) **9**:271
"The Hemingway Hero" (Yevtushenko) **40**:345
"Un hémisphere dans un chevelure" (Baudelaire) **106**:89, 121
"Hemlocks" (Dorn) **115**:57
"Hemmed-in Males" (Williams) **7**:369
"The Hemp" (Benét) **64**:18-19
"Hen" (Herbert) **50**:4
"The Hen Flower" (Kinnell) **26**:243, 249-50, 252, 266, 274
"Henceforth, from the Mind" (Bogan) **12**:105, 113
"The Henchman" (Whittier) **93**:229, 235, 239, 249
"Hendecasyllabics" (Swinburne) **24**:320
"Hendecasyllable" (Parra)
See "Endecasílabo"
"Hengist Cyning" (Borges) **32**:48, 94
"Hengist quiere hombres (449 A.D.)" (Borges) **32**:89-90
"Henley-on-Thames" (Betjeman) **75**:20, 77, 79, 81
"Henri Matisse: 'Asphodèles'" (Benn) **35**:67
"Henri Rousseau and Friends" (Ondaatje) **28**:298
"Henry" (Berryman) **64**:99
Henry and Emma (Prior) **102**:309, 317-19, 321
"Henry and Mary" (Graves) **6**:141
"Henry C. Calhoun" (Masters) **36**:229
"Henry Howard" (Drayton) **98**:6
"Henry James" (Thomas) **99**:356
"The Henry Manley Blues" (Kumin) **15**:208
"Henry Manley Living Alone Keeps Time" (Kumin) **15**:208
"Henry Phipps" (Masters) **36**:230-31
"Henry Purcell" (Hopkins) **15**:144, 168
"Henry Tripp" (Masters) **36**:190
Henry's Fate and Other Poems, 1967-1972 (Berryman) **64**:168, 171, 185
"The Henyard Round" (Hall) **70**:34
"Heptonstall" (Hughes) **89**:114, 121-23
"Her and It" (Berryman) **64**:93
"Her Becoming" (Roethke) **15**:269, 272-74
"Her Confession" (Hardy) **92**:241, 248, 250
"Her Daughter's Eyes" (Tapahonso) **65**:224, 258
"Her Dead Brother" (Lowell) **3**:205-06
"Her Death and After" (Hardy) **8**:99; **92**:267, 274, 277-78, 285
"Her Definition" (Hardy) **92**:241-42, 245-46, 257
"Her Dilemma" (Hardy) **92**:241, 243, 245, 247
"Her Early Work" (Swenson) **14**:276-77
"Her Eyes" (Robinson) **1**:459
"Her Father" (Hardy) **92**:366
"Her Final Show" (Doty) **53**:72
"Her/Flesh" (Cummings) **5**:95
"Her Garden" (Belloc) **24**:38-9
"Her Hair" (Riley) **48**:323
"Her Husband" (Hughes) **89**:103
"Her Immortality" (Hardy) **8**:131; **92**:248-49, 300
"Her Initials" (Hardy) **92**:236-37, 239
"Her Kind" (Sexton) **2**:359; **79**:190, 276, 312, 332-33, 335, 337
"Her Lips Are Copper Wire" (Toomer) **7**:320, 332, 340
"Her Management" (Swenson) **14**:248
"Her Mime of the Lame Seagull" (Heaney) **100**:264
"Her Muffe" (Lovelace) **69**:224
"Her Music" (Belloc) **24**:29
"Her Name" (Cowley) **90**:27
"Her Nativity" (Southwell) **83**:255, 283
"Her Reproach" (Hardy) **92**:241, 248, 250
"Her Right Eye Catches the Lavender" (Stern) **115**:272
"Her Second Weight" (Ríos) **57**:325
"Her Spousals" (Southwell) **83**:283
"Her Triumph" (Jonson) **17**:180
"Her Unbelief" (Cowley) **90**:27
"Her Vertical Smile" (Kinsella) **69**:129, 137-38
Her Vertical Smile (Kinsella) **69**:129, 137-38
"Her Voice Could Not Be Softer" (Clarke) **112**:108
"Her, Whom I Must Stil Honour in the Dust" (Raleigh) **31**:238
"Hera of Samos" (Clampitt) **19**:87
"Heraclitus on Rivers" (Mahon) **60**:144, 172, 195, 204, 214, 217-18, 224-25
Herald of the Autochthonic Spirit (Corso) **33**:35-7, 44, 50; **108**:3, 17, 19-20, 23-25, 32, 34, 60
"Heraldic: Deborah and Horse in Morning Forest" (Dickey) **40**:211
"Heraldos" (Darío) **15**:96
"Herba Santa" (Melville) **82**:148
"Herbert Street Revisited" (Montague) **106**:288, 298, 316
"Herbseele" (Trakl) **20**:265
"Herbst" (Benn) **35**:69
"Herbstlied" (Werfel) **101**:350
Hercule Chrestien (Ronsard) **11**:273
"Hercules and Antaeus" (Heaney) **18**:203, 207-210; **100**:211, 298
"A Herd of Does" (MacDiarmid) **9**:156
"The Herds" (Merwin) **45**:35, 86
"Here" (Abse) **41**:10
"Here" (Creeley) **73**:44
"Here" (Kenyon) **57**:2, 26
"Here" (Larkin) **21**:238-39, 253-55
"Here" (Niedecker) **42**:140
"Here" (Paz)
See "Aqui"
"Here" (Yamada) **44**:324, 346
"Here Again" (Creeley) **73**:100
"Here Among the Bones" (Seferis) **66**:179
"Here and Now" (Stryk) **27**:211
Here and Now (Levertov) **11**:159, 163, 188
"Here and There" (Werfel)
See "Dort und Hier"
Here Begynnis the Traitie of Orpheus Kyng . . . (Henryson) **65**:12, 14, 29, 58, 100, 104-6
"Here Come the Saints" (Gunn) **26**:206-207
"Here in Katmandu" (Justice) **64**:249-50, 253, 290
"Here Is" (Char)
See "Voici"
"Here Lies a Lady" (Ransom) **61**:269, 273, 301, 306-7, 311
"Here, Rattler, Here" (Brown) **55**:149
"Here she lies, a pretty bud" (Herrick)
See "Upon a Child That Died"
"Here the Legion Halted" (Masefield) **78**:44
"Here then, an aged shepherd dwelled" (Thoreau) **30**:202
"The Here-and Never" (MacNeice) **61**:120-22
"Heredity" (Hardy) **8**:129
"The Hereford Speech" (Masefield) **78**:64
"La herencia" (Guillén) **23**:118-19
"Here's a Health to Them That's Awa" (Burns) **114**:46, 56
"Here's to Opening and upward, to Leaf and to Sap" (Cummings) **5**:106

"Here's to the Mice!" (Lindsay) **23**:269
Here's What is Happening to Me (Yevtushenko) **40**:356-57
"The Heretic's Tragedy" (Browning) **2**:37, 59, 88
"Heriot's Ford" (Kipling) **3**:181
"Heritage" (Cullen) **20**:52-54, 57, 64-65, 72, 82, 87
"Heritage" (Hogan) **35**:255
"Herman and Dorothea" (Goethe)
See *Hermann und Dorothea*
Hermann und Dorothea (Goethe) **5**:223, 225-26, 236, 239, 257-59, 261
"Hermaphroditus" (Swinburne) **24**:308-11, 317, 361-63
"Hermes" (H. D.) **5**:273
Hermes, Dog and Star (Herbert)
See *Hermes, pies i gwiazda*
"Hermes of The Ways" (H. D.) **5**:303
Hermes, pies i gwiazda (Herbert) **50**:4-7, 24-26
"Hermetic Definition" (H. D.) **5**:281, 283, 285, 289, 297, 299
"Hermetic Poem" (Kunitz) **19**:172
"The Hermit" (Apollinaire)
See "L'ermite"
"The Hermit" (Mahon) **60**:208
"The Hermit" (McKay) **2**:222
The Hermit (Goldsmith) **77**:184
"The Hermit at Outermost House" (Plath) **1**:389; **37**:182, 188
"The Hermit Goes Up Attic" (Kumin) **15**:190
"Hernani" (Meredith) **60**:250
The Herne's Egg (Yeats) **20**:335
"The Hero" (Kavanagh) **33**:79, 121; **105**:96
"Hero" (Madhubuti) **5**:342
"The Hero" (Moore) **4**:265; **49**:92, 100-101, 161
"The Hero" (Sassoon) **12**:242, 263, 277, 280, 283, 285
"The Hero" (Thoreau) **30**:218
"Hero and Leander" (Hood) **93**:67-68, 74-77, 117
"Hero and Leander" (Hunt) **73**:148-49
Hero and Leander (Chapman) **96**:20, 33, 35-36, 58, 66-67, 69-70, 87, 89, 94-95, 120, 124
Hero and Leander (Marlowe) **57**:50-168
Hero and Leander, and Bacchus and Ariadne (Hunt) **73**:136
"The Hero Leaves His Ship" (Guest) **55**:212
"The Hero, the Girl and the Fool" (Yeats) **51**:108
"The Hero With One Face" (Wagoner) **33**:327, 369
"Herodes Atticus" (Cavafy) **36**:46
Hérodiade (Mallarmé) **4**:188, 190, 196-97, 199-203, 208, 213, 218-25; **102**:19-23, 56, 63, 72, 87, 100, 126-27, 135
Herodias (Mallarmé)
See *Hérodiade*
"Heroes and Worms" (Barker) **77**:14, 20
"Heroes Are Gang Leaders" (Baraka) **4**:10
"Heroic" (Boland) **58**:41
Heroic and Elegiac Song for the Lost Second Lieutenant of the Alb nian Campaign (Elytis)
See *Ázma iroikó ke pénthimo yia ton haméno anthipolohaghó tis Alvanías*
"Heroic Bronze, Silver Stars" (Quintana) **36**:272
"A Heroic Death" (Baudelaire)
See "Une Mort héroïque"
"Heroic Poem in Praise of Wine" (Belloc) **24**:13, 20, 22, 33, 39
"Heroic Sculpture" (O'Hara) **45**:200
"Heroic Simile" (Hass) **16**:198
"Heroic Stages" (Guest) **55**:185, 212
Heroical Epistles (Drayton)
See *Englands Heroicall Epistles*
"Heroics" (Wylie) **23**:324
Heroides (Ovid) **2**:234, 238-9, 241, 243-46, 253-55
Heroines (Ovid)
See *Heroides*
"Heroique Stanzas to the Glorious Memory of Cromwell" (Dryden) **25**:101
"Heroism" (Cowper) **40**:74-6, 81
"Heroism" (Montale)
See "L'eroismo"
"The Heron Ballads" (Burns) **114**:22
"A Heron for Mrs. Altroochi" (Spicer) **78**:299
"Heron Rex" (Ondaatje) **28**:332, 334
"Herons in Winter in the Frozen Marsh" (Oliver) **75**:334
"Hero's Portion" (Montague) **106**:327
"Herramientas" (Mistral) **32**:287
"Herrin" (Goethe) **5**:249
"Hers is the Noise, Also, of the Dogs Asleep and in Dreams" (Ríos) **57**:325
"Herself" (Cervantes) **35**:116
"Hertfordshire" (Betjeman) **75**:26, 79
"Hertha" (Swinburne) **24**:308, 312, 343
"Das Herz" (Trakl) **20**:235-36
"das herz von gröuland" (Enzensberger) **28**:138
"Her-zie" (Smith) **12**:339
"Hesperia" (Carducci) **46**:28
"Hesperia" (Swinburne) **24**:313, 316, 318, 323
"The Hesperides" (Tennyson) **6**:351; **101**:141-42, 247
Hesperides: or, The Works Both Humane & Divine of Robert Herrick, Esq. (Herrick) **9**:85, 87, 89, 90, 92-6, 100, 102, 104-06, 108-10, 116-17, 122, 125, 127-29, 132-35, 138, 140, 143-46
"L'Heure de se taire" (Éluard) **38**:87, 91
"Hevyn and erth" (Wyatt) **27**:349-50
"He-Who-Came-Forth" (Levertov) **11**:177
"Hex" (Brathwaite) **56**:96
"The Hex" (Sexton) **79**:216
"Hey tutie tatey" (Burns) **114**:161
"Hey Yu" (Bissett) **14**:7
"Hey-Hey Blues" (Hughes) **1**:240
"Hi!" (de la Mare) **77**:94, 97
Hi no tori (Yosano) **11**:308
"Hi Plane: A Saga of the Crossing" (Dorn) **115**:223
"Hiawatha" (Longfellow)
See *The Song of Hiawatha*
Hiawatha (Longfellow)
See *The Song of Hiawatha*
"Hiawatha's Photographing" (Carroll) **18**:46; **74**:29, 72
"Hibernaculum" (Ammons) **16**:10, 12, 20, 23, 29, 47-49, 60
"Hibiscus on the Sleeping Shores" (Stevens) **6**:294-95, 305
"Les Hiboux" (Péret) **33**:210
"Hic Jacet" (Walcott) **46**:248, 286-87
"The Hidalgo's Hat and a Hawk's Bell of Gold" (Espada) **74**:137-38
"Hidden Door" (Ferlinghetti) **1**:166
"Hidden Ice" (MacNeice) **61**:137
"The Hidden Love" (Clough) **103**:142
"Hidden Things" (Cavafy) **36**:39, 41, 74-75, 101
"The Hidden Treasure" (Vaughan) **81**:306
"Hidden Within Walls" (Cernuda) **62**:170
"Hiding the Skeleton" (Meredith) **60**:312
Hiding the Universe: Poems by Wang Wei (Wang Wei) **18**:382, 390
"Hier ist kein Trost" (Benn) **35**:8
Hier régnant désert (Bonnefoy) **58**:109, 126, 150, 154-55, 167
"Hieroglyphic" (Harjo) **27**:66
"Hieronymus Bosch" (Melville)
See "Homage to Hieronymus Bosch"
"Hierro" (Martí) **76**:105, 133
High and Low (Betjeman) **75**:13, 25-26, 32, 64, 83
"High and Low Tide Compromise" (Sachs) **78**:226, 232
"High Dive" (Empson) **104**:84, 90-91, 101, 106, 108, 110, 134
"High Diver" (Francis) **34**:255
"The High Green Hill" (Bissett) **14**:20
The High Green Hill (Bissett) **14**:14, 16, 18-21
"High in the Mountains, I Fail to Find the Wise Man" (Li Po) **29**:176
"The High Malady" (Pasternak)
See "Vysokaya bolesn"
"High Noon" (Clampitt) **19**:97
"The High Oaks Barking Hall July 19th 1896" (Swinburne) **24**:318-20
"The High Priest to Alexander" (Tennyson) **101**:193
"High Provence" (Rexroth) **95**:268
"High Quality Information" (Snyder) **21**:326
"High Street, 1786" (Heaney) **100**:334
"High Summer" (Heaney) **100**:240
"High Talk" (Yeats) **20**:336
"High Tension Lines across a Landscape" (Ciardi) **69**:35
"The High Tide" (Das) **43**:92
"High to Low" (Hughes) **1**:258, 267
High West Rendezvous (Dorn) **115**:230, 232-33, 235
"High Windows" (Larkin) **21**:238, 259
High Windows (Larkin) **21**:250, 259
"The Higher Criticism" (Hardy) **92**:232
The Higher Mathamatics (Chesterton) **28**:99
"The Higher Pantheism in a Nutshell" (Swinburne) **24**:320
"The Higher Unity" (Chesterton) **28**:94
"The Highest Wind that Ever Blew" (Chappell) **105**:18, 44
"Highland Laddie" (Burns) **114**:62
"The Highland Widow's Lament" (Burns) **114**:62
The Highlander: A Poem in Six Cantos (Macpherson) **97**:172, 175, 250, 344
"High-mindedness of an English Poet" (Enright) **93**:23
"A High-Toned Old Christian Woman" (Stevens)
See "To a High-Toned Old Christian Woman"
"Highway 61 Revisited" (Dylan) **37**:48, 51
Highway 61 Revisited (Dylan) **37**:44, 46, 50-1, 60-1
"Highway Barns, the Children of the Road" (Koch) **80**:341
The Highway Enthusiasts (Yevtushenko) **40**:341
"Highway: Michigan" (Roethke) **15**:246, 294
"Highway Patrol" (Ferlinghetti) **1**:187
"Highway Poems" (Mueller) **33**:189
"The Highwayman" (Noyes) **27**:133, 136
"El hijo" (Storni) **33**:261, 295, 301
Hijo del Pueblo (Quintana)
See *Hijo del pueblo: New Mexico Poems*
Hijo del pueblo: New Mexico Poems (Quintana) **36**:248-50, 260, 262, 264, 268
"Hiking on the Coast Range" (Rexroth) **20**:215; **95**:259, 270, 306-7
"Hilda" (Ransom) **61**:271
"The Hill" (Brooke) **24**:72, 77
"The Hill" (Creeley) **73**:122
"A Hill" (Hecht) **70**:77, 83, 92
"The Hill" (Masefield) **78**:56, 99
"The Hill" (Masters) **1**:345; **36**:181, 190, 201-02, 220, 241
"The Hill" (Tomlinson) **17**:314, 316, 337
"The Hill and Grove at Bill-Borrow" (Marvell)
See "Upon the Hill and Grove at Billborow"
"Hill at Parramatta" (Shapiro) **25**:269
"Hill Burial" (Winters) **82**:317
"The Hill Farmer Speaks" (Thomas) **99**:241
"Hill Field" (Montague) **106**:313, 327
"Hill in Kikineis" (Mickiewicz)
See "Góra Kikineis"
"The Hill Wife" (Frost) **1**:195, 202, 229; **39**:L232, 253
The Hilliad (Smart) **13**:333
"Hills Brothers Coffee" (Tapahonso) **65**:222, 226, 257
"Hill-Stone Was Content" (Hughes) **7**:149
"The Hilltop" (Hugo) **68**:290

"Himne for the Circumcision Day" (Crashaw) **84**:48
"Himno a la tristeza" (Cernuda) **62**:197, 213
"Himno al árbol" (Mistral) **32**:155
"Himno del mar" (Borges) **22**:92; **32**:37, 122
"Himno entre ruinas" (Paz) **1**:353, 360-61, 363; **48**:187
The Hind and the Panther (Dryden) **25**:81-2
The Hind and the Panther, Transvers'd to the Story of the Country Mouse and the City-Mouse (Prior) **102**:311-13
"Hindola" (Kabīr) **56**:342, 346
Hinge and Sign: Poems, 1968-1993 (McHugh) **61**:201-2, 206-7
Hinge Picture (Howe) **54**:52-53, 71, 87, 107, 109
"Hinges" (Silverstein) **49**:323, 328
"L'hinne de Bacus" (Ronsard) **11**:230, 232-33
"The Hinterland" (Clampitt) **19**:90
"Hip Hop" (Snodgrass) **74**:331
"Hippios Colonus" (Seferis) **66**:212
"Hippocrene" (Clampitt) **19**:92
"Hippolytus" (H. D.) **5**:267
"The Hippophagi" (Clarke) **112**:57-58, 69
"The Hippopotamus" (Carroll) **18**:31
"The Hippopotamus" (Eliot) **5**:187
"The Hippopotamus" (Nash) **21**:280
"Hippo's Hope" (Silverstein) **49**:335
"Hippy-Mo" (Smith) **12**:314, 327, 339
"Hir Face, Hir Tong, Hir Wit" (Raleigh) **31**:201
"Hiraeth" (Thomas) **99**:268
"The Hired Boy" (Kavanagh) **33**:156
"Hiroshima, Watts, My Lai" (Hayden) **6**:190
"His Age, Dedicated to His Peculiar Friend, M. John Wickes, under the Name Posthumus" (Herrick) **9**:103, 107, 114-15
"His Animal Is Finally a Kind of Ape" (Stern) **115**:248
"His Anthem, to Christ on the Crosse" (Herrick) **9**:121
"His Bargain" (Yeats) **20**:332
"His Bathrobe Pockets Stuffed with Notes" (Carver) **54**:18, 26
"His Blindness" (Barrett Browning) **6**:16
"His Carpets Flowered" (Niedecker) **42**:104
"His Circumcision" (Southwell) **83**:283
"His Confession" (Herrick) **9**:109, 117
"His Confidence" (Yeats) **20**:314, 332-33
"His Creed" (Herrick) **9**:104
"His Death" (Barrett Browning) **6**:16
"His Death" (Wright) **36**:396-97
"His Dream" (Wagoner) **33**:360
"His Embalming to Julia" (Herrick) **9**:127, 129
"His Est Locus Patriae" (Bonnefoy) **58**:130, 132-33, 174
"His farwell unto Poetrie" (Herrick)
See "Farewell to Poetry"
"His Figure Passes" (Spender) **71**:217
"His Grange, or Private Wealth" (Herrick) **9**:89
"His Horn" (Kaufman) **74**:195, 246
"His Lachrimae, or Mirth, Turn'd to Mourning" (Herrick) **9**:108
"His Majesty at His Passage into England" (Philips) **40**:268
"His Master's Voice" (Cohen) **109**:101
"His Meditation upon Death" (Herrick) **9**:109
His Noble Numbers: or, His Pious Pieces, Wherein (amongst Other Things) He Sings the Birth of His Christ: and Sighes for His Saviours Suffering on the Crosse (Herrick) **9**:85, 87, 90-2, 94-5, 100-01, 104, 106, 109-10, 117-18, 122, 140-41
"His Own Epitaph" (Herrick) **9**:131
"His Parting from Her" (Donne)
See "Elegie XII: His parting from her"
"His Perennial" (Barker) **77**:7
"His Phoenix" (Yeats) **20**:329
"His Poetry His Pillar" (Herrick) **9**:89, 106
"His Prayer for Absolution" (Herrick) **9**:94, 109, 117, 141
"His Prayer to Ben Jonson" (Herrick)
See "Prayer to Ben Jonson"
"His Returne to London" (Herrick) **9**:89, 98, 108
"His Reverie of Water" (Heaney) **100**:342
"His Shield" (Moore) **4**:247-48, 261; **49**:100, 119, 132, 134
"His Shining Helmet: Its Horsehair Crest" (Gallagher) **9**:62
"His Smell" (Olds) **22**:326
"His Smile" (Warren) **37**:363
"His Song of the Green Willow" (Stern) **115**:271
"His Stillness" (Olds) **22**:321, 340
"His Story" (Cisneros) **52**:153, 160
"His Tears to Thamasis" (Herrick) **9**:108
"His Terror" (Olds) **22**:324
"His Tomb in Ohio" (Wright) **36**:396
His Toy, His Dream, His Rest: 308 Dream Songs (Berryman) **64**:92, 121-22, 130-33, 138
"His Vigil" (Riley) **48**:303
"His Winding-Sheet" (Herrick) **9**:109
"His Words to Christ, Going to the Crosse" (Herrick) **9**:121
Hispanics (Quintana) **36**:254
"Hispaniola" (Clampitt) **19**:102
"Hisperica Famina" (Spicer) **78**:277
"Histoire du Régent" (Perse) **23**:230
Historia de Gloria (Fuertes) **27**:20-5, 34-42, 44-7
"Historia de la noche" (Borges) **32**:67
Historia de la noche (Borges) **22**:95-6; **32**:63-7, 86, 90, 112
Historia del corazón (Aleixandre) **15**:3-4, 7, 11, 15-16, 22, 41
"Historias de loca" (Mistral) **32**:181
Las historias prohibidas del pulgarcito (Dalton) **36**:128
"Historic Evening" (Rimbaud)
See "Soir historique"
Historical and Literary Lectures (Carducci)
See *Discorsi storici e letterari*
"Historical Associations" (Stevenson) **84**:328, 344
"L'Historienne" (Char) **56**:134
"Histories" (Jackson) **44**:7, 11
"Histories" (Tomlinson) **17**:326, 344, 350
"Histories of Modern Poetry" (Meynell)
See "'The Return to Nature': Histories of Modern Poetry"
"History" (Berry) **28**:8
"History" (Francis) **34**:243, 250
"History" (Graham) **59**:152
"History" (Heaney) **100**:248
"History" (Hughes) **53**:150-51
"History" (Lawrence) **54**:169, 183
"History" (Ní Chuilleanáin) **34**:360
"History" (Simic) **69**:286, 318, 337-39
"History" (Soto) **28**:378
History (Lowell) **3**:224, 226, 228-29, 231-32
"History: 13" (Olds) **22**:319
"History among the Rocks" (Warren) **37**:275, 278, 284, 289, 319-21, 331
"History During Nocturnal Snowfall" (Warren) **37**:379
"History is the Memory of Time" (Olson) **19**:271
"History is What a Man Does" (Ciardi) **69**:31
"History Lesson" (Kumin) **15**:194, 202
"History of a Literary Movement" (Nemerov) **24**:258
"The History of Fire" (Hogan) **35**:257
"History of Ideas" (Cunningham) **92**:136, 173, 181, 191
"The History of Karate" (Soto) **28**:400
"History of My Heart" (Pinsky) **27**:176
History of My Heart (Pinsky) **27**:163-4, 173, 176
History of Peter I (Pushkin)
See *The History of Peter the Great*
The History of Peter the Great (Pushkin) **10**:394
The History of Plants (Cowley)
See *Plantarum*
"The History of Poetry" (Strand) **63**:197-98
"The History of Red" (Hogan) **35**:278
The History of the Heart (Aleixandre)
See *Historia del corazón*
"A History of the Night" (Borges)
See "Historia de la noche"
A History of the Night (Borges)
See *Historia de la noche*
"History of the Poet as a Whore" (Madhubuti) **5**:329
"The History of the Twentieth Century" (Brodsky) **9**:19
"The History of the World: A T.V. Docu-Drama" (Ferlinghetti) **1**:184
"History on Wheels" (Baraka) **4**:29
"The History Teacher" (Collins) **68**:220
"History Walk" (Montague) **106**:316
"Hitchhiker" (Baca) **41**:47
"Hitherto Uncollected" (Moore) **4**:259; **49**:149
Hitler (Cohen)
See *Flowers for Hitler*
"Hitler" (Cohen) **109**:89
"Hitler the Brain-Mole" (Cohen) **109**:89
"The Hitlerian Spring" (Montale)
See "La primavera Hitleriana"
"Hitler's First Photograph" (Szymborska)
See "Pierwsza fotografia Hitlera"
"Hitoyo enishi" (Hagiwara) **18**:168-69
"Hits and Runs" (Sandburg) **2**:316
"The Hive at Gettysburg" (Whittier) **93**:275
"L'Hiver" (Jaccottet) **98**:174
"Hiver" (Verlaine) **32**:400-02, 405-06
"L'Hiver qui vient" (Laforgue) **14**:72-4, 78, 90
"L'hiver sur la prairie" (Éluard) **38**:71
H'm: Poems (Thomas) **99**:256, 281, 284, 286, 288, 290, 296, 315-17, 355-56, 359
"I' ho già fatto un gozzo in questo stento" (Michelangelo) **103**:342
"The Hoarder" (Sexton) **79**:233
"The Hobo's Lullaby" (Service) **70**:150
"Hochbeglückt in deiner Liebe" (Goethe) **5**:247
"The Hock-Cart, or Harvest Home" (Herrick) **9**:141-42
"Hod Putt" (Masters) **1**:345; **36**:179, 181, 190, 244
"Hoeing" (Soto) **28**:378
"Hoelderlin's Old Age" (Spender) **71**:225
"Hog" (Sexton) **79**:240
"Hohe Gemeinschaft" (Werfel) **101**:347
"Hohenlinden" (Hood) **93**:72
"Hohensalzburg: Fantastic Variations on a Theme of Romantic Character" (Jarrell) **41**:163, 169, 179, 186, 192-93, 196, 208
Hojas de Parra (Parra) **39**:292-93, 301, 303
"¡Hojas nuevas! risa siento" (Castro) **41**:115
"Hojoki" (Rexroth) **95**:260, 272, 321
"Hokusai" (Carson) **64**:221
"Hold, Hard, These Ancient Minutes in the Cuckoo's Mouth" (Thomas) **52**:284
"Hold Me" (Levine) **22**:217
"Hölderlin" (Schwartz) **8**:316
"Holderlin's Journey" (Muir) **49**:207, 243, 270, 288
"The Holdfast" (Herbert) **4**:123
"Holding On" (Levine) **22**:214
"Holding Out" (Rich) **5**:357
"Holding the Mirror up to Nature" (Nemerov) **24**:291
"Holding the Sky" (Stafford) **71**:287
"Hold-Up" (MacNeice) **61**:125
"A Hole in the Floor" (Wilbur) **51**:209-10, 301
Holes in the Sky (MacNeice) **61**:157-58
"Holiday" (Elliott) **96**:164
"Holiday" (Sitwell) **3**:311-12, 326
"Holiday Inn Blues" (Ferlinghetti) **1**:187
The Hollow Men (Eliot) **5**:163, 171, 174, 180, 185, 191, 193, 198, 206, 209; **31**:111, 117, 133, 138, 156
"The Hollow Wood" (Thomas) **53**:274, 277-78, 289, 291
"Holly Berry and Mistletoe" (Braithwaite) **52**:106

"Hollowind" (Chappell) **105**:81
"Hollywood" (Kaufman) **74**:259
"Hollywood" (Shapiro) **25**:295
"Holofernes" (Deloney)
See "Judith and Holofernes"
"Holy Angels, I Don't Envy You" (Stampa) **43**:296
"Holy Baptisme I" (Herbert) **4**:120
"The Holy Child's Song" (Merton) **10**:330, 340
"The Holy City" (Very) **86**:141
"The Holy Communion" (Vaughan) **81**:295, 297, 333, 367
"Holy Cross Day" (Browning) **2**:38, 63
"The Holy Fair" (Burns) **6**:49, 53, 57, 83-4, 86-8, 91, 94; **114**:5, 41, 60, 67, 69, 90, 157
"The Holy Grail" (Tennyson) **6**:407; **101**:196-97, 233, 289-90
The Holy Grail (Spicer) **78**:244, 275, 281, 286, 289-90, 292, 298, 308, 311, 313, 328, 354, 363
The Holy Grail, and Other Poems (Tennyson) **101**:272
"A Holy Hymn" (Southwell) **83**:279, 323
"The Holy Nativity" (Crashaw)
See "To the Holy Nativity"
"holy night" (Clifton) **17**:18, 24, 38
"Holy Orders" (Erdrich) **52**:191
"The Holy Places" (Yeats) **51**:86
"Holy Saturday" (Carducci)
See "Sabato Santo"
"Holy Satyr" (H. D.) **5**:268
"Holy Scriptures" (Vaughan)
See "H. Scriptures"
"Holy Scriptures I" (Herbert) **4**:126
"Holy Scriptures 2" (Herbert) **4**:133
"Holy Sonnet 11" (Donne) **43**:149
"Holy Sonnet VI" (Donne) **43**:128, 133, 149
"Holy Sonnet VII" (Donne) **43**:132
"Holy Sonnet XIV: Batter my heart, three-person'd God" (Donne) **1**:138; **43**:115, 117-18, 130, 133, 148, 160, 162-63
"Holy Sonnet XVII" (Donne) **43**:128
Holy Sonnets (Donne) **1**:128, 136, 138-40; **43**:113-18, 122, 159-64
"Holy Spring" (Thomas) **2**:382, 390
"Holy Table" (Betjeman) **75**:67
"Holy Thursday" (Blake) **12**:5, 7, 23-24, 34-35; **63**:11-12, 15, 41-47, 49, 68, 70, 76, 79, 82-83, 92, 101, 105-06, 121-22, 126, 133
"Holy Trinity, Sloane Street" (Betjeman) **75**:96
"The Holy Tulzie" (Burns) **114**:20, 157
Holy Virgin (Mickiewicz)
See *Panno święta*
"Holy Willie's Prayer" (Burns) **6**:53, 65, 83, 85-6, 88-9, 96; **114**:4, 9, 39, 41, 66-68, 92, 118, 128-29, 157
"Homage" (Viereck) **27**:284
Homage and Desecrations (Paz)
See "Homenaje y profanaciones"
"Homage and Lament for Ezra Pound" (Duncan) **75**:175
"Homage and Valediction" (Tomlinson) **17**:338
Homage: Joining of Lives (Guillén)
See *Homenaje*
"Homage to Clichés" (MacNeice) **61**:135-37
Homage to Clio (Auden) **1**:17
"Homage to Diana Toy" (Chin) **40**:9
"Homage to Emerson, on Night Flight to New York" (Warren) **37**:367, 374
"Homage to Flanders" (Sarton) **39**:334, 336, 345
"Homage to Hieronymus Bosch" (Melville) **82**:7, 9, 15, 27, 29, 37, 50, 53-54
"Homage to Jack Yeats" (Melville) **82**:36, 54
"A Homage to John Keats" (Clampitt) **19**:91
"Homage to Li Po" (Melville) **82**:37, 54
"Homage to Literature" (Rukeyser) **12**:211
"Homage to Malcolm Lowry" (Mahon) **60**:215-16
"Homage to Marcel Proust" (Melville) **82**:35, 38, 40, 48, 54
"Homage to Mayakofsky" (Berrigan) **103**:13
"homage to mine" (Clifton) **17**:24
Homage to Mistress Bradstreet (Berryman) **64**:71-73, 77, 79-80, 88, 90, 98-99, 106-7, 110-12, 117, 121, 126-27, 129, 142, 154-56, 159, 168-70, 172, 175-76, 179, 182, 188-91
Homage to Mistress Bradstreet (Cunningham) **92**:157
"Homage to Paul Mellon, I.M. Pei, Their Gallery, and Washington City" (Meredith) **28**:198
"Homage to Paul Robeson" (Hayden) **6**:192, 195
"Homage to R.F." (Wilbur) **51**:288
"Homage to Rimbaud" (Montale)
See "Omaggio a Rimbaud"
"Homage to Ruteboeuf" (Melville) **82**:48-49
"Homage to Sextus Propertius" (Pound) **4**:317-18, 333, 363-66; **95**:100
"Homage to Sextus Propertius" (Ungaretti) **57**:359
"Homage to the British Museum" (Empson) **104**:119, 122, 125
"Homage to the Empress of the Blues" (Hayden) **6**:188, 196
"Homage to the Memory of Wallace Stevens" (Justice) **64**:271, 276
"Homage to the Tree" (Tagore)
See "Vriksha-vandana"
"Homage to Theodore Dreiser" (Warren) **37**:305, 340, 366
"Homage to Vercingetorix" (Melville) **82**:12, 39, 54-55
"Homage to William Cowper" (Davie) **29**:104
"Homage to Yalta" (Brodsky) **9**:7
"El hombre" (Storni) **33**:283
"El Hombre" (Williams) **109**:238-39, 268
"Hombre Ciego" (Alurista) **34**:10
"El Hombre de la esquina rosada" (Borges) **32**:87
"El hombre imaginario" (Parra) **39**:294-95
"Hombre pequeñito" (Storni) **33**:237, 241, 251-52, 275-76, 298, 305, 309, 318, 320
"El hombre sereno" (Storni) **33**:251, 307
Hombres (Verlaine) **32**:370
"Hombres de las orillas" (Borges)
See "El Hombre de la esquina rosada"
"Hombres necios" (Juana Inés de la Cruz)
See "Hombres necios que acusáis"
"Hombres necios que acusáis" (Juana Inés de la Cruz) **24**:220
"Home" (Brooke) **24**:57
"Home" (Herbert) **50**:18
"Home" (Herbert) **4**:102, 130-31
"Home" (Lorde) **12**:138-39
"Home" (Sandburg) **41**:336
"Home" (Thomas) **53**:279, 281-82, 331-32
"Home after Three Months Away" (Lowell) **3**:206, 209, 216, 221
"Home After Three Months Away" (Sexton) **2**:350
Home Again (Montague) **106**:249, 251, 284, 318, 338, 340-41
Home at Grasmere (Wordsworth) **4**:414
Home Ballads and Poems (Whittier) **93**:167, 266, 346-47, 350
The Home Book: Prose and Poems, 1951-1970 (Schuyler) **88**:187, 189, 200-201
"Home Burial" (Frost) **1**:193, 195, 229; **39**:246-47, 253
Home Coming: Poems (Sanchez)
See *Homecoming*
Home Course in Religion (Soto) **28**:394, 396, 398-400, 403
"Home for Old Ladies" (Wagoner) **33**:364, 367
"Home for Thanksgiving" (Merwin) **45**:8
"Home for the Holidays" (Nemerov) **24**:295
"Home for the Imagination" (Wickham) **110**:288
"The Home Front" (Mahon) **60**:141
"Home Home Home" (Ferlinghetti) **1**:180
"Home Is So Sad" (Larkin) **21**:242
"Home Is Where the Music Is" (Cruz) **37**:31
"Home, James" (Viereck) **27**:264
"The Home of Taste" (Elliott) **96**:156, 163, 176
"Home Revisited: Midnight" (Ciardi) **69**:35
"Home Sweet Home" (Castro)
See "Miña casiña"
"Home Thoughts" (Sandburg) **2**:309
"Home Town" (Ní Chuilleanáin) **34**:369
"Home Town" (Snodgrass) **74**:284, 302, 304
"The Home Voyage" (Riley) **48**:326
"Home Wounded" (Dobell) **100**:139
Homeage to the American Indians (Cardenal)
See *Homenaje a los indios americanos*
"Homecoming" (Brathwaite) **56**:10, 31, 68
"Homecoming" (Goodison) **36**:143
"The Homecoming" (Hardy) **8**:99
"Homecoming" (Hölderlin)
See "Heimkunft"
"Homecoming" (Mahon) **60**:132
"Homecoming" (Merwin) **45**:24
"Homecoming" (Sanchez) **9**:207, 209, 223
"Homecoming" (Shapiro) **25**:273
"Homecoming" (Viereck) **27**:265, 280
"Homecoming" (Yamada) **44**:325, 334
Homecoming (Heine)
See *Die Heimkehr*
Homecoming (Sanchez) **9**:204, 206-07, 210-13, 215-16, 218-19, 222, 224, 229, 231-34, 237-38, 242
"The Homecoming" (Wickham) **110**:260, 286
"Homecoming: Anse La Raye" (Walcott) **46**:286
"Homecoming, from Tillie Olsen" (Yamada) **44**:353
"Homecomings" (Heaney) **18**:244
"Home-Folks" (Riley) **48**:352
Homegirls and Hand Grenades (Sanchez)
See *homegirls & handgrenades*
homegirls & handgrenades (Sanchez) **9**:228, 230-31, 234-36, 238, 244
"Homeland" (Bely)
See "Rodine"
"Homeland" (Clampitt) **19**:100, 102
"Homeland" (Merwin) **45**:46
"The Homeless" (Merwin) **45**:46
Homenaje (Guillén) **35**:140, 189, 195, 198, 200-205, 227, 228, 229, 234, 239, 241
Homenaje a los indios americanos (Cardenal) **22**:103, 124-26, 128, 131-32
Homenaje a Pablo Neruda de los poetas espanoles: Tres cantos materiales (Neruda) **4**:277, 306
"Homenaje y profanaciones" (Paz) **1**:356-57
"Homer in Basic" (Rexroth) **95**:254, 274
Homer Prince of Poets (Chapman) **96**:37
"Homeric Simile" (Meredith) **28**:174, 182, 187
"Homes" (Montague) **106**:246
"Homesick" (Kenyon) **57**:40
"Homesick in Heaven" (Holmes) **71**:94
"The Homestead" (Lanier) **50**:91
"The Homestead" (Whittier) **93**:238-39
The Homestead Called Damascus (Rexroth) **20**:182, 209-12, 214; **95**:247-48, 253-54, 261-62, 264-65, 271, 275-76, 281-82, 332
"Home-Thoughts" (McKay) **2**:228
"Hometown Piece for Messers Alston and Reese" (Moore) **4**:256, 259; **49**:132, 141, 147
"Hometown Piece for Messrs. Alston and Reese" (Moore)
See "Hometown Piece for Messers Alston and Reese"
"Homeward" (Ciardi) **69**:25
Homeward to America (Ciardi) **69**:3-4, 6, 23-25, 28, 35, 49
"The Homework Machine" (Silverstein) **49**:328
"Homily" (Tate) **50**:293
"Homily" (Viereck) **27**:280
"Homily on the Piety of All Herd Animals (A Mammoth Idyll)" (Viereck) **27**:280
"L'homme" (Lamartine) **16**:275, 285, 290-91, 297-98
L'homme approximatif (Tzara) **27**:234, 237-38, 240-42, 249

"L'homme et la mer" (Baudelaire) **106**:71
"L'homme juste" (Rimbaud) **57**:174, 205, 290, 296
"Homo Sap" (Dorn) **115**:200
"Homo Will Not Inherit" (Doty) **53**:54-55, 63
"Homosexuality" (O'Hara) **45**:156, 224
"Homuneulue Artifex" (Merrill) **28**:248
"The Hon. Sec." (Betjeman) **75**:77
El hondero entusiasta, 1923-1924 (Neruda) **4**:276
"Honest Lover Whosoever" (Suckling) **30**:140
"Honey" (Wright) **36**:393
"Honey" (Yevtushenko) **40**:345
Honey and Salt (Sandburg) **2**:336, 339; **41**:303-6, 308-11, 319, 321
"The Honey Bee and the Thistle" (Hughes) **89**:205
"Honey Bud" (Tagore)
See "Madhumanjari"
"Honey Mah Love" (Brown) **55**:115
"Honeymoon" (Berssenbrugge) **115**:22, 24, 40
"Honeymoon" (Seifert) **47**:324
"The Honeysuckle" (Marie de France)
See "Chevrefoil"
A Hong Kong House: Poems, 1951-1961 (Blunden) **66**:7
"Honky Tonk in Cleveland, Ohio" (Sandburg) **41**:297
"Honoria" (Patmore) **59**:229
"Hoods Own" (Hood) **93**:89
"Hook" (Wright) **36**:314, 378, 383-84, 401-3
"The Hooks of a Corset" (Milosz) **8**:182, 197, 210
"Hooriyya's Teaching" (Darwish) **86**:26-27
"Hop o' My Thumb" (Ashbery) **26**:127, 160
"Hope" (Clare) **23**:44
"Hope" (Cowper) **40**:47, 51
"Hope" (Crashaw) **84**:31, 73
"Hope" (Hughes) **53**:101
"The Hope" (Ignatow) **34**:277, 293
"Hope" (Jarrell) **41**:168, 195
"Hope" (Milosz) **8**:187-88, 192
"Hope" (Mueller) **33**:174
"Hope" (Very) **86**:135
"Hope Atherton's Wanderings" (Howe) **54**:47, 60, 62, 64, 66, 93-94, 113
"Hope Dieth: Love Liveth" (Morris) **55**:340
"Hope Is a Subtle Glutton" (Dickinson) **1**:111
Hopelessly (Storni)
See *Irremediablemente*
Hopes and Impediments: Selected Essays (Achebe) **6**:1015
"Hope's Despari" (Tagore)
See "Ashar nairashya"
"The Hop-Garden" (Smart) **13**:330-31, 333, 342
"Hopi Basketweaver Song" (Berssenbrugge) **115**:9
"Hopi Overlay" (Rose) **13**:233
Hoping for a Hoopoe (Updike)
See *The Carpentered Hen and Other Tame Creatures*
"Hopper: Confessions" (Carson) **64**:221, 229
"La hora 19" (Storni) **33**:239, 271
"La hora cero" (Cardenal)
See "La hora O"
"La hora O" (Cardenal) **22**:111
la hora 0 (Cardenal) **22**:103-4, 124-25, 131
Horace (Smart)
See *The Works of Horace, Translated into Verse*
"Horace, Lib. 2 Sat. 6. Part of It Imitated" (Swift) **9**:297
"Horace to Leuconoë" (Robinson) **1**:459
"A Horacio Quiroga" (Storni) **33**:235, 261
"Horae Beatae Inscriptio" (Pound) **95**:122
"Horae Canonicae" (Auden) **1**:17
Horae Canonicae (Auden) **92**:14-16, 43-48, 129
"Horatian Epode to the Duchess of Malfi" (Tate) **50**:229, 246, 258, 319
"An Horatian Ode upon Cromwell's Return from Ireland" (Marvell) **10**:259, 261-62, 264, 267-71, 275, 277, 289, 292, 294-95, 305-09, 311, 317-18; **86**:184, 210, 257, 267
"Horatio Alger Uses Scag" (Baraka) **4**:30
"Horizon" (Graham) **59**:175
"Horizons and Rains" (Ortiz) **17**:227
"Horizons Home" (Ortiz) **17**:226
"Horizonte" (Pessoa) **20**:155
"Horizontes en círculo" (Guillén) **35**:154
"L'Horloge" (Baudelaire) **106**:71, 84, 88
"The Horn" (Vigny)
See "Le cor"
"The Horn of Egremont Castle" (Wordsworth) **4**:377
"Horned Purple" (Williams) **7**:368; **109**:293-94, 296-98
"The Horned Rampion" (Clampitt) **19**:102
"Hornet" (Sexton) **79**:240
"Hornpipe" (Sitwell) **3**:297, 303
"Horoscope" (Cunningham) **92**:190
"L'horreur sympathique" (Baudelaire) **1**:55; **106**:83
"A Horrible Religious Error" (Hughes) **7**:144
"Horror Eroticus" (Shvarts) **50**:142, 145-46
"Hors des jours étrangers" (Césaire) **25**:31
"Horse" (Glück) **16**:164
"Horse" (Hugo) **17**:67
"The Horse" (Wright) **36**:278-79, 335-36
"Horse and Swan Feeding" (Swenson) **14**:246, 262, 277
"The Horse Chestnut Tree" (Eberhart) **76**:25, 59
"A Horse for the Stranger" (Darwish) **86**:27
"The Horse Show" (Williams) **7**:391, 394
"The Horse That Died of Shame" (Momaday) **25**:189, 213
"Horse Weebles" (Brathwaite) **56**:96
The Horse-Eaters: Poems and Satires (Clarke) **112**:31, 34, 37, 47, 50-51, 56, 62, 68, 80
"Horseman in Rain" (Neruda) **4**:282
"Horses" (Alexie) **53**:3, 24
"Horses" (Berry) **28**:9
"Horses" (Hughes) **7**:118, 143
"The Horses" (Hughes) **89**:211, 216, 225-26
"Horses" (Merwin) **45**:48
"Horses" (Muir) **49**:227-28, 238, 258, 274, 287, 290-91, 293, 298
"Horses" (Sandburg) **2**:324
"Horses" (Walker)
See *Horses Make a Landscape Look More Beautiful*
"The Horses" (Wilbur) **51**:273
Horses (Harjo)
See *She Had Some Horses*
"Horses and Men in Rain" (Sandburg) **41**:297
"Horses and Prisoners" (Dickey) **40**:257
Horses Don't Bet on People and Neither Do I (Bukowski) **18**:15
Horses Make a Landscape Look More Beautiful (Walker) **30**:343-44, 346, 349, 370
"The horses of Achilles" (Cavafy) **36**:53
"The Horses of Achilles" (Sikelianos) **29**:368-69
"The Horsewoman" (Kumin) **15**:194
"Hortus" (Marvell) **10**:284, 286, 288
"Horus" (Nerval) **13**:180-81, 187-91
"Hosanna" (Traherne) **70**:238, 288
"Hosea" (Walker) **20**:278-79
"Hospes Comesque Corporis" (Wylie) **23**:310
"The Hospital" (Kavanagh) **33**:62, 67, 72, 79, 88, 103, 120, 147; **105**:96-97, 138, 153
"Hospital" (de la Mare) **77**:77
"The Hospital" (Lermontov) **18**:284-85
"Hospital Barge at Cérisy" (Owen) **19**:342; **102**:143, 210-13, 225
"Hospital Journal" (Enright) **93**:32
"A Hospital named 'Hotel Universe'" (Viereck) **27**:263
"Hospital / poem (for etheridge 9/26/69)" (Sanchez) **9**:225
"The Hospital Window" (Dickey) **40**:161, 176, 179, 181, 185, 211, 262
"Host" (Wickham) **110**:309
"The Hostage" (Smith) **12**:329-30, 333
Hosties noires (Senghor) **25**:231, 233, 235, 238, 248, 254-55
"The Hosting of the Sidhe" (Yeats) **20**:344, 346
"Hot" (Bukowski) **18**:24
"Hot Day at the Races" (Raworth) **107**:274
"Hot Dog" (Stern) **115**:275-78, 283, 285
"A Hot Noon in Malabar" (Das) **43**:80
"The Hot Season" (Holmes) **71**:68
"Hot Springs" (Birney) **52**:28, 98
"Hotdog" (Stern)
See "Hot Dog"
"Hôtel" (Apollinaire) **7**:48
"Hotel" (McGuckian) **27**:76, 100
"Hotel Bed" (Graves) **6**:143-44
"Hotel Breakfast" (MacLeish) **47**:214
"Hotel Confidential" (Randall) **86**:339
"Hotel de l'Univers et Portugal" (Merrill) **28**:234
"Hotel Genève" (Song) **21**:335-36, 338-41
"Hotel Insomnia" (Simic) **69**:367
Hotel Insomnia (Simic) **69**:278-80, 299, 304-5, 307, 311, 317-20, 340, 366
"Hotel Ivoire" (Randall) **86**:339
Hotel Lautreamont (Ashbery) **26**:161-164, 166
"Hotel Merlin" (Creeley) **73**:93
"Hotel nights" (Abse) **41**:31
"The Hotel Normandie Pool" (Walcott) **46**:247-48
"The Hotel of Lost Light" (Kinnell) **26**:273
"Hotel of Two Worlds" (Guillén) **335**:221
"Hotel Steinplatz" (Olson) **19**:305
"Houdini" (Baraka) **113**:15
"The Hounds of Hell" (Masefield) **78**:14-15, 49-50, 62
"The Hour and the Ghost" (Rossetti) **7**:280
"The Hour of Cowdust" (Ondaatje) **28**:337
"The Hour of Fate" (Lindsay) **23**:281
"Hour of Proof" (Sarton) **39**:342
"The hourglass" (Borges)
See "La clepsidra"
"Hourglass" (Jacobsen) **62**:319-20, 323
Hours of Idleness: A Series of Poems, Original and Translated (Byron)
See *Fugitive Pieces*
Hous of Fame (Chaucer)
See *House of Fame*
"House" (Browning) **2**:59, 66
"The House" (Creeley) **73**:33
"The House" (Douglas) **106**:186
"The House" (Hogan) **35**:257
"The House" (Jordan) **38**:121
"The House" (McHugh) **61**:190
"The House" (Merrill) **28**:273
"The House" (Sexton) **2**:361-62
"The House" (Spark) **72**:217
"The House" (Williams) **109**:193
"House and Land" (Curnow) **48**:5, 20, 28
"House and Man" (Thomas) **53**:329
"The House and the Vineyard" (Lamartine)
See "La vigne et la maison"
House, Bridge, Fountain, Gate (Kumin) **15**:192, 194, 202, 208
"The House Builders" (Das) **43**:79
"House by the Sea" (Montale)
See "Casa sul mare"
"A House Divided" (Ondaatje) **28**:293
"House Down" (Enright) **93**:5
"House (fires)" (Alexie) **53**:30
"The House Fly" (Merrill) **28**:282-83, 285-87
"House Guest" (Bishop) **3**:56; **34**:139
"The House in Main St." (Lowell) **13**:84
"A House in Taos" (Hughes) **53**:94
"The House in the West" (Clarke) **112**:84-85
"The House in the Wood" (Jarrell) **41**:194
"House in This World" (Hughes) **53**:180
"The House in Winter" (Sarton) **39**:345
House of Creation (Akhmadulina)
See *Dom tvorchestva*

"House of Dream" (de la Mare) **77**:112
"House of Dreams" (Teasdale) **31**:356
The House of Dust: A Symphony (Aiken) **26**:4, 6, 8, 13, 22, 27, 31, 36, 50, 72
The House of Falling Leaves (Braithwaite) **52**:106
House of Fame (Chaucer) **19**:5, 10, 14, 17-18, 20-3, 73
"The House of God" (Hope) **56**:266
"House of Horrors" (Snodgrass) **74**:324, 334
"The House of Idiedaily" (Carman) See "In the House of Idiedaily"
"The House of Life" (Rossetti) **44**:166-67, 169, 173, 185, 198, 202-6, 214, 220-21, 223-24, 227, 230, 238, 250, 253-57, 259, 261, 263
House of Light (Oliver) **75**:295
"A House of Mercy" (Smith) **12**:326, 334-35
"The House of Over-Dew" (Smith) **12**:330, 332-33
"The House of Silence" (Hardy) **92**:209, 370
"The House of Splendour" (Pound) **95**:121-22
House of the Customs Men (Montale) See *La casa dei doganieri e altri versi*
"The House of the Dead" (Apollinaire) See "La maison des mortes"
"The House of the Heart" (Wakoski) **15**:348, 354
"The House on Bishop Street" (Dove) **6**:113
The House on Marshland (Glück) **16**:125-30, 132-33, 136, 139-44, 147-49, 151, 153-54, 157
"House on the Cliff" (MacNeice) **61**:111
House on the Corner (Dove) See *The Yellow House on the Corner*
"The House on the Hill" (Robinson) **1**:459
"The House on the Hill" (Snodgrass) **74**:286
"House Party to Celebrate the Destruction of the Roman Catholic Church in Ireland" (Kavanagh) **33**:63, 79, 81; **105**:92, 100
"The House, The Environment: The Emperor" (Piercy) **29**:325
"House Under Construction" (Pavese) See "Casa in costruzione"
"A House with a History" (Hardy) **92**:275
Houseboat Days: Poems (Ashbery) **26**:140, 144-45, 153, 155, 162, 172
"Housecleaning" (Giovanni) **19**:140
"Household Poems" (Thomas) **53**:305
"Household Spirits" (Kinsella) **69**:133-34, 140
"The Householder" (Browning) **2**:59
"The Housekeeper" (Frost) **1**:193
"The Housemaid" (Wickham) **110**:267
"Houseman" (Brown) **55**:164
"The Houses" (Kipling) **91**:90
"Houses at Edge of Railway Lines" (Spender) **71**:166, 186, 225
"The Houses of Old Moscow" (Tsvetaeva) See "Domiki staroi Moskvy"
"The House-Top" (Melville) **82**:133, 191, 200, 203, 211
"The Housewife" (Gilmore) **87**:302
"Housewife" (Sexton) **2**:346, 370; **79**:194
"Houston 6 PM" (Zagajewski) **27**:402
"The Hovel of the Historian" (Char) See "Le Bouge de l'historien"
"How" (Atwood) **8**:24
"The How and the Why" (Tennyson) **6**:347
"How Annandale Went Out" (Robinson) **1**:461
"How Aunt Maud Took to Being a Woman" (Stone) **53**:234, 237, 245
"How can one teach 'Spring and Fall: To a Young Child' in the Hawaiian Islands?" (Mueller) **33**:191
"How Come?" (Ignatow) **34**:275, 277, 287
"How Cruel Is the Story of Eve" (Smith) **12**:309
"How do I love thee?" (Barrett Browning) **62**:84
"How Do I Love Thee" (Owen) **102**:227-28
"How Do You See?" (Smith) **12**:325, 332-33, 352
"How Do You Tell a Story?" (Wakoski) **15**:372
"How doth the little crocodile" (Carroll) **74**:24, 72
"How easl'y wert thou chained" (Campion) **87**:53
"How Everything Happens (Based on a Study of the Wave)" (Swenson) **14**:271
"How Faltering You Are, My Speech" (Yevtushenko) **40**:348
"How Few, of All the Hearts That Loved" (Brontë) **8**:50, 74
"How gently it rained" (Castro) See "Cómo llovía, suaviño"
"How Happy" (Corso) **108**:16
"How Happy I Used to Be" (Corso) **33**:48
"How Hill-Billy Jim Won the Great Fiddlers' Prize" (Benét) **64**:40, 43
"How I Came to Be a Graduate Student" (Rose) **13**:232
"How I Got That Name: An Essay on Assimilation" (Chin) **40**:8-9, 19, 21, 24, 31-2, 34
"How I See Things" (Komunyakaa) **51**:53
"How it feels to be touching you" (Piercy) **29**:301
"How It Goes On" (Kumin) **15**:207
"How It Is" (Kumin) **15**:204, 218-20
"How It Strikes a Contemporary" (Browning) **2**:80
"How John Quit the Farm" (Riley) **48**:319
"How Josette Takes Care of It" (Erdrich) **52**:193
"How 'Kaddish' Happened" (Ginsberg) **47**:27, 62-63
"How Like the Sound" (Kenyon) **57**:47
"How Lilies Came White" (Herrick) **9**:143
"How Lisa Loved the King" (Eliot) **20**:124
"How Love Looked for Hell" (Lanier) **50**:56
"How Lucy Backslid" (Dunbar) **5**:122, 146
"How Many Bards" (Keats) **1**:313
"How Many Devils Can Dance on the Point" (Enright) **93**:21, 35
"How Many Ham Have Twenty Pigs?" (Kipling) **91**:169
"How Many Heavens" (Sitwell) **3**:312
"How Many Nights" (Kinnell) **26**:257
"How Marigolds Came Yellow" (Herrick) **9**:102
"How Moss..." (Wagoner) **33**:348
"How Much Can It Hurt" (Levine) **22**:215
"How Much Earth" (Levine) **22**:219
"How My Fever Left" (Wright) **36**:340
"How Naked, How without a Wall" (Millay) **6**:238
"How Not to Die" (Corso) **108**:19
"How Not to Have to Dry the Dishes" (Silverstein) **49**:311, 328
"How Not to Settle It" (Holmes) **71**:120
"How Piaf Departed" (Yevtushenko) **40**:347
"How Pleasant to Know Mr. Lear" (Lear) **65**:146, 161, 186
"How Poems Are Made/ A Discredited View" (Walker) **30**:347
"How Potchikoo Got Old" (Erdrich) **52**:193
"How Raven Stole Light" (Wagoner) **33**:353
"How Right They Were, The Chinese Poets" (Enright) **93**:9, 18, 35
"How Roses Came Red" (Herrick) **9**:143
"How Roses Get Black" (O'Hara) **45**:164
"How Samson Bore Away the Gates of Gaza" (Lindsay) **23**:276
"How Shall I Woo Thee" (Dunbar) **5**:126
"How Shall My Animal" (Thomas) **52**:237, 316
"How She Was Given Her Name" (Tapahonso) **65**:258
"How Sigurd awoke Brynhild upon Hindfell" (Morris) **55**:333
"How Sleep the Brave . . ." (Collins) **72**:46, 51-52, 54, 61, 83, 87-88, 91, 94, 98, 119
"How Sleep the Brave" (Thoreau) **30**:203
"How sould I rewill me or in quhat wys" (Dunbar) **67**:13
"How Stone Held His Breath" (Wagoner) **33**:348, 353-54
"How strangely this sun reminds me of my love" (Spender) **71**:221
"How Stump Dreamed of Earthmaker" (Wagoner) **33**:348, 353
"How sweet I roam'd from field to field" (Blake) **12**:32, 36; **63**:27
"How the Ant Takes Part" (Bly) **39**:44
"How the Job Gets Done" (Chappell) **105**:38
"How the Old Horse Won the Bet" (Holmes) **71**:68, 85, 93, 112
"How the Wallflower Came First" (Herrick) **9**:102
"How the Women Went from Dover" (Whittier) **93**:225, 247-48, 250
"How They Don't Let Potchikoo into Heaven" (Erdrich) **52**:193
"How They Got Her to Quiet Down" (Stone) **53**:245-46, 249, 257
"How to Be Old" (Swenson) **14**:250, 288
"How to Build the Earthly Paradise" (Chappell) **105**:27, 46, 71, 75
"How to Die" (Sassoon) **12**:267, 285
"How to Enter a Big City" (Merton) **10**:337, 344
"How to Get On in Society" (Betjeman) **75**:38
"How to Get There" (O'Hara) **45**:125
"How to Kill" (Douglas) **106**:200, 203, 205, 210
"How to Live. What to Do" (Stevens) **110**:168
"How to Make a Good Chili Stew" (Ortiz) **17**:228, 233
"How to Pass, Kick, Fall, and Run" (Cage) **58**:202
"How to Regain Your Soul" (Stafford) **71**:334-35
"How to Write the Great American Indian Novel" (Alexie) **53**:34
"How Very Often at a Fashionable Ball" (Lermontov) **18**:297
"How We Are Spared" (Merwin) **45**:21
"how we avoid prayr" (Bissett) **14**:32
"How We Danced" (Sexton) **2**:366; **79**:202, 207
"How Yesterday Looked" (Sandburg) **2**:305
"How You Feel" (Cruz) **37**:5
"Howard at Atlanta" (Whittier) **93**:316, 318
"Howard Lamson" (Masters) **1**:338
"Howarth Churchyard" (Arnold) **5**:33-4, 52
"Howl" (Ginsberg) **4**:44-9, 51, 57-61, 63-5, 67-70, 73-5, 79; **47**:1-76
Howl, and Other Poems (Ginsberg) **4**:73, 87; **47**:3-5, 7-12, 30-37
Howl: Original Draft Facsimile (Ginsberg) **47**:49, 54-55, 57-60
Howling at the Moon (Hagiwara) See *Tsuki ni hoeru*
"The Howling of Wolves" (Hughes) **7**:137, 142, 159; **89**:114
Howls and Whispers (Hughes) **89**:188, 193, 206, 212, 234-35
"Hříšné město" (Seifert) **47**:331
Hristos voskres (Bely) **11**:7, 24, 28, 31, 33
"Hsiang Consort" (Li Ho) **13**:51-2
"Hsin-i Village" (Wang Wei) **18**:362
"Huckleberry Woman" (Merwin) **45**:46
"A Huddle of Need" (Berryman) **64**:100
"Hudson Ferry" (Schuyler) **88**:180, 213
The Hudson Letter (Mahon) **60**:229-30, 235-36
"The Hudsonian Curlew" (Snyder) **21**:292, 297, 308
"Hue, carcan!" (Laforgue) **14**:93
"La huella" (Mistral) **32**:186
"Los huesos de los muertos" (Mistral) **32**:175-76
"Hug o' War" (Silverstein) **49**:313
"Hugh, 1599" (Montague) **106**:344
Hugh Selwyn Mauberley (Pound) **4**:318-21, 330, 338-39, 341-42, 348; **95**:73, 96-97, 100, 102, 119-20, 122, 128-29, 155, 162-63, 176
"Hughie At The Inn" (Wylie) **23**:311
"Hugo at Théophile Gautier's Grave" (Lowell) **3**:224
"Huhediblu" (Celan) **10**:124

"L'Huillier, si nous perdons ceste belle Princess" (Ronsard) **11**:250
"L'huître" (Ponge) **107**:130, 153, 185, 190
"The Human Abstract" (Blake) **12**:10, 34; **63**:4, 10, 28, 48, 76, 79, 83-84, 92, 94-95, 105, 109, 120, 129
"Human Affection" (Smith) **12**:310
"Human Applause" (Cernuda)
See "Aplauso humano"
"Human Applause" (Hölderlin)
See "Menschenbeifall"
"Human Balloon" (Silverstein) **49**:342
"The Human Being Is a Lovely Creature" (Eberhart) **76**:23, 51
"Human Burning" (Aleixandre) **15**:19, 21
The Human Climate (Jacobsen) **62**:320
"Human Condition" (Gunn) **26**:185
"A Human Condition" (Stafford) **71**:293
"Human Cylinders" (Loy) **16**:322
"The Human Fold" (Muir) **49**:228
"Human Grief" (Trakl)
See "Menschliche Trauer"
"The Human Heart" (Riley) **48**:302
"Human Life" (Prior) **102**:306
"The Human Sacrament" (Koch) **80**:327
"Human Sacrifice" (Whittier) **93**:356-57, 359
Human Shows, Far Phantasies, Songs, and Trifles (Hardy) **8**:89; **92**:212, 241, 291
"The Human Situation" (Spender) **71**:166, 186, 210, 227-28
"Human Ties" (Storni)
See "Ligadura humana"
"Human to Spirit Humanism for Animals" (Baraka) **113**:17
"Human Torch" (Snodgrass) **74**:324, 332, 334
Human Wishes (Hass) **16**:215-17, 221-22
"A Humane Materialist . . ." (Smith) **12**:331
"L'humanitè" (Lamartine) **16**:266, 281, 293
"L'Humanité chaussait le vaste enfant Progrès" (Rimbaud) **57**:253
"The Humanities Building" (Shapiro) **25**:322
"Humanity I Love You" (Cummings) **5**:90
"Humanity Outfitted the Vast Child Progress" (Rimbaud)
See "L'Humanité chaussait le vaste enfant Progrès"
"Humanly Speaking" (Davie) **29**:110
"Humble Jar" (Song) **21**:344-48
"The Humble Petition of Frances Harris" (Swift) **9**:251, 296
"The humble Petition of poore Ben: To . . . King Charles" (Jonson)
See *The Under-Wood LXXVI*
"The Humble-Bee" (Emerson) **18**:79, 84-85, 93, 99
"Humildad" (Storni) **33**:279
"Humiliation" (Blok) **21**:5, 15
"Humility" (Chappell) **105**:19
"Humility" (Storni)
See "Humildad"
"The Humming-Bird" (Dickinson) **1**:79
"The Humming-Bird" (Very) **86**:127
"Hummingbirds" (Oliver) **75**:334
"Hummingbirds" (Stone) **53**:241
"Humor" (Yevtushenko) **40**:343-44
"The Humours" (Bradstreet)
See "Of the Four Humours in Man's Constitution"
"Humpbacks" (Oliver) **75**:285-86, 295
"Humpty-Dumpty" (Sarton) **39**:332
"Hunchback Girl: She Thinks of Heaven" (Brooks) **7**:53, 69, 80
"The Hunchback in the Park" (Thomas) **2**:394; **52**:281
"Der Hund" (Werfel) **101**:337
"A Hundred Collars" (Frost) **1**:215
A Hundred Joys (Szymborska)
See *Sto pociech*
"Hunger" (Cullen) **20**:63, 76
"Hunger" (Rich) **5**:374
"Hunger" (Simic) **69**:264
Hunger (Hogan)
See *The Book of Medicines*
Hunger and the Book of Medicines (Hogan)
See *The Book of Medicines*
"A Hunger Camp at Jaslo" (Szymborska)
See "Obóz glodowy pod Jaslem"
"Hunger in the South" (Neruda) **4**:282
"Hungerfield" (Jeffers) **17**:129, 136
Hungerfield and Other Poems (Jeffers) **17**:123, 136
"Hungry and Laughing Men" (Sandburg) **41**:313
"Hung-Up Age" (Corso) **33**:36, 38
"The Hunt" (Jones) **116**:83-85, 118, 162-63, 185, 238
"The Hunt By Night" (Mahon) **60**:146, 148, 150, 174, 202, 213
The Hunt by Night (Mahon) **60**:145-50, 154-56, 172-74, 186, 189-92, 194, 196-97, 201
"A Hunt in the Black Forest" (Jarrell) **41**:179, 192
"Hunt the Thimble" (Abse) **41**:14, 28-30
"The Hunter" (Macpherson) **97**:344
"The Hunter" (O'Hara) **45**:164
"The Hunter" (Williams) **7**:360
"The Hunter of the Black" (Gilmore) **87**:288, 301
"The Hunter of the Prairies" (Bryant) **20**:23
"Hunters" (Erdrich) **52**:172, 189, 191
"Hunter's Moon—Eating the Bear" (Oliver) **75**:294, 300-301
"The Hunters of Men" (Whittier) **93**:207, 243, 343
"The Hunter's Serenade" (Bryant) **20**:15
"Hunting Civil War Relics at Nimblewill Creek" (Dickey) **40**:155-57, 176, 226
Hunting herbs (Char)
See *Aromates chasseurs*
"The Hunting of the Hare" (Leapor) **85**:276
The Hunting of the Snark (Carroll)
See *The Hunting of the Snark: An Agony in Eight Fits*
The Hunting of the Snark: An Agony in Eight Fits (Carroll) **18**:30-33, 40-49; **74**:3-5, 7, 9-14, 25, 27-28, 35-41, 45, 53-58, 60-61, 63, 66-67, 72, 75, 77-79, 82-85, 107-8
"Hunting Pheasants in a Cornfield" (Bly) **39**:79-80, 82
"Hunting Watch" (Wang Wei) **18**:389
"Huntress" (H. D.) **5**:269
"The Huntress and Her Dogs" (MacDiarmid) **9**:191
"Huntsman, My Constellation" (Sachs)
See "Jäger, mein Sternbild"
Huntsman, What Quarry? (Millay) **6**:230-31, 233-24, 242; **61**:240
"The Huntsman's Apology" (Montague) **106**:232, 277
"The Huntsmen" (de la Mare) **77**:73
"Hurk" (Silverstein) **49**:329
"Hurrah for Karamazov!" (Viereck) **27**:279
"Hurrah for Positive Science" (Whitman) **3**:384
"Hurrah for Thunder" (Okigbo) **7**:235, 247
"The Hurricane" (Bryant) **20**:15
"The Hurricane" (Crane) **99**:20
"The Hurricane" (Finch)
See "A Pindarick Poem upon the Hurricane"
Hurricane Poem (Brathwaite)
See *Shar*
"Hurry Up Please It's Time" (Sexton) **2**:367-68; **79**:200, 209, 218, 237, 239, 282, 284-90, 292, 298-99, 332-35, 337-38, 340
"Hurrying Away from the Earth" (Bly) **39**:13
"Hurt Hawks" (Jeffers) **17**:117, 129
"Hurt Hawks II" (Jeffers) **17**:110
"The Hurt Trees" (Bell) **79**:3-4
"Hurucan" (Walcott) **46**:247
"Husband and Wife" (Patmore) **59**:231, 234
"Husband in the grave, son in prison" (Akhmatova)
See "Muzh v mogile, syn v tiur'me"
"The Husbands" (Hall) **70**:31
"Hush Gentle Streams" (Dobell) **100**:165
"Hush'd Be the Camps To-day" (Whitman) **3**:418
"The Huskers" (Whittier) **93**:172
"Huswifery" (Taylor) **63**:296-97, 316, 346, 351-52
"The Huxter" (Thomas) **53**:300-301, 303
"The Hyacinth Symphony" (Elytis) **21**:131
Hybrids of Plants and of Ghosts (Graham) **59**:131-32, 145, 168-70, 174-76, 183, 185
"Hydra" (Erdrich) **52**:189
"The Hydra" (Merwin) **45**:9, 25
"Hydrangeas" (Sandburg) **41**:234
"L'hydre Univers tordant son corps écaillé d'astres" (Hugo) **17**:90
"Hylas" (Carman) **34**:208-09
"L'hylas" (Ronsard) **11**:235
"A Hymb of Faith" (Riley) **48**:333, 335
"Hyme" (Donne)
See "Hymne to God my God, in my sicknesse"
Hymen (H. D.) **5**:266-70
"Hymme to God My God, in My Sicknesse" (Donne)
See "Hymne to God my God, in my sicknesse"
"Hymmnnl" (Ginsberg) **47**:71
"Hymn" (Ammons) **16**:27, 40, 57-8, 60, 63-5
"Hymn" (Betjeman) **75**:67, 81
"Hymn" (Boland) **58**:45, 53
"Hymn" (Dunbar) **5**:137
"Hymn" (Poe) **1**:446
"Hymn" (Randall) **86**:290, 298, 334
"Hymn" (Walker) **30**:340
"Hymn among the Ruins" (Paz)
See "Himno entre ruinas"
"Hymn before Action" (Kipling) **91**:66, 88-90
"Hymn before Sunrise in the Vale of Chamouni" (Coleridge) **11**:48-9, 53, 55-8, 92; **39**:156-57
"Hymn for Lanie Poo" (Baraka) **4**:15; **113**:92, 95-99, 148
"Hymn for My Brother's Ordination" (Longfellow) **30**:46
"A Hymn for the Ascension of the Holy Virgin" (Mickiewicz) **38**:162
"Hymn for the Blessed Sacrament" (Crashaw) **84**:29
"Hymn for the Celebration of Emancipation at Newburyport" (Whittier) **93**:213
"Hymn for the Dedication of a Cemetery" (Tuckerman) **85**:333
"Hymn from a Watermelon Pavilion" (Stevens) **6**:292
"Hymn III" (Pound) **95**:115
"Hymn in Adversity" (Cunningham) **92**:165-66, 186
"Hymn in the Holy Nativity" (Crashaw)
See "To the Holy Nativity"
"Hymn IV" (Ammons) **16**:22
Hymn No. IV (Evans) **40**:56
Hymn No. V (Evans) **40**:56
Hymn No. VIII (Cowper)
See "O Lord, I Will Praise Thee"
Hymn No. IX (Cowper)
See "The Contrite Heart"
Hymn No. II (Cowper)
See "Jehovah Our Righteousness"
Hymn No. I4 (Evans) **40**:56
Hymn No. II4 (Evans) **40**:56
Hymn No. II9 (Evans) **40**:56
Hymn No. III8 (Evans) **40**:56
Hymn No. IV1 (Evans) **40**:56
Hymn No. V8 (Cowper)
See "The New Convert"
Hymn No. LXVII (Cowper)
See "I will praise the Lord at all times"
"Hymn of Apollo" (Shelley) **14**:167, 170
"Hymn of Death" (Lamartine)
See "Hymne de la mort"
"Hymn of Not Much Praise for New York City" (Merton) **10**:344

"Hymn of Pan" (Shelley) **14**:167, 177
"Hymn of St. Thomas" (Crashaw) **84**:9
"Hymn of the Church in Meditation of the Day of Judgment" (Crashaw) **84**:31
"Hymn of the Great Return" (Sikelianos)
See "The Great Homecoming"
"Hymn of the Holy Cross" (Crashaw)
See "Vexilla Regis: the Hymn of the Holy Cross"
"Hymn of the Morning" (Lamartine)
See "L'hymne du matin"
"A Hymn of the Sea" (Bryant) **20**:3, 13
"Hymn of the Waldenses" (Bryant) **20**:5
"Hymn of Trust" (Holmes) **71**:62
Hymn on the Morning of Christ's Nativity (Milton) **29**:220-21
"Hymn to Adversity" (Gray)
See "Ode to Adversity"
"Hymn to Aphrodite" (Sappho)
See "Ode to Aphrodite"
"Hymn to Artemis Orthia" (Sikelianos) **29**:372
"Hymn to Beauty" (Baudelaire)
See "Hymne à la beauté"
"Hymn to Beauty" (Spenser)
See "An Hymne in Honour of Beautie"
"A Hymn to Christ, at the Authors Last Going into Germany" (Donne) **43**:131, 163
"Hymn to Colour" (Meredith) **60**:246, 278-81, 284, 299, 330
"Hymn to Death" (Bryant) **20**:4, 10, 13, 16, 18
"Hymn to death" (Ungaretti)
See "Inno alla morte"
"An Hymn to Diana" (Jonson) **17**:171, 182, 207
"Hymn to Dispel Hatred at Midnight" (Winters) **82**:344
"Hymn to Earth" (Wylie) **23**:304-306, 308, 311, 323
"An Hymn to God the Father" (Jonson) **17**:172
"Hymn to Heavenly Beauty" (Spenser)
See "An Hymne of Heavenly Beautie"
"An Hymn to Humanity" (Wheatley) **3**:338, 340-41, 348, 361, 363
"Hymn to Hymen" (Chapman) **96**:59
"Hymn to Ignorance" (Gray) **2**:143, 155
"Hymn to Intellectual Beauty" (Shelley) **14**:166, 169, 177-8, 187, 217, 234, 237-8; **67**:136, 139, 166, 202
"Hymn to Life" (Schuyler) **88**:181-82, 187-89, 191, 198, 201, 207, 223
Hymn to Life: Poems (Schuyler) **88**:179-80, 182, 187, 194, 197, 201, 206, 210, 221, 224
"Hymn to Love Ended" (Williams) **109**:286
"Hymn to Pan" (Chapman) **96**:71
"Hymn to Physical Pain" (Kipling) **3**:192
"Hymn to Priapus" (Lawrence) **54**:167, 169, 176, 241, 244
"Hymn to Proserpine" (Swinburne) **24**:316, 320, 338, 345-48
Hymn to Satan (Carducci)
See *Inno a Satana*
"Hymn to St. Teresa" (Crashaw) **84**:10, 19, 32, 49, 108-9, 120-21, 128, 153, 177
"An Hymn to the Evening" (Wheatley) **3**:361, 363
"Hymn to the Honor and Name of the Admirable Sainte Teresa" (Crashaw)
See "Hymn to St. Teresa"
"An Hymn to the Morning" (Leapor) **85**:249, 255
"Hymn to the Name above Every Name, the Name of Jesus" (Crashaw)
See "To the Name above Every Name"
"Hymn to the Name and Honor of the Admirable Sainte Teresa" (Crashaw)
See "Hymn to St. Teresa"
Hymn to the New Omagh Road (Montague) **106**:215, 237, 244, 251, 253-54, 256, 258, 262, 279, 292, 340
"An Hymn to the Morning" (Wheatley) **3**:361
"Hymn to the Night" (Longfellow) **30**:26, 45
"Hymn to the Penates" (Southey) **111**:193-94, 244, 252
"Hymn to the Seal" (Smith) **12**:295
"Hymn to the Sun" (Prior) **102**:309
"Hymn to the Supreme Being, on Recovery from a Dangerous Fit of Illness" (Smart) **13**:346
"Hymn to the Virgin" (Bishop) **34**:94
"Hymn to Venus" (Morris) **55**:329
Hymnarium (Werfel) **101**:325
"Hymne" (Baudelaire) **1**:63; **106**:130
"Eine Hymne" (Benn) **35**:26
"Hymne à la Beauté" (Baudelaire)
See "La Beauté"
"Hymne à la beauté" (Baudelaire) **1**:71
"Hymne au Christ" (Lamartine) **16**:280, 293
"L'hymne au soleil" (Lamartine) **16**:277
Hymne de Bacus, avec la version latine de Iean Dorat (Ronsard) **105**:274
"Hymne de Calaïs et de Zetes" (Ronsard) **11**:287
L'hymne de France (Ronsard) **105**:219
"Hymne de la mort" (Lamartine) **16**:283
"Hymne de la Mort" (Ronsard) **11**:226-27, 244, 269, 272-74
"L'hymne de la nuit" (Lamartine) **16**:262, 266, 292
"Hymne de l'ange de la terre apres la destruction de globe" (Lamartine) **16**:265, 281, 287
"Hymne de l'autonne" (Ronsard) **11**:230, 232-34, 267, 279
Hymne de l'Esté (Ronsard) **105**:213
"L'Hymne de l'hiver" (Ronsard) **11**:266
"Hymne de Pollux et de Castor" (Ronsard) **11**:284, 287
"L'hymne du matin" (Lamartine) **16**:267, 279, 292
"Hymne du printemps" (Ronsard) **11**:242
"An Hymne in Honour of Beautie" (Spenser) **8**:331, 337
"An Hymne in Honour of Love" (Spenser) **8**:337
"Hymne in the Glorious Epiphanie" (Crashaw)
See "To the Glorious Epiphany"
"Hymne of Beauty" (Spenser)
See "An Hymne in Honour of Beautie"
"An Hymne of Heavenly Beautie" (Spenser) **8**:332, 336-37, 345
"An Hymne of Heavenly Love" (Spenser) **8**:329, 332, 336-37, 345
"Hymne of Love" (Spenser)
See "An Hymne in Honour of Love"
"Hymne of the Nativity" (Crashaw)
See "To the Holy Nativity"
"A Hymne to Christ, at the authors last going into Germany" (Donne) **1**:139
"Hymne to God my God, in my sicknesse" (Donne) **1**:140, 158; **43**:179
"A Hymne to God the Father" (Donne) **1**:138-39; **43**:113, 133
"Hymne to St. Teresa" (Crashaw)
See "Hymn to St. Teresa"
Hymnes (Ronsard) **11**:248
Hymnes (Spenser)
See *Fowre Hymnes*
Les hymnes de P. de Ronsard a tresillustre et reverendissime Odet, cardinal de Chastillon (Ronsard) **105**:273
"Hymnes in Honor of Love and Beauty" (Spenser) **8**:331
Hymnos Aumnos (Clough) **103**:141
Hymns (Donne) **43**:115
Hymns (Ronsard)
See *Hymnes*
Hymns and Spiritual Songs for the Fasts and Festivals of the Church of England (Smart) **13**:332, 340-42, 368
Hymns for Children (Smart)
See *Hymns for the Amusement of Children*
Hymns for the Amusement of Children (Smart) **13**:340, 349, 361
Hymns for the Fasts and Festivals (Smart)
See *Hymns and Spiritual Songs for the Fasts and Festivals of the Church of England*
"Hymns to Death" (Ginsberg) **4**:58
"Hymns to the Sun, Moon, and the Elements" (Coleridge) **39**:131
"Hymnus in Cynthiam" (Chapman) **96**:28-29, 32, 46, 77, 114-15, 117-18, 122-24
"Hymnus in Noctem" (Chapman) **96**:22, 32, 77-79, 118, 120, 132-33
"Hyōhakusha no uta" (Hagiwara) **18**:183
Hyōtō (Hagiwara) **18**:176, 181, 183-84
Hyperion (Keats) **1**:278-79, 281-82, 284, 287-91, 305, 309; **96**:196-98, 216-17, 246-47, 282, 285, 288-90, 309, 339-40, 349
Hyperion: A Fragment (Keats)
See *Hyperion*
Hyperions Schiksalslied (Hölderlin) **4**:151
"Hypersonnet" (Zanzotto)
See "Ipersonetto"
"Hypocrite Auteur" (MacLeish) **47**:192
"Hypocrite lecteur" (Baudelaire)
See "Au lecteur"
"Hypocrite Swift" (Bogan) **12**:95, 101, 125
"Hysteria" (Eliot) **90**:300
"I" (Borges)
See "Yo"
"I" (Creeley) **73**:42, 85, 120
"I" (Thomas) **99**:309
I. 3 (Pindar)
See *Isthmian 3*
I. 4 (Pindar)
See *Isthmian 4*
"I abide and abide" (Wyatt) **27**:302
"i accuse us" (Birney) **52**:42
"I am" (Borges)
See "Soy"
"I Am" (Clare) **23**:22
"I Am" (Smith) **12**:314
"I Am a Beggar Always" (Cummings) **5**:100
"I Am a Camera" (Kaufman) **74**:184
"I Am a Cowboy in the Boat of Ra" (Reed) **68**:321, 323-24, 329-30, 332, 337-38, 347, 349
"I am a little world made cunningly" (Donne) **43**:160, 162
"I Am a Lonesome Hobo" (Dylan) **37**:70
"I Am a Most Fleshly Man" (Duncan) **75**:225
"I Am a Parcel of Vain Strivings Tied" (Thoreau) **30**:181, 188, 193, 199, 240, 245, 252, 254, 258, 293
"I Am a Sioux Brave, He Said in Minneapolis" (Wright) **36**:319, 403
"I Am a Victim of Telephone" (Ginsberg) **4**:85
"I Am an Old Town Square" (Viereck) **27**:280
"I Am as I Am" (Wyatt) **27**:317
"I Am Becoming My Mother" (Goodison) **36**:142, 144-45, 148, 154
I Am Becoming My Mother (Goodison) **36**:141, 143-44, 147, 149, 158
"I am Black" (Kaufman) **74**:272
"'I Am Cherry Alive,' the Little Girl Sang" (Schwartz) **8**:318
"I Am Dreaming of a White Christmas: The Natural History of a Vision" (Warren) **37**:301, 304-5, 307, 333
"I Am Guided in the Darkest Night" (Thoreau) **30**:258, 271
I Am in the Unstable Hour (Paz)
See *Vrindaban*
"I am Ireland" (Boland)
See "Mise Eire"
"I am Marilyn Mei Ling Chin" (Chin) **40**:31
"I Am Mortal" (Guillén) **35**:217, 220, 221
"I Am Not Afraid" (Duncan) **75**:124
"I Am Not Even Dust" (Borges)
See "Ni siquiera soy polvo"
"I Am Not Yours" (Teasdale) **31**:379
"I Am of Ireland" (Yeats) **20**:328
"I am Raftery" (Mahon) **60**:134, 196
"I Am She" (Giovanni) **19**:143

"I Am Sick and Tired of My Separateness" (Shvarts)
See "Mne moia otdel'nost' nadoela"
"I Am the Autumnal Sun" (Thoreau) **30**:180, 240, 254, 258, 265
"I Am the Bread of Life" (Very) **86**:138
"I Am the Hounded Slave" (Whitman) **91**:255
"I am the Individual" (Parra) **39**:277
"I am the Land, Surrounding Sea" (Barker) **77**:7
"I Am the Little Irish Boy" (Thoreau) **30**:182, 236, 258
"I am the One" (Hardy) **92**:210
"I Am the People, the Mob" (Sandburg) **41**:274, 315-16, 329, 332, 348, 364-65, 367
"I Am the Way" (Meynell) **112**:159
"I am the Way" (Very) **86**:136, 139
"I Am to My Own Heart Merely a Serf" (Schwartz) **8**:306
"I am too close for him" (Szymborska)
See "Jestem za blisko"
"I Am Untrue Yet I" (Jordan) **38**:120
"I Am Useless" (Storni)
See "Inútil soy"
"I am writing to you" (Lermontov) **18**:303
"I and Not I" (Muir) **49**:242
"I and Your Eyes" (Knight) **14**:39-40, 46
I Apologize for the Eyes in My Head (Komunyakaa) **51**:6, 15, 18-20, 30, 33, 52-54, 56, 62
"I Ask My Mother to Sing" (Lee) **24**:245
"I at creation" (Clifton) **17**:35
"i belong with th wind" (Bissett) **14**:34
"I Brought to Art" (Cavafy) **36**:75, 77, 91, 107
"I Built Myself a House of Glass" (Thomas) **53**:287-88
"I Came out of the Mother Naked" (Bly) **39**:16, 18, 22, 28, 55, 70, 94, 101, 103
"I Can Be Seen" (Ignatow) **34**:282
"An 'I' Can Never Be a Great Man" (Spender) **71**:179-80, 186, 217
"I Cannot Forget the High Spell" (Bryant) **20**:29
"I Cannot Stand Tears" (Bukowski) **18**:4
"I Can't" (Alurista) **34**:9, 46
"I care not for these Ladies" (Campion) **87**:41, 43-45, 65, 85, 107
"I climb the mossy bank of the glade" (Bridges) **28**:86
"I Climbed into the Tousled Hayloft" (Mandelstam) **14**:118, 122
I Colloqui (Gozzano) **10**:173, 176-81, 183-86
"I come and go" (Brutus) **24**:116
"i come from halifax" (Bissett) **14**:31
"I Come to Speak for Your Dead Mouths" (Wright) **36**:319
"I confess" (Chin) **40**:4
"I Congratulate You, Mamma" (Yevtushenko) **40**:341
"I Could Believe" (Levine) **22**:234
"I Cry, Love! Love!" (Roethke) **15**:248, 284, 298-301
"I Decided" (Cohen) **109**:22
"I Did Not Know the Spoils of Joy" (Schwartz) **8**:299
"I Die Alive" (Southwell) **83**:236-39, 280
"I Do Confess Thou Art Sae Fair" (Burns) **6**:81
"I Do Not Fear" (Thoreau) **30**:192
"I don't believe in the peaceful way" (Parra) **39**:311
"I Don't Know Why You Think" (Guillén)
See "No sé por qué piensas tú"
"I don't love you" (Baraka) **4**:19; **113**:139, 141
"I don't understand" (Yevtushenko) **40**:345
"I Dream" (Ignatow) **34**:324
"I Dream a World" (Hughes) **1**:259
"I dreamed" (Masefield) **78**:92
"I Dreamed I Saw St. Augustine" (Dylan) **37**:61-2
"I Dreamed in a Dream" (Whitman) **91**:198, 218
"I Dreamed My Genesis" (Thomas) **52**:237, 256
"I Dreamed that I Was Old; in Stale Declension" (Kunitz) **19**:175
"I Drive Westward" (Cunningham) **92**:161
"I due Titani" (Carducci) **46**:54
"I dut chaoy i dhi i gody" (Blok) **21**:17
"I Dwell in Possibility" (Dickinson) **1**:102
"I Dwelled in Hell on Earth to Write This Rhyme" (Ginsberg) **4**:79
"I Dye without desert" (Southwell) **83**:252
"I Exist, Well I Know It" (Cernuda) **62**:170
"I Experiment" (Douglas) **106**:191
"I Explain a Few Things" (Neruda)
See "Explico algunas cosas"
"I Explain the Silvered Passing of a Ship at Night" (Crane) **80**:52
"I Fellowed Sleep" (Thomas) **52**:245
"I Felt" (Ignatow) **34**:313, 317
"I find no peace, and all my war is done" (Wyatt)
See "I fynde no peace"
"I Foretell the Days of Yore" (Amichai) **38**:48
"I Found Her Out There" (Hardy) **8**:134; **92**:314-15
"I Found the Words to Every Thought" (Dickinson) **1**:102
"i found the world outside of me" (Alurista) **34**:38
"I from my window where the meuse is wide" (Belloc) **24**:11
"I fynde no peace" (Wyatt) **27**:342, 358
"I Gather the Limbs of Osiris" (Pound) **95**:219
"I Gave Away . . ." (Corso) **108**:4, 30
"I gift you this notebook" (Akhmadulina)
See "Dariu tebe siiu tetrad"
"I Give You Back" (Harjo) **27**:57, 61
"I Go Back to May 1937" (Olds) **22**:318
"I Had a Dream . . ." (Smith) **12**:295, 305-06, 318, 345
"I Had a Future" (Kavanagh) **33**:59-60, 62, 76
"I had eight birds hatcht in one nest" (Bradstreet)
See "In Reference to her Children, 23 June 1659"
"I Had No Human Fears" (Wordsworth) **4**:420
"I Hate America" (Ginsberg) **4**:74
"I Hate the Sea" (Martí)
See "Odio al mar"
"I Have" (Guillén)
See "Tengo"
I Have (Guillén)
See *Tengo*
"I Have a Friend" (Spencer) **77**:332
"I Have a Handsome Profile" (Auden) **92**:127
I Have a Name (Ignatow) **34**:344-45
"I Have Been Taught" (Muir) **49**:226, 299
"I Have Been Through the Gates" (Mew) **107**:56
"I Have Believed That I Prefer to Live" (Wylie) **23**:314
"i have evn herd uv thee" (Bissett) **14**:33
"I Have Folded My Sorrows" (Kaufman) **74**:212
"I Have Forgotten the Word I Wanted to Say" (Mandelstam) **14**:116, 155
"I Have Found my Flesh" (Alurista) **34**:23, 29, 47
"I Have Had to Learn to Live With My Face" (Wakoski) **15**:326, 330
"I Have Heard the Sunset Song of the Birches" (Crane) **80**:40
"I have known the hissing assemblies" (Kinsella) **69**:138-39
"I Have Lived in England" (Bukowski) **18**:5
"I Have Lived with Shades" (Hardy) **92**:221
"I Have Longed to Move Away" (Thomas) **2**:379, 389; **52**:236
"I Have Not Lingered in European Monasteries" (Cohen) **109**:52
"I Have Outlived My Desires" (Pushkin)
See "Ia Perezhil Svoi Zhelan'ia"
"I Have Seen the Spring" (Teasdale) **31**:336
"I Have Taken You" (Cohen) **109**:25
"I have the secret of wondrous blooming" (Akhmadulina)
See "Est' tajna u menja ot cudnogo cvetenija"
"I Have Three Daughters" (Stone) **53**:228
"I Have Written You Off" (Ignatow) **34**:345
"I Hear an Army" (Joyce)
See "XXXVI"
"I hear the cries of evening" (Spender) **71**:152, 180-81, 219
"I Heard" (Niedecker) **42**:147
"I Heard Immanuel Singing" (Lindsay) **23**:284, 288
"I Heard Wild Geese" (Ekeloef) **23**:87
"i herd ya laffin in th water" (Bissett) **14**:33
"I Hoed and Trenched and Weeded" (Housman) **2**:192; **43**:240, 248
"I, in My Intricate Image" (Thomas) **52**:226, 237, 241, 245
"I Jehova Decree" (Parra)
See "Yo Jehová decreto"
I kalosíni stis likoporiés (Elytis) **21**:128
"I Keep repeating the first line" (Tsvetaeva)
See "Vse Povtoryayv pervyi stikh"
"I Keep to Myself Such Measures . . ." (Creeley) **73**:38, 44, 48, 105, 125-28
"I knew a clean man" (Niedecker) **42**:183
"I Knew a Man by Sight" (Thoreau) **30**:181
"I Knew a Woman" (Roethke) **15**:275, 286, 289
"I Knew I'd Sing" (McHugh) **61**:196-97, 205
"I Knew Not 'Twas So Dire a Crime" (Brontë) **8**:72
"I Know" (Bely)
See "Znayu"
"I Know a Man" (Creeley) **73**:4, 7, 59-61, 63, 66, 69, 123
"I Know All This When Gipsy Fiddles Cry" (Lindsay) **23**:275, 280, 287
"I Know I Am but Summer to Your Heart" (Millay) **6**:225
"I Know This Vicious Minute's Hour" (Thomas) **2**:405
I, Laminarian (Césaire)
See *moi, Laminaire*
"I Lay Next to You All Night Trying Awake to Understand the Watering Places of the Moon" (Wakoski) **15**:364
"I Learned to Sew" (Yamada) **44**:346
"I Left a Woman Waiting" (Cohen) **109**:68
"I Like Rats" (Koch) **80**:319
"I Like the Way You Opposed Me" (Cohen) **109**:25
"I like to Sleep" (Alurista) **34**:23, 29, 42
"I live in a proper kitchen garden" (Mandelstam)
See "Ia zhivu na vazhnykh ogorodakh"
"I Live in Subtraction" (Jordan) **38**:118
"I Live Up Here" (Merwin) **45**:22
"I Look at My Hand" (Swenson) **14**:281
"I Look at the Future With Fear" (Lermontov) **18**:281
"I Look into My Glass" (Hardy) **8**:90; **92**:212, 285
"I love all beauteous things" (Bridges) **28**:84
I Love Artists: New and Selected Poems (Berssenbrugge) **115**:46
"I love frosty breath . . . and reality is reality" (Mandelstam)
See "Liubliu moroznoe dykhan'e"
"I Love Music" (Baraka) **113**:60, 63, 68
"I love thee" (Hood) **93**:78
"I love thee, mournful, sober-suited Night" (Smith) **104**:182
"I Love to Fly" (Ignatow) **34**:323
"I Love You" (Chappell) **105**:51
"I Loved You Once" (Randall) **86**:291, 340, 343
"I Lovve Loyyd" (Wyatt) **27**:371
"I, Maister Andro Kennedy" (Dunbar) **67**:5, 7
"I Make This in a Warring Absence" (Thomas) **52**:263, 316
"I Make Ye An Offer" (Thoreau) **30**:193, 216

"I married" (Niedecker) **42**:100, 137, 183-84
I Marry You: A Sheaf of Love Poems (Ciardi) **69**:25, 29, 36, 39-41, 52, 55
"I, Maximus of Glouster, to You" (Olson) **19**:276, 280-81
"I May, I Might, I Must" (Moore) **4**:256; **49**:110, 123, 126, 140
"I May Reap" (Kavanagh) **33**:99
"I Meet the Motion of Summer Thinking Guns" (Ciardi) **69**:14
"I Meet Them" (Stone) **53**:258
"I Met This Guy Who Died" (Corso) **33**:44; **108**:4
"I Might Have Seen It" (Ashbery) **26**:133
"I Miss My Dear Cats" (Corso) **33**:41
"I misteri della pedagogia" (Zanzotto) **65**:270
"I must complain" (Campion) **87**:25, 27, 32, 35, 71-72
"I must live, though I've already died twice" (Mandelstam)
See "Ia dolzhen zhit', khotia ia dvazhdy umer"
"I must repress" (Spender) **71**:216
"I Need Help from the Philosophers" (Stern) **115**:248
"I Need, I Need" (Roethke) **15**:252, 272-73, 277, 298
"I Never Hear That One Is Dead" (Dickinson) **1**:94
"I Never Saw a Moor" (Dickinson) **1**:101
"I Never Saw That Land Before" (Thomas) **53**:307, 309, 317, 319
"I nuovi credenti" (Leopardi) **37**:92-93
"I Only Am Escaped Alone to Tell Thee" (Nemerov) **24**:261
"I paesaggi primi" (Zanzotto) **65**:274
"I Plant in Your Favor This Tree of Cybele" (Ronsard)
See "Je plante en la faveur cest arbre de Cybelle"
"I Poeti di Parte Bianca" (Carducci) **46**:52
"I Pressed My Hands Together..." (Akhmatova) **2**:11
"I Pursue a Form" (Darío)
See "Yo persigo una forma"
"I re magi" (Leopardi) **37**:165, 169
"I Read Yeats" (Dorn) **115**:156
"I Reckon—When I Count at All—/First—Poets" (Dickinson) **1**:96
"I Remember" (Boland) **58**:47
"I Remember" (Smith) **12**:314, 320
"I Remember Galileo" (Stern) **115**:248, 270
"I Remember, I Remember" (Hood) **93**:62, 79, 103, 117
"I Remember, I Remember" (Larkin) **21**:228, 231, 246
"I Rode with My Darling" (Smith) **12**:327
"I rose from marsh mud" (Niedecker) **42**:136, 169
"I rose up as my custom is" (Hardy) **92**:236
"I Said" (H. D.) **5**:305
"I Said It" (Baraka) **4**:13
"I Said to Poetry" (Walker) **30**:344
"I Sailed Up a River with a Pleasant Wind" (Thoreau) **30**:192, 195
"I Save Your Coat, but You Lose It Later" (Gallagher) **9**:44, 60
"I Saw a Delicate Flower" (Thoreau) **30**:236
"I Saw a Man" (Crane) **80**:40, 52, 57-58
"I Saw Eternity" (Bogan) **12**:89, 100, 121
"I Saw Here Here" (Masefield) **78**:90
"I Saw in Louisiana a Live-Oak Growing" (Whitman) **3**:402
"I Saw Thee on Thy Bridal Day" (Poe)
See "Song"
"I Saw While Sitting" (Cernuda)
See "Veía sentado"
"I See a Truck" (Ignatow) **34**:305
"I See around Me Tombstones Grey" (Brontë) **8**:74
"I See the Boys of Summer" (Thomas) **2**:384; **52**:232, 322
"I See What I Want" (Darwish) **86**:11
"I Seek the Present Time" (Thoreau) **30**:227
"I Seek the Word" (Szymborska) **44**:292
"I Shall Be Free" (Dylan) **37**:60
"I Shall Be Released" (Dylan) **37**:55
"I Shall Never See You Again" (Masters) **1**:333, 338
I Shall Not Be Moved (Angelou) **32**:25, 30
"I Shall Not Care" (Teasdale) **31**:345, 379, 387-88
"I Shall Say How You Were Born" (Cernuda)
See "Diré como nacisteis"
"I Shall Some Day" (Das) **43**:76, 85
"I Showed Him My Wound" (Ignatow) **34**:306, 350
"i shun like the owl" (othersAlurista) **34**:32
"I Sing of Olaf Glad and Big" (Cummings) **5**:88
"I Sing the Body Electric" (Whitman) **3**:385, 396; **91**:206-8, 216, 230-31, 258, 260
"I Sing to the Sea" (Parra)
See "Se canta al mar"
"I sing when my throat is moist . . ." (Mandelstam)
See "Poiu kngda gortan' syra . . ."
"I Sit and Look Out" (Whitman) **91**:214
"I Sit by the Window" (Brodsky) **9**:8, 13
"I Sit in My Room" (Toomer) **7**:337
"I sonetti del ritorno" (Gozzano) **10**:188
"I Speak of the City" (Paz)
See "Hablo de la ciudad"
I Sterna (Seferis) **66**:93, 99, 105, 111, 147, 182, 184-85
"I Stood Musing in a Black World" (Crane) **80**:80, 84
"I Stood on a High Place" (Crane) **80**:82
"I Stood on Tiptoe" (Keats)
See "I Stood Tip-Toe"
"I Stood Tip-Toe" (Keats) **1**:291, 313; **96**:222, 265, 349
"I Stood upon a Highway" (Crane) **80**:77
"I Stop Writing the Poem" (Gallagher) **9**:65
"I Struck a Diminished Seventh" (Ammons) **16**:39
"I Studied All Men" (Das) **43**:84
"I Substitute for the Dead Lecturer" (Baraka) **113**:12, 27, 29, 41
"I swear" (Akhmadulina) **43**:9
"I swive as well as others do" (Wilmot)
See "The Mock Song"
"I Swore to Stab the Sonnet" (Shapiro) **25**:322
"I Take Back Everything I've Said" (Parra)
See "Me retracto de todo lo dicho"
"I Take Care of You: A Lantern Dashes by in the Glass" (Gallagher) **9**:50
"I Taste a Liquor Never Brewed" (Dickinson) **1**:80
"I Taste the Ashes of Your Death" (Bukowski) **18**:7
"I Tell You for Several Years of My Madness I Heard the Voice of Lilith Singing in the Trees of Chicago" (Carruth) **10**:85
"I that in heill wes and gladnes" (Dunbar) **67**:5, 10-11
"I' the Glooming Light" (Tennyson)
See "Song"
"I the Woman" (Cisneros) **52**:160
"I Think" (Schuyler) **88**:189
"I Think Continually of Those Who Were Truly Great" (Spender) **71**:135, 139, 158, 168, 180, 219-20, 251
"I think: how stupid I have been" (Akhmadulina)
See "La dumaiu: kak ia byla glupa"
"I think, yes, a leopard in Duty blue would" (Villa) **22**:355
"I Thirst" (Harper) **21**:198
"I Thought of You" (Teasdale) **31**:360
"I to My Perils" (Housman) **2**:180
"I Told Susan Reyna" (Cisneros) **52**:159, 164
"I, Too" (Hughes) **53**:94, 106, 109
I Too Am a Painter (Apollinaire)
See *Et moi aussi je suis peintre*
"I, Too, Have Been to the Huntington" (Cunningham) **92**:179
"I, Too, Know What I Am Not" (Kaufman) **74**:181, 183, 261, 271
"I, Too, Sing America" (Hughes) **1**:241, 258-59
"I took from its glass" (Tuckerman) **85**:334
"I Travel as a Phantom Now" (Hardy) **8**:89; **92**:207
"I Uncork Another Bottle" (Parra) **39**:263
"I Used to Be But Now I Am" (Berrigan) **103**:45
"I Vecchi" (Pound) **4**:317
"I visit the graves" (Niedecker) **42**:99
"I Visited Again" (Pushkin)
See "Vnov' Ya Posetil"
"I' vo pensando" (Petrarch) **8**:227
"I. W. to Her Unconstant Lover" (Whitney) **116**:277-78
"I Wahodd Dyddgu" (Dafydd ap Gwilym) **56**:207, 238, 247
"I Wake Up at Dawan" (Parra) **39**:262-63
"I Walked out to the Graveyard to See the Dead" (Eberhart) **76**:51, 58
"I Walked over the Grave of Henry James" (Eberhart) **76**:49
"I walkt the other day" (Vaughan) **81**:278, 281, 367
"I Wandered Lonely as a Cloud" (Wordsworth) **4**:388, 400
"I Want" (Ignatow) **34**:305
"I Want, I Want" (Plath) **37**:182
"I Want New York" (Nash) **21**:263
"I Want You" (Dylan) **37**:51
"I Wanted to be There When My Father Died" (Olds) **22**:325-26, 341-42
"I wanted to stay in September" (Cassian) **17**:5
"I Was" (Cernuda) **62**:171
"I Was a Middle-Aged Corrupter of Youth" (Enright) **93**:33
"I Was a Poet in the House of Frankenstein" (Yau) **61**:337, 358
"I Was Afraid of Dying" (Wright) **36**:332
"I Was Angry" (Ignatow) **34**:282, 345
"I Was Born in Lucerne" (Levine) **22**:226
"I was Born Upon Thy Bank River" (Thoreau) **30**:216
"I was born with an unlined palm" (Shvarts) **50**:142, 144, 146
"i was just cummin" (Bissett) **14**:34
"I Was Made Erect and Lone" (Thoreau) **30**:245
"I was not born to hate" (Castro)
See "Yo no he nacido para odiar"
"I was not young long; I met the soul early" (Villa) **22**:351
"I Was Reading a Scientific Article" (Atwood) **8**:13
"I Was Sick and in Prison" (Very) **86**:152
"I Was Taught Three" (Graham) **59**:131, 183
"I Was Washing Outside in the Darkness" (Mandelstam) **14**:122
"I Wasn't One of the Six Million" (Amichai) **38**:47-49
"I Watched a Snake" (Graham) **59**:132, 148, 151, 174
"I Went" (Cavafy) **36**:74, 108
"I Went into the Maverick Bar" (Snyder) **21**:293, 296-97
"I Where I Stand" (Corso) **33**:37; **108**:6
"I Will Be" (Cummings) **5**:93
"I will break God's seamless skull" (Villa) **22**:352
"I Will Lie Down" (Swenson) **14**:286
"I Will Love the Twenty-First Century" (Strand) **63**:188
"I will praise the Lord at all times" (Cowper) **40**:55
"I Will Put Chaos into Fourteen Lines" (Millay) **6**:243, 246
"I Will Sing You One-O" (Frost) **1**:195
"I Will Wade Out" (Cummings) **5**:91
"I Wish" (Kaufman) **74**:216

"I Wish I Had Great Knowledge or Great Art" (Schwartz) **8**:294
"I Wish I My Never Hear of the United States Again" (Wright) **36**:358
"I Wisht I was Unwed Again" (Gilmore) **87**:302
"I wonder by my troth" (Donne)
See "The good-morrow"
"I Would Have Been a Trumpet Player If I Hadn't Gone to College" (Baraka) **4**:36
"I Would I Were a Careless Child" (Byron) **16**:73, 86-8
"I Would Live in Your Love" (Teasdale) **31**:388
"I would not be thought less than a man" (Brutus) **24**:116
"I Would Not Paint—a Picture" (Dickinson) **1**:102
"I Would Return South" (Neruda)
See "Quiero volver a sur"
"I Would Steal Horses" (Alexie) **53**:41
I Would Steal Horses (Alexie) **53**:3
I Wouldn't Have Missed It: Selected Poems of Ogden Nash (Nash) **21**:277
"i10 de Octubre!" (Martí) **76**:99
"Ia dolzhen zhit', khotia ia dvazhdy umer" (Mandelstam) **14**:151
"Ia Perezhil Svoi Zhelan'ia" (Pushkin) **10**:412
"Ia zhivu na vazhnykh ogorodakh" (Mandelstam) **14**:152
"Iago Prytherch" (Thomas) **99**:233
Iambics and Epodes (Carducci)
See *Giambi ed epodi*
"Ibadan Lagos Kano London 5 Jan 72" (Brutus) **24**:123
Ibis (Ovid) **2**:238, 242, 244
IBM (Bissett) **14**:15
"Ibo" (Hugo) **17**:83, 89
"Ibsen" (Muir) **49**:243
"Icarian Bird" (Thoreau) **30**:216
"Icarian Wings" (Cullen) **20**:67
"Icarium Mare" (Wilbur) **51**:249, 309
Ice Cod Bell or Stone (Birney) **52**:11-14, 17, 44-46, 67, 74, 94
"Ice Cream at Blaunberg" (Tomlinson) **17**:353
"The Ice Eagle" (Wakoski) **15**:324, 363
"Ice Handler" (Sandburg) **41**:261, 365
The Ice Land (Hagiwara)
See *Hyōtō*
"Ice Shall Cover Nineveh" (Rexroth) **95**:262, 271
"Ice Storm" (Hayden) **6**:193-4
"Ice Storm" (Kenyon) **57**:4, 43
"The Iceberg" (Merwin) **45**:7
"Iceboy's Bolero" (Espada) **74**:133
"The Ice-Cream Wars" (Ashbery) **26**:136
"Iceland First Seen" (Morris) **55**:340
"Iceland Revisited" (Auden) **92**:67-68
"The Ice-Storm" (Pinsky) **27**:174
"Ich" (Stramm) **50**:175
"Ich habe eine gute Tat getan" (Werfel) **101**:345
"Ich staune" (Werfel) **101**:360
"Ichabod" (Whittier) **93**:177, 185, 210, 235, 239, 264-68, 280-81, 335, 344
"Ich-Gefühl" (Benn) **35**:50
Ichiaku no suna (Ishikawa) **10**:193, 200-02, 204-05, 210-11, 216
"Ichigatsu" (Nishiwaki) **15**:231-32
"Ich-Zerfall" (Benn) **35**:50
"Icicles" (Pinsky) **27**:158
Ici-haut. Pamyati Maksimilian Voloshin (Tsvetaeva) **14**:324
Iconographs (Swenson) **14**:268-72, 274, 281, 285-86
"The Icosasphere" (Moore) **49**:101, 126
"Ida Chicken" (Masters) **36**:230, 244
"Idaho" (Ashbery) **26**:137
"Idaho" (Winters) **82**:315, 319, 322
Idaho Out (Dorn) **115**:85
"Idaho Out" (Dorn) **115**:58-60, 62-63, 66, 74, 79, 92, 102, 108, 122, 126, 128, 134-35, 137-38, 140, 159, 228
Idea (1594) (Drayton)
See *Ideas Mirrour. Amours in Quatorzains*
Idea (1599) (Drayton)
See *Ideas Mirrour. Amours in Quatorzains*
Idea (1619) (Drayton)
See *Ideas Mirrour. Amours in Quatorzains*
"The Idea of Ancestry" (Knight) **14**:39, 41, 43-4, 52-3
"The Idea of Order at Key West" (Stevens) **6**:305, 307, 325, 327; **110**:94-95, 147-48, 150-51
"The Idea of Order at the Józef Attila Estate" (Szirtes) **51**:178
"The Idea of Trust" (Gunn) **26**:207, 220
Idea. The Shepheards Garland, Fashioned in Nine Eglogs. Rowlands Sacrifice to the Nine Muses (Drayton) **98**:26, 38, 50, 57, 65, 68, 93, 125
"The Ideal Father" (Olds) **22**:322
"Ideal Landscape" (Rich) **5**:393
"Ideal Love" (Amichai) **38**:19
"Ideas" (Merrill) **28**:267
Ideas Mirrour. Amours in Quartorzains (Drayton) **98**:7, 53, 119-29
Ideas of Order (Stevens) **6**:296-97, 318-19, 330-32, 335, 337; **110**:93, 141-42, 156, 168
"L'idee de Dieu" (Lamartine) **16**:265-66, 293
"L'Idée du devenir" (Éluard) **38**:96-97
"Lo idéntico" (Paz) **48**:207
"Identity" (Ammons) **16**:27, 29
"Identity: A Poem" (Stein) **18**:334
"Identity and Argument for Prayer" (Warren) **37**:313
"Identity Card" (Darwish)
See "Bitaqat Huwiyya"
"The Ides of March" (Cavafy) **36**:28
"Idillio di Maggio" (Carducci) **46**:49-50
"Idillio maremmano" (Carducci) **46**:11, 36-37, 50, 56-58, 62-66, 79-80
"The Idiocy of Human Aspiration" (Mahon) **60**:237
Idiom (Zanzotto)
See *Idioma*
Idioma (Zanzotto) **65**:289, 296-99, 303, 338
"Idiot" (Tate) **50**:228, 280, 311-13
"The Idiot Boy" (Wordsworth) **4**:372, 374, 381, 416-18, 426-27; **67**:261-63, 276, 278, 282-83, 287-88, 295, 297-98, 304, 311-13, 316, 319-20, 327-28, 330, 346-48, 365, 368-69
"Idiot Wind" (Dylan) **37**:56
"The Idle Shepherd-boys" (Wordsworth) **67**:328, 351
"An Idle Visitation" (Dorn) **115**:54, 87, 123, 154, 216-18
"The Idler" (Very) **86**:113
"The Idols of the Tribe" (Tolson) **88**:329, 344
"Idoto" (Okigbo) **7**:223, 225
Idut belye snegi (Yevtushenko) **40**:359, 363
"Idyl" (Parker) **28**:355
"An Idyl of the King" (Riley) **48**:312, 340
"Idyll" (Roethke) **15**:246
"Idyll of the Maremma" (Carducci)
See "Idillio maremmano"
"Idylls in Colour Film" (Curnow) **48**:45
Idylls of the Bible (Harper) **21**:185
Idylls of the Hearth (Tennyson)
See *Enoch Arden, and Other Poems*
Idylls of the King (Tennyson) **6**:358, 360, 369, 374, 376, 379, 406-08; **101**:120-21, 134, 192, 194, 196, 199, 202-5, 208-10, 215-18, 220-21, 223-25, 228-29, 237, 240, 245, 265, 284-90, 292
"Idylls of the King: Balin and Balan" (Tennyson) **6**:376-77
"Idylls of the King: Gareth and Lynette" (Tennyson) **6**:373, 376
"Idylls of the King: Pelleas and Ettarre" (Tennyson) **6**:376
"Idylls of the King: The Coming of Arthur" (Tennyson) **6**:408
"Idylls of the King: The Last Tournament" (Tennyson) **6**:376
"If" (Kipling) **3**:176, 183-84, 188; **91**:111
"If" (Thomas) **53**:296
"If a Man Could Only Say" (Cernuda) **62**:171, 173
"If Actually Dead" (Cavafy) **36**:112
"If any hath the heart to kill" (Campion) **87**:71
"If Anyone Had Told Me" (Aleixandre)
See "If Someone Could Have Told Me"
"If Anything Will Level with You Water Will" (Ammons) **16**:54
"If Blood Were Not as Powerful as It Is" (Gallagher) **9**:59
"If Cynthia be a Queen, a Princes, and Supreme" (Raleigh)
See "If Synthia be a Queene, a princes, and supreame"
"If Dead Indeed" (Cavafy) **36**:20, 38
"If Death is Kind" (Teasdale) **31**:334
"If Ever You Go to Dublin Town" (Kavanagh) **33**:63, 81, 89, 147; **105**:100, 110, 136, 155, 164
"If faithfull soules be alike glorifi'd" (Donne) **43**:164
"If Fun Is Fun Isn't That Enough?" (Nash) **21**:274
"If I Am Too Brown or Too White for You" (Rose) **13**:241
"If I Could Only Live at the Pitch That Is Near Madness" (Eberhart) **76**:12, 23-24, 34, 36, 50, 58, 68-69
"If I Had Children" (Swenson) **14**:279
"if i have made, my lady, intricate" (Cummings) **5**:87
"If I Knew What Poets Know" (Riley) **48**:325
"If I Leave You" (Ríos) **57**:329
"If I Should Cast off This Tattered Coat" (Crane) **80**:80
"If I Think About You Again It Will Be the Fifty-Third Monday of Next Year" (Harjo) **27**:70
"If I Were Dead" (Patmore) **59**:209
"If I Were God I'd" (Randall) **86**:345
"If I Were Four-and-Twenty" (Yeats) **51**:147
"If I Were Lord of Tartary" (de la Mare)
See "Tartary"
"If I were Paris" (Johnson) **24**:144
"If I Were President of Chile" (Parra)
See "Si yo fuera presidente de Chile"
"If I Were Tickled by the Rub of Love" (Thomas) **2**:384, 386, 401; **52**:227
"If I Were to Own" (Thomas) **53**:328
"If in Beginning Twilight of Winter Will Stand" (Cummings) **5**:109-10
"If It All Went Up In Smoke" (Oppen) **35**:304
"If It Be Your Will" (Cohen) **109**:100
"If It Chance Your Eye Offend You" (Housman) **2**:184
"If It Should Ever Come" (Dorn) **115**:106
"If It Were Spring" (Cohen) **109**:52, 56, 58
"If It Were You" (Page) **12**:179
"If Love loves truth" (Campion) **87**:25, 59
"If love may perswade" (Campion) **87**:68
"If mine eyes can speake" (Sidney) **32**:235
"If, My Darling" (Larkin) **21**:236, 248
"If My Head Hurt a Hair's Foot" (Thomas) **2**:386, 407; **52**:262
"If Now You Desperately Call the One Name" (Sachs)
See "Rufst de nun den einen Namen verzweifelt"
"If Only" (Rossetti) **7**:280
"If Only We Could Communicate" (Hall) **70**:32
"If perchance, my Fabio" (Juana Inés de la Cruz)
See "Si acaso, Fabio mío"
"If poysonous mineralls, and if that tree" (Donne) **43**:160, 162, 164
"If Snakes Were Blue" (Warren) **37**:378
"If Someone Could Have Told Me" (Aleixandre) **15**:4
"If Synthia be a Queene, a princes, and supreame" (Raleigh) **31**:218, 239, 304

"If the Pope Doesn't Break with the U.S.A." (Parra)
See "Si el Papa no rompe con el USA"
"If There are Any Heavens My Mother Will (All by Herself) Have" (Cummings) **5**:88
"If They Come in the Night" (Piercy) **29**:311
"If This Is the Way It Is" (Warren) **37**:326, 341
"If thou longst" (Campion) **87**:58, 71-72, 91, 120
"If waker care if sudden pale colour" (Wyatt) **27**:368
"If We Must Die" (McKay) **2**:206-07, 211, 217, 220, 229
"If We Take All Gold" (Bogan) **12**:122
"If, When Don Cupid's Dart" (Suckling) **30**:138
"If Words Are Signs" (Waldrop) **109**:122
"If yet I have not all thy love" (Donne)
See "Lovers infinitenesse"
"If You" (Creeley) **73**:55-57, 90
If You (Creeley) **73**:3
If You Call This Cry a Song (Carruth) **10**:77
"If You Got a Notion" (Kennedy) **93**:144
"If You Had Known" (Hardy) **92**:328
"If You Only Knew..." (Guillén)
See "Ay negra, si tu supiera"
"If You Saw a Negro Lady" (Jordan) **38**:126
"If You See Her, Say Hello" (Dylan) **37**:54
"If You See Me in L.A. It's Because I'm Looking for the Airport" (Cruz) **37**:30
"IFF" (Nemerov) **24**:289
"If-ing" (Hughes) **53**:115
Igitur; ou, la folie d'Elbehnon (Mallarmé) **4**:199, 201-03, 208; **102**:62, 87-90, 100, 135
Ignatius His Conclave (Donne) **43**:119, 125
"Ignis Fatuus" (Tate) **50**:229, 286, 318
"Ignorance" (Larkin) **21**:227, 246
"Ignorance of Death" (Empson) **104**:85
"L'Ignorant" (Jaccottet) **98**:158, 174-76
L'Ignorant: Poèmes (Jaccottet) **98**:148-49, 170-75, 179-84, 186, 195
"I,it,was,that,saw" (Villa) **22**:355
"Ikarus" (Benn) **35**:47, 48, 49, 68, 77
"Ike" (Dove) **6**:109
"Ike Walton's Prayer" (Riley) **48**:302
"Ikey (Goldberg)'s Worth I'm" (Cummings) **5**:82
"Il bove" (Carducci) **46**:11, 49, 75
"Il canto dell' amore" (Carducci) **46**:6, 11, 53, 55, 73, 89
"Il comune rustico" (Carducci) **46**:53, 76, 81, 84, 88
"Œil de sourd" (Éluard) **38**:69
Il dolore (Ungaretti) **57**:338-39, 360, 377
Il galateo in bosco (Zanzotto) **65**:263, 266, 269-71, 277-86, 289, 296-301, 303, 338
"Il Liuto e la Lira" (Carducci) **46**:52
"Il mio paese è l'Italia" (Quasimodo) **47**:284
"Il nini muart" (Pasolini) **17**:251, 256, 281, 284
"Il n'y a rien d'incompréhensible" (Éluard) **38**:96
"Il Passero Solitario" (Leopardi) **37**:81-82, 124, 139
"Il penseroso" (Gray) **2**:141
"Il Penseroso" (Milton) **19**:193, 201-02, 226, 229-33, 249, 255; **29**:232, 240-41
"Il Pensiero Dominante" (Leopardi) **37**:92, 103, 110, 123-24
"Il piccolo Rifiuto" (MacNeice) **61**:166
"Il plebiscito" (Carducci) **46**:56
"Il pleure dans mon coeur" (Verlaine) **32**:362-63
"Il pleut" (Apollinaire) **7**:20, 34
"Il poeta" (Carducci) **46**:81
"Il Ponte Vecchio Di Firenze" (Longfellow) **30**:51
Il Porto Sepolto (Ungaretti) **57**:338, 375
"Il Primo Amore" (Leopardi) **37**:78, 81, 84, 111, 123
"Il reduce" (Gozzano) **10**:184-85, 190
"Il Risorgimento" (Leopardi) **37**:109, 142, 145
"Il sabato del villaggio" (Leopardi) **37**:102, 115, 120
"Il Sogno" (Leopardi) **37**:82, 102, 123
"Il Sonetto" (Carducci) **46**:75
Il Taccuino del Vecchio (Ungaretti) **57**:339
"Il tramonto della luna" (Leopardi) **37**:102, 124, 126, 133, 138
"Il y a" (Apollinaire) **7**:22
Iliad (Homer) **23**:149, 151-53, 155-57, 159-63, 165-72, 175-89, 191
Iliads (Homer)
See *Iliad*
The Iliads of Homer (Chapman) **96**:13, 23-25, 36-37, 45, 133
Ilias (Homer)
See *Iliad*
Ílios o prótos (Elytis) **21**:119-20, 124, 127
"I'll Be Your Baby Tonight" (Dylan) **37**:49
"I'll Come Back" (Ignatow) **34**:277
"Ill Humor" (Werfel)
See "Unmut"
"(Ill Ill)" (Zanzotto)
See "(ILL) (ILL)"
"(ILL ILL)" (Zanzotto)
See "(ILL) (ILL)"
"(ILL) (ILL)" (Zanzotto) **65**:269
"Ill Ill" (Zanzotto)
See "(ILL) (ILL)"
"ILL ILL" (Zanzotto)
See "(ILL) (ILL)"
"I'll never forget it" (Castro)
See "Jamás lo olvidare!"
"I'll Run Wild in the Dark Streets Gypsy Camp" (Mandelstam) **14**:119
"I'll tell thee everything I can . . ." (Carroll) **74**:29
"I'll tell thee now (dear love) what thou shalt doe" (Donne)
See "A Valediction: of the booke"
"I'll Tell You a Tale of a Wife" (Burns) **114**:129
"Illic Jacet" (Housman) **2**:184
"Illileo" (Riley) **48**:322
"Illinois Farmer" (Sandburg) **2**:316
"The Illiterate" (Meredith) **28**:188
"Illumination" (Hecht) **70**:108
"The Illumination" (Kunitz) **19**:174-75, 178
"Illuminations" (Glück) **16**:151
Illuminations (Rimbaud)
See *Les illuminations*
Les illuminations (Rimbaud) **3**:249, 254, 259-65, 279; **57**:191, 197, 214, 224-25, 227-30, 234-36, 238-41, 243-44, 246-47, 251, 253-54, 260, 266, 269, 271-74, 276-77, 280-82, 284-87, 293-94, 296, 300
"Les *Illuminations* à l'Opéra-Comique" (Ponge) **107**:72
"The Illusion of Eternity" (Eberhart) **76**:45
The Illustrated Wilfred Funk (Ferlinghetti) **1**:186
"Illustration" (Ashbery) **26**:123, 137
"The Illustration" (Levertov) **11**:168
"Illustrations of the Poetic as a Sense" (Stevens) **110**:202
"Illustrative Lines" (Duncan) **75**:232
"Ilu, the Talking Drum" (Knight) **14**:39, 41, 44-6
I'm a Stranger Here Myself (Nash) **21**:264
"I'm Clean, How about You" (Dorn) **115**:201
"Im Feuer" (Stramm) **50**:171, 188
"Im Geheimnis" (Sachs) **78**:122
Im Geschweige der Liebe (Stramm) **50**:176
"I'm Guided in the Darkest Night" (Thoreau) **30**:227, 268
"Im Hafen" (Heine) **25**:157-58, 160, 163-64
"I'm Here" (Ignatow) **34**:310
"I'm Here" (Roethke) **15**:270, 272, 279
"Im Osten" (Trakl) **20**:225-26, 250, 255-56
"I'm Still Not Patriarch" (Mandelstam) **14**:122
"I'm Sure of It" (Baca) **41**:37
"I'm Thankful that My Life doth not Deceive" (Thoreau) **30**:193
"I'm Unwilling" (Ammons) **16**:44
"I'm Wife....I'm Woman Now" (Dickinson) **1**:93
"Im winterlichen Hospital" (Werfel) **101**:330
"I'm Working on the World" (Szymborska) **44**:299
I'm Your Man (Cohen) **109**:29-30, 32, 35, 80
"The Image" (Day Lewis) **11**:146
"The Image" (Ignatow) **34**:328
The Image and the Law (Nemerov) **24**:255, 260, 264, 285, 288-89, 298
"An Image from a Past Life" (Yeats) **20**:328
"An Image from Beckett" (Mahon) **60**:134, 144, 192, 195, 198
The Image Marker (Merrill) **28**:270
"The Image of God" (Barrett Browning) **6**:20
"Image of her whom I love" (Donne) **43**:194
"An Image of Leda" (O'Hara) **45**:117, 201, 206-7
"Image of Man as a Gardener after Two World Wars" (Ciardi) **69**:55
"Image of the Engine" (Oppen) **35**:297, 308, 338
"Imagen" (Storni) **33**:239
"The Images" (Rich) **5**:385, 396
"Images à Crusoe" (Perse) **23**:210, 217, 228, 230, 234-35, 247, 254, 256-57
"Images d'un sou" (Verlaine) **32**:378
"Images for Godard" (Rich) **5**:366, 391
"Images in place of logging" (Birney) **52**:37
"Images of Angels" (Page) **12**:168-69, 177, 190
"Images of Crusoe" (Perse)
See "Images à Crusoe"
"Images of Elspeth" (Berryman) **64**:102
"Images of Perfection" (Tomlinson) **17**:349
"An Imaginable Conference" (Updike) **90**:350
"Imaginary Elegies" (Spicer) **78**:253, 288, 301-3
"The Imaginary Iceberg" (Bishop) **34**:79, 188-89
"The Imaginary Jew" (Berryman) **64**:80
"The Imaginary Man" (Parra)
See "El hombre imaginario"
"Imaginary Prisons" (Schnackenberg) **45**:330, 336, 342, 346-47, 349
"Imaginary Translation" (Hacker) **47**:80
"Imagination" (Wheatley)
See "On Imagination"
"The Imagination's Pride" (de la Mare) **77**:77, 83, 125
Imagine the Angels of Bread (Espada) **74**:139, 144-46, 149, 156, 158, 169
"Imagining How It Would Be to Be Dead" (Eberhart) **76**:40, 49
"Imago" (Boland) **58**:38, 40
"Imago" (Clampitt) **19**:82
"Imbécile habitant" (Éluard) **38**:85
"Imenos" (Cavafy) **36**:110, 111
"Imitation" (Behn)
See "In Imitation of Horace"
L'imitation de Notre-Dame la lune (Laforgue) **14**:57, 61, 70-1, 80, 97
"Imitation from the Armenian" (Akhmatova) **55**:7
"Imitation of Boileau" (Shvarts) **50**:138
"Imitation of Byron" (Lermontov) **18**:302
Imitation of Horace, Epistle I, i (Pope)
See *Satires and Epistles of Horace, Imitated*
Imitation of Horace, Epistle II, i (Pope)
See *Satires and Epistles of Horace, Imitated*
Imitation of Horace, Satire II, i (Pope)
See *Satires and Epistles of Horace, Imitated*
"An Imitation of Spenser" (Blake) **12**:31
Imitation of the Second Epistle of the Second Book of Horace (Pope)
See *Satires and Epistles of Horace, Imitated*
"An Imitation of the Sixteenth Ode of the Third Book of Horace" (Duck) **89**:10
Imitations (Lowell) **3**:213, 223, 228, 232
Imitations (Pope)
See *Satires and Epistles of Horace, Imitated*

"Imitations of Drowning" (Sexton) **2**:363
"Imitations of Horace" (Swift) **9**:265
Imitations of Horace (Pope)
See *Satires and Epistles of Horace, Imitated*
Imitations of Horace, The First Epistle of the Second Book (Pope)
See *Satires and Epistles of Horace, Imitated*
L'immaculée conception (Éluard) **38**:91, 96-7
"Immanence" (Warren) **37**:326
"Immanuel Kant and the Hopi" (Stern) **115**:248
"Immature Pebbles" (Zukofsky) **11**:355
"The Immeasurable Expanses of Despair" (Barker) **77**:2
"Immer hinter den Rändern der Welt" (Sachs) **78**:208
The Immigrant Iceboy's Bolero (Espada) **74**:112-14, 122, 127-28, 133-35, 139-40, 145, 149, 152, 158, 167
"The Immigrants" (Atwood) **8**:38
Immigrants in our Own Land (Baca) **41**:37-8, 55, 70
"The Immigration Department" (Cassian) **17**:5-6
The Immobile Wind (Winters) **82**:313, 334
"Immobilism" (Graham) **59**:175-76
"Immoderately Mourning My Brother's Untimely Death" (Lovelace) **69**:159, 177, 237-38
"Immolated" (Melville) **82**:78
"The Immoral Proposition" (Creeley) **73**:7, 28, 39, 88
The Immoral Proposition (Creeley) **73**:3
"The Immortal" (Simic) **69**:278, 307
"Immortal Autumn" (MacLeish) **47**:126-27, 188, 213, 253
"Immortal Helix" (MacLeish) **47**:130, 156, 197, 213
The Immortal Husband (Merrill) **28**:227
"Immortal Ode" (Wordsworth)
See "Ode: Intimations of Immortality from Recollections of Early Childhood"
"The Immortal Part" (Housman) **2**:179, 192; **43**:256-58, 261
"L'immortalité" (Lamartine) **16**:275, 279, 291, 300, 302
"Immortality" (Lamartine)
See "L'immortalité"
"Immortality" (Reese) **29**:333
"Immortality Ode" (Wordsworth)
See "Ode: Intimations of Immortality from Recollections of Early Childhood"
"Immortality over the Dakotas" (Warren) **37**:366, 377
"The Immortals" (Parker) **28**:360
"Immortelle" (Carman) **34**:202
Immortelle maladie (Péret) **33**:220, 223-24, 230-31
"Immutable Moods" (Corso) **33**:49; **108**:13
"The Impalpabilities" (Tomlinson) **17**:327, 357
"Impasse" (Hughes) **1**:260
"Impasse" (Sandburg) **41**:310
"L'Impatient" (Éluard) **38**:69, 87
"L'impenitent" (Verlaine) **2**:417
"Imperator Victus" (Crane) **99**:111, 114
"Imperatrix" (Wickham) **110**:298
"The Impercipient" (Hardy) **8**:107-08, 112; **92**:289, 319
"The Imperfect Enjoyment" (Wilmot) **66**:267, 269-70, 290, 324, 329, 342-43, 354, 367
"The Imperfect Lover" (Sassoon) **12**:258
Imperfect Thirst (Kinnell) **26**:288, 290, 293-94
"Imperia" (Gautier) **18**:125
"Imperial Adam" (Hope) **56**:270, 286, 288
"The Imperial Bison is" (Guillén)
See "Está el bisonte imperial"
"Imperialism" (Graham) **59**:131, 134, 152, 157-58
"The Implements of Augury" (Simic) **69**:287
"Important" (Silverstein) **49**:328
"Impossibilità della parola" (Zanzotto) **65**:265, 275
"The Impossibility of the Word" (Zanzotto)
See "Impossibilità della parola"
"L'impossible" (Rimbaud) **57**:191, 195, 243, 249, 251
"The Impossible Indispensibility of the Ars Poetica" (Carruth) **10**:86
"Impossible to Tell" (Pinsky) **27**:174-6
"The Impossible Woman/Ideal" (Jiménez)
See "Quimérica"
"Impotence" (Bell) **79**:3
"Impotence of the Heart" (Werfel)
See "Trägheit des Herzens"
"Impression of Exile" (Cernuda) **62**:169, 172
"Impressionism" (Mandelstam) **14**:118
"The Impressionist" (Wickham) **110**:265
"Impressionist Picture of a Garden" (Lowell) **13**:95
"L'Imprévu" (Baudelaire) **106**:126
"Imprint for Rio Grande" (Toomer) **7**:337
"Imprisonment of Queene Elenor" (Deloney) **79**:57
"Impromptu" (Benn) **35**:26
"Impromptu In a Low Key" (Curnow) **48**:19, 42-43, 45
"Impromptu on Lord Holland's House" (Gray)
See "On Lord Holland's Seat near Margate, Kent"
"Impromptu on the English Court" (Wilmot) **66**:324
"Impromptu: The Suckers" (Williams) **109**:195
"Impromptus (Thoughts About Zasha)" (Randall) **86**:346
"Improprieties" (Jackson) **44**:68
"The Improvement" (Traherne) **70**:189, 268, 288, 291-92, 314
"An Improvisation" (Ignatow) **34**:300
"An Improvisation for the Stately Dwelling" (Ammons) **16**:32, 63
"Improvisations" (Williams) **109**:231-32
"Improvisations: Lights and Snow" (Aiken) **26**:50
"The Improvisatore" (Coleridge) **11**:105
"L'impuissance est vaincue" (Mallarmé) **102**:19
"Impute me righteous, thus purg'd of evil" (Donne) **43**:149
"In 1864" (Tapahonso) **65**:248, 257
"In 1929" (Spender) **71**:180, 217, 241
"In a Back Alley" (Sandburg) **41**:314
"In a Bad Light" (Boland) **58**:25, 60, 96-97
"In a Bad Time" (Stevens) **110**:181
"In a Bath Teashop" (Betjeman) **75**:7, 28
"In a Bird Sanctuary" (Wilbur) **51**:188
In a Blue River (Berrigan) **103**:31, 34-35
"In a Boat" (Belloc) **24**:5
"In a Buggy at Dusk" (Milosz) **8**:205
"In a Burying Ground" (Teasdale) **31**:356
"In a Bye-Canal" (Melville) **82**:86, 97, 149
"In a Caledonian Forest" (MacDiarmid) **9**:176
"In a Castle" (Lowell) **13**:70
"In a Cemetery" (Aleixandre) **15**:18
"In a Church of Padua" (Melville) **82**:97, 106, 150
"In a Churchyard" (Wilbur) **51**:259
"In a Clearing" (Merwin) **45**:15
"In a Copy of Browning" (Carman) **34**:203
"In a Country Church" (Thomas) **99**:235, 348-49
"In a Country Churchyard" (Blunden) **66**:7-9
"In a Cuban Garden" (Teasdale) **31**:360
"In a Dark Time" (Roethke) **15**:268, 276, 278, 281, 306, 313
"In a Darkening Garden" (Teasdale) **31**:339, 373
"In a Deserted Rest Home" (Akhmadulina)
See "V opustevshem dome otdykha"
"In a District of Asia Minor" (Cavafy) **36**:33
"In a Dry Land" (Sarton) **39**:323
"In a Eweleaze near Weatherbury" (Hardy) **92**:341
"In a Garden" (Carman) **34**:219
"In a Garret" (Melville) **82**:74, 174
"In a Glass of Water Before Retiring" (Benét) **64**:22
"In a Gondola" (Browning) **2**:26
"In a Gothic Cathedral" (Carducci)
See "In una Chiesa Gotica"
"In a Gothic Church" (Carducci)
See "In una Chiesa Gotica"
"In A Grand Pré Garden" (Carman) **34**:225
"In a Green Night" (Walcott) **46**:229-33, 238, 247, 270-74, 276, 285, 322-25
"In a Hard Intellectual Light" (Eberhart) **76**:34, 51, 67
"In a Hospital" (Teasdale) **31**:358
In a Marine Light (Carver)
See *Ultramarine*
"In a Museum" (Hardy) **92**:214, 326
"In a Myrtle Shade" (Blake) **63**:4
"In A Poem" (Frost) **39**:357
"In a Prominent Bar in Secaucus One Day" (Kennedy) **93**:129, 138, 148, 153
"In a redneck bar down the street" (Cisneros) **52**:147, 153, 160
"In a Rosary" (Swinburne) **24**:322, 324
"In a Ship Recently Raised from the Sea" (Page) **12**:168, 184
"In a Spanish Garden" (Stryk) **27**:187
"In a Station of the Metro" (Pound) **4**:355; **95**:116
"In a Strange House" (Kunitz) **19**:148
"In a Subway Station" (Teasdale) **31**:331
"In a Time of Dearth" (Lowell) **13**:83
"In a Time of Revolution for Instance" (Ferlinghetti) **1**:188
In a Time of Violence (Boland) **58**:17-21, 47-50, 68, 85, 92, 96-98, 100
"In a Township of Asia Minor" (Cavafy) **36**:40
"In a Train" (Bly) **39**:79
"In a Troubled Key" (Hughes) **1**:254-55
In a Vast Dominion (Aleixandre)
See *En un vasto dominio*
"In a Waiting-Room" (Hardy) **8**:107
"In a Whispering Gallery" (Hardy) **8**:108; **92**:214
"In a Wood" (Hardy) **92**:327
"In Absence" (Lanier) **50**:71
"In Absentia" (Ignatow) **34**:202
"In Amicum Foeneratorem" (Vaughan) **81**:358
"In Africa" (Randall) **86**:343
"In Amorem divinum" (Crashaw) **84**:52
"In an Act of Pity" (Creeley) **73**:41
"In an Artist's Studio" (Rossetti) **7**:284-85
"In an Iridescent Time" (Stone) **53**:227
In an Iridescent Time (Stone) **53**:215-18, 220, 227-28, 230, 239, 242
"In an Old Book" (Cavafy) **36**:75, 76
"In an Open Palm" (Ignatow) **34**:323
"In & Out" (Berryman) **64**:100
"In Another Fashion" (Ondaatje) **28**:298, 318
"In Answer of an Elegiacal Letter, upon the Death of the King of Sweden, from Aurelian Townsend, inviting me to write on that subject" (Carew) **29**:13, 50, 74
"In Answer of Sir John Suckling's Verse" (Waller) **72**:335
"In Arden" (Tomlinson) **17**:326, 343, 346-48, 353
"In Arthur's House" (Morris) **55**:261, 306
"In August" (Soto) **28**:380
"In Autumn" (Merwin) **45**:20-1
"In Autumn" (Meynell) **112**:157, 287
In Autumn (Ekeloef) **23**:71
"In Bed" (Koch) **80**:342
"In Bed with Joan & Alex" (Berrigan) **103**:35
"In Belfast" (Mahon) **60**:171, 182
"In Blood" (Berrigan) **103**:34
"In Blood's Domaine" (Duncan) **2**:120; **75**:209, 250, 258-59
"In Bretonem" (Campion) **87**:5
"In Broad Daylight" (Szymborska) **44**:297
In Broken Country (Wagoner) **33**:349, 352, 362

"In Broken Images" (Graves) **6**:134-35, 137, 151, 153
"In Buque-Escuela" (Storni) **33**:305
"In California" (Stafford) **71**:267
"In Carrowdore Churchyard" (Mahon) **60**:157, 190, 193, 215, 220, 223
"In casa del sopravissuto" (Gozzano) **10**:180, 183, 185, 189
"In Celebration" (Strand) **63**:152, 161
"In Celebration of My Uterus" (Sexton) **2**:352-53; **79**:248, 253, 317
"In celebration of the yearely Preserver of the Games" (Davenant) **99**:175
"In Chains" (Williams) **109**:197
"In Chopin's Garden" (Davie) **29**:110
"In Church" (Cavafy) **36**:38
"In Church" (Thomas) **99**:241, 256, 349-50, 357
"In circumcisionem" (Crashaw)
See "On the Circumcision"
"In City Gardens Grow No Roses as We Know Them" (Goodison) **36**:154
In Cold Hell, in Thicket (Olson) **19**:284
"In Context" (Thomas) **99**:259, 337
"In Country Heaven" (Thomas) **2**:395; **52**:274-76, 283, 313, 316-17, 324
"In Country Sleep" (Thomas) **2**:395; **52**:274-76, 281, 303, 315-18, 320-22, 324
"In court to serve" (Wyatt) **27**:367
"In Danger from the Outer World" (Bly) **39**:48, 51
"In Dear Detail, by Ideal Light" (Stafford) **71**:264, 362
"In Death, Cannot Reach What Is Most Near" (Ginsberg) **47**:38
"In Defense of Metaphysics" (Tomlinson) **17**:315
In Defense of the Earth (Rexroth) **20**:181, 186, 188, 190, 192, 194, 209; **95**:247-48, 254, 258, 273, 314, 319, 334, 348
"In den Wohnungen des Todes" (Sachs) **78**:117
In den Wohnungen des Todes (Sachs) **78**:110-11, 113-14, 128, 130, 161, 164-65, 167-68, 170, 193, 198, 200-201, 203, 207, 225
"In der Fremde" (Bridges) **28**:77, 81
"In deserto" (Gautier) **18**:156
"In 'Designing a Cloak to Cloak His Designs,' You Wrested from Oblivion a Coat of Immortality for Your Own Use" (Moore) **49**:115, 117
"In Despair" (Cavafy) **36**:75, 77
"In die Passionis Dominicæ" (Crashaw)
See "On the Day of the Master's Passion"
"In Distrust of Merits" (Moore) **4**:236, 238, 240, 249, 261, 267-69; **49**:93, 101, 126, 134, 144
"In Dock" (Guest) **55**:195
In Dreams Begin Responsibilities, and Other Stories (Schwartz) **8**:281-82, 291, 294, 300-01, 305-07, 319
"In Drear Nighted December" (Keats) **96**:204, 213, 260
"In Durance" (Pound) **95**:121
"In Early Spring" (Meynell) **112**:189, 284-85, 295
"In England" (Brodsky) **9**:8
"In Eternum I was ons Determed" (Wyatt) **27**:318, 324
"In Europe they grow a new bean while here" (Niedecker) **42**:151
"In Evening Air" (Roethke) **15**:275, 281
"In Examination" (Brooke) **24**:57
"In Excelsis" (Lowell) **13**:91, 97
"In Excelsis" (Sexton) **79**:245
"In Exchange for Haiku" (Niedecker) **42**:96, 102, 137-38
"In Exile" (Boland) **58**:88
"In Explanation of Our Times" (Hughes) **1**:258
"In Extremis: Poems about My Father" (Berry) **28**:30
In Fact (Ciardi) **69**:13
"In Fear and Valor" (Stafford) **71**:377
"In Fear of Harvests" (Wright) **36**:340
"In February" (Meynell) **112**:231
"In Florida" (Swenson) **14**:272
"In Fog" (Stafford) **71**:288-89
"In Freiburg Station" (Brooke) **24**:62, 66
"In Front of the Landscape" (Hardy) **92**:260
"In Fur" (Stafford) **71**:297
"In Gallarus Oratory" (Heaney) **18**:201, 223
"In Galleries" (Jarrell) **41**:185
In Gemäldegalerien (Heine) **25**:131
In Glad Thanksgiving (Masefield) **78**:49, 73, 85, 88, 99
"In Glenelly Valley" (Heaney) **100**:263
"In Gold Lacquer" (Carman) **34**:211
"In Golden Gate Park That Day" (Ferlinghetti) **1**:183
"In Gratitude to Beethoven" (Wakoski) **15**:345
"In Great Waters" (Thomas) **99**:274
"In Guernsey" (Swinburne) **24**:325-26
"In Harmony with Nature" (Arnold) **5**:31, 38, 49
"In Haste" (Guillén) **35**:218
"In Her Own Image" (Boland) **58**:13
In Her Own Image (Boland) **58**:5-6, 12, 29-30, 33, 37, 41, 44-45, 51, 72-73, 77, 91, 98
"In Her Praise" (Graves) **6**:171-72
"In Him We Live" (Very) **86**:42, 126
"In Honor of David Anderson Brooks, My Father" (Brooks) **7**:62
"In Honor of Those the Negroes Are Revolting Again" (Corso) **108**:22
"In Honour of America, 1917" (Meynell) **112**:174, 177
"In Honour of Du Bartas" (Bradstreet) **10**:2, 6, 52
"In Honour of that High and Mighty Princess, Queen Elizabeth" (Bradstreet) **10**:37, 56
"In Hospital" (Pasternak)
See "V bol'nitse"
"In Imitation of Boileau" (Shvarts) **50**:135
"In Imitation of Horace" (Behn) **88**:16, 150, 152
"In Innocence" (Cunningham) **92**:146, 166
"In Ireland" (Meynell) **112**:303
"In Isolation" (Jacobsen) **62**:331
"In Italy" (Brodsky) **9**:23
"In January" (Brooke) **24**:61, 82
"In Just-" (Cummings) **5**:88, 104
"In Kashmir" (Sarton) **39**:345-6
"In Kovalchick's Garden" (Stern) **115**:250
"In Laughter" (Hughes) **7**:159
"In Lieu" (MacNeice) **61**:176
"In Lieu of the Lyre" (Moore) **4**:259; **49**:145, 149
"In Limbo" (Wilbur) **51**:236-38, 247, 280, 335-36
"In limine" (Montale) **13**:114-15, 165
"In Llandough Hospital" (Abse) **41**:14, 19
In London (Creeley) **73**:117, 120
"In Love" (Das) **43**:72, 85
"In Love for Long" (Muir) **49**:232, 245, 250-51, 298
"In Love Made Visible" (Swenson) **14**:274, 284
"In Love with You" (Koch) **80**:300, 310
"In Loving Memory of the Late Author of Dream Songs" (Meredith) **28**:180, 199, 202, 205, 216-17
"The Lybian Hunter, a Fable" (Leapor)
See "The Libyan Hunter, A Fable"
"In Lycium et Clytham" (Campion) **87**:100
"In Lyric Season" (Carman) **34**:210
In Mad Love and War (Harjo) **27**:66-7
"In Medias Res" (Stafford) **71**:276, 289, 368
"In meiner Kammer" (Sachs) **78**:136
"In Melleam" (Campion) **87**:35
"In Memoriam" (Brodsky) **9**:23
"In Memoriam" (Bryant) **20**:45
"In Memoriam" (Carruth) **10**:85
"In Memoriam" (Enright) **93**:33
"In memoriam" (Mistral) **32**:154
"In Memoriam" (Reese) **29**:349
"In Memoriam" (Roethke) **15**:279
"In Memoriam" (Sarton) **39**:358
"In Memoriam" (Seferis) **66**:119, 124-25
"In Memoriam" (Ungaretti) **57**:365
In Memoriam (Tennyson) **6**:354, 359-60, 362-64, 367-71, 379, 388, 392-94, 398-99, 403, 405-08, 412, 416; **101**:124, 130-34, 145, 161-62, 172, 177-81, 183-85, 215-17, 219-25, 237, 242, 244, 251, 257-65, 269, 274-80
"In memoriam A. G." (Cernuda) **62**:266
"In Memoriam (Easter, 1915)" (Thomas) **53**:325
"In Memoriam F. A. S." (Stevenson) **84**:307, 326
"In Memoriam: Gertrud Kolmar, 1943" (Hope) **56**:277
In Memoriam James Joyce: From A Vision of World Language (MacDiarmid) **9**:163-66, 173, 180, 182-84, 186
"In Memoriam Mae Noblitt" (Ammons) **16**:62
"In Memoriam N. K. M. (1889-1947)" (Meredith) **28**:190
"In Memory of the Vertuous and Learned Lady Madre de Teresa" (Crashaw) **84**:20, 27, 48, 96
"In Memoriam PW Jr 1921-1980" (Kumin) **15**:221
"In Memoriam, R. L. M. G." (Curnow) **48**:5, 9
"In Memoriam Stratton Christensen" (Meredith) **28**:185, 209
"In Memoriam: Wallace Stevens" (Duncan) **2**:114; **75**:145
"In Memory" (Kinsella) **69**:82, 131
"In Memory: After a Friend's Sudden Death" (Levertov) **11**:206
"In Memory of A. I. Odoevsky" (Lermontov) **18**:268, 298
"In Memory of a Spanish Poet" (Wright) **36**:319, 338
"In Memory of Ann Jones" (Thomas)
See "After the Funeral: In Memory of Anne Jones"
"In Memory of Arthur Winslow" (Lowell) **3**:218
"In Memory of Charles Coffin" (Wright) **36**:377
In Memory of David Archer (Barker) **77**:40
"In Memory of Dylan Thomas" (Curnow) **48**:12
"In Memory of Elena" (Forché)
See "The Memory of Elena"
"In Memory of Eva Gore-Booth and Con Markiewicz" (Yeats) **20**:349
"In Memory of Jack" (Kenyon) **57**:35
"In Memory of Leopardi" (Wright) **36**:320
"In Memory of Lost Brain Cells" (Snodgrass) **74**:332
"In Memory of Major Robert Gregory" (Tomlinson) **17**:307
"In Memory of Major Robert Gregory" (Yeats) **20**:321, 327; **51**:98
"In Memory of My Dear Grandchild Elizabeth Bradstreet" (Bradstreet) **10**:27, 45
"In Memory of My Feelings" (O'Hara) **45**:120, 128, 130, 141-43, 147, 154, 168, 192, 225
"In Memory of My Mother" (Kavanagh) **33**:63, 73, 81, 96, 143, 147-8; **105**:99, 154
"In Memory of Radio" (Baraka) **4**:14; **113**:5, 33, 39-40, 96, 126-27, 148
"In Memory of Robert Frost" (Meredith) **28**:195, 202, 216
"In Memory of the Ottomans" (Wright) **36**:378
"In Memory of Vachel Lindsay" (Teasdale) **31**:346
"In Memory of W. B. Yeats" (Auden) **1**:14
"In Memory of W. H. Auden" (Stern) **115**:258, 283
"In Memory of Walter Savage Landor" (Swinburne) **24**:335
"In Michigan" (Masters) **1**:329; **36**:175-76
"In Mind" (Levertov) **11**:211-13
"In mine one Monument" (Lovelace) **69**:219
"In Montgomery" (Brooks) **7**:82
"In Monument Valley" (Merrill) **28**:255
"In morte del realismo" (Pasolini) **17**:259
"In Morte di G. B. Niccolini" (Carducci) **46**:51
"In Morte di Giovanni Cairoli" (Carducci) **46**:51

"In Morton's Grille" (Berrigan) **103**:26
"In Mr. Minnit's House" (Ransom) **61**:274
"In Mundum" (Campion) **87**:5
"In My Chamber" (Sachs)
See "In meiner Kammer"
"In My Craft or Sullen Art" (Thomas) **2**:383
"In My Day We Used to Call It Pussy-Whipped" (Bukowski) **18**:15
"In My Dreams" (Smith) **12**:343
"In My Father's House There Are a Few Mansions, More Hovels, and Probably Even More Ranch Houses" (Ciardi) **69**:13
"In My First Hard Springtime" (Welch) **62**:339, 355, 370, 372
In My Honor (Rilke) **2**:280
"In My Land" (Baca) **41**:37
"In My Life, On My Life" (Amichai) **38**:48
"In My Lifetime" (Welch) **62**:338, 361-62, 370, 372
"In My Room" (Berrigan) **103**:38
In My Secret Life (Cohen) **109**:79
"In My Solitary Hours" (Bradstreet) **10**:62-3
"In Nature There Is Neither Right Nor Left Nor Wrong" (Jarrell) **41**:217
"In Neglect" (Frost) **1**:192
"In Nine Sleep Valley" (Merrill) **28**:223
"In Nineteen Twenty-Seven" (Jackson) **44**:6, 8, 10, 59-62
"In No Man's Land" (Spender) **71**:227
"in nova scotia th peopul" (Bissett) **14**:32
"In Nunhead Cemetery" (Mew) **107**:5, 28-30, 35-36, 39, 41
"In Ohio" (Wright) **36**:340
"In 'Othello'" (Meynell) **112**:231, 303
In Other Words (Swenson) **14**:272-74, 277, 279-80, 283, 287
In Our Terribleness (Some Elements and Meaning in Black Style) (Baraka) **4**:19-21; **113**:19-20, 73, 77, 79-80
"In Our Time" (Rukeyser) **12**:216
In Parallel (Verlaine)
See *Parallèlement*
In Parenthesis (Jones) **116**:61-68, 71, 73-77, 79, 82-91, 97, 108, 120, 123, 125-27, 129, 141-43, 147-48, 150-51, 153-54, 156-57, 159, 161, 172, 183-87, 190-92, 194, 196-97, 199, 215, 218-24, 226-27, 234, 243-46
"In Paris in a Loud Dark Winter" (Ferlinghetti) **1**:165
"In Parte Ove Non E Che Luca" (Chappell) **105**:31, 36, 45
"In Passing" (Mueller) **33**:197
"In Passing with My Mind" (Williams) **109**:296
"In Paths Untrodden" (Whitman) **91**:244, 247
"In Place of an Introduction" (Akhmatova) **55**:4
"In Place of Love" (Ignatow) **34**:305
"In Plaster" (Plath) **37**:201, 254
"In Plaster, with a Bronze Wash" (Meredith)
See "Thoughts on One's Head"
"In Portugal, 1912" (Meynell) **112**:224
"In Prais of Wemen" (Dunbar) **67**:25, 38
"In Praise of California Wines" (Winters) **82**:310
"In Praise of Cities" (Gunn) **26**:186, 231
"In Praise of Darkness" (Borges)
See "Elogio de la sombra"
In Praise of Darkness (Borges)
See *Elogio de la sombra*
"In Praise of Dreams" (Szymborska) **44**:298, 320
"In Praise of Feeling Bad about Yourself" (Szymborska)
See "Pochwala zlego o sobie mniemania"
"In Praise of Johnny Appleseed" (Lindsay) **23**:280, 288
In Praise of Krishna (Levertov) **11**:181
"In Praise of Lessius" (Crashaw)
See "Temperance"
"In Praise of Limestone" (Auden) **1**:17, 20; **92**:14-15, 36
"In Praise of Marriages" (Wright) **14**:342, 365
"In Praise of My Lady" (Morris) **55**:302
"In Praise of My Sister" (Szymborska) **44**:290
"In Praise of Nurses" (Masefield) **78**:83
In Praise of Peace (Gower) **59**:20, 25-33
"In Praise of Self-Deprecation" (Szymborska)
See "Pochwala zlego o sobie mniemania"
"In Praise of Surfaces" (Mueller) **33**:181
"In Praise of the Fool" (Olson) **19**:283
"In Prison" (Bishop) **34**:66, 68
"In Process of a Noble Alliance" (Ransom) **61**:271
"In Procession" (Graves) **6**:138
"In Quest of the Tao in An-Ling, I Met Kai Huan Who Fashioned for Me a Register of the Realized Ones; (This Poem) Left Behind As a Present When About to Depart" (Li Po) **29**:169
"In railway halls" (Spender) **71**:220
"In Rain" (Berry) **28**:16
In Reckless Ecstasy (Sandburg) **2**:334; **41**:273, 293, 360-1
"In Reference to her Children, 23 June 1659" (Bradstreet) **10**:13, 26-7, 34-5, 43, 59
In renovationem votorum, festis natalis Domini (Southwell)
See *For the renewing of his vows at Christmas-time*
"In Reply When Lesser Officials of Chung-tu Brought a Pot of Wine and Two Fish to My Inn as Gifts" (Li Po) **29**:146
"In Response to a Manifesto Circulated by the Union of Concerned Scientists" (Jackson) **44**:38
"In Response to a Question" (Stafford) **71**:270, 297
"In Response to a Rumor that the Oldest Whorehouse in Wheeling, West Virginia, Has Been Condemned" (Wright) **36**:296, 319, 329, 341, 354-55, 358, 375
"In Response to 'Tongtang Tune' by Censor Lu" (Li Po) **29**:179-80, 182
"In Rome" (Ní Chuilleanáin) **34**:356, 380
"In Santa Maria del Popolo" (Gunn) **26**:186, 201, 219
"In School-Days" (Whittier) **93**:238-39, 252-53
"In Search of Egyptics" (Corso) **108**:11
"In Secreit Place" (Dunbar) **67**:3, 46-47, 49
"In Seditionem Horrendam" (Cowper) **40**:101
"In Shadow" (Crane) **3**:98-9
"In Shame and Humiliation" (Wright) **36**:372, 374
"In Sickness" (Swift) **9**:295
"In Silence" (Merton) **10**;347, 349
"In Silence We Sat Across the Table" (Ignatow) **34**:309
"In Sleep" (Meynell) **112**:223
"In Sleep" (Montale)
See "Nel sonno"
"In Sligo and Mayo" (MacNeice) **61**:108
"In Society" (Ginsberg) **4**:71
"In Some Doubt but Willingly" (Ciardi) **69**:56
"In Sparta" (Cavafy) **36**:58
"In Spring, Santa Barbara" (Teasdale) **31**:359
"In St. Paul's a While Ago" (Hardy) **92**:370
"In Stafford Country" (Hugo) **68**:245
"In Strange Cities" (Zagajewski) **27**:394
"In Strasbourg in 1349" (Ammons) **16**:39
"In Suffolk" (Sarton) **39**:367
"In Summer" (Dunbar) **5**:139
"In Tall Grass" (Sandburg) **2**:324; **41**:260, 297
"In Tenebris (I)" (Hardy) **8**:94, 110
"In Terror of Hospital Bills" (Wright) **36**:314, 341-42, 365-66
"In Testament" (Gilmore) **87**:283
"In Texas" (Sarton) **39**:336, 357
"In Thankful Remembrance for My Dear Husband's Safe Arrival" (Bradstreet) **10**:60-1, 64
"In That Deep Wood" (Sarton) **39**:321
"In That Time when It Was Not the Fashion" (Gallagher) **9**:60
"In that time where a villain" (Akhmadulina) **43**:56
"In the Alley" (Simic) **69**:289
"In the Aran Islands" (Mahon) **60**:142
"In the Arboretum" (Stone) **53**:230, 244, 257-58
"In the Badlands" (Wagoner) **33**:344
"In the Baggage Room at Greyhound" (Ginsberg) **47**:5, 37
"In the Bahamas" (Hass) **16**:217
"In the Balance" (Tomlinson) **17**:346
"In the Bamboo Hut" (Kinnell) **26**:260
"In the Beach House" (Sexton) **2**:363
"In the Beauty Created by Others" (Zagajewski) **27**:381, 383
"In the Beginning" (Sanchez) **9**:228-29
"In the Beginning" (Thomas) **2**:403; **52**:232, 290, 293, 295
"In the Blackwater Woods" (Oliver) **75**:287
"In the Bodies of Words" (Swenson) **14**:287
"In the Bomly Village" (Cavafy) **36**:78
"In the cathedral" (Castro)
See "N'a catredal"
"In the Cemetery" (Parra) **39**:278
"In the Cities" (Lawrence) **54**:198
In the Clearing (Frost) **1**:212-13, 224; **39**:239-40; **71**:43
"In the Cold" (Stafford) **71**:293
"In the Cold House" (Wright) **36**:340
"In the Constellations" (Darío)
See "En las constelaciones"
"In the Courtroom" (Sanchez) **9**:225
"In the Crevice of Time" (Jacobsen) **62**:277-78, 309, 316, 320
In the Crevice of Time: New and Collected Poems (Jacobsen) **62**:306, 319-20, 322-4, 326, 329, 334
"In the Dark" (Duncan) **75**:259-60
"In the Dark" (Lawrence) **54**:187
"In the Dark and Cloudy Day" (Housman) **2**:193
"In the Dark Violin of the Valley" (Hughes) **89**:135
"In the Days of Prismatic Color" (Moore) **4**:251-52, 257-58; **49**:96, 101, 107, 121
"In the Deep Channel" (Stafford) **71**:257, 278, 296, 361
"In the Deep Museum" (Sexton) **2**:346, 348, 351, 360-61
"In the Desert" (Melville) **82**:76
"In the desert soul are many, many" (Shvarts) **50**:134
"In the Dock" (de la Mare) **77**:64, 77
"In The Duomo" (Curnow) **48**:16-18, 36, 50
"In the Dwellings of Death" (Sachs)
See "In den Wohnungen des Todes"
In the Dwellings of Death (Sachs)
See *In den Wohnungen des Todes*
"In the Ear of Christ" (Mistral)
See "Al oído de Cristo"
"In the Early Morning" (Corso) **33**:46
In the Early Morning Rain (Berrigan) **103**:33-36, 41
"In the East" (Trakl)
See "Im Osten"
"In the Elegy Season" (Wilbur) **51**:188, 278
"In the End" (Teasdale) **31**:360
"In the Face of Hatred" (Wright) **36**:340
"In the Field" (Wilbur) **51**:235, 305, 312
"In the Fields" (Mew) **107**:6, 56, 58
"In the 51st State" (Berrigan) **103**:35
"In the Fleeting Hand of Time" (Corso) **33**:9, 40, 43, 47
"In the Forest" (Pasternak)
See "V lesu"
"In the friendly dark" (Brutus) **24**:122
"In the Fullness of Time" (Tomlinson) **17**:312, 321, 341
"In the Funk World" (Baraka) **113**:114
"In the Garden" (Boland) **58**:13-14
"In the Garden at Swainston" (Tennyson) **101**:229
"In the Glass of Fashion" (Nemerov) **24**:289, 291

"In the Glorious Epiphany" (Crashaw)
See "To the Glorious Epiphany"
"In the Great Migration, I Love You More" (Darwish) **86**:26
"In the great snowfall before the bomb" (Niedecker) **42**:106-7, 137
"In the Greenhouse" (Montale)
See "Nella serra"
"In the Greenroom" (Justice) **64**:270
In the Habitations of Death (Sachs)
See *In den Wohnungen des Todes*
"In the Hall of Marbles" (Melville) **82**:109
"In the Hall of Mirrors" (Merrill) **28**:242, 244
"In the Hands of a Blindman" (Gallagher) **9**:60
"In the Heart of Contemplation" (Day Lewis) **11**:144
"In the Heart of the Hills" (Carman) **34**:211, 220
"In the Hills" (Bely) **11**:5
"In the Hills" (Niedecker) **42**:101-2
"In the Hole" (Ciardi) **69**:48-49, 57
"In the Hostelry" (Melville) **82**:77
"In the Hotel" (Graham) **59**:138, 177
"In the Hotel of Lost Light" (Kinnell) **26**:251, 267
"In the House of Idiedaily" (Carman) **34**:201, 207, 219
"In the House of the Soul" (Wickham) **110**:303
In the Houses of Death (Sachs)
See *In den Wohnungen des Todes*
In the Illusion of the Threshhold (Bonnefoy)
See *Dans le leurre du seuil*
"In the Isle of Brittain" (Wilmot) **66**:350
"In the Kitchen of the Old House" (Hall) **70**:31
"In the Land of..." (Silverstein) **49**:343
"In the Lobby of the Hotel del Mayo" (Carver) **54**:22
"In the Lupanar at Pompeii" (Dickey) **40**:181
In the Lure of the Threshold (Bonnefoy)
See *Dans le leurre du seuil*
"In the M5 Restaurant" (Hughes) **7**:162
"In the Manner of G. S." (Seferis) **66**:144, 200
"In the Marble Quarry" (Dickey) **40**:261
"In the Market-Place" (Nemerov) **24**:291
"In the Marshes of the Blood River" (Piercy) **29**:314
"In the Matter of One Compass" (Kipling) **91**:153
"In the Mecca" (Brooks) **7**:78, 81-2, 88-91
In the Mecca (Brooks) **7**:62-3, 66, 81-3, 88, 90-1, 94, 105, 107
"In the Memory of Andrée Rexroth" (Rexroth) **95**:257, 259, 269, 328
"In the Middle of the Easel" (Guest) **55**:212
"In the Midst of the Throng" (Cernuda)
See "En medio de la multitud"
"In the Month of Athyr" (Cavafy) **36**:3, 4, 75, 89-90, 91-92, 105
"In the Month of March" (Viereck) **27**:278
"In the month of May" (Akhmadulina)
See "V tot mesiats Mai"
"In the Moonlight" (Hardy) **8**:124
"In the Morning" (Dorn) **115**:126
"In the Mountain Tent" (Dickey) **40**:186, 207, 212, 258
"In the mountains" (Wang Wei) **18**:376, 380, 383
"In the Mountains of Jerusalem" (Amichai) **38**:25
"In the Movies" (O'Hara) **45**:166
"In the Murhaka" (Amichai) **38**:24-25
"In the Museum" (Stafford) **71**:263, 298
"In the Museum Gardens" (Seferis) **66**:184
"In the Naked Bed, in Plato's Cave" (Schwartz) **8**:291, 297, 301-02, 308-09, 311, 316
"In the Neolithic Age" (Kipling) **3**:167; **91**:81, 86
"In the Night" (Crane) **80**:53, 80
"In the Night" (Smith) **12**:345
"In the Night Desert" (Stafford) **71**:263
"In the Night Fields" (Merwin) **45**:18
"In the Nursing Home" (Kenyon) **57**:19-20, 47
"In the old age black was not counted fair" (Shakespeare)
See "Sonnet 127"
"In the Old Days" (Stafford) **71**:290
"In the Open Season" (Wagoner) **33**:335
"In the Oregon Country" (Stafford) **71**:259, 326, 328
"In the Outhouse" (Yamada) **44**:342
"In the Park" (Kumin) **15**:209-11
"In the Park" (Montale) **13**:151
"In the Park" (Smith) **12**:345, 352-54
"In the Past" (Zagajewski) **27**:383
"In the Pasture" (Graham) **59**:163-64, 168
"In the Pauper's Turnip Field" (Melville) **82**:107
"In the Pink" (Sassoon) **12**:242, 262
"In The Plaza" (Aleixandre)
See "En la plaza"
"In the Pocket" (Dickey) **40**:229, 254
In the Presence of the Sun: A Gathering of Shields (Momaday) **25**:220-22
"In the Prison Pen" (Melville) **82**:84
"In the Public Garden" (Moore) **4**:259; **49**:142
In the Quarried Rain (Char)
See *Dans la pluie giboyeuse*
"In the Rain" (H. D.) **5**:304
In the Residences of Death (Sachs)
See *In den Wohnungen des Todes*
"In the Restaurant" (Blok) **21**:3
"In the Restaurant" (Hardy) **8**:124
"In the Ringwood" (Kinsella) **69**:117-18, 122
"In the Ruins of New York City" (Merton) **10**:344, 349
"In the Same Boat" (Kipling) **3**:183
"In the Savile Club" (Clarke) **112**:123
"In the Sconset Bus" (Williams) **7**:409
"In the Secret Room" (Wakoski) **15**:348
"In the Shelter" (Day Lewis) **11**:151
"In the Smoking Car" (Wilbur) **51**:301
"In the Square" (Aleixandre)
See "En la plaza"
"In the Stopping Train" (Davie) **29**:115, 124, 126, 129
"In the Street" (Cavafy) **36**:74, 76, 78
"In the Street" (Spender) **71**:225
"In the Streets" (Sachs) **78**:226, 231
"In the Summertime" (Dylan) **37**:66
"In the Survivor's Home" (Gozzano)
See "In casa del sopravissuto"
"In the Tank" (Gunn) **26**:203
"In the Tavernas" (Cavafy) **36**:75, 108
"In the Tents of Akbar" (Dunbar) **5**:138
"In the Theatre" (Abse) **41**:11, 14, 25, 32
"In the Theatre: A True Incident" (Abse)
See "In the Theatre"
"In the Time of the Blossoms" (Merwin) **45**:16, 26
"In the Tradition" (Baraka) **4**:40; **113**:26, 36-37, 43, 45
"In the Tree House at Night" (Dickey) **40**:155, 164, 175-76, 226, 256
"In the Tunnel Bone of Cambridge" (Corso) **33**:14
"In the Turpitude of Time: N.D." (Warren) **37**:381
"In the Turret" (Melville) **82**:270
"In the Underworld" (Rukeyser) **12**:220
"In the Valley of Cauteretz" (Tennyson) **101**:250, 281
"In the Waiting Room" (Bishop) **3**:59, 69-70; **34**:56, 58, 61, 68, 73-74, 77-78, 82, 84, 86-87, 97, 101-02, 109, 120, 139-41, 144-46, 151, 170
"In the Ward: The Sacred Wood" (Jarrell) **41**:171, 173, 175, 177, 185
"In the Waxworks" (Shapiro) **25**:273, 308, 312
"In the Wheel" (Berrigan) **103**:34
"In the White Giant's Thigh" (Thomas) **2**:395, 404; **52**:255-56, 274-76, 311, 313, 316-17
"In the Wilderness" (Graves) **6**:128-29
"In the winter in Paris" (Guillén) **23**:103
"In the Winter of My Thirty-Eighth Year" (Merwin) **45**:9, 21, 24-5
"In the Wood" (Pasternak) **6**:252-53, 259
"In the Woods" (Meredith) **60**:286-91
"In These Days" (Walker) **30**:344, 349
"In These Dissenting Times" (Walker) **30**:338, 367
In Thirty-three Pieces (Char)
See *En trente-trois morceaux*
"In This Age of Hard Trying, Nonchalance Is Good and" (Moore) **4**:229, 270; **49**:229, 270
"In Those Days" (Jarrell) **41**:146
"In those days you were like a mother to me" (Tsvetaeva)
See "V ony dni, ty mne byla kak mat'"
"in ths forest" (Bissett) **14**:27
"In Time Like Air" (Sarton) **39**:326, 333, 365, 369
In Time Like Air (Sarton) **39**:321, 324, 326, 329, 337-38, 340, 342-43
"In Time of Mourning" (Swinburne) **24**:319
"In Time of Plague" (Gunn) **26**:231
"In Time of 'The Breaking of Nations'" (Hardy) **8**:115, 121; **92**:268
"In Time of War" (Auden) **1**:18; **92**:101, 103
"In to Thir Dirk and Drublie Dayis" (Dunbar) **67**:7, 105
"In Two Poets" (Meynell) **112**:193, 229, 303
"In una Chiesa Gotica" (Carducci) **46**:24, 30, 54
"In Vain I See the Morning Rise" (Thoreau) **30**:254
"In vain with eye a with a nail" (Tsvetaeva)
See "Naprasno glazom kak gvozdem"
"In Valleys Green and Still" (Housman) **2**:180; **43**:211, 245
"In Vision I Roamed" (Hardy) **92**:207, 241, 244, 248
"In Wagga Wagga, Long Ago" (Gilmore) **87**:299
"In War-Time: A Psalm of the Heart" (Dobell) **100**:183, 188
In War Time, and Other Poems (Whittier) **93**:181, 347-48
"In Warm Rooms Before a Blue Light" (Kumin) **15**:211
"In Warsaw" (Milosz) **8**:192
"In Weather" (Hass) **16**:196, 200, 202-03
"In Westminster Abbey" (Betjeman) **75**:7, 18, 28, 45, 91-92
In What Hour (Rexroth) **20**:177, 183, 192-93, 198, 214-15, 217; **95**:248, 253-54, 257-58, 270-71, 305-6, 332
"In What Manner the Body Is United with the Soule" (Graham) **59**:147, 178
"In what torne ship" (Donne)
See "A Hymne to Christ, at the authors last going into Germany"
"In Which I Write My Feelings to be Sent to My Cousin Li Zhao of Binzhou" (Li Po) **29**:179, 183
"In Which the Ancient History I Learn is Not My Own" (Boland) **58**:19, 22
"In Which We Are Paid the Dubious Political Compliment of Opposing Messages" (Dorn) **115**:160
"In Whose Will Is Our Peace?" (Cunningham) **92**:162, 187
"In Willesden Churchyard" (Betjeman) **75**:97-98
"In Yonder Grave a Druid Lies" (Collins)
See "An Ode Occasion'd by the Death of Mr. Thomson"
"In Your Bad Dream" (Hugo) **68**:271
"In Your Big Dream" (Hugo) **68**:273
"In Your Dream After Falling in Love" (Hugo) **68**:271
"In Your Dream on the Eve of Success" (Hugo) **68**:271
"In Your Fucking Utopias" (Berrigan) **103**:27
"In Your Fugitive Dream" (Hugo) **68**:271
"In Your Good Dream" (Hugo) **68**:293

"In Your War Dream" (Hugo) **68**:271
"In Your Wild Dream" (Hugo) **68**:271
"In Yüeh Viewing the Past" (Li Po) **29**:145
"Inam" (Brathwaite) **56**:71
"The Inanimate Object" (Simic) **69**:319
Inaugual Odes (Horace) **46**:117, 122
"Inaugural Rose" (Jordan) **38**:127
"Inauguration Day: January 1953" (Lowell) **3**:214, 218, 222
"Inauguration Poem #2" (Dorn) **115**:85, 126
"Incantation" (Akhmadulina)
See "Zaklinanie"
"Incantation" (Milosz) **8**:202
"Incantation" (Pinsky) **27**:166
"Incantation at Assisi" (Viereck) **27**:267
Incantations (Werfel)
See *Beschwörungen*
"Incantesimo" (Montale) **13**:110
"Incarnate Devil" (Thomas) **52**:227
"The Incarnate One" (Muir) **49**:290, 294-95
"Incarnation" (Rexroth) **20**:206, 216; **95**:260, 320
"Incarnations" (Jackson) **44**:11
Incarnations: Poems, 1966-1968 (Warren) **37**:299, 301, 303-4, 307, 328, 347, 353, 355, 358, 361, 367, 371, 380
"Incense of the Lucky Virgin" (Hayden) **6**:195
"Incespicare" (Montale) **13**:134
"Incident" (Cullen) **20**:61
"An Incident in the Early Life of Ebenezer Jones, Poet, 1828" (Betjeman) **75**:43
"Incident on a Journey" (Gunn) **26**:218
Incidental Numbers (Wylie) **23**:311, 321, 325-26, 331
Incidentals (Sandburg) **41**:293-94
"Incidents in the Life of My Uncle Arly" (Lear) **65**:146, 161-62, 165, 204
"Inclusions" (Barrett Browning) **6**:5-6, 15
"The Incomparable Light" (Eberhart) **76**:5, 38, 46, 60, 69-70
"Incomparable Marriage" (Hughes) **89**:195, 199
"Incompatibilities" (Hughes) **7**:113; **89**:138
"An Incomplete List of People I Wish Were Indian" (Alexie) **53**:23
"Inconstancy of Luve" (Dunbar) **67**:38
"The Inconstant" (Cowley) **90**:14, 116
"Incontro" (Montale) **13**:165
"Incontro" (Pavese) **13**:217
"Incorporeal Voluptuousness" (Shvarts) **50**:132
"The Incorrigible Dirigible" (Carruth) **10**:88
An Incorrigible Music (Curnow) **48**:13-16, 18-19, 23, 47-48, 50, 52
"Incredible Buys In" (Stone) **53**:257-58
"Indentured" (Wylie) **23**:305
"Independence" (Cavafy) **36**:55
"Independence" (Thoreau) **30**:216, 219, 281-82, 295
"Independence Day" (Bukowski) **18**:15
"The Independent Man" (Brooks) **7**:53
"An Indian at the Burial-Ground of His Father" (Bryant) **20**:36
"Indian Boarding School: The Runaways" (Erdrich) **52**:181-82
"Indian Boy Love Song (#4)" (Alexie) **53**:39
"Indian Boy Love Song (#3)" (Alexie) **53**:39
"Indian Bread" (Kinnell) **26**:238
"The Indian Cave Jerry Ramsey Found" (Stafford) **71**:342
"Indian Caves in the Dry Country" (Stafford) **71**:342
"Indian Dances" (Sarton) **39**:321
"Indian Education" (Alexie) **53**:3
"The Indian Girl's Lament" (Bryant) **20**:10, 17
"Indian Graves at Jocko" (Hugo) **68**:270
Indian Journals, March 1962-May 1963 (Ginsberg) **4**:53, 56, 60
"Indian Noël" (Mistral)
See "Noël indio"
"Indian Pipe" (Eberhart) **76**:12
"Indian Procession" (Mistral)
See "Procesión India"
"Indian Serenade" (Montale)
See "Serenata indiana"
"Indian Summer" (Parker) **28**:347
"Indian Summer" (Pavese)
See "Estate di San Martino"
"The Indian to His Love" (Yeats) **20**:343
"Indiana" (Crane) **3**:88, 106-07
"Indians" (Baraka) **113**:18
"The Indians Visit the Museum" (Oliver) **75**:298
"TH INDIANS WERE WELCOMED AS BRIDGEBUILDERS" (Bissett) **14**:33
L'Indicateur des chemins de coeur (Tzara) **27**:229, 231, 234
"The Indictment" (Wickham) **110**:294
"Indictment of Senior Officers" (Olds) **22**:307
"Indifference" (Arnold)
See "Euphrosyne"
"The Indifferent" (Donne) **1**:125
"The Indifferent One" (Spender) **71**:225
"Indignation Jones" (Masters) **36**:182
"The Indigo Glass in the Grass" (Stevens) **6**:324
"Indigone" (Brathwaite) **56**:91
"Indisciplina" (Pavese) **13**:214, 226
"Indispensability of Eyes" (Olds) **22**:307
"The Individual Man" (Duncan) **2**:118
"Individuality" (Lanier) **50**:54, 56, 105
"The Indivisible Incompatibles" (Swenson) **14**:284
"Indolence" (Bridges) **28**:48, 83
"Indolence" (Hecht) **70**:108
"Indolence" (Keats)
See "Ode on Indolence"
"Indolence in Early Winter" (Kenyon) **57**:45
"The Indolent Monk" (Baudelaire)
See "Le mauvais moine"
"Les indolents" (Verlaine) **32**:351, 390, 393
"Indoor Games New Newbury" (Betjeman) **75**:105
"Indulgence" (Li Po) **29**:177
"The Indweller" (Tagore)
See "Antaryami"
Inebriety (Crabbe) **97**:78-79
"Inelegant Evangelist" (Wickham) **110**:264
"Inevitability" (Tolson) **88**:349
"Infancy—A Fragment" (Crabbe) **97**:156
"Infant" (Smith) **12**:310, 326
"Infant Boy at Mid-Century" (Warren) **37**:300
"The Infant Jesus of Prague" (Schuyler) **88**:200
"Infant Joy" (Blake) **12**:7, 9, 33-34; **63**:5-6, 30, 73, 75, 102, 113, 115, 119-20, 125
"Infant Sorrow" (Blake) **12**:7, 31, 34; **63**:4-5, 30, 70, 76, 95, 109-10
"Infanta Marina" (Stevens) **6**:311; **110**:94
"El infante" (Guillén) **35**:174
"Infant-Ey" (Traherne) **70**:243, 257-58, 288
"The Inference" (Traherne) **70**:198, 288
"An Inference of Mexico" (Hayden) **6**:194, 198
Inferno (Dante) **21**:53, 56, 59-67, 69-72, 75-7, 81-5, 89, 95-6, 98-9, 101, 103-08
Infidels (Dylan) **37**:60, 65
"Infiltration of the Universe" (MacLeish) **47**:192
"L'infini dans les cieux" (Lamartine) **16**:266, 280, 284-85
"Les Infiniments Petits" (Béranger) **112**:20
"The Infinite" (Leopardi)
See "L'Infinito"
"The Infinite" (Simic) **69**:304
"The Infinite Reason" (MacLeish) **47**:192
"L'Infinito" (Leopardi) **37**:82, 84, 102, 105, 109-11, 123-30, 134, 139-40, 143
"The Infirm Love of Day" (Zanzotto) **65**:321
"Inflation Blues" (Walker) **20**:294
"The Influence Coming into Play: The Seven of Pentacles" (Piercy) **29**:325
"The Influence of Channing" (Very) **86**:61
"The Influence of the Night on Faith and Imagination" (Very) **86**:113
"The Influence Passing: The Knight of Swords" (Piercy) **29**:324
"The Influx" (Traherne) **70**:318
"The Informant" (Ní Chuilleanáin) **34**:360, 362
"Informer" (Randall) **86**:329, 336
"El ingenuo" (Borges) **22**:97, 99; **32**:90
"Les ingénus" (Verlaine) **32**:349, 391, 393
"Ingoldsby Legends" (Browning) **2**:36
"Ingrateful Beauty Threatened" (Carew) **29**:3, 9, 18, 32, 34, 71
Ingrowing Thoughts (Thomas) **99**:305, 307-8, 336
The Inhabitant and His Hope (Neruda)
See *El habitante y su esperenza*
"The Inheritance" (Das) **43**:89
"The Inheritance" (Lawrence) **54**:240
"Inheritances" (Hacker) **47**:80
"Inheritor" (Wright)
See "Eroded Hills"
"Inhuman World" (Aleixandre) **15**:20
"The Inhumanist" (Jeffers) **17**:136
"The Iniquity of the Fathers upon the Children" (Rossetti) **7**:266, 289-90
"Initial Conditions" (Bell) **79**:33
"Initial, Daemonic, and Celestial Love" (Emerson) **18**:93
"The Initiate" (Merwin) **45**:35
"Initiations" (Okigbo) **7**:224-25, 232, 237
"Injudicious Gardening" (Moore) **4**:266; **49**:91, 114
"Injuria Anicitiae" (Philips) **40**:296
"The Injury" (Williams) **7**:360; **109**:197
"Inland Sea" (Blunden) **66**:24, 28-30
"The Inlet" (Glück) **16**:125
"Inmate Torres Sings Waiting for the Parole Board" (Espada) **74**:122
"Lo inmenso del mar" (Guillén) **35**:229
The Inn Album (Browning) **2**:68, 96
"The Inn of Earth" (Teasdale) **31**:364
"The Inner Kingdom" (Darío)
See "El reino interior"
Inner Landscape (Sarton) **39**:309-12, 334-35, 341, 344, 348, 353-54, 356-57, 364
The Inner Room (Merrill) **28**:281
"Inner Space" (Raworth) **107**:323
"Inner Voice" (Herbert) **50**:20-21
"Innisfree" (Yeats) **51**:103
"The Inniskeen Hellions" (Kavanagh) **33**:91
"Inniskeen Road: July Evening" (Kavanagh) **33**:74, 92, 97, 99-100, 102, 142, 150
"Inno a Nettuno" (Leopardi) **37**:165-66, 168, 170-71
Inno a Satana (Carducci) **46**:5, 16, 21, 23, 28, 37, 47, 56-57, 69, 76, 81, 84, 88
"Inno ai patriarchi" (Leopardi) **37**:171
"Inno alla morte" (Ungaretti) **57**:348
Innocence (Blake)
See *Songs of Innocence and of Experience: Shewing the Two Contrary States of the Human Soul*
"The Innocence" (Creeley) **73**:5, 7
"Innocence" (Gunn) **26**:197, 201
"Innocence" (Kavanagh) **33**:74, 81, 100, 118, 128, 145; **105**:99, 103, 110, 145
"Innocence" (Levine) **22**:228
"Innocence" (Traherne) **70**:169, 185-86, 223, 228, 266, 268, 288, 314
"The Innocent" (Stone) **53**:229
"The Innocent Ill" (Cowley) **90**:31-32
"Innocent Landscape" (Wylie) **23**:305-306, 333-34
"The Innocents" (Wylie) **23**:302-303, 310
"Inns" (Crabbe) **97**:103
"¡No hay salida?" (Paz) **48**:232
"Inochi no fune" (Ishikawa) **10**:213, 215
"L'inoffensif" (Char) **56**:120, 134, 154
"The Inoffensive One" (Char)
See "L'inoffensif"
"Inquest" (Snodgrass) **74**:291
La inquietud del rosal (Storni) **33**:234, 236, 241, 244, 267, 272-74, 297, 310-11
"Inquiry into a December Because" (Kaufman) **74**:184
"Inquiry into the Nature of Cruelty" (Cohen) **109**:52

"ins lesebuch für die oberstufe" (Enzensberger) **28**:135
"Insane Buildings" (Alurista) **34**:48
"Insatiableness" (Traherne) **70**:198, 330
"Inscription" (Melville) **82**:77
Inscription (Herbert)
See *Napis*
"Inscription Facing Western Sea" (Merwin) **45**:44
"Inscription for a Graveyard" (Winters) **82**:344-45
"Inscription for a Headstone" (Clarke) **112**:54, 92, 118-19
"Inscription for the Entrance into a Wood" (Bryant) **20**:4, 17, 19, 35, 40, 47
"Inscription for the Tank" (Wright) **36**:182, 317, 341-42, 366, 375
"Inscriptions" (Boland) **58**:25, 61
"Inscriptions After Fact" (Kennedy) **93**:142
"Insects" (Enright) **93**:9
"Insensibility" (Owen) **19**:327, 337, 340, 347-48, 355, 357, 369-70; **102**:144, 148, 151, 167, 169, 171-73, 181, 187-91, 197-98, 211, 213, 257-58, 263
"Inside a mountain idles an idol" (Mandelstam)
See "Vnutri gory bezdeistvuet kumir"
"Inside and Outside" (Tate) **50**:256
"The Inside Dance" (Piercy) **29**:311
"Inside News" (Yamada) **44**:339
Inside the Blood Factory (Wakoski) **15**:324-25, 341, 348, 350-51, 362-63, 365
"Inside the River" (Dickey) **40**:156, 262
"Inside the Story" (Strand) **63**:143
"The Insidious Dr. Fu Man Chu" (Baraka) **4**:15; **113**:4
"L'insinuant" (Valéry) **9**:395
"Insipidities" (Verlaine) **32**:386
"Insomnia" (Bishop) **34**:66, 146
"Insomnia" (Borges)
See "Insomnio"
"Insomnia" (Empson) **104**:101
"Insomnia" (MacLeish) **47**:164
"Insomnia" (Paz)
See "Insomnio"
Insomnia (Tsvetaeva) **14**:299, 301
"Insomnia at the Solstice" (Kenyon) **57**:15
"Insomnia. Homer. Tautly Swelling Sails. . ." (Mandelstam) **14**:141
"Insomniac" (Plath) **1**:399
"Insomnio" (Borges) **22**:92; **32**:39, 58, 85
"Insomnio" (Paz) **48**:176
"Insonnia" (Quasimodo) **47**:270
"Inspection" (Owen) **19**:335, 354, 356; **102**:170, 172, 181, 187, 204, 207-8, 225
"Inspiration" (Lowell) **3**:245
"Inspiration" (Thoreau) **30**:180, 190, 192, 223, 239-40, 254, 268, 281-82, 284, 295
"Inspiration" (Tuckerman) **85**:319, 335
"Inspiration for a Burned Bridge" (Merwin) **45**:8
"Installation" (Brossard) **80**:24
"Installation of the Duke of Grafton as Chancellor of Cambridge" (Gray) **2**:143
Installations: Avec et sans pronoms (Brossard) **80**:22-26
"Instances of Communication" (Jacobsen) **62**:320-22, 331
"The Instant" (Levertov) **11**:166, 168
Instant Chronicles (Enright) **93**:22-23, 33
"Instead of a Foreword" (Akhmatova)
See "Instead of a Preface"
"Instead of a Preface" (Akhmatova) **55**:8, 36, 57-58, 63-64
"Instead of Camargue" (Swenson) **14**:249
"Instinct" (Pavese)
See "L'istinto"
"Institutio" (Kipling) **91**:87
"The Instruction" (Traherne) **70**:169, 188-89, 239, 268, 276, 312, 314
"The Instruction Manual" (Ashbery) **26**:111, 129, 159, 164
Instructions to a Painter (Waller) **72**:297, 303, 305, 330
"Instructions to a princess" (Reed) **68**:325
Instructions to his Son and to Posterity (Raleigh) **31**:273
"Instructions to the Double" (Gallagher) **9**:58, 60
Instructions to the Double (Gallagher) **9**:35-7, 43, 53-4, 58
"Instructions to the Orphic Adept" (Graves) **6**:133
"The Instructor" (Kipling) **91**:174
"Insufficiency" (Barrett Browning) **6**:15
"Insularum Ocelle" (Swinburne) **24**:326
"An Insult" (Kavanagh) **33**:101
"The Insulted and Injured" (Viereck) **27**:279
Intact Wind (Paz)
See *Viento entero*
"The Intangible" (Kavanagh) **33**:91
Integer uitae (Horace) **46**:94, 98
"The Intellectual" (Shapiro) **25**:270, 312
Intellectual Things (Kunitz) **19**:147-48, 153, 155, 159-61, 163, 185
"The Intellectuals" (Randall) **86**:290, 299, 336
"Inter & Outer Rhyme" (Corso) **33**:50
"Interborough Rapid Transit Co." (Williams) **109**:294
"The Intercepter" (Muir) **49**:284
"Intercettazione telefonica" (Montale) **13**:133
"Interdeterminancy" (Cage) **58**:195
"Interface" (Wright) **14**:373
"Interference" (Ammons) **16**:6
"Intérieur" (Éluard) **38**:69
"Intérieur" (Valéry) **9**:365, 396
"Interim" (Levertov) **11**:176, 195-96
"Interim" (Millay) **6**:205-07, 214; **61**:212, 225, 254
"Interior" (Crane) **99**:114
"Interior" (Guillén) **35**:157
"Interior" (Sandburg) **41**:240
"Interior Decorator" (Betjeman) **75**:37
"Interior (with Jane)" (O'Hara) **45**:201
"Interjection Number" (Warren) **37**:378
"Interjection Number 7" (Warren) **37**:306
"Interjection Number Four: Bad Year, Bad War: A New Year's Card, 1969" (Warren) **37**:306
"Interjection Number Three: I Know a Place Where All Is Real" (Warren) **37**:305
"Interjection Number Two: Caveat" (Warren) **37**:304, 380
"Interlude" (Longfellow) **30**:62, 65-6
"The Interlude" (Shapiro) **25**:303, 326
"Interlude: in a Bar" (Eliot) **90**:329
"Interlude in London" (Eliot) **90**:329
"An Interlude of Winter Light" (Duncan) **75**:135, 146, 204, 256
"Intermezzo" (Carducci) **46**:23, 27
"Intermezzo" (Heine)
See "Lyrisches Intermezzo"
"Intermezzo" (Montale) **13**:106
"Intermezzo" (Schnackenberg) **45**:345
"Intermezzo No 1" (Heine) **25**:141
"Intermission 3" (Brooks) **7**:58, 62, 91, 104
"Intermission with Peanuts" (Kennedy) **93**:137
"Intermittence" (Spark) **72**:263-64
"International Ode" (Holmes) **71**:96
"Interoffice Communications" (Rexroth) **95**:269
"Interplay" (Wright) **14**:348
"Interpreting Nature" (Very) **86**:89
"Interrignum" (Muir) **49**:240
"Interrogaciones" (Darío) **15**:100
"Interrogaciones" (Mistral) **32**:161, 176
"Interrogate the Stones" (MacLeish) **47**:186
"The Interrogation" (Muir) **49**:199, 213, 229, 256, 264, 282-83
"The Interrogation of the Man of Many Hearts" (Sexton) **2**:352
Interrogations (Quintana) **36**:257, 260-61, 263, 265-67, 270-72, 275
"The Interrupted" (Jacobsen) **62**:322
"Interruption" (Cavafy) **36**:46, 53, 86
"An Interruption" (Ciardi) **69**:58
"Interruption" (Graves) **6**:137, 143-44
"Interruptions From the West" (Paz) **48**:256
"Interstices" (Berrigan) **103**:29
"Interval" (Paz) **48**:273
"Interval of Joy" (Seferis) **66**:170
"The Interview" (Creeley) **73**:5
"Interview" (Ekeloef) **23**:86-7
"Interview" (Parker) **28**:361
"Interview" (Randall) **86**:290
"Interview with a Policeman" (Ai) **72**:16
"Interview with a Spirit Healer" (Abse) **41**:19
"Interview with a Tourist" (Atwood) **8**:14
"Interview with Doctor Drink" (Cunningham) **92**:147, 150, 168
"An Interview with John Cage" (Berrigan) **103**:45
"Intifada" (Jordan) **38**:127
"Intima" (Mistral) **32**:151, 176-77
"Intimacy of Tone" (Guest) **55**:201
"Intimate Parnassus" (Kavanagh) **33**:63, 72, 88, 100, 103, 115, 119; **105**:96, 120
"Intimates" (Lawrence) **54**:185
"Intimation" (Mistral)
See "Intima"
"Intimation of Immortality" (Smith) **12**:313
"Intimations Ode" (Hall) **70**:9
"The Intimations Ode" (Wordsworth)
See "Ode: Intimations of Immortality from Recollections of Early Childhood"
"Intimations of Immorality" (Sappho) **5**:418
"Intimations of Immortality" (Thomas) **2**:392
"Intimations of Immortality" (Wordsworth)
See "Ode: Intimations of Immortality from Recollections of Early Childhood"
"Intimations of Mortality" (Meynell) **112**:231
"Intimidation" (Heaney) **100**:334
Intimité marine (Césaire) **25**:22
"Into Her Lying Down Head" (Thomas) **52**:316, 333, 335
"Into My Heart and Air That Kills" (Housman) **2**:192; **43**:245
"Into My Own" (Frost) **1**:213; **39**:237, 240-41, 246
"Into the ark" (Szymborska) **44**:296
"Into the Arteries of the Republic poured" (Tolson) **88**:231
"Into the Golden Vessel of Great Song" (Millay) **6**:211
"Into the Matter" (Paz) **48**:274
"Into the Salient" (Blunden) **66**:59
"Into the Shandy Westerness" (Rexroth) **20**:196
"Into the Stone" (Dickey) **40**:180, 225
Into the Stone and Other Poems (Dickey) **40**:154, 166, 175-76, 179, 181, 184-85, 187, 189, 195, 204, 212, 229-30, 240, 261-62
"Into the Tree" (Milosz) **8**:198
"Into the Twilight" (Yeats) **20**:346
"Into these Loves, who but for Passion lookes" (Drayton) **98**:127
"Into Thirty Centuries Born" (Muir) **49**:297
"Intoxication" (Dickinson)
See "I Taste a Liquor Never Brewed"
"Intrigue" (Crane) **80**:84, 97, 109
Intrigues (Crane) **80**:108
"introducing a new loa" (Reed) **68**:332, 348
"Introduction" (Akhmatova)
See "Vstuplenie"
"Introduction" (Blake) **12**:7, 32, 34-35, 43-47; **63**:16, 20-24, 76, 88, 90, 99, 104-05, 120, 123, 134
"An Introduction" (Das) **43**:72, 85
"The Introduction" (Finch) **21**:155-57, 159, 161, 181
"Introduction" (Lawrence) **54**:207
"The Introduction" (MacNeice) **61**:178
"Introduction au galet" (Ponge) **107**:251
"Introduction to Native American Literature" (Alexie) **53**:8
"Introduction to Poetry" (Collins) **68**:221, 224
"An Introduction to Some Poems" (Stafford) **71**:295

"Introduction to the Hoh" (Hugo) **68**:287
"Introitus" (Longfellow) **30**:65
"Introvert" (Birney) **52**:8
"Intruding" (Piercy) **29**:311
"The Intrusion" (Graves) **6**:156
"El intruso" (Cernuda) **62**:173, 256, 258
"Inútil soy" (Storni) **33**:280
"Invaders" (Douglas) **106**:197
"The Invaders" (Winters) **82**:338-41
"Les Invalides" (Kinnell) **26**:260
"Invasion Exercise on the Poultry Farm" (Betjeman) **75**:83
"The Invasion of the Sleep Walkers" (Ciardi) **69**:49
"Invasion on the Farm" (Thomas) **99**:268
"Invasion Spring" (Birney) **52**:4
"Invasions" (Kunitz) **19**:148
"Invective Against Swans" (Stevens) **6**:294
Invectives (Verlaine) **2**:419
"Les Inventeurs" (Char) **56**:154
"L'invention" (Éluard) **38**:69
"Invention of Nothing" (Simic) **69**:315
"Invention of the Cross" (Gower) **59**:31
Inventions of the March Hare: Poems 1909-1917 (Eliot) **90**:285-86, 299, 329-30
"Inventory" (Carver) **54**:29
"Invernal" (Darío) **15**:117
"Inverno in bosco—osterie—cippi" (Zanzotto) **65**:285
"Inversely" (Rexroth) **95**:260, 271
"Invictus" (Parker) **28**:355
"De invierno" (Darío) **15**:107-08, 110
"The Inviolate" (Blunden) **66**:24, 28-29
"INVISIBLE" (Villa) **22**:356
"The Invisible Hunter" (Shvarts) **50**:131, 144-45
"El invisible muro" (Cernuda) **62**:221
"invisible presence" (Ekeloef)
See "osynlig närvaro"
Invisible Reality (Jiménez)
See *La realidad invisible*
"The Invisible Wall" (Cernuda)
See "El invisible muro"
"The Invitation" (Behn) **88**:148-49, 152
"The Invitation" (Clare) **23**:23
"The Invitation" (Very) **86**:120
"L'invitation au voyage" (Baudelaire) **1**:69; **106**:8, 57, 86, 88-90, 108, 120, 122, 172, 176
"L'Invitation au voyage" (Char) **56**:197
"An Invitation of my learned Friends at Cambridge" (Barker) **91**:17, 23, 28, 32
"The Invitation to Daphnis" (Finch) **21**:139, 153-54, 161
"Invitation to Dyddgu" (Dafydd ap Gwilym)
See "I Wahodd Dyddgu"
"Invitation to Juno" (Empson) **104**:94, 119, 122, 135
"Invitation to Miss Marianne Moore" (Bishop) **3**:44; **34**:146
"Invitation to Miss Moore" (Bishop)
See "Invitation to Miss Marianne Moore"
"Invitation to the Country" (Bridges) **28**:66, 69
"Invitations to the Dance" (Kennedy) **93**:150-51
"Invite to Eternity" (Clare) **23**:22-4, 26
Invocaciones (Cernuda) **62**:171, 200, 203, 213, 222, 248, 250, 254
"Invocation" (Hacker) **47**:117
"Invocation" (Hope) **56**:268, 272
"The Invocation" (Hope) **56**:268, 270-71, 286-87, 306
"Invocation" (Kennedy) **93**:152, 158
"L'invocation" (Lamartine) **16**:277, 279, 290
"Invocation" (Lamartine)
See "L'invocation"
"Invocation" (Levertov) **11**:177
"L'Invocation" (Sainte-Beuve) **110**:48
"Invocation" (Sitwell) **3**:312
"Invocation" (Spender) **71**:178, 216
"The Invocation" (Suckling) **30**:130
"Invocation to Kali" (Sarton) **39**:320, 328, 339-40, 342, 344, 366
"The Invocation to Kali 4: The Time of Burning" (Sarton) **39**:328
"An Invocation to Sleep" (Finch) **21**:143, 146, 179-80
"Invocation to the Social Muse" (MacLeish) **47**:164, 166, 190, 197, 240-41, 254
Invocations (Cernuda)
See *Invocaciones*
Inward Companion (de la Mare) **77**:92, 94
"The Inward Morning" (Thoreau) **30**:181, 191, 193, 198-99, 203, 213, 222, 241, 267
"Inward Morning" (Very) **86**:92
"Io" (Koch) **80**:328
"Io crederrei, se tu fussi di sasso" (Michelangelo) **103**:210
"Io non pensava che lo cor giammai" (Cavalcanti) **114**:234
"Io poeta delle Ceneri" (Pasolini) **17**:292
"Iodine" (Cohen) **109**:68
"Iola, Kansas" (Clampitt) **19**:95-96
"Iona" (Housman) **43**:255-57
"Ione" (Dunbar) **5**:125
"Ionic" (Cavafy) **36**:73, 86, 112
"Iork" (Brodsky)
See "York: In Memoriam W. H. Auden"
"Iota" (Tolson) **88**:237-38, 261-62, 272, 304, 332
"A ioyfull songe of the Roiall Receauing of the queenes maiestie into her camp at Tilbery: the 8 and 9 of August 1588" (Deloney) **79**:55
"Ipersonetto" (Zanzotto) **65**:270, 277, 282
"Irapuato" (Birney) **52**:77, 98
"An Irate Host" (Surrey) **59**:286, 353
"Ireland" (Meynell)
See "In Ireland"
"The Ireland of the Bombers" (Davie)
See "1969, Ireland of the Bombers"
"Ireland with Emily" (Betjeman) **75**:66-67, 83, 85-86
"Iride" (Montale) **13**:109, 111, 121-22, 130-31, 152, 166
"Iris" (Melville) **82**:153
"Iris" (Montale)
See "Iride"
"Iris, her Book" (Holmes) **71**:67-68
Iris of Creation: Poems (Bell) **79**:41
"Irises" (Berssenbrugge) **115**:15
"Irises" (Lee) **24**:240
"An Irish Airman Foresees His Death" (Yeats) **20**:304
"Irish-American Dignitary" (Clarke) **112**:56
"Irish Boy" (Wordsworth) **67**:306
"An Irish Childhood in England: 1951" (Boland) **58**:3
"The Irish Cliffs of Moher" (Stevens) **6**:304
"The Irish Schoolmaster" (Hood) **93**:52, 72
"Irish Stew" (Kavanagh) **33**:86; **105**:110
"Irish Street Scene, with Lovers" (Montague) **106**:298, 302
"The Irish Tradition" (Kavanagh) **33**:132
"The Irish Unionist's Farewell to Greta Hellstrom in 1922" (Betjeman) **75**:84
"The Irish Writer" (Kinsella) **69**:88
"An Irishman in London" (Mahon) **60**:182, 185
"Iron" (Sandburg) **41**:269
"Iron" (Zagajewski) **27**:381, 387
"Iron Age Burial" (Szirtes) **51**:161
"the Iron Characters" (Nemerov) **24**:262, 279
The iron coin (Borges)
See *La moneda de hierro*
"The Iron Gate" (Holmes) **71**:65, 68, 82, 94
"Iron Hans" (Sexton) **2**:365-68; **79**:190
"The Iron Horse" (Riley) **48**:283
"Iron Landscapes (and the Statue of Liberty)" (Gunn) **26**:197-198, 206, 214
"Iron Thunder" (Quintana) **36**:272
"Iron Train" (Zagajewski) **27**:402
"Ironing Grandmother's Tablecloth" (Kenyon) **57**:12
"Irregular Dance" (Storni)
See "Danza irregular"
"L'irrémédiable" (Baudelaire) **1**:55; **106**:10-11, 96-97
"L'Irrémédiable" (Char) **56**:197
Irremediablemente (Storni) **33**:236-37, 244, 247, 251-52, 275-77, 297, 307, 311, 318
"L'Irréparable" (Baudelaire) **1**:68
"Is" (Kavanagh) **33**:63, 96, 119-20; **105**:153, 176
is 5 (Cummings) **5**:77, 92, 95, 104
"Is it possible?" (Wyatt) **27**:353
"Is It True?" (Sexton) **2**:368, 374; **79**:211, 215-16, 222, 237, 288, 336
"Is It Wise" (Smith) **12**:343
"Is My Team Ploughing" (Housman) **2**:180, 193, 196; **43**:214, 245, 261
I's (Pronounced Eyes) (Zukofsky) **11**:357
"Is That What You Are" (Merwin) **45**:25
"Is There for Honest Poverty" (Burns) **6**:58, 83; **114**:23, 44, 47, 51, 57-58, 91, 104, 147; **114**:171
"Is There No Way Out?" (Paz)
See "No hay salida?"
"Is This Feeling About the West Real?" (Stafford) **71**:373
"IS. W. Beyng Wery of Writyng" (Whitney) **116**:292
"Is Your Town Nineveh?" (Moore) **49**:116-17
"Isaac and Abraham" (Brodsky)
See "Isaak i Avraam"
"Isaac and Archibald" (Robinson) **1**:467, 486-87, 496
"Isaacs Marriage" (Vaughan) **81**:363
"Isaak i Avraam" (Brodsky) **9**:4, 6
"Isabel" (Dobell) **100**:166
"Isabel" (Tennyson) **6**:387
"Isabella" (Hood) **93**:67
"Isabella" (Keats) **1**:279, 282, 288-89, 296
"Isabella" (Morris) **55**:247
"Isabella; or, The Pot of Basil" (Keats)
See "Isabella"
Isabella (Keats) **96**:209, 236, 284, 340-41
"Isaiah" (Walker) **20**:278
"Isaiah LXII: 1-8" (Wheatley) **3**:357
"Isaiah Beethoven" (Masters) **36**:183, 190-91
"Isba Song" (McGuckian) **27**:103
"Ischia" (Lamartine) **16**:287, 291
"Ishmael's Dream" (Stern) **115**:258
"Ishtar" (Wright) **14**:363
"La isla" (Guillén) **35**:181
Isla ignorada (Fuertes) **27**:10, 19, 21
"Isla ignorado" (Fuertes) **27**:43
"The Islam" (Borges) **32**:58
"The Island" (Dickey) **40**:160
"The Island" (Forché) **10**:138, 152, 161, 166
"Island" (Hughes) **1**:244, 248; **53**:119, 129
"The Island" (Jarrell) **41**:146
"The Island" (Muir) **49**:196, 200, 205, 298-99
"An Island" (Robinson) **1**:465, 467
"The Island" (Thomas) **99**:257, 316-17
The Island (Allard) **24**:116
The Island (Byron) **16**:86, 88, 90, 109
Island and Time (Curnow) **48**:3, 11, 23-29
"Island Bulletin" (Cohen) **109**:89
"The Island Hawk" (Noyes) **27**:122
"Island in the Works" (Merrill) **28**:268, 270-71
"Island of Night" (Kinnell) **26**:257
"The Island of Statues" (Yeats) **20**:343, 346, 353
"Island of Summer" (Warren) **37**:301
"The Islanders" (Kipling) **3**:179, 192; **91**:72-73, 77-80, 111, 115-17, 119, 173
"Islandmen" (Thomas) **99**:273
"Islands" (Brathwaite) **56**:14
"The Islands" (H. D.) **5**:268
"The Islands" (Hayden) **6**:191, 193, 200
"Islands" (Merwin) **45**:87
"Islands" (Walcott) **46**:238
Islands (Brathwaite) **56**:8-11, 14-15, 17-18, 22, 24, 26, 31, 33-34, 49, 53, 59, 64-68, 70-71, 73-75, 77, 86-88, 94-95, 98, 100
"Islands and Exiles" (Brathwaite) **56**:39, 83
"Islands and Towers" (Zagajewski) **27**:389

"Islands of the Blest" (Yeats) **51**:103
Ismaelillo (Martí) **76**:79-82, 84-85, 88, 96, 100-101, 115, 132-36, 138
"Ismaïl Bey" (Lermontov) **18**:278, 300
"Isola" (Quasimodo) **47**:302
"Isola di Ulisse" (Quasimodo) **47**:302-3
"Isola mattutina" (Quasimodo) **47**:301
"I S O L A T E" (Berrigan) **103**:36
"Isolation: To Marguerite" (Arnold) **5**:13, 18
"Isolation: To Marguerite—Continued" (Arnold) **5**:13, 42-5, 49, 64
"Isolationist" (Page) **12**:170
"L'isolement" (Lamartine) **16**:265, 274-77, 290, 298-301
"Ispoved" (Lermontov) **18**:300
"Israel" (Borges) **32**:58
"Israel" (Shapiro) **25**:283, 285, 297-98, 307, 320, 325
"Israeli Travel" (Amichai) **38**:48-49
"Israfel" (Poe) **1**:438, 447-48
"L'issue" (Char) **56**:120
"The Issue" (Whittier) **93**:321
"The Issues" (Olds) **22**:313
"Ister Bank Song" (Sidney) **32**:237, 243
Isthm. VII (Pindar)
See *Isthmian 7*
Isthmian 3 (Pindar) **19**:426
Isthmian 4 (Pindar) **19**:426
Isthmian 6 (Pindar) **19**:398, 414, 421-22
Isthmian 7 (Pindar) **19**:425
Isthmian 8 (Pindar) **19**:398, 424
"L'istinto" (Pavese) **13**:205, 213
"Isto" (Pessoa) **20**:172
"It becomes dark at midnight and light shortly after" (Akhmadulina) **43**:56
"It breaks" (Piercy) **29**:314
It Catches My Heart in Its Hands: New and Selected Poems, 1955-1963 (Bukowski) **18**:5, 21
"It Could Well Be..." (Storni)
See "Bien pudiera ser"
"It fell on a sommers day" (Campion) **87**:36, 44, 65, 96, 99-100, 104
"It fortifies my soul to know" (Clough) **103**:81
"It Has Always Been This Way" (Tapahonso) **65**:237-38, 257
"It hurts him to think" (Thomas) **99**:250
"It Is" (Alurista) **34**:45, 47
"It Is a Big Red House" (Berrigan) **103**:13
"It Is a Living Coral" (Williams) **7**:369
"It Is a Spring Afternoon" (Sexton) **2**:352
"It Is Everywhere" (Toomer) **7**:337, 340
"It Is Forbidden to Look" (Spicer) **78**:269
"It Is March" (Merwin) **45**:19-20
"It Is Much" (Sandburg) **41**:336
"It Is My Thoughts That Color My Soul" (Wylie) **23**:322
"It Is Necessary to Know" (Cernuda)
See "Hace falta saber"
"It Is No Dream of Mine" (Thoreau) **30**:216
"It Is No Longer Possible" (Aleixandre) **15**:20
"It is no spirit" (Wordsworth) **67**:269
"It Is Not Always May" (Longfellow) **30**:26
"It Is Not Dead" (Warren) **37**:380
"It is over" (Guillén)
See "Se acabó"
"It Is Poetry" (Enright) **93**:25
"It Is Said" (Alurista) **34**:43
"It Is So" (Neruda)
See "Es así"
"It Is the First Mild Day of March" (Wordsworth)
See "Lines on the First Mild Day of March"
"It Is the Time You Think" (Stafford) **71**:337
"It Is Too Late" (Curnow) **48**:11
"It Is Well" (Brooke) **24**:71-2
"It may be good, like it who list" (Wyatt) **27**:316, 329, 341
"It Must Be Done" (Service) **70**:152-53
"It Must Be Sophisticated" (Ashbery) **26**:161
"It Must Be the Milk" (Nash) **21**:278-79
"It Must Give Pleasure" (Stevens) **6**:329; **110**:113
"It Nods and Curtseys and Recovers" (Housman) **2**:192-93
"It Out-Herods Herod. Pray You, Avoid It" (Hecht) **70**:78, 102
"It Rains" (Thomas) **53**:286
"It Rolls On" (Rexroth) **95**:259
"It Was" (Corso) **108**:17
"It Was a Face Which Darkness Could Kill" (Ferlinghetti) **1**:183
"It Was a' for Our Rightfu' King" (Burns) **6**:99; **114**:62
"It Was a Funky Deal" (Knight) **14**:46
"It Was a Gentle Breeze" (Darío)
See "Era un aire suave"
"It Was a Soft Air" (Darío)
See "Era un aire suave"
"It Was All Very Tidy" (Graves) **6**:142, 144
"It Was Black Black Took" (Stein) **18**:328
"It Was in Vegas" (Cunningham) **92**:150, 168
"It Was That Indian" (Ortiz) **17**:234
"It Was Upon" (Thomas) **53**:266
It Was When (Snyder) **21**:289
"It Was Winter" (Milosz) **8**:194
"'It Was Wrong to Do This,' Said the Angel" (Crane) **80**:52
"It weeps away" (Piercy) **29**:315
"It Will Not Change" (Teasdale) **31**:332, 359
"L'Italia" (Pasolini) **17**:270, 272
"Italia mia" (Petrarch) **8**:267, 270
"Italian Cantos" (Pound) **95**:151-52, 155-56, 234
"Italian Extravaganza" (Corso) **33**:6, 14, 41, 43; **108**:15
"Italian Garden" (Sarton) **39**:332
"The Italian Kitchen" (Ní Chuilleanáin) **34**:350
"Italian Morning" (Bogan) **12**:106
An Italian Visit (Day Lewis) **11**:150
"Italie" (Sainte-Beuve) **110**:57
"Italy" (Whittier) **93**:269
"Italy and France" (Browning) **2**:26
"Itching Heels" (Dunbar) **5**:146
"Ite, missa est" (Darío) **15**:113
"Item" (Williams) **109**:284-86
"Ithaca" (Cavafy) **36**:3, 28, 41, 50, 51, 73, 74, 76, 78, 86, 108
"Ithaca" (Glück) **16**:172
"Ithaka" (Cavafy)
See "Ithaca"
"Itinerary" (Kumin) **15**:220
"Itinerary of an Obession" (Kumin) **15**:220
"The Itinerary of Ua Cleirigh" (Clarke) **112**:83
"'It's a Cold Night,' Said Coney to Coney" (Jacobsen) **62**:320
"It's a New Day" (Sanchez) **9**:229
It's a New Day: Poems for Young Brothas and Sistuhs (Sanchez) **9**:207, 211-12, 215, 229, 237
"It's a Woman's World" (Boland) **58**:4, 12, 15, 45
"It's both boring and sad" (Lermontov) **18**:268-69
"It's Cold" (Parra)
See "Hace frio"
"Its Course" (Carver) **54**:13
"It's Dull and Dreary" (Lermontov) **18**:281
"Its Everlasting Possibility" (Pinsky) **27**:153
"Its Great Emptiness" (Pinsky) **27**:153-4
"It's Half an Hour Later Before" (Ammons) **16**:25
"Its Many Fragments" (Pinsky) **27**:153
"It's Miller Time" (Cruz) **37**:30
"It's Nation Time" (Baraka) **4**:19, 26, 40; **113**:19
It's Nation Time (Baraka) **4**:19, 20, 26; **113**:19, 26, 55, 73, 77-78, 80
"It's Not Going to Happen Again" (Brooke) **24**:84-5, 93
"It's Oblivion" (Parra)
See "Es olvido"
"It's over a (See Just" (Cummings) **5**:108
"It's Probably Spring" (Cohen) **109**:71
"It's Raining" (Apollinaire)
See "Il pleut"
"It's Time, My Friend, It's Time" (Pushkin)
See "Pora, Moi Drug, Pora"
"It's Unbecoming" (Pasternak) **6**:265
Iustum et tenacem (Horace) **46**:104
"Iuvenes Dum Sumus" (Hall) **70**:30
"Iva" (Akhmatova) **55**:39
I've Been a Woman (Sanchez)
See *I've Been a Woman: New and Selected Poems*
I've Been a Woman: New and Selected Poems (Sanchez) **9**:207, 211-12, 215-16, 218-22, 227, 229, 232, 238, 242
"I've Been Asleep" (Levine) **22**:218
"I've Been Thinking" (Moore)
See "Occasionem Cognosce"
"I've Come to See" (Cernuda) **62**:171
"I've Looked So Much" (Cavafy) **36**:74, 107
"I've Nothing to Offer" (Ignatow) **34**:344-45
I-VI (Cage) **58**:212, 214
"The Ivory Statuette" (Wylie) **23**:321
IX Ecloghe (Zanzotto) **65**:262, 265-67, 270, 276, 278, 287-88, 295, 315, 338
IX Ecologues (Zanzotto)
See *IX Ecloghe*
Iz shesti knig (Akhmatova) **2**:18
Izbrannoe. Stikhi (Akhmadulina) **43**:33
Izbrannyye proizvedeniya (Yevtushenko) **40**:359, 363
Izya Kramer, Inspector of Lights (Yevtushenko) **40**:357
J. B. (MacLeish) **47**:167-70, 174, 177, 179-80, 197, 208, 212, 215, 228-30, 232, 234, 261-62
"J. G. Whittier to the 'Rustic Bard'" (Whittier) **93**:200
"J. T. on his Travels" (Enright) **93**:33
"Ja dumala, cto ty moj vrag..." (Akhmadulina) **43**:59-62
"Ja k vam pishu" (Lermontov) **18**:303
"Jabberers" (Sandburg) **41**:270
"Jabberwocky" (Carroll) **18**:36, 38-40, 48-50, 52, 59-60; **74**:4, 9, 24-25, 29, 31, 58-60, 62-63, 67, 69, 74-76, 83, 94, 100, 106
Jablko z klína (Seifert) **47**:316, 325, 333
"Jack Hall" (Hood) **93**:52
Jack Kelso: A Dramatic Poem (Masters) **1**:339
"Jack Roy" (Melville) **82**:144, 163
"Jack Straw's Castle" (Gunn) **26**:205, 213, 228
"The Jackal-Headed Cowboy from Ra" (Reed) **68**:323, 331
"Jacke and Jone" (Campion) **87**:65
"Jacket Notes" (Reed) **68**:335, 338, 348
"Jacklight" (Erdrich) **52**:176, 189, 192
Jacklight (Erdrich) **52**:170-80, 182, 184-87, 189-91, 193
"Jack's Final Wire" (Yau) **61**:333
Jack's Straw Castle, and Other Poems (Gunn) **26**:194-197, 204-206, 208, 210, 213, 219-220, 229
"Jackson, Mississippi" (Walker) **20**:283
"Jacob" (Clough) **103**:55
"The Jacob's Ladder" (Glück) **16**:171
The Jacob's Ladder (Levertov) **11**:168, 193, 206
"Jacobs Pillow, and Pillar" (Vaughan) **81**:306
"Jacob's Wives" (Clough) **103**:55, 138
"Jacobson" (Rexroth)
See "For Eli Jacobson"
"The Jacquerie" (Lanier) **50**:90, 107-8
"Jactancia de quietud" (Borges) **22**:72; **32**:38, 123, 139
"Jadis" (Rimbaud)
See "Jadis, si je me souviens bien . . ."
Jadis et naguère (Verlaine) **2**:416; **32**:355, 369, 375, 377-78, 385-86, 400-01
"Jadis, si je me souviens bien . . ." (Rimbaud) **57**:246, 251
"Jäger, mein Sternbild" (Sachs) **78**:117
"The Jaguar" (Hughes) **7**:118, 151, 163; **89**:207, 223

"Jah" (Brathwaite) **56**:53-54, 75, 86, 100
"Jah Music" (Goodison) **36**:143, 154
Jah Music (Brathwaite) **56**:45, 51, 71
"J'ai Mal à Nos Dents" (Ní Chuilleanáin) **34**:360, 362, 364
"J'ai plus de souvenirs" (Baudelaire) **1**:67
"Jail Poems" (Kaufman) **74**:178-79, 183, 195, 199
"The Jailer" (Plath) **37**:230, 232-34
"Jailhouse Blues" (Randall) **86**:289, 338
"The Jain Bird Hospital in Delhi" (Meredith) **28**:215
"Jaisurya" (Das) **43**:73
"Jam Session" (Hughes) **1**:245; **53**:192
"The Jam Trap" (Tomlinson) **17**:314
"Jamaica 1980" (Goodison) **36**:153-54
"Jamāl al-mawt" (Gibran) **9**:78
"Jamás lo olvidare!" (Castro) **41**:116
"James Lee's Wife" (Browning) **61**:88
"James Stephens" (Clarke) **112**:93
"James Wetherell" (Robinson) **1**:467
"Jamestown" (Jarrell) **41**:146, 169
"jamming naked" (Cruz)
See "descarga en cueros"
"jamming with drums" (Cruz)
See "descarga en cueros"
"The Jam-Pot" (Kipling) **3**:190
"Jan Kubelik" (Sandburg) **41**:318, 321, 365
"Jan, the Son of Thomas" (Sandburg) **41**:302
"Jane" (Masefield) **78**:49
"Janet Waking" (Ransom) **61**:271, 301, 313, 323
"January" (Belloc) **24**:29
"January" (Hass) **16**:216
"January" (Nishiwaki)
See "Ichigatsu"
"January" (Song) **21**:341
"January" (Thomas) **99**:245, 286
"January and May" (Chaucer)
See "Miller's Tale"
"January Morning" (Williams) **109**:241-42, 277-79
"A January Night" (Hardy) **8**:110
"January 1918" (Pasternak) **6**:261
"January 1919" (Pasternak) **6**:252
"January 1904" (Cavafy) **36**:109
"January 10, 1973" (Walker) **30**:354
"A Japanese Elegy" (Yakamochi)
See "Nihon no Banka"
Japanese Garland (Blunden) **66**:14, 17-18, 23-24, 31, 44
"Japanese Lament" (Yakamochi)
See "Nihon no Banka"
"Japanese Prints" (Sarton) **39**:339, 345, 349, 351
"Japanese Prints: Tourist" (Sarton) **39**:327
"Japanese River Tales" (Hughes) **89**:144
"Jaquet et Robine" (Ronsard) **105**:281
"Jardín" (Cernuda) **62**:174, 181
"Jardín antiguo" (Cernuda) **62**:203, 220
"El jardin botánico" (Borges) **32**:60
"Jardín de invierno" (Neruda) **4**:287, 289-90
"El jardín triste se pierde" (Jiménez) **7**:199
"Jardín zoológico de nubes" (Storni) **33**:295
Jardines lejanos (Jiménez) **7**:209
"Jarmark cudó" (Szymborska) **44**:280
Jarmark cudó (Szymborska) **44**:317, 230
Jaro sbohem (Seifert) **47**:323, 325, 333-34
"Jarrama" (Ekeloef) **23**:76
"La Jarre" (Éluard) **38**:67-68
"Jasmine Arbour" (Tagore)
See "Chameli-vitan"
"Jason" (MacLeish) **47**:182
"Jaufré Rudel" (Carducci) **46**:52
"Jaws" (Sandburg) **2**:330; **41**:269
"Jaybird" (Dunbar) **5**:144
"Jazbo" (Sandburg) **41**:270
"Jazz Band in a Parisian Cabaret" (Hughes) **53**:82
"Jazz Chick" (Kaufman) **74**:244, 268
"Jazz Fantazia" (Sandburg) **41**:297
"Jazz te deum for Inhaling a Mexican Bonfires" (Kaufman) **74**:188, 195, 240
"Jazzonia" (Hughes) **1**:246, 261; **53**:80, 82, 86, 91, 117
Je ne mange pas de ce pain-là (Péret) **33**:220, 230
"Je ne suis pas seul . . ." (Char) **56**:120
"Je ne veux point la mort" (Ronsard) **105**:197
"Je plaings le temps de ma jeunesse" (Villon) **13**:388-89
"Je plante en la faveur cest arbre de Cybelle" (Ronsard) **11**:277
Je sublime (Péret) **33**:202, 204, 206-07, 214-15, 220, 225, 231
"Je suis bruslé, Le Gast, d'une double chaleur" (Ronsard) **11**:250
"Je suis l'empire à la fin de la décadence" (Verlaine) **2**:416
"Je Suis Une Table" (Hall) **70**:32
"Je suis venu, calme orphelin" (Verlaine) **32**:379
"Je te dirais" (Péret) **33**:208
"Je te donne ces vers . . ." (Baudelaire) **106**:84
"Je veux chanter en ces vers ma tristesse" (Ronsard) **105**:185-86, 188-91
"Je vous envoye un bouquet que ma main" (Ronsard) **105**:194, 197
"The Jealous Man" (Graves) **6**:142, 144
"Jealousy" (Brooke) **24**:56
"Jealousy—A Confessional" (Wakoski) **15**:356
"Jean de Nivelle" (Verlaine) **32**:378
"Jeanne d'Arc" (Glück) **16**:140
"Jean's TV" (Carver) **54**:12, 14
"jed bi kor benkst trik" (Bissett) **14**:34
"Jede Schönheit" (Werfel) **101**:350
"Jedwab duszy" (Herbert) **50**:5
"Jeffereidos" (Davenant) **99**:177, 195, 197-201, 218
"Jefferson" (Shapiro) **25**:270
"Jefferson Cantos" (Pound) **95**:80
"Jefferson Howard" (Masters) **36**:230, 232
"Jehova" (Lamartine) **16**:280, 293
"Jehovah Our Righteousness" (Cowper) **40**:54
"Jehuda ben Halevy" (Heine) **25**:149
"A Jellyfish" (Moore) **49**:104, 140, 184-85
"Jem and Nancy" (Elliott) **96**:175
"Jemez" (Tomlinson) **17**:355
"Jen jedno jsem spatřil..." (Seifert) **47**:335
"Jener" (Benn) **35**:69
"Jenny" (Rossetti) **44**:165, 167, 175-77, 180, 191, 201-3, 237, 239-42, 252
"Jenny Kissed Me" (Hunt) **73**:162, 167-68
"Jephthah's Daughter" (Vigny)
See "La Fille de Jephte"
"The Jerboa" (Moore) **4**:233, 236, 243; **49**:94, 97-98, 100, 119, 129, 142, 144, 149, 155
"Jeremiah" (Walker) **20**:278
"Jerome" (Jarrell) **41**:208
"Jeronimo's House" (Bishop) **3**:37, 47; **34**:130
"Jerusalem" (Douglas) **106**:203
"Jerusalem" (Rich) **5**:383
"Jerusalem 1967" (Amichai) **38**:8, 54
"Jerusalem Is Everywhere" (Sachs)
See "Überall Jerusalem"
"Jerusalem, Jerusalem, Why Jerusalem" (Amichai) **38**:47, 49
Jerusalem: The Emanation of the Giant Albion (Blake) **12**:13, 20, 27, 29-32, 34-40, 43-44, 51-59, 61-75, 80; **63**:17, 54, 73, 85, 104, 117
"Jesse and Colin" (Crabbe) **97**:95, 98
"Jessie Cameron" (Rossetti) **7**:280
"Jessie Mitchell's Mother" (Brooks) **7**:58, 62, 68, 96, 99-100, 102
"The Jest" (Clarke) **112**:71
"Jestem za blisko" (Szymborska) **44**:269, 286
"The Jester" (Gower) **59**:58
"The Jester" (Hughes) **1**:235; **53**:85
"The Jester, A Ballad" (Bely)
See "Shut, Bellada"
"Jester, A Flame" (Bely)
See "Shut: Plamen"
"Jester above It" (Bely)
See "Shut Nad ney"
"Jesu" (Herbert) **4**:100
"The Jesus" (Hughes) **53**:115
"Jesus and Isolt" (Pinsky) **27**:157, 175
"Jesus and the Carrion-Path" (Werfel)
See "Jesus und der Äser-Weg"
"Jesus Asleep" (Sexton) **79**:218
"Jesus Awake" (Sexton) **79**:218
"Jesus Cooks" (Sexton) **79**:219
"Jesus Dies" (Sexton) **79**:219
"The Jesus Papers" (Sexton) **2**:360; **79**:218-19, 252
"Jesus Raises Up the Harlot" (Sexton) **79**:218
"Jesus Suckles" (Sexton) **79**:218
"Jesus Summons Forth" (Sexton) **79**:219
"Jesus, the Actor, Plays the Holy Ghost" (Sexton) **79**:238
"Jesus Unborn" (Sexton) **79**:219
"Jesus und der Äser-Weg" (Werfel) **101**:302, 320, 338-40, 347, 357
"Jesus Walking" (Sexton) **2**:360-61, 373
"Jesus Weeping: S. Luke 19. ver. 41" (Vaughan) **81**:313-14
"Le jet d'eau" (Baudelaire) **1**:61
"Le Jeu" (Baudelaire) **106**:103
"Le jeu de construction" (Éluard) **38**:79
"Jeu de lettres" (Brossard)
See "Character/Jeu de lettres"
"Jeu sublime" (Péret) **33**:215
"Jeune, avide, inconnu, j'ai désiré la gloire" (Sainte-Beuve) **110**:44
"Jeune ménage" (Rimbaud) **57**:183, 219, 253
"La jeune mère" (Ponge) **107**:137, 142
La jeune parque (Valéry) **9**:346-48, 351-58, 361, 363-67, 369-74, 379-85, 387, 390-96, 401-03
"La jeune prêtre" (Valéry) **9**:391
"Jeunesse" (Rimbaud) **3**:261, 263; **57**:239, 246, 250, 269, 271, 275
Jeux à vendre (Christine de Pizan) **68**:96
"Jew" (Abse) **41**:3, 8
"Jew" (Shapiro) **25**:296-97
"The Jew" (Very) **86**:88
"The Jew at Christmas Eve" (Shapiro) **25**:283, 286, 300
"The Jewel" (Wright) **36**:305, 313, 340, 355, 357, 374, 398-99
"The Jewels" (Baudelaire)
See "Les Bijoux"
"The Jewels" (Clarke) **112**:48, 50
"The Jeweled Stairs' Grievance" (Li Po) **29**:144
"Jewelled Bindings" (Wylie) **23**:320
"Jewels" (Teasdale) **31**:356
"The Jewish Cemetery at Newport" (Longfellow) **30**:36
"Jewish Emigrant" (Mistral)
See "Emigrada judía"
"The Jewish Problem" (Shapiro) **25**:323
"The Jewish Time Bomb" (Amichai) **38**:51
"Jewish Travel" (Amichai) **38**:50
"The Jews" (Vaughan) **81**:313
"J'habite une douleur" (Char) **56**:157
"Jhesu and his moder Marie" (Dunbar) **67**:18
The Jig of Forslin: A Symphony (Aiken) **26**:5-7, 16, 21-22, 35
Jill (Larkin) **21**:225, 232
"Jillain the box" (Piercy) **29**:314
"Jim and Arabel's Sister" (Masters) **1**:328; **36**:175
"Jim at Sixteen" (McKay) **2**:223
"Jim Brown on the Screen" (Baraka) **4**:19
Jim Crow's Last Stand (Hughes) **1**:250, 253; **53**:145, 153
"jimi hendrix" (Alurista) **34**:39
"Jimmy" (Baca) **41**:68
"Jimmy Jet and His TV Set" (Silverstein) **49**:308, 311
"Jin'a jiiai bun" (Yakamochi) **48**:136, 139
"Jinny the Just" (Prior) **102**:297, 308, 319
Th Jinx Ship nd Othr Trips (Bissett) **14**:14
"Jitterbugs" (Baraka) **4**:12, 18; **113**:16

"Jivan devata" (Tagore) **8**:408
"Jivan madhyahna" (Tagore) **8**:407
"Jiving" (Dove) **6**:114, 117
"The Joachim Quartet" (Bridges) **28**:88
"Joal" (Senghor) **25**:241, 243-44, 246
"Joan and Darby" (Graves) **6**:156
"Joan Miró" (Éluard) **38**:71
"Joan of Arc" (Coleridge) **11**:80, 83, 97
Joan of Arc, an Epic Poem (Southey) **111**:191, 205, 207-8, 213-14, 240-41, 244-45, 253
"Joasaph and Fatumeh" (Ekeloef) **23**:67
"Job" (Blake) **12**:38
"Job" (Sachs) **78**:110
"A Job for Poetry: Notes on an Impulse" (Curnow) **48**:26
"Job Work" (Riley) **48**:299
"Job's Answer" (Wagoner) **33**:334
Jocelyn: Épisode; Journal trouvé chez un curé de village (Lamartine) **16**:257-61, 263-64, 269-70, 273-74, 286-87, 293, 297
"Jochanan Hakkadosh" (Browning) **2**:75
"A Jocular Retort" (Clarke) **112**:120-21
"Joe Harris" (Birney) **52**:8, 35-37, 39-40
"Joel" (Walker) **20**:278-79
"Joe's Jacket" (O'Hara) **45**:133, 145-47, 154, 193
"Joggin' Erlong" (Dunbar) **5**:145
"Johann" (Walker) **30**:340, 352, 357, 365
"A Johannes Brahms" (Borges) **22**:96
"Johannesburg Mines" (Hughes) **53**:111, 169-70
"John" (Thumboo) **30**:333
"John and Anne" (Meredith) **28**:199, 205
"John Anderson" (Douglas) **106**:186, 197
"John Anderson, My Jo" (Burns) **6**:78, 98
"John Barleycorn" (Burns) **6**:52
"John Brown" (Hayden) **6**:192, 195
"John Brown" (Lindsay) **23**:264-65, 275, 279, 286
"John Brown" (Robinson) **1**:468
"John Brown" (Spencer)
See "A Dream of John Brown: On His Return Trip Home"
"John Brown's Body" (Benét) **64**:3-6, 8-10, 13-15, 17-20, 26-27, 33, 36, 50, 52-53, 55-59, 63
"John Brown's Kiss" (Whittier) **93**:281
"John Burke" (Olson) **19**:305
"John Cabanis" (Masters) **36**:230, 233
"John Chapman" (Wilbur) **51**:246, 283-84
"John Coltrane Arrived with An Egyptian Lady" (Mackey) **49**:4
"John Cowper Powys" (Masters) **1**:343
John Deth: A Metaphysical Legend and Other Poems (Aiken) **26**:12, 53
"John Donne in California" (Clampitt) **19**:92
"John Dryden" (Carruth) **10**:74
John Endicott (Longfellow) **30**:73
"John Gilpin" (Cowper)
See "The Diverting History of John Gilpin"
John Gilpin (Cowper)
See "The Diverting History of John Gilpin"
"John Gorham" (Robinson) **1**:462, 468, 478
"John Greenleaf Whittier tie-clip" (Berrigan) **103**:39
"John Hancock Otis" (Masters) **36**:171
"John Henry" (Tolson)
See "The Birth of John Henry"
"John I:4" (Borges)
See "Juan I, 4"
"John I, 4" (Borges)
See "Juan I, 4"
"John L. Sullivan, the Strong Boy of Boston" (Lindsay) **23**:265, 270, 273, 276
"John MacLean (1879-1923)" (MacDiarmid) **9**:179
"John Marr" (Melville) **82**:71-72, 103, 142-44, 160, 163
John Marr and Other Sailors, with Some Sea-Pieces (Melville) **82**:71-74, 77, 86, 90, 96-97, 100, 103-4, 141-45, 151, 156, 158, 164, 166, 182, 199, 211, 269
"John Maydew; or, The Allotment" (Tomlinson) **17**:326, 341
"John Mouldy" (de la Mare) **77**:122
John Wesley Harding (Dylan) **37**:49, 61-2
"Johnnie Cope" (Burns) **114**:61
"Johnny Appleseed" (Masters) **1**:330
"Johnny Spain's White Heifer" (Carruth) **10**:74
"Johnny Thomas" (Brown) **55**:73, 156
"Johnson's Cabinet Watched by Ants" (Bly) **39**:9
"Joilet" (Sandburg) **2**:324
"Joke" (Bely)
See "Shutka"
"The Joke" (Creeley) **73**:10
"A Joker" (Baudelaire)
See "Un plaisant"
Jokes to Mislead the Police (Parra)
See *Chistes parra desorientar a la policia*
"La jolie rousse" (Apollinaire) **7**:3, 9, 49
"Jollie Gleeman" (Viereck) **27**:282
"The Jolly Beggars" (Burns) **6**:55-6, 58, 78, 90-6; **114**:10, 12-13, 15, 17, 38, 71, 75
"The Jolly Company" (Brooke) **24**:58
"Jo-Mama" (Berrigan) **103**:27
"Jonah" (Jarrell) **41**:174
"Jonah" (Sarton) **39**:342
"Jonas Keene" (Masters) **36**:171, 182
"Jonathan Edwards" (Lowell) **3**:212
"Jonathan Edwards in Western Massachusettes" (Lowell) **3**:216
"Jonathan Swift Somers" (Masters) **36**:222
"Jones' Private Argument" (Lanier)
See "Jones's Private Argyment"
"Jones's Private Argyment" (Lanier) **50**:107
Jones Very: Selected Poems (Very)
See *Selected Poems*
Jones Very: The Complete Poems (Very) **86**:151, 165-66
"Jordan" (Herbert) **4**:102, 107, 113
"Jordan I" (Herbert) **4**:114, 129
"Jordan II" (Herbert) **4**:100, 114
Jorge Luis Borges: Selected Poems 1923-1969 (Borges) **22**:71
"Jorge the Church Janitor Finally Quits" (Espada) **74**:124, 126, 139
"Josef Weinheber" (Auden) **92**:14, 17
Joseffy: An Appreciation (Sandburg) **41**:341
"Joseph" (Forché) **10**:144, 156-57
Joseph Delorme (Sainte-Beuve)
See *Vie, poésies et pensées de Joseph Delorme*
"Joseph Pockets" (Stern) **115**:246
"Joseph to His Brothers" (Baraka) **113**:133, 139-40
"Josepha" (Meredith) **60**:308
"Joseph's Amazement" (Southwell) **83**:279, 281
"Joseph's Coat" (Herbert) **4**:130
"Jose's Country" (Winters) **82**:314
"Joshua on Eighth Avenue" (Ciardi) **69**:14, 43
"Joshua Tree" (Ammons) **16**:5
"Joue et dors" (Char) **56**:151
"Le joueur généreux" (Baudelaire) **106**:92-93
Jouga (Stevens) **110**:150, 154
"Le joujou du pauvre" (Baudelaire) **1**:58
"Jouncer's Trump" (Masefield) **78**:45, 98-99
"Le jour au fond du jour sauvera-t-il . . ." (Bonnefoy) **58**:118
"Jour et nuit" (Césaire) **25**:30
"Journal Night Thoughts" (Ginsberg) **4**:52, 69
"Journal of an Airman" (Auden) **1**:5
Journal on Deck, I (Seferis)
See *Logbook I*
Journal on Deck, II (Seferis)
See *Logbook II*
Journal on Deck, III (Seferis)
See *Logbook III*
"Journal the 6th" (Chatterton) **104**:52
Journalism (Mahon) **60**:220
"The Journalist Reader and Writer" (Lermontov) **18**:268-69, 281
Journals: Early Fifties, Early Sixties (Ginsberg) **4**:60, 69
The Journals of Susanna Moodie (Atwood) **8**:10-12, 15, 21, 29, 31, 33, 35-6, 40
"Journey" (Auden) **92**:63
"The Journey" (Boland) **58**:6-7, 30-32, 35, 47-48, 51, 68, 70
"The Journey" (Kumin) **15**:198, 203
"The Journey" (de la Mare) **77**:73
"Journey" (Millay) **6**:206; **61**:212
"Journey" (Olds) **22**:322
"Journey" (Seferis) **66**:125
"The Journey" (Southey) **111**:185
"The Journey" (Spender) **71**:139
"Journey" (Stafford) **71**:336
"The Journey" (Thomas) **99**:235, 245
"The Journey" (Winters) **82**:346
"The Journey" (Wright) **36**:348, 360, 366, 378, 400
The Journey (Boland) **58**:3, 5-7, 11, 15-16, 47-48, 66-67, 80, 87, 96
The Journey and Other Poems (Winters) **82**:313, 334, 337-38, 345
"The Journey Back" (Heaney) **18**:256
"The Journey Back" (Muir) **49**:198, 200, 221, 296
"Journey for Love" (Dafydd ap Gwilym)
See "Taith i Garu"
"Journey Home" (MacLeish) **47**:164
"Journey Home" (Page) **12**:178
Journey into Dustlessness (Sachs)
See *Fahrt ins Staublose*
Journey into the Beyond (Sachs)
See *Fahrt ins Staublose*
A Journey into Worcestershire (Davenant) **99**:214-15
"Journey North" (Tu Fu) **9**:332
"The Journey of Life" (Bryant) **20**:10
"Journey of the Magi" (Eliot) **5**:171, 177, 194, 197, 203, 205, 209
Journey to a Known Place (Carruth) **10**:70
"Journey to an Unknown Destination" (Tagore)
See "Niruddesh yatra"
A Journey to Kashima (Matsuo Basho)
See *Kashima kikō*
Journey to Love (Williams) **7**:371, 403; **109**:261
A Journey to Sarashina (Matsuo Basho)
See *Sarashina kikō*
"Journey to the Interior" (Atwood) **8**:36
"Journey to the Interior" (Roethke) **15**:279, 310, 314
"Journey toward Poetry" (Sarton) **39**:323
"Journeys" (Brathwaite) **56**:5, 49
"Journeys and Faces" (Abse) **41**:3
Journeys and Places (Muir) **49**:228-29, 242-43, 246, 270, 278, 288-89
"Jouvence des Névons" (Char) **56**:126
"Jouvert" (Brathwaite) **56**:68, 74-75, 88
"El joven marino" (Cernuda) **62**:203
"La joven noche" (Borges) **32**:91
"Jóvenes" (Parra) **39**:309
"Joy" (Creeley) **73**:12, 53
"Joy" (Enzensberger) **28**:142
"Joy" (Jeffers) **17**:106
"Joy" (Levertov) **11**:192
"Joy" (Mueller) **33**:191, 193
"Joy" (Sandburg) **41**:243, 267, 338
"Joy" (Teasdale) **31**:321, 388
"The Joy and Agony of Improvisation" (Carruth) **10**:73
"Joy and Margaret" (Blunden) **66**:9
"Joy in Russia" (Bely) **11**:6
"Joy of My Life" (Vaughan) **81**:271, 306, 328, 330
"Joy of Shipwrecks" (Berrigan) **103**:25
"The Joy of Writing" (Szymborska)
See "Radosc pisania"
"Joy sweetest lifeborn joy" (Bridges) **28**:89
"Joyce Carol Oates Plays the Saturn Piano" (Wakoski) **15**:368
"The Joycentenary Ode" (Mahon) **60**:171
"Joyeuse Garde" (Swinburne) **24**:355
"The Joyful Black Demon of Sister Clara Flies through the Midnight Woods on Her

Snowmobile" (Wakoski) **15**:332
"The Joyous Wanderer" (Meynell) **112**:191
"Joys Faces Friends" (Cummings) **5**:110
"The Joys of the Road" (Carman) **34**:201, 206
"Juan Diego" (Alurista) **34**:41
"Juan Figueroa, Casa del Yodo 'Maria Elena,' Antofagasta" (Neruda) **4**:294
"Juan Figueroa, Iodine Factory 'Maria Elena,' Antofagasta" (Neruda)
See "Juan Figueroa, Casa del Yodo 'Maria Elena,' Antofagasta"
"Juan I, 4" (Borges) **22**:75, 96; **32**:58, 92
"Juan's Song" (Bogan) **12**:90, 92, 100
"Jubal" (Eliot) **20**:101, 117, 119-20, 124, 134-37, 144
Jubilate Agno (Smart) **13**:339-40, 342-44, 346-48, 350-52, 355, 357-58, 360-69
Jubilation (Tomlinson) **17**:361
"The Jubilee of a Magazine" (Hardy) **92**:328
"The Jubilee Singers" (Whittier) **93**:318
"Jubilo" (Tate) **50**:252, 256
Judarieh (Darwish) **86**:28
"Judas Iscariot" (Cullen) **20**:55-56, 67, 86
"Judas Iscariot" (Spender) **71**:188
"Judas Kiss" (Kinnell) **26**:286-87
"Judería" (Borges) **32**:80
"The judge" (Hughes) **89**:198, 233
The Judge Is Fury (Cunningham) **92**:135-37, 139, 180, 188, 191
"Judge Somers" (Masters) **36**:230
"The Judgement Day" (Johnson) **24**:128-29, 164-65, 169
"Judgement Day" (Thomas) **99**:237
"The Judgement of Paris" (Merwin) **45**:19, 26
Judges (Vigny) **26**:368
"Judging Logs" (Wagoner) **33**:352
"The Judgment" (Akhmatova) **2**:15
"Judgment" (Crabbe) **97**:77
"Judgment" (Herbert) **4**:129
"Judgment of God" (Morris) **55**:238, 267, 302
"The Judgment of Midas" (Smart) **13**:348
"Judith" (Hecht) **70**:108
"Judith and Holofernes" (Deloney) **79**:55, 57
"Judith of Bethulia" (Ransom) **61**:296
"Le Jugement d'Octobre" (Char) **56**:153, 182
"Le Jugement originel" (Éluard) **38**:96
"Juggler" (Wilbur) **51**:208, 219, 242
"Juggling Jerry" (Meredith) **60**:262, 293-94, 328
"Juice Joint: Northern City" (Hughes) **1**:243
"Juke Box Love Song" (Hughes) **53**:124-25
"Jukebox" (Randall)
See "A Poet Is Not a Jukebox"
"Julia" (Wordsworth) **4**:399
"Julian and Maddalo" (Shelley) **14**:173, 175, 182, 240
Julian and Maddalo (Shelley)
See "Julian and Maddalo"
"Julian and the Citizens of Antioch" (Cavafy) **36**:33, 39
"Julian at Nicodemia" (Cavafy) **36**:33
"Julian at the Mysteries" (Cavafy) **36**:39, 54, 58
"Julian M. and A. G. Rochelle" (Brontë) **8**:52
"Julian seeing Negligence" (Cavafy) **36**:33
"Julia's Petticoat" (Herrick) **9**:143
"Julio" (Lermontov)
See "Dzhulio"
"Julius and Ethel" (Dylan) **37**:65
"July" (Belloc) **24**:29
"July 8, 1656" (Bradstreet) **10**:60
"July, 1773" (Berry) **28**:38
"July 1914" (Akhmatova) **55**:36
"July, 1964" (Davie) **29**:124
"July 1968" (Levertov) **11**:194
"July, Against Hunger" (Kumin) **15**:207
"July in Vallombrosa" (Loy) **16**:313
"July in Washington" (Lowell) **3**:214
"July Midnight" (Lowell) **13**:64
"A July Night" (Ekeloef) **23**:58
"July's Farewell" (Clough) **103**:140
"The Jumblies" (Lear) **65**:146-47, 149-51, 154, 157, 160
"Jumbo" (Stevens) **110**:190, 192
"Jump to Glory Jane" (Meredith) **60**:262, 293
Jumping Out of Bed (Bly) **39**:70
"Jumping Rope" (Silverstein) **49**:347
"June" (Bryant) **20**:9, 14, 16, 18
"June" (Riley) **48**:315
"June" (Sandburg) **41**:348
"June 6, 1967" (Sexton) **79**:196-97
"June 30, 1974" (Schuyler) **88**:189, 200
"June, 1915" (Mew) **107**:31, 60, 64-65
"June 1940" (Spender) **71**:154, 188
"June, 1968" (Borges)
See "Junio, 1968"
"June Dreams in January" (Lanier) **50**:68
"June: Dutch Harbor" (Meredith) **28**:170, 172, 185, 187
"June Light" (Wilbur) **51**:188, 335
"June Night" (Teasdale) **31**:360
"June Thunder" (MacNeice) **61**:115, 117, 119, 137
"June Twilight" (Masefield) **78**:69
"Der junge Hebbel" (Benn) **35**:48
"Junge Leiden" (Heine) **25**:139
"The Jungle" (Kavanagh) **33**:95, 118
"The Jungle and the Sea" (Aleixandre) **15**:3, 14
The Jungle Book (Kipling) **91**:83-84, 135, 190, 193
The Jungle Books (Kipling) **3**:162, 185, 188-89
"Jungle Knot" (Ammons) **16**:4
"Jungle Surrender" (Komunyakaa) **51**:28, 41-42
"Jungle Warfare" (Spicer) **78**:271
"Das jüngste Gericht" (Rilke) **2**:277
"Junín" (Borges) **32**:61
"Junio, 1968" (Borges) **32**:88
"Juniper-Tree" (Behn)
See "On a Juniper-Tree"
Junjo shokyoku shu (Hagiwara) **18**:176, 182
"Junk" (Wilbur) **51**:198, 202, 204, 209, 217, 222, 268, 273
"Junk Ball" (Chappell) **105**:34
"The Junk Man" (Sandburg) **41**:338
"Junkie Monkey Reel" (Angelou) **32**:28
"Junkman's Obbligato" (Ferlinghetti) **1**:165-66, 173
"Junta" (Walcott) **46**:286
"Just a Smack at Auden" (Empson) **104**:89, 137
"Just Don't Never Give Up on Love" (Sanchez) **9**:234, 238, 244
"Just For Starters" (Ashbery) **26**:165
"Just Friends" (Creeley) **73**:5, 30
Just Give me a Cool Drink of Water 'fore I Diiie (Angelou) **32**:3, 10-11, 26-7, 29
"Just Like a Woman" (Dylan) **37**:55
"Just like Tom Thumb's Blues" (Dylan) **37**:42-4, 46-9, 54-6
"Just Lost, When I Was Saved!" (Dickinson) **1**:97
"Just Lying on the Grass at Blackwater" (Oliver) **75**:342-43
"The Just Made Perfect" (Thoreau) **30**:254, 268
"The Just Man" (Rimbaud)
See "L'homme juste"
"The Just Man And" (Moore) **49**:113, 116
"Just over There" (Paredes)
See "Ahí nomás"
"The Just Remained Upright . . ." (Rimbaud)
See "Le Juste restait droit . . ."
Just So Stories (Kipling) **91**:132, 153
"Just Whistle a Bit" (Dunbar) **5**:137
"Le Juste restait droit . . ." (Rimbaud) **57**:244, 246
"Justice" (Herbert) **4**:102
"Justice" (Hughes) **1**:252; **53**:150
"Justice" (Kipling) **91**:173
"Justice II" (Herbert) **4**:131
"Justice at Midnight" (Barker) **77**:19-20
"Justice Denied in Massachusetts" (Millay) **6**:223
"Justice Is Reason Enough" (Wakoski) **15**:336
"The Justice of the Peace" (Belloc) **24**:28
"La justicia por la mano" (Castro) **41**:116
"Juvat ire jugis" (Arnold) **5**:36
"Juveniles" (Stone) **53**:217
"Juvenilia" (Kavanagh) **105**:154-55
Juvenilia (Carducci) **46**:4, 8, 18, 36, 48, 50-52, 64, 69
Juvenilia; or, A Collection of Poems Written between the Ages of Twelve and Sixteen (Hunt) **73**:134, 144-45, 162-63
"Juventud" (Cernuda) **62**:178, 201
"Juventudes" (Storni) **33**:262, 294-96
"K Liciniju" (Pushkin) **10**:408
"K Likomedu, na Skiros" (Brodsky) **9**:5
"K moriu" (Pushkin) **10**:413
"K Muze" (Blok) **21**:6, 40
"K*** Ne dumaj chtob ja byl dostoin sozhalen'ja" (Lermontov) **18**:301, 304
"K pustoi zemle nevol'no pripadaia" (Mandelstam) **14**:155-56
"K smerti" (Akhmatova) **55**:29
K Uranii (Brodsky)
See *To Urania: Selected Poems 1965-1985*
"Ka 'Ba" (Baraka) **4**:18; **113**:18
"Kabekona Lake" (Bly) **39**:45, 60
"Kabi kahini" (Tagore) **8**:405
The Kabir Book (Kabīr) **56**:323
Kabìr-granthavalì (Kabīr) **56**:344-46
Kabir's Sayings (Kabīr)
See *Sayings of Kabir*
Kabìr's Words (Kabīr) **56**:342
Kabìr-vanis (Kabīr)
See *Sayings of Kabir*
Kabìr-yanis (Kabīr)
See *Sayings of Kabir*
"Lo kabrosh" (Amichai) **38**:51
"Kaddish" (Ginsberg) **4**:49-50, 53, 59, 61, 64-5, 72, 74, 81, 83-6, 91; **47**:16-19, 21-27, 33, 46-47, 49-54, 61-73
Kaddish, and Other Poems (Ginsberg) **4**:47
"Kaeru no shi" (Hagiwara) **18**:168, 179
"Kaeru yo" (Hagiwara) **18**:180
"Kafka and His Precursors" (Borges)
See "Los precursores de Kafka"
"Kafka y sus precursores" (Borges)
See "Los precursores de Kafka"
"Kahara" (Kabīr) **56**:342
Kahini (Tagore) **8**:410
Kai oi (Matsuo Basho) **3**:24
"Kai, Today" (Snyder) **21**:289
"Kairos and Logos" (Auden) **92**:63
"Kaisarion" (Cavafy) **36**:42, 109-10
"Kak svetoteni muchenik Rembrandt" (Mandelstam) **14**:154
"Kalaloch" (Forché) **10**:133-35, 168
"Kalamazoo" (Lindsay) **23**:270
"Kaleidoscope" (Verlaine) **32**:369
Kaleidoscopes Baroque: A Poem (Atwood) **8**:11
"Kali" (Clifton) **17**:23
"Kalimpong" (Tagore) **8**:426
"Kali's Galaxy" (Reed) **68**:330
"Kallundborg Church" (Whittier) **93**:176, 249
"Kally" (Lermontov) **18**:300
"The Kallyope Yell" (Lindsay) **23**:266, 272, 274-76, 280, 284, 289, 296
Kalpana (Tagore) **8**:410-11, 415
Kamen' (Mandelstam) **14**:106, 108, 112-15, 117-18, 122, 135, 142
Kamennyi gost' (Pushkin) **10**:394
Kamenný most (Seifert) **47**:335
"Kampfflur" (Stramm) **50**:173, 202
"Kamyk" (Herbert) **50**:4-6
"Kanashi Tsukio" (Hagiwara) **18**:168
Kanashiki gangu (Ishikawa) **10**:195-97, 200-01, 205, 210-11, 217
"Kansas" (Lindsay) **23**:273, 286
"Kansas City" (Harjo) **27**:55, 65, 72
"Kansas City to St. Louis" (Ginsberg) **4**:54, 57
"The Kansas Emigrants" (Whittier) **93**:211
"Kantian Lyrics I" (Tomlinson) **17**:346
"Kanun Blagoveshchen'ia" (Tsvetaeva) **14**:319-20, 322
"Das kapital" (Baraka) **4**:30, 38

"Das Kapitäl" (Rilke) **2**:275; **113**:24
"Kaplan" (Herbert) **50**:7
"Kappa" (Tolson) **88**:238-39, 263, 273, 304, 312
"Kapuzinerberg (Saltzberg)" (Bogan) **12**:100
"Karamojans" (Walker) **30**:346
Kari o komal (Tagore) **8**:406-7, 415
"Karma" (Hughes) **89**:102, 112, 141
Kartofa (Mickiewicz)
See "Kartofel"
"Kartofel" (Mickiewicz) **38**:162
Kartofla (Mickiewicz)
See "Kartofel"
"Karyatide" (Benn) **35**:20, 45, 46, 47, 48, 49, 50, 54, 67, 77
Kashima kikō (Matsuo Basho) **3**:27
Katha (Tagore) **8**:410
"Katharinal" (Heine) **25**:135
"Käthe Kollwitz" (Rukeyser) **12**:228-30
"Die Kathedrale" (Rilke) **2**:275
"Katherine's Dream" (Lowell) **3**:201
"Kathleen" (Whittier) **93**:172, 223, 239, 245, 267
"Katun 8 Ahau" (Cardenal) **22**:129, 131
"Katun 11 Ahau" (Cardenal) **22**:128-29
Kavanagh's Weekly (Kavanagh) **33**:95
Kavkazsky plennik (Pushkin) **10**:357-58, 364-65, 371, 386-88, 395, 415-21
"Kay Rutledge" (Masters) **1**:334
"Kayanerenhkowa" (Cardenal) **22**:128-29, 131
"Kazach'ja kolybel'naja pesnja" (Lermontov) **18**:304
"Kazan University" (Yevtushenko) **40**:369
"Keats House" (Stryk) **27**:203
"Kednaminsha" (Kavanagh) **33**:150, 154, 157
"Keel, Ram, Stauros" (Jones) **116**:176
"Keen" (Millay) **6**:225
"Keep a Pluggin' Away" (Dunbar) **5**:119
"Keep in a Cool Place" (Curnow) **48**:10-11
"keep on th grass" (Bissett) **14**:33
"Keeper of the Flocks" (Pessoa)
See "O Guardador de Rebanhos"
"The Keepers" (Wagoner) **33**:336
"Keeping Going" (Heaney) **100**:247-49, 305
"Keeping Informed in D.C." (Nemerov) **24**:262
"Keeping Their World Large" (Moore) **4**:236, 268; **49**:93
"Keeping Things Whole" (Strand) **63**:140, 151, 172-73, 175, 180, 190-91
"Keepsake Mill" (Stevenson) **84**:315-16, 344
Kehama (Southey)
See *The Curse of Kehama*
"Keith of Ravelston" (Dobell) **100**:139
"Kelche" (Benn) **35**:66
"Keller Gegen Dom" (Williams) **7**:378; **109**:236
"Kellyburn Braes" (Burns) **6**:78
"Ken" (Mew) **107**:19, 35, 41, 47-49, 51
"Kenrick" (Chatterton) **104**:71
The Kensington Mass (Jones) **116**:107, 147, 167-68
"A Kensington Notebook" (Mahon) **60**:196, 199, 214
"Kent and Christendome" (Wyatt) **27**:331
"Kentucky Blues" (Brown) **55**:76, 154
"Kentucky Mountain Farm" (Warren) **37**:275, 286, 288, 319, 329, 331, 333, 354, 376, 378, 380-81
"Kenyon Review, After the Sandstorm" (Bukowski) **18**:15
"Kept" (Bogan) **12**:105, 122
"Kéramos" (Longfellow) **30**:37, 49, 71
"Kerhonah" (Elliott) **96**:161
"Kerk str. Oost, Pretoria, Transvaal" (Seferis) **66**:210
"Kerouac / *continued*" (Berrigan) **103**:36
"Kerr's Ass" (Kavanagh) **33**:73, 81, 100, 102-3, 119, 147; **105**:99, 111, 153
"Die Kerze" (Sachs) **78**:197, 199
"Kew Gardens" (Chatterton) **104**:4, 32, 68
A Key into the Language of America (Waldrop) **109**:125, 148-50, 167, 169-72, 174-75, 180, 182
"The Key of Water" (Paz) **48**:192
"The Key to Everything" (Swenson) **14**:247
"Key West" (Bishop) **34**:123
"Key West: An Island Sheaf" (Crane) **3**:90
"The Keys of Morning" (de la Mare) **77**:72
Kezfogasok (Illyés) **16**:231, 235
"Khadji Abrek" (Lermontov) **18**:285, 300
"Khalil al-kāfir" (Gibran) **9**:78
"Khalil the Heretic" (Gibran)
See "Khalil al-kāfir"
"Khalil the Unbeliever" (Gibran)
See "Khalil al-kāfir"
"The Khan's Devil" (Whittier) **93**:222
"Khansky polon" (Tsvetaeva) **14**:314-15
Khas Granth (Kabīr) **56**:341
Kheya (Tagore) **8**:412-13, 415
"Khilaf Ghayr Lughawi ma'Imru' al-Qays" (Darwish) **86**:20-21, 24
"Khristos Voskres" (Pushkin) **10**:411-12
"Kicking the Leaves" (Hall) **70**:9, 11-12, 14-16, 27-28, 38
Kicking the Leaves (Hall) **70**:6, 14-16, 19, 27, 30, 33-34, 43-44
"The Kid" (Ai) **72**:6
"The Kid" (Aiken) **26**:16, 41-2
"Kid" (Creeley) **73**:78
"Kid" (Hayden) **6**:196
The Kid (Aiken) **26**:24, 30, 45
"Kid Sleepy" (Hughes) **53**:100
"Kidnapped!" (Silverstein) **49**:313, 334, 344
"The Kids in School with Me" (Hughes) **53**:115
"The Kids Who Die" (Hughes) **1**:243
"Kierkegaard" (Thomas) **99**:321
"Kierkegaard on Hegel" (Zagajewski) **27**:383, 385
"A Kike is the Most Dangerous" (Cummings) **5**:82, 84
"The Kill" (Hall) **70**:31-32
"Killala" (Davie) **29**:110
"Killauea" (Kinnell) **26**:286
"Killed at the Ford" (Longfellow) **30**:47
"The Killer and the Dove" (Viereck) **27**:282
"KILLER WHALE" (Bissett) **14**:10-11, 17-18, 34
"Killers" (Sandburg) **41**:235, 238, 269
"Killiecrankie" (Burns) **6**:78
"Killing a Bug" (Randall) **86**:348
Killing Floor (Ai) **72**:3-5, 7, 27
"Killing the Love" (Sexton) **79**:241
"Killing the Plants" (Kenyon) **57**:45
"Killing the Spring" (Sexton) **2**:365
"Killingworth" (Longfellow) **30**:72
"Kilmarnock Burns" (Burns) **114**:3
"The Kiln" (Blunden) **66**:27
"Kilroy" (Viereck) **27**:263
Kimako's Story (Jordan) **38**:112
"Kimi Shinitamô koto nakare" (Yosano) **11**:320-26, 328-29
"Kimon Learchou, Aged 22, Student of Greek Letters (at Cyrene)" (Cavafy)
See "Kimon, Son of Learchos, 22, Student of Greek Literature in Kyrene"
"Kimon, Son of Learchos, 22, Student of Greek Literature in Kyrene" (Cavafy) **36**:89, 109
"Kin" (Sandburg) **41**:228
"Kin to Sorrow" (Millay) **6**:205; **61**:213
The Kind Act of (Creeley) **73**:3
"Kind are her answers" (Campion) **87**:8, 59
"The Kind Ghosts" (Owen) **19**:343; **102**:151, 181
"The Kind Master and Dutiful Servant" (Hammon) **16**:177-78, 180-82, 190
"Kind of an Ode to Duty" (Nash) **21**:272
"A Kind of Ethics" (Gunn) **26**:206
"A Kind of People" (Mahon) **60**:141, 189
The Kind of Poetry I Want (MacDiarmid) **9**:180, 182, 184, 185-86
"Kind Regards" (Waldrop) **109**:179, 186
"Kind Sir: These Woods" (Sexton) **2**:358
"Kind Words" (Very) **86**:166
Kindai no Guwa (Nishiwaki) **15**:231
"Kindergarten After Thirty Years" (Shvarts)
See "Detskii sad cherez 30 let"
"Kindliness" (Brooke) **24**:56, 77
"Kindness" (Plath) **1**:391, 393
Kindness in the Wolfpasses (Elytis)
See *I kalosíni stis likoporiés*
"Kinds of Water: An Essay on the Road to Compostela" (Carson) **64**:216, 230
"Kinds of Wind" (Sarton) **39**:324
"The King" (Kipling) **3**:161, 166; **91**:86
"King Alleluiah" (Empson) **104**:95
"The King and His Steward's Wife" (Gower) **59**:5, 109
"King Arthur's Men Have Come Again" (Lindsay) **23**:283
"King Arthur's Tomb" (Morris) **55**:238, 240, 257, 264-65, 299-302, 348-49
"King Arthur's Tomb" (Swinburne) **24**:355
"King Ban" (Swinburne) **24**:355
King Bolo (Eliot) **5**:174
"King Claudius" (Cavafy) **36**:39, 40, 53, 54
King Cole (Masefield) **78**:49, 51-52, 56, 58, 62-63
"King Crow" (Corso) **33**:3
"King David" (Benét) **64**:10, 19-21
"King David Dances" (Berryman) **64**:120
"King Demetrios" (Cavafy)
See "King Demetrius"
"King Demetrius" (Cavafy) **36**:7, 29
"King Edward the Confessor and His Ring" (Masefield) **78**:49
"King Edward the Second Tells His Story" (Masefield) **78**:49
"King Edward the Third" (Blake) **12**:11, 61
"King Edward the third, and the faire Countesse of Salisbury" (Deloney) **79**:56
"King Hamlet's Ghost" (Smith) **12**:311, 353
"King Harald's Trance" (Meredith) **60**:251, 263
"King Haydn of Miami Beach" (Duncan) **75**:173-74
"A King in a Funeral Procession" (Smith) **12**:315
King Jasper (Robinson) **1**:479, 483; **35**:368
"King John's Castle" (Kinsella) **69**:88, 90, 122
"King Kong Meets Wallace Stevens" (Ondaatje) **28**:327, 333
The King Maiden (Tsvetaeva)
See *Tsar-devitsa*
"The King of Asini" (Seferis) **66**:90, 94, 112, 118, 136, 141, 148, 179, 220
"The King of Books" (Espada) **74**:154
"King of Carrion" (Hughes) **7**:153
"The King of Denmark's Sons" (Morris) **55**:340
"The King of Harlem" (García Lorca) **3**:139
"The King of Owls" (Erdrich) **52**:192
"King of Swords" (Goodison)
See "Ceremony for the Banishment of the King of Swords"
"The King of the Ditchbacks" (Heaney) **18**:213
The King of the Great Clock Tower (Yeats) **20**:348
"King of the River" (Kunitz) **19**:157-59, 163, 168, 172-73, 175, 180
"The King of Yellow Butterflies" (Lindsay) **23**:281
"King Robert of Sicily" (Longfellow) **30**:25, 62
"King Solomon and the Ants" (Whittier) **93**:222
"King Solomon and the Queen of Sheba" (Lindsay) **23**:264, 280
"King Volmer and Elsie" (Whittier) **93**:167, 221, 249
"King Witlaf's Drinking-Horn" (Longfellow) **30**:27
"The Kingdom" (MacNeice) **61**:133, 141
"The Kingdom of Poetry" (Schwartz) **8**:289, 308-09
"The Kingfisher" (Clampitt) **19**:82, 84
"King-fisher" (Montale) **13**:139
The Kingfisher (Clampitt) **19**:82-3, 85-91, 93
"Kingfishers" (Hopkins)
See "As kingfishers catch fire"
"The Kingfishers" (Olson) **19**:286, 308

"The Kings" (Hope) **56**:266
"The Kings are Gone" (Bukowski) **18**:5
The King's Daughter (Bely) **11**:32
"Kings daughter of France, Patient Grissel" (Deloney) **79**:55
"The King's Missive" (Whittier) **93**:174, 177, 198, 247
The King's Missive, and Other Poems (Whittier) **93**:177
"King's Ransom" (Wylie) **23**:320
"Kings River Canyon" (Rexroth) **95**:290-91
"A King's Soliloquy" (Hardy) **92**:326
"The King's Task" (Kipling) **3**:183
"The King's Treasure-House" (Morris) **55**:306
"Kinsale" (Mahon) **60**:210
"Kinsey Keene" (Masters) **36**:218, 230, 232
"Kinship" (Heaney) **18**:195-96, 204, 210; **100**:214, 220-22, 291
"Kinship" (Wright) **14**:379
Kiosk (Enzensberger) **28**:166
"The Kirillovnas" (Akhmadulina)
See "Kirillovny"
"Kirillovny" (Akhmadulina) **43**:18
"The Kirk o' Scotland's Garland" (Burns) **114**:157
"The Kirk's Alarm" (Burns) **6**:78
"The Kiss" (Patmore) **59**:269, 271
"The Kiss" (Rossetti) **44**:203-4
"The Kiss" (Sassoon) **12**:262
"The Kiss" (Sexton) **2**:353
"The Kiss" (Tagore)
See "Chumban"
"The Kiss" (Teasdale) **31**:363, 379
"The kiss at Bayreuth" (Gunn) **26**:212
"Kissee Lee" (Walker) **20**:286
"Kisses" (Cassian) **17**:12-13
"Kisses from the Moon" (Berssenbrugge) **115**:47
"Kisses in the Train" (Lawrence) **54**:168
"The Kissing Place" (Szirtes) **51**:159
"Kissing Stieglitz Goodbye" (Stern) **115**:263
A Kist of Whistles: New Poems (MacDiarmid) **9**:182
"Kita no umi" (Ishikawa) **10**:213
"The Kitchen" (Carver) **54**:18
"Kitchener's School" (Kipling) **91**:66, 90
"Kitchenette Building" (Brooks) **7**:79
"The Kite" (Eberhart) **76**:16, 31-32
"The Kite" (Elytis) **21**:131
"The Kite" (Strand) **63**:154
"Kite Flying" (McKay) **2**:223
"A Kite is a Victim" (Cohen) **109**:17
"The Kites" (Patmore) **59**:204, 231
"The Kitten and the Falling Leaves" (Wordsworth) **67**:248
"Kitty Hawk" (Frost) **1**:213
"Kitty Stobling" (Kavanagh)
See "Come Dance with Kitty Stobling"
Kitty Stobling (Kavanagh)
See *Come Dance with Kitty Stobling, and Other Poems*
"Kiwis" (Birney) **52**:79
"KKK" (Guillén) **23**:121
"Klage" (Trakl) **20**:229, 236-37, 244, 250, 255-56, 258
"Klage II" (Trakl) **20**:250-51, 253
"Klagemauer Nacht" (Sachs) **78**:114
"Klarisu yunosha lyubil" (Lermontov) **18**:288
"Klasyk" (Herbert) **50**:5
"Kleenex" (Shapiro) **25**:324
"Kleine Aster" (Benn) **35**:30, 36, 53, 67, 68
"Eine Kleine Nachtmusik" (Jarrell) **41**:169
"Eine Kleine Snailmusik" (Sarton) **39**:345
"Kleiner herbst dämon" (Enzensberger) **28**:140
"Kleitos Illness" (Cavafy)
See "The Sickness of Kleitos"
"Knacker Rhymes" (Clarke) **112**:39, 57, 68-69
"Knee-Deep in June" (Riley) **48**:292, 334, 340
"Kneeling Down to Look into a Culvert" (Bly) **39**:100
"The Kneeling One" (Gallagher) **9**:57
"The Knife" (Douglas) **106**:199, 203
"Knife" (Simic) **69**:314
"The Knight" (Hughes) **7**:126; **89**:195-97
"The Knight" (Rich) **5**:370
"The Knight, Death, and the Devil" (Jarrell) **41**:139, 171, 178, 181, 189, 196, 208
"The Knight Fallen on Evil Days" (Wylie) **23**:326
"Knight of the Swan" (Guest) **55**:221
"Knight's" (Chaucer)
See "Knight's Tale"
"Knights of the White Camelia & Deacons of Defense" (Komunyakaa) **51**:32
"Knight's Tale" (Chaucer) **19**:13, 56, 60, 70, 75
"The Knight's to the Mountain" (Scott) **13**:305
"Knives" (Welch) **62**:340, 370
"A Knocker" (Herbert)
See "Kolatka"
"The Knocker" (Herbert)
See "Kolatka"
"Knockin' On Heaven's Door" (Dylan) **37**:59, 64
"Knocking Around" (Ashbery) **26**:133
"Knocking Donkey Fleas off a Poet from the Southside of Chi" (Madhubuti) **5**:323, 344
"Knot" (Hughes) **89**:234
"The Knot" (Kumin) **15**:202
"The Knot" (Kunitz) **19**:176
"Knotted Letter" (Gallagher) **9**:63
"Know Deeply, Know Thyself More Deeply" (Lawrence) **54**:185-87
"Know Thyself" (Johnson) **81**:236
"The Knowing Heart" (Roethke) **15**:293
"Knowing Rubén Darío" (Aleixandre) **15**:6
"Knowledge" (Bogan) **12**:101, 103, 120
Knowledge, Acquaintance, Resort, Favour with Grace (Skelton) **25**:344-45
"Knowledge of Himself, Latin Verses at Eton" (Gray) **80**:137
"Known World" (Heaney) **100**:240, 242
"Knox" (Parker) **28**:362
"Knoxville, Tennessee" (Giovanni) **19**:139-41
"Knucks" (Sandburg) **2**:308, 324; **41**:240
"Knut Hamsun in Old Age" (Mahon) **60**:148-49, 180
Ko; or, A Season on Earth (Koch) **80**:294-97, 300-301, 303, 305-6, 309, 312, 315, 319-20, 328, 333
"Kobiety Rubensa" (Szymborska) **44**:313
"Kodachromes of the Island" (Hayden) **6**:183, 193, 196, 198
"Kofejnyj certik" (Akhmadulina) **43**:17, 36, 39-40, 43
"Kôgao no shi" (Yosano) **11**:324-26, 328
"Kogda b v pokornosti neznan'ja" (Lermontov) **18**:302
Kogda razglyaetsya (Pasternak) **6**:266-69, 284-85
"Kogda v mrachneyshey iz stolits" (Akhmatova) **2**:12
"The Koh-i-Noor" (Patmore) **59**:232, 259
"Koi wo koi suru hito" (Hagiwara) **18**:168, 180
"Koide shidō" (Hagiwara) **18**:183
Koigoromo (Yosano) **11**:306-07
"Kokain" (Benn) **35**:49, 50
"Koker" (Brathwaite) **56**:61
Kokin Wakashu (Tsurayuki)
See *Kokinshu*
Kokinshu (Tsurayuki) **73**:240-370
Kokinshu "1" (Tsurayuki) **73**:294-95
Kokinshu "2" (Tsurayuki) **73**:281, 313
Kokinshu "6" (Tsurayuki) **73**:287
Kokinshu "9" (Tsurayuki) **73**:313-14, 317
Kokinshu "11" (Tsurayuki) **73**:300, 357
Kokinshu "14" (Tsurayuki) **73**:291
Kokinshu "25" (Tsurayuki) **73**:314
Kokinshu "27" (Tsurayuki) **73**:245
Kokinshu "30" (Tsurayuki) **73**:319
Kokinshu "31" (Tsurayuki) **73**:298-300, 320
Kokinshu "39" (Tsurayuki) **73**:314
Kokinshu "41" (Tsurayuki) **73**:309
Kokinshu "42" (Tsurayuki) **73**:283
Kokinshu "43" (Tsurayuki) **73**:298-99
Kokinshu "44" (Tsurayuki) **73**:298-99
Kokinshu "55" (Tsurayuki) **73**:287
Kokinshu "56" (Tsurayuki) **73**:288-89, 317
Kokinshu "57" (Tsurayuki) **73**:303
Kokinshu "59" (Tsurayuki) **73**:317, 319
Kokinshu "60" (Tsurayuki) **73**:306
Kokinshu "61" (Tsurayuki) **73**:298-99
Kokinshu "68" (Tsurayuki) **73**:300
Kokinshu "76" (Tsurayuki) **73**:286-87
Kokinshu "84" (Tsurayuki) **73**:256, 307
Kokinshu "86" (Tsurayuki) **73**:309
Kokinshu "88" (Tsurayuki) **73**:285
Kokinshu "89" (Tsurayuki) **73**:317
Kokinshu "91" (Tsurayuki) **73**:286
Kokinshu "95" (Tsurayuki) **73**:287
Kokinshu "96" (Tsurayuki) **73**:287
Kokinshu "102" (Tsurayuki) **73**:289, 319
Kokinshu "103" (Tsurayuki) **73**:295
Kokinshu "109" (Tsurayuki) **73**:288
Kokinshu "113" (Tsurayuki) **73**:253, 283
Kokinshu "115" (Tsurayuki) **73**:312, 314, 316-17, 355
Kokinshu "116" (Tsurayuki) **73**:355
Kokinshu "117" (Tsurayuki) **73**:257, 355
Kokinshu "118" (Tsurayuki) **73**:355
Kokinshu "119" (Tsurayuki) **73**:286
Kokinshu "127" (Tsurayuki) **73**:309
Kokinshu "129" (Tsurayuki) **73**:297
Kokinshu "130" (Tsurayuki) **73**:295
Kokinshu "132" (Tsurayuki) **73**:307-8
Kokinshu "139" (Tsurayuki) **73**:259, 283
Kokinshu "142" (Tsurayuki) **73**:306-7
Kokinshu "153" (Tsurayuki) **73**:306-7
Kokinshu "154" (Tsurayuki) **73**:306
Kokinshu "155" (Tsurayuki) **73**:291, 318
Kokinshu "157" (Tsurayuki) **73**:300, 318
Kokinshu "159" (Tsurayuki) **73**:283
Kokinshu "160" (Tsurayuki) **73**:257
Kokinshu "162" (Tsurayuki) **73**:314
Kokinshu "164" (Tsurayuki) **73**:308
Kokinshu "165" (Tsurayuki) **73**:245
Kokinshu "167" (Tsurayuki) **73**:307-9
Kokinshu "168" (Tsurayuki) **73**:309
Kokinshu "169" (Tsurayuki) **73**:294
Kokinshu "180" (Tsurayuki) **73**:309-10
Kokinshu "190" (Tsurayuki) **73**:309-10
Kokinshu "193" (Tsurayuki) **73**:274, 291
Kokinshu "194" (Tsurayuki) **73**:300
Kokinshu "195" (Tsurayuki) **73**:295
Kokinshu "197" (Tsurayuki) **73**:292
Kokinshu "206" (Tsurayuki) **73**:296
Kokinshu "207" (Tsurayuki) **73**:304, 307, 318
Kokinshu "214" (Tsurayuki) **73**:303
Kokinshu "218" (Tsurayuki) **73**:292, 318
Kokinshu "219" (Tsurayuki) **73**:307-8
Kokinshu "225" (Tsurayuki) **73**:284
Kokinshu "226" (Tsurayuki) **73**:245, 286
Kokinshu "228" (Tsurayuki) **73**:292
Kokinshu "232" (Tsurayuki) **73**:316-17
Kokinshu "235" (Tsurayuki) **73**:303
Kokinshu "236" (Tsurayuki) **73**:301
Kokinshu "239" (Tsurayuki) **73**:292
Kokinshu "240" (Tsurayuki) **73**:283
Kokinshu "241" (Tsurayuki) **73**:287
Kokinshu "244" (Tsurayuki) **73**:287
Kokinshu "249" (Tsurayuki) **73**:246
Kokinshu "250" (Tsurayuki) **73**:285
Kokinshu "257" (Tsurayuki) **73**:292-93
Kokinshu "258" (Tsurayuki) **73**:301
Kokinshu "260" (Tsurayuki) **73**:314
Kokinshu "261" (Tsurayuki) **73**:294-95
Kokinshu "265" (Tsurayuki) **73**:307
Kokinshu "269" (Tsurayuki) **73**:293
Kokinshu "270" (Tsurayuki) **73**:304
Kokinshu "271" (Tsurayuki) **73**:291
Kokinshu "275" (Tsurayuki) **73**:304
Kokinshu "277" (Tsurayuki) **73**:311-12
Kokinshu "283" (Tsurayuki) **73**:245
Kokinshu "284" (Tsurayuki) **73**:289
Kokinshu "293" (Tsurayuki) **73**:288
Kokinshu "295" (Tsurayuki) **73**:292-93
Kokinshu "296" (Tsurayuki) **73**:301

Kokinshu "297" (Tsurayuki) **73**:316-17
Kokinshu "300" (Tsurayuki) **73**:297
Kokinshu "301" (Tsurayuki) **73**:289
Kokinshu "305" (Tsurayuki) **73**:308
Kokinshu "310" (Tsurayuki) **73**:289
Kokinshu "312" (Tsurayuki) **73**:312, 314, 317
Kokinshu "313" (Tsurayuki) **73**:309
Kokinshu "326" (Tsurayuki) **73**:290, 318
Kokinshu "327" (Tsurayuki) **73**:301, 303
Kokinshu "329" (Tsurayuki) **73**:309
Kokinshu "330" (Tsurayuki) **73**:297
Kokinshu "331" (Tsurayuki) **73**:315, 317
Kokinshu "334" (Tsurayuki) **73**:245
Kokinshu "336" (Tsurayuki) **73**:315-17
Kokinshu "338" (Tsurayuki) **73**:309, 311
Kokinshu "339" (Tsurayuki) **73**:295, 318
Kokinshu "357" (Tsurayuki) **73**:245
Kokinshu "360" (Tsurayuki) **73**:309-11, 317
Kokinshu "399" (Tsurayuki) **73**:308, 310-11
Kokinshu "404" (Tsurayuki) **73**:313-14
Kokinshu "409" (Tsurayuki) **73**:245, 260
Kokinshu "415" (Tsurayuki) **73**:314-15
Kokinshu "416" (Tsurayuki) **73**:310
Kokinshu "420" (Tsurayuki) **73**:289
Kokinshu "421" (Tsurayuki) **73**:289, 319
Kokinshu "422" (Tsurayuki) **73**:293
Kokinshu "423" (Tsurayuki) **73**:293
Kokinshu "437" (Tsurayuki) **73**:304
Kokinshu "453" (Tsurayuki) **73**:284
Kokinshu "459" (Tsurayuki) **73**:298-99
Kokinshu "460" (Tsurayuki) **73**:312, 317
Kokinshu "462" (Tsurayuki) **73**:302, 305, 334
Kokinshu "470" (Tsurayuki) **73**:288, 317
Kokinshu "471" (Tsurayuki) **73**:313, 315
Kokinshu "473" (Tsurayuki) **73**:295
Kokinshu "474" (Tsurayuki) **73**:295-96
Kokinshu "478" (Tsurayuki) **73**:302, 305
Kokinshu "479" (Tsurayuki) **73**:313, 315-16
Kokinshu "480" (Tsurayuki) **73**:294
Kokinshu "481" (Tsurayuki) **73**:311
Kokinshu "482" (Tsurayuki) **73**:314
Kokinshu "552" (Tsurayuki) **73**:246, 282
Kokinshu "558" (Tsurayuki) **73**:294
Kokinshu "559" (Tsurayuki) **73**:293-94
Kokinshu "564" (Tsurayuki) **73**:304, 307
Kokinshu "565" (Tsurayuki) **73**:305
Kokinshu "566" (Tsurayuki) **73**:302
Kokinshu "567" (Tsurayuki) **73**:290
Kokinshu "568" (Tsurayuki) **73**:290
Kokinshu "569" (Tsurayuki) **73**:290
Kokinshu "572" (Tsurayuki) **73**:315, 317, 355
Kokinshu "573" (Tsurayuki) **73**:315, 317, 355
Kokinshu "574" (Tsurayuki) **73**:355
Kokinshu "577" (Tsurayuki) **73**:292
Kokinshu "578" (Tsurayuki) **73**:294
Kokinshu "579" (Tsurayuki) **73**:315, 317
Kokinshu "581" (Tsurayuki) **73**:296
Kokinshu "582" (Tsurayuki) **73**:354, 358-61, 365
Kokinshu "583" (Tsurayuki) **73**:359-61, 365
Kokinshu "584" (Tsurayuki) **73**:311, 354, 356, 359-61, 365
Kokinshu "585" (Tsurayuki) **73**:318, 359-60, 365
Kokinshu "586" (Tsurayuki) **73**:303, 359-61, 365
Kokinshu "587" (Tsurayuki) **73**:355, 359, 361, 364-65
Kokinshu "588" (Tsurayuki) **73**:355, 359, 361, 363, 366
Kokinshu "589" (Tsurayuki) **73**:316, 355, 358-59, 361, 366
Kokinshu "590" (Tsurayuki) **73**:361, 366
Kokinshu "591" (Tsurayuki) **73**:361, 366
Kokinshu "592" (Tsurayuki) **73**:302, 305, 366
Kokinshu "593" (Tsurayuki) **73**:303, 305, 355, 359, 366
Kokinshu "594" (Tsurayuki) **73**:305, 354-55, 359, 366
Kokinshu "595" (Tsurayuki) **73**:355, 359, 366
Kokinshu "596" (Tsurayuki) **73**:304, 355, 359, 367
Kokinshu "597" (Tsurayuki) **73**:315, 355, 359, 367
Kokinshu "598" (Tsurayuki) **73**:355, 359, 367
Kokinshu "599" (Tsurayuki) **73**:316, 354-55, 359, 361, 367
Kokinshu "600" (Tsurayuki) **73**:311
Kokinshu "601" (Tsurayuki) **73**:302
Kokinshu "602" (Tsurayuki) **73**:300
Kokinshu "604" (Tsurayuki) **73**:355
Kokinshu "605" (Tsurayuki) **73**:313-15, 355
Kokinshu "606" (Tsurayuki) **73**:355
Kokinshu "607" (Tsurayuki) **73**:305
Kokinshu "609" (Tsurayuki) **73**:301
Kokinshu "613" (Tsurayuki) **73**:296
Kokinshu "615" (Tsurayuki) **73**:256
Kokinshu "616" (Tsurayuki) **73**:254
Kokinshu "617" (Tsurayuki) **73**:293-94
Kokinshu "625" (Tsurayuki) **73**:303
Kokinshu "626" (Tsurayuki) **73**:295-96
Kokinshu "628" (Tsurayuki) **73**:301-2
Kokinshu "633" (Tsurayuki) **73**:312
Kokinshu "639" (Tsurayuki) **73**:294
Kokinshu "643" (Tsurayuki) **73**:292
Kokinshu "644" (Tsurayuki) **73**:246
Kokinshu "645" (Tsurayuki) **73**:253, 282
Kokinshu "646" (Tsurayuki) **73**:253
Kokinshu "656" (Tsurayuki) **73**:253
Kokinshu "657" (Tsurayuki) **73**:283
Kokinshu "658" (Tsurayuki) **73**:253, 283
Kokinshu "661" (Tsurayuki) **73**:305, 307
Kokinshu "665" (Tsurayuki) **73**:296-97
Kokinshu "667" (Tsurayuki) **73**:256
Kokinshu "668" (Tsurayuki) **73**:306
Kokinshu "679" (Tsurayuki) **73**:319
Kokinshu "681" (Tsurayuki) **73**:298
Kokinshu "684" (Tsurayuki) **73**:305
Kokinshu "685" (Tsurayuki) **73**:296
Kokinshu "686" (Tsurayuki) **73**:311
Kokinshu "691" (Tsurayuki) **73**:286
Kokinshu "708" (Tsurayuki) **73**:244
Kokinshu "715" (Tsurayuki) **73**:305, 307
Kokinshu "722" (Tsurayuki) **73**:288
Kokinshu "733" (Tsurayuki) **73**:298
Kokinshu "735" (Tsurayuki) **73**:247, 285
Kokinshu "741" (Tsurayuki) **73**:298
Kokinshu "745" (Tsurayuki) **73**:290
Kokinshu "747" (Tsurayuki) **73**:246, 254, 283
Kokinshu "751" (Tsurayuki) **73**:294
Kokinshu "756" (Tsurayuki) **73**:298
Kokinshu "770" (Tsurayuki) **73**:285
Kokinshu "771" (Tsurayuki) **73**:285
Kokinshu "787" (Tsurayuki) **73**:304
Kokinshu "791" (Tsurayuki) **73**:258
Kokinshu "797" (Tsurayuki) **73**:246, 252
Kokinshu "799" (Tsurayuki) **73**:286-87
Kokinshu "802" (Tsurayuki) **73**:287
Kokinshu "804" (Tsurayuki) **73**:314
Kokinshu "810" (Tsurayuki) **73**:298
Kokinshu "838" (Tsurayuki) **73**:256
Kokinshu "842" (Tsurayuki) **73**:312
Kokinshu "846" (Tsurayuki) **73**:246
Kokinshu "859" (Tsurayuki) **73**:291
Kokinshu "861" (Tsurayuki) **73**:254, 281
Kokinshu "874" (Tsurayuki) **73**:293
Kokinshu "879" (Tsurayuki) **73**:246
Kokinshu "899" (Tsurayuki) **73**:247
Kokinshu "920" (Tsurayuki) **73**:300
Kokinshu "921" (Tsurayuki) **73**:284
Kokinshu "926" (Tsurayuki) **73**:298-99, 318
Kokinshu "938" (Tsurayuki) **73**:247
Kokinshu "942" (Tsurayuki) **73**:281
Kokinshu "947" (Tsurayuki) **73**:287
Kokinshu "957" (Tsurayuki) **73**:308, 310-11, 320
Kokinshu "968" (Tsurayuki) **73**:299
Kokinshu "976" (Tsurayuki) **73**:310
Kokinshu "983" (Tsurayuki) **73**:246, 285
Kokinshu "991" (Tsurayuki) **73**:304
Kokinshu "998" (Tsurayuki) **73**:291
Kokinshu "1012" (Tsurayuki) **73**:288
Kokinshu "1013" (Tsurayuki) **73**:293
Kokinshu "1015" (Tsurayuki) **73**:310
Kokinshu "1021" (Tsurayuki) **73**:297
Kokinshu "1030" (Tsurayuki) **73**:252
Kokinshu "1031" (Tsurayuki) **73**:290
Kokinshu "1035" (Tsurayuki) **73**:310
Kokinshu "1036" (Tsurayuki) **73**:301, 305
Kokinshu "1051" (Tsurayuki) **73**:299
Kokinshu "1062" (Tsurayuki) **73**:296
Kokinshu "1064" (Tsurayuki) **73**:290
Kokinshu "1065" (Tsurayuki) **73**:292
Kokinshu "1067" (Tsurayuki) **73**:310-11
Kokinshu "1086" (Tsurayuki) **73**:285
Kokinshu "1110" (Tsurayuki) **73**:247
"Kolatka" (Herbert) **50**:8, 38
"Kolbel'naya treskovogo mysa" (Brodsky) See "A Cape Cod Lullaby"
"Koliaska, zabytaia u magazina" (Shvarts) **50**:153-54
"Komboloi" (Merrill) **28**:256
"Komedyjki" (Szymborska) **44**:308-9
Koncert na ostrově (Seifert) **47**:327-28, 335
"Koncert na vokzale" (Mandelstam) **14**:115, 129
Konec prekrasnoj èpox (Brodsky) See *Konets prekrasnoy epokhi*
Konets prekrasnoy epokhi (Brodsky) **9**:7
Koniec i poczatek (Szymborska) **44**:280, 286, 292, 298, 302-06, 308
"the konkreet pome is on its hed" (Bissett) **14**:32
"konkreet vizual" (Bissett) **14**:33-4
Konrad Wallenrod (Mickiewicz) **38**:149, 158, 166-67, 172-77, 184, 191, 194-95
"Kootenay Still Life" (Birney) **52**:27, 58
Köp den blindes sång (Ekeloef) **23**:76
Kora in Hell: Improvisations (Williams) **7**:344, 349, 374-75, 377, 379-81, 383-84, 394, 400, 405, 410; **109**:203, 231-32, 234, 236, 246-51, 253-57, 273-74, 277, 279, 321
"Kora wo omou uta" (Yakamochi) **48**:101, 131, 133-34, 139
"Kore" (Creeley) **73**:32
"Kore" (Merwin) **45**:52, 54-5, 87-8
"The Korean Emergency" (Kennedy) **93**:142
"Korean Mums" (Schuyler) **88**:204, 224
"A Korean Woman Seated by a Wall" (Meredith) **28**:177-78, 190
"Koroleva" (Akhmadulina) **43**:60
Körper des Sommers (Elytis) **21**:116
"Korsar" (Lermontov) **18**:299
"Kossuth" (Whittier) **93**:266
"Kostroma—Dionysus" (Shvarts) **50**:143
"Kot w pustym mieszkaniu" (Szymborska) **44**:283-94, 306, 308
"Koumfort" (Brathwaite) **56**:70, 97
"The Kraken" (Tennyson) **6**:360, 389, 391, 406-10; **101**:221, 246
"Kral Majales" (Ginsberg) **4**:82, 85
"Krasnopresnenskaya Station" (Momaday) **25**:202
"Krasnyi bychok" (Tsvetaeva) **14**:325
"Krebsbarack" (Benn) **35**:30, 35, 36
"Kreisler" (Sandburg) **41**:321
"Kremlin of Smoke" (Schnackenberg) **45**:335, 346
"Kretische Vase" (Benn) **35**:8, 46, 47
"Kreutzer Sonata" (Hughes) **89**:114, 208
"Krieg" (Stramm) **50**:175, 207, 219
"Der Krieg" (Werfel) **101**:330, 348
"Krieggrab" (Stramm) **50**:170, 188, 218, 223
"Kronos; To Coachman Kronos" (Goethe) See "An Schwager Kronos"
"Kropka" (Herbert) **50**:7
Krug (Shvarts) **50**:131
"Krysolov" (Tsvetaeva) **14**:325-26
Kshanikā (Tagore) **8**:411
Księgi narodu polskiego i pielgrzymastwa polskiego (Mickiewicz) **38**:169-70, 180, 186, 194-95
"Kubla Khan" (Coleridge) **11**:41-47, 51, 59, 73, 75-79, 84-88, 90, 104, 107, 110; **39**:118-227

"Kubla Khan: A Vision" (Coleridge)
See "Kubla Khan"
Kubla Khan, a Vision (Coleridge) **100**:6, 19-20, 22-23, 25-26, 54, 80, 124
Kubok metelej: Chetviortiia simfoniia (Bely) **11**:3, 6-7, 14-17, 22
"Kubota" (Hongo) **23**:197
"küchenzettel" (Enzensberger) **28**:135, 140
"Kuda mne det'sia v etom Ianvare?" (Mandelstam) **14**:154
"Kudzu" (Dickey) **40**:171-72, 259
Kumārasambhava (Kālidāsa) **22**:178, 180, 182, 185, 188, 191-93, 196-206
"Kung Canto" (Pound) **4**:325
"Kure no kane" (Ishikawa) **10**:214
"Kurkonzert" (Benn) **35**:46
"Kuroi fūkin" (Hagiwara) **18**:178, 182-83
"The Kursaal at Interlaken" (Rich) **5**:359
"Kutir-vasi" (Tagore) **8**:416
"Kutoa Umoja" (Baraka) **4**:26
"kwa mama zetu waliotuzaa" (Sanchez)
See "Kwa Mamu Zetu Waliotuzaa (for our mothers who gave us birth)"
"Kwa Mamu Zetu Waliotuzaa (for our mothers who gave us birth)" (Sanchez) **9**:215-16, 221, 227, 229, 243
"The Kykes" (Kîpling) **91**:172
"Kynd Kittok" (Dunbar) **67**:26, 101, 103-5
"Kyoko" (Ishikawa) **10**:213
Kyomō no seigi (Hagiwara) **18**:176, 182
"A Kyōto Garden" (Enright) **93**:5
Kypron, hou m'ethespisen . . . (Seferis) **66**:92
"La" (Tolson) **88**:331
Le La (Breton) **15**:54
"A la Ausencia" (Fuertes) **27**:44
"A la Coconut School" (Koch) **80**:327
"À la Colonne de la Place Vendôme" (Hugo) **17**:88-89
"À la désespérade" (Char) **56**:171
"A la flamme des fouets" (Éluard) **38**:71, 85
"A la luna" (Castro) **41**:81, 84
"À La Malade" (Waller) **72**:335, 361
"A la muerte" (Fuertes) **27**:39, 45
"À la musique" (Rimbaud) **3**:258, 276, 283; **57**:191, 194, 202, 205-6, 210, 241, 245, 289, 294
A la orilla del mundo (Paz) **48**:184, 244
"La: Pen" (Carew)
See "An Elegie on the La: Pen: sent to my Mistresse out of France"
"A la Petra Camara" (Gautier) **18**:125
"A la recherche de l'innocense" (Éluard) **38**:91
"A la recíproca'" (Guillén) **35**:229
A la santé du serpent (Char) **56**:112, 132
"A la sombra te sientas de las desnudas rocas" (Castro) **41**:115
"L.A. to Wichita" (Ginsberg) **4**:54
"A la Virgen de la colina" (Mistral) **32**:174
Laberinto (Jiménez) **7**:200-01, 211
"Labor and Management" (Baraka) **4**:13
Laboratories of the Spirit (Thomas) **99**:259, 261-63, 266-67, 274, 276, 282, 286, 290, 315, 318-19, 339, 348, 355-58
"The Laboratory" (Browning) **2**:60; **61**:88
"Laboratory Poem" (Merrill) **28**:241, 243
"The Laboring Skeleton" (Baudelaire)
See "Le squelette laboureur"
"The Labors of Hercules" (Moore) **49**:93
"A Labourer" (Thomas) **99**:241
"The Labourer" (Thomas) **99**:268-69
"The Labyrinth" (Muir) **49**:195, 200, 223-4, 228-9, 233-4, 256, 265, 272, 284, 289
Labyrinth (Jiménez)
See *Laberinto*
The Labyrinth (Muir) **49**:198, 213, 224-25, 229, 233, 235, 249, 256, 270, 273, 276-78, 282, 284, 289
"The Labyrinth of Life" (Walker) **20**:294
Labyrinths, with Path of Thunder (Okigbo) **7**:231, 233-35, 241-43, 248-49, 251-52, 254-56
"Le lac" (Lamartine) **16**:265, 268, 271, 276-77, 283, 290, 298, 301-02
"Lace" (Boland) **58**:96-97
"Lachin Y Gair" (Byron) **16**:86
"Lachrymae Christi" (Crane) **3**:82, 96-7, 102; **99**:11, 16, 24, 36-37, 84-85
"Lack of Discipline" (Pavese)
See "Indisciplina"
"Lack of Faith" (Pushkin)
See "Bezverie"
"Lackawanna" (Kinnell) **26**:294
"Lackawanna" (Merwin) **45**:45
"The Lacking Sense" (Hardy) **92**:326
"Laconic" (Elytis) **21**:116
"Lacrime" (Pasolini) **17**:265
"The Lad Made King" (Clarke) **112**:84
"Ladder of St. Augustine" (Longfellow) **30**:27
Ladera este (Paz) **1**:354, 346, 361-63, 374, 376; **48**:191, 206-7, 211, 214, 264
"The Ladies" (Kipling) **3**:164, 166, 174
Ladies and Gentlemen (Belloc) **24**:27
"Ladies First" (Silverstein) **49**:311, 333
"Ladies Looking for Lice" (Kennedy) **93**:137, 148
"Ladies' Praise" (Patmore) **59**:219, 240
"The Ladle" (Prior) **102**:299, 313-15
"The Lads in Their Hundreds" (Housman) **2**:192; **43**:245
"The Lads of the Village" (Smith) **12**:330, 333
"Lady" (Carruth) **10**:74
"Lady" (Cunningham) **92**:169
"The Lady A. L., My Asylum in a Great Extremity" (Lovelace) **69**:159, 213, 215, 217-19, 229
"Lady Acheson Weary of the Dean" (Swift) **9**:295-96
"The Lady and the Unicorn" (Sarton) **39**:322, 333, 364-65
"Lady Bank Dick" (Wakoski) **15**:363
"Lady Barbara; or, the Ghost" (Crabbe) **97**:115;
"Lady Bates" (Jarrell) **41**:139, 154, 171, 177, 191
"Lady Constance" (Dobell) **100**:139
"Lady Geraldine's Courtship" (Barrett Browning) **6**:10, 17-18, 26, 38-9, 42
"Lady Hsi" (Wang Wei) **18**:388-89
"The Lady in Kicking Horse Reservoir" (Hugo) **68**:266, 274, 293, 311
The Lady in Kicking Horse Reservoir (Hugo) **68**:248, 250-54, 259, 261, 271, 281, 284, 288
"Lady in the Leopard Coat" (Niedecker) **42**:122
"The Lady in the Pink Mustang" (Erdrich) **52**:172, 175
"The Lady in the Shingle" (Glück) **16**:139
"Lady, Lady" (Spencer) **77**:346
"Lady Lazarus" (Cunningham) **92**:157
"Lady Lazarus" (Plath) **1**:382, 386, 391, 395-97, 400-01, 406-07, 410, 413-14; **37**:196-98, 232-34, 241, 243, 257, 260-61, 268
"Lady Lost" (Ransom) **61**:274, 307, 322
"Lady Luncheon Club" (Angelou) **32**:3
"Lady of Cowrie Palace" (Li Ho) **13**:51-4
Lady of Miracles (Cassian) **17**:13
"A Lady of Quality" (Kinsella) **69**:119, 137
"The Lady of Shalott" (Swinburne) **24**:357
"The Lady of Shalott" (Tennyson) **6**:350, 358-59, 378, 380, 395, 409-10; **101**:128, 138, 140, 142, 187, 189, 224, 226
"The Lady of the Highest Prime" (Li Po) **29**:164
The Lady of the Lake (Scott) **13**:257-58, 261, 267-68, 270-71, 273, 276-79, 281, 283, 285, 289, 291, 293, 304, 310-11, 319-20
"The Lady of the Lambs" (Meynell) **112**:159, 164
"The Lady of the Land" (Morris) **55**:249, 268, 310
"The Lady of the Pool" (Jones) **116**:174, 180, 216
"The Lady of the Well-Spring" (Smith) **12**:304, 306, 329, 341
"The Lady Poverty" (Meynell) **112**:154, 159, 231
"Lady reservd by the heav'ns to do pastors company honnor" (Sidney) **32**:235, 247
"A Lady Thinks She Is Thirty" (Nash) **21**:274
"Lady Wentworth" (Longfellow) **30**:62
"The Lady Who Drove Me to the Airport" (Wakoski) **15**:369
"The Lady Who Offers Her Looking-Glass to Venus" (Prior) **102**:306
"Lady Wife" (Lawrence) **54**:182
"Lady with a Falcon" (Sarton) **39**:325
"A Lady with a Falcon on her fist" (Lovelace) **69**:252
"Ladyis Solistaris" (Dunbar)
See "Of the Ladyis Solistaris at Court"
"Lady's Boogie" (Hughes) **1**:266
"The Lady's Dream" (Hood) **93**:87, 102
"The Lady's Dressing Room" (Swift) **9**:257, 262, 268, 270, 273, 279, 281, 286-89, 291-92, 295, 298-99, 302-03
"A Ladys Lament for her Lover Overseas" (Surrey) **59**:286
"The Lady's Tower" (Ní Chuilleanáin) **34**:349
"Laes Gertrude Hoffman Girls" (Éluard) **38**:71
"Laeti et Errabundi" (Verlaine) **2**:417
"Lafayette" (Whittier) **93**:193
"À l'Afrique" (Césaire) **25**:5, 30, 32
"The Lag" (Rich) **5**:363
Lagar (Mistral) **32**:164-66, 170, 176, 179, 182, 185, 187-91
"Il lago di Annecy" (Montale) **13**:138
"Una lágrima" (Storni) **33**:240, 262-63
"Lai des Deuz Amanz" (Marie de France)
See "Les Dous Amanz"
"Laid in my quyett bedd" (Surrey) **59**:314-15
"Lair" (Pinsky) **27**:153
"Lais" (H. D.) 5:268
Lais (Marie de France) **22**:246, 254-55, 260-62, 264-65, 268-75, 278, 281, 283-84, 287-88, 300 -303
Les Lais (Villon) **13**:374-75, 377, 387, 396-99, 402, 404-05, 408-10, 412-13
"The Lake" (Lamartine)
See "Le lac"
"The Lake" (Merwin) **45**:45
"The Lake" (Wright) **14**:348, 379
"Lake Boats" (Masters) **1**:330, 333
"Lake Chelan" (Stafford) **71**:328
"Lake District" (Betjeman) **75**:20
"Lake Dwelling: Crannog" (Montague)
See "Crannog"
Lake Effect Country (Ammons) **16**:63
"The Lake Isle of Inisfree" (Kavanagh) **105**:163
"The Lake Isle of Innisfree" (Yeats) **20**:310
"Lake Mapourika" (Curnow) **48**:29
"The Lake of Gaube" (Swinburne) **24**:312-20, 322, 341, 348
"A Lake Scene" (Swenson) **14**:262
"Lake Superior" (Niedecker) **42**:94, 96-7, 102, 106
"Lake Yi" (Wang Wei) **18**:379
De l'Allemagne (Heine)
See *Deutschland: Ein Wintermärchen*
"Lamarck" (Mandelstam) **14**:129
"Lamarck Elaborated" (Wilbur) **51**:188, 237
"The Lamb" (Blake) **12**:7, 9, 32, 62; **63**:10-11, 14, 17, 53, 60, 68, 72, 75, 100, 113-14, 120, 123-24, 134
"Lambda" (Tolson) **88**:238-39, 273, 304, 311-13, 316, 324
"Lambert Hutchins" (Masters) **36**:230
"Lambkin: A Fable" (Hope) **56**:266
"The Lambs of Grasmere" (Rossetti) **7**:266
"The Lambs on the Boulder" (Wright) **36**:311
"The Lame Boy and the Fairy" (Lindsay) **23**:281
"The Lament" (Burns) **6**:53
"Lament" (Ginsberg) **47**:71
"Lament" (Hardy) **8**:135
"Lament" (Millay) **6**:211
"Lament" (Montague) **106**:241, 247

"Lament" (Plath) **1**:410
"Lament" (Sexton) **2**:350
"Lament" (Thomas) **52**:233, 276, 311, 313, 326-28
"Lament" (Trakl)
See "Klage"
Lament and Triumph (Barker) **77**:46
"Lament, beside an Acéquia, for the Wife of Awatsireh" (Winters) **82**:313-14
"Lament for Damon" (Milton) **19**:212
"Lament For Glasgerion" (Wylie) **23**:310
Lament for Ignacio Sánchez Mejías (García Lorca)
See *Llanto por Ignacio Sánchez Mejías*
"Lament for My Brother on a Hayrake" (Wright) **36**:335-36, 373
"Lament for Pasiphae" (Graves) **6**:144
Lament for the Death of a Bullfighter (García Lorca)
See *Llanto por Ignacio Sánchez Mejías*
Lament for the Death of a Bullfighter, and Other Poems (García Lorca)
See *Llanto por Ignacio Sánchez Mejías*
"Lament for the Makaris" (Dunbar) **67**:77, 122-23
"Lament for the Makers" (Pinsky) **27**:164
Lament for the Makers (Spicer) **78**:239, 241, 250, 275-76, 279, 294
"A Lament for the Martyrs" (Wright) **36**:310
"Lament for the Poles of Buffalo" (Hass) **16**:195, 197
"Lament for Weldon Kees" (Stryk) **27**:204
"Lament for Yin Yao" (Wang Wei) **18**:379
"The Lament of a Husband after the Death of His Wife" (Dobell) **100**:165
"Lament of a lovesick lizard" (Char)
See "Complainte du lézard amoureux"
"The Lament of a New England Mother" (Eberhart) **76**:44
"The Lament of Fortinbras" (Herbert)
See "Tren Fortynbrasa"
"Lament of Mary Queen of Scots" (Burns) **6**:78
The Lament of Tasso (Byron) **16**:76; **95**:35, 38
"Lament of the Belle Heaulmiere" (Villon)
See "Les Regrets de la belle Heaulmière"
"Lament of the Drums" (Okigbo) **7**:224, 229-30, 244, 247, 254
"Lament of the Lavender Mist" (Okigbo) **7**:229, 248
"The Lament of the Masks: For W. B. Yeats: 1865-1939" (Okigbo) **7**:230, 245
"Lament of the Silent Sisters" (Okigbo)
See "Silences: Lament of the Silent Sisters"
"Lament over Love" (Hughes) **53**:124
"The lamentable death of King John; Of Edward the second, being poysoned" (Deloney) **79**:57
"Lamentatio Davidis super Saulum & Jonathanem" (Prior) **102**:307
"Lamentation" (Hölderlin)
See "Menons Klagen um Diotima"
"Lamentation of Beccles" (Deloney) **79**:55, 57
"Lamentation of Mr. Pages Wife" (Deloney)
See "Lamentation of Pages Wife of Plymouth, the Death and Execution of Fourteen most wicked Traitors"
"Lamentation of Pages Wife of Plymouth, the Death and Execution of Fourteen most wicked Traitors" (Deloney) **79**:55, 57
"Lamentation of Shores Wife" (Deloney) **79**:57
"Lamentationen" (Heine) **25**:131
"Lamentations" (Glück) **16**:151, 154
"Lamentations" (Sassoon) **12**:267, 286
Lamentations (Glück) **16**:129
Lamentations (Jeremiah) **44**:109-61
"The Lamentations of Jeremy, for the most part according to Tremelius" (Donne) **1**:139
"Lamentations of the Peruvians" (Tennyson) **101**:193
"Lamenting the Terms of Modern Praise" (Jackson) **44**:38-9, 55
"Laments" (Berrigan) **103**:34
"Laments for a Dead Companion" (Jaccottet) **98**:198-99
"Lamia" (Hood) **93**:65, 79
Lamia (Keats) **96**:196, 212-13, 215, 217, 236, 242, 272, 299-300, 340, 348, 355
Lamia, Isabella, The Eve of St. Agnes, and Other Poems (Keats) **1**:276, 279, 281, 296, 307-09, 311; **96**:298, 301, 303
"Lamia's Song" (Melville) **82**:76, 148
"Lamium" (Glück) **16**:132, 171
"A Lammas Tiding" (Duncan) **75**:133, 203
"The Lamp" (Teasdale) **31**:335
"The Lamp and the Jar" (Hope) **56**:268, 301
"La lámpara en la tierra" (Neruda) **64**:344, 350
"La lampe du temple" (Lamartine) **16**:292
"La Lampe sur la Table" (Scève) **111**:7
"Lampfall" (Walcott) **46**:272
"The Lamplighter" (Stevenson) **84**:315
The Lamplit Answer (Schnackenberg) **45**:329-31, 335, 339, 342-43, 345-46
"The Lamp's Shrine" (Rossetti) **44**:204
"Lana Turner has Collapsed!" (O'Hara) **45**:145, 162, 243
"Lancelot" (Swinburne) **24**:355
Lancelot (Robinson) **1**:465, 468-70, 489, 491; **35**:362
"Lancelot and Elaine" (Tennyson) **101**:128, 189-90, 195, 205, 240, 244
"Lancer" (Housman) **2**:162
"Land" (Heaney) **18**:201; **100**:233
"The Land" (Kipling) **3**:171
"Land" (Ungaretti)
See "Terra"
"The Land Behind the Wind" (Wagoner) **33**:359
"The Land Below" (Dorn) **115**:51, 54, 56, 74, 92, 121-22, 126, 128, 134, 138, 212, 219
"The Land Betrayed" (Neruda)
See "La arena traicionada"
"Land East of the Sun and West of the Moon" (Morris) **55**:250, 285, 292, 308
"The Land Is You" (Barker) **77**:7
"The Land of Beyond" (Service) **70**:153
"The Land of Dreams" (Blake) **12**:35
"The land of four o'clocks is here" (Niedecker) **42**:140
"The Land of Happy" (Silverstein) **49**:347
"Land of Israel" (Sachs) **78**:219
"The Land of Silence" (Sarton) **39**:323, 332
The Land of Silence and Other Poems (Sarton) **39**:321, 331, 337, 341-42, 347
"The Land of Story-Books" (Stevenson) **84**:314, 317, 328, 344
"The Land of the Counterpane" (Stevenson) **84**:316, 344
Land of the Free—U.S.A. (MacLeish) **47**:148-49, 152, 191, 243, 257
"The Land of Two Mists" (Clarke) **112**:85
Land of Unlikeness (Graham)
See *Region of Unlikeness*
Land of Unlikeness (Lowell) **3**:199, 202, 213, 216-17, 232
"The Land Where All Is Gained" (Tagore)
See "Sab-peyechhir desh"
Land Workers (Masefield) **78**:89, 97
"Landcrab II" (Atwood) **8**:43
Landesprcahe (Enzensberger) **28**:133-35, 141, 143, 165
"Landfall" (Wagoner) **33**:356-57
Landfall (Wagoner) **33**:354, 356, 359, 361-62
"Landfall in Unknown Seas" (Curnow) **48**:4, 11, 23
"The Landing" (Tomlinson) **17**:353
"Landing on the Moon" (Swenson) **14**:257
"Landlady, Count the Lawin" (Burns) **6**:81
"The Landlord's Wife" (Chin) **40**:3
"The Landmark" (Rossetti) **44**:173
Landor's Poetry (Pinsky) **27**:153
"Land's End" (MacLeish) **47**:126, 130, 143, 196
"Landscape" (Baudelaire)
See "Paysage"
"The Landscape" (Masters) **1**:333, 344
"Landscape" (Merton) **10**:349
"Landscape" (Oliver) **75**:290-91
"Landscape" (Parker) **28**:362
"Landscape" (Parra)
See "Paisaje"
"Landscape" (Sarton) **39**:320
"Landscape after a Battle" (Neruda)
See "Paisaje después de una batalla"
"Landscape as a Nude" (MacLeish) **47**:189, 254
"Landscape for the Disappeared" (Komunyakaa) **51**:34
"Landscape I" (Pavese)
See "Paesaggio I"
"Landscape in Spring" (Soto) **28**:382
"The Landscape Near an Aerodrome" (Spender) **71**:134, 147, 180, 218, 220
"Landscape of a Dead Love" (Storni)
See "Paisaje del amor muerto"
"A Landscape of Cries" (Sachs)
See "Landschaft aus Schreien"
"Landscape of Cries" (Sachs)
See "Landschaft aus Schreien"
"Landscape of Patagonia" (Mistral)
See "Paisajes de la Patagonia"
"Landscape of Screams" (Sachs)
See "Landschaft aus Schreien"
"Landscape of the Heart" (Jiménez)
See "Paisaje del corozon"
"Landscape of the Star" (Rich) **5**:362
"Landscape of the Urinating Multitudes (Battery Place Nocturne)" (García Lorca)
See "Paisaje de la multitud que orina"
"Landscape of the Vomiting Multitudes (Coney Island Dusk)" (García Lorca)
See "Paisaje de la multitud que vomita"
"Landscape VI" (Pavese)
See "Paesaggio VI"
"Landscape VII" (Pavese)
See "Paesaggio VII"
Landscape West of Eden (Aiken) **26**:24, 29-30
"Landscape Winter" (Sexton) **79**:241
"Landscape with Boat" (Stevens) **110**:114-17, 151
"Landscape with Figures" (Ammons) **16**:6
"Landscape with Figures" (Douglas) **106**:186
"Landscape with Little Figures" (Justice) **64**:259
"Landscape with Serifs" (Page) **12**:183
"Landscapes" (Eliot) **5**:166, 183
"Landscapes" (Wright) **14**:339, 342-43
Landscapes of Living and Dying (Ferlinghetti) **1**:180-81, 187
"Landscapes of My Name" (Ciardi) **69**:11
"Landschaft aus Schreien" (Sachs) **78**:117, 133-34, 137, 140-41, 143, 161
"The Lane" (Thomas) **53**:348
"The Lane of the Sky-Blue Waters" (Meredith) **28**:196
"The Lang Coortin" (Carroll) **18**:46
"Le langage des saints" (Péret) **33**:230
"Langaig" (Hugo) **68**:292
Langour (Storni)
See *Languidez*
"Langston Blues" (Randall) **86**:290, 338, 343
"The Language" (Creeley) **73**:12, 52-53, 89, 102
"Language" (Ortiz) **17**:231
Language (Spicer) **78**:244, 281, 286, 288-89, 292, 311-12, 326-29, 332, 335, 338, 341, 343, 354, 362-63
"Language as an Escape from the Discrete" (Jacobsen) **62**:301
Language Lattice (Celan)
See *Sprachgitter*
"The Language of Love and Tea with Roasted Almonds" (Amichai) **38**:47
"A Language of New York" (Oppen) **35**:312, 322, 340, 343
"The Language of Shadows" (Koch) **80**:290-92
"The Language of the Brag" (Olds) **22**:328

language of the land (Enzensberger)
See *Landesprcahe*
"The Language of the Present Moment" (Wright) **36**:311
"Language-Mesh" (Celan)
See "Sprachgitter"
"Langue" (Brossard) **80**:25
"Languedoc Variorum: A Defense of Heresy and Heretics" (Dorn) **115**:215, 223, 231-35
Languidez (Storni) **33**:236-37, 241, 244, 247-48, 252-53, 277-79, 282-83, 297-98, 307
"The Lantern" (Merwin) **45**:35
"The Lantern Out of Doors" (Hopkins) **15**:145, 156
"A Lantern Song" (Crane) **80**:40
"Lanval" (Marie de France) **22**:241-45, 250-51, 254-55, 258, 260, 267-69, 271-72, 275, 282, 294, 29 7, 300-303
"The Lanyard" (Collins) **68**:226
"Laocoön Dream Recorded in Diary Dated 1943" (Swenson) **14**:288
"Laodamia" (Wordsworth) **4**:394, 399, 406-07
Laon and Cythna (Shelley)
See *Laon and Cythna; or, The Revolution of the Golden City: A Vision of the Nineteenth Century*
Laon and Cythna; or, The Revolution of the Golden City: A Vision of the Nineteenth Century (Shelley) **3**:267, 270, 292-96, 298, 300, 331-32, 334, 336, 338, 340-41, 355; **67**:136, 159, 161, 163-64, 167-79, 183, 190, 231
"Laostic" (Marie de France)
See "Laüstic"
"Lápida filial" (Mistral) **32**:161
"Lapis Lazuli" (Yeats) **20**:314, 333; **51**:112, 142
"A lápiz" (Guillén) **35**:211
"Un lápiz" (Storni) **33**:240, 262, 295
"Lapraik II" (Burns)
See "Second Epistle to John Lapraik"
"Lapse" (Dunbar) **5**:126
"Laquelle est la vraie?" (Baudelaire) **106**:77-78, 90
Lara (Byron) **16**:92, 109
"Larceny" (Berrigan) **103**:34
"La larga busca" (Borges) **22**:95
"Large Bad Picture" (Bishop) **3**:37, 70-1; **34**:192
"Large Jigsaw Puzzle" (Mueller) **33**:192
"A Large Number" (Szymborska)
See "Wielka liczba"
A Large Number (Szymborska)
See *Wielka liczba*
"Large Red Man Reading" (Stevens) **110**:100, 190, 192, 229
"The Large Starfish" (Bly) **39**:23
Large Testament (Villon)
See *Le Testament*
"The Largess" (Eberhart) **76**:12
"The Lark" (Merwin) **45**:95
"The Lark Ascending" (Meredith) **60**:252, 254, 296-97, 332-33
"The Lark now leaves his watry Nest" (Davenant) **99**:176
"Larks" (Bridges) **28**:85
"Larks" (Hughes) **89**:259, 262, 264
"The Lark's Nest: A Fable from Esop" (Smith) **104**:182
"Larme" (Rimbaud) **3**:271; **57**:177
Larmes de Racine (Sainte-Beuve) **110**:34
"Lasalle" (Davie) **29**:96
"Lassitude" (Verlaine) **32**:386-87
"The Last" (Kinsella) **69**:135
"Last" (Kipling) **3**:160
"Last Act" (Hughes) **89**:133
"Last Acts" (Olds) **22**:318, 323, 326, 337
Last and Lost Poems of Delmore Schwartz (Schwartz) **8**:311, 319
"The Last Banquet" (Benét) **64**:18
"The Last Battle" (Parra) **39**:310-11
"Last Before America" (MacNeice) **61**:110
"The Last Blossom" (Holmes) **71**:68
"The Last Bus" (Strand) **63**:158
"Last Canto of Childe Harold" (Lamartine)
See "Le dernier chant de pèlerinage de Childe Harold"
"The Last Chantey" (Kipling) **3**:161; **91**:86-87
"Last Child" (Kennedy) **93**:140, 143, 149
"The Last Chrysanthemum" (Hardy) **92**:261
"A Last Confession" (Rossetti) **44**:164, 166-67, 176, 202, 246, 261-63
"The Last Contention" (Meredith) **60**:254
"The Last Covenant" (Jackson) **44**:8, 69, 79
"Last Dance at the Four Penny" (Cohen) **109**:55-56
"The Last Dane" (Mahon) **60**:132
"The Last Day" (Olds) **22**:33-37
"The Last Day" (Seferis) **66**:99, 165-67
"The Last Day" (Stafford) **71**:292
"Last Day in Viet Nam" (Quintana) **36**:272
"Last Day There" (Hugo) **68**:253
"The Last Days of Alice" (Tate) **50**:230, 234-35, 242, 257, 280, 289, 301, 306
"Last Declamation" (Taylor) **63**:281
The Last Ditch (MacNeice) **61**:138, 141
"The Last Drunk" (Wright) **36**:308
"The Last Duchess" (Browning) **2**:30
The Last Epiphany (Aleixandre)
See *Nacimiento último*
Last Foray in Lithuania (Mickiewicz)
See *Pan Tadeusz; czyli, Ostatni zajazd na Litwie*
"The Last Gangster" (Corso) **33**:41
"Last Harmony" (Lawrence) **54**:235
The Last Harvest (Tagore)
See *Chaitāli*
"The Last Hiding Places of Snow" (Kinnell) **26**:259, 271-72
"Last Hill in a Vista" (Bogan) **12**:104
"The Last Instructions to a Painter" (Marvell) **10**:275
"The Last Invocation" (Whitman) **3**:378
"Last Kiss" (Olds) **22**:321
"The Last Laugh" (Betjeman) **75**:36
"The Last Laugh" (Owen) **19**:366
"The Last Laugh" (Warren) **37**:340
"The Last Leaf" (Holmes) **71**:68, 70, 88, 95, 114, 125-26
"Last Letter" (Glück) **16**:164-65
"Last Lines" (Brontë) **8**:59
"Last Load" (Hughes) **7**:166
"Last Looks at the Lilacs" (Stevens) **6**:292; **110**:95
The Last Lunar Baedeker (Loy) **16**:330, 333
"The Last Man" (Gunn) **26**:203
"The Last Man" (Hood) **93**:52-53, 72-73, 81, 117-19
"The Last Meeting" (Sassoon) **12**:262
"The Last Metaphor" (Warren) **37**:319, 331
"The Last Mowing" (Frost) **1**:206
"The Last Mummer" (Heaney) **18**:201; **100**:194, 232
"Last Night" (Hughes) **89**:135
"Last Night I Drove a Car" (Corso) **33**:6, 43; **108**:22
The Last Night of the Earth Poems (Bukowski) **18**:16, 19
"Last Night Train" (Book-Senninger) **37**:379
Last Octave (Tagore)
See *Shesh saptak*
"The Last of Autumn" (Blunden) **66**:5
"The Last of Saturdays" (Elytis) **21**:135
"The Last of the Fire Kings" (Mahon) **60**:135, 139, 152, 183-84, 193-94, 210-11, 214, 235
"The Last of the Flock" (Wordsworth) **4**:373, 415, 418; **67**:261-62, 277, 279, 282, 300, 312, 328, 339-40, 347-48, 368
"The Last of the Light Brigade" (Kipling) **91**:118
"The Last One" (Merwin) **45**:9, 21-2, 42, 45, 49, 64-66
"The Last Oracle" (Swinburne) **24**:320, 347
"The Last Pain" (Empson)
See "This Last Pain"
"The Last People" (Merwin) **45**:37-8
"Last Poem" (Berrigan) **103**:3, 6-8, 35-36, 40
"Last Poem" (Kennedy) **93**:147
"Last Poems" (Tagore)
See "Śesh lekhā"
Last Poems (Barrett Browning) **6**:23-4, 38, 40
Last Poems (Berryman) **64**:81
Last Poems (Celan) **10**:120
Last Poems (Housman) **2**:161-67, 173-76, 180-81, 186, 191, 196, 199-201; **43**:210, 220-21, 223-27, 235-36, 243, 245-47, 249-51, 253-55, 258-61
Last Poems (Lawrence) **54**:171, 173, 195, 197-203, 214, 218, 226-27, 232, 249-50
Last Poems (Schuyler) **88**:190
"Last Poems: XX— The Night Is Freezing Fast" (Housman) **2**:196
Last Poems and Two Plays (Yeats) **20**:307, 311, 314, 332; **51**:152
The Last Poems of Alice Meynell (Meynell) **112**:162, 171, 174, 177, 181, 184, 193, 229, 233, 240, 291, 295, 299, 303
The Last Poems of Elinor Wylie (Wylie) **23**:321
"Last Prelude" (Teasdale) **31**:380
"The Last Quatrain of the Ballad of Emmett Till" (Brooks) **7**:62
"The Last Question" (Parker) **28**:362
"The Last Reader" (Holmes) **71**:114
The Last Remains (Suckling)
See *The Last Remains of Sir John Suckling*
The Last Remains of Sir John Suckling (Suckling) **30**:125-26
"The Last Revolutionary" (Baraka) **113**:26
"The Last Rhyme of True Thomas" (Kipling) **3**:181-82; **91**:86
"The Last Ride of Wild Bill" (Brown) **55**:80, 113, 118, 120, 122
The Last Ride of Wild Bill and Eleven Narrative Poems (Brown) **55**:111, 114, 116-17, 121, 157
"The Last Ride Together" (Browning) **2**:75
"The Last River" (Kinnell) **26**:255, 257, 262, 290, 293
The Last Septet (Tagore)
See *Shesh saptak*
"The Last Sheaf" (Montague) **106**:227
"The Last Signal" (Hardy) **8**:131; **92**:203, 321
Last Song (Harjo) **27**:59, 64
"The Last Song of Lucifer" (Lindsay) **23**:284
Last Songs From Vagabondia (Carman) **34**:205, 218, 220-21
Last Songs of Vagabondia (Carman)
See *Last Songs From Vagabondia*
"Last Stop" (Cavafy) **36**:111
"The Last Stop" (Seferis) **66**:90, 99, 125, 179, 219
"The Last Supper" (Service) **70**:141
"Last Supper" (Wylie) **23**:303, 308, 310
"The Last Survivor" (Holmes) **71**:65, 68
"The Last Suttee" (Kipling) **3**:183
"The Last Thing I Say" (Bell) **79**:29
"The Last Time" (Hardy) **92**:328
"The Last Tournament" (Tennyson) **101**:199, 228-29, 231-32, 234-35
"Last Tree" (Mistral)
See "Ultimo árbol"
"The Last Turn of the Screw" (Smith) **12**:295
"The Last Verses Written by Chatterton" (Chatterton) **104**:30-32
"The Last Visit" (Winters) **82**:344
Last Volume (Swift) **9**:255
The Last Voyage (Noyes) **27**:133
"The Last Walk in Autumn" (Whittier) **93**:231, 239, 263
"Last Walk of Season" (Warren) **37**:367, 378
"The Last War" (Muir) **49**:257-58, 284, 300
"The Last Warmth of Arnold" (Corso) **33**:25, 39-40; **108**:34-35
"The Last Will" (Herbert) **50**:24

"The Last Will and Testament of Thomas Chatterton" (Chatterton) **104**:5, 28
"The Last Word" (Tagore)
See "Shesh katha"
"Last Words" (Olds) **22**:324
"Last Words" (Plath) **1**:396, 407
"Last Words of the Dying Recruit" (McKay) **2**:226
"Last Words of the Human Fly" (Wagoner) **33**:334
"Last Words to Miriam" (Lawrence) **54**:175
"Last Year the Piñons Were Plentiful" (Tapahonso) **65**:215
"Lastness" (Kinnell) **26**:252, 274-75
"Late" (Bogan) **12**:122
"Late" (de la Mare) **77**:116
"Late" (Olds) **22**:318
"Late a Night During a Visit of Friends" (Bly) **39**:7
"Late Abed" (MacLeish) **47**:197, 207
"Late Afternoon in Manzanilla" (Birney) **52**:22, 99
Late Arrival on Earth (Ekeloef) **23**:66, 85, 88-90
"A Late Aubade" (Wilbur) **51**:215
"Late August" (Atwood) **8**:28-9, 42
"Late August Letter" (Hacker) **47**:88
"Late Beethoven" (Zagajewski) **27**:384-85
"Late Cantos" (Pound) **95**:192, 196
"Late Echo" (Ashbery) **26**:140
Late Epigrams (Cunningham) **92**:175, 192
"Late Feast" (Zagajewski) **27**:395
"Late Fragment" (Carver) **54**:19, 24
"Late half moon" (Rexroth) **95**:282
The Late Hour (Strand) **63**:150, 157, 181-82
"Late Hours" (Mueller) **33**:193
"Late Last Night" (Hughes) **1**:243
"Late Leaves" (Justice) **64**:291
Late Lyrics and Earlier with Many Other Verses (Hardy) **8**:89, 123; **92**:217, 241, 245, 266, 295
"Late Moon" (Bly) **39**:87
"Late Movies With Skyler" (Ondaatje) **28**:338
"Late November in a Field" (Wright) **36**:345, 357
"Late Poem to My Father" (Olds) **22**:324
Late Settings (Merrill) **28**:266-68, 281
"The Late Snow & Lumber Strike of the Summer of Fifty-four" (Snyder) **21**:322
"Late Spring" (Hass) **16**:216, 222
"Late Spring Evening" (Bridges) **28**:85
"Late Subterfuge" (Warren) **37**:331
"Late Thinker" (Stafford) **71**:264
"Late-Comer" (Montague) **106**:257-58, 261
"Lately" (Baraka) **113**:15
"Lately, Alas, I Knew A Gentle Boy" (Thoreau) **30**:203, 216, 251, 270
"Lately, at Night" (Kumin) **15**:200
"Latencies" (Chappell) **105**:17
"Later" (Stafford) **71**:333
Later (Creeley) **73**:84, 87, 92
"A Later Alexandrian" (Meredith) **60**:252
Later Collected Verse (Service) **70**:140, 144, 148, 161
"Later Life" (Rossetti) **7**:278
Later Lyrics (Howe) **81**:63
Later Poems (Bridges) **28**:65
Later Poems (Carman) **34**:230
Later Poems (Clarke) **112**:31, 34, 47-48, 50, 58, 79-80
Later Poems (Meynell) **112**:159-60, 171, 184, 186, 190-93, 229, 299
Later Poems (Rexroth) **95**:290
Later Poems (Sachs)
See *Späte Gedichte*
Later Poems: A Selection (Thomas) **99**:270, 274, 299, 351, 360
Later Poems—Ancient Lights (Clarke)
See *Ancient Lights*
The Later Poems of John Clare 1837-1864 (Clare) **23**:46
The Latest Decalogue (Clough) **103**:54
"Latest Face" (Larkin) **21**:236
"The Latest Freed Man" (Stevens) **110**:201
"The Latest Hotel Guest Walks over Particles That Revolve in Seven Other Dimensions Controlling Latticed Space" (Stone) **53**:235-36
"Lathmon" (Macpherson) **97**:265
"Latin America" (Dalton) **36**:125
"latin and soul" (Cruz) **37**:11
"The Latin Lesson" (Boland) **58**:47
"Latin Night at the Pawnshop" (Espada) **74**:126, 128
"Latter-Day Warnings" (Holmes) **71**:66, 68
"The Latter-day Saint" (Tuckerman) **85**:340
"The Latter Rain" (Very) **86**:42, 165-66
"Lauda" (Milosz) **8**:201
"Lauda" (Paz) **1**:361
"Lauda Sion Salvatorem" (Crashaw) **84**:19, 93-95, 98
"Laudantes Decern Pulchritudinis Johannae Templi" (Pound) **95**:115-16
"Lauds" (Auden) **92**:43
"The Laugh" (Graves) **6**:156
Laughable Lyrics (Lear)
See *Laughable Lyrics: A Fourth Book of Nonsense Poems, Songs, Botany, Music, Etc.*
Laughable Lyrics: A Fourth Book of Nonsense Poems, Songs, Botany, Music, Etc. (Lear) **65**:141-43, 146-47, 149-51, 154, 156, 158-61, 169
"The Laughers" (Francis) **34**:244
"Laughers" (Hughes)
See "My People"
"Laughing Corn" (Sandburg) **2**:316; **41**:241, 286, 326
"Laughing Gas" (Ginsberg) **4**:74, 81; **47**:22
"The Laughing Hyena by Hokusai" (Enright) **93**:8, 32
Laughing Lost in the Mountains: Poems of Wang Wei (Wang Wei) **18**:391
"The Laughing Song" (Blake) **12**:4, 7, 23; **63**:6, 14, 68, 121
"Laughing with One Eye" (Schnackenberg) **45**:329
"Laughter in the Senate" (Lanier) **50**:107-8
"Launcelot and Elaine" (Masters)
See "The Ballad of Launcelot and Elaine"
"The Launch" (Meynell) **112**:161
"The Laundress" (Kinsella) **69**:95, 121
"Laundromat" (Niedecker) **42**:109
"Laura and Francisca" (Jackson) **44**:7, 11
"Laura Gray" (Wickham) **110**:271
"The Laureate" (Graves) **6**:142, 144
"Laus Deo" (Whittier) **93**:186, 213, 239, 304, 348
"Laus Veneris" (Swinburne) **24**:308, 360-61
Laus Veneris, and Other Poems and Ballads (Swinburne)
See *Poems and Ballads*
"Lausanne" (Mickiewicz) **38**:215
"Laüstic" (Marie de France) **22**:237, 258, 260, 264-66, 269-72, 301
"Lava" (Kinnell) **26**:260
"Lava" (Zagajewski) **27**:387
"Lava Cameo: A brooch carved on volcanic rock" (Boland) **58**:100
"Laval, Pomeret, Petain" (Niedecker) **42**:140
"The Lavender Woman-A Market Song" (Reese) **29**:329
"Laventille" (Walcott) **46**:284-85
"Lavorare stanca" (Pavese) **13**:203, 213, 225-27
Lavorare stanca (Pavese) **13**:201-02, 204-05, 210-14, 216-19, 222, 224-26, 228
"The Law" (Duncan) **75**:196-97
"Law" (Lowell) **3**:214
"The Law for George" (Brown) **55**:164
"The Law I Love Is Major Mover" (Duncan) **2**:124; **75**:147
"The Law of the Jungle" (Kipling) **91**:83
"The Law of the Yukon" (Service) **70**:114, 125, 155, 160
"Lawn Design" (Wagoner) **33**:365, 367
Lawn of the Excluded Middle (Waldrop) **109**:125, 137-38, 142-43, 153-58, 175, 179-82
"Lawn of the Excluded Middle" (Waldrop) **109**:155-56, 159
"A lawnmower's one of the babies I'd have" (Niedecker) **42**:151
"The Laws of God, the Laws of Man" (Housman) **2**:162, 179
"The Laws of Verse" (Meynell) **112**:154, 173, 236, 240-43
The Lawyers Know Too Much (Sandburg) **41**:277
"The Lawyer's Second Tale" (Clough) **103**:98, 156
"Lax though the Longing May Wear" (Barker) **77**:7
"Lay Down Your Weary Tune" (Dylan) **37**:65-6
"Lay le Freyne" (Marie de France)
See "Le Fraisne"
"Lay of Guigemar" (Marie de France) **22**:239-45, 258, 263-66, 268-76, 278, 293-94, 301
"Lay of the Jabberwocky" (Carroll) **74**:6
"The Lay of the Labourer" (Hood) **93**:87, 102, 105, 119
The Lay of the Last Minstrel (Scott) **13**:246, 248-51, 256, 258, 266, 269, 271, 273, 274-76, 279-83, 285, 303, 311-12, 315, 317-18
The Lay of the Laureate. Carmen Nuptiale (Southey) **111**:177, 250, 255-56
"The Layers" (Kunitz) **19**:180-81
"Laying Down the Law" (Hood) **93**:100
Laying Down the Tower (Piercy) **29**:323, 327
"Laying the Dust" (Levertov) **11**:165
Lays (Marie de France)
See *Lais*
Lays of My Home, and Other Poems (Whittier) **93**:266
Lays of Twilight (Hugo) **17**:44
"Lazarillo and the Beggar" (Aleixandre) **15**:4, 6
"Lázaro" (Cernuda) **62**:169, 219, 255-56, 258
"Lazarus" (Cernuda)
See "Lázaro"
"Lazarus" (Robinson) **1**:468
"Lazarus" (Sarton) **39**:341
"Lazarus (First Draft)" (Carson) **64**:221, 229
"Lazarus Standup" (Carson) **64**:222
"Lazarus's place" (Guillén) **35**:221-22
"Lead Soldiers" (Lowell) **13**:78
"Leadbelly Gives an Autograph" (Baraka) **113**:17, 69
"The Leaden Echo and the Golden Echo" (Hopkins) **15**:130-31, 143-44, 161
"The Leaden-Eyed" (Lindsay) **23**:268, 276, 281, 296
"The Leader" (Belloc) **24**:11
"The Leaders" (Brooks) **7**:63, 90
"The Leaders of the Crowd" (Yeats) **51**:75
"A Leaf" (Curnow) **48**:9-10
"The Leaf" (Warren) **37**:353-55, 360, 362
"Leaf Eater" (Kinsella) **69**:96
"Leaf Mould" (Hughes) **89**:146
"Leaf of Faces" (Whitman) **91**:314-15
"A Leaf Treader" (Frost) **39**:232; **71**:56
"The Leaf-House" (Dafydd ap Gwilym)
See "Y Deildy"
"Leaflets" (Rich) **5**:396
Leaflets: Poems, 1965-1968 (Rich) **5**:357, 365, 370-72, 383, 388-89, 396, 399
"A Lean and Hungry Look" (Nemerov) **24**:291
"The Leap" (Dickey) **40**:158, 226, 258
"Leaping Falls" (Kinnell) **26**:238
The Leaping Fire (Montague) **106**:215, 250-51, 266, 340
"The Leaping Laughers" (Barker) **77**:7, 44
Lear in the Original: Drawings and Limericks (Lear) **65**:144, 168
"Lear Is Gay" (Hayden) **6**:187
"The Lea-Rig" (Burns) **6**:82
"The Learned Boy" (Crabbe) **97**:96, 102

"A Learned Man Came to Me Once" (Crane) **80**:77
"The Learned Men" (MacLeish) **47**:197
"Learning a Dead Language" (Merwin) **45**:4, 1, 13-14, 24
"Learning About the Indians" (Oliver) **75**:298-99
"Learning About Water" (Sarton) **39**:328, 339
"Learning By Doing" (Nemerov) **24**:270
"Learning the Trees" (Nemerov) **24**:285
"Learning to Read" (Harper) **21**:192, 198, 200, 213
"Learning to Write" (Lorde) **12**:136
"The Least of Love" (Carman) **34**:226
"Leather Jacket" (Page) **12**:172
"Leather Leggings" (Sandburg) **2**:302; **41**:240, 270
"Leave" (Jarrell) **41**:155
"Leave me, O Love, which reaches but to dust" (Sidney) **32**:239
"Leave of Absence" (Kennedy) **93**:137-38
"Leave to the Wind" (Char)
See "Congé au vent"
"Leaves" (Hughes) **89**:125
"Leaves" (Mahon) **60**:140, 167, 211-12
"Leaves and Men" (Elliott) **96**:165
"Leaves before the Wind" (Sarton) **39**:324
"Leaves Compared with Flowers" (Frost) **39**:233
"Leaves of a Magazine" (Moore) **49**:109
Leaves of Grass (Whitman) **3**:370, 378-79, 382, 384, 386-87, 389, 397-99, 401, 404-08, 410-14, 416-17; **91**:197-203, 205, 211-18, 220-21, 223-25, 227-33, 238-41, 243-52, 254-60, 263, 271-73, 278-81, 286, 289-99, 301, 304, 307-12, 321, 329, 337, 339, 341-50
Leaves of Hypnos (Char)
See *Feuillets d'Hypnos*
The Leaves of the Tree (Sarton) **39**:335, 337
"Leaves that Talk" (Sexton) **79**:198-99, 210, 241
"Leave-taking Near Shoku" (Pound) **4**:331
"Leaving" (Song) **21**:333, 335, 342-43
"Leaving" (Wilbur) **51**:249-50, 274
"Leaving Barbados" (Kenyon) **57**:40, 45
"Leaving Barra" (MacNeice) **61**:135, 137
"Leaving Early" (Plath) **37**:254
"Leaving Inishmore" (Heaney) **100**:264
"Leaving Ithaca" (Snodgrass) **74**:293, 309
"Leaving L'Atelier-Aix-en-Provence" (Rexroth) **20**:196
"Leaving Modernity" (Guest) **55**:196, 199
"Leaving Mt. Baldy" (Cohen) **109**:101
"Leaving New York with Harry" (Stone) **53**:224
"Leaving the Atocha Station" (Ashbery) **26**:113
"Leaving the Door Open" (Ignatow) **34**:334
Leaving the Door Open (Ignatow) **34**:324-25, 327, 332
"Leaving the Motel" (Snodgrass) **74**:293
"Leaving the Temple at Nimes" (Wright) **36**:387
"Leaving Town" (Kenyon) **57**:39
"Leavings" (Heaney) **100**:274
"LEBANON VOICES" (Bissett) **14**:32
lebanon voices (Bissett) **14**:2
Lebediny stan (Tsvetaeva) **14**:313-14
"lebenslanf" (Enzensberger) **28**:135
"Lebenslauf" (Hölderlin) **4**:147
"Ein Lebenslied" (Werfel)
See "A Song of Life"
"Lebensweisheitspielerei" (Stevens) **110**:95
Leçons (Jaccottet) **98**:151, 168, 181-83, 191, 196, 198
"Lector Aere Perennoir" (Cunningham) **92**:138, 148, 154
"Lectura" (Guillén) **35**:175
"Lecture" (Milosz) **8**:200
"Lecture" (Montague) **106**:262
"Lecture I" (Milosz) **8**:202
"Lecture IV" (Milosz) **8**:203
"Lecture VI" (Milosz) **8**:199
"Lecture VII" (Milosz) **8**:202
"Lecture on Commitment" (Cage) **58**:205
"Lecture on Mystery" (Zagajewski) **27**:400
"Lecture on Nothing" (Cage) **58**:219
"A Lecture on Practical Aesthetics" (Spicer) **78**:304
"Lecture on the Weather" (Cage) **58**:188, 212-13, 215
"A Lecture upon the Shadow" (Donne) **1**:135, 145, 147; **43**:133
"A Lecturer" (Thomas) **99**:253
"Leda and the Swan" (Montale) **13**:150
"Leda and the Swan" (Yeats) **20**:315, 319; **51**:74
"Ledyard: The Exhaustion of Sheer Distance" (Dorn) **115**:121
Lee: A Dramatic Poem (Masters) **1**:339
"Lee in the Capitol" (Melville) **82**:72, 83, 85, 93, 138, 200, 206, 270
"Leech Gatherer" (Wordsworth) **4**:390, 394
"Leffingwell" (Robinson) **1**:466
"Left Behind" (Lowell) **13**:97
"Left Behind" (Mew) **107**:33
"The Leg" (Shapiro) **25**:268, 288, 297, 300-301
"Legacies" (Barrett Browning) **6**:16
"Legacies" (Giovanni) **19**:111
"Legacies" (Mahon) **60**:133
"Legacy" (Harjo) **27**:71
"A Legacy" (Quintana) **36**:257
"Legacy: My South" (Randall) **86**:318, 343
"Legal Fiction" (Empson) **104**:88-89, 101
"The Legal System" (Hogan) **35**:257
"Legend" (Crane) **3**:101; **99**:11, 15, 19, 21, 24, 37, 54, 57-61, 64, 74, 139
"Legend" (Wright) **14**:338
Legend (Chaucer)
See *Legend of Good Women*
Legend (Longfellow)
See *The Golden Legend*
"The Legend Beautiful" (Longfellow) **30**:62
Legend of Good Women (Chaucer) **19**:7, 10, 21, 23-4, 34, 60, 64, 74; **58**:295
The Legend of Jubal, and Other Poems (Eliot) **20**:116, 123, 125, 131-32
"The Legend of Language" (Werfel)
See "Legende von der Sprache"
"A Legend of Porcelain" (Lowell) **13**:61, 65
"The Legend of St. Mark" (Whittier) **93**:221
The Legend of the Centuries (Hugo)
See *La légende des siècles*
"The Legend of the One-Eyed Man" (Sexton) **79**:269-70
"A Legend of Versailles" (Tolson) **88**:349-50
"A Legend of Viable Women" (Eberhart) **76**:65
"Legende" (Celan) **10**:126
"Lègende" (Laforgue) **14**:74
La légende des siècles (Hugo) **17**:49, 54-57, 60-61, 65, 68, 78, 80, 83-86, 89, 91
Legende of Good Women (Chaucer)
See *Legend of Good Women*
"Légende théologique" (Gautier) **18**:162
"Legende von der Sprache" (Werfel) **101**:325
"Legender" (Ekeloef) **23**:69, 71
Legends (Lowell) **13**:60-3, 65, 74, 83, 93
"Legends and Dirges" (Ekeloef) **23**:69
"Legends like This" (Welch) **62**:340
Legends of New England in Prose and Verse (Whittier) **93**:170, 193, 243, 260
"La Leggenda di Teodorico" (Carducci) **46**:52
"The Legion Club" (Swift) **9**:281
"The Legions of Caesar" (Wright) **36**:310
"The Legs" (Graves) **6**:151
"Das leichte und das schwere Herz" (Werfel) **101**:330
"Leisure" (Blunden) **66**:4
"Leisure" (Teasdale) **31**:328, 371
"The Leisure of the Theory Class" (Howe) **54**:150
"Le Lejanía" (Dorn) **115**:132
"The Lemming: O Sweden" (Spencer) **77**:328-29
"Lemonade" (Carver) **54**:18, 28
"The Lemons" (Montale) **13**:149
"Lemons" (Walcott) **46**:289
"Lemuel's Blessing" (Merwin) **45**:33-4, 72-3, 82, 85
"Lengas dai frus di sera" (Pasolini) **17**:256
"Length of Days" (Meynell) **112**:153, 174, 177, 218
"Leningrad" (Akhmadulina) **43**:55
"Lenore" (Poe) **1**:434, 438, 445; **54**:260, 311
"Lenox Avenue: Midnight" (Hughes) **1**:265; **53**:101
"Lenses" (Eberhart) **76**:54
"Lent" (Herbert) **4**:100
"The Lent Lily" (Housman) **2**:184, 192
"Lenten Thoughts of a High Anglican" (Betjeman) **75**:34, 98
"Lenteur de l'avenir" (Char) **56**:137
"Leo Blue's and the Tiger Rose" (Espada) **74**:121
"Leon" (Cardenal) **22**:110
"Leonainie" (Riley) **48**:283, 287
"A Leone Traverso" (Montale) **13**:139
"Léonides" (Char) **56**:149
"Leonine Elegiacs" (Tennyson) **6**:385-86
"The Leopard" (Brathwaite) **56**:64
"Leopardi" (Strand) **63**:181-82
"Leopardi—L'Infinito" (Rexroth) **95**:272
"Lepanto" (Chesterton) **28**:94, 99-100, 108, 125, 128-30
"The Leper" (Swinburne) **24**:307, 337
"Lepidopterist" (Goodison) **36**:143
"Lerici" (Gunn) **26**:218
"leroy" (Baraka) **4**:19, 23; **113**:41
The Lesbians (Baudelaire)
See *Les fleurs du mal*
"Lesbienne" (Brossard) **80**:22
Les Lesbiennes (Baudelaire)
See *Les fleurs du mal*
"Lesbos" (Baudelaire) **106**:23-24
"Lesbos" (Plath) **1**:394; **37**:256, 269
"The Less Deceived" (Larkin) **21**:222
The Less Deceived (Larkin) **21**:224, 226-27, 230, 233, 235, 251-52, 255, 256, 259
Lesser Testament (Villon)
See *Les Lais*
"La lessiveuse" (Ponge) **107**:78, 139, 192
"The Lesson" (Collins) **68**:220
"The Lesson" (Kipling) **91**:63, 118-19, 172
"The Lesson" (Levertov) **11**:167
"The Lesson" (Lowell) **3**:211
"A Lesson in Geography" (Rexroth) **20**:215; **95**:253, 271
"Lessons" (Teasdale) **31**:355
"Lessons in Hunger" (Sexton) **79**:245-46
"Lestnitsa" (Tsvetaeva)
See "Poèma lestnitsy"
"Lestrygonians" (Boland) **58**:20
"Let America Be America Again" (Hughes) **1**:250, 253; **53**:109-10, 148
Let Each Man Remember (Jacobsen) **62**:290, 303, 307, 311, 320
"Let Evening Come" (Kenyon) **57**:31-33, 37
Let Evening Come (Kenyon) **57**:5-6, 11, 19, 23, 36, 38, 40-41, 45
"Let It Be Forgotten" (Teasdale) **31**:323, 335, 357
"Let It Go" (Empson) **104**:85, 88, 111, 136
"Let Koras and Balafong Accompany Me" (Senghor)
See "Que m'accompagnent Kôras et Balafong"
"Let Me Begin Again" (Levine) **22**:219, 225
"Let Me Enjoy" (Hardy) **8**:98
"Let me go, Voronezh . . ." (Mandelstam)
See "Pusti menia, Voronezh . . ."
"Let Me Live with Marriage" (Jordan) **38**:119, 122
"Let Me Rest" (Elliott) **96**:166
"let me tell yu a story of how they met" (Bissett) **14**:17
"Let My People Go" (Johnson) **24**:128-29, 139, 144, 166, 169
"Let No Charitable Hope" (Wylie) **23**:314, 323-24, 333-34

"Let not Love go to" (Noyes) **27**:134
"Let Pure Hate Still Underprop" (Thoreau) **30**:180, 192, 203, 247, 265, 273, 293
"Let Something Good Be Said" (Riley) **48**:304
"Let the Light Enter! The Dying Words of Goethe" (Harper) **21**:210
"Let There be Light" (Lawrence) **54**:249
Let Us Be Great (Yevtushenko) **40**:344
Let Us Compare Mythologies (Cohen) **109**:3, 11-14, 17, 19, 28, 31, 34, 43, 46-54, 81-82, 88, 100, 106, 108-9
"Let us gather at the river" (Piercy) **29**:303, 315
"Let Us Never Try to Love" (Cernuda) See "No intentemos el amor nunca"
"Let Us Prepare" (Swenson) **14**:268
"Let Yourself Be Sidetracked by Your Güiro" (Alurista) **34**:23
"Letanía de los montes de la vida" (Fuertes) **27**:39
"Letanía de nuestro Señor Don Quijote" (Darío) **15**:96
"Letanías de la tierra muerts" (Storni) **33**:254
"Letchworth" (Betjeman) **75**:20
"Leter 20: not a pastoral letter" (Olson) **19**:274
"Le lethe" (Baudelaire) See "Léthé"
"Léthé" (Baudelaire) **1**:72
"Lethe" (H. D.) **5**:287, 304
"Lethe" (Yamada) **44**:351
"Let's Beat Down the Poor" (Baudelaire) See "Assommons les pauvres"
"Let's beat up the poor!" (Baudelaire) See "Assommons les pauvres"
"Let's, from Some Loud Unworld's Most Rightful Wrong" (Cummings) **5**:109
"A Letter" (Berry) **28**:6
"A Letter" (Bogan) **12**:95, 127
"Letter" (Cohen) **109**:13
"The Letter" (Creeley) **73**:5
"A Letter" (Cunningham) **92**:185
"The Letter" (Elliott) **96**:159
"Letter" (Hass) **16**:196
"A Letter" (Hecht) **70**:108
"The Letter" (Kenyon) **57**:6, 42
"Letter" (Montale) See "Lettera"
"The Letter" (Owen) **19**:347, 363-65; **102**:229-30
"A Letter" (Simic) **69**:310-11, 320
"The Letter" (Thomas) **99**:335-36
Letter (Whitney) See *The Copy of a Letter, Lately Written in Meter, by a Young Gentlewoman: To Her Unconstant Lover*
"Letter I" (Empson) **104**:99, 107, 119, 122
"Letter I" (Olson) **19**:282, 284
"Letter II" (Empson) **104**:88, 93, 112, 127
"Letter 2" (Olson) **19**:277, 281-82
"Letter 3" (Olson) **19**:273, 280, 282, 284
Letter 3 (Brutus) **24**:106, 115
"Letter IV" (Empson) **104**:119
"Letter 4" (Olson) **19**:283
"Letter 5" (Brutus) **24**:101, 106
"Letter V" (Empson) **104**:99, 122, 124
"Letter 5" (Olson) **19**:266, 271, 282-83
"Letter 6" (Olson) **19**:280, 282-83
Letter 6 (Brutus) **24**:115
Letter 7 (Brutus) **24**:115
"Letter 8" (Olson) **19**:280, 283
"Letter 9" (Olson) **19**:267, 281, 283-84
Letter 9 (Brutus) **24**:115
"Letter 10" (Brutus) **24**:115
"Letter 10" (Olson) **19**:267, 281, 283-84
"Letter 11" (Olson) **19**:296
Letter 13 (Brutus) **24**:99, 106, 115
"Letter 14" (Brutus) **24**:100
"Letter 14" (Olson) **19**:273
"Letter 15" (Olson) **19**:277
"Letter 16" (Brutus) **24**:101
Letter 17 (Brutus) **24**:106, 115
"Letter for Jan" (Lorde) **12**:152
"Letter for Melville" (Olson) **19**:297
"Letter for Those Who Grew Up Together" (Ciardi) **69**:5
"Letter from a Coward to a Hero" (Warren) **37**:277, 284, 289, 321, 332
"Letter from a Death Bed" (Ciardi) **69**:41
"A Letter from a Girl to Her Own Old Age" (Meynell) **112**:158, 165, 181, 184-85, 191, 245, 271, 275-76, 279-80, 284
"Letter from a Metaphysical Countryside" (Ciardi) **69**:31
"Letter: From a Missionary of the Methodist Episcopal Church South in Kansas to a Distinguished Politician" (Whittier) **93**:211, 239, 265-66, 344
"Letter from a Rubber Raft" (Ciardi) **69**:24, 31
"Letter from an Empty House" (Ciardi) **69**:41
Letter from Artemisia in the Towne to Chloe in the Country (Wilmot) **66**:237, 260-61, 263, 268-69, 283-85, 329, 336, 348, 351-53, 356
"Letter from Chicago for Virginia Woolf" (Sarton) **39**:329
"Letter from Costa Brava" (Tomlinson) **17**:315
"A Letter from Gussie" (Merwin) **45**:24
"A Letter from Li Po" (Aiken) **26**:45, 56-7
A Letter from Li Po, and Other Poems (Aiken) **26**:24, 29-30
"Letter from New York" (Mahon) **60**:218
"Letter from Oregon" (Stafford) **71**:360
"Letter from Our Man in Blossomtime" (Glück) **16**:124
"A Letter from Phillis Wheatley" (Hayden) **6**:189, 192, 195
"Letter from Pontus" (Masefield) **78**:91
A Letter from Pontus and Other Verse (Masefield) **78**:49, 62, 98-101
"Letter from Prague, 1968-78" (Forché) **10**:144, 156, 168-69
"A Letter from Rome" (Hope) **56**:278, 302-3
"Letter from San Francisco" (Rexroth) **95**:338
"Letter from the End of the World" (Mueller) **33**:198
"Letter from the Line" (Hope) **56**:295-96
"Letter from the North" (Bukowski) **18**:4
"A Letter Home" (Sassoon) **12**:262
"A Letter in a Bottle" (Brodsky) **9**:3, 4
"A Letter, in the Meantime, Not to Be Mailed Tonight" (Dorn) **115**:126-27
"Letter, May 2, 1959" (Olson) **19**:306
"Letter Number Forty-One" (Olson) **19**:306
"Letter of a Mother" (Warren) **37**:320, 331
"Letter of Advice to a Young Poet" (Swift) **9**:272
The Letter of Cupid (Christine de Pizan) See *L'epistre au dieu d'amours*
"Letter of Mathios Pakallis" (Seferis) **66**:163
"Letter of Recommendation" (Amichai) **38**:46
"Letter of Testimony: Cantata" (Paz) **48**:273, 275
Letter of the Prodigal Son (Southwell) **83**:229-30
"Letter of the Seer" (Rimbaud) See "Lettre du voyant"
"Letter on August 15" (Hacker) **47**:86
"Letter Perfect Is Not Perfect" (Moore) **49**:134
"Letter" poems (Empson) **104**:99
"Letter Sycorax" (Brathwaite) **56**:61
"Letter III" (Empson) **104**:121
"Letter to a Bourgeois Friend Whom Once I Loved (and Maybe Still Do If Love Is Valid)" (Giovanni) **19**:115
"Letter to a Boy at School" (Wickham) **110**:263, 266
"A Letter to a Brother of the Pen in Tribulation" (Behn) **13**:7, 30; **88**:83, 149, 152
"Letter to a Conceivable Great-Grandson" (Birney) **52**:28
"Letter to a Cuzco Priest" (Birney) **52**:41-42, 99
"Letter to a Friend" (Barker) **77**:38
"Letter to a Friend" (Warren) **37**:288
"Letter to a Friend" (Wright) **14**:336, 338
"Letter to a Friend: Who Is Nancy Daum?" (Schuyler) **88**:187
"Letter to a Psychiatrist" (Sarton) **39**:340
"Letter to a Psychiatrist: The Fear of Angels" (Sarton) **39**:342
"Letter to a Wound" (Auden) **1**:22
"Letter to a Wound" (Hacker) **47**:107
"Letter to a Young Poet" (Barker) **77**:18
"A Letter to Alex Comfort" (Abse) **41**:11, 16, 18
"A Letter to An Aspiring Junkie" (Angelou) **32**:28
"Letter to an Indian Friend" (Sarton) **39**:322-23, 332
"Letter to Ann Landers" (Ondaatje) **28**:328
"Letter to Annick from Boulder" (Hugo) **68**:278
"A Letter to Basil" (Brutus) **24**:106, 108
"Letter to Birch from Deer Lodge" (Hugo) **68**:271, 275, 278
"Letter to Blessing from Missoula" (Hugo) **68**:278, 293
"Letter to Bob Kaufman" (Komunyakaa) **51**:34
"Letter to California" (Mueller) **33**:191
"A Letter to Dafnis April: 2nd 1685" (Finch) **21**:165
"Letter to Dante" (Ciardi) **69**:4
"A Letter to Dr. Martin Luther King" (Sanchez) **9**:244
"Letter to E. Franklin Frazier" (Baraka) **113**:13
"A Letter to Franz Wright" (Wright) **36**:311-12, 366
"Letter to Gale from Ovando" (Hugo) **68**:278
"Letter to G.N. from Wrest" (Carew) **29**:7-8, 11, 41-43, 46-48
"Letter to Goldbarth from Big Fork" (Hugo) **68**:270, 278, 290, 293
"Letter to Graham and Anna" (MacNeice) **61**:124, 135
"Letter to Haislip from Hot Springs" (Hugo) **68**:279
"Letter to Her" (Bly) **39**:103
"A Letter to Her Husband, Absent upon Public Employment" (Bradstreet) **10**:8, 28, 30, 34, 40, 65
"Letter to Hill from St. Ignatius" (Hugo) **68**:279
"Letter to His Brother" (Berryman) **64**:82, 90
"Letter to Hona" (Cisneros) **52**:161
"Letter to J . . ." (Prior) **102**:311
"Letter to J. R. R., the Last Transcendentalist" (Ciardi) **69**:24-25
"A Letter to Jack Johnson" (Duncan) **75**:252
"A Letter to James Stephens" (Sarton) **39**:320-21, 335, 348
"Letter to Jean-Paul Baudot, at Christmas" (Stryk) **27**:182, 196, 200, 202, 204-5, 215, 218
"Letter to John Franco—Venice" (Cisneros) **52**:154, 161
"Letter to Kizer from Seattle" (Hugo) **68**:277
"Letter to León Felipe" (Paz) **48**:273
"Letter to Levertov from Butte" (Hugo) **68**:265, 270, 272-73
"Letter to Logan from Milltown" (Hugo) **68**:278
"Letter to Lord Byron" (Auden) **92**:75
"Letter to Lord Byron" (MacNeice) **61**:123
Letter to Lord Byron (Auden) **1**:22, 34
A Letter to Lucian and Other Poems (Noyes) **27**:135
"A Letter to Lucian the Sceptic Dated from the Island of Cos in the year AD 165" (Noyes) **27**:136
"Letter to Mantsch from Havre" (Hugo) **68**:279
"Letter to Mastre Canynge" (Chatterton) **104**:5-6, 22, 28
"Letter to Matthews from Barton Street Flats" (Hugo) **68**:271, 277, 285-86, 291
"Letter to Maxine Sullivan" (Carruth) **10**:87

"Letter to Miguel Otero Silva, in Caracas, 1948" (Neruda)
See "Carta a Miguel Otero Silva, en Caracas, 1948"
"Letter to Mother" (Ciardi) **69**:23, 50
"A Letter to Mr. Creech" (Behn) **88**:22, 71-72, 118, 136, 145, 148, 151
"A Letter to my Aunt Discussing the Correct Approach to Modern Poetry" (Thomas) **52**:263
"Letter to My Father from 40,000 Feet" (Olds) **22**:324-25
"A Letter to My Friends" (Merton) **10**:346-47
"Letter to My Sister" (Spencer) **77**:332, 341, 345
"Letter to My Sisters at Home" (Ciardi) **69**:24
"Letter to No One" (Cervantes) **35**:135
"Letter to Oberg from Pony" (Hugo) **68**:278, 293
"Letter to Peterson from the Pike Place Market" (Hugo) **68**:271
"A Letter to Sara Hutchinson" (Coleridge) **11**:69-72, 91
"Letter to Sister Madeline from Iowa City" (Hugo) **68**:271, 279, 293
"Letter to the Academy" (Hughes) **53**:110, 115
"Letter to the Countesse of Huntingdon" (Donne) **1**:130
"Letter to the Dygne Mastre Canynge" (Chatterton)
See "Letter to Mastre Canynge"
"Letter to the Front" (Rukeyser) **12**:228, 231-34
"A Letter to the Honorable Lady Mrs. Margaret Candish Harley" (Prior) **102**:316
"Letter to the Local Police" (Jordan) **38**:117
"A Letter to the Same Person" (Finch) **21**:160, 164
"Letter to V-" (Wylie) **23**:324
"Letter to Vincent Van Gogh" (Goodison) **36**:158
"Letter to Virginia Johnson" (Ciardi) **69**:4, 32
"Letter to Wagoner from Port Townsend" (Hugo) **68**:257, 262
"A Letter to William Carlos Williams" (Rexroth) **20**:193; **95**:257, 260
"A Letter to Yvor Winters" (Rexroth) **95**:270
"Letter Written during a January Northeaster" (Sexton) **2**:351; **79**:204, 208, 210-11
"Letter Written on a Ferry Crossing Long Island Sound" (Sexton) **2**:351, 361
"Letter Written on a Ferry While Crossing Long Island Sound" (Sexton) **79**:257, 261-62, 264, 266-67
"Lettera" (Montale) **13**:161
"Lettera" (Quasimodo) **47**:285
"Lettera amorosa" (Char) **56**:110, 115-16, 169
"Letters" (Cassian) **17**:5
Letters (Donne) **43**:113-14, 120
Letters (Duncan) **2**:106
Letters (Ovid)
See *Heroides*
Letters (Riley) **48**:343
"Letters and Other Worlds" (Ondaatje) **28**:315-16, 327, 329, 331
"Letters for the Dead" (Levine) **22**:220, 223
"Letters for the Next Time" (Ciardi) **69**:23, 25
"Letters from a Land of Sinners" (Rich) **5**:354
Letters from a Traveller's Pannier (Matsuo Basho)
See *Oi no obumi*
Letters from Iceland (Auden) **1**:9, 13; **92**:61, 63-64, 68
Letters from Iceland (MacNeice) **61**:181
"Letters from Maine" (Sarton) **39**:361, 369
Letters from Maine: New Poems (Sarton) **39**:361-62, 368-69
"Letters from the Island" (Cruz) **37**:31
"Letters from the Ming Dynasty" (Brodsky) **9**:29
"Letters from the Poet Who Sleeps in a Chair" (Parra) **39**:308-10
"Letters from Yadoo" (Raworth) **107**:324
The Letters of Carl Sandburg (Sandburg) **41**:351
Letters of Elizabeth Barrett Browning to Mary Russell Mitford 1836-1854 (Barrett Browning) **62**:75
The Letters of John Keats (Keats) **96**:206, 221
"Letters of the Dead" (Szymborska) **44**:279
Letters of the Heroines (Ovid)
See *Heroides*
Letters: Poems 1953-1956 (Duncan) **75**:138, 176, 181-82, 226, 229, 232
"Letters to a Cuzco Priest" (Birney) **52**:16
"Letters to Dead Imagists" (Sandburg) **41**:360
Letters to Martha and Other Poems from a South African Prison (Brutus) **24**:99-100, 102, 104-09, 112, 114-15, 118-20
Letters to Martha II (Brutus) **24**:100
"Letters to the Egyptian" (Goodison) **36**:143
"Lettre" (Verlaine) **32**:351, 390, 392, 394
"Lettre à une femme" (Hugo) **17**:100
"Lettre du vingt-six juin" (Jaccottet) **98**:174
"Lettre du voyant" (Rimbaud) **57**:211-13, 216, 283-85
"Lettre-Océan" (Apollinaire) **7**:18, 25-9, 32, 34-7
"Lettres de l'Hivernage" (Senghor) **25**:232-33, 235, 247-51
Lettres du voyant (Rimbaud) **57**:232
"Lettres d'un Soldat" (Stevens) **110**:184
"lettrs (for a passing comet)" (Bissett) **14**:20
Letzte Gedichte und Gedanken (Heine) **25**:172
"Letzter Abend" (Rilke) **2**:267
"Letzter Frühling" (Benn) **35**:71
Leurs yeux toujours purs (Éluard) **38**:71
"Levántate y Rie" (Alurista) **34**:46
"Levedad" (Jiménez) **7**:201
"The Levee: Letter to No One" (Cervantes) **35**:133, 134
"The Level at Which Sky Began" (Soto) **28**:370, 378
"Level Light" (Stafford) **71**:299
"Le Lever du soleil" (Breton) **15**:48
"Levet" (Johnson)
See "On the Death of Dr. Robert Levet"
Levia gravia (Carducci) **46**:4, 8, 11, 13, 37, 47, 49-51
"Leviathan" (Curnow) **48**:17, 36-37
"Leviathan" (Merwin) **45**:6-7, 9
"Leviathan" (Neruda) **4**:282
"Leviathan" (Oppen) **35**:333
"Leviathan" (Shvarts) **50**:142
"Levkoienwelle" (Benn) **35**:46, 70
"Lewd Love Is Loss" (Southwell) **83**:279
"Lews estoilles envoyées à Monsieur de Pibrac en Polonne" (Ronsard) **11**:236-37, 239
"Lewti" (Coleridge) **67**:304
"Lexington" (Holmes) **71**:71, 96
"Le lézard" (Ponge) **107**:79, 140
"Li occi dolenti" (Dante) **21**:73
"The Liar" (Baraka) **4**:17; **113**:151-53
"The Liars (March, 1919)" (Sandburg) **2**:304; **41**:298, 329
"Libation" (Ammons) **16**:4
"Libation" (Brathwaite) **56**:84
"Libation" (Levertov) **11**:197
"Libel Summons" (Burns) **114**:125-29
Liber Spectaculorum (Martial) **10**:230
"Libera II" (Char) **56**:147
liberating skies (Bissett) **14**:7-8, 16
"Liberation" (Glück) **16**:156
"Liberation" (Stone) **53**:219
"Liberation" (Winters) **82**:316, 325
"Liberation Poem" (Sanchez) **9**:209
"The Liberators" (Neruda)
See "Los libertadores"
"La libertad" (Paredes) **83**:30
Libertad bajo palabra (Paz) **1**:353; **48**:183, 244, 258, 267
"Libertad sin Lágrimas" (Alurista) **34**:10, 46
"Los libertadores" (Neruda) **4**:292
"La liberte, ou une nuit a Rome" (Lamartine) **16**:278, 291
"The Liberties" (Howe) **54**:126, 129-30, 134
The Liberties (Howe) **54**:42-43, 52, 57, 59, 90
"The Libertine" (Behn) **13**:4
"The Libertine" (MacNeice) **61**:141
"Liberty" (Pushkin)
See "Vol'nost': Oda"
"Liberty" (Thomas) **53**:296, 317-18
"Liberty. An Ode" (Pushkin)
See "Vol'nost': Oda"
Liberty behind the Words (Paz)
See *Libertad bajo palabra*
Liberty on Parole (Paz)
See *Libertad bajo palabra*
Liberty under parole (Paz)
See *Libertad bajo palabra*
"Liberty without Tears" (Alurista)
See "Libertad sin Lágrimas"
"Liberty's Twilight" (Mandelstam)
See "The Twilight of Freedom"
"Libido" (Brooke) **24**:53
"The Librarian" (Olson) **19**:280
"The Library" (Williams) **109**:193
The Library. A Poem (Crabbe) **97**:70, 75-79, 163-67
"The Library Is on Fire" (Char) **56**:146
"A Library of Law" (MacLeish) **47**:182
Libretto (Jaccottet) **98**:201
Libretto for the Republic of Liberia (Tolson) **88**:231-34, 254-55, 267, 269, 281, 296-97, 303, 317, 323, 330-31, 336-46, 353
Libri Plantarum (Cowley)
See *Plantarum*
"El libro" (Darío) **15**:99, 101-02
Libro de las preguntas (Neruda) **4**:287, 290
El Libro de los Gorriones (Bécquer) **113**:162, 168, 228, 241, 243, 247, 252
Libro de poemas (García Lorca) **3**:117-18, 147-49
"Un libro di Ecloghe" (Zanzotto) **65**:265
Un libro levemente odioso (Dalton) **36**:128
Un libro rojo para Lenin (Dalton) **36**:131-32
Libros inéditos de poesía (Jiménez) **7**:201
"The Libyan Hunter, A Fable" (Leapor) **85**:212, 214, 249
The Lice (Merwin) **45**:5, 9-10, 15, 18-21, 23-7, 30-2, 34-5, 38, 41-4, 49, 52, 54, 57, 59, 61, 63, 70-1, 75, 81, 83-8, 90, 93, 100
"Licentiousness" (Cassian) **17**:5
Lichee Nuts (Masters) **1**:338
"Les Lichens" (Char) **56**:151
"Das Licht und das Schweigen" (Werfel) **101**:324, 349
"Lichtenberg" (Kipling) **91**:142-43, 174
Lichtzwang (Celan) **10**:96, 98, 121
"Liddy's Orange" (Olds) **22**:315
"Lidice" (Day Lewis) **11**:146
"The Lie" (Raleigh) **31**:202, 212-13, 219, 234, 259, 277-78, 281, 285, 304
"Liebe" (Benn) **35**:8
"Liebesgedichte" (Stramm) **50**:189
"Liebeskampf" (Stramm) **50**:168, 193-95, 208-9
"(Liebeslied.)" (Celan) **10**:123-24
"Liebeslied" (Stone) **53**:230
"Liebestod" (Parker) **28**:362
"Liebhaber in allen Gestalten" (Goethe) **5**:246, 251
"Die Liedenschaftlichen" (Werfel) **101**:349
"Lieder" (Pasolini) **17**:256
Lieder (Heine) **25**:155
"Liens" (Apollinaire) **7**:28, 49
"Lieu de la salamandre" (Bonnefoy) **58**:134, 147, 174
"Lieu du combat" (Bonnefoy) **58**:123
Lieutenant Schmidt (Pasternak) **6**:265, 272
"Life" (Aleixandre) **15**:25-6
"Life" (Bryant) **20**:16
"Life" (Cowley) **90**:104, 138
"Life" (Dunbar) **5**:121, 124-26, 130
"Life" (Herbert) **4**:100, 113
"A Life" (Thomas) **99**:283
"Life" (Very) **86**:42, 152
"The Life" (Wright) **36**:328, 345, 397

Life (Crabbe)
See *The Poetical Works of the Rev. George Crabbe; with His Letters and Journals and His Life, by His Son*
Life (Hejinian)
See *My Life*
"Life After Death" (Hughes) **89**:160, 162
Life and Death (Creeley) **73**:109, 118, 124
"Life and Death at Sunrise" (Hardy) **8**:124
The Life and Death of Jason (Morris) **55**:240-42, 248-49, 251-52, 254, 259, 274, 305, 328-30
"Life and Fame" (Cowley) **90**:104
"The Life and Genuine Character of Dr. Swift" (Swift) **9**:280, 295
"Life and Letters" (Enright) **93**:17
"Life and Letters" (Rich) **5**:352
"Life and Song" (Lanier) **50**:54, 67, 98
"Life as a Visionary Spirit" (Eberhart) **76**:45
"Life at War" (Levertov) **11**:176, 194
"The Life Beyond" (Brooke) **24**:57
"Life Class" (Montague) **106**:233, 244
"Life Cycle of Common Man" (Nemerov) **24**:283
"A Life History: in Harmonies and Discords" (Lawrence) **54**:235-36
"Life in a Love" (Browning) **61**:88
Life in the Forest (Levertov) **11**:205, 207-10
"Life Is a Battlefield" (Corso) **108**:40
"Life Is a Summer's Day" (Thoreau) **30**:187, 189
"Life Is but Loss" (Southwell) **83**:238, 280
"Life is More True than Reason Will Decieve" (Cummings) **5**:108
"Life Is Motion" (Stevens) **6**:333
"Life Is Trying to Be Life" (Hughes) **89**:129
"Life Laughs Onward" (Hardy) **92**:295
"A Life Lesson" (Riley) **48**:309
"Life, Love, and Death" (Rossetti) **44**:255
"Life of a Man" (Berrigan) **103**:34
Life of a Man (Ungaretti)
See *Vita d'un uoma*
"The life of Borodin" (Bukowski) **18**:22
"Life of Life" (Patmore) **59**:201
"Life of Life" (Shelley) **14**:181
"The Life of Lincoln West" (Brooks) **7**:85, 91-2
"The Life of My Friend" (Blok) **21**:6, 20
"The Life of the Dead" (Jackson) **44**:7, 11, 44-5, 102
"Life of the Poet" (Thomas) **99**:282
"The Life of Towns" (Carson) **64**:201, 204-7
"Life on Earth" (O'Hara) **45**:156
Life, Poems, and Thoughts of Joseph Delorme (Sainte-Beuve)
See *Vie, poésies et pensées de Joseph Delorme*
Life Sentence (Cassian) **17**:10-13
"Life Story" (Wickham) **110**:288-89
Life Studies (Lowell) **3**:205-09, 211-14, 216-19, 221, 223, 227, 230, 232-33, 242-43
Life Studies: Secular Love (Ondaatje) **28**:316
"Life Support System" (Welch) **62**:343
"The Life That Is" (Bryant) **20**:8
"The Life They Lead" (Ignatow) **34**:324
"Life Work" (Stafford) **71**:371
"Lifeboat" (Silverstein) **49**:349
"The Lifeguard" (Dickey) **40**:150, 166, 175, 180, 257
"Life-in Love" (Rossetti) **44**:204
"Life-Long, Poor Browning" (Spencer) **77**:341, 343-44
"Life's Death, Love's Life" (Southwell) **83**:239, 280
"Life's Noonday" (Tagore)
See "Jivan madhyahna"
"Life's Rendezvous" (Cullen) **20**:77
"Life's Work" (Kumin) **15**:202
"Life-Size is Too Large" (Jackson) **44**:89
"A Lifetime" (Bryant) **20**:8, 12, 46
"A Lifetime Later" (Ferlinghetti) **1**:183
"The Liffey Hill" (Kinsella) **69**:72-73
"Lift Every Voice and Sing" (Johnson) **24**:136, 130-31, 143-44, 146, 154, 159-60, 166, 170
"Lift up to heav'n, sad wretch, thy heavy spright" (Campion) **87**:66, 98
"The Lifting" (Olds) **22**:318, 325, 334-36, 340
"Lifting Belly" (Stein) **18**:327, 341-42
"th lifting hands" (Bissett) **14**:34
"Lifting Illegal Nets By Flashlist" (Wright) **36**:322, 351
"Lifting my forehead and lowering my eyes" (Tsvetaeva)
See "Zakinuv golovu i opustiv glaza"
"Lifting Stone" (Sarton) **39**:324
"Ligadura humana" (Storni) **33**:278
"The Light" (Ferlinghetti) **1**:183
"Light" (Ondaatje) **28**:339-40
"Light" (Wakoski) **15**:369
"Light a Candle" (Tapahonso) **65**:258
"Light against Darkness" (Williams) **7**:385
"The Light and Glory of the Word" (Cowper) **40**:84
Light and Serious Verse (Carducci)
See *Levia gravia*
"Light and Silence" (Werfel)
See "Das Licht und das Schweigen"
The Light around the Body (Bly) **39**:8-15, 17, 22, 27, 37, 42, 47-50, 52, 63, 66, 71, 83-4, 90-1, 94, 100-01
"Light Baggage" (Walker) **30**:354
"Light Becomes Darkness" (Williams) **7**:384, 388
"Light Becomes Where No Sun Shines" (Thomas)
See "Light Breaks Where No Sun Shines"
Light Beyond the Darkness (Harper) **21**:189
"Light Breaks Where No Sun Shines" (Thomas) **2**:304; **52**:245, 256, 262, 271
"A Light Breather" (Roethke) **15**:268, 309
Light Compulsion (Celan)
See *Lichtzwang*
Light Conceits of Lovers (Campion) **87**:7, 12, 25, 32, 42, 51, 56-57, 65, 67, 71-72, 111
"Light from Above" (Eberhart) **76**:45, 73
"The Light from Within" (Very) **86**:166
"Light in Darkness" (Harper) **21**:197
"A Light in the Attic" (Silverstein) **49**:323
A Light in the Attic: Poems and Drawings (Silverstein) **49**:305-6, 309-13, 322-24, 327-29, 331, 333-36, 338-41, 343-44, 346-48
"The Light in the Hallway" (Wright) **36**:342
"Light is Speech" (Moore) **49**:134
"Light Love" (Rossetti) **7**:289
"Light Music" (Mahon) **60**:143, 195
"The Light of Day" (Parra)
See "La Luz del día"
"Light of My Eyes" (Walcott) **46**:262
"The Light of Stars" (Longfellow) **30**:22, 26, 36, 96, 103, 108-09
"The Light of the World" (Walcott) **46**:266
"Light on earth" (Neruda)
See "La lámpara en la tierra"
"The Light on the Pewter Dish" (Rexroth) **20**:196; **95**:272
"Light on the Subject" (Komunyakaa) **51**:29
"Light Sleeping" (Gunn) **26**:218
"A Light Snow-Fall after Frost" (Hardy) **8**:124; **92**:375
"The Light Tree" (Elytis) **21**:123
The Light Tree and the Fourteenth Beauty (Elytis) **21**:123, 133
"Light Verse on a Rock" (Wang Wei) **18**:358-59
"The Light Years" (Sarton) **39**:325
"A Lighted Cigar That Is Smoking" (Apollinaire)
See "Paysage"
"The Lighted House" (Day Lewis) **11**:145-46
"The Lighted Window" (Teasdale) **31**:335, 351
"Lighten heavy hart" (Campion) **87**:55-56, 66
"Lightenings" (Heaney) **18**:259; **100**:252
"The Lighthouse" (Longfellow) **30**:42
"A Lighthouse in Maine" (Mahon) **60**:146, 170, 198, 214
"Lighthouse with Dead Leaves" (McGuckian) **27**:104
"Lighting a Candle" (Shvarts)
See "Zazhigaia svechu"
"Lighting a Candle for W. H. Auden" (Wright) **36**:359
"Lighting of the Penitentiary" (Char)
See "L'Eclairage du pénitencier"
"Lightness" (Jiménez)
See "Levedad"
"Lightness" (Wilbur) **51**:193, 281, 292
"Lightnin' Blues" (Dove) **6**:117
"The Lightning" (Berryman) **64**:79, 90
"Lightning" (Lawrence) **54**:174-5, 206-7
"The Lightning" (Swenson) **14**:285
"Lightning Bugs Asleep in the Afternoon" (Wright) **36**:370, 378
"The Lightning Speed of the Past" (Carver) **54**:11
"Lightning Storm on Fuji" (Nemerov) **24**:295
"Lights" (Boland) **58**:45
"The Lights in the Sky Are Stars" (Rexroth) **95**:250, 260, 273
"Lights of my Eyes" (Guest) **55**:194
"Lights Out" (Thomas) **53**:271, 275, 293, 297-98, 309, 317, 349
"Light-Winged Smoke, Icarian Bird" (Thoreau) **30**:192, 205, 208-09, 211, 216, 221, 235, 257, 267, 294
"Like a Bird on the Wire" (Cohen) **109**:82
"Like a Bulwark" (Moore) **49**:112, 129, 136
Like a Bulwark (Moore) **4**:257; **49**:125, 133, 136
"Like a Message on Sunday" (Dorn) **115**:54, 110, 125
"Like a Rolling Stone" (Dylan) **37**:50, 56, 62-3, 65, 70
"Like a Sitting Breeze" (Viereck) **27**:267-68, 283
"Like a Slight Sound" (Cernuda) **62**:171
"Like Africa" (Spark) **72**:245
"Like an Eddy" (Birney) **52**:46, 76, 82
"Like Ankle-rings" (Ekeloef) **23**:87
"Like Decorations in a Nigger Cemetery" (Stevens) **6**:308, 318
"Like Dolmens Round My Childhood, the Old People" (Montague) **106**:276, 285, 292-94, 309, 321, 325, 331-38, 344-45
"Like Father, Like Sun" (Kaufman) **74**:183, 195-96, 262, 271
"Like Ghosts of Eagles" (Francis) **34**:244, 247, 249
Like Ghosts of Eagles (Francis) **34**:244-45
"Like one who in her third widdowhood" (Donne) **43**:108
"Like Rembrandt, martyr of chiaroscuro" (Mandelstam)
See "Kak svetoteni muchenik Rembrandt"
"Like Skin" (Cernuda)
See "Como la piel"
"Like Snow" (Graves) **6**:144, 172
Like Someone Waiting for the Dawn (Cernuda)
See *Como quien espera el alba*
"Like the Inner Wall of a House" (Amichai) **38**:42
"Like the Thistledown" (Aleixandre) **15**:15
"Like the Touch of Rain" (Thomas) **53**:338
"Like, This Is What I Meant" (Baraka) **4**:38; **113**:23, 57
"Like This Together" (Rich) **5**:364, 382
"Like Three Fair Branches from One Root Deriv'd" (Hass) **16**:199
"Like to a Hermite Poore in Place Obscure" (Raleigh) **31**:201, 216, 266, 269-71
"Like Truthles Dreames" (Raleigh) **31**:201, 219, 266, 268, 271, 297
"Likewise" (Hughes) **53**:193
"Lilacs" (Lowell) **13**:64, 67, 84-5, 98-9
"Lilacs" (Schuyler) **88**:175

"Lilacs" (Whitman)
See "When Lilacs Last in the Dooryard Bloom'd"
"Lilacs in New York City" (Doty) **53**:61
"Lilian" (Patmore) **59**:218-19, 239-40
"Lilian" (Tennyson) **6**:359
"The Lilies" (Mickiewicz)
See "Lilje"
"Lilis Park" (Goethe) **5**:246
"Lilje" (Mickiewicz) **38**:151
"The Lillies Break Open over the Dark Water" (Oliver) **75**:342
"The Lilly" (Blake) **12**:34-35; **63**:16, 28, 54-55, 68-71, 73, 75-76, 107
"The Lilly in a Christal" (Herrick) **9**:112-13, 115, 137-38, 144
"The Lily" (Williams) **109**:275
"Lily, Rosemary, and the Jack of Hearts" (Dylan) **37**:54, 56-57
Limadha Tarakta al-Hisana Wahidan (Darwish) **86**:20, 26, 33-34
Limatha Tarakta al-Hissana Waheedan (Darwish)
See *Limadha Tarakta al-Hisana Wahidan*
"Limbes" (Verlaine) **32**:356
Les Limbes (Baudelaire)
See *Les fleurs du mal*
"Limbo" (Brathwaite) **56**:23, 86
"Limbo" (Cernuda) **62**:257
"Limbo" (Coleridge) **11**:52, 85
"Limbo" (Graves) **6**:166
"Limbo" (Heaney) **100**:203, 205
"The Limbo Dancer" (Jacobsen) **62**:320
The Lime Orchard Woman (Ríos) **57**:323, 325-26
"Lime Trees in Winter, Retouched" (McGuckian) **27**:102-104
Lime-Tree Bower (Coleridge)
See *This Lime-Tree Bower My Prison*
"The Limit" (Aleixandre) **15**:6
"Limitation of Perfection" (Tagore)
See "Purner abhav"
"Limitations" (Sassoon) **12**:245
"Limited" (Sandburg) **2**:312; **41**:236, 239, 254, 314, 321
"Limited Access" (Hugo) **68**:236
"Limites" (Borges) **32**:58
"Límites y espejo" (Aleixandre) **15**:42-3
"Limits" (Borges)
See "Limites"
"Limits" (Brathwaite) **56**:7, 29, 85
"Limits" (Okigbo) **7**:241-42
Limits (Okigbo) **7**:223-28, 233-34, 246-48, 250-51
"Limits and mirror" (Aleixandre)
See "Límites y espejo"
Limits and Renewals (Kipling) **91**:134-37
"I limoni" (Montale) **13**:114, 119, 122
"Limosna" (Storni) **33**:242, 313
"The Lincoln Relics" (Kunitz) **19**:175, 178-80
"A Lincolnshire Church" (Betjeman) **75**:37, 95
"A Lincolnshire Tale" (Betjeman) **75**:22, 83
"Lindau" (Montale) **13**:146
"The Linden Branch" (MacLeish) **47**:192-93
"A Line from St. David's" (Thomas) **99**:253
"Line of Work" (Akhmadulina) **43**:45
"The Line Up" (Randall) **86**:289, 338
"Lineage" (Hughes) **7**:159; **89**:216
"Lineage" (Walker) **20**:281
"Linen Town" (Heaney) **18**:202; **100**:197-98, 292, 321
"Liner Notes For the Poetically Unhep" (Hughes) **53**:115
"The Liner She's a Lady" (Kipling) **3**:161; **91**:86
"Lines" (Cowper)
See "Lines Written during a Period of Insanity"
"Lines" (Hardy) **92**:327
"Lines" (Harper) **21**:190, 218
"Lines" (Sainte-Beuve) **110**:20
"Lines" (Williams) **7**:351-52
"Lines about the Unknown Soldier" (Mandelstam)
See "Stikhi o neizvestnom soldate"
"Lines Above Tintern Abbey" (Wordsworth)
See "Lines Composed a Few Miles above Tintern Abbey, on Revisiting the Banks of the Wye during a Tour, July 13, 1798"
"Lines Addressed to Miss Roberts on Her Departure for India" (Hood) **93**:54
"Lines & Circularities" (Nemerov) **24**:288, 301
"Lines Composed a Few Miles above Tintern Abbey, on Revisiting the Banks of the Wye during a Tour, July 13, 1798" (Wordsworth) **4**:373, 387, 391, 409-12, 418-19, 425-26, 428; **67**:247-48, 263, 269, 271, 279, 281-83, 285-87, 294-95, 302-4, 313, 319-22, 324, 329, 343-48, 370
"Lines Composed in Passing through a Forest in Germany" (Smith) **104**:225
"Lines Composed Over Three Thousand Miles from Tintern Abbey" (Collins) **68**:215
"Lines Composed While Climbing the Left Ascent of Drockley Coomb, Somersetshire, May 1795" (Coleridge) **11**:82
"Lines for a Book" (Gunn) **26**:185, 189
"Lines for a Picture of St. Dorothea" (Hopkins) **15**:144
"Lines for a Prologue" (MacLeish) **47**:156, 164, 167
"Lines for Akhmatova" (Kenyon) **57**:15
"Lines for an Album" (Montale)
See "Per album"
"Lines for an Internment" (MacLeish) **47**:145, 190
"Lines for an Ode-Threnody on England" (Brooke) **24**:89
"Lines for an Old Man" (Eliot) **5**:170
"Lines from My Grandfather's Journal" (Cohen) **109**:51, 55
"Lines in a Country Churchyard" (Shelley) **14**:166
"Lines in New England" (Walcott) **46**:322
"Lines Left upon a Seat in a Yew-tree" (Wordsworth) **4**:373, 418; **67**:277, 295, 310, 339, 366, 369-70
"Lines Left upon a Seat in a Yew-Tree, Which Stands near the Lake of Esthwaite, on a Desolate Part of the Shore, Commanding a Beautiful Prospect" (Wordsworth)
See "Lines Left upon a Seat in a Yew-tree"
"Lines Lost Among Trees" (Collins) **68**:209
"Lines on a Fly-Leaf" (Whittier) **93**:176
"Lines on a Young Lady's Photograph Album" (Larkin) **21**:236
"Lines on an Autumnal Evening" (Coleridge) **11**:106
"Lines on Revisiting the Country" (Bryant) **20**:37-8
"Lines on Stirling" (Burns) **114**:91
"Lines on the First Mild Day of March" (Wordsworth) **4**:418
"Lines on the Loss of the Royal George" (Cowper) **40**:44
"Lines on the Mermaid Tavern" (Keats) **96**:268
"Lines on the Portrait of a Celebrated Publisher" (Whittier) **93**:239, 314, 319
"Lines Spoken by the Ghost of John Dennis at the Devil Tavern" (Gray) **80**:136
"Lines Suggested by Reading a State Paper" (Whittier) **93**:266
"Lines to a Don" (Belloc) **24**:11, 29, 38
"Lines to a Favourite Laurel" (Peacock) **87**:334
"Lines to a Lady on Her Departure for India" (Hood) **93**:54
"Lines to a Movement in Mozart's E-Flat Symphony" (Hardy) **8**:114; **92**:255
"Lines to a Nasturtium" (Spencer) **77**:341, 343-44
"The Lines to a Spider" (Hunt) **73**:137
"Lines to Accompany Flowers for Eve" (Kizer) **66**:67
"Lines to Lady Denbigh" (Crashaw)
See "To the Noblest and Best of Ladyes, the Countesse of Denbigh"
"Lines to Miles O'Reilly" (Harper) **21**:197
"Lines to Mr. Henry Vaughan, Silurist, on His Poems" (Philips) **40**:270
"Lines to Myself" (Heaney) **18**:191
"Lines to Olga" (Pound) **95**:167, 171
"Lines to Sour-Faced Gila" (Juana Inés de la Cruz) **24**:176
"Lines to Walpole" (Chatterton) **104**:30-31
"Lines Written" (Corso) **108**:11, 21, 43
"Lines written a few miles above Tintern Abbey" (Wordsworth)
See "Lines Composed a Few Miles above Tintern Abbey, on Revisiting the Banks of the Wye during a Tour, July 13, 1798"
"Lines Written after Detecting in Myself a Yearning toward the Large, Wise, Calm, Richly Resigned, Benignant Act Put on by a Great Many People after Having Passed the Age of Thirty Five" (Bogan) **12**:115
"Lines Written among the Euganean Hills" (Shelley) **14**:171, 177, 235; **67**:228, 231
"Lines Written at a Small Distance from My House" (Wordsworth)
See "Lines Written at a Small Distance from My House, and Sent by My Little Boy to the Person to Whom They Are Addressed"
"Lines Written at a Small Distance from My House, and Sent by My Little Boy to the Person to Whom They Are Addressed" (Wordsworth) **4**:418; **67**:282, 365
"Lines Written at Burnham" (Gray) **80**:136
"Lines Written during a Period of Insanity" (Cowper) **40**:46
"Lines Written in an Asylum" (Carruth) **10**:84, 89
"Lines Written in Anticipation of a London Paper Attaining a Guaranteed Circulation of Ten Million Daily" (Sassoon) **12**:251-52
"Lines Written in Early Spring" (Wordsworth) **4**:418; **67**:277, 279, 282, 301-2, 310, 329
"Lines Written in Kensington Gardens" (Arnold) **5**:19, 35, 49
"Lines Written in Ridicule of Thomas Warton's Poems" (Johnson) **81**:244
"Lines Written in the Blue Ridge" (Tuckerman) **85**:339
"Lines Written in the Highlands after a Visit to Burns's Country" (Keats) **96**:284
"Lines Written in the Library of Congress after the Cleanth Brooks Lecture" (Kumin) **15**:222
"Lines Written near Richmond" (Wordsworth) **67**:247, 295, 369-70
"Lines Written Nov. 22, 23—1963—In Discord" (Corso) **33**:49
"Lines Written on a Seat on the Grand Canal, Dublin" (Kavanagh) **33**:63, 96, 103, 120; **105**:120, 137-38, 179
"Lines Written on a Window at the King's Arms Tavern, Dumfries" (Burns) **114**:21
"Lines, Written on Being Told There Was Too Much of Levity in My Later Writings" (Whittier) **93**:200
"Lines Written on My Nineteenth Birthday" (Owen) **19**:371
"Lines, Written on Reading Several Pamphlets Published by Clergymen Against the Abolition of the Gallows" (Whittier)
See "The Gallows"
"Lines Written on Windows of the Globe Tavern, Dumfries" (Burns) **114**:27
"À l'infini" (Éluard) **38**:84
"The Lingam and the Yoni" (Hope) **56**:287, 304
"Lingard and the Stars" (Robinson) **1**:464
"Lingua" (Pasolini) **17**:272
"Links" (Apollinaire)
See "Liens"

"The Linnet and the Goldfinch" (Leapor) **85**:251
"The Linnet in the Rocky Dells" (Brontë) **8**:68-9
"Linoleum" (Gallagher) **9**:44, 56, 60
"Linterna roja" (Cernuda) **62**:200, 230
"The Lion" (Belloc) **24**:24
"Lion" (Wright) **14**:346
"Lion & Honeycomb" (Nemerov) **24**:262
"The Lion and the Lamb" (Wylie) **23**:309, 324
"The Lion and the Mouse" (Henryson) **65**:7, 13-14, 21, 23, 29, 31, 34-35, 55, 59, 61-64, 79-80
"The Lion and the Rose" (Sarton) **39**:321, 323-24, 340
The Lion and the Rose (Sarton) **39**:318, 321-22, 331, 335-37, 339-40, 342-43, 353, 356-59
"The Lion in Love" (Moore) **4**:261
Lion, Lion (Raworth) **107**:309, 316
"Lion Under Maples" (Jacobsen) **62**:326, 330
"Lions" (Borges) **32**:66
"The Lions" (Hayden) **6**:194, 197
The Lion's Tail and Eyes: Poems Written Out of Laziness and Silence (Bly) **39**:13, 73-4
"Lip" (Cunningham) **92**:166, 169
"Liquid Metal Fast Breeder Reactor" (Snyder) **21**:293
Lirici greci (Quasimodo) **47**:293, 295-98
"Lis" (Cummings) **5**:100
"Lisa" (Eliot) **20**:102
"Lisa May" (Dunbar) **5**:137
"Lisbon Revisited, 1923" (Pessoa) **20**:158, 169
Lisettes (Béranger) **112**:17
"Listen" (Nash) **21**:274
"Listen" (Tapahonso) **65**:224
"Listen Carefully" (Levine) **22**:234
"listen children" (Clifton) **17**:26
"Listen Here Blues" (Hughes) **1**:270
"Listen, Lord—A Prayer" (Johnson) **24**:144, 164
"Listen. This Is the Noise of Myth" (Boland) **58**:20, 48
"Listen to the Mustn'ts" (Silverstein) **49**:339
"Listenen to Big Black at S.F. State" (Sanchez) **9**:225
"The Listeners" (de la Mare) **77**:62, 99-103, 105, 108-9, 116, 135-36, 148
The Listeners, and Other Poems (de la Mare) **77**:59-60, 70-74, 80, 82, 84, 94, 142
"Listening" (Lawrence) **54**:244
"Listening" (Stafford) **71**:258, 265, 269, 280, 290, 377
Listening Deep (Stafford) **71**:334, 337
"Listening to a Cricket in the Wainscoting" (Bly) **39**:53, 69
"Listening to Bach" (Bly) **39**:43, 71
"Listening to Foxhounds" (Dickey) **40**:175, 182, 185
"Listening to Music of Arsenio Rodríquez is Moving Closer to Knowledge" (Cruz) **37**:12
"Listening to Presiden Kennedy Lie about the Cuban Invasion" (Bly) **39**:12
"Listening to the Mourners" (Wright) **36**:400
Le lit la table (Éluard) **38**:74
"The Litanie" (Donne) **1**:136-39, 147, 150; **43**:112-14, 134, 164
"Les litanies de satan" (Baudelaire) **1**:45, 71; **106**:96-97, 123, 125, 128
"The Litanies of Satan" (Baudelaire)
See "Les litanies de satan"
"Litany" (Ashbery) **26**:131-135, 140-143, 145, 156, 169-170, 172
"Litany" (Collins) **68**:212
"Litany" (Sandburg)
See "The Long Shadow of Lincoln: A Litany"
"Litany for Dictatorships" (Benét) **64**:6-7, 9, 13-14, 25
"A Litany for Survival" (Lorde) **12**:137
"A Litany of Friends" (Randall) **86**:291, 301, 324, 349
A Litany of Friends: New and Selected Poems (Randall) **86**:285, 287, 289, 291, 301, 324, 333, 342-48
"The Litany of the Dark People" (Cullen) **20**:57, 75
"The Litany of the Heroes" (Lindsay) **23**:266, 272, 285, 295
"Literary Adventures" (Kavanagh) **33**:96
"Literary Critic" (Chappell) **105**:50-51
"A Literary Discovery" (Betjeman) **75**:17, 20
"The Literary Life" (Hughes) **89**:162, 273
"Literary Statement On Struggle!" (Baraka) **4**:30
The Literary Works of Matthew Prior (Prior) **102**:306-16, 318-20
"The Literate Farmer and the Planet Venus" (Frost) **1**:210; **39**:233
"Literature" (Chappell) **105**:39
"The Lithuanian" (Lermontov)
See "Litvinka"
"Lithuanian Dance Band" (Ashbery) **26**:145
"Lithuanian Nocturne" (Brodsky) **9**:22-4, 27
"Litovskii noktyurn" (Brodsky)
See "Lithuanian Nocturne"
"Little Abigail and the Beautiful Pony" (Silverstein) **49**:312, 332
"Little Aster" (Benn) **35**:54
"The Little Beauty That I Was Allowed" (Wylie) **23**:314
"A Little Bit of a Tumbler" (Stein) **18**:321, 334, 353
"The Little Black Boy" (Blake) **12**:7-8; **63**:6, 9, 11-13, 15, 53, 59, 68, 80-81, 103, 114, 119-21, 125-27, 129
"The Little Black Door on the Left" (Corso) **108**:16
"Little Blond Head of Hair" (Cernuda)
See "Pequeña cabellera rubia"
"The Little Blue Engine" (Silverstein) **49**:312
A Little Book on the Human Shadow (Bly) **39**:85
"The Little Box of Olinalá" (Mistral)
See "La cajita de Olinalá"
"Little Boy and Lost Shoe" (Warren) **37**:306
"The Little Boy and the Old Man" (Silverstein) **49**:308, 313, 325-26
"The Little Boy Found" (Blake) **12**:7; **63**:7, 11, 102, 121
"A Little Boy Lost" (Blake) **12**:7, 23, 33-5
"Little Boy Lost" (Smith) **12**:321, 325, 332; **63**:7-8, 16, 21, 102, 109-10
"Little Boy Sick" (Smith) **12**:318
"Little Boy Stanton" (García Lorca) **3**:143
"Little Breeches" (Riley) **48**:299
"Little Brown Baby" (Dunbar) **5**:142
"A Little Called Pauline" (Stein) **18**:331
"The Little Canticles of Asturias" (Heaney) **100**:240, 321
"A Little Child Shall Lead Them" (Harper) **21**:187
The Little Children of the Snow (Bryant)
See "The Little People of the Snow"
"Little Clown, My Heart" (Cisneros) **52**:147
"The Little Coat" (Riley) **48**:340
"The Little Coat" (Spender) **71**:211, 228
"A Little Dawn Song for My Companion" (Guillén) **35**:217
"A little demon in wet fur crept in" (Mandelstam)
See "Vlez besenok v mokroi sherstke"
"The Little Dog's Day" (Brooke) **24**:59
"Little Elegy" (Kennedy) **93**:129, 138
"Little Elegy" (O'Hara) **45**:172
"Little Elegy" (Wylie) **23**:314-15
"Little Exercise" (Bishop) **3**:49; **34**:52-53, 130
"Little Fanfare for Felix MacGowan" (Merrill) **28**:253
A Little Fleet (Masefield) **78**:42
"The Little Friend" (Barrett Browning) **6**:14
Little Friend, Little Friend (Jarrell) **41**:137, 139, 146, 178-80, 218
"Little Fugue" (Hughes) **89**:179
"Little Fugue" (Plath) **1**:390; **37**:214, 218-21, 246, 249
"The Little General" (Muir) **49**:289
"The Little Ghost" (Millay) **6**:206; **61**:212
"Little Gidding" (Eliot) **5**:165-67, 169-70, 181-83, 185, 193, 204-05, 208, 210-11; **31**:169
"Little Gidding" (Wilbur) **51**:209
Little Gidding (Eliot) **90**:226, 298, 304, 306
"The Little Girl Found" (Blake) **12**:7, 33-34, 61; **63**:8, 16, 54, 90, 100, 114, 132
"The Little Girl Lost" (Blake)
See "A Little Girl Lost"
"A Little Girl Lost" (Blake) **12**:7, 33-34, 61; **63**:4, 8, 16, 24, 54, 90-91, 95, 100, 102, 105, 110, 114-15, 132
"Little Girl, My String Bean, My Lovely Woman" (Sexton) **2**:363; **79**:192, 228, 230-32, 249
"Little Girl Wakes Early" (Warren) **37**:367, 375
"Little Girls" (Page) **12**:176-77
"The Little Girl's Song" (Dobell) **100**:139
"The Little Good-Fellows" (Melville) **82**:107
"The Little Green Orchard" (de la Mare) **77**:123
"Little Green Sea" (Elytis) **21**:123
"Little Green Tree" (Hughes) **1**:243
Little Henrietta (Reese) **29**:337, 339, 348, 353
"The Little Hill" (Millay) **6**:214, 233
"Little Horse" (Merwin) **45**:98
The Little House of Kolomna (Pushkin)
See *Domik v Kolomne*
"Little Jim" (McKay) **2**:216, 222
"The Little June Book" (Stevens) **6**:332-33
"Little Lamentation" (Traherne) **70**:284
"The Little Land" (Stevenson) **84**:343, 346-47
"The Little Larousse" (Zagajewski) **27**:401
"Little Letter" (Eliot)
See "Petit Epître"
"Little Lion Face" (Swenson) **14**:280
"Little Lobeila's Song" (Bogan) **12**:100-01, 111
"The Little Lost Orphans" (Stafford) **71**:283
"The Little Love" (Wickham) **110**:267
"A Little Love of Life" (Stein) **18**:313
"Little Lyric" (Hughes) **1**:240; **53**:102
"Little Man" (Storni)
See "Hombre pequeñito"
"Little Mandy's Christmas-Tree" (Riley) **48**:302
The Little Mariner (Elytis)
See *O Mikrós naftilos*
"Little Marvel Stove" (Bishop) **34**:91
"Little Mattie" (Barrett Browning) **6**:24
"Little Miss Muffet Sat on a Prophet" (Nash) **21**:265
The Little Old House (Wickham) **110**:260, 275
"The Little Old House" (Wickham) **110**:255, 270
"Little Old Letter" (Hughes) **1**:243
"The Little Old Log Cabin" (Service) **70**:150, 152
"The Little Old Women" (Baudelaire)
See "Les petites vielles"
"The Little Ones" (Soto) **28**:371
"Little Orphant Annie" (Riley) **48**:309, 340
"Little Owl Who Lives in the Orchard" (Oliver) **75**:334
"The Little Passion" (Eliot) **90**:298, 300
"The Little Peasant" (Sexton) **2**:364, 368
"The Little People of the Snow" (Bryant) **20**:15-16
"De Little Pikaninny's Gone to Sleep" (Johnson) **24**:162
"The Little Pins of Memory" (Simic) **69**:300, 309
"Little Poems" (Updike) **90**:352
Little Poems in Prose (Baudelaire)
See *Le spleen de Paris, petits poèmes en prose*
"The Little Portress" (Mew) **107**:3
"The Little Rapids" (Swenson) **14**:262
"Little Red Riding Hood" (Mistral)
See "Caperucita Roja"
"The Little Robber Girl Gets on in the Wide World" (Hacker) **47**:82

The Little Sailor (Elytis)
See *O Mikrós naftilos*
"Little Salamander" (de la Mare) **77**:74
"A Little Scraping" (Jeffers) **17**:117
The Little Seafarer (Elytis)
See *O Mikrós naftilos*
"The Little Serving Maid" (Belloc) **24**:5
"Little Shakespeare in a Bonnet" (Wickham) **110**:283
"Little Sleep's-Head Sprouting Hair in the Moonlight" (Kinnell) **26**:251, 283, 291
"Little Songs for Gaia" (Snyder) **21**:301
"Little Sonnet" (Wylie) **23**:332
"The Little Straw" (Mistral)
See "La pajita"
"Little Summer Poem Touching the Subject of Faith" (Oliver) **75**:330
"Little T. C." (Marvell)
See "The Picture of Little T. C. in a Prospect of Flowers"
"A Little Testament" (Montale)
See "Piccolo testamento"
The Little That Is All (Ciardi) **69**:25, 31, 50, 53
"The Little Tower" (Morris) **55**:299, 302
"The Little Town" (Hall) **70**:32
"The Little Town o' Tailholt" (Riley) **48**:329, 332, 334
"Little Tree" (Cummings) **5**:93
"A Little Uncomplicated Hymn" (Sexton) **2**:363; **79**:227-28, 284
"The Little Utopia" (Graham) **59**:166
"The Little Vagabond" (Blake) **12**:7; **63**:108
"A Little While" (Teasdale) **31**:340, 359
"The Little White Rose" (MacDiarmid) **9**:154, 176, 186
"Little Word, Little White Bird" (Sandburg) **41**:309
"Little Words" (Parker) **28**:363
"Little Worker" (Mistral)
See "Obrerito"
"Littleblood" (Hughes) **7**:153, 168-69
"Littoral" (Brathwaite) **56**:69, 74
Liturgies intimes (Verlaine) **2**:417-18
"Litvinka" (Lermontov) **18**:300
"Liubliu moroznoe dykhan'e" (Mandelstam) **14**:154
"Live" (Sexton) **2**:351, 364; **79**:189, 196, 229, 232, 269
Live Another Day (Ciardi) **69**:3-4, 6, 24-25, 27, 29-31, 33, 36, 49
"Live Niggers—Stop Bullshitting" (Baraka) **4**:18
"Live Oak" (Whitman) **91**:314
Live or Die (Sexton) **2**:349, 351, 356, 362-65; **79**:187, 190, 192, 196, 204, 212, 222, 227-29, 231-32, 234, 248-49, 310, 315, 337
Live Songs (Cohen) **109**:35
"The lively sparks that issue from those eyes" (Wyatt) **27**:357
"Liverpool, 1890" (Masefield) **78**:101
"Liverpool, 1930" (Masefield) **78**:102
"Lives" (Mahon) **60**:139, 150, 155, 178, 193, 195
"Lives" (Rimbaud)
See "Vies"
"Lives" (Rukeyser) **12**:207, 217, 228
Lives (Mahon) **60**:132-34, 138, 140-41, 144, 154, 183, 200-201, 203
Lives of X (Ciardi) **69**:31, 33-34, 47, 49, 51, 53-55
"The Livid Lightnings Flashed in the Clouds" (Crane) **80**:79
"Living" (Guillén) **35**:221
"Living" (Levertov) **11**:186
"Living by the Red River" (Wright) **36**:355
"Living Earth" (Toomer) **7**:336-37
"The Living God" (Very) **86**:114, 158
"Living in Sin" (Rich) **5**:351, 369
"Living in the City" (Ignatow) **34**:305
"Living in the Country" (Kavanagh) **33**:87
"Living in the Country: I" (Kavanagh) **33**:102
"Living in the Country: II" (Kavanagh) **33**:120
"Living in the Moment" (Hacker) **47**:104
"Living in the Mountain on an Autumn Night" (Wang Wei) **18**:391
"Living in the Open" (Piercy) **29**:310
Living in the Open (Piercy) **29**:304, 310-11
"Living Near the Water" (Song) **21**:345-46
"Living Off the Land" (Wagoner) **33**:352
"Living on Sin" (Clarke) **112**:62, 80
"Living on the Plains" (Stafford) **71**:375
"A Living Pearl" (Rexroth) **20**:186-87, 216, 218; **95**:250, 260, 273
Living Room (Jordan) **38**:123, 127
"The Living Temple" (Holmes) **71**:63, 118
"The Living Values" (Spender) **71**:224
"Living with Chris" (Berrigan) **103**:6
"LIVING WITH TH VISHYUN" (Bissett) **14**:34
living with th vishyun (Bissett) **14**:16-17
Living without Being Alive (Cernuda)
See *Vivir sin estar viviendo*
"Livingshayes" (Davie) **29**:115
Le livre de la mutacion de fortune (Christine de Pizan) **68**:3, 34, 37, 57, 59-63, 68, 73-77, 81-83, 87-88, 104, 106-7, 111, 114, 119, 121-22, 138, 145, 160-65, 170-75, 178
Livre d'amour (Sainte-Beuve) **110**:43-49, 51, 54-56
Le Livre de l'Espurgatorie (Marie de France)
See *L'Espurgatoire Saint Patrice*
"Le livre des morts" (Jaccottet) **98**:147, 177, 179-84
Le Livre des Trois jugemens (Christine de Pizan) **68**:3, 23-24, 37, 98, 139, 142, 144, 148-50, 153, 172
Le livre du chemin de long estude (Christine de Pizan) **68**:3, 26, 61, 77, 138, 178
Le livre du duc des vrais amans (Christine de Pizan) **68**:4, 9, 21-22, 35-36, 83, 96, 98-99, 145, 151, 153, 179, 181-82, 187, 192
Le livre ouvert, 1938-1940 (Éluard) **38**:63, 74
"Le livre, pour vieillir" (Bonnefoy) **58**:118-19, 167-68
Le livret de folastries à Janot Parisien (Ronsard) **105**:272, 279-85, 326-28, 331-32
"Lix" (Brathwaite) **56**:51
"LIX" (Carman) **34**:224-25
"A Liz Town Humorist" (Riley) **48**:288
"The Lizard" (Hardy) **92**:322
"Lladrata Merch" (Dafydd ap Gwilym) **56**:232
Llanto por Ignacio Sánchez Mejías (García Lorca) **3**:121-22, 124, 126, 128
"Llegada" (Guillén) **23**:99, 105-106
"Llewellyn and the Tree" (Robinson) **1**:462, 468
"Llovizna" (Storni) **33**:239, 261
"La lluvia lenta" (Mistral) **32**:144, 179
"Llychwino Pryd y Ferch" (Dafydd ap Gwilym) **56**:232
"Lo! A Child Is Born" (MacDiarmid) **9**:178-79
"Lo lo lógico" (Fuertes) **27**:22
"El lo sabe" (Fuertes) **27**:15
"Lo These Are Parts of His Ways" (Curnow) **48**:21
"Lo What It is to Love" (Wyatt) **27**:317, 346
"The Load of Sugar-Cane" (Stevens) **6**:293
"Loam" (Sandburg) **41**:242, 297, 339
"Loan Exhibit" (Francis) **34**:250
"The Loaning" (Heaney) **100**:205
"Lob" (Thomas) **53**:267, 301-4, 332, 349
"Lobster" (Sexton) **79**:240
"Local Complainer" (Clarke) **112**:55
"Localities" (Sandburg) **41**:240
"Locas letanías" (Mistral) **32**:159, 161, 181
"Le Locataire" (Jaccottet) **98**:174
The Location of Things (Guest) **55**:183, 196, 207-8, 210, 225
"Loch Derg" (Kavanagh)
See *See "Lough Derg"*
"Loch Torridon" (Swinburne) **24**:313
"lock lied" (Enzensberger) **28**:138-39
"Lockerbie Fair" (Riley) **48**:326
"Lockerbie Street" (Riley) **48**:292, 326
"The Locket" (Montague) **106**:289, 292, 294, 355
"The Lockless Door" (Frost) **1**:218
"Locks" (Bukowski) **18**:15
"Locks" (Koch) **80**:318
"Locksley Hall" (Auden) **92**:110
"Locksley Hall" (Tennyson) **6**:354, 357, 359-60, 363; **101**:130, 141-42, 161, 281
"Locus" (Hayden) **6**:189, 194, 196
"The Locust Tree in Flower" (Williams) **7**:363; **109**:283, 286-87
"The Locusts" (Merrill) **28**:231, 243
"Locutions des Pierrots, I" (Laforgue) **14**:81
"Locutions des Pierrots XIV" (Laforgue) **14**:89
"The Lode" (Dickey) **40**:228, 236
"The Lodger" (Carman) **34**:212
"The Lodger" (Hughes) **89**:161
"The Lodging-House Fuchsias" (Hardy) **92**:328
"Loe when backe mine eyes" (Campion) **87**:55-56, 66
"Lofty in the Palais de Danse" (Gunn) **26**:220
"A Lofty Sky" (Thomas) **53**:287
"Log" (Merrill) **28**:221-2, 256
Logbook I (Seferis) **66**:90, 92, 94, 142, 165-66, 177, 200, 206-7, 209-10
Logbook II (Seferis) **66**:90, 92, 94-95, 164, 177-79, 207, 210
Logbook III (Seferis) **66**:90, 152, 164, 177, 179, 194-95, 206, 211-12
"Logging 2" (Larkin) **21**:322
"Logic and 'The Magic Flute'" (Moore) **49**:126, 130-31, 134, 139, 145, 161
"Logical Appointments; or Giving the People What They Want by Way of Giving Them What They Deserve" (Dorn) **115**:200
Logical Consequences/Succession (Brossard)
See *Suite logique*
"Logos" (Hughes) **7**:120, 159; **89**:101, 103, 155
"Logos" (Muir) **49**:237-38
"Logos Logos Logos" (Corso) **108**:6, 22
"Lohengrin" (Cavafy) **36**:53
"Loi de formation du progrès" (Hugo) **17**:100
"Loin Cloth" (Sandburg) **2**:329
Loin de nos cendres (Char) **56**:189
"Loin des oiseaux" (Rimbaud) **3**:274
"Loin du pigeonnier" (Apollinaire) **7**:18, 21, 23
"Loisaida" (Cruz) **37**:31
"Les loisirs de la poste" (Mallarmé) **102**:29, 97
"Loitering with a Vacant Eye" (Housman) **2**:193
Lola (Dorn)
See *Yellow Lola*
Lollingdon Downs, and Other Poems (Masefield) **78**:12-13, 35, 44, 55, 62-63, 72, 91
"Lollocks" (Graves) **6**:137, 142, 144
"London" (Jarrell) **41**:127
"London" (Johnson)
See "London: A Poem, In Imitation of the Third Satire of Juvenal"
"London" (Pinsky) **27**:150
London (Blake) **12**:7, 25, 34; **63**:18, 29, 38, 44-49, 52, 54, 68, 84, 92-95, 102, 105, 108-9, 115, 119-20, 134
"London: A Poem, In Imitation of the Third Satire of Juvenal" (Johnson) **81**:72, 85, 87, 90, 108-11, 115, 119-23, 138, 147, 152-54, 157, 163-65, 169-70, 172-76, 178, 227-34, 236, 238-39
"London Bridge" (Robinson) **1**:466, 468
"London, hast thou accused me" (Surrey) **59**:306-10
"London Rain" (MacNeice) **61**:138
"London Snow" (Bridges) **28**:51, 61, 70, 83
"London Town" (Masefield) **78**:56
"Lone Founts" (Melville) **82**:76, 148
"The Lone Ranger" (Hall) **70**:31
"The Lone Trail" (Service) **70**:115, 148
"Loneliness" (Betjeman) **75**:35, 92, 97
"Loneliness" (Whittier) **93**:195

Loneliness (Paz)
See *Soledad*
"Lonely" (Wright) **36**:395-96
"A Lonely Character" (Hagiwara)
See "Sabishii jinkaku"
"Lonely Love" (Blunden) **66**:22-23, 27
"Lonely Particular" (Walker) **30**:339
"The Lonely Street" (Williams) **7**:362
"Lonesome" (Dunbar) **5**:119
"Lonesome Valley" (Brown) **55**:143-44
"Long Afternoons" (Zagajewski) **27**:395
"Long Ages Past" (Owen) **19**:351
"Long Ago" (Cavafy) **36**:75
Long Ago and A Short While Ago (Verlaine)
See *Jadis et naguère*
Long Ago and Not So Long Ago (Verlaine)
See *Jadis et naguère*
"The Long Alley" (Roethke) **15**:248, 254
Long and Short Poems (Shvarts)
See *Stikhotvoreniia i poemy*
"Long and Sluggish Lines" (Stevens) **110**:230
The Long Approach (Kumin) **15**:214, 221
"The Long Death" (Piercy) **29**:311
"Long Distance" (Stafford) **71**:299
Long Division: A Tribal History (Rose) **13**:232
"A Long Dress" (Stein) **18**:349
"The Long Drive" (Masefield) **78**:62
"The Long Garden" (Kavanagh) **33**:81, 152, 154, 160-1; **105**:99, 104, 150
"Long Gone" (Brown) **55**:89, 108, 110-11, 174
"The Long Hill" (Teasdale) **31**:323, 334, 336
"The Long Home" (Berryman) **64**:89
"Long Hot Summer" (MacLeish) **47**:197
"The Long Hunter" (Berry) **28**:38
"Long John Brown & Little Mary Bell" (Blake) **12**:35
"Long John Nelson and Sweetie Pie" (Walker) **20**:286
Long Live Man (Corso) **33**:15, 34-8, 44, 48-9; **108**:3-5, 8-9, 16-18, 20-23, 25, 31, 34, 38, 41
"Long Live the Cordillera of the Andes / Death to the Cordillera of the Coast!" (Parra)
See "Viva la cordillera de los Andes / Muera la cordillera de la Costa!"
"The long love" (Wyatt)
See "The longe love that in my thought doth harbour"
"Long Nose" (Stern) **115**:249
"Long Past Moncada" (Rukeyser) **12**:231-32
"The Long River" (Hall) **70**:55
The Long Road of Learning (Christine de Pizan)
See *Le livre du chemin de long estude*
"Long Screams" (Hughes) **7**:150
"Long Shadow at Dulce" (Momaday) **25**:219
"The Long Shadow of Lincoln: A Litany" (Sandburg) **2**:334; **41**:301-2
"The Long Small Room" (Thomas) **53**:285-86, 329
"A Long Story" (Gray) **2**:143, 152-53; **80**:121-23
"A Long Time" (Guillén) **35**:218
"Long To'ds Night" (Dunbar) **5**:147
"Long Track Blues" (Brown) **55**:80, 95-96, 114, 177
"The Long Trail" (Kipling) **91**:82
"The Long Tunnel Ceiling" (Hughes) **7**:148; **89**:122
"The Long Vacation in London" (Davenant) **99**:177-78
"Long walk" (Borges)
See "Caminata"
"The Long Waters" (Roethke) **15**:310, 316-17
"A Long Way" (Ungaretti) **57**:359
"The longe love" (Wyatt)
See "The longe love that in my thought doth harbour"
"The longe love that in my thought doth harbour" (Wyatt) **27**:340, 355, 358
Longer Poems (Rexroth)
See *The Collected Longer Poems*
Longer Poems: Third World Express/Come and Hope with Me (Serote) **113**:286
"Longing" (Arnold) **5**:42-3
"Longing" (Brutus) **24**:114
"The Longing" (Roethke) **15**:272, 274, 310, 312-15
"Longing" (Teasdale) **31**:325
Longing (Ishikawa)
See *Akogare*
"Longing for Heaven" (Bradstreet) **10**:27, 30, 42
"Longing for Lermontov" (Akhmadulina) **43**:52
A Longing for the Light: Selected Poems of Vicente Aleixandre (Aleixandre) **15**:24
"Longing Is Like the Seed" (Dickinson) **1**:111
"Longings" (Cavafy) **36**:66, 73, 76
"Long-Legged Fly" (Yeats) **20**:315
Longshot Poems for Broke Players (Bukowski) **18**:3-4
Longshot Pomes for Brave Players (Bukowski) **18**:5
"The Look" (Olds) **22**:342
"Look!" (Smith) **12**:342
"The Look" (Teasdale) **31**:332, 334, 337-38
"Look at Us Play with Our Meat" (Stern) **115**:248
"Look Back" (Snyder) **21**:300
"Look Deep" (Hecht) **70**:108
"Look Down from the High Terrace Seeing Off Reminder Li" (Wang Wei) **18**:370
"Look for You Yesterday, Here You Come Today" (Baraka) **4**:14-15; **113**:5, 96, 138, 148
"Look Hart That Horse You Ride Is Wood" (Viereck) **27**:284
"Look Home" (Southwell) **83**:281, 286, 336-37
"The Look of the Hedge" (Reese) **29**:334
"Look on This Picture and on This" (Rossetti) **7**:277
"A Look Returned" (Stafford) **71**:264
"Look Stranger, at This Island Now" (Auden) **92**:62
"Look, Stranger, on This Island Now" (Auden) **1**:7-8, 12, 22, 30
Look! We Have Come Through! (Lawrence) **54**:169-70, 175, 182-83, 186, 189, 197-98, 207, 212-13, 232, 237, 240, 244
"Look What You Did, Christopher!" (Nash) **21**:275
"Look You, I'll Go Pray" (Lindsay) **23**:281
"Looking across the Fields and Watching the Birds Fly" (Stevens) **110**:229-31
"Looking at a Map" (Abse) **41**:13
"Looking at a Picture on an Anniversary" (Hardy) **8**:137-38
"Looking at My Father" (Olds) **22**:321
"Looking at Pictures to be Put Away" (Snyder) **21**:287
"Looking at Sheep" (Thomas) **99**:253
"Looking at Some Flowers" (Bly) **39**:21
"Looking at Stars" (Kenyon) **57**:35
"Looking at the Fall" (Ní Chuilleanáin) **34**:350
"Looking Backwards" (Vaughan) **81**:340
"Looking Book" (Merwin) **45**:48
Looking for Luck (Kumin) **15**:213, 216, 221, 223-24
"Looking for Luck in Bangkok" (Kumin) **15**:214
"Looking for Mushrooms at Sunrise" (Merwin) **45**:21, 26, 87
"Looking for Nothing" (Snyder) **21**:310
"Looking for th Lammas" (Bissett) **14**:7
"Looking for the Buckhead Boys" (Dickey) **40**:166, 200, 220
"Looking for Work" (Carver) **54**:19
"Looking Forward" (Rossetti) **7**:277
"Looking Forward" (Stevenson) **84**:315, 348
"Looking Forward to See Jane Real Soon" (Schuyler) **88**:215
"Looking from Oregon" (Birney) **52**:42
"Looking Glass" (Gunn) **26**:206, 218
"Looking Glass" (Thomas) **99**:282
"Looking in a Mirror" (Atwood) **8**:32, 38
"Looking into History" (Wilbur) **51**:227, 229, 266-67
"Looking Out" (Yamada) **44**:344-45
"Looking Up at the Top of a Blue Tree" (Hagiwara) **18**:177
"The Looking-Glass Dictionary" (Szirtes) **51**:173
"Looking-Glass River" (Stevenson) **84**:316, 348
"Look-Out Mountain. The Night Fight" (Melville) **82**:133
"The Loom" (Masters) **1**:333
The Loon (Bly) **39**:45, 67, 69-71
"loon about to laugh" (Birney) **52**:33, 83
"The Loon's Cry" (Nemerov) **24**:257, 292-93, 295, 299-300
"Loons Mating" (Wagoner) **33**:361
"The Loop" (Masters) **1**:329; **36**:175-76
"Loop" (Ondaatje) **28**:331
The Loop in Lone Kauri Road: Poems: 1983-85 (Curnow) **48**:21, 32
"The Loose Box" (Heaney) **100**:242-43, 324-25, 327
"A Loose Gown" (Ignatow) **34**:328
"A Loose Mountain Telescopic" (Frost) **39**:233
"A Loose Saraband" (Lovelace) **69**:168, 179, 198, 228
Loose Woman (Cisneros) **52**:146-47, 151, 156
"The Loosening" (Eberhart) **76**:54
"Loot" (Kipling) **3**:160, 163, 174, 187
Lord Byron: The Complete Poetical Works (Byron) **95**:8, 22-23, 29
"Lord Forgive a Spirit" (Stern) **115**:269
"Lord I Owe Thee a Death" (Meynell) **112**:177
"The Lord in the Air" (Dickey) **40**:200
"Lord Lundy" (Belloc) **24**:18
"Lord of Elbë, on Elbë Hill" (Brontë) **8**:73
The Lord of the Isles (Scott) **13**:277, 281, 288, 294, 296, 304, 311-12, 318, 321
Lord Weary's Castle (Lowell) **3**:200, 202-03, 206-07, 211-12, 216-18, 224, 230-33
The Lords of Misrule: Poems, 1992-2001 (Kennedy) **93**:150, 152
"Lord's Prayer" (Lawrence) **54**:250
"The Lord's Prayer" (Meynell) **112**:177, 217-18, 223
"Lord's Prayer" (Parra)
See "Padre nuestro"
"Lore" (Stafford) **71**:288
"Lorelei" (Plath) **1**:388-89; **37**:179-82, 238, 241
"L'lorloge de demain" (Apollinaire) **7**:32
"Lorna" (Zanzotto) **65**:274
"The Los Cities" (Cardenal)
See "Las ciudades perdidas"
"De los periódicos" (Fuertes) **27**:12
"The Loser" (Stryk) **27**:201
"Losing a Language" (Merwin) **45**:93
"The Losing of the Child" (Tennyson) **101**:248-49
"Losing Track" (Levertov) **11**:160, 169
"Loss" (H. D.) **5**:303
"Loss" (Jarrell) **41**:139, 174
"Loss" (Stone) **53**:229
"Loss in Delays" (Southwell) **83**:281, 327
"Loss, of Perhaps Love, in Our World of Contingency" (Warren) **37**:309, 333
"Loss of Sounds" (Jacobsen) **62**:323
"The Loss of Strength" (Clarke) **112**:31, 39, 55, 90, 122, 124
"The Loss of the Eurydice" (Hopkins) **15**:147, 162
"The Loss of The Nabara" (Day Lewis)
See "The Nabara"
"The Losse" (Finch) **21**:146, 179
"Losses" (Jarrell) **41**:144, 188, 195, 202, 218
"Losses" (Sandburg) **41**:313
Losses (Jarrell) **41**:136-39, 146, 178-79
"Lost" (Bukowski) **18**:24
"Lost" (Sandburg) **2**:303; **41**:225, 238, 244, 267, 285, 318, 350, 364

"Lost" (Spender) **71**:160
"The Lost" (Very) **86**:93, 115
"Lost and Found" (Levine) **22**:224
"Lost and Found" (Mueller) **33**:192-93
"The Lost Angel" (Levine) **22**:213
lost angel mining company (Bissett) **14**:6-7, 9, 17, 19
Lost Body (Césaire)
See *Corps perdu*
"The Lost Bower" (Barrett Browning) **6**:7
"Lost Box" (Yau) **61**:330
"The Lost Boy" (Holmes) **71**:124
"Lost Child" (Wright) **14**:349, 352
"The Lost Children" (Jarrell) **41**:186, 217-18
"The Lost Children" (Oliver) **75**:299
"Lost Christmas" (Thomas) **99**:272
"Lost Commagene" (Elytis) **21**:135
Lost Copper (Rose) **13**:235, 237-38, 240
"The Lost Dancer" (Toomer) **7**:336
"Lost Days" (Rossetti) **44**:174
"The Lost Federation" (Walcott) **46**:234, 274
"The Lost Girls" (Hogan) **35**:256
"Lost Gnostic Poem" (Melville)
See "Fragments of a Lost Gnostic Poem"
"The Lost Heifer" (Clarke) **112**:85, 101
"Lost Horizon" (Ashbery) **26**:127
"Lost in Heaven" (Frost) **39**:233
Lost in the Bonewheel Factory (Komunyakaa) **51**:29, 33, 35, 49
"Lost in Translation" (Merrill) **28**:227, 232, 242, 260, 269
"The Lost Ingredient" (Sexton) **2**:350, 359
"The Lost Kiss" (Riley) **48**:297
"The Lost Land" (Boland) **58**:38, 50
"The Lost Land" (Muir) **49**:287
The Lost Land (Boland) **58**:38, 40, 47-48, 50-51, 65
"The Lost Lilies" (Brooke) **24**:81
"Lost Love" (Graves) **6**:129
"Lost Love" (Hardy) **92**:235
"The Lost Love" (Jarrell) **41**:168
"The Lost Man" (Wright) **14**:339, 346
"The Lost Mistress" (Browning) **2**:38
"The Lost Money" (Szirtes) **51**:178
"Lost My Voice? Of Course" (Walker) **30**:339, 341
"The Lost Occasion" (Whittier) **93**:177
"The Lost Pyx" (Hardy) **92**:273
"Lost Sheep" (Storni)
See "Oveja descarriada"
"Lost Sister" (Song) **21**:331-32, 343, 350
"The Lost Son" (Roethke) **15**:248, 250, 255, 262-63, 267-68, 270, 272, 275-76, 278, 284, 298-99, 301-02
The Lost Son, and Other Poems (Roethke) **15**:246-50, 260, 282-83, 290-91, 296-97, 304, 308-09
"A Lost Tradition" (Montague) **106**:310
"The Lost Wife" (Benét) **64**:8
"The Lost Wine" (Valéry)
See "Le vin perdu"
"The Lost World" (Jarrell) **41**:169, 177, 189, 217-18
The Lost World (Jarrell) **41**:142, 156, 162, 181, 206, 211, 217
"Lot and His Daughters" (Hope) **56**:271, 285
"A Lot of Night Music" (Hecht) **70**:96
"The Lotos-Eaters" (Tennyson) **6**:352, 358-60, 409-12; **101**:121, 124, 127, 130, 141-43, 226, 251, 281
"Lots: I" (Cervantes) **35**:106
"Lots: II" (Cervantes) **35**:106
"Lots II: Herself" (Cervantes) **35**:123
"Lot's Wife" (Hecht) **70**:108
"Lot's Wife" (Nemerov) **24**:255
"Lot's Wife 1988" (Clifton) **17**:29
Lotto-Poems (Cassian) **17**:6
"Lotus and Frost" (Lawrence) **54**:175
"The Lotus and the Rose" (Lindsay) **23**:292
"Loud Posters" (Das) **43**:85
"Louenge a la court" (Villon) **13**:394-95
"The louer lamentes the deth of his loue" (Wyatt) **27**:340
"Lough Derg" (Kavanagh) **105**:169, 172
Lough Derg (Kavanagh) **33**:121, 158, 167, 169-71; **105**:114, 155
"A Lough Neagh Sequence" (Heaney) **18**:201; **100**:212, 243, 349
"Louis Curel de la Sorgue" (Char) **56**:155, 157, 171
"Louis MacNeice" (Spender) **71**:246
"Louise" (O'Hara) **45**:155
"Le loup criait" (Rimbaud) **57**:250
"Love" (Boland) **58**:19, 49
"Love" (Brooke) **24**:85
"Love" (Char)
See "L'amour"
"Love" (Coleridge) **39**:180; **67**:288
"Love" (Collins) **68**:213, 226
"Love" (Cowley) **90**:15
"Love" (Creeley) **73**:111-12
"Love" (Das) **43**:85, 90
"Love" (Hagiwara)
See "Airen"
"Love" (Herbert) **4**:100, 114
"Love" (Thoreau) **30**:258, 272-73
"Love" (Traherne) **70**:190, 192, 194, 204, 259, 275-76, 317
Love (Verlaine)
See *Amour*
"Love" (Very) **86**:46, 58, 151
Love: A Building on Fire (Byrne) **46**:279
"Love, a Greeting" (Montague) **106**:298
Love, A Poem, in Three Parts. To Which Is Added, The Giaour, A Satirical Poem (Elliott) **96**:181
"Love a woman? You're an ass!" (Wilmot) **66**:270, 306-9, 311, 344
"Love Again" (Larkin) **21**:259
"Love America" (Neruda) **64**:328, 330
"Love among the Ruins" (Browning) **2**:88; **61**:88
"Love and Death" (Barker) **77**:17
"Love and Death" (Leopardi)
See "Amore e Morte"
"Love and Debt Alike Troublesome" (Suckling) **30**:127, 161
"Love and Duty" (Tennyson) **101**:243, 251
Love and Fame (Berryman) **64**:74, 76-77, 79-80, 88, 92-95, 97-103, 115, 118-19, 130, 152, 154, 161, 165, 168, 170-71
"Love & Fame & Death" (Bukowski) **18**:5
"Love and Friendship" (Brontë) **8**:51
"Love and Harmony Combine" (Blake) **12**:32
"Love and Honour" (Belloc) **24**:29
"Love and Liberty" (Burns) **114**:10, 12, 14-15, 38, 75-76, 117, 161
"Love and Life" (Wilmot) **66**:286, 324
"Love and Money" (Stone) **53**:224
"Love and Music" (Guillén) **35**:219
"The Love and the Hate" (Jeffers) **17**:136
"Love and the Times" (Davie) **29**:110
Love and War, Art and God (Shapiro) **25**:318, 322
"Love Arm'd" (Behn) **13**:4, 7, 15, 23-5; **88**:148-149, 152
Love as Love (Jackson) **44**:59
"Love at First Sight" (Szymborska)
See "Milosc od pierwszego wejrzenia"
"Love Calls Us to the Things of This World" (Wilbur) **51**:188, 197, 210-11, 213-14, 217, 244, 248, 257-59, 261, 267-68, 272, 299, 302, 314, 323-24
"Love Came Back at Fall of Dew" (Reese) **29**:333
"Love Comes Quietly" (Creeley) **73**:6-7, 33
Love, Death, and the Changing of the Seasons (Hacker) **47**:83, 85-88, 90-92, 96-97, 100, 108
"Love Despoiled" (Dunbar) **5**:125
"Love 8" (Spicer)
See "Love VIII"
Love Elegies (Donne)
See *Elegies*
"A Love for Four Voices" (Hecht) **70**:80, 92
"The Love for October" (Merwin) **45**:88
"Love Fossil" (Olds) **22**:310, 317
"Love from the North" (Rossetti) **7**:260, 278, 280, 289
"Love Fulfilled" (Morris) **55**:340
"The Love Gift" (Masefield) **78**:46-47, 51, 62
"Love Given Over" (Cowley) **90**:13-14
"Love in a Life" (Browning) **61**:88
"Love in a Meadow" (Kavanagh) **33**:104; **105**:164
"Love in a Valley" (Betjeman) **75**:20, 81
"Love in America?" (Moore) **49**:149
"Love in Barrenness" (Graves) **6**:172
"Love in Blood Time" (Olds) **22**:316
"Love in Exile" (Howe) **81**:49
"Love in Fantastic Triumph Sat" (Behn)
See "Love Arm'd"
"Love in Idleness" (Patmore) **59**:233
"Love in Its Separate Being" (Jarrell) **41**:127
"Love in Moonlight" (Glück) **16**:169
"Love in the Museum" (Rich) **5**:393
Love in the Turning Year: One Hundred More Poems from the Chinese (Rexroth) **95**:251
"Love in the Valley" (Meredith) **60**:243-44, 246, 250, 254-55, 259, 263, 293, 295, 328
"Love Is" (Swenson) **14**:283
"Love Is a Deep and a Dark and a Lonely" (Sandburg) **41**:303
Love Is a Dog From Hell (Bukowski) **18**:19
"Love Is a Piece of Paper Torn to Bits" (Bukowski) **18**:6
"Love Is an Art of Time" (Rexroth) **95**:281
"Love is Enough" (Morris) **55**:259-60
Love Is Enough (Morris) **55**:273-74, 276-78, 329-33, 337-39, 343
"Love is More Thicker than Forget" (Cummings) **5**:108
"Love is the Only God" (Cummings) **5**:107
"Love Joy" (Herbert) **4**:122-23, 125
"Love Justified" (Patmore) **59**:228, 232
"Love Lamp" (Snodgrass) **74**:334
"A Love Letter" (Dunbar) **5**:147
"Love Letter" (Meredith) **28**:170-71, 185
"Love Letter" (Schnackenberg) **45**:337
"A Love Letter" (Wickham) **110**:267, 310
Love Letter from an Impossible Land (Meredith) **28**:170, 172, 177, 182-87, 194, 209-10, 216
"Love Letter From an Impossible Lane" (Meredith) **28**:190
"Love Letter Postmarked Van Beethoven" (Wakoski) **15**:326, 331
"Love Letter Written in a Burning Building" (Sexton) **79**:246
"Love Lies Sleeping" (Bishop) **34**:119-20
Love, Like Pronouns (Waldrop) **109**:175, 180, 187
"Love Me!" (Smith) **12**:346
"Love Me" (Teasdale) **31**:338
"Love me or not" (Campion) **87**:97
"Love Medicine" (Erdrich) **52**:176, 184
"The Love Nut" (Ferlinghetti) **1**:187
"The Love of Alcestis" (Morris) **55**:310
"The Love of Christ which Passeth Knowledge" (Rossetti) **7**:268, 290
"A Love of Death" (Pinsky) **27**:154
"LOVE OF LIFE, the 49th parallel" (Bissett) **14**:7, 10, 18
"The Love of Narcissus" (Meynell) **112**:192, 229, 295
"Love of the Puppets" (Wilbur) **51**:188, 289-90
"The Love of Two Seasons" (Corso) **33**:25
"The Love of Windows" (Szirtes) **51**:169
"Love on my hear from heaven fell" (Bridges) **28**:59
"Love on the Farm" (Lawrence) **54**:221, 236-37
"Love Passes Beyond the Incredible Hawk of Innocence" (Wakoski) **15**:351
"The Love Plant" (Sexton) **79**:241
"Love Poem" (Barker) **77**:3
"Love Poem" (Glück) **16**:150

"Love Poem" (Lorde) **12**:158
"Love Poem" (Page) **12**:177
"Love Poem" (Raworth) **107**:324
"Love Poem" (Stryk) **27**:197, 203
"Love Poem For Real" (Giovanni) **19**:126
"Love Poem for the Forty-Second Street Library" (Ignatow) **34**:287, 335
"Love Poems" (Spicer) **78**:337-39, 341
Love Poems (Barker) **77**:9
Love Poems (Sanchez) **9**:207, 212, 216, 218-21, 227, 229, 234, 237, 242
Love Poems (Sexton) **2**:349, 351-53, 355, 364-65; **79**:205, 228, 231-33, 241, 245, 249-50
Love Poems, and Others (Lawrence) **54**:161-62, 174, 236, 240
The Love Poems of Marichiko (Rexroth) **20**:203, 218; **95**:281-84
The Love Poems of May Swenson (Swenson) **14**:274-75, 280, 283-84
"Love, Reason, Hate" (Suckling) **30**:119-20
Love Respelt (Graves) **6**:154, 156
"Love Reveng'd" (Behn) **88**:150
"Love II" (Spicer) **78**:274
"Love Sex and Romance" (Wakoski) **15**:357
"Love Song" (Amichai) **38**:46
"Love Song" (Eliot)
See "The Love Song of J. Alfred Prufrock"
"Love Song" (Levertov) **11**:159, 171
"Love Song" (Randall) **86**:338
"Love Song" (Sexton) **2**:363
"Love Song" (Williams) **7**:345, 406-07
"Love Song" (Wylie) **23**:314
"Love Song from the Gaelic" (Yeats) **20**:345-46
"A Love Song in the Modern Taste" (Swift) **9**:252, 268
"The Love Song of J. Alfred Prufrock" (Eliot) **5**:153-54, 157, 160, 206; **31**:91-198; **90**:239, 304, 326, 328
"Love Song of Prufrock Junior" (Viereck) **27**:264
"The Love Song of St. Sebastian" (Eliot) **90**:286, 298, 301, 329
"Love Song to Eohippus" (Viereck) **27**:280
Love Songs (Dorn)
See *Twenty-Four Love Songs*
Love Songs (Loy) **16**:310, 314-15, 320-21, 323, 325-26, 328
Love Songs (Teasdale) **31**:322, 324, 330-31, 337, 339,-40, 347, 355, 369-70, 388
"Love Songs I" (Loy) **16**:306
"Love Songs in Age" (Larkin) **21**:229, 258
Love Songs to Joannes (Loy) **16**:316, 332
"Love Songs VI" (Loy) **16**:307
"Love Sorrow" (Hafiz) **116**:15-16
"Love Story" (Dalton) **36**:136
"A Love Story" (Graves) **6**:129, 133, 136-37, 144, 163, 172
"Love III" (Herbert) **4**:121
"Love III" (Spicer) **78**:274
"Love the Butcher Bird Lurks Everywhere" (Stafford) **71**:293
"Love Thy Neighbour" (Lawrence) **54**:249
"Love to a Woman" (Wilmot) **66**:355, 362, 365-68
"The Love Tree" (Cullen) **20**:85
"Love Turn'd to Hatred" (Suckling) **30**:146
"Love Undiscovered" (Cowley) **90**:14
"Love Unknown" (Herbert) **4**:109, 112, 123, 129
"Love VII" (Spicer) **78**:274
"Love VIII" (Spicer) **78**:274
"Love whets the dullest wittes" (Campion) **87**:62
"The love which is imprinted in my soule" (Sidney) **32**:250
"Love Winter When the Plant Says Nothing" (Merton) **10**:334
"Love without Hope" (Graves) **6**:141, 144, 149-50
Love You (Randall) **86**:286, 289, 333
"Love You Right Back" (Brooks) **7**:94
"The Love-Letters" (Patmore) **59**:230, 234, 258
"Loveliest of Trees" (Housman) **2**:184-85, 192, 194-95; **43**:261
"Lovely Chance" (Teasdale) **31**:358
"Lovely Flowers and White as Became Him Well" (Cavafy) **36**:81
"Lovely Ladies" (Tu Fu) **9**:330
"The Lovely Lady" (Tu Fu) **9**:322
"A Lovely Love" (Brooks) **7**:81, 96, 100-01
"Lovely White Flowers" (Cavafy) **36**:75, 76, 79, 80-81
Love-Poems (Ovid)
See *Amores*
"The Lover" (Borges)
See "El enamorado"
"The Lover" (Creeley) **73**:36-37
"The Lover" (Douglas) **106**:207
"The Lover" (Montagu) **16**:337
"The Lover After All" (Cohen) **109**:25
"The Lover hopeth of better chance" (Wyatt) **27**:338
"The lover lamentes the death of his love" (Wyatt)
See "The louer lamentes the deth of his loue"
"The Lover of a Subversive is Also a Subversive" (Espada) **74**:138
"The Lover of Love" (Hagiwara)
See "Koi wo koi suru hito"
"The Lover Pleads with His Friend for Old Friends" (Yeats) **20**:330
"The Lover Seweth how He is Forsaken of Fortune who Sometime Favoured Him" (Wyatt) **27**:309
"A Lover since Childhood" (Graves) **6**:129
"The Lover Tells of the Rose in His Heart" (Morris) **55**:284
"The Lover Tells of the Rose in His Heart" (Yeats) **20**:338
"The Lover Urges the Better Thrift" (Meynell) **112**:164
"Lovers" (Cohen) **109**:92
"The Lovers" (Graham) **59**:132, 173
"The Lovers" (Jacobsen) **62**:277-78
"The Lovers" (Merrill) **28**:239, 243
"A Lover's Affliction" (Dafydd ap Gwilym)
See "Cystudd Cariad"
A Lover's Complaint (Shakespeare) **84**:255; **101**:1-116
"Lovers' Death" (Baudelaire)
See "La mort des amants"
"The lovers Elesium, Or Fools Paradice: a dream" (Barker) **91**:5-7, 44
"Lovers infinitenesse" (Donne) **1**:130, 153
"The Lover's Journey" (Crabbe) **97**:75, 95, 102
"The Lovers of Gudrun" (Morris) **55**:245, 250, 259-60, 262, 285, 307, 309, 329, 332
"Lovers of the Poor" (Brooks) **7**:86, 88, 96
"A Lovers' Quarrel" (Browning) **61**:88
"The Lover's Secret" (Holmes) **71**:94
"The Lover's Song" (Yeats) **20**:308
"The Lover's Tale" (Tennyson) **6**:358, 373-74, 379-80; **101**:217, 237
The Lover's Watch (Behn)
See *La Montre; or, The Lover's Watch*
The Lover's Watch: Or, the Art of Making Love (Behn)
See *La Montre; or, The Lover's Watch*
"Loves Alchymie" (Donne) **1**:147, 159; **43**:125, 130, 132, 183
"Love's Apology" (Patmore) **59**:219, 240
"Love's Causes" (Barrett Browning) **6**:17
"Love's Clock" (Suckling) **30**:162
"Loves Deitie" (Donne) **43**:174
"Love's Deity" (Cowley) **90**:112-13
"Love's Diet" (Donne) **1**:127; **43**:128
"Love's Draft" (Dunbar) **5**:126
"Love's Expression" (Barrett Browning) **6**:17
"Love's Farewell" (Brontë) **8**:57
"Loves Fire" (Behn)
See "To Lysander, who made some Verses on a Discourse of Loves Fire"
"Love's Garden Grief" (Southwell) **83**:279-80
"Love's Gleaning Tide" (Morris) **55**:340
"Loves Growth" (Donne) **1**:153; **43**:129, 182
"Loves Invalides" (Thoreau) **30**:245
"Love's Loneliness" (Yeats) **20**:333
"Love's Map" (Justice) **64**:267
"Love's New Creation" (Barrett Browning) **6**:17
"Love's Nocturn" (Rossetti) **44**:257-60
"Love's Nocturne" (Rossetti) **44**:257-60
"Love's Obstacles" (Barrett Browning) **6**:16
"The Loves of the Plants" (Noyes) **27**:129
"Love's Parable" (Warren) **37**:286, 288, 322, 332
"Love's Philosophy" (Shelley) **14**:167
"Love's Power" (Behn) **88**:87
"Loves Progress" (Donne) **43**:129, 191-92, 194-98, 201-3
"Love's Progress" (Roethke) **15**:289
"Love's Refuge" (Barrett Browning) **6**:17
"Love's Repetitions" (Barrett Browning) **6**:17
"Love's Reward" (Morris) **55**:340
"Love's Riddle" (Cowley) **90**:4
"Loves Riddles" (Donne) **1**:153
"Love's Sacrifice" (Barrett Browning) **6**:17
"Love's Servile Lot" (Southwell) **83**:279
"Loves Siege" (Suckling) **30**:145
"Love's Tears" (Dafydd ap Gwilym)
See "Dagrau Serch"
"Love's Trappist" (Chesterton) **28**:95
"Love's Triumph" (Cowley) **90**:117
"Love's Visibility" (Cowley) **90**:117
"Love's World" (Suckling) **30**:118, 142
Lovesick (Stern) **115**:255-56, 260-65, 271
"Love-Sick" (Vaughan) **81**:367
"The Lovesick Monk" (Cohen) **109**:101
"(Lovesong.)" (Celan)
See "(Liebeslied.)"
"Lovesong" (Hughes) **89**:142-44, 209
"The Love-Song of a Leprechaun" (Noyes) **27**:136
"Love-Sweetness" (Rossetti) **44**:166
Lovhers (Brossard)
See *Amantes*
"Loving a Noble Girl" (Dafydd ap Gwilym)
See "Caru Merch Fonheddig"
Loving a Woman in Two Worlds (Bly) **39**:74, 84, 98, 100-04
"Loving an Honest Man" (Piercy) **29**:309
"Loving and Beloved" (Suckling) **30**:140, 146
"Loving him secretly" (Char)
See "L'amoureuse en secret"
"The Loving Shepherdess" (Jeffers) **17**:110, 131
"Loving the Killer" (Sexton) **2**:352-53; **79**:241, 245
"Low Barometer" (Bridges) **28**:77
"Low down" (Brown) **55**:150
"The Low Sky" (Jeffers) **17**:117
"Low Tide" (Carman)
See "Low Tide on Grand Pré"
"Low Tide" (Millay) **6**:236
"Low Tide at Grand Pré" (Carman)
See "Low Tide on Grand Pré"
"Low Tide at Schoodic" (Clampitt) **19**:86, 90
"Low Tide on Avon" (Carman) **34**:236
"Low Tide on Grand Pré" (Carman) **34**:203-05, 210, 214, 235-37
Low Tide on Grand Pré: A Book of Lyrics (Carman) **34**:198, 205, 208, 210, 212, 214-15, 217-18, 224, 235, 237-38
"Low to High" (Hughes) **1**:258, 267
"Low-anchored Cloud" (Thoreau) **30**:190, 194, 207, 216
"A Lowden Sabbath Morn" (Stevenson) **84**:301, 330
"The Lower East Side of Manhattan" (Cruz) **37**:31
"Lower Field—Enniscorthy" (Olson) **19**:293
"The Lowest Place" (Rossetti) **7**:274, 291
"The Lowest Room" (Rossetti)
See "The Lowest Place"
"The Lowestoft Boat" (Kipling) **3**:183
"A Loyal Mother" (Hughes) **89**:196, 199
Les Loyaux Adversaires (Char) **56**:186

"A Lu Mountain Song for the Palace Censor Empty-Boat Lu" (Li Po) **29**:156
"Lub O' Mine" (McKay) **2**:221
"Lucas XXIII" (Borges) **32**:48
"Lucasia" (Philips) **40**:295
"Lucasta" (Lovelace)
See "To Lucasta: Going to the Warres"
Lucasta: Epodes, Odes, Sonnets, Songs, & c. To Which Is Added Aramantha, A Pastorall (Lovelace) **69**:155, 157, 159, 164, 186, 195-96, 198-99, 203, 206, 208, 212, 234, 236, 251
"Lucasta: Going to the Warres" (Lovelace) **69**:239
Lucasta: Posthume Poems of Richard Lovelace, Esq. (Lovelace) **69**:155, 158, 196, 198-99, 209, 219, 231-32, 234, 236, 238
"Lucasta, Taking the Waters at Tunbridge" (Lovelace) **69**:159
"Lucasta's Fan, with a Looking-Glass in It" (Lovelace) **69**:197
"Lucasta's World" (Lovelace) **69**:225
"Lucca" (Ungaretti) **57**:347
"Lucien Létinois" (Verlaine) **2**:416
"Lucifer" (Lawrence) **54**:218
"Lucifer in Starlight" (Meredith) **60**:253, 262, 295, 326, 335-36, 338-40
"Lucifer in the Train" (Rich) **5**:354, 362, 393
"lucifer speaks in his own voice" (Clifton) **17**:37
"lucifer understanding at last" (Clifton) **17**:30
"Lucifer's Feast" (Noyes) **27**:122
"Lucina Schynning in Silence of the Nicht ..." (Ní Chuilleanáin) **34**:348
"Lucinda Matlock" (Masters) **36**:183, 185
"Luck" (Carver) **54**:31
"Lucknow" (Whittier)
See "The Pipes of Lucknow"
"Lucks my fair falcon and your fellows all" (Wyatt) **27**:367
The Lucky Bag (MacDiarmid) **9**:158
"The Lucky Coin" (Clarke) **112**:36, 47, 49
Lucky Life (Stern) **115**:246, 248-49, 251, 253-54, 258, 261-64, 269-70, 277, 281-82, 285
"Lucky Life" (Stern) **115**:253, 283
"Lucrece" (Gower) **59**:55, 58, 60-61
Lucrece (Shakespeare)
See *The Rape of Lucrece*
"Lucrece and Nara" (Jackson) **44**:29, 62-3
"Lucretius" (Tennyson) **6**:358, 360, 378, 380; **101**:119, 123, 225
"Lucretius, III, 1053-1076" (Rexroth) **95**:260
"Lucretius versus the Lake Poets" (Frost) **71**:9
"Luctus in Morte Infantis" (Barker) **77**:5, 29
"lucy and her girls" (Clifton) **17**:13
"Lucy Gray" (Coleridge) **11**:73-4
"Lucy Gray" (Wordsworth) **4**:398, 404, 428
"Ludzie na moście" (Szymborska) **44**:313, 315
Ludzie na moscie (Szymborska) **44**:274, 279, 293
Lueurs des tirs (Apollinaire) **7**:22
"Lufis Inconstance" (Dunbar) **67**:25
"Lugar da Lázaro" (Guillén) **35**:215
"Luis Cernuda 1902-1963" (Paz) **48**:184
"Luis de Baviera escucha Lohengrin" (Cernuda) **62**:173, 270
"Luke Havergal" (Robinson) **1**:467, 475, 490-94
"Luke 2. *Quœrit* Jesum *Suum* Maria" (Crashaw)
See " *Quœrit* Jesum"
"Luke 11. Blessed be the Paps which Thou hast sucked" (Crashaw)
See "Blessed be the Paps"
"The Lull" (Hecht) **70**:65, 79, 86
"Lull" (Roethke) **15**:246-50, 282
"Lull" (Wagoner) **33**:367
"Lull (November, 1939)" (Roethke) **15**:250
"Lullaby" (Dunbar) **5**:122
"Lullaby" (Glück) **16**:170
"Lullaby" (Goodison)
See "A Lullaby for Jean Rhys"
"The Lullaby" (Jackson) **44**:5
"A Lullaby" (Jarrell) **41**:200
"Lullaby" (de la Mare) **77**:112
"Lullaby" (Sexton) **2**:359
"Lullaby" (Sitwell) **3**:309, 311, 326
"Lullaby" (Stone) **53**:221
"Lullaby" (Yeats) **20**:328
"Lullaby" (Zagajewski) **27**:389
"A Lullaby for Jean Rhys" (Goodison) **36**:143, 154
"Lullaby for Jumbo" (Sitwell) **3**:303
"The Lullaby of Broadway" (Szirtes) **51**:178
"The Lullaby of Charles V" (Carducci)
See "Nina Nanna di Carlo V"
Lullay Lullay like a Child (Skelton) **25**:345
"Lully" (de la Mare) **77**:112
"Lulu Gay" (Stevens) **110**:90
"Lulu Morose" (Stevens) **110**:90
"Lumb Chimneys" (Hughes) **89**:150-51
"Lumber Yard Pools at Sunset" (Sandburg) **41**:322
"Lumb's Remains" (Hughes) **89**:129
"The Lumens" (Olds) **22**:340
"La lumière, changée" (Bonnefoy) **58**:118-19
"La Lumière du soir" (Bonnefoy) **58**:167-68
"Luminol" (Das) **43**:85
"Lumuba's Grave" (Hughes) **53**:111
"La luna" (Borges) **22**:100; **32**:42, 74, 132
"Luna bez golovy" (Shvarts) **50**:161
Luna de enfrente (Borges) **22**:71-2, 93-4; **32**:37-8, 57, 60, 83-4, 95, 124
"Luna de marzo sobre el mar" (Storni) **33**:239, 269, 271
"Luna do utra" (Akhmadulina) **43**:19, 41
"Luna Habitabilis" (Gray) **2**:155
"Luna llena" (Alurista) **34**:28
Luna silvestre (Paz) **1**:367; **48**:176, 243
"Luna v Taruse" (Akhmadulina) **43**:17, 36-37, 43
"Lunar Baedecker" (Loy) **16**:306-08, 321
Lunar Baedecker (Loy) **16**:306, 310, 316, 321-22, 330
Lunar Baedecker and Time-tables (Loy) **16**:306, 316
"The Lunar Cycle" (Piercy) **29**:311
The Lunar Cycle (Piercy) **29**:300, 303
"The Lunar Probe" (Kumin) **15**:180
"Lunch" (Koch) **80**:318
"Lunch" (Stein) **18**:328
"The Lunch Hour FYI" (O'Hara) **45**:170
"Lunch in the Sun" (Mistral)
See "Almuerzo al sol"
Lunch Poems (O'Hara) **45**:116, 132, 135, 145, 214, 216, 218-19
"Lunch with Buns" (Duncan) **75**:175
"Lundi rue Christine" (Apollinaire) **7**:18, 36
"Lune de miel" (Eliot) **5**:185, 191
"La lune est sterile" (Laforgue) **14**:61
"Lune ot revnivtsa" (Akhmadulina) **43**:37
Lupercal (Hughes) **7**:115, 118-20, 123, 135-38, 140-41, 150, 158, 162-63, 165, 169; **89**:101-2, 109, 114, 130, 137-40, 150, 155, 163-64, 210, 221
"Lupercalia" (Hughes) **89**:139
"The Lure" (Montague) **106**:261, 335, 345
"The Lure of Little Voices" (Service) **70**:115
Lusiad (Camões)
See *Os Lusíadas*
Os Lusíadas (Camões) **31**:5-15, 17-21, 24, 26-29, 31-32, 34-40, 43-51, 53-54, 56-62, 64-70, 72-84,
The Lusiads (Camões)
See *Os Lusíadas*
"Lust" (Brooke) **24**:53, 56, 85
"Lustra" (Okigbo) **7**:221, 225, 232, 239, 250
Lustra (Pound) **4**:320, 365; **95**:95-96, 121, 123, 131, 214
"Lusts" (Verlaine)
See "Luxures"
"The Lute and the Lyre" (Carducci)
See "Il Liuto e la Lira"
"Lute Music" (Rexroth) **95**:260
"Luto" (Mistral) **32**:170
"Lux" (Hugo) **17**:54
"Luxures" (Verlaine) **2**:416
"La Luz del día" (Parra) **39**:294
"Luz natal" (Guillén) **35**:174, 229
"La luz sobre el monte" (Guillén) **35**:158
"LVIII" (Carman) **34**:228
"LXI" (Storni) **33**:287, 290
"LXVII" (Carman) **34**:210
"LXVII" (Storni) **33**:287
"LXVIII" (Carman) **34**:211
"LXXIX" (Carman) **34**:210
"LXXXIV" (Carman) **34**:211
"Lycambes Talks to John" (Tate) **50**:319
"Lyceia" (Graves) **6**:156
"Lycidas" (Arnold) **5**:7
"Lycidas" (Hall) **70**:9
"Lycidas" (Milton) **19**:193, 202, 211-13, 217, 219-26, 242, 250-53; **29**:212, 214, 241, 243, 272
Lycidas (Milton)
See "Lycidas"
Lycidus; or, The Lover in Fashion (Behn) **88**:69, 71-75, 103-6, 110, 125
"Lycus the Centaur" (Hood) **93**:42, 55, 57-58, 64, 67-68, 74, 76-77, 79, 117
"Lydia" (Smith) **104**:167, 224
"Lydia Is Gone This Many a Year" (Reese) **29**:333, 347
"Lyell's Hypothesis Again" (Rexroth) **20**:216, 218; **95**:259, 272, 333
"Lying" (Wilbur) **51**:249, 311, 315, 335
"Lying in a Hammock at William Duffy's Farm in Pine Island, Minnesota" (Wright) **36**:283, 285, 300, 309, 326, 339-40, 350, 352, 364, 374, 396
"Lying Spying" (Jackson) **44**:5
"Lynch I" (Césaire) **25**:30
"The Lynching" (McKay) **2**:205-06, 212, 217
"Lynching Song" (Hughes) **1**:241; **53**:114
"Lyndon Libre" (Ai) **72**:14-15
"Lyon" (Melville) **82**:132
"Lyonnesse" (Plath) **37**:208
"The Lyoun and the Mous" (Henryson)
See "The Lion and the Mouse"
"La Lyre" (Ronsard) **11**:266; **105**:189-91, 213
Lyres (Ponge)
See *Le Grand Recueil*
"A Lyric" (Carman) **34**:202, 208
"The Lyric" (Howe) **81**:8
"The Lyric Beasts" (Dickey) **40**:228
"Lyric Intermezzo" (Heine)
See *Lyrisches Intermezzo*
"Lyric LIII" (Carman) **34**:227
"Lyric LIV" (Carman) **34**:211, 227, 233
"Lyric LXIII" (Carman) **34**:226
"Lyric V" (Carman) **34**:227
"Lyric VI" (Carman) **34**:227
"Lyric XXXIX" (Carman) **34**:228
"The Lyric Year" (Darío)
See "El año lírico"
Lyrical Ballads (Coleridge) **11**:37, 59-60, 68, 91; **39**:169, 182; **67**:245-374
Lyrical Ballads (Wordsworth) **4**:372-73, 375, 378, 380, 400, 412, 415-19, 425-29; **67**:245-374
Lyrical Ballads, with a Few Other Poems (Coleridge) **100**:19-22, 31, 38, 41, 57, 74, 85
Lyrical Campaigns: Selected Poems (Jordan) **38**:126
"Lyrical intermezzo" (Heine)
See "Lyrisches Intermezzo"
"Lyrical Letter to Another Woman" (Storni)
See "Carta lírica a otra mujer"
Lyrical Poems (de la Mare) **77**:59
"A Lyrick to Mirth" (Herrick) **9**:94, 103
Lyrics, 1962-1985 (Dylan) **37**:59-65
Lyrics of a Lowbrow (Service) **70**:134, 140-41, 161
Lyrics of Life and Love (Braithwaite) **52**:106, 110, 122

Lyrics of Love and Laughter (Dunbar) **5**:119, 139
Lyrics of Lowly Life (Dunbar) **5**:117-18, 132, 136, 140
"Lyrisches Intermezzo" (Heine) **25**:131
Lyrisches Intermezzo (Heine) **25**:130-31, 139, 141, 143, 161
"Lyrisches Intermezzo No 10" (Heine) **25**:142
"Lyrisches Intermezzo No 39" (Heine) **25**:144
"Lyrisches Intermezzo No.33" (Heine) **25**:142
"Lysander...Loves Fire (Behn)
See "To Lysander, who made some Verses on a Discourse of Loves Fire"
"Lysergic Acid" (Ginsberg) **4**:74, 81
"Lyubil i ya v bylye gody" (Lermontov) **18**:293
"Lyubka" (Pasternak) **6**:253-54
"M AA l'anti-philosophe" (Tzara) **27**:235
"A M Alphonse de Lamartine" (Hugo) **17**:75, 90
"M Anti-psychologue" (Tzara) **27**:235
"M Antipyrine" (Tzara) **27**:235
"M Antitête" (Tzara) **27**:235
"M. Crashaw's Answer for Hope" (Crashaw) **84**:10
"A M de Chateaubriand" (Hugo) **17**:90
M: Writings, '67-'72 (Cage) **58**:195, 205-7, 217-19
"Ma bohème" (Rimbaud) **3**:271, 276, 283; **57**:173, 178, 191, 196, 202, 208-9, 253
"Ma Man" (Hughes) **1**:270
Ma Muse (Sainte-Beuve) **110**:39
"Ma Rainey" (Brown) **55**:72, 76, 90, 94, 102, 113-14, 142, 145, 151-52, 154, 178-79
"Ma Vocation" (Béranger) **112**:21
"Mabel Martin, a Harvest Idyll" (Whittier) **93**:227, 239
"Mablethorpe" (Tennyson) **101**:230
"Macarius and the Pony" (Merton) **10**:351
"Macaw" (Bogan) **12**:86
Macchu Picchu (Neruda)
See *Alturas de Macchu Picchu*
MacFlecknoe; or, A Satire upon the Trew-Blew-Protestant Poet, T. S. (Dryden) **25**:70, 114-16, 118, 120-23
"Machine" (Ciardi) **69**:56
"The Machine Gun" (Jarrell) **41**:213
"Macho" (Cervantes) **35**:134
"Machu Picchu" (Birney) **52**:15-16, 45, 57, 96, 98
"Mackinnon's Boat" (Tomlinson) **17**:344
"MacMoransbridge" (Ní Chuilleanáin) **34**:354
"Macpherson's Farewell" (Burns) **6**:55
"MacStatesman and Co." (MacDiarmid) **9**:176
"Mad As the Mist and the Snow" (Yeats) **20**:328-29
"The Mad Druggist" (Warren) **37**:350
"The Mad Farmer Manifesto: The First Amendment" (Berry) **28**:13
"Mad Gardener's Song" (Carroll) **74**:108
"Mad Judy" (Hardy) **8**:102
Mad Love (Harjo)
See *In Mad Love and War*
"The Mad Maid's Song" (Herrick) **9**:87
"The Mad Monk" (Coleridge) **11**:69
"The Mad Mother" (Wordsworth) **4**:374, 380; **67**:277, 282, 300, 304, 368-69
"A Mad Negro Soldier Confined at Munich" (Lowell) **3**:205, 218, 222
"The Mad Prince" (de la Mare) **77**:73
"The Mad Scene" (Merrill) **28**:254
"Mad Song" (Blake) **12**:31-32; **63**:101
"Mad Song" (Wickham) **110**:264
"Mad Yak" (Corso) **33**:25, 40-41; **108**:33
"Madagascar" (Davenant) **99**:170, 177-78, 216, 218-19, 221-22, 224-26
Madagascar; With Other Poems (Davenant) **99**:174-75, 190-93, 217
"Madam and Her Might-Have Been" (Hughes) **1**:243
"Madam and the Army" (Hughes) **53**:115
"Madam and the Movies" (Hughes) **53**:115
"Madam and the Wrong Visitor" (Hughes) **1**:243
"Madam, Your Man Said Thai wald Ryd" (Dunbar) **67**:4, 128
"Madame de Soubise" (Vigny) **26**:410-11
"Madame Decrepitude" (Cassian) **17**:13
"Madame, il est donc vrai" (Sainte-Beuve) **110**:65, 68
"Madame La Fleurie" (Stevens) **110**:95, 185
"Madame, Man to God's image..." (Donne) **43**:131
"A Madame Sand" (Nerval) **13**:178
"Madame Withouten Many Wordes" (Wyatt) **27**:316, 328, 330
"Madame, Ye Heff a Dangerous Dog" (Dunbar) **67**:4, 8
"Madcaps" (Melville) **82**:154, 156
"Das Mädchen spricht" (Goethe) **5**:249
"Made Sober" (Spender) **71**:216
"Madeleine" (Apollinaire) **7**:32
"Madeleine in Church" (Mew) **107**:6-8, 12, 16-18, 30, 35, 39, 41, 52, 56, 58, 64
"Mademoiselle Bistouri" (Baudelaire) **1**:58; **106**:90
"A Mademoiselle Louise B" (Hugo) **17**:93
"Mademoiselle Veronique" (Brodsky) **9**:10
"Madhouse Cells" (Browning) **2**:26, 30
"Madhumanjari" (Tagore) **8**:416
"Madih al-Zill al-'Ali" (Darwish) **86**:20
"The Madison Experience" (Jordan) **38**:126
"Madison in the Mid-Sixties" (Stone) **53**:243
The Madman, His Parables and Poems (Gibran) **9**:69, 71, 75, 77-80, 82
"Madman's Song" (Wylie) **23**:301, 309, 326, 328
"Madness" (Baraka) **4**:27; **113**:20
"Madness" (Dickey) **40**:176, 183-84, 199-200, 244, 246
"The Madness of King Goll" (Yeats) **20**:344, 354
Madoc (Southey) **111**:190, 212-18, 220, 225, 239-42, 244-46, 253, 259-61, 279
"Madoc in Aztlan" (Southey) **111**:217-19
"Madoc in Wales" (Southey) **111**:217
"A Madona Poesía" (Storni) **33**:257, 262, 285, 294
"Madonna" (Kinsella) **69**:138-39, 141
"Madonna" (Sexton) **79**:193
"The Madonna" (Tennyson) **6**:353
Madonna and Other Poems (Kinsella) **69**:134, 138, 143, 145-46
"Madonna of the Evening Flowers" (Lowell) **13**:60, 64, 67, 96
"La madre" (Carducci) **46**:32, 49, 64-65
"La madre granada" (Mistral) **32**:179-80
"Madre Sofia" (Ríos) **57**:312
"La madre triste" (Mistral) **32**:201
"Madre Tumba Soledad" (Alurista) **34**:28, 47
"Madrid 1937" (Neruda) **4**:310
"Madrigal" (Nemerov) **24**:256
"Madrigal triste" (Baudelaire) **1**:61
"Madrigali privati" (Montale) **13**:106, 167
"Madrugada" (Fuertes) **27**:7
"Madurai" (Paz) **1**:361
"The Madwoman's Miracle" (Wylie) **23**:321
"Maenad" (Plath) **37**:243
Maeoniae (Southwell) **83**:253
"La maestra rural" (Mistral) **32**:208
"Le maestrine" (Pavese) **13**:221
"Mag" (Sandburg) **41**:272-73, 334, 364
"Magadalena" (Gautier) **18**:163-64
"Magasins du Louvre" (Loy) **16**:312, 328
Magazine Verse (Spicer)
See *Book of Magazine Verse*
The Magdalene Sermon (Ní Chuilleanáin) **34**:350, 352, 354, 360-62, 373, 380, 382
The Magdalene Sermon and Earlier Poems (Ní Chuilleanáin) **34**:360
"The Magellanic Clouds" (Wakoski) **15**:325, 363
The Magellanic Clouds (Wakoski) **15**:350-51, 363, 365-66
"The Magellanic Heart" (Neruda)
See "El corazón magellanico"
"Les mages" (Hugo) **17**:83, 87
"Maggie, a Lady" (Rossetti) **7**:291
"Maggiolata" (Carducci)
See "Idillio di Maggio"
"The Magi" (Glück) **16**:125, 140, 149
"Magian Wine" (Melville) **82**:75, 148
"Magias parciales del Quijote" (Borges) **32**:60
"Magic" (Dove) **6**:113
"Magic" (Levertov) **11**:209
"Magic" (Spicer) **78**:242
"Magic Carpet" (Silverstein) **49**:332
"Magic Carpet" (Montague) **106**:356
Magic City (Komunyakaa) **51**:21-22, 29, 31-34, 56, 58
"The Magic Flute" (Carman) **34**:208
"Magic Fox" (Welch) **62**:337, 339, 346, 359, 367, 370
"Magic Island" (Song) **21**:344
The Magic Lantern (Tsvetaeva)
See *Volshebny fonar*
"TH MAGIC LURE OF SEA SHELLS" (Bissett) **14**:34
"The Magic Morning" (Smith) **12**:331
"Magic Psalm" (Ginsberg) **47**:22
"The Magical" (Eberhart) **76**:11
"Magical Dangers" (Hughes) **89**:141
"Magician" (Shapiro) **25**:309
The Magician (Abse) **41**:3-4
The Magician's Feastletters (Wakoski) **15**:356
"The Magician's Retreat" (Moore) **49**:150, 161
Magique (Césaire) **25**:36
"Magna est Veritas" (Smith) **12**:333
"Magnanimity" (Kinsella) **69**:97
"Magnanimity Baffled" (Melville) **82**:135
"The Magnet" (Sarton) **39**:322
"The Magnet" (Stone) **53**:217
The Magnetic Fields (Breton)
See *Les Champs Magnétiques*
The Magnetic Mountain (Day Lewis) **11**:123-26, 128-30, 135, 138-39, 143-45, 148, 151-52
"Magnetic Water" (Raworth) **107**:333-34
"Magnets" (Cullen) **20**:60
Magnificat (Mallarmé) **102**:53
"The Magnifying Glass" (de la Mare) **77**:111
"Magnitudo parvi" (Hugo) **17**:89
"Le magnolia" (Ponge) **107**:138-39
"Magnolia Flower" (Hughes) **1**:237
"The Magnolia Shadow" (Montale)
See "L'ombra della magnolia"
"Magnolias" (Mueller) **33**:193
"Magnolias in Snow" (Hayden) **6**:194, 196
"The Magpie's Advice" (Dafydd ap Gwilym)
See "Cyngor y Biogen"
The Magpie's Shadow (Winters) **82**:313-14, 316
"Magpie's Song" (Snyder) **21**:297
"Magpiety" (Milosz)
See "Śroczość"
"Magritte Dancing" (Stern) **115**:263
"The Magus" (Dickey) **40**:176, 179
"Mahmound" (Hunt) **73**:137
"Mahomets Gesang" (Goethe) **5**:247
Mahua (Tagore) **8**:415-16
"Mai Village" (Brathwaite) **56**:93
"The Maid Servant at the Inn" (Parker) **28**:353
"The Maiden" (Duncan) **75**:170
"A Maiden" (Teasdale) **31**:363, 379
"The Maiden Marriage" (Swinburne) **24**:357
"Maiden May" (Rossetti) **7**:277
"Maiden, Open" (Randall) **86**:291
"Maiden Song" (Rossetti) **7**:264, 274-6, 289
"The Maiden without Hands" (Sexton) **2**:365; **79**:205
"Maidenhead" (Cowley) **90**:115
"Maidenhood" (Howe) **81**:51
"Maidenhood" (Longfellow) **30**:13-14, 21, 45
"A Maiden's Pledge" (Hardy) **8**:98
"Maiden's Sorrow" (Bryant) **20**:15
"The Maiden's Virtues" (Dafydd ap Gwilym)
See "Campau Bun"

"The Maid's Story" (Crabbe) **97**:114, 119
"The Maid's Thought" (Jeffers) **17**:117
The Maid's Tragedy Alter'd (Waller) **72**:344, 356
"Maifest" (Goethe) **5**:251
"Maighdean Mara" (Heaney) **100**:203
"The Mail" (Carver) **54**:12
"Mail Boxes" (Duncan) **75**:175
"Mail Call" (Jarrell) **41**:189, 200
"Mail Order" (Quintana) **36**:275
"Mailied" (Goethe) **5**:245
"Mailie's Dying Words and Elegy" (Burns)
See "The Death and Dying Words of Poor Mailie, the Author's Only Pet Yowe, an Unco Mournfu' Tale"
"Maillol" (Tomlinson) **17**:311, 314, 335
"The Mailman" (Strand) **63**:155
"The Maim'd Debauchee" (Wilmot)
See "The Disabled Debauchee"
"The Maimed Man" (Tate) **50**:268, 290-96, 329, 331-33
"A Maine Roustabout" (Eberhart) **76**:21, 30, 42, 59
Mainland (Cruz) **37**:10, 12, 16, 25, 33-4
"Mainly by the Music" (Randall) **86**:337
"Mairegen" (Stramm) **50**:175, 205
"Maisie" (Merrill) **28**:228, 254
"La maison des mortes" (Apollinaire) **7**:47
"La Maison D'Or (Bar Harbor)" (Holmes) **71**:127
"Maison doyenne" (Char) **56**:150
"La maison du Berger" (Vigny) **26**:370, 377, 386-87, 391-94, 396, 402, 404, 406, 409, 413
"La Maison d'Yves" (Breton) **15**:63-7
"Maison flake" (Tzara) **27**:233
"Maithuna" (Paz) **1**:361, 368
"The Maja and the Old Woman" (Aleixandre) **15**:5-6
"Majeski Plays the Saxophone" (Espada) **74**:120
"A Majestic Love Song" (Amichai) **38**:46
"Le Majeur Ydow" (Smith) **12**:331
"Major Macroo" (Smith) **12**:309, 317
"A Major Work" (Meredith) **28**:201
Majors and Minors (Dunbar) **5**:115, 117-18, 128, 132, 135-36, 142
"Make Big Money at Home! Write Poems in Spare Time!!" (Nemerov) **24**:267
"The Maker" (Auden) **92**:38
"The Maker" (Borges)
See "El hacedor"
"The Maker" (Illyés)
See "Teremteni"
The Maker (Borges)
See *El hacedor*
"The Maker to Posterity" (Stevenson) **84**:330
"The Makers" (Nemerov) **24**:289-90
"Making" (Thomas) **99**:257, 288-89, 291-93
"Making a Living" (Sexton) **2**:367; **79**:217
"Making a Sacher Torte" (Wakoski) **15**:355, 372
"Making, Camp" (Wagoner) **33**:359
"Making Certain It Goes On" (Hugo) **68**:292
Making Certain It Goes On: Collected Poems (Hugo) **68**:238
"Making Marks" (Raworth) **107**:299
"The Making of an Irish Goddess" (Boland) **58**:12, 14, 31-35, 48, 56-58, 88, 93
The Making of Personality (Carman) **34**:205
"the making of poems" (Clifton) **17**:27
"The Making of the Drum" (Brathwaite) **56**:50, 75, 84
The Making of the Pré (Ponge)
See *La Fabrique du Pré*
"Making the Connection" (Kumin) **15**:208
"Making Up" (Boland) **58**:4, 29, 35, 44, 98
"Le mal" (Rimbaud) **3**:283; **57**:244
"Malabaress" (Baudelaire)
See "À une Malabaraise"
"Malachowski's Ravine" (Herbert)
See "Wawóz Malachowskiego"
"Malachy Deagan" (Masters) **1**:343
"Malade" (Lawrence) **54**:175
"Mal'akhei goral" (Amichai) **38**:7
"Malarz" (Herbert) **50**:5
"Malcolm" (Sanchez) **9**:224, 231
"Malcolm" (Walker) **20**:277
"Malcolm Spoke/Who listened? (This Poem Is for My Consciousness Too)" (Madhubuti) **5**:328, 341
"The Maldive Shark" (Melville) **82**:73, 86, 97, 99, 103, 142
"Il male di vivere" (Montale) **13**:105
"Male Gorillas" (Stone) **53**:247, 257
"La malédiction" (Éluard) **38**:70
"Malediction Upon Myself" (Wylie) **23**:303, 310
Malherbe (Ponge)
See *Pour un Malherbe*
Les Malheurs des immortels (Éluard) **38**:88-89, 92-93
"Malinconia" (Ungaretti) **57**:346
"Le maline" (Rimbaud) **3**:283
"Malines" (Verlaine) **32**:395
"The Malingerer" (McKay) **2**:226
"'Mallorca,' un poema en el olvido" (Borges) **22**:92
"Malmaison" (Lowell) **13**:71, 78, 84
"Malourène" (Apollinaire) **7**:48
"Malvern Hill" (Melville) **82**:102, 133
"Mama and Child" (Serote) **113**:275, 278-79
"Mama Don't Want U" (Alurista) **34**:27
"Maman" (Walcott) **46**:239
"Mamie" (Sandburg) **41**:234, 261, 273, 295, 318
Maminka (Seifert) **47**:326, 335
"Mammon" (Brathwaite) **56**:67, 76
"Mammorial Stunzas for Aimee Simple McFarcin" (Birney) **52**:11, 20, 26-27, 62, 79
"the mammoth corridors" (Birney) **52**:36, 38, 72
"Mammy Hums" (Sandburg) **2**:324; **41**:270
"Mammy Songs" (Hughes) **53**:101
"Man" (Brooke) **24**:71, 75
"Man" (Corso) **33**:35, 37-8, 44, 48-9; **108**:4, 20, 34
"Man" (Herbert) **4**:100-01, 103
"Man" (Lamartine)
See "L'homme"
"Man!" (MacLeish) **47**:127
"Man" (Seferis) **66**:118, 163, 185
"The Man" (Storni)
See "El hombre"
"Man" (Vaughan) **81**:367
"A Man Adrift on a Slim Spar" (Crane) **80**:52, 59, 62, 68-69, 80
"The Man against the Sky" (Robinson) **1**:462, 471, 490, 492-94
The Man against the Sky (Robinson) **1**:462-63, 467-68, 474; **35**:368
"Man and Bat" (Lawrence) **54**:187, 236
"Man and Bird" (Mahon) **60**:163-64, 167, 169
"Man and Dog" (Sassoon) **12**:255
"Man and Dog" (Thomas) **53**:326
"The Man and the Echo" (Yeats) **20**:314, 335
"Man and Wife" (Lowell) **3**:206, 209, 221, 245
"Man and Wife" (Sexton) **2**:363; **79**:279
"Man and Woman Go through a Cancer Ward" (Benn)
See "Mann und Frau gehn durch die Krebsbaracke"
"The Man beneath the Tree" (Wright) **14**:343, 345, 347
"Man Bites Dog-Days" (Nash) **21**:265
"Man Born to Be King" (Morris) **55**:242, 259
The Man Born to be King (Morris) **55**:249
"The Man Born to Farming" (Berry) **28**:26
"Man Carrying Thing" (Stevens) **110**:209
"The Man Closing Up" (Justice) **64**:253, 288
"Man Coming of Age" (Warren) **37**:284, 331
Man Does, Woman Is (Graves) **6**:154
"Man Doesn't Exist" (Aleixandre) **15**:20, 22
"Man Eating" (Kenyon) **57**:14, 38, 47
"Man Entering the Sea, Tangier" (Corso) **108**:8
"A Man Feared That He Might Find an Assassin" (Crane) **80**:52
"The Man from Athabaska" (Service) **70**:130
"The Man from Eldorado" (Service) **70**:116
"The Man from Washington" (Welch) **62**:343-44, 346-47, 356, 370, 373, 378
"The Man Gardener's Song" (Carroll) **74**:107
"The Man Has Lost His Shadow" (Alurista) **34**:10
"The Man He Killed" (Hardy) **8**:102-03; **92**:326
"A Man I Am" (Smith) **12**:295
"Man in Black" (Plath) **1**:389; **37**:179-80
"A Man in Blue" (Schuyler) **88**:207
"Man in Darkness" (Vaughan) **81**:273
"Man in Harmony with Nature" (Very) **86**:81, 88
"Man in Majesty" (Jarrell) **41**:170
"Man in Moonlight" (Warren) **37**:295
The Man in the Black Coat Turns (Bly) **39**:63, 65-6, 98-104
"The Man in the Dead Machine" (Hall) **70**:7, 25
A Man in the Divided Sea (Merton) **10**:338, 346-47, 350
"The Man in the Manmade Moon" (Kennedy) **93**:138
"The Man in the Mirror" (Strand) **63**:140, 152, 156, 160, 178-79
The Man in the Moone (Drayton)
See *Endimion and Phoebe. Ideas Latmus*
"The Man in the Street Is Fed" (Sandburg) **41**:332
"The Man in the Yellow Terry" (Walker) **30**:361
"The Man Inside" (Tolson) **88**:343
"Man into Men" (Hughes) **1**:241, 243
"Man is a Snow" (Birney) **52**:8, 39, 47, 51-52, 54
"Man is a Spirit" (Smith) **12**:297, 316
"Man Listening to Disc" (Collins) **68**:215
"A Man May Change" (Bell) **79**:31
"A Man Meets a Woman on the Street" (Jarrell) **41**:169, 178, 180-81, 189
"The Man of Fashion" (Peacock) **87**:321
"Man of Lawe's Tale" (Chaucer)
See "Man of Law's Tale"
"Man of Law's Tale" (Chaucer) **19**:13, 15, 24, 26, 45, 54-6, 59-60, 62
"The man of life upright" (Campion) **87**:54-55, 63-65, 101-3
"A Man of the Middle Class" (Brooks) **7**:62
"The Man of Tyre" (Lawrence) **54**:187, 197, 199-201, 250
"Man of Words" (Ashbery) **26**:126
"Man on a Tractor" (Birney) **52**:8, 36-37, 39-40
"The Man on His Death Bed" (Aleixandre) **15**:8
"The Man on the Dump" (Ashbery) **26**:153
"The Man on the Dump" (Stevens) **110**:141, 151, 208
"The Man on the Hotel Room Bed" (Kinnell) **26**:286
"Man on the Pink Corner" (Borges)
See "El Hombre de la esquina rosada"
"Man Ray" (Éluard) **38**:86
Man Root (Paz)
See *Raíz del hombre*
"A Man Said to the Universe" (Crane) **80**:52
"the man say we making noise" (Alurista) **34**:35
"The Man Seeking Experience Enquires His Way of a Drop of Water" (Hughes) **7**:116, 118
"Man, sen thy lyfe is ay in weir" (Dunbar) **67**:13
"Man Sleeping" (Kenyon) **57**:47
"Man Splitting Wood in the Daybreak" (Kinnell) **26**:293
"Man Spricht Deutsch" (Enzensberger) **28**:142
"Man Stranded" (Ciardi) **69**:24
"Man, the Man-Hunter" (Sandburg) **2**:308
"Man the Master" (Merton) **10**:345
"Man the Monarch" (Leapor) **85**:205-6, 233, 253, 276, 287, 294

"man thinks you just began it" (Alurista) **34**:39
"Man to the Wound in Christ's Side" (Southwell) **83**:239, 241, 279, 281
"A Man Toiled on a Burning Bed" (Crane) **80**:80
"Man Waking" (Kenyon) **57**:20, 47
"A Man Walking and Singing" (Berry) **28**:3-4, 7, 18
"Man Was Made to Mourn" (Burns) **6**:68; **114**:92, 113, 182
"Man Watching a Woman" (Ní Chuilleanáin) **34**:367
"The Man Who Came to the Last Floor" (Cruz) **37**:10, 18
"The Man Who Died" (Lawrence) **54**:230, 234
The Man Who Died Twice (Robinson) **1**:469, 472, 475, 477, 483, 489-90
"The Man Who Dreamed of Fairyland" (Yeats) **20**:343, 354
"A Man Who Loves Love" (Hagiwara)
See "Koi wo koi suru hito"
"The Man Who Married Magdalene: Variation on a Theme by Louis Simpson" (Hecht) **70**:75
"The Man Who Never Laughed Again" (Morris) **55**:305
The Man Who Shook Hands (Wakoski) **15**:366
"The Man Who Writes Ants" (Merwin) **45**:50
"The Man Whose Pharynx Was Bad" (Stevens) **6**:294
"The Man with a Hammer" (Wickham) **110**:268
The Man with a Hammer: Verses (Wickham) **110**:259-60, 295, 307
"The Man with a Past" (Hardy) **8**:93
Man with a Sling (Neruda)
See *El hondero entusiasta, 1923-1924*
The Man with Night Sweats (Gunn) **26**:224, 228, 230-231
"Man with One Small Hand" (Page) **12**:170
The Man with Seven Toes (Ondaatje) **28**:298-302, 318, 322, 326-27
"The Man with the Blue Guitar" (Stevens) **6**:298, 323-24, 326, 337, 339; **110**:92, 97, 122, 131-36, 148-49, 153, 215
The Man with the Blue Guitar, and Other Poems (Stevens) **6**:304
"Man Without Sense of Direction" (Ransom) **61**:275, 289
"A Man Writes to a Part of Himself" (Bly) **30**:7, 18, 79-80, 84, 94, 102-03
"A Man Young and Old" (Yeats) **20**:328
"The Manager" (Ignatow) **34**:273
"Una mañana de 1649" (Borges) **32**:116
"Mañana gris" (Storni) **33**:268
"Mañanas de verano" (Cernuda) **62**:177
"El manantial" (Guillén) **35**:155, 157, 232
"Manas-sundari" (Tagore) **8**:408
"La manca" (Mistral) **32**:180
Manchester Square (Dorn) **115**:123
"Manchouli" (Empson) **104**:90, 104
"Manciple's Tale" (Chaucer) **19**:11, 13, 48; **58**:336
"Mandalay" (Kipling) **3**:158, 160, 162, 167, 188-89, 192; **91**:97-105
"The Mandolin, the Carnation and the Bamboo" (Apollinaire)
See "La mandoline, l'oeillet et le bambou"
"Mandoline" (Verlaine) **32**:350-51, 370-71, 390-91
"La mandoline, l'oeillet et le bambou" (Apollinaire) **7**:18, 20-2, 34, 36
"The Maner of Her Wyll" (Whitney) **116**:292-95, 298, 300, 302, 308
"Maner of Passing to Confessioun" (Dunbar) **67**:17
"Manet: 'The Execution of the Emperor Maximilian'" (Snodgrass) **74**:315
"Manfred" (Meredith) **60**:250
Manfred (Byron) **16**:68-72, 82-4, 86-90, 108, 111; **95**:55, 57, 62
"Mangham" (Dickey) **40**:200
Mango (Cervantes) **35**:132
"Mango Grove" (Tagore)
See "Amravan"
"Mango of Poetry" (Goodison) **36**:158
"The Mango on the Mango Tree" (Warren) **37**:331
"Manhattan: Grace Church" (Clampitt) **19**:100
"Manhattan: Luminism" (Doty) **53**:69
"Manhattan May Day Midnight" (Ginsberg) **4**:84
"Manhood" (Thoreau) **30**:180, 197
"Mania di solitudine" (Pavese) **13**:225
"Mania for solitude" (Pavese)
See "Mania di solitudine"
"Manicure" (Brooks) **7**:53
"Manie" (Éluard) **38**:69
"Manifest Destiny" (Graham) **59**:135, 138, 159, 177
"Manifesto" (Lawrence) **54**:185-86, 194-95, 211, 214, 232-33
"Manifesto" (Parra) **39**:275-76, 293, 295, 305-6, 309-10
"Manifesto" (Thomas)
See "Poetic Manifesto"
"Manitoba Childe Roland" (Sandburg) **41**:240
"Mankind" (Trakl)
See "Menschheit"
"The Man-Moth" (Bishop) **3**:37, 65; **34**:79, 82, 95, 97, 146, 160, 163-64, 189
"Mann und Frau gehn durch die Krebsbaracke" (Benn) **35**:4, 30
"The Manner of Her Will" (Whitney)
See "The Maner of Her Wyll"
"The Manner of the World Nowadays" (Skelton) **25**:337
Mannerly Margery Milk and Ale (Skelton) **25**:345
"Manners" (Bishop) **34**:69, 95
"The Manners: An Ode" (Collins) **72**:18, 50, 52, 54, 83, 94-95, 97, 120, 122-23, 126, 128, 148
"The Manor Farm" (Thomas) **53**:329; **53**:267, 274, 349
"The Manor Garden" (Plath) **1**:389; **37**:182-83
"Manos de obreros" (Mistral) **32**:187
Las manos del día (Neruda) **4**:288
"A Man's a Man" (Burns) **114**:78, 117
"A Man's a Man for a' That" (Burns) **6**:60
"Man's Civille Warre" (Southwell) **83**:331-32, 334, 336-37
"Mans Fall and Recovery" (Vaughan) **81**:340
"A Man's Last Word" (Carman) **34**:226
"Man's Medley" (Herbert) **4**:101, 127
"A Man's Night with his Demon" (Cernuda)
See "Noche del hombre y su demonio"
"Mans perplexity when called to an account" (Taylor) **63**:264
"A Man's Requirements" (Barrett Browning) **62**:80
"Manscape" (Tomlinson) **17**:351-52
"Mansion" (Ammons) **16**:16, 20
"Le Manteau de Pascal" (Graham) **59**:185-87
"Mantis" (Zukofsky) **11**:341, 347, 356, 392-99
"'Mantis,' an Interpretation" (Zukofsky) **11**:341, 356, 394
"Manual System" (Sandburg) **2**:304
"Manuel Comnenus" (Cavafy) **36**:3, 35
"Manuelzinho" (Bishop) **3**:59-60; **34**:139
"Manuscript Found in a Book of Joseph Conrad" (Borges)
See "Manuscrito hallado en un libro de Joseph Conrad"
"Manuscrito hallado en un libro de Joseph Conrad" (Borges) **32**:83
"Many Farms Notes" (Ortiz) **17**:231
"Many Handles" (Sandburg) **41**:302
Many Happy Returns (Berrigan) **103**:16, 30, 32-33, 35, 37, 43
"Many Happy Returns" (Berrigan) **103**:4, 43
"Many Have" (Corso) **108**:17
"Many Have Fallen" (Corso) **33**:50
Many Inventions (Kipling) **3**:160
Many Long Years Ago (Nash) **21**:266
"Many Loves" (Ginsberg) **47**:54
"The Many Mansions" (Levertov) **11**:201
"Many of Our Waters: Variations on a Poem by a Black Child" (Wright) **36**:301, 309, 317, 320-21, 366, 371
"Many Swans" (Lowell) **13**:61, 64-5, 83
"The Many Things" (Werfel)
See "Die vielen Dinge"
Manyo (Yakamochi)
See *Man'yōshū*
Manyo Anthology (Yakamochi)
See *Man'yōshū*
"Manyone Flying" (Swenson) **14**:283
Manyōshiu Kogi (Yakamochi) **48**:72
The Manyōshū (Yakamochi)
See *Man'yōshū*
Man'yōshū (Yakamochi) **48**:72-146
Manyoshu (Yakamochi)
See *Man'yōshū*
The Manyoshu: One Thousand Poems Selected and Translated from the Japanese (Yakamochi)
See *Man'yōshū*
"Manzanita" (Snyder) **21**:297
"The Map" (Bishop) **3**:37, 50-2; **34**:54, 63, 67, 81, 115, 122, 146, 149, 161
"The Map" (Stryk) **27**:203
"Map for Despair" (Sarton) **39**:321
"A Map of Love" (Justice) **64**:267-70
The Map of Love (Thomas) **2**:381, 390
"A Map of the Antilles" (Walcott) **46**:231, 272-73, 322
"A Map of the City" (Gunn) **26**:219
"Map of the Peninsula" (Hugo) **68**:262
"Maple" (Frost) **39**:235; **71**:24, 34
"Maple and Sumach" (Day Lewis) **11**:144
"Maple Syrup" (Hall) **70**:27, 33
"Mappemounde" (Birney) **52**:9, 21-22, 44-47, 56-57, 79, 91
"La Máquina a Houston" (Dorn) **115**:133
"Las máquinas" (Guillén) **35**:142
"El mar" (Borges) **22**:99
"El mar" (Paz) **48**:181
"Mar de pantalla" (Storni) **33**:262, 294, 296
"Mar de Sangres" (Alurista) **34**:46, 46
"Mar Portuguese" (Pessoa) **20**:170
El mar y las campanas (Neruda) **4**:287-88
"Mar y noche" (Aleixandre) **15**:16
"Mara" (Jeffers) **17**:146
"La Marais du Cygne" (Whittier) **93**:212
"Marathon" (Glück) **16**:152, 164, 166-67
"Marble" (Warren) **37**:336
"marbles and calluses" (Alurista)
See "las canicas y mis callos"
"Marburg" (Pasternak) **6**:270-71, 281
"Marc Chagall 'Lilac above the River'" (Thomas) **99**:307
Marcel Duchamp, James Joyce, Erik Satie: An Alphabet (Cage) **58**:219
"March" (Bryant) **20**:12
"March" (Housman) **43**:236
"March" (Kavanagh) **33**:132
"March" (MacLeish) **47**:127
"March" (Thomas) **53**:328, 332
"March" (Wilbur) **51**:280
"March" (Williams) **109**:236-37, 239-40
"March 1, 1847. By the First Post" (Boland) **58**:25, 60-61
"March 14, 1964" (Sexton) **79**:196
"March 18, 1871-1921" (Rexroth) **95**:270
"March 21 1987" (Brutus) **24**:110
"A March Calf" (Hughes) **89**:125
"March Dusk" (Winters) **82**:316
"March Hares" (de la Mare) **77**:114
"The March into Virginia" (Melville) **82**:84, 92, 132-33, 194-96, 201-2
"March is a Silversmith" (Kavanagh) **33**:140
"March Moon" (Hughes) **53**:85
"March Morning Unlike Others" (Hughes) **89**:125
The March of Coxey's Army (Wagoner) **33**:337

"The March of the Cameron Men" (Robinson) **1**:476
"The March of the Dead" (Service) **70**:151
"The March to the Sea" (Melville) **82**:133-34
"March Twilight" (Bogan) **12**:111
"March Wind" (Berssenbrugge) **115**:9
Marcha triunfal (Darío) **15**:79-80, 85, 111
"Marchas pawnees" (Cardenal) **22**:131
"Marché aux Oiseaux" (Wilbur) **51**:298
"Marche de funèbre pour la mort de la terre" (Laforgue) **14**:95
"Marche Funèbre" (Seifert) **47**:328
"La marche impériale" (Valéry) **9**:391
"The Märchen" (Jarrell) **41**:157-60, 168, 185-86, 194
"Marchenbilder" (Ashbery) **26**:127, 150
"The Marching Morrows" (Carman) **34**:219
"Marching Song" (Stevenson) **84**:316-17, 344, 346
"Marching Song" (Wang Wei) **18**:389
"The Marchioness of Brinvilliers" (Melville) **82**:145
"Marcia funebre" (Pasolini) **17**:264
Marconi's Cottage (McGuckian) **27**:84, 91-92, 94-95, 99, 104-105, 110
"The Mare and Foal at Grass" (Masefield) **78**:100
"Mare Bred from Pegasus" (Wickham) **110**:285, 297
"Maremma Idyl" (Carducci)
See "Idillio maremmano"
"Mares escarlatas" (Cernuda) **62**:231
"Margaret" (Sandburg) **2**:303; **41**:335
"Margaret" (Wordsworth) **4**:399
"Margaret Fuller Slack" (Masters) **36**:182, 222
"Margaret's Bridal Eve" (Meredith) **60**:328
"Margarita" (Castro) **41**:80, 82, 99
"Margarita Debayle" (Darío) **15**:80, 95
"Margate 1940" (Betjeman) **75**:20
"The Margin" (Berssenbrugge) **115**:11
"Marginal Employment" (Clampitt) **19**:81, 88
"The Marginal Field" (Spender) **71**:226
"Marginalia" (Wilbur) **51**:266, 281
"Margite, Marguerite and Margherita" (Stein) **18**:325, 334
"Margites" (Tuckerman) **85**:302, 311, 340
Margots (Béranger) **112**:17
"Margrave" (Jeffers) **17**:142
"The Margrave's Birthright" (Melville) **82**:75, 145-46
"Marguerite" (Whittier) **93**:267
"I mari del sud" (Pavese) **13**:210, 212, 216, 220-26, 228
Mari Magno; or, Tales on Board (Clough) **103**:51, 54, 58, 76, 98, 116, 133, 155-58
"Maria" (Gautier) **18**:126
Maria Neféli (Elytis) **21**:130-31
Maria Nephele (Elytis)
See *Maria Neféli*
"Maria Stuart" (Pasternak) **6**:267
"Maria Wentworth" (Carew) **29**:59
"Maria Who Made Faces and a Deplorable Marriage" (Belloc) **24**:24
"The Mariachis—A Glimpse" (Wakoski) **15**:332
"Le Mariage des feuilles" (Péret) **33**:212, 230
"Marian" (Meredith) **60**:308
"Marian Drury" (Carman) **34**:203-04
"Mariana" (Mallarmé) **102**:128-29
"Mariana" (Tennyson) **6**:359, 364, 387, 389, 391, 406-09, 411; **101**:128, 130, 138-39, 143, 187, 226, 242, 244, 281
"Mariana in the South" (Tennyson) **6**:350; **101**:128, 243-44
A Marianne Moore Reader (Moore) **49**:92, 136
"Marianne, My Mother, and Me" (Kumin) **15**:210-12
"Mariano Explains Yanqui Colonialism to Judge Collins" (Espada) **74**:115, 139
"Maria's Return" (Peacock) **87**:321
"Marichika" (Tagore) **8**:407
Marichiko (Rexroth)
See *The Love Poems of Marichiko*
"Marie Vaux of the Painted Lips" (Service) **70**:141
"Marietta, Minnesota" (Bly) **39**:69
"Marijuana Notation" (Ginsberg) **4**:79
Marilyn Monroe and Other Poems (Cardenal)
See *Oracion por Marilyn Monroe y otros poemas*
"Marina" (Brooke) **24**:58
"Marina" (Eliot) **5**:164, 195, 205-06, 210
"Marine" (Rimbaud) **3**:261; **57**:239, 273-74, 284
"Marine" (Verlaine) **32**:387
Mariner (Coleridge)
See *The Rime of the Ancient Mariner: A Poet's Reverie*
"Los marineros son las alas del amor" (Cernuda) **62**:235, 237, 240
"Marines USA" (Guillén) **23**:126
Marino Faliero: Doge of Venice (Byron) **16**:103
"The Marionettes" (de la Mare) **77**:58
"Mariposa de obsidiana" (Paz) **1**:364
"Maritime Ode" (Pessoa)
See "Ode Marítima"
"The Mark" (Bogan) **12**:87-8, 98, 106, 121
"Mark Atherton" (Tuckerman) **85**:302, 305, 319, 340
"Market" (Hayden) **6**:194, 196
"Market at Turk" (Gunn) **26**:186, 219
"Market Day" (Hacker) **47**:87
"Market Street Woman" (Brown) **55**:150
"Markings" (Heaney) **100**:244, 246-48, 287
"Mark's Sheep" (MacLeish) **47**:214
"The Marlon Brando Memorial Swimming Pool" (Alexie) **53**:4
Marmion (Scott) **13**:249-51, 256, 258, 261, 264, 266-68, 270-71, 273, 275-76, 279, 281-85, 287-90, 304, 311-12, 317-18
Marmor Norfolciense; or, An Essay on an Ancient Prophetical Inscription, in Monkish Rhyme, Lately Discover'd Near Lynn in Norfolk (Johnson) **81**:161-62, 164, 170, 234
"The Marmozet" (Belloc) **24**:24
"Marquis de Carabas" (Béranger) **112**:22
Marquis de Grandvin (Melville) **82**:77
"Marrana Placa" (Alurista) **34**:47
"Marriage" (Clarke) **112**:117-19
"Marriage" (Corso) **33**:5-7, 15-6, 23, 25, 34-6, 42-44, 47, 52-4; **108**:21, 24-25, 30, 34
"A Marriage" (Creeley) **73**:5, 29
"Marriage" (Ignatow) **34**:282, 286
"Marriage" (Moore) **4**:230-31, 233, 243, 249, 251-52, 254-55, 258, 260-61; **49**:88, 91-92, 101, 103, 112, 131, 155
"A Marriage" (Randall) **86**:341, 344
"Marriage" (Thomas) **99**:312
"The Marriage" (Wickham) **110**:268
"The Marriage" (Winters) **82**:346-47
"Le marriage d'André Salmon" (Apollinaire)
See "Poème lu au mariage d'André Salmon"
"The Marriage II" (Levertov) **11**:167
"A Marriage in the Sixties" (Rich) **5**:363
"The Marriage of Faustus and Helen" (Crane)
See "For the Marriage of Faustus and Helen"
"The Marriage of Geraint" (Tennyson) **101**:240
The Marriage of Heaven and Hell (Blake) **12**:12, 28, 36, 39-41, 47-51, 60-61, 64; **63**:4, 52, 56-57, 85, 95, 104-5, 112, 117, 125, 132, 134
"The Marriage of Hector and Andromache" (Sappho) **5**:414, 418
"The Marriage of Lord Fauconberg and Lady Mary Cromwell" (Marvell) **10**:270
"The Marriage Ring" (Blake) **12**:34
"Marriage Was a Foreign Country" (Yamada) **44**:334
"Marri'd" (Gilmore) **87**:302
Marri'd and Other Verses (Gilmore) **87**:283, 298-99, 301
"The Married Lover" (Patmore) **59**:250
"The Married Man" (Kipling) **3**:192
"The Marring of Malyn" (Carman) **34**:202, 213
"The Marrow" (Roethke) **15**:277, 281
"La Marseillaise" (Éluard) **38**:85
"The Marsh" (Snodgrass) **74**:285, 300-301
"Marsh Leaf" (Wagoner) **33**:324, 364-65
"Marsh Song at Sunset" (Lanier) **50**:55
"Marshall Washer" (Carruth) **10**:74
"The Marshes of Glynn" (Lanier) **50**:54, 56, 62, 79-81, 83-86, 92, 98-100
"Marston" (Spender) **71**:216
"Marsyas" (Masters) **1**:329; **36**:176
Le marteau sans maître (Char) **56**:112, 115, 127-30, 134, 158, 161, 184-85, 189
"The Marten" (Clare) **23**:7
"Martha" (Holmes) **71**:96
"Martha" (Lorde) **12**:140, 157
"Martha Blake" (Clarke) **112**:36, 47, 49, 80, 91, 120, 124
"Martha Blake at Fifty-One" (Clarke) **112**:80, 91, 98, 120
"Marthe Away" (Rexroth) **95**:349
"A Martial Law Carol" (Brodsky) **9**:26-7
"Martial—XII, LII" (Rexroth) **95**:260
"Martín" (Baca) **41**:39-40, 45, 65, 68, 70-1, 73
Martín and Meditations (Baca)
See *Martín and Meditations on the South Valley*
Martín and Meditations on the South Valley (Baca) **41**:39-40, 61, 63, 65-7, 70, 74
"Martín VIII" (Baca) **41**:42
"Martín V" (Baca) **41**:42
"Martín IV" (Baca) **41**:42
"Martín IX" (Baca) **41**:42
"Martín I" (Baca) **41**:41
"Martín VII" (Baca) **41**:42
"Martín VI" (Baca) **41**:42
"Martín II" (Baca) **41**:40-1
"Martino Lutero" (Carducci) **46**:52
"Martin's Puzzle" (Meredith) **60**:262, 294
"Martire, Primavera" (Zanzotto) **65**:290-91
"Martirio de Santa Olalla" (García Lorca) **3**:132, 146
"Martock Moor" (Hardy)
See "On Martock Moor"
"The Martyr" (Melville) **82**:93, 138
"The Martyr" (Whittier) **93**:192
"The Martyr of Alabama" (Harper) **21**:190
The Martyr of Alabama, and Other Poems (Harper) **21**:189
"The Martyr Poets Did Not Tell" (Dickinson) **1**:96
"A Martyr: The Vigil of the Feast" (Rossetti) **7**:285
"The Martyrdom of Bishop Farrar" (Hughes) **7**:112; **89**:208
"Martyrdom of Saint Eulalia" (García Lorca)
See "Martirio de Santa Olalla"
"Martyrdom, Springtime" (Zanzotto)
See "Martire, Primavera"
"Une martyre" (Baudelaire) **1**:45, 48, 62; **106**:24, 26, 29
"Le Marvais moine" (Baudelaire) **106**:68
"The Marvel" (Douglas) **106**:197, 200
"Marvella, for Borrowing" (Ríos) **57**:325
"Marvelous" (Berrigan) **103**:18
The Marvelous Arithmetics of Distance (Lorde) **12**:153
"The Marvels of the City" (Simic) **69**:284, 302
A Marvin Bell Reader: Selected Poetry and Prose (Bell) **79**:34-35
"Mary" (Blake) **12**:35, 43
"Mary and Gabriel" (Brooke) **24**:59, 78, 84
"Mary and Mildred" (Patmore) **59**:228-29
"Mary and the Seasons" (Rexroth) **20**:209; **95**:249-50, 260
"Mary at the Feet of Christ" (Harper) **21**:191
"Mary Bly" (Wright) **36**:340, 351
"Mary Desti's Ass" (O'Hara) **45**:133, 141
"Mary Garvin" (Whittier) **93**:170, 172, 267
"The 'Mary Gloster'" (Kipling) **3**:161, 167, 181; **91**:86-87
"Mary Kroger" (Erdrich) **52**:186, 188

"Mary Magdalen's Blush" (Southwell) **83**:281, 296
"Mary Magdalen's Complaint at Christ's Death" (Southwell) **83**:280, 322
"Mary Morison" (Burns)
See "Ye Are Na Mary Morison"
"Mary, Pity Women" (Kipling) **3**:161, 192
"Mary Rowlandson" (Howe)
See "The Captivity and Restoration of Mrs. Mary Rowlandson"
"Mary seeks her own Jesus" (Crashaw)
See " *Quœrit* Jesum"
"Mary Sheffield" (Dickey) **40**:226
"Mary Winslow" (Lowell) **3**:206, 217-18
"mary's dream" (Clifton) **17**:19
"Mary's Ghost" (Hood) **93**:52
"Mary's Song" (Plath) **37**:230, 232-33
"Más allá" (Guillén) **35**:186, 187, 191, 204, 227, 229, 230, 234
"Más esplendor" (Guillén) **35**:179, 181, 182, 183
"Más verdad" (Guillén) **35**:228
Mascarilla y trébol (Storni) **33**:239, 242, 255-59, 261-62, 269, 272, 284-85, 291-97, 305
"Mascha riait aux anges" (Éluard) **38**:70
"The Mask" (Baudelaire)
See "Le masque"
"Mask" (Illyés) **16**:245, 250
"The Mask" (Spender) **71**:187, 228
The Mask (Raworth) **107**:285, 324
Mask and Clover (Storni)
See *Mascarilla y trébol*
A Mask for Janus (Merwin) **45**:3, 10-11, 18-19, 24, 29, 52, 74, 89-90, 93, 99
The Mask of Anarchy (Shelley)
See *The Masque of Anarchy*
Mask of Anarchy (Shelley)
See *The Masque of Anarchy*
Mask of Comus (Milton)
See *Comus: A Maske*
A Mask of Motion (Hejinian) **108**:253, 288
"The Masked Face" (Hardy) **8**:119; **92**:214
"Masked Woman's Song" (Bogan) **12**:100-01
"The Mask-Maker" (Abse) **41**:4, 8
"Masks" (Brathwaite) **56**:7
"Masks" (Moore) **49**:114, 121
"Masks" (Stryk) **27**:191, 197
Masks (Brathwaite) **56**:3, 5-8, 11-12, 17-18, 21-23, 26, 29-30, 33-34, 49-50, 59, 65, 67, 70, 73-75, 77, 84-86, 88, 98
"Masks of Dawn" (Paz) **1**:359
Masks of Time (Blunden) **66**:17
"Masks of Woman" (Yamada) **44**:351
Masnavi (Rumi)
See *Mathnawi*
Masnavi-yi Ma'navi (Rumi) **45**:293-302
"Mas'ot Binyamin ha'aharon mitudela" (Amichai) **38**:5, 8-9, 13-14, 16, 19, 26
"Le masque" (Baudelaire) **1**:45, 65, 72; **106**:22, 86
A Masque for Janus (Merwin)
See *A Mask for Janus*
"Masque funèbre" (Char) **56**:157
"Masque nègre" (Senghor) **25**:224
The Masque of Anarchy (Shelley) **14**:171, 175, 210; **67**:214, 226
A Masque of Mercy (Frost) **1**:211
The Masque of Pandora (Longfellow) **30**:23, 51
"The Masque of Plenty" (Kipling) **3**:181
A Masque of Reason (Frost) **1**:203-04, 206, 217
The Masque of Snow (Blok)
See *Snezhnye maski*
"Masque of Tsars" (Viereck) **27**:280
"Masquerada" (Snodgrass) **74**:333
"Masquerade in the Park" (Akhmatova) **2**:6
"Masqueraders" (Page) **12**:178
"Mass for the Day of St. Thomas Didymus" (Levertov) **11**:198, 200-01
"Mass Man" (Walcott) **46**:286
Mass for Hard Times (Thomas) **99**:340
"The Mass of the Grove" (Dafydd ap Gwilym)
See "Offeren Y Llwyn"
"Massachusetts to Virginia" (Whittier) **93**:209, 239, 264, 315
"The Massacre of Glencoe" (Dobell) **100**:166
"Massacre of the Innocents" (Hope) **56**:270-71
"The Massage" (Kinnell) **26**:286
"Masses" (Sandburg) **41**:239, 269, 349
"Le Masseur de Ma Soeur" (Hecht) **70**:89, 91
"Masseuse and Prostitute" (Rexroth)
See "For a Masseuse and Prostitute"
"Mastectomy" (Boland) **58**:37
"Master" (Abse) **41**:7-8
"The Master" (H. D.) **5**:306
"The Master" (Merwin) **45**:18
"The Master" (Robinson) **1**:461, 465, 467; **35**:362, 368
"Master and Man" (Brown) **55**:168
"Master and Mistress" (Kunitz) **19**:148
"Master Herrick's Farewell unto Poetry" (Herrick)
See "Farewell to Poetry"
"Master Hugues of Saxe-Gotha" (Browning) **2**:37, 61, 88
"The Master Image" (Eberhart) **76**:29, 31
"The Master of Ceremonies" (Simic) **69**:308
"Master Rabbit" (de la Mare) **77**:114
Master Thaddeus; or, The Last Foray in Lithuania (Mickiewicz)
See *Pan Tadeusz; czyli, Ostatni zajazd na Litwie*
"Masterpiece" (Corso) **33**:49
"The Masters of the Heart Touched the Unknown" (Schwartz) **8**:292
"Masters of War" (Dylan) **37**:71
"Mastery" (Teasdale) **31**:355
"Masts at Dawn" (Warren) **37**:299, 302, 307, 347-48, 362, 365, 375
"The Matachines" (Tomlinson) **17**:328-29
"The Match" (Blunden) **66**:25, 51
"The Match" (Marvell) **10**:271, 300
"The Match" (Vaughan) **81**:263, 296-97, 332-33, 368
"Matchbox with a Fly in It" (Simic) **69**:281
"Mateo XXV, 30" (Borges) **22**:73-5; **32**:38, 58, 60, 86, 93
"Materia humana" (Aleixandre) **15**:34
Materialism (Graham) **59**:137-38, 145, 150-53, 155, 157-59, 161, 163, 168-69, 175-78, 186
The Materials (Oppen) **35**:284, 292, 295, 297, 308, 310, 312, 314, 315, 320, 321, 322, 325, 326, 330, 331, 333, 338
"Materias" (Mistral) **32**:160
"Maternità" (Pavese) **13**:213
"Maternity" (Meynell) **112**:165, 186
"Mathew VIII, 28ff" (Wilbur) **51**:215-16, 281
"Mathilde in Normady" (Rich) **5**:352, 359
Mathnavi (Rumi)
See *Mathnawi*
Mathnawi (Rumi) **45**:273-80, 294-96, 298-302, 305-10, 312-13, 320-22
"La Matière et nos épaules" (Brossard) **80**:28
"La Matière harmonieuse manoeuvre encore" (Brossard) **80**:31
Matilda (Drayton) **98**:7, 53
"Le Matin" (Baudelaire) **106**:88
"Un Matin" (Péret) **33**:231
"Matin" (Rimbaud) **57**:246
"Matinal and Nocturne" (Carducci)
See "Mattutino e notturno"
The Matinals (Char)
See *Les matinaux*
Les matinaux (Char) **56**:126, 131, 134-38, 144, 146, 149-51, 154-55, 166, 170, 173-74, 176-78, 184-86, 188-89
"Matinée d'ivresse" (Rimbaud) **3**:261, 263, 271-73, 281-82; **57**:249-50, 265-66, 268-70, 275, 282-83
"Matinees" (Merrill) **28**:285-87
"Matins" (Berryman) **64**:171
"Matins" (Glück) **16**:170-71
"Matins" (Levertov) **11**:166
"Matins" (Montague) **106**:303, 314
"Matisse: Blue Interior with Girls etc. etc." (Hecht) **70**:94
"Matisse: Blue Interior with Two Girls—1947" (Hecht) **70**:100
"Matka" (Herbert) **50**:7, 9
"Matoaka" (Clampitt) **19**:101-02
"Matrimony" (Erdrich) **52**:191
"Matrix" (Clampitt) **19**:102
"Matronhood" (Howe) **81**:51
"Matros v Moskve" (Pasternak) **6**:283
"Mattens" (Herbert) **4**:119
"Mattens, or Morning Prayer" (Herrick) **9**:118
"Matter Harmonious" (Brossard) **80**:31, 33
Matter Harmonious (Brossard) **80**:32
"The Matter of the Bees" (Duncan) **75**:180
"Matthew V. 29-30" (Mahon) **60**:135, 186, 188
"Matthew VIII, 28ff" (Wilbur)
See "Mathew VIII, 28ff"
"Matthew XXV: 30" (Borges)
See "Mateo XXV, 30"
Matthias at the Door (Robinson) **1**:473-74, 479; **35**:368
"Mattinata" (Carducci) **46**:50
"Mattino" (Pavese) **13**:230
"Mattutino e notturno" (Carducci) **46**:42, 48
"Maturity" (Ginsberg) **4**:87
"Mauberley, 1920" (Pound)
See *Hugh Selwyn Mauberley*
"Maud" (Howe) **81**:49
Maud (Tennyson) **101**:130-31, 134, 161-65, 167-68, 170-72, 191, 196, 216-18, 220-25, 241, 268-70, 275, 282
Maud, and Other Poems (Tennyson) **6**:354, 356-57, 360, 363, 366, 373, 379-80, 383, 385, 387, 407
"Maud Muller" (Whittier) **93**:167, 170, 172-73, 233, 239, 250, 266-67, 344
"Maude Clare" (Rossetti) **7**:260, 280, 291
"Maumee Ruth" (Brown) **55**:73, 75, 80
"Maundy Thursday" (Owen) **19**:352, 358
"Mausfallen-Sprüchlein" (Mörike) **1**:114
Mausoleum (Enzensberger) **28**:148-50, 154-55, 158, 165
"Le mauvais moine" (Baudelaire) **1**:59
"Mauvais sang" (Rimbaud) **57**:182-83, 189-91, 194-99, 244-46, 248-49, 251-53, 277-78
"Le mauvais vitrier" (Baudelaire) **1**:67; **106**:98
"Mauve" (Brossard) **80**:15
Mauve (Brossard) **80**:14-15
"Mawl i'r Haf" (Dafydd ap Gwilym) **56**:233
"Mawu" (Lorde) **12**:143
"Max" (Sexton) **79**:194
"Max Ernst" (Éluard) **38**:69, 71
"Maximian, Elegy V" (Rexroth) **95**:272
Maximilian (Masters) **36**:189
"Maximus" (Lawrence) **54**:197, 199
"Maximus at the Harbor" (Olson) **19**:312-13
"Maximus From Dogtown—IV" (Olson) **19**:306
"Maximus of Gloucester" (Olson) **19**:294, 304
The Maximus Poems (Olson) **19**:266-67, 270-71, 273-75, 277, 279-83, 285-87, 294, 296-98, 304-7, 316
"Maximus, to Himself" (Olson) **19**:269
Maximus, Vol. II (Olson) **19**:306
Maximus, Vol. III (Olson) **19**:285, 287-88, 295, 305-7
"May" (Heaney) **100**:206
"May" (Oliver) **75**:287
"May" (Rossetti) **7**:265
"May, 1915" (Mew) **107**:59-61, 63-65
"May 5, 1970" (Sexton) **79**:195-98
"May 20, 1928" (Borges) **22**:76
"May 23" (Thomas) **53**:302, 304, 349
"May 24, 1980" (Brodsky) **9**:24
"May 24th or so" (Schuyler) **88**:195
"May 30th" (Sexton) **79**:199
"May 1943" (H. D.) **5**:307
"May 1954" (Thumboo) **30**:332
"May 1968" (Olds) **22**:339
"May, 1972" (Schuyler) **88**:197, 200
"may all thes blessings" (Bissett) **14**:30

"May and December: A Song" (Randall) **86**:291, 344-45
"May and June" (Carman) **34**:208
"May Banners" (Rimbaud)
See "Bannières de mai"
"May Day" (Rexroth) **95**:254
"May Day" (Teasdale) **31**:331, 340
"May Day Sermon to the Women of Gilmer County, Georgia, by a Woman Precher Leaving the Baptist Church" (Dickey) **40**:158, 166, 183, 191-92, 195-96, 201, 208, 224, 232, 241-42, 248, 255
"May Festival" (Goethe)
See "Maifest"
"May It Be" (Pasternak) **6**:261
"The May Magnificat" (Hopkins) **15**:124-25, 165
"May Morning" (Thoreau) **30**:181, 233-34
"May Night" (Carducci)
See "Notte di Maggio"
The May Queen (Tennyson) **6**:359
"May Song" (Carducci)
See "Idillio di Maggio"
"Maya" (Muir) **49**:237
Maya Angelou: Poems (Angelou) **32**:25
A Mayan Astronomer in Hell's Kitchen (Espada) **74**:157-58, 169
"The Mayan Ground" (Oppen) **35**:316, 349
"Mayapán" (Cardenal) **22**:128, 131
"Mayavada" (Tagore) **8**:408
"Maybe this is a sign of madness" (Mandelstam) **14**:155
"Maybe this is the beginning of madness" (Mandelstam)
See "Mozhet byt' eto tochka bezumiia"
"May-Day" (Emerson) **18**:76, 88, 111
May-Day and Other Pieces (Emerson) **18**:75, 113
"Mayday on Holderness" (Hughes) **89**:163
"May-Day Song for North Oxford" (Betjeman) **75**:21-22, 83
"Maydes are simple" (Campion) **87**:58, 69, 72, 89
"Mayflies" (Wilbur) **51**:334
Mayflies (Wilbur) **51**:331-35
"Mayflower" (Aiken) **26**:41-2, 45
"Mayfly" (MacNeice) **61**:131, 170
"Mayo nuestro" (Guillén) **35**:182, 183
"The Mayo Tao" (Mahon) **60**:142-43, 167, 238
"The Mayor of Gary" (Sandburg) **2**:304, 308
"The Maypole Is Up" (Herrick) **9**:102, 145
"May's Love" (Barrett Browning) **6**:24
"Maze" (Eberhart) **76**:13, 34-36
"A Maze of Sparks of Gold" (Rexroth) **20**:190
"Mazeppa" (Hugo) **17**:75
Mazeppa (Byron) **16**:83
"Mazurka" (McGuckian) **27**:101
"M.B." (Brodsky) **9**:10
"McAndrew's Hymn" (Kipling) **3**:161, 167, 170, 186, 192; **91**:81, 86-88, 154
"Mcyri" (Lermontov)
See *Mtsyri*
"Me Again" (Rexroth) **20**:218
Me Again: Uncollected Writings of Stevie Smith (Smith) **12**:314, 333-34, 340, 343-44, 346-47
"Me an' Rome we come to town" (Gilmore) **87**:295
"Me centuplant Persée" (Césaire) **25**:31
"Me crucé con un entierro" (Fuertes) **27**:11
"Me from Myself to Banish" (Dickinson) **1**:94
"Me retiro con mis Sueños" (Alurista) **34**:31, 46
"Me retracto de todo lo dicho" (Parra) **39**:264, 278, 306-7, 309-10
"Me tuviste" (Mistral) **32**:202
"Me Whoppin' Big-Tree Boy" (McKay) **2**:226
Me'adam (Amichai) **38**:22-23, 32-35
"The Meadow" (Carver) **54**:11
Meadow (Raworth) **107**:302, 325, 336
"Meadow Milk" (Bogan) **12**:110
Meadowlands (Glück) **16**:171-73
"Meadowlands 3" (Glück) **16**:171
"Meadowlarks" (Teasdale) **31**:340, 359
"The Meadows in Spring" (FitzGerald) **79**:68, 108, 175
"Mean Gnome Day" (Kennedy) **93**:141
"Mean Old Yesterday" (Hughes) **53**:115
"Meaning" (Milosz)
See "Sens"
"The Meaning of Death" (Tate) **50**:243-45, 251
"The Meaning of Fall" (McHugh) **61**:190
"The Meaning of Life" (Tate) **50**:231, 243-45, 251, 259
"The Meaning of the Shovel" (Espada) **74**:156
"Meaningless Poem" (Eberhart) **76**:54, 72-73
"Meanwhile" (Chappell) **105**:20
"The Measure" (Stone) **53**:217
"The Measure of Memory (The Navigator)" (Baraka) **113**:10
"The Measure of Poetry" (Nemerov) **24**:303
"Meat without Mirth" (Herrick) **9**:98
"Mecanique" (Brossard) **80**:14
"Mechanism" (Ammons) **16**:40
"Meciendo" (Mistral) **32**:201-02
"Médaillon" (Char) **56**:156-57
"Le médaillon toujours ferme" (Apollinaire) **7**:22
The Medall. A Satire Against Sedition (Dryden) **25**:74
"Medallion" (Plath) **37**:182
The Medea, and Some Poems (Cullen) **20**:60-62, 66
Medea the Sorceress (Wakoski) **15**:372-73
Le médecin malgré lui (Williams) **7**:349
"A Mediaeval Legend" (Hardy) **92**:273
"La medianoche" (Mistral) **32**:181
"Medical Missionary of Mary" (Clarke) **112**:68
Medicamina Faciei (Ovid) **2**:238-39, 243, 251, 253, 258
"Medicine" (Bissett) **14**:20
MEDICINE my mouths on fire (Bissett) **14**:16, 19, 27
Médieuses (Éluard) **38**:84
"A Medieval Miniature" (Szymborska) **44**:277
Medieval Scenes (Duncan) **2**:109; **75**:124, 126, 129, 175-76, 181, 203, 227-28, 252
Medieval Welsh Lyrics (Dafydd ap Gwilym) **56**:221
"Médiocriteé" (Laforgue) **14**:88
"Mediocritie in love rejected" (Carew) **29**:25, 32
"Meditation 1.1" (Taylor) **63**:228, 269, 315-16
"Meditation 1.2" (Taylor) **63**:232
"Meditation 1.4" (Taylor) **63**:206, 249, 252, 316, 319, 321, 345
"Meditation 1.5" (Taylor) **63**:316, 344
"Meditation 1.6" (Taylor) **63**:207, 269-70, 301
"Meditation 1.7" (Taylor) **63**:253, 267, 270, 332-33, 337
"Meditation 1.8" (Taylor) **63**:347
"Meditation 1.10" (Taylor) **63**:348, 352
"Meditation 1.11" (Taylor) **63**:346, 350
"Meditation 1.12" (Taylor) **63**:353
"Meditation 1.17" (Taylor) **63**:270, 350
"Meditation 1.18" (Taylor) **63**:271
"Meditation 1.19" (Taylor) **63**:350
"Meditation 1.20" (Taylor) **63**:350
"Meditation 1.21" (Taylor) **63**:352
"Meditation 1.22" (Taylor) **63**:220-21, 268, 271, 347-48, 351
"Meditation 1.23" (Taylor) **63**:207
"Meditation 1.24" (Taylor) **63**:317, 351
"Meditation 1.25" (Taylor) **63**:230, 345, 348
"Meditation 1.27" (Taylor) **63**:350, 353
"Meditation 1.28" (Taylor) **63**:342
"Meditation 1.29" (Taylor) **63**:345, 350
"Meditation 1.30" (Taylor) **63**:267, 342-43
"Meditation 1.31" (Taylor) **63**:267, 347, 351, 354
"Meditation 1.34" (Taylor) **63**:207, 349
"Meditation 1.36" (Taylor) **63**:348, 351
"Meditation 1.37" (Taylor) **63**:227
"Meditation 1.38" (Taylor) **63**:334-35
"Meditation 1.39" (Taylor) **63**:252, 334-36
"Meditation 1.40" (Taylor) **63**:207, 267, 334-36, 348
"Meditation 1.41" (Taylor) **63**:351
"Meditation 1.42" (Taylor) **63**:301, 345
"Meditation 1.43" (Taylor) **63**:316
"Meditation 1.45" (Taylor) **63**:267, 344, 348
"Meditation 1.46" (Taylor) **63**:267, 346
"Meditation 1.48" (Taylor) **63**:348
"Meditation 1.49" (Taylor) **63**:345
"Meditation 2" (Taylor) **63**:267-71, 316, 318, 321, 337
"Meditation 2.1" (Taylor) **63**:207, 319, 322
"Meditation 2.4" (Taylor) **63**:316, 345
"Meditation 2.5" (Taylor) **63**:349
"Meditation 2.6" (Taylor) **63**:336-37
"Meditation 2.10" (Taylor) **63**:317, 320, 345
"Meditation 2.17" (Taylor) **63**:207, 250, 344
"Meditation 2.21" (Taylor) **63**:349
"Meditation 2.23" (Taylor) **63**:348
"Meditation 2.26" (Taylor) **63**:348, 351
"Meditation 2.27" (Taylor) **63**:337-38
"Meditation 2.28" (Taylor) **63**:317
"Meditation 2.31" (Taylor) **63**:316
"Meditation 2.32" (Taylor) **63**:228
"Meditation 2.33" (Taylor) **63**:345, 349
"Meditation 2.34" (Taylor) **63**:317-18, 337
"Meditation 2.35" (Taylor) **63**:266, 350
"Meditation 2.40" (Taylor) **63**:316
"Meditation 2.44" (Taylor) **63**:348
"Meditation 2.46" (Taylor) **63**:345
"Meditation 2.47" (Taylor) **63**:321
"Meditation 2.50" (Taylor) **63**:345
"Meditation 2.51" (Taylor) **63**:348
"Meditation 2.53" (Taylor) **63**:346
"Meditation 2.54" (Taylor) **63**:316
"Meditation 2.56" (Taylor) **63**:301, 318, 345-46
"Meditation 2.58-61" (Taylor) **63**:316
"Meditation 2.59" (Taylor) **63**:316
"Meditation 2.60B" (Taylor) **63**:348
"Meditation 2.61" (Taylor) **63**:252-53, 321
"Meditation 2.62" (Taylor) **63**:346
"Meditation 2.63" (Taylor) **63**:316, 344
"Meditation 2.67B" (Taylor) **63**:250-51, 348
"Meditation 2.68B" (Taylor) **63**:250, 353
"Meditation 2.69" (Taylor) **63**:227, 316, 348
"Meditation 2.70" (Taylor) **63**:230
"Meditation 2.71" (Taylor) **63**:230, 346
"Meditation 2.72" (Taylor) **63**:351
"Meditation 2.77" (Taylor) **63**:317
"Meditation 2.78" (Taylor) **63**:231, 318
"Meditation 2.79" (Taylor) **63**:231, 269
"Meditation 2.80" (Taylor) **63**:318
"Meditation 2.82" (Taylor) **63**:315
"Meditation 2.83" (Taylor) **63**:316, 344
"Meditation 2.84" (Taylor) **63**:316
"Meditation 2.85" (Taylor) **63**:344
"Meditation 2.86" (Taylor) **63**:316, 347
"Meditation 2.89" (Taylor) **63**:319-20
"Meditation 2.92" (Taylor) **63**:267
"Meditation 2.93" (Taylor) **63**:317
"Meditation 2.99" (Taylor) **63**:322
"Meditation 2.100" (Taylor) **63**:315
"Meditation 2.104" (Taylor) **63**:228
"Meditation 2.106" (Taylor) **63**:266, 271
"Meditation 2.108" (Taylor) **63**:347
"Meditation 2.110" (Taylor) **63**:347
"Meditation 2.111" (Taylor) **63**:303
"Meditation 2.115" (Taylor) **63**:345
"Meditation 2.121" (Taylor) **63**:348
"Meditation 2.123A" (Taylor) **63**:227
"Meditation 2.126" (Taylor) **63**:348
"Meditation 2.128" (Taylor) **63**:346
"Meditation 2.129" (Taylor) **63**:344, 348
"Meditation 2.130" (Taylor) **63**:344
"Meditation 2.131" (Taylor) **63**:316
"Meditation 2.132" (Taylor) **63**:344
"Meditation 2.138" (Taylor) **63**:232, 347
"Meditation 2.142" (Taylor) **63**:348
"Meditation 2.143" (Taylor) **63**:346
"Meditation 2.144" (Taylor) **63**:344
"Meditation 2.145" (Taylor) **63**:227

"Meditation 2.147" (Taylor) **63**:318
"Meditation 2.149" (Taylor) **63**:250
"Meditation 2.155" (Taylor) **63**:228
"Meditation 2.156" (Taylor) **63**:347
"Meditation 2.159" (Taylor) **63**:346-47
"Meditation 2.160" (Taylor) **63**:345
"Meditation 2.161A" (Taylor) **63**:345
"Meditation 2.161B" (Taylor) **63**:345
"Meditation 2.164" (Taylor) **63**:346
"Meditation 11:104" (Taylor) **63**:266
"Meditation 32" (Taylor) **63**:264
"Meditation" (Baudelaire)
See "Recueillement"
"Meditation" (Berryman) **64**:82
"A Meditation" (Eberhart) **76**:38, 41
"A Meditation" (Ignatow)
See "A Meditation on Violence"
"Meditation" (Lermontov)
See "Duma"
"A Meditation" (Melville) **82**:72, 85, 91-92, 138, 200, 206
"Meditation" (Tate) **50**:250
"Meditation" (Thomas) **99**:266
"Meditation at Kew" (Wickham) **110**:268, 270-71
"Meditation at Lagunitas" (Hass) **16**:200, 209, 211, 219
"Meditation at Oyster River" (Roethke) **15**:265, 276, 310, 313, 316
"A Meditation for His Mistresse" (Herrick) **9**:101
"Meditation in Sunlight" (Sarton) **39**:321, 357
"Meditation in the Spring Rain" (Berry) **28**:6
"A Meditation in Time of War" (Yeats) **20**:314
"A Meditation in Tuscany" (Barrett Browning) **6**:16
"The Meditation of the Old Fisherman" (Yeats) **20**:337
"Meditation on a June Evening" (Aiken) **26**:7, 50
"Meditation on a Memoir" (Cunningham) **92**:137
"A Meditation on John Constable" (Tomlinson) **17**:341-42
"A Meditation on Philosophy" (Bly) **39**:64
"Meditation on Saviors" (Jeffers) **17**:142, 144-45
"Meditation on Statistical Method" (Cunningham) **92**:135-37, 156, 177, 183, 191
"A Meditation on Violence" (Ignatow) **34**:279
"Meditation One" (Eberhart) **76**:32
"Meditation under Stars" (Meredith) **60**:261, 280, 327
"Meditations 1.8-11" (Taylor) **63**:347
"Meditations 2.1-2.30" (Taylor) **63**:230
"Meditations 2.58-60B" (Taylor) **63**:230
"Meditations 2.84-86" (Taylor) **63**:344
"Meditations 2.104-109" (Taylor) **63**:303
"Meditations" (Baca)
See "Meditations on the South Valley"
"Meditations" (Eberhart) **76**:32
"Meditations" (Schwerner) **42**:209
Meditations (Taylor)
See *Preparatory Meditations before My Approach to the Lords Supper. Chiefly upon the Doctrin Preached upon the Day of Administration*
Les meditations (Lamartine) **16**:256-62, 265, 268-69
"Meditations in an Emergency" (O'Hara) **45**:158, 190, 228-29
Meditations in an Emergency (O'Hara) **45**:116, 132, 205
"Meditations in Time of Civil War" (Yeats) **20**:314, 342, 349; **51**:73, 102, 111
"Meditations of an Old Woman" (Roethke) **15**:262, 264-65, 273
"Meditations on the National Problem" (Herbert)
See "Meditations on the Problem of the Nation"
"Meditations on the Problem of the Nation" (Herbert) **50**:18
Meditations on the Six Days of the Creation (Traherne) **70**:197
"Meditations on the South Valley" (Baca) **41**:39-40, 42, 65, 69, 72-3
"Meditations on the South Valley III" (Baca) **41**:42
"Meditations on the South Valley XXVIII" (Baca) **41**:43
"Meditations on the South Valley XXV" (Baca) **41**:67
"Meditations on the South Valley XXI" (Baca) **41**:42
"Meditations on the South Valley XXVII" (Baca) **41**:43
Méditations poétiques (Lamartine) **16**:270, 272-82, 284-85, 287, 289-93, 302
"Mediterranean" (Sarton) **39**:324, 343
"The Mediterranean" (Tate) **50**:250, 270, 272, 274, 279, 289, 295, 301, 320-21, 335
The Mediterranean (Tate) **50**:230-31
"Mediterranean Basin" (Warren) **37**:337
"Mediterraneo" (Montale) **13**:115
"Medium for Stasis" (Stone) **53**:224
"Medley: Mortal Love Watches the Dance" (Snodgrass) **74**:335
Medny Vsadnik (Pushkin) **10**:367-68, 373-74, 385, 390-400, 414
"Medusa" (Bogan) **12**:85, 104-06, 111-12, 115, 117
"Medusa" (Cullen) **20**:69
"Medusa" (Dove) **6**:123
"Medusa" (Gower) **59**:88, 91-92
"Medusa" (Merrill) **28**:229
"Medusa" (Plath) **37**:255
"The Meehoo with an Exactlywatt" (Silverstein) **49**:335
"Meer- und Wandersagen" (Benn) **35**:49, 74
"Meet the Family" (Thomas) **99**:233, 237
"The Meeting" (Abse) **41**:4
"Meeting" (Arnold) **5**:42
"The Meeting" (Hope) **56**:287, 299
"Meeting" (Hughes) **89**:150
"The Meeting" (Longfellow) **30**:103
"The Meeting" (Mistral)
See "El encuentro"
"A Meeting" (Montague) **106**:232, 288
"Meeting" (Montale)
See "Incontro"
"A Meeting" (Pasternak)
See "Vstrecha"
"The Meeting" (Rukeyser) **12**:231
"Meeting" (Spender) **71**:188
"The Meeting" (Whittier) **93**:198
"Meeting a Bear" (Wagoner) **33**:336, 339, 373
"Meeting among the Mountains" (Lawrence) **54**:186
"Meeting in Winter" (Morris) **55**:340
"Meeting Mescalito at Oak Hill Cemetery" (Cervantes) **35**:106, 116, 117
"A Meeting of Minds" (Lorde) **12**:135
"Meeting of Strangers" (Birney) **52**:16, 23, 97
"Meeting of the Alumni of Harvard College" (Holmes) **71**:92
"The Meeting of the Dryads" (Holmes) **71**:68, 92
"Meeting of two Smiles" (Éluard) **38**:90-91
"Meeting Point" (MacNeice) **61**:138
"Meeting the Minister for Culture" (Enright) **93**:21
"A Meeting with Despair" (Hardy) **92**:364-67
"A Meeting with My Father" (Amichai) **38**:26, 28
"Meeting-House Hill" (Lowell) **13**:67
"Megalopolis" (Cruz) **37**:10
Meghadūta (Kālidāsa) **22**:177-78, 182, 185, 188-89, 192, 194-95, 204-05, 207-08
La meglio gioventù (Pasolini) **17**:250-51, 254, 262, 264-67, 275, 279, 281-83, 293
"A Mehinaku Girl in Seclusion" (Song) **21**:344
Me-horei Kol Zeh Mistater Osher Gadol (Amichai) **38**:16, 19, 43, 45-6, 51
"mehrere elstern" (Enzensberger) **28**:139
"Mein Karren knarrt nicht mehr" (Celan) **10**:124
"A Mei-p'i Lake Song" (Tu Fu) **9**:330-31, 333
"Meirion" (Peacock)
See "Farewell to Meirion"
"Melampus" (Meredith) **60**:330, 332
"Melancholia" (Gautier) **18**:135
"Melancholia" (Verlaine) **32**:386-87
"Melancholia en Orizba" (Neruda) **4**:281
"Melancholy" (Bely) **11**:6
"Melancholy" (Bridges) **28**:76
"Melancholy" (Hunt) **73**:134
"Melancholy" (Thomas) **53**:285-86
"Melancholy" (Ungaretti)
See "Malinconia"
Melancholy (Peacock)
See *The Philosophy of Melancholy: A Poem in Four Parts with a Mythological Ode*
"Melancholy in Orizaba" (Neruda)
See "Melancholia en Orizba"
"A Melancholy Moon" (Baudelaire)
See "Les tristesses de la lune"
"Melancholy Ode" (Hood)
See "Ode to Melancholy"
"Melancholy of Jason Cleander" (Cavafy)
See "Melancholy of Jason, son of Cleander, poet in Syria Commagene, A.D. 595"
"Melancholy of Jason Kleander, Poet in Kommagini, A.D. 595" (Cavafy)
See "Melancholy of Jason, son of Cleander, poet in Syria Commagene, A.D. 595"
"Melancholy of Jason, son of Cleander, poet in Syria Commagene, A.D. 595" (Cavafy) **36**:34, 46, 69, 111
Melancolía (Jiménez) **7**:211
"Melancthon" (Moore) **4**:251, 254; **49**:90, 100, 180, 185-87
"Mélange adultère de tout" (Eliot) **5**:185
"Melbourne" (Shapiro) **25**:269
"Melchior Vulpius" (Moore) **49**:142
"Melibea's Orchard" (Guillén) **35**:220
"Melibee" (Chaucer)
See "Tale of Melibee"
"Melinda on an Insipid Beauty in imitation of a fragment of Sapho's" (Finch) **21**:167
"Mellow" (Hughes) **53**:191
"Melodien" (Benn) **35**:20, 24, 25, 26, 27
"Melo-Drama: Taurassdes" (Elliott) **96**:181
"Melody" (Tomlinson) **17**:341
"The Melongene" (Wilbur) **51**:295
"Melpomene in Manhattan" (Ignatow) **34**:310, 343
"Melville's Marginalia" (Howe) **54**:105-6
"Memento, homo, quod cinis es!" (Dunbar) **67**:11
"Mementos, 1" (Snodgrass) **74**:292
"Mementos, 2" (Snodgrass) **74**:292
"Meminisse Horret" (Carducci) **46**:29, 71
"Memo" (Jordan) **38**:127
"Memo: For the Race Orators" (Brown) **55**:82, 114
"Memo from the Cave" (Glück) **16**:147-48
"Memo: Preliminary Draft of a Prayer to God the Father" (Ciardi) **69**:56
"Memo to Non-White People" (Hughes) **53**:110, 116
"Memoir" (Pinsky) **27**:157
"Memoir of a Proud Boy" (Sandburg) **41**:240, 274
"Mémoire" (Rimbaud) **3**:262, 268; **57**:171, 175, 177, 216-18, 222, 245
"Memoirs" (Meredith) **28**:199
"The Memoirs of Glükel of Hameln" (Jarrell) **41**:171
"Memoirs of the World" (Gunn) **26**:203
"Memorabilia" (Masters) **1**:343
"Memoranda to Horace" (MacNeice) **61**:118, 143-44, 176, 178
"Memorandum Confided by a Yucca to a Passion-Vine" (Lowell) **13**:61, 64

"À Memória do President Rei Sidónio" (Pessoa) **20**:154
"Memorial" (Gilmore) **87**:302
"Memorial" (Pinsky) **27**:153
"Memorial" (Sanchez) **9**:224
"Memorial Candle" (Shvarts)
See "Pominal'naia svecha"
Memorial Day (Berrigan) **103**:33, 40, 43
"Memorial Day" (Niedecker) **42**:147
"Memorial Day, 1950" (O'Hara) **45**:127, 135, 181-82, 200, 223, 238
A Memorial for Dylan Thomas (Rexroth)
See *Thou Shalt Not Kill: A Memorial for Dylan Thomas*
"A Memorial for My Mother" (Stafford) **71**:378
"Memorial for the City" (Auden) **1**:23; **92**:14-15, 19, 97
"Memorial Rain" (MacLeish) **47**:190, 197
"A Memorial: Son Bret" (Stafford) **71**:375
"Memorial Tablet" (Sassoon) **12**:269
"Memorial Thresholds" (Rossetti) **44**:221
"Memorial II" (Lorde) **12**:140, 157
"Memorial Wreath" (Randall) **86**:343
"Memories" (Cohen) **109**:68-69
"Memories..." (Jiménez)
See "Recuerdos..."
"Memories" (Thomas) **99**:268
"Memories" (Whittier) **93**:197
"Memories Are Made of This" (Berrigan) **103**:36
"Memories of Mortalities" (Jackson) **44**:8, 11-12, 57, 63-64, 76
"Memories of Mortalities 2: My Father and My Childhood" (Jackson) **44**:8
"Memories of My Father" (Kinnell) **26**:286
"Memories of the Forest" (Ishikawa)
See "Mori no omoide"
"Memories of West Street and Lepke" (Lowell) **3**:206, 208, 220, 223, 237
"Memories of Youth" (Parra) **39**:278
"Memory" (Benét) **64**:8, 14, 21-22
"Memory" (Bogan) **12**:101, 120, 122
"A Memory" (Brooke) **24**:85-6
"A Memory" (Gilmore) **87**:300
"Memory" (Hecht) **70**:108
"A Memory" (Pavese) **13**:203
"Memory" (Rimbaud)
See "Mémoire"
"Memory" (Roethke) **15**:275
"Memory" (Sassoon) **12**:269
"Memory" (Smith) **104**:190
"Memory" (Tennyson) **101**:249
"Memory" (Walker) **20**:283
"Memory" (Wright) **14**:376
"Memory I" (Rossetti) **7**:277
"Memory and I" (Hardy) **92**:221, 295, 375
Memory and Other Poems (de la Mare) **77**:94
Memory for Forgetfulness: August, Beirut, 1982 (Darwish)
See *Dhakirah lil-nisyan: al-zaman, Bayrout, al-makan, ab 1982*
"Memory Green" (MacLeish) **47**:126, 165
"Memory I" (Seferis) **66**:195-96, 206
"Memory II" (Seferis) **66**:118, 195, 215
"Memory of a Strange Refreshment" (Shvarts)
See "Vospominanie o strannom ugoshchenii"
"Memory of Africa" (Ungaretti) **57**:360
"Memory of Brother Michael" (Kavanagh) **33**:157; **105**:102
"The Memory of Cock Robin Dwarfs W. D." (Snodgrass) **74**:334
"The Memory of Elena" (Forché) **10**:136, 139, 152-53, 166, 169
"A Memory of Love—Terms and Conditions" (Amichai) **38**:32
"memory of my crickets" (Alurista) **34**:34
"Memory of My Father" (Kavanagh) **33**:75, 93, 149; **105**:163
"Memory of Radio" (Baraka)
See "In Memory of Radio"
"Memory of Spring" (Merwin) **45**:16
"The Memory of Swans" (Sarton) **39**:321
"Memory of V. I. Ulianov" (Zukofsky) **11**:396
"Memory of W. H. Auden" (Kinsella) **69**:137
"A Memory Picture" (Arnold) **5**:49
"Memphis Blues" (Brown) **55**:73, 76, 82, 110, 153-54, 174, 177
"Men" (Angelou) **32**:28
"Men" (MacLeish) **47**:126, 130, 166
"The Men" (Neruda) **64**:329
"Men" (Parker) **28**:347, 354
"Men" (Parra) **39**:289
"Men" (Toomer) **7**:336
Men (Verlaine)
See *Hombres*
"Men Alone" (Hall) **70**:34
Men and Women (Browning) **2**:66, 77, 94; **61**:57, 87
"Men at Forty" (Justice) **64**:270-71
"Men Improve with the Years" (Yeats) **20**:314
Men in the Off Hours (Carson) **64**:221, 223, 227, 229-32, 237, 244
"Men Loved Wholly beyond Wisdom" (Bogan) **12**:104, 126
"Men Marry What They Need; I Marry You" (Ciardi) **69**:40, 52
"The Men of New Australia" (Gilmore) **87**:300
"The Men of Sheepshead" (Oppen) **35**:308
"Men of the High North" (Service) **70**:114
"Men of the North" (Harper) **21**:190
"The Men of War" (Vaughan) **81**:306
"The Men that Are Falling" (Stevens) **6**:310
"The Men That Don't Fit In" (Service) **70**:115, 164
"Men Who March Away" (Hardy) **92**:200
Men, Women, and Ghosts (Lowell) **13**:63, 71, 73, 76, 79, 85, 93
"The Menace" (Gunn) **26**:228
"Menaces du témoin" (Bonnefoy) **58**:124
"The Mendicants" (Carman) **34**:199, 201, 207, 220
"El mendigo que entregaba un papel" (Fuertes) **27**:30
"Mending Wall" (Frost) **1**:225, 227, 229; **39**:230, 237, 240, 246, 253, 256; **71**:34, 43
"Mendocino Rose" (Hongo) **23**:199
"Menelaus" (Walcott) **46**:266
"Menelaus and Helen" (Brooke) **24**:56, 65, 76, 79, 82
"Meng Tzu's Song" (Merwin) **45**:24
"Menippus in Sussex" (Douglas) **106**:186
"Menons Klagen um Diotima" (Hölderlin) **4**:141-2
"Meno's Lamentation for Diotima" (Hölderlin)
See "Menons Klagen um Diotima"
"Men's Confessions" (Heaney) **100**:263
"Mens Creatrix" (Kunitz) **19**:159
"The Men's Room in the College Chapel" (Snodgrass) **74**:291
Mensagem (Pessoa) **20**:154-57, 159-63, 165, 168, 170
"Mensaje" (Aleixandre) **15**:6, 10
"Menschenbeifall" (Hölderlin) **4**:165
"Die Menschheit" (Stramm) **50**:170-71, 173, 175-76, 201, 206, 214
"Menschheit" (Trakl) **20**:250, 253-55
"Menschliche Trauer" (Trakl) **20**:253
"Menschliches Elend" (Trakl) **20**:253
"Menses" (Boland) **58**:37
"Menses" (Millay) **6**:233
"Menstruation at Forty" (Sexton) **2**:363; **79**:232, 249, 317-18
"Mental Cases" (Owen) **19**:330, 336, 340-41, 343, 347, 353, 355, 359, 365, 368, 370-71; **102**:167, 169-70, 190, 202, 225
"The Mental Traveller" (Blake) **12**:36, 46, 48
"The Mental Traveller" (Hardy) **92**:207
"Mentana" (Dobell) **100**:136
"Menthol Sweets" (Amichai) **38**:46
"Mentre n'atrista e duol" (Michelangelo) **103**:274
"Merch ac Aderyn" (Dafydd ap Gwilym) **56**:247
"The Merchantmen" (Kipling) **3**:161
"Merchant's Tale" (Chaucer) **19**:13, 15, 28, 33, 62-3; **58**:246, 248-9, 344, 351, 365
"Merched Llanbadarn" (Dafydd ap Gwilym) **56**:249
"Mercifully" (Moore) **49**:150
"Mercury and Cupid" (Prior) **102**:314
"Mercury and the Elephant" (Finch) **21**:159, 161
"Mercy" (Dickey) **40**:219-20, 242-43, 246
"The Mercy Killers" (Randall)
See "To the Mercy Killers"
"Mercy on Broadway" (Doty) **53**:60-61, 63
"Merely Statement" (Lowell) **13**:86
"Mericano" (Ortiz) **17**:228
"Meridian" (Clampitt) **19**:83
"Meriggiare pallido e assorto" (Montale) **13**:105
"The Merle and the Nightingale" (Dunbar) **67**:25, 95, 109
"Merlin" (Emerson) **18**:81-82, 88, 99, 104, 106
"Merlin" (Muir) **49**:209, 247
Merlin: A Poem (Robinson) **1**:462-63, 465, 468-71, 482-83, 488-89, 491; **35**:362
"Merlin and the Gleam" (Tennyson) **6**:389, 407; **101**:199
"Merlin and Vivien" (Tennyson) **101**:192, 195-97, 204, 237
"Merlin Enthralled" (Wilbur) **51**:189, 227
"Mermaid of Margate" (Hood) **93**:44, 52
"Mermaid Tavern" (Kavanagh) **105**:136
"The Mermaid's Children" (Lowell) **3**:241
Mermaids in the Basement: Poems for Women (Kizer) **66**:63-64, 78
"The Mermen" (Crane) **3**:90
Merope (Arnold) **5**:8, 12, 35, 37, 45, 47, 58-60, 62-3
"Merrow Down" (Kipling) **91**:153
"The Merry Guide" (Housman) **2**:180, 192
"Merry Margaret" (Skelton) **25**:336
The Merry Muses of Caledonia (Burns) **114**:50, 122, 126-31
"The Merry Muses" (Burns) **6**:96
"Merry-Go-Round" (Hughes) **53**:126-27
"The merry-go-round at night" (Abse) **41**:31
"Mersa" (Douglas) **106**:200, 203
"Meru" (Yeats) **20**:326
"Merveilles de la guerre" (Apollinaire) **7**:3, 22
"Mes bouguins refermés" (Mallarmé) **4**:199; **102**:102
"Mes deux Filles" (Hugo) **17**:82
"De Mes Haras" (Césaire) **25**:10
Mes Livres (Sainte-Beuve) **110**:37
"Mes petites amoureuses" (Rimbaud) **3**:262, 284; **57**:202-4, 209-10, 212, 214, 292, 295
"Mes Sources" (Péret) **33**:220
"Mesa Blanca" (Cruz) **37**:18
"Mesa Blanca/White Table" (Cruz) **37**:18
"Mescaline" (Ginsberg) **4**:74, 81
"Un mese fra i bambini" (Montale) **13**:134
"Meseta" (Guillén) **35**:156
Les meslanges (Ronsard) **11**:247, 266
"Mess Hall Discipline" (Yamada) **44**:341, 343
"Mess Occupation" (Berrigan)
See "Sonnet XXXIX"
"Message" (Aleixandre)
See "Mensaje"
"Message" (Berryman) **64**:80, 93, 99, 102
"Message" (Chappell) **105**:26
"Message" (Forché) **10**:139, 144, 154-55
"The Message" (Levertov) **11**:171
Message (Pessoa)
See *Mensagem*
"The Message" (Sassoon) **12**:248
"The Message" (Very) **86**:98, 136, 138
"A Message All Blackpeople Can Dig (& A Few Negroes Too)" (Madhubuti) **5**:329, 341
"Message at Sunset for Bishop Berkeley" (McHugh) **61**:202
"Message for the Sinecurist" (Gallagher) **9**:62
"Message from Abroad" (Tate) **50**:248-50
"Message from the NAACP" (Baraka) **4**:11

"Message from Your Toes" (Stone) **53**:230, 255, 258
"A Message Hidden in an Empty Wine Bottle That I Threw into a Gulley of Maple Trees One Night at an Indecent Hour" (Wright) **36**:319, 340
"the message of crazy horse" (Clifton) **17**:25
"The Message of the March Wind" (Morris) **55**:329, 338
"Message to a Black Soldier" (Madhubuti) **5**:339
"Messages" (Dickey) **40**:200, 219
"Messages" (Senghor) **25**:255
"A Messenger" (Atwood) **8**:18
"The Messenger" (Gunn) **26**:219, 226
"Messenger" (Herbert) **50**:14
"The Messenger" (Kinsella) **69**:80
"The Messenger" (Merton) **10**:339
"The Messenger" (Sassoon) **12**:259
The Messenger (Kinsella) **69**:130, 137, 143
"A Messenger from the Horizon" (Merton) **10**:334
"The Messenger of Love" (Hafiz) **116**:15
"The Messengers" (Creeley) **73**:120
"Messengers" (Glück) **16**:127, 133, 142
"The Messiah" (Pope) **26**:314, 319, 322
"Messiah (Christmas Portions)" (Doty) **53**:61
"Messianic Eclogue" (Vergil)
See "Eclogue 4"
"Messias" (Shapiro) **25**:284, 317
"Messina 1908" (Meynell) **112**:153
Město v slzách (Seifert) **47**:315, 330-31
"The Metal and the Flower" (Page) **12**:168, 178
The Metal and the Flower (Page) **12**:167, 171, 193
Die Metamorphose der Pflanzen (Goethe) **5**:239-40
Metamorphoses (Ovid) **2**:233, 238-241, 244-45, 260
"Les métamorphoses du vampire" (Baudelaire) **1**:48, 71; **106**:8, 23, 26, 77, 166-67
"The Metamorphoses of the Vampire" (Baudelaire)
See "Les métamorphoses du vampire"
"Metamorphosis" (Glück) **16**:163
"Metamorphosis" (Sitwell) **3**:304
"Metamorphosis" (Stone) **53**:218, 221, 256
"Metamorphosis" (Walcott) **46**:286
Metamorphosis (Ovid)
See *Metamorphoses*
"Métaphore" (Brossard) **80**:22
"Metaphors of a Magnifico" (Stevens) **6**:311-12; **110**:109
"Metaphors of the Arabian Nights" (Borges) **32**:66
"The Metaphysical Amorist" (Cunningham) **92**:135, 175, 182
"The Metaphysical Automobile" (Nemerov) **24**:284
"The Metaphysical Garden" (Sarton) **39**:325, 332
Metaphysical Ironies (Abse) **41**:3
"Metaphysical Poem" (O'Hara) **45**:119
"Metaphysics" (Ginsberg) **47**:38
"Meta-Rhetoric" (Jordan) **38**:121-22, 126
Metel' (Akhmadulina) **43**:33
"Metempsicosis" (Darío) **15**:101
Meteo (Zanzotto) **65**:338
"Meteor of August 13" (Char)
See "Météore du 13 août"
"Météore du 13 août" (Char) **56**:132
"The Meteorite" (Jarrell) **41**:154
"Metho Drinker" (Wright) **14**:333, 341
Méthodes (Ponge)
See *Le Grand Recueil*
The Methow River Poems (Stafford) **71**:373-74
"Metric Figure" (Williams) **109**:278
A Metrical History of Christianity (Taylor)
See *A Transcript of Edward Taylor's Metrical History of Christianity*
"Metro" (Szirtes) **51**:160-61, 167, 171
Metro (Szirtes) **51**:160, 169
"Metro North" (Doty) **53**:61
"The Metropolis" (Clampitt) **19**:90
"Métropolitain" (Rimbaud) **3**:265; **57**:232, 238-39, 247, 282, 284-86
"Metropolitan Ice Co." (Ciardi) **69**:6
"Metropolitan Melancholy" (Stevens) **110**:93
"Metropolitan Nightmare" (Benét) **64**:25-26
"The Metropolitan Railway" (Betjeman) **75**:19, 22
"The Metropolitan Tower" (Teasdale) **31**:331
"Metropolitan Water Bawd" (Enright) **93**:36
"Mexican Child" (Mistral)
See "Niño mexicano"
"Mexican Divertimento" (Brodsky) **9**:12
"Mexican Divertissement" (Brodsky)
See "Mexican Divertimento"
"Mexican Impressions" (Corso) **33**:5, 24, 41, 43, 47
"The Mexican Peacock" (Jacobsen) **62**:317, 320
"Mexicans Begin Jogging" (Soto) **28**:387
"The Mexican-Texan" (Paredes) **83**:34, 38
"Mexico" (Birney) **52**:46
"Mexico" (Cervantes) **35**:118, 124, 126
"Mexico" (Dalton) **36**:127
"Mexico Is a Foreign Country: Five Studies in Naturalism" (Warren) **37**:287, 332
"México, La Ilusión de Continente" (Paredes) **83**:40
"Mexico, The Dream of the Continent" (Paredes)
See "México, La Ilusión de Continente"
"Mezzo Cammin" (Longfellow) **30**:50, 64
"Mezzo Forte" (Williams) **7**:405
"Mezzogiorno alpino" (Carducci) **46**:48, 61, 88
"M.G. to O.B." (Wilmot)
See "An Epistolary Essay from M.G. to O.B."
"Mi" (Tolson) **88**:331
"Mi Abuelo" (Ríos) **57**:311
"A mi barrio, El Cuatro Veintiuno" (Paredes) **83**:30
"Mi caballero" (Martí) **76**:88
"Mi chiquita" (Guillén) **23**:142
"Mi Pueblo" (Paredes) **83**:30, 35
"Mi reyecillo" (Martí) **76**:135
"I' mi son caro assai piu ch'i' non soglio" (Michelangelo) **103**:192
"Mi suerte" (Fuertes) **27**:14, 27
"Mi vida entera" (Borges) **22**:93; **32**:57-8, 83, 99
"Mi voz" (Aleixandre) **15**:40
"Mía" (Darío) **15**:107, 113
"La mia musa" (Montale) **13**:139
"Mia vita a te non chiedo lineamenti" (Montale) **13**:139
"Miami You Are About to be Surprised" (Merton) **10**:351
"MIA's" (Sanchez)
See "MIA's (Missing in Action and Other Atlantas)"
"MIA's (Missing in Action and Other Atlantas)" (Sanchez) **9**:230, 235, 244
"Micah" (Walker) **20**:278
"Micah" (Whittier) **93**:195
"Micene" (Quasimodo) **47**:293
"Michael" (Service) **70**:133
"Michael" (Wordsworth) **4**:380-81, 394, 399, 402, 412, 414, 425, 428; **67**:247, 263-64, 288, 328, 330, 366
Michael (Crabbe) **97**:82
Michael Angelo (Longfellow) **30**:23, 43, 67, 72-3
"Michael Gallagher" (Masters) **36**:211
Michael Robartes and the Dancer (Yeats) **20**:310, 314
"Michel et Christine" (Rimbaud) **3**:264, 281; **57**:177, 203
"Michelangelo the Elder" (Kaufman) **74**:213, 235
"The Microbe" (Belloc) **24**:15, 25
Microcosme (Scève) **111**:11, 26-27, 29-31, 41, 43, 45, 51, 53, 63-65, 103, 120, 148
"Mid/Life" (Brathwaite) **56**:97
"Midas" (Winters) **82**:333
"Midas Among Goldenrod" (Merrill) **28**:239
"Mid-August at Sourdough Mountain Lookout" (Snyder) **21**:286
"Midday in the Alps" (Carducci)
See "Mezzogiorno alpino"
"Middle Age" (Das) **43**:81
"Middle Distance" (Graham) **59**:188
"Middle Flight" (Meredith) **28**:174, 186
"Middle of a Long Poem on 'These States'" (Ginsberg) **4**:47
"Middle of Life" (Hölderlin)
See "Hälfte des Lebens"
"The Middle of the World" (Lawrence) **54**:227
"Middle Passage" (Hayden) **6**:176-81, 183, 187-88, 194, 196-200
Middle Passages (Brathwaite) **56**:55-56, 61, 66, 71
"Middle Sea and Lear Sea" (Jones) **116**:168
"The Middle-Aged" (Rich) **5**:362-63, 367, 369
"The Middleness of the Road" (Frost) **39**:233
"Middlesex" (Betjeman) **75**:22
"The Midlands Express" (Spender) **71**:225
"Midnight" (Creeley) **73**:37
"Midnight" (Heaney) **18**:192; **100**:197
"Midnight" (Howe) **81**:28
"Midnight" (Martí) **76**:97
"Midnight" (Mistral)
See "La medianoche"
"Midnight" (Parker) **28**:351, 364
"Midnight" (Vaughan) **81**:324, 363
"Midnight" (Wright) **14**:337
"The Midnight Carnival" (Snodgrass) **74**:330, 334
"Midnight Chippie's Lament" (Hughes) **1**:255
"Midnight II <27" (Ignatow) **34**:342
"Midnight in Early Spring" (Merwin) **45**:96
"Midnight in Moscow" (Mandelstam) **14**:122
"A Midnight Interior" (Sassoon) **12**:246
"Midnight Mass for the Dying Year" (Longfellow) **30**:45
"Midnight Nan at Leroy's" (Hughes) **1**:246
"Midnight on the Great Western" (Hardy) **8**:107; **92**:213
"The Midnight Scene" (Whittier) **93**:193
"The Midnight Show" (Ríos) **57**:324
"Midnight Show" (Shapiro) **25**:295
"Midnight Snack" (Merrill) **28**:249
"Midnight Verses" (Akhmatova) **2**:16
Midnight Verses (Akhmatova) **55**:48
"Midnight Wind" (Winters) **82**:335-36
"A Midnight Woman to the Bobby" (McKay) **2**:224
"Midpoint" (Updike) **90**:352-57
Midpoint, and Other Poems (Updike) **90**:352-55, 358
Midquest (Chappell) **105**:3, 5-6, 9, 16-19, 22-37, 39-41, 45-48, 50-54, 57-75, 78-79, 81-82, 85-86
"Midsummer" (Kinsella) **69**:117
"Midsummer" (Mahon) **60**:141, 199
"Midsummer" (Spender) **71**:188
Midsummer (Walcott) **46**:241-42, 244-45, 259, 322-23
The Midsummer Cushion (Clare) **23**:45
"Midsummer, England" (Walcott) **46**:237
"A Midsummer Holiday" (Swinburne) **24**:313, 329
"Midsummer Night" (Masefield) **78**:62
Midsummer Night and Other Tales in Verse (Masefield) **78**:46-48, 62, 73, 92
"Mid-Term Break" (Heaney) **18**:189; **100**:268
"Midway" (Graves) **6**:143
"Midwinter Blues" (Hughes) **53**:140
"Midwinter Notes" (Mueller) **33**:196
"A Midwinter Prayer" (Ní Chuilleanáin) **34**:348
"Midwinter, Presolstice" (Atwood) **8**:2
"The Midwives" (Enzensberger) **28**:142
"Miedo" (Storni) **33**:279
"Miedo divino" (Storni) **33**:258
"La miej zoventút" (Pasolini) **17**:281

"Mientras dura vida, sobra el tiempo" (Forché) **10**:135
"Mientras la Gracia me excita" (Juana Inés de la Cruz) **24**:188
"Might These be Thrushes Climbing through Almost (Do They" (Cummings) **5**:108
"The Mighty Flight" (Baraka) **4**:26
"Mignonne, allons voir si la rose" (Ronsard)
See "Ode à Cassandre: 'Mignonne, allons voir'"
"A Migrating Dialogue" (Cohen) **109**:75-76, 89, 92
"Migration" (Boland) **58**:42
"Migration" (Carver) **54**:13
"Migration, 1902" (Alexie) **53**:24
"Migratory" (Doty) **53**:66
"Mike" (Schuyler) **88**:187
"El milagro secreto" (Borges) **32**:50
"Milan Cathedral" (Melville) **82**:97, 106
"Milczenie roslin" (Szymborska) **44**:320
"The Mild Despair of Tremayne" (Justice) **64**:266
"Mildred's Thoughts" (Stein) **18**:346
"Mildred's Umbrella" (Stein) **18**:334
"A Mild-Spoken Citizen Finally Writes to the White House" (Meredith) **28**:206
Mileposts I (Tsvetaeva)
See *Vyorsty I*
Mileposts II (Tsvetaeva)
See *Vyorsty II*
Miles Standish (Longfellow)
See *The Courtship of Miles Standish*
"A Milesian Encounter on the Sligachan" (Hughes) **89**:218-19
"Milestone Mountain" (Rexroth)
See "Climbing Milestone Mountain, August 22, 1937"
"Militant" (Hughes) **53**:110, 113
"Military Band" (O'Hara) **45**:130
"The Militant Black Poet" (Randall) **86**:299, 329, 335
"Military Cemetery" (O'Hara) **45**:224
"Military Review" (Mickiewicz) **38**:168
"Milk" (Stein) **18**:323, 330
"The Milk Factory" (Heaney) **18**:237
"A Milkweed" (Wilbur) **51**:289
"Milkweed" (Wright) **36**:326-27, 329-30, 369, 374
"Milk-Wort and Bog Cotton" (MacDiarmid) **9**:160, 176, 199
"The Mill" (Robinson) **1**:468, 475, 478; **35**:368
"The Mill" (Wickham) **110**:269, 271
"The Mill" (Wilbur) **51**:312
"The Mill Field at Aetnaville, Ohio: 1960" (Wright) **36**:390
"Mill Mountain" (Brown) **55**:114
"Mill Song" (Ekeloef) **23**:54
"Mill-Doors" (Sandburg) **41**:239, 243, 349, 364
"Mille fois" (Péret) **33**:216, 231
"Millennium" (Cohen) **109**:18, 89
"Miller's" (Chaucer)
See "Miller's Tale"
"The Miller's Daughter" (Tennyson) **6**:350; **101**:215, 243
"Miller's Tale" (Chaucer) **19**:11, 13-14, 40, 44, 54, 61; **58**:248-9, 266, 346
"Millibars of the Storm" (Césaire) **25**:17
"Millibars of the Storn" (Césaire) **25**:17
"Millie's date" (Abse) **41**:31
"A Million Laughs, A Bright Hope" (Szymborska) **44**:277
"A Million Young Workmen, 1915" (Sandburg) **41**:297
"The Millionaire" (Bukowski) **18**:13
"The Millionaires at Marine Drive" (Das) **43**:75, 81
Millions of Strange Shadows (Hecht) **70**:63, 65, 71, 77-78, 81-82, 84, 86-88, 92
"Millpond Lost" (Warren) **37**:336
"The Mills" (Hughes) **53**:111
"The Mills of the Kavanaughs" (Lowell) **3**:204, 206-07, 215, 217, 224, 226, 231
The Mills of the Kavanaughs (Lowell) **3**:204, 206-07, 215, 217, 224, 226, 231
"The Mill-Stream" (Howe)
See "Mind versus Mill-Stream"
"The Milltown Union Bar" (Hugo) **68**:250, 252
"The Mill-Water" (Thomas) **53**:328-29
"Milly; ou, La terre natale" (Lamartine) **16**:280, 286, 293
"Milonga de Calandria" (Borges) **32**:87
"Milonga del forastero" (Borges) **32**:66
"Milosc od pierwszego wejrzenia" (Szymborska) **44**:285, 308
"Milpa" (Cardenal) **22**:131
"Milton" (Muir) **49**:219
Milton (Blake) **12**:13, 27, 30, 36-8, 42, 44-5, 50, 62-5, 73, 75-80; **63**:54, 85, 95
"Milton: A Sonnet" (Warren) **37**:379
"Milun" (Marie de France) **22**:258, 264, 266, 268, 270-75, 295-96
"Mima: Elegía pagana" (Darío) **15**:110-11
"Mimnermos: The Brainsex Paintings" (Carson) **64**:207, 229
"Le mimosa" (Ponge) **107**:73, 128, 236
"Miña casiña" (Castro) **41**:89
Minashi Guri (Matsuo Basho) **3**:11
"Mind" (Graham) **59**:181
"Mind" (Wilbur) **51**:209, 304-5, 307, 311
"Mind Breaths" (Ginsberg) **47**:59, 73
Mind Breaths: Poems, 1972-1977 (Ginsberg) **4**:61, 82
"The Mind for Al Its Reasoning" (Kaufman) **74**:235
"The Mind Hesitant" (Williams) **7**:390
"The Mind, Intractable Thing" (Moore) **4**:243; **49**:145, 157
"The Mind is an Enchanted Thing" (Moore)
See "The Mind Is an Enchanting Thing"
"The Mind Is an Enchanting Thing" (Moore) **4**:261; **49**:127, 130, 134, 144-45, 161
"The Mind of the Frontispiece to a Book" (Jonson)
See *The Under-Wood XXVI*
"Mind versus Mill-Stream" (Howe) **81**:26-27, 47-48, 50-51
Mindfield (Corso) **33**:42-4, 53; **108**:19-20, 23, 25, 39, 43, 45, 47
"The Mind-Reader" (Wilbur) **51**:231-34, 260-61, 276, 278, 285, 303, 305, 308, 335
The Mind-Reader: New Poems (Wilbur) **51**:234, 236, 238, 245, 247, 250, 260-61, 287, 289-90, 301
"The Mind's Own Place" (Oppen) **35**:336, 349, 357
Mindwheel (Pinsky) **27**:157, 171
"Mine and Thine" (Morris) **55**:325
"Mine Own John Poins" (Wyatt)
See "Myne owne John Poynts sins ye delight to know"
"Mine own John Poyntz" (Wyatt)
See "Myne owne John Poynts sins ye delight to know"
Mine the Harvest (Millay) **6**:226, 231-33, 237, 242
"The Mine: Yamaguchi" (Stryk) **27**:185-86, 191, 202, 214
"Mined Country" (Wilbur) **51**:192, 289-91, 315, 317-20
"Mineral" (Page) **12**:170
"Los Mineros" (Dorn) **115**:54, 81, 126
"Miners" (Owen) **19**:342-43, 346, 348, 365, 370; **102**:143, 148, 181, 225, 238-39, 263
"Miners" (Wright) **36**:319, 340, 385-86, 390, 399
"The Miner's Revenge" (Parra)
See "La venganza del minero"
"Minesweepers" (Kipling) **3**:183
"Mingus" (Kaufman) **74**:240
"The Mini Skirt" (Randall) **86**:291, 293, 297, 343
"Miniature" (Meredith) **28**:171
"Minicursi" (Fuertes) **27**:23
The Minimus Poems (Kennedy) **93**:151-52
"The Minister" (Thomas) **99**:239-45, 258, 290
The Minister (Thomas) **99**:323
"Le Ministre" (Ponge) **107**:137
"The Ministry of Fear" (Heaney) **100**:224, 267, 272
"Miniver Cheevy" (Robinson) **1**:462, 467, 478, 487, 496; **35**:362, 377
"The Minneapolis Poem" (Wright) **36**:319-20, 324, 328-29, 341, 345, 353-54, 360, 366, 384, 392
"Minneapolis Story" (Warren) **37**:326
"Minnesbilder" (Ekeloef) **23**:69
"Minnesota Recollection" (Warren) **37**:376
"Minnesota Thanksgiving" (Berryman) **64**:97
"Minnie and Mattie" (Rossetti) **7**:274
Minnie Maylow's Story (Masefield) **78**:46-47, 49, 51, 62, 73
"Minnie Mooch" (Quintana) **36**:256
"Minor Litany" (Benét) **64**:23
"A Minor Prophet" (Eliot) **20**:123, 140-41
"Minor Works of Camoens" (Camões) **31**:32
"Minority Report" (Updike) **90**:357
"Minotaur" (Wylie) **23**:302-303, 306, 323
"The Minstrel Man" (Hughes) **53**:85
Minstrels (Sitwell) **3**:290
"Minstrel's Song, on the Restoration of Lord Clifford the Shepherd" (Wordsworth) **4**:377
The Minstrelsy of the Scottish Border (Scott) **13**:249, 269, 278, 281, 306
"Minus 18 Street" (McGuckian) **27**:80
"The Minute" (Shapiro) **25**:306
"The Minute before Meeting" (Hardy) **8**:90; **92**:250, 370
"Minutes from the Meeting" (Jordan) **38**:122
"La minutieuse" (Char) **56**:150
"Minutius. Artemisia. A Dialogue" (Leapor) **85**:213
Mira Bai and Her Padas (Mirabai) **48**:164-69
"Mira to Octavia" (Leapor) **85**:214-17
"Mirabeau Bridge" (Apollinaire)
See "Le pont Mirabeau"
"Mirabel" (Mallarmé) **102**:30
Mirabell: Books of Numbers (Merrill) **28**:233, 235-38, 240, 251, 260-64, 275-77, 279, 281
"The Miracle" (Bukowski) **18**:5
"Miracle" (Carver) **54**:15, 18, 28-29
"The Miracle" (Gunn) **26**:220
"Miracle" (Randall) **86**:340
"The Miracle" (Stone) **53**:230
"Miracle Fair" (Szymborska)
See "Jarmark cudó"
Miracle Fair: Selected Poems (Szymborska)
See *Jarmark cudó*
"A Miracle for Breakfast" (Bishop) **3**:46, 57; **34**:78, 124-27, 137, 190-91
"A Miracle for Breakfast" (Curnow) **48**:44
"Miracle Glass Co." (Simic) **69**:309
"Miracles" (Abse) **41**:21
"The Miracles" (Kipling) **91**:86
"Miracles" (Whitman) **3**:381
"Miraculous Weapons" (Césaire)
See "Les armes miraculeuses"
"una mirada" (Storni) **33**:271
"El mirador" (Cernuda) **62**:216
"Mirage" (Tagore)
See "Marichika"
"Mirage des Aiguilles" (Char) **56**:112, 135, 152
"Mirage of the Desert" (Masters) **1**:344
"Mirage of the Peaks" (Char)
See "Mirage des Aiguilles"
"The Mirages" (Hayden) **6**:193, 197
"Miramar" (Carducci) **46**:9, 26, 52, 85-86
"Miramar" (Walcott) **46**:238
"Miranda Dies in the Fog, 1816" (Neruda)
See "Miranda muere en la niebla, 1816"
"Miranda muere en la niebla, 1816" (Neruda) **4**:295
"Miranda's Supper" (Wylie) **23**:302, 307, 314-15, 321
"Mira's Picture" (Leapor) **85**:196-98, 206, 234, 252, 254, 262, 287, 295-96

"Mira's Will" (Leapor) **85**:260-61
"El mirasol" (Storni) **33**:294
"Miravalle" (Cernuda) **62**:216
"Miriam" (Whittier) **93**:176, 188, 222
"Miriam Tazewell" (Ransom) **61**:274, 323
"Miriam's Song" (Harper) **21**:194-95
"Miró Celi una rosa que en el prado" (Juana Inés de la Cruz) **24**:225
"Le miroir d'un moment" (Éluard) **38**:71, 105
Mirour de l'Omme (Gower) **59**:20, 41-45, 113, 117-19
"The Mirror" (Borges) **32**:66
"Mirror" (Merrill) **28**:225, 242, 245-47
"Mirror" (Paz)
See "Espejo"
"The Mirror" (Rossetti) **44**:238, 255-56
"Mirror" (Updike) **90**:347
"Mirror Image" (Glück) **16**:162-63
"Mirror in February" (Kinsella) **69**:80, 141
"The Mirror in the Roadway" (Tomlinson) **17**:334
"The Mirror in the Woods" (Rexroth) **20**:181; **95**:248
"The Mirror in Which Two Are Seen as One" (Rich) **5**:368
"Mirror Mirror on the Wheel" (Raworth) **107**:297-300
"The Mirror Of Madmen" (Chesterton) **28**:108
"Mirror Sermon" (Brutus) **24**:99
"The Mirror Speaks" (Stevenson) **84**:303
"Mirrors" (Borges)
See "Los espejos"
"The Mirrors" (Williams) **7**:370
Mirrors (Creeley) **73**:118
"Mirrors & Windows" (Nemerov) **24**:292
Mirrors and Windows (Nemerov) **24**:256, 261, 264, 295-96
"Mirrors at 4 A.M." (Simic) **69**:309
"The Mirth of Shipwrecks" (Ungaretti) **57**:358
"Mis libros" (Mistral) **32**:149-50
"Mis queridos difuntos" (Fuertes) **27**:12
"Mis versos" (Martí) **76**:106
"Misanthropos" (Gunn) **26**:188-190, 192-193, 214, 223, 225-226
Misanthropos (Gunn) **26**:203
"Misapprehension" (Traherne) **70**:222, 288
Miscellaneous Poems (Harper)
See *Poems on Miscellaneous Subjects*
Miscellaneous Poems (Longfellow) **30**:26
Miscellaneous Poems (Marvell) **10**:257, 277, 311; **86**:239
Miscellanies (Cowley) **90**:7, 15, 18, 21, 98
Miscellanies (Swift) **9**:251, 253, 255, 275
Miscellanies in Verse and Prose (Chatterton) **104**:8
"Miscellany" (Castro)
See "Varia"
Miscellany (Surrey)
See *Tottel's Miscellany*
Miscellany: Being a Collection of Poems by Several Hands. Together with Reflections on Morality, or Seneca Unmasqued (Behn) **88**:42, 48, 69-73, 75, 106, 110
A Miscellany of New Poems (Behn) **13**:7
Miscellany Poems on Several Occasions, Written by a Lady, 1713 (Finch) **21**:140, 148, 161, 163-64, 172-73
"Mischief" (Thomas) **99**:326
"Mise Eire" (Boland) **58**:4-5, 15, 37, 48-49, 66, 69, 87
"Mise en Scene" (Lowell) **13**:96
"Misericords" (Szirtes) **51**:157
"Miserie" (Herbert) **4**:108, 121
"The Miseries of St. Germains" (Barker) **91**:6, 18, 44
"Misery" (Hughes) **1**:328; **53**:113, 124
"Misery" (Vaughan) **81**:266, 335, 342, 368
"The Misery of the Heathen" (Stevenson) **84**:342
"The Misfit" (Day Lewis) **11**:147
"Misfortune" (Cernuda) **62**:206
"Misgiving" (Frost) **1**:195; **39**:232
"Misgiving at Dusk" (Enright) **93**:35
"Misgivings" (Melville) **82**:83, 91, 130-31, 134, 207-8
"Misiricords" (Szirtes)
See "Misericords"
"Miss B—" (Clare) **23**:25
"Miss Book World" (Abse) **41**:10, 14-15
"Miss Drake Proceeds to Supper" (Plath) **1**:398-99
"Miss Gada-Nigi" (Seifert) **47**:333
"Miss Gee" (Auden) **1**:30; **92**:55-56
Miss Kilmansegg and Her Precious Leg: A Golden Legend (Hood) **93**:61-62, 81, 83, 102, 104-5, 115, 118-19
"Miss Loo" (de la Mare) **77**:70
"Miss Marnell" (Clarke) **112**:55
"Miss Nostradamus" (Simic) **69**:320
"Miss Own" (Brathwaite) **56**:96
"Miss Rosie" (Clifton) **17**:32-33
"Miss T" (de la Mare) **77**:113
"Miss Universe" (Kavanagh) **33**:88, 136; **105**:164
"Missel Thrush" (de la Mare) **77**:112
"The Missing" (Gunn) **26**:224
"Missing Dates" (Empson) **104**:80, 84-85, 88, 122
"The Missing Knot" (Herbert) **50**:20-21
Missing Link (Kennedy) **93**:147-48
The Missing Piece Meets the Big O (Silverstein) **49**:305
"Missing the Mountains" (Goodison) **36**:154
"Missing the Trail" (Wagoner) **33**:337, 340
"The Mission" (Warren) **37**:313
"Mississippi Anatomy" (Jacobsen) **62**:325
"Mississippi Levee" (Hughes) **1**:256
"Mississippi Mother" (Brooks) **7**:96
"Mississippi Winter" (Walker) **30**:343
"Mississippi Winter III" (Walker) **30**:370
"Missoula Softball Tournament" (Hugo) **68**:285, 288, 305
"Missus Dorra" (Niedecker) **42**:140
"the missyun" (Bissett) **14**:24, 34
"Mist in the Valley" (Noyes) **27**:134
"The Mist of Pornography" (Cohen) **109**:98, 102
"The Mistaken Lover" (Leapor) **85**:211, 248, 285, 293
"Míster no!" (Guillén) **23**:126
"Mister Samuel and Sam" (Brown) **55**:155
"The Mistress" (Thomas) **99**:309
"The Mistress" (Wilmot) **66**:324
Mistress Bradstreet (Berryman)
See *Homage to Mistress Bradstreet*
The Mistresse (Cowley) **90**:6, 13-16, 20-24, 26-33, 35, 41, 60, 82, 98, 111-20, 179
"Mistris, since you so much desire" (Campion) **87**:63, 71, 97
"Misty Dawn at Feeding Time" (Tapahonso) **65**:225, 258
"Mithridates" (Emerson) **18**:71
"Mithridates at Chios" (Whittier) **93**:314
"Mito" (Pavese) **13**:210, 228-29
"Mitotera" (Quintana) **36**:273
"Mixed Feelings" (Ashbery) **26**:124, 127
"The Mixer" (MacNeice) **61**:141
"Mne moia otdel'nost' nadoela" (Shvarts) **50**:162
"Mnemonic" (Lee) **24**:243
"The Mnemonic Demigod" (Barker) **77**:19
Mnemosyne Lay in Dust (Clarke) **112**:50, 67-68, 80, 82, 87, 89, 93-94, 98, 105-8, 110, 113, 116, 122, 126, 129, 134
"Może to wszystko" (Szymborska) **44**:308
"The Mob" (Brutus) **24**:108
Mock Beggar Hall (Graves) **6**:127-28
"Mock Confessional" (Ferlinghetti) **1**:187
"Mock Orange" (Glück) **16**:145, 164
"A Mock Song" (Lovelace) **69**:167, 185, 243, 254
"The Mock Song" (Wilmot) **66**:266, 278-81, 310, 329
"The Mocking Bird" (Lanier) **50**:56, 77
"The Mockingbird" (Jarrell) **41**:162
Mockingbird, Wish Me Luck (Bukowski) **18**:19
"Mockingbirds" (Oliver) **75**:313
"Models" (Clampitt) **19**:99
"Models" (Nemerov) **24**:290
"Modern Craft" (Crane) **99**:37, 46, 70
"Modern Elegy of the Motif of Affectation" (Guillén)
See "Elegía moderna del motivo cursi"
Modern Fable Poems (Nishiwaki)
See *Kindai no Guwa*
"Modern Love" (Keats) **1**:311
Modern Love (Meredith) **60**:246, 252, 258, 263-71, 274-76, 280, 286, 290-92, 294, 299-310, 312-13, 315, 317-26, 328, 341-42, 344-46
"Modern Love-Letter" (Leapor)
See "Strephon to Celia. A Modern Love-Letter"
"The Modern Mother" (Meynell) **112**:165, 186
"The Modern Patriot" (Cowper) **40**:102-3
"The Modern Poet" (Meynell) **112**:156
"Modern Poetry Is Prose (But It Is Saying Plenty)" (Ferlinghetti) **1**:182-83
"A Modern Sappho" (Arnold) **5**:12
"Modern Times" (Parra) **39**:11
The Modern Traveller (Belloc) **24**:25-7, 35
"Moderna" (Storni) **33**:251
"A Modernist Ballade" (Belloc) **24**:39
"Modes of Being" (Levertov) **11**:197-98
"Modes of Pleasure" (Gunn) **26**:186, 219
"A Modest Meane for Maides" (Whitney) **116**:265, 268-70, 278, 284, 286, 312
"A Modest Mound of Bones" (Updike) **90**:352
"Modest Proposal" (Enzensberger) **28**:158, 161
"A Modest Proposal" (Hughes) **7**:118
"A Modest Request" (Holmes) **71**:64, 68, 86
"Modlitwa Pana Cogito-Podróznika" (Herbert) **50**:40-41
"Modulations for a Solo Voice" (Levertov) **11**:209
A Moelna Elegy (Ekelöf)
See *En Mölna-elegi*
Moeoniae; or, Certain Excellent Poems and Spirituall Hymnes: Omitted in the Last Impression of "Peters Complaint" (Southwell) **83**:279, 281
"Moesta et Errabunda" (Baudelaire) **1**:70; **106**:127
Mogg Megone (Whittier) **93**:171, 221
"Mogiły haremu" (Mickiewicz) **38**:222
"La Moglie del Gigante" (Carducci) **46**:52, 54
"Mogollon Morning" (Momaday) **25**:221
"Moharram" (Stryk) **27**:214
Mohn und Gedächtnes (Celan) **10**:95
moi, Laminaire (Césaire) **25**:33, 41, 45
"Moia rodoslovnaia" (Akhmadulina) **43**:2, 45
"Moira McCavendish" (Betjeman) **75**:84
"Moïse" (Vigny) **26**:369, 380-81, 384, 391, 398, 401, 410-11
"Mój ojciec" (Herbert) **50**:7
"Mole" (Stryk) **27**:199-200
"Moles" (Oliver) **75**:287
"Moling's Gloss" (Heaney) **100**:238
"El Molino Rojo" (Ríos) **57**:312-13
"Molitva" (Tsvetaeva) **14**:312
"Molitvy" (Lermontov) **18**:303
Moll Pitcher and The Minstrel Girl (Whittier) **93**:170, 221
"Le Mollusque" (Ponge) **107**:100-102
"Molly Gone" (Hardy) **92**:235
"Molly Means" (Walker) **20**:291-92
En Mölna-elegi (Ekeloef) **23**:50-8, 62-3, 77-87
"Moloch in State Street" (Whittier) **93**:211
Molodets (Tsvetaeva) **14**:313, 325-26
"Molti anni fassi qual felice, in una" (Michelangelo) **103**:306
"Molto diletta al gusto intero e sano" (Michelangelo) **103**:277
Moly (Gunn) **26**:192, 196-197, 203-204, 206-207, 209, 212, 214-215, 219, 221, 226, 228-229
"The Moment" (Abse) **41**:13, 27-28

"Moment" (Nemerov) **24**:264
"The Moment" (Stafford) **71**:284
"Moment" (Zagajewski) **27**:381, 396
"The Moment Cleary" (Kursh) **15**:179
"Moment of Eternity" (MacDiarmid) **9**:193
"The Moment of Grace" (Amichai)
See "She'at ha-Hesed"
"Moment On the Canal" (Kavanagh) **33**:161
"Momento" (Storni) **33**:251
"Momento epico" (Carducci) **46**:49, 77
"Moments Musicaux" (Melville) **82**:39, 55
"Moments of Glory" (Jeffers) **17**:141
"Moments of Minnie" (Ransom) **61**:271
Moments of the Italian Summer (Wright) **36**:308-09
"Moments of Vision" (Hardy) **92**:205
Moments of Vision and Miscellaneous Verses (Hardy) **92**:290-91
"Momma and the Neutron Bomb" (Yevtushenko) **40**:358, 366, 370
"Momma Welfare Roll" (Angelou) **32**:3, 29
"Momus" (Sandburg) **41**:313
"Mon Allas, Mona Lisa" (Yau) **61**:335
"Mon Dieu m'a dit" (Verlaine) **2**:415; **32**:341
"Mon Enfance" (Hugo) **17**:75
Mon Habit (Béranger) **112**:8
"Mon héroïsme, quelle farce" (Césaire) **25**:56
"Mon petit mont blanc" (Éluard) **38**:91
"Mon rêve familier" (Verlaine) **32**:341, 386
"Monadnoc" (Emerson) **18**:71, 74, 102-3, 111
"Monadnock from Wachusett" (Whittier) **93**:239
"Monaghan Hills" (Kavanagh) **105**:151
"The Monarch of the Id" (Birney) **52**:8
Monarchia (Dante)
See *De monarchia*
"Monarchies" (Bradstreet)
See "The Four Monarchies"
"Monarchs" (Olds) **22**:307
"Monax" (Pushkin) **10**:407
"Monday" (Dalton) **36**:136
"Monday" (Seferis) **66**:151, 170, 186, 206
"Monday Morning" (Collins) **68**:215
"Monday Morning" (Cunningham) **92**:166, 191
"Monday: Roxana; or The Drawing-room" (Montagu) **16**:338, 348
"Mondblick" (Stramm) **50**:189, 202, 207
"Mondschein" (Stramm) **50**:171-72, 189
La moneda de hierro (Borges) **22**:96-7; **32**:64, 69, 86
"Monet 'Lady with a Parasol'" (Thomas) **99**:3063
"Monet 'Portrait of Mme Gaudibert'" (Thomas) **99**:306
"Monet Refuses the Operation" (Mueller) **33**:196
"Monet's 'Waterlilies'" (Hayden) **6**:183, 195
"Money" (Jarrell) **41**:135-36
"Money" (Nemerov) **24**:262, 281
"Money and Grass" (Ignatow) **34**:286
"Money Goes Upstream" (Snyder) **21**:300
"Money, Honey, Money" (Walker) **20**:294
"Money/Love" (Corso) **33**:37
"Mongo" (Lermontov) **18**:281
"Mongolian Idiot" (Shapiro) **25**:300, 325
"La monja gitana" (García Lorca) **3**:132
"La monja y el ruiseñor" (Darío) **15**:107-08
"The Monk" (Kinsella) **69**:66, 121
"The Monk" (Pushkin)
See "Monax"
"Monkey" (Enright) **93**:14
"The Monkey Puzzle" (Moore) **49**:89, 97, 99-100
"The Monkeys" (Moore) **4**:270; **49**:93, 121, 161
The Monkey's Cloak (Matsuo Basho)
See *Sarumino*
The Monkey's Raincoat (Matsuo Basho)
See *Sarumino*
Monkey's Straw Raincoat (Matsuo Basho)
See *Sarumino*
"Monkhood" (Berryman) **64**:101
"The Monks of Casal-Maggiore" (Longfellow) **30**:43, 63
The Monks of St. Mark (Peacock) **87**:322, 346, 350
"Monk's Tale" (Chaucer) **19**:13, 42, 45, 56, 63; **58**:336
"The Monk's Walk" (Dunbar) **5**:121, 137-38, 141
"Monna Innominata" (Rossetti) **7**:271, 275, 280-1
"Le monocle de mon oncle" (Stevens) **6**:292, 295, 303, 327
"Monody" (Melville) **82**:90, 98, 145-47, 151
"Monody" (Zukofsky) **11**:368
"Monody on a Century" (Birney) **52**:3, 39
"Monody on the Death of a Platonist Bank Clerk" (Betjeman) **75**:78, 83
"Monody on the Death of Aldersgate Street Station" (Betjeman) **75**:27, 45, 94
"Monody on the Death of Chatterton" (Coleridge) **11**:49, 52
The Monogram (Elytis) **21**:123
"The Monoliths" (Momaday) **25**:219
"Monolog" (Benn) **35**:23, 24
"The Monologue" (de la Mare) **77**:58
"Monologue at Midnight" (Warren) **37**:284, 288, 322, 332, 377, 380
"Monologue of a Broadway Actress" (Yevtushenko) **40**:357
"Monologue of a Fox on an Alaskan Fur Farm" (Yevtushenko) **40**:357
"Monologue of a Mother" (Lawrence) **54**:175, 244
"Monologue of a Polar Fox on an Alaskan Fur Farm" (Yevtushenko)
See "Monologue of a Fox on an Alaskan Fur Farm"
"Monologue of a Silver Fox on a Fur Farm in Alaska" (Yevtushenko)
See "Monologue of a Fox on an Alaskan Fur Farm"
Monologue of a Spanish Guide (Yevtushenko) **40**:357
"Monologue of the Beatniks" (Yevtushenko) **40**:345
"Monologue of the Husband" (Barker) **77**:20
"Monologue of the Wife" (Barker) **77**:20
"The Monosyllable" (Jacobsen) **62**:296, 305, 316
"Monotone" (Sandburg) **2**:303; **41**:261
"Monotony" (Boland) **58**:14, 53
"Monotony" (Cavafy) **36**:57
"Monsieur Jean" (Sainte-Beuve) **110**:20, 56, 69
"Monsieur Prudhomme" (Verlaine) **32**:374, 376
"Monsieur qui Passe" (Mew) **107**:17-18, 51, 57
"The Monster" (Shvarts)
See "Chudishche"
"The Monster of Mr. Cogito" (Herbert)
See "Potwór Pana Cogito"
"Monsters From the Ozarks" (Reed) **68**:330
"Le Monstre" (Verlaine) **32**:392
"Mont Blanc" (Brathwaite) **56**:93
"Mont Blanc" (Shelley) **14**:206, 211-12, 217, 241; **67**:166-67, 196-200, 204-5, 215, 224, 228
"Le mont des Oliviers" (Vigny) **26**:367-68, 370, 380, 383, 385, 391, 401, 412
"Montage of a Dream Deferred" (Hughes) **53**:94
Montage of a Dream Deferred (Hughes) **1**:244-45, 247-48, 251, 253, 258, 261, 263, 265-68, 270; **53**:108, 114, 121, 123, 126, 129, 140, 145, 152, 156-64, 176-78, 183-85, 188-93, 197
"Montana" (Hugo) **68**:259
"Montana" (Zanzotto) **65**:264
"Montana Eclogue" (Stafford) **71**:333, 362
"Montana Fifty Years Ago" (Cunningham) **92**:177
"Montana Pastoral" (Cunningham) **92**:159, 166, 173, 186
"Montana Ranch Abandoned" (Hugo) **68**:234, 251
"La montaña rusa" (Parra) **39**:251, 254, 260, 278, 305-6, 308
"Montcalm" (Davie) **29**:96
"Montesano Revisited" (Hugo) **68**:283
"Montesano Unvisited" (Hugo) **68**:311-12
"Montevideo" (Borges) **32**:83
"Montezuma" (Whittier) **93**:198
"Montezuma's Revenge" (Berrigan) **103**:26
"Montgomery Hollow" (Hugo) **68**:251, 284-85, 305
"Montgomery's Return" (Whittier) **93**:193
"A Month among Children" (Montale)
See "Un mese fra i bambini"
"A Month in Summer" (Kizer) **66**:74
"The Month of August" (Leapor) **85**:247, 254-55, 289
"The Months: A Pageant" (Rossetti) **7**:280
"The Month's Calendar" (Hardy) **92**:327
"Montparnasse" (Apollinaire) **7**:34
La Montre; or, The Lover's Watch (Behn) **13**:3; **88**:82, 85, 111, 138
Une montre sentimentale (Nishiwaki) **15**:237
"The Monument" (Bishop) **3**:37, 41-3, 48-9, 72; **34**:66, 109, 136-37, 144-45, 189
"A Monument" (Hughes) **89**:125, 151
"Monument" (Oppen) **35**:311, 312
"Monument" (Pushkin)
See "Pamjatnik"
The Monument (Strand) **63**:150, 156, 159, 165-70, 172-74, 180, 189-90, 195-96
"The Monument" (Strand) **63**:168
"A Monument in Utopia" (Schnackenberg) **45**:334, 348, 350
"The Monument Maker" (Hardy) **92**:258-60
"Monument Mountain" (Bryant) **20**:14, 29, 47
"Monument of Love" (Jiménez) **7**:184
"The Monument to Peter the Great" (Mickiewicz) **38**:168
"Monuments for a Friendly Girl at a Tenth Grade Party" (Stafford) **71**:379
"The Monuments of Hiroshima" (Enright) **93**:14, 19
"Mood" (Cullen) **20**:63, 75
"The Mood of a Day" (Seferis) **66**:122, 125, 128, 143-45, 170
Moods, Conjectures and Fancies (Blunden) **66**:21, 23
"The Moon" (Borges)
See "La luna"
"The Moon" (Carruth) **10**:71
"The Moon" (Duncan) **75**:216
"The Moon" (Hall) **70**:31
"The Moon" (Ignatow) **34**:279, 292, 319
"Moon" (Schuyler) **88**:176, 222-23
"The Moon" (Stevenson) **84**:344
"Moon" (Walcott) **46**:286
Moon across the Way (Borges)
See *Luna de enfrente*
"Moon and Insect Panorama: Love Poem" (García Lorca) **3**:141
"Moon and Oatgrass" (Chin) **40**:25, 27, 31, 33-5
"The Moon and the Night and the Men" (Berryman) **64**:78, 83, 85
"The Moon and the Yew Tree" (Plath) **1**:390, 409
"The Moon Being the Number 19" (Wakoski) **15**:364
"Moon Compasses" (Frost) **39**:246
Moon Crossing Bridge (Gallagher) **9**:62-5
"Moon Down Elphinstone" (Birney) **52**:40
"The Moon Explodes in Autumn as a Milkweed Pod" (Wakoski) **15**:364
"The Moon Has a Complicated Geography" (Wakoski) **15**:364
"Moon in Hydra" (Cisneros) **52**:153
"The Moon in Lleyn" (Thomas) **99**:259
"The Moon in Your Hands" (H. D.) **5**:275
"The Moon is Always Female" (Piercy) **29**:311
The Moon Is Always Female (Piercy) **29**:311, 323

"The Moon Is the Number Eighteen" (Olson) **19**:293-94, 321
"Moon Landing" (Auden) **92**:98
"Moon Lines, after Jiminez" (Ondaatje) **28**:335
"The Moon Looks In" (Hardy) **92**:208
"The Moon Moves Up her Smooth and Sheeny Path" (Thoreau) **30**:192
"The Moon Now Rises to Her Absolute Rule" (Thoreau) **30**:266
"The Moon over Tarusa" (Akhmadulina)
See "Luna v Taruse"
"Moon over the Gasworks" (Seifert) **47**:324
"Moon Poems" (Lindsay) **23**:281
"Moon Tiger" (Levertov) **11**:177
"The Moon to the Sun" (Meynell) **112**:158, 192, 298, 300-302
"The Moon until Morning" (Akhmadulina) **43**:36, 43-44
"The Moon upon the Waters" (Raworth) **107**:336
"The Moondial" (Carman) **34**:212
The Moone-Calfe (Drayton) **98**:77-79
"Moonlight" (Apollinaire)
See "Clair de lune"
"Moonlight" (Harjo) **27**:56
"Moonlight" (Ransom) **61**:293
"Moonlight" (Teasdale) **31**:360, 380, 388
"Moonlight" (Verlaine)
See "Clair de lune"
"Moonlight Alert" (Winters) **82**:334
"Moonlight and Jellyfish" (Hagiwara) **18**:168
"Moonlight and Maggots" (Sandburg) **41**:322
"Moonlight Night" (Tu Fu) **9**:321
"Moonlight Night: Carmel" (Hughes) **1**:240
"Moonrise" (Lawrence) **54**:169
"Moonrise" (Plath) **1**:406; **37**:176, 184
"Moonrise" (Sappho) **5**:416
"Moonrise" (Winters) **82**:318, 344-45
Moons (Oliver)
See *Twelve Moons*
"The Moon's Funeral" (Belloc) **24**:49
"Moon's Revenge" (Carducci)
See "Vendette della luna"
"Moon-Set" (Carruth) **10**:85
"Moonset Glouster" (Olson) **19**:322-23
"Moonshine and Sunny Beams" (Snodgrass) **74**:305
"Moon-Skin" (Wagoner) **33**:354
"Moonstruck" (MacDiarmid) **9**:160
"Moonwalk" (Hughes) **89**:181
"The Moor" (Thomas) **99**:245, 258, 315, 318, 320
The Moor of Peter the Great (Pushkin)
See *Arap Petra Velikogo*
"Moorland" (Thomas) **99**:320
"Moortown" (Hughes) **7**:162
Moortown (Hughes) **7**:157-58, 162-63, 165, 171; **89**:119, 124-25, 128-31, 134, 144, 150-52, 157, 168, 188, 192, 216-17
Moortown Diary (Hughes)
See *Moortown*
Moortown Elegies (Hughes)
See *Moortown*
"The Moose" (Bishop) **3**:58-60, 73, 75; **34**:54, 56, 58, 62, 72, 78, 82, 100, 104, 107-13, 143, 146, 187, 193
"The Moose" (Bly) **39**:72
"Moose in the Morning" (Sarton) **39**:368
"The Moose Wallow" (Hayden) **6**:194-95
"Mopsus; or, The Castle-Builder" (Leapor) **85**:252
A Moral Alphabet (Belloc) **24**:16-18, 26
"The Moral Bully" (Holmes) **71**:66, 68, 108
"Moral Clothing" (Lawrence) **54**:249
Moral Emblems (Stevenson) **84**:302, 320, 335
Moral Essays (Pope) **26**:320, 340
Moral Fables (Henryson)
See *The Morall Fabillis of Esope the Phrygian*
"A Moral Poem" (Cunningham) **92**:166, 185
"Moral Reflections on the Cross of St. Paul's" (Hood) **93**:122
"Moral Songs" (Hood) **93**:72
"Moral Tales" (Clarke) **112**:123
Moral Tales (Laforgue)
See *Moralités légendaires*
Moral Teachings and Proverbs (Christine de Pizan)
See *Enseignemens et Proverbes moraux*
"The Moral Vision" (Leapor) **85**:186, 259
"Morale" (Gautier) **18**:158
"The Moralists" (Winters) **82**:338-40, 342
"La moralité" (Mickiewicz) **38**:180
Moralités légendaires (Laforgue) **14**:70
Moralities (Kinsella) **69**:115, 122
"Morality" (Arnold) **5**:42
"The Morality of Poetry" (Wright) **36**:299, 315-16, 338, 340, 380-81
"Morality Play" (Oppen)
See "A Morality Play: Preface"
"A Morality Play: Preface" (Oppen) **35**:336, 337
The Morall Fabillis of Esope the Phrygian (Henryson) **65**:3, 5, 10-15, 19-20, 22-23, 25-31, 33-35, 49, 53-55, 58-65, 69, 79-81, 83, 104, 124
"Un morceau en forme de poire" (Wakoski) **15**:372
Morceaux choisis (Tzara) **27**:223-4
"More" (Stein) **18**:319, 330
"A More Ancient Mariner" (Carman) **34**:201, 207
More Beasts—For Worse Children (Belloc) **24**:24-6, 35
"More Clues" (Rukeyser) **12**:225
More Collected Verse (Service) **70**:140, 143-44, 161
"More Extracts from a Diary of Dreams" (Clarke) **112**:69, 139
"More Foreign Cities" (Tomlinson) **17**:318
"More Light! More Light!" (Hecht) **70**:78, 81, 84, 86, 102, 109
"More Love Lyrics" (Hardy) **92**:242
"The More Loving One" (Auden) **92**:104
"More Memories of Underdevelopment" (Enright) **93**:27
More Nonsense, Pictures, Rhymes, Botany, Etc. (Lear) **65**:141-43, 166, 168-69
More Pansies (Lawrence) **54**:184-85, 224, 249
More Peers (Belloc) **24**:26-7, 41, 43, 49
More Poems (Housman) **2**:167, 171-74, 176, 182-83, 188; **43**:220, 223, 227, 245-46, 253-54, 257-61, 264
More Poems in Scots (Stevenson) **84**:335
More Poems, 1961 (Graves) **6**:154-56
More Poems to Solve (Swenson) **14**:276
More Songs From Vagabondia (Carman) **34**:200, 207, 218, 237-38
"More Sonnets at Christmas" (Tate) **50**:240, 251-53, 255, 261
"More Than a Fool's Song" (Cullen) **20**:57
More to Remember: Poems of Four Decades (Randall) **86**:285, 289, 291, 296, 298, 306, 328-29, 333-39
More Verse and Prose by the Corn-law Rhymer (Elliott) **96**:158, 181
"Morfudd a Dyddgu" (Dafydd ap Gwilym) **56**:245
"Morfudd and Dyddgu" (Dafydd ap Gwilym)
See "Morfudd a Dyddgu"
"Morfudd Fel yr Haul" (Dafydd ap Gwilym) **56**:246
"Morfudd Like the Sun" (Dafydd ap Gwilym)
See "Morfudd Fel yr Haul"
"Der Morgen" (Stramm) **50**:171-72, 175
"Morgue II" (Benn) **35**:50
Morgue und andere Gedichte (Benn) **35**:3, 7, 8, 22, 23, 24, 29, 30, 46, 47, 50, 53, 54, 83
"Mori no michi" (Ishikawa) **10**:213
"Mori no omoide" (Ishikawa) **10**:212-13
Morituri salutamus (Longfellow) **30**:49, 73, 103
"Moriturus" (Millay) **6**:236
"Morning" (Blake) **63**:17
"A Morning" (Dickey) **40**:189, 224, 227-28
"Morning" (Glück) **16**:152
"Morning" (Ransom) **61**:307
"Morning" (Rimbaud)
See "Matin"
"The Morning" (Schuyler) **88**:216
"Morning" (Seferis) **66**:165
"Morning" (Teasdale) **31**:325
"The Morning" (Very) **86**:113
"Morning" (Wheatley)
See "An Hymn to the Morning"
"Morning" (Williams) **7**:352
"Morning After" (Hughes) **1**:256; **53**:120
"The Morning after the Moon" (Akhmadulina)
See "Utro posle luny"
"Morning at Blackwater" (Oliver) **75**:343
"Morning at the Window" (Eliot) **31**:159
"The Morning Baking" (Forché) **10**:142
"The Morning before Christmas" (Hughes) **89**:132, 134
"The Morning Bell" (Ishikawa)
See "Akatsuki no kane"
"The Morning Call" (Patmore) **59**:228-29
"Morning Coffee" (Kinsella) **69**:134, 138-42
"The Morning Dream" (Cowper) **40**:105, 119
"Morning Exercises" (Cassian) **17**:11
"Morning Express" (Sassoon) **12**:275
"Morning Glories" (Oliver) **75**:342
The Morning Glory, Another Thing That Will Never Be My Friend (Bly) **39**:22, 24, 29, 37, 43, 69
"Morning Glory Pool" (Plath) **37**:257
"Morning Hymn to a Dark Girl" (Wright) **36**:315, 335-36, 375
"A Morning Imagination of Russia" (Williams) **7**:350
"Morning in the Square" (Szirtes) **51**:158
The Morning Line (Berrigan) **103**:35-36
"The Morning Moon" (Walcott) **46**:236-37
"The Morning News" (Berry) **28**:11
"Morning, Noon, and Night" (Page) **12**:173
"Morning of Intoxication" (Rimbaud)
See "Matinée d'ivresse"
"The Morning of the Poem" (Schuyler) **88**:176, 181-82, 189-92, 198-99, 201, 203, 225-26
The Morning of the Poem (Schuyler) **88**:176, 188-90, 201
"Morning Poem" (Oliver) **75**:293
Morning Poems (Bly) **39**:116
Morning Poems (Yevtushenko) **40**:344
"Morning Purpose" (Baraka) **113**:18
"Morning Radio" (Mahon) **60**:150
"A Morning Ride" (Kipling) **3**:194
"The Morning road with the electric trains" (Spender) **71**:219
"Morning Sea" (Cavafy) **36**:50
"Morning Song" (Carducci)
See "Mattinata"
"Morning Song" (Plath) **1**:390; **37**:256
"Morning Song" (Teasdale) **31**:360, 370
"The Morning Song of Lord Zero" (Aiken) **26**:15, 24
Morning Songs (Tagore)
See *Prabhat sangit*
"The Morning Star" (Pavese)
See "Lo steddazzu"
The Morning Star (Rexroth) **95**:268, 281-84, 326, 328
"Morning Sun" (MacNeice) **61**:123, 126
"Morning, the Horizon" (Ortiz) **17**:245
"The Morning They Shot Tony Lopez" (Soto) **28**:375
"A Morning Wake among Dead" (Kinnell) **26**:256-57
"The Morning Watch" (Very) **86**:113
"Morning with Broken Window" (Hogan) **35**:257
"Morning-Land" (Sassoon) **12**:240
"Mornings and Aprils" (Masefield) **78**:63
"Mornings in a New House" (Merrill) **28**:221
"Mornings in various years" (Piercy) **29**:315
"The Morning-watch" (Vaughan) **81**:369

"Moro Assassinato" (Curnow) **48**:12, 15-19, 43, 46, 49-51
Morový sloup (Seifert) **47**:317, 319-20, 328-29, 336
"Mors" (Carducci) **46**:6, 54
"Mors" (Hugo) **17**:83
"Morskaya tsarevna" (Lermontov) **18**:292
"La Mort" (Baudelaire) **106**:126
"La mort" (Leopardi) **37**:169-70
"Mort!" (Verlaine) **32**:396
"La mort dans la conversation" (Éluard) **38**:69
"La Mort dans la vie" (Gautier) **18**:131, 155
"La Mort de Narcisse" (Ronsard) **11**:251
"La mort des amants" (Baudelaire) **1**:54, 73; **106**:22, 32, 34-36, 38, 77, 129
"La mort des artistes" (Baudelaire) **1**:45; **106**:22
"La Mort des pauvres" (Baudelaire) **106**:6, 22, 77
"La mort du Diable" (Béranger) **112**:18, 20
"Mort du duc de Berry" (Hugo) **17**:75
"La mort du loup" (Vigny) **26**:367, 369-70, 380-81, 401-402, 412-15
"La Mort du Soldat est près des choses naturelles (5 Mars)" (Stevens) **6**:294
La mort en ce jardin (Bunuel) **15**:207, 218
"Une Mort héroïque" (Baudelaire) **106**:72, 137
"Le mort joyeux" (Baudelaire) **1**:45
"La Mort l'amour la vie" (Éluard) **38**:78
"La mort rose" (Breton) **15**:52
"Mortal" (Jackson) **44**:28
Mortal Acts, Mortal Words (Kinnell) **26**:257, 260-61, 271, 280, 292
"Mortal Enemy" (Parker) **28**:362
"The Mortal Face" (Bonnefoy)
See "Le visage mortel"
"Mortal Girl" (Rukeyser) **12**:231
"Mortal Landscape" (Kennedy) **93**:147
"Mortal Limit" (Warren) **37**:364, 366, 376-77
"Mortal Pride" (Clarke) **112**:47-48
"Mortality" (Betjeman) **75**:13
"Le morte chitarre" (Quasimodo) **47**:286-88
"Morte d'Arthur" (Tennyson) **6**:354, 358-59, 409; **101**:121, 168, 195, 199, 210, 238, 240, 248, 265, 272, 286, 288, 291-92
La morte de Socrate (Lamartine) **16**:263, 266, 273, 278-79, 291
"La morte di Dio" (Montale) **13**:133
La morte meditata (Ungaretti) **57**:347
"Mortel Lay" (Christine de Pizan) **68**:100
"Le Mortel Partenaire" (Char) **56**:155
"I morti" (Montale) **13**:105, 112
"The Mortician's Twelve-Year-Old Son" (Ai) **72**:28
"Mortification" (Herbert) **4**:100-01, 120, 127, 133
Mortimeriados. The Lamentable Civell Warres of Edward the Second and the Barrons (Drayton) **98**:6, 53-54, 125, 132, 134, 137
"Mortmain" (Robinson) **1**:470
"Mortmain" (Warren) **37**:307, 360, 367
"Morts de quatre-vingt-douze" (Rimbaud)
See "Morts de quatre-vingt-douze et de quatre-vingt-treize"
"Morts de quatre-vingt-douze et de quatre-vingt-treize" (Rimbaud) **3**:283; **57**:249
"A Mortul Prayer" (Riley) **48**:300
"Mosaic of the Nativity: Serbia, Winter 1993" (Kenyon) **57**:20, 46
"Moscow Freight Station" (Yevtushenko) **40**:342-43
Moscow Mansions (Guest) **55**:183-85, 214
Moscow Notebooks (Mandelstam) **14**:150
"Moses" (Muir) **49**:197, 298
"Moses" (Nemerov) **24**:295
"Moses" (Shapiro) **25**:296
Moses: A Story of the Nile (Harper) **21**:185, 187-89, 191-98, 201
"Mosquito" (Hughes) **89**:150
"Mosquito" (Lawrence) **54**:187
"The Mosquito and the Moon" (Raworth) **107**:336
"Mossbawn: Sunlight" (Heaney) **18**:197, 232; **100**:210-11, 262, 295, 337
"The Most Humble Poem" (Seifert)
See "Básežn nejpokornější"
"Most like an Arch This Marriage" (Ciardi) **69**:41
"Most Likely You'll Go Your Way and I'll Go Mine" (Dylan) **37**:51
"Most of a Dialogue in Cuzco" (Birney) **52**:16, 42, 96, 99
"The Most of It" (Frost) **1**:205-06, 230-31; **39**:238
"Most Things at Second Hand through Gloves We Touch" (Schwartz) **8**:293
"Most wretched heart" (Wyatt) **27**:353
"Mostly Hospital and Old Age" (Viereck) **27**:294
"Mostru o pavea" (Pasolini) **17**:253
"Mot" (Césaire) **25**:31
Mot (Césaire) **25**:38
"Le mot joie" (Jaccottet) **98**:182, 196-98
"The Mote" (Carman) **34**:207
"The Motel" (Olds) **22**:341
"A Motel in Troy, New York" (Jacobsen) **62**:308, 318
"Motet" No. 1 (Montale) **13**:120-22
"Motet" No. 2 (Montale) **13**:120, 122
"Motet" No. 3 (Montale) **13**:118-20
"Motet" No. 4 (Montale) **13**:120
"Motet" No. 5 (Montale) **13**:118, 121-22, 125, 127
"Motet" No. 6 (Montale) **13**:121-22, 150
"Motet" No. 7 (Montale) **13**:119, 122
"Motet No. 8" (Montale)
See "Mottetto No. 8"
"Motet" No. 9 (Montale) **13**:119, 122-24
"Motet" No. 10 (Montale) **13**:123
"Motet" No. 11 (Montale) **13**:124-25
"Motet" No. 12 (Montale) **13**:124
"Motet" No. 13 (Montale) **13**:124
"Motet" No. 14 (Montale) **13**:124
"Motet" No. 15 (Montale) **13**:125
"Motet" No. 17 (Montale) **13**:125-26
"Motet" No. 18 (Montale) **13**:125, 127
"Motet" No. 19 (Montale) **13**:126
"Motet" No. 20 (Montale) **13**:126
"Motet XX" (Montale) **13**:136
"The Moth" (de la Mare) **77**:77
"The Mother" (Brooks) **7**:67
"The Mother" (Chappell) **105**:65-66
"The Mother" (Crabbe) **97**:97, 99
"The Mother" (Gilmore) **87**:302
"Mother" (Hacker) **47**:80
"The Mother" (Olds) **22**:309
"Mother" (Shvarts)
See "Vospominanie o strannom ugoshchenii"
"Mother" (Smith) **12**:326
"The Mother" (Snodgrass) **74**:289, 309, 312
Mother (Seifert)
See *Maminka*
"Mother, among the Dustbins" (Smith) **12**:352
"Mother and Child" (Clarke) **112**:54, 62
"Mother and Child" (Ignatow) **34**:272
"Mother and Daughter" (Sexton) **2**:365; **79**:193, 230
"Mother and Jack and the Rain" (Sexton) **79**:206
The Mother and Other Poems (Sitwell) **3**:299, 302, 319
"Mother and Poet" (Barrett Browning) **6**:30-1
"Mother and Son" (Morris) **55**:338-39
"Mother and Son" (Tate) **50**:230-31, 255, 302
"Mother and Son" (Thomas) **99**:309
"Mother Cat" (Montague) **106**:353
"Mother Dear" (McKay) **2**:222
"Mother Earth: Her Whales" (Snyder) **21**:293, 297
"Mother Farewell!" (Johnson) **24**:145
"Mother Goose" (Niedecker) **42**:95, 98, 141, 152
"Mother Goose" (Rexroth) **20**:195, 218; **95**:250, 254, 258, 260, 274
"Mother Goose Up-to-date; John Masefield Related the Story of Tom, Tom, the Piper's Son" (Masefield) **78**:104
"Mother Goose's Garland" (MacLeish) **47**:130
"Mother Hubberd's Tale" (Spenser)
See "Prosopopoia; or, Mother Hubberds Tale"
"mother i am mad" (Clifton) **17**:19
"Mother in Wartime" (Hughes) **1**:252
"Mother Marie Therese" (Lowell) **3**:205
"Mother Mind" (Howe) **81**:13, 46
"The Mother Mourns" (Hardy) **92**:262, 299-302
"Mother Night" (Johnson) **24**:127, 137, 159, 166
"Mother of God" (Sikelianos) **29**:366
"Mother of God I Shall Pray in Humility" (Lermontov) **18**:296
"Mother of Hermes" (Keats) **96**:213
Mother Poem (Brathwaite) **56**:34-35, 41-45, 50-51, 61-62, 70-71, 89-90, 96-98, 100
"Mother Pomegranae" (Mistral)
See "La madre granada"
"Mother Rosarine" (Kumin) **15**:191
"Mother Stone" (Stone) **53**:258
"Mother the Great Stones Got to Move" (Goodison) **36**:153
"Mother to Son" (Hughes) **1**:241, 248-49, 262; **53**:84, 125, 187
"The Mother Tongue" (Boland) **58**:38, 62
"Mother Tongue" (Simic) **69**:371
Mother, What Is Man? (Smith) **12**:326
"The Mothering Blackness" (Angelou) **32**:29
"Motherland" (Lermontov)
See "Rodina"
"Mother-Right" (Rich) **5**:384
"Mothers" (Giovanni) **19**:140
"The Mother's Blessing" (Harper) **21**:197
"Mother's Day" (Stafford) **71**:378
"A Mother's Heroism" (Harper) **21**:194, 206, 217
"The Mother's Lesson" (Dobell) **100**:139
"The Mother's Secret" (Holmes) **71**:94
"The Mother's Story" (Clifton) **17**:29
"The Mother's Tale" (Ai) **72**:24
"Mother's Things" (Creeley) **73**:78
"Mother's Voice" (Creeley) **73**:79
"Moths" (Boland) **58**:19, 49
"The Moths" (Merwin) **45**:22
"The Moth-Signal" (Hardy) **8**:99; **92**:206
"The Motion" (Jacobsen) **62**:301
"Motion and Rest" (Toomer) **7**:338
"The Motion of Songs Rising" (Tapahonso) **65**:242
"Motion of Wish" (Kunitz) **19**:160
"The Motions" (Ammons) **16**:5
"The Motive for Metaphor" (Stevens) **6**:312-13, 340
Motivos de son (Guillén) **23**:97-98, 104-08, 110, 133, 141-45
"Motley" (de la Mare) **77**:58, 73
Motley, and Other Poems (de la Mare) **77**:59, 71; 74, 77, 94, 142
"A Motor" (Bell) **79**:22
"Motor Lights on a Hill Road" (Lowell) **13**:60
"A Motorbike" (Hughes) **7**:162
The Motorcycle Betrayal Poems (Wakoski) **15**:325-26, 331-32, 345, 350, 363, 366, 369-70
"Motoring" (Brooke) **24**:68
"Les mots 'Andalou,' 'Andalousie'" (Jaccottet) **98**:201
"Motteti" (Montale) **13**:105
"Mottetto No. 8" (Montale) **13**:105, 113, 122, 127
"The Motto" (Cowley) **90**:14, 51, 54, 83, 117, 154, 170, 180
"Motto" (Hughes) **1**:267; **53**:150-52, 159
"The Motto on the Sundial" (Rexroth) **20**:192; **95**:270

"Motto to the Songs of Innocence and of Experience" (Blake) **12**:10
"Moules à la Marinière" (Curnow) **48**:36, 38
Moulin premier (Char) **56**:121, 129-30, 142, 158-59, 185
"Moulin Rouge" (Mueller) **33**:193
"The Mound Builders" (Kunitz) **19**:158
"La Mounine" (Ponge) **107**:112, 175
"Mount Chungnan" (Wang Wei) **18**:362-63
"Mount Eagle" (Montague) **106**:271, 290
Mount Eagle (Montague) **106**:281-82, 289, 302-3, 305, 313
"Mount Kearsarge" (Hall) **70**:32
"Mount Kikineis" (Mickiewicz)
See "Góra Kikineis"
"Mount Mary" (Wright) **14**:343
"Mount of Olives" (Vaughan) **81**:334
"The Mount of Olives" (Vigny)
See "Le mont des Oliviers"
"Mount Zion" (Hughes) **7**:147; **89**:122
Mount Zion; or, In Touch with the Infinite (Betjeman) **75**:6, 59-60, 69, 106
"th mountain" (Bissett) **14**:20
"The Mountain" (Frost) **1**:226
"The Mountain" (Merwin) **45**:18, 29
"Mountain Blueberries" (Francis) **34**:261
"The Mountain Chapel" (Thomas) **53**:326
"Mountain Daisy" (Burns)
See "To a Mountain Daisy"
"A Mountain Gateway" (Carman) **34**:229
Mountain Interval (Frost) **1**:197, 202, 207, 215; **39**:232-33, 235; **71**:29, 40, 55
"Mountain Lion" (Hogan) **35**:276
"Mountain Pictures" (Whittier) **93**:231
"Mountain Plateau" (Warren) **37**:330
"The Mountain Spirit" (Wang Wei) **18**:382
Mountain Talk (Ammons) **16**:14
"The Mountain Village of Bastundzhi" (Lermontov)
See "Aul Bastundzi"
"The Mountain Whippoorwill" (Benét) **64**:19
"The Mountaineers" (Abse) **41**:7
"The Mountaineer's Ballard" (Wylie) **23**:311
"Mountains" (Auden) **1**:17
"Mountains" (Hayden) **6**:194, 196
"Mountains" (Hughes) **7**:137; **89**:110-11
"The Mountains" (Muir) **49**:243, 297
Mountains and Rivers without End (Snyder) **21**:299
"The Mountains in the Desert" (Creeley) **73**:10, 12, 45, 48, 54
"The Mountains in the Horizon" (Thoreau) **30**:285-87, 293
"A Mounted Umbrella" (Stein) **18**:334, 349
Mourir de ne pas mourir (Éluard) **38**:60, 73, 103
"The Mourner" (Merwin) **45**:9, 49
"The Mourners" (Service) **70**:132, 151
"The Mourner's Bench" (Masters) **1**:339, 343; **36**:194
"Mournin' for Religion" (Masters) **1**:344; **36**:194
"Mourning" (Marvell) **10**:271, 301, 314
"Mourning Dove" (Niedecker) **42**:143-44, 147-48
"A Mourning Forbidding Valediction" (Ashbery) **26**:161
"Mourning Letter, March 29, 1963" (Dorn) **115**:54, 57, 110, 156
"Mourning Pablo Neruda" (Bly) **39**:64
"Mourning to Do" (Sarton) **39**:362
"La Mousche" (Scève) **111**:3
"The Mouse" (Snodgrass) **74**:290
"The Mouse's Nest" (Clare) **23**:7
"La Mousse" (Ponge) **107**:110-12
"Mouth" (Hall) **70**:32
"The Mouth of the Hudson" (Lowell) **3**:215
"The Mouth of Truth" (Ferlinghetti) **1**:183
"Les moutons" (Éluard) **38**:91
"Mouvement" (Rimbaud) **57**:183, 234
"Mouvement" (Tzara) **27**:227
"Move the Meeting Be Adjourned" (Parra)
See "Pido que se levante la sesión"
"The Move to California" (Stafford) **71**:266, 304, 325
"Move Un-noticed to be Noticed: A Nationhood Poem" (Madhubuti) **5**:345
"The Movement of Fish" (Dickey) **40**:182, 190
"Movement to Establish My Identity" (Wakoski) **15**:350
"Movements" (Tomlinson) **17**:327
"Movements II" (Tomlinson) **17**:343
"Movements IV" (Tomlinson) **17**:326, 341
"Movies" (Hughes) **1**:266; **53**:162, 190
"Moving" (Jarrell) **41**:174, 198, 200
Moving (Raworth) **107**:316
"Moving Books to a New Study" (Bly) **39**:53
"The Moving Floor" (Szirtes) **51**:159
"Moving Fred's Outhouse/Geriatrics of Pine" (Ondaatje) **28**:335
"The Moving Image" (Wright) **14**:337, 362
The Moving Image (Wright) **14**:334-35, 338-41, 345-51, 353, 357, 368
"Moving into the Garden" (Wagoner) **33**:348
"Moving Right Along" (Stone) **53**:230
"Moving South" (Wright) **14**:373
The Moving Target (Merwin) **45**:3, 5, 8, 10, 14, 18-19, 24, 26-8, 30, 32-3, 50, 52, 58, 61, 63-4, 71-4, 78-9, 81-3, 85, 87-8, 90, 97
"Moving the Moving Image" (Duncan) **75**:217, 277
"Moving through the silent crowd" (Spender) **71**:220
"The Moving to Griffin" (Ondaatje) **28**:291
Moving Towards Home: Political Essays (Jordan) **38**:140
"The Mower against gardens" (Marvell) **10**:266, 293, 297
"The Mower to the Glo-Worms" (Marvell) **10**:266, 296-97, 315
"The Mower Upon Gardens" (Marvell) **86**:183
"The Mower's Song" (Marvell) **10**:266, 296-97
"Mowing" (Frost) **71**:55
Moya Rodoslovnaya (Pushkin) **10**:391
"Moyulla" (Heaney) **100**:331
"Mozart, 1935" (Stevens) **6**:296
Mozart in Prague (Seifert) **47**:320
"Moze byc bez tytulu" (Szymborska) **44**:304
"Mozhet byt' eto tochka bezumiia" (Mandelstam) **14**:152
"Mr. and Mrs. Discobbolos" (Lear) **65**:156-57, 159
"Mr. and Mrs. Spikky Sparrow" (Lear) **65**:151-52, 157-59
"Mr. Bleaney" (Larkin) **21**:228-29, 241, 247-48
"Mr. Brodsky" (Tomlinson) **17**:311, 353
"Mr. Burnshaw and the Statue" (Stevens) **6**:297, 321; **110**:191
Mr. Cogito (Herbert)
See *Pan Cogito*
Mr Cogito (Herbert)
See *Pan Cogito*
"Mr. Cogito About the Magic" (Herbert)
See "Pan Cogito o magii"
"Mr. Cogito and Longevity" (Herbert)
See "Pan Cogito a dlugoniecznosc"
"Mr. Cogito and Maria Rasputin-An Attempt at Contact" (Herbert)
See "Pan Cogito a pop"
"Mr. Cogito and Pop Music" (Herbert)
See "Pan Cogito a pop"
"Mr. Cogito and Pure Thought" (Herbert)
See "Pan Cogito a mysl czysta"
"Mr. Cogito and the Imagination" (Herbert) **50**:13, 24, 42
"Mr. Cogito and the Movement of Thoughts" (Herbert)
See "Pan Cogito a ruch mysli"
"Mr. Cogito and the Poet of Certain Age" (Herbert)
See "Pan Cogito a poeta w pewnym wieku"
"Mr. Cogito Bemoans the Pettiness of Dreams" (Herbert)
See "Pan Cogito biada nad maloscia snów"
"Mr. Cogito Considers the Difference between the Human Voice and the Voice of Nature" (Herbert)
See "Pan Cogito rozwaza róznice miedzy glosem ludzkim a glosem przyrody"
"Mr. Cogito Laments the Pettiness of Dreams" (Herbert)
See "Pan Cogito biada nad maloscia snów"
"Mr. Cogito looks at his own face in the mirror" (Herbert)
See "Pan Cogito obserwuje w lustrze swoja twarz"
"Mr. Cogito observes his dead friend" (Herbert)
See "Pan Cogito obserwuje zmarlego przjaciela"
"Mr. Cogito on the Need for Precision" (Herbert) **50**:13, 15
"Mr. Cogito on Upright Attitudes" (Herbert)
See "Pan Cogito o postawie wyprostowanej"
"Mr. Cogito on Virtue" (Herbert)
See "Pan Cogito o cnocie"
"Mr. Cogito Seeks Advice" (Herbert)
See "Pan Cogito szuka rady"
"Mr. Cogito Tells about the Temptation of Spinoza" (Herbert)
See "Pan Cogito oponiada o kuszeniu Spinozy"
"Mr. Cogito Thinks about Returning to his Native Town" (Herbert)
See "Pan Cogito mysli o powrocie . . ."
"Mr. Cogito's Adventures with Music" (Herbert)
See "Pana Cogito przygody z muzyka"
"Mr. Cogito's Game" (Herbert)
See "Gra Pana Cogito"
"Mr. Cogito's Precipice" (Herbert)
See "Przepasc Pana Cogito"
"Mr. Cogito's Reflections About Suffering" (Herbert)
See "Pan Cogito rozmysla o cierpieniu"
"Mr. Cogito's Soul" (Herbert)
See "Dusza Pana Cogito"
"Mr. Cogito-The Return" (Herbert)
See "Pan Cogito-Powrót"
"Mr. Death" (Sexton)
See "For Mr. Death Who Stands with His Door Open"
"Mr. Edwards and the Spider" (Lowell) **3**:215
"Mr. Eliot's Sunday Morning Service" (Eliot) **5**:184
"Mr. Evil Disguises Himself as Herself—with Murder in Her heart for W. D." (Snodgrass) **74**:333
"Mr. Flood's Party" (Robinson) **1**:478; **35**:377
"Mr. Francis Finch" (Philips) **40**:296
"Mr. Grinhil" (Behn)
See "On the Death of Mr. Grinhil, the Famous Painter"
"Mr. High-mind" (Updike) **90**:351
"Mr. Longfellow and His Boy" (Sandburg) **41**:301
"Mr. M. L." (Vaughan)
See "To Mr. M. L. upon his reduction of the Psalms into Method"
"Mr. Mahoney" (Jacobsen) **62**:301, 318, 324
"Mr. Mammon I" (Ignatow) **34**:273
"Mr. Mammon II" (Ignatow) **34**:273
"Mr. McMirty" (Jacobsen) **62**:313
"Mr. Mine" (Sexton) **2**:352
"Mr. Moneybag's Lament" (Corso) **108**:6
"Mr. Nixon" (Pound) **4**:320
"Mr. Over" (Smith) **12**:297, 339
"Mr. Pope" (Tate) **50**:228, 246, 282-83, 304, 306, 309
Mr. Pope and Other Poems (Tate) **50**:229, 231, 282, 285, 309, 311, 318

"Mr. Seurat's Sunday Afternoon" (Schwartz)
See "Seurat's Sunday Afternoon along the Seine"
"Mr. Silberberg" (Riley) **48**:340
"Mr. Sludge, 'The Medium'" (Browning) **2**:72, 82
"Mr. Stratis Thalassinos Describes a Man" (Seferis) **66**:117-18, 123, 143-44, 163, 170-72, 184-85
"Mr. Styrax" (Pound) **4**:317
"Mr. Tambourine Man" (Dylan) **37**:45-9
"Mr. Wakeville on Interstate 90" (Hall) **70**:22, 34
"Mr. Withering's Cure" (Hood) **93**:99
"Mrs. Alfred Uruguay" (Stevens) **6**:304
"Mrs Arbuthnot" (Smith) **12**:314
"Mrs. Báez Serves Coffee on the Third Floor" (Espada) **74**:114, 119, 139
"Mrs. Benjamin Pantier" (Masters) **1**:347; **36**:169, 182
"Mrs. Hempel and her Katz" (Stone) **53**:218
"Mrs. Kessler" (Masters) **36**:239
"Mrs. Mandrill" (Nemerov) **24**:259, 268
"Mrs. Purkapile" (Masters) **36**:182
"Mrs. Simpkins" (Smith) **12**:344
"Mrs. Small" (Brooks) **7**:62, 69, 96-8
"Mrs. Throckmorton's Bulfinch" (Cowper)
See "On the Death of Mrs. Throckmorton's Bulfinch"
"Mrs. Walpurga" (Rukeyser) **12**:204
"Mrs. Williams" (Masters) **1**:347
"Mrs. Zen" (Seferis) **66**:116, 140
"Mt. Gabriel" (Mahon) **60**:190
"Mt. Tamalpais" (Rexroth) **95**:290-91
"Mtsiri" (Lermontov)
See *Mtsyri*
"Mtsyri" (Lermontov)
See *Mtsyri*
Mtsyri (Lermontov) **18**:279, 282-83, 298, 302
"mu" (Mackey) **49**:25, 30
"Mu" (Tolson) **88**:238-39, 258-60, 273, 304, 312, 316, 324
"Muchacha recién crecida" (Guillén) **23**:126
"Muchas gracias, adiós" (Guillén) **35**:184
"The Muck Farmer" (Thomas) **99**:233
"Muckers" (Sandburg) **41**:273
"Mud" (Cassian) **17**:4
"Mud" (Kumin) **15**:182
"The Mud Turtle" (Nemerov) **24**:274
"The Mud Vision" (Heaney) **18**:227-28, 230, 237
"A Muddy Cup" (Montague) **106**:279, 281, 312, 353-54
"Muerte de Antoñito el Camborio" (García Lorca) **3**:131
"La muerte y la brújula" (Borges) **32**:69
"Muerto de amor" (Guillén) **35**:182
"El muerto huyente" (Storni) **33**:295
"Los Muertos" (Fuertes) **27**:12
"The Muezzin" (Winters) **82**:313, 315
"Mugging" (Ginsberg) **4**:85
"Mugitusque Boum" (Hugo) **17**:83
"Muiopotmos; or, the Fate of the Butterflie" (Spenser) **8**:365, 367-68, 371
"Una mujer" (Mistral) **32**:184
"Una mujer de movimientos de rio" (Paz) **48**:251
"Mujer de prisionero" (Mistral) **32**:186
La mujer desnuda (1918-1923) (Jiménez) **7**:213-14
"La mujer fuerte" (Mistral) **32**:174
"Mujer nueva" (Guillén) **23**:105
"Mujeres" (Martí) **76**:106-8
"Mujeres" (Parra) **39**:286
"Mulatá" (Guillén) **23**:110, 142
"The Mulatta and the Minotaur" (Goodison) **36**:143, 147
"The Mulatta as Penelope" (Goodison) **36**:143, 147, 152
"Mulatta Song" (Goodison) **36**:143, 154
"Mulatta Song II" (Goodison) **36**:154
"Mulatto" (Hughes) **1**:238, 263-64, 270
"The Mulch" (Kunitz) **19**:159
"Mule Team and Poster" (Justice) **64**:280
"Mulholland's Contract" (Kipling) **3**:161
"Multiplication" (Wickham) **110**:267, 310
Multitudes, Multitudes (Clampitt) **19**:87-8
"The Multiversity" (Duncan) **2**:116; **75**:115, 254, 277
"Mummer" (Spicer) **78**:271
"The Mummer" (Wickham) **110**:296-97, 311
"Mummia" (Brooke) **24**:77
Mundo a solas (Aleixandre) **15**:3, 18-24, 32-3
"Mundo continuo" (Guillén) **35**:196, 198
"El mundo de siete pozos" (Storni) **33**:235, 272
"Mundo en claro" (Guillén) **35**:180, 181
"Mundus and Paulina" (Gower) **59**:68, 88, 108
"The Munich Mannequins" (Plath) **1**:384, 391; **37**:258, 269
"The Municipal Gallery Revisited" (Yeats) **20**:322, 324
Muoyce (Cage) **58**:204-05
"La muraglia" (Quasimodo) **47**:283
Muraka (Amichai) **38**:24
"Murano" (Doty) **53**:60
"The Murder" (Brooks) **7**:68
"The Murder" (Page) **12**:178
"Murder Mystery" (Wagoner) **33**:333, 371
The Murder of Lidice (Millay) **6**:220
"The Murder of William Remington" (Nemerov) **24**:258, 280
"Murder Poem No. 74321" (Rexroth) **20**:187
"The Murdered Traveller" (Bryant) **20**:40
"The Murderer" (Ignatow) **34**:286
"The Murderess" (Glück) **16**:126
Mureau (Cage) **58**:183-85, 188, 192, 195, 205
"Les mûres" (Ponge) **107**:127, 169, 184, 190, 213, 252
A Muriel Rukeyser Reader (Rukeyser) **12**:234
"Murmurings in a Field Hospital" (Sandburg) **41**:239, 249, 351
"Murphy in Manchester" (Montague) **106**:242
"Musa" (Holmes) **71**:67-68, 73
"Musa traviesa" (Martí) **76**:133-35
"The Muse" (Akhmatova)
See "Muza"
"The Muse" (Cowley) **90**:104, 180
"The Muse among the Motors" (Kipling) **91**:154
"The Muse as Donkey" (Sarton) **39**:362-63, 369
"The Muse as Medusa" (Sarton) **39**:342, 365-6
"The Muse for Hire" (Baudelaire)
See "La muse vénale"
"La muse malade" (Baudelaire) **106**:134
"La muse vénale" (Baudelaire) **106**:134
"A Muse of Water" (Kizer) **66**:70, 75-76
"Musée des Beaux Arts" (Auden) **92**:40
The Muses Elizium, Lately Discovered, by a New Way over Parnassus. The Passages Therein, Being the Subject of Ten Sundry Nymphalls (Drayton) **98**:17, 21, 24, 26, 31-37, 49, 51-53, 57, 64, 72-73, 79-83
"The Muses Embassy" (Leapor) **85**:284
"Muses No More But Mazes Be Your Names" (Raleigh) **31**:305
"Museum" (Kinsella) **69**:84-87, 89
"Museum" (Szymborska) **44**:296-97, 299
Museum (Dove) **6**:104-07, 109, 115-16, 118, 121
"The Museum at Tillamook" (Stafford) **71**:263, 328
"Museum Guards (London)" (Stryk) **27**:214
The Museum of Clear Ideas (Hall) **70**:52
"Museum of Cruel Days" (Hugo) **68**:274
"Museum Piece" (Wilbur) **51**:192, 210, 326
"Museum Pieces" (Heaney) **100**:334
"Museum Vase" (Francis) **34**:244
"The Mushroom Gatherers" (Davie) **29**:95
"Mushrooms" (Atwood) **8**:43
"Mushrooms" (Plath) **1**:389, 404, 406, 408
"Mushrooms" (Tomlinson) **17**:334, 347, 354
"A Music" (Berry) **28**:4
"Music" (Herbert) **4**:100
"Music" (O'Hara) **45**:127, 135-37, 139-40, 243
"Music" (Pasternak)
See "Muzyka"
"Music" (Stone) **53**:251
"Music" (Thoreau) **30**:182, 195, 227
"Music as a Woman Imperfectly Perceived" (Chappell) **105**:18, 37
"The Music Box" (Montague) **106**:286, 304, 321
"The Music Crept by Us" (Cohen) **109**:89
"The Music Grinders" (Holmes) **71**:68
"the music in my veins travels" (Alurista)
See "la musica en mis venas navega"
"Music in the Bush" (Service) **70**:152
"Music Is an Oversimplification of the Situation We're in" (Waldrop) **109**:187
Music Lessons (Akhmadulina)
See *Uroki muzyki*
"The Music of Anatomy" (Espada) **74**:138
"The Music of Poetry" (Kinnell) **26**:288
"The Music of Time" (Larkin) **21**:227
The Music: Reflections on Jazz and Blues (Baraka) **113**:43, 60-61, 63-64, 66-67, 69
"Music Swims Back to Me" (Sexton) **2**:359; **79**:276, 281, 338
"The Music That Hurts" (Komunyakaa) **51**:18-19
"la musica en mis venas navega" (Alurista) **34**:38
"Música, sólo música" (Guillén) **35**:185
"A Musical Comedy Thought" (Parker) **28**:354
"A Musical Instrument" (Barrett Browning) **6**:23
"Musical Moments" (Abse) **41**:32
"The Musical Voice" (Ishikawa)
See "Gakusei"
"The Music-Healers" (Clarke) **112**:29, 89
"Musician" (Bogan) **12**:124
"The Musician" (Thomas) **99**:236
"The Musician's Wife" (Clarke) **112**:84-86, 96
"Musick-Meeting" (Behn)
See "To Lysander at the Musick-Meeting"
"Musicks Duell" (Crashaw)
See "Music's Duel"
"Musicks Empire" (Marvell) **10**:313
"Music's Duel" (Crashaw) **84**:7, 21, 49, 107
"Musing allone this hinder nicht" (Dunbar) **67**:13
"A Musing on Victory" (Dobell) **100**:166
"La Musique" (Char) **56**:197-98
"Musketaquid" (Emerson) **18**:88, 91, 111
"Mussel Hunter at Rock Harbour" (Plath) **1**:388, 407; **37**:180, 182
"Mussels" (Oliver) **75**:302
"Muszla" (Herbert) **50**:5
"Mutabilitie Cantos" (Spenser)
See "Two Cantos of Mutabilitie"
"Mutability" (Brooke) **24**:56-7, 72, 85
"Mutability" (Shelley) **14**:166
Mutacion de Fortune (Christine de Pizan)
See *Le livre de la mutacion de fortune*
"Mutation" (Bryant) **20**:34, 44
"Mutation of the Spirit" (Corso) **33**:24-6, 36, 49
"Mutations" (MacNeice) **61**:140
"Mutations of the Spirit" (Corso) **108**:13
Mute Objects of Expression (Ponge)
See *La Rage de l'expression*
"Mute Phenomena" (Mahon) **60**:167, 178
"Muted Music" (Warren) **37**:365, 378
"Muteness" (Akhmadulina)
See "Nemota"
"Mutilateurs" (Char) **56**:155
"Mutilation" (Lawrence) **54**:187
"The Mutiny" (Vaughan) **81**:269, 271
"Mutra" (Paz) **1**:369; **48**:232, 264
"Mutterings over the Crib of a Deaf Child" (Wright) **36**:290, 335, 338
"Mutton" (Stein) **18**:323-24
"Mutual Trust" (Merrill) **28**:257
"Muza" (Akhmatova) **55**:14
"Muzh v mogile, syn v tiur'me" (Akhmatova) **55**:55

"Muzhestvo" (Akhmatova) **2**:19
"Muzyka" (Pasternak) **6**:288
"Mwilu/or Poem for the Living" (Madhubuti) **5**:346
"My Aged Uncle Arly" (Lear)
See "Incidents in the Life of My Uncle Arly"
"My Alba" (Ginsberg) **47**:52
My Alexandria (Doty) **53**:45-47, 49, 52-53, 61-63, 65, 72
"My Apish Cousins" (Moore) **49**:121
"My Aunt" (Holmes) **71**:68, 91
"My Autumn Walk" (Bryant) **20**:5, 46
"My Aviary" (Holmes) **71**:68, 94
"My Beard Rough as the Beginning" (Ignatow) **34**:308
"My Bed Is a Boat" (Stevenson) **84**:317, 344, 347
My Best Poems (Aleixandre) **15**:18
"My Birth Day" (Prior) **102**:309
"My boddy in the walls captived" (Raleigh) **31**:218, 239, 251, 301, 303-04
"My Bohemian Life" (Rimbaud)
See "Ma bohème"
"My Books" (Longfellow) **30**:51
"My Books I'd Fain Cast Off" (Thoreau) **30**:181, 192, 194, 203, 214-15, 225, 235, 240, 258
"My Books I'd Fain Cast Off, I Cannot Read" (Thoreau)
See "My Books I'd Fain Cast Off"
"My Boots" (Thoreau) **30**:182, 229, 287
"My Brothers the Silent" (Merwin) **45**:23
"My Buddy" (Hugo) **68**:255
"My Butterfly" (Frost) **71**:10
"My Career" (Cohen) **109**:102
"My Cats" (Smith) **12**:339
"My Children at the Dump" (Updike) **90**:357
"My Chili" (Ríos) **57**:329
"My Church" (Very) **86**:119, 136
"My Cicely" (Hardy) **92**:264
"My City" (Johnson) **24**:144, 154
"My Coat" (Béranger) **112**:14
"My coat threadbare" (Niedecker) **42**:150-51
"My Comforter" (Burroughs) **8**:51
"My Community's Corner" (Paredes)
See "Esquinita de mi pueblo"
"My Corn-cob Pipe" (Dunbar) **5**:133
"My Country in Darkness" (Boland) **58**:61-62
"My Cousin in April" (Glück) **16**:154
"My Cousin Muriel" (Clampitt) **19**:97
My Creative Method (Ponge) **107**:177
"My Daughter Is Coming!" (Walker) **30**:370
"My Daughter the Junkie on a Train" (Lorde)
See "To My Daughter the Junkie on a Train"
"My Daughter's Aquarium" (Stryk) **27**:204
"My Day's Delight, My Springtime Joys Foredone" (Raleigh) **31**:217
"My Dear and Loving Husband" (Bradstreet)
See "To My Dear and Loving Husband His Goeing into England"
"My Death" (Strand) **63**:177-78
"My delight and thy delight" (Bridges) **28**:70
"My Dove, My Beautiful One" (Joyce)
See "XIV"
"My Doves" (Barrett Browning) **6**:21
"my dream about being white" (Clifton) **17**:36
"My Dreams Are a Field Afar" (Housman) **2**:182
"My Dreams, My Work, Must Wait till after Hell" (Brooks) **7**:74
"My Dyet" (Cowley) **90**:28, 34, 116, 119
"My Enemy" (Lawrence) **54**:249
"My Entire Life" (Borges)
See "Mi vida entera"
"My Erotic Double" (Ashbery) **26**:133
"My Fairy Godmother" (Hyde) **7**:147
My Farish Street Green (Walker) **20**:294
"My Fate" (Cowley) **90**:14, 32, 180
"My Father Allergic to Fire" (Chappell) **105**:27, 35, 40, 46, 69-70
"My Father Burns Washington" (Chappell) **105**:43-44, 62
"My Father Died Imperfect as a Man" (Ciardi) **69**:9, 51, 53
"My Father Fought their War for Four Years" (Amichai) **38**:27-28
"My Father Laughing in the Chicago Theater" (Wagoner) **33**:374
"My Father Moved through Dooms of Feel" (Cummings)
See "My Father Moved through Dooms of Love"
"My Father Moved through Dooms of Love" (Cummings) **5**:81, 89
"My Father: October 1942" (Stafford) **71**:280
"My Father Paints the Summer" (Wilbur) **51**:188, 192-93, 269
"My Father Speaks to Me from the Dead" (Olds) **22**:323, 325, 338
"My Father Washes His Hands" (Chappell) **105**:45, 62, 69
"My Father's Breasts" (Olds) **22**:328
"My Fathers Came from Kentucky" (Lindsay) **23**:265
"My Father's Eyes" (Olds) **22**:332
"My Father's Funeral" (Shapiro) **25**:305
"My Father's Hurricane" (Chappell) **105**:31, 35, 58, 69-70, 75
"My Father's Irish Setters" (Merrill) **28**:284
"My Father's Love Letters" (Komunyakaa) **51**:23
"My Father's Wedding" (Bly) **39**:65, 99-100
"My Fire" (Wagoner) **33**:355
"My first borne love unhappily conceived" (Raleigh) **31**:201
"My First Weeks" (Olds) **22**:338
"My 5 Favorite Records" (Berrigan) **103**:36
"My Foe" (Riley) **48**:304
"My Friend" (Gibran) **9**:77
"My Friend Felix" (Hall) **70**:34
My Friend Tree (Niedecker) **42**:94, 102, 106, 134-35, 152, 183
"My Friends" (Merwin) **45**:5
"My Friends" (Service) **70**:115
"My Friends, Why Should We Live" (Thoreau) **30**:254-55
"My galley charged with forgetfulness" (Wyatt) **27**:323-324, 357-358
"My Garden" (Emerson) **18**:76, 88
"My Garden, My Daylight" (Graham) **59**:147-48
"My Geneaology" (Akhmadulina)
See "Moia rodoslovnaia"
My Geneology (Pushkin)
See *Moya Rodoslovnaya*
"My General's Face" (Ciardi) **69**:34
"My Gentlest Song" (Viereck) **27**:263, 278, 281
"My Grandfather Dishes the Dirt" (Chappell) **105**:45
"My Grandfather Gets Doused" (Chappell) **105**:58-59, 71
"My Grandfather's Church Goes Up" (Chappell) **105**:18, 35, 58-59, 74-75
"My Grandmother Washes Her Feet" (Chappell) **105**:24, 42, 45-46, 56, 69
"My Grandmother Washes Her Vessels" (Chappell) **105**:41-42, 58
"My Grandmother's Dream of Plowing" (Chappell) **105**:27, 45, 81
"My Grandmother's Ghost" (Wright) **36**:338, 373
"My Grandmother's Gold Pin" (Mueller) **33**:178-79
"My Grandmother's Hard Row to Hoe" (Chappell) **105**:75
"My Grandmother's House" (Das) **43**:80, 85
"My Grandmother's Love Letters" (Crane) **3**:98; **99**:72, 100, 133-34
"My Granny's Hieland Hame" (Burns) **6**:98
"My Grave" (Levine) **22**:228
"My Great & Only" (Kipling) **91**:68
"My Ground is High" (Thoreau) **30**:195
My Hair Turning Gray among Strangers (Quintana) **36**:273-74
"My Hartis Tresure and Swete Assured Fo" (Dunbar) **67**:105
"My Hat" (Smith) **12**:331
"My Heart" (O'Hara) **45**:164
"My Heart and I" (Barrett Browning) **6**:23
"My Heart, Being Hungry" (Reese) **29**:332
"My Heart Discovered" (Cowley) **90**:14
"My Heart Goes Out" (Smith) **12**:318, 325
"My Heart is Heavy" (Teasdale) **31**:359
"My Heart Shall Be Thy Garden" (Meynell) **112**:158
"My Heart Was Full" (Smith) **12**:333
"My Heart's in the Highlands" (Burns) **114**:168
"My Heid Did Yak" (Dunbar) **67**:4, 8
"My Hermitage in the Bamboo Grove" (Wang Wei) **18**:358
"My Heroes Have Never Been Cowboys" (Alexie) **53**:7-9
"My Hero's Genealogy" (Pushkin)
See "Rodoslovnaya Moego Geroya"
"My home" (Ungaretti)
See "Casa mia"
"My Honey" (Guillén)
See "Mi chiquita"
"My House" (Giovanni) **19**:112-13, 116, 140, 142-43
My House (Giovanni) **19**:107, 110-14, 116, 118, 121-25, 136-37, 140-41, 144
"My 'I don't Believe" (Amichai)
See "Ha'ani lo ma'amin sheli"
"My Indigo" (Lee) **24**:240, 244
"My Issei Parents, Twice Pioneers, Now I Hear Them" (Yamada) **44**:346
"My Jacket Old" (Melville) **82**:109
"My Kate" (Barrett Browning) **6**:23
"My Kingdom" (Stevenson) **84**:298, 314, 346-47
"My Lady of the Castle Grand" (Dunbar) **5**:134, 138
"My Lady's Lamentation and Complaint against the Dean" (Swift) **9**:295-96
"My Lady's Lips Are Like de Honey" (Johnson) **24**:141
"My Lai soldier" (Sexton) **79**:243
"My Last Afternoon with Uncle Devereux Winslow" (Lowell) **3**:219, 222
"My Last Dance" (Howe) **81**:24
"My Last Duchess" (Browning) **2**:37, 94; **61**:88; **97**:1-66
"My Last Poem" (Goodison) **36**:141
"My Lecture" (Howe) **81**:30
"My Library" (Service) **70**:140
"My Library: Volume One" (Masefield) **78**:45
My Life (Hejinian) **108**:243-51, 253-58, 262, 267-85, 287-93, 295-99, 301, 303-4, 306, 309, 314
"My Life" (Strand) **63**:177-78
"My Life By Somebody Else" (Strand) **63**:177-80
"My Life By Water" (Niedecker) **42**:107, 138-39, 165
"My Life in Art" (Cohen) **109**:24
"My Life in Robes" (Cohen) **109**:101
"My Life Is Full of Weary Days" (Tennyson) **101**:282
"My Life with the Wave" (Paz) **1**:354
"My Light with Yours" (Masters) **1**:333
"My Little Lovers" (Rimbaud)
See "Mes petites amoureuses"
"My Lord" (Bishop) **34**:161
"My Lord" (Crabbe) **97**:105
"My Lost Youth" (Longfellow) **30**:27, 34, 40, 46-7, 71
"My Love" (Hafiz) **116**:21-24
"My love bound me with a kisse" (Campion) **87**:62
"My love hath vow'd" (Campion) **87**:64
"My Love Must Be As Free" (Thoreau) **30**:192, 216
"My Loved Subject" (Jeffers) **17**:131

"My lute awake" (Wyatt) **27**:328, 339, 349, 357, 362
"My Luve Is Like a Red, Red Rose" (Burns) **6**:75, 77, 99; **114**:41
"My Mate" (Service) **70**:132
"My Meat and Drink" (Very) **86**:114, 139
"My mistress' eyes are nothing like the sun" (Shakespeare)
See "Sonnet 130"
"My most. My most. O my lost!" (Villa) **22**:349
"My Mother" (McGuckian) **27**:96
"My Mother at Sixtysix" (Das) **43**:81
"My Mother Remembers That She Was Beautiful" (Gallagher) **9**:58
"My Mother Said" (Stafford) **71**:378
"My Mother Shoots the Breeze" (Chappell) **105**:44, 69, 81
"My Mother Was A Soldier" (Stafford) **71**:378
"My Mother Would Be a Falconress" (Duncan) **2**:127; **75**:133, 147, 203, 229, 232, 250, 256, 261, 263
"My Mother's Hard Row to Hoe" (Chappell) **105**:35, 45
"My Mother's Life" (Meredith) **28**:182
"My Mother's Maids" (Wyatt)
See *My mothers maydes when they did sowe and spynne*
My mothers maydes when they did sowe and spynne (Wyatt) **27**:304, 371
"My Mother's Sea Chanty" (Goodison) **36**:158
"My Mother's Voice" (Very) **86**:72
"My Mountain Home" (McKay) **2**:222
"My Muse" (Montale)
See "La mia musa"
"My Muse" (Randall) **86**:345-46
"My Muse" (Smith) **12**:312, 324, 336
"My Muse, what ailes this Ardoure?" (Sidney) **32**:235
"My nacali vmeste: rabocie, ja i zima" (Akhmadulina) **43**:17, 46
My Name Is William Tell (Stafford) **71**:372-73
"My Name It Is Sam Hall" (Jarrell)
See "O My Name It Is Sam Hall"
"My Namesake" (Whittier) **93**:239, 261
"My Native Costume" (Espada) **74**:147
"My Native Land" (Ignatow) **34**:318
"My Native Land" (Lermontov)
See "Rodina"
"My Native Land" (Randall) **86**:317
"My Native Land, My Home" (McKay) **2**:216, 224
"My Neighbor" (Ignatow) **34**:314
"My Neighbor, the Literary Scholar" (Akhmadulina) **43**:32
"My New-Cut Ashlar" (Kipling) **3**:183
"My nocturnal torments" (Shvarts) **50**:134
"My Non-Credo" (Amichai)
See "Ha'ani lo ma'amin sheli"
"My Nose Garden" (Silverstein) **49**:347
Nosgay (Whitney)
See *A Sweet Nosgay, or Pleasant Posye: Contayning a Hundred and Ten Phylosophicall Flowers*
"My Nurses" (Williams) **109**:196
"My Olivetti Speaks" (Koch) **80**:326, 328, 340
"My Own" (Parker) **28**:350-51
"My Own Sweet Good" (Brooks) **7**:55
"My Parents Kept Me From Children Who Were Rough" (Spender) **71**:150, 180, 219, 221, 250
"My Parents' Lodging Place" (Amichai) **38**:50
"My parents quarrel in the neighbour room" (Spender) **71**:181, 189-90, 221
"My pen take payn" (Wyatt) **27**:339, 341
"My People" (Hughes) **1**:270; **53**:93, 108-9
"My People" (Kavanagh) **33**:156
"My People" (Paredes)
See "Mi Pueblo"
"My People" (Sandburg) **41**:330
"My Philosofy" (Riley) **48**:299, 334-35, 352
"My Physics Teacher" (Wagoner) **33**:361
"My Picture" (Cowley) **90**:115
"My Playmate" (Whittier) **93**:235, 252-53, 267, 347
"My Poem" (Giovanni) **19**:111
"My Poets" (Levine) **22**:212
"My Portrait" (Pushkin) **10**:407
"My Powers" (Kavanagh) **33**:120
"My President Weeps" (Ignatow) **34**:323, 325
"My Pretty Dan" (McKay) **2**:221
"My Pretty Rose Tree" (Blake) **12**:34; **63**:4, 16, 26-28, 107
"My Psalm" (Whittier) **93**:347
"My Quarrel with the Infinite" (Simic) **69**:305
"My Religion" (Carson) **64**:234
"My Ruthers" (Riley) **48**:302
"My s koshkoi dremlem den' i noch" (Shvarts) **50**:162
"My Sad Captains" (Gunn) **26**:186, 197
My Sad Captains, and Other Poems (Gunn) **26**:181, 186, 189, 194-195, 197, 201-202, 207, 209, 211, 216, 218-219, 221, 223, 225-226
"My Sea-ward Window" (Howe) **81**:24-25, 47
"My Secret Identity Is" (Simic) **69**:298
"My Senses Do Not Deceive Me" (Moore) **49**:105
"My Shadow" (Stevenson) **84**:312, 345
"My Ship and I" (Stevenson) **84**:315
"My Shy Hand" (Owen) **19**:336
"My Silks in Fine Array" (Blake) **12**:31
My Sister, Life (Pasternak)
See *Sestra moia zhizn*
"My Sisters, O My Sisters" (Sarton) **39**:318, 322, 337, 342, 358-59, 364
"My Sister's Sleep" (Rossetti) **44**:174, 227
"My Soldier Lad" (McKay) **2**:223
"My Son, My Executioner" (Hall) **70**:12, 30, 32
"My Son the Haiku Writer" (Raworth) **107**:324
"My Son Was Drafted" (Amichai) **38**:47-48, 55-56
"My Song" (Brooke) **24**:62, 72, 76
"My Songs" (Yosano)
See "Waga Uta"
"My Sort O' Man" (Dunbar) **5**:131
"My Soul Accused Me" (Dickinson) **1**:94
"My Soul and I" (Whittier) **93**:270, 272
"My soul is dark" (Lermontov) **18**:202
"My Soul, Rejoice Thou in Thy God" (Bradstreet) **10**:60-1
"My Spectre around Me" (Blake) **12**:13
"My Spirit" (Traherne) **70**:172, 183, 190, 208-9, 211, 243, 258-59, 264, 269-70, 313, 315
"My spirit kisseth thine" (Bridges) **28**:85
"My Spirit Will Not Haunt the Mound" (Hardy) **8**:118; **92**:295
"My Star" (Browning) **2**:59
"My Students" (Randall) **86**:291
"My Surgeons Are a Savage Band" (Kunitz) **19**:151
"My sweet Ann Foot, my bonny Ann" (Clare) **23**:25
"My Sweet Brown Gal" (Dunbar) **5**:119
"My sweetest Lesbia" (Campion) **87**:24-25, 30, 44-45, 54, 64, 84-86, 117
"My Tale" (Clough) **103**:156-57
"My Treasures" (Stevenson) **84**:299, 347
"My Tribe" (Ciardi) **69**:12
"My Trip in a Dream to the Lady of Heaven Mountain" (Li Po)
See "My Trip in a Dream to the Lady of Heaven Mountain: A Farewell to Several Gentlemen of Eastern Lu"
"My Trip in a Dream to the Lady of Heaven Mountain: A Farewell to Several Gentlemen of Eastern Lu" (Li Po) **29**:153
"My Triumph" (Whittier) **93**:349
"My true love hath my hart" (Sidney) **32**:260
"My Two Springs" (Lanier) **50**:56, 91
"My Uncle a Child" (Jacobsen) **62**:320
"My Vegetarian Friend" (Eliot) **20**:123
"My Verse That Once Was Tender" (Randall) **86**:345
"My Vision of Summer" (Riley) **48**:293
"My Voice" (Aleixandre)
See "Mi voz"
"My Voice Not Being Proud" (Bogan) **12**:101, 120
"My Whole Life" (Borges)
See "Mi vida entera"
"My Wicked Uncle" (Mahon) **60**:132
My Wicked Wicked Ways (Cisneros) **52**:137, 144, 148, 151-52, 156-57, 160-62, 164
"My Wife" (Carver) **54**:15
"My Wife and My Mother-In-Law" (Merwin) **45**:74
"My Will" (Goodison) **36**:150
"The Myall in Prison" (Gilmore) **87**:301
"Mycenae" (Seferis) **66**:90, 109, 124, 127, 148
"Mycenae Lookout" (Heaney) **100**:338-42, 344-45
"Mycerinus" (Arnold) **5**:13, 33-4, 37, 39, 48
"Mye Love toke Skorne" (Wyatt) **27**:316
"Myfanwy at Oxford" (Betjeman) **75**:71, 77
Mylo Jones (Riley) **48**:306
"Mylo Jones's Wife" (Riley) **48**:315, 318-19
"Myne owne Iohn poyntz" (Wyatt)
See "Myne owne John Poynts sins ye delight to know"
"Myne owne John Poynts sins ye delight to know" (Wyatt) **27**:333-337, 341
"Myne owne John Poyntz" (Wyatt)
See "Myne owne John Poynts sins ye delight to know"
"My-ness" (Milosz) **8**:179
"Myopia: A Night" (Lowell) **3**:215
"Myra's Picture" (Leapor)
See "Mira's Picture"
"Myres: Alexandria, A.D. 340" (Cavafy) **36**:8, 41, 75, 79
The Myriad Leaves Collection (Yakamochi)
See *Man'yōshū*
"Le myrte" (Bonnefoy) **58**:118-19, 148
"Myrtho" (Nerval) **13**:180
"Myself I Sing" (Oppen) **35**:293
"Myself Was Formed—a Carpenter" (Dickinson) **1**:96
"Le mystère dans les lettres" (Mallarmé) **102**:40
"Le mystère des trois cors" (Laforgue) **14**:73
"Mysteries" (Abse) **41**:10
"The Mysteries" (H. D.) **5**:305
"The Mysterious Visitor" (Holmes) **71**:68, 91
"The Mystery" (Braithwaite) **52**:107
"Mystery" (Hughes) **53**:117
"The Mystery" (Teasdale) **31**:359
"'Mystery Boy' Looks for Kin in Nashville" (Hayden) **6**:196
"The Mystery of Gilgal" (Riley) **48**:299
"The Mystery of the Fall" (Clough) **103**:83, 135, 138
"Mystic" (Lawrence) **54**:247
"The Mystic" (Muir) **49**:239
"The Mystic" (Noyes) **27**:138
"Mystic" (Plath) **37**:258, 260
"The Mystic" (Tennyson) **101**:246
"Mystic River" (Ciardi) **69**:31, 33-34
Mysticism for Beginners (Zagajewski) **27**:396, 398-401
Mystics and Zen Masters (Merton) **10**:352
"Mystique" (Rimbaud) **3**:260; **57**:236, 246, 250, 272
"The Myth" (Muir) **49**:207, 210, 246-49, 298
"Myth" (Pavese)
See "Mito"
"Myth" (Rukeyser) **12**:228
"Myth" (Sarton) **39**:342
"Myth of Mountain Sunrise" (Warren) **37**:359-60, 380
Myth of the Blaze (Oppen) **35**:324
"Myth on Mediterranean Beach: Aphrodite as Logos" (Warren) **37**:301, 307
Myth-History (Seferis)
See *Mythistorema*
"The Mythical Journey" (Muir) **49**:215, 243, 270, 295

Mythical Story (Seferis)
See *Mythistorema*
Mythistorema (Seferis) **66**:89-90, 92-94, 99, 105, 111-12, 114, 118, 139, 144-50, 152, 162-63, 165, 171-72, 183-84, 187, 191-95, 197, 206-7, 214-16
"Mythological Ode to the Spirit of Fire" (Peacock) **87**:307, 349
Mythologies (Cohen)
See *Let Us Compare Mythologies*
"Mythology" (Hacker) **47**:96
"A Mythology Reflects its Region" (Stevens) **6**:306
"Myths" (Erdrich) **52**:189, 191
Myths and Texts (Snyder) **21**:290-92, 297, 299, 322
N. 4 (Pindar)
See *Nemean 4*
N. 7 (Pindar)
See *Nemean 7*
N. 9 (Pindar)
See *Nemean 9*
"N'a catredal" (Castro) **41**:94, 105
"A na fruta" (Pasolini) **17**:274-77
"Na krasnom kone" (Tsvetaeva) **14**:315
"Na pokoj grecki w eomu księżnej Zeneidy Wøkońskiej w Moskwie" (Mickiewicz) **38**:226-27, 229-31
Na rannikh poezdakh (Pasternak) **6**:282
Na vlnách T. S. F. (Seifert) **47**:316, 324, 332, 348
"The Nabara" (Day Lewis) **11**:127, 130-31, 144
"Nachlied" (Trakl) **20**:259
"Nacht" (Benn) **35**:50, 68, 75, 77
"Nachtcafé" (Benn) **35**:7, 23, 24, 25, 36, 46, 50, 53, 54
Nachtgesänge (Hölderlin) **4**:142, 146, 148, 166
"Nachtmusik" (Szirtes) **51**:169
"Nachtregen" (Werfel) **101**:349
"nachts wird kälter" (Enzensberger) **28**:140
"Nachwort" (Heine) **25**:172-75, 177, 179
"Nachzeichnung" (Benn) **35**:71
"Naci en una buhardilla" (Fuertes) **27**:49
"Nací para poeta o para muerto" (Fuertes) **27**:49
"Nacimiento de Cristo" (García Lorca) **3**:141
Nacimiento último (Aleixandre) **15**:9, 16
"Nada" (Jiménez) **7**:202
"Nadezhdoi Sladostnoi" (Pushkin) **10**:412
"Nadgrobie" (Tsvetaeva) **14**:325, 327
"Nadie" (Aleixandre) **15**:20, 22
"Nadie" (Guillén) **23**:125
"Nadie me estorba" (Guillén) **35**:229
"Nafsī muthqa ah bi athmāriha" (Gibran) **9**:82
"Nah, im Aortenbogen" (Celan) **10**:101
"Nähe des Todes" (Trakl) **20**:248
"Naia and Edward" (Masefield) **78**:62
"La naîade" (Gautier) **18**:141
"The Nail" (Hughes) **7**:143
"The Nailhead" (Ignatow) **34**:277
"The Nails" (Merwin) **45**:18, 83
"Naissance du duc de Bordeaux" (Hugo) **17**:75
"The naïve person" (Borges)
See "El ingenuo"
"A Naive Poem" (Milosz)
See "The World"
Naivedya (Tagore) **8**:411-13
"Naked and Essential" (Montale) **13**:141
"Naked Girl and Mirror" (Wright) **14**:356, 362
Nakedness Lost (Char)
See *Le Nu perdu*
"Nam" (Brathwaite) **56**:93
"Nam Samiran" (Kabīr) **56**:333
"The Name" (Creeley) **73**:11, 33
"A Name for All" (Crane) **3**:90, 104; **99**:6-7, 122-23
"The Name I Call You" (Piercy) **29**:311, 315
"The Name of Old Glory" (Riley) **48**:325-26
"The Nameless" (Abse) **41**:26
"Nameless" (Pasternak)
See "Bez nazvaniya"
"Nameless Flower" (Wright) **14**:347, 379
Nameless Songs (Parra)
See *Cancionero sin nombre*
"Nameless Thing" (Warren) **37**:341
"The Names" (Collins) **68**:226
"Names" (Guillén)
See "Los nombres"
"Names" (Hayden) **6**:194
"Names" (Stone) **53**:230, 244
"Names" (Walcott) **46**:275, 279-80, 290
"Names of Horses" (Hall) **70**:28, 34
The Names of the Lost (Levine) **22**:223-24
"Names Scarred at the Entrance to Chartres" (Wright) **36**:318
"Naming" (Brathwaite) **56**:87
Naming Our Destiny (Jordan)
See *Naming Our Destiny: New and Selected Poems*
Naming Our Destiny: New and Selected Poems (Jordan) **38**:126, 132, 137, 139, 144
"Naming the Animals" (Hecht) **70**:80
"Naming the Animals" (Hogan) **35**:276, 277
"The Nana-Hex" (Sexton) **2**:365
"Nancy" (Wylie) **23**:301, 318-19, 324
"The Nancy's Pride" (Carman) **34**:213
"Nani" (Das) **43**:88
"Nani" (Ríos) **57**:316, 324
"Nanny" (Goodison) **36**:141
"Nano-Knowledge" (McHugh) **61**:204
"The Nap Taker" (Silverstein) **49**:342
"The Nape of the Neck" (Graves) **6**:166
Napis (Herbert) **50**:5, 7, 9, 19-20, 25
"Naples, August 1849" (Clough)
See "Easter Day"
"Naples in the Time of Bomba" (Melville) **82**:77, 108
"Napoleon" (de la Mare) **77**:105
"Napoléon" (Meredith) **60**:247
Napoleon III in Italy, and Other Poems (Barrett Browning)
See *Poems before Congress*
"Napoleon in 1814" (Spender) **71**:210, 228
"Napoleon na El'be" (Pushkin) **10**:409, 421
"Napoleon on the Elba" (Pushkin)
See "Napoleon na El'be"
"Naprasno glazom kak gvozdem" (Tsvetaeva) **14**:325
"Naptha" (O'Hara) **45**:137
"När man kommit så långt" (Ekeloef) **23**:76
"Narcisse parle" (Valéry) **9**:350, 356, 363, 365, 385, 392, 395
"Narcissus" (Gower) **59**:88, 92-93, 95, 102
"Narcissus" (Lawrence) **54**:232-34
"Narcissus and the Women" (Kavanagh) **33**:73
"Narcissus I" (Barker) **77**:3, 6, 23
"Narcissus II" (Barker) **77**:6
"Narcissus III" (Barker) **77**:6
"Narcissus Moving" (Berryman) **64**:69
"Narcissus Speaks" (Valéry)
See "Narcisse parle"
"Narikel" (Tagore) **8**:416
"Narita" (Curnow) **48**:53
Narraciones (García Lorca) **3**:148
"Narragansett Park" (Berrigan) **103**:42
"Narration" (Seferis) **66**:99
"A Narrative" (Oppen) **35**:315, 317, 322, 340, 343, 350
"Narrative" (Stein) **18**:313
"Narrative Bridges for Adams Way" (Duncan) **75**:134
"A Narrow Escape" (Merrill) **28**:239, 243
"The Narrow Place" (Muir) **49**:255, 258
The Narrow Place (Muir) **49**:224, 228-29, 231, 245-46, 250, 254-56, 270, 272-73, 276-77, 279, 282-84, 289
The Narrow Pond (Matsuo Basho)
See *Oku no hosomichi*
The Narrow Road to the Deep North (Matsuo Basho)
See *Oku no hosomichi*
"The Narrow Valley" (Amichai) **38**:25
"The Narrow Way" (Cowper) **40**:42
"Narva and Mored" (Chatterton) **104**:8, 74
"Nascita del canto" (Quasimodo) **47**:301-3
"I nascondigli" (Montale) **13**:138
"Nashedshij podkovu" (Mandelstam) **14**:121, 125, 130
Nashville Skyline (Dylan) **37**:60
"Nasse Zäune" (Benn) **35**:71
"Natal'ia Shishigina—instrument dlia proiavleniia dukhov, perchatka, i telefon" (Shvarts) **50**:153
"Natalie Maisie" (Masefield) **78**:51
"The Nation Is Like Ourselves" (Baraka) **4**:19; **113**:21, 77-78
"National Security" (MacLeish) **47**:205, 261
"National Song" (Hunt) **73**:195
"National Thoughts" (Amichai) **38**:45
"National Trust" (Heaney) **100**:263
"Nationalist" (Randall) **86**:329, 336
"Nationality" (Gilmore) **87**:286, 291, 300
"Nationality in Drinks" (Browning) **2**:59
Nationchild Plumaroja (Alurista) **34**:4, 15-16, 21, 23, 24, 26-29, 31, 39-43, 45, 47
"The Native American Broadcasting System" (Alexie) **53**:31
"The Native Born" (Kipling) **3**:161-62
"A Native Hill" (Berry) **28**:39
Native Land (Blok) **21**:16
Native Land (Rich)
See *Your Native Land, Your Life*
"The Nativitie of Christ" (Southwell) **83**:256, 283, 334, 336-38, 340-41
"Nativity" (Sarton) **39**:326, 334-35, 343
"The Nativity" (Spark) **72**:215, 220, 226, 229-32, 234, 246, 255, 257-59, 264
"Nativity" (Vaughan)
See "Christs Nativity"
"A Nativity" (Yeats) **20**:319
"Nativity Hymn" (Crashaw)
See "To the Holy Nativity"
"A Nativity (1914-18)" (Kipling) **3**:183, 189
"Nativity Ode" (Milton)
See "On the Morning of Christ's Nativity"
"Nativity Poem" (Glück) **16**:125, 141
"Nativity Scene" (Szirtes) **51**:156
"Natrabach i na cytrze" (Milosz) **8**:186, 214
"Natura Naturans" (Clough) **103**:73
"The Natural" (Oppen) **35**:304
"Natural History" (Plath) **37**:254
"Natural History" (Walcott) **46**:237
"Natural History II" (Walcott) **46**:279
"Natural Music" (Jeffers) **17**:134-35
Natural Numbers: New and Selected Poems (Rexroth) **20**:209; **95**:247, 253, 255, 258-59, 274, 289, 314
"Natural or Divine" (Guillén)
See "Naturaleza con altavoz"
"Natural Resources" (Rich) **5**:374, 380, 384-85
"Naturaleza con altavoz" (Guillén) **35**:185, 241
"Naturaleza viva" (Guillén) **35**:193, 228
"Naturalism" (Berssenbrugge) **115**:24
"Naturally" (Gallagher) **9**:43
"Naturally the Foundation Will Bear Your Expenses" (Larkin) **21**:223
"Nature" (Longfellow) **30**:51
"Nature" (Masters) **1**:336
"Nature" (Traherne) **70**:190-91, 272, 316, 318
"Nature" (Very) **86**:41, 80, 98, 137
"Nature and Free Animals" (Smith) **12**:323
"Nature and Necessity" (Tuckerman) **85**:305
"Nature Doth Have Her Dawn" (Thoreau) **30**:191, 193, 268, 271, 293
"Nature morte" (Brodsky) **9**:4, 12
"Nature Morte" (MacNeice) **61**:139
"The Nature of a Mirror" (Warren) **37**:304
"The Nature of an Action" (Gunn) **26**:185
The Nature of Things (Ponge)
See *Le Parti pris des choses*
"The Nature of This Flower Is to Bloom" (Walker) **30**:341
"Nature Poem" (Tomlinson) **17**:345, 348
Nature: Poems Old and New (Swenson) **14**:283, 287-88

"Nature that gave the bee so feet a grace" (Wyatt) **27**:346-47
"Nature that washt her hands in milke" (Raleigh) **31**:201, 215, 235, 302
"Nature II" (Emerson) **18**:102
"Nature's Gentleman" (Corso) **108**:8, 22
"Nature's Lineaments" (Graves) **6**:150-51
"Nature's Nation" (Wagoner) **33**:360
"Nature's Questioning" (Hardy) **8**:96; **92**:209, 229, 289, 292, 300-303
"Naughty Boy" (Creeley) **73**:7, 28
"Navidad en el Hudson" (García Lorca) **3**:141
"Navigation" (Thomas) **99**:349
"Navigator" (Sarton) **39**:322, 337
"The Navigators" (Curnow) **48**:4
"The Navigators" (Hacker) **47**:79
"Nayarit" (Birney) **52**:78
Ne forte credas (Horace) **46**:97
"Ne muchnistoi babochkoiu beloi" (Mandelstam) **14**:152, 156
"Ne pisat' o groze" (Akhmadulina) **43**:8
"Ne plus partager" (Éluard) **38**:70
"Ne Plus Ultra" (Coleridge) **11**:52
"Ne ris point des sonnets" (Sainte-Beuve) **110**:74
"Ne s'entend pas" (Char) **56**:131, 157
"Ne sravnivai: zhivushchii nesravnim" (Mandelstam) **14**:154
"Ne udeljaj mne mnogo vremeni" (Akhmadulina) **43**:60
"Neap-tide" (Swinburne) **24**:313, 341, 343
"Near" (Stafford) **71**:269-70, 286
"Near a Monastery" (Carducci)
See "Presso Una Certosa"
Near and Far (Blunden) **66**:23, 31, 44-45
Near and Far: New Poems (Blunden)
See *Near and Far*
"Near, as All That Is Lost" (Gallagher) **9**:64
"Near Avalon" (Morris) **55**:279, 282, 301-2
Near False Creek Mouth (Birney) **52**:15-16, 44, 46, 74, 79
"Near Kalalock" (Hugo) **68**:270
"Near Keokuk" (Sandburg) **2**:332
Near Klamath (Carver) **54**:3
"Near Lanivet, 1872" (Hardy) **8**:97, 125-26
"Near Mullingar" (Davie)
See "1977, Near Mullingar"
"Near Perigord" (Stern) **115**:284
"Near the Ocean" (Lowell) **3**:226-28, 233
Near the Ocean (Lowell) **3**:232
"Nearing Forty" (Walcott) **46**:237
"Nearing La Guarira" (Walcott) **46**:231, 273
"Nearly a Valediction" (Hacker) **47**:107
"Nearness of Death" (Trakl)
See "Nähe des Todes"
"Nebraska" (Shapiro) **25**:313
"Nebuchadnezzar's Punishment" (Gower) **59**:9
"Necessities" (Mueller) **33**:189
Necessities of Life: Poems, 1962-1965 (Rich) **5**:356, 363-64, 370-71, 382, 388-89, 397
"Necessity" (Eberhart) **76**:7, 48
"The Necessity for Belief" (Warren) **37**:380
"The Necessity of Fate" (Barker) **91**:42
"The Neckan" (Arnold) **5**:12
The Necklace (Tomlinson) **17**:299, 302-04, 317-18, 320-22, 327, 334-35, 341
"The Necktie and the Watch" (Apollinaire)
See "La cravate et la montre"
"Necrological" (Ransom) **61**:267, 299, 308
"Necropolis" (Kinsella) **69**:104
"Necropolis" (Shapiro) **25**:279, 297, 318
"Need: A Chorale for Black Women's Voices" (Lorde) **12**:144, 154, 156, 158
"The Need of Being Versed in Country Things" (Frost) **1**:229, 231
"The Need to Confide" (Jackson) **44**:90
The Need to Hold Still (Mueller) **33**:175-76, 178-79, 188
"A Needed Poem for My Salvation" (Sanchez) **9**:208-09
"Needle" (Simic) **69**:272
Needle's Eye (Oppen)
See *Seascape: Needle's Eye*
"Nefertiti" (Yevtushenko) **40**:343, 347, 352
"Negative" (Szymborska)
See "Negatyw"
"Negative Information" (Douglas) **106**:199, 209
"Negative Love" (Donne) **43**:131
"Negatives" (Walcott) **46**:234
"Negatyw" (Szymborska) **44**:319
"Negli anni molti e nelle molote pruove" (Michelangelo) **103**:344
"Negro" (Hughes) **53**:108, 122
"The Negro Artist and the Racial Mountain" (Hughes) **53**:94, 108
"Negro bembón" (Guillén) **23**:98, 142
"Un negro canta en Nueva York" (Guillén) **23**:127
"A Negro Cemetery Next to a White One" (Nemerov) **24**:281
"Negro Dancers" (Hughes) **1**:236; **53**:80, 82, 86, 117
"Negro Ghetto" (Hughes) **53**:115
"The Negro Hero" (Brooks) **7**:86
"A Negro Love Song" (Dunbar) **5**:132, 142
"Negro Mask" (Senghor) **25**:227-30
Negro Mask (Senghor)
See "Masque nègre"
"The Negro Mother" (Hughes) **53**:114, 119, 122, 125
The Negro Mother (Hughes) **53**:114
The Negro of Peter the Great (Pushkin)
See *Arap Petra Velikogo*
"The Negro Scholar" (Tolson) **88**:341
"Negro Servant" (Hughes) **1**:247
"Negro Song" (Guillén) **23**:131
"A Negro Speaks of Rivers" (Hughes) **1**:241-42, 248, 258-59, 263, 268; **53**:84, 89, 93-94, 105, 108-9, 118, 142
"Negro Spiritual" (McKay) **2**:214
"The Negro's Complaint" (Cowper) **40**:105, 119
"Negus" (Brathwaite) **56**:10, 74-75, 87-88
Nehez fold (Illyés) **16**:233, 238-39, 245
"La neige" (Vigny) **26**:401-402, 410-11
"Neige sur Paris" (Senghor) **25**:227, 239
"Neiges" (Perse) **23**:213, 216-18, 220-21, 232, 234, 250, 253, 256-57
"Neighbor" (Hughes) **53**:129
"Neighbor" (Hugo) **68**:287
"Neighborhood Bully" (Dylan) **37**:70
Neighborly Poems and Dialect Sketches (Riley) **48**:327, 332
"Neighbors" (Sandburg) **41**:320
"Neighbors" (Spencer) **77**:341
"Neither" (Thomas) **99**:324
"Neither Brings Charges" (McHugh) **61**:203
"Neither buskin now nor bay" (Campion) **87**:7
"Neither Out Far nor in Deep" (Frost) **1**:197, 218, 227-28; **39**:248
"Neither Sweet Pity, nor Lamentable Weeping" (Ronsard)
See "Ny la douce pitie, ny le pleur lamentable"
"Neither Wanting More" (Swenson) **14**:284
"Neko" (Hagiwara) **18**:181
"Neko no shigai" (Hagiwara) **18**:182
"Nel giusto tempo umano" (Quasimodo) **47**:277
"Nel Mezzo" (Melville) **82**:45-46, 50
"Nel Mezzo del Cammin di Nostra Vita" (Duncan) **75**:198, 223
"Nel Mezzo del Commin di Nostra Vita" (Duncan) **2**:103
"Nel mio paese" (Zanzotto) **65**:265
"Nel parco di Caserta" (Montale) **13**:127
"Nel sonno" (Montale) **13**:107, 128, 150
"Nele de Kantule" (Cardenal) **22**:127, 132
"Nell' annuale della fondazione di Roma" (Carducci) **46**:44, 52, 82, 84, 87
"Nella Piazza di San Petronio in una Sera d'Inverno" (Carducci) **46**:6, 54, 84, 87-89
"Nella serra" (Montale) **13**:110
"Nella valle" (Zanzotto) **65**:264
"Nell'antica" (Quasimodo) **47**:276, 301
"Nelly Gray" (Hood)
See "Faithless Nelly Gray"
"Nelly Meyers" (Ammons) **16**:5, 19
Nem. IV (Pindar)
See *Nemean 4*
Nem. VIII (Pindar)
See *Nemean 8*
Nemean 1 (Pindar) **19**:398, 412
Nemean 2 (Pindar) **19**:425
Nemean 3 (Pindar) **19**:425
Nemean 4 (Pindar) **19**:387, 391
Nemean V (Pindar)
See *Nemean 5*
Nemean 5 (Pindar) **19**:388, 420, 424
Nemean 7 (Pindar) **19**:388, 413, 425
Nemean 8 (Pindar) **19**:388, 413, 420, 425
Nemean 9 (Pindar) **19**:405, 425
Nemean 10 (Pindar) **19**:398, 405, 412
Nemean 11 (Pindar) **19**:405
"Nemota" (Akhmadulina) **43**:7, 65
"A Neoclassicist" (Rexroth) **95**:271
"The Neo-HooDoo Aesthetic" (Reed) **68**:333, 338, 348
"Neo-HooDoo Manifesto" (Reed) **68**:323-24, 329, 332, 347
"Neon Signs" (Hughes) **53**:190-91
Neon Vernacular: New and Selected Poems (Komunyakaa) **51**:24, 29, 31-33, 35, 45, 52, 56-57, 62-63
"Neophyte" (Meynell) **112**:158
"Nepenthe" (Smith) **104**:187-91
"Les Néréides" (Gautier) **18**:129, 141
"The Nereids of Seriphos" (Clampitt) **19**:92
"Nero's Term" (Cavafy) **36**:32
"Nerthus" (Heaney) **100**:352
"Neruda" (Wright) **36**:312
"Nerve Gas part II" (Bissett) **14**:7
"Nervous Prostration" (Wickham) **110**:255, 270, 274, 296, 311
"Nervous Songs" (Berryman) **64**:81, 88, 90, 122, 189, 191
Nest (Berssenbrugge) **115**:47
"Nest" (Berssenbrugge) **115**:3, 5
The Nesting Ground (Wagoner) **33**:327, 329, 333, 347, 367, 369, 373
"Nestor's Bathtub" (Dove) **6**:109
"Nestus Gurley" (Jarrell) **41**:154, 165, 168-69, 181, 185, 188
"The Net" (Teasdale) **31**:359
"Net, eto ne ia" (Akhmatova) **55**:25
"Net Menders" (Plath) **37**:177
"Nether, Nether, Netherland" (Alurista) **34**:21
Nets to Catch the Wind (Wylie) **23**:300-301, 306, 309, 311, 324-34
Nettles (Lawrence) **54**:171, 173, 220, 224, 249
Netzahualcóyotl (Cardenal) **22**:128, 130-31
Neue Gedichte (Heine) **25**:129-132
Neue Gedichte (Rilke) **2**:266-68, 275, 280-81
Neue Gedichte (Werfel) **101**:350, 360
Der neue Pausias und sein Blumenmädchen (Goethe) **5**:239-40
Neuer Frühling (Heine) **25**:129-31
"Neuf merci" (Char) **56**:120
"The Neurotic" (Day Lewis) **11**:147
"Neutral Tones" (Hardy) **8**:88, 126, 130; **92**:241, 248-49, 291, 342, 346-47, 352-54, 359-62, 365, 367
"Neutrality" (MacNeice) **61**:109, 141, 160-61, 181
"Nevada" (Cernuda) **62**:169, 171
"Never" (Silverstein) **49**:334
"Never" (Stone) **53**:258-59
"Never Again Would Birds' Song Be the Same" (Frost) **1**:231
"Never Give a Bum an Even Break" (Welch) **62**:339, 341, 346, 370, 375
"Never love unlesse you can" (Campion) **87**:59
"Never Offer Your Heart" (Walker) **30**:355
"Never seek to tell thy love . . ." (Blake) **63**:28
"Never Such Love" (Graves) **6**:137
"Never to Dream of Spiders" (Lorde) **12**:143

"Never weather-beaten Saile" (Campion) **87**:12, 42, 44, 52, 55-56, 66
"Nevermore" (Verlaine) **32**:368, 386-89
"Nevermore Baltimore" (Corso) **108**:31
"Nevertheless" (Moore) **49**:102, 130
Nevertheless (Moore) **49**:106, 126
"Never-to-Be" (de la Mare) **77**:116
"Nevesta" (Akhmadulina) **43**:60
"Nevicata" (Carducci) **46**:51
New Addresses (Koch) **80**:330
"The New Age" (Smith) **12**:313, 316
"The New America" (Blok) **21**:8, 26, 29
New and Collected Poems (Wilbur) **51**:247-50, 257, 261, 264, 266, 274, 276-85, 303, 309, 315-18, 322, 333
New and Collected Poems, 1917-1976 (MacLeish) **47**:193, 195, 197, 207
New and Selected (Viereck) **27**:275, 279, 280-82, 284
New and Selected Poems (Bell) **79**:31-33, 41
New & Selected Poems (Kenyon)
See *Otherwise*
New and Selected Poems (Meredith) **28**:210, 215
New and Selected Poems (Nemerov) **24**:258, 260, 262, 264, 266, 268, 284, 286
New and Selected Poems (Oliver) **75**:310-12, 317, 321
New and Selected Poems (Soto) **28**:404
New and Selected Poems: 1923-1985 (Warren) **37**:364-67
New and Selected Poems, 1940-1986 (Shapiro) **25**:318-22
New and Selected Things Taking Place (Swenson) **14**:274, 277, 280-81, 287
"New Animals" (Hall) **70**:34
New Arcadia (Sidney) **32**:316, 322
The New Arcadia (Sidney)
See *The Countess of Pembroke's Arcadia*
"The New Bathroom Policy at English High School" (Espada) **74**:146, 161
New Bats in Old Belfries (Betjeman) **75**:5, 61, 66, 84-88, 107
"The New Belfry of Christ Church, Oxford" (Carroll) **74**:72
The New Belfry of Christ Church, Oxford (Carroll) **74**:72
"The New Believers" (Leopardi)
See "I nuovi credenti"
"New Birth" (Morris) **55**:338
"The New Birth" (Very) **86**:46, 58, 89, 98, 126, 135, 151
"The New Body" (Very) **86**:115
"New Brunswick" (Birney) **52**:48-49, 51
New Cautionary Tales (Belloc) **24**:27
New Collected Poems (Graves) **6**:166
"The New Congo" (Brown) **55**:114, 164
"The New Convert" (Cowper) **40**:56
"New Dawn" (Warren) **37**:335, 377
"A New Day" (Levine) **22**:223-24
New Days (Jordan)
See *New Days: Poems of Exile and Return*
New Days: Poems of Exile and Return (Jordan) **38**:114, 120
New Desire (Hagiwara)
See *Atarashiki yokujō*
"A New Diary" (Abse) **41**:10, 15
"The New Eden" (Holmes) **71**:92
"New England" (Whittier) **93**:260
"New England, 1967" (Borges) **32**:88
"A New England Bachelor" (Eberhart) **76**:21, 30, 42, 65
"New England November" (Hall) **70**:30
New England Tragedies (Longfellow) **30**:23, 39, 59, 65-6
New Found Land: Fourteen Poems (MacLeish) **47**:125, 127-28, 137, 188, 194, 253
"New Georgia" (Jarrell) **41**:174, 209
New Goose (Niedecker) **42**:94, 97, 102, 105, 134-35, 139, 148-52, 167, 174
"New Granddaughter" (Abse) **41**:33
"New Grown Girl" (Guillén)
See "Muchacha recién crecida"
"A New Guide" (Koch) **80**:322
"New Hampshire" (Eliot) **5**:166, 169
"New Hampshire" (Frost) **39**:234-35, 243-44, 254
"New Hampshire" (Hall) **70**:7
New Hampshire (Frost) **1**:215, 224; **39**:233-35, 243, 245, 254-55; **71**:42
"New Hampshire, February" (Eberhart) **76**:4-5, 12, 42
"New Haven" (Stevens)
See "An Ordinary Evening in New Haven"
"New Heaven and Earth" (Lawrence) **54**:170, 176, 213-14, 232-34
"New Heaven, New Warre" (Southwell) **83**:257-58, 275-76, 286-88, 341
"New Heavens for Old" (Lowell) **13**:85, 88
"The New House" (Thomas) **53**:269, 286, 294
"New Jerusalem" (MacNeice) **61**:176-78
"The New Jerusalem" (Very) **86**:96
"New Koide Road" (Hagiwara)
See "Koide shidō"
"The New Leader" (Cohen) **109**:13, 89
New Leaves (Castro)
See *Follas novas*
"New leaves! I feel like laughing" (Castro)
See "¡Hojas nuevas! risa siento"
"New Legends" (Graves) **6**:149
New Life (Dante)
See *La vita nuova*
"The New Little Larousse" (Zagajewski) **27**:401
"The New Love" (Parker) **28**:356
"New Love and Old" (Teasdale) **31**:365, 379
A New Lovesong for Stalingrad (Neruda)
See *Nuevo canto de amor a Stalingrado*
"The New Mariner" (Thomas) **99**:260
New Mexico Poems (Quintana)
See *Hijo del pueblo: New Mexico Poems*
"The New Mistress" (Housman) **43**:234
"New Moon in January" (Hughes) **89**:112, 114
"New Moon in November" (Merwin) **45**:20
"New Morality" (Coleridge) **11**:102-03
"New Mother" (Olds) **22**:312
New Music-New Poetry (Baraka) **113**:26
"A New Notebook" (Akhmadulina) **43**:3
"New Objectives, New Cadres" (Rexroth) **20**:215; **95**:270
"New Orleans" (Harjo) **27**:65
"New Orleans 30 Oct 71" (Brutus) **24**:124
"The New Pastoral" (Boland) **58**:45
A New Path to the Waterfall (Carver) **54**:15, 20-21, 26
"A New Poem" (Duncan) **75**:200, 223
"New Poems" (Wright) **36**:350
New Poems (Arnold) **5**:12, 43, 50
New Poems (Bridges) **28**:51, 67, 69
New Poems (Heine)
See *Neue Gedichte*
New Poems (Kinsella) **69**:72-73, 128
New Poems (Lawrence) **54**:207, 217, 225, 232, 239-40
New Poems (Montale) **13**:143-46
New Poems (Rexroth) **20**:197, 204 **95**:253-54, 268, 274, 281-82
New Poems (Rilke)
See *Neue Gedichte*
New Poems (Werfel)
See *Neue Gedichte*
New Poems and Variant Readings (Stevenson) **84**:334
New Poems by George Crabbe (Crabbe) **97**:90, 123
New Poems, 1962 (Graves) **6**:154
"The New Poetry Handbook" (Strand) **63**:198
"New Prince, New Pompe" (Southwell) **83**:257, 259, 276, 286-88
"The New Proletarian" (Morris) **55**:338
"New Prologue Spoken at the Representation ofComus" (Johnson) **81**:235
"A New Psalm for the Chapel of Kilmarnock" (Burns) **6**:89
"A New Reality Is Better Than a New Movie!" (Baraka) **4**:30; **113**:24, 43, 55, 126
"A New Record" (Duncan) **2**:103
New Rhymes (Carducci)
See *Rime nuove*
"The New Saddhus" (Pinsky) **27**:176
"New Season" (Levine) **22**:223
New Selected Poems (Levine) **22**:220-221, 223-24, 226, 228
New Selected Poems 1957-1981 (Hughes)
See *Selected Poems 1957-1981*
New Selected Poems 1957-1994 (Hughes) **89**:187, 190, 212, 233
New Selected Poems: 1966-1987 (Heaney) **100**:231-34, 252
"The New Sheriff" (Baraka) **4**:10, 15
"The New Ships" (Brathwaite) **56**:67
A New Siege (Montague) **106**:216-17, 250, 252, 262, 265, 279, 285, 308, 310, 314, 326, 340
"The New Sirens" (Arnold) **5**:5, 39
New Skins for the Old Ceremony (Cohen) **109**:35
"A New Song" (Heaney) **18**:202, 241; **100**:197
A New Song (Hughes) **1**:242, 250, 253-54, 268; **53**:111-13, 115
New Songs (Béranger)
See *Chansons nouvelles*
"The New Spirit" (Ashbery) **26**:108, 130, 169-70
The New Spoon River (Masters) **1**:333-34, 344-45; **36**:184, 190, 194, 209-12, 215, 220, 238, 243
"New St. Louis Blues" (Brown) **55**:74, 80, 110, 144, 150-51, 154, 160
"New Stanzas" (Montale)
See "Nuove stanze"
"New Stanzas to Augusta" (Brodsky)
See "Novye stansy k Avguste"
"New Steps" (Brown) **55**:174-75
"A New Story" (Ortiz) **17**:234
"New Territory" (Boland) **58**:42
New Territory (Boland) **58**:42-43, 91
"A New Theme" (Ignatow) **34**:305
"New Thoughts on Old Subjects" (Coleridge) **11**:105
New Time (Scalapino) **114**:297, 299, 313-14, 334, 336, 338, 341
"New Vestments" (Lear) **65**:146, 153-54, 156-57, 160
"New Vows" (Erdrich) **52**:177
"The New Warden" (Baca) **41**:37
"New Warre" (Southwell) **83**:258-59
"New Weather" (Sandburg) **41**:310
"New Wife and the Old" (Whittier) **93**:223, 244
"The New Woman" (Guillén)
See "Mujer nueva"
"The New Woman" (Randall) **86**:291-92, 295, 343
"New World" (Brathwaite) **56**:22, 86
"New World" (Momaday) **25**:199, 216
"New World" (Walcott) **46**:290
"The New World" (Very) **86**:132
The New World (Masters) **1**:339
"New World A-Comin" (Brathwaite) **56**:4, 26, 38, 75, 99
"New Year" (Spender) **71**:219, 221
"The New Year" (Thomas) **53**:322
"The New Year" (Whittier) **93**:206, 314, 317
The New Year (Mickiewicz) **38**:157
"New Year Letter" (Auden) **92**:38, 41, 44, 64-65, 94, 102-3, 105, 129
"New Year Letter" (Brathwaite) **56**:65
"New Year Letter" (Rexroth) **95**:332
New Year Letter (Auden) **1**:16, 21, 23-24, 34
"New Year Resolve" (Sarton) **39**:369
"New Year Wishes" (Sarton) **39**:322, 343
"The New Yeares Gift, or Circumcision Song" (Herrick)
See "Another New-yeeres Gift; or song for the Circumcision"
"New Year's Address" (Whittier) **93**:193, 199
"New Year's Dawn, 1947" (Jeffers) **17**:141

"New Year's Eve" (Berryman) **64**:90
"New Year's Eve" (Hardy) **8**:104, 119
"New Year's Eve" (Lawrence) **54**:169
"New Year's Eve" (Tennyson) **101**:237
"New Year's Eve 1959" (Kursh) **15**:224
"A New Year's Eve in War Time" (Hardy) **92**:215, 269
"New Year's Gift" (Herrick)
See "A New-Yeares Gift Sent to Sir Simeon Steward"
"New Year's Greetings" (Tsvetaeva)
See "Novogodnee"
"New Year's Song" (Seifert) **47**:325
"New York" (Gunn) **26**:209, 220
"New York" (Moore) **49**:90-91, 94, 96, 128
"New York" (Senghor) **25**:255
"New York" (Viereck) **27**:274
"New York: 5 March 1957" (Cunningham) **92**:137, 166, 169
"New York 1962: Fragment" (Lowell) **3**:215
"New York at Night" (Lowell) **13**:79
"New York City 1970" (Lorde) **12**:146, 158
New York Head Shop and Museum (Lorde) **12**:146-47, 154
"New York in August" (Davie) **29**:97, 110
"New York: Office and Denunciation" (García Lorca)
See "Nueva York: Oficina y denuncia"
"The New York Times" (Kumin) **15**:200
"The New Yorkers" (Giovanni) **19**:142
"New Yorkers" (Hughes) **53**:161
"Los New Yorks" (Cruz) **37**:33-34
The New Youth (Pasolini)
See *La nuova gioventù*
"New Zealand City" (Curnow) **48**:26
"New Zealand Poems" (Wright) **14**:377
"The New Zealot to the Sun" (Melville) **82**:105
"Newark Abbey" (Peacock) **87**:334, 342, 351
"Newborn Death" (Rossetti) **44**:254
"Newborn Girl-Child" (Guillén) **23**:132
"Newcomer" (Okigbo) **7**:233, 240
"The Newer Vainglory" (Meynell) **112**:162
"The Newest Bath Guide" (Betjeman) **75**:33
The Newly Fallen (Dorn) **115**:82, 122, 125, 135, 152, 154, 219
"Newport Beach 1979" (Komunyakaa) **51**:34
"Newport Jazz Festival" (Jordan) **38**:126
"Newtown" (Berrigan) **103**:34, 41
"News" (Niedecker) **42**:98
"The News" (Stone) **53**:222
"News" (Traherne) **70**:288
"The News and the Weather" (Stevens) **110**:113, 159
"The News Carried To Macedonia" (Carver) **54**:28
"News for the Delphic Oracle" (Yeats) **20**:312-13, 316, 334-35
"News from China" (Hood) **93**:99
"News from Mount Amiata" (Montale)
See "Notizie dall'Amiata"
News from Plymouth (Davenant) **99**:176
"News from the Cabin" (Swenson) **14**:253-54
"News Item" (Kavanagh) **33**:79
"News Item" (Parker) **28**:347, 359
"News of the Assassin" (Merwin) **45**:9, 22
News of the Universe (Bly) **39**:54, 58, 100
News of the World (Barker) **77**:8, 10, 13-14
"News of the World II" (Barker) **77**:14
"News of the World III" (Barker) **77**:14
"News Photo" (Warren) **37**:304
"News Report" (Ignatow) **34**:273, 284, 308
"News Report" (Randall) **86**:339
The Newspaper: A Poem (Crabbe) **97**:79-80, 101
"A Newspaper Is a Collection of Half-Injustices" (Crane) **80**:52
"Newspaper Readers" (Tsvetaeva)
See "Chitateli gazet"
"The News-Reel" (MacNeice) **61**:142
"Newsreel: Man and Firing Squad" (Atwood) **8**:23
"A New-Yeares Gift Sent to Sir Simeon Steward" (Herrick) **9**:102, 145
"A New-yeares gift. To the King" (Carew) **29**:52
"A New-yeares-Gift to the Queen, in the Year 1643" (Davenant) **99**:177
"Next!" (Nash) **21**:270
"Next Day" (Jarrell) **41**:185, 189, 191, 200
Next: New Poems (Clifton) **17**:24, 26-28, 35-36
"Next, Please" (Larkin) **21**:226-27, 230, 235, 242, 246
The Next Room of the Dream (Nemerov) **24**:259, 262, 264, 266, 289
"Next Summer" (Jacobsen) **62**:323
"The Next Time" (Strand) **63**:183, 186-88
"Next to of Course God America I" (Cummings) **5**:89
Next-to-Last Things: New Poems and Essays (Kunitz) **19**:186
"The Next War" (Owen) **102**:205, 209, 263
Neypayasam (Das) **43**:84
"Nezabudka" (Lermontov) **18**:188-89
Nezhnost (Yevtushenko) **40**:344-46, 350
Neznakomka (Blok) **21**:4, 24
"Ni siquiera soy polvo" (Borges) **32**:66
Ni tiro (Fuertes) **27**:17
Ni tiro ni veneno (Fuertes) **27**:16
"Niagara" (Lindsay) **23**:275
"Nic Darowane" (Szymborska) **44**:298, 308
"Nic dwa razy" (Szymborska) **44**:285, 293
"Nic ladnego" (Herbert) **50**:5
"Nicaraguan canto" (Cardenal)
See "Canto nacional"
"Niccolò" (Carducci) **46**:52
"A nice day" (Bukowski) **18**:23
"Nice Guy" (Ignatow) **34**:305
"Nice Mountain" (Stern) **115**:271
"A Nice Shady Home" (Stevens) **6**:292
"Night Watchman, Look to My Flashlight" (Dorn) **115**:133, 162
"Nicholas Bindle" (Masters) **36**:170
"Nicholas Nye" (de la Mare) **77**:94
"Nichóri" (Cavafy) **36**:52
"Nick and the Candlestick" (Plath) **1**:390; **37**:257
"Nicodemus" (Robinson) **1**:476, 485
"Nicou" (Chatterton)
See "The Death of Nicou"
"Nido en una estatua" (Storni) **33**:294
"Niebla" (Guillén) **35**:154
"Niebo" (Szymborska) **44**:284, 303-4, 308-9
"Niedzwiedzie" (Herbert) **50**:8
"Niektórzy lubia poezje" (Szymborska) **44**:292, 305
Die Niemandsrose (Celan) **10**:95, 98-99, 113, 117, 121
"Nienawisc" (Szymborska) **44**:295, 305
"Niespodziane spotkanie" (Szymborska) **44**:269
"Nieve" (Guillén) **23**:109
"La nieve" (Guillén) **35**:186-87, 188
"Nigerian Unity/or Little Niggers Killing Little Niggers" (Madhubuti) **5**:329, 341-42
"Nigger" (Sanchez) **9**:223, 232
"Nigger" (Sandburg) **41**:337, 365
"Nigger" (Shapiro) **25**:270
The Nigger of Peter the Great (Pushkin)
See *Arap Petra Velikogo*
"Nigger Song: An Odyssey" (Dove) **6**:105
"Niggerlips" (Espada) **74**:126, 162
"Nigger's Leap: New England" (Wright) **14**:335-36, 338, 340, 349-50, 368, 374
"Niggy the Ho" (Baraka) **4**:29, 38; **113**:24
"Night" (Akhmadulina)
See "Noch"
"Night" (Blake) **12**:7-8, 23, 33, 61; **63**:8, 10, 14-16, 24, 83, 102, 118, 121-22
"Night" (Bogan) **12**:96, 104
"Night" (Celan) **10**:112
"Night" (Giovanni) **19**:141
"Night" (Jeffers) **17**:107, 131, 145
"Night" (Lovelace) **69**:168
"Night" (Pasternak)
See "Noch'"
"Night" (Pavese)
See "La notte"
"Night" (Rilke) **2**:275
"The Night" (Vaughan) **81**:272-74, 281-83, 303-5, 307-8
"Night" (Very) **86**:44, 113, 163
Night, A Descriptive Poem (Elliott) **96**:181-82
"Night, a street, a lamp, a chemist's" (Blok)
See "Noch' ulitsa fonar' apteka"
"Night and Day" (Lanier) **50**:56
"Night and Day" (Stevenson) **84**:299
"Night and Day in 1952" (O'Hara) **45**:163, 189
"Night and Morning" (Clarke) **112**:47-48
Night and Morning: Poems (Clarke) **112**:30-32, 34-35, 37, 47, 53, 65-68, 80, 82, 87-88, 90-91, 97-99, 110, 113
"Night and Sleep" (Patmore) **59**:258
"Night and the Child" (Wright) **14**:352
"Night and the City" (Berryman) **64**:70, 83
"A Night at the Napi in Browning" (Hugo) **68**:251
"Night Bear Which Frightened Cattle" (Atwood) **8**:39
"The Night Before" (Robinson) **1**:460
"The Night before Goodbye" (Yamada) **44**:330-34, 343, 347
"The Night before Great Babylon" (Sitwell) **3**:310
"The Night before the Night before Christmas" (Jarrell) **41**:139, 163, 171-73, 180, 194, 216-17
"Night Café" (Benn)
See "Nachtcafé"
"Night City" (Bishop) **34**:160
"The Night Comes On" (Cohen) **109**:101
"Night Conference, Wood Quay: 6 June 1979" (Kinsella) **69**:130
Night Crossing (Mahon) **60**:132-34, 137-38, 154, 171, 181, 199
"The Night Dances" (Plath) **1**:388, 390
"Night, Death, Mississippi" (Hayden) **6**:194, 196
"The Night Dream" (MacLeish) **47**:190
"Night Feed" (Boland) **58**:13, 46, 52-53, 57
Night Feed (Boland) **58**:12, 14-15, 44-45, 47, 52, 66-67
"Night, Four Songs" (Hughes) **1**:240
"The Night Game" (Pinsky) **27**:159, 176
"Night Hawk" (Welch) **62**:354
"Night Hours" (Blok) **21**:5
"Night in Arizona" (Teasdale) **31**:365, 379
"A Night in Four Parts" (Spicer) **78**:302
"Night in Maine" (Lowell) **3**:226
"Night in the Forest" (Kinnell) **26**:240
"Night in the Old Home" (Hardy) **8**:105; **92**:317
"The Night Is Freezing Fast" (Housman)
See "Last Poems: XX— The Night Is Freezing Fast"
"Night is Personal" (Warren) **37**:302
"The Night Journey" (Brooke) **24**:60
"Night Journey" (Roethke) **15**:246
"Night Journey in the Cooking Pot" (Bly) **39**:25, 27-8, 84-5
"Night Journeys" (Ní Chuilleanáin) **34**:351, 353, 380
"Night Launch" (Kumin) **15**:209
"Night Letter" (Kunitz) **19**:154, 157, 161, 169
"The Night Lies" (Ciardi) **69**:24
"The Night Life" (Ignatow) **34**:323
Night Light (Justice) **64**:249, 251-53, 257, 275, 280, 288-90
"The Night My Father Got Me" (Housman) **2**:191
"Night of Frost in May" (Meredith) **60**:248, 280, 284, 295
"Night of Hell" (Rimbaud)
See "Nuit de l'enfer"
"Night of Sine" (Senghor)
See "Nuit de Sine"
"The Night of the Dance" (Hardy) **92**:329

"The Night of the Falling Apples" (Akhmadulina)
See "Noc' upadan'ja jablok"
"Night of the Shirts" (Merwin) **45**:51
"Night on the Downland" (Masefield) **78**:106
"Night Operations Coastal Command RAF" (Nemerov) **24**:287
"A Night Out" (Abse) **41**:9, 18-19, 25
"Night Out" (Harjo) **27**:55
"Night People" (Ignatow) **34**:273
"Night Piece" (Heaney) **18**:201, 217
"A Night Piece" (Smart) **13**:341, 347
"Night Piece for My Twenty-seventh Birthday" (Ciardi) **69**:27-28
"The Night Piece: To Julia" (Herrick)
See "The Night-Piece to Julia"
"Night Pieces" (Strand) **63**:181
"Night Pleasures" (Pavese)
See "Piaceri notturni"
"Night Practice" (Swenson) **14**:266
"Night Rain" (Werfel)
See "Nachtregen"
"Night Scenes" (Duncan) **75**:195-96, 199-200
"Night Shift" (Plath) **1**:388; **37**:176
"Night Sky" (Erdrich) **52**:175, 178, 192
"Night Sky" (Thomas) **99**:257, 337-38, 356
"Night Song" (Glück) **16**:145-47
"Night Song at Amalfi" (Teasdale) **31**:322, 379
"Night Song for Amalfi" (Teasdale) **31**:364
"Night Song of an Asiatic Wandering Shepherd" (Montale)
See "Canto notturno di un pastore errante nell'Asia"
"Night Songs" (Kinsella) **69**:118
"Night steals upon the world" (Whittier) **93**:201
"Night Storm" (Sarton) **39**:342
"Night Sung Sailor's Prayer" (Kaufman) **74**:195
"Night Taxi" (Gunn) **26**:231
"The Night that Lorca Comes" (Kaufman) **74**:214
"The Night, the Porch" (Strand) **63**:194-95
"Night Thoughts" (Smith) **12**:337
"Night Train" (Hagiwara)
See "Yogisha"
"Night Transfigured" (Tomlinson) **17**:319, 342
"Night Visits with the Family" (Swenson) **14**:281
"Night Watch in the City of Boston" (MacLeish) **47**:205, 211
"The Night Watchman" (Jacobsen) **62**:315, 323
"The Night-Blooming Cereus" (Hayden) **6**:194-95, 198
The Night-Blooming Cereus (Hayden) **6**:182, 184, 187, 190, 194
"Nightbreak" (Rich) **5**:358
"Nightfall" (de la Mare) **77**:60, 134
"Nightfishing" (Schnackenberg) **45**:345
"Night-Flowering Cactus" (Merton) **10**:334
"The Nightingale" (Coleridge) **11**:85, 106; **67**:277, 280, 295, 304, 339
"The Nightingale" (Finch)
See "To the Nightingale"
"Nightingale" (Keats)
See "Ode to a Nightingale"
"The Nightingale" (Marie de France)
See "Laüstic"
"The Nightingale" (Ronsard)
See *See "Le Rossignol"*
"The Nightingale and Glow-worm" (Cowper) **40**:124
"The Nightingale Garden" (Blok) **21**:20
The Nightingale of the Catholic Church (Pasolini)
See *L'usignuolo della Chiesa Cattolica*
"The Nightingale on the Stone" (Cernuda) **62**:174
The Nightingale Sings Badly (Seifert)
See *Slavík zpíváśpatně*
The Nightingale Sings out of Tune (Seifert)
See *Slavík zpíváśpatně*
The Nightingale Sings Poorly (Seifert)
See *Slavík zpíváśpatně*
"Nightingales" (Bridges) **28**:64, 66, 70, 75-6
"The Nightingales" (Williams) **7**:345
Nightingales (Robinson)
See *The Glory of the Nightingales*
"The Nightingales Nest" (Clare) **23**:4-5
"The Night-March" (Melville) **82**:75
"Nightmare" (Kumin) **15**:198
"Nightmare" (Lowell) **13**:78
"Nightmare" (Page) **12**:168
"Nightmare at Noon" (Benét) **64**:9, 25-26
The Nightmare Factory (Kumin) **15**:190, 200, 208
"Nightmare for Future Reference" (Benét) **64**:25-26
"Nightmare Number Three" (Benét) **64**:25-26
"Nightmare of Peace" (Muir) **49**:257
"Nightmare, with Angels" (Benét) **64**:25
"Nightmares" (Benét) **64**:6
"Nightmares" (Heaney) **100**:225
"Night-Music" (Rukeyser) **12**:209, 211
"Night-piece" (Cunningham) **92**:169
"Night-Piece" (Kunitz) **19**:148, 153
"Night-Piece" (Sassoon) **12**:240
"The Night-piece" (Waller) **72**:335
"A Night-Piece" (Wordsworth) **67**:269-70
"The Night-Piece to Julia" (Herrick) **9**:94, 132
"Night-Ride on Ariel" (Hughes) **89**:274-75
"Nights and Days" (Rich) **5**:375
Nights and Days (Merrill) **28**:220, 225-28, 230-32, 234, 240, 250, 252-54, 281
"Nights of '57" (Heaney) **100**:244
"Nights of 1962: The River Merchant's Wife" (Hacker) **47**:87, 105, 114
"Nights of 1964-1966: The Old Reliable" (Hacker) **47**:87-88, 105
"Nightsong: City" (Brutus) **24**:113
"Night-Time in the Cemetery" (Smith) **12**:316
"Nightwalker" (Kinsella) **69**:68-69, 71, 83, 85-89, 92, 95, 98, 104-5, 107-9, 127, 129, 131, 135
Nightwalker and Other Poems (Kinsella) **69**:66, 80, 82-92, 95-100, 102-5, 107, 109, 121, 130
Nightworks: Poems 1962-2000 (Bell) **79**:38-40, 42, 44
"The Nihilist as Hero" (Lowell) **3**:229
"Nihon no Banka" (Yakamochi) **48**:99-100, 132-33, 137-39
"Nijinski" (Seferis) **66**:182-83, 185
"Nikki-Rosa" (Giovanni) **19**:139
"Nilamanilata" (Tagore) **8**:416
"The Nile" (Hunt) **73**:136, 162
"Nils Lykke" (Pound) **95**:115, 117
"Nimm fort die Amarylle" (Benn) **35**:69
"Nimmo" (Robinson) **1**:468
"Nimphe aus beaus yeus" (Ronsard) **105**:201
Nimphidia, the Court of Fayrie (Drayton) **98**:14, 45, 49, 51
"Nimrod in September" (Sassoon) **12**:278
"La niña de Guatemala" (Martí) **76**:79, 101
"Nina Nanna di Carlo V" (Carducci) **46**:52
"Nina Replies" (Rimbaud)
See "Les reparties de Nina"
"Nina's Replies" (Rimbaud)
See "Les reparties de Nina"
"IX" (Joyce) **22**:160, 167
"Nine Charms against the Hunter" (Wagoner) **33**:333
Nine Entertainments (Spender) **71**:146
Nine Experiments: Being Poems Written at the Age of Eighteen (Spender) **71**:178, 215-16, 218
"9 from 8" (Lanier) **50**:106-7
Nine Horses (Collins) **68**:225-26
"Nine Lives" (Merrill) **28**:283
"Nine Nectarines" (Moore)
See "Nine Nectarines and Other Porcelain"
"Nine Nectarines and Other Porcelain" (Moore) **49**:94, 98, 146
"Nine Poems for the Unborn Child" (Rukeyser) **12**:228
"Nine Sleep Valley" (Merrill) **28**:254-55
"Nine Variations in a Chinese Winter Setting" (Tomlinson) **17**:299, 331
"Nine Verses of the Same Song" (Berry) **28**:5
"XIX" (Joyce) **22**:145, 169, 171
"1914" (Owen) **19**:352
1914, and Other Poems (Brooke) **24**:61, 63, 80, 85, 87-8
"1909" (Apollinaire) **7**:46-7
"1984" (Komunyakaa) **51**:62
"1954" (Kavanagh) **33**:59
"1959" (Corso) **33**:43, 49
"1953" (Corso) **33**:48
"1940" (Betjeman) **75**:37
"1945-1985: Poem for the Anniversary" (Oliver) **75**:312
"1941" (Stone) **53**:243, 258
"1914" (Jarrell) **41**:169
"MCMXIV" (Larkin) **21**:229, 234
"Nineteen Hadley Street" (Schnackenberg) **45**:329, 342, 345, 349
"Nineteen Hundred and Nineteen" (Yeats) **20**:314, 325, 350-51
"Nineteen Hundred Nineteen" (Walcott) **46**:307
"1975" (Kinsella) **69**:131
"1975" (Spencer) **77**:326, 330, 339
"1975 (an alternative)" (Kinsella) **69**:131
"1977, Near Mullingar" (Davie) **29**:105, 108
"1977: Poem for Mrs. Fannie Lou Hamer" (Jordan) **38**:127
"1964" (Borges) **32**:64
"1969" (Warren) **37**:306
"1969, Ireland of the Bombers" (Davie) **29**:105-06, 108, 120
"1967" (Hardy) **92**:241-42, 245
"1966 and All That" (Montague) **106**:265, 337
"1963" (Dove) **6**:106
"1930's" (Oppen) **35**:327
"The Nineteen-thirties" (Kennedy) **93**:140
"1934" (Eberhart) **76**:34
"Nineteen Thirty-eight" (Berryman) **64**:83
"1937" (Niedecker) **42**:140
"1936" (Benét) **64**:14
"1933" (Levine)
See *1933*
1933 (Levine) **22**:217-18, 223
"1933" (MacLeish) **47**:130, 150-51
"1912-1952 Full Cycle" (Viereck) **27**:264
1921-1925 (Mandelstam) **14**:151, 155
"The Nineteenth Century and After" (Yeats) **20**:314
"Ninetieth Birthday" (Thomas) **99**:236
"90 North" (Jarrell) **41**:127, 188, 191-92, 213-14
95 Poems (Cummings) **5**:109-10
"96 Tears" (Hongo) **23**:199
Ninfeas (Jiménez) **7**:197, 199
"Niño" (Guillén) **35**:157
"Niño mexicano" (Mistral) **32**:161
"El niño solo" (Mistral) **32**:174, 179
"los niños crecen" (Alurista) **34**:38
"Ninth Elegy" (Hope) **56**:275
"Ninth Elegy" (Rilke) **2**:281, 286-87
"Ninth Elegy: The Antagonists" (Rukeyser) **12**:223
Ninth Nemean (Pindar)
See *Nemean 9*
"Ninth Psalm" (Sexton) **2**:367; **79**:231
Ninth Pythian (Pindar)
See *Pythian 9*
"The Ninth Symphony of Beethoven Understood at Last as a Sexual Message" (Rich) **5**:360, 370
"Niobe in Distress for Her Children Slain by Apollo" (Wheatley) **3**:338, 355, 357-60
Niobjeta ziemia (Milosz) **8**:179, 211
A Nip in the Air (Betjeman) **75**:32, 39, 64
"Nipping Pussy's Feet in Fun" (Smith) **12**:339
"Nirbhay" (Tagore) **8**:415
"Nirjharer svapnabhanga" (Tagore) **8**:406
"Niruddesh yatra" (Tagore) **8**:408
"Nirvâna" (Lanier) **50**:56, 67
"Nishikigizuka" (Ishikawa) **10**:213

"Nitrate" (Levine) **22**:224
"Niwatori" (Hagiwara) **18**:174, 180
"Nixon's the One" (Meredith) **28**:176, 206
"Nixt that a turnament wes tryid" (Dunbar) **67**:15-16
"No" (Kenyon) **57**:20, 42
"No" (Stein) **18**:327
"No" (Thomas) **99**:336
"No. 54, chicano infante" (Alurista) See "chicano infante"
"No. 57, sacred robe" (Alurista) **34**:13
"No Answer" (Ignatow) **34**:274
No Baby Must Weep (Serote) **113**:297
"No Bed" (de la Mare) **77**:112
"No Believers in the Resurrection" (Mandelstam) **14**:120
"No Bell-Ringing. A Ballad of Durnover" (Hardy) **92**:272, 277
"No Better than 'a withered daffodil'" (Moore) **49**:142
"No Boy Knows When He Goes to Sleep" (Riley) **48**:299
"No Buyers: A Street Scene" (Hardy) **8**:101
"No Coward Soul Is Mine" (Brontë) **8**:51, 60, 69-70
"No decía palabras" (Cernuda) **62**:235
"No dejan escribir" (Fuertes) **27**:49
"No Difference" (Silverstein) **49**:313
"No Doubt What he Saw" (Corso) **33**:25
No End of Fun (Szymborska) See *Sto pociech*
"No Feeble Dream ..." (Barker) **77**:3
"No Foe Shall Gather Our Harvest" (Gilmore) **87**:303
"No Grown-ups" (Silverstein) **49**:342
"No hay salida?" (Paz) **1**:364
"No Hearing (Discovering)" (Lowell) **3**:228
No Hiding Place (Brown) **55**:81, 89, 94, 111, 113-15, 117, 158, 164, 166-69, 172
"No Ideas but in Things" (Creeley) **73**:27
"No intentemos el amor nunca" (Cernuda) **62**:230
"No Lamp Has Ever Shown Us Where to Look" (MacLeish) **47**:186
"No Lilies for Lisette" (Service) **70**:141
"No Loser, No Weeper" (Angelou) **32**:27
"No Man Believes" (Thomas) **52**:292-93, 298
"No Man's Land" (Heaney) **18**:202; **100**:199, 297
"No Matter, Never Mind" (Snyder) **21**:297
"No more" (Milosz) **8**:190, 193
"No More Access to Her Underpants" (Updike) **90**:359
"No More Ghosts" (Graves) **6**:132
"No More Marching" (Madhubuti) **5**:339
"No More Mozart" (Abse) **41**:15
"No More Sacrifices" (Ortiz) **17**:223, 234
"No Music" (Montague) **106**:288
No Nature: New and Selected Poems (Snyder) **21**:324-25
"No Need" (Carver) **54**:15, 19
"No Neutral Stone" (Kennedy) **93**:149
"No No No No" (Angelou) **32**:12
"No Noon at My Village Home" (Das) **43**:80
"No One Remembers" (Levine) **22**:223
"No One Sentence" (Stein) **18**:313
"No One So Much As You" (Thomas) **53**:271-72, 275-76
The No One's Rose (Celan) See *Die Niemandsrose*
"No Orpheus, No Eurydice" (Spender) **71**:187
"No Particular Day" (Strand) **63**:157
"No Particular Reason" (Tapahonso) **65**:224, 258
"¡No pasarán" (Paz) **48**:178-79, 243
"NO PEACE / BLACK HOLES / EARTH CRACKS" (Raworth) **107**:276
"No Poetic Authorisation" (Kavanagh) **105**:176
"No Possom, No Sop, No Taters" (Stevens) **6**:302
"No Recompense" (Clarke) **112**:29-30, 37, 50, 87
"No renunciation" (Char) **56**:131
"No Resurrection" (Jeffers) **17**:141
"No retiring summer stroke" (Niedecker) **42**:149
"No Road" (Larkin) **21**:230, 235
"No Sanctuary" (Heaney) **18**:202; **100**:199
"No sé por qué piensas tú" (Guillén) **23**:140
"No Second Coming" (Curnow) **48**:28
"No Speech from the Scaffold" (Gunn) **26**:202
"No Steps" (Kenyon) **57**:45
"No Succour!" (Stern) **115**:259
"No Swan So Fine" (Moore) **49**:172, 176, 178
"No, Thank You, John!" (Rossetti) **7**:267, 281, 291
No Thanks (Cummings) **5**:106-07
"No, That Is Not I" (Akhmatova) See "Net, eto ne ia"
"No Theory" (Ignatow) **34**:277, 309, 323, 325
"No Through Road" (Thomas) **99**:245
"No Time" (Collins) **68**:225
"No Title Required" (Szymborska) See "Moze byc bez tytulu"
No Truce with the Furies (Thomas) **99**:321-22, 324-26, 330, 349
"No Way of Knowing" (Ashbery) **26**:124, 144
"No Way of Knowing When This Song Began" (Mandelstam) **14**:118
"No, we didn't suffer together in vain" (Akhmatova) **55**:35
"No Word" (Corso) **33**:42
"No Word" (Kunitz) **19**:170, 186
"No Worst, There Is None" (Hopkins) **15**:175
Noah and the Waters (Day Lewis) **11**:127-28, 144, 152-53
"Noah Built the Ark" (Johnson) **24**:128-29, 144, 155, 164-65, 169
"Noah's Raven" (Merwin) **45**:8, 14, 32, 34
"The Nobel Prize" (Pasternak) See "Nobelevskaya premiya"
"Nobelevskaya premiya" (Pasternak) **6**:268, 284
"The Noble Acts of Arthur of the Round Table" (Deloney) **79**:58-59, 61
"The Noble Lady's Tale" (Hardy) **8**:99; **92**:271
"The Noble Lord" (Belloc) **24**:41
Noble Numbers, or Pious Pieces (Herrick) See *His Noble Numbers: or, His Pious Pieces, Wherein (amongst Other Things) He Sings the Birth of His Christ: and Sighes for His Saviours Suffering on the Crosse*
"Noble Peasant" (Crabbe) **97**:150
"Noble Sisters" (Rossetti) **7**:272, 274, 276, 280
"The Nobleman Orsha" (Lermontov) **18**:300
"The Noble Radiant Man" (Werfel) See "Der schöne strahlende Mensch"
"The Noblest Service" (Riley) **48**:301
Nobodaddy (MacLeish) **47**:175-76, 178, 183-87, 192, 253
"Nobody" (Aleixandre) See "Nadie"
"Nobody" (Guillén) See "Nadie"
"Nobody" (Silverstein) **49**:327
"Nobody Comes" (Hardy) **8**:101, 125
"Nobody Owns th Earth" (Bissett) **14**:10
Nobody Owns th Earth (Bissett) **14**:10-12, 18
"Nobody Riding the Roads Today" (Jordan) **38**:118
"Nobody Sings Anymore" (Baraka) **113**:54
"Nobody's Lookin' but de Owl and de Moon" (Johnson) **24**:141
The Nobody's Rose (Celan) See *Die Niemandsrose*
"Noc' upadan'ja jablok" (Akhmadulina) **43**:18-19
Les Noces d'Hérodiade (Mallarmé) See *Hérodiade*
"Noch" (Akhmadulina) **43**:6
"Noch'" (Pasternak) **6**:285
Noch feiert Todd das Leben (Sachs) **78**:111, 157, 159, 161, 169, 175-76
"Noch' na 30 marta" (Akhmadulina) **43**:37
"Noch' I" (Lermontov) **18**:302
"Noch' II" (Lermontov) **18**:302
"Noch' ulitsa fonar' apteka'" (Blok) **21**:44
"La Noche" (Creeley) **73**:7
"De noche" (Guillén) **35**:157
"La noche cíclica" (Borges) **22**:73; **32**:39, 63, 85-6
"Noche de luna" (Guillén) **35**:153
"Noche de Mayo" (Martí) **76**:104
"Noche de resurrecciones" (Paz) **48**:181
"Noche del Caballero" (Guillén) **35**:233, 234, 237, 238-39, 240
"Noche del gran estío" (Guillén) **35**:157
"Noche del hombre y su demonio" (Cernuda) **62**:172, 176
"Noche encendida" (Guillén) **35**:158
"La noche es la propicia" (Martí) **76**:96
"La noche, la calle, los astros" (Guillén) **35**:156, 157
"Nocturnal Beacon" (Storni) See "Faro en la noche"
"Nocturnal Pleasures" (Pavese) See "Piaceri notturni"
"A Nocturnal Reverie" (Finch) **21**:140-41, 143, 146, 157, 160, 173-75
"Nocturnal Song of a Wandering Shepherd in Asia" (Leopardi) See "Canto notturno di un pastore errante dell'Asia"
"A Nocturnal upon S. Lucies day, Being the shortest day" (Donne) **1**:130, 134, 149-50, 154; **43**:105, 125
"A nocturnall upon S. Lucies day" (Donne) See "A Nocturnal upon S. Lucies day, Being the shortest day"
"Nocturne" (Ignatow) **34**:315
"Nocturne" (de la Mare) **77**:141
"Nocturne" (MacLeish) **47**:156, 185
"Nocturne" (Mistral) See "Nocturno"
"Nocturne" (Mueller) **33**:192
"Nocturne" (Pavese) See "Notturno"
"Nocturne" (Paz) See "Nocturno"
"Nocturne" (Winters) **82**:318-19
"Nocturne among Grotesqueries" (Cernuda) See "Nocturno entre las musarañas"
"Nocturne in a Deserted Brickyard" (Sandburg) **2**:301, 303; **41**:228, 234, 257, 259, 276, 298, 312, 322, 337
"Nocturne in Black and Gold" (Doty) **53**:51, 54
"Nocturne of a Wandering Shepherd in Asia" (Leopardi) See "Canto notturno di un pastore errante dell'Asia"
Nocturne of Remembered Spring and Other Poems (Aiken) **26**:50, 72
"Nocturne of San Ildefonso" (Paz) See "Nocturno de San Ildefonso"
"Nocturne of the Descent" (Mistral) See "Nocturno del descendimiento"
"Nocturne of the Self-Evident Presence" (Melville) **82**:4, 6, 8, 10, 29, 32, 35, 38
"Nocturne of the Void" (García Lorca) See "Nocturno del hueco"
"Nocturne Parisien" (Verlaine) **32**:375
"Nocturne vulgaire" (Rimbaud) **3**:264; **57**:239, 275
Nocturnes (Senghor) **25**:231-33, 238-40, 255
"Nocturnes of Consummation" (Mistral) See "Nocturnos de la Consumacíón"
"Nocturno" (Mistral) **32**:155, 161, 174, 176, 183, 190-94
"Nocturno" (Paz) **48**:176
"Nocturno" (Storni) **33**:237, 307
"Nocturno de San Ildefonso" (Paz) **1**:370-72, 375; **48**:191, 204, 233
"Nocturno del descendimiento" (Mistral) **32**:181
"Nocturno del hueco" (García Lorca) **3**:139
"Nocturno en los muelles" (Guillén) **23**:106

"Nocturno entre las musarañas" (Cernuda) **62**:232
"Nocturnos de la Consumacíón" (Mistral) **32**:181
"Nod" (de la Mare) **77**:93, 99
"Nodier raconte" (Pound) **4**:317
"Noel: Christmas Eve" (Bridges) **28**:77, 81
"Noël indio" (Mistral) **32**:185
"no(h)-setting" (Scalapino) **114**:288
"Noise Day" (Silverstein) **49**:341
"The Noise of Myth" (Boland)
See "Listen. This Is the Noise of Myth"
"A Noiseless Patient Spider" (Whitman) **3**:390; **91**:270, 273, 276
"Noli Me Tangere" (Lawrence) **54**:249
"Nollekans" (Jarrell) **41**:174
"Un nom" (Lamartine) **16**:287
"Nomad Exquisite" (Stevens) **6**:293
"Nomad Songs" (Merwin) **45**:48
No-man's Rose (Celan)
See *Die Niemandsrose*
"Los nombres" (Guillén) **35**:193, 210-11, 229-30
"Nomenclature" (Benét) **64**:21
"Le non godute" (Gozzano) **10**:184
"Non ha l'ottimo artista alcun concetto" (Michelangelo) **103**:181, 189, 207, 333, 343-44
"Non Omnis Moriar" (Tate) **50**:319
"Non posso altra figura immaginarmi" (Michelangelo) **103**:219
Non Serviam (Ekeloef) **23**:51, 58-9, 63, 76
"Non Sum Dignus" (Jacobsen) **62**:331
"The Nonconformist" (Davie) **29**:102
The Nonconformist's Memorial (Howe) **54**:82, 84-85, 87, 95, 97, 105-6, 125-27, 134-35, 137
"None with Him" (Rossetti) **7**:276, 284
"Nones" (Auden) **92**:43
"Nones" (Berryman) **64**:119
Nones (Auden) **1**:23
"A Non-Linguistic Dispute with Imru' al-Qays" (Darwish)
See "Khilaf Ghayr Lughawi ma'Imru' al-Qays"
"Nonne Preestes Tale" (Chaucer)
See "Nun's Priest's Tale"
"Nonsense Rhyme" (Wylie) **23**:305
"Nonsense Song" (Benét) **64**:22
Nonsense Songs, Stories, Botany, and Alphabets (Lear) **65**:141-43, 146, 149, 151-52, 154, 157-58, 160-61, 169
"Nonsun Blob a" (Cummings) **5**:109
"The Noodle-Vendor's Flute" (Enright) **93**:9, 20
"Noom" (Brathwaite) **56**:54, 56
"Noon" (Cunningham) **92**:138
"Noon" (Levine) **22**:214, 219, 222
"Noon" (Thoreau) **30**:234
"NOON May 29th. 1970" (Raworth) **107**:275
"Noon Hour" (Sandburg) **41**:335, 364
"Noon of the Sunbather" (Piercy) **29**:308
"Noon Walk on the Asylum Lawn" (Sexton) **2**:359
"Noonday Grace" (Ransom) **61**:292-93
"Noone' Autumnal This Great Lady's Gaze" (Cummings) **5**:107
"A Noon-Piece" (Smart) **13**:347
"Noons of Poppy" (Carman) **34**:213
"Nor We of Her to Him" (Smith) **12**:326, 330
"Nora" (Toomer) **7**:317
"Die Nordsee" (Heine) **25**:139, 145, 158, 160, 162, 163
"Norfolk Sprang Thee" (Surrey) **59**:327
"Noria" (Césaire) **25**:33
"Norma" (Sanchez) **9**:234
"Norma y paraíso de los negros" (García Lorca) **3**:150
"Norman Macleod" (Williams)
See "A Poem for Norman Macleod"
"A Norman Simile" (Heaney) **100**:243
"A Norse Child's Requiem" (Carman) **34**:220
"North" (Heaney) **18**:203; **100**:213-14, 222, 268, 354
North (Heaney) **18**:194-95, 197-99, 203, 205, 208-11, 215, 230, 238-39, 241, 246, 255; **100**:209-27, 231, 266-67, 271-72, 274, 278, 282, 284, 293, 295, 298-99, 309, 325, 334, 341, 344, 349, 351, 354
"North Africa Breakdown" (Raworth) **107**:275
"th north aint easy to grow food in" (Bissett) **14**:25, 33
"North American Sequence" (Roethke) **15**:309-10, 312
"North American Time" (Rich) **5**:395
The North American Turbine (Dorn)
See *The North Atlantic Turbine*
"North and South" (McKay) **2**:207
North & South (Bishop) **3**:37, 39, 50; **34**:52, 67, 125, 127, 153, 161, 164, 174
The North Atlantic Turbine (Dorn) **115**:54-55, 63, 104, 109, 112-13, 119, 123, 129, 137, 140, 154-55, 203, 220, 237
"The North Atlantic Turbine" (Dorn) **115**:51, 74, 91-92, 113, 115, 119, 129-30
"North Central" (Niedecker) **42**:107
North Central (Niedecker) **42**:90, 94, 100, 102, 106-7, 111
"North Coast Recollections" (Betjeman) **75**:20
"The North Country" (Lawrence) **54**:222
"North Dakota North Light" (Momaday) **25**:219
"North Dublin" (Davie) **29**:95, 108, 120
"North Haven" (Bishop) **34**:113
"North Labrador" (Crane) **3**:83
North of Boston (Frost) **1**:193-95, 202, 207, 214, 217, 223-26; **71**:55
"North of Superior" (Birney) **52**:20, 38
"North of Time" (Kaufman) **74**:218
"North Palisades, the End of September, 1939" (Rexroth) **95**:270
"The North Sea" (Davie) **29**:113
The North Sea (Heine)
See "Die Nordsee"
"North Sea" (Montague) **106**:243
"The North Sea Undertaker's Complaint" (Lowell) **3**:216
The North Ship (Larkin) **21**:224-26, 230, 232-33, 235, 241, 251, 257, 259
"North Star West" (Birney) **52**:21, 58
"North Wind" (Montale)
See "Tramontana"
"North Wind in October" (Bridges) **28**:67
"North Wind: Portrush" (Mahon) **60**:146, 152, 207, 232
"The North Wind to a Dutiful Beast Midway Between the Dial and the Foot of a Garden Clock" (Moore) **49**:114, 118
North Winter (Carruth) **10**:70-71
"A Norther—Key West" (Bishop) **34**:69
Northern Birds in Color (Bissett) **14**:25
"Northern Door" (Ortiz) **17**:234
"Northern Elegies" (Akhmatova) **2**:4, 18
"The Northern Farmer" (Tennyson) **6**:358, 360
"The Northern Farmer—Old Style" (Tennyson) **6**:406
Northern Heroic (Bely)
See *Severnaia simfoniia: Pervia geroicheskaia*
"A Northern Hoard" (Heaney) **18**:202-3; **100**:194, 199, 201, 208, 220
"Northern Liberal" (Hughes) **1**:252; **53**:115
"Northern Pike" (Wright) **36**:324, 360, 376
"Northern River" (Wright) **14**:340
"The Northern Sea" (Ishikawa)
See "Kita no umi"
Northern Symphony (Bely)
See *Severnaia simfoniia: Pervia geroicheskaia*
"A Northern Vigil" (Carman) **34**:203-04, 210-11, 216
Northfield Poems (Ammons) **16**:4-5, 28
"Northumberland, Bound Down" (Barker) **77**:7
"Northumberland House" (Smith) **12**:296
"Northwest Airlines" (Chappell) **105**:67
Northwest Ecolog (Ferlinghetti) **1**:187
"Northwest Passage" (Stevenson) **84**:344-45
"Northwood Path" (Glück) **16**:126
De nos oiseaux (Tzara) **27**:233
"The Nose" (Stone) **53**:228, 254
"Nossis" (H. D.) **5**:268
"Nostalgia" (Carducci) **46**:50
"Nostalgia" (Collins) **68**:220
"Nostalgia" (Jiménez)
See "Nostaljia"
"Nostalgia" (Shapiro) **25**:269, 288, 325
"Nostalgia for India" (Sarton) **39**:327
"Nostalgias" (Mahon) **60**:141, 183
"Nostalgic Catalogue" (Hongo) **23**:198-99
"Nostalgies d'obélisques" (Gautier) **18**:158, 163
"Nostaljia" (Jiménez) **7**:201
"The Nostomaniac" (Service) **70**:153
"Not a fighter for two positions, but— if I'm a casual guest" (Tsvetaeva)
See "Dvukh stanov ne beots, a— esli gost sluchainyi"
"Not a Movie" (Hughes) **53**:162, 191
"Not a Prayer" (McHugh) **61**:202-3, 206-7
"Not a Suicide Poem" (Jordan) **38**:119
"Not Adlestrop" (Abse) **41**:19
"Not Both" (Meredith) **28**:208
"La not di maj" (Pasolini) **17**:252
"Not Dying" (Strand) **63**:142
"Not Every Day Fit for Verse" (Herrick) **9**:114
"Not Fair" (Cowley) **90**:14-15
"Not Feeling" (Graham) **59**:166
"Not for Charity" (Cunningham) **92**:180, 182
Not for the Sake of Remembering (Amichai)
See *Ve-Lo al Menat Lizkor*
"Not Going to New York: A Letter" (Hass) **16**:198-99
Not I, and Other Poems (Stevenson) **84**:302
"Not Ideas about the Thing but the Thing Itself" (Stevens) **110**:153-54, 232
"The Not Impossible Him" (Millay)
See "To the Not Impossible Him"
Not In Narrow Seas: Poems with Prose (Curnow) **48**:23-29
"Not Joining the Wars" (Bell) **79**:31
Not Just to Remember (Amichai)
See *Ve-Lo al Menat Lizkor*
"Not Leaving the House" (Snyder) **21**:289
"Not Like a Cypress" (Amichai)
See "Lo kabrosh"
"Not like a floury white butterfly" (Mandelstam)
See "Ne muchnistoi babochkoiu beloi"
"Not Like Dante" (Ferlinghetti) **1**:182
"Not Looking" (Jordan) **38**:119
"Not Marble Nor the Gilded Monuments" (MacLeish) **47**:165, 188, 196, 209
"Not Palaces" (Spender)
See "Not palaces, an era's crown"
"Not palaces, an era's crown" (Spender) **71**:135, 164-67, 180-81, 221
"Not Planning a Trip Back" (Ashbery) **26**:165
Not So Deep as a Well (Parker) **28**:365
"Not So Far as the Forest" (Millay) **6**:238
"Not So, Not So" (Sexton) **2**:373
"Not That From Life, and All Its Woes" (Bryant) **20**:16
Not That He Brought Flowers (Thomas) **99**:267, 270, 321, 336
"Not There" (Gallagher) **9**:59
Not This Pig (Levine) **22**:212-13, 215-17, 220, 223, 226
Not Wanting To Say Anything About Marcel (Cage) **58**:183
"Not Waving but Drowning" (Smith) **12**:293, 300, 307, 319-21, 324, 328, 331, 333, 337, 347, 349, 354
Not Waving but Drowning (Smith) **12**:292-93
"Not with libations, but with Shouts and Laughter" (Millay) **6**:211, 244-46
"Not Yet, My Soul" (Stevenson) **84**:301
"Nota biográfica" (Fuertes) **27**:18, 48-9
"Notas de viaje" (Parra) **39**:283-84

"A Notation on the Evening of November 27, 1966" (Dorn) **115**:217
"A Note" (Ní Chuilleanáin) **34**:361
"Note" (Stafford) **71**:321
"Note" (Thomas) **52**:222
"Note from Capri to Richard Ryan on the Adriatic Floor" (Hugo) **68**:237
"A Note Left in Jimmy Leonard's Shack" (Wright) **36**:281, 337
"A Note Left on the Mantelpiece" (Abse) **41**:12
"Note on Local Flora" (Empson) **104**:84, 86, 90, 119
"Note on Moonlight" (Stevens) **110**:117-19, 231
"Note on Rhyme" (Wickham) **110**:264
"Note sibérienne" (Char) **56**:154, 173
"note to myself" (Clifton) **17**:30
"Note with the Gift of Bird's Nest" (Wagoner) **33**:356
"Notebook" (Levertov)
See "From a Notebook, October '68—May '69"
"Notebook" (Raworth) **107**:323-24, 326-27
Notebook 1967-68 (Lowell) **3**:223-26, 231-32, 239-40
"The Notebook in the Gate-legged Table" (Lowell) **13**:84
"Notebook of a Return to the Native Land" (Césaire)
See *Cahier d'un retour au pays natal*
The Note-Book of William Blake (Blake) **12**:11, 34-5
"Noted in the New York Times" (Kumin) **15**:209
"Notes after" (Corso) **108**:18
"Notes after Blacking Out" (Corso) **33**:43, 48
"Notes at Edge" (Wright) **14**:375, 377
Notes for a Guidbook (Stryk) **27**:181, 183, 191-94, 197, 210, 214, 216, 218
"Notes for a Guidebook" (Stryk) **27**:186, 195
"Notes for a Little Play" (Hughes) **7**:130, 152; **89**:141
"Notes for a Speech" (Baraka) **4**:5; **113**:8, 18, 20
"Notes for a Week" (Seferis) **66**:150-51, 163, 170, 186-87, 206
"Notes for an Elegy" (Meredith) **28**:170, 173, 181, 184-85, 187, 210
"Notes for CXVII et seq." (Pound) **95**:184-85
"Notes for the Legend of Salad Woman" (Ondaatje) **28**:329
Notes from a Diary (Das)
See *Dayarikkurippukal*
"Notes from a Nonexistent Himalayan Expedition" (Szymborska) **44**:296, 318
"Notes from India" (Sarton) **39**:345
Notes from New York, and Other Poems (Tomlinson) **17**:333-34, 336, 353-54
"Notes From Robin Hill Cottage" (Carruth) **10**:85
"Notes From the Air" (Ashbery) **26**:163
Notes from the Land of the Dead, and Other Poems (Kinsella) **69**:76, 80, 92-93, 96, 99-100, 104, 110, 139
"Notes from the Other Side" (Kenyon) **57**:12, 35
"Notes Made in the Piazzo San Marco" (Swenson) **14**:261
"Notes on a Conspiracy" (Rose) **13**:241
Notes on Literature (Guest) **55**:222
"Notes on the 1930s" (Jones) **116**:171
"Notes on the Reality of the Self" (Graham) **59**:138, 150, 152-53, 158-59, 176
"Notes pour le petit jour" (Jaccottet) **98**:176
"Notes pour un coquillage" (Ponge) **107**:139
"Notes premières de l'Homme" (Ponge) **107**:137
"Notes prises pour un oiseau" (Ponge) **107**:117
"Notes to Be Left in a Cornerstone" (Benét) **64**:14, 24-26
"Notes toward a Poem That Can Never Be Written" (Atwood) **8**:18, 43
"Notes toward a Supreme Fiction" (Hope) **56**:286
Notes toward a Supreme Fiction (Stevens) **6**:310, 314, 324, 326-37, 329, 335, 337; **110**:116, 138, 143, 227
"Notes toward a Supreme Fiction" (Stevens) **110**:94-95, 162, 164, 167, 175, 182-84, 190, 193-94, 198, 200-201, 221, 225-28
"Notes toward Time" (Jacobsen) **62**:320-21
"Notes Towards Home" (Jordan) **38**:127
"Nothin' to Say, My Daughter" (Riley) **48**:288-89, 292, 297, 314, 362
"Nothing" (Abse) **41**:19
"Nothing and Something" (Harper) **21**:187, 191
"Nothing but Color" (Ai) **72**:5
Nothing but Love (Seifert)
See *Samá láska*
"Nothing Down" (Dove) **6**:110, 112
"Nothing Endures" (Cullen) **20**:59
Nothing for Tigers: Poems, 1959-1964 (Carruth) **10**:70
Nothing for You (Berrigan) **103**:31, 35, 41
"Nothing Gold Can Stay" (Frost) **1**:194; **39**:239
"Nothing in Heaven Functions As It Ought" (Kennedy) **93**:131, 142
"Nothing Is Really Hard but to Be Real" (Ciardi) **69**:8, 10, 48
"Nothing is Right" (Walker) **30**:365
"Nothing Makes Sense" (Giovanni) **19**:112
"Nothing Significant Was Really Said" (Larkin) **21**:259
"Nothing Special" (Herbert)
See "Nic ladnego"
"Nothing Stays Put" (Clampitt) **19**:94
"Nothing to Be Said" (Larkin) **21**:227
"Nothing Twice" (Szymborska)
See "Nic dwa razy"
"(Nothing Whichful About" (Cummings) **5**:108
"Nothing Will Cure the Sick Lion but to Eat an Ape" (Moore) **49**:134
"Nothing Will Die" (Tennyson) **101**:245
"Nothing will yield" (Nemerov) **24**:262
"Nothing's a Gift" (Szymborska)
See "Nic Darowane"
"Notice" (Parra)
See "Aviso"
"Noticia de la lengua española" (Guillén) **35**:230
"Notificazione di presenza" (Zanzotto) **65**:270
"Notizia di cronaca" (Quasimodo) **47**:289
"Notizie dall'Amiata" (Montale) **13**:106, 121, 127
"Notre Dame de Chartres" (Meredith) **28**:171, 188-89
"Notre Nuit meilleure que nos jours" (Éluard) **38**:83, 87
"Notre vie" (Éluard) **38**:78
"Notre-Dame" (Gautier) **18**:144-46
"La notte" (Pavese) **13**:230
"Notte di Maggio" (Carducci) **46**:23, 49
"Una notte di settembre" (Quasimodo) **47**:289
"Notturno" (Benn) **35**:26, 70
"Notturno" (Pavese) **13**:230
"Noubousse" (Apollinaire) **7**:48
"Noun" (Shapiro) **25**:276
"Nourish the Crops" (Ignatow) **34**:319-20
"Nous n'osons plus chanter les roses" (Cavafy) **36**:108
"Nous prenions par ces prés" (Bonnefoy) **58**:167
"Nous sommes" (Éluard) **38**:79
"Nous tombons" (Char) **56**:120
Nouveau Recueil (Ponge) **107**:79, 104, 114, 129-30, 134-35, 142, 164, 203, 213, 253
Nouveaux Poèmes (Éluard) **38**:70
"La Nouvelle Araignée" (Ponge) **107**:100, 161-62, 209
"nouvelle bonte" (Césaire) **25**:45
Nouvelle confidences (Lamartine) **16**:293
Nouvelle continuation des amours (Ronsard) **105**:279, 284
"Les Nouvelles du Soir" (Jaccottet) **98**:173
Nouvelles méditations poétiques (Lamartine) **16**:266, 271, 273-74, 277-79, 287, 290-09
Nouvelles Odes (Hugo) **17**:88
"Nouvelles Variations sur le Point-du-Jour" (Verlaine) **32**:378
"Nova" (Jeffers) **17**:130
"A Novel" (Glück) **16**:158, 161
"Novel" (Rimbaud)
See "Roman"
"The Novel" (Stevens) **110**:82
"A Novelette" (Williams) **109**:277
"Novelettes" (MacNeice) **61**:138-39, 141
"November" (Belloc) **24**:34
"November" (Bryant) **20**:37, 44
"November" (Hughes) **7**:119, 132-33, 136
"November" (MacLeish) **47**:197
"November" (Merwin) **45**:53
"November" (Ransom) **61**:294
"November" (Teasdale) **31**:336
"November" (Thomas) **53**:325
"November 22, 1983" (Alexie) **53**:39
November and May (Szirtes) **51**:157
"November Blue" (Meynell) **112**:257
"November Cotton Flower" (Toomer) **7**:319, 333-34
"November Graveyard" (Plath) **37**:177, 184
"A November Night" (Teasdale) **31**:331
"November Sun" (Walcott) **46**:283
"November Surf" (Jeffers) **17**:117, 120, 132
"November Walk near False Creek Mouth" (Birney) **52**:17-19, 22, 36, 49, 57-58, 62, 71-74
The Novice (Lermontov)
See *Mtsyri*
"The Novices" (Levertov) **11**:169
"Novices" (Moore) **49**:93, 101
"Los novios" (Paz) **48**:198
"Novissima verba" (Lamartine) **16**:268, 280, 283, 292-93, 297
"Novogodnee" (Tsvetaeva) **14**:325
"Novye stansy k Avguste" (Brodsky) **9**:4
"Now" (Jacobsen) **62**:309
"Now" (Sexton) **2**:352
"Now" (Stafford) **71**:283
"Now" (Walker) **20**:276
"Now Air Is Air and Thing Is Thing: No Bliss" (Cummings) **5**:110
"Now and in Other Days" (Amichai) **38**:14
Now and in Other Times (Amichai)
See *'Akhshav 'vayamim ha'aherim*
Now and Then: Poems, 1976-1978 (Warren) **37**:310, 312, 317, 330, 334-35, 338, 341, 350, 355, 357-58, 365, 367, 380
"Now Close the Windows" (Frost) **1**:197
"Now Does Our World Descend" (Cummings) **5**:111
"Now hath Flora robbed her bowers" (Campion) **87**:7
"Now He Knows All There Is to Know. Now He Is Acquainted with the Day and Night" (Schwartz) **8**:319
"Now Hollow Fires" (Housman) **2**:189
"Now I Become Myself" (Sarton) **39**:324, 345
"Now I Hear" (Ignatow) **34**:324
Now in Wintry Delights (Bridges) **28**:76-7
"Now Is the Air Made of Chiming Balls" (Eberhart) **76**:34, 48, 58-59
Now Is Time (Birney) **52**:4, 11, 37, 39, 45, 67
"Now It Is Clear" (Merwin) **45**:66
"Now It Is You I Praise, Banner" (Rilke) **2**:273
"Now let her change" (Campion) **87**:32-34, 58
"Now lufferis cummis" (Dunbar) **67**:16
"Now Lythis of ane Gentill Knycht" (Dunbar) **67**:5
"Now of Wemen" (Dunbar) **67**:7
"Now Pine-Needles" (Smith) **12**:318
"Now Returned Home" (Jeffers) **17**:141
Now Sheba Sings the Song (Angelou) **32**:25
"Now Sleeps the Crimson Petal" (Tennyson) **101**:152-53
"Now that Holocaust and Crucifixion are

Coffee-Table Books" (Viereck) **27**:293-94, 296
"Now That I Am Never Alone" (Gallagher) **9**:62
"Now that the shapes of mist" (MacNeice) **61**:160, 183-84
"Now That We Live" (Kenyon) **57**:29
"Now the Record Now Record" (Duncan) **2**:103
"Now This Cold Man" (Page) **12**:168, 170, 178, 184
"Now Voyager" (Sarton) **39**:322
"Now we have present made" (Raleigh) **31**:259, 299
"Now Westlin Winds" (Burns) **114**:94
"Now winter nights enlarge" (Campion) **87**:8, 12, 48, 58, 70-71, 75, 85-86, 117
"Now with My Hand I Cover Africa" (Spender) **71**:230
"Nowhere" (Zanzotto)
See "Gnessulùogo"
"Nox" (Hugo) **17**:54
Nozarashi Diary (Matsuo Basho) **3**:6
Nozarashi kikō (Matsuo Basho) **3**:11, 28
"Nozze" (Carducci) **46**:21
"Le Nozze del Mare" (Carducci) **46**:5
"Nu" (Tolson) **88**:238-40, 258, 260, 304, 314, 324
Le Nu perdu (Char) **56**:113, 130, 134-35, 137-40, 144, 149-57, 185-89, 198
Las nubes (Cernuda) **62**:172, 175, 178-79, 203, 248-50, 252-55
"NUCLEAR CICULAR" (Bissett) **14**:6, 24, 32
"Nuda Natens" (Updike) **90**:357
"Nude" (Cassian) **17**:4
"The Nude" (Guest) **55**:185
"Nude Descending a Staircase" (Kennedy) **93**:136, 147, 150
Nude Descending a Staircase: Poems, Songs, A Ballad (Kennedy) **93**:128, 133, 136-38, 141-42, 148, 152
"Nude Interrogation" (Komunyakaa) **51**:55
"Nude Photograph" (Clifton) **17**:29
"Nude Pictures" (Komunyakaa) **51**:8
"The Nude Swim" (Sexton) **2**:352
"Nude Young Dancers" (Hughes) **1**:246; **53**:83, 143
"Nudite de la vérité" (Éluard) **38**:70, 103
"Nudity of Truth" (Éluard)
See "Nudite de la vérité"
"La Nue" (Gautier) **18**:125, 129
"Nue nue comme ma maîtresse" (Péret) **33**:216, 230
"Les Nuées" (Bonnefoy) **58**:168
Les nues, ou nouvelles (Ronsard) **105**:272
"Nuestra Casa" (Alurista) **34**:40
"Nuestra Casa—Denver '69" (Alurista) **34**:24, 39-40
"Nueva York: Oficina y denuncia" (García Lorca) **3**:141, 151
Nuevo canto de amor a Stalingrado (Neruda) **4**:279-80
Nuevos sermones y prédicas del Cristo de Elqui (Parra) **39**:292
"The Nuisance" (Piercy) **29**:309
"La nuit blanche" (Kipling) **3**:172
"Nuit blanche" (Lowell) **13**:89-90
"La nuit d'Avril, 1915" (Apollinaire) **7**:3
"Nuit de l'enfer" (Rimbaud) **57**:190, 247-49, 252
"Nuit de Sine" (Senghor) **25**:224, 227, 255
"Nuit du Walpurgis classique" (Verlaine) **32**:388
La Nuit I (Char)
See *La nuit talismanique*
La Nuit II (Char)
See *La nuit talismanique*
La nuit talismanique (Char) **56**:120-24, 126, 134, 137-38, 140-41, 143-44, 161, 187-88, 196
La Nuit talismanique qui brillait dans son cercle (Char)
See *La nuit talismanique*
La Nuit verte du Parc Labyrinthe (Brossard) **80**:19-22, 28
"Nuits de juin" (Hugo) **17**:64
"Nuits partagées" (Éluard) **38**:67-8, 73
"Nul I" (Éluard) **38**:69
"Nul II" (Éluard) **38**:69
"Nullo" (Toomer) **7**:320, 330-31, 334
"Number" (Hughes) **53**:115
"number 18" (Baca) **41**:76
"Number 57" (Villa) **22**:346
"Number Man" (Sandburg) **2**:322
"Number 68" (Villa) **22**:347
"Number Three on the Docket" (Lowell) **13**:79, 84-5
"The Numbers" (Ammons) **16**:5
"Numbers" (Creeley) **73**:38, 115
"Numbers" (Hughes) **1**:267; **53**:159
"Numbers" (Smith) **12**:317
"Numbers, Letters" (Baraka) **4**:19; **113**:13-14, 152-53
"The Numerous Blood" (Guillén)
See "La sangre numerosa"
"Numpholeptos" (Browning) **2**:86, 88
"The Nun" (Hunt) **73**:138
"The Nun" (Wagoner) **33**:324
"Nun of Nidaros" (Longfellow) **30**:20
"Nunc dimittis" (Brodsky) **9**:5
"Nunca se sabe" (Fuertes) **27**:17
"Nuns at Lunch on the Bus" (Stone) **53**:223, 254
"A Nun's Complaint" (Rilke) **2**:270
"Nuns in the Wind" (Rukeyser) **12**:211
"Nuns Painting Water-Lilies" (Stevens) **110**:230
"Nun's Priest's Tale" (Chaucer) **19**:6, 13-15, 26, 31-2, 48, 52, 57, 75
La nuova gioventù (Pasolini) **17**:282-83, 287
"Nuova poesia in forma di rose" (Pasolini) **17**:274, 278
Nuove odi barbare (Carducci) **46**:8, 47
Nuove poesie (Carducci) **46**:13, 47
Nuove poesie (Quasimodo) **47**:279, 300, 302-4
Nuove Rime (Carducci)
See *Rime nuove*
"Nuove stanze" (Montale) **13**:106, 120-21
The Nuptial Countenance (Char)
See *Le visage nuptial*
"Nuptial Sleep" (Rossetti) **44**:164, 166, 203-4, 206
"A Nuptiall Song, or Epithalamie on Sir Clipseby Crew and His Lady" (Herrick) **9**:86, 102, 139
"Nuptials" (Tate) **50**:319
"The Nuptials of Attila" (Meredith) **60**:247, 250, 263-64, 294, 328
"Nuremberg" (Longfellow) **30**:46
"Nürnberge Rede" (Enzensberger) **28**:164
"Nurse Edith Cavell" (Meynell) **112**:174-75, 177-78
"Nurse Whitman" (Olds) **22**:322, 328
"The Nurse-Mother" (Sandburg) **41**:267
"The Nursery" (Howe) **81**:49
"A Nursery Rhyme" (Brooke) **24**:66
"Nursery Rhyme" (Niedecker) **42**:140
"Nursery Rhyme" (Stone) **53**:254
"Nursery Rhyme for a Seventh Son" (Wright) **14**:338
"Nursery Rhymes for Little Anglo-Indians" (Kipling) **3**:190
Nursery Rhymes from Mother Stone (Stone) **53**:221
"Nurse's Song" (Blake) **12**:7, 21-22, 34; **63**:5, 7, 16, 30, 49, 54, 70, 72-73, 76, 102, 106, 120-22, 133
"Nurse's Song" (Glück) **16**:148
"Nurse's Songs" (Thomas) **52**:330
"Nursing Home" (Page) **12**:176
"Nurture" (Kumin) **15**:209, 211
Nurture (Kumin) **15**:209-14, 221, 223
"Nusch" (Éluard) **38**:68
"Nutcracker" (Updike) **90**:347
"The Nutcrackers and the Sugar-Tongs" (Lear) **65**:149-53, 160
Nux (Ovid) **2**:244
"Nux Postcœnatica" (Holmes) **71**:68, 92
"N.W. 5 and N. 6" (Betjeman) **75**:30, 49, 92
"Ny la douce pitie, ny le pleur lamentable" (Ronsard) **11**:278
Nye and Riley's Railway Guide (Riley) **48**:346
"The Nymph and the Faun" (Marvell)
See "The Nymph Complaining for the Death of Her Faun"
"The Nymph Complaining for the Death of Her Faun" (Marvell) **10**:260-62, 266-67, 271, 274, 277, 290, 294, 297, 301-02, 309-10, 315-16, 319, 325; **86**:178, 190, 198, 263, 267
Nymphidia (Drayton)
See *Nimphidia, the Court of Fayrie*
"A Nympholept" (Swinburne) **24**:312-319, 322, 326, 341, 348
"The Nymphs" (Hunt) **73**:145, 148-50, 157, 211
"Nymph's Reply to the Shepherd" (Raleigh) **31**:235, 269
"O" (Wilbur) **51**:295
O. 1 (Pindar)
See *Olympian 1*
O. 7 (Pindar)
See *Olympian 7*
O. 8 (Pindar)
See *Olympian 8*
O. 9 (Pindar)
See *Olympian 9*
O. 14 (Pindar)
See *Olympian 14*
"O Africans" (Goodison) **36**:154
"O Be a Fine Girl" (Hope) **56**:277
"O Black and Unknown Bards" (Johnson) **24**:127, 137, 142, 146, 152, 160, 166
"O Breath" (Bishop) **34**:84, 88-90, 105
"O Captain! My Captain!" (Whitman) **3**:404, 418, 422; **91**:214, 304, 329
"O Carib Isle!" (Crane) **3**:90; **99**:52, 54, 106
"O Cheese" (Hall) **70**:27, 33
"O Daedalus, Fly Away Home" (Hayden) **6**:176, 179, 189
"O das Quinas" (Pessoa) **20**:155
"O Desejado" (Pessoa) **20**:156
"O, desesperement sous l'aile echevelée" (Mallarmé) **102**:20
"O Deus immense" (Gower) **59**:25
"O Didn't He Ramble" (Johnson) **24**:151, 170
"O die Schornsteine" (Sachs) **78**:146, 200-202, 219, 227, 232
O die Schornsteine (Sachs) **78**:188-89, 192, 196, 198-202
"O dos Castelos" (Pessoa) **20**:155
"O Dreams O Destinations" (Brathwaite) **56**:28, 84
"O Dreams, O Destinations" (Day Lewis) **11**:145
"O encanta da Pedra Chan" (Castro) **41**:93
"O Florida, Venereal Soil" (Stevens) **6**:305, 339; **110**:97
O fons Bandusiae (Horace) **46**:107
"O for a Muse of Fire" (Smith) **104**:210
"O Geist" (Benn) **35**:50
"O Gloriosa Domina" (Crashaw) **84**:9, 96
"O Glorious France" (Masters) **1**:342
"O Great Exploit of Gentle Cavalier" (Stampa) **43**:296
"O griefe, O spight" (Campion) **87**:58, 69-71
"O Guardador de Rebanhos" (Pessoa) **20**:151-52
"O happie dames" (Surrey) **59**:297, 306, 307, 310, 315, 334
"O Happy Dogs of England" (Smith) **12**:318, 330
"O Hell" (Loy) **16**:316
"O Infante" (Pessoa) **20**:155
"O Krytykach i Recenzentach" (Mickiewicz) **38**:156, 167
"O lady, leave thy silken thread" (Hood) **93**:78
"O Lady, when the Tipped Cup of the Moon Blessed You" (Hughes) **7**:113

"O Land of Empire, Art and Love" (Clough) **103**:71, 73-75
"O Lapwing . . ." (Blake) **63**:26
"O Lay Thy Loof in Mine, Lass" (Burns) **6**:76
"O Leave Novels" (Burns) **114**:19
"O, Let Me in This Ae Night" (Burns) **6**:81
"O Lord, I Will Praise Thee" (Cowper) **40**:55
"O lothsome place" (Surrey) **59**:297, 353
"O Love, my muse" (Bridges) **28**:59
"O Love, Sweet Animal" (Schwartz) **8**:313
"O Love, the Interest Itself in Thoughtless Heaven..." (Auden) **1**:22
"O Love, where are thy Shafts, thy Quiver, and thy Bow?" (Campion) **87**:89
O Lovely England (de la Mare) **77**:142
"O Lull Me, Lull Me" (Roethke) **15**:261, 273, 299, 302
"O May I Join the Choir Invisible" (Eliot) **20**:123, 131, 136, 139, 143
"O May They Morn" (Burns) **114**:168
"O me donzel" (Pasolini) **17**:252
"O might those sighes and teares returne againe" (Donne) **43**:160, 162
O Mikrós naftilos (Elytis) **21**:134-35
"O moj zastencivyj geroj" (Akhmadulina) **43**:60
"O Mon Dieu, vous m'avez blessé d'amour" (Verlaine) **2**:416
"O Mostrengo" (Pessoa) **20**:155
"O muse contiens-toi! muse aux hymnes d'airain" (Hugo) **17**:97
"O my blacke Soule!" (Donne) **43**:148
"O my companions, O my sister Sleep" (Belloc) **24**:38
"O my joy" (Bridges) **28**:63
"O My Name It Is Sam Hall" (Jarrell) **41**:136
"O my thoughtes" (Sidney) **32**:235
"O my vague desires" (Bridges) **28**:59
"O Nacht" (Benn) **35**:50
"O Night O Trembling Night" (Spender) **71**:158
"O notte" (Stampa) **43**:287
"O notte, o dolce tempo" (Michelangelo) **103**:255-56, 274
"O Omega, Invocation" (Spender) **71**:188
"O Pastor Amoroso" (Pessoa) **20**:152
"O Pinions" (Spencer) **77**:339
"O Pug!" (Smith) **12**:301
"Ó Riada's Farewell" (Montague) **106**:246-47, 280
"O saisons, ô châteaux!" (Rimbaud) **3**:275; **57**:252-53
"O Saisons! O Châteaux!" (Sarton) **39**:322
"O ship, ship, ship" (Clough) **103**:97
"O Sion of my heart" (Kunitz) **19**:175
"O Sleepless Night" (Schuyler) **88**:176, 189
"O Southland!" (Johnson) **24**:137, 142, 147, 160
"O Swallow, Swallow" (Tennyson) **101**:150, 153
"O Sweet Spontaneous" (Cummings) **5**:105
"O sweete woodes" (Sidney) **32**:235
"O Taste and See" (Levertov) **11**:169
O Taste and See (Levertov) **11**:159, 169, 171, 211
"O Tempora" (Tolson) **88**:236
"O, Tempora! O Mores!" (Poe) **1**:449
"O the Chimneys" (Sachs)
See "O die Schornsteine"
O the Chimneys: Selected Poems, Including the Verse Play,Eli (Sachs)
See *O die Schornsteine*
"O, Thou Opening, O" (Roethke) **15**:284, 300, 302-03
"O Thou that sleep'st like 'Pigg' in Straw, Thou Lady dear, arise" (Davenant) **99**:176
"O tlumaczeniu wierszy" (Herbert) **50**:5
"O to Be a Dragon" (Moore) **4**:249; **49**:107, 146, 161
O to Be a Dragon (Moore) **49**:136, 140, 184
"O Troi" (Herbert) **50**:7
"O Virtuous Light" (Wylie) **23**:311, 315
"O Wander Not So Far Away!" (Burroughs) **8**:73
"O Wha's Been Here afore Me, Lass" (MacDiarmid) **9**:155, 160
"O, what unhop't for sweet supply" (Campion) **87**:56
"O Wife Unmasked" (Cohen) **109**:25, 68
"O Word I Love to Sing" (McKay) **2**:217, 219
"O World of Many Worlds" (Owen) **19**:352; **102**:149, 184
"O wreche, be war! this warld will wend the fro" (Dunbar) **67**:11
"O Ye Tongues" (Sexton) **2**:367, 372-73; **79**:219, 221-22, 239, 253, 284, 291, 340
Oak and Ivy (Dunbar) **5**:128, 132
"The Oak and the Broom" (Wordsworth)
See "The Oak and the Broom, A Pastoral"
"The Oak and the Broom, A Pastoral" (Wordsworth) **67**:328
"The Oak and the Olive" (Barker) **77**:40
"The Oak and the Rose" (Silverstein) **49**:327
"Oak Hill Cemetery" (Cervantes) **35**:104
"The Oak Leaf" (Lermontov) **18**:281
"Oaks" (Castro)
See "Los robles"
"Oasis" (Stryk) **27**:187
"Oat" (Hughes) **89**:156
"The Oath" (Tate) **50**:231, 235, 244, 251, 257, 260
"Oatmeal" (Kinnell) **26**:286
"Oaxaca, 1974" (Cervantes) **35**:108, 118, 130, 131, 133
"Oaxaca 1925" (Rexroth) **95**:255, 268
"Obedience" (Herbert) **4**:119, 125-26
"Obéissez à vos porcs qui existent . . ." (Char) **56**:120, 145
"Obermann Once More" (Arnold) **5**:19, 63-4
"Oberon's Chappell" (Herrick)
See "The Fairie Temple: or, Oberons Chappell. Dedicated to Mr. John Merrifield, Counsellor at Law"
"Oberon's Feast" (Herrick) **9**:90
"Oberon's Palace" (Herrick) **9**:86, 90, 137
"Obit Dean, September 30, 1955" (O'Hara) **45**:172
"Obituary" (Dorn) **115**:120
"Obituary" (Tate) **50**:246
"Obituary for a Living Lady" (Brooks) **7**:66-7, 69
"The Objection to Being Stepped On" (Frost) **1**:215
"Objects" (Herbert)
See "Przedmioty"
"Objects" (Wilbur) **51**:186-88, 192-93, 220-21, 237
"Objects and Apparitions" (Paz) **48**:274
"Objet d'Art" (Stryk) **27**:204
"Oblation" (Cernuda)
See "Ofrenda"
"Oblique Prayers" (Levertov) **11**:198, 201
Oblique Prayers (Levertov) **11**:198, 200-02, 209
"Oblivion" (Smith) **12**:317, 354
"Oboe sommerso" (Quasimodo) **47**:301
Oboe sommerso (Quasimodo) **47**:268, 275, 278, 297, 300-303
"O-Bon: Dance for The Dead" (Hongo) **23**:199
"Oboroniaet son moiu donskuiu son" (Mandelstam) **14**:154
"Obóz glodowy pod Jaslem" (Szymborska) **44**:299
Obra gruesa (Parra) **39**:364, 370, 372, 392, 301-4, 311
Obra Poetica (Paz) **48**:258
Obra poetica, 1923-1964 (Borges) **32**:60, 81-6, 88, 90, 94, 112, 135
Obra poética 1923-1967 (Borges) **22**:72, 96
Obra poética: 1923-1976 (Borges) **22**:95; **32**:86-7
Obras (Castro) **41**:107, 110-19
Obras completas (Aleixandre) **15**:7, 18, 34
Obras completas (Bécquer)
See *see Obras de Gustavo Adolfo Bécquer*
Obras completas (Borges) **32**:69, 102, 124, 126, 133
Obras completas (Juana Inés de la Cruz) **24**:202, 233
Obras completas (Neruda) **64**:309-12, 314-17, 338
Obras de Gustavo Adolfo Bécquer (Bécquer) **113**:162-63, 214, 242-43, 251
Obras de Luis de Camões (Camões) **31**:13
Obras incompletas (Fuertes) **27**:3-5, 19-21, 23-5, 33-47
"Obrerito" (Mistral) **32**:179
"El obrero" (Storni) **33**:279
"Obscure Beginnings" (Simic) **69**:305, 367
L'Obscurité (Jaccottet) **98**:186
"Obsequies for a Poetess" (Cunningham) **92**:165-66
"Obsequies to the Lady Anne Hay" (Carew) **29**:6, 36, 38, 59-60, 66, 74
"Obsequies to the Lord Harrington" (Donne) **43**:131
"Observation" (Larkin) **21**:259
"An Observation" (Sarton) **39**:329
"Observation Car" (Hope) **56**:268, 270, 276, 302
"Observation of Facts" (Tomlinson) **17**:299, 315, 335
Observations (Moore) **4**:229-30, 244, 249-52; **49**:88-90, 92, 95-96, 105, 113-14, 117, 134, 150, 152, 159, 180, 185-86
"Observations From the Outer Edge" (Wagoner) **33**:331
"The Observatory" (Noyes) **27**:128
"The Observer" (Rich) **5**:370
"Observers" (Chappell) **105**:20
"La obsesión" (Mistral) **32**:161, 176
"Obsessed by Her Beauty" (Viereck) **27**:263
"Obsession" (Baudelaire) **106**:7
"An Obsessive Combination of Ontological Inscape, Trickery and Love" (Sexton) **79**:288, 290, 296, 298-300, 303, 305
"Obsidian Butterfly" (Paz)
See "Mariposa de obsidiana"
"Obsolescence" (Ciardi) **69**:57
"Obsolete" (Ignatow) **34**:323
Obus couleur de lune (Apollinaire) **7**:22
Occasional Poems (Cowley)
See *Verses, Lately Written upon Several Occasions*
"Occasional Verses" (Hacker) **47**:80
Occasional Verses (Cowley)
See *Verses, Lately Written upon Several Occasions*
"Occasioned by Sir William Temple's Late Illness and Recovery" (Swift) **9**:250
"Occasionem Cognosce" (Moore) **49**:133, 149
Le occasioni (Montale) **13**:103-05, 108-09, 113-14, 117-21, 126-28, 131-32, 136, 141 , 160, 165-66
The Occasions (Montale)
See *Le occasioni*
"Gli occhi di quella gentil foresetta" (Cavalcanti) **114**:234
"L'occident" (Lamartine) **16**:266
"The Occulation" (Hardy) **92**:207
"The Occultation of Orion" (Longfellow) **30**:82
"The Occupation" (Abse) **41**:3
"Occupations" (Whitman)
See "A Song for Occupations"
"The Occurrences" (Oppen) **35**:286, 295, 312, 317, 335, 336, 343
"Ocean" (Whittier) **93**:195
The Ocean (Raleigh)
See *The Ocean to Cynthia*
"Ocean on Monday" (Hugo) **68**:234
The Ocean to Cynthia (Raleigh) **31**:201, 211-16, 218-22, 225-28, 230-32, 237-44, 246-47, 249, 251-60, 264, 278, 285-90, 292, 297, 313
"Ocean Waves" (Tagore)
See "Sindhu-taranga"

"Ocean-Letter" (Apollinaire)
See "Lettre-Océan"
"Oceano Nox" (Hugo) **17**:64
The Ocean's Love to Cynthia (Raleigh)
See *The Ocean to Cynthia*
"Ocean's Love to Ireland" (Heaney) **18**:196; **100**:215, 224
"Los Ochentas" (Dorn) **115**:161, 199-200
Ocher (Storni)
See *Ocre*
"Ocho Perritos" (Mistral) **32**:184
"Ocho Rio" (Goodison) **36**:156
"Ocho Rios I" (Goodison) **36**:150
"Ocho Rios II" (Goodison) **36**:150, 155, 157
Ochre (Storni)
See *Ocre*
"Ocio" (Cernuda) **62**:216
Ocnos (Cernuda) **62**:175, 177, 182, 195, 214, 216, 218, 220-24, 226
Ocre (Storni) **33**:236-37, 244-45, 256, 266, 277, 279-82, 290-92, 297, 299
Octavie: L'illusion (Nerval) **13**:177
"The Octets" (Mandelstam) **14**:152
"October" (Frost) **1**:225
"October" (Hayden) **6**:193, 195
"October" (Kavanagh) **33**:81, 96, 120; **105**:96, 100, 111, 175
"October" (Komunyakaa) **51**:64
"October" (Lorde) **12**:154
"October" (Mahon) **60**:143
"October" (Oliver) **75**:311, 318, 343
"October" (Sassoon) **12**:240
"October" (Thomas) **53**:275, 290
"October" (Winters) **82**:316
"October Arriving" (Simic) **69**:365
"October at Hellbrünn" (Muir) **49**:238, 287
October Blast (Yeats) **51**:92, 108
"October Dawn" (Hughes) **7**:115
"October Frost" (Bly) **39**:86
"October in Bloomsbury" (MacNeice) **61**:176-77
"October in Hyde Park" (Mahon) **60**:210, 215
"October Journey" (Walker) **20**:284, 289
October Journey (Walker) **20**:284, 287, 289
"October Judgment" (Char)
See "Le Jugement d'Octobre"
"October Maples, Portland" (Wilbur) **51**:209, 291-92
"October, 1973" (Kizer) **66**:68
"The October Redbreast" (Meynell) **112**:163, 231
"An October Salmon" (Hughes) **89**:135-36, 152, 187
"October Thought" (Heaney) **18**:191
"October Trees" (Sassoon) **12**:248, 254
"October 26 1952 10:30 o'clock" (O'Hara) **45**:227
"Octobre, Elle est à Bièvre" (Sainte-Beuve) **110**:46
"The Octopus" (Merrill) **28**:239, 242
"An Octopus" (Moore) **4**:233, 252, 254-55, 264; **49**:94, 97, 102, 112, 128, 155
"Od konca" (Herbert) **50**:8
"Oda" (Cernuda) **62**:202
"Oda a España" (Paz) **48**:179-80
"Oda a Salvador Dali" (García Lorca) **3**:136, 138, 143
"Oda a Walt Whitman" (García Lorca) **3**:121, 127, 150
"Oda al edificio" (Neruda) **4**:285
"Oda al santísimo sacramento del altar: exposición y mundo" (García Lorca) **3**:136, 138, 143
"Oda al sueño" (Paz) **48**:179, 181-82
"Oda compuesta en 1960" (Borges) **32**:111
"Oda escrita en 1966" (Borges) **32**:111
"Oda inicial" (Guillén) **35**:146
"Oda k nuzhniku" (Lermontov) **18**:284-85
"Oda o Mlodości" (Mickiewicz) **38**:150, 154, 157, 162, 189
"Oda solar al ejérito del pueblo" (Neruda) **4**:309
Odas elementales (Neruda) **4**:285, 287
Odas Mínimas (Guillén) **23**:100
"Odd" (Abse) **41**:6, 13
Odd Mercy (Stern) **115**:275-78, 283
"Oddjob, a Bull Terrier" (Walcott) **46**:236, 240
"The Odds" (Hecht) **70**:86-87
"Ode" (Eliot) **90**:285
"Ode" (Lamartine) **16**:291
"Ode" (MacNeice) **61**:145
"Ode" (Marvell)
See "An Horatian Ode upon Cromwell's Return from Ireland"
"Ode" (Tennyson) **6**:357
"Ode" (Wordsworth) **4**:377, 399, 403-04, 407
"Ode à Cassandre: 'Mignonne, allons voir'" (Ronsard) **11**:218-21, 234, 240
Ode à Charles Fourier (Breton) **15**:52, 61
"Ode a Jacques Peletier des beautez qu'il voudroit en s'amie" (Ronsard) **105**:218
"Ode à Joachim du Bellay" (Ronsard) **11**:280
"Ode à l'Amitié" (Hugo) **17**:87-88
"Ode à Michel de l'Hospital" (Ronsard) **11**:258, 287-91
Ode à Michel de L'Hospital (Ronsard) **105**:236, 238
"Ode à Victor Hugo" (Gautier) **18**:144
"Ode Against St. Cecilia's Day" (Barker) **77**:13
"Ode at the Grave of Jackson Pollock" (O'Hara) **45**:148, 143
"Ode de la Paix" (Ronsard) **11**:283, 286, 289-91
Ode de la paix (Ronsard) **105**:234-36, 238
"An Ode (Dedicated to the Under-Secretary for India in expectation of his immediate promotion to Cabinet rank through the Postmaster-General)" (Belloc) **24**:41
"An Ode: Fired into Being by Life's 48-Star Editorial" (Updike) **90**:350-51
"Ode for a Social Meeting" (Holmes) **71**:66, 68, 118
"Ode for All Rebels" (MacDiarmid) **9**:171, 176
"Ode for Dick Brown" (Duncan) **75**:227
"Ode for General Washington's Birthday" (Burns) **114**:42-43, 47, 52-53, 58, 115, 177
"An Ode for Him" (Herrick) **9**:86
"Ode for Music" (Gray) **2**:153, 155; **80**:140, 164-65, 241
"Ode for School Convocation" (Ciardi) **69**:6
"Ode for St. Cecilia's Day" (Pope) **26**:315
"Ode for the Burial of a Citizen" (Ciardi) **69**:6
"Ode for the Spring of 1814" (Hunt) **73**:155, 197-98
"Ode inachevée à la boue" (Ponge) **107**:78, 108, 131-33
"An Ode. Inscribed to the Memory of the Honble Col. George Villiers" (Prior) **102**:307, 310
"Ode Inscribed to W. H. Channing" (Emerson) **18**:88, 111
"Ode: Intimations of Immortality from Recollections of Early Childhood" (Wordsworth) **4**:387-88, 390, 395, 401, 403, 411; **67**:301
"Ode Marítima" (Pessoa) **20**:166, 169
"Ode: My Twenty-Fourth Year" (Ginsberg) **4**:73
"Ode: O Bosky Brook" (Tennyson) **6**:388-89
"An Ode Occasion'd by the Death of Mr. Thomson" (Collins) **72**:57, 65, 71, 89, 97-98, 121, 126-27, 129-30, 144, 148, 177, 179-80, 182, 195
"Ode: Of Wit" (Cowley) **90**:7, 18, 21
"Ode on a Distant Prospect of Eton College" (Gray) **2**:133-34, 137, 149-50, 153; **80**:119, 123, 138, 180, 238, 283
"Ode on a Drop of Dew" (Marvell) **10**:269, 271, 277, 296, 313-14; **86**:188-89, 222, 257
"Ode on a Grecian Urn" (Keats) **1**:281-82, 290-98, 300, 303-04, 307, 313-15; **96**:205, 211, 215, 236, 242, 279, 283, 317-18, 327, 362-63, 365-68, 370-71
"Ode on Causality" (O'Hara) **45**:130, 148-49, 243-45
"Ode on Immortality" (Wordsworth)
See "Ode: Intimations of Immortality from Recollections of Early Childhood"
"Ode on Indolence" (Keats) **1**:302-04, 307-08, 314; **96**:211-12, 260, 303, 352, 354
"Ode on Lust" (O'Hara) **45**:147-48
"Ode on Melancholy" (Keats) **1**:298-300, 306-07, 309, 312; **96**:205, 256, 259-60, 272, 309-10
"Ode on Mercy" (Leapor) **85**:268
"Ode on Spring" (Gray) **2**:133, 135, 143, 145, 152; **80**:119, 123, 136, 138, 159, 166-68, 180, 193-94, 232, 236, 238, 250, 279
"Ode on the Bells of Arragon" (Collins) **72**:41, 47, 116
Ode on the Coronation of King Edward (Carman) **34**:205, 211
"Ode on the Death of a Favourite Cat" (Gray) **80**:119, 123
"Ode on the Death of a Favourite Cat, Drowned in a Tub of Gold Fishes" (Gray) **2**:133, 146, 148, 152
"Ode on the Death of the Duke of Wellington" (Tennyson) **101**:265
"Ode on the Departing Year" (Coleridge) **67**:306
"Ode on the Morning of Christ's Nativity" (Milton)
See "On the Morning of Christ's Nativity"
"Ode on the Pleasure Arising from Vicissitude" (Gray) **2**:143, 152-53; **80**:125
"Ode on the Poetical Character" (Collins) **72**:53, 56-58, 61, 83, 85-86, 94, 97, 106, 118-20, 123, 125-27, 129, 131-32, 134, 137, 139-43, 145-46, 148, 151, 153-57, 161-62, 167, 170, 172-73, 176, 200, 202
Ode on the Popular Superstitions of the Highland of Scotland (Collins) **72**:208
"Ode on the Popular Superstitions of the Highlands of Scotland, Considered as the Subject of Poetry" (Collins) **72**:41, 43, 46, 48, 50-51, 60-61, 63, 80-81, 98-100, 116, 126, 147, 182-83, 190-93, 196-98, 200-202
"Ode on the Progress of Poesy" (Gray)
See "The Progress of Poesy"
"Ode on the Recollections of Early Childhood" (Wordsworth)
See "Ode: Intimations of Immortality from Recollections of Early Childhood"
"Ode on the Spring" (Gray)
See "Ode on Spring"
"Ode on Vicissitude" (Gray)
See "Ode on the Pleasure Arising from Vicissitude"
"Ode on Washington's Birthday" (Burns)
See "Ode for General Washington's Birthday"
"An Ode. Presented to the King, on His Majesty's Arrival in Holland, After the Queen's Death. 1695" (Prior) **102**:307
"Ode: Salute to the French Negro Poets" (O'Hara) **45**:165
"Ode secrète" (Valéry) **9**:394-96
"Ode sur la naissance du duc de Bordeaux" (Lamartine) **16**:291
"Ode: The Medusa Face" (Merwin) **45**:93
"An Ode: The Merchant, to Secure His Treasure" (Prior) **102**:316
"Ode to a Beloved Woman" (Sappho)
See "Ode to Anactoria"
"Ode to a Colt" (Corso) **108**:17
"Ode to a Dead Aeronaut" (Barker) **77**:2, 4
"Ode to a Friend on his Return etc." (Collins) **72**:14, 118, 147-49, 151, 191-92
"The Ode to a Girl" (Sappho) **5**:408
"Ode, to a Lady on the Death of Colonel Charles Ross in the Action of Fontenoy" (Collins) **72**:46, 51, 57, 83, 87-88, 90, 117, 129, 145, 184-85, 194
"Ode to a Nightingale" (Keats) **1**:281-83, 295-98, 301, 303, 305, 307-09, 314-15; **96**:206,

210-11, 214-15, 217, 222, 236, 242, 301, 306, 314, 362-65, 367-72, 375
"Ode to Adversity" (Gray) **2**:133, 135, 138-39, 141, 152; **80**:123-24, 180, 188, 235, 238
"Ode to Anactoria" (Sappho) **5**:407, 411, 413
"Ode to Aphrodite" (Sappho) **5**:408, 411, 413, 431
"Ode to Apollo" (Keats) **1**:313
"Ode to Arnold Schoenberg" (Tomlinson) **17**:308, 317, 328, 337
"Ode to Atthis" (Sappho) **5**:416
"Ode to Autumn" (Hood) **93**:42, 62, 65-66, 78, 117
"Ode to Autumn" (Keats) **1**:282-83, 298-302, 314-15; **96**:200-201, 205-6, 213-14, 217-18, 230, 242, 245, 258-59, 297-307
"Ode to Beauty" (Emerson) **18**:81
"Ode to Bill" (Ashbery) **26**:135, 159
Ode to Charles Fourier (Breton)
See *Ode à Charles Fourier*
"Ode to Coit Tower" (Corso) **33**:15, 36, 39, 46-8
"Ode to Dr. Kitchener" (Hood) **93**:42, 47
"Ode to Dr. William Sancroft" (Swift) **9**:250
"Ode to dream" (Paz)
See "Oda al sueño"
"Ode to Duty" (Wordsworth) **4**:401, 406-07
"Ode to Ethiopia" (Dunbar) **5**:124, 129, 131-34, 143
"Ode to Evening" (Collins) **72**:40, 43, 49, 51-54, 56-58, 60, 63, 74-76, 82-83, 88, 91-94, 97-98, 108, 117-18, 122, 126-30, 139, 143, 162-63, 180-83
"Ode to Fame" (Masters) **1**:332
"Ode to Fancy" (Collins) **72**:70
"Ode to Fear" (Collins) **72**:53, 82-84, 95, 97, 118, 121, 129-30, 149, 155, 161-62, 167-68, 170, 172-73, 177, 197, 201-2
"Ode to Fear" (Day Lewis) **11**:147
"Ode to Fear" (Tate) **50**:243-44
"Ode to France" (Coleridge) **11**:92, 94, 99-101; **39**:167; **100**:21
"ode to frank silvera" (Bissett) **14**:34
"Ode to Freedom" (Collins) **72**:63
"Ode to Freedom" (Pushkin)
See "Vol'nost': Oda"
"Ode to Gaea" (Auden) **92**:66
"Ode to General Draper" (Smart) **13**:342
"Ode to George Colman the Younger" (Hood) **93**:48
"The Ode to Hesperus" (Sappho) **5**:418
"Ode to Himself" (Jonson) **17**:166, 174
"Ode to Indolence" (Hughes) **89**:259-62, 264
"Ode (to Joseph LeSueur) on the Arrow That Flieth by Day" (O'Hara) **45**:134-35, 147-48
"Ode to Joy" (O'Hara) **45**:147-49
"Ode to Liberty" (Collins) **72**:40, 43, 54, 56-57, 63, 66-67, 69, 83, 89-91, 100, 120-21, 127, 129, 132, 137, 193, 198
"Ode to Liberty" (Pushkin)
See "Vol'nost': Oda"
"Ode to Liberty" (Shelley) **14**:178; **67**:187
"An Ode to Love" (Behn) **13**:30; **88**:150
"Ode to Mæcenas" (Wheatley) **3**:333, 340-41, 344-45, 348, 354, 356-57, 361-62
"Ode to Melancholy" (Hood) **93**:44, 62, 65-67, 78, 117
"Ode to Memory" (Tennyson) **6**:347, 359-60; **101**:249
"Ode to Mercy" (Collins) **72**:88-89, 120, 130, 194
"Ode to Michael Goldberg's Birth and Other Births" (O'Hara) **45**:142-43, 164, 171
"Ode to Miss Kelly on Her Opening the Strand Theater" (Hood) **93**:64
"Ode to Mr. Graham" (Hood) **93**:48
"Ode to Mr. John Home" (Collins) **72**:47
"Ode to Myself and Her" (Corso) **108**:7
"Ode to Neptune" (Wheatley) **3**:354, 357, 361
"Ode to Our Young Pro-Consuls of the Air" (Tate) **50**:252-53, 322, 335
"Ode to Peace" (Collins) **72**:83, 88, 90, 94, 196
"Ode to Phœbus" (Carducci) **46**:4
"Ode to Pity" (Collins) **72**:53, 59, 82-84, 97, 108, 120, 127-28, 130, 177
"Ode to Plurality" (Zagajewski) **27**:381, 383, 385, 395-96
"Ode to Prized Koi and Baby Finches" (Chin) **40**:11
"Ode to Psyche" (Keats) **1**:295, 301, 305, 308-09, 314; **96**:211, 252-53, 260, 314
"Ode to Rae Wilson" (Hood) **93**:118
"Ode to Rhyme" (Carducci)
See "Alla rima"
"Ode to Rome" (Carducci)
See "Roma"
"Ode to Salvador Dali" (García Lorca)
See "Oda a Salvador Dali"
"Ode to San Francisco" (Tomlinson) **17**:361
"Ode to Simplicity" (Collins) **72**:52-54, 67, 83-84, 97, 126, 128, 207-8
"An Ode to Sir Clipsebie Crew" (Herrick) **9**:103
"Ode: To Sir William Sydney, on his Birth-day" (Jonson) **17**:158-59
"Ode to Sir William Temple" (Swift) **9**:250
"Ode to Spain" (Paz)
See "Oda a España"
Ode to Stalin (Mandelstam) **14**:133, 148-49, 153-55
"Ode to Suburbia" (Boland) **58**:43
"Ode to Sura" (Corso) **33**:25, 44
"Ode to the Athenian Society" (Swift) **9**:250
"Ode to the Austrian Socialists" (Benét) **64**:6, 15, 25
"An Ode to the Birth of Our Saviour" (Herrick) **9**:119-20
"Ode to the Clitumnus" (Cardozo-Freeman) **46**:7
"Ode to the Comic Spirit" (Meredith) **60**:261
"Ode to the Confederate Dead" (Tate) **50**:228, 230-31, 243, 251-52, 262, 264, 271-74, 277, 280, 288, 295-96, 300, 304-7, 313-16, 318, 326, 335, 337-38, 340-41
"Ode to the Departing Year" (Coleridge) **11**:49, 54, 93-4; **39**:167
"Ode to the Latrine" (Lermontov)
See "Oda k nuzhniku"
"Ode to the Moon" (Hood) **93**:66
"Ode to the Most Blessed Sacrament" (García Lorca)
See "Oda al santísimo sacramento del altar: exposición y mundo"
"Ode to the Most Holy Eucharist: Exposition and World" (García Lorca)
See "Oda al santísimo sacramento del altar: exposición y mundo"
"Ode to the Nightingale" (Keats)
See "Ode to a Nightingale"
"Ode to the Sacrament" (García Lorca)
See "Oda al santísimo sacramento del altar: exposición y mundo"
"Ode to the Sky Lark" (Shelley) **14**:167, 171, 175, 196, 198, 207, 212
"Ode to the Spirit of Earth in Autumn" (Meredith) **60**:296, 327
"Ode to the Spleen" (Finch) **21**:140-41, 145-46, 150, 152, 156-57, 159, 163, 165-66, 168, 172, 180-81
"Ode to the Spring" (Gray)
See "Ode on Spring"
"Ode to the Springs of Clitumnus" (Carducci)
See "Alle fonti del Clitumno"
"Ode to the Virginian Voyage" (Drayton)
See "To the Virginian Voyage"
"Ode to the West Wind" (Barker) **77**:18
"Ode to the West Wind" (Rexroth) **95**:292
"Ode to the West Wind" (Shelley) **14**:167-9, 171, 177, 196, 205-6, 208, 211-12, 234, 236-37, 239-40; **67**:180, 188, 208, 222, 224, 226, 228, 231
"Ode to Truth" (Hunt) **73**:134
"Ode to Venus" (Sappho)
See "Ode to Aphrodite"
"Ode to Walt Whitman" (Benét) **64**:7, 9, 13, 24-25
"Ode to Walt Whitman" (García Lorca)
See "Oda a Walt Whitman"
"Ode to Willem de Kooning" (O'Hara) **45**:147
"Ode to Youth" (Mickiewicz)
See "Oda o Mlodości"
"Ode Triunfal" (Pessoa) **20**:169
"Ode upon Dr. Harvey" (Cowley)
See "Upon Dr. Harvey"
"Ode upon His Majesties Restauration and Return" (Cowley) **90**:146-47
"Ode Written by Mr. Abraham Cowley for Her Majesty, Queen to King Charles I" (Cowley) **90**:15
"Ode Written in the Beginning of the Year 1746" (Collins) **72**:56-57, 83, 87, 128, 177-78, 192-97, 200
Odes (Drayton) **98**:68
Odes (Gray) **2**:135
Odes (Horace) **46**:95, 97-99, 102, 104-5, 108, 114, 117-18, 126, 128-32, 135, 138-40, 149-52, 155, 157-58, 160-63, 168-71, 173-74, 177-78, 181-85, 194, 204-5, 207, 211-14, 221-22
Odes (Hugo) **17**:55, 70, 87-90
Odes (O'Hara) **45**:147, 165
Odes (Pindar) **19**:380
Odes (Ronsard) **11**:230, 234, 280, 287, 289, 291-92; **105**:213-15, 218-20, 238
Odes (Valéry) **9**:365
Odes and Addresses to Great People (Hood) **93**:41-43, 46-51, 54, 64, 72, 114, 116, 118
Odes en son honneur (Verlaine) **32**:407
Odes et ballades (Hugo) **17**:45, 62, 74-75, 90-91
Odes et poésies diverses (Hugo) **17**:62
Odes, 1550 (Ronsard)
See *See Les quatre premiers livres des odes de Pierre de Ronsard, ensemble son bocage*
Odes, 1560-87 (Ronsard) **105**:234-35, 237
Odes in Contribution to the Song of French History (Meredith) **60**:259-60, 292, 335
The Odes of Horace (Horace)
See *Odes*
Odes on Several Descriptive and Allegoric Subjects (Collins) **72**:46, 56, 69, 83, 85, 91, 97-98, 117-18, 121, 123, 125, 142-43, 165, 184, 207-8
Odes to Simple Things (Neruda)
See *Odas elementales*
"Ode-Thnrenody on England" (Brooke) **24**:70
"Les Odeurs de l'amour" (Péret) **33**:218
Odi barbare (Carducci) **46**:4, 6-8, 11, 13, 16, 23, 26-27, 35, 37, 47, 50, 62, 64-65, 73
"Odi et Amo" (Carson) **64**:224
"Odio al mar" (Martí) **76**:88, 93, 104, 116
"Odious Scenery" (Hagiwara) **18**:177
"Odlegtose" (Milosz) **8**:189
Odlévání ní zvonů (Seifert) **47**:317, 328, 335
"Odnazhdy, pokanuvshis' na kraiu" (Akhmadulina) **43**:8
"The Odor of Verbena" (Whittier) **93**:274
"The Odour" (Herbert) **4**:102, 134
"The Odour" (Traherne) **70**:292-93
Odysseis (Homer)
See *Odyssey*
Odysses (Homer)
See *Odyssey*
"Odysseus Tells" (Masefield) **78**:91
"Odysseus to Telemachus" (Brodsky) **9**:4
Odyssey (Homer) **23**:151-53, 155-58, 161, 165-66, 176-79, 186, 188-91
"Odyssey, Book Twenty-Three" (Borges) **32**:65
"Odyssey of Big Boy" (Brown) **55**:72, 74, 80, 87-90, 101, 108, 110-11, 123, 125, 156, 160, 174
"The Odyssey of 'Erbert 'Iggins" (Service) **70**:130
"Oeconomic divina" (Milosz) **8**:186-87
"Oedipal '48" (Seferis) **66**:208

"Oedipus" (Muir) **49**:229, 233-35, 278-79
"Oedipus and the Riddle" (Borges) **32**:62
"Oedipus Crow" (Hughes) **7**:138
Oedipus Tyrannus; Or Swellfoot the Tyrant (Shelley) **14**:175, 202
"The Oedipus Within" (Wakoski) **15**:324
"L'œillet" (Ponge) **107**:73, 144, 195
"Oenone" (Tennyson) **6**:359, 410-12; **101**:125-26, 128, 138, 215, 224, 226, 240
"Oenone to Paris" (Behn)
See "A Paraphrase on Oenone to Paris"
"Oeuvre" (Stryk) **27**:193, 195, 201
Œuvres (Éluard) **38**:101, 103-7
Oeuvres (Rimbaud) **57**:257, 282-83
Oeuvres (Ronsard) **11**:247, 254, 269, 272, 276
Oeuvres complètes (Césaire) **25**:33
Oeuvres complètes (Char) **56**:147, 149, 158-59, 161-62, 164, 184-90, 196-201
Oeuvres complètes (Mallarmé) **4**:198
Oeuvres completes (Perse) **23**:254
Oeuvres complètes (Rimbaud) **57**:243-54, 264
Oeuvres Complètes (Ronsard)
See *See Pierre de Ronsard: Œvres complètes*
Oeuvres complètes (Tzara) **27**:232
Oeuvres Complètes, 1560-1587 (Ronsard)
See *See Les œuvres de P. de Ronsard, gentilhomme vandomois*
Les Oeuvres de Francois Villon (Villon) **13**:373, 394, 412
Les œuvres de P. de Ronsard, gentilhomme vandomois (Ronsard) **105**:235, 237, 241-42, 249, 276
Oeuvres poétiques (Apollinaire) **7**:36
Oeuvres poétiques (Verlaine) **32**:409
Oeuvres poetiques completes (Lamartine) **16**:268
"Of 1826" (Berryman)
See "Dream Song 22"
"Of a Dance in the Quenis Chalmer" (Dunbar)
See "Dance in the Quenis Chalmer"
"Of a Lady Who Can Sleep When She Pleases" (Waller) **72**:333
"Of a Lady Who Writ in Praise of Mira" (Waller) **72**:361
"Of a Tree Cut in Paper" (Waller) **72**:347
"Of a War with Spain, and a Fight at Sea" (Waller) **72**:288, 303, 321
"Of an Elegy Made by Mrs. Wharton on the Earl of Rochester" (Waller) **72**:364
"Of Ane Blak-Moir" (Dunbar) **67**:39, 41
"Of Beginning Light" (Tomlinson) **17**:333
"Of Being" (Levertov) **11**:199, 202
"Of Being Numerous" (Oppen) **35**:287-88, 312, 322-23, 337, 341, 342, 343-45, 354-55, 357
Of Being Numerous (Oppen) **35**:287-88, 293, 294, 301-02, 307, 308, 310, 323, 324, 325, 333, 334, 337, 340, 343-45, 354
"Of De Witt Williams on His Way to Lincoln Cemetery" (Brooks) **7**:85
"Of Distress Being Humiliated by the Classical Chinese Poets" (Carruth) **10**:87-88
"Of Divine Love" (Waller) **72**:363-64
"Of Divine Poesy" (Waller) **72**:364
"Of Dying Beauty" (Zukofsky) **11**:368
"Of English Verse" (Waller) **72**:295-96, 329, 343-48, 355-56, 361
"Of Forced Sightes and Trusty Ferefulness" (Graham) **59**:158
"Of Goats and Monkeys" (Walcott)
See "Goats and Monkeys"
"Of Greatness" (Cowley) **90**:13
"Of Havens" (Sarton) **39**:328
"Of heaven and hell" (Borges)
See "Del infierno y del cielo"
"Of Her Chamber" (Waller) **72**:322, 353
"Of Her Passing Through a Crowd of People" (Waller) **72**:371
Of his Ladies not Coming to London (Drayton) **98**:63
"Of his love called Anna" (Wyatt) **27**:342
"Of His Majesty's Receiving the News of the Duke of Buckingham's Death" (Waller) **72**:305-8
"Of Hours" (Oppen) **35**:324
"Of Itzig and His Dog" (Abse) **41**:25
"Of Liberation" (Giovanni) **19**:108
"Of Love" (Waller) **72**:38
"Of Loving At First Sight" (Waller) **72**:323
"Of Lufe" (Dunbar)
See "Of Lyfe"
"Of Luve Erdly and Divine" (Dunbar) **67**:38
"Of Lyfe" (Dunbar) **67**:11, 19
"Of Margaret" (Ransom) **61**:271, 306
"Of Marriage" (Waldrop) **109**:148
"Of Men and Cities" (Tolson) **88**:231, 329
"Of Modern Poetry" (Stevens) **6**:324; **110**:96, 150-51
"Of Myself" (Cowley) **90**:16
"Of Neptune's empire let us sing" (Campion) **87**:3
"Of Night" (Guillén)
See "De noche"
"Of others fained sorrow and the lovers fained mirth" (Wyatt) **27**:340
"Of Pacchiarotto, and How He Worked in Distemper" (Browning)
See "Pacchiarotto"
Of Pen and Ink and Paper Scraps (Stryk) **27**:214
Of Poets and Poesie (Drayton) **98**:140
"Of Rabbi Yose" (Abse) **41**:25
Of Reformation Touching Church-Discipline in England (Milton) **29**:238
"Of Suicide" (Berryman) **64**:100
"Of Swine" (Kipling) **91**:169-70
"Of Sylvia" (Waller) **72**:337, 374
"OF TH LAND DIVINE SERVICE" (Bissett) **14**:30
OF TH LAND DIVINE SERVICE (Bissett) **14**:2, 10
"Of the Blessed Sacrament of the Altar" (Southwell) **83**:279, 294, 340
"Of the Contention betwixt the Queens" (Morris) **55**:334
"Of the Danger His Majesty (while Prince) Escaped . . . at St. Andere" (Waller) **72**:305
"Of the Four Humours in Man's Constitution" (Bradstreet) **10**:17, 41
"Of the foure Elements" (Bradstreet)
See "The Four Elements"
"Of the Invasion and Defeat of the Turks" (Waller) **72**:305
"Of the Jews A.D. 50" (Cavafy) **36**:31
"Of the Ladyis Solistaris at Court" (Dunbar) **67**:38, 41
"Of the last Verses in the Book" (Waller) **72**:335, 356, 360-63, 365
"Of the Marriage of the Dwarfs" (Waller) **72**:333
"Of the Muse" (Sarton) **39**:369
"Of the Nativitie of Christ" (Dunbar) **67**:20
"Of the Paraphrase on the Lord's Prayer, Written by Mrs. Wharton" (Waller) **72**:364
Of the Progres of the Soule (Donne)
See *The Second Anniversarie. Of the Progres of the Soule. Wherein, By Occasion Of the Religious death of Mistris Elizabeth Drury, the incommodities ofthe Soule in this life, and her exaltation in the next, are Contemplated*
"Of the Terrible Doubt of Appearances" (Whitman) **91**:248
"Of the Vanity of All Worldly Creatures" (Bradstreet)
See "The Vanity of All Worldly Things"
Of the War: Passages 22-27 (Duncan) **2**:104
"Of the Warldis Instabilitie" (Dunbar)
See "This waverand warldis wretchidnes"
"Of the West" (Jeffers) **17**:130
"Of Thee (kind boy)" (Suckling) **30**:146-47
"Of Their Numbers" (Waldrop) **109**:171
"Of Their Paintings" (Waldrop) **109**:149, 172
"Of Travel" (Waldrop) **109**:171
"Of Wit" (Cowley)
See "Ode: Of Wit"
"The Ofay-Watcher Looks Back" (Serote) **113**:290-91
"Ofay-Watchers, Throbs-Phase" (Serote) **113**:282
"Off Cape Colonna" (Melville) **82**:77, 106
"off d pig" (Reed) **68**:325, 330
"Off Februar the fyiftene nycht" (Dunbar) **67**:14
"Off from swing shift" (Hongo) **23**:196-97, 203
"Off Lentren in the first mornyng" (Dunbar) **67**:13, 17
"Off Point Lotus" (Kunitz) **19**:171
"Off Shore" (Swinburne) **24**:313
"Off Spectacle Island" (Eberhart) **76**:59
"Off The Campus: Wits" (Brutus) **24**:106, 114
"Off the Peg" (MacNeice) **61**:176
"Off the Turnpike" (Lowell) **13**:78, 85
"The Offending Eel" (Carver) **54**:18
"The Offensive 1" (Douglas) **106**:199
"Offeren Y Llwyn" (Dafydd ap Gwilym) **56**:210
"Offering" (Tagore)
See "Utsarga"
"An Offering for Mr. Bluehart" (Wright) **36**:293-94, 306, 337
"Offering of Man to God" (Alurista) **34**:41
An Offering to the Lares (Rilke) **2**:280
"Offerings" (Clarke) **112**:53
"Offerings" (Heaney) **100**:334
"The Offers" (Hughes) **89**:234
"Offhand Compositions" (Wang Wei) **18**:370, 374
"Office for the Dead" (Kinsella) **69**:83
"The Office of the Holy Cross" (Crashaw) **84**:9, 28, 33, 37, 69-72, 102
"An Officers' Prison Camp Seen from a Troop-Train" (Jarrell) **41**:178-79
"Offices" (Page) **12**:173
"Official Inquiry Among the Grains of Sand" (Simic) **69**:300
"Official Piety" (Whittier) **93**:239
"Ofrenda" (Cernuda) **62**:178
"Oft have I sigh'd" (Campion) **87**:58, 120, 125
"Often I Am Permitted to Return to a Meadow" (Duncan) **2**:120, 127; **75**:147, 164, 169-70, 230, 250, 255-57, 263
"Often Rebuked, yet Always Back Returning" (Brontë) **8**:50
"Ogier the Dane" (Morris) **55**:250, 261, 286, 329
"Ogni cosa a morte arriva" (Michelangelo) **103**:274
"Ogni van chiuso, ogni coperto loco" (Michelangelo) **103**:221, 260
"The Ogre" (Williams) **7**:349, 378, 393; **109**:236
"Ogres and Pygmies" (Graves) **6**:139, 142, 144, 151
"Ogun" (Brathwaite) **56**:69, 74, 100
"Oh" (Sexton) **2**:365
"Oh" (Stern) **115**:298
"Oh Brave New Bull" (Heaney) **100**:263
"Oh Chatterton! How very sad thy fate" (Keats) **96**:291, 293
"Oh Christianity, Christianity" (Smith) **12**:325, 352
"Oh, Dear! Oh Dear! A Sonnet" (Brooke) **24**:52
"Oh death shall find me" (Brooke) **24**:52, 72, 76
"Oh do not die" (Donne)
See "A Feaver"
"Oh Don't Ask Why" (Dorn) **115**:126
"Oh Fair Enough Are Sky and Plain" (Housman) **2**:193
"Oh Fairest of the Rural Maids" (Bryant) **20**:35
"Oh general en tu Pentágono!" (Guillén) **23**:126
"Oh General in Your Pentagon!" (Guillén)
See "Oh general en tu Pentágono!"
"Oh Happy Day" (Parra)
See "Hay un día feliz"

Oh, Hell (Silverstein) **49**:314-17
"Oh, how painful are all those other troubles" (Akhmadulina) **43**:4
"Oh Irene" (Ignatow) **34**:328
"Oh ivy green" (Niedecker) **42**:96
"Oh! laissez-vous aimer" (Sainte-Beuve) **110**:65, 68
"Oh, Look - I can Do It, Too" (Parker) **28**:354
Oh Mercy (Dylan) **37**:60
"Oh n'insultez jamais une femme qui tombe!" (Hugo) **17**:66
"Oh, oh, you will be sorry for that word!" (Millay) **61**:242
"Oh! Place Me Where the Burning Noon" (Smith)
See "Sonnet 13"
Oh Pray My Wings Are Gonna Fit Me Well (Angelou) **32**:3, 11, 26
"Oh seasons, oh castles" (Rimbaud)
See "O saisons, ô châteaux!"
"Oh, See How Thick the Gold Cup Flowers" (Housman) **2**:183, 185, 196
"Oh So Dear from Far and Near" (Mallarmé) **102**:77
"Oh, Tell Us" (Elliott) **96**:166
"Oh Think Not I Am Faithful to a Vow" (Millay) **6**:211
"Oh, to vex me, contraryes meete in one" (Donne) **43**:163
"Oh, What Damned Age Do We Live In" (Wilmot) **66**:234
"Oh You Are Coming" (Teasdale) **31**:359, 388
"Oh You Sabbatarians!" (Masters) **1**:344
"Oh young men, oh young comrades" (Spender) **71**:157, 180, 220
"Ohio Valley Swains" (Wright) **36**:309, 317, 348, 377
"Ohio Winter" (Walcott) **46**:240
"Ohioan Pastoral" (Wright) **36**:347
"Ohnedaruth's Day Begun" (Mackey) **49**:4
"Ŏi" (Seifert) **47**:349
Oi no kobumi (Matsuo Basho) **3**:6
Oi no obumi (Matsuo Basho) **3**:12
"Oil" (Hogan) **35**:254
"Oil Painting of the Artist as the Artist" (MacLeish) **47**:189
"Oil Refinery" (Birney) **52**:38
"Oina-Morul" (Macpherson) **97**:233
"Un oiseau a fienté sur mon veston salaud" (Péret) **33**:202
"L'oiseau spirituel" (Char) **56**:120
Oiseaux (Perse) **23**:239-41, 247-48, 253-54, 256-57
"Oitaru mi ni yamai wo kasane, toshi wo hete tashinami, kor wo omou ni itaru uta" (Yakamochi) **48**:131, 134, 139
"Oithona" (Macpherson) **97**:246, 319, 321
"O-Jazz-O" (Kaufman) **74**:247, 250, 275
"O-Jazz-O War Memoir: Jazz, Don't Listen to it at Your Own Risk" (Kaufman) **74**:275
"Ojo" (Storni) **33**:269, 282-83
"Ojos de agua" (Cernuda) **62**:239
"Okay, First . . ." (Berrigan) **103**:27
Oktyabr' (Yevtushenko) **40**:362-63
Oku no hosomichi (Matsuo Basho) **3**:13, 27-30
Ol. IX (Pindar)
See *Olympian 9*
Ol. XI (Pindar)
See *Olympian 11*
"The Ol' Tunes" (Dunbar) **5**:122, 145
"The Old Adam" (Levertov) **11**:170
"Old Age Compensation" (Wright) **36**:328, 341, 345
"The Old Age of Queen Maeve" (Yeats) **51**:73
"Old Amusement Park" (Moore) **49**:145
Old and Modern Poems (Vigny)
See *Poèmes antiques et modernes*
"Old and New Art" (Rossetti) **44**:227, 250
Old and New Poems (Hall) **70**:44-45, 49, 55
"The Old and the New Masters" (Jarrell) **41**:160-61, 163, 184
Old Arcadia (Sidney) **32**:235, 246, 281-82, 314-15
"The Old Author" (de la Mare) **77**:99
"The Old Bachelor" (Crabbe) **97**:114
The Old Band (Riley) **48**:292
"The Old Beau" (FitzGerald) **79**:70
"Old Bill Pheasant" (Stone) **53**:219
"Old Boards" (Bly) **39**:85
"Old Botany Bay" (Gilmore) **87**:286
"The Old Burying Ground" (Whittier) **93**:239
"Old Cambridge" (Holmes) **71**:68
"The Old Canal" (Masefield) **78**:30
"The Old Chartlist" (Meredith) **60**:262
"The Old Clock on the Stairs" (Longfellow) **30**:21, 46
"Old Communists and Guerillas" (Dalton) **36**:130
"Old Counsel" (Melville) **82**:73
"Old Countryside" (Bogan) **12**:87, 94, 113
"An Old Cracked Tune" (Kunitz) **19**:158
"The Old Cumberland Beggar" (Wordsworth) **4**:411-12, 428
"Old Dog Dead" (Warren) **37**:377
"Old Dogs" (Smith) **12**:331-32
"Old Dominion" (Hass) **16**:198
"Old Dwarf Heart" (Sexton) **2**:361; **79**:203, 216
"Old England" (McKay) **2**:225
"Old-fashioned Air" (Berrigan) **103**:40-41
"Old Fashioned Pilgrimage" (Clarke) **112**:68, 89-90, 94
Old-Fashioned Pilgrimage and Other Poems (Clarke) **112**:120
"An Old Field Mowed for Appearances' Sake" (Meredith) **28**:194
"Old Flag" (Merwin) **45**:49, 86
"The Old Flagman" (Sandburg) **41**:330
"Old Flame" (Lowell) **3**:212, 215
"An Old Flame" (Snodgrass) **74**:333
"Old Flame" (Warren) **37**:337
"Old Florist" (Roethke) **15**:295
"Old Folks Home" (Stryk) **27**:210
"Old Folk's Home, Jerusalem" (Dove) **6**:123
"Old Friends" (Betjeman) **75**:30
"The Old Front Gate" (Dunbar) **5**:122
"Old Furniture" (Hardy) **8**:105; **92**:317
"Old Garden" (Cernuda) **62**:172
"The Old Gods" (Muir) **49**:210
"Old Goldenrod at Field's Edge" (Oliver) **75**:342
"The Old Gray Couple" (MacLeish) **47**:197, 207
"The Old Gray Couple II" (MacLeish) **47**:207
"The Old Gray Wall" (Carman) **34**:229
"The Old Hamer Place" (Stafford) **71**:263
"Old Harry" (Kinsella) **69**:95
"Old Hills" (Ortiz) **17**:231
"Old Home Day" (Hall) **70**:6
The Old Home Folks (Riley) **48**:349
"The Old Horsefly" (Shapiro) **25**:324
The Old Horsefly (Shapiro) **25**:323
"Old House" (Wright) **14**:348-49, 353
The Old House in the Country (Reese) **29**:337-339, 348, 352
"The Old Huntsman" (Sassoon) **12**:240, 242, 250, 252-53, 275-76
The Old Huntsman and Other Poems (Sassoon) **12**:249, 252, 256-57, 260, 263-64, 269, 272, 277
"Old Ironsides" (Holmes) **71**:68, 70, 88, 91, 114, 124-25
"The Old Issue" (Kipling) **91**:66-67
"The Old Italians Dying" (Ferlinghetti) **1**:182
"Old King Cole" (Robinson) **1**:468; **35**:362
"Old King Cotton" (Brown) **55**:110
"The Old King's New Jester" (Robinson) **1**:487
"An Old Lady's Winter Words" (Roethke) **15**:272, 278
"Old Laughter" (Brooks) **7**:61
"Old Lem" (Brown) **55**:80-81, 83, 94, 113-14, 140, 152-53, 168
"The Old Liberals" (Betjeman) **75**:17-18
"The Old Life" (Kinnell) **26**:277
Old Lights for New Chancels: Verses Topographical and Amatory (Betjeman) **75**:5, 7, 60, 84, 87, 107
"Old Lines" (Montale)
See "Vecchi versi"
"The Old Lovers" (Aleixandre)
See "Los amantes viejos"
"The Old Maid" (Teasdale) **31**:388
"An Old Man" (Cavafy) **36**:95
"Old Man" (Thomas) **53**:276-77, 280, 291-92, 296-97, 300-301, 309-10, 332, 347-48
"The Old Man and Jim" (Riley) **48**:297, 325, 327
"Old Man at the Beach" (Wagoner) **33**:324
"An Old Man Awake in His Own Death" (Strand) **63**:189
"The Old Man Dreams" (Holmes) **71**:68
"Old Man Feeding Hens" (Francis) **34**:252
"Old Man Hoppergrass" (Benét) **64**:14
"The Old Man Is Like Moses" (Aleixandre) **15**:4, 24
"Old Man of Coblenz" (Lear)
See "There Was an Old Man of Coblenz"
"The Old Man of Dunluce" (Lear) **65**:172, 183, 185
"An Old Man of the Dee" (Lear) **65**:172, 185
"The Old Man of the Sea" (Holmes) **71**:66, 68, 93
"Old Man of Vesuvius" (Lear) **65**:168
"Old Man, Old Man" (Wagoner) **33**:334
"An Old Man on the River Bank" (Seferis) **66**:122, 157, 160, 179, 189
"Old Man Playing with Children" (Ransom) **61**:305, 311-12
"Old Man Potchikoo" (Erdrich) **52**:174, 178, 193
Old Man Rubbing His Eyes (Bly) **39**:85
"The Old Man to the Lizard" (MacLeish) **47**:165
"The Old Man Travelling" (Wordsworth) **4**:374, 416; **67**:277, 295, 312, 337, 370
Old Man Whiskery-Whee-Kum-Wheeze (Riley) **48**:292
"Old Man who seined" (Niedecker) **42**:169
"The Old Man's Counsel" (Bryant) **20**:35, 41
"The Old Man's Funeral" (Bryant) **20**:10
"An Old Man's Winter Night" (Frost) **39**:246
"Old Mansion" (Ransom) **61**:268, 275, 311
"The Old Marlborough Road" (Thoreau) **30**:233, 236, 242
"Old Marrieds" (Brooks) **7**:53, 69, 79
"Old Mary" (Brooks) **7**:106
"The Old Masters" (Herbert) **50**:31
"Old Medium" (Enzensberger) **28**:167
"An Old Memory" (Dunbar) **5**:140
"The Old Men" (Kipling) **91**:71, 73
"The Old Men" (de la Mare) **77**:75
"Old Men" (Nash) **21**:263, 274
Old Men and Comets (Enright) **93**:31-32
"Old Mother turns blue and from us" (Niedecker) **42**:140, 182
"An Old Mountain Woman Reading the Book of Job" (Chappell) **105**:22
Old Mythologies: A Poem (Montague) **106**:275, 313, 316
"The Old Neighbour and the New" (Hardy) **8**:104
"Old Nigger on One-Mule Cart Encountered Late at Night When Driving Home from Party in the Back Country" (Warren) **37**:330, 380
"Old Oak of Summer Chace" (Tennyson) **6**:356
"Old Oats" (Hughes) **89**:217
"Old, Old, Old, Old Andrew Jackson" (Lindsay) **23**:280, 288
"Old Osawatomie" (Sandburg) **41**:297
"Old Paint, Old Partner" (Kumin) **15**:220
"Old Park" (Jiménez) **7**:183
"The Old Peasant" (Kavanagh) **105**:179
"The old people" (Paz)
See "Los viejos"

"Old People on the Nursing Home Porch" (Strand) **63**:151
"The Old Peppermint Ladies" (Francis) **34**:258
"An old Photograph" (Nemerov) **24**:255
"An Old Photograph of strangers" (Meredith) **28**:193
"Old Photograph of the Future" (Warren) **37**:366, 376
"Old Pictures in Florence" (Browning) **2**:37
"Old Pictures in Florence" (Rossetti) **44**:250
The Old Playhouse and Other Poems (Das) **43**:73-74, 76, 80, 85, 93
"The Old Playhouse" (Das) **43**:74-75, 88-89
"Old poet" (Bukowski) **18**:22
"The Old Poet" (Shapiro) **25**:304
"The Old Poet Moves to a New Apartment 14 Times" (Zukofsky) **11**:353
"The Old Pond" (Matsuo Basho) **3**:32
"An Old Portrait" (Akhmadulina)
See "Starinnyi portret"
Old Possum's Book of Practical Cats (Eliot) **6**:174
"The Old Prison" (Wright) **14**:359
"The Old Prometheus" (Herbert)
See "Stary Prometeusz"
"The Old Quarry, I & II" (Jones) **116**:167
Old Raiger and Other Verse (Masefield) **78**:49, 63, 73, 85, 91
"The Old Reliable" (Hacker)
See "Nights of 1964-1966: The Old Reliable"
"Old Revolution" (Enzensberger) **28**:166
"Old Rhyme" (Montague) **106**:267
"Old Roses" (Hall) **70**:28
"The Old Sceptic" (Noyes) **27**:139
The Old Sceptic (Noyes) **27**:139
"The Old Seer" (Tennyson)
See "The Ancient Sage"
"Old Shepherd's Prayer" (Mew) **107**:18, 56
Old Shirts and New Skins (Alexie) **53**:3-5, 8, 11-15, 24, 26, 29-31, 39-40
Old Shirts & New Skins (Alexie) **53**:3-5, 8, 11-15, 24, 26, 29-31, 39-40
"The Old Soldier's Story" (Riley) **48**:331, 350
"Old Song" (Crane) **3**:90
"An Old Song" (Jarrell) **41**:169
"An Old Song" (Thomas) **53**:227
"The Old Song and Dance" (Rexroth) **95**:260
"An Old Song Ended" (Rossetti) **44**:202
"The Old South" (Whittier) **93**:198
"Old Spring" (Winters) **82**:314
"An Old Steel Engraving" (Boland) **58**:58, 85
"The Old Steps of the Passaic General Hospital" (Williams) **109**:196
"The Old Stoic" (Brontë) **8**:60
"The Old Stone House" (de la Mare) **77**:112, 149
"An Old Story" (Robinson) **1**:459; **35**:368
"An Old Sweetheart of Mine" (Riley) **48**:308, 323-24, 336, 350
"The Old Swimmin' Hole" (Riley) **48**:284, 312, 329, 332, 340
The Old Swimmin' Hole, and 'Leven More Poems (Riley) **48**:282, 284, 328, 339, 342, 347, 356
"Old Timers" (Sandburg) **2**:302; **41**:240, 270
"Old Timer's Day at Fenway" (Hall) **70**:34
"Old Trails" (Robinson) **1**:462
"The Old Trundle Bed" (Riley) **48**:324
"The Old Vicarage, Grantchester" (Brooke) **24**:54, 58, 63-5, 68, 78, 86, 93
"Old Walt" (Hughes) **1**:257; **53**:104
"The Old Warrior Terror" (Walker) **30**:339, 365
"Old Weavers" (Mistral)
See "Tejedores viejos"
"Old West Vancouver Ferry" (Birney) **52**:58
"Old Witherington" (Randall) **86**:302, 343, 348
"Old Woman" (Pinsky) **27**:160-1
"Old Woman" (Sandburg) **41**:323
"An Old Woman" (Sitwell) **3**:312, 326
"The Old Woman and the Statue" (Stevens) **6**:297; **110**:95
"An Old Woman Passes" (Werfel)
See "Eine alte Frau geht"
"An Old Woman Remembers" (Brown) **55**:81, 114, 166
"Old Woman's Old Man" (Rimbaud)
See "Vieux de la vieille"
"Old Words" (Sanchez) **9**:221
"An Old World Thicket" (Rossetti) **7**:277
"The Old WPA Swimming Pool in Martin's Ferry, Ohio" (Wright) **36**:304, 358, 363, 377, 392, 396, 398
The Oldest Killed Lake in North America (Carruth) **10**:91
"The Oldest Place" (Kinsella) **69**:134
"Old-Fashioned Roses" (Riley) **48**:290, 315, 317, 319, 327, 356
"Olena's Feet" (Yevtushenko) **40**:347
"Oleszkiewicz" (Mickiewicz) **38**:169
"Olfactory Pursuits" (Abse) **41**:25, 28
"Olive Branch" (Meredith) **60**:245
"Olive Grove" (Merrill) **28**:228
"The Olive Grove" (Sarton) **39**:324, 340
"The Olive in Its Orchard" (Housman) **2**:189-90
"Olive Mandate" (Raworth) **107**:277
"The Olive Wood Fire" (Kinnell) **26**:278
"Les olives" (Ponge) **107**:102, 133, 184
Olney Hymns (Cowper) **40**:42, 53
Olor Iscanus. A Collection of Some Select Poems, and Translations, Formerly Written by Mr. Henry Vaughan, Silurist (Vaughan) **81**:257, 259, 336, 341, 346-47, 350, 355-59, 364, 366, 368
"Olson as Oracle" (Curnow) **48**:56-57
"Oltranza oltraggio" (Zanzotto) **65**:264, 269, 277, 311
"The Olympian" (Dickey) **40**:230
Olympian 1 (Pindar) **19**:380-81, 388-89, 396, 398, 400, 402, 407, 413-17, 420, 422
Olympian 2 (Pindar) **19**:381, 423
Olympian 3 (Pindar) **19**:425
Olympian 6 (Pindar) **19**:381, 389-90, 398, 414, 420
Olympian 7 (Pindar) **19**:396, 401, 406, 414
Olympian VII (Pindar)
See *Olympian 7*
Olympian 8 (Pindar) **19**:422-23
Olympian 9 (Pindar) **19**:390
Olympian 10 (Pindar) **19**:387-88
Olympian 11 (Pindar) **19**:389, 412
Olympian 13 (Pindar) **19**:387, 391, 398
Olympian 14 (Pindar) **19**:421-23
Olympian Odes 1 (Pindar)
See *Olympian 1*
"The Olympic Girl" (Betjeman) **75**:11
"A Olympio" (Hugo) **17**:76
"Olympus" (Berryman) **64**:79, 95, 102, 115
Om hösten (Ekeloef) **23**:76
"Omaggio a Rimbaud" (Montale) **13**:111, 157
"Omagh Hospital" (Montague) **106**:215, 278
El Ombligo de Aztlán (Alurista) **34**:31, 34
"Ombra" (Ungaretti) **57**:347
"L'ombra della magnolia" (Montale) **13**:109-10, 118, 126
"Ombra mai fu" (Wilbur) **51**:282
"L'ombre aux soupirs" (Éluard) **38**:69
"Ombre Chinoise" (Lowell) **13**:94
"L'Ombre du cheval" (Ronsard) **105**:190-91
"Omega" (Tolson) **88**:244-45, 256, 283, 285, 304, 315, 319
"Omero" (Carducci) **46**:52
Omeros (Walcott) **46**:249, 254, 257-63, 265-69, 287, 292, 294-98, 300, 304-16, 324-26
"Omicron" (Tolson) **88**:241, 275, 304, 315-17, 320
Ommateum with Doxology (Ammons) **16**:4-5, 20, 24, 27, 39-44, 52-3
"Omnibus" (Birney) **52**:44
"Omnibus" (Hood) **93**:99
"Omnibus" (Tsvetaeva)
See "Avtobus"
Omniscience (Smart)
See *On the Omniscience of the Supreme Being*
"Omoide" (Ishikawa) **10**:213
"On" (Kaufman) **74**:195
"On a Biographical Dictionary" (Blunden) **66**:26
"On a Bust" (Masters) **1**:342
"On a Canaanite Stone at the Dead Sea" (Darwish) **86**:26, 28
"On a Celebrated Ruling Elder" (Burns) **114**:89
"On a Certain Engagement South of Seoul" (Carruth) **10**:84, 89
"On a Child's Death" (Blok) **21**:15
"On a Clean Book" (Dunbar) **5**:125
"On a Conventicle" (Behn) **13**:7
"On a Copy of Verses made in a Dream" (Behn) **88**:16, 148, 151
"On a Copy of Verses Made in a Dream, and Sent to Me in a Morning before I Was Awake" (Behn) **13**:31
"On a Discovered Curl of Hair" (Hardy) **8**:137
"On a Distant Prospect of Eton College" (Gray)
See "Ode on a Distant Prospect of Eton College"
"On a Drawing by Flavio" (Levine) **22**:223
"On a Dream" (Owen) **102**:211
"On a Drop of Dew" (Marvell)
See "Ode on a Drop of Dew"
"On a Fine Morning" (Hardy) **8**:108
"On a Foreign Verse" (Seferis)
See "Reflections on a Foreign Line of Verse"
"On a Friend's Escape from Drowning" (Barker) **77**:20
"On a Gift in the Shape of a Heart" (Kinsella) **69**:101
"On a Girdle" (Waller) **72**:271, 333
"On a Goldfinch Starved to Death in His Cage" (Cowper) **40**:126
"On a Heath" (Hardy) **8**:93
"On a Juniper Tree, Cut Down to Make Busks" (Behn) **13**:7, 27-8
"On a Juniper-Tree" (Behn) **88**:27, 30, 87, 138-39, 147-49, 151-53
"On a Leander Which Miss Reynolds, My Kind Friend, Gave Me" (Keats) **96**:346
"On a Lock of Milton's Hair" (Hunt) **73**:137
"On a Locket of Hair Wove in a True-Loves Knot" (Behn) **88**:149, 151-52
"On a March Day" (Teasdale) **31**:341
"On a Midsummer Eve" (Hardy) **92**:254, 259
"On a Month's Reading of the English Newspapers" (Corso) **33**:26
"On a Mountainside" (Wagoner) **33**:373
"On a Name for Black Americans" (Randall)
See "An Answer to Lerone Bennett's Questionnaire on a Name for Black Americans"
"On a New Year's Eve" (Jordan) **38**:122-23
"On a night without ornament" (Char)
See "Sur une nuit sans ornement"
"On a Photo of Sgt. Ciardi a Year Later" (Ciardi) **69**:14, 27, 50, 55
"On a Photography of a Friend, Dead" (Spender) **71**:191
"On a Phrase from Southern Ohio" (Wright) **36**:313, 322, 404
"On a Pietà of Tintoretto" (Bonnefoy) **58**:147
"On a Political Prisoner" (Yeats) **20**:314, 349
"On a Prayer-Book" (Whittier) **93**:239
"On a Prayer Booke Sent to Mrs. M. R." (Crashaw) **84**:20-21, 23-26, 73-74, 96, 103
"On a Presentation of Two Birds to My Son" (Wright) **36**:335, 337
"On a Raised Beach" (MacDiarmid) **9**:157, 172, 176, 180
"On a Red Steed" (Tsvetaeva)
See "Na krasnom kone"
"On a Return from Egypt" (Douglas) **106**:183, 193, 202

"On a Rocky Spur of Peoria" (Mandelstam) **14**:117
"On a Sentence by Pascal" (Schwartz) **8**:285, 292
"On a September Day" (Baca) **41**:37
"On a Side Street" (Simic) **69**:304
"On a Side Street" (Zagajewski) **27**:389
"On a Singing Girl" (Wylie) **23**:324
"On a Sledge, Overlaid with Straw" (Mandelstam) **14**:119
"On a Sleeping Friend" (Belloc) **24**:9
"On a small Dog, thrust out in a Tokyo street soon after his birth, and rescued in vain" (Blunden) **66**:18, 24, 51
"On a Solemn Music" (Milton) **19**:211, 253; **29**:238-40
"On a Starry Night" (Dunbar) **5**:125-27
"On a Theme by Frost" (Francis) **34**:244
"On a Tree Fallen Across the Road" (Frost) **1**:213
"On a View of Pasadena from the Hills" (Winters) **82**:310, 346, 348
"On a Winter Night" (Sarton) **39**:332
"On a winter's night long time ago" (Belloc) **24**:34
"On acquiring an encyclopedia" (Borges)
See "Al adquirir una Enciclopedia"
"On Acrocorinth" (Sikelianos) **29**:372
"On Aesthetics" (Koch) **80**:302-3
"On Affliction" (Finch) **21**:144, 146
"On an Anthology of Chinese Poems" (Jeffers) **17**:140
"On an Early Photograph of My Mother" (Hope) **56**:277
"On an Engraving by Casserius" (Hope) **56**:281
"On an Old Horn" (Stevens) **110**:149-50
"On an Old Photograph of My Son" (Carver) **54**:18, 29
"On an Old Roundel" (Swinburne) **24**:324-25, 328-29
"On an Old-Fashioned Water-Colour of Oxford" (Betjeman) **75**:22
"On an Un-named Mountain" (Stafford) **71**:337
"On Anactoria" (Sappho)
See "Ode to Anactoria"
"On Angels" (Milosz) **8**:201
"On Annunciation Day" (Tsvetaeva)
See "V den' Blagoveshchen'ia"
"On Another Politician" (Belloc) **24**:36-7
"On Another's Sorrow" (Blake) **12**:7, 33; **63**:10, 24, 33, 102, 115, 121, 125, 127-28
"On Aspalathoi . . ." (Seferis) **66**:200, 205, 212
"On Badon Hill" (Masefield) **78**:92
On Ballycastle Beach (McGuckian) **27**:80, 83-85, 90, 92-95, 99-102, 104
"On Barbara's Shore" (Wakoski) **15**:333
"On Beauty" (Koch) **80**:303
"On Becoming a Mermaid" (Goodison) **36**:143, 145-46
"On Becoming a Tiger" (Goodison) **36**:154
"On Beginning the Study of Anglo-Saxon Grammar" (Borges)
See "Al iniciar el estudio de la gramática anglosajona"
"On Being Asked to Write a Poem Against the War in Vietnam" (Carruth) **10**:77
"On Being Brought from Africa to America" (Wheatley) **3**:338, 340, 346, 349, 353, 362-63
"On Being Cautioned against Walking on an Headland Overlooking the Sea, Because It was Frequented by a Lunatic" (Smith)
See "Sonnet 70"
"On Being Forgotten" (Waldrop) **109**:120
"On Being Given Time" (Sarton) **39**:325
"On Being Yanked from a Favorite Anthology" (Shapiro) **25**:323
"On Blake's Victory over the Spaniards" (Marvell)
See "On the Victory Obtained by Blake over the Spaniards"
"On byl v krayu svyatom" (Lermontov) **18**:289
"On Cartagena de Indias, His Native City" (Birney) **52**:15
"On Cheating the Fiddler" (Parker) **28**:362
"On Childhood" (Bradstreet) **10**:38
"On Certain Incredible Nights" (Cohen) **109**:13
"On Christmas Eve" (Lowell) **13**:85
"On Court-worme" (Jonson) **17**:197
"On Death" (Clare) **23**:44
"On Deism" (Wheatley) **3**:354
"On Desire" (Behn) **88**:22
"On Desire. A Pindarick" (Behn) **13**:8, 10, 14
"On Diverse Deviations" (Angelou) **32**:17
"On Don Surly" (Jonson) **17**:197
"On Duelling" (Graves) **6**:144
"On Each Journey" (Merwin) **45**:48, 101
On Early Trains (Pasternak)
See *Na rannikh poezdakh*
"On Elgin Marbles" (Keats) **1**:279
"On Exodus iii. 14" (Prior) **102**:310, 319, 328
"On Falling Asleep by Firelight" (Meredith) **28**:189-90, 213
"On Falling Asleep to Bird Song" (Meredith) **28**:192, 213
"On Fame" (Keats) **96**:354
"On Fields O'er Which the Reaper's Hand has Passed" (Thoreau) **30**:207
"On Finding the Slide of John in the Garden" (Cervantes) **35**:134
"On Finding the Truth" (Very) **86**:141
"On First Looking into Chapman's Homer" (Keats) **96**:196, 251-53, 255, 349
"On Fleet: Shepheards Taking Away a Childs Bread and Butter" (Prior) **102**:311
"On Flower Wreath Hill" (Rexroth) **20**:220-21; **95**:281-82, 290, 326, 328, 339
"On Food" (Belloc) **24**:17
"On Freedom" (Ignatow) **34**:342
"On Freedom's Ground" (Wilbur) **51**:250, 302
"On Friendship" (Wheatley) **3**:363
"On Fugitives and Flight" (Sachs)
See "Von Flüchtlingen und Flucht"
"On Getting a Natural (For Gwendolyn Brooks)" (Randall) **86**:290, 301, 337
"On Going Back to the Street after Viewing and Art Show" (Bukowski) **18**:5
"On Going to the Wars" (Birney) **52**:38
"On Going Unnoticed" (Frost) **1**:205; **39**:241
"On Gorse. . ." (Seferis)
See "On Aspalathoi . . ."
"On Growing Old" (Masefield) **78**:63, 89
"On Gut" (Jonson) **17**:174
"On Handling Some Small Shells from the Windward Islands" (Swenson) **14**:287
"On Having Mis-identified a Wild Flower" (Wilbur) **51**:301
"On Hearing a New Escalation" (Hugo) **68**:255
"On Hearing of Love" (Cavafy) **36**:41
"On Hearing the Full Peal of Ten Bells from Christ Church, Swindon, Wilts" (Betjeman) **75**:93
"On Hearing Wild Geese Cry" (Kokinshu) (Tsurayuki) **73**:338
"On Her Loving Two Equally" (Behn)
See "Song: On Her Loving Two Equally"
"On Himselfe" (Herrick) **9**:87, 89, 131
"On his being arrived at the age of twenty-three" (Milton)
See "Sonnet 7"
"On His Blindness" (Borges) **32**:89
"On His Books" (Belloc) **24**:31
"On His Having Arrived at the Age of Twenty-Three" (Milton)
See "Sonnet 7"
"On His Mistris" (Donne)
See "Elegie XVI: On his mistris"
"On his mistris Singing" (Davenant) **99**:165, 167
"On His Work in the English Tongue" (Heaney) **100**:239
"On Hope" (Crashaw)
See "Hope"
"On Hope, by Way of Question and Answer, between A. Cowley and R. Crashaw" (Cowley) **90**:6
"On Huntingdon's 'Miranda'" (Lanier) **50**:69
"On Imagination" (Wheatley) **3**:335-36, 338, 353-55
"On Indolence" (Keats)
See "Ode on Indolence"
"On Installing an American Kitchen in Lower Austria" (Auden) **1**:24
"On Jenkins' Hill" (Meredith) **28**:206
"On Julia's Clothes" (Herrick)
See "Upon Julia's Clothes"
"On Leaping over the Moon" (Traherne) **70**:181, 293
"On Leaving a Part of Sussex" (Smith)
See "Sonnet 45"
"On Leaving Some Friends" (Keats) **1**:313; **73**:311; **96**:221
"On Leaving Wantage, 1972" (Betjeman) **75**:35, 93
"On Lending a Punch-Bowl" (Holmes) **71**:68
"On Liberty and Peace" (Wheatley) **3**:337, 341, 363
"On Lieutenant Shift" (Jonson) **17**:197
"On Looking at a Copy of Alice Meynell's Poems Given to Me Years Ago by a Friend" (Lowell) **13**:85, 89-90, 99-100
"On Looking into E. V. Rieu's Homer" (Kavanagh) **33**:100, 118
"On Looking Up by Chance at the Constellations" (Frost) **39**:233
"On Lookout Mountain" (Hayden) **6**:180, 194
"On Lord Holland's Seat near Margate, Kent" (Gray) **2**:143
"On Losing One's Coolant" (Dorn) **115**:157
"On Lucy Countesse of Bedford" (Jonson)
See "Epigram LXXVI"
"On Madison" (Tomlinson) **17**:353
"On Major General Lee" (Wheatley)
See "Thoughts on His Excellency Major General Lee"
"On Making Certain Anything Has Happened" (Frost) **39**:233
"On Malvern Hill" (Masefield) **78**:44, 55
"On Marriage" (Crashaw) **84**:99
"On Martock Moor" (Hardy) **92**:267-68
"On Minding One's Own Business" (Wright) **36**:288
"On Moral Leadership as a Political Dilemma" (Jordan) **38**:127
"On Mount Marius" (Carducci)
See "Su Monte Mario"
"On Mr. F.S. Killing the French K . . ." (Prior) **102**:311
"On Mr. G. Herberts Booke Intituled the *Temple* " (Crashaw) **84**:74
"On Mr. J. H. in a Fit of Sickness" (Behn) **13**:8; **88**:150-51
"On Mr. Pope's *Universal Prayer* " (Leapor) **85**:212, 214, 217, 235-36, 288
"On Mr. Walpole's Cat" (Gray)
See "Ode on the Death of a Favourite Cat"
"On Mrs. Willis" (Wilmot) **66**:268, 270
"On Music" (Duck) **89**:9
"On My First Daughter" (Jonson) **17**:172, 197
"On My First Son" (Jonson) **17**:172, 177, 197
"On my Mother and my lady W— who both lay sick at the same time under the Hands of Dr. Paman" (Barker) **91**:24
"On My Own" (Levine) **22**:226
"On My Picture Left in Scotland" (Jonson)
See *The Under-Wood II*
"On My Songs" (Owen) **102**:151
"On My Son's Return out of England" (Bradstreet) **10**:36, 60
"On My Way Out I Passed over You and the Verrazano Bridge" (Lorde) **12**:138-39
"On Myselfe" (Finch) **21**:146, 155, 165
"On Neal's Ashes" (Ginsberg) **4**:74
"On no work of words" (Thomas) **52**:304

"On Not Being Listened To" (McGuckian) **27**:90
On Nothing (Wilmot)
See *Upon Nothing, A Poem*
"On Obedience" (Duncan) **2**:114
"On Observing Some Names of Little Note in the Biographia Britannica" (Cowper) **40**:124
"On One Month's Reading of English Newspapers" (Corso) **108**:11, 43
"On Open Form" (Merwin) **45**:39
"On Palatine" (Corso) **33**:37
"On Parting with My Wife, Jamina" (Milosz) **8**:211
"On Passing over a Dreary Tract of Country, and near the Ruins of a Deserted Chapel, during a Tempest" (Smith) **104**:165
"On Passing the New Menin Gate" (Sassoon) **12**:246
"On Patience. To Stella" (Leapor) **85**:186
"On Patmos" (Sarton) **39**:341
On Poetry (Char)
See *Sur la poésie*
"On Poetry: A Rhapsody" (Swift) **9**:249
"On Police Brutality" (Walker) **20**:294
"On Ponkawtasset, Since We Took Our Way" (Thoreau) **30**:181, 202, 266
"On Ponkawtasset, since, with such delay" (Thoreau)
See "On Ponkawtasset, Since We Took Our Way"
"On Portents" (Graves) **6**:149, 172-73
"On Poverty" (Duck) **89**:67
"On Prime Ministers" (Belloc) **24**:37
"On Providence" (Duck) **89**:5
"On Rachmaninoff's Birthday #158" (O'Hara) **45**:226
On Radio Waves (Seifert)
See *Na vlnách T. S. F.*
"On Raglan Road" (Kavanagh) **105**:164
"On Reaching Forty" (Angelou) **32**:27
"On Reading a Book of Common Wild Flowers" (Kavanagh) **33**:100, 119, 121
"On Reading an Anthology of Postwar German Poetry" (Mueller) **33**:175, 197
"On Reading an Old Baedeker in Schloss Leopoldskron" (Kumin) **15**:209, 212
"On Reading Christopher Marlowe" (Carducci) **46**:26
"On Reading John Cage" (Paz) **1**:355, 363, 374
"On Reading Omar Khayyam" (Lindsay) **23**:283
"On Reading William Blake's 'The Sick Rose'" (Ginsberg) **4**:55
"On Receiving a Curious Shell" (Keats) **96**:221; **96**:221
"On Recollection" (Wheatley) **3**:332, 340, 361
"On Restless River" (Brown) **55**:112
"On Returning to Detroit" (Forché) **10**:144, 156
"On Richmond Park" (Duck) **89**:28, 67
"On Righteous Indignation" (Chesterton) **28**:114
"On San Gabriel Ridges" (Snyder) **21**:291
"On Sannazar's being honoured with six hundred ducats by the Clarissimi of Venice, for composing an Elegiac Hexastich of the City. A Satire" (Lovelace) **69**:199
"On Sark" (Sarton) **39**:362
"On Scratchbury Camp" (Sassoon) **12**:259
"On Seeing a Piece of Our Artillery Brought into Action" (Owen) **19**:336
"On Seeing a Wounded Hare Limp by Me" (Burns) **114**:101
"On Seeing an Old Poet in the Café Royal" (Betjeman) **75**:22
"On Seeing an X-Ray of my Head" (Wagoner) **33**:328
"On Seeing Diana go Maddddddddd" (Madhubuti) **5**:344
"On Seeing the Elgin Marbles" (Keats) **96**:252
"On Seeing Two Lovers in the Street" (Muir) **49**:245
"On Sickness" (Leapor) **85**:284
"On Sir Voluptuous Beast" (Jonson) **17**:174, 212
"On Skysails" (Masefield) **78**:90
"On Spies" (Jonson)
See "Epigram LIX"
"On Squaw Peak" (Hass) **16**:217
On St. James's Park, as Lately Improved by His Majesty (Waller) **72**:305, 328, 330, 340
"On Stage" (Seferis) **66**:149, 152
"On Stillpoint Hill at Midnight" (Chappell) **105**:42, 62-63
"On Stripping the Bark from Myself" (Walker) **30**:349
"On Sublimity" (Tennyson) **101**:139-40
"On Swimming" (Zagajewski) **27**:396
"On Sylvia Plath" (Carson) **64**:201
"On Teaching the Young" (Winters) **82**:333
"On That Day" (Lawrence) **54**:239, 243
"On the Aisle" (Kenyon) **57**:23, 40
"On the Alliance of Education and Government" (Gray)
See "Essay on the Alliance of Education and Government"
"On the Anniversary of the Founding of Rome" (Carducci)
See "Nell' annuale della fondazione di Roma"
"On the Apothecary's Filling my Bills amongst the Doctors" (Barker) **91**:42
"On the Approaching Birth of a Child to Friends" (Barker) **77**:10
On the Art of Poetry (Horace)
See *Ars Poetica*
"On the Assumption" (Crashaw) **84**:48, 96-99
"On the Asylum Road" (Mew) **107**:6, 19, 48-49, 51
"On the Author of . . . The Way to Health . . ." (Behn) **13**:8
"On the Balcony" (Lawrence) **54**:206-7
"On the Banks o' Deer Crick" (Riley) **48**:334
On the Banks of the River Sar (Castro)
See *En las orillas del Sar*
"On the Battle of Kulikovo Field" (Blok) **21**:8, 26, 29
"On the Beach" (Birney) **52**:15-16, 22, 28, 78
"On the Beach at Fontana" (Joyce) **22**:136
"On the Beach at Night" (Whitman) **3**:401
"On the Beach at Ostia" (Ferlinghetti) **1**:184
"On the Benefit Received by His Majesty from Sea-Bathing in the Year 1789" (Cowper) **40**:98, 120
"On the Birth of a Black/Baby/Boy" (Knight) **14**:43
"On the Bleeding Body of Our Crucified Lord" (Crashaw)
See "The Wounds of our Crucified Lord"
"On the Bleeding Wounds of Our Crucified Lord" (Crashaw)
See "The Wounds of our Crucified Lord"
"On the Blood of the Lord's Circumcision" (Crashaw) **84**:178
On the Boiler (Yeats) **20**:311
"On the Building of Springfield" (Lindsay) **23**:277, 281, 296
"On the Burning of Lord Mansfield's Library" (Cowper) **40**:101
"On the Calculus" (Cunningham) **92**:135, 166
"On the Circumcision" (Crashaw) **84**:178-79
"On the Cliffs" (Swinburne) **24**:313, 315, 317, 319-20, 343
"On the Coming of Arthur" (Masefield) **78**:48, 62
"On the Coming Victory" (Brutus) **24**:117
"On the Cosawattee" (Dickey) **40**:191, 258
"On the Day of the Master's Passion" (Crashaw) **84**:178-79
"On the Death" (Corso) **108**:20
"On the Death of a Favourite Old Spaniel" (Southey) **111**:193
"On the Death of a Justly Admir'd Author" (Leapor) **85**:212, 249, 295
"On the Death of Dr. Robert Levet" (Johnson) **81**:93, 97, 99, 116, 163, 190, 212, 214-16, 218, 235, 237, 239, 241, 247-48
"On the Death of E. Waller, Esq." (Behn) **88**:48, 145-46
"On the Death of Friends in Childhood" (Justice) **64**:272, 278
"On the Death of G. B. Niccolini" (Carducci)
See "In Morte di G. B. Niccolini"
"On the Death of Giovanni Cairoli" (Carducci)
See "In Morte di Giovanni Cairoli"
"On the Death of Joseph DjugashvilialiasStalin" (Melville) **82**:11-12, 39
"On the Death of Little Mahala Ashcraft" (Riley) **48**:334-35
"On the Death of Marschal Keith" (Macpherson) **97**:344
"On the Death of Mr. Crashaw" (Cowley) **90**:53, 153-54
"On the Death of Mr. Grinhil, the Famous Painter" (Behn) **88**:14, 45, 147-48, 151
"On the Death of Mr. Grinhill, the Famous Painter" (Behn) **13**:8
"On the Death of Mr. Richard West" (Gray)
See "Sonnet on the Death of Mr. Richard West"
"On the Death of Mr. William Hervey" (Cowley) **90**:41
"On the Death of Mrs. Throckmorton's Bulfinch" (Cowper) **40**:123, 126-27
"On the Death of My Dear Friend and Play-Fellow, Mrs. E. D. Having Dream'd the night before I heard thereof, that I had lost a Pearl" (Barker) **91**:29
On the Death of Pushkin (Lermontov)
See "Smert' poeta"
"On the Death of Sir W. Russell" (Cowper) **40**:46
"On the Death of the Late Earl of Rochester" (Behn) **13**:8; **88**:31, 48, 70, 79
"On the Death of the Lucky Gent" (Corso) **33**:25, 41
"On the Death of the Noble Prince King Edward the Fourth" (Skelton) **25**:339
"On the Death of the Queen" (Finch) **21**:171-72
"On the Death of the Rev. Mr. George Whitefield" (Wheatley)
See "An Elegiac Poem on the Death of George Whitefield"
"On the Death of the Reverend Dr. Sewall" (Wheatley) **3**:342
"On the Debt My Mother Owed to Sears Roebuck" (Dorn) **115**:54, 83, 120, 163
"On the Decline of Oracles" (Plath) **37**:238, 243
"On The Dedication of Dorothy Hall" (Dunbar) **5**:131, 134
"On the Departure of the Nightingale" (Smith)
See "Sonnet 7"
"On the Departure Platform" (Hardy) **8**:90; **92**:328
"On the Desert" (Crane) **80**:41
"On the Difficulty of Conjuring Up a Dryad" (Plath) **37**:237, 254
"On the Double Ninth Remembering My Brothers" (Wang Wei) **18**:365, 386
"On the Downs" (Chesterton) **28**:98
"On the Downs" (Masefield) **78**:55
"On the Duke of Buckingham" (Carew) **29**:61
"On the Dunes" (Teasdale) **31**:325, 334
"On the Eastern Front" (Trakl)
See "Im Osten"
"On the Edge" (Levine) **22**:212
"On the Edge" (Lorde) **12**:137
On the Edge (Koch) **80**:309
On the Edge (Levine) **22**:211-12, 216
"On the End" (Carson) **64**:200

"On the Escalator" (Zagajewski) **27**:381
"On the Esplanade" (Hardy) **92**:208
On the Eternity of God (Smart)
See *On the Eternity of the Supreme Being*
On the Eternity of the Supreme Being (Smart) **13**:328, 343
"On the Extinction of the Venetian Republic" (Wordsworth) **4**:377
"On the Eyes of an SS Officer" (Wilbur) **51**:250, 317
"On the Fair Weather Just at the Coronation" (Philips) **40**:268, 271, 295, 318
"On the Famous Voyage" (Jonson)
See "Epigram CXXXIII"
"On the Far Edge of Kilmer" (Stern) **115**:277
"On the Farm" (Thomas) **99**:237
"On the Fear of God" (Waller) **72**:362-63
"On the Ferry across Chesapeake Bay" (Bly) **39**:7
"On the Field of Kulikovo" (Blok)
See "On the Battle of Kulikovo Field"
"On the Fields of Marengo" (Carducci)
See "Sui Campi di Marengo"
"On the First Discovery of Falseness in Amintas. By Mrs. B." (Behn) **13**:20-1
"On the First of January 1657" (Philips) **40**:317
"On the Foreclosure of a Mortgage in the Suburbs" (Wright) **36**:390-91
"On the Fragility of Mind" (Eberhart) **76**:23
"On the Glass Ice" (Stafford) **71**:296-97
On the Goodness of the Supreme Being (Smart) **13**:340, 359-60
"On the Grasshopper and Cricket" (Keats) **96**:204, 213
On the Great Atlantic Rainway: Selected Poems, 1950-1988 (Koch) **80**:302, 323
"On the Grecian Room in Princess Zeneida Volkonskaia's House in Moscow" (Mickiewicz)
See "Na pokoj grecki w eomu księżnej Zeneidy Wøkońskiej w Moskwie"
"On the Hall at Stowey" (Tomlinson) **17**:341, 344
"On the Happ Life" (Martial)
See "Vitam quae faciunt beatiorem"
"On the Highest Pillar" (Montale)
See "Sulla colonna più alta"
On the Hill (Masefield) **78**:45, 47, 49, 56, 73, 91, 98
"On the Hill and Grove at Billborow" (Marvell)
See "Upon the Hill and Grove at Billborow"
"On the Honourable Sir Francis Fane . . ." (Behn) **13**:8
"On the Horizon the Peaks Assembled" (Crane) **80**:52
"On the Idle Hill of Summer" (Housman) **2**:185
On the Immensity of the Supreme Being (Smart) **13**:343
"On the Island" (Brutus) **24**:115
"On the Lack of Sleep" (Spark) **72**:264
"On the Lake" (Goethe)
See "Auf dem See"
"On the Last Performance of" (Hongo) **23**:197
"On the Late Capt. Grose's Peregrination thro' Scotland, Collecting the Antiquities of that Kingdom" (Burns) **114**:62
"On the Liberation of Woman" (Wright) **36**:377
"On the London Train" (Berryman) **64**:81
"On the Loss of the Royal George" (Cowper)
See "Lines on the Loss of the Royal George"
"On the Mantelpiece" (Lowell) **13**:83
"On the Millennium" (Waldrop) **109**:143
"On the Monument of Dante to be erected in Florence" (Leopardi)
See "Sopra il monumento di Dante"
"On the Morning of Christ's Nativity" (Milton) **19**:209, 251-54; **29**:212, 214, 229, 232, 238-41, 272
On the Motion and Immobility of Douve (Bonnefoy)
See *Du mouvement et de l'immobilité de Douve*
"On the Mountain" (Amichai) **38**:28
"On the Mountain" (Merwin) **45**:100
"On the Mountain Tops" (Clarke) **112**:62
"On The Move" (Abse) **41**:4
"On the Move" (Gunn) **26**:184-5, 188-9, 196, 200, 202, 206-9
"On the Murder of Lieutenant José Del Castillo by the Falangist Bravo Martinez, July 12, 1936" (Levine) **22**:223, 225
"On the Name of Jesus" (Crashaw) **84**:50
"On the Night Shift" (Hope) **56**:292
"On the Ninth" (Li Po) **29**:185
"On the numerous accesse of the English to waite upong the King in Holland" (Philips) **40**:318
"On the Occasion of National Mourning" (Nemerov) **24**:289
"On the Ocean Floor" (MacDiarmid) **9**:191
On the Omniscience of the Supreme Being (Smart) **13**:344
"On the Orthodoxy and Creed of My Power Mower" (Ciardi) **69**:56
"On the Outskirts of Antioch" (Cavafy) **36**:33, 52, 63
"On the Pechora" (Yevtushenko) **40**:347
"On the Platform" (Nemerov) **24**:262
"On the Plethora of Dryads" (Plath) **37**:237
"On The Portrait of a Beautiful Woman" (Leopardi) **37**:124
On the Power of the Supreme Being (Smart) **13**:344
"On the Present Unhappy Situation of the Queen of France, and Her Son" (Smith) **104**:210
"On the Promotion of Edward Thurlow, Esq. to the Lord High Chancellorship of England" (Cowper) **40**:100
"On the Pulse of Morning" (Angelou) **32**:23-4, 30-2
"On the Queen's Grotto" (Duck) **89**:87, 89
"On the Queen's Visit to London" (Cowper) **40**:98, 120
"On the Question of God's Tolerance" (Dorn) **115**:234
On the Radio Waves (Seifert)
See *Na vlnách T. S. F.*
"On the Republic" (Elytis) **21**:123
"On the Reservations" (Hughes) **89**:146
"On the Resurrection of Christ" (Dunbar) **67**:20
"On the Rhine" (Arnold) **5**:19, 43
"On the River" (Levine) **22**:228
"On the River Adda" (Carducci)
See "Su l'Adda"
"On the River Encountering Waters Like the Sea, I Wrote a Short Poem on the Spot" (Tu Fu) **9**:326
"On the Road" (Heaney) **18**:214
"On the Road" (McKay) **2**:205, 220
"On the Road Again" (Dylan) **37**:51
"On the Road Home" (Stevens) **6**:311-12; **110**:116, 223
"On the Road to Delphi" (Herbert)
See "W drodze do Delf"
"On the Road to Woodlawn" (Roethke) **15**:291, 293-95
"On the Same" (Cowper) **40**:101
On the Scale of One to One (Cassian) **17**:6, 9
"On the Ship" (Cavafy) **36**:75
On the Shore of the World (Paz)
See *A la orilla del mundo*
On the Sick-Bed (Tagore)
See *Rogsajyae*
On the Side of Things (Ponge)
See *Le Parti pris des choses*
"On the Skeleton of a Hound" (Wright) **36**:279, 335-36, 371, 373
"On the Slain Collegians" (Melville) **82**:72, 85, 92, 135, 194
"On the South Coast" (Swinburne) **24**:313, 329
"On the Spring" (Gray)
See "Ode on Spring"
"On the Spur of the Moment" (Tu Fu) **9**:323
"On the Square" (Aleixandre)
See "En la plaza"
"On the Stage of Ghosts a Pale Gleaming" (Mandelstam) **14**:120
"On the Stairs" (Cavafy) **36**:41, 42, 74, 76, 81
"On the Statue of King Charles I" (Waller) **72**:347
"On the Street" (Stone) **53**:257
"On the Subject of Poetry" (Merwin) **45**:92
"On the Subway" (Olds) **22**:314
"On the Sussex Downs" (Teasdale) **31**:333, 379
"On the Tennis Court at Night" (Kinnell) **26**:260
"On the Threshold" (Gozzano) **10**:174
"On the Threshold of His Greatness, the Poet Comes Down with a Sore Throat" (Nemerov) **24**:267
"On the Translation of the House of Loretto" (Crashaw) **84**:168-69
"On the Treatise of Charity" (Crashaw) **84**:32
"On the Verge of the Path" (Guest) **55**:183
"On the Victory Gained by Sir George Rodney" (Cowper) **40**:103
"On the Victory Obtained by Blake over the Spaniards" (Marvell) **10**:270-71
On the Waves of the Wireless (Seiler)
See *Na vlnách T. S. F.*
On the Waves of Wireless Telegraphy (Seifert)
See *Na vlnách T. S. F.*
"On the Way" (Robinson) **1**:468; **35**:368
"On the Way" (Sandburg) **41**:341, 364
"On the Way to Lycomedes of Scyrus" (Brodsky)
See "K Likomedu, na Skiros"
"On the Way to School" (Aleixandre) **15**:24
"On the Wide Heath" (Millay) **6**:215, 232, 238
"On the windshield of a new Fiat for James Klosty (who had not made up his mind where to go) and Carolyn Brown" (Cage) **58**:218
"On the Women about Town" (Wilmot) **66**:320, 329
"On the Works of Providence" (Wheatley)
See "Thoughts on the Works of Providence"
On the World's Shore (Paz)
See *A la orilla del mundo*
On These I Stand: An Anthology of the Best Poems of Countee Cullen (Cullen) **20**:75-76, 79, 82-83
"On These Islands" (MacNeice) **61**:137
On This Island (Auden)
See "Look, Stranger, on This Island Now"
"On Those That Hated 'The Playboy of the Western World'" (Yeats) **20**:320
"On Torture, a Public Singer" (Belloc) **24**:34
"On Translating Poetry" (Herbert)
See "O tlumaczeniu wierszy"
"On Troy" (Herbert) **50**:18
"On Two Ministers of State" (Belloc) **24**:33, 41
"On Universalism" (Knight) **14**:37-8
"On Vacation" (Creeley) **73**:39
"On Virtue" (Wheatley) **3**:361
"On Visiting the Tomb of Burns" (Keats) **1**:314; **96**:283
"On voit" (Jaccottet) **98**:196-99
"On Walking into a Dark Alley" (Ignatow) **34**:274
"On Walking Slowly After an Accident" (Smith) **12**:314, 316
"On Warsaw Critics and Reviewers" (Mickiewicz)
See "O Krytykach i Recenzentach"
"On Watching a World Series Game" (Sanchez) **9**:210, 225
"On Wee Johnie" (Burns) **114**:89
"On Wenlock Edge" (Housman)
"On Wenlock Edge the wood's in trouble" (Housman) **2**:180; **43**:211, 245
"On What He Was" (Masefield) **78**:41

"On Working White Liberals" (Angelou) **32**:28
"On Young Men" (Spender) **71**:219
"Once" (Celan) **10**:97
"Once" (Thomas) **99**:281-82
Once (Walker) **30**:337, 340, 342, 344-47, 349-50, 352-59, 362, 365
Once Again (Tagore)
See *Punascha*
"Once again the metaphor" (Borges)
See "Otra vez la metáfora"
"Once and Again" (Carruth) **10**:91
"the once and future dead" (Clifton) **17**:19
"Once by the Pacific" (Frost) **1**:221
"Once I Pass'd through a Populous City" (Whitman) **91**:306
"Once I Wrote Now and in Other Days" (Amichai) **38**:49
"Once in May" (Levine) **22**:217-18
"Once it was the colour of saying" (Thomas) **52**:264
"Once More At Chartres" (Sarton) **39**:339
"Once More, the Round" (Roethke) **15**:302
"Once There Was a Man" (Crane) **80**:80
"Once, rocking on the edge" (Akhmadulina)
See "Odnazhdy, pokanuvshis' na kraiu"
"Once upanza time" (Quintana) **36**:267
"The Once-in-Passing" (MacNeice) **61**:121-22
"L'Ondine et le pêcheur" (Gautier) **18**:141
"Une" (Éluard) **38**:71, 84
"I" (Joyce) **22**:138, 144, 158, 162, 164, 166, 168
"On-Ej" (Akhmadulina) **43**:62
"The One" (Kavanagh) **33**:64, 120, 138, 162; **105**:96
One (Kinsella) **69**:76, 80, 107, 132, 134, 137
"One and the same" (Paz)
See "Lo idéntico"
"One Art" (Bishop) **3**:62-3, 66-8; **34**:59, 74-75, 82, 102, 109, 134, 141, 146, 148, 161, 185, 187, 193
"One at One with his Desire" (Ammons) **16**:50
"One by One" (Levine) **22**:218
"One Day" (Brooke) **24**:86
"One Day" (Corso) **108**:13
"One Day" (Creeley) **73**:41
The One Day: A Poem in Three Parts (Hall) **70**:14-19, 29-30, 34-39, 45-49
"One Day I'll Sit on the Sidewalk" (Darwish) **86**:27
"One Day in Spring" (Sitwell) **3**:311
"One Day We Play a Game" (Cullen) **20**:67
"One Ear to the Ground" (Wagoner) **33**:334
"187" (Quintana) **36**:275
"One Evening" (Stafford) **71**:375
"One Fond Embrace" (Kinsella) **69**:81-82
One Fond Embrace (Kinsella) **69**:109, 125, 128-32, 134, 136, 138, 140, 142, 146
"One Foot in Eden" (Muir) **49**:196, 261-62, 280
One Foot in Eden (Muir) **49**:208, 215, 225, 233, 235, 250, 253, 270, 273, 277, 280, 290, 295
"One Foot in the River" (Stern) **115**:283
One for the Rose (Levine) **22**:220, 226
"The One Girl at the Boys' Party" (Olds) **22**:311; **42**:163
"One grief of thine" (Bridges) **28**:86
One Handful of Sand (Ishikawa)
See *Ichiaku no suna*
"One Home" (Stafford) **71**:257, 265
"The 151st Psalm" (Shapiro) **25**:285
One Hundred French Poems (Rexroth) **95**:251
One Hundred Poems from the Chinese (Rexroth) **20**:188, 204; **95**:251, 319
One Hundred Poems from the Japanese (Rexroth) **95**:251
100 Selected Poems (Cummings) **5**:86
"164 East 72nd Street" (Merrill) **28**:285
"125th Street" (Hughes) **53**:162
"125th Street and Abomey" (Lorde) **12**:155, 160
"1 Jan." (Ammons) **16**:21
"1 January 1924" (Mandelstam) **14**:121, 134
"One Last Look at the Adige: Verona in the Rain" (Wright) **36**:312, 320
"One Leaf" (Ignatow) **34**:329
"One: Many" (Ammons) **16**:6
"One More" (Carver) **54**:18
"One More Brevity" (Frost) **1**:213
"One More Car Poem for Julie" (Hacker) **47**:107
"One More New Botched Beginning" (Spender) **71**:191, 246
"One More Round" (Angelou) **32**:2
"One More 'S' in the U.S.A." (Hughes) **53**:115
"One More Shiprock Night" (Tapahonso) **65**:225
One More Shiprock Night: Poems (Tapahonso) **65**:221, 240, 256, 258
"One Morning in New Hampshire" (Swenson) **14**:249, 275
"One ne peut me connaître" (Éluard) **38**:73
"One Need Not Be a Chamber to Be Haunted" (Dickinson) **1**:94
"One Night" (Cavafy) **36**:74, 108
"One Night in a Familiar Room" (Ríos) **57**:325
"One Night Stand" (Baraka) **4**:6; **113**:134
"One Night Stand" (Spicer) **78**:302
One Night Stand, and Other Poems (Spicer) **78**:302, 304, 307
"One Night's Bond" (Hagiwara) **18**:168-69
"One O'Clock at Night" (Loy) **16**:312, 327
"One of Many" (Smith) **12**:314, 331, 333
"One of the Bo'sun's Yarns" (Masefield) **78**:70
"One of the Inhabitants of the West" (Stevens) **110**:230
"One of the Rooming Houses" (Doty)
See "One of the Rooming Houses of Heaven"
"One of the Rooming Houses of Heaven" (Doty) **53**:61
"One of Their Gods" (Cavafy) **36**:32, 50, 73, 112
"One of These Nights" (Mahon) **60**:150, 178, 207
"One of Those Springs" (Seifert) **47**:328
"One of Us Must Know (Sooner or Later)" (Dylan) **37**:51
"1.1.87" (Heaney) **18**:258
"One or Two I've Finished" (Stein) **18**:342
"One Perfect Rose" (Parker) **28**:361
"One Person" (Wylie) **23**:304-305, 311, 314, 317-18, 321-24
"One Ralph Blossom Soliloquizes" (Hardy) **8**:124
"One Ran Before" (Winters) **82**:335
"The One Remains" (Owen) **19**:368
"One self" (Jackson) **44**:97
"1 septembre" (Sainte-Beuve) **110**:45, 49
"1 September 1939" (Berryman) **64**:85
"One Should Not Talk to a Skilled Hunter about What is Forbidden by the Buddha" (Snyder) **21**:292
"One Sided Shoot-Out" (Madhubuti) **5**:321, 345
"One Soldier" (Rukeyser) **12**:231
"The One Song" (Strand) **63**:177
"One Spring Day" (Abse) **41**:3, 5, 8
"One Spring Morning" (Niedecker) **42**:164
"One Springtime" (Storni)
See "En una primavera"
"One Stick Song" (Alexie) **53**:20
One Stick Song (Alexie) **53**:23-24
"One Tennis Shoe" (Silverstein) **49**:349
"The One Thing in Life" (Stern) **115**:246
"The One Thing That Can Save America" (Ashbery) **26**:127, 148
"1.31 PM. JUNE 5th. 1970" (Raworth) **107**:275
"One Thousand Fearful Words for Fidel Castro" (Ferlinghetti) **1**:187
1x1 (Cummings) **5**:83, 107-08
One Train (Koch) **80**:302, 318-19, 322, 328
"One Train May Hide Another" (Koch) **80**:318
"One Version of Events" (Szymborska)
See "Wersja wydarzen"
"One Viceroy Resigns" (Kipling) **3**:181, 186
"One View of the Question" (Kipling) **3**:184
"One Volume Missing" (Dove) **6**:114
"One Way" (Thomas) **99**:360
One Way Ticket (Hughes) **1**:241, 243, 247, 252, 260-61, 268; **53**:114, 153, 185
"One We Knew" (Hardy) **8**:99, 132; **92**:254, 317
"One Who Used To Beat His Way" (Kinnell) **26**:240
"The One Who Was" (Aleixandre) **15**:4
One Winter Night in August and Other Nonsense Jingles (Kennedy) **93**:129-30, 133
"One Woman to All Women" (Lawrence) **54**:183
"One Word" (Benn)
See "Ein Wort"
"One Word More" (Browning) **2**:66, 71, 95
"One World" (Tomlinson) **17**:333
"One year" (Illyés)
See "Egy ev"
"One Year" (Olds) **22**:341
"The One-Armed" (Mistral)
See "La manca"
"One-Eye" (Merwin) **45**:28
"One-Eye, Two-Eyes, Three-Eyes" (Sexton) **2**:365
"The One-Eyed King" (Levine) **22**:213
Onegin's Journey (Pushkin) **10**:400-01
"One-Legged Man" (Sassoon) **12**:242, 263
One-Legged on Ice (Abse)
See *Way Out in the Centre*
"The One-Legged stool" (Komunyakaa) **51**:41
"One-Night Homecoming" (Kennedy) **93**:140
"One's-Self I Sing" (Whitman)
See "Song of Myself"
"The One-Year-Old" (Updike) **90**:351
"The Onion" (Szymborska)
See "Cebula"
"Onion Days" (Sandburg) **41**:226, 234, 239, 274, 349, 351, 365
"Onion Fields" (Francis) **34**:244
"Onirocritique" (Apollinaire) **7**:12
"Only a Boche" (Service) **70**:130
"Only a Curl" (Barrett Browning) **6**:24, 30
"Only a Few Left" (Madhubuti) **5**:340
"Only a Little Sleep, a Little Slumber" (Hughes) **7**:154
"The Only Bar in Dixon" (Welch) **62**:346-47, 350, 352, 367-68, 370-71
"The Only Card I Got on My Birthday Was from an Insurance Man" (Stafford) **71**:264
"Only Child" (Page) **12**:170, 175-76
"Only in the Dream" (Eberhart) **76**:34
Only Love (Seifert)
See *Samá láska*
"Only Once I Caught a Glimpse..." (Seifert)
See "Jen jedno jsem spatřil..."
"The Only One" (Hölderlin)
See "Der Einzige"
Only the Soul Knows How to Sing (Das) **43**:93
"Only Those Above 55, Obsessed with Sex" (Das) **43**:84
"Only Years" (Rexroth) **95**:260
"Ons As Me Thought" (Wyatt) **27**:316
"The Onset" (Frost) **1**:222; **39**:233
"Otho the Great" (Keats) **96**:252
"Ontological Episode of the Asylum" (Carruth) **10**:89
"The Oon Olympian" (MacDiarmid) **9**:197
"Oonts" (Kipling) **3**:158
"The Open Boat" (Levine) **22**:223
"Open Books" (Alexie) **53**:24
Open Closed Open (Amichai) **38**:47-51, 54-56
"Open Court" (Kinsella) **69**:82, 145
Open Court (Kinsella) **69**:138, 143, 146
Open Eye, Open Heart (Ferlinghetti) **1**:186-88
"Open House" (Roethke) **15**:291, 293, 302
Open House (Roethke) **15**:245-46, 248, 250, 256, 259, 282, 287, 290-91, 293-95, 298, 304
"Open It, Write" (Ekeloef) **23**:62, 64

"An Open Letter to George Bush" (Quintana) **36**:272
"Open Rose" (McGuckian) **27**:105
"The Open Sea" (Meredith) **28**:182, 190, 212
"Open Sea" (Neruda) **4**:282
The Open Sea (Masters) **1**:333, 335
The Open Sea (Meredith) **28**:171, 174-75, 177, 181, 187-92, 194, 200-01, 210-11, 213, 215
"Open the Door to Me, O" (Burns) **6**:75
"Open the Gate" (Corso) **108**:24
"Open the Gates" (Kunitz) **19**:155, 162, 173-74, 176-77, 186
"Open to Huge Light" (Hughes) **89**:122
"Open Windows" (Hacker) **47**:81
Opened Ground: Selected Poems, 1966-1996 (Heaney) **100**:261, 266, 275-78, 297, 342-43, 351
The Opening of the Field (Duncan) **2**:103-04, 106, 113-14, 120, 122, 124-25, 127-28; **75**:125, 149-50, 152, 157, 160-62, 164, 167-71, 180-82, 187-88, 192, 203-4, 226, 229-30, 255, 257-58, 260-61
Opening the Hand (Merwin) **45**:97
"The Opening World" (Betjeman) **75**:25
Openings (Berry) **28**:5, 15-16
"L'Opera di Dante" (Carducci) **46**:55
"An Opera House" (Lowell) **13**:79
"The Operation" (Creeley) **73**:41, 122
"The Operation" (Sexton) **2**:348, 350, 353, 361, 365; **79**:258
"The Operation" (Snodgrass) **74**:285, 301, 312
"The Operation" (Tomlinson) **17**:360
"Operation Bootstrap: San Juan, 1985" (Espada) **74**:117, 152
"Das Opfer" (Werfel) **101**:331
"Ophelia" (Hughes) **89**:135
"Ophélie" (Rimbaud) **3**:283; **57**:255, 283
"Opiário" (Pessoa) **20**:166
"An Opinion on a Matter of Public Safety" (Dorn) **115**:160
"Opinions politiques de Shakespeare" (Ponge) **107**:142
"Opium and Hitler" (Cohen) **109**:89
Opposites (Wilbur) **51**:243
"Opposition" (Lanier) **50**:56
"Oppositions" (Wright) **14**:379
"Oppositions debate with Mallarmé" (Tomlinson) **17**:338-39
"Oppression" (Hughes) **53**:149
"oppressive chains" (Alurista)
See "Cadenas rotas"
"An Oppressive Climate, a Populous Neighbourhood" (Curnow) **48**:45-46
"Opredelenyie poezii" (Pasternak) **6**:272, 285
"The Optimist's Salutation" (Darío)
See "Salutación del optimista"
"Opulence" (Eberhart) **76**:71-73
"Opulence" (Graham) **59**:150, 177, 182-83
"Opus Dei" (Berryman) **64**:119
Opus incertum (Ekeloef) **23**:63, 76
Opus incertum II (Ekeloef) **23**:77
Opus Posthumous (Stevens) **6**:306, 339; **110**:90-93, 95, 126-27, 152-53, 155, 159, 161, 169-71, 173-75, 177, 191, 200-201, 203-4, 227, 230
"Òpyt análiza chetyryokhstópnogo yàmba" (Bely) **11**:18
"... Or a Wind" (Birney) **52**:39
Or Else: Poem/Poems, 1968-1974 (Warren) **37**:308, 329, 333, 335, 347, 356, 366, 378, 380
"Or, Solitude" (Davie) **29**:122-24
"Or suis je vers vous venu" (Christine de Pizan) **68**:191
"Or When Your Sister Sleeps Around for Money" (Knight)
See "The Violent Space (or when your sister sleeps around for money)"
"Oración" (Fuertes) **27**:5, 11, 30
"Oracion" (Neruda) **4**:278
"La oración de la maestra" (Mistral) **32**:208
"Oración para altas horas de la madrugada" (Fuertes) **27**:39
Oracion por Marilyn Monroe y otros poemas (Cardenal) **22**:125
"Oracle" (Heaney) **18**:201, 203; **100**:196, 199, 295, 337
"The Oracle" (Merton) **10**:339
"Oracle over Managua" (Cardenal)
See "Oráculo sobre Managua"
"The Oracles" (Housman) **2**:164
"Les oracles" (Vigny) **26**:369, 403, 405
"Oráculo sobre Managua" (Cardenal) **22**:103-06
"Oraculos" (Cardenal) **22**:131
"Oraison du soir" (Rimbaud) **57**:174, 209-10, 245, 253, 295, 299
"The Oral Tradition" (Boland) **58**:48, 92, 95
Oral Tradition (Sikelianos)
See "Agraphon"
"L'orange" (Ponge) **107**:101, 116, 130, 137, 169
"An Orange Clock" (Berrigan) **103**:5
"Orange Drums, Tyrone, 1966" (Heaney) **100**:225, 267
"Orange In" (Stein) **18**:318, 328
"Orange of Midsummer" (Lowell) **13**:97
"The Orange Picker" (Ignatow) **34**:273, 284
"Orange Poem Praising Brown" (Stone) **53**:229
"The Orange Tree" (Levertov) **11**:169
"Orangerie" (Bonnefoy) **58**:130
"Oranges" (Cervantes) **35**:119
"Oranges" (O'Hara) **45**:116, 130, 156, 177, 224
"Oranges: 12 Pastorals" (O'Hara)
See "Oranges"
"Orange-Tree" (Wright) **14**:341
"Oration" (Ciardi) **69**:12
"Oration on Death" (Bryant) **20**:13
The Orators: An English Study (Auden) **1**:4-5, 8-11, 16, 22, 25, 30-31, 37
"The Orb Weaver" (Francis) **34**:242, 250, 257, 261-62
The Orb Weaver (Francis) **34**:243, 245, 248, 265
"Orbits" (Cassian) **17**:11
"Orchard" (Eberhart) **76**:5-6, 42, 50, 58, 63-64
"Orchard" (H. D.)
See "Priapus"
"Orchard" (Stone) **53**:216-17
"The Orchard of the Dreaming Pigs" (Wagoner) **33**:350
"The Orchard Pit" (Rossetti) **44**:237
"Orchestra (Donne) **43**:137
"The Orchid House" (McGuckian) **27**:97
The Order of Nature (Bryant) **20**:5
"An Order Prescribed by I. W. to Two of Her Younger Sisters Serving in London" (Whitney)
See "A Modest Meane for Maides"
"Order to View" (MacNeice) **61**:139
"Orders" (Duncan) **2**:125; **75**:117, 232, 271, 273-76
"The Ordinariness of the Soul" (Herbert)
See "Codziennosc duszy"
"The Ordinary" (Stryk) **27**:208, 214
"An Ordinary Evening in New Haven" (Stevens) **6**:338; **110**:152-53, 161, 173, 176, 227, 229, 232
"An Ordinary Girl" (Sirkis) **8**:417
"An Ordinary Morning" (Levine) **22**:224
An Ordinary Woman (Clifton) **17**:21, 23-24, 26, 34, 37
"Ordinary Women" (Stevens) **6**:295
Ordinary Words (Stone) **53**:239, 243-49, 252, 255, 259
"The Ordination" (Burns) **6**:83, 88
L'Ordre des Oiseaux (Perse) **23**:254, 256
"Ore calanti I, II, III" (Zanzotto) **65**:291
"Oread" (H. D.) **5**:268, 275, 304
"Gli orecchini" (Montale) **13**:108, 128
"Oregon" (Kaufman) **74**:214, 217-19, 249
An Oregon Message (Stafford) **71**:322, 324, 329, 333-34, 349-50, 371, 378
"Una oreja" (Storni)
See "La oreja"
"La oreja" (Storni) **33**:240, 259, 262
"Orestes at Tauris" (Jarrell) **41**:135
"Orestes-Theme" (H. D.) **5**:305
"Orfeo" (Spicer) **78**:256-57, 271, 354
"The Organ-Blower" (Holmes) **71**:68
"Organelle" (Swenson) **14**:247
"Organic Bloom" (Kunitz) **19**:148
"Organic Philosophy" (Rexroth)
See "Toward an Organic Philosophy"
"Organization Men in Affluent Society" (Rexroth) **95**:255-56
"Organo ad Libitum" (Curnow) **48**:12, 19, 52-53
"Organon" (Rexroth) **95**:262
"Organs" (Swenson) **14**:276
"L'orgie Parisienne; ou, Paris se Repeuple" (Rimbaud) **3**:281; **57**:202, 205-6, 208, 210, 246
"Orgueil du soir" (Mallarmé)
See "Tout Orgueil fume-t-il du soir"
"Oriana" (Tennyson)
See "The Ballad of Oriana"
"The Orient" (Borges) **32**:58
"Orient and Immortal Wheat" (Walcott) **46**:247
"The Orient Express" (Jarrell) **41**:139, 153, 177, 196, 208
"The Oriental Ballerina" (Dove) **6**:113
Oriental Eclogues (Collins)
See *Persian Eclogues*
"Oriental Maxims" (Whittier) **93**:187
"Oriental phase" (Ungaretti)
See "Fase d'oriente"
"Oriental Politics" (Enright) **93**:15
Les orientales (Hugo) **17**:45, 50-52, 55, 62-63, 70, 74-76, 87, 90-91
Orientations (Elytis)
See *Prosanatolizmí*
"Origin" (Harjo) **27**:64
An Origin Like Water: Collected Poems 1967-1987 (Boland) **58**:42, 48, 91-92, 98-99
"The Origin of Centaurs" (Hecht) **70**:91
"The Origin of Cities" (Hass) **16**:199
"The Origin of Laughter" (Updike) **90**:356
"Origin of the Haiku" (Enright) **93**:27
"Original Child Bomb" (Merton) **10**:337
"Original Memory" (Harjo) **27**:68
"The Original Place" (Muir) **49**:265
"Original Sin" (Cisneros) **52**:141
"Original Sin" (Cunningham) **92**:191
"Original Sin" (Jeffers) **17**:132
"Original Sin" (O'Hara) **45**:162
"Original Sin: A Short Story" (Warren) **37**:285, 287-88, 313, 322-23, 332-33
"Original Sin on the Sussex Coast" (Betjeman) **75**:26
"The Originators" (Merton) **10**:345
"Origins" (Ignatow) **34**:204
"Origins" (Stafford) **71**:298, 336
"Origins and History of Consciousness" (Rich) **5**:374
"O'Riley's Late-Bloomed Little Son" (Kennedy) **93**:139
Orillas (Castro)
See *En las orillas del Sar*
Orillas del Sar (Castro)
See *En las orillas del Sar*
"Orinda to Lucasia" (Philips) **40**:312, 325
"Orinda Upon Little Hector Philips" (Philips) **40**:293, 296
"Orion" (Cohen) **109**:25
"Orion" (Elytis) **21**:118
Orlando furioso di Ludovico Ariosto de Ferrara (Ariosto) **42**:3-4, 7, 8, 9-15, 17-22, 24-5, 27, 29-43, 45, 47-58, 60-4, 73-5, 81, 85-7
"Orlovu" (Pushkin) **10**:409
"Ormai" (Zanzotto) **65**:274
"Ornamentations" (Blunden) **66**:18, 24

"Ornières" (Rimbaud) **3**:264; **57**:232, 238, 241, 247, 282, 284
El oro de los tigres (Borges) **22**:79-81, 93, 95; **32**:52, 56, 61, 63, 65-6, 86, 89-91
"Orophernes" (Cavafy) **36**:73, 75
"Une oroyson de la vie et passion de Nostre Seigneur" (Christine de Pizan) **68**:62-63
"Orozco's Christ" (Erdrich) **52**:190
The Orphan Angel (Wylie) **23**:329
"The Orphan Reformed" (Smith) **12**:326
"Orphans' New Year's Gifts" (Rimbaud)
See "Les étrennes des orphelins"
"L'Orphée" (Ronsard) **11**:251
"Orphée" (Valéry) **9**:351
"L'orphelin" (Mallarmé) **4**:202
"Orpheus" (Hope) **56**:292
"Orpheus" (Meredith) **28**:191-92
"Orpheus" (Snodgrass) **74**:284-85, 298-301
Orpheus (Hope) **56**:290-92
Orpheus (Rukeyser) **12**:207, 213-14, 220
"Orpheus and Eurydice" (Graham) **59**:173
"Orpheus and Eurydice" (Noyes) **27**:118, 134
"Orpheus and Eurydice" (Shvarts) **50**:142
Orpheus and Eurydice (Henryson)
See *Here Begynnis the Traitie of Orpheus Kyng . . .*
"Orpheus' Dream" (Muir) **49**:280
"Orpheus. Eurydike. Hermes" (Rilke) **2**:295
"Orpheus in Hell" (Spicer) **78**:256-57, 296
"Orpheus to Beasts" (Lovelace) **69**:234
"Orphic Scenario" (Nemerov) **24**:257, 294-97
Orphide and Other Poems (Clarke) **112**:76
"Orphische Zellen" (Benn) **35**:70
"L'orto" (Montale) **13**:109-10, 113, 121-22, 133, 151
Orts (Hughes) **89**:124, 129-30
"Orts #3" (Hughes) **89**:129
"Orts #5" (Hughes) **89**:130
"Orts #6" (Hughes) **89**:130
"Orts #7" (Hughes) **89**:130
"Orts #9" (Hughes) **89**:130
"Orts #11" (Hughes) **89**:130
"Orts #19" (Hughes) **89**:130
"Orts #23" (Hughes) **89**:130
"Oscillation" (Paz)
See "Vaivén"
"Osen' v Taruse" (Akhmadulina) **43**:18
"Osgar" (Pushkin) **10**:407
"Osiris and Set" (Duncan) **2**:103; **75**:195, 197
"Osiris, Come to Iris" (Thomas) **2**:402
Osiris Jones (Aiken) **26**:12, 29
Osm dnů (Seifert) **47**:325, 334
"Osobny zeszyt" (Milosz) **8**:186-87, 199, 204
Osorio (Coleridge)
See *Remorse*
"Ospreys in Cry" (Eberhart) **76**:49, 59
Ossi di seppia (Montale) **13**:103, 105-07, 109, 112-17, 119, 122, 126-27, 131, 133-34, 139, 141, 143, 160, 162-66
"Ossian" (Masefield) **78**:41
"Ossian's Grave" (Jeffers) **17**:117
"Ostanovka v pustyne" (Brodsky) **9**:3, 5, 7
"Osterinsel" (Benn) **35**:8, 33, 35, 36, 49, 50, 73, 74, 75, 76, 77
"L'ostessa di Gaby" (Carducci) **46**:88
"Ostia Antica" (Hecht) **70**:97
"Ostriches & Grandmothers" (Baraka) **4**:15; **113**:96
"osynlig närvaro" (Ekeloef) **23**:88-92
"The Other" (Borges)
See "El otro, el mismo"
"The Other" (Dickey) **40**:175, 184, 204-6, 210
"The Other" (Hughes) **89**:190
"The Other" (Sexton) **2**:365; **79**:216-17
"Other" (Stone) **53**:222-23
"The Other" (Thomas) **53**:269, 297, 305, 308-9, 322, 329, 337; **99**:257, 295-96
"The Other" (Wagoner) **33**:357
"The Other Alamo" (Espada) **74**:138
"Other Countries" (Cisneros) **52**:153, 161
"Other Days (1900-1910)" (Sandburg) **41**:227
"The Other Dublin" (Melville) **82**:35, 38
Other Exiles (Brathwaite) **56**:34, 36, 49, 65, 88
"The Other Friend" (Storni)
See "La otra amiga"
The Other Half (Wright) **14**:349, 355-56, 362, 366
"The other, himself" (Borges)
See "El otro, el mismo"
"An Other Letter Sent to IS. W." (Whitney) **116**:290
"The Other Noah" (Elytis) **21**:123
"The Other Oedipus" (Muir) **49**:235, 278
"The Other One" (Borges)
See "El otro, el mismo"
"The Other One" (Mistral)
See "La otra"
"Other people" (Zanzotto)
See "Altri papaveri"
Other Poems (Meynell) **112**:159, 171-72, 191, 295, 301
"Other Poetry Bed" (Koch) **80**:342
"The Other Side" (Heaney) **18**:205; **100**:198-99, 297, 353
Other Skies (Ciardi) **69**:3, 5-6, 25-27, 29, 49-50
The other, the same (Borges)
See *El otro, el mismo*
"The Other Tiger" (Borges)
See "El otro tigre"
"Other Times Have Come" (Yevtushenko) **40**:347
"Other Travellers to the River" (Merwin) **45**:45
"The Other Whitman" (Borges)
See "El otro Whitman"
"Other Yellow Tulips" (Cernuda)
See "Otros tulipanes amarillos"
"Others" (Guest) **55**:200-201
"Others I Am Not the First" (Housman) **2**:179, 195
"Otherwise" (Kenyon) **57**:12, 18, 34, 38, 40-41
"Otherwise" (Stone) **53**:252
Otherwise (Kenyon) **57**:12-13, 15-16, 18-19, 21, 25-26, 28, 34, 38, 41, 44-46
Otho the Great (Keats) **1**:279
Otkuda vy? (Yevtushenko) **40**:364
"Otoño" (Neruda) **4**:290
"Otoño" (Paz) **48**:176
El otoño (Guillén) **35**:231
"El otoño: isla" (Guillén) **35**:153, 156, 157, 182
"La otra" (Mistral) **32**:183
"La otra amiga" (Storni) **33**:245
"Otra vez la metáfora" (Borges) **32**:125
"Otro Cementerio" (Cernuda) **62**:197
"El otro, el mismo" (Borges) **22**:74
El otro, el mismo (Borges) **22**:71, 73-4, 95-6, 98, 100; **32**:38-40, 56, 58, 64-6, 69, 93, 95, 111, 117, 139
"Otro poema de los dones" (Borges) **32**:38
"El otro tigre" (Borges) **22**:73, 96-7; **32**:43, 66, 139
"El otro Whitman" (Borges) **32**:100
"Otrok" (Tsvetaeva) **14**:315-16
"Otros tulipanes amarillos" (Cernuda) **62**:180
"Otryvok" (Akhmadulina) **43**:62
"Otryvok-A Fragment" (Lermontov) **18**:302
"The Otter" (Heaney) **18**:217, 239, 245; **100**:321
"An Otter" (Hughes) **7**:136, 140
"Où es-tu" (Péret) **33**:207-08, 215
"Là où retombe la flèche" (Bonnefoy) **58**:150
"L'Ouest derrière soi perdu" (Char) **56**:155
"Ougadougou" (Brathwaite) **56**:29, 85
"Ouija" (Hughes) **89**:246
"Ouija" (Plath) **37**:208-10, 213, 236
"Our Bodies" (Levertov) **11**:169
"Our Bog Is Dood" (Smith) **12**:331, 333
"our bread" (Alurista)
See "el pan nuestro"
"Our Cabal" (Behn) **13**:7, 20; **88**:22, 39, 139, 147-48, 150, 152
"Our Camp" (Dorn) **115**:125
"Our City Is Guarded by Automatic Rockets" (Stafford) **71**:293, 329
"Our Cottage" (Hunt) **73**:154
"Our Country" (Thoreau) **30**:287
"Our Countrymen in Chains!" (Whittier) **93**:239
Our Dead Behind Us (Lorde) **12**:137-39, 141-43, 148, 154-55, 157-58
"Our Dead Singer" (Holmes) **71**:96
"Our Dear Mother" (Very) **86**:53
"Our English Friends" (Harper) **21**:198
"Our Father" (Parra)
See "Padre nuestro"
"Our Forefathers Literary" (Birney) **52**:28
"Our Forward Shadows" (Swenson) **14**:276
"Our Friends in Jail" (Bissett) **14**:7
"Our Government-in-Exile" (Cohen) **109**:25
"Our Grandmothers" (Angelou) **32**:28
Our Ground Time Here Will Be Brief (Kumin) **15**:214, 217, 221
"Our Hearts" (Koch) **80**:290-91
"Our Home Is in the Rocks" (Rexroth) **95**:249
"Our Insufficiency to Praise God Suitably, for his Mercy" (Taylor) **63**:283
"Our Kind" (Stafford) **71**:378
"Our Kind of a Man" (Riley) **48**:301
"Our Lady of the Rocks" (Rossetti) **44**:172, 214
"Our Lady of the Sackcloth" (Kipling) **3**:183
"Our Lady of the Snows" (Kipling) **91**:64-65, 89-90, 142
"Our Lady of the Snows" (Stevenson) **84**:325
"Our Lady of Youghal" (Ní Chuilleanáin) **34**:383
"Our Land" (Hughes) **53**:84
"Our Long Sweet Sommers Day" (Raleigh) **31**:238-39
"Our Lord and Our Lady" (Belloc) **24**:5
"Our Lord in his Circumcision to His Father" (Crashaw) **84**:48
"Our Love Was Incorruptible" (Clarke) **112**:125
"Our Master" (Whittier) **93**:235, 239
"Our Masterpiece is the Private Life" (Strand) **63**:183-84, 186, 188-89
"Our Mother" (Kinsella) **69**:83, 99-100
"Our Mother Pocahontas" (Lindsay) **23**:288
"Our Mothers" (Rossetti) **7**:286
"Our Mothers Depart" (Yevtushenko) **40**:343
"Our Names" (Ortiz) **17**:245
"Our Need" (Walker) **20**:283
"Our Old Friend Dualism" (Hardy) **92**:205
"Our People" (Stafford) **71**:264
"Our Prayer of Thanks" (Sandburg) **2**:316; **41**:334
"Our Storm" (Pasternak) **6**:271
"Our Sun" (Seferis) **66**:99, 165, 209-10
"Our Times" (Ciardi) **69**:32
"Our Whole Life" (Rich) **5**:391
"Ourselves or Nothing" (Forché) **10**:137, 143-44, 148, 154, 158-59, 161, 168
"Ourselves We Do Inter with Sweet Derision" (Dickinson) **1**:102
"Out" (Hughes) **7**:123, 149; **89**:99, 102
"Out in the Dark" (Thomas) **53**:271-72, 274, 309, 349
"Out Is Out" (Nash) **21**:268
"Out of a Sudden" (Raworth) **107**:338-43
"Out of Debt" (McKay) **2**:222
Out of Ireland (Kinsella) **69**:126, 134
"Out of My Head" (Swenson) **14**:255, 266, 282
"Out of my soules deapth" (Campion) **87**:55, 65
"Out of Stupidity" (Seferis) **66**:200, 203
"Out of Superstition" (Pasternak)
See "From Superstition"
"Out of the Aegean" (Elytis) **21**:118
"Out of the Bag" (Heaney) **100**:238, 320
"Out of the Black" (Duncan) **75**:188
"Out of the Cradle" (Hall) **70**:9
"Out of the Cradle Endlessly Rocking" (Whitman) **3**:378, 382, 391-92, 397, 401; **91**:207, 278-79, 309, 312, 314, 317-19, 321-22
"Out of the Hills" (Thomas) **99**:240-41
"Out of the Land of Heaven" (Cohen)

109:56-57
"Out of the Picture" (Raworth) **107**:307, 342
"Out of the Rainbow End" (Sandburg) **41**:303
"Out of the Sea, Early" (Swenson) **14**:264
"Out of the Sighs" (Thomas) **52**:228
"Out of the Watercolored Window, When You Look" (Schwartz) **8**:301
"Out of Three of four in a Room" (Amichai) **38**:42
"Out of Work" (Hughes) **53**:139-40
"Out on the Lawn I Lie in Bed..." (Auden) **1**:22
"OUT ON THE TOWN JOY RIDIN" (Bissett) **14**:31
"Out, Out—" (Frost) **1**:227
"Out Picking Up Corn" (Bly) **39**:87
"Out the Alley Our Soul Awaits Us" (Alurista) **34**:40
"Out to Old Aunt Mary's" (Riley) **48**:328, 336
"Out to the Hard Road" (Lorde) **12**:138
"Out Upon It" (Suckling) **30**:137, 156
"Out Walking" (Zagajewski) **27**:396
"Out West" (Stafford) **71**:328
"Outbound" (Carman) **34**:213
"Outcast" (McKay) **2**:213, 217, 221
The Outcasts (Sitwell) **3**:321
"The Outcome of Mr. Buck's Superstition" (Nash) **21**:267
"The Outcome of the Matter: The Sun" (Piercy) **29**:326
"The Outdoor Concert" (Gunn) **26**:195, 208
Outdoor Show (Cassian) **17**:6
"Outer and Inner" (Meredith) **60**:298
"The Outer Banks" (Rukeyser) **12**:224
"Outer Egypt" (Mackey) **49**:4
"Outgoing, Incoming" (Eberhart) **76**:54
Outlantish (Mackey) **49**:17
"The Outlaw" (Heaney) **18**:200; **100**:263
"The Outlaw" (Whittier) **93**:201
Outline of the Air (Cernuda)
See *Perfil del aire*
"Outlines" (Lorde) **12**:137
"Outrance Outrage" (Zanzotto)
See "Oltranza oltraggio"
"Outside" (Stafford) **71**:297, 334
"Outside a Dirtroad Trailer" (Simic) **69**:287, 319
"Outside a Gate" (Lowell) **13**:94
"Outside Armagh Jail, 1971" (Montague) **106**:314, 327
"Outside Eden" (Muir) **49**:264
"Outside Fargo, North Dakota" (Wright) **36**:300, 344
"Outside History" (Boland) **58**:8, 17, 48, 51, 55-56, 59, 61, 82, 85, 87
Outside History: Selected Poems, 1980-90 (Boland) **58**:8, 12-21, 26, 29-30, 33, 47-49, 51, 67, 84-85, 87-89, 91-92, 96, 98
"Outside my window" (Viereck) **27**:278
"Outside of Wedlock" (Stevens) **110**:95
"Outside or Underneath?" (Silverstein) **49**:332
"outside, over there" (Alurista)
See "allá ajüera"
"Outside the Crowd" (Meredith) **60**:263
"Outside the Diner" (Gunn) **26**:214
"Outside the Gates" (Goodison) **36**:154
"Outside the House" (Cavafy) **36**:74
"Outside the Monastery of Bologna" (Carducci)
See "Furi alla Certosa di Bologna"
"Outside the Operating Room of the Sex-Change Doctor" (Olds) **22**:316
"The Outskirts of the Capital" (Mickiewicz) **38**:168
"L'Ouverture ancienne" (Mallarmé) **102**:19-21, 23
"Ouvriers" (Rimbaud) **57**:241, 243, 275
"Ovando" (Hugo) **68**:250
"Ovation for Spring" (Spender) **71**:178, 215
"Oveja descarriada" (Storni) **33**:274
"The Oven Bird" (Frost) **1**:222; **39**:253
"Ovenstone" (Guillén) **23**:102
"Over 2,000 Illustrations and a Complete Concordance" (Bishop) **3**:67; **34**:54, 78, 97, 108, 113, 187
Over All the Obscene Boundaries: European Poems & Transitions (Ferlinghetti) **1**:183-85
"Over Brooklyn Bridge" (Tomlinson) **17**:359
"Over Cities" (Milosz) **8**:186
"Over Denver Again" (Ginsberg) **4**:57
"Over Sir John's Hill" (Thomas) **2**:395, 404; **52**:224, 259, 266-67, 270, 274-76, 316-17
"Over St. John's Hill" (Thomas)
See "Over Sir John's Hill"
"Over the Hills" (Schuyler) **88**:190
"Over the Sea to Skye" (Stevenson) **84**:332
"Over the Water to Ch______lie" (Burns) **114**:164
"Over these brookes" (Sidney) **32**:266
"Over Troubled Water" (Sarton) **39**:363
"Over Us If (as what Was Dusk Becomes" (Cummings) **5**:109
"Overcrowding" (Baca) **41**:38
"Overdues" (Silverstein) **49**:333
"The Overgrown Pasture" (Lowell) **13**:60, 78, 85
"Overheard" (Kipling) **3**:193
"Overheard" (Levertov) **11**:160
"Overheard in the Louvre" (Kennedy) **93**:138
"The Over-Heart" (Whittier) **93**:188
"Overland to the Islands" (Levertov) **11**:188, 192, 196
Overland to the Islands (Levertov) **11**:166, 188, 202
"Overlooking the River Stour" (Hardy) **8**:116-17
"Overnights" (Walker) **30**:343
"Overpopulation" (Ferlinghetti) **1**:167, 175, 187
"Overture to a Dance of Locomotives" (Williams) **7**:345, 410
"Overtures to Death" (Day Lewis) **11**:144
Overtures to Death and Other Poems (Day Lewis) **11**:127-30, 144
"Ovid in Exile" (Graves) **6**:164
"Ovid in Tomis" (Mahon) **60**:146, 151, 178, 188, 196-97
"Ovid, Old Buddy, I Would Discourse with You a While" (Carruth) **10**:88
"Ovid to Julia. A Letter, by an unknown Hand" (Behn) **88**:72
Ovids Banquet of Sense. A Coronet for His Mistresse Philosophie, and His Amorous Zodiacke. With a Translation of a Latine Coppie, Written by a Fryer, Anno Dom. 1400 (Chapman) **96**:16-17, 19-22, 24-26, 32-35, 41-42, 46-48, 55, 66-67, 74, 77-79, 112-15, 122-24, 131-32
Ovnis (Cardenal)
See *Los ovnis de oro*
Los ovnis de oro (Cardenal) **22**:126, 132
"Owatari Bridge" (Hagiwara)
See "Ōwatari-bashi"
"Ōwatari-bashi" (Hagiwara) **18**:183
"Owen Ahern and His Dancers" (Yeats) **20**:328
"The Owl" (Hughes) **89**:162, 178
"Owl" (Stafford) **71**:288-89
"The Owl" (Thomas) **53**:295, 317, 320
"The Owl and the Pussycat" (Lear) **65**:144, 147-49, 151-52, 156-57, 165
"The Owl in the Sarcophagus" (Stevens) **6**:304; **110**:226, 229
"The Owl King" (Dickey) **40**:149-50, 155-56, 163-64, 166, 176-77, 180-81, 183, 185, 190, 201, 230
"Owl Song" (Atwood) **8**:25
Owls and Other Fantasies (Oliver) **75**:334
Owl's Clover (Stevens) **6**:297-98, 317-20; **110**:137, 150, 156, 190, 226
"Owl's Song" (Hughes) **7**:160-61; **89**:142
"Ownership" (Reese) **29**:336, 344
"Owning" (Hughes) **89**:235
"Owning Everything" (Cohen) **109**:4
"The Ox" (Carducci)
See "Il bove"
"Ox Cart Man" (Hall) **70**:7-8, 15, 17, 19, 28, 34, 39-40, 45
"The Ox Tamer" (Whitman) **3**:377
"The Oxen" (Hardy) **8**:112, 121; **92**:227, 274, 290
"Oxen: Ploughing at Fiesole" (Tomlinson) **17**:311
"Oxford" (Auden) **1**:30; **92**:74-75, 77-79
"Oxford" (Dorn) **115**:54, 57, 108, 113-14, 123
"Oxford: Sudden Illness at the Bus-Stop" (Betjeman) **75**:28
Oxota: A Short Russian Novel (Hejinian) **108**:267, 307, 310, 315-16
"Oysters" (Heaney) **18**:217, 239, 241
"Oysters" (Sexton) **2**:365; **79**:207, 209-10
"Oysters" (Snyder) **21**:292
"Oznob" (Akhmadulina) **43**:13-15, 18, 61, 65
Oznob. Izbrannye proizvedeniia (Akhmadulina) **43**:33, 41
"Ozone" (Dove) **6**:121-23
"P. N. in the heart" (Paz)
See "Pablo Neruda en el corazón"
"P. P. C." (Wickham) **110**:281
"Pablo Casals" (MacLeish) **47**:197
"Pablo Neruda" (Clarke) **112**:93
"Pablo Neruda en el corazón" (Paz) **48**:183
"A Pablo Picasso" (Éluard) **38**:71, 86
"Pacchiarotto" (Browning) **2**:63, 71, 75
"Pachuchan Miners" (Birney) **52**:22, 99
"The Pachuco's Wedding" (Quintana) **36**:254
"Pacific Beach" (Rexroth) **95**:254, 274
"Pacific Door" (Birney) **52**:35, 92
"Pacific Epitaphs" (Randall) **86**:285, 289-91, 295, 334
"Pacific Gazer" (Warren) **37**:331
"Pacific Letter" (Ondaatje) **28**:316
"Pacific Sonnets" (Barker) **77**:48
"A Pacific State" (Milosz) **8**:205
"The Pacifist's Song" (Berryman) **64**:79, 86
"A Packet of Letters" (Bogan) **12**:94
"A Pact" (Pound) **95**:80
"A Pact with Faustus" (Chappell) **105**:60
"The Paddiad" (Kavanagh) **33**:62, 74, 79, 86, 95-96, 102, 111, 118; **105**:95, 110, 120, 143, 173
"The Paddock and the Mouse" (Henryson) **65**:17, 26-27, 35, 55, 64, 79-80, 83
"Padre nuestro" (Parra) **39**:272, 301
Paean 8 (Pindar) **19**:396
"Paean to Place: And the Place Was Water" (Niedecker) **42**:96, 99, 104-5, 132, 137
"Paesaggio I" (Pavese) **13**:204, 212, 220, 225-26
"Paesaggio II" (Pavese) **13**:212
"Paesaggio III" (Pavese) **13**:212
"Paesaggio V" (Pavese) **13**:212
"Paesaggio VI" (Pavese) **13**:228
"Paesaggio VII" (Pavese) **13**:204, 212
"Paesaggio VIII" (Pavese) **13**:212, 230
"Paestum" (Dickey) **40**:254
"The Pagan Isms" (McKay) **2**:219-20
"Pagan Prayer" (Cullen) **20**:65, 72
"Page d'ascendants pour l'an 1964" (Char) **56**:196, 199
"Page Eglantine" (Owen) **102**:149, 227
"Page of Gaspé" (Birney) **52**:21
"The Pageant" (Whittier) **93**:349
A Pageant, and Other Poems (Rossetti) **7**:270
The Pageant of Seasons (Anonymous)
See *Rtusamhāra*
Pages (Mallarmé) **102**:66, 135
"Pages bis" (Ponge) **107**:89, 138
Pages from Parra (Parra)
See *Hojas de Parra*
"Pages: Port Townsend" (Bell) **79**:32
"Pagett, M. P." (Kipling) **3**:190
"La página blanca" (Darío) **15**:103-04
"Página musical" (Storni) **33**:294
"Página para recordaral coronel Suárez, vencedor en Junín" (Borges) **32**:107

Paginas (Jiménez) **7**:208, 212
"The Pahty" (Dunbar) **5**:116, 119, 122-23, 146
Paid on Both Sides (Auden) **1**:5, 8, 20, 30, 34
Paid on Both Sides: A Charade (Auden) **92**:53-54, 61, 101, 113
"The Pail" (Bly) **39**:29
"Le pain" (Ponge) **107**:133, 173, 187, 239, 253
"Pain and Time Strive Not" (Morris) **55**:340
"Pain for a Daughter" (Sexton) **2**:363; **79**:228-29, 231
"Pain Tells You What to Wear" (McGuckian) **27**:103
"The Pains of Sleep" (Coleridge) **11**:41, 44; **39**:164, 170, 176, 179, 224-25
"The Painted Columbine" (Very)
See "To the Painted Columbine"
"The Painted Cup" (Bryant) **20**:23
"Painted Head" (Ransom) **61**:301-3
Painted Lace and Other Pieces (1914-1937) (Stein) **18**:341
"Painted Steps" (Gallagher) **9**:45
"The Painter" (Ashbery) **26**:112, 167
"Painter" (Herbert)
See "Malarz"
"The Painter Dreaming in the Scholar's House" (Nemerov) **24**:285, 300
The Painter Went Poor into the World (Seifert)
See *Šel malíř chudě do světa*
"The Painters" (Kenyon) **57**:45
"Painters of Angels and Seraphim" (Simic) **69**:289-90
"The Painting" (Williams) **7**:394
"Painting the North San Juan School" (Snyder) **21**:300
"The Pair He Saw Pass" (Hardy) **92**:266-67, 277-78
"Pairing Time Anticipated" (Cowper) **40**:124
"PAIS" (Cernuda) **62**:204
"Paisaje" (Parra) **39**:276
"Paisaje de la multitud que orina" (García Lorca) **3**:140
"Paisaje de la multitud que vomita" (García Lorca) **3**:140
"Paisaje del amor muerto" (Storni) **33**:239
"Paisaje del corozon" (Jiménez) **7**:199
"Paisaje después de una batalla" (Neruda) **4**:309
"Paisajes de la Patagonia" (Mistral) **32**:174
"Paisant Chronicle" (Stevens) **110**:82, 85
"La Paix à la campagne" (Éluard) **38**:91
La paix, au Roy (Ronsard) **105**:232-35
"Los Pájaros Anidan" (Fuertes) **27**:51
"Pajaros sin descenso" (Aleixandre) **15**:19-21
"La pajita" (Mistral) **32**:180
"Palabras" (Aleixandre) **15**:39
"Las palabras" (Paz) **1**:358
"Las palabras del poeta" (Aleixandre) **15**:41
"Palabras en el trópico" (Guillén) **23**:106
"Palabras manidas a la luna" (Storni) **33**:295
"Palabras serenas" (Mistral) **32**:159, 174
"Palace" (Apollinaire)
See "Palais"
"The Palace" (Ondaatje) **28**:337
"The Palace of Art" (Tennyson) **6**:353, 359-60, 370, 375, 378-80, 382, 409, 412; **101**:139-40, 142, 144, 281
"The Palace of Humbug" (Carroll) **74**:69
"The Palace of Pan" (Swinburne) **24**:313
"Palace of Pleasure" (Hunt) **73**:134
"Palace of the Babies" (Stevens) **6**:293
"Palais" (Apollinaire) **7**:45-6, 48
"Palais des Arts" (Glück) **16**:130, 150
"Palam" (Das) **43**:85
"Palamon and Arcite" (Chaucer)
See "Knight's Tale"
Palātakā (Tagore) **8**:415
"The Palatine" (Whittier) **93**:247-48
"Palau" (Benn) **35**:8, 33, 35-6, 49-50, 73-7
Palayanam (Das) **43**:84
"A Pale Arrangement of Hands" (Song) **21**:334, 341-42
"Pale Horse" (Hagiwara) **18**:176-77
"Pale, Intent Noontide" (Montale)
See "Meriggiare pallido e assorto"
"The Pale Light" (Montague) **106**:243
"The Pale Panther" (MacNeice) **61**:175
"Pale Tepid Ode" (Justice) **64**:291
"Palec na gubax" (Akhmadulina) **43**:18
The Palfrey (Hunt) **73**:138, 150
"Palimpsest" (Komunyakaa) **51**:63
"Pâline" (Apollinaire) **7**:48
"Palinodia al marchese Gino Capponi" (Leopardi) **37**:92-93, 103, 105
"Palinodie à Denise" (Ronsard) **105**:272
Palinodies (Ronsard) **105**:275
"Palladium" (Arnold) **5**:8
"Pallas Athene" (Masters) **1**:344
"Palm" (Valéry)
See "Palme"
"Palm and Pine" (Kipling) **3**:179
The Palm at the End of the Mind (Stevens) **110**:205-6, 208-9, 212, 215-16
"Palme" (Valéry) **9**:363, 365, 367, 393-94
"Palms, Victory, Triumph, Excellence" (Dorn) **115**:120
"Palm-Sunday" (Vaughan) **81**:306
Palmyra, and Other Poems (Peacock) **87**:307-8, 310, 318-19, 322-26, 328, 330-31, 337, 340-41, 346-49
"Palo Alto: The Marshes" (Hass) **16**:218
"Una paloma" (Storni) **33**:239
La paloma de vuelo popular: Elegiás (Guillén) **23**:100, 124, 128, 133
"Pals" (Sandburg) **2**:303
"The Paltry Nude Starts on a Spring Voyage" (Stevens) **6**:295
"Pamiatnik" (Pushkin)
See "Pamjatnik"
"Pamjatnik" (Pushkin) **10**:408, 412, 415
Pamphilia to Amphilanthus (Wroth) **38**:242-47, 249-51, 254-56, 258-59, 262, 264, 268, 275, 296-300, 304-5, 307-11, 313-19, 324, 328, 332
"Pan" (Hugo) **17**:91
"Pan" (Mistral) **32**:160
"Pan" (Riley) **48**:328
"Pan" (Sikelianos) **29**:369
"Pan and Luna" (Browning) **2**:88-9
"Pan and Thalassius" (Swinburne) **24**:315
Pan Cogito (Herbert) **50**:5, 7, 9, 19-20, 22, 25, 36-37, 39-40, 42
"Pan Cogito a dlugoniecznosc" (Herbert) **50**:36
"Pan Cogito a mysl czysta" (Herbert) **50**:37-38
"Pan Cogito a poeta w pewnym wieku" (Herbert) **50**:41
"Pan Cogito a pop" (Herbert) **50**:39
"Pan Cogito a ruch mysli" (Herbert) **50**:38-39
"Pan Cogito biada nad maloscia snów" (Herbert) **50**:38
"Pan Cogito mysli o powrocie . . ." (Herbert) **50**:37
"Pan Cogito o cnocie" (Herbert) **50**:23, 39
"Pan Cogito o magii" (Herbert) **50**:39
"Pan Cogito o postawie wyprostowanej" (Herbert) **50**:14, 21, 38-39
"Pan Cogito o potrzebie scisloscí" (Herbert) **50**:40
"Pan Cogito obserwuje w lustrze swoja twarz" (Herbert) **50**:37
"Pan Cogito obserwuje zmarlego przjaciela" (Herbert) **50**:39
"Pan Cogito oponiada o kuszeniu Spinozy" (Herbert) **50**:41, 45
"Pan Cogito rozmysla o cierpieniu" (Herbert) **50**:37
"Pan Cogito rozwaza róznice miedzy glosem ludzkim a glosem przyrody" (Herbert) **50**:9
"Pan Cogito szuka rady" (Herbert) **50**:41
"Pan Cogito z Maria Rasputin-Próba Kontaktu" (Herbert) **50**:41
"Pan Cogito-Powrót" (Herbert) **50**:40
"Pan in Vermont" (Kipling) **91**:83
"Pan is Dead" (Barrett Browning)
See "The Dead Pan"
"Pan is Dead" (Pound) **95**:96
"el pan nuestro" (Alurista) **34**:35
Pan Tadeusz; czyli, Ostatni zajazd na Litwie (Mickiewicz) **38**:149, 160-61, 169-71, 180-82, 185-88, 192, 194-203, 205-7, 210, 212-16, 218-20, 231, 233, 237
"Pan with Us" (Frost) **39**:231, 246
"Pana Cogito przygody z muzyka" (Herbert) **50**:40
"Pana/Ramas" (Cruz) **37**:17
"Panamá" (Guillén) **23**:126
"Panchishe vaisakh" (Tagore) **8**:415
"A Panegerick to Sir Lewis Pemberton" (Herrick) **9**:102
"A Panegyrick on the Dean in the Person of a Lady in the North" (Swift) **9**:262, 274, 295
"A Panegyrick to my Lord Protector" (Waller) **72**:289-90, 292-93, 305, 310-11, 313, 315, 354, 360-61
"Panegyrique de la Renommée" (Ronsard) **11**:243
"Pangloss's Song" (Wilbur) **51**:191, 301
"The Pangolin" (Moore) **4**:235; **49**:99, 155, 160
Panic: A Play in Verse (MacLeish) **47**:134, 139-40, 150-51, 241-42, 255
"Panicz i dziewczyna" (Mickiewicz) **38**:153
Panno święta (Mickiewicz) **38**:197
"Panorama" (Éluard) **38**:84
"Panorama" (Guillén) **35**:154
"Panorama" (Whittier) **93**:239, 316-23, 326, 328-30, 343
The Panorama, and Other Poems (Whittier) **93**:266
"Panorama ceigo de Nueva York" (García Lorca) **3**:141
Panoramas (Cruz) **37**:30-1
Pansies (Lawrence) **54**:171, 173, 175, 185-86, 220, 224, 231, 248-49
"La pantera" (Borges) **32**:90
"The panther" (Borges)
See "La pantera"
"Panther" (Hughes) **53**:148
"The Panther" (Hunt) **73**:136
The Panther and the Lash: Poems of Our Times (Hughes) **1**:251-52, 257-58, 260, 262, 268; **53**:94, 110-11, 117, 147-53
"Panther-Ballade" (Werfel) **101**:338-39, 342
"Pantomime" (Verlaine) **2**:430; **32**:348-51, 353, 364, 390
"Paolo e Virginia" (Pavese) **13**:221
"The Papa and Mama Dance" (Sexton) **2**:349, 352-53
"Papà beve sempre" (Pavese) **13**:214
"Papa Love Baby" (Smith) **12**:315, 322, 325-26, 343
"El papagayo" (Mistral) **32**:180
"Papageno" (Snodgrass) **74**:285, 299-300
"Paper and Sticks" (Thomas) **52**:239-40
"Paper Cities" (Schnackenberg) **45**:337-38
"The Paper Cutter" (Ignatow) **34**:273
Paper Money Lyrics, and Other Poems (Peacock) **87**:351
"The Paper Nautilus" (Moore) **4**:255
"The Paper on the Floor" (Bukowski) **18**:3
"Paper Thin Hotel" (Cohen) **109**:69-70
"The Paper Wind Mill" (Lowell) **13**:78
"The Paperweight" (Schnackenberg) **45**:342
"The Paphian Ball" (Hardy) **92**:273-74
"Le papillon" (Lamartine) **16**:278
"Le papillon" (Ponge) **107**:132, 191
Papo Got His Gun (Cruz) **37**:16, 25, 29
"Pappel" (Benn) **35**:49
"Par la bouche de l'engoulevent" (Char) **56**:134
Para las seis cuerdas (Borges) **22**:71; **32**:86-7
"¿Para quién escribo?" (Aleixandre) **15**:41
"Para un mejor amor" (Dalton) **36**:131
"Para una calle del Oeste" (Borges) **32**:39
"Para unos vivir" (Cernuda) **62**:212
"Parable" (Wilbur) **51**:188, 192

"Parable of Cervantes and Don Quixote" (Borges) **32**:66
"Parable of the Hostages" (Glück) **16**:171
"The Parable of the Old Man and the Young" (Owen) **19**:335, 354, 356, 359, 370; **102**:146, 148, 207, 225
"The Parabolic Ballad" (Yevtushenko) **40**:343
Paracelsus (Browning) **2**:26-31, 34, 42-3, 48, 65-6, 73, 82, 91-3, 96
"Parachutes, My Love, Could Carry Us Higher" (Guest) **55**:211, 232
"Parade" (Hughes) **53**:190
"Parade" (Rimbaud) **57**:241, 247, 275, 278, 296
"Parade of Painters" (Swenson) **14**:253
"Parades Parades" (Walcott) **46**:234, 274
"The Paradigm" (Tate) **50**:243
Les paradis artificiels: Opium et haschisch (Baudelaire) **106**:7-8, 66, 151
"Paradis Perdu" (Nishiwaki) **15**:237
"Paradise" (Gallagher) **9**:64
"Paradise" (Glück) **16**:161
"Paradise" (Herbert) **4**:114, 130
"Paradise" (Mistral)
See "Paraíso"
Paradise (Dante)
See *Commedia*
Paradise Illustrated (Enright) **93**:22, 27-28, 36
Paradise Lost (Milton) **19**:193-200, 203-12, 219, 224, 234-36, 238, 240-49, 252, 254, 258; **29**:194-292
"Paradise of Tears" (Bryant) **20**:10
"The Paradise of the Theologians" (Herbert)
See "Raj teologów"
"Paradise on the Roofs" (Pavese) **13**:204
Paradise Poems (Stern) **115**:251-54, 257-58, 261, 263, 265, 268-71, 273, 277, 283-84
Paradise Regain'd (Milton)
See *Paradise Regained*
Paradise Regained (Milton) **19**:204-06, 208, 214-16, 219; **29**:212, 218, 244, 261, 266-68
"Paradise Saved" (Hope) **56**:284
'Paradise': Selected Poems (Shvarts) **50**:140, 146-47
"Paradisiacal Bird" (Barker) **77**:5
Paradiso (Dante) **21**:49-50, 53-5, 57-8, 67, 69, 72, 75-7, 81-2, 92, 94, 96, 103-06, 109-11
"Paradox" (Francis) **34**:258
"A Paradox" (Lovelace) **69**:159
"Paradox" (Lowell) **13**:85
The Paradox (Noyes) **27**:138
"Paradox of Time" (Warren) **37**:326
Paradoxes (Donne) **43**:119-20, 134, 138
"Les Parages d'Alsace" (Char) **56**:118
"The Paragon" (Patmore) **59**:228
"Paragraphs" (Carruth) **10**:74-5, 83, 85
"Paragraphs from a Daybook" (Hacker) **47**:117
"Paraíso" (Mistral) **32**:181
"Parajaya sangīt" (Tagore) **8**:405
"Paralipomeni della Batracomiomachia" (Leopardi) **37**:91-97, 103, 122
Parallel Destinies (Cassian) **17**:6
Parallèlement (Verlaine) **2**:414, 416-17, 419, 425-26; **32**:359, 366, 378, 385-86
"Paralysis" (Brooke) **24**:56, 77
"Paralytic" (Plath) **1**:391; **37**:232, 258
"Paranoia in Crete" (Corso) **33**:6, 35; **108**:30
"Paranoid" (Page) **12**:175
"Paraphrase" (Crane) **3**:102; **99**:11, 133-34, 138
"A Paraphrase on Oenone to Paris" (Behn) **88**:87, 137, 150-52
"A Paraphrase on the Eleventh Ode Out of the first Book of Horace" (Behn) **88**:145, 150
Paraphrases (Surrey) **59**:297
"The Parasceve, or Preparation" (Herrick) **9**:117, 119
Parasites of Heaven (Cohen) **109**:19, 88, 111
"Parasites of Heaven" (Cohen) **109**:18
"Paratile of a Certain Virgin" (Parker) **28**:348
"The Parcel" (Boland) **58**:49
"A Parcel of Rogues in a Nation" (Burns)
See "Such a Parcel of Rogues in a Nation"
"Pardners" (Brown) **55**:110
"Pardon" (Éluard) **38**:85-86
"Pardon" (Thomas) **99**:261
"The Pardon" (Wilbur) **51**:188, 223, 266
"Pardon Keeps the Sun" (Ignatow) **34**:286, 313
"Pardoner's Prologue" (Chaucer) **19**:26, 46; **58**:365, 368
"Pardoner's Tale" (Chaucer) **19**:13, 30, 46, 49, 51-2, 68
"Parentage" (Meynell) **112**:165, 171-74, 176, 178, 186, 231, 299
"Parentage" (Stafford) **71**:280, 290-91
"A Parental Ode to My Son, Aged Three Years and Five Months" (Hood) **93**:122
"Paréntesis pasional" (Borges) **22**:92
"Parents" (Meredith) **28**:180, 208
"The Parents: People Like Our Marriage, Maxie and Andrew" (Brooks) **7**:80
"Le Parfum" (Baudelaire) **106**:70
"Parfum exotique" (Baudelaire) **1**:45; **106**:8, 70, 153
"Parfum exotique" (Char) **56**:197
"Paring the Apple" (Tomlinson) **17**:331
"Paris" (Corso) **33**:41; **108**:22
"Paris" (Ondaatje) **28**:298-99
"Paris" (Stern) **115**:292
"Paris" (Stryk) **27**:214
"Paris" (Vigny) **26**:402, 411-12
"Paris, 7 a.m." (Bishop) **34**:78-79
"París, 1856" (Borges) **32**:114
"Paris 1954" (Hughes) **89**:234
"Paris and Helen" (Schwartz) **8**:311
"Paris at Nightfall" (Baudelaire)
See "Le crépuscule du soir"
"Paris Commune" (Rexroth)
See "From the Paris Commune to the Kronstadt Rebellion"
"Paris in the Snow" (Senghor) **25**:241
Paris Spleen (Baudelaire)
See *Le spleen de Paris, petits poèmes en prose*
"The Parish" (Thomas) **99**:244
"The Parish-Clerk" (Crabbe) **97**:107-8, 110, 128
The Parish Register (Crabbe) **97**:69, 71, 74, 76, 82-83, 88-89, 101, 124, 129, 138, 144, 148-50, 152
"A Parisian Dream" (Baudelaire)
See "Rêve parisien"
"Parisian Orgy or Paris Repopulated" (Rimbaud) **57**:246
The Parisian Prowler (Baudelaire)
See *Le spleen de Paris, petits poèmes en prose*
"Parisien, mon frère" (Verlaine) **32**:375
"Parisina" (Byron) **16**:109
"The Park" (Stryk) **27**:211
"Park Bench" (Hughes) **1**:242
"The Parklands" (Smith) **12**:317
Parlement (Chaucer)
See *Parlement of Foules*
Parlement of Foules (Chaucer) **19**:10, 12, 20-3, 38, 74
"Parle-moi" (Péret) **33**:231
"Parleying with Charles Avison" (Browning) **2**:83
"Parleying with Gerard de Lairesse" (Browning) **2**:81, 83, 86
Parleyings (Browning)
See *Parleyings with Certain People of Importance in Their Day*
Parleyings with Certain People of Importance in Their Day (Browning) **2**:64, 85, 95-6
"Parlez-vous français" (Schwartz) **8**:302-03
"Parliament Hill Fields" (Betjeman) **75**:20, 26, 77, 89
"Parliament Hill Fields" (Plath) **1**:391
Parliament of Fowls (Chaucer)
See *Parlement of Foules*
"Parlour-Piece" (Hughes) **7**:140
"Le Parnasse" (Ponge) **107**:166
"Parnell's Funeral" (Yeats) **20**:326, 348
"Parochial Theme" (Stevens) **110**:201
"Parodos" (Glück) **16**:159-62
"A Parody" (Southwell) **83**:280
"Parola" (Quasimodo) **47**:297, 301-2
"La Parole" (Éluard) **38**:69, 83-84
"Le parole" (Montale) **13**:134
"La Parole aux Oricous" (Césaire) **25**:12
La parole en archipel (Char) **56**:113-15, 120, 138, 149-52, 154, 156, 161, 167, 176, 184, 202
"La parole étouffée sous les roses" (Ponge) **107**:195, 231
"Paroles dans l'air" (Jaccottet) **98**:174
"Paroles sur la dune" (Hugo) **17**:64
"Parom" (Akhmadulina) **43**:18
"A Parrot" (Sarton) **39**:345
"A Parrot at Sea" (Shvarts) **50**:141
"Parrots" (Wright) **14**:348
"The Parrots at Karekare" (Curnow) **48**:14
"The Parrott" (Mistral)
See "El papagayo"
"Parsifal" (Verlaine) **32**:341
"Parsley" (Dove) **6**:105, 110
"Parson Turell's Legacy" (Holmes) **71**:92, 118
"The Parson's Daughter and the Seminarist" (Bely) **11**:3
"Parson's Prologue" (Chaucer) **58**:368
"The Parson's Son" (Service) **70**:116
"Parson's Tale" (Chaucer) **19**:37, 45, 47; **58**:235, 246, 266-7
A Part (Berry) **28**:4, 9-10
"Part of a Bird" (Cassian) **17**:4, 12-13
"Part of a Letter" (Wilbur) **51**:187
"Part of a True Story" (Hacker) **47**:82, 87
"Part of Mandevil's Travels" (Empson) **104**:90, 94, 101
"A Part of Speech" (Brodsky)
See "Chast' rechi"
A Part of Speech (Brodsky)
See *Chast' rechi: Stikhotvoreniia 1972-76*
A Part of Speech: Poems 1972-76 (Brodsky)
See *Chast' rechi: Stikhotvoreniia 1972-76*
"Part of the Doctrine" (Baraka) **4**:18
"Part of the Seventh Epistle of the First Book of Horace Imitated and Addressed to the Earl of Oxford" (Swift) **9**:296
"Part of the Vigil" (Merrill) **28**:221, 224
"Part Song" (Wagoner) **33**:326, 370, 372
Partage formel (Char) **56**:112, 121, 132, 164
"Parted" (Dunbar) **5**:125, 140
"Parted" (Meynell) **112**:189, 287
"Partenza per il Vaud" (Zanzotto) **65**:290
"Párthen" (Cavafy) **36**:39, 40, 86
"Parthenissa's Answer to the Pocket-Book's Soliloquy" (Leapor) **85**:284
"The Parthenon" (Melville) **82**:74
Le Parti pris des choses (Ponge) **107**:70, 72, 80, 98, 100-101, 107, 127, 129-31, 133, 136, 142, 144, 170, 177, 182-83, 185-86, 189, 191-92, 206, 213-14, 222-23, 228, 237, 239, 251-55
"Partial Accounts" (Meredith) **28**:205, 215
Partial Accounts: New and Selected Poems (Meredith) **28**:211-16
"Partial Comfort" (Parker) **28**:362
"Partial Eclipse" (Snodgrass) **74**:292
"Partial Enchantments of the Quixote" (Borges)
See "Magias parciales del Quijote"
"Partial Magic in the Quixote" (Borges)
See "Magias parciales del Quijote"
"Particularité des fraises" (Ponge) **107**:169
"Partida" (Storni) **33**:246
La Partie pour le tout (Brossard) **80**:18
"Parting" (Ammons) **16**:63
"Parting" (Arnold) **5**:43, 55
"The Parting" (Cowley) **90**:13
"The Parting" (Harper) **21**:194
"The Parting" (Li Po) **29**:140
"A Parting" (Meynell) **112**:156
"Parting as Descent" (Berryman) **64**:88
"Parting at Dawn" (Ransom) **61**:301, 307, 309
"Parting Gift" (Wylie) **23**:321
"A Parting Health" (Holmes) **71**:68

"The Parting Hour" (Crabbe) **97**:95-96, 102, 105-6, 112, 132
"The Parting of the Columns" (Kipling) **91**:69, 141, 172
"Parting, Without a Sequel" (Ransom) **61**:288, 307
"The Parting Word" (Holmes) **71**:92
Partitur (Ekeloef) **23**:68-9, 78
"Partly from the Greek" (Belloc) **24**:32
"The Partner" (Roethke) **15**:256
"The Partner's Desk" (McGuckian) **27**:105
"Parts" (Creeley) **73**:96, 103
Parts of a World (Stevens) **6**:299, 311, 318; **110**:137-38, 142, 159, 201, 203
"A Part-Sequence for Change" (Duncan) **2**:103
"Parturition" (Loy) **16**:313-14, 318, 320, 325, 329, 333
"The Party" (Dunbar)
See "The Pahty"
"The Party" (Hafiz) **116**:24-26
"Party on Shipboard" (Oppen) **35**:342
"The Party Wall" (Ní Chuilleanáin) **34**:361
"Les pas" (Valéry) **9**:366, 374, 396
Pasado en claro (Paz) **1**:369, 371-72, 374; **48**:174, 188, 245, 258, 273
"Pascuas sangrientas de 1956" (Guillén) **23**:128
"El Paseo de Julio" (Borges) **32**:60
"Pasión" (Storni) **33**:239, 269, 283
Pasión de la tierra (Aleixandre) **15**:3, 10, 18, 29-32, 34, 40
"Pasión por pasión" (Cernuda) **62**:235
"Pasiphae" (Hope) **56**:298-99
"Paso a la aurora" (Guillén) **35**:228, 234
"La Pasqua a Pieve di Soligo" (Zanzotto) **65**:263-64, 269-70
"Pasqua di maggio" (Zanzotto) **65**:268-69
Pasque (Zanzotto) **65**:263-64, 266-70, 273, 277-78, 301-2
"Pass on by" (Guillén)
See "Sigue"
Pass th Food Release th Spirit Book (Bissett) **14**:15-16, 24
"Pass through Fleeting Words" (Darwish) **86**:15, 29
"Passage" (Ammons) **16**:6
"Passage" (Brossard) **80**:22, 25
"Passage" (Crane) **3**:82; **99**:11, 16, 27-29, 32-33, 84
"Passage" (Levertov) **11**:202
"Passage" (Okigbo) **7**:223-24, 231, 236-39, 248-49, 251, 255
"Passage de l'oiseau divin" (Breton) **15**:49
"Passage over Water" (Duncan) **75**:127
"Passage to India" (Whitman) **3**:378, 394-98; **91**:273
Le Passager du transatlantique (Péret) **33**:223, 230
"Passagers de seconde classe et leurs cheveux" (Péret) **33**:230
"Passages" (Duncan) **75**:147, 156, 158, 171, 173, 189-90, 204, 212, 214-16, 232, 250, 254, 261, 275-77
"Passages 1" (Duncan)
See "Tribal Memories"
"Passages 2" (Duncan)
See "At the Loom"
"Passages 4" (Duncan)
See "Where It Appears"
"Passages 8" (Duncan) **75**:216
"Passages 13" (Duncan)
See "The Fire"
"Passages 16" (Duncan)
See "The Currents"
"Passages 17" (Duncan)
See "Moving the Moving Image"
"Passages 18" (Duncan)
See "The Torso"
"Passages 21" (Duncan)
See "The Multiversity"
"Passages 23" (Duncan) **75**:133
"Passages 25" (Duncan)
See "Up Rising"
"Passages 26" (Duncan)
See "The Soldiers"
"Passages 27" (Duncan) **2**:116
"Passages 29" (Duncan) **2**:116
"Passages 31" (Duncan) **2**:117
"Passages 35 (Tribunals)" (Duncan) **2**:116, 118
"Passages 36" (Duncan) **2**:115-17; **75**:171
The Passages of Joy (Gunn) **26**:208-209, 211-212, 214, 216-217, 220, 230-231
"Le Passe" (Hugo) **17**:64
"La Passe de Lyon" (Char) **56**:151
"Passe forth my wonted cryes" (Wyatt) **27**:362
"Passer mortuus est" (Millay) **6**:228
"A Passer-By" (Bridges) **28**:67, 70
"Passers-By" (Sandburg) **41**:340
"Passers-By on a Snowy Night" (Warren) **37**:380
"Passing Between the Passing Words" (Darwish)
See "Pass through Fleeting Words"
"Passing by San Guido" (Carducci)
See "Davanti San Guido"
"Passing Chao-ling Again" (Tu Fu) **9**:322
"The Passing Cloud" (Smith) **12**:339
"Passing, men are sorry for the birds in cages" (Spender) **71**:219, 221
"The Passing Night" (Winters) **82**:316
"The Passing of Arthur" (Tennyson)
See "Morte d'Arthur"
"The Passing of the Hawthorn" (Swinburne) **24**:313, 317
"Passing Over in Silence" (Ní Chuilleanáin) **34**:367, 373, 383-84
"Passing Remark" (Stafford) **71**:259, 280
"The Passing Strange" (Masefield) **78**:51-52, 55
"Passing Things to John Ashbery" (O'Hara)
See "Choses Passagères à John Ashbery"
"Passing Through" (Cavafy) **36**:74, 108
"Passing Through" (Kunitz) **19**:187
"Passing Through Little Rock" (Ortiz) **17**:227
Passing Through: The Later Poems New and Selected (Kunitz) **19**:186
"Passing Time in Skansen" (Koch) **80**:319
"Passing Visit to Helen" (Lawrence) **54**:168
"Passion" (Cunningham) **92**:140, 177
"Passion" (Trakl) **20**:269
"The Passion" (Vaughan) **81**:295, 333
Passion Flowers (Howe) **81**:11-13, 17-19, 21, 23, 29-30, 46-52, 62-63
"A Passion For Travel" (Curnow) **48**:20, 51
Passion: New Poems, 1977-1980 (Jordan) **38**:112, 117-19, 122-23, 127, 131
"The Passion of Christ" (Dunbar) **67**:128
The Passion of Claude McKay: Selected Poetry and Prose, 1912-1948 (McKay) **2**:218
Passion of the Earth (Aleixandre)
See *Pasión de la tierra*
"The Passion of the Mad Rabbit" (Sexton) **79**:219, 242
The Passionate Heart (Gilmore) **87**:283, 298, 302
"The Passionate Man's Pilgrimage..." (Raleigh) **31**:210, 217, 236
"The Passionate Ones" (Werfel)
See "Die Liedenschaftlichen"
"La passione" (Pasolini) **17**:288
Passione e ideologia (Pasolini) **17**:250, 252, 263-64, 291, 295
"The Passions" (Coleridge) **39**:213
"The Passions" (Cowley) **90**:115
"Passions" (Komunyakaa) **51**:35
"The Passions: An Ode for Music" (Collins) **72**:40, 42-43, 46, 52, 54-55, 58, 61-63, 78, 83, 95-97, 117, 123, 126, 128-29, 131, 143-44, 148, 164, 173, 177
Passovers (Zanzotto)
See *Pasque*
Passport to the War (Kunitz) **19**:148, 154, 160-62
The Pass-Times and Diversions of a Countrey-Muse (Vaughan)
See *Thalia Rediviva: The Pass-Times and Diversions of a Countrey-Muse, in Choice Poems on Several Occasions. With Some Learned Remains of the Eminent Eugenius Philalethes. Never Made Publick Till Now*
Passwords (Stafford) **71**:369-72, 374
"The Past" (Bryant) **20**:9
"The Past" (Emerson) **18**:76
"Past" (Sanchez) **9**:219
The Past (Kinnell) **26**:277-78, 292-93
"Past and Future" (Barrett Browning) **6**:16, 41
"Past and Future Turn About" (Rexroth) **95**:257, 259, 262, 271, 333
"Past and Present" (Clarke) **112**:29
"Past and Present" (Masters) **1**:343
The past clarified/copied out (Paz)
See *Pasado en claro*
"Past Days" (Swinburne) **24**:327, 329
"The Past Is the Present" (Moore) **4**:237; **49**:92, 115, 117, 122
"The Past Reordered" (Ignatow) **34**:283
"Past Tense" (Francis) **34**:251
"The Past Values" (Spender) **71**:208, 224
"Pastime" (Schuyler) **88**:216
"Pastor hacia el puerto" (Aleixandre) **15**:35
"Pastoral" (Dove) **6**:120-21
"Pastoral" (Simic) **69**:274-76, 370
"The Pastoral" (Soto) **28**:370
"Pastoral" (Tate) **50**:231
"Pastoral" (Viereck) **27**:271
"Pastoral" (Williams) **7**:367, 378; **109**:241
Pastoral (Williams) **7**:349
"Pastoral Dialogue" (Swift) **9**:261
"A Pastoral Dialogue between Alexis and Strephon" (Wilmot) **66**:267, 329
A Pastoral Elegy (Duck) **89**:5
"A Pastoral Fetish" (Corso) **33**:46; **108**:38-39
"Pastoral II" (Meredith) **60**:287
"The Pastoral Letter" (Whittier) **93**:314, 337
"A Pastoral Pindaric . . ." (Behn) **13**:8
"Pastoral Poesy" (Clare) **23**:4
"A Pastoral to Mr. Stafford" (Behn) **13**:8, 32
"A Pastoral to Mr. Stafford, under the name of Silvio, on his Translation of the Death of Camilla: out of Virgil. By Mrs. Behn. Thirsis and Amarillis" (Behn) **88**:72
"Pastoral VI" (Meredith) **60**:287
"Pastorale" (Crane) **3**:98-9
Pastorales (Jiménez) **7**:184
"A Pastorall Song to the King" (Herrick) **9**:86
"Pastorals" (Montague) **106**:293
Pastorals (Pope) **26**:319, 321
Pastorals (Vergil)
See *Georgics*
"Pastorela di Narcis" (Pasolini) **17**:253, 282
Pastoure (Christine de Pizan)
See *Le dit de la pastoure*
"The Pasture" (Frost) **1**:197, 212, 225; **39**:236, 256-57
Pastures and Other Poems (Reese) **29**:336-337, 339, 348
"Pat Rack Sieve" (Berssenbrugge) **115**:9
"Patagonian Lullaby" (Mistral)
See "Arrullo patagón"
"Patch and Mend" (Hope) **56**:276
"Patch Patch Patch" (Raworth) **107**:299
"Patchwork" (Boland) **58**:45, 53, 59
"Patent Leather" (Brooks) **7**:58, 68, 79
"The Patent of a Lord" (Crane) **80**:52, 68-70, 80
"Pater Filio" (Bridges) **28**:89
"Paternità" (Pavese) **13**:213, 229
"Paternity" (Pavese)
See "Paternità"
"Paterson" (Ginsberg) **4**:73-5
Paterson (Williams) **7**:350, 354-60, 362, 364-65, 370-75, 377, 379, 392-95, 402-03, 408-10; **109**:191-93, 202, 215, 217, 225-26, 237, 276-77, 282, 290, 309-11, 313-18, 337

Paterson I (Williams) **7**:354, 357-58, 360, 365
Paterson II (Williams) **7**:363, 391-92
Paterson IV (Williams) **7**:363, 392
Paterson V (Williams) **7**:364-65, 370-71, 393
"Paterson: Episode 17" (Williams) **7**:360
"The Path" (Dunbar) **5**:125
"The Path" (Thomas) **53**:328, 348
"The Path Among the Stones" (Kinnell) **26**:252, 269, 273, 275-76
"Path of the Chameleon" (Wylie) **23**:330
"Path of Thunder" (Okigbo) **7**:228, 246-47, 255
Path of Thunder (Okigbo)
See *Labyrinths, with Path of Thunder*
"Pathfinders" (Brathwaite) **56**:6, 29, 85
"Pathology of Colours" (Abse) **41**:11, 25, 28
The Paths and the Roads of Poetry (Éluard)
See *Les sentiers et les routes de la poésie*
"Paths and Thingscape" (Atwood) **8**:36
"Patience" (Chappell) **105**:21
"Patience" (Éluard) **38**:63
"Patience" (Graves) **6**:154
"Patience" (Lowell) **13**:60
"Patience" (Stone) **53**:244, 257
Patience (Anonymous) **76**:226-27, 229
"La patience, Le ciel" (Bonnefoy) **58**:118, 167
"Patient" (Owen) **102**:160
"Un patio" (Borges) **32**:53, 81
"El Patio" (Cernuda) **62**:221
"Patmos" (Hölderlin) **4**:148, 150-51, 153, 155-57, 159, 166, 172
Patria o muerte! The Great Zoo, and Other Poems by Nicolás Guillén (Guillén)
See *El gran zoo*
"Patricia's Poem" (Jordan) **38**:126
"The Patriot" (Thomas) **99**:253-54
"The Patriot Engineer" (Meredith) **60**:250
"Patriot Virtue" (Smith) **104**:239
"Patriotic Ode on the Fourteenth Anniversary of the Persecution of Charlie Chaplin" (Kaufman) **74**:259
"Patriotic Poem" (Wakoski) **15**:358
Patriotic Suite (Montague) **106**:252, 261, 264-66, 279, 285, 309, 317, 320, 331, 334-41, 344-45
"The Patroit" (Browning) **2**:60
"The Patron" (Crabbe) **97**:97, 105, 112
"Patrouille" (Stramm) **50**:172, 175, 209, 220
"Patterns" (Lowell) **13**:60, 71, 76-7, 84-5, 89, 96
"Patterns" (Wright) **14**:376
"Paul" (Niedecker) **42**:169
"Paul" (Wright) **36**:359, 363
"Paul and Virginia" (Gozzano) **10**:176, 178, 180-84
Paul Celan: Poems (Celan) **10**:95-6, 107-08, 114
"Paul Klee" (Éluard) **38**:71
"Paul Revere's Ride" (Longfellow) **30**:25, 44, 48, 61-2
"Paul Robeson" (Brooks) **7**:92-3
"Paul Valéry Stood on the Cliff and Confronted the Furious Energies of Nature" (Warren) **37**:353
"Paula Becker To Clara Westhoff" (Rich) **5**:379
Pauline (Browning)
See *Pauline: A Fragment of a Confession*
Pauline: A Fragment of a Confession (Browning) **2**:25-6, 42-3, 48, 66, 90-2, 94; **97**:32
"Pauline Barrett" (Masters) **36**:183
"Paulo Purganti and His Wife: An Honest, but a Simple Pair" (Prior) **102**:314-15
"Paul's Wife" (Frost) **1**:194; **39**:235
"Paumanok" (Clampitt) **19**:102
"Paumanok" (Whitman)
See "Starting from Paumanok"
"The Pauper Witch of Grafton" (Frost) **39**:235
"The Pauper's Christmas Carol" (Hood) **93**:47, 85, 101-2, 118
"Pause au château cloaque" (Char) **56**:137-38
"A Pause for Thought" (Rossetti) **7**:280, 297
"Pausilippo" (Melville) **82**:149
"Pauvre Lélian" (Verlaine) **2**:416
"Les pauvres à l'église" (Rimbaud) **3**:255; **57**:203, 205, 250
"Les pauvres gens" (Hugo) **17**:61
"Pavilastukay" (Masefield) **78**:51
"Pavilion" (Collins) **68**:217
"Pavitra prem" (Tagore) **8**:407
"The Paw" (Merwin) **45**:29
"Pawn to Bishop's Five" (Masefield) **78**:91
"The Pawnbroker" (Kumin) **15**:180, 192, 200
"The Pawnee Brave" (Whittier) **93**:198
"Pax" (Darío) **15**:82, 115
"Pax" (Lawrence) **54**:250
"Pay Day" (Hughes) **1**:255
"Pay Day" (McKay) **2**:226
"Pay Up or Else" (Tapahonso) **65**:225, 259
"Paying a Debt" (Dafydd ap Gwilym)
See "Talu Dyled"
"Paying Calls" (Hardy) **8**:105
"The Payne Whitney Poems" (Schuyler) **88**:205
"Pays Natal" (Walcott) **46**:272
"Paysage" (Apollinaire) **7**:32, 34-5
"Paysage" (Baudelaire) **106**:60, 136
"Paysage" (Verlaine) **32**:378
"Paysage Moralisé" (Auden) **1**:23
"Le Paysage nu" (Éluard) **38**:87
"Paysages belges" (Verlaine) **2**:415
"Paz" (Storni) **33**:251
"Peace" (Berrigan) **103**:5-6, 46
"Peace" (Brooke) **24**:59, 74, 79-80, 87-9
"Peace" (Clare) **23**:44
"Peace" (Darío)
See "Pax"
"Peace" (Das) **43**:90
"Peace" (Herbert) **4**:101, 134
"Peace" (Hopkins) **15**:127
"Peace" (Kavanagh) **33**:73, 81, 100; **105**:99, 109, 151
"Peace" (Levine) **22**:219
"Peace" (Yeats) **20**:329
"Peace, babbling Muse!" (Waller) **72**:339-40
"The Peace of Cities" (Wilbur) **51**:187
"The Peaceable Kingdom of Emerald Windows" (Chappell) **105**:30, 45-46, 59, 68, 72-74
"The Peaceful Island" (Enright) **93**:15, 17
"The peaceful western wind" (Campion) **87**:12
"The Peace-Offering" (Hardy) **8**:93
"Peach" (Lawrence) **54**:187, 225-27
"Peach Blossom Spring" (Wang Wei) **18**:374
"The Peaches" (Thomas) **52**:284
"Peachstone" (Abse) **41**:10, 14
"Peacock" (Merrill) **28**:234
Peacock Pie (de la Mare) **77**:58, 71, 73-74, 81-82, 94, 97, 99, 122-24, 129, 142, 144
"The Peacock Room" (Hayden) **6**:193-95, 198
"The Peal of Bells" (Thoreau)
See "The Peal of the Bells"
"The Peal of the Bells" (Thoreau) **30**:193, 254
"The Pear" (Kenyon) **57**:23, 40, 43
"The Pear" (Stone) **53**:227
"The Pear Tree" (Gilmore) **87**:291
"Pear Tree" (H. D.) **5**:275
"The Pearl" (Herbert) **4**:100, 128
"The Pearl" (Patmore) **59**:232
Pearl (Anonymous) **76**:175, 197, 211, 226, 229, 276, 279-80
"The Pearl Diver" (Wylie) **23**:321
"Pearl Fog" (Sandburg) **41**:364
"Pearl Harbor" (Howe) **54**:37
"Pearl Horizons" (Sandburg) **2**:307
"Peasant" (Kavanagh) **33**:156; **105**:132
"A Peasant" (Thomas) **99**:241
"Peasant Greeting" (Thomas) **99**:241, 269
"Peasant: His Prayer to the Powers of the World" (Merwin) **45**:23
"The Peasant Whore" (Pavese)
See "La puttana contadina"
"The Peasant's Confession" (Hardy) **8**:124
The Peasant's Wake: For Fellini's Casanova (Zanzotto)
See *Filò: per il Casanova di Fellini*
"The Peau de Chagrin of State Street" (Holmes) **71**:96
"Pebble" (Herbert)
See "Kamyk"
"The Pebble" (Ponge)
See "Le galet"
"Pebbles" (Brathwaite) **56**:68
"Pebbles" (Melville) **82**:73-74, 97, 144, 199
"Pécheresse" (Mew) **107**:16, 35, 49-50
Peculiar Motions (Waldrop) **109**:179
"Pedantic Literalist" (Moore) **4**:229; **49**:114, 116-17, 120, 155
"Pedestrian" (Oppen) **35**:284
"The Pedlar" (Clarke) **112**:83
"The Pedlar" (Mew) **107**:36, 57
"Pedro as el cuando..." (Neruda) **4**:288
"Peekaboo, I Almost See You" (Nash) **21**:269-70
"Peekaboo Miss Human Soap" (Cohen) **109**:76
"Peele Castle" (Wordsworth)
See "Stanzas on Peele Castle"
"The Peephole" (Valenzuela)
See "La ventana"
"Peers" (Toomer) **7**:336-37
Peers (Belloc) **24**:49
"Pegasus" (Kavanagh) **33**:62, 75, 77, 85, 93-4, 96; **105**:94
"Pegasus in Pound" (Longfellow) **30**:88
"Pegli occhi fere un spirito sottile" (Cavalcanti) **114**:216-17
Le Peintre à l'étude (Ponge) **107**:142
"Peinture" (Lovelace) **69**:232-33, 237
Peirs Gaveston, Earle of Cornwall. His Life, Death, and Fortune (Drayton) **98**:7, 53-54
"Pelagos" (Ponge) **107**:130
"A pelear" (Alurista) **34**:27
"The Pelican" (Wilbur) **51**:190
"The Pelican Chorus" (Lear) **65**:144, 146, 159-60
"Pelleas and Ettarre" (Tennyson) **101**:230
"Pellín and Nina" (Espada) **74**:139
"Pelota en el agua" (Storni) **33**:293-96
"The Pen" (Carver) **54**:14
"The Pen" (Kinnell) **26**:293
"Penal Law" (Clarke) **112**:108, 117, 119, 125
"Penal Rock / Altamuskin" (Montague) **106**:260-64, 266
"Penance" (Erdrich) **52**:191
"A Pencil" (Hass) **16**:196
"Pencils" (Sandburg) **41**:302
"Pendulum" (Updike) **90**:347
"Penelope" (Boland) **58**:20
"Penelope" (Parker) **28**:362
"Penelope at Her Loom" (Graham)
See "Self-Portrait as Hurry and Delay"
"Penelope's Song" (Glück) **16**:172
"Penetra" (Alurista) **34**:27
"The Peninsula" (Heaney) **18**:200, 222-23
"The Penitent" (Leapor) **85**:286
"The Penitent" (Millay) **6**:211
"Penmanship" (Graham) **59**:170, 175
Penniless Painter Goes Out into the World (Seifert)
See *Šel malíř chudě do světa*
"A Penniless Painter Went Out into the World" (Seifert)
See *Šel malíř chudě do světa*
"Penniwit, the Artist" (Masters) **36**:182
"Pennsylvania Letter" (Whittier) **93**:314
"The Pennsylvania Pilgrim" (Whittier) **93**:176, 225-26, 238-39, 253
Penny Wheep (MacDiarmid) **9**:151, 158, 166, 179, 188
"The Penny Whistle" (Thomas) **53**:300
Penny Whistles (Stevenson) **84**:325
"The Pennycandystore beyond the El" (Ferlinghetti) **1**:187
"Penobscot" (Oppen) **35**:314
"Pénombre" (Char) **56**:155
"The Pens" (Merwin) **45**:77
"El Pensador de Rodin" (Mistral) **32**:154
"Pensar, dudar" (Hugo) **17**:92, 96-97

Pensées d'août (Sainte-Beuve) **110**:3, 9, 13, 15, 20, 39, 43, 49, 51, 54-56, 58, 61, 63, 69-70
"Pensées d'août" (Sainte-Beuve) **110**:55
Pensées de Joseph Delorme (Sainte-Beuve)
See *Vie, poésies et pensées de Joseph Delorme*
"Pensées des morts" (Lamartine) **16**:280
"The Pensées of Pascal" (Eliot) **90**:240
Pensées sous les nuages: Poèmes (Jaccottet) **98**:182, 188, 194-200, 207, 209
"Pensées sur les nuages" (Jaccottet) **98**:199, 205-6, 208
"Penshurst Place" (Mahon) **60**:142
"Pensieri di Deola" (Pavese) **13**:214
"The Pensioners" (Carman) **34**:203, 210, 217
"Pente" (Tzara) **27**:229-31
"La pente de la rêverie" (Hugo) **17**:48, 91, 93
"Penthesilea" (Noyes) **27**:115
"Penúltima canción de Don Simón" (Fuertes) **27**:40
"Penumbra" (Lowell) **13**:64
"Peonies" (Oliver) **75**:320
"People" (Toomer) **7**:336-37
"The People" (Yeats) **20**:328
"People Are Sick of Pretending That They Love the Boss" (Wright) **36**:390-91
"People Asking Me" (Alurista) **34**:21-22
"THE PEOPLE BURNING" (Baraka) **4**:12; **113**:12-13
"People Getting Divorced" (Ferlinghetti) **1**:183
"People of the Eaves, I Wish You Good Morning" (Sandburg) **41**:287
"People of the South Wind" (Stafford) **71**:321, 336
"People of Unrest" (Walker) **20**:282
"People on a Bridge" (Szymborska)
See "Ludzie na moście"
People on a Bridge (Szymborska)
See *Ludzie na moscie*
"The People People" (Oppen) **35**:316
"People Were Laughing Behind A Wall" (Yevtushenko) **40**:347
"People Who Change Their Names" (Berrigan) **103**:26
"People Who Died" (Berrigan) **103**:15, 40
"People Who Don't Understand" (Pavese)
See "Gente che non capisce"
"People Who Have No Children" (Brooks) **7**:75
"People Who've Been There" (Pavese) **13**:218
"The People Will Live On" (Sandburg) **41**:332
"The People, Yes" (Sandburg) **41**:279, 330, 332-33, 346
The People, Yes (Sandburg) **2**:317-18, 320-23, 325-26, 328, 330, 333, 335-39, 341; **41**:279, 330, 332-33, 346
A Peopled Landscape (Tomlinson) **17**:305, 309, 317-18, 327, 333, 335, 337, 341
"The People's Anthem" (Elliott) **96**:180
"People's Surroundings" (Moore) **49**:93-94, 112
Pepel' (Bely) **11**:3-4, 6-7, 24, 30-2
Peppercanister Poems, 1972-1978 (Kinsella) **69**:74, 77-78, 80
Pequeña antología de Gabriela Mistral (Mistral) **32**:166
"Pequeña cabellera rubia" (Cernuda) **62**:239
"La Pequeña oda a un negro boxeador cubano" (Guillén) **23**:98-99, 103, 105-107
"El pequeño burgués" (Parra) **39**:277
"Per album" (Montale) **13**:130
"Per Eduardo Corrazzini" (Carducci) **46**:51
"Per fido esemplo all mia vocazione" (Michelangelo) **103**:307, 342-43
"Per Giuseppe Monti e Gaetano Tognetti" (Carducci) **46**:51
"Per il Santo Natale" (Leopardi) **37**:169
"Per il Trasporto delle Relique di Ugo Foscolo in Santa Croce" (Carducci) **46**:51
"Per la Morte di Eugenio Napoleone" (Carducci) **46**:52, 84
"Per la Proclamazione del Regno d'Italia" (Carducci) **46**:51
"Per la Rivoluzione di Grecia" (Carducci) **46**:5, 51
"Per lumina, per limina" (Zanzotto) **65**:266
"Per molti donna, anzi per mille amanti" (Michelangelo) **103**:318
"Per quella via che la bellezza corre" (Dante) **21**:74
"Per un ritorna al paese" (Pasolini) **17**:266
"Perch" (Heaney) **100**:237-38, 327, 329
"The Perch" (Kinnell) **26**:287
"Perché Febo non torce" (Michelangelo) **103**:256
"Perché non fuoro a me gli occhi dispenti" (Cavalcanti) **114**:209, 225
"Perché siamo" (Zanzotto) **65**:265
"Perch-fishing" (Blunden) **66**:4
"Perdidi Diem" (Tennyson) **101**:243
"Lo perdido" (Borges) **22**:80
"Perdition" (Césaire) **25**:29
"Perdón si por mis ojos..." (Neruda) **4**:288
"Peregrinaciones" (Darío) **15**:82
"Peregrinations" (Darío)
See "Peregrinaciones"
"Peregrine" (Wylie) **23**:307, 310, 324
"El peregrino" (Parra) **39**:283-84
"Perekop" (Tsvetaeva) **14**:326-27
"Peremena" (Pasternak) **6**:285
"The Perennial Answer" (Rich) **5**:351-52
"Perennials" (Levine) **22**:228
Pereulochki (Tsvetaeva) **14**:325-26
"Perfección del círculo" (Guillén) **35**:154, 211
"Perfect" (MacDiarmid) **9**:177
"The Perfect Forms" (Hughes) **89**:101
"The Perfect Husband" (Nash) **21**:278
"The Perfect Sky" (Gallagher) **9**:59
"Perfection" (Walker) **30**:339
"Perfection of the Cirlce" (Guillén)
See "Perfección del círculo"
"El Perfecto" (Chappell) **105**:51
"La perfezione della neve" (Zanzotto) **65**:276, 314-16
Perfil del aire (Cernuda) **62**:227, 229
"Perforation, Concerning Genius" (Pinsky) **27**:144
"The Performance" (Dickey) **40**:159, 166-67, 175, 181, 183, 189, 192, 258
"The Performers" (Hayden) **6**:195
"El perfume" (Cernuda) **62**:270-71
"The Perfume" (Donne)
See "Elegie IV: The Perfume"
"Perhaps" (Spender) **71**:190, 219, 221
"Perhaps" (Thomas) **99**:259, 261, 338, 358
"Perhaps Because I Love You" (Alurista)
See "Tal vez porque te quiero"
"Perhaps No Poem But All I Can Say and I Cannot Be Silent" (Levertov) **11**:198
"Perhaps the Best Time" (Meredith) **28**:174
"Peripeteia" (Hecht) **70**:62-63, 81-82, 84-85, 87
"Peripeurperal Insanity" (Das) **43**:81
"Perjury Excused" (Suckling) **30**:127
"The Permanent Hell" (Ignatow) **34**:283
"Permanent invisible" (Char) **56**:152
"The Permanent Tourists" (Page) **12**:178, 181-89
"Permanently" (Koch) **80**:320
"The perpetual migration" (Piercy) **29**:303
"Perpetual Motion" (Raworth) **107**:324-25
"Perpetuum Mobile: The City" (Williams) **7**:350
"Perplexities" (Kennedy) **93**:153
"Le Perroquet" (Perse) **23**:228, 254-56
"Persée et Andromède" (Laforgue) **14**:93
"Persephone" (Duncan) **75**:168
"Persephone" (Heaney) **100**:264
"Persephone" (Smith) **12**:331-32
"Perseus" (Owen) **102**:146, 149-50
"Perseus" (Plath) **37**:254
"Pershore Station; or, A Liverish Journey First Class" (Betjeman) **75**:14, 26
"Persia" (Tennyson) **101**:142
"The Persian" (Smith) **12**:330
Persian Eclogues (Collins) **72**:39, 42-44, 47-48, 50, 57, 60-61, 78-82, 126, 133
"Persian Song" (Hafiz) **116**:44
"A Persian Suite" (Stryk) **27**:186-87
"The Persian Version" (Graves) **6**:143, 152
Persimmon (Viereck) **27**:282, 284
The Persimmon Tree (Viereck) **27**:271
"Persimmons" (Lee) **24**:243, 246
"Persistences" (Hecht) **70**:87
"Persistent Explorer" (Ransom) **61**:289
"The Person" (Hejinian) **108**:296, 304, 313-14
"The Person" (Traherne) **70**:191, 258-59, 273, 316
"A Person from Porlock" (Thomas) **99**:334-36
Person, Place, and Thing (Shapiro) **25**:261-64, 267-69, 276, 285, 288, 295, 308, 318-19, 322, 324
Person to Person (Ciardi) **69**:13
Personae (Pound) **4**:317; **95**:72, 114-15, 120
Personae: The Collected Poems of Ezra Pound (Pound) **95**:80, 83, 95-96, 116, 121-22, 128, 159, 161-62, 193
"Personae Separatae" (Montale) **13**:106, 126
"Personal" (Hughes) **1**:241, 259
Personal Anthology (Borges)
See *Antologia personal*
A Personal Anthology (Borges)
See *Antologia personal*
"Personal Helicon" (Heaney) **18**:200, 217; **100**:264, 349
"Personal Landscape" (Page) **12**:178, 190
"Personal Letter No. 2" (Sanchez) **9**:224, 232-33
"Personal Letter No. 3" (Sanchez) **9**:225
A Personal Library (Borges)
See *Antologia personal*
Personal Places (Kinsella) **69**:82, 128-33, 136, 138, 140-41, 146
"Personal Poem" (O'Hara) **45**:145, 184, 189, 227-28, 243
"Personal Poem #9" (Berrigan) **103**:3, 6, 16
"Personal Problem" (Kavanagh) **33**:74, 81, 89; **105**:100
"Personism" (Mahon) **60**:229
"Persons Half Known" (Sandburg) **41**:241
"Perspectives" (MacNeice) **61**:176
"Persuasions to Love" (Carew)
See "To A.L. Perswasions to Love"
"Perswasions to Enjoy" (Carew) **29**:36
"La perte de l'anio" (Lamartine) **16**:292
"El Peru / Cheyenne Milkplane" (Dorn) **115**:230
Pervaja simfonija (Bely) **11**:17
"Pervaya pesenka" (Akhmatova) **2**:9
"Perversity" (Dickey) **40**:201
"Perversity" (Owen) **102**:211
Pervoe svidanie (Bely) **11**:3, 7-11, 17-21, 28-9, 31-3
"La Pesadilla" (Borges) **32**:77
Peschiera (Clough) **103**:140
"Pesnia poslednei vstrechi" (Akhmatova) **2**:11; **55**:48
Pesnja pro kuptsa Kalashinikova (Lermontov)
See *Pesnya pro tsarya Ivana Vasilievicha, molodogo oprichnika i undalogo kuptsa Kalashnikova*
Pesnya pro tsarya Ivana Vasilievicha, molodogo oprichnika i undalogo kuptsa Kalashnikova (Lermontov) **18**:278, 281-82, 304
"Peso ancestral" (Storni) **33**:243, 252
"Pet Shop" (MacNeice) **61**:178
"Peter" (Moore) **4**:257; **49**:99-100, 180, 185-88
"Peter" (Ondaatje) **28**:292-93, 298-99, 318, 321
"Peter" (Wilbur) **51**:281
"Peter and John" (Wylie) **23**:324
Peter Bell (Wordsworth)
See *Peter Bell: A Tale in Verse*
Peter Bell: A Tale in Verse (Wordsworth) **4**:399, 420; **67**:262, 264, 276-77, 282, 296, 298-99, 308, 328, 354-60
Peter Bell the Third (Shelley) **14**:175
Peter Faultless to his Brother Simon, Tales of Night, in Rhyme, and Other Poems (Elliott) **96**:157, 181

"Peter Goole" (Belloc) **24**:18
"Peter Grimes" (Crabbe) **97**:106-7, 109-10, 127, 165
"Peter Kipp to the High School" (Williams) **109**:196
"Peter Lorre Dreams He Is the Third Reincarnation of a Geisha" (Yau) **61**:358
"Peter Lorre Improvises Mr. Moto's Monologue" (Yau) **61**:336, 358
"Peter Lorre Records His Favorite Walt Whitman Poem for Posterity" (Yau) **61**:346, 358
"Peter Lorre Speaks to the Spirit of Edgar Allan Poe During a Séance" (Yau) **61**:358
"Peter Quince at the Clavier" (Stevens) **6**:293, 295, 300-01; **110**:93
"Peterhot Holiday" (Lermontov) **18**:285
"Petersburg" (Akhmadulina) **43**:55
"Petersburg" (Mickiewicz) **38**:168
"Petersburg Tale" (Akhmatova) **55**:3, 24
"Petit Air I" (Mallarmé) **102**:10
"The Petit Bourgeois" (Parra)
See "El pequeño burgués"
"Petit Epître" (Eliot) **90**:304, 306
"Petit Paul" (Hugo) **17**:56
"Petit Poème en Prose" (O'Hara) **45**:178
"Le Petit Roi de Galicie" (Hugo) **17**:61
Le Petit Testament (Villon)
See *Les Lais*
"Petit, the Poet" (Masters) **36**:167, 199, 211
"La petite Enfance de Dominique" (Éluard) **38**:84, 86
Petite prière sans prétentions (Laforgue) **14**:63
"Petite Ville" (Tzara) **27**:223
"Petite Ville en Sibérie" (Tzara) **27**:223
"Les petites vielles" (Baudelaire) **1**:45, 64; **106**:5, 22, 102, 146
"Petition" (Auden) **92**:65
"Pétition" (Laforgue) **14**:73
"Petition" (Raleigh)
See "Petition to Queen Anne"
"The Petition for an Absolute Retreat" (Finch) **21**:142-43, 145-48, 156-57, 164, 170, 172, 175
"Petition to Queen Anne" (Raleigh) **31**:201, 210, 217, 221
"Petition to the Queen" (Raleigh)
See "Petition to Queen Anne"
Petits poèmes lycanthropes (Baudelaire)
See *Le spleen de Paris, petits poèmes en prose*
Petits poems en prose: Le spleen de Paris (Baudelaire) **106**:87-90, 112, 152-54
"The Pet-Lamb: A Pastoral" (Wordsworth) **67**:328, 331
"Petrarca" (Carducci) **46**:52
"Petrificada petrificante" (Paz) **1**:367
"The Petrifying Petrified" (Paz)
See "Petrificada petrificante"
"Petrou his name was sorrow" (Niedecker) **42**:140
"Pettichap's Nest" (Clare) **23**:5
"A Petticoat" (Stein) **18**:330, 341
"Pevitsa" (Tsvetaeva) **14**:325, 327
"Phaedo" (Rexroth) **95**:255
"Phaedra" (H. D.) **5**:267
"Phaestos is a Village with 25 Families" (Corso) **33**:11
"Phaeton" (Meredith) **60**:260
"Phaetons" (Hughes) **89**:222, 226
"Phaius Orchid" (Wright) **14**:346, 361
"Phallomeda" (Clarke) **112**:61
"Phallus" (Hope) **56**:301, 306
"A Phansie turned to a sinner's complaint" (Southwell) **83**:249, 297, 327, 336
"Phantasia for Elvira Shatayev" (Rich) **5**:377
"Phantasmagoria" (Carroll) **74**:7, 71
"Phantasmagoria" (Komunyakaa) **51**:55
Phantasmagoria (Carroll) **18**:46, 48; **74**:3, 10, 35, 64, 70-72
"Phantasy" (Meredith) **60**:262
"A Phantom" (Baudelaire)
See "Une Fantôme"
"The Phantom" (de la Mare) **77**:111
Phantom Dwelling (Wright) **14**:374-75, 379
"The Phantom Horsewoman" (Hardy) **8**:91, 136
The Phantom Ice Cream Man: More Nonsense Verse (Kennedy) **93**:130, 133
"The Phantom Light of All Our Day" (Mackey) **49**:5-6
"Phantom or Fact" (Coleridge) **39**:170
"The Phantoms of Desire" (Cernuda)
See "Los fantasmas del deseo"
"Pharaoh" (Kenyon) **57**:12, 15, 24
"Pharaoh and the Sergeant" (Kipling) **91**:66, 90
"Les Phares" (Baudelaire) **106**:120, 122
"Les Phares" (Char) **56**:199
"The Phase after History" (Graham) **59**:136, 152, 156, 180, 184-85
"Phase Four" (Berryman) **64**:168
"The Phases of the Moon" (Yeats) **51**:151
"Ph.D." (Hughes) **53**:115, 171
"Phèdre" (Smith) **12**:331-32
"Phénix" (Bonnefoy) **58**:174
Le phénix (Éluard) **38**:78
"Phénix" (Mallarmé) **102**:95
"Phenomenal Survivals of Death in Nantucket" (Glück) **16**:131, 135, 139
"Phenomenal Woman" (Angelou) **32**:23, 25, 27-28
"Le phénomène futur" (Mallarmé) **102**:10
"The Phenomenology of Anger" (Rich) **5**:371-72, 384, 394
"The Phenomenon" (Carver) **54**:22
"Phi" (Tolson) **88**:243-44, 260, 304, 315-17, 324, 333
"Philai Te Kou Philai" (Oppen) **35**:314, 340
The Philanthropist (Werfel)
See *Der Weltfreund*
"Philemon and Baucis" (Gunn) **26**:214
"Philhellene" (Cavafy) **36**:40, 46, 49
Philip Sparow (Skelton)
See *Boke of Phyllyp Sparowe*
Philip Sparrow (Skelton)
See *Boke of Phyllyp Sparowe*
Philip the King and Other Poems (Masefield) **78**:8, 11-12, 25
Phillip Sparrow (Skelton)
See *Boke of Phyllyp Sparowe*
"Phillis; or, The Progress of Love, 1716" (Swift) **9**:253
"Philological" (Updike) **90**:351
"Philomela" (Arnold) **5**:37-8, 41, 46-7
"Philomela" (Ransom) **61**:274, 319
"The Philosopher and His Mistress" (Bridges) **28**:87
"The Philosopher and the Lover: to a Mistress dying" (Davenant) **99**:175
"The Philosopher to His Mistress" (Bridges) **28**:87
"The Philosophers" (Merton) **10**:337
"The Philosophers Disquisition to the Dying Christian" (Davenant) **99**:172, 176, 179
"Philosophical Poem" (Ciardi) **69**:14, 31
"Philosoph-Master and Poet-Aster" (Howe) **81**:47, 50
"Philosophy" (Dunbar) **5**:144
"Philosophy" (Parker) **28**:361
"Philosophy in Warm Weather" (Kenyon) **57**:16, 43
"The Philosophy of Composition" (Poe) **54**:263-64, 268-71, 278-79, 282, 284, 292, 294-99, 307-9, 311-17, 320-24, 326, 334-35, 341-42
The Philosophy of Melancholy: A Poem in Four Parts with a Mythological Ode (Peacock) **87**:307, 313, 315, 317-18, 325-26, 329-33, 336, 346, 348-50
"Phoebus with Admetus" (Meredith) **60**:259, 330-31
"Phoebus to Artemisia" (Leapor) **85**:252, 286
"The Phoenix" (Cunningham) **92**:135, 137, 139, 147, 159, 162, 165-66, 170, 173, 177, 188
"Phoenix" (Kavanagh) **105**:163
"The Phoenix" (Sarton) **39**:326, 332, 342
The Phoenix (Éluard)
See *Le phénix*
Phoenix (Lawrence) **54**:197, 203, 218, 251
"The Phoenix Again" (Sarton) **39**:362
"The Phoenix and the Tortoise" (Rexroth) **20**:178
The Phoenix and the Tortoise (Rexroth) **20**:180, 182-84, 192-94, 198-202, 210, 212-13, 217; **95**:248-50, 254-55, 257-59, 262, 264, 271, 273, 275, 277-79, 281, 332-33, 340, 347
The Phoenix and Turtle (Shakespeare) **101**:10, 46
"The Phoenix Gone, The Terrace Empty" (Chin) **40**:11, 13, 16, 19, 21-3, 31-5
The Phoenix Gone, The Terrace Empty (Chin) **40**:8-9, 11-13, 27-9, 34
"Phoenix Park" (Kinsella) **69**:69, 71-73, 76, 80, 83, 85-86, 88-93, 95, 101, 104, 106-7, 142
"Phone Call from Mexico" (Page) **12**:198
"Phoning from Sweathouse Creek" (Hugo) **68**:292, 305
Phosphenes (Zanzotto)
See *Fosfeni*
"The Photograph" (Akhmadulina) **43**:32
"The Photograph" (Cavafy) **36**:41, 76
"The Photograph" (Cohen) **109**:71
"The Photograph" (Smith) **12**:308, 346
"Photograph of My Father in His 22nd Year" (Carver) **54**:6
"Photograph of My Room" (Forché) **10**:144, 156
"Photograph of the Girl" (Olds) **22**:313
"The Photograph of the Unmade Bed" (Rich) **5**:366
"The Photograph on My Father's Desk" (Boland) **58**:12, 58
"The Photographer in Winter" (Szirtes) **51**:171
"Photographs Courtesy of the Fall River Historical Society" (Olds) **22**:307
"Photographs of China" (Hall) **70**:27, 33
"Photomontage of the Urban Parks" (Viereck) **27**:280
"Photos of a Salt Mine" (Page) **12**:167-68, 189
"Phrases" (Rimbaud) **3**:263; **57**:234-35, 253, 285
"Phrases in Common Use" (Jacobsen) **62**:316
"Phronesis" (Rexroth) **95**:269
"P.H.T." (Thomas) **53**:305, 307-8
Phyllyp Sparowe (Skelton)
See *Boke of Phyllyp Sparowe*
Phyllyp Sparrow (Skelton)
See *Boke of Phyllyp Sparowe*
"Physcial Union" (Tagore)
See "Deher milan"
"Physical Love" (Ignatow) **34**:282
"Physician's Tale" (Chaucer) **19**:15, 62; **58**:291
"A Physics of Sudden Light" (Ríos) **57**:329
"Pi" (Tolson) **88**:241, 275-76, 304, 315-17, 319-20, 329
"Piaceri notturni" (Pavese) **13**:205, 226
"I' piango" (Michelangelo) **103**:295
"Piano" (Lawrence) **54**:167-68, 176
"Piano" (Shapiro) **25**:269
"A Piano" (Stein) **18**:318, 350
"Piano after War" (Brooks) **7**:73
"Piano Practice at the Academy of Holy Angels" (Strand) **63**:189
"Le piano que baise une main frê" (Verlaine) **32**:360-63
"Piano Solo" (Parra)
See "Solo de piano"
"The Piano Tuner's Wife" (Shapiro) **25**:303
"Pianto antico" (Carducci) **46**:51, 56, 76, 78
"Piazza di Spagna" (Jacobsen) **62**:331
"Piazza di Spagna, Early Morning" (Wilbur) **51**:189, 209
"Piazza Piece" (Ransom) **61**:271, 301, 306-7
"Piazzas" (Guest) **55**:185, 212
"Pibroch" (Hughes) **89**:114, 142, 152, 166-67, 169, 216
"La pica" (Fuertes) **27**:30

"Picasso" (Pasolini) **17**:295
"The Picasso Poem" (Stern) **115**:263
Piccadilly (Seifert)
See *Deštník z Piccadilly*
"Piccola commedia" (Wilbur) **51**:279, 285
"Piccolini" (Wright) **36**:311
"Piccolo testamento" (Montale) **13**:104, 113, 165-66, 168
The Pickering Manuscript (Blake) **12**:35-7, 43; **63**:25
"Picking and Choosing" (Moore) **49**:96
"Picking Blueberries, Austerlitz, New York, 1957" (Oliver) **75**:322
"Picking Piñons" (Baca) **41**:47
"Pickthorn Manor" (Lowell) **13**:60, 77, 84
"Picnic Boat" (Sandburg) **41**:321, 365
Picnic, Lightning (Collins) **68**:203, 205-6, 208, 215-17, 223
"Picnic Remembered" (Warren) **37**:284, 286, 288, 307, 322, 331-32, 377
"Picnic Weather" (Welch) **62**:370-71
"Picomegan" (Tuckerman) **85**:302
"A Pict Song" (Kipling) **91**:115-16, 165, 167
"Pictor Ignatus" (Browning) **2**:30
"The Picture" (Coleridge) **39**:223
"Picture" (Leapor)
See "Mira's Picture"
"A Picture" (Nemerov) **24**:281
"The Picture" (Tagore)
See "Chhabi"
"Picture Bride" (Song) **21**:334-36, 347-48, 350
Picture Bride (Song) **21**:331-38, 340-41, 343-44, 346-50
"Picture Galleries" (MacNeice) **61**:139
"Picture of a 23-Year-Old Painted by his Friend of the Same Age, an Amateur" (Cavafy) **36**:75, 76
"Picture of a Black Child with a White Doll" (Merton) **10**:341, 345
"The Picture of J. T. in a Prospect of Stone" (Tomlinson) **17**:326
"A Picture of Lee Ying" (Merton) **10**:341
"The Picture of Little J A" (Ashbery) **26**:172
"The Picture of Little T. C. in a Prospect of Flowers" (Marvell) **10**:271, 274, 277, 289, 294, 303-04; **86**:222, 263
"A Picture of Otto" (Hughes) **89**:178, 242, 272
"Picture Puzzle Piece" (Silverstein) **49**:334-35
Picture Show (Sassoon) **12**:257-58, 269
"Pictures" (Whitman) **91**:258
"Pictures By Vuillard" (Rich) **5**:350
Pictures from Brueghel, and Other Poems (Williams) **7**:371-72, 374, 377, 392-93, 403, 408; **109**:192, 282, 301, 325
"Pictures in the Smoke" (Parker) **28**:361
"Pictures of Philippa" (Hall) **70**:32
Pictures of the Floating World (Lowell) **13**:73-4, 93-4, 96
Pictures of the Gone World (Ferlinghetti) **1**:167-69, 171-75, 186
"Pido que se levante la sesión" (Parra) **39**:271
"Pie de árbol" (Storni) **33**:257-58, 305
"A Piece" (Creeley) **73**:46
"A Piece of Coffee" (Stein) **18**:333, 349
"A Piece of the Storm" (Strand) **63**:194-95
Pieces (Creeley) **73**:8, 20, 26-27, 35-36, 38, 41, 46, 58-59, 64, 89-90, 93, 104, 106, 115-17
Pièces (Ponge)
See *Le Grand Recueil*
Pièces du Bocage (Ronsard)
See *See Le bocage*
"Pièces finales" (Sainte-Beuve) **110**:45
"Pied Beauty" (Hopkins) **15**:133, 158
"The Pied Piper" (Tsvetaeva)
See "Krysolov"
"The Pied Piper of Akashi" (Enright) **93**:18
"Pied Piper of Hamelin" (Browning) **2**:36, 63
"Piedmont" (Carducci)
See "Piemonte"
"Piedra" (Soto) **28**:378, 383
"Piedra de sol" (Paz)
See *Piedra de sol*
Piedra de sol (Paz) **1**:353, 355-56, 358-59, 368-69, 371, 373, 375-77; **48**:180, 191, 193, 212, 229, 231, 233, 235, 244-45, 272, 274-75
"Piedra Miserable" (Storni) **33**:251
"Piedra roca niebla" (Alurista) **34**:28
"Pielgrzym" (Mickiewicz) **38**:160
"Piemonte" (Carducci) **46**:26, 52, 56
"The Pier" (Hongo) **23**:201
"The Pier" (Merrill) **28**:267
"Pierce Street" (Gunn) **26**:231
Pierce-Arrow (Howe) **54**:118-22, 149-54
"The Pier-Glass" (Graves) **6**:137, 142, 172
The Pier-Glass (Graves) **6**:128, 147, 150
"Une Pierre" (Bonnefoy) **58**:168
Pierre de Ronsard: Œvres complètes (Ronsard) **105**:195-201, 213-16, 218-21, 224-25, 231, 283-85
Pierre écrite (Bonnefoy) **58**:109, 118, 123, 156, 165-68, 170
"Pierre Menard, Author of Don Quixote" (Borges)
See "Pierre Menard, autor del Quijote"
"Pierre Menard, Author of the Quixote" (Borges)
See "Pierre Menard, autor del Quijote"
"Pierre Menard, autor del Quijote" (Borges) **32**:107
"Pierrot" (Teasdale) **31**:332, 336
"Pierrot" (Verlaine) **32**:365
Pierrot fumiste (Laforgue) **14**:81
"Pierrot's Soliloquy" (Kennedy) **93**:145
Piers Gaveston (Drayton)
See *Peirs Gaveston, Earle of Cornwall. His Life, Death, and Fortune*
"Pierwsza fotografia Hitlera" (Szymborska) **44**:284, 298
"Piet" (Kipling) **91**:173
"Pietà" (Glück) **16**:130
"La pietà" (Ungaretti) **57**:376
Pietà (Thomas) **99**:241, 268, 270, 315, 320-21, 328, 355, 357
"Pig" (Hecht) **70**:108
"Pig Cupid" (Loy) **16**:314-15, 326
"Pig Game" (Stone) **53**:228
"Pig Glass, 1973-1978" (Ondaatje) **28**:327, 335, 337, 339-40
"The Pig-boy" (Ní Chuilleanáin) **34**:351
"Le pigeon" (Hugo) **17**:100
"Le pigeon" (Ponge) **107**:133
"The Pigeon Shooting" (Service) **70**:134
"Pigeon Woman" (Swenson) **14**:265
"Pigeons" (Moore) **49**:120, 129
"Pigeons, Sussex Avenue" (Ondaatje) **28**:292
"Piggy to Joey" (Smith) **12**:321
"Pig's Eye View of Literature" (Parker) **28**:348, 353, 362
"A Pig-Tale" (Carroll) **74**:107-8
"Pike" (Hughes) **7**:136, 158; **89**:163, 169, 185, 188, 207, 211, 257
"The Pike" (Lowell) **13**:69
"Pike Place Market" (Hugo) **68**:236
"Pile of Feathers" (Stern) **115**:249
"Pileup" (Kennedy) **93**:150
"The Pilgrim" (Boland) **58**:42
"A Pilgrim" (Bradstreet)
See "As Weary Pilgrim"
"Pilgrim" (Mickiewicz)
See "Pielgrzym"
"A Pilgrim Dreaming" (Levertov) **11**:209
"Pilgrim Fish Heads" (Bly) **39**:73
"Pilgrimage" (Clarke) **112**:29, 79, 90, 105, 119
"The Pilgrimage" (Herbert) **4**:109
"Pilgrimage" (Olds) **22**:309
"Pilgrimage" (Pinsky) **27**:158
"Pilgrimage" (Wickham) **110**:312
Pilgrimage (Byron)
See *Childe Harold's Pilgrimage*
Pilgrimage (Southey)
See *The Poet's Pilgrimage to Waterloo*
Pilgrimage and Other Poems (Clarke) **112**:27, 31, 34-35, 47, 66, 74, 76, 78-79, 85, 90, 96-97, 113, 116, 120
The Pilgrimage of Festus (Aiken) **26**:13, 22
"Pilgrimages" (Thomas) **99**:274, 338, 358, 360
The Pilgrims of Hope (Morris) **55**:326, 329, 332, 338-39, 343
"A Pilgrim's Progress Through Inniskeen in the Thirties" (Kavanagh) **33**:143
Pili's Wall (Levine) **22**:226
"The Pill" (Clarke) **112**:124
"The Pillar of Fame" (Herrick) **9**:106
"Pillar of Glory" (Whittier) **93**:196
"Pillar of Salt" (Mueller) **33**:196-97
"The pillar perished is" (Wyatt)
See "The piller pearisht is whearto I Lent"
"Pillars" (Paz) **48**:273
"The piller pearisht is whearto I Lent" (Wyatt) **27**:357-58
"Pillow" (Hogan) **35**:257
"A Pilot from the Carrier" (Jarrell) **41**:202
"Pilot Snake" (Oliver) **75**:329
"Pilots, Man Your Planes" (Jarrell) **41**:136, 148, 185, 202
"Le pin" (Ronsard) **11**:277; **105**:265-70, 273-75
"The Piñata Painted With a Face Like Mine" (Espada) **74**:147
"Pin'd I am, and like to die" (Campion) **87**:56, 71
Pindaric Odes (Cowley)
See *Pindarique Odes*
Pindaric Odes, 1550 (Ronsard)
See *See Les quatre premiers livres des odes de Pierre de Ronsard, ensemble son bocage*
A Pindaric on the Death of Our Late Sovereign (Behn) **13**:8
A Pindaric Poem on the Happy Coronation of . . . James II (Behn) **13**:8
"Pindaric Poem to the Reverend Doctor Burnet" (Behn) **13**:32
"A Pindaric to Mr. P. Who Sings Finely" (Behn) **13**:8
"Pindaric to the Rev. Dr. Gilbert Burnet" (Behn) **88**:26
"A Pindarick Poem upon the Hurricane" (Finch) **21**:163, 180
Pindarics (Cowley)
See *Pindarique Odes*
Pindarique Odes (Cowley) **90**:56, 74, 98-100, 104, 106, 118, 128
"Pine" (Dickey) **40**:241-42, 244-46
"The Pine" (Ronsard)
See "Le pin"
The Pine Apple and the Bee (Cowper) **40**:70
"The Pine Planters (Marty South's Reverie)" (Hardy) **8**:101
"The Pine Trees and the Sky" (Brooke) **24**:76
"The Pine with Pine Cones" (Mistral)
See "El piño de piñas"
"The Pineys" (Stern) **115**:258-59
The Pink Church (Williams) **7**:370
"The Pink Corner Man" (Borges)
See "El Hombre de la esquina rosada"
"Pink Dog" (Bishop) **3**:65; **34**:105, 119
"The Pink Dress" (Wakoski) **15**:345, 374-75
"Pink Hands" (Soto) **28**:398-99
"Pink Melon Joy" (Stein) **18**:346
"Pink Moon the Pond" (Oliver) **75**:286
"The pinks along my garden walks" (Bridges) **28**:85
"El piño de piñas" (Mistral) **32**:179-80
"Piñones" (Quintana) **36**:256-57
"Pinos de Navidad" (Mistral) **32**:185
"Pinoy at The Coming World" (Hongo) **23**:198
"Pinup" (Collins) **68**:219
"Pio Nono" (Howe) **81**:30
"Pioggia d'agosto" (Gozzano) **10**:184-85
"Pioneers" (Niedecker) **42**:94, 151
"Pioneers! O Pioneers!" (Whitman) **91**:207, 209
"The Piper" (Blake) **12**:9
Pipes O' Pan at Zekesbury (Riley) **48**:290

"The Pipes of Lucknow" (Whittier) **93**:175, 268-69
"The Pipes of Pan" (Carman) **34**:208, 222
The Pipes of Pan (Carman) **34**:205, 208, 210, 214, 221, 224
Pippa Passes (Browning) **2**:28, 30, 35, 37, 67
"Pirate Story" (Stevenson) **84**:313, 316-18, 344, 346
"The Pirates in England" (Kipling) **91**:116
"Il Pirla" (Montale) **13**:138
The Pisan Cantos (Pound) **4**:320, 337, 344-48, 352, 357-58, 360; **95**:80, 102, 151-52, 156, 170-71, 175-77, 183, 185, 188, 219, 222, 224, 230-31, 234-35, 237-40
"Pisane w hotelu" (Szymborska) **44**:300
"Pisa's Leaning Tower" (Melville) **82**:97, 143
"Pisces" (Thomas) **99**:235, 284-87
"Píseň o lásce" (Seifert) **47**:334
Píseň o Viktorce (Seifert) **47**:321, 323, 326-27, 335
"The Pit" (Roethke) **15**:302
"The Pit" (Stryk) **27**:195, 202
The Pit and Other Poems (Stryk) **27**:181, 183, 190, 193-94, 198, 214, 216
"Pit Viper" (Momaday) **25**:188, 193-94, 199
"Pitcher" (Francis) **34**:242, 244, 246, 253, 255
"The Pitchfork" (Heaney) **18**:256; **100**:247, 322
"Pitching the Potatoes" (Espada) **74**:158
La Pitié suprême (Hugo) **17**:65
"Le pitre châtié" (Mallarmé) **4**:202; **102**:95, 100, 116
"Pity for Poor Africans" (Cowper) **40**:105, 119-20
"Pity Me" (Wylie) **23**:321, 324
"Pity Me Not" (Millay) **6**:225
"Pity the Deep in Love" (Cullen) **20**:57
"Pity 'Tis, 'Tis True" (Lowell) **13**:84
"A Pity. We Were Such a Good Invention" (Amichai) **38**:43, 53
"Pjatnadcat' mal'cikov" (Akhmadulina) **43**:60
Placard pour un chemin des écoliers (Char) **56**:159-62, 169
Placard pour un chemin des écoliers suivi de Dehors la nuit est gouvernée (Char)
See *Dehors la nuit est gouvernée*
"A Place" (Creeley) **73**:44
"The Place" (Warren) **37**:366, 378
"Place; & Names" (Olson) **19**:296
"Place and Time" (Mueller) **33**:196
"Place for a Third" (Frost) **1**:194, 221
"A Place for Lazarus" (Guillén)
See "Lazarus's place"
"Place of a Skull" (MacNeice) **61**:144
"Place of combat" (Bonnefoy)
See "Lieu du combat"
"Place and Displacement" (Heaney) **100**:214
"The Place of Light and Darkness" (Muir) **49**:269, 288-89
The Place of Love (Shapiro) **25**:267, 269, 309, 311, 315
"The Place of Pain in the Universe" (Hecht) **70**:93
"Place of the Salamander" (Bonnefoy)
See "Lieu de la salamandre"
"The Place of Value" (Nemerov) **24**:255
"Place Pigalle" (Wilbur) **51**:317, 320
"The Place Rumored to Have Been Sodom" (Duncan) **75**:263
"The Place That Is Feared I Inhabit" (Forché) **10**:143
"A Place to Stand" (Wagoner) **33**:370-71
A Place to Stand (Wagoner) **33**:325-27, 333, 347, 366, 368-70, 372-73
"Place We Have Been" (Ortiz) **17**:228
"A Place Where Nothing Is" (Warren) **37**:302
"Placed and Punctuation: The Coast" (Stafford) **71**:337
"The Placeless Heaven: Another Look at Kavanaugh" (Heaney) **18**:233
Los placeres prohibidos (Cernuda) **62**:171, 173, 200, 203, 206, 209, 212, 220-21, 230, 235-42, 247, 254, 256
"Places" (Hardy) **8**:91, 104, 135-36
"Places" (Teasdale) **31**:323, 357, 359
"Places and Ways to Live" (Hugo) **68**:253
"Places, Loved Ones" (Larkin) **21**:246
The Plague Column (Seifert)
See *Morový sloup*
The Plague Monument (Seifert)
See *Morový sloup*
"A Plague of Starlings" (Hayden) **6**:185, 195
"The Plagues of Egypt" (Cowley) **90**:104, 106-8
"The Plaid Dress" (Millay) **6**:234
"The Plain Sense of Things" (Stevens) **110**:226, 228, 230-32
"A Plain Song for Comadre" (Wilbur) **51**:220, 268
"La Plaine" (Sainte-Beuve) **110**:39, 57
"Plaint" (Elliott) **96**:154
"Plaint" (Williams) **109**:196
The Plaint of a Rose (Sandburg) **41**:293
"The Plain of Blood" (Montague) **106**:326
"A Plaint to Man" (Hardy) **92**:290
"Plainte d'automne" (Mallarmé) **4**:187; **102**:127
"The plaintiff" (Hughes) **89**:200, 233
"Plainview: 1" (Momaday) **25**:195, 203, 207, 213
"Plainview: 2" (Momaday) **25**:189, 195-96, 200, 213
"Plainview: 3" (Momaday) **25**:196, 213-14
"Plainview: 4" (Momaday) **25**:196, 213-14
Plainwater: Essays and Poetry (Carson) **64**:200-2, 204-7, 210, 212, 214, 219, 229-30, 238
"Un plaisant" (Baudelaire) **1**:59
"Les plaisirs de la porte" (Ponge) **107**:254
"Das Plakat" (Benn) **35**:45, 50
"The Plan" (Creeley) **73**:7
"The Plan" (Stone) **53**:232
Plan (Alurista)
See *El Plan Espiritual de Aztlán*
El Plan Espiritual de Aztlán (Alurista) **34**:17
"Plan for the Young English King" (Pound) **4**:364
"Plan of Future Works" (Pasolini) **17**:257
"The Planctus" (Hope) **56**:289
"Planes" (Merwin) **45**:18
Planet News: 1961-1967 (Ginsberg) **4**:51-2, 65-6; **47**:50
"The Planet on the Table" (Stevens) **110**:95
Planet Waves (Dylan) **37**:63
"Planetarium" (Rich) **5**:366, 370
"Planh" (Pound) **95**:115
"Planh for the Young English King" (Pound) **4**:364
"Planning the Garden" (Lowell) **13**:64
"Planning the Perfect Evening" (Dove) **6**:106
"Planos de un crepúsculo" (Storni) **33**:294-95
"Plans for Altering the River" (Hugo) **68**:253
"The Planster's Vision" (Betjeman) **75**:7, 12, 24, 27, 88
Plant and Phantom (MacNeice) **61**:139
Plant Dreaming Deep (Sarton) **39**:333
Plantain (Akhmatova)
See *Podorozhnik*
Plantarum (Cowley) **90**:45-46, 56, 60, 63, 165, 169, 176
"The Plantation" (Heaney) **18**:201, 225
"A Plantation Bacchanal" (Johnson) **24**:153
"A Plantation Portrait" (Dunbar) **5**:147
"The Planted Skull" (Viereck) **27**:265
"The Planters" (Atwood) **8**:36
"Planting a Cedar" (Hogan) **35**:256
"Planting a Magnolia" (Snodgrass) **74**:315
"Planting Strawberries" (Stern) **115**:249
"Planting Trees" (Berry) **28**:37
"The Plaster" (Merwin) **45**:25
"Plat de poissons frits" (Ponge) **107**:182
"Platane" (Ponge) **107**:78
Platero and I (Jiménez)
See *Platero y Yo*
Platero and I: An Andalusion Elegy (Jiménez)
See *Platero y Yo*
Platero y Yo (Jiménez) **7**:185-89, 191, 199-201, 203
"The Platform Man" (Snodgrass) **74**:293
"Plato Elaborated" (Brodsky) **9**:19, 20
"Platonic Lady" (Wilmot) **66**:324, 347
"Platonic Lassitude" (Warren) **37**:378
"Platonic Love" (Cowley) **90**:14, 116
"Platypus" (Wright) **14**:372
"The Play" (Sexton) **79**:254, 335
"Play Again" (Ignatow) **34**:318
"A Play of Memory" (Updike) **90**:355-56
"The Play Way" (Heaney) **18**:187
"The Player Piano" (Jarrell) **41**:180-81, 188
"Player Piano" (Updike) **90**:350
The Player Queen (Yeats) **20**:353
"Playing Cards" (Atwood) **8**:5, 7
"Playing the Inventions" (Nemerov) **24**:285-87
"Playing the Machine" (Nemerov) **24**:301
"The Playmate" (Whittier) **93**:267
"Plaza en invierno" (Storni) **33**:239, 246
"A Plea" (Randall) **86**:345
"Plea for a Captive" (Merwin) **45**:8
"The Plea of the Midsummer Fairies" (Hood) **93**:42, 56-57, 59, 62, 67, 74, 77, 80, 117
The Plea of the Midsummer Fairies, Hero and Leander, Lycus the Centaur, and Other Poems (Hood) **93**:46, 55, 65, 74, 77, 79-81, 89, 117
"Plea to Those Who Matter" (Welch) **62**:339, 345-46
"Pleading" (McKay) **2**:223
Pleasant Butter (Raworth) **107**:316
"Please" (Komunyakaa) **51**:24, 64
"Please, Master" (Ginsberg) **4**:54, 90; **47**:41
"pleases Davie no end" (Niedecker) **42**:130
"Pleasure Bay" (Pinsky) **27**:157-58, 161, 164-65, 169, 174, 176
Pleasure Dome: New and Collected Poems (Komunyakaa) **51**:50, 57
"The Pleasure of Princes" (Hope) **56**:268-69, 286, 288
"Pleasures" (Levertov) **11**:159, 164, 189
"Pleasure's Lament" (Tagore)
See "Sukher vilap"
"The Pleasures of Peace" (Koch) **80**:311, 319-20
The Pleasures of Peace and Other Poems (Koch) **80**:302
"The Pleasures of Reading" (Simic) **69**:308
"Pleasures of Spring" (Clare) **23**:14
"Plebiscitum" (Carducci)
See "Il plebiscito"
"A Pledge" (Hecht) **70**:95
"Pledge" (Merrill) **28**:284
"Plegaria" (Jiménez) **7**:198
"Plegaria de la traición" (Storni) **33**:306
"Plegaria por el nido" (Mistral) **32**:155
"Pleiades from the Cables of Genocide" (Cervantes) **35**:134
"Plein Ciel" (Hugo) **17**:62, 87
"Pleine Mer" (Hugo) **17**:62, 89
"Plennyi rytsar" (Lermontov) **18**:291
"Pleno amor" (Guillén) **35**:180, 183
"Plenum and Vacuum" (Empson) **104**:122-23
"Plessy vs. Ferguson: Theme and Variations" (Merton) **10**:345
"Pleurs dans la nuit" (Hugo) **17**:89
"Plighted to Shame" (Jackson) **44**:69
"Ploja fòur di dut" (Pasolini) **17**:287
"Ploja tai cunfins" (Pasolini) **17**:250-52, 265, 287
"Plokhaia vesna" (Akhmadulina) **43**:7
"The Plot" (Clarke) **112**:92-93
"The Plots" (Davenant) **99**:175, 177
The plotters (Borges)
See *Los conjurados*
"Plough Horses" (Kavanagh) **33**:77; **105**:151-52
"Ploughing" (Pasternak) **6**:267
"Ploughing on Sunday" (Stevens) **6**:297, 333; **110**:103
"Ploughman" (Kavanagh) **33**:65, 68-9, 77, 113, 155; **105**:102, 151

Ploughman and Other Poems (Kavanagh) **33**:60, 68-71, 82, 92, 113, 117, 167; **105**:90, 98, 102, 171-72
"Plowboy" (Sandburg) **41**:321
Plowman (Kavanagh)
See *Ploughman and Other Poems*
"Plugging In" (Silverstein) **49**:340
"Pluie" (Ponge) **107**:132, 168-73, 190, 222-23
"Pluies" (Perse) **23**:211, 213-14, 221, 232, 233-34, 247, 249-51, 253
"Plumbing" (Stone) **53**:253
"The Plumet Basilisk" (Moore) **4**:243; **49**:94, 98, 107-8, 144, 160-61
"The Plum's Heart" (Soto) **28**:381
"Plunking the Skagit" (Hugo) **68**:235, 259, 284
"Plurality" (MacNeice) **61**:139
"Plus Intra" (Swinburne) **24**:324
Le plus jeune (Éluard) **38**:71
Le Plus Long Jour de l'année (Sainte-Beuve) **110**:38
"Plus près de nous" (Éluard) **38**:69
"Plus Ultra" (Swinburne) **24**:324
Pluseurs Balades de Divers Propos (Christine de Pizan)
See *Autres balades*
Plusieurs sonnets (Mallarmé) **4**:214-15
"Pluto Incognito" (Viereck) **27**:296
"Plutonian Ode" (Ginsberg) **4**:61-2
Plutonian Ode: Poems, 1977-1980 (Ginsberg) **4**:61-2
"The PMLA Biblio, is Limited to Certain Printed Works" (Stafford) **71**:329
"Pnomes, Jukollages, and Other Stunzas" (Birney) **52**:31, 46, 78, 82, 102
"Po' Boy Blues" (Hughes) **1**:254, 270; **53**:82
"Po' Little Lib" (Spencer) **77**:328, 330, 339
Po Pechore (Yevtushenko) **40**:364
"The Pobble Who Has No Toes" (Lear) **65**:144, 149, 156-57, 165
"Pochwala zlego o sobie mniemania" (Szymborska) **44**:290
"Počitadlo" (Seifert) **47**:332, 348
"The Pocket-Book's Petition to Parthenissa" (Leapor) **85**:252
"Pocomania" (Walcott) **46**:273
"Pocta Vladimíru Holanovi" (Seifert) **47**:336
"Pod jedna gwiazdka" (Szymborska) **44**:273, 286, 296, 300
"Poderoso Quienseas" (Fuertes) **27**:38
"Podolie" (Apollinaire) **7**:48
Podorozhnik (Akhmatova) **2**:3, 13, 18
"Podrazhanije Bajronu" (Lermontov) **18**:302
"Podziekowanie" (Szymborska) **44**:319
"Les poêles" (Ponge) **107**:131
"Poem" (Alexie) **53**:30
"The Poem" (Amichai) **38**:35
"Poem" (Berrigan) **103**:28
"Poem" (Bishop) **3**:54-5, 70; **34**:54, 75, 155, 158, 185
"Poem" (Cohen) **109**:49
"Poem" (Corso) **108**:33
"Poem" (Enzensberger) **28**:151
"Poem" (Glück) **16**:142
"Poem" (Hughes) **53**:84
"Poem" (Justice) **64**:263, 267, 272
"The Poem" (Kinnell) **26**:240-41
"Poem" (Kunitz) **19**:147
"The Poem" (Lowell) **13**:83
"Poem" (Meredith) **28**:199
"Poem" (Merton) **10**:349
"The Poem" (Merwin) **45**:3
"Poem" (Rukeyser) **12**:233
"Poem" (Sanchez) **9**:232
"Poem" (Schuyler) **88**:182, 202-3, 206
"A Poem" (Stein) **18**:313
"Poem" (Thomas) **99**:309
"Poem" (Tomlinson) **17**:315, 323, 328, 332, 339, 342, 345
"The Poem" (Williams) **7**:399; **109**:266, 269
"Poem 1" (Akhmatova) **55**:27, 29-30, 37, 42-44, 57-58, 61
"Poem 1" (Ferlinghetti) **1**:167
"Poem 2" (Akhmatova) **55**:29-30, 37, 42-44, 59, 61
"Poem 2" (Ferlinghetti) **1**:173
"Poem 3" (Akhmatova) **55**:28-30, 38, 61
"Poem 3" (Ferlinghetti) **1**:174
"Poem 4" (Akhmatova) **55**:27-30, 38, 42-43, 50-52, 55-56, 58, 61
"Poem IV" (Auden) **1**:10
"Poem 4" (Ferlinghetti) **1**:174
"Poem 5" (Akhmatova) **55**:27-28, 30, 38, 52, 57, 60-61
"Poem 5" (Ferlinghetti) **1**:168, 172
"Poem V" (Rich) **5**:378
"Poem 6" (Akhmatova) **55**:27, 29-30, 38, 52, 61
"Poem 6" (Ferlinghetti) **1**:168, 173-74
"Poem 7" (Akhmatova) **55**:28-30, 38, 42, 61
"Poem 7" (Ferlinghetti) **1**:187
"Poem VII" (Rich) **5**:378-79
"Poem 8" (Akhmatova) **55**:27-31, 38, 42-44, 55, 61
"Poem 8" (Ferlinghetti) **1**:174
"Poem 9" (Akhmatova) **55**:27-30, 32, 38, 42, 61-62
"Poem IX" (Auden) **1**:10
"Poem 10" (Akhmatova) **55**:29, 38, 43-44, 51, 61
"Poem 10" (Ferlinghetti) **1**:172-73
"Poem 11" (Ferlinghetti) **1**:174-75
"Poem 13" (Ferlinghetti) **1**:169, 174
"Poem XIII" (Rich) **5**:379
"Poem 14" (Ferlinghetti) **1**:168, 170
"Poem 15" (Ferlinghetti) **1**:175
"Poem 16" (Ferlinghetti) **1**:175
"Poem 17" (Ferlinghetti) **1**:176
"Poem 18" (Ferlinghetti) **1**:174
"Poem 19" (Ferlinghetti) **1**:173, 175
"Poem 20" (Ferlinghetti) **1**:174, 176
"Poem XX" (Larkin) **21**:242
"Poem XX" (Rich) **5**:379
"Poem 21" (Ferlinghetti) **1**:175
"Poem 22" (Ferlinghetti) **1**:169, 176
"Poem 23" (Ferlinghetti) **1**:172, 174
"Poem 24" (Ferlinghetti) **1**:168, 171, 175
"Poem XXV" (Auden) **1**:10
"Poem 25" (Ferlinghetti) **1**:169, 174-75
"Poem 26" (Ferlinghetti) **1**:174-75
"Poem 27" (Ferlinghetti) **1**:174
"Poem 143: The Festival Aspect" (Olson) **19**:306
"Poem 214" (Dickinson)
See "I Taste a Liquor Never Brewed"
"Poem 287" (Dickinson)
See "The Clock"
"Poem 512" (Dickinson)
See "The Soul Has Bandaged Moments"
"Poem 657" (Dickinson)
See "I Dwell in Possibility"
"Poem 712" (Dickinson)
See "Because I Could Not Stop for Death"
"Poem 1463" (Dickinson)
See "A Route of Evanescence"
"Poem: A View of the Mountain" (Ignatow) **34**:308
"Poem about a Ball in the Nineteenth Century" (Empson) **104**:106
"A Poem about George Doty in the Death House" (Wright) **36**:315, 335, 337, 399
"Poem about Morning" (Meredith) **28**:214
"Poem About My Rights" (Jordan) **38**:116-18, 123-26, 128-29, 131-32, 145
"Poem about People" (Pinsky) **27**:161-2, 173-4, 176
"Poem About Police Violence" (Jordan) **38**:117
"Poem about the Future" (Enzensberger) **28**:142
"Poem about the Imperial Family" (Tsvetaeva)
See "Poema o tsarskoi sem'e"
"Poem after Carlos Drummond de Andrade" (Bell) **79**:34-35
"Poem after Leopardi" (Strand)
See "Leopardi"
"Poem Against the Rich" (Bly) **39**:90
"Poem (All the Mirrors in the World)" (O'Hara) **45**:120
"The Poem as Mask: Orpheus" (Rukeyser) **12**:228
"Poem (At night Chinamen jump)" (O'Hara) **45**:163, 226
"Poem at Thirty" (Sanchez) **9**:224, 232-33, 240
"poem beginning in no and ending in yes" (Clifton) **17**:30
"Poem Beginning 'The'" (Zukofsky) **11**:366-69, 373-74, 381, 383-86, 390, 395
"Poem Beginning with a Line by Cavafy" (Mahon) **60**:196
"A Poem Beginning with a Line by Pindar" (Duncan) **2**:121-22, 127; **75**:203, 230, 250, 256, 258, 261
"The Poem Begins in Silence" (Waldrop) **109**:188
"A Poem Boldly Expressing My Own Feelings" (Yakamochi) **48**:101
"Poem by the Sub-Official Otomo no Sukune Minaka When Hasetsukabe no Tatsumaro, Clerk with the Office of Land Allotment in the Province of Settsu, Strangled Himself in the First Year of the Tempyo Era" (Yakamochi) **48**:132
"Poem Catching Up with an Idea" (Carruth) **10**:88
"A Poem, composed when the Tenno ascended Kagu Hill to behold the country" (Yakamochi) **48**:99
Poem Counterpoem (Randall) **86**:286-88, 333-34
"Poem Dedicatory" (MacLeish) **47**:126
"Poem en Forme de Saw" (O'Hara) **45**:218
"A Poem entreating of Sorrow" (Raleigh) **31**:261
"A Poem for 3rd World Brothers" (Knight) **14**:42
"Poem for a Birthday" (Plath) **1**:381, 390
"Poem for a Decorative Panel" (Hughes) **53**:84
"A Poem for a Poet" (Madhubuti) **5**:327, 344
"A Poem for Anna Russ and Fanny Jones" (Baraka) **4**:39; **113**:25
"Poem for Aretha" (Giovanni) **19**:110
"Poem for Benn's Graduation from High School" (Ciardi) **69**:53
"A Poem for Bhain" (Berryman) **64**:88
"A Poem for Black Hearts" (Baraka) **4**:18-19
"A Poem for Black Relocation Centers" (Knight) **14**:39, 52
"Poem (For BMC No. 2)" (Giovanni) **19**:139
"A Poem for Children, with Thoughts on Death" (Hammon) **16**:177-78, 180, 183, 187-89
"Poem (for DCS 8th Graders—1966-67)" (Sanchez) **9**:224
"A Poem for Democrats" (Baraka) **113**:139
"Poem for Don Cherry" (Mackey) **49**:4
"Poem for Etheridge" (Sanchez) **9**:225, 242
A Poem for Farish Street (Walker)
See *My Farish Street Green*
"A Poem for Halfwhite College Students" (Baraka) **113**:41, 126
"A Poem for Julia" (Hecht) **70**:65
"A Poem for Max 'Nordau" (Robinson) **1**:459
"Poem for Maya" (Forché) **10**:142, 157
"Poem for My Birthday" (Mueller) **33**:192
"A Poem for My Father" (Sanchez) **9**:220, 225, 240
"Poem for My Son" (Kumin) **15**:199, 201
"Poem for My Thirtieth Birthday" (Ciardi) **69**:27, 29
"Poem for My Thirty-ninth Birthday" (Ciardi) **69**:9, 27, 36
"Poem for My Thirty-Second Birthday" (Ciardi) **69**:27
"Poem for My Twentieth Birthday" (Koch) **80**:316
"Poem for My Twenty-ninth Birthday" (Ciardi) **69**:12, 27-28, 50
"A Poem for Myself" (Knight) **14**:39

"A Poem for Negro Intellectuals (If There Bes Such a Thing)" (Madhubuti) **5**:329
"Poem (For No Name No. 2)" (Giovanni) **19**:108
"A Poem for Norman Macleod" (Williams) **109**:286-87
"Poem for Personnel Managers" (Bukowski) **18**:4, 6
"Poem for South African Women" (Jordan) **38**:128
"A Poem for Speculative Hipsters" (Baraka) **113**:99, 139
"A Poem for Sterling Brown" (Sanchez) **9**:229
"A Poem for the Birth-day of the Right HonBLE the Lady Catherine Tufton" (Finch) **21**:164
"A Poem for the Blue Heron" (Oliver) **75**:287
"A Poem for the End of the Century" (Milosz) **8**:213
"POEM For the portrait of an African boy after the manner of Gauguin" (Hughes) **53**:83
"Poem for the Young White Man Who Asked Me How I, an Intelligent, Well-Read Person Could Believe in the War Between Races" (Cervantes) **35**:104, 110, 113, 117, 131
"A Poem for Willie Best" (Baraka) **4**:10-11; **113**:8-9, 18, 41
"Poem From Taped Testimony in the Tradition of Bernhard Goetz" (Jordan) **38**:124
"Poem (Hate is only one of many responses)" (O'Hara) **45**:223
A Poem Humbly Dedicated to the Great Pattern of Piety and Virtue Catherine Queen Dowager (Behn) **13**:8
"poem I" (Storni) **33**:287, 289
"Poem (I lived in the first century of world wars. . . .)" (Rukeyser) **12**:222
"poem II" (Storni) **33**:287
"Poem in C" (Toomer) **7**:333
"Poem in Lieu of a Preface" (Alurista) **34**:17
"Poem in October" (Thomas) **2**:382, 392, 404; **52**:218, 247, 258-59, 271, 281-83, 314-15, 324
"poem in praise of menstruation" (Clifton) **17**:29-30, 36
"Poem in Prose" (Bogan) **12**:100, 107, 112
"Poem in Prose" (MacLeish) **47**:209
"Poem in Three Parts" (Bly) **39**:7, 11, 79-80
"Poem in Which I Refuse Contemplation" (Dove) **6**:120
"Poem Instead of a Columbus Day Parade" (Jordan) **38**:127
"The Poem Itself" (Jacobsen) **62**:300
"poem IV" (Storni) **33**:286
"Poem Jottings in the Early Morn" (Corso) **33**:50
"Poem (Khrushchev Is Coming on the Right Day!)" (O'Hara) **45**:141, 219
"poem L" (Storni) **33**:287
"poem LIV" (Storni) **33**:289
"Poem LIX" (Storni) **33**:287
"A Poem Looking for a Reader" (Madhubuti) **5**:323
"poem LX" (Storni) **33**:288
"poem LXIV" (Storni) **33**:287
"poem LXV" (Storni) **33**:290
"Poem No. 2" (Sanchez) **9**:220
"Poem No. 8" (Sanchez) **9**:242
"Poem No. 13" (Sanchez) **9**:213
"Poem (Now it is light, now it is the calm)" (O'Hara) **45**:225
"Poem #19 in the Old Manner" (Li Po) **29**:146
"Poem of Apparitions in Boston in the 73rd Year of These States" (Whitman) **3**:386
"Poem of Autumn" (Darío)
See "Poema de otoño"
Poem of Autumn, and Other Poems (Darío)
See *Poema del otoño y otros poemas*
"The Poem of Flight" (Levine) **22**:225
"A Poem of 'Good Departure, Good Return'" (Yakamochi) **48**:99
The Poem of Joan of Arc (Christine de Pizan)
See *Le Ditié de Jehanne d'Arc*
"Poem of Lament for the Transience of the Mundane World" (Yakamochi)
See "Zokudo no, kari ni ai sunawachi hanare, sariyasuku todomarigataki koto wo kanashiburu shi"
"The Poem of Life" (Stern) **115**:277
"Poem of Memory" (Akhmatova) **2**:16
"A Poem of Praise" (Sanchez) **9**:242
"Poem of the Air" (Tsvetaeva)
See "Poema vozdukha"
"Poem of the Body" (Whitman) **3**:385
Poem of the Cante Jondo (García Lorca)
See *Poema del cante jondo*
"Poem of the Daily Work of the Workmen and Workwomen of These States" (Whitman) **3**:385
The Poem of the Deep Song (García Lorca)
See *Poema del cante jondo*
Poem of the Deep Song (García Lorca)
See *Poema del cante jondo*
"Poem of the End" (Tsvetaeva)
See "Poèma kontsa"
"A Poem of the Forty-Eight States" (Koch) **80**:341
"Poem of the Fourth Element" (Borges)
See "Poema del cuarto elemento"
"Poem of the Gifts" (Borges)
See "Poema de los dones"
"Poem of the Hill" (Tsvetaeva)
See "Poèma gory"
"Poem of the Land" (Darwish)
See "Qasuhidat al-Arduh"
"Poem of the Mountain" (Tsvetaeva)
See "Poèma gory"
"Poem of the Poet" (Whitman) **3**:386
"Poem of the Singers and of the Works of Poems" (Whitman) **3**:386
Poem of the Son (Mistral)
See "Poema del hijo"
"Poem of the Staircase" (Tsvetaeva)
See "Poèma lestnitsy"
"Poem of These States" (Ginsberg) **4**:66
"A Poem of Towers" (Wright) **36**:306
"A Poem of Walt Whitman, an American" (Whitman) **3**:384, 414
"Poem of Welcome" (Holmes) **71**:81
"A Poem Off Center" (Giovanni) **19**:116
"Poem on a Dream" (Barker) **77**:3
"Poem on a Japanese Paulownia Zither" (Yakamochi) **48**:102
"A Poem on her Brother's Death" (Barker) **91**:17
"Poem on His Birthday" (Thomas) **2**:391; **52**:237-38, 276-77, 301, 303-5, 322, 332
"Poem on Ireland" (Barker) **77**:46-47
"Poem on Life" (Burns) **114**:156-57
A Poem on the Late Civil War (Cowley)
See *The Civil War*
"Poem on the Road" (Jordan) **38**:126
"Poem on Thinking of His Children" (Yakamochi)
See "Kora wo omou uta"
"A Poem Once Significant Now Happily Not" (Cullen) **20**:85
"Poem, or Beauty Hurts Mr. Vinal" (Cummings) **5**:96
"Poem out of Childhood" (Rukeyser) **12**:231, 235
"Poem Read at Joan Mitchell's" (O'Hara) **45**:178-79, 226
"Poem Read at the Dinner Given to the Author by the Medical Profession" (Holmes) **71**:93
"Poem, Small and Delible" (Kizer) **66**:65
"A Poem Some People Will Have to Understand" (Baraka) **4**:16
"The Poem that Took the Place of a Mountain" (Justice) **64**:282
"A Poem to Complement Other Poems" (Madhubuti) **5**:329, 342
"A Poem to Detain Me" (Cohen) **109**:55
"Poem to Galway Kinnell" (Knight) **14**:38
"A Poem to My Daughter" (Pinsky) **27**:153
"Poem to My Husband from My Father's Daughter" (Olds) **22**:322
"A Poem to Peanut" (Brooks) **7**:90
"Poem to Set a Confused Heart Straight" (Yakamochi) **48**:100, 129
"Poem to the Reader of the Poem" (Spicer) **78**:253, 258
"Poem Toward the Bottom Line" (Jordan) **38**:123
"Poem (Twin spheres full of fur and noise)" (O'Hara) **45**:150
"A Poem Upon the Death of His Late Highness the Lord Protector" (Marvell)
See "Poem upon the Death of O. C."
"Poem upon the Death of O. C." (Marvell) **10**:270-71, 305, 312
"Poem Upon the Lisbon Disaster" (Hecht) **70**:108
"Poem V (F) W" (O'Hara) **45**:222
"poem VI" (Storni) **33**:287
"A Poem with Children" (Guillén)
See "Poema con niños"
"A Poem with No Ending" (Levine) **22**:221, 224
"Poem with One Fact" (Hall) **70**:32
"Poem With Refrains" (Pinsky) **27**:175
Poem without a Hero (Akhmatova)
See *Poema bez geroya*
Poem without a Hero: Triptych (Akhmatova)
See *Poema bez geroya*
"Póem Without a Title" (Simic) **69**:263, 299, 335
"Poem Written in a Copy of Beowulf" (Borges)
See "Composición escrita en un ejemplar de la gesta de Beowulf"
"Poem Written on One of my Yearly Visits Home form California" (Quintana) **36**:274
"poem XI" (Storni) **33**:287-88
"poem XL" (Storni) **33**:289
"Poem XLIX" (Storni) **33**:288-90
"poem XLVI" (Storni) **33**:289
"poem XV" (Storni) **33**:287
"Poem XVII" (Storni) **33**:287-88
"poem XX" (Storni) **33**:287
"Poem XXII" (Storni) **33**:287-88
"poem XXIII" (Storni) **33**:287
"Poem XXIV" (Storni) **33**:288
"poem XXIX" (Storni) **33**:290
"Poem XXV" (Storni) **33**:288
"poem XXVI" (Storni) **33**:288
"poem XXXIII" (Storni) **33**:290
"poem XXXVIII" (Storni) **33**:289
"Poema" (Mistral) **32**:166-67, 169-70
"Poema a la eñe" (Fuertes) **27**:37
Poema bez geroia (Akhmatova)
See *Poema bez geroya*
Poema bez geroya (Akhmatova) **2**:4, 6-8, 16, 18-21; **55**:3, 5, 13, 24, 38, 48-49, 64
"Poema Chicano" (Cruz) **37**:31
"Poema con niños" (Guillén) **23**:139
"Poema conjetural" (Borges) **32**:49, 61, 85-6, 115-17
"Poema de amor" (Dalton) **36**:132
"Poema de Chile" (Mistral) **32**:165-66, 170
"Poema de los dones" (Borges) **32**:42, 131
"Poema de otoño" (Darío) **15**:81-2, 91, 96
Poema del cante jondo (García Lorca) **3**:118, 123, 127, 129, 135, 137
"Poema del cuarto elemento" (Borges) **22**:74; **32**:85
"Poema del hijo" (Mistral) **32**:153, 164-65, 176
Poema del otoño y otros poemas (Darío) **15**:86
"Poema en ón" (Fuertes) **27**:37
"Poèma gory" (Tsvetaeva) **14**:325
"Poema komnaty" (Tsvetaeva) **14**:325

"Poèma kontsa" (Tsvetaeva) **14**:301-02, 306, 316, 325
"Poèma lestnitsy" (Tsvetaeva) **14**:325
"Poema o tsarskoi sem'e" (Tsvetaeva) **14**:326-27
"Poèma para los Californios Muertos" (Cervantes) **35**:131, 135
"Poema para un cuerpo" (Cernuda) **62**:173, 222
"Poema vozdukha" (Tsvetaeva) **14**:325
Poemas (1935-1975) (Paz) **48**:175-77, 179-84, 229, 232-33
Poemas de amor (Guillén) **23**:100, 133
Poemas de la consumación (Aleixandre) **15**:4, 6-7, 12, 16-17, 25, 39, 41-4
"Poemas de las madres" (Mistral) **32**:208
Poemas de transición (Guillén) **23**:108
Poemas y antipoemas (Parra) **39**:260, 263, 266-67, 269-72, 276, 279, 282-82, 285, 287-88, 292, 295, 297, 300-2, 304, 306-9
Poemata (Campion)
See *Thomae Campiani Poemata. Ad Thamesin. Fragmentum Umbra. Liber Elegiarum. Liber Epigrammatum*
Poemata Latina (Cowley) **90**:60, 63
"Poème" (Rimbaud) **57**:174
Poeme à l'étrangèr (Perse) **23**:211-13, 217, 232, 234, 250, 256-57
"Poème de la femme" (Gautier) **18**:125, 129-30, 139, 157
"Le poème de la mer" (Rimbaud) **3**:272
"Poème liminaire" (Senghor) **25**:247
"Poème lu au mariage d'André Salmon" (Apollinaire) **7**:48
"Poème pour M Valery Larbaud" (Perse) **23**:223-24
Le poême pulverisé (Char) **56**:114, 170, 173, 189-90
Poémes (Breton) **15**:53
Poèmes (Éluard) **38**:69
Poèmes (Ronsard) **11**:249
Poèmes (Senghor) **25**:232
Poëmes (Vigny) **26**:401, 410
Poèmes antiques et modernes (Vigny) **26**:367, 372, 374, 398-99, 401-402, 404, 410-12
Poemes bibliques et modernes (Vigny) **26**:391
Poèmes des deux années (Char) **56**:108
Poëmes en prose (Baudelaire)
See *Le spleen de Paris, petits poèmes en prose*
Poèmes et prose choisis (Char) **56**:113, 115
Poèmes militants (Char) **56**:129, 158, 186
Poèmes nocturnes (Baudelaire)
See *Le spleen de Paris, petits poèmes en prose*
Poemes Philosophiques (Vigny)
See *Les destinées: Poèmes philosophiques*
Les Poèmes saturniens (Verlaine) **2**:413-15, 430-32; **32**:340, 346, 361, 368, 375-77, 384-87, 389, 393, 399, 407
Poèmes variés (Villon)
See *Poésies diverses*
Poèmes: Yves Bonnefoy (Bonnefoy) **58**:148
"Poemo" (Fuertes) **27**:49
"Poem-Painting" (Guest) **55**:223
"Poems" (Cooke) **6**:348, 394, 416
"Poems" (Shapiro) **25**:294, 320
"Poems" (Stein) **18**:313
Poems (Akhmadulina)
See *Stikhi; Stikhotvoreniia*
Poems (Arnold) **5**:12, 43, 50
Poems (Auden) **1**:4, 8, 10; **92**:53, 64, 81, 86, 109
Poems (Barker) **77**:3-8, 31, 44, 74
Poems (Barrett Browning) **6**:14, 16-17, 19, 21, 25-27, 32, 36-38, 41-42; **62**:61
Poems (Berry) **28**:14-15
Poems (Berryman) **64**:81, 84, 154
Poems (Bishop) **34**:167
Poems (Brooke) **24**:55, 83
Poems (Clough) **103**:54, 104-5, 112
Poems (Cowley) **90**:23, 26-29, 31-36, 44, 59-61, 63, 67, 98-99, 112-13, 115, 117
Poems (Crabbe) **97**:80, 107, 122
Poems (Dorn)
See *Collected Poems: 1956-1974*
Poems (Drayton) **98**:125
Poems (Emerson) **18**:82, 84, 100
Poems (Empson) **104**:89-90, 97, 119, 125, 134
Poems (Harper) **21**:185, 189, 193, 196-97, 209
Poems (Hope) **56**:265, 269, 271
Poems (Ignatow) **34**:271, 274, 279-80, 286, 311
Poems (Kavanagh)
See *See Collected Poems*
Poems (Kinsella) **69**:100, 115-17, 119, 122
Poems (Koch) **80**:299
Poems (Longfellow) **30**:38, 45-6, 50, 53, 62-5, 67-8
Poems (MacNeice) **61**:181
Poems (Mandelstam) **14**:106, 135
Poems (Melville) **82**:6-7, 11-12, 15, 20, 25, 38, 43-44, 49, 52-54, 57-58, 102, 122, 182-85, 188-89
Poems (Meredith) **60**:250, 292, 308, 328
Poems (Meynell) **112**:156, 181, 184-86, 227, 235, 238, 285-87, 291, 294, 296, 298-99, 304
Poems (Milton) **19**:221, 249-50
Poems (Moore) **4**:228, 239, 250-51, 264; **49**:88, 96, 111
Poems (Owen) **19**:325; **102**:236-38, 246-47, 250
Poems (Pasolini)
See *Poesi*
Poems (Poe) **1**:428, 437, 441
Poems (Rimbaud)
See *Poésies*
Poems (Ronsard)
See *Poèmes*
Poems (Rossetti) **44**:165, 201-6, 257-8
Poems (Rossetti) **7**:265
Poems (Southey) **111**:190, 193, 244
Poems (Spender) **71**:138-39, 146, 164, 166-73, 180-81, 183, 186, 189-90, 199, 207, 216, 218-22, 236, 239-43, 246
Poems (Stevens) **110**:191-94
Poems (Stevenson) **84**:335
Poems (Tennyson) **101**:137-38, 243, 270
Poems (Thomas) **53**:264
Poems (Tuckerman) **85**:302-03, 307, 324, 330-34, 337
Poems (Very) **86**:65, 84, 102
Poems (Werfel)
See *Gedichte*
Poems (Williams) **7**:367, 374, 395, 398; **109**:283
Poems (Wordsworth) **4**:375, 401, 415
Poems (Wroth) **38**:305-7, 309-15
Poems (Yeats) **20**:347
The Poems: A New Edition (Yeats) **51**:108, 110
Poems About Abroad (Yevtushenko) **40**:344
Poems about God (Ransom) **61**:267, 273, 291-92, 294, 305-6, 312-15
"Poems about Having Disease Added to His Aged Body, Suffering through the Years, and Coming to Long for His Children" (Yakamochi) **48**:131, 134, 139
Poems about Moscow (Tsvetaeva) **14**:299
"Poems about St. Petersburg, II" (Akhmatova) **2**:12
Poems and Antipoems (Parra)
See *Poemas y antipoemas*
Poems and Ballads (Masefield)
See *Ballads and Poems*
Poems and Ballads (Swinburne) **24**:309, 314, 321, 324, 334, 337, 345, 347, 358, 362-63
Poems and Ballads, Second Series (Swinburne) **24**:319
Poems and Drawings (Bukowski) **18**:5
Poems and Essays (Very) **86**:96-98, 102
Poems and Fragments (Hölderlin) **4**:171
The Poems and Letters of Andrew Marvell (Marvell) **10**:277
Poems and Lyrics of the Joy of Life (Meredith) **60**:329
Poems and Lyrics of the Joy of the Earth (Meredith) **60**:289-90, 292, 294, 295, 298, 328, 333, 336, 339
Poems and New Poems (Bogan) **12**:89, 91, 107, 120, 124-26
Poems and Poem Outlines (Lanier) **50**:118
The Poems and Prose Remains of Arthur Hugh Clough (Clough) **103**:51, 93, 97, 108, 133, 141-43
Poems and Satires (Graves) **6**:135
The Poems and Songs of Robert Burns (Burns) **114**:65-67, 69-72, 87-90, 92, 94-95, 97-98, 113, 116-21, 125, 129-30, 134-35, 140, 144-47, 155-57, 160
Poems and Translations (Kinsella) **69**:115-18, 122
Poems Barbarous (Nishiwaki) **15**:237
Poems before Congress (Barrett Browning) **6**:6, 23, 27, 36
Poems by Currer, Ellis, and Acton Bell (Brontë) **8**:46
Poems by George Crabbe (Crabbe) **97**:119
Poems by George Meredith (Meredith) **60**:287
Poems by Jones Very (Very)
See *Poems*
Poems by Mr. Gray (Gray) **80**:165
"Poems by Ships at Sea" (Koch) **80**:302
Poems, by S. T. Coleridge, Esq. (Coleridge) **100**:21
Poems. By the Incomparable Mrs. K.P. (Philips) **40**:272, 280, 295-99, 312, 318, 328
Poems by the Way (Morris) **55**:325, 329, 338, 340
Poems by Thomas Carew, Esquire (Carew) **29**:64, 87
Poems by Two Brothers (Tennyson) **6**:358; **101**:119, 236
Poems by William Cowper, of the Inner Temple, Esq. (Cowper) **40**:70, 111
Poems, Chiefly in the Scottish Dialect (Burns) **6**:49; **114**:50, 135, 160, 182
Poems, Chiefly Lyrical (Tennyson) **6**:347, 385, 406-09; **101**:119, 242, 245, 249
"Poems Continual" (Jackson) **44**:7, 11
Poems Descriptive of Rural Life and Scenery (Clare) **23**:38-44
"Poems Done on a Late Night Car" (Sandburg) **41**:321, 336
Poems etc. on Several Occasions (Wilmot) **66**:259
"Poems for a Body" (Cernuda)
See "Poema para un cuerpo"
"Poems for a Woman" (Amichai) **38**:54
"Poems for My Cousin" (Jacobsen) **62**:320
Poems for People Who Don't Read Poems (Enzensberger) **28**:141, 143-44, 156
Poems for the Times (Heine)
See *Zeitgedichte*
Poems for Young Ladies. In Three Parts: Devotional, Moral, and Entertaining (Goldsmith) **77**:184, 219
Poems: Four Canzones (Okigbo)
See "Four Canzones"
"Poems from a Cycle Called 'Patriotic Songs'" (Amichai) **38**:44-5
Poems from Algiers (Brutus) **24**:112, 115, 117
Poems from Centre City (Kinsella) **69**:79, 81-82, 97, 109, 128, 131-33, 135-38, 140, 143, 146
Poems from Prison (Knight) **14**:38, 41, 46, 48, 52-3
Poems from the Book of Hours (Rilke)
See *Das Stundenbuch*
Poems from the Greek Anthology (Rexroth) **95**:251
"Poems from the Margins of Thom Gunn's Moly" (Duncan) **75**:160, 206
"Poems from the Margins of Thom Gunn's 'Moly'" (Duncan) **2**:127
"Poems from the Plum Blossom Banquet" (Yakamochi) **48**:103, 106

Poems from the Portuguese of Luis De Camõens (Camões) **31**:24-25, 28-32, 49-53
Poems from the Years 1908-1945 (Werfel)
See *Gedichte aus den Jahren 1908-1945*
Poems from Thirty Years (Werfel)
See *Gedichte aus dreβig Jahren*
Poems, Golders Green (Abse) **41**:2-4, 6, 9-10, 16, 22, 25
Poems Here at Home (Riley) **48**:286, 290
Poems Hitherto Unpublished (Stevenson) **84**:325, 333
"The Poems I Have Lost" (Ortiz) **17**:227
"Poems in Classical Prosody" (Bridges) **28**:65
"Poems in Imitation of the Fugue" (Schwartz) **8**:289, 305
"Poems in Praise of Wine" (Yakamochi) **48**:100
Poems in Prose from Charles Baudelaire (Baudelaire)
See *Le spleen de Paris, petits poèmes en prose*
Poems in the Porch (Betjeman) **75**:12
Poems in the Shape of a Rose (Pasolini)
See *Poesia in forma di rosa*
Poems, in Two Volumes (Wordsworth) **67**:248, 305, 308, 328
Poems in Wartime (Day Lewis) **11**:145
Poems, New and Collected 1957-1997 (Szymborska) **44**:317
Poems, 1909-1925 (Eliot) **90**:234, 261
Poems 1911 (Brooke) **24**:52-4, 61, 80
Poems, 1914-1926 (Graves) **6**:132
Poems, 1922-1947 (Tate) **50**:241, 255, 337
Poems, 1923-1954 (Cummings) **5**:85, 89
Poems, 1924-1933 (MacLeish) **47**:128, 131, 142-44, 147-48, 153, 165, 184, 190, 213, 222
Poems, 1924-1946 (Seferis)
See *Collected Poems, 1924-1946*
Poems, 1926-1930 (Graves) **6**:132
Poems: 1928-1931 (Tate) **50**:230, 242, 256, 293
Poems, 1930-1940 (Blunden) **66**:44-45
Poems, 1934-1969 (Ignatow) **34**:295, 301, 307, 310-11, 313, 319, 322-23, 329, 335
Poems, 1938-1945 (Graves) **6**:129
Poems, 1940-1953 (Shapiro) **25**:285, 297, 313, 317
Poems, 1943-1947 (Day Lewis) **11**:147
Poems, 1943-1956 (Wilbur) **51**:186, 191
Poems, 1949-1957 (Curnow) **48**:3, 6, 12, 24
Poems 1950-65 (Creeley) **73**:8
Poems, 1953 (Graves) **6**:154-55
Poems, 1956-1973 (Kinsella) **69**:74-76, 78
Poems, 1957-1967 (Dickey) **40**:150, 154, 180-82, 185, 192, 195, 197, 226, 239, 241, 259
Poems, 1962-1978 (Mahon) **60**:138-39, 145, 154, 157, 165, 170-72, 175, 181-84, 186-97, 199-200, 203, 205
Poems, 1965-1975 (Heaney) **18**:206, 211; **100**:266
"Poems 1978-1980" (Wright) **14**:377-78
Poems of a Jew (Shapiro) **25**:282, 285, 287, 290, 297-302, 320
Poems of Akhmatova (Akhmatova) **2**:16
Poems of André Breton: A Bilingual Anthology (Breton) **15**:54
The Poems of Arthur Hugh Clough (Clough) **103**:133-40
The Poems of Charlotte Smith (Smith) **104**:151, 282, 286, 293, 301, 338
Poems of Consummation (Aleixandre)
See *Poemas de la consumación*
The Poems of Coventry Patmore (Patmore) **59**:218, 225, 237, 239-45
Poems of Dedication (Spender) **71**:139, 146, 187-88, 190
The Poems of Edmund Waller (Waller) **72**:353
The Poems of Edward Taylor (Taylor) **63**:203, 228, 302
Poems of Felicity (Traherne) **70**:280
Poems of Ferdinand Pessoa (Pessoa) **20**:168
"Poems of Final Occasion" (Jackson) **44**:7, 10
The Poems of Francois Villon (Villon)
See *Les Oeuvres de Francois Villon*
The Poems of George Chapman (Chapman) **96**:65, 74-76
Poems of Gerard Manley Hopkins (Hopkins) **15**:129, 133
Poems of Hart Crane (Crane) **99**:36-37, 39, 42-50, 55, 57-60
"Poems of Imagination" (Wordsworth)
See "Poems of the Imagination"
"Poems of Immediate Occasion" (Jackson) **44**:7, 10
The Poems of J. V. Cunningham (Cunningham) **92**:171-72, 185-92
The Poems of Jane Barker: The Magdalen Manuscript (Barker) **91**:42, 44
The Poems of John Clare (Clare) **23**:3, 9, 11-14
The Poems of John Keats (Keats) **96**:221-23, 225-27, 263, 265-67, 284-85, 294, 337, 342-43, 345-46, 348-49, 353
The Poems of Laura Riding: A New Edition of the 1938 Collection (Jackson) **44**:5-12, 42, 44-45, 51-53, 57-58, 61-63, 65, 68-74, 77-79, 83, 86-87, 89-90, 96, 101-2, 107
"Poems of Longing for the Boy Called Furuhi" (Yakamochi) **48**:131-33, 136, 139
Poems of Many Years (Blunden) **66**:7, 44
"Poems of Mythical Occasion" (Jackson) **44**:7, 10
Poems of Nature (Thoreau) **30**:197, 281
Poems of Night (Kinnell) **26**:257
Poems of 1912-1913 (Hardy) **8**:91-94, 132, 137-38; **92**:225-26, 304-5, 307-09, 311, 315, 319, 367
The Poems of Ossian and Related Works (Macpherson) **97**:306-10
The Poems of Ossian, &c. Containing the Poetical Works of James Macpherson, Esq. (Macpherson) **97**:239-43, 249-55
The Poems of Ossian, in the original Gaelic, with a literal translation into Latin by the Late Robert Macfarlan, A. M. (Macpherson) **97**:199-201, 205, 210-12, 214, 243, 248, 253, 255, 291-92
The Poems of Ossian, the Son of Fingal: Translated by James Macpherson, Esq. (Macpherson)
See *The Works of Ossian, the Son of Fingal, in two volumes. Translated from the Galic language by James Macpherson. The third Edition. To which is subjoined a critical dissertation on the poems of Ossian. By Hugh Blair, D.D.*
The Poems of Ossian. Translated by James Macpherson, Esq., in two volumes. A new edition, carefully corrected, and greatly improved (Macpherson)
See *The Works of Ossian, the Son of Fingal, in two volumes. Translated from the Galic language by James Macpherson. The third Edition. To which is subjoined a critical dissertation on the poems of Ossian. By Hugh Blair, D.D.*
"The Poems of Our Climate" (Stevens) **6**:299; **110**:116, 198-202
Poems of Paul Celan (Celan)
See *Paul Celan: Poems*
Poems of Places and People (Barker) **77**:40
The Poems of Robert Southwell (Southwell) **83**:278-81, 284, 294, 298
The Poems of Samuel Taylor Coleridge (Coleridge) **11**:70, 81, 83, 104
Poems of Shadow (Jiménez) **7**:183
The Poems of Sir Walter Ralegh (Raleigh) **31**:228, 245, 249, 258
The Poems of Stanley Kunitz, 1928-1978 (Kunitz) **19**:175-76, 186
The Poems of Tennyson (Tennyson) **101**:237
"Poems of the Imagination" (Wordsworth) **67**:269
Poems of the Past and Present (Hardy) **8**:121, 123, 125
Poems of the Past and Present: Retrospect (Hardy) **92**:221, 225, 241, 261, 264-65, 286, 340, 371
Poems of Tragic Life (Meredith) **60**:298
Poems of Various Years (Yevtushenko)
See *Stikhi raznykh let*
The Poems of William Dunbar (Dunbar) **67**:26
Poems on Affairs of State (Marvell) **10**:311
Poems on Miscellaneous Subjects (Harper) **21**:184-6, 188, 193, 196-7, 203, 206, 208-9, 215, 217-8
"poems on my fortieth birthday" (Clifton) **17**:18
Poems on Several Occasions (Duck)
See *Poems on Several Subjects*
Poems on Several Occasions (Prior) **102**:283-87, 289, 294-96, 298-300, 317, 326
Poems on Several Occasions By the Right Honourable The E. of R— (Wilmot) **66**:255, 265, 278, 289
Poems on Several Occasions, Never before Printed (Davenant)
See *The Works of Sir William D'avenant, Knight; Consisting of Those Which Were Formerly Printed, and Those Which He Design'd for the Press; Now Published out of the Authors Originall Copies*
Poems on Several Subjects (Duck) **89**:4, 11-12, 14, 26, 30, 36, 41, 88-89
Poems on Slavery (Longfellow) **30**:80-1
Poems on Various Subjects (Coleridge) **100**:20, 25
Poems on Various Subjects, Religious and Moral, by Phillis Wheatley, Negro Servant to Mr. John Wheatley of Boston, in New England, 1773 (Wheatley) **3**:332-34, 336, 338, 345, 349-52, 356
"Poems Referring to the Times" (Barker) **91**:52
Poems Retrieved (O'Hara)
See *Poems Retrieved: 1950-1966*
Poems Retrieved: 1950-1966 (O'Hara) **45**:127, 130, 153, 155, 157-58
Poems Selected and New (Page) **12**:180
Poems: Selected and New, 1950-1974 (Rich) **5**:384, 387
"Poems Speaking of Buddha" (Lindsay) **23**:283
Poems, Supposed to Have Been Written at Bristol, by Thomas Rowley, and Others, in the Fifteenth Century (Chatterton) **104**:3, 6-8, 12, 22
Poems: The Empty Purse (Meredith) **60**:292, 294
Poems: The Location of Things, Archaics, the Open Skies (Guest) **55**:211-12, 214, 217-18, 227
"Poems to a Brown Cricket" (Wright) **36**:301, 329-30, 355
Poems to Akhmatova (Tsvetaeva)
See "Stikhi K Akhmatovoi"
Poems to Blok (Tsvetaeva)
See *Stikhi K Blok*
"Poems to Bohemia" (Tsvetaeva)
See "Stikhi k Chekhii"
"Poems to my Son" (Tsvetaeva)
See "Stikhi k synu"
"Poems to Pushkin" (Tsvetaeva)
See "Stikhi k Pushkinu"
Poems to Solve (Swenson) **14**:276
Poems Upon Several Occasions, by Mrs. Leapor of Brackley in Northamptonshire, Volume 1 (Leapor) **85**:183-88, 190, 193
Poems Upon Several Occasions, by the late Mrs. Leapor of Brackley in Northamptonshire, the Second and Last Volume (Leapor) **85**:183-84, 186, 190, 196
"Poems upon several occasions, by several hands: On the Death of the late Earl of Rochester. By Mrs. A. B." (Behn)
See "On the Death of the Late Earl of Rochester"
Poems upon Several Occasions, with a Voyage to the Island of Love (Behn) **13**:3, 7-8, 16, 18; **88**:27, 29, 39, 45, 70, 72-73, 111,

121, 136, 138-40, 142, 144-47, 160, 163-64; **88**:72, 87, 139, 146-47, 149-51, 153, 160
Poems, with the Tenth Satyre of Juvenal Englished, by Henry Vaughan, Gent. (Vaughan) **81**:318, 336, 355, 363, 366, 368
Poems written before jumping out of an 8 story window (Bukowski) **18**:13
Poems Written during the Progress of the Abolition Question in the United States, Between the Years 1830 and 1838 (Whittier) **93**:318, 336-39
"Poemsicle" (Silverstein) **49**:335
"poemXXXII" (Storni) **33**:290
Poesi (Pasolini) **17**:278
"Poesi i sak" (Ekeloef) **23**:77
"La Poesía" (Borges) **32**:74
"La Poesía" (Cernuda) **62**:224, 226
"La poesía" (Paz) **1**:353; **48**:182, 184
Poesía (Jiménez) **7**:183, 202
"La poesía castellana" (Darío) **15**:95
Poésia Completa (Martí) **76**:132-33
Poesia in forma di rosa (Pasolini) **17**:249, 273-74, 276-77, 286
La poesía juvenil (Borges) **22**:92-3
Poesía, moral, público (Aleixandre) **15**:9
Poesia política (Parra) **39**:292, 301, 304
Poesía superrealista (Aleixandre) **15**:3, 22, 24
Poesía y literatura (Cernuda) **62**:174
Poesías completas (Darío) **15**:93, 107
Poesías últimas escojidas (1918-1958) (Jiménez) **7**:214
"Poésie" (Valéry) **9**:366, 394
Poesie (Carducci) **46**:4, 47
Poesie (Pavese) **13**:207, 210, 215, 220-21, 223-30
Poesie (Quasimodo) **47**:293
Poesie (Ungaretti) **57**:343-45, 347-49, 352
Poésie, 1946-1967 (Jaccottet) **98**:157-59, 171-79, 181, 186
Poesie, 1938-1973 (Zanzotto) See *A che valse? Versi, 1938-1942*
Poesie a Casarsa (Pasolini) **17**:252, 254, 257, 262, 264-67, 279-82
Poesie e prose (Gozzano) **10**:184-85
Poesie edite e inedite (Pavese) **13**:208, 219, 230
"Poesie incivili" (Pasolini) **17**:273
"Poésie ininterrompue" (Éluard) **38**:64
"Poésie; ou, Le paysage dans le Golfe de Glafenes" (Lamartine) **16**:262
"Poesie, ou Paysage dans le Golfe de Genes" (Lamartine) **16**:292
"Poésie sacrée" (Lamartine) **16**:274, 290
Poèsies (Gautier) **18**:126
Poésies (Mallarmé) **102**:66, 98, 102, 135
Poésies (Rimbaud) **57**:205, 237, 244-45, 249, 252-54, 289
Poésies (Valéry) **9**:399
Poésies complètes (Gautier) **18**:147
Poésies complètes (Laforgue) **14**:72
Poésies complétes (Mallarmé) **4**:206; **102**:66, 98, 102, 135
Poésies complètes (Sainte-Beuve) **110**:18, 20, 69
Poésies de Joseph Delorme (Sainte-Beuve) See *Vie, poésies et pensées de Joseph Delorme*
Poésies diverses (Villon) **13**:394-95, 397, 402-03, 407, 411
"A Poet" (Akhmatova) **55**:48
"The Poet" (Aleixandre) See "El poeta"
"The Poet" (Bryant) **20**:11, 33
"The Poet" (Carducci) See "Il poeta"
"The Poet" (Carruth) **10**:84
"The Poet" (Cullen) **20**:85
"The Poet" (Darío) See "El poeta"
"The Poet" (Day Lewis) **11**:146
"The Poet" (Dunbar) **5**:121, 136
"The Poet" (Emerson) **18**:88-89
"The Poet" (H. D.) **5**:306
"A Poet" (Hardy) **8**:90
"The Poet" (Kaufman) **74**:181, 214, 254
"Poet" (Kavanagh) **33**:161
"The Poet" (Lermontov) **18**:281, 298
"Poet" (MacLeish) **47**:197
"The Poet" (Muir) **49**:217
"The Poet" (Rilke) **2**:280
"The Poet" (Randall) **86**:296, 324, 327, 334, 343
"Poet" (Shapiro) **25**:283, 286, 311
"The Poet" (Tennyson) **6**:369
"The Poet" (Tolson) **88**:254, 340
"Poet" (Viereck) **27**:259, 263, 272, 282
"The Poet" (Werfel) See "Der Dichter"
"Poet: A Lying Word" (Jackson) **44**:44, 71, 77-8
"The Poet acquires speech from afar. . ." (Tsvetaeva) See "Poèt—izdaleka zovodit rech'. . ."
"The Poet and His Book" (Meynell) **112**:193, 228-29
"The Poet and His Book" (Millay) **6**:220
"The Poet and His Myths" (Cernuda) **62**:223
"The Poet and His Song" (Dunbar) **5**:118, 121, 134
"The Poet and the Grey Friar" (Dafydd ap Gwilym) See "Y Bardd a'r Brawd Llwyd"
"The Poet and the Muse" (Cavafy) **36**:52
"The Poet at Forty" (Nemerov) **24**:267
"Poet at Seventy" (Milosz) **8**:180, 197, 209
"The Poet Egan O'Rahilly, Homesick in Old Age" (Kinsella) **69**:97, 132
Poet in New York (García Lorca) See *Poeta en Nueva York*
Poet in New York, and Other Poems (García Lorca) See *Poeta en Nueva York*
Poet in Our Time (Montale) **13**:146
"The Poet in Pain" (Owen) **102**:151
"The Poet in Residence" (Mahon) **60**:193
"Poet in Residence" (Sarton) **39**:335-6
"The Poet in Retirement" (Enright) **93**:7
"The Poet in the Machine Age" (Viereck) **27**:284
"The Poet in the World" (Levertov) **11**:172-74
"The Poet Is a Hospital Clerk" (Ignatow) **34**:281, 286
"The Poet Laments the Coming of Old Age" (Sitwell) **3**:317
"The Poet of Ignorance" (Sexton) **2**:368; **79**:237, 317
"A Poet of One Mood" (Meynell) See "Sonnet"
"A Poet Is Not a Jukebox" (Randall) **86**:292, 301, 324, 327-28, 330, 346, 349
"A Poet of the Thirteenth Century" (Borges) See "Un poeta del siglo XIII"
"A Poet Recognizing the Echo of the Voice" (Wakoski) **15**:350
"The Poet Reflects on Her Solitary Fate" (Cisneros) **52**:148
"Poet School" (MacDiarmid) See "Gairmscoile"
"The Poet Sings to Her Poet" (Meynell) See "The Spring to the Summer"
"The Poet Speaks to Her Poet" (Meynell) See "The Moon to the Sun"
"The Poet, the Oyster and Sensitive Plant" (Cowper) **40**:124
"A Poet to His Baby Son" (Johnson) **24**:144
"The Poet, to His Book" (Merton) **10**:337
"The Poet to His Childhood" (Meynell) **112**:271-73, 275-76, 279-80
"The Poet to the Birds" (Meynell) **112**:193, 228, 233
"Poet to Tiger" (Swenson) **14**:280
"El poeta" (Aleixandre) **15**:3, 15, 38, 40
"El Poeta" (Cernuda) **62**:215
"El poeta" (Darío) **15**:99
Poeta de guardia (Fuertes) **27**:13, 15-8, 21, 25, 27-31, 50
"Un poeta del siglo XIII" (Borges) **32**:106
Poeta en Nueva York (García Lorca) **3**:120-21, 125, 136-38, 140, 143, 148-51
"El poeta pregunta por Stella" (Darío) **15**:113
"Los poetas celestes" (Neruda) **4**:293
"Le Poète" (Hugo) **17**:91
"La poéte Mourant" (Lamartine) **16**:271, 273-74, 278
"Les poètes de sept ans" (Rimbaud) **3**:258; **57**:173-77, 184, 216, 234, 246, 249-50, 253
Les poètes maudites (Verlaine) **32**:355
"The Poetess" (Guest) **55**:185-86, 188
"Poetess" (Updike) **90**:351
The Poetic Art (Horace) See *Ars Poetica*
Poetic Contemplations (Lamartine) See *Les recueillements poétiques*
"Poetic Manifesto" (Thomas) **52**:297
"The Poetic Principle" (Poe) **54**:265, 268, 275-76, 331, 342-43
Poetic works (Borges) See *Obra poética: 1923-1976*
The Poetic Year for 1916: A Critical Anthology (Braithwaite) **52**:106, 109
"Poetica" (Pavese) **13**:228
Poetical Blossoms (Cowley) See *Poeticall Blossomes*
"Poetical Epistle to a Tailor" (Burns) See "Epistle from a Taylor to Robert Burns"
Poetical Epistles, with a Preface by the learned Martinus Scriblerus (Crabbe) **97**:157
The Poetical Meditations of M. Alphonse de La Martine (Lamartine) See *Méditations poétiques*
Poetical Recreations: Consisting of Original Poems, Songs, Odes, &c. with Several New Translations. In Two Parts, Part I. Occasionally Written by Mrs. Jane Barker. Part II. By Several Gentlemen of the Universities, . . . (Barker) **91**:11-12, 14-16, 21-33, 42-44, 47
Poetical Sketches (Blake) **12**:31-32, 36, 43, 60-61; **63**:14, 27-28, 65, 69, 98-99, 104, 119
Poetical Works (Coleridge) **100**:103
Poetical Works (Goldsmith) **77**:250
Poetical Works (Hunt) **73**:135, 138, 212
Poetical Works (Montagu) **16**:338, 341
The Poetical Works (Southey) **111**:219, 225, 239, 241, 251-53, 274
The Poetical Works of Abraham Cowley (Cowley) **90**:60
The Poetical Works of Christina Georgina Rossetti (Rossetti) **7**:282-83
The Poetical Works of Ebenezer Elliott (Elliott) **96**:174, 178, 181
The Poetical Works of Edward Taylor (Taylor) **63**:237, 295-99, 301, 303
The Poetical Works of John Greenleaf Whittier (Whittier) **93**:266, 318
The Poetical Works of Mr. William Collins (Collins) **72**:50, 60
The Poetical Works of Rupert Brooke (Brooke) **24**:61, 75-6, 80-1, 89
The Poetical Works of S. T. Coleridge (Coleridge) **11**:75; **39**:169-70, 222; **100**:19-23, 124
The Poetical Works of Samuel Taylor Coleridge Including the Dramas of Wallenstein, Remorse, and Zapolya (Coleridge) **100**:19-23
The Poetical Works of Sydney Dobell (Dobell) **100**:151, 176-77, 179
The Poetical Works of the Rev. George Crabbe; with His Letters and Journals and His Life, by His Son (Crabbe) **97**:76, 90, 119-20, 147, 161
The Poetical Works of Thomas Chatterton (Chatterton) **104**:7, 21, 31

The Poetical Works of Thomas Traherne (Traherne) **70**:183, 186, 189, 193-94, 216, 222, 295, 312, 333-34
The Poetical Works of William Wordsworth (Wordsworth) **67**:248, 251-58, 309-10
Poeticall Blossomes (Cowley) **90**:3, 5, 82, 137, 169
"Poetics" (Ammons) **16**:21-2, 28
"Poetics" (Pavese)
See "Poetica"
"The Poetics of the Physical World" (Kinnell) **26**:289
"Poeticus Eficacciae" (Dalton) **36**:127
"Poetik" (Ekeloef) **23**:77
"Poèt—izdaleka zovodit rech'. . ." (Tsvetaeva) **14**:323
"Poetry" (Arnold) **5**:41
"Poetry" (Goethe) **5**:227
"Poetry" (Kaufman) **74**:218
"Poetry" (Moore) **4**:232, 235, 249, 251, 254, 270-71; **49**:95-96, 161
"Poetry" (O'Hara) **45**:170, 183-84, 227
"Poetry" (Pasternak) **6**:252, 262, 272, 279, 282
"Poetry" (Paz)
See "La poesía"
"Poetry" (Yevtushenko) **40**:338, 346
Poetry (Crashaw) **84**:9
Poetry (Pavese)
See *Poesie*
Poetry (Szymborska)
See *Poezje*
Poetry, 1948-1962 (Amichai)
See *Shirim, 1948-1962*
"Poetry: A Metrical Essay" (Holmes) **71**:83, 89
"Poetry and Happiness" (Wilbur) **51**:254
"Poetry and Landscape" (Wilbur) **51**:255
Poetry and Literature (Cernuda)
See *Poesía y literatura*
"Poetry and Pleasure" (Pinsky) **27**:165
"Poetry and Politics" (Oppen) **35**:340
Poetry and Prose (Blake)
See *The Complete Poetry and Prose of William Blake*
"Poetry and Religion" (Corso) **33**:35
"Poetry and the Landscape" (Wilbur)
See "Poetry and Landscape"
Poetry and the World (Pinsky) **27**:156-58, 160-61, 176
"Poetry = Anger x Imagination" (Alexie) **53**:3, 15
"Poetry by the People" (Elliott) **96**:183
"Poetry Days" (Yevtushenko) **40**:350
"Poetry dusint have to be" (Bissett) **14**:13, 27
"Poetry Festival" (Enzensberger) **28**:162
"Poetry Finished Me Off" (Parra) **39**:264
Poetry for Supper (Thomas) **99**:232-33, 235, 239, 269, 271, 335
"Poetry for the Advanced" (Baraka) **4**:31, 39; **113**:25
Poetry Is (Hughes) **7**:158
"Poetry Is a Destructive Force" (Stevens) **110**:198, 201
"Poetry is Not a Luxury" (Lorde) **12**:143
"Poetry is the Smallest" (Ammons) **16**:43
"Poetry of Departures" (Larkin) **21**:229
The Poetry of Life (Carman) **34**:205-06, 230-31
The Poetry of Luis Cernuda (Cernuda) **62**:169, 176, 178-79
"The Poetry of Milton" (Meredith) **60**:336
"Poetry of the Present" (Lawrence) **54**:184
"Poetry Perpetuates the Poet" (Herrick) **9**:146
"Poetry the True Fiction" (Guest) **55**:196
"The Poets" (Boland) **58**:42
"Poets" (Herrick) **9**:91, 106
"Poets" (Kennedy) **93**:139
"The Poets" (Meynell) **112**:156, 158
"Poets and Painters: Rivals or Partners" (Birney) **52**:76
"The Poets are Silent" (Smith) **12**:354
The Poet's Calendar (Longfellow) **30**:99
"The Poet's Chair" (Heaney) **100**:234
"The Poet's Death" (Lermontov)
See "Smert' poeta"
"The Poet's Death Is His Life" (Gibran) **9**:73
"The Poet's Delay" (Thoreau) **30**:193, 203, 226, 240, 251, 276
"Poet's Epitaph" (Burns) **114**:108
"A Poet's Epitaph" (Elliott) **96**:183
"Poet's Epitaph" (Paz) **48**:250
"The Poet's Epitaph" (Wordsworth) **67**:287, 366
"Poets Hitchhiking on the Highway" (Corso) **33**:5, 23, 31-2, 43, 48; **108**:23, 30
"The Poets Lament for His Lost Boyhood" (Surrey) **59**:352
"The Poets of Seven Years" (Rimbaud)
See "Les poètes de sept ans"
"The Poets of the Nineties" (Mahon) **60**:156
"The Poets of the White Faction of Dante's Florence" (Carducci)
See "I Poeti di Parte Bianca"
The Poet's Pilgrimage to La Belle Alliance (Southey)
See *The Poet's Pilgrimage to Waterloo*
The Poet's Pilgrimage to Waterloo (Southey) **111**:180, 182-86, 250, 252-56, 260, 268
"The Poet's Portion" (Hood) **93**:62, 66-67, 79
"A Poet's Sonnet" (Meynell) **112**:156
"The Poet's Story" (Tagore)
See "Kabi kahini"
"Poets Survive in Fame" (Cunningham) **92**:134-35, 137
"A Poet's Thought" (Hardy) **92**:209
"Poets Tribute to Philip Guston" (Berrigan) **103**:23-24
"The Poet's Vow" (Barrett Browning) **6**:38-9
"A Poet's Welcome to His Love-Begotten Daughter" (Burns) **114**:67-68, 119
"A Poet's Wife" (Meynell) **112**:191, 193, 228
"The poet's words" (Aleixandre)
See "Las palabras del poeta"
"Poet's Work" (Niedecker) **42**:106, 136, 181
"Poet-Tree 1" (Birney) **52**:31, 82
Poezje (Herbert) **50**:17, 19, 21-22, 25
Poezje (Szymborska) **44**:269
"Poins" (Crabbe) **97**:123
"The Point" (Hayden) **6**:193
"The Point" (Montague) **106**:241, 247
"The Point" (Soto) **28**:371
"Le Point du Jour" (Verlaine)
See "Point du Jour de Paris"
"Point du Jour de Paris" (Verlaine) **32**:378
"Point Joe" (Jeffers) **17**:130, 136
"Point No Point" (Hugo) **68**:248
"A Point of Age" (Berryman) **64**:81-82
"A Point of Origin" (McHugh) **61**:200
Point Reyes Poems (Bly) **39**:22-3
"Point Shirley" (Plath) **1**:389; **37**:177, 181-82
"Point-of-View" (Graham) **59**:166
"Le poison" (Baudelaire) **1**:45, 61; **106**:7, 102-3
"Poison" (Tagore)
See "Halahal"
"A Poison Tree" (Blake) **12**:7; **63**:18, 28, 54, 56-57, 68, 70, 83, 92, 105, 109
"The Poisoned Glass" (Martí)
See "La copa envenenada"
Poisoned Lands and Other Poems (Montague) **106**:218-19, 226, 234-35, 242, 275-76, 278, 284, 291, 294, 298, 312, 325, 333
"The Poisoned Man" (Dickey) **40**:192
Poisson soluble (Breton) **15**:48, 63, 68, 70
"Poiu kngda gortan' syra . . ." (Mandelstam) **14**:150, 154
"Pokeberries" (Stone) **53**:230
Pokerface (Collins) **68**:203, 208, 215
Polar Bear Hunt (Bissett) **14**:16-17, 19
"Polar Exploration" (Spender) **71**:207, 223
"Polarballade" (Werfel) **101**:339, 341
"Polder" (Heaney) **18**:245
"Pole Star" (MacLeish) **47**:179, 190, 255
"Polémica" (Dalton) **36**:129
"Police" (Corso) **33**:15, 25, 47-8; **108**:16, 30
"A Police Manual" (Wagoner) **33**:334
"The Policeman's Ball" (Espada) **74**:120, 123
"Policía" (Guillén) **23**:101
"A Polish Dictionary" (Zagajewski) **27**:381
"Polish Pilgrims" (Mickiewicz)
See "Pielgrzym"
"A Polished Performance" (Enright) **93**:13, 25
Politica Poetry (Parra)
See *Poesia política*
"A Political Cartoon" (Ignatow) **34**:318
"Political Meeting" (Enright) **93**:21, 35
"Political Poem" (Baraka) **4**:10
"A Political Poem" (Oppen) **35**:300, 302
"Political Relations" (Lorde) **12**:141
"Politics" (Meredith) **28**:206, 214
"Pollen" (Berssenbrugge) **115**:16
"Pollice Verso" (Martí) **76**:78
"Pollock and Canvas" (Graham) **59**:133, 150, 173, 189-90, 194
"Polonius Passing Through a Stage" (Nemerov) **24**:294-95
Poltava (Pushkin) **10**:366-69, 371, 373, 390-91, 394, 409, 411
Poly-Olbion; or, a Chorographicall Description of Tracts, Rivers, Mountaines, Forrests, and Other Parts of This Renowned Isle of Great Britaine, with Intermixture of the Most Remarkable Stories, Antiquities, Wonders, Rarityes, Pleasures and Commodities of the Same: Digested in a Poem (Drayton) **98**:11-16, 18, 24, 26-29, 31, 38-45, 57, 61-70, 76, 78, 80, 85-87, 89, 91-93, 95, 104-5, 110-14, 116-17
"Pomade" (Dove) **6**:111, 113
"The Pomegranate" (Boland) **58**:19, 48
"Pomegranate" (Glück) **16**:126, 140-41
"Pomegranates" (Valéry)
See "Les grenades"
Pomes for Yoshi (Bissett) **14**:11, 17-18
"Pominal'naia svecha" (Shvarts) **50**:163
"La Pomme de terre" (Ponge) **107**:78, 104
"Les Pommes" (Bonnefoy) **58**:152
"Pomona" (Morris) **55**:323, 325-27
"Pompeii" (Updike) **90**:357
"Pompey's Ghost" (Hood) **93**:99
"Pompilia" (Browning) **2**:41
"The Pond" (Glück) **16**:134
"The Pond" (Nemerov) **24**:261
"The Pond at Dusk" (Kenyon) **57**:15, 26, 37
"Pondicherry Blues" (Jacobsen) **62**:301, 316, 320, 324, 327
"The Ponds" (Oliver) **75**:310-11
"Pondy Woods" (Warren) **37**:287
"Le pont Mirabeau" (Apollinaire) **7**:11, 21
"Pont Mirabeau" (Kennedy) **93**:145-46, 150
"Ponte Veneziano" (Tomlinson) **17**:342, 347, 349
"Ponti Profundis" (Johnson) **81**:117, 236-37
"Pontoosuce" (Melville) **82**:78, 87, 101, 109
"Les ponts" (Rimbaud) **3**:264; **57**:232, 236, 239, 254, 274
"Pony Hill" (MacLeish) **47**:213
"The Poodler" (Merrill) **28**:234, 242
"The Pool" (Creeley) **73**:7
"The Pool and the Star" (Wright) **14**:346
"The pool that swims in us" (Piercy) **29**:316, 318
"Poor" (Brooke) **24**:59
"The Poor" (Very) **86**:46, 88
"The Poor and their Poetry" (Elliott) **96**:183
"Poor Art" (Montale)
See "L'arte povera"
"The Poor at Church" (Rimbaud)
See "Les pauvres à l'église"
"The Poor Bastard" (Corso) **108**:11
"Poor Birds" (Hughes) **89**:168
"The Poor Child's Toy" (Baudelaire)
See "Le joujou du pauvre"
"A Poor Christian Looks at the Ghetto" (Milosz) **8**:191-92, 214
"Poor Clare" (Erdrich) **52**:186, 188
"Poor Dumb Butch" (Randall) **86**:291, 347
"Poor Girl" (Angelou) **32**:27

"The Poor House" (Teasdale) **31**:321
"The Poor in Church" (Rimbaud)
See "Les pauvres à l'église"
"Poor Mailie's Elegy" (Burns)
See "The Death and Dying Words of Poor Mailie, the Author's Only Pet Yowe, an Unco Mournfu' Tale"
"The Poor Man's Pig" (Blunden) **66**:4
"A Poor Man's Wealth" (Riley) **48**:302
"The Poor of London" (Belloc) **24**:28
"The Poor Old Deaf Woman" (Castro)
See "¡A probiña qu' esta xorda . . . !"
"Poor Pierrot" (Masters) **1**:330, 333
"Poor Poll" (Bridges) **28**:77-9
"Poor Poll" (Montague) **106**:329
"Poor Susan" (Wordsworth) **4**:374
"The Poor Washed Up by Chicago Winter" (Wright) **36**:319, 366, 391
"Poor Women in a City Church" (Heaney) **18**:200
"A Poor Young Shepherd" (Verlaine) **32**:399
"The Pope" (Browning) **2**:41, 72
"Pope to Bolingbroke" (Montagu) **16**:342
"The Pope's Penis" (Olds) **22**:316
"Poplar Memory" (Kavanagh) **33**:149
"Poplar, Sycamore" (Wilbur) **51**:187, 204
"Poplars" (Kavanagh) **105**:154
"Poplars" (Sandburg) **41**:324
"Poppa Chicken" (Walker) **20**:273, 276, 286
"Poppies" (Oliver) **75**:319
"Poppies" (Sandburg) **2**:303
"Poppies in July" (Plath) **1**:381, 388
"Poppies in October" (Plath) **1**:384; **37**:257
"A Poppy" (Bridges) **28**:67
Poppy and Memory (Celan)
See *Mohn und Gedächtnes*
"Poppy Flower" (Hughes) **1**:240
"The Poppy Trembling" (Barker) **77**:7
"Poppycock" (Francis) **34**:248
"The Popular Cupid" (Hood) **93**:52
"Popular Demand" (Merrill) **28**:284-85
"Popular Songs" (Ashbery) **26**:162
"Population Census" (Szymborska)
See "Census"
"Population Drifts" (Sandburg) **41**:239, 243, 325-27, 329, 364
"Populist" (Oppen) **35**:301
"Populist Manifesto" (Ferlinghetti) **1**:176, 182, 188
"Popytka komnaty" (Tsvetaeva) **14**:308, 325
"Popytka revnosti" (Tsvetaeva) **14**:306, 308
"Por boca cerrada entran moscas" (Neruda) **4**:290
"Por de pronto" (Guillén) **35**:221
"Pora, Moi Drug, Pora" (Pushkin) **10**:410
"Porcelain Bowl" (Glück) **16**:150
"The Porch" (Thomas) **99**:319, 356
"Porch Swing" (Kumin) **15**:215
"The Porcupine" (Kinnell) **26**:240-42, 244, 257, 262, 291
"Porcupine" (Oliver) **75**:313
"the pores of my skin" (Alurista) **34**:32
"Pornographer" (Hass) **16**:195
"Porphyria's Lover" (Browning) **61**:88; **97**:9, 41-43; **100**:176
"Porphyro in Akron" (Crane) **99**:8, 131, 138
"The Port" (Merwin) **45**:37-9
"The Port" (Spender) **71**:180-81, 217
"Port Bou" (Spender) **71**:205, 207, 227
"Port of Call" (Abse) **41**:3
"Port of Embarkation" (Jarrell) **41**:144
"Port Townsend" (Hugo) **68**:235, 258-60, 262, 282-83, 287, 314
"Port Townsend '274" (Hugo) **68**:260, 262
"Portail" (Gautier) **18**:143-45, 155-56
"Porte ouverte" (Éluard) **38**:69
"The Portent" (Melville) **82**:91, 99, 130, 134, 191-92, 194-95, 206
"Porter" (Hughes) **1**:242
"Pórtico" (Darío) **15**:113
"A Portion of History" (Kenyon) **57**:12, 45
"Portionless" (Gilmore) **87**:301
"Portland, 1968" (Glück) **16**:129, 150, 154
"The 'Portland' Going Out" (Merwin) **45**:7
"Portovenere" (Jaccottet) **98**:172
"Portovenere" (Montale) **13**:151
"Le Portrait" (Baudelaire) **106**:104
"Portrait" (Bogan) **12**:87, 101, 103
"Portrait" (Éluard) **38**:87
"The Portrait" (Graves) **6**:144
"The Portrait" (Kunitz) **19**:176-77, 179
"A Portrait" (Parker) **28**:360
"Portrait" (Pound) **95**:117
"A Portrait" (Rossetti) **7**:296-7
"The Portrait" (Rossetti) **44**:174, 176, 195, 238-39, 244-45, 250-52
"Portrait" (Wright) **14**:356, 362
"Portrait by a Neighbor" (Millay) **6**:233
"Portrait de Paul Éluard" (Péret) **33**:230
"A Portrait in Greys" (Williams) **7**:409
"Portrait of a Girl" (Aiken) **26**:24, 72
"Portrait of a Lady" (Eliot) **5**:153, 161, 183, 185-86; **31**:131, 134, 137, 140, 162, 166, 190; **90**:294, 304, 316, 325
"Portrait of a Lady" (Williams) **109**:325
"A Portrait of a Modern Lady" (Swift) **9**:259
"Portrait of a Women in Bed" (Williams) **7**:348, 367
"Portrait of a Young Artist as a Middle-aged Man" (Abse) **41**:19
"Portrait of an Artist" (Kavanagh) **33**:76, 98-9
"Portrait of an Engineer" (Kinsella) **69**:121
"Portrait of an Old Woman on the College Tavern Wall" (Sexton) **2**:358
"Portrait of García Lorca" (Storni)
See "Retrato de García Lorca"
"Portrait of Georgia" (Toomer) **7**:310, 320, 334
"Portrait of Marina" (Page) **12**:168, 176, 189-90
"Portrait of Mrs Spaxton" (Tomlinson) **17**:311
"Portrait of My Father in an English Landscape" (Szirtes) **51**:173, 178
Portrait of My Father in an English Landscape (Szirtes) **51**:172
"Portrait of the Artist" (Kavanagh) **105**:136
"A Portrait of the Artist" (Kinsella) **69**:133-34
"A Portrait of the Artist" (Mahon) **60**:179, 199
"Portrait of the Artist" (Parker) **28**:351, 361
"Portrait of the Artist" (Sarton) **39**:319
"Portrait of the Artist" (Tomlinson) **17**:320
"Portrait of the Artist as a Prematurely Old Man" (Nash) **21**:279
"Portrait of the Artist as a Young Chicana" (Cisneros) **52**:148
"Portrait of the Author" (Pavese) **13**:205
"Portrait of the Author as a Young Anarchist" (Rexroth) **20**:187
"A Portrait of the Reader with a Bowl of Cereal" (Collins) **68**:207
"A Portrait of the Self as Nation, 1990-1991" (Chin) **40**:9, 19-20, 23-4
"A Portrait of the Times" (Williams) **109**:287
"Portrait of Three Conspirators" (Nemerov) **24**:292
"Portraits" (Cummings) **5**:94
Portraits (Tolson)
See *A Gallery of Harlem Portraits*
Portraits and Elegies (Schnackenberg) **45**:329, 336, 338-39, 342-43, 345
Portraits with a Name (Aleixandre)
See *Retratos con nombre*
"Portret blokady cherez zhanr, natiurmort, i peizazh" (Shvarts) **50**:162
"The Portuguese Sea" (Pessoa)
See "Mar Portuguese"
"Die posaunenstelle" (Celan) **10**:98, 111
"Pose After the painting Mrs. Badham by Ingres" (Boland) **58**:45
"Poseidonians" (Cavafy) **36**:40
"Poseidon's Law" (Kipling) **91**:86-87
"La posesión" (Cernuda) **62**:223
"Posesión del ayer" (Borges) **22**:95
"The Posie" (Burns) **6**:76
"The Posie" (Herbert) **4**:129
Positives (Gunn) **26**:202, 208, 219, 226
"Positives: For Sterling Plumpp" (Madhubuti) **5**:346
"Posle grozy" (Pasternak) **6**:267-68, 285
Posle razluki (Bely) **11**:3, 25, 32-3
Posle Rossii (Tsvetaeva) **14**:298, 306, 310-11, 315, 317, 324-25, 327
"The Possessed" (Berryman) **64**:83, 88
"Possessing Eden" (Kavanagh) **33**:142
"Possession" (Brathwaite) **56**:23-24, 88
"The Possession" (Thomas) **99**:357
"Possessions" (Crane) **3**:83; **99**:11, 58, 68, 73
"Possessions extérieures" (Char) **56**:138
"Possessive Case" (Stein) **18**:327
"Possibili prefazi I" (Zanzotto) **65**:314
"Possibili prefazi II" (Zanzotto) **65**:312-13, 317
"Possibili prefazi IV" (Zanzotto) **65**:315, 318
"Possibili prefazi IX" (Zanzotto) **65**:316, 318-20
"Possibili prefazi o represe o conclusioni V" (Zanzotto) **65**:269
"Possibili prefazi V" (Zanzotto) **65**:317
"Possibili prefazi VII" (Zanzotto) **65**:319
"Possibili prefazi VIII" (Zanzotto) **65**:316
"Possibili prefazi X" (Zanzotto) **65**:312-13, 316
"Possibilities" (Szymborska) **44**:300
"Possible prefaces II" (Zanzotto)
See "Possibili prefazi II"
"Possom Trot" (Dunbar) **5**:133
"Possum Song (A Warning)" (Johnson) **24**:163
"Post aetatem nostram" (Brodsky) **9**:4
"Post mortem" (Jeffers) **17**:117, 141
"The Post Office Clerk and His Daily Duty" (Williams) **109**:196
"POST RESSURECTION CITY BLUES" (Bissett) **14**:31-2
"Post the Lake Poets Ballad" (O'Hara) **45**:186
"A Postcard from Berlin" (Mahon) **60**:148, 150, 198
"Postcard from Cornwall" (Abse) **41**:3
"Postcard from Flamingo" (Oliver) **75**:302
"Postcard from Picadilly Street" (Ondaatje) **28**:329
"A Postcard from the Volcano" (Stevens) **6**:297
"Postcard to the Lace Man—The Old Market, Antibes" (Cisneros) **52**:161
"Postcards for Bert Meyers" (Hongo) **23**:197
"Posted" (Masefield) **78**:101
"Post-Graduate" (Parker) **28**:362
Posthume Poems (Lovelace)
See *Lucasta: Posthume Poems of Richard Lovelace, Esq.*
Posthumous Cantos (Pound)
See *Canti postumi*
Posthumous Poems of Percy Bysshe Shelley (Shelley) **67**:146, 148
"Posthumous Remorse" (Baudelaire) **106**:154
Posthumous Tales (Crabbe) **97**:71, 87, 89, 124-25
"Postilla" (Zanzotto) **65**:283-85
"A Post-Impressionist Susurration for the First of November, 1983" (Carruth) **10**:88
"Postlude" (Williams) **7**:345; **109**:232, 234-36
"Postlude Home" (Brathwaite) **56**:5, 28
"Postman Cheval" (Breton)
See "Facteur Cheval"
"Postmark" (Abse) **41**:3
"Postmeridian" (Cassian) **17**:12
"Postmistress" (Montague) **106**:313
"A Post-Mortem" (Sassoon) **12**:248
Poštovní holub (Seifert) **47**:324-25, 332
"Postponement" (Hardy) **92**:241
"Postponement of Self" (Jackson) **44**:29
"Post-Prandial" (Holmes) **71**:65, 68, 92
"Postscript" (Heaney) **100**:237, 242
"Postscript" (Kunitz) **19**:147
"Postscript" (Seferis) **66**:210, 221
Postscripts (Tagore)
See *Punascha*
"Posvyashchenie" (Akhmatova) **55**:4-5, 8-9, 13, 15-19, 27-30, 36, 41, 43-44, 49, 57-60, 63
"The Posy" (Herbert)
See "The Posie"

"The Pot of Earth" (MacLeish) **47**:125, 127, 129, 132, 136-37, 140, 150, 156, 164, 175, 177, 183-85, 187, 191-92, 222
"The Pot of Flowers" (Williams) **7**:388
"A Pot of Tea" (Service) **70**:121-23
"Pot Roast" (Strand) **63**:158-59
"Potato" (Kenyon) **57**:12
"The Potato" (Mickiewicz)
See "Kartofel"
"Potato" (Viereck) **27**:279
"Potato" (Wilbur) **51**:187, 193, 266-67, 295
"Potato Blossom Songs and Jigs" (Sandburg) **2**:316; **41**:240, 270
"The Potatoes' Dance" (Lindsay) **23**:281
"Potchikoo Greets Josette" (Erdrich) **52**:193
"Potchikoo Marries" (Erdrich) **52**:193
"Potchikoo Restored" (Erdrich) **52**:193
"Potchikoo's Detour" (Erdrich) **52**:193
"Potchikoo's Life after Death" (Erdrich) **52**:188, 193
"Potchikoo's Mean Twin" (Erdrich) **52**:193
"Potega smaku" (Herbert) **50**:13, 22, 24, 40
"Potluck at the Wilmot Flat Baptist Church" (Kenyon) **57**:39, 43
"Potpourri" (Stern) **115**:248
"Potter" (Ondaatje) **28**:318
"Pottery Class" (Kennedy) **93**:139
"Potwór Pana Cogito" (Herbert) **50**:19, 32-33, 38, 40, 46
"Un Pouacre" (Verlaine) **32**:378
"Poui" (Goodison) **36**:142-43, 149-50
"Pouir fêter des oiseaux" (Perse) **23**:254
Pour feter une enfance (3) (Perse) **23**:217, 221, 257
"Pour le livre d'amour" (Laforgue) **14**:80
"Pour Prende Congé" (Parker) **28**:362
"Pour saluer le tiers monde" (Césaire) **25**:13
"Pour se prendre au piège" (Éluard) **38**:69-70
"Pour un anniversaire" (Éluard) **38**:75
Pour un Malherbe (Ponge) **107**:74, 78-79, 81, 91, 99, 102, 104, 115-17, 120, 126, 129, 135, 144, 147-48, 162, 167, 201, 206, 210, 222, 224, 239
"Pouring Milk Away" (Rukeyser) **12**:224
"Pourquoi mon âme est-elle triste?" (Lamartine) **16**:280
"Poussin" (MacNeice) **61**:124
Poverkh barierov (Pasternak) **6**:263, 268-69
"Poverty" (Ammons) **16**:32
"Poverty" (Thoreau) **30**:181
"P.O.W" (Yamada) **44**:334
"Powder Monkey" (Carver) **54**:11
"Power" (Corso) **33**:6, 9, 15, 25, 36, 44-5, 47-8; **108**:19, 22, 26, 34
"Power" (Lorde) **12**:155
"Power" (Rich) **5**:377
"Power" (Rukeyser) **12**:210
"Power" (Wright) **14**:362
"Power and Light" (Dickey) **40**:151-52, 154, 161, 168-70, 175, 255, 258, 260
"The Power and the Glory" (Sassoon) **12**:246
"The Power of God" (Ransom) **61**:294
"The Power of Maples" (Stern) **115**:247, 277
"The Power of Perez" (Guillén) **35**:241
"The Power of Taste" (Herbert)
See "Potega smaku"
"Power of the Many" (Curnow) **48**:24
Power Politics (Atwood) **8**:9, 12, 14-16, 21-4, 26, 31, 44
"Power to the People" (Walker) **20**:294
"Powers" (Milosz) **8**:202, 211
"Powhatan's Daughter" (Crane) **3**:86, 88, 105
"Powrót prokonsula" (Herbert) **50**:32, 36
"Powroty" (Szymborska) **44**:269, 277
"Powwow" (Snodgrass) **74**:291
"Powwow Love Songs" (Alexie) **53**:25
"Powwow Polaroid" (Alexie) **53**:11
"Pow-Wow in Geneva" (Dorn) **115**:201
"A pox upon thy needful scorn" (Behn) **88**:111-12
Prabhat sangit (Tagore) **8**:405-6
"Practical People" (Jeffers) **17**:117
"A Practical Program for Monks" (Merton) **10**:334
"The Prado: Bosch: S. Antonio" (Hugo) **68**:251
"Praesentatio B. Virginis" (Southwell)
See "The Presentation"
"Praeteritio" (Ní Chuilleanáin) **34**:358
Praeteritio (Ní Chuilleanáin) **34**:373
Prague (Seifert)
See *Praha*
"Prague in a Dream" (Seifert)
See "Praha ve snu"
Praha (Seifert) **47**:335
"Praha ve snu" (Seifert) **47**:341
"The Prairie" (Clampitt) **19**:93, 96-7
"Prairie" (Sandburg) **2**:303, 304, 307, 314, 316, 339; **41**:242, 260-1, 270, 274, 296-7, 327
"Prairie Waters" (Sandburg) **41**:270
"Prairie Waters by Night" (Sandburg) **2**:316
"The Prairies" (Bryant) **20**:14, 19, 23-4, 29, 34, 40-1, 47
"Praise" (Ciardi) **69**:54
Praise (Hass) **16**:197-201, 210, 212, 215-16, 222, 226
"Praise II" (Herbert) **4**:121
"Praise III" (Herbert) **4**:125
"Praise Be" (Kumin) **15**:214
"Praise for an Urn" (Crane) **3**:90, 100; **99**:73, 84
"Praise for Sick Women" (Snyder) **21**:325
"Praise for the fountain open'd" (Cowper) **40**:55
"Praise Him" (Walcott) **46**:262
"Praise in Summer" (Wilbur) **51**:188, 193, 267, 283
"The Praise of Pindar" (Cowley) **90**:104
"Praise of the Lofty Shadow" (Darwish)
See "Madih al-Zill al-'Ali"
"Praise to the End!" (Roethke) **15**:254, 272, 274, 284, 298-99, 301-02, 304, 307
Praise to the End! (Roethke) **15**:248-51, 256, 282-84, 298-99, 301-03, 309
"Praise to the Rich" (Akhmadulina) **43**:9
"Praised be Dianas faire and harmles light" (Raleigh) **31**:202, 219, 238, 248-50, 253, 259
Prāntik (Tagore) **8**:422-24
"Pratidhyani" (Tagore) **8**:406
"Pratique de la littérature" (Ponge) **107**:79
"Pravahini" (Tagore) **8**:415
"Pray to What Earth Does This Sweet Cold Belong" (Thoreau) **30**:267
"The Prayer" (Barrett Browning) **6**:19
"Prayer" (Boland) **58**:34
"Prayer" (Cavafy) **36**:53, 79
"Prayer" (Enright) **93**:29, 36
"The Prayer" (Herbert) **4**:102, 130
"Prayer" (Hughes) **1**:240
"Prayer" (Jiménez)
See "Plegaria"
"A Prayer" (Lermontov) **18**:303
"The Prayer" (Mistral)
See "El ruego"
"Prayer" (Olds) **22**:316, 328
"Prayer" (Ransom) **61**:294
"Prayer" (Roethke) **15**:260
"A Prayer" (Tapahonso) **65**:224, 257
"A Prayer" (Teasdale) **31**:322
"Prayer" (Thomas) **99**:360
"Prayer" (Toomer) **7**:320-22, 334-35
"A Prayer" (Tsvetaeva)
See "Molitva"
"The Prayer" (Very) **86**:88, 135, 160, 166
"Prayer" (Wright) **14**:356, 366
"Prayer I" (Herbert) **4**:115
"Prayer at Sunrise" (Johnson) **24**:145, 153
"Prayer before Birth" (MacNeice) **61**:126, 142
The Prayer Before the Poem (Yevtushenko) **40**:356
"Prayer Before Work" (Sarton) **39**:320, 341, 344, 356
"Prayer for a Prayer" (Parker) **28**:351, 364
"Prayer for a Second Flood" (MacDiarmid) **9**:155-56, 197-98
"Prayer for Change" (Yamada) **44**:346
"Prayer for Evening" (Vaughan) **81**:293
"A Prayer for Faith" (Kavanagh) **33**:162
"Prayer for His Lady's Life" (Pound) **95**:220
A Prayer for Marilyn Monroe and other poems (Cardenal)
See *Oracion por Marilyn Monroe y otros poemas*
"Prayer for my Daughter" (Spicer) **78**:294
"A Prayer for my Daughter" (Tomlinson) **17**:307
"A Prayer for My Daughter" (Yeats) **20**:320, 328, 336, 338-39, 342; **51**:98, 134, 142
"A Prayer for My Son" (Winters) **82**:342
"A Prayer for My Son" (Yeats) **20**:336, 339-40; **51**:84
"A Prayer for Old Age" (Yeats) **51**:137
"Prayer for Peace" (Senghor)
See "Prière de paix"
"Prayer for Purity" (Werfel)
See "Gebet um Reinheit"
"A Prayer for Slowness" (Chappell) **105**:26
"Prayer for Sunset" (Cohen) **109**:49
"Prayer for the Great Family" (Snyder) **21**:297
"A Prayer for the King's Reign" (Masefield) **78**:77
"Prayer for the Messiah" (Cohen) **109**:17, 48
"A Prayer for the Mountains" (Chappell) **105**:26
"Prayer for the Pest" (Henryson) **65**:10, 37
"A Prayer for the Year, 1745" (Leapor) **85**:184
"A Prayer for Truth" (Chappell) **105**:14, 26
"Prayer in Mid-Passage" (MacNeice) **61**:142
"Prayer in Prospect of Death" (Burns) **114**:67
"A Prayer of Columbus" (Whitman) **3**:379, 384, 395; **91**:281
"Prayer of Descending Order" (Stone) **53**:259
"The Prayer of Miriam Cohen" (Kipling) **91**:153
"Prayer of Mr. Cogito—Traveler" (Herbert)
See "Modlitwa Pana Cogito-Podróznika"
"The Prayer of Nature" (Byron) **16**:87
"The Prayer of the Understanding" (Dobell) **100**:139
"Prayer to Ben Jonson" (Herrick) **9**:86, 96
"A Prayer to Escape from the Market Place" (Wright) **36**:326-27, 332, 350
"A Prayer to Go to Paradise with the Donkeys" (Wilbur) **51**:190
"Prayer to Love" (Wickham) **110**:309
"Prayer to Masks" (Senghor)
See "Prière aux Masques"
"Prayer to My Mother" (Pasolini) **17**:289
"Prayer to the Father of Heaven" (Skelton) **25**:337, 339
"Prayer to the Good Poet" (Wright) **36**:335, 377, 391, 393
"A Prayer to the Lord Ramakhrishna" (Wright) **36**:341-42, 355
"Prayers and Meditations" (Crabbe) **97**:76
"Prayers for a Dead Bridegroom" (Sachs)
See "Gebete für den toten Bräutigam"
"Prayers for the People of the World" (Dorn) **115**:125
"Prayers of Steel" (Sandburg) **2**:302, 311; **41**:240, 262, 270, 329
"Praying on a 707" (Sexton) **2**:373
"Prayrs for th One Habitation" (Bissett) **14**:20
"Praze" (Seifert) **47**:316
"Le pré" (Ponge) **107**:90-96, 123-24, 129-30, 134, 161, 174, 197, 206, 264, 266-67
"The Pre World Now" (Corso) **108**:11
"The Preacher" (Whittier) **93**:176, 188-89, 251
"The Preacher at the Corner" (Stafford) **71**:287, 289, 319
"The Preacher: Ruminates behind the Sermon" (Brooks) **7**:53, 87, 94
"Preaching" (Howe) **81**:4
"A Preaching from a Spanish Young Princess" (Meredith) **60**:263-64
"The Preaching of the Swallow" (Henryson) **65**:13-14, 26-27, 33-34, 54, 61, 64, 80, 110
"Preamble" (Rukeyser) **12**:209

"Pre-Cambrian" (Thomas) **99**:262, 264, 266, 274, 353
"Precaution" (Frost) **71**:10
"Precautions" (Clarke) **112**:64
"Prece" (Pessoa) **20**:155-56
"Precedent" (Dunbar) **5**:133
"Precession of the Equinoxes" (Rexroth) **20**:193, 196; **95**:259
"The Precinct. Rochester" (Lowell) **13**:83
"The Precincts of February" (Winters) **82**:315
"Preciosa and the Wind" (García Lorca)
See "Preciosa y el aire"
"Preciosa y el aire" (García Lorca) **3**:146
"Precious Angel" (Dylan) **37**:59
"Precious Guilt" (Warren) **37**:376
"Precious Little" (Strand) **63**:188
"Precious Moments" (Sandburg) **2**:331
"Precious Yeast of the World" (Mandelstam)
See "Drozhzhi mira dorogie"
"The Precipice" (Wright) **14**:354
"Precise Techniques" (Baraka) **113**:16
"A Precise Woman" (Amichai) **38**:54
"The Precision" (Winters) **82**:321
"Los precursores de Kafka" (Borges) **32**:47
"Predestination" (Prior) **102**:311, 319, 334-36
"Preface" (Behn) **88**:71
"Preface" (Cisneros) **52**:148
"Préface" (Gautier) **18**:154, 156
"La préface" (Olson) **19**:318-21, 323
"Preface of the Galaxy" (Matsuo Basho)
See "Ginga no jo"
"Preface to a Love Poem" (Mahon) **60**:163, 165-67, 190, 193
Preface to a Twenty Volume Suicide Note (Baraka) **4**:5-6, 14-17, 27, 31, 37; **113**:4, 7-8, 10, 13, 21, 23, 40, 54-55, 77, 92, 96, 126, 147-48
"Preface to an Excursion to the Matsura River" (Yakamochi) **48**:102-3
"Preface to Lyrical Ballads" (Wordsworth) **67**:259-63, 265, 269-70, 277-78, 282-83, 286, 289-91, 294-95, 299, 301, 304, 308-10, 315, 319, 329-31, 335, 338, 340, 348-50, 354-55, 360-62, 366, 370
"Prefatory Poem to My Brother's Sonnets" (Tennyson) **101**:235-36
"The Preferred Voice" (Baudelaire)
See "La Voix"
"Preguntas Frente al lago" (Cardenal) **22**:111
Preguntas y respuestas (Parra) **39**:297
"Prehistoric" (Silverstein) **49**:334
"Prelenstnitse" (Lermontov) **18**:303
Preliminary Poems (Barker)
See *Thirty Preliminary Poems*
"Prelude" (Brathwaite) **56**:26, 49, 67, 75, 82, 98
"Prélude" (Hugo) **17**:91-93
"Prelude" (Kavanagh) **33**:63, 86, 95, 121-2, 148-9
"Prelude" (Longfellow) **30**:19, 26, 44, 62
"Prelude" (Mallarmé) **102**:19-21
"Prelude" (Serote) **113**:292
"Prelude" (Swinburne) **24**:313, 355, 357
"A Prelude" (Tomlinson) **17**:327, 333
"Prelude" (Tomlinson) **17**:328
"Prelude" (Walcott) **46**:272-73, 279, 322
"The Prelude" (Whittier) **93**:239, 267, 275, 345, 349
Prelude (Kavanagh) **105**:96
The Prelude (Wordsworth)
See *The Prelude; or, Growth of a Poets Mind: Autobiographical Poem*
"Prélude au savon" (Ponge) **107**:81
The Prelude; or, Growth of a Poets Mind: Autobiographical Poem (Wordsworth) **4**:397, 402-09, 412, 414, 421-27; **67**:261, 263, 267, 269-71, 281-82, 284-85, 287, 291, 315, 320, 350, 356-57, 364
"Prelude: The Troops" (Sassoon) **12**:264
"Prelude to a Fairy Tale" (Sitwell) **3**:295, 300, 304
"Prelude to an Evening" (Ransom) **61**:276-77, 298
"Prelude to Objects" (Stevens) **110**:159-60, 162, 201
"Prelude to Our Age: A Negro History Poem" (Hughes) **53**:115
"Preludes" (Eliot) **5**:153; 31; 131, 133-34, 159; **90**:329-30
"Les préludes" (Lamartine) **16**:278
Preludes (Aiken) **26**:23, 29-30
Preludes (Meynell) **112**:155-57, 159-60, 181, 228, 235, 252, 270-73, 275-76, 280, 284-92, 294-99, 301, 304
"Préludes autobiographiques" (Laforgue) **14**:66, 95
Preludes for Memnon; or, Preludes to Attitude (Aiken) **26**:23, 29-30, 33, 38, 52-3, 57-69, 72
Preludes to Attitude (Aiken) **26**:38-39
Preludes to Definition (Aiken) **26**:38-9
"Premature Rejoicing" (Blunden) **66**:58
"Premier Amour" (Sainte-Beuve) **110**:39, 64
"Le Premier Jour" (Péret) **33**:231
Premier livre des amours (Ronsard) **11**:246
Premier Livre des Odes (Ronsard)
See *See Les quatre premiers livres des odes de Pierre de Ronsard, ensemble son bocage*
Le premier livre des poemes (Ronsard) **11**:280
"Le premier regret" (Lamartine) **16**:293
"Premier sourire du printemps" (Gautier) **18**:128
La Première Aventure céleste de Mr Antipyrine (Tzara) **27**:227
"Première du monde" (Éluard) **38**:71, 76-7
"Première soirèe" (Rimbaud) **3**:258, 283; **57**:202, 236
Premières alluvions (Char) **56**:129
"Les premières communions" (Rimbaud) **3**:260; **57**:184, 202-3, 205, 250, 253, 294
"Les Premiers Instants" (Char) **56**:156
"Premonition" (Carman) **34**:207
"Premonition" (Montague) **106**:285
"The Premonition" (Roethke) **15**:293
"Prendimiento de Antoñito el Camborio" (García Lorca) **3**:131
"PREPAID CATASTROPHE COVERAGE" (Birney) **52**:79
"Preparations for Victory" (Blunden) **66**:55-57
"The Preparative" (Traherne) **70**:169, 171, 175-76, 180-81, 186-88, 228, 268, 288, 312, 314
"Preparatory Exercise (Dyptych with Votive Tablet)" (Paz) **1**:374; **48**:192
Preparatory Meditations before My Approach to the Lords Supper. Chiefly upon the Doctrin Preached upon the Day of Administration (Taylor) **63**:203, 206-8, 210, 227-28, 230-32, 247, 249, 252, 256, 260, 264, 266-70, 278, 284-85, 287, 295-98, 300-304, 306-7, 315-19, 321-22, 330-31, 333, 335-37, 344-45, 348-51, 353
"Prepare Thy Self" (Roethke) **15**:293
"Préparons" (Ponge) **107**:93
"Prepiratel'stva i primirenija" (Akhmadulina) **43**:17, 20, 36, 43, 53
"The Prepositions" (Olds) **22**:320
"Pres Spoke in a Language" (Baraka) **4**:39; **113**:25
"Presagios" (Guillén) **35**:155, 156
"Prescription of Painful Ends" (Jeffers) **17**:141-144-45
"The Prescriptive Stalls As" (Ammons) **16**:25, 44
"The Presence" (Graves) **6**:137
"The Presence" (Kumin) **15**:181
"The Presence" (Very) **86**:43, 97, 114
"Presence" (Zagajewski) **27**:389, 393
"Presence of an External Master of Knowledge" (Stevens) **110**:230
"The Presences" (Jacobsen) **62**:309
"Presences" (Justice) **64**:252, 274
Presences (Creeley) **73**:23, 79
"Presencia del aire" (Guillén) **35**:157
"Présense" (Césaire) **25**:10
"The Presense" (Elytis) **21**:130
"Present" (Cage) **58**:218
"Present" (O'Hara) **45**:150
"Present" (Sanchez) **9**:219
"Present" (Thomas) **99**:356
"Present, Afterwards" (Aleixandre)
See "Presente, después"
"The Present Age" (Harper) **21**:190
"A Present for the Queen of France" (Cowper) **40**:103
"The Presentation" (Southwell) **83**:257, 278-79, 282-83, 344-45
"The Presentation of the Blessed Virgin" (Southwell)
See "The Presentation"
Presentation Piece (Hacker) **47**:79-80, 88, 90, 115
"Presente, después" (Aleixandre) **15**:6
Presented to Ch'en Shang (Li Ho) **13**:44
"Presented to Wang Lun" (Li Po) **29**:146
"Presented to Wei Pa, Gentleman in Retirement" (Tu Fu) **9**:322
"Presenza: F. T. Marinetti" (Pound)
See "Canto 72"
"Preseul, ovile regis" (Gower) **59**:25
"The President About to Address the Nation in the Eighth Year of the Vietnam War" (Bly) **39**:51
"President Harding's Tomb in Ohio" (Wright) **36**:396
"President Lincoln's Proclamation of Freedom" (Harper) **21**:197
"The Presidentiad" (Hall) **70**:26, 32
"Prèsomptif" (Perse) **23**:230
"Press Release" (Merriman) **28**:284-85
"A Pressed Flower" (Raworth) **107**:308
"The Pressed Gentian" (Whittier) **93**:275
"Presso l'Urna di Percy Bysshe Shelley" (Carducci) **46**:9, 16, 26, 54, 87
"Presso Una Certosa" (Carducci) **46**:31
"Pressure to Grow" (Baraka) **4**:30
"Pressures" (Wright) **14**:375
"Preston North End" (Szirtes) **51**:179
"Prestupnik" (Lermontov) **18**:289
"The Presumptions of Death" (Hecht) **70**:92, 94-95, 100-101, 108
"Pretend You Live in a Room" (Stafford) **71**:373
"Pretiolae" (Moore) **49**:126
"Pretty" (Smith) **12**:301, 318, 321, 328
"The Pretty Bar-Keeper of the Mitre" (Smart) **13**:341, 347
"The Pretty Barmaid" (Smart)
See "The Pretty Bar-Keeper of the Mitre"
"The Pretty Redhead" (Apollinaire)
See "La jolie rousse"
"The Pretty Redhead, from the French of Apollinaire" (Wright) **36**:308-9
"A Pretty Woman" (Browning) **61**:90
"Pretty Words" (Wylie) **23**:314, 324
"Prevalent at One Time" (Moore) **49**:150
"Priapus" (H. D.) **5**:275, 303
Priapus and the Pool and Other Poems (Aiken) **26**:46
"Pricing" (Ignatow) **34**:305
"La prière" (Lamartine) **16**:276-77, 291, 299-301
"Prière aux Masques" (Senghor) **25**:224, 227, 229-30, 241
"Prière de paix" (Senghor) **25**:231, 254
"Prière du matin" (Verlaine) **2**:416
"La prière pour tous" (Hugo) **17**:45
"The Priest" (H. D.) **5**:306
"Priest" (Herbert) **50**:18, 25
"The Priest" (Thomas) **99**:267
"Priest and Peasant" (Thomas) **99**:246
"The Priest and the Matador" (Bukowski) **18**:4
"Priest of the Temple of Serapis" (Cavafy) **36**:32
"The Priest Says Goodbye" (Cohen) **109**:4, 54-55

"A Priest to his People" (Thomas) **99**:243-44
"Prigovor" (Akhmatova) **2**:8-9; **55**:5, 10, 25-26, 28, 42, 58, 60, 62
"Prikljucenie v antikvarnom magazine" (Akhmadulina) **43**:7, 14-15
Přilba hlíny (Seifert) **47**:316, 326, 335
"Prima del viaggio" (Montale) **13**:134
"Prima persona" (Zanzotto) **65**:278
"Primal Death" (Stramm)
See "Urtod"
"Primal Landscapes" (Zanzotto)
See "I paesaggi primi"
"Primal Vision" (Benn) **35**:8
Primal Vision (Benn) **35**:7, 8, 9
"Primäre Tage" (Benn) **35**:67
"Primary Colors" (Song) **21**:333-34, 343, 350
"A Primary Ground" (Rich) **5**:361
"La primavera" (Jiménez) **7**:193-94
"Primavera" (Winters) **82**:323
"Primavera classica" (Carducci) **46**:48, 77-78, 80
"Primavera delgada" (Guillén) **35**:186, 188
"La primavera Hitleriana" (Montale) **13**:104, 109, 145, 148, 165-66
"Primaveral" (Darío) **15**:117
"Primavere Dorica" (Carducci) **46**:40, 42, 86
"Primavere elleniche" (Carducci) **46**:23, 37, 43, 54, 58, 64, 78, 86
"Prime" (Auden) **92**:43, 45-46, 48
"Prime" (Hughes) **53**:150
"Prime" (Lowell) **13**:64, 67
"Prime Minister" (Enright) **93**:21
Primer for Blacks (Brooks) **7**:83, 86
Primer for Blacks—Three Preachments (Brooks)
See *Primer for Blacks*
"A Primer of the Daily Round" (Nemerov) **24**:257, 283
Primer romancero gitano (García Lorca) **3**:119-21, 127, 130, 133-34, 136-38, 145-49
Primeras poesías (Cernuda) **62**:170, 181, 212, 245-46, 251
Primeras poesias (Jiménez) **7**:209
"Primero sueño" (Juana Inés de la Cruz)
See *El Sueño*
Primero sueño (Juana Inés de la Cruz)
See *El Sueño*
"Primeros Sonidos" (Cruz) **37**:31
"The Primitive" (Madhubuti) **5**:322
"Primitive" (Olds) **22**:307
"Primitive" (Oppen) **35**:300-01
"The Primitive" (Swenson) **14**:264
Primitive (Oliver)
See *American Primitive: Poems*
Primitive (Oppen) **35**:300-01, 302, 303, 304, 324, 325, 335, 338
"A Primitive Like an Orb" (Stevens) **6**:314, 335; **110**:94, 226, 229
"Primitives" (Randall) **86**:288, 336
"'Primitivism' Exhibit" (Kumin) **15**:209
"Primo vere" (Carducci) **46**:87
"The Primrose" (Donne) **1**:126, 130
"Primrose" (Herrick) **9**:125
"Primrose" (Kavanagh) **33**:97, 118, 162; **105**:152
"Primrose" (Williams) **7**:345
The Primrose Path (Nash) **21**:263
"The Prince" (de la Mare) **77**:113-14
"The Prince" (Wald) **46**:230
"Prince Athanase" (Shelley) **14**:189, 192, 202, 234-35
"Prince Henry" (Donne) **43**:125
Prince Hohenstiel-Schwangau (Browning) **2**:43, 47, 82, 95
"Prince Meow" (Cassian) **17**:3
"The Prince of Darkness Passing through this House" (Wakoski) **15**:363
"Prince Tank" (Viereck) **27**:260, 280
"The Prince's Progress" (Rossetti) **7**:262-4, 279-80, 287, 289, 293-4, 296-8
The Prince's Progress, and Other Poems (Rossetti) **7**:261, 263, 266, 296
The Princess: A Medley (Tennyson) **6**:354, 360, 364-65, 371, 409; **101**:145, 147-56, 188-89, 215-16, 218-20, 222-24, 238-39, 241, 243, 248-49, 269-70, 274, 280-81
The Princess and the Knights (Bely) **11**:24
"Princesse Loysa drawing" (Lovelace) **69**:233-34
"Principalities of June" (Doty) **53**:69
"Príncipe enano" (Martí) **76**:133-34
"De Principiis" (Gray)
See *De principiis cogitandi*
De principiis (Gray)
See *De principiis cogitandi*
De principiis cogitandi (Gray) **2**:154; **80**:234-36, 238-39, 249, 251, 261
Principle in Art (Crabbe) **97**:121
"Prinkin' Leddie" (Wylie) **23**:301
"Printemps" (Tzara) **27**:223
"Printemps" (Verlaine) **32**:400-05
"Prioress's Tale" (Chaucer) **19**:13, 15, 54-6
"The Priory of St. Saviour, Glendalough" (Davie) **29**:108-09
"The Prism" (Hughes) **89**:162
"La Prison" (Vigny) **26**:380, 401-403, 410
"The Prison Cell" (Darwish) **86**:34
"The Prisoner" (Barrett Browning) **6**:26
"The Prisoner" (Brontë)
See "Julian M. and A. G. Rochelle"
"The Prisoner" (Das) **43**:89-90
"The Prisoner" (Douglas) **106**:186
"The Prisoner" (Paz)
See "El prisonero"
"The Prisoner" (Tagore)
See "Bandi"
"The Prisoner" (Thomas) **99**:348
"The Prisoner" (Very) **86**:97
The Prisoner of Chillon, and Other Poems (Byron) **16**:87
"The Prisoner of the Caucasus" (Lermontov) **18**:278
The Prisoner of the Caucasus (Pushkin)
See *Kavkazsky plennik*
"The Prisoner of Zenda" (Wilbur) **51**:285
"El prisonero" (Paz) **1**:364-65
"Prisoners" (Boland) **58**:44
"The Prisoners" (Hayden) **6**:194-95
"Prisoners" (Komunyakaa) **51**:61
"The Prisoners" (Spender) **71**:147, 180, 219
"The Prisoner's Complaint" (Scott) **13**:292
"The Prisoner's Dream" (Montale)
See "Il Sogno del prigioniero"
"The Prisoner's Woman" (Mistral)
See "Mujer de prisionero"
"Le Prisonnier" (Béranger) **112**:21
"Privacy" (Rexroth) **20**:221
"A Private" (Thomas) **53**:326
"A private bestiary" (Piercy) **29**:314
The Private Dining Room (Nash) **21**:270-71
"The Private Life" (Graham) **59**:166
"The Private Life" (Mueller) **33**:180
The Private Life (Mueller) **33**:175-76, 178-80, 186
"Private Madrigals" (Montale)
See "Madrigali privati"
"A Private Man on Public Men" (Hardy) **92**:209, 222
"Private Means is Dead" (Smith) **12**:309, 333
A Private Mythology (Sarton) **39**:321, 326-28, 333, 338-43, 345
"The Private Place" (Muir) **49**:242
The Privilege (Kumin) **15**:180-81, 200, 208
"The Prize" (Muir) **49**:232
"Prize Fighter" (Hughes) **53**:181
"A Prize Poem submitted by Mr. Lambkin of Burford to the Examiners of the University of Oxford on the Prescribed Poetic Theme Set by Them in 1893, 'The Benefits of the Electric Light'" (Belloc) **24**:4
"Pro femina" (Kizer) **66**:68-69, 71, 77-78
"Pro Nobis" (Oppen) **35**:307
A Probable Volume of Dreams (Bell) **79**:39
"The Probationer" (Page) **12**:176
"Probity" (Graham) **59**:186, 190
"A Problem" (Borges) **32**:46
"The Problem" (Emerson) **18**:74, 79, 84, 100-2
"A Problem from Milton" (Wilbur) **51**:193
"A Problem in Spatial Composition" (Warren) **37**:331, 356, 366, 380
"The Problem of Anxiety" (Koch) **80**:290
"The Problem of the Poem for My Daughter, Left Unsolved" (Dorn) **115**:54, 56, 74, 83, 85, 114, 127, 192, 220
"Problemas del subdesarrollo" (Guillén) **23**:121
Problems (Donne) **43**:118-20
"Problems of Knowledge" (Warren) **37**:381
"Problems of Underdevelopment" (Guillén)
See "Problemas del subdesarrollo"
"Problems With Hurricanes" (Cruz) **37**:23
"Procedure" (Stone) **53**:253
"Procedures for Underground" (Atwood) **8**:13, 19
Procedures for Underground (Atwood) **8**:2-3, 12, 15-16, 21
"Le Procès à la Révolution" (Hugo) **17**:102
"Procesión India" (Mistral) **32**:185
"Process" (Montague) **106**:256, 270, 292
"A Process" (Tomlinson) **17**:323, 331, 339
"A Process in the Weather of the Heart" (Thomas) **52**:310, 322
"Processe of tyme worketh suche wounder" (Wyatt) **27**:317, 320
"Processes" (Tomlinson) **17**:322, 327, 337-40
"Procession" (Tate) **50**:256
"A Procession at Candlemas" (Clampitt) **19**:82-3, 89, 98
"A Procession of Dead Days" (Hardy) **92**:328
"Procession Poem" (Wakoski) **15**:324
"Processional" (Enright) **93**:34
"Processionals, II" (Duncan) **2**:101; **75**:156
"The Proclamation" (Whittier) **93**:213, 348
"Procrastination" (Crabbe) **97**:94-95, 97, 103, 110, 125-27, 134, 138
"Proda di Versilia" (Montale) **13**:112, 148
"The Prodigal" (Simic) **69**:307
"The Prodigal Son" (Bishop) **34**:82, 97
"The Prodigal Son" (Bly) **39**:63-4, 100
"The Prodigal Son" (Johnson) **24**:128-29, 133, 156, 164, 169
"The Prodigal Son" (Merwin) **45**:11-12, 14-15, 24
"The Prodigal-Child's Soul-Wrack" (Southwell) **83**:281
"The Prodigal's Return" (Harper) **21**:208
"Prodigy" (Simic) **69**:269, 295, 312
"The Produce District" (Gunn) **26**:203, 231
"Product" (Oppen) **35**:284, 293
"Proem" (Chappell) **105**:49
"Proem" (Hughes) **53**:84
"Proem" (Patmore) **59**:261, 275
"Proem" (Whittier) **93**:198, 239, 347
"Proem: To Brooklyn Bridge" (Crane) **3**:85, 88, 90, 107, 109; **99**:105
Proêmes (Ponge) **107**:78, 88-89, 130, 136-37, 142-43, 161, 166, 173, 177, 192, 213, 225, 236-37
Profane Proses (Darío)
See *Prosas profanas, y otros poemas*
"Profer'd Love Rejected" (Suckling) **30**:126
"Profession" (Akhmadulina)
See "Rod zanjatij"
"The Professional" (Ignatow) **34**:273
"Professor Eucalyptus" (Stevens) **110**:141
"Professor Gratt" (Hall) **70**:32
"Professor of Middle English Confronts Monster" (Birney) **52**:15
"A Professor's Song" (Berryman) **64**:88
"Profezie" (Pasolini) **17**:277
"Profezie I" (Zanzotto) **65**:320
"Profezie III" (Zanzotto) **65**:318
"Profezie IX" (Zanzotto) **65**:312-13, 316-17
"Profezie o memorie o giornali murali XVI" (Zanzotto) **65**:263
"Profezie V" (Zanzotto) **65**:312-14, 317

"Profezie X" (Zanzotto) **65**:317
"Profezie XI" (Zanzotto) **65**:319
"Profezie XIII" (Zanzotto) **65**:314
"Profezie XV" (Zanzotto) **65**:314
"Profezie XVIII" (Zanzotto) **65**:316
"The Proffer" (Vaughan) **81**:348-51
"Profile" (Hope) **56**:278
Profile of the Wind (Cernuda)
See *Perfil del aire*
"The Profile on the Pillow" (Randall) **86**:289, 301, 343-44
Profiles (Waldrop)
See *The Reproduction of Profiles*
"Profit Is a Dead Weight" (Moore) **49**:146
"Les profondeurs" (Apollinaire) **7**:32, 34
The profound rose (Borges)
See *La rosa profunda*
"De profundis" (Barrett Browning) **6**:5, 23
"De Profundis" (Trakl) **20**:261-62
"Profundity and Levity" (Melville) **82**:152
"Profusion du soir" (Valéry) **9**:391
"Prognosis" (Kenyon) **57**:15
"Prognosis" (MacNeice) **61**:138
"Programme" (Holmes) **71**:92
"Progress" (Gilmore) **87**:301
"Progress" (Kumin) **15**:214
"Progress" (Moore)
See "I May, I Might, I Must"
"The Progress of Beauty, 1720" (Swift) **9**:253, 257, 298-99
"The Progress of Error" (Cowper) **40**:51, 70-71
"The Progress of Faust" (Shapiro) **25**:296
"Progress of Painting" (Hunt) **73**:134
"The Progress of Poesy" (Gray) **2**:133, 135, 137, 139, 143-44, 146, 148-49, 151-55; **80**:235
"The Progress of Poetry" (Gray)
See "The Progress of Poesy"
"The Progress of Poetry" (Hope) **56**:292
"The Progress of Poetry" (Swift) **9**:249
"Progress Report" (Ammons) **16**:45
"Progress Report" (Kumin) **15**:204, 208, 219
The Progresse of the Soule (Donne)
See *The Second Anniversarie. Of the Progres of the Soule. Wherein, By Occasion Of the Religious death of Mistris Elizabeth Drury, the incommodities ofthe Soule in this life, and her exaltation in the next, are Contemplated*
"Progression" (Niedecker) **42**:145
"Progression" (Smith) **12**:316
"Progressive Insanities of a Pioneer" (Atwood) **8**:4
"Progulka" (Akhmadulina) **43**:11
"Prohibido para mayores" (Dalton) **36**:128
"The Prohibition" (Donne) **1**:130
"Projected Slide of an Unknown Soldier" (Atwood) **8**:7
"Projection" (Hughes) **53**:123, 191
"Projection" (Nemerov) **24**:268
"Les Projets" (Baudelaire) **106**:88
A Prolegomenon to a Theodicy (Rexroth) **20**:179, 183, 210-11; **95**:255, 262, 264, 269, 275-77, 281, 332
"Prolija memoria" (Juana Inés de la Cruz) **24**:180
"Prolog" (Benn) **35**:72
"Prolog" (Heine) **25**:131
"Prolog" (Herbert) **50**:12, 19
"Prólogo" (Borges) **22**:95
"El prólogo" (Guillén) **35**:153, 193
"Prólogo" (Guillén) **23**:127
"Prologue" (Akhmatova) **55**:36, 55-56, 58, 60, 63
"The Prologue" (Bradstreet) **10**:2, 6, 11, 52
"Prologue" (Chaucer)
See "General Prologue"
"Prologue" (Henryson) **65**:20-25, 28, 30-31, 49, 59-65, 79-80, 83
"Prologue" (Herbert)
See "Prolog"
"Prologue" (Holmes) **71**:68
"Prologue" (Hughes) **7**:154
"Prologue" (Hugo) **17**:97
"Prologue" (Ignatow) **34**:282, 286
"Prologue" (Lorde) **12**:156
"Prologue" (MacLeish) **47**:185, 189, 201
"Prologue" (Marie de France) **22**:246-48, 260, 264-66, 283-85, 293, 298
"Prologue" (Noyes) **27**:119, 128
"Prologue" (Taylor) **63**:296
"Prologue" (Thomas)
See "Author's Prologue"
"Prologue" (Verlaine) **2**:432
"Prologue" (Williams) **109**:321
"Prologue" (Yevtushenko) **40**:338-39, 342
"Prologue: An Interim" (Levertov)
See "Interim"
"Prologue at Sixty" (Auden) **1**:20; **92**:70
"Prologue for a Play" (Ciardi) **69**:4
"Prologue in Six Parts" (Schwerner) **42**:196
"A Prologue Intended to the Play of Chit Chat, but Never Finished" (Prior) **102**:310
"Prologue Spoken by Mr. Garrick at the Opening of the Theatre in Drury-Lane, 1747" (Johnson) **81**:205, 235-37
"Prologue Spoken by Mr. Woods on His Benefit Night" (Burns) **114**:177
"Prologue to a Saga" (Parker) **28**:363-64
"Prologue to Hugh Kelly's A Word to the Wise" (Johnson) **81**:96, 235
"Prologue to King John" (Blake) **12**:31
"Prologue to the Wife of Bath's Tale" (Chaucer) **19**:26; **58**:230-1, 233-7, 246-9, 252, 256-60, 262, 265-7, 270-5, 277-84, 288-9, 292, 294-5, 299, 305-7, 310, 313, 321-8, 334-7, 339-40, 342-5, 348, 350, 353-5, 362-3, 365, 367-9
"Prologue toThe Good Natur'd Man" (Johnson) **81**:235
"Prologue"(Vox Clamantis) (Gower)
See *Vox Clamantis*
Prolusion (Milton) **29**:228
"Promenade" (Ignatow) **34**:275
"Promenade" (Sainte-Beuve) **110**:39, 61
"La promenade à la fin de l'été" (Jaccottet) **98**:174-75
"Promenade à Trois" (Melville) **82**:38
"La Promenade dans nos serres" (Ponge) **107**:177, 179-80, 213
"Promenade on Any Street" (Kunitz) **19**:147-48
"Proměny" (Seifert) **47**:334
"Promethean Aspiration: To Be a Pythagorean and a Woman" (Howe) **54**:37
"Prometheus" (Carducci) **46**:26
"Prometheus" (Dunbar) **5**:146
"Prometheus" (Goethe) **5**:247, 254
"Prometheus" (Graves) **6**:137
"Prometheus" (Longfellow) **30**:103
"Prometheus" (Meynell) **112**:291
"Prometheus" (Tomlinson) **17**:315, 319, 322, 325-27, 341
Prometheus Bound (Barrett Browning) **62**:112
Prometheus Bound, and Miscellaneous Poems (Barrett Browning) **6**:16, 18
"Prometheus in Straits" (Ransom) **61**:275
"Prometheus #1" (Hughes) **89**:127
"Prometheus #2" (Hughes) **89**:127
"Prometheus #3" (Hughes) **89**:127
"Prometheus #4" (Hughes) **89**:127
"Prometheus #7" (Hughes) **89**:127
"Prometheus #9" (Hughes) **89**:127
"Prometheus #11" (Hughes) **89**:127
"Prometheus #13" (Hughes) **89**:127
"Prometheus #15" (Hughes) **89**:127
"Prometheus #17" (Hughes) **89**:127
"Prometheus #18" (Hughes) **89**:127
"Prometheus #19" (Hughes) **89**:127
"Prometheus #20" (Hughes) **89**:127
Prometheus on His Crag (Hughes) **7**:155-56
Prometheus on His Crag: 21 Poems (Hughes) **89**:124, 126-27, 188
"Prometheus Unbound" (Yeats) **20**:333, 336
Prometheus Unbound (Shelley) **14**:166-67, 171-75, 177, 183, 186-91, 193, 196-97, 202, 206, 212-13, 215-16, 218-21, 224-28, 232, 240-41; **67**:131-244
Prometheus Unbound: A Lyrical Drama in Four Acts, with Other Poems (Shelley)
See *Prometheus Unbound*
"The Promise" (Toomer) **7**:338
"The Promise" (Very) **86**:138
Promise (Yevtushenko) **40**:341
"Promise and Fulfillment" (Dunbar) **5**:121
"Promise Me" (Kunitz) **19**:147
"Promise Me a Long Night" (Tapahonso) **65**:225
"Promise of a Brilliant Funeral" (Niedecker) **42**:145
"The Promise of the Hawthorn" (Swinburne) **24**:313, 317
The Promised Land (Ungaretti) **57**:339
"The Promised One" (Wright) **14**:337
"The Promisers" (Owen) **19**:336, 343
"Promises" (Warren) **37**:307
Promises: Poems, 1954-1956 (Warren) **37**:296-97, 299-300, 307, 310, 328-30, 332, 347, 349, 354, 361, 370, 373, 380
"Promising Author" (Kizer) **66**:66
"La promisión en alta mar" (Borges) **32**:38, 57
"Promontoire" (Rimbaud) **3**:264; **57**:234, 236, 239, 241, 254, 276, 280-81
"Promontory" (Rimbaud)
See "Promontoire"
"The Pronouncement" (Dorn) **115**:113, 135, 220
"Pronouns of This Time" (Spender) **71**:191
"The Proof" (Winters) **82**:338, 341-42
The Proof (Winters) **82**:312, 317-18, 324-26, 334, 337, 343, 345-46
"Prooimion" (Viereck) **27**:259
"The Propagandists of War" (Werfel)
See "Die Wortemacher des Krieges"
Propertius (Pound)
See *Homage to Sextus Propertius*
"Property" (Shapiro) **25**:295
"Property is Poverty" (Niedecker) **42**:138
"Prophecies V" (Zanzotto)
See "Profezie V"
"Prophecy" (Wylie) **23**:310, 323
"The Prophecy of Samuel Sewall" (Whittier) **93**:173, 227, 229, 239, 251-52, 271, 346
"Prophecy on Lethe" (Kunitz) **19**:162, 173-75
"The Prophet" (Cowley) **90**:12, 28-29, 34
"The Prophet" (Lermontov) **18**:281
"The Prophet" (Pushkin)
See "Prorok"
"The Prophet" (Very) **86**:153
The Prophet (Gibran) **9**:69-75, 80-2
"The Prophet Lost in the Hills at Evening" (Belloc) **24**:30
"Prophetic Soul" (Parker) **28**:357, 360
"Prophetie" (Césaire) **25**:9, 19, 30
"The Prophets" (Amichai) **38**:35
"Prophets for a New Day" (Walker) **20**:278, 288
Prophets for a New Day (Walker) **20**:275, 278-79, 283, 287-89, 292
"Prophets Who Cannot Sing" (Patmore) **59**:222
"Propogation House" (Roethke) **15**:296
"A propos d'Horace" (Hugo) **17**:64
"Proposal" (Carver) **54**:17, 19
"The Proposal" (Leapor) **85**:286
"The Propositions" (Duncan) **75**:229, 261
"The Propositions, 2" (Duncan) **75**:151
"Propriety" (Moore) **49**:130
"Prorok" (Pushkin) **10**:409, 414
Prosanatolizmí (Elytis) **21**:118-19, 124, 127, 134
Prosas profanas, y otros poemas (Darío) **15**:78, 80, 82-4, 87-9, 91-2, 94-5, 97, 103-05, 109, 112-14, 117-20
Prosas profanos, and Other Poems (Darío)
See *Prosas profanas, y otros poemas*
"Prose à l'éloge d'Aix" (Ponge) **107**:128

"Prose de profundis à la gloire de Claudel" (Ponge) **107**:74, 142
"Prose Poem" (Tomlinson) **17**:338, 340
Prose Poems (Baudelaire)
See *Le spleen de Paris, petits poèmes en prose*
"Prosopopoia; or, Mother Hubberds Tale" (Spenser) **8**:335, 365, 368-71, 390
"Prospective Immigrants Please Note" (Rich) **5**:370
"The Prospector" (Service) **70**:114
"Prospectors of the Future" (Yevtushenko) **40**:341
"Prospects" (Hecht) **70**:95
Prospectus to the Excursion (Wordsworth)
See *The Excursion, Being a Portion of "The Recluse"*
"Prosperity in Poza Rica" (Birney) **52**:37, 98
"Prospice" (Browning) **2**:51, 66
"Prostitute" (Ai) **72**:29
"Protection of Moveable Cultural Heritage" (Komunyakaa) **51**:34
"Protest" (Cullen) **20**:57
"Protest" (Kennedy) **93**:143
"Protest" (Montague) **106**:241
Protest Against Apartheid (Brutus) **24**:100
"A Protest from Italy" (Howe) **81**:30
"Protestant Easter" (Sexton) **2**:363
"The Protestant View" (Dorn) **115**:161, 199, 230
"Proteus" (Sarton) **39**:342
"Prothalamion" (Kumin) **15**:180
"Prothalamion" (Schwartz) **8**:290-91, 299, 301-02, 304-05
Prothalamion (Spenser)
See *Prothalamion; or, A Spousall Verse*
Prothalamion; or, A Spousall Verse (Spenser) **8**:336, 390
"Protocols" (Jarrell) **41**:198, 218
"Prototype" (Collins) **68**:215
"The Proud Farmer" (Lindsay) **23**:287
"Proud King" (Morris) **55**:308
"A Proud Lady" (Wylie) **23**:309, 321, 332
"Proud Maisie" (Scott) **13**:272, 278, 280
"A Proud Poem" (O'Hara) **45**:160
"Proud Songsters" (Hardy) **92**:213, 326
"Proust on Skates" (Hecht) **70**:94
Provença (Pound) **95**:118
"Provence" (MacNeice) **61**:139
"La Provence Point Oméga" (Char) **56**:136
"Proverbs of Hell" (Blake) **12**:36, 49-50
"Provide, Provide" (Frost) **1**:227-28, 231
"Providence" (Herbert) **4**:102, 134
"La providence à l'homme" (Lamartine) **16**:276, 283, 291, 293
"Providence in Winter" (Waldrop) **109**:121
"The Provider" (Jacobsen) **62**:324
Provinces (Milosz) **8**:212, 214-15
"Provincia deserta" (Pound) **4**:366
"The Provincial" (Thomas) **99**:253
"Provision" (Merwin) **45**:21, 24
"Provisional Conclusions" (Montale)
See "Conclusioni provvisorie"
Provisional Conclusions: A Selection (Montale) **13**:135
"A Provisional Fragment" (Dorn) **115**:213
"Provisions for the Return" (Char) **56**:162
"Provoda" (Tsvetaeva) **14**:309, 311, 315
"Proximity" (Corso) **33**:44, 50; **108**:3
"Proxozij mal'cik, cto ty, mimo..." (Akhmadulina) **43**:62, 64, 66
"prozession" (Enzensberger) **28**:135-36
"Prufrock" (Boland) **58**:12
"Prufrock" (Eliot)
See "The Love Song of J. Alfred Prufrock"
Prufrock and Other Observations (Eliot) **5**:152, 173, 184-85, 195, 204, 206; **31**:101, 120-21,; **90**:313, 317, 320
"Przeczucia eschatologiczne Pana Cogito" (Herbert) **50**:35, 39
"Przedmioty" (Herbert) **50**:4-5
"Przepasc Pana Cogito" (Herbert) **50**:37
"Przeslanie Pana Cogito" (Herbert) **50**:12, 15, 22-24, 33, 38-39
"Przylot" (Szymborska) **44**:294, 299
"P.S. 42" (Corso) **108**:8
"The Psalm" (Bridges) **28**:80
"Psalm" (Celan) **10**:98, 101, 118, 120
"A Psalm" (Merton) **10**:332
"Psalm" (Oppen) **35**:298, 323
"Psalm" (Simic) **69**:264
"Psalm II" (Ginsberg) **4**:81
"Psalm 2" (Smart) **13**:330
"Psalm 72: Man Declared a Treasure" (Enright) **93**:6
"Psalm 94" (Smart) **13**:362
"Psalm 104" (Smart) **13**:332
"Psalm 105" (Smart) **13**:362
"Psalm 120" (Smart) **13**:363
"Psalm Concerning the Castle" (Levertov) **11**:177
"Psalm for Supersunday" (Enright) **93**:24, 29, 34
"Psalm of Death" (Longfellow) **30**:21, 45
"A Psalm of Life" (Hardy) **92**:295
"A Psalm of Life" (Longfellow) **30**:21-2, 26-7, 34, 36-9, 45, 47, 95-8, 103, 105-11
"Psalm of the West" (Lanier) **50**:54-56, 75, 77, 80, 106
"Psalm of Those Who Go Forth before Daylight" (Sandburg) **41**:259, 270, 321
"Psalm: Our Fathers" (Merwin) **45**:16-17, 27
"Psalm Praising the Hair of Man's Body" (Levertov) **11**:171
"Psalms" (Smart)
See *A Translation of the Psalms of David, Attempted in the Spirit of Christianity, and Adapted to the Divine Service*
"Psalms" (Stern) **115**:249, 282
Psalms (Sidney) **32**:225, 247-50, 293-96
Psalms (Smart)
See *A Translation of the Psalms of David, Attempted in the Spirit of Christianity, and Adapted to the Divine Service*
Psalms of David (Smart)
See *A Translation of the Psalms of David, Attempted in the Spirit of Christianity, and Adapted to the Divine Service*
"Pseudodoxia Epidemica" (Hope) **56**:289
Pseudo-Martyr (Donne) **43**:118-19
"Psi" (Tolson) **88**:244-45, 283, 285, 304, 316, 334
"Psyche and Eros" (Waldrop) **109**:179
"Psyche's Discontent" (Patmore) **59**:207, 267
"Der Psychiater" (Benn) **35**:50, 68
"The Psychiatrist's Song" (Bogan) **12**:101, 115
"Psychoanalysis: An Elegy" (Spicer) **78**:247, 258, 302, 335
"Psychology" (Seferis) **66**:185
"Der Ptolemäer" (Benn) **35**:33, 34
"Public Bar TV" (Hughes) **7**:120, 122; **89**:101, 210
"Public Garden" (Lowell) **3**:199-200, 215
The Public Rose (Éluard)
See *La rose publique*
Public Speech: Poems (MacLeish) **47**:139-40, 148-49, 151, 190, 241, 255
The Public World/Syntactically Impermanence (Scalapino) **114**:331, 335, 340
Published and Unpublished Poems (Pavese)
See *Poesie edite e inedite*
"Publius Vergilius Maro, The Madison Avenue Hick" (Updike) **90**:352
"Puck of Pook's Hill" (Kipling) **3**:192
Puck of Pook's Hill (Kipling) **91**:109, 115, 117-18, 134, 152, 165
"Puck's Song" (Kipling) **3**:183, 192; **91**:109
"La Pudeur bien en vue" (Éluard) **38**:91
"Pueblo Pot" (Millay) **6**:215
"Puedes?" (Guillén) **23**:116, 124, 127
Puella (Dickey) **40**:205, 210-12, 228, 235, 237-40, 259
"Puella Mea" (Cummings) **5**:104
"Puella Parvula" (Stevens) **110**:229
"Puerta Rica" (Cruz) **37**:22
"Puerto Rican Autopsy" (Espada) **74**:128
"Puesto del Rastro" (Fuertes) **27**:22, 45-6
"the pull" (Bissett) **14**:22
"The Pulley" (Herbert) **4**:102
"The Pulling" (Olds) **22**:318, 323, 326, 340
"Pulse-Beats and Pen-Strokes" (Sandburg) **41**:293
The pulverised poem (Char)
See *Le poême pulverisé*
"Pulvis et umbra" (Carman) **34**:202, 211, 215
"Puma in Chapultepec Zoo" (Corso) **33**:39, 43, 47; **108**:40
"El puñal" (Borges) **32**:87
Punascha (Tagore) **8**:417
Punch: The Immortal Liar, Documents in His History (Aiken) **26**:22
"Puncture" (Ransom) **61**:311
"Punishment" (Heaney) **18**:196, 204, 210-11, 238; **100**:214, 216-18, 274, 298, 341-42, 344, 354
"The Puppets" (Page) **12**:184
Purabi (Tagore) **8**:415
"Purchas His Pilgrimes" (Enright) **93**:4
"Purdah" (Plath) **37**:241
"Pure Death" (Graves) **6**:137, 151
"The Pure Fury" (Roethke) **15**:258, 272, 277, 290
"The Pure Good of Theory" (Stevens) **110**:124-25, 173, 198, 202
"Pure Love" (Tagore)
See "Pavitra prem"
"The Pure Ones" (Hass) **16**:198
"The Pure Spirit" (Vigny)
See "L'Esprit pur"
"Purely" (Villa) **22**:353
"Purely Local" (Rich) **5**:352
Purgatorio (Dante) **21**:49, 52-4, 58, 62-3, 69-82, 84-6, 91, 95-6, 104-05, 107-09
"Purgatory" (Lowell) **3**:241
"A Purgatory" (Merwin) **45**:49
Purgatory (Dante)
See *Purgatorio*
Purgatory (Marie de France)
See *L'Espurgatoire Saint Patrice*
The Purgatory of St. Patrick (Marie de France)
See *L'Espurgatoire Saint Patrice*
"The Puritan" (Shapiro) **25**:270, 286
"The Puritan and the Papist" (Cowley) **90**:63-64, 71
"A Puritan Lady" (Reese) **29**:331
"The Puritan's Ballard" (Wylie) **23**:310
Purity (Anonymous)
See *Cleanness*
"Purner abhav" (Tagore) **8**:414
"Puro Mejicano" (Quintana) **36**:252
"Purple Grackles" (Lowell) **13**:64, 67, 87, 98-9
"The Purpose of Altar Boys" (Ríos) **57**:324
"The Purpose of Time Is to Prevent Everything from Happening at Once" (Kennedy) **93**:152
"Les Pur-Sang" (Césaire) **25**:8-9, 18
"The Purse of Aholibah" (Huneker) **27**:165
"The Purse Seine" (Jeffers) **17**:117
"Pursuit" (H. D.) **5**:287-88
"Pursuit" (Plath) **37**:236, 241, 260
"Pursuit" (Warren) **37**:284, 287, 289, 323, 332
"Pursuit from Under" (Dickey) **40**:183, 196, 258
"Purveyors General" (Pound) **95**:117
"La Push" (Hugo) **68**:233
"Pushkin Pass" (Yevtushenko) **40**:350
"Pushkinskomu domu" (Blok) **21**:44
"Puss in Boots" (Moore) **49**:161
"Pusti menia, Voronezh . . ." (Mandelstam) **14**:152
"Put Off the Wedding Five Times and Nobody Comes to It" (Sandburg) **41**:298
Put Out the Lights (Seifert)
See *Zhasněte světla*
"Put Something In" (Silverstein) **49**:330

"Put Your Muzzle Where Your Mouth Is (Or Shut Up)" (Randall) **86**:329-30, 336-37
Putem vseia zemli (Akhmatova) **55**:53
"La puttana contadina" (Pavese) **13**:210, 219
"Puttin' on Dog" (Brown) **55**:114
"Putting to Sea" (Bogan) **12**:123
"Puzzle" (Parra)
See "Rompecabezas"
P.W. (Hunt) **73**:169-70
"Pygmalion" (H. D.) **5**:270, 304
"Pygmalion" (Hope)
See "The Invocation"
"Pygmalion" (Meynell) **112**:156, 158
"Pygmalion's Image" (Ní Chuilleanáin) **34**:354, 373
"Pygmies Are Pygmies Still, Though Percht on Alps" (Brooks) **7**:55
"The Pylons" (Spender) **71**:142, 167, 180, 220
"The Pyramids" (Brooke) **24**:66, 80
"Pyramis; or, The House of Ascent" (Hope) **56**:268, 272, 275
"Pyrotechnics" (Bogan) **12**:117
"Pyrotechnics" (Lowell) **13**:83
Pytania zadawane sobie (Szymborska) **44**:268, 281, 318
Pyth. III (Pindar)
See *Pythian 3*
Pyth. X (Pindar)
See *Pythian 10*
Pyth XI (Pindar)
See *Pythian 11*
"Pythagorean Lines" (Mahon) **60**:178-79
Pythagorean Silence (Howe) **54**:37-40, 45, 68, 99-100, 102, 141, 151
Pythian 1 (Pindar) **19**:381, 389, 392-93, 400, 411-12, 424-25
Pythian 2 (Pindar) **19**:402, 410, 420
Pythian 3 (Pindar) **19**:390, 398, 402, 410, 412
Pythian 4 (Pindar) **19**:381, 390, 396, 398-99, 405, 413, 420, 425
Pythian 5 (Pindar) **19**:396, 408-11, 422-23, 425
Pythian 6 (Pindar) **19**:400, 406
Pythian 7 (Pindar) **19**:412
Pythian 8 (Pindar) **19**:381, 391, 400, 406-07, 413, 426
Pythian 9 (Pindar) **19**:391, 398, 400, 412-13
Pythian 10 (Pindar) **19**:411-12, 425-26
Pythian 11 (Pindar) **19**:413
Pythian Odes 10 (Pindar)
See *Pythian 10*
"La pythie" (Valéry) **9**:353, 365-66, 369, 373, 379, 393
"Qasidat Beirut" (Darwish) **86**:20
"Qasuhidat al-Arduh" (Darwish) **86**:11
"The QPP" (Walker) **30**:339
"Quack-Hunting" (de la Mare) **77**:114
Quaderno de quattro anni (Montale) **13**:128, 153, 156, 160, 168
"The Quadroon Girl" (Longfellow) **30**:48
"Quaerendo Invenietis" (Nemerov) **24**:288
Quaerimoniae (Southwell) **83**:251
" *Quœrit* Jesum" (Crashaw) **84**:140-41, 144-47
"Quai d'Orléans" (Bishop) **3**:37; **34**:63-66
"The Quail" (Wright) **36**:280, 362
"The Quake" (Stryk) **27**:203, 211
"Quake Theory" (Olds) **22**:309
"The Quaker Alumni" (Whittier) **93**:198
"The Quaker Graveyard at Nantucket (for Warren Winslow, Dead at Sea)" (Lowell) **3**:200-02, 204, 212, 217, 223, 233, 235-38
"Quaker Hill" (Crane) **3**:86, 90, 106
"Quality Time" (Silverstein) **49**:342
"Qualm" (Ashbery) **26**:152
"Quand vous serez bien vieille" (Ronsard) **11**:218-21
Quando caddreo gli alberi e le mura (Quasimodo) **47**:287
"Quando de minhas magoasa comprida" (Camões) **31**:24
"Quando il soave mio fido conforto" (Petrarch) **8**:235
"The Quangle Wangle's Hat" (Lear) **65**:160
"Quante dirne si de' non si può dire" (Michelangelo) **103**:318
"Quarant' Ore" (Ní Chuilleanáin) **34**:360
"The Quarrel" (Aiken) **26**:24
"The Quarrel" (Kunitz) **19**:175
"Quarrel" (Stramm)
See "Zwist"
"Quarrel in Old Age" (Yeats) **20**:328-31
"The Quarry" (Clampitt) **19**:82, 89
The Quarry: New Poems (Eberhart) **76**:27-32, 35, 40, 42, 59
"Quarry Pigeon Cove" (Kumin) **15**:181
Quarry West (Cervantes) **35**:132
"Le quart d'une vie" (Péret) **33**:229-30
"Quartär" (Benn) **35**:4, 8, 67
"A Quartet" (Blunden) **66**:31
"Quartets" (Eliot) **31**:99
"Quashie to Buccra" (McKay) **2**:215, 223
"Quasi un madrigale" (Quasimodo) **47**:284-86
"Quasi-Slum" (Curnow) **48**:26
"Quatrains" (Emerson) **18**:77
"Quatre à quatre" (Péret) **33**:220-22, 230
Quatre de P. de Ronsard aux injures et calomnies (Ronsard) **11**:291
"Quatre Dols" (Marie de France)
See "Le Chaitivel"
Les quatre premiers livres de la Franciade (Ronsard) **11**:226, 234, 246, 271, 283, 286-87, 290; **105**:214-15
Les quatre premiers livres des odes de Pierre de Ronsard, ensemble son bocage (Ronsard) **105**:249, 272, 279, 283, 288, 292, 325
Les quatre vents de l'esprit (Hugo) **17**:65
"¿... Qué?" (Storni) **33**:251
"Los que a través de sus lágrimas" (Castro) **41**:103
"La que comprende" (Storni) **33**:246, 307-08
"Que de fois près d'Oxford" (Sainte-Beuve) **110**:65, 69
"Lo que el difunto dijo de sí mismo" (Parra) **39**:285
Que estás en la tierra (Fuertes) **27**:44
"Que font les olives" (Péret) **33**:202
"Que m'accompagnent Kôras et Balafong" (Senghor) **25**:255
"Los que no danzan" (Mistral) **32**:175
"Que no me quiera Fabio, al verse amado" (Juana Inés de la Cruz) **24**:183
"Los que no miraban los ojos de los otros" (Cernuda) **62**:214
"Que nous avons le doute en nous" (Hugo) **17**:92-93
"De qué país" (Cernuda) **62**:235
"De qué país eres tú?" (Cernuda) **62**:220, 235
"Qué ruido tan triste" (Cernuda) **62**:220, 235
"¿Qué Te?" (Castro) **41**:95
"¿Qué tiene?" (Castro) **41**:116
Que van a dar a la mar (Guillén) **35**:214-16
"Que vient-elle me dire, aux plus tendres instants" (Sainte-Beuve) **110**:45
"quebec bombers" (Bissett) **14**:21-2
"Quechua Song" (Mistral)
See "La canción que chua"
"The Queen and the Young Princess" (Smith) **12**:326, 352
"Queen Anne's Lace" (Jordan) **38**:122
"Queen Jane Approximately" (Dylan) **37**:55
"Queen Mab" (Hood) **93**:45
Queen Mab (Shelley) **14**:170, 173, 178, 185-86, 212-17, 219, 222; **67**:134, 158-59, 163, 172, 177, 185, 222, 224, 228, 230-33
Queen Mab: A Philosophical Poem, with Notes (Shelley)
See *Queen Mab*
"Queen of Bubbles" (Lindsay) **23**:277
"The Queen of Hearts" (Rossetti) **7**:272, 274
"The Queen of pentacles" (Piercy) **29**:323
"The Queen of the Night Walks Her Thin Dog" (Wakoski) **15**:363
"The Queen of the North" (Morris) **55**:306
"Queen Worship" (Browning) **2**:26
"Queen Yseult" (Swinburne) **24**:355
"Queen-Anne's Lace" (Williams) **7**:374
"The Queen's Bearing" (Char) **56**:162
"The Queen's Room" (Patmore) **59**:230
"Queja" (Storni) **33**:253
"Quelle soie aux baumes de temps . . ." (Mallarmé) **102**:102
"Quelque bonté" (Éluard) **38**:68
"Quelques Complaintes de la vie" (Laforgue) **14**:95
"Qu'en dis-tu, voyageur" (Verlaine) **32**:375
"The Quene" (Dunbar) **67**:38
"Querencia" (Stafford) **71**:333
"Querent's Attitude as It Bears Upon the Matter: The Three of Cups" (Piercy) **29**:325
"The Quest" (Montague) **106**:275-76, 281
"The Quest" (Wright) **36**:346
The Quest of Cynthia (Drayton) **98**:50
"The Quest of the Purple-Fringed" (Frost) **1**:218
"Qu'est-ce pour nous" (Rimbaud) **57**:182-84, 250, 302, 304-6
"Qu'est-ce pour nous, mon coeur . . ." (Rimbaud)
See "Qu'est-ce pour nous"
"Questing" (Spencer) **77**:341, 346
"A Question" (Arnold) **5**:38
"The Question" (Duncan) **75**:187
"The Question" (Meynell) **112**:163
"The Question" (Muir) **49**:245, 251
"The Question" (Rukeyser) **12**:225
"Question" (Swenson) **14**:250, 252, 282, 286
"The Question" (Thomas) **99**:242-43
"Question and Answer" (Barrett Browning) **6**:5
"Question and Answer" (Warren) **37**:322, 332
"Question and Answer: A Tale of Sutton Walls" (Masefield) **78**:49
"Question at Cliff-Thrust" (Warren) **37**:366-67, 380
"Question au clerc du quichet" (Villon) **13**:394
"Question in Red Ink" (Koch) **80**:316
"A Question of Climate" (Lorde) **12**:136
"A Question of Essence" (Lorde) **12**:140
"The Question of Loyalty" (Yamada) **44**:339
"Question to Life" (Kavanagh) **33**:103, 120; **105**:121
"The Question Whither" (Meredith) **60**:290, 299
"Questioni di etichetta e anche cavalleresche" (Zanzotto) **65**:299
"Questions" (Thomas) **99**:318, 351-53
Questions About Angels (Collins) **68**:203, 205-6, 208, 215, 219
Questions and Answers (Parra)
See *Preguntas y respuestas*
Questions Asked of Oneself (Szymborska)
See *Pytania zadawane sobie*
"Questions Beside the Lake" (Cardenal)
See "Preguntas Frente al lago"
"Questions of Life" (Whittier) **93**:170, 172, 267
"Questions of Travel" (Bishop) **3**:55, 67; **34**:106, 158
Questions of Travel (Bishop) **3**:48, 53, 59; **34**:58, 61, 66-67, 91, 94, 155, 160, 174, 189-90
Questions Put to Myself (Szymborska)
See *Pytania zadawane sobie*
"A questo punto" (Montale) **13**:158
"Quetzalcóatl" (Cernuda) **62**:180, 219
"Quhone He List to Feyne" (Dunbar) **67**:25, 38, 41
"Quhy will Ye, Merchantis of Renoun" (Dunbar) **67**:3
"A qui la faute?" (Hugo) **17**:101
"Qui regna amore" (Carducci) **46**:77
"Qui sait—" (Benn) **35**:75
"Qui S'Excuse, S'Accuse" (Moore) **49**:105, 109, 121, 134
Quia pawper amavi (Pound) **4**:317
"The Quick and the Dead" (Blunden) **66**:24, 26, 28

"Quick I the Death of Thing" (Cummings) **5**:108
"Quick Trip" (Silverstein) **49**:324
"A Quickening: A Song for the Visitation" (Merton) **10**:339
"The Quickening of St. John Baptist" (Merton) **10**:339
"Quickly Delia" (Finch) **21**:178
"Quickness" (Vaughan) **81**:367
"Quick-Step" (Creeley) **73**:66-67, 69, 73
"The Quids" (Jackson) **44**:5
"A quien leyere" (Borges) **22**:94
"Quién seré?" (Guillén) **35**:229
"Quiero saber" (Aleixandre) **15**:31
"Quiero volver a sur" (Neruda) **4**:281
"Quiet!" (Castro)
See "¡Silencio!"
"The Quiet After the Storm" (Leopardi)
See "La quiete dopo la tempesta"
"Quiet Evening" (Glück) **16**:172
"Quiet Evenings" (Hunt) **73**:154
"The Quiet House" (Mew) **107**:6, 9, 35, 39, 41-42, 48, 51, 60
"A Quiet Normal Life" (Stevens) **110**:230
The Quiet of the Land (Stafford) **71**:311
A Quiet Road (Reese) **29**:329-330, 335-336, 339, 345-346
"The Quiet Thing" (Francis) **34**:251
"Quiet Town" (Stafford) **71**:293
"Quiet Work" (Arnold) **5**:12, 36, 38, 49
"La quiete dopo la tempesta" (Leopardi) **37**:102, 120, 124
"Quietly" (Rexroth) **95**:349
"Quietness" (Williams) **7**:382; **109**:293-94, 298
"Qu'il vive" (Char) **56**:184
Quill, Solitary, APPARITION (Guest) **55**:196, 199
"A Quilt Pattern" (Jarrell) **41**:158, 173, 176-77, 186, 194
"Quilted Spreads" (Ammons) **16**:44
Quilting: Poems 1987-1990 (Clifton) **17**:28-29, 36
"Quimérica" (Jiménez) **7**:197
"Quinnapoxet" (Kunitz) **19**:175, 178-79
A Quinzaine for This Yule (Pound) **95**:114
"The Quip" (Herbert) **4**:100, 102, 108, 119, 130
Quitter (Char) **56**:117
"Quod tegit omnia" (Winters) **82**:312, 336
"Quoth the Duchess of Cleveland to Counselor Knight" (Wilmot) **66**:329
"R. A. F." (H. D.) **5**:307
R. L. S. Teuila (Stevenson) **84**:335
"The Rabbi" (Hayden) **6**:195, 198
"Rabbi Ben Ezra" (Browning) **2**:51, 75, 95; **97**:13
"Rabbi Ismael" (Whittier) **93**:221
"The Rabbi's Song" (Kipling) **3**:183; **91**:154
"The Rabbit" (Millay) **6**:238
"The Rabbit Catcher" (Hughes) **89**:162, 177
"The Rabbit Catcher" (Plath) **37**:232, 264
"Räber-Schiller" (Benn) **35**:48
"Race" (Darío)
See "Raza"
"The Race" (Olds) **22**:319, 323, 326
"The 'Race Line' Is a Product of Capitalism" (Baraka) **113**:36
"A Race of Sound" (Corso) **108**:7
"Race Relations" (Kizer) **66**:65
"The Racer" (Masefield) **78**:26
"The Racer's Widow" (Glück) **16**:139
"Rachunek Elegijny" (Szymborska) **44**:220, 306, 308
"The Racist" (Baraka) **113**:19
"Rack" (Ammons) **16**:39
"Radar" (Spicer) **78**:256
"Radha Krishna" (Das) **43**:73
"Radiance Draws the Moth's Desire" (Hafiz) **116**:55
Radiant Silhouette: New and Selected Work 1974-88 (Yau) **61**:334, 340, 348
"Radical" (Moore) **49**:100, 113, 185-86
"The Radical Poets" (Elliott) **96**:183
"Radio" (Benn) **35**:70
"Radio" (Duncan) **75**:175
"La radio" (Ponge) **107**:133
"A radio made of seawater" (Villa) **22**:356-57
"Radiometer" (Merrill) **28**:267
"Radosc pisania" (Szymborska) **44**:295, 314-15
"Raft" (Ammons) **16**:20, 27
"The Raft" (Lindsay) **23**:273
Rag and Bone Shop (Birney) **52**:72, 75, 83
The Rag and Bone Shop of the Heart: Poems for Men (Bly) **39**:98
"Rag & Bone" (Birney) **52**:32
"The Rag Man" (Hayden) **6**:195
"The Rag Rug" (Hughes) **89**:162, 179
"Raga Malkos" (Ekeloef) **23**:87
"The Rag-and-bone Man's Wine" (Baudelaire)
See "Le Vin des chiffonniers"
"Rage" (Oliver) **75**:285, 294
La Rage de l'expression (Ponge) **107**:109, 124, 142, 161, 175, 230, 236
"Rage for Order" (Mahon) **60**:168, 172, 187, 194, 200, 233, 235
The Rage for the Lost Penny (Jarrell) **41**:179, 183, 213
"Rages de césars" (Rimbaud) **3**:283
"Ragged ending" (Piercy) **29**:313
"Ragged Point" (Brathwaite) **56**:65
"The Ragged Schools of London" (Barrett Browning)
See "A Song for the Ragged Schools of London"
"The Ragged Stocking" (Harper) **21**:191
"The Raggedy Man" (Riley) **48**:292, 306, 340
Raghuvamśa (Kālidāsa) **22**:180, 182, 185, 188-90, 198, 204-07
"La ragion meco si lamenta e dole" (Michelangelo) **103**:218
"A Rail Road Cutting near Alexandria in 1855" (Melville) **82**:109
"The Railing" (Yevtushenko) **40**:345
"Railing Rimes Returned upon the Author by Mistress Mary Wrothe" (Wroth) **38**:258
"Railroad Avenue" (Hughes) **1**:237
"Railroad Bill, a Conjure Man" (Reed) **68**:329, 332, 336
"The Railway Children" (Heaney) **100**:335
The Railway Timetable of the Heart (Tzara) **27**:250
"Rain" (Borges) **32**:140
"Rain" (Brown) **55**:74
"The Rain" (Creeley) **73**:7
"Rain" (Giovanni) **19**:109
"The Rain" (Herbert)
See "Deszcz"
"Rain" (Hogan) **35**:257
"Rain" (Hughes) **89**:125
"The Rain" (Levertov) **11**:176
"Rain" (Oliver) **75**:318, 322
"Rain" (Ponge)
See "Pluie"
"Rain" (Ransom) **61**:309
"Rain" (Soto) **28**:370, 377
"Rain" (Stevenson) **84**:299, 314
"Rain" (Stryk) **27**:201
"Rain" (Thomas) **53**:278, 285-86, 288-89, 295, 317, 328
"Rain" (Williams) **7**:349
"Rain" (Wright) **36**:391
"Rain at Bellagio" (Clampitt) **19**:87
"Rain at Night" (Merwin) **45**:93
"Rain Charm for the Duchy, a Blessed, Devout Drench for the Christening of a Prince Harry" (Hughes) **7**:171
"Rain Downriver" (Levine) **22**:224-25
"Rain Festival" (Tagore)
See "Varsha-mangal"
Rain Five Days and I Love It (Hugo) **68**:262
"The Rain Guitar" (Dickey) **40**:223, 232, 256
"The Rain Horse" (Hughes) **89**:107
"Rain in January" (Kenyon) **57**:3, 13, 19, 43
The Rain in the Trees (Merwin) **45**:89, 93-4, 97-8
"The Rain, It Streams on Stone and Hillock" (Housman) **2**:162
"Rain on a Grave" (Hardy) **8**:134; **92**:312-15
"Rain on the Borders" (Pasolini) **17**:287
"Rain or Hail" (Cummings) **5**:88
"Rain Outside of Everything" (Pasolini) **17**:287
"The Rain Stick" (Heaney) **100**:243, 245
"Rain Towards Morning" (Bishop) **34**:89
"The Rainbow" (Kinnell) **26**:259-60
"The Rainbow" (Vaughan) **81**:338
"rainbow mewsik" (Bissett) **14**:24
"La Rainette" (Char) **56**:152
"Rainforest" (Wright) **14**:375, 377
"The Rainmaker" (Cassian) **17**:4
"Rains" (Perse)
See "Pluies"
"Rain-Songs" (Dunbar) **5**:125
"The Rainy Day" (Longfellow) **30**:45, 64
"Rainy Mountain Cemetery" (Momaday) **25**:190, 197
"The Rainy Season" (Meredith) **28**:187
"Rainy Season: Sub-Tropics" (Bishop) **34**:116
"Rainy Summer" (Meynell) **112**:159
"Raise a Song" (Brown) **55**:114
"raise the shade / will youse dearie" (Cummings) **5**:89
"The Raisin" (Hall) **70**:33
"Raisin Eyes" (Tapahonso) **65**:225, 241, 259
"Raison de plus" (Éluard) **38**:69
Raíz del hombre (Paz) **48**:179, 243
"Raj teologów" (Herbert) **50**:5
"Raleigh" (Cardenal) **22**:107, 110
"Raleigh Was Right" (Williams) **7**:360
Ralentir travaux (Char) **56**:168
"Ralph Rhodes" (Masters) **36**:231
"Rama del otoño" (Guillén) **35**:153, 154
"A Ramble in St. James's Park" (Wilmot) **66**:234, 267-68, 270-71, 279-82, 290-91, 293, 320, 324, 329, 342, 353, 362-63, 365-68
The Rambling Sailor (Mew) **107**:5, 9, 36, 47
"La rameur" (Valéry) **9**:367, 395-96
"Rammon" (Melville) **82**:78
"El ramo azul" (Paz) **48**:230
"Rampart of Twigs" (Char)
See "Le Rempart de Brindilles"
"Randolph of Roanoke" (Whittier) **93**:263
Random Possession (Berssenbrugge) **115**:3, 38, 46
"R-and-R Centre" (Enright) **93**:33
"The Range in the Desert" (Jarrell) **41**:171
"Rank and File" (Noyes) **27**:122
"Rano Raraku" (Breton) **15**:53-4
"Ransom" (Ní Chuilleanáin) **34**:349, 351
"Ransom" (Warren) **37**:284, 287-88, 321, 331-32
"A Rant" (O'Hara) **45**:164
"The Ranter" (Elliott) **96**:156, 161, 181, 183
"Rap of a Fan..." (Apollinaire)
See "Coup d'evential..."
"Rape" (Rich) **5**:361
"Rape is Not a Poem" (Jordan) **38**:123, 126, 128
"The Rape of Aurora" (Meredith) **60**:244, 294
The Rape of Lucrece (Shakespeare) **84**:183-295 **89**:306, 313-14, 318, 320, 333-36; **98**:241; **101**:4, 32, 42, 44, 56-58, 64-65, 71, 75, 90-91
"Rape of the Leaf" (Kunitz) **19**:147
The Rape of the Lock (Pope) **26**:303, 307-309, 314-19, 322-23, 326-27, 340, 346-51
"The Raper from Passenack" (Williams) **7**:353, 368, 399; **109**:260
"Rapids" (Ammons) **16**:63
"Rapids by the Luan Trees" (Wang Wei) **18**:370
"Raport z oblezonego miasta" (Herbert) **50**:11, 14, 22, 41
Raport z oblezonego miasta (Herbert)
See *Raport z oblezonego miasta i inne wiersze*

Raport z oblezonego miasta i inne wiersze (Herbert) **50**:11-12, 15, 17, 20, 22-24, 36, 39-41
"A Rapture" (Carew) **29**:10, 18, 27-28, 32, 34, 36-38, 48, 71-72, 75-76, 87-88
"The Rapture" (Traherne) **70**:170, 189, 288, 293-94, 302, 314
"Rapunzel" (Morris) **55**:238, 267-68, 272, 282, 300, 302
"Rapunzel" (Sexton) **2**:368; **79**:191-92
"The Rare Birds" (Baraka) **113**:132
"Raree Show" (MacLeish) **47**:186
"Raspiatie" (Akhmatova) **2**:15; **55**:10, 27, 31-32, 38, 51-52, 57
"Rasshchelina" (Tsvetaeva) **14**:306-08
Rat Jelly (Ondaatje) **28**:294, 327-35
"Ratbert" (Hugo) **17**:59
"The Ratcatcher" (Tsvetaeva)
See "Krysolov"
"Rathlin Island" (Mahon) **60**:146, 192, 194, 220, 232
"Rational Anthem" (Kaufman) **74**:212
"Rational Man" (Rukeyser) **12**:220, 230
The Rationale of Verse (Poe) **54**:264
"The Rats" (Levine) **22**:213
"The Rat's Dance" (Hughes) **89**:209
"Rats Live On No Evil Star" (Sexton) **79**:216-17
"The Rat's Vision" (Hughes) **89**:113
"ratschlag auf höchster ebene" (Enzensberger) **28**:136
"The Rattle Bag" (Dafydd ap Gwilym)
See "Y Rhugl Groen"
"rattle poem" (Bissett) **14**:21
"Rattlesnake Country" (Warren) **37**:305, 308, 340
"Rattlin' Roarin' Willie" (Burns) **114**:127
"The Ravaged Face" (Plath) **37**:206
"The Ravaged Villa" (Melville) **82**:75, 151
"Ravel and Unravel" (Graham) **59**:191-93
"Raveling through the Dark" (Stafford) **71**:262
"The Raven" (Poe) **1**:419-20, 424, 427, 429-34, 436, 439-40, 443-44, 447, 452-53; **54**:256, 258, 260, 263-66, 268-82, 284-312, 314-16, 320-27, 330-32, 334-37, 339, 341-43
"Raven" (Seferis) **66**:170
"The Raven: A Christmas Tale" (Coleridge) **11**:109-17
The Raven, and Other Poems (Poe) **1**:437, 449; **54**:293, 305, 330
"Ravenna" (MacNeice) **61**:178
"Ravens" (Hughes) **89**:262
"The Ravine" (Carruth) **10**:85, 90
"Raving Mad" (Césaire) **25**:15
"Rawhead and Bloody Bones" (Hope) **56**:285
"Ray-Flowers" (Dickey) **40**:211-12, 237
Les rayons et les ombres (Hugo) **17**:45, 50-53, 63-64, 67, 76-77, 87, 91-92, 97
"Les Rayons jaunes" (Sainte-Beuve) **110**:34, 38, 53, 62
"Raza" (Darío) **15**:115
"Razgovor s geniem" (Tsvetaeva) **14**:325
Rbaiyyat (Khayyam)
See *Rubáiyát*
"Re" (Tolson) **88**:331
Re:Creation (Giovanni) **19**:108-11, 114, 118, 122, 128, 136-37, 140-41
"Reaching Out" (Stone) **53**:228
"The reaching out of warmth is never done" (Viereck) **27**:278
"Reaching Out with the Hands of the Sun" (Wakoski) **15**:363
"Re-Act for Action" (Madhubuti) **5**:338
"Read by Moonlight" (Hardy) **92**:329
"The Reader" (Chappell) **105**:39
Reader (Bell)
See *A Marvin Bell Reader: Selected Poetry and Prose*
"The Reader over My Shoulder" (Graves) **6**:143, 151
"Reading" (Stone) **53**:257
"Reading Aloud" (Gallagher) **9**:60
"Reading Aloud to My Father" (Kenyon) **57**:12, 27, 47-48
"Reading an Anthology of Chinese Poems of the Sung Dynasty, I Pause to Admire the Length and Clarity of Their Titles" (Collins) **68**:221
"Reading Apollinaire by the Rouge River" (Ferlinghetti) **1**:181, 187
"Reading at the Old Federal Courts Building, St. Paul" (Hugo) **68**:254
"Reading History" (Simic) **69**:309
"Reading Holderlin on the Patio with the Aid of a Dictionary" (Dove) **6**:109
"Reading in the Fall Rain" (Bly) **39**:86
"Reading in Wartime" (Muir) **49**:195, 232, 252
"Reading Late of the Death of Keats" (Kenyon) **57**:4
"Reading my poems from World War II" (Meredith) **28**:180, 195
"Reading Myself" (Lowell) **3**:229
A Reading of Earth (Meredith) **60**:257, 289-90, 298, 333
A Reading of Life (Meredith) **60**:287, 289-90, 292, 294
"The Reading of the Psalm" (Francis) **34**:244
"Reading on the Beach" (Jacobsen) **62**:320
"Reading Plato" (Graham) **59**:133, 152
"Reading the Brothers Grimm to Jenny" (Mueller) **33**:175
"Reading the Headlines" (Ignatow) **34**:310
"Reading the Japanese Poet Issa" (Milosz) **8**:189
"Reading the Landscape" (Wagoner) **33**:352
"Reading the Sky" (Wagoner) **33**:358
Reading the Spirit (Eberhart) **76**:6, 35-36, 38
"Reading the Will" (Kipling) **3**:190
"Reading Time: 1 Minute 26 Seconds" (Rukeyser) **12**:206
"Reading Trip" (Kennedy) **93**:139
"Reading with Little Sister: A Recollection" (Stafford) **71**:370
"Readings of History" (Rich) **5**:355
"Ready for Goodbye" (Cassian) **17**:3
"Ready to Kill" (Sandburg) **41**:347
"Reah habenzin 'oleh be'api" (Amichai) **38**:6, 33-5
"The Real Construction" (Baraka) **113**:64
"The Real Estate Agents Tale" (Lowell) **13**:84
"A Real Irishman" (Montague) **106**:313, 316
"Real Life" (Baraka) **4**:30
"Real Life" (Enzensberger) **28**:159
Real Live (Dylan) **37**:59
"Real Mammy Song" (Brown) **55**:164
"The Real Names" (Heaney) **100**:239
"The Real Revolution Is Love" (Harjo) **27**:70
"The Real Southwest by Greyhound" (Stone) **53**:223
"The Real Thing" (Ní Chuilleanáin) **34**:361, 371
"A Real Toad in a Real Garden" (Mueller) **33**:189
"The Real Work" (Snyder) **21**:324-25
The Real World (Snyder) **21**:291
La realidad invisible (Jiménez) **7**:207
La realidad y el deseo (Cernuda) **62**:168-69, 174-81, 183-84, 191, 193, 198-200, 202, 204-5, 212, 216, 220-22, 224, 229, 245, 248-49, 251, 254-56
"Realities" (MacLeish) **47**:182
"Reality" (Pasolini) **17**:258
Reality and Desire (Cernuda)
See *La realidad y el deseo*
"Reality Demands" (Szymborska)
See "Rzeczywistość wymaga"
"Reality Is an Activity of the Most August Imagination" (Stevens) **110**:152, 230
"Reality! Reality! What Is It?" (Eberhart) **76**:4-5, 42
Reality Sandwiches (Ginsberg) **4**:67, 81; **47**:16
"The Realization" (Winters) **82**:318, 338-41
"A Reaper and the Flowers" (Longfellow) **30**:21, 26, 45
"Reapers" (Toomer) **7**:319, 333-34
"Reaping" (Lowell) **13**:60
"Reaping in Heat" (Heaney) **18**:191
"The Rear-Guard" (Sassoon) **12**:266
"Rearmament" (Jeffers) **17**:117, 121-22
"The Reason" (Thomas) **99**:340
"Reason and Imagination" (Smart) **13**:341, 347
"Reason and Nature" (Cunningham) **92**:134, 182
"A Reason for Moving" (Strand) **63**:140, 172
The Reason of Church Government (Milton) **29**:272
"A Reason of Numbers" (Jacobsen) **62**:317
"Reason tell me thy mind" (Sidney) **32**:235
"A Reasonable Affliction" (Prior) **102**:306
"A Reasonable Constitution" (Melville) **82**:200
"Reasons for Attendance" (Larkin) **21**:223, 229, 244, 247
Reasons for Moving (Strand) **63**:139-41, 144, 159-61, 169, 172, 174-75, 178-80
"Reasons for Music" (MacLeish) **47**:192
"Reawakening" (Pavese)
See "Risveglio"
"The Rebel" (Belloc) **24**:12, 30, 38
"Rebel Color-Bearers at Shiloh" (Melville)
See "Shiloh"
"Le rebelle" (Baudelaire) **1**:55
"Rebellion" (Brathwaite) **56**:23-24, 31, 87
"Rebellion" (Lowell) **3**:318
"Rebellion Is the Circle of a Lover's Hands" (Espada) **74**:133, 147
Rebellion Is the Circle of a Lover's Hands (Espada) **74**:14, 127-29, 131, 133-34, 139, 144-45, 149, 153-54, 158-59, 162, 168
"Rebellions Antidote: or a Dialogue Between Coffee and Tea" (Behn) **88**:22-24
"The Rebels" (Ferlinghetti) **1**:184
"Rebirth" (Pushkin) **10**:408
"Rebuke of the Rocks" (Warren) **37**:319, 380
"A Rebus by I. B." (Wheatley) **3**:338
"Recado de Chile" (Mistral) **32**:165
"Recado sobre Chile" (Mistral)
See "Recado de Chile"
"Recado terrestre" (Mistral) **32**:188
"Recall to Earth" (Curnow) **48**:26
"Recalling War" (Graves) **6**:137, 142, 144, 165
"The Recantation: An Ode. By S. T. Coleridge" (Coleridge) **11**:94, 99
"The Recapitulation" (Eberhart) **76**:33
"Recapitulations" (Shapiro) **25**:272-73, 285, 296-97, 319-20, 324
"Receive Thy Sight" (Bryant) **20**:6
"The Recent Past" (Ashbery) **26**:143
Recent Poems (Curnow) **48**:24
Recent Songs (Cohen) **109**:35
"The Reception" (Jordan) **38**:125
"Réception d'Orion" (Char) **56**:137, 145
"Recessional" (Kipling) **91**:61, 67, 73, 90, 93, 95-96, 113, 134, 154, 158-59, 172, 175, 190
"Recessional" (Masters) **1**:333
"Recessional" (Melville) **82**:15, 26, 35, 38, 44, 53
"Rechauffe" (MacNeice) **61**:178
Recherche de la base et du sommet (Char) **56**:108-9, 112, 114, 120, 128, 132, 134, 136, 139-40, 148, 191, 195
"Recipe for Happiness in Khaboronsky" (Ferlinghetti) **1**:183
"Récit" (Brossard) **80**:25
"Récit à Adèle" (Sainte-Beuve) **110**:45, 47
"The Recital" (Ashbery) **26**:130, 149
"Rècitation à l 'Éloge d'une Reine" (Perse) **23**:230
"Recitative" (Berssenbrugge) **115**:11, 25
"Recitative" (Crane) **3**:81, 83; **99**:11-12, 24, 71, 74
"Recitativo di Palinuro" (Ungaretti) **57**:339
"Recitativo veneziano" (Zanzotto) **65**:268, 323, 325, 328-29
Recklings (Hughes) **7**:120, 122-23; **89**:98, 102
"Reclamation at Coloma" (Hugo) **68**:249
"The Recluse" (Smith) **12**:299, 331, 333

The Recluse (Wordsworth)
See *The Recluse; or Views on Man, Nature, and on Human Life*
The Recluse; or Views on Man, Nature, and on Human Life (Wordsworth) **4**:406-7, 409; **67**:355
"The Recognition" (Wagoner) **33**:370, 372
"Recoil" (Stafford) **71**:299
"La Recoleta" (Borges) **32**:59
"Recollection" (Wheatley)
See "On Recollection"
"Recollection in Upper Ontario, from Long Before" (Warren) **37**:336
"Recollection of Childhood" (Eberhart) **76**:12
"A Recollection of School Days" (Carducci)
See "Rimembranze di Scuola"
"The Recollections" (Leopardi)
See "Le ricordanze"
"Recollections" (Swinburne) **24**:329
"Recollections of Bellagio" (Meredith) **28**:198, 215
Recollections of Gran Apacheria (Dorn) **115**:51, 53-54, 56, 119-20, 132-33, 160, 221-22, 225, 240
"Recollections of Solitude" (Bridges) **28**:60
"Recollections of the Arabian Nights" (Tennyson) **6**:347, 359, 389, 406, 408-09; **101**:144, 238, 245-46
Recollections of Tsarskoe-Selo (Pushkin)
See "Vospominanie v Tsarskom Sele"
"The Recommendation" (Crashaw) **84**:9
"The Recompense" (Tomlinson) **17**:349
"Reconciliation" (Day Lewis) **11**:147
"Reconciliation" (Milosz) **8**:213
"Reconciliation" (Sassoon) **12**:289
"Reconciliation" (Whitman) **3**:378
"Reconstructions" (Snodgrass) **74**:292
"The Record" (Berry) **28**:30
Record of a Journey to Sarashina (Matsuo Basho)
See *Sarashina kikō*
"Records" (Tate) **50**:255-56
The Records of a Travel-worn Satchel (Matsuo Basho)
See *Oi no kobumi*
Records of a Weather Exposed Skeleton (Matsuo Basho)
See *Nozarashi kikō*
"Recours au ruisseau" (Char) **56**:137, 157, 171
"Recourse to the river" (Char)
See "Recours au ruisseau"
"Recovered from the Storm" (Graham) **59**:153-55, 158-59, 161
"Recovering" (Rukeyser) **12**:225
"Recovery" (Ammons) **16**:6
"The Recovery" (Pushkin) **10**:408
"The Recovery" (Traherne) **70**:192, 275, 317
Recovery (Tagore)
See *Ārogya*
"Recovery of Sexual Desire after a Bad Cold" (Chappell) **105**:38
"Recreaciones arqueológicas" (Darío) **15**:96
"Re-creating the Scene" (Komunyakaa) **51**:38
"The Recruit" (Housman) **2**:196
"A Recruit on the Corpy" (McKay) **2**:226
"Recruiting Team" (Yamada) **44**:339
"The Recruit's Ball" (Dobell) **100**:139
"Reçu" (Péret) **33**:231
Recueil des Pièces retranchées (Ronsard) **105**:303
"Recueillement" (Baudelaire) **1**:65; **106**:129
Les recueillements poétiques (Lamartine) **16**:263, 268, 284-85
"Recuerdo" (Millay) **6**:215
"El Recuerdo" (Storni) **33**:306
"Recuerdos..." (Jiménez) **7**:199
"Recuerdos de juventud" (Parra) **39**:283, 286
"The Recurrence" (Muir) **49**:196
"Red" (Hughes) **89**:162, 183
"Red Armchair" (McGuckian) **27**:105
"The Red Balloon" (Abse) **41**:6-7
Red Beans (Cruz) **37**:15-16, 20, 25, 31
"Red Blues" (Alexie) **53**:12-13
"Red Buzzard of Light Circling in the 25th Precinct" (Espada) **74**:128
"A Red Carpet for Shelley" (Wylie) **23**:322, 333
"Red Clay" (Hogan) **35**:258
Red Clay (Hogan) **35**:257, 263, 264
"Red Clay Blues" (Hughes) **53**:116, 200
The Red Coal (Stern) **115**:252, 259, 262-63, 269-70, 277
"The Red Coal" (Stern) **115**:268
"The Red Dance" (Sexton) **79**:241, 245
Red Dirt (Cervantes) **35**:132
Red Dust (Levine) **22**:211, 213-15, 217-18, 222-23, 227-28
"Red Eye" (Baraka) **113**:16
"A Red Flower" (Moore) **49**:105, 110
"Red Geranium and Godly Mignonette" (Lawrence) **54**:199, 227
"Red Guard" (Borges)
See "Guardia roja"
"Red Harvest" (Service) **70**:130
"Red Island" (Montague) **106**:320
"The Red Knight" (Lowell) **13**:84
"The Red Lacquer Music Stand" (Lowell) **13**:78
"Red Lantern" (Cernuda)
See "Linterna roja"
"Red Maple Leaves" (Rexroth) **20**:221
"Red Maples" (Teasdale) **31**:360
"The Red Mullet" (Warren) **37**:299, 302, 362
"Red Poppy" (Gallagher) **9**:64
"A Red, Red Rose" (Burns)
See "My Luve Is Like a Red, Red Rose"
"The Red Retreat" (Service) **70**:119
"Red Riding Hood" (Sexton) **2**:354, 364; **79**:191, 205
"Red Rising" (Brathwaite) **56**:51
"Red Roses" (Hughes) **53**:115
Red Roses for Bronze (H. D.) **5**:270-71, 304
"Red Shift" (Berrigan) **103**:6, 30, 36, 42
"Red Silk Stockings" (Hughes) **1**:269
"The Red Sleep of Beasts" (Erdrich) **52**:192
"Red Slippers" (Lowell) **13**:79
"Red Son" (Sandburg) **41**:227
"The Red Steer" (Tsvetaeva)
See "Krasnyi bychok"
Red Wagon: Poems (Berrigan) **103**:29, 31, 34-35, 41
"The Red Wheelbarrow" (Williams) **7**:378, 401-02, 409-10; **109**:223, 246, 266-67, 269, 279, 289-93, 295-96, 298
The Red Wheelbarrow (Spicer) **78**:241, 258, 273, 275, 305-6
"Red, White and Blue" (Heaney) **100**:243
"Red, White and Blue" (Quintana) **36**:272
"The Red Wolf" (Carman) **34**:213
"Redbirds" (Teasdale) **31**:359
"The Redbreast and the Butterfly" (Wordsworth) **4**:376; **67**:248
"Redcap" (Brown) **55**:164
"Red-Cotton Nightcap Country" (Browning) **2**:46, 96
"Rededication" (Cohen) **109**:49
"A Redeemer" (Jeffers) **17**:131, 141
"The Redeemer" (Sassoon) **12**:242, 249-51, 261-62, 276, 278, 287
"Redemption" (Herbert) **4**:119, 130
"Redeployment" (Nemerov) **24**:287, 290
"Red-Headed Restaurant Cashier" (Sandburg) **41**:286, 318
"Rediscovering America" (Alexie) **53**:9
"Redness of the Dawn Breakers" (Char)
See "Rougeur des Matinaux"
Redo (Hejinian) **108**:304
"Redondillas" (Pound) **95**:122
"Redonnez-leur . . ." (Char) **56**:134
"Redrift" (Jones) **116**:141
"Red-Tail Hawk and Pyre of Youth" (Warren) **37**:310-12, 336, 355, 357, 360, 370
"Redwing" (Gallagher) **9**:62
"Redwing Blackbirds" (Warren) **37**:326
"Redwings" (Wright) **36**:311
"Redwood-Tree" (Whitman)
See "Song of the Redwood Tree"
"The Reed" (Lermontov) **18**:304
"A Reed Boat" (Komunyakaa) **51**:55
"The Reedbeds of the Hackensack" (Clampitt) **19**:87
"The Reefy Coast" (Ishikawa)
See "Ariso"
"The Re-Enactment" (Hardy) **92**:275, 277
"Reeve's Tale" (Chaucer) **19**:10, 13-14, 61; **58**:265, 363
"Reference" (Raworth) **107**:309
"Reference Back" (Larkin) **21**:228
"The Refiner's Gold" (Harper) **21**:189
"The Refinery" (Pinsky) **27**:158, 171-2, 176
"The Reflecting Trees of Being and Not Being" (Rexroth) **95**:258, 327
"The Reflection" (Behn) **88**:149, 152
"Reflection" (Creeley) **73**:95
"The Reflection: A Song" (Behn) **13**:18, 20-1
"Reflection by a Mailbox" (Kunitz) **19**:154
"Reflection from Anita Loos" (Empson) **104**:117
"Reflection in a Forest" (Auden) **1**:17
"Reflection in a Green Arena" (Corso) **33**:49; **108**:5, 18
"Reflection in an Ironworks" (MacDiarmid) **9**:155
"Reflection on Ice-Breaking" (Nash) **21**:279
"Reflections" (Duncan) **75**:126
"Reflections" (MacNeice) **61**:125
"Reflections" (Thomas) **99**:330
"Reflections" (Tomlinson) **17**:316, 324
"Reflections at Lake Louise" (Ginsberg) **4**:84
"Reflections in a Double Mirror" (Sarton) **39**:325
"Reflections in a Forest" (Auden) **92**:6
"Reflections in a Slum" (MacDiarmid) **9**:181
"Reflections in an Old House" (Tate) **50**:284-86
"Reflections on a Foreign Line of Verse" (Seferis) **66**:97, 144-45, 149, 163, 178, 184
"Reflections on Having Left a Place of Retirement" (Coleridge) **11**:81; **67**:280-81
Reflections on Having Left a Place of Retirement (Coleridge) **100**:23
Reflections on Morality, or Seneca Unmasqued (Behn) **88**:70-71, 83
"Reflections on Some Drawings of Plants" (Smith)
See "Sonnet 91"
"Reflections While Oiling a Machine Gun" (Ciardi) **69**:26
"Reflective" (Ammons) **16**:6
"Reflexion" (Lamartine) **16**:266, 285
"The Reflexion" (Taylor) **63**:206, 250, 252, 300, 303, 315-17, 321, 346
"Reflexions" (Meynell) **112**:193, 228-29, 231, 303
"Réflexions en lisant 'L'essai sur l'absurde'" (Ponge) **107**:129, 137
"Reformation" (Finch) **21**:166
"The Reformer" (Whittier) **93**:167
"Refrain" (Dove) **6**:117
"Refrain" (Montague) **106**:288
"Refuge" (Teasdale) **31**:322
"Refugee Blues" (Auden) **92**:103, 115-16
"Refugee in America" (Hughes) **53**:94, 149-50
"Refugee Ship" (Cervantes) **35**:108, 118, 130, 131
"The Refugees" (Jarrell) **41**:169
"Refugees" (MacNeice) **61**:139
"The Refugees" (Muir) **49**:251, 256, 273, 277, 282-83, 296, 299
"Refugees" (Zagajewski) **27**:402
"The Refusal" (Wright) **36**:337
"Refusal Song" (Char) **56**:131
"A Refusal to Mourn" (Mahon) **60**:132, 134, 193
"A Refusal to Mourn" (Thomas)
See "A Refusal to Mourn the Death, by Fire, of a Child in London"

"A Refusal to Mourn the Death, by Fire, of a Child in London" (Thomas) **2**:382-83, 386, 388, 390, 398, 400; **52**:218, 264-65, 268, 278, 280-81, 313, 322, 335-36
"The Refuse Man" (Ignatow) **34**:310
"Regarding Wave" (Snyder) **21**:297, 304-06
Regarding Wave (Snyder) **21**:285, 288-92, 300, 304-08, 310, 317, 322
"The Regatta" (Wilbur) **51**:255-58, 261
"Regeneration" (Vaughan) **81**:274-75, 283, 295, 306, 324, 338, 341-43
"Regent's Park Sonnets" (Hacker) **47**:81
Regina Cœli (Patmore) **59**:223
The Region November (Stevens) **110**:153-54
Region of Unlikeness (Graham) **59**:131, 133-39, 143-45, 155-59, 161, 163, 168-69, 175-76, 178, 184
"Règle" (Tzara) **27**:230-31
"Régles de l'Ode" (Hugo) **17**:90
"Regreso a la cordura" (Storni) **33**:257-58, 295
"Regreso a mis pájaros" (Storni) **33**:257, 259, 294
"Regreso en sueños" (Storni) **33**:268, 284
"Regressiv" (Benn) **35**:68
"Regret Not Me" (Thomas) **52**:283
"Regrets" (Meynell) **112**:189, 287
"Les Regrets de la belle Heaulmière" (Villon) **13**:389-90
"Regrets of the Belle Heaumiere" (Villon)
See "Les Regrets de la belle Heaulmière"
"Regulus" (Tuckerman) **85**:309
"Rehabilitation & Treatment in the Prisons of America" (Knight) **14**:53
"The Rehearsal" (Smith) **12**:330
"Reincarnation I" (Dickey) **40**:155, 176, 197, 248
"Reincarnation II" (Dickey) **40**:158, 166, 197, 202, 248, 255, 259
"El reino interior" (Darío) **15**:79-80, 92, 96, 114
"Re-interment: Recollection of a Grandfather" (Warren) **37**:376
"Reise" (Benn) **35**:49, 74
"Reisen" (Benn) **35**:70
"The Rejected Lover" (Dafydd ap Gwilym)
See "Y Cariad a Wrthodwyd"
"Rejoice in the Abyss" (Spender) **71**:189
Rejoice in the Lamb (Smart)
See *Jubilate Agno*
"Rejoice, Liars" (Jackson) **44**:101
Rejoicings: Selected Poems 1966-72 (Stern) **115**:246, 248-50, 259, 261-63, 265, 271, 277, 285
"Rejoinder" (Chappell) **105**:50
Rekviem: Tsikl stikhotvorenii (Akhmatova) **2**:4, 7, 9, 15-16, 19-20; **55**:3-67
The Relation Ship (Raworth) **107**:273-76, 278, 301, 316, 324
"Relations" (Thomas) **99**:273
Relations and Contraries (Tomlinson) **17**:317, 342
"A Relationship" (Das) **43**:85
"Relatives" (Stone) **53**:240-41, 248
"Relearning the Alphabet" (Levertov) **11**:195-98
Relearning the Alphabet (Levertov) **11**:176-78, 180, 193-94
"Release" (Lawrence) **54**:168
"The Release" (MacLeish) **47**:190
"A Reliable Service" (Curnow) **48**:19-20
"Relic" (Hughes) **89**:152
"Relief" (Curnow) **48**:25
"Relief" (Very) **86**:132
"Religio" (Hugo) **17**:66
Religio Laici; or, A Layman's Faith (Dryden) **25**:79-82, 97, 101
"Religion" (Dunbar) **5**:125
"Religion" (Vaughan) **81**:298, 304-5, 337-38, 342-43
"The Religion of My Time" (Pasolini) **17**:257-59
The Religion of My Time (Pasolini) **17**:285
"Religion, Queen of Virtues" (Cowley) **90**:7
La religione del mio tempo (Pasolini) **17**:264-66, 270, 272-73, 295
"Religious Articles" (Hall) **70**:31
"Religious Isolation" (Arnold) **5**:42
"A Religious Man" (Smith) **12**:352
"Religious Musings" (Coleridge) **11**:49-51, 53, 80-2, 93-6; **39**:128, 152, 155-56, 163, 167, 179-81; **100**:31, 34, 82-83, 91-93
"Religious Phase" (Enright) **93**:28
"Religious Propaganda" (Tagore)
See "Dharma prachar"
Le Reliquare (Rimbaud) **57**:298
"The Relique" (Donne) **1**:126, 130; **43**:126, 133
"Reliques" (Spencer) **77**:339
"Relocation" (Ortiz) **17**:231
"El reloj de arena" (Borges) **32**:60
"Reluctance" (Frost) **39**:246
Reluctant Gravities (Waldrop) **109**:142-43, 175, 178-80
Remains (Snodgrass) **74**:289, 291, 326-27
"The Remains" (Strand) **63**:141, 156, 174-77
Remains of Elmet (Hughes) **7**:146, 149, 162
Remains of Elmet: A Pennine Sequence (Hughes) **89**:119-24, 131, 150-51, 193, 232-33
"Rémanence" (Char) **56**:157
"Remarques" (Jaccottet) **98**:201
"Rembrandt to Rembrandt" (Robinson) **1**:487
"Remember" (Harjo) **27**:59
"Remember" (Rossetti) **7**:269, 280
"Remember" (Stafford) **71**:268
"Remember?" (Walker) **30**:348
"Remember Graham" (Hugo) **68**:253, 255
"Remember Me" (Peacock) **87**:308
"Remember my little granite pail?" (Niedecker) **42**:98, 106-7, 140, 176-77
"Remember the Days" (Hafiz) **116**:24
"Rememberance" (Hölderlin)
See "Andenken"
"A Remembered Beat" (Kaufman) **74**:195, 253, 259
"Remembered Spring" (Winters) **82**:312
"Remembering a Strange Treat" (Shvarts) **50**:142, 144, 146
"Remembering Althea" (Stafford) **71**:379
"Remembering Dam Myra Hess" (Masefield) **78**:89
"Remembering in Osolo the Old Picture of the Magna Carta" (Bly) **39**:79
"Remembering into Sleep" (Waldrop) **109**:120-21
"Remembering Nat Turner" (Brown) **55**:114, 166
"Remembering Old Wars" (Kinsella) **69**:101
"Remembering Pearl Harbor at the Tutankhamen Exhibit" (Kumin) **15**:196, 206, 208
"Remembering Robert Lowell" (Meredith) **28**:177, 180
"Remembering Teheran" (Hughes) **89**:187, 190
"Remembering the Thirties" (Davie) **29**:98
"Remembering Watching Romy Schneider" (Ríos) **57**:325
"Remembering Wind Mountain at Sunset" (Chappell) **105**:44, 70
"Remembrance" (Angelou) **32**:16
"Remembrance" (Brontë) **8**:52, 56, 60, 65, 68, 74-5
"A Remembrance" (Carman) **34**:229
"Remembrance" (Hölderlin)
See "Andenken"
"Remembrance" (Muir) **49**:287
"Remembrance Has a Rear and Front" (Dickinson) **1**:94
"Remembrance in Tsarskoe Selo" (Pushkin)
See "Vospominanie v Tsarskom Sele"
Remembrance of Crimes Past (Abse) **41**:32
"Remembrance Sunday" (Enright) **93**:28
"Remembrances" (Leopardi)
See "Le ricordanze"
Remeslo (Tsvetaeva) **14**:315, 318, 324-25
"Remind Me of Apples" (Francis) **34**:249, 253-54
"Reminiscence" (Ishikawa)
See "Omoide"
"Réminiscence" (Mallarmé)
See "L'orphelin"
"Reminiscences at Tsarskoe Selo" (Pushkin)
See "Vospominanie v Tsarskom Sele"
"Reminiscences of Childhood" (MacNeice) **61**:169
"Reminiscene" (Niedecker) **42**:43
"Reminiscent of a Wave at the Curl" (Moore) **49**:150
"Remission" (Hughes) **89**:162
"Remittance Man" (Wright) **14**:340, 348, 368
"Remodeling the Hermit's Cabin" (Chappell) **105**:39
"Remonstrance" (de la Mare) **77**:61
"Remonstrance" (Lanier) **50**:55
"Remordimiento" (Borges)
See "Remordimiento por cualquier defunción"
"Remordimiento en traje de noche" (Cernuda) **62**:230, 239
"Remordimiento por cualquier defunción" (Borges) **32**:64
"Remords posthume" (Baudelaire) **1**:45
"Remorse" (Betjeman) **75**:11, 29
"Remorse" (Sassoon) **12**:282
Remorse (Coleridge) **11**:58
"Remorse for Intemperate Speech" (Yeats) **20**:328, 333
"Remorse in Evening Dress" (Cernuda)
See "Remordimiento en traje de noche"
"Remorse Is Memory Awake" (Dickinson) **1**:111
"Remote-a-Dad" (Silverstein) **49**:319, 340
"The Removal" (Merwin) **45**:45-6
"Removing the Plate of the Pump on the Hydraulic System of the Backhoe" (Snyder) **21**:307
"Le Rempart de Brindilles" (Char) **56**:108
Ren'aimeikashū (Hagiwara) **18**:170, 172
"Renaissance" (Lawrence) **54**:235-36
"Renaming the Kings" (Levine) **22**:215
"Renascence" (Lawrence) **54**:235-36
"Renascence" (Millay) **6**:204-05, 207-08, 211, 214-15, 217, 221, 224, 226-27, 242
Renascence, and Other Poems (Millay) **6**:204-06, 225, 240; **61**:209-58
"Rencontre de deux sourires" (Éluard) **38**:90-91, 93
"Rendezvous" (Kumin) **15**:213, 224
Le Rendez-vous (Sainte-Beuve) **110**:39
"Rendezvous with America" (Tolson) **88**:329, 337-39, 343, 348
Rendezvous with America (Tolson) **88**:231, 254-55, 330, 336, 340, 343-44, 347-50, 355, 360
"The Rendition" (Whittier) **93**:167, 210-11
"The Renegade Wants Words" (Welch) **62**:340, 357, 372
"The Renewal" (Roethke) **15**:275
"Renewal" (Thumboo) **30**:313
"Renewal of Strength" (Harper) **21**:189
Renga (Paz) **48**:221-26
"Le Reniement de Saint Pierre" (Baudelaire) **106**:101
"Renka" (Nishiwaki) **15**:238
"Renouncement" (Meynell) **112**:156-57, 164, 181, 189, 286, 297-98, 300-301, 304
"Rent Day Blues" (Brown) **55**:178
"Repentance" (Clarke) **112**:32, 36, 47, 49, 90, 116, 119
"Renunciation" (Curnow) **48**:24-25
"Renunciation" (Parker) **28**:360
"Reparation" (Reese) **29**:335
"Les reparties de Nina" (Rimbaud) **3**:271; **57**:191, 202, 204, 241, 244-45, 249, 252
"El reparto" (Mistral) **32**:184-85
"Repas" (Valéry) **9**:391
"Repent" (Kumin) **15**:209, 211
"Repent, England, Repent" (Deloney) **79**:55

"Repentance" (Herbert) **4**:120
"Repentance" (Vaughan) **81**:306, 366
Répétitions (Éluard) **38**:88, 101-2, 105-6
"Repetitions of a Young Captain" (Stevens) **110**:181
"The Repetitive Heart" (Schwartz) **8**:292-93, 302
"Repining" (Rossetti) **7**:287
Replication (Skelton)
See *A Replycacion*
"Reply" (Benét) **64**:14
"Reply" (Bridges) **28**:66, 69
"Reply" (Thomas) **99**:266, 297, 300
"Reply to Censure" (Roethke) **15**:291
"A Reply to Impromptu Verses by Baretti" (Johnson) **81**:240
"A Reply to Matthew Arnold" (Wright) **36**:369
"Reply to Mr. Wordsworth" (MacLeish) **47**:192
"Reply to the Warsaw Critics" (Mickiewicz)
See "O Krytykach i Recenzentach"
A Replycacion (Skelton) **25**:374, 385
A Replycacion Against Certayne Yong Scolars Abjured of Late (Skelton)
See *A Replycacion*
"A Replye to the same" (Whitney) **116**:312
"Reponse aux adieux de Sir Walter Scott" (Lamartine) **16**:283
"Report" (Harper) **21**:207, 216
"Report" (Illyés) **16**:243
"Report from Paradise" (Herbert) **50**:34
"Report from the Besieged City" (Herbert)
See "Raport z oblezonego miasta"
Report from the Besieged City (Herbert)
See *Raport z oblezonego miasta i inne wiersze*
Report from the Besieged City and Other Poems (Herbert)
See *Raport z oblezonego miasta i inne wiersze*
"Report from the Skull's Diorama" (Komunyakaa) **51**:28, 41
"Report on Experience" (Blunden) **66**:45
"Report to the Mother" (Knight) **14**:52
"Reporting Back" (Stafford) **71**:298
"Repos d'été" (Éluard) **38**:75
"Repose of Rivers" (Crane) **3**:83, 90, 96; **99**:20, 27-30, 32, 107
"Representing Far Places" (Stafford) **71**:262, 269, 350, 362
"Repression of War Experience" (Sassoon) **12**:264, 267, 288
"The Reprimand" (Bishop) **34**:160-61
"The Reproach" (Glück) **16**:152, 156, 164
"Reproach" (Graves) **6**:140, 144
"Reproach to Dead Poets" (MacLeish) **47**:126, 167
The Reproduction of Profiles (Waldrop) **109**:121, 123-25, 142-43, 175, 179-81
"A Reproof of Gluttony" (Belloc) **24**:17
"The Republic" (Ondaatje) **28**:298
"Republican Living Rooms" (Olds) **22**:307
"Repulse Bay" (Chin) **40**:4
"The Request" (Cowley) **90**:13, 26
"Request" (Sarton) **39**:319, 347
"Request for Blanca" (Mistral)
See "Encargo a Blanca"
"Request for Offering" (Eberhart) **76**:36
"Request for Requiems" (Hughes) **1**:243
"Request of Blanca" (Mistral)
See "Encargo a Blanca"
"Request to a Year" (Wright) **14**:375
"A Request to the Divine Being" (Leapor) **85**:187, 262
"A Request to the Graces" (Herrick) **9**:88
"Requeste à Monseigneur de Bourbon" (Villon)
See "Requête à Monseigneur de Bourbon"
"Requête à Monseigneur de Bourbon" (Villon) **13**:413
"Requiem" (Akhmatova)
See *Rekviem: Tsikl stikhotvorenii*
"Requiem" (Berry) **28**:16-17
"Requiem" (Ignatow) **34**:324, 344
"Requiem" (Nash) **21**:273
"Requiem" (Stafford) **71**:262
"Requiem" (Stevenson) **84**:308-9, 324, 326, 329, 335
Requiem (Rilke) **2**:267, 279
Requiem: A Cycle of Poems (Akhmatova)
See *Rekviem: Tsikl stikhotvorenii*
"Requiem for 'Bird' Parker, Musician" (Corso) **33**:46
"A Requiem for My Father" (Das) **43**:81
"Requiem for the Croppies" (Heaney) **100**:212, 219, 291
"Requiem for the Death of a Boy" (Rilke) **2**:279
"A Requiem for the Memory of Bees, Lake Michigan" (Winters) **82**:313-14
"Requiem for the Spanish Dead" (Rexroth) **20**:192; **95**:257, 259, 270, 306-7
"Requiescat" (Arnold) **5**:12
"Requiescat" (Mew) **107**:58
"Requiescat" (Tennyson) **101**:245
"Le Requin et al mouette" (Char) **56**:156
Rerum vulgarium fragmenta (Petrarch)
See *Canzoniere*
"Resaca en Sansueña" (Cernuda) **62**:249
"The Rescue" (Hughes) **89**:99, 103
"Rescue" (Stafford) **71**:371
"Rescue Poem" (Wakoski) **15**:324, 361
"Rescue the Dead" (Ignatow) **34**:286-87, 294, 298, 309, 313, 320, 324, 341
Rescue the Dead (Ignatow) **34**:277, 279, 281, 289-93, 318-19, 321, 323-24, 344
"Rescue with Yul Brynner" (Moore) **4**:242, 256, 259; **49**:147
"The Rescued Year" (Stafford) **71**:265, 290, 302
The Rescued Year (Stafford) **71**:258, 264-66, 271-72, 275-78, 280, 286-88, 296, 302, 320-22, 326, 329, 339, 341, 349, 378, 380
"The Research Team in the Mountains" (Stafford) **71**:2 :59, 258
"Resentment" (Crabbe) **97**:103-4, 106, 112
"Resentments of Orpheus" (Wickham) **110**:301
"Reservation Drive-In" (Alexie) **53**:8
"Reservation Mathematics" (Alexie) **53**:10
"A Reservation Table of Elements" (Alexie) **53**:6
"Reservations" (Dorn) **115**:133
"Reservoirs" (Thomas) **99**:250
Residence on Earth (Neruda)
See *Residencia en la tierra*
Residence on Earth and Other Poems (Neruda)
See *Residencia en la tierra*
Residencia en la tierra (Neruda) **4**:277, 2809, 282-83, 285, 293, 295, 300-01, 304, 306; **64**:298, 300, 305, 313-14, 329, 332-33, 337-38, 340, 343, 345, 349-50
Residencia en la tierra, Vol. 1, 1925-31 (Neruda)
See *Residencia en la tierra*
Residencia en la tierra, Vol. 2, 1931-35 (Neruda)
See *Residencia en la tierra*
Residencia I (Neruda)
See *Residencia en la tierra*
Residencia II (Neruda)
See *Residencia en la tierra*
Residencia III (Neruda)
See *Residencia en la tierra*
"Residue of Song" (Bell) **79**:3
Residue of Song (Bell) **79**:32, 39
"Resignation" (Arnold) **5**:6, 18, 32, 34, 37-41, 43, 47, 49-51, 54
"Resignation" (Dunbar) **5**:133
"Resignation" (Longfellow) **30**:21, 49
"Resistance Principle" (Zanzotto)
See "Retorica su"
"Resistenza" (Zanzotto)
See "Retorica su"
"Resolution" (Berrigan) **103**:33
"Resolution" (Warren) **37**:289
"Resolution and Independence" (Snodgrass) **74**:285
"Resolution and Independence" (Wordsworth) **4**:399, 404, 406, 411-12, 426; **67**:264
"Resolution of Dependence" (Barker) **77**:38
"The Resolve" (Levertov) **11**:170
"Resolve" (Plath) **1**:406; **37**:184
"The Resolve" (Vaughan) **81**:306, 368
"Resolved never to Versifie more" (Barker) **91**:28
"Resolved to Be Beloved" (Cowley) **90**:13-14, 16, 32
"Resolved to Love" (Cowley) **90**:13, 35, 114
"The Resource" (Wickham) **110**:300
"Respect" (Montague) **106**:313
"Respectability" (Browning) **2**:95
"The Respectable Burgher on 'The Higher Criticism'" (Hardy) **8**:124
"The Respectable Folks-/Where Dwell They?" (Thoreau) **30**:201
Responce aux injures (Ronsard) **11**:234
"Responde tú" (Guillén) **23**:117, 127
"Respondez!" (Whitman) **3**:405
"Response" (Dunbar) **5**:139
"Résponse" (Sainte-Beuve) **110**:56
"Résponse à une acte d'accusation" (Hugo) **17**:64, 82
Responsibilities, and Other Poems (Yeats) **20**:311, 320, 323, 342; **51**:81
"Responsibilities of the Poet" (Pinsky) **27**:160, 170
"Responsibility: The Pilots Who Destroyed Germany, Spring, 1945" (Spender) **71**:169
"Responso a Verlaine" (Darío) **15**:98
"A Responsory, 1948" (Merton) **10**:333
"Respontio Regis" (Dunbar) **67**:16
"Respuesta a un cónsul" (Paz) **48**:184
"Ressouvenir du lac Leman" (Lamartine) **16**:286
"Ressurection, Imperfect" (Donne) **1**:147
"Rest" (Rossetti) **7**:277, 280
"The Rest I Will Tell to Those Down in Hades" (Cavafy) **36**:39, 41
"Le Restaurant Lemeunier, rue de la Chaussée d'Antin" (Ponge) **107**:214-17
"Restless" (Tagore)
See "Chanchal"
"Restless Night" (Tu Fu) **9**:319, 323
"Restoration Ode" (Cowley)
See "Ode upon His Majesties Restauration and Return"
"Restore To Them . . ." (Char)
See "Redonnez-leur . . ."
"Restraint" (Curnow) **48**:25-26
"Restricted Area" (Birney) **52**:8
"Results of a Lie Detector Test" (Kaufman) **74**:234
"Résumé" (Parker) **28**:347, 363
"Resumen" (Guillén) **35**:202
"Resumption" (Carducci)
See "Ripresa"
"Resurgam" (Carman) **34**:203, 229
"Resurgam" (Tate) **50**:228
"Resurgir" (Storni) **33**:241, 306
"Resurrection" (Atwood) **8**:40
"The Resurrection" (Cowley) **90**:104
"Resurrection" (Jeffers) **17**:141
"The Resurrection" (Ransom) **61**:294
"The Resurrection" (Schnackenberg) **45**:333, 337
"The Resurrection" (Winters) **82**:314
"Resurrection and Immortality" (Vaughan) **81**:296, 320, 370
"The Resurrection of Jesus" (Harper) **21**:189
"Resurrection of the Right Side" (Rukeyser) **12**:225
"Le Rétablissement de la Statue de Henri IV" (Hugo) **17**:88
"The Retaliatarians" (Bell) **79**:33
Retaliation (Blok)
See *Vozmezdie*
Retaliation (Goldsmith) **77**:161, 193, 226-27, 253

"A Retir'd Friendship To Ardelia" (Philips) **40**:295
"Retired Ballerina, Central Park West" (Ferlinghetti) **1**:183
"The Retired Colonel" (Hughes) **7**:140; **89**:189
"The Retired Postal Clerk" (Betjeman) **75**:38
"Retirement" (Cowper) **40**:44-5, 49, 111-12, 130
"Retirement" (Hunt) **73**:134
"Retirement" (Philips) **40**:269
"Retirement" (Stafford) **71**:375
"Retorica su" (Zanzotto) **65**:269-71, 319-20
"Retort" (Dunbar) **5**:125, 127
"The Retort Discourteous (Italy—sixteenth century)" (Benét) **64**:52
"Retort to Jesus" (Lawrence) **54**:249
"Le retour" (Lamartine) **16**:286
"Retour à la poésie" (Sainte-Beuve) **110**:38, 65
Retour amont (Char) **56**:110-13, 115, 117-19
Retour au pays natal (Césaire)
See *Cahier d'un retour au pays natal*
"Retraction" (Chaucer) **58**:284
"Retractions" (Chaucer)
See "Retraction"
"Retrato de García Lorca" (Storni) **33**:240, 269
"Retrato de poeta" (Cernuda) **62**:215
"Retrato de un muchacho que se llama Sigfrido" (Storni) **33**:240
Retratos con nombre (Aleixandre) **15**:4, 12, 16
Retreat (Blunden) **66**:17-18, 44
"The Retreate" (Vaughan) **81**:262, 269-74, 283, 340, 362
"Retribution" (Blok) **21**:31
"Retribution" (Harper) **21**:190
Retribution (Blok)
See *Vozmezdie*
The Retrieval System (Kumin) **15**:203-09, 217, 221
"Retrievers in Translation" (Doty) **53**:60
"Retroduction to American History" (Tate) **50**:228-29, 243, 246, 248, 274, 316
"Retrospect" (Brooke) **24**:62, 64, 86
"The Retrospect" (Southey) **111**:252
"The Retrospective Review" (Hood) **93**:58, 79
"Return" (Alurista) **34**:29
"The Return" (Behn) **88**:148, 152
"Return" (Blunden) **66**:30
"The Return" (Brathwaite) **56**:7, 20, 62, 83, 85
"The Return" (Brooke) **24**:61
"Return" (Brown) **55**:110
"Return" (Corso) **33**:50
"Return" (Creeley) **73**:38, 91
"The Return" (Eberhart) **76**:69
"Return" (Forché) **10**:136-41, 144-45, 152, 154-56, 162, 167
"The Return" (Hayden) **6**:194
"Return" (Heaney) **18**:201
"Return" (Jeffers) **17**:117, 119, 131, 141, 147
"The Return" (Kipling) **91**:70, 142-43, 175-76
"Return" (Lawrence) **54**:168
"Return" (MacLeish) **47**:126, 188
"The Return" (MacNeice) **61**:139
"The Return" (Mahon) **60**:140, 142, 152, 184-85, 192-93
"Return" (Montague) **106**:243
"The Return" (Muir) **49**:202, 206, 260-61, 289, 297
"The Return" (Oppen) **35**:310, 333
"Return" (Paz)
See "Vuelta"
"The Return" (Pound) **4**:355-56, 365; **95**:95
"The Return" (Roethke) **15**:274
"Return" (Sarton) **39**:325
"The Return" (Sikelianos)
See "The Great Homecoming"
"The Return" (Teasdale) **31**:334
"The Return" (Traherne) **70**:223, 288
"Return" (Wright) **14**:342
The Return (Bely)
See *Vozvrat: Tretiia simfoniia*
Return (Paz)
See *Vuelta*
"The Return: an Elegy" (Warren) **37**:276, 279, 286, 288, 320, 329, 331-33, 376
"Return from England" (Clarke) **112**:31, 54, 92, 122
"Return from Greece" (Cavafy)
See "Returning Home from Greece"
"Return from the Freudian Isles" (Hope) **56**:286
"Return in Dreams" (Storni)
See "Regreso en sueños"
"Return in Hinton" (Tomlinson) **17**:311, 327-28
"The Return of Aphrodite" (Sarton) **39**:343
"The Return of Helen" (McGuckian) **27**:77, 100
"The Return of Icarus" (Wagoner) **33**:348
"The Return of Odysseus" (Muir) **49**:252, 264, 279, 289
"The Return of Persephone" (Hope) **56**:268, 273, 278, 281
"The Return of Robinson Jeffers" (Hass) **16**:195, 203, 228
"Return of Spring" (Winters) **82**:314
"The Return of the Birds" (Bryant) **20**:46
"The Return of the Exile" (Seferis) **66**:165, 210
"The Return of the Goddess" (Graves) **6**:137, 144
"The Return of the Greeks" (Muir) **49**:245, 251-52, 297
"The Return of the Muses" (Guest) **55**:219
"The Return of the Proconsul" (Herbert)
See "Powrót prokonsula"
"Return of the Sun" (Brathwaite) **56**:91
Return: Poems Collected and New (Alurista) **34**:45-48
"Return to a Country House" (Teasdale) **31**:335, 341
"Return to a Place Lit by a Glass of Milk" (Simic) **69**:301
Return to a Place Lit by a Glass of Milk (Simic) **69**:264, 301, 371
"Return to Cardiff" (Abse) **41**:3, 5
"Return to Chartres" (Sarton) **39**:343, 345
"Return to DeKalb" (Stryk) **27**:214
"Return to D'Ennery, Rain" (Walcott) **46**:234, 272
"Return to Hiroshima" (Stryk) **27**:187, 202, 216
"Return to Kraków in 1880" (Milosz) **8**:204
"A Return to Me" (Neruda)
See "Se vuelve a yo"
Return to My Native Land (Césaire)
See *Cahier d'un retour au pays natal*
"'The Return to Nature': Histories of Modern Poetry" (Meynell) **112**:169, 291, 294-95, 303
"Return to Oneself" (Neruda)
See "Se vuelve a yo"
"Return to Solitude" (Bly) **39**:7, 11
"Return to the River" (Wagoner) **33**:352
"Return to the Swamp" (Wagoner) **33**:356
"Return to Wang River" (Wang Wei) **18**:392
"The Return to Work" (Williams) **7**:369
"The Return Trip" (Ekeloef) **23**:54
"Returned to Frisco, 1946" (Snodgrass) **74**:284, 295, 297, 300
"Returned to Say" (Stafford) **71**:260-61, 264, 275, 292, 299, 327
"Returning" (Lowell) **3**:226
"Returning" (Quintana) **36**:273
"Returning a Lost Child" (Glück) **16**:124
"Returning Birds" (Szymborska)
See "Przylot"
"Returning Home from Greece" (Cavafy) **36**:40, 74, 76
"Returning North of Vortex" (Ginsberg) **4**:76
"Returning to Mount Sung" (Wang Wei) **18**:371
"Returning to the Rhetoric of an Earlier Mode" (Duncan) **75**:175, 189
"Returning to the Rhetoric of an Early Mode" (Duncan) **2**:109, 113
"Returning to Vienna, 1947" (Spender) **71**:189
"Returns" (Szymborska)
See "Powroty"
"Reuben Bright" (Robinson) **1**:467, 496
"Reuben Pantier" (Masters) **1**:347; **36**:169
"Reunion" (Forché) **10**:137, 142-44, 147, 157, 168
"The Reunion" (Harper) **21**:200, 214
"Reunion" (Owen) **102**:149, 152
"A Reunion" (Szirtes) **51**:157
"Reunión bajo las nuevas banderas" (Neruda) **64**:313, 315
"The Rev. Abner Peet" (Masters) **36**:230
"Le rêve d'un curieux" (Baudelaire) **1**:54; **106**:22, 103
"Rêve Expérimental" (Tzara) **27**:242
"Rêve parisien" (Baudelaire) **1**:47, 54
"Rêve pour l'hiver" (Rimbaud) **57**:196, 245
"The Revealer" (Robinson) **35**:368
"Reveillé" (Housman) **2**:164
"Reveille" (Hughes) **7**:123, 159; **89**:113
"Reveille for My Twenty-eighth Birthday" (Ciardi) **69**:27-28
"The Reveillon" (Belloc) **24**:11
"Revelation" (Amichai) **38**:8
"The Revelation" (Service) **70**:130-31
"Revelation" (Warren) **37**:284, 287, 289, 322, 332-33, 376
"The Revelation" (Wright) **36**:288
"The Revelation of the Spirit through the Material World" (Very) **86**:89
"Revelations" (Brown) **55**:110, 174, 178
"The Revenant" (de la Mare) **77**:116
"The Revenant" (Meredith) **28**:181
The Revenant (MacNeice) **61**:141
"Revenge Fable" (Hughes) **7**:132, 143; **89**:142
"The Revenge of Hamish" (Lanier) **50**:56
"Revenir dans une ville" (Éluard) **38**:71
"Reverdure" (Berry) **28**:8-9
"Reverend Friend Mr. H." (Barker) **91**:25
"Reverend Magistracy" (Hunt) **73**:152
"Les Reverends Pères" (Béranger) **112**:17
"Reverie" (Browning) **2**:96
"Reverie" (Muir) **49**:287
"Reveries" (Castro)
See "Vaguedás"
"Reversibilité" (Baudelaire) **1**:56, 67
"Reversionary" (Smith) **12**:314
"A Revery" (Philips) **40**:271
"The Review" (Traherne) **70**:198
"The Review II" (Traherne) **70**:289
"Revision" (Thomas) **99**:264-65, 310, 325
Revised Arcadia (Sidney) **32**:314-15
"The Revisitation" (Hardy) **92**:264
"Revisiting the MacDowell Colony" (Kumin) **15**:222
"The Revival" (Tennyson) **101**:245
"The Revolt" (Carducci) **46**:26
"Revolt against the Crepuscular Spirit in Modern Poetry" (Pound) **95**:121
The Revolt of Islam (Shelley)
See *Laon and Cythna; or, The Revolution of the Golden City: A Vision of the Nineteenth Century*
The Revolt of Islam; A Poem, in Twelve Cantos (Shelley)
See *Laon and Cythna; or, The Revolution of the Golden City: A Vision of the Nineteenth Century*
"Revolution" (Housman) **43**:225
"Revolution" (Hughes) **53**:110
"The Revolution at Market Hill" (Swift) **9**:260
"Revolution in the Revolution in the Revolution" (Snyder) **21**:306
"The Revolutionary" (Stryk) **27**:208
"Revolutionary Dreams" (Giovanni) **19**:111
"Revolutionary Music" (Giovanni) **19**:110
"Revolutionary Petunias" (Walker) **30**:339, 363-65
Revolutionary Petunias (Walker) **30**:337, 340, 342, 343, 346-47, 349-53, 355-56, 363, 365
"Revolutionary Spanish Lesson" (Espada) **74**:161
"Revolutions" (Arnold) **5**:51
"Les revolutions" (Lamartine) **16**:280-81, 293
"Revolutionsaufruf" (Werfel) **101**:330
Le revolver á cheveux blancs (Breton) **15**:50-2

"Revolving Meditation" (Kunitz) **19**:174, 178
"Revulsion" (Hardy) **8**:91; **92**:241, 247-49
"The Revulsion" (Patmore) **59**:228, 234
Rewards and Fairies (Kipling) **3**:184; **91**:109, 111, 133, 152
"Reyerta" (García Lorca) **3**:131
Reynard the Fox (Masefield) **78**:16-17, 22-23, 26, 30, 38-39, 51-52, 56-58, 60-63, 70, 80, 92, 104
"A Rhapsodie" (Vaughan) **81**:337-38, 341, 356-57
"Rhapsody" (O'Hara) **45**:137, 218, 243
Rhapsody in Plain Yellow (Chin) **40**:36
"The Rhapsody of Life's Progress" (Barrett Browning) **6**:6
"Rhapsody on a Windy Night" (Eliot) **5**:153, 155, 171; **31**:131, 133,-34, 140
"A Rhapsody on Irish Themes" (Jarrell) **41**:158, 160
"A Rhapsody on Poetry" (Swift) **9**:281
"Der Rhein" (Hölderlin) **4**:143, 148, 153, 155, 173-4
"Rhénane d'automne" (Apollinaire) **7**:42
"Rhetorical Exercises" (Parra)
See "Ejercicios retóricos"
"The Rhine" (Hölderlin)
See "Der Rhein"
"Rho" (Tolson) **88**:241-43, 277, 304, 316-17, 320, 324, 333
Rhododaphne: or The Thessalian Spell. A Poem (Peacock) **87**:307, 318-19, 323, 325, 328, 331-32, 334-38, 346, 349-51
"Rhododendrons" (Gallagher) **9**:60
"The Rhodora" (Emerson) **18**:74, 82, 94, 96, 98-100, 102
"Rhotruda" (Tuckerman) **85**:302-3, 306, 319, 330-31, 333
R-hu (Scalapino) **114**:335-36
"Rhum des fougères" (Ponge) **107**:131
"Rhyme" (Seferis) **66**:110, 124
"A Rhyme about an Electrical Advertising Sign" (Lindsay) **23**:296
Rhyme? And Reason? (Carroll) **74**:3
"A Rhyme for All Zionists" (Lindsay) **23**:283
"Rhyme for My Tomb" (Service) **70**:147
"The Rhyme of Reb Nachman" (Pinsky) **27**:175
"The Rhyme of the Duchess May" (Barrett Browning) **6**:28
"The Rhyme of the Remittance Man" (Service) **70**:115
"The Rhyme of the Roughrider" (Service) **70**:151
"The Rhyme of the Three Captains" (Kipling) **3**:181-82
"The Rhyme of the Three Sealers" (Kipling) **3**:182
"Rhymed Address to All Renegade Campbellites Exhorting Them to Return" (Lindsay) **23**:265
Rhymed Ruminations (Sassoon) **12**:252
Rhymes (Elliott)
See *Corn Law Rhymes. The Ranter, Written and Published by Order of the Sheffield Mechanics' Anti-Bread Tax Society*
Rhymes (Jiménez)
See *Rimas*
Rhymes and Rhythms (Carducci)
See *Rime e ritmi*
Rhymes For My Rags (Service) **70**:140, 143-44
Rhymes of a Rebel (Service) **70**:140-42, 161
Rhymes of a Red Cross Man (Service) **70**:118-20, 123, 127, 129-33, 151, 158-60
Rhymes of a Rolling Stone (Service) **70**:153, 158-59
Rhymes of a Roughneck (Service) **70**:140-41, 147, 161
Rhymes of Childhood (Riley) **48**:290, 346-47, 357
Rhyming Poems (Lawrence) **54**:207, 232
"The Rhythm" (Creeley) **73**:37, 89
"Rhythm & Blues" (Baraka) **113**:9, 41
"Rhythm & Blues 1" (Baraka) **4**:16
Rhythm, Content & Flavor: New & Selected Poems (Cruz) **37**:16, 25, 31
"Rhythm, etc." (Cage) **58**:219
"Rhythm of Autumn" (García Lorca)
See "Ritmo de otoño"
"The Rib" (Dickey) **40**:185, 225
Rib of Earth (Thumboo) **30**:299
"A Ribban" (Carew)
See "Upon a Ribband"
"La ricchezza" (Pasolini) **17**:270, 273, 295
"Rice Coming Into Town" (Enright) **93**:13
Rice Pudding in Ghee (Das)
See *Neypayasam*
"The Rich Rival" (Cowley) **90**:13
"Richard Bone" (Masters) **1**:324
"Richard Cory" (Robinson) **1**:467, 475, 486; **35**:361-78
"Richard Hunt's 'Arachne'" (Hayden) **6**:186
"Richard Roe and John Doe" (Graves) **6**:141
"Richard the second to Queen Isabel" (Drayton) **98**:3
"Riche de larmes" (Char) **56**:163, 165, 190, 194-95
"Riches" (Teasdale) **31**:357
"A Richland County Lyric for Elizabeth Asleep" (Jordan) **38**:144
"The Rick of Green Wood" (Dorn) **115**:57, 105, 110, 119
"Le ricordanze" (Carducci) **46**:63
"Le ricordanze" (Leopardi) **37**:102, 109-11, 123-25, 127, 141, 143, 165
"The Riddle" (Auden) **1**:34
"The Riddle" (Heaney) **18**:229, 232, 237
"Riddle" (Prior) **102**:306
"Riddle" (Snodgrass) **74**:284-85, 302
"A Riddle" (Wilbur) **51**:301
"Riddle in the Garden" (Warren) **37**:301, 307, 362
"Riddles" (Guillén) **23**:131
"Riddles" (Parra)
See "Rompecabezas"
"The Ride" (Smith) **12**:315
"The Ride" (Wilbur) **51**:249, 302, 309-10, 335
"The Ride of Paul Revere" (Longfellow)
See "Paul Revere's Ride"
"A Ride on the Swan-Boats" (Bishop) **34**:96
"Ride to Aix" (Browning) **2**:35
"The Rider at the Gate" (Masefield) **78**:91
"The Rider-Garden" (Akhmadulina)
See "Sad-vsadnik"
"Rider Victory" (Muir) **49**:232
"The Ridge Farm" (Ammons) **16**:46-7, 50-1
"Riding in cars" (MacNeice) **61**:137
"Riding the Earthboy 40" (Welch) **62**:352, 370
Riding the Earthboy 40: Poems (Welch) **62**:337, 340, 342-6, 350-4, 356, 358-9, 361-3, 367-71, 374, 377-8
"Riding the Elevator into the Sky" (Sexton) **2**:373; **79**:237
"Riding through Mádrid" (Dorn) **115**:132
"Riding Together" (Morris) **55**:238, 248, 252, 302, 344-47
"Rien d'autre" (Éluard) **38**:85
"Riflemen Form!" (Tennyson) **101**:269
"Rigamarole" (Williams) **7**:383, 389
"Right Apprehension" (Traherne) **70**:222, 254
"Right in the Trail" (Snyder) **21**:327
The Right Madness on Skye (Hugo) **68**:271, 286-88, 294
"Right Now" (Stafford) **71**:288
"The Right of Way" (Williams) **7**:387, 409, 411; **109**:283, 319-25
Right Royal (Masefield) **78**:26, 45, 51, 55, 58, 60-63
"The Right Thing Happens to the Happy Man" (Roethke) **15**:270
"Right to Die" (Stafford) **71**:374
"The Right to Grief" (Sandburg) **41**:234, 262, 334, 338, 364
"Right Wing Sympathies" (Davie) **29**:97
"The Righteous" (Francis) **34**:246
"The Righteous Ones" (Borges) **32**:58
"The Rightful One" (Ignatow) **34**:213, 282, 313, 317
Rights of Passage (Brathwaite) **56**:3-8, 17-18, 20, 22-23, 26, 29-30, 33-34, 37-41, 43, 49, 59, 62, 64-68, 73, 75, 77, 79, 82-84, 88, 95-96, 98-99
"Right's Security" (Dunbar) **5**:127
"Rigor" (Guillén) **35**:146
"Rigorists" (Moore) **49**:91, 143
Riley Farm-Rhymes (Riley) **48**:315, 318
Riley Love Lyrics (Riley) **48**:323
"Rillons, Rillettes" (Wilbur) **51**:285
"Rima" (Seferis)
See "Rhyme"
"Rima 1" (Bécquer) **113**:169, 184, 225, 228, 232, 235, 241, 251-52
"Rima 2" (Bécquer) **113**:163, 169, 190, 210, 225, 232, 267, 270
"Rima 3" (Bécquer) **113**:169, 199, 202, 209, 225, 232
"Rima 4" (Bécquer) **113**:163, 184, 195, 205, 225, 232, 235
"Rima 5" (Bécquer) **113**:163, 169, 177, 182-84, 190, 208, 225-27, 232, 235
"Rima 6" (Bécquer) **113**:225, 232
"Rima 7" (Bécquer) **113**:169, 208, 225, 232, 239
"Rima 8" (Bécquer) **113**:169, 189, 209, 225, 232, 247, 252
"Rima 9" (Bécquer) **113**:169, 225, 232, 252
"Rima 10" (Bécquer) **113**:169, 214, 225, 252, 268-70
"Rima 11" (Bécquer) **113**:163, 169, 206, 222, 225, 238
"Rima 12" (Bécquer) **113**:169-70, 184, 225
"Rima 13" (Bécquer) **113**:163, 170, 184
"Rima 14" (Bécquer) **113**:170, 203, 222
"Rima 15" (Bécquer) **113**:163, 170, 177, 183, 206, 210, 216-17, 222
"Rima 16" (Bécquer) **113**:170, 177, 180, 187, 190
"Rima 17" (Bécquer) **113**:238, 252
"Rima 18" (Bécquer) **113**:170
"Rima 20" (Bécquer) **113**:170
"Rima 21" (Bécquer) **113**:170, 205, 214, 238, 241
"Rima 22" (Bécquer) **113**:170
"Rima 23" (Bécquer) **113**:163
"Rima 24" (Bécquer) **113**:163, 170-71, 181, 190
"Rima 25" (Bécquer) **113**:171, 183
"Rima 26" (Bécquer) **113**:163, 171, 180-81, 210
"Rima 27" (Bécquer) **113**:163, 212
"Rima 28" (Bécquer) **113**:180-81
"Rima 29" (Bécquer) **113**:171, 247
"Rima 30" (Bécquer) **113**:171
"Rima 31" (Bécquer) **113**:171, 260
"Rima 32" (Bécquer) **113**:171
"Rima 33" (Bécquer) **113**:171
"Rima 34" (Bécquer) **113**:171, 188
"Rima 35" (Bécquer) **113**:171-72
"Rima 37" (Bécquer) **113**:172, 214
"Rima 38" (Bécquer) **113**:172, 184
"Rima 39" (Bécquer) **113**:172, 217
"Rima 40" (Bécquer) **113**:172
"Rima 41" (Bécquer) **113**:172, 183
"Rima 42" (Bécquer) **113**:172
"Rima 43" (Bécquer) **113**:172
"Rima 45" (Bécquer) **113**:172, 186
"Rima 46" (Bécquer) **113**:172
"Rima 47" (Bécquer) **113**:172-73
"Rima 49" (Bécquer) **113**:173, 212, 260
"Rima 50" (Bécquer) **113**:173, 213
"Rima 51" (Bécquer) **113**:173
"Rima 53" (Bécquer) **113**:173, 239
"Rima 55" (Bécquer) **113**:255-62
"Rima 56" (Bécquer) **113**:187
"Rima 59" (Bécquer) **113**:173
"Rima 60" (Bécquer) **113**:173, 206, 255-56, 259-62
"Rima 61" (Bécquer) **113**:163, 173

"Rima 62" (Bécquer) **113**:174, 266-68, 270
"Rima 68" (Bécquer) **113**:199
"Rima 69" (Bécquer) **113**:163
"Rima 71" (Bécquer) **113**:174, 199, 222
"Rima 74" (Bécquer) **113**:174, 207, 222
"Rima 75" (Bécquer) **113**:198, 222, 253
"Rima 76" (Bécquer) **113**:174, 236
"Rima 77" (Bécquer) **113**:162
"Rima 78" (Bécquer) **113**:162
"Rima 79" (Bécquer) **113**:162, 174
"Rima 81" (Bécquer) **113**:212
"Rima 85" (Bécquer) **113**:255-58, 261-62
Rimas (Bécquer) **113**:161-68, 174, 178, 184-85, 189, 191, 195, 201, 204, 213, 215, 225, 229-30, 232, 235-37, 239-40, 243-45, 249, 252, 260-61, 265, 269-70
Rimas (Jiménez) **7**:197, 199
"Rimbaud Fire Letter to Jim Applewhite" (Chappell) **105**:5, 35, 43-44, 48, 60, 70, 79, 82-83
"The Rime" (Coleridge)
See *The Rime of the Ancient Mariner: A Poet's Reverie*
Rime (Carducci) **46**:13, 16, 35, 46
Rime (Petrarch)
See *Canzoniere*
Rime d'amore (Stampa) **43**:278, 280-81, 285, 287-92, 296-98, 301, 303, 305, 307, 310-12, 319, 324-25, 327, 329, 331-34, 339-45
"Rime d'Amore" (Stampa) **43**:288
Rime de Michelagnolo Buonarroti, racolte de Michelagnolo suo nipote (Michelangelo) **103**:183, 185-96, 199, 202, 205-8, 222, 226-28, 231, 254-55, 267, 275, 281, 283-84, 286-87, 289, 292-93, 315, 325-29, 331-32, 340-41, 343-44, 346
Rime e ritmi (Carducci) **46**:26, 48, 54, 76, 81
Rime nuove (Carducci) **46**:8, 35, 37, 47, 50, 56, 64-65, 69, 73-75, 81, 88
"The Rime of the Ancient Mariner" (Coleridge)
See *The Rime of the Ancient Mariner: A Poet's Reverie*
The Rime of the Ancient Mariner: A Poet's Reverie (Coleridge) **11**:37-42, 44, 51, 53, 55, 58-69, 81, 84, 88-9, 92-7, 104, 106, 110, 117; **39**:123, 131, 135, 140, 153, 156-57, 160, 169, 171, 175-76, 178-81, 185, 187, 203, 215; **67**:262, 265, 276, 278-80, 282, 287-88, 293-96, 298, 304, 327-28, 331, 345-48, 355-56, 358, 361, 365; **100**:1-133
The Rime of the Ancyent Marinere (Coleridge)
See *The Rime of the Ancient Mariner: A Poet's Reverie*
"The Rime of the Youthful Mariner" (Owen) **102**:149
Rime sparse (Petrarch)
See *Canzoniere*
Rime Varie (Stampa) **43**:281, 291-92, 319
"Rime Varie" (Stampa) **43**:288-90
"Rimembranze di Scuola" (Carducci) **46**:23, 34, 37
"Un rimorso" (Gozzano) **10**:188
The Ring and the Book (Browning) **2**:39-40, 42-4, 46-7, 53, 56, 63, 66-7, 73, 76-7, 82-3, 85, 88, 95; **61**:1-103; **97**:11, 33, 49
"The Ring and the Castle" (Lowell) **13**:60-1
"The Ring Cycle" (Merrill) **28**:285-87
"The Ring Given to Venus" (Morris) **55**:249, 323
"The Ring of the Unicorn" (Char)
See "L'anneau de la licorne"
"Ring out your belles" (Sidney) **32**:250-51
"Ringing the Bells" (Sexton) **2**:350, 353
"Ringless" (Wakoski) **15**:324
The Rings of Saturn (Wakoski) **15**:368-69
"Río de la Plata en celeste nebliplateado" (Storni) **33**:294
"Río de la Plata en gris áureo" (Storni) **33**:294-95
"Río de la Plata en Lluvia" (Storni) **33**:260, 295
"Río de la Plata en negro y ocre" (Storni) **33**:294
Un río, un amor (Cernuda) **62**:170, 186, 189, 191, 200-201, 206, 212, 220-21, 230-32, 234-35, 237-39, 241, 247, 251, 254-55
"Río Vespertino" (Cernuda) **62**:174, 182, 196-97, 202
"Los ríos del canto" (Neruda) **4**:293
"Riot" (Brooks) **7**:82, 88-9, 91
Riot (Brooks) **7**:63-4, 66, 82, 88, 91, 94
"Riots in Algeria, in Cypress, in Alabama" (Snodgrass) **74**:323
"Rip" (Wright) **36**:320
"Rip Van Winkle, M.D.—An after-dinner prescription taken by the Massachusetts Medical Society at their meeting, held May 25, 1870" (Holmes) **71**:65, 68
"Rip Van Winkle's Lilac" (Melville) **82**:107, 155-56
"Ripeness is All" (Cunningham) **92**:168
"Riposo dell'erba" (Quasimodo) **47**:301-2
Ripostes of Ezra Pound (Pound) **4**:317, 355; **95**:91, 95-96, 119, 123
"The Ripple" (Levertov) **11**:171
"A Ripple Song" (Kipling) **3**:183
"Riprap" (Snyder) **21**:284, 299, 302
Riprap (Snyder) **21**:286-87, 290-91, 297, 300, 322
"Ripresa" (Carducci) **46**:50
"Rise" (Alexie) **53**:25
"The Risen" (Hughes) **89**:195, 198
"The Risen Lord" (Lawrence) **54**:249
"The Risen One" (Rilke) **2**:271
"Rising" (Berry) **28**:16, 18-19
"The Rising of the Sun" (Milosz)
See "Gdzie wschodzi slonce i kêdy zapada"
"The Rising Out" (McGuckian) **27**:102-104
"The Rising Sun" (Jarrell) **41**:155
"Risks and Possibilities" (Ammons) **16**:3, 29, 40
"Risveglio" (Pavese) **13**:229
"Rita and the Rifle" (Darwish) **86**:28
"The Rite" (Randall) **86**:329
"Rite of Passage" (Olds) **22**:312
"Rites" (Brathwaite) **56**:69, 76, 87
"Rites" (Cohen) **109**:49
"Rites and Ceremonies" (Hecht) **70**:69, 78, 84, 86, 97-98, 108
"The Rites for Cousin Vit" (Brooks) **7**:66, 78, 81
"Rites for the Extrusion of a Leper" (Merton) **10**:345
"Rites of Passage" (Gunn) **26**:204
"Rites of Passage" (Stryk) **27**:204, 210
"Ritmo de otoño" (García Lorca) **3**:125
"Ritner" (Whittier) **93**:206
"Ritorno di Deola" (Pavese) **13**:229
"Ritratto" (Pound) **4**:317
"Ritratto d'autore" (Pavese) **13**:213
"Ritter" (Rilke) **2**:266-67
"The Ritual" (Erdrich) **52**:186, 188
"Ritual" (Ignatow) **34**:291-92, 313, 321
"Ritual" (Stone) **53**:223
"Ritual for Singing Bat" (Ciardi) **69**:5
"Ritual of Departure" (Kinsella) **69**:67, 69, 83, 104, 107, 130
"The Ritual of Memories" (Gallagher) **9**:60
"Ritual Three" (Ignatow) **34**:287
"A Ritual to Read to Each Other" (Stafford) **71**:383
"Ritual Two" (Ignatow) **34**:298
"Rituals" (Ignatow) **34**:308
"A Rival" (Hughes) **89**:133
"The Rival" (Plath) **1**:390
"The Rival Brothers" (Leapor) **85**:250
"The Rivals" (Dunbar) **5**:122
"The Rivals" (Johnson) **24**:141
The Rivals (Davenant) **99**:176
"The River" (Arnold) **5**:19, 43
"The River" (Carver) **54**:14, 26
River (Chappell) **105**:25, 28, 34-35, 39, 41-44, 47, 53, 58, 61, 67, 72
"The River" (Ciardi) **69**:34
"The River" (Crane) **3**:84-6, 88-90, 95
"The River" (Emerson) **18**:97
"The River" (Masefield) **78**:11-12, 71-72
"The River" (Muir) **49**:197, 272-73, 282
"The River" (Patmore) **59**:218, 239-40, 257
"The River" (Tagore)
See "Pravahini"
"River" (Viereck) **27**:277
River (Hughes) **89**:119, 124, 131-36, 144, 149-50, 152, 156, 193, 217-18, 232
The River (Hughes) **7**:163, 171
A River, A Love (Cernuda)
See *Un río, un amor*
"The River Awakening" (Chappell) **105**:43, 62-63, 72
"River Barrow" (Hughes) **89**:133
"The River, By Night" (Bryant) **20**:17
"The River Down Home" (Wright) **36**:319, 329, 366
"The River God" (Smith) **12**:331, 337
"River in Spate" (MacNeice) **61**:125, 129, 132
"The River Merchant's Wife" (Hacker)
See "Nights of 1962: The River Merchant's Wife"
"The River Merchant's Wife: A Letter" (Amichai) **38**:43
"The River of Bees" (Merwin) **45**:20-1, 23, 25, 35
The River of Heaven (Hongo) **23**:198-99, 201, 204
"River Roads" (Sandburg) **2**:316; **41**:241, 270
"River Rouge: 1932" (Berryman) **64**:81, 84
"The River Seeks Again the Sea" (Chappell) **105**:43
"River Sound Remembered" (Merwin) **45**:7
"River Stop" (Tu Fu) **9**:319
The River Styx, Ohio, and Other Poems (Oliver) **75**:298
"The River Swelleth More and More" (Thoreau) **30**:180, 195, 198, 241
"River Village" (Tu Fu) **9**:319
"River, with Boats" (Ní Chuilleanáin) **34**:350, 366
"Riverbank Blues" (Brown) **55**:110, 154
Riverbed (Wagoner) **33**:333-34, 347-48
"The Riverman" (Bishop) **34**:84, 91, 116
"The River-Merchant's Wife: A Letter" (Li Po) **29**:144, 176
Rivers and Mountains (Ashbery) **26**:107-108, 113-114, 116, 129, 142-143, 148, 154-155, 167, 173-174
"The Rivers of Song" (Neruda)
See "Los ríos del canto"
"The River's Story" (Tagore)
See "Tatinir katha"
Rivers to the Sea (Teasdale) **31**:321, 324-25, 330-31, 337, 345, 347, 351, 354-55, 359, 370, 379
"Rivers Unknown to Song" (Meynell) **112**:163
The Riverside Chaucer (Chaucer) **58**:302, 363
"La rivière" (Éluard) **38**:69, 105-7
"Riviere" (Montale) **13**:162
"La Rivière de Cassis" (Rimbaud) **57**:244, 250
"The Rivulet" (Bryant) **20**:12, 14-15
"Rizpah" (Tennyson) **6**:372-73, 377, 379, 381, 411; **101**:225
"Rizpah, the Daughter of Ai" (Harper) **21**:191, 209, 218
"The Road" (Aiken) **26**:24, 46
"The Road" (Muir) **49**:229-30, 243, 273, 289
"The Road" (Pinsky) **27**:168
"The Road" (Sassoon) **12**:242
"Road along the Precipice in Czufut-Kale" (Mickiewicz)
See "Droga nad przepascic w Czufut-Kale"
"The Road and the End" (Sandburg) **2**:300; **41**:225, 242
"The Road Between Here and There" (Kinnell) **26**:292
"Road Ends at Tahola" (Hugo) **68**:236, 287
"The Road from Delphi" (Stryk) **27**:214

The Road Is Everywhere, or Stop This Body (Waldrop) **109**:127, 177, 179-80
"The Road Not Taken" (Frost) **1**:202, 205, 213, 221, 230; **39**:230, 232, 254; **71**:1-57
"The Road of the Dread" (Goodison) **36**:140-41, 153
"The Road to Damascus" (Hecht) **70**:108
"The Road to Hate" (Kavanagh) **33**:118; **105**:143
"The Road to Kerity" (Mew) **107**:59
"Road to Mandalay" (Kipling) **3**:179
"The Road to Nijmegen" (Birney) **52**:22, 37, 44-45, 47, 60
The Road to Ruin (Sassoon) **12**:252, 270
"The Road to Russia" (Mickiewicz) **38**:168
"The Road to Shelter" (Gozzano) **10**:177
The Road to Shelter (Gozzano)
See *La via del refugio*
"Road Up" (Smith) **12**:317
"Roads" (Darío)
See "Caminos"
"Roads" (Thomas) **53**:271, 296, 317, 327, 330
"The Roads Also" (Owen) **19**:343
"The Road's End" (Montague) **106**:242, 340
"Roadways" (Masefield) **78**:70
"Roaming in Thought" (Whitman) **91**:205
"Roan Stallion" (Jeffers) **17**:107, 111, 113, 116, 127, 130, 135, 146
Roan Stallion, Tamar, and Other Poems (Jeffers) **17**:106, 122, 132, 135-37
Roaratorio (Cage) **58**:219
"Roarers in a Ring" (Hughes) **7**:123
"The Roaring Frost" (Meynell) **112**:299
"Roast Opossum" (Dove) **6**:111
"Roastbeef" (Stein) **18**:327
"The Roasted Englishman in Moscow" (Shvarts)
See "Zharenyi anglichanin v Moskve"
"Robben Island" (Brutus) **24**:120
"The Robber" (MacDiarmid) **9**:155
"The Robber Bridegroom" (Tate) **50**:256
The Robber Brothers (Pushkin)
See *Bratya Razboiniki*
"Robbery" (Shapiro) **25**:312
"Robbing Myself" (Hughes) **89**:162
"The Robe" (Very) **86**:152
"Robe of Love" (Yosano)
See *Koigoromo*
"Robene and Makyne" (Henryson) **65**:124-29, 131
"Robert Bruce's March to Bannockburn" (Burns)
See "Bruce to His Men at Bannockburn"
"Robert Burns's Answer" (Burns)
See "Answer"
"Robert Carpenter" (Masters) **36**:210
"(Robert) Duncan Spoke of a Process" (Baraka) **113**:139
"Robert Frost" (Clarke) **112**:93
"Robert Frost at Bread Loaf His Hand against a Tree" (Swenson) **14**:247, 253
"Robert Fulton Tanner" (Masters) **36**:222
"Robert G. Ingersoll" (Masters) **1**:343
"Robert Gould Shaw" (Dunbar) **5**:121
"Robert Louis Stevenson" (Reese) **29**:346
Robert Louis Stevenson: Collected Poems (Stevenson) **84**:309, 333-35
"Robert Lowell" (Shapiro) **25**:323
Robert of Normandy (Drayton) **98**:53
"Robert Schumann, Or: Musical Genius Begins with Affliction" (Dove) **6**:108
"Robert Sitting in My Hands" (Wright) **36**:396
Robert Southey, Poetical Works, 1793-1810 (Southey)
See *The Poetical Works*
"Roberta Lee" (Brown) **55**:164
"The Robin" (Very) **86**:40, 163
"Robin and Ben: or, the Pirate and the Apothecary" (Stevenson) **84**:320-21, 323
"Robin Hood. To a Friend" (Keats) **96**:268
"Robin Hood's Heart" (Wylie) **23**:311
"Robin Song" (Hughes) **7**:134
"Los robles" (Castro) **41**:84, 117
"A Robyn" (Wyatt)
See "A Robyn Joly Robyn"
"A Robyn Joly Robyn" (Wyatt) **27**:315
"Rocaille" (Gautier) **18**:141
"Un rocher" (Ponge) **107**:139
"Rochester Extempore" (Wilmot) **66**:325
"The Rock" (Creeley) **73**:12
"The Rock" (Merwin) **45**:54
"The Rock" (Stevens) **6**:303, 313; **110**:114, 160, 168, 230-31
The Rock (Stevens) **110**:225-26, 229-32
Rock and Hawk (Jeffers) **17**:137
"The Rock Below" (Graves) **6**:128-29
Rock Drill Cantos (Pound)
See *Section: Rock Drill, 85-95 de los cantares*
"Rock Music" (Mahon) **60**:147, 172, 174, 179, 205, 211
"Rock 'N' Roll Band" (Silverstein) **49**:334
"The Rock of Rubies and the Quarry of Pearls" (Herrick) **9**:146
"Rock Study with Wanderer" (Berryman) **64**:90
"Rockabye" (Silverstein) **49**:325-26
"Rockefeller is yo vice president, & yo mamma don't wear no drawers" (Baraka) **4**:30
"The Rocker" (Hall) **70**:34
"Rocket" (Seferis) **66**:119, 123-24, 143-44
"Rockets and Carts" (Yevtushenko) **40**:343-44
"Rockpool" (Wright) **14**:376
Rocks on a Platter: Notes on Literature (Guest) **55**:200-202, 204-5, 215, 221-22, 231
"Rocky Acres" (Graves) **6**:151
"Rod zanjatij" (Akhmadulina) **43**:17
Roderick, the Last of the Goths (Southey) **111**:250, 253
"Rodina" (Lermontov) **18**:281, 297
"Rodine" (Bely) **11**:24
"Rodoslovnaya Moego Geroya" (Pushkin) **10**:391, 394
"Rodrigo" (Heine) **25**:159, 161
"Rodrigo de Barro" (Cisneros) **52**:163
The Rodrigo Poems (Cisneros) **52**:156, 163
"Rodriguez Street" (Ríos) **57**:312
"Roe Deer" (Hughes) **89**:126
"The Roe Deer" (Tomlinson) **17**:335, 343
"Roger Bacon" (Thomas) **99**:261-62, 266
"Roger Bernard" (Char) **56**:191
"Roger Clay's Proposal" (Merrill) **28**:234, 250
"Roger Heston" (Masters) **36**:182
Rogsajyae (Tagore) **8**:424-26
Le Roi d'Ivetot (Béranger) **112**:3, 16
"Roi's New Blues" (Baraka) **113**:5
Rokeby (Scott) **13**:265, 267-68, 277-78, 281, 285, 304, 307, 311, 318
"Roland Hayes Beaten" (Hughes) **1**:241, 243, 252
"The Roll of the Ages" (Noyes) **27**:136
"Roller Coaster" (Parra)
See "La montaña rusa"
"Rolling in at Twilight" (Snyder) **21**:288
"Rolling, Rolling" (Toomer) **7**:337
"Rolling the Lawn" (Empson) **104**:92
"Roma" (Carducci) **46**:52
Roma 1950 diario (Pasolini) **17**:260
"Roma o morte" (Carducci) **46**:51
"Roman" (Rimbaud) **3**:271, 276; **57**:174, 234, 244
The Roman: A Dramatic Poem (Dobell) **100**:136-40, 145-46, 148, 150, 160
Roman Bartholow (Robinson) **1**:479, 483, 489; **35**:368
"Roman Cadences" (Viereck) **27**:278
The Roman Calendar (Ovid)
See *Fasti*
"The Roman Centurion's Song" (Kipling) **91**:152
Roman Elegies (Goethe)
See *Römische Elegien*
Roman Elegies II (Brodsky) **9**:21
"Roman Fountain" (Bogan) **12**:99
"A Roman Holiday" (Hecht) **70**:97
"Roman Poem I" (Barker) **77**:40
"Roman Portrait Busts" (Updike) **90**:357
"The Roman Quarry" (Jones) **116**:118, 159-60, 167-68
The Roman Quarry and Other Sequences (Jones) **116**:100, 107-9, 114, 118, 132, 142, 158, 162-69, 218, 221
"The Roman Road" (Smith) **12**:346
"Romance" (Cassian) **17**:4
"Romance" (Peacock) **87**:326
"Romance" (Reese) **29**:335
"Romance" (Robinson) **1**:495
"Romance" (Stone) **53**:258
Romance 48 (Juana Inés de la Cruz) **24**:215, 217-18
"Romance de la Guardia Civil Española" (García Lorca) **3**:131, 148
"Romance de la luna, luna" (García Lorca) **3**:133
"Romance de la pena negra" (García Lorca) **3**:133
"Romance del emplazado" (García Lorca) **3**:133
"Romance for a Demoiselle Lying in the Grass" (Stevens) **110**:93
"Romance moderne" (Williams) **7**:345
"A Romance of the Age" (Barrett Browning)
See "Lady Geraldine's Courtship"
"Romance of the Spanish Civil Guard" (García Lorca)
See "Romance de la Guardia Civil Española"
"The Romance of the Swan's Nest" (Barrett Browning) **6**:32
"Romance sonámbulo" (García Lorca) **3**:131, 133, 147
Romancero (Heine)
See *Romanzero*
Romancero (Pasolini) **17**:253-54, 279, 281
Romancero gitano (García Lorca)
See *Primer romancero gitano*
Romances sans paroles (Verlaine) **2**:414-15, 418-19, 424, 431-32; **32**:340, 342, 359, 361, 378, 382, 385, 394-96, 399-402, 407, 409-12
Romanees and Ballads (Mickiewicz)
See *Ballady i Romanse*
"Romans Angry about the Inner World" (Bly) **39**:13
"The Romantic" (Bogan) **12**:87, 100-01, 103
"Romantic Sonnet" (Simic) **69**:280
Romanticism (Mickiewicz)
See *Romantycznoś*
Romantycznoś (Mickiewicz) **38**:156-57
"Romantyczność" (Mickiewicz) **38**:162-64
"The Romany Girl" (Emerson) **18**:77
Romanzen (Heine) **25**:131, 158-59
Romanzero (Heine) **25**:167
"The Romaunt of Margret" (Barrett Browning) **6**:32
"The Romaunt of the Page" (Barrett Browning) **6**:30, 37-8, 42-3, 45
"Rome" (Hecht) **70**:97
"Rome" (Howe) **81**:19-21, 46
Rome 1950 A Diary (Pasolini) **17**:260-61
"Rome, Anno Santo" (Montague) **106**:275
"Rome: Building a Street in the Old Quarter" (Hardy) **92**:233
"Rome-Sickness" (Arnold) **5**:19
Römische Elegien (Goethe) **5**:239-40, 249, 255, 257
"Römische Sarkophage" (Rilke) **2**:278
"Romney's Remorse" (Tennyson) **101**:225
"Rompecabezas" (Parra) **39**:292, 307
"Ronda de la ceiba equatoriana" (Mistral) **32**:175, 180
"Rondalla" (Gautier) **18**:125
"Rondeau" (Hunt) **73**:155, 162
"Rondeau" (Kennedy) **93**:137
"Rondeau 4" (Christine de Pizan) **68**:182

A Roof of Tiger Lilies (Hall) **70**:6, 26, 31-32, 55
"Roofers" (Hass) **16**:248
"The Roofwalker" (Rich) **5**:363, 392-93, 395
"The Room" (Aiken) **26**:24
"The Room" (Ignatow) **34**:291-92, 321
"The Room" (Merwin) **45**:20
"The Room" (Reese) **29**:330
"The Room" (Strand) **63**:143, 162
"The Room above the Square" (Spender) **71**:160, 225
"Room Next Door" (Cernuda)
See "Habitación de al lado"
"The Room of Mirrors" (Masters) **1**:344
"The Room of My Life" (Sexton) **2**:373
"Room Tone" (Graham) **59**:130, 139, 171
"A Room with a View" (Wagoner) **33**:330, 333
"The Room with the Tapestry Rug" (Giovanni) **19**:143
"Rooming-house, Winter" (Atwood) **8**:14
"Rooms" (Stryk) **27**:215, 218
"The Rooms of Other Women Poets" (Boland) **58**:18, 30, 92, 94-95
"Roosevelt" (Lindsay) **23**:288
"Rooster" (Hagiwara)
See "Niwatori"
"The Roosters" (Bishop) **3**:37, 46-8, 56-7, 60, 66; **34**:52, 68, 78, 137, 139, 146, 165, 170, 189, 192
"Root Cellar" (Roethke) **15**:260, 295
"The Root of All Evil" (Lawrence) **54**:249
Root of Man (Paz)
See *Raíz del hombre*
"Root, Stem, Leaf" (Hughes) **89**:106
"Root-Light; or, The Lawyer's Daughter" (Dickey) **40**:210, 222
"Roots" (Heaney) **18**:202; **100**:199, 334
"Roots" (Hongo) **23**:198
"Roots" (Meredith) **28**:171, 175, 192, 194
"Roots" (Walcott) **46**:270, 272, 323, 325
"Roots and Branches" (Duncan) **2**:103, 110; **75**:231, 256
Roots and Branches (Duncan) **2**:102, 105-06, 109, 113-14, 119, 125; **75**:123, 134, 160-61, 171, 175, 187-89, 194-95, 197-200, 203, 223, 230-31, 245-46, 262-67
"Roots and Leaves Themselves Alone" (Whitman) **91**:247
"The Ropewalk" (Longfellow) **30**:43, 71
"Rorate Celi Desuper" (Dunbar) **67**:5
"Rory" (Mahon) **60**:141
"Ros Mary" (Dunbar) **67**:37
"La rosa" (Guillén) **35**:157
"La rosa blanca" (Martí) **76**:101
"Rosa divina que en gentil cultura" (Juana Inés de la Cruz) **24**:225
"Rosa Mundi" (Rexroth) **95**:258, 272-73
"Rosa Mystica" (Hopkins) **15**:148, 159, 165
La rosa profunda (Borges) **22**:97; **32**:63, 86, 90, 95, 108
La rosa separada: obra póstuma (Neruda) **4**:287
"Una rosa y Milton" (Borges) **32**:114, 117
Rosalind and Helen (Shelley) **14**:173, 175, 192, 234
"Rosamund's Bower" (Tennyson) **101**:244
"Rosania's private marriage" (Philips) **40**:298
The Rosary (Akhmatova)
See *Chyotki*
"A Rosary of Your Names" (Goodison) **36**:147, 151, 153
"A Rosary of Your Names II" (Goodison) **36**:147, 153
"Rosary Songs" (Trakl)
See "Rosenkranzlieder"
"Rosas" (Borges) **32**:80
Rosas (Masefield) **78**:58, 63
"Rosas de elegía" (Guillén) **23**:100
"Roscoe Purkapile" (Masters) **36**:182, 199
"The Rose" (Cohen) **109**:24
"The Rose" (Creeley) **73**:10, 33
"Le Rose" (Gautier) **18**:125
"The Rose" (Lovelace) **69**:156
"The Rose" (Roethke) **15**:310-11
Rose (Sainte-Beuve) **110**:39-40
"The Rose" (Very) **86**:46
"The Rose" (Williams) **7**:386, 410
"The Rose" (Yeats) **20**:310
Rose (Lee) **24**:239-44
The Rose (Yeats) **20**:326, 328, 343, 347
"The Rose and the Cross" (Blok) **21**:31
"The Rose and the Eagle" (Piercy) **29**:300
"The Rose and the Fern" (Holmes) **71**:96
"The Rose and the Rod" (Barker) **77**:14
"La rose de l'infant" (Hugo) **17**:60-61, 65
"La rose des vents" (Wilbur) **51**:193, 217-18
"The Rose Farmer" (Melville) **82**:78, 107, 155
"Rose in fiamme" (Ungaretti) **57**:347
"The Rose Marble Table" (Guest) **55**:185
"The Rose of Marion" (Schuyler) **88**:175
"The Rose of the World" (Masefield) **78**:49
"The Rose of the World" (Patmore) **59**:205
"The Rose of the World" (Yeats) **20**:329
"Rose on the Heath" (Goethe)
See "Heidenröslein"
La rose publique (Éluard) **38**:62, 68, 73
"Rose, Rose" (Bukowski) **18**:5
"rose th night nd th green flowr" (Bissett) **14**:28, 33
"The Rose Tree" (Blake)
See "My Pretty Rose Tree"
"The Rose Trellis" (McGuckian) **27**:94
"Rose Window" (Melville) **82**:154
"Roseamond" (Apollinaire)
See "Rosemonde"
"Rosebud" (Alexie) **53**:14
"Rose-Cheekt Lawra" (Campion) **87**:104
The Rose-Geranium (Ní Chuilleanáin) **34**:360-61, 380
"Rosemary" (Moore) **49**:126, 128, 138
"Rosemonde" (Apollinaire) **7**:45, 47-8
"Rosen" (Benn) **35**:71
"Rosenkranzlieder" (Trakl) **20**:233, 248
"Rosenschimmer" (Celan) **10**:122
"Roses" (Dove) **6**:109
"Roses" (Guest) **55**:185
"Roses" (Hunt) **73**:138
"Roses" (Sandburg) **2**:324
"Roses and Revolutions" (Randall) **86**:288, 315, 343
"Roses in flames" (Ungaretti)
See "Rose in fiamme"
"Roses Only" (Moore) **49**:89, 91-92, 94, 114
"Rosilla nueva" (Martí) **76**:134
"Le rossignol" (Lamartine) **16**:293
"Le Rossignol" (Ronsard) **105**:289
"Le Rossignol" (Verlaine) **32**:387
"Röster under jorden" (Ekeloef) **23**:76
"Rostro tras el cristal (Mirada del viejo)" (Aleixandre) **15**:43
"Rosy" (Glück) **16**:138
"The Rosy Bosom'd Hours" (Patmore) **59**:267
"Rosy Ear" (Herbert) **50**:4
"Rosy-Checked Death" (Yosano)
See "Kôgao no shi"
"Rot" (Benn) **35**:70, 73
"A Rotten Carcass" (Baudelaire)
See "Une Charogne"
"Rotten Sample" (Stone) **53**:225
"Rotting Clam" (Hagiwara) **18**:167, 177
"A Rotting Corpse" (Baudelaire)
See "Une charogne"
"Rouge" (Berrigan) **103**:36
"Rougeur des Matinaux" (Char) **56**:121, 174, 185
"Rough" (Thomas) **99**:257, 261, 286-88, 292-93, 318
The Rough Field (Montague) **106**:215, 217-18, 226-28, 233-39, 244-46, 248-51, 253-54, 256, 261-67, 270-73, 278, 281, 284-86, 292, 295, 298-99, 306-7, 309-19, 321-22, 325-26, 329, 333, 337-41, 345-46, 351, 353, 356
"Rough Outline" (Simic) **69**:313-14, 317
The Rough Rider, and Other Poems (Carman) **34**:205, 211, 228
"The Rough Sketch" (Howe) **81**:49-50
"Rough times" (Piercy) **29**:303, 305
"Round About Midnight" (Kaufman) **74**:195, 243-44
"A Round & A Canon" (Olson) **19**:281
"Round Dance Somewhere Around Oklahoma City/November Night" (Harjo) **27**:69
"The Round of Grief" (Jordan) **38**:120
"The Round of the Ecuadorian Ceiba Tree" (Mistral)
See "Ronda de la ceiba equatoriana"
The Round Table; or, King Arthur's Feast (Peacock) **87**:332, 350
"Round the Corner" (MacNeice) **61**:177-78
"Round the Turning" (Pasternak) **6**:267
"Round Time" (McHugh) **61**:204
"Round Trip" (Page) **12**:163
"The Roundel" (Swinburne) **24**:319, 322-23
A Roundhead's Rallying Song (Noyes) **27**:138
"Rounding the Horn" (Masefield) **78**:106
"The Rout" (Spark) **72**:217, 229
"Route" (Oppen) **35**:289, 293, 337, 340, 341, 346, 357
"De Route March" (McKay) **2**:225
"Route Marchin'" (Kipling) **3**:160
"A Route of Evanescence" (Dickinson) **1**:104
"The Route of the Táin" (Kinsella) **69**:72
"Route Six" (Kunitz) **19**:175
"Rover" (Kunitz) **19**:175
"A Rover's Song" (Carman) **34**:207
Roving Across Fields (Stafford) **71**:317, 336
"A Row of Thick Pillars" (Crane) **80**:70
"The Rowers" (Kipling) **91**:107
"Rowing" (McGuckian) **27**:104
"Rowing" (Sexton) **2**:373; **79**:209, 216, 221, 238
"The Rowing Endeth" (Sexton) **2**:371; **79**:209-11, 221-22, 238-39
"The Rowley Mile" (Kavanagh) **105**:164
Rowley Poems (Chatterton)
See *Poems, Supposed to Have Been Written at Bristol, by Thomas Rowley, and Others, in the Fifteenth Century*
"Rows of Cold Trees" (Winters) **82**:315, 320, 336
"A Roxbury Garden" (Lowell) **13**:77-8, 96
"Roxy" (Schuyler) **88**:180
"Royal Aristocrat" (Collins) **68**:226
Royal Benevolence: A Poem (Duck) **89**:5
"The Royal Guest" (Howe) **81**:24, 47
"The Royal Palms" (Walcott) **46**:271
"A Royal Princess" (Rossetti) **7**:272, 291
"Royauté" (Rimbaud) **3**:261-63
"Rozhdenie ulybki" (Mandelstam) **14**:152-53
"Rozmowa" (Mickiewicz) **38**:196
"Rozmyslania o ojcu" (Herbert) **50**:37
"R.T.S.L." (Walcott) **46**:247
Rtusamhāra (Kālidāsa) **22**:177, 182, 184-85, 208
Ruba'iyat (Khayyam)
See *Rubáiyát*
Rubáiyát (Khayyam) **8**:143-45, 151-53, 157-70
"Rubáiyát of Doc Sifers" (Riley) **48**:304, 351
Rubáiyát of Omar Khayyám (FitzGerald) **79**:68, 73-79, 82-83, 86-95, 97, 99, 106-17, 127-30, 132-38, 142-50, 155-68, 170-72, 175-80
Rubáiyát of Omar Khayyám, Astronomer Poet of Persia (FitzGerald)
See *Rubáiyát of Omar Khayyám*
"Ruba'yat" (Darwish) **86**:26
"Rubbings of Reality" (Stevens) **110**:201
"Rubens' Women" (Szymborska)
See "Kobiety Rubensa"
"Rubies" (Emerson) **18**:77
"Ruby Brown" (Hughes) **1**:249
"Ruby Daggett" (Eberhart) **76**:44, 59
Ruce Venušiny (Seifert) **47**:316, 325-26, 333
"Rückenfigur" (Howe) **54**:151-54
"Rückfall" (Benn) **35**:50

Rudyard Kipling: Complete Verse (Kipling) **91**:169
"Rue de Belleyme" (Hacker) **47**:118
La rueda dentada (Guillén) **23**:109, 127, 133
"Rueful Associations" (Surrey) **59**:357-58
"El ruego" (Mistral) **32**:153, 155, 164, 175-76
"Rufst de nun den einen Namen verzweifelt" (Sachs) **78**:212
"Rugaroo" (Erdrich) **52**:177
"Rugby Chapel" (Arnold) **5**:33
"Rugby Football Excursion" (MacNeice) **61**:137
"Ruin" (García Lorca)
See "Ruina"
"The Ruin" (Tomlinson) **17**:325-26, 335
"Ruina" (García Lorca) **3**:139
"Las ruinas" (Cernuda) **62**:172, 177, 196, 202
"Las ruinas circulares" (Borges) **32**:60
"The Ruined Cottage" (Muir) **49**:299
"The Ruined Cottage" (Wordsworth) **4**:416, 418; **67**:263-64, 277, 293
"The Ruined Maid" (Hardy) **92**:241, 246-47, 286, 370
"The Ruined Temple" (Tagore)
See "Bhagna mandir"
"The Ruines of Time" (Spenser) **8**:366-67, 371
The Ruins (Cernuda)
See "Las ruinas"
Ruins and Visions (Spender) **71**:139, 146, 187-89
"Ruins of a Great House" (Walcott) **46**:271, 275, 285, 313, 325
"El ruiseñor sobre la piedra" (Cernuda) **62**:204
"Ruit hora" (Carducci) **46**:50, 86
Ruka a plamen (Seifert) **47**:335
"Rules and Lessons" (Vaughan) **81**:295, 297-98, 306, 333, 354, 370
"Rules and Regulations" (Carroll) **74**:67
"A Ruminant" (Hecht) **70**:94
"Ruminants" (Joyce) **22**:149
"Rumination" (Eberhart) **76**:14, 49
"Rumor at Twilight" (Warren) **37**:376
Rumor Verified: Poems, 1979-1980 (Warren) **37**:325-36, 335, 340-42, 345, 350, 358, 367, 380
"Rumors from an Aeolian Harp" (Thoreau) **30**:180, 192-93, 202-03, 227, 259
"Rumour" (Tomlinson) **17**:317
"Rumpelstiltskin" (Sexton) **2**:364; **79**:191, 323, 325
A Run of Jacks (Hugo) **68**:233, 235-38, 250-51, 258, 265, 271, 281, 286-87
"run tonight" (Bissett) **14**:16-17
Run with the Hunted (Bukowski) **18**:4-5
"Runagate, Runagate" (Hayden) **6**:176, 178-80, 183, 185, 188, 194, 197-98
"The Runaway" (Frost) **1**:194
"Runaway" (Rexroth) **95**:271
The Runaway, and Other Stories (Tagore)
See *Palātakā*
"Runaway Colors" (Sandburg) **41**:311
"The Runaway Slave at Pilgrim's Point" (Barrett Browning) **6**:30, 37-8, 42-3, 45
"Runaways" (Erdrich) **52**:172, 189
"Runaways Café I" (Hacker) **47**:85
"Runaways Café II" (Hacker) **47**:86
"Rune of the Finland Woman" (Hacker) **47**:119
"Runes" (Nemerov) **24**:262, 265, 268, 291
"Runes on Weland's Island" (Kipling) **3**:171
"Running Away from Home" (Kizer) **66**:78-79
"Running on the Shore" (Swenson) **14**:288
"Running Water Music" (Snyder) **21**:306
"Rupture" (Pasternak) **6**:260
The Rural Muse (Clare) **23**:44
"Rural Objects" (Ashbery) **26**:124
"Rus in Urbe" (Meredith) **28**:171, 190
"Rusalka" (Lermontov) **18**:289-90, 292
Rush/What Fuckan Theory (Bissett) **14**:13
"Rusia en 1931" (Hass) **16**:224
Ruslan and Lyudmila (Pushkin)
See *Ruslan i Lyudmila*
Ruslan i Lyudmila (Pushkin) **10**:357-58, 363-64, 375, 381-82, 386-88, 398, 404-09
"Russell Kincaid" (Masters) **36**:191
"Russia" (Borges) **32**:121
"Russia" (Williams) **7**:370
"Russia comes into Poland" (Zagajewski) **27**:389, 394
"The Russian Quote" (Dorn) **115**:157
Russian Songs (Parra)
See *Canciones rusas*
"Russian Sonia" (Masters) **1**:327; **36**:168, 182
"A Russian Tale" (Herbert) **50**:31
"Russian Tanks in Prague" (Yevtushenko) **40**:369-70
"Russians" (Douglas) **106**:186, 197
"The Rustic Commune" (Carducci)
See "Il comune rustico"
Rustic Elegies (Sitwell) **3**:294-95, 319
Rustic moon (Paz)
See *Luna silvestre*
"A Rustic Walk and Dinner" (Hunt) **73**:138, 154
"Rusty Crimson (Christmas Day, 1917)" (Sandburg) **2**:331
"Ruth" (Hood) **93**:58, 66, 78, 117-18
"Ruth" (Wordsworth) **4**:380, 402; **67**:285, 287, 328
"Ruth and Naomi" (Harper) **21**:191, 194, 209, 218
"Ruts" (Rimbaud)
See "Ornières"
"Ru'ya'" (Gibran) **9**:79
"Ryemeadows" (Masefield) **78**:49, 91
"Ryght True It is" (Wyatt) **27**:318
"Ryojō" (Hagiwara) **18**:178
"Rzeczywistość wymaga" (Szymborska) **44**:300, 305
"S morya" (Tsvetaeva) **14**:325
"S. Peter's Remorse" (Southwell)
See "St. Peter's Remorse"
s th story i to (Bissett) **14**:3, 5, 7-8
"Sa fosse est fermée" (Mallarmé) **102**:129
"Saadi" (Emerson) **18**:81, 87-88, 98, 104, 107
Sáanii Dahataal: The Women Are Singing (Tapahonso) **65**:234, 240, 244, 250, 253, 255-59
"Sab: Lost" (Wilmot) **66**:320
"Sábado" (Borges) **32**:102
"Sábado" (Storni) **33**:274
"Sábado de gloria" (Guillén) **35**:176
"Sábados" (Borges) **22**:93; **32**:82, 102-03
"Sabala" (Tagore) **8**:415
"Sabás" (Guillén) **23**:103
"Sabato Santo" (Carducci) **46**:51
"The Sabbath" (Auden) **92**:98
"A Sabbath Morning at Sea" (Barrett Browning) **6**:14
"Sabbath Park" (McGuckian) **27**:101
"A Sabbath Scene" (Whittier) **93**:210, 333-36, 339, 344
Sabbaths (Berry) **28**:34, 38-39, 43-44
"Sabishii jinkaku" (Hagiwara) **18**:177, 181
Sabotage (Baraka) **4**:38; **113**:12-13, 16-18, 24, 74-75
"Sab-peyechhir desh" (Tagore) **8**:412
"El sacamuelas" (Fuertes) **27**:35
"La Sacra di Enrico Quinto" (Carducci) **46**:52
"Sacrament" (Cullen) **20**:85
"The Sacraments" (Erdrich) **52**:191
"Le Sacré-Coeur" (Mew) **107**:16, 27-29, 34
"The Sacré-Coeur CAfé" (Corso) **33**:37
"Le sacre de Charles le Simple" (Béranger) **112**:20
"Sacred Chant for the Return of Black Spirit and Power" (Baraka) **4**:27
"The sacred disease" (Abse) **41**:31
"Sacred Elegies" (Barker) **77**:11
"Sacred Elegy V" (Barker) **77**:17
"The Sacred Order" (Sarton) **39**:365
"sacred robe" (Alurista)
See "No. 57, sacred robe"
"The Sacred Way" (Hope) **56**:277
"The Sacred Way" (Sikelianos) **29**:366, 368, 370-71, 373
"The Sacred Wood" (Sarton) **39**:323
"The Sacrifice" (Crashaw) **84**:72
"Sacrifice" (Hecht) **70**:108
"The Sacrifice" (Herbert) **4**:107, 117, 120
"Sacrifice" (Hughes) **89**:146, 189
"Sacrifice" (Whittier)
See "Human Sacrifice"
"The Sacrifice. An Epistle to Celia" (Leapor) **85**:258
"A Sacrifice in the Orchard" (Bly) **39**:67
"The Sacrifice of Er-Heb" (Kipling) **3**:181
"The Sacrilege" (Hardy) **8**:99
"Sad" (Akhmadulina) **43**:18
Sad Airs (Jiménez)
See *Arias tristes*
"Sad Cowboy" (Baraka) **113**:15
"A Sad Distant View" (Hagiwara) **18**:176
The sad field-hand (Illyés)
See *Szomoru beres*
"The Sad Garden Dissolves" (Jiménez)
See "El jardín triste se pierde"
"Sad Indian" (Crane) **99**:111
Sad Ires and Others (Enright) **93**:27-28
"Sad Moments" (Gallagher) **9**:64
"Sad Moonlit Night" (Hagiwara)
See "Kanashi Tsukio"
Sad. Novye stikhi (Akhmadulina) **43**:32-34, 36, 40, 42-43, 45
"The sad ones" (Castro)
See "Los tristes, IV"
"The Sad Shepherd" (Yeats) **20**:354
"Sad Song" (Kunitz) **19**:147, 155
"Sad Steps" (Larkin) **21**:229-30
"Sad Strains of a Gay Waltz" (Stevens) **6**:296-97; **110**:157
"The Sad Supper" (Pavese)
See "La cena triste"
Sad Toys (Ishikawa)
See *Kanashiki gangu*
"The Sad Voice of the Hubble" (Stone) **53**:224
"Sad Wine" (Pavese)
See "Il vino triste"
"Sadako" (Soto) **28**:385
"Sad-Eyed Lady of the Lowlands" (Dylan) **37**:56, 60
"Sadie and Maude" (Brooks) **7**:67, 69
Sadness and Happiness: Poems (Pinsky) **27**:143-44, 153, 156, 160-62, 173, 175-76
"The Sadness of Brothers" (Kinnell) **26**:260
"The Sadness of Lemons" (Levine) **22**:211
"The Sadness of the Sea" (Williams) **109**:283, 286
"Sadness Sits Around Me" (Jordan) **38**:118
"Sad-vsadnik" (Akhmadulina) **43**:18
"Saethu'r Ferch" (Dafydd ap Gwilym) **56**:247
"Safe Flights" (Guest) **55**:209-11
"Safe Subjects" (Komunyakaa) **51**:35
"Safety" (Brooke) **24**:59, 80, 88
"Safety" (Wright) **36**:396
"Saffron" (Smith) **12**:295
"Saga" (Viereck) **27**:265
Saga Diary (Matsuo Basho)
See *Saga nikki*
Saga nikki (Matsuo Basho) **3**:29
"The Saga of King Olaf" (Longfellow) **30**:19, 25, 61-2
Sagan om Fatumeh (Ekeloef) **23**:60, 65-6, 68-71, 77-8, 85
"The Sage Enamoured and the Honest Lady" (Meredith) **60**:261, 335
"Sagesse" (H. D.) **5**:275
"Sagesse" (Hugo) **17**:77-78, 97
Sagesse (H. D.) **5**:282, 285
Sagesse (Verlaine) **2**:413, 415-19, 425-26, 430; **32**:343, 359, 361, 363, 369, 374-75, 379, 382, 386, 402
"Saggi di un canto alle Muse" (Carducci) **46**:47
"Sahara" (Patmore) **59**:231
"Said Not a Word" (Cernuda) **62**:171
"Said Song" (Ammons) **16**:19
"Said the Poet to the Analyst" (Sexton) **2**:358-59; **79**:187, 195, 274, 281

"The Sail" (Lermontov) **18**:297
"The Sail of Ulysses" (Stevens) **6**:326, 328; **110**:210
"Sailboat, Your Secret" (Francis) **34**:255
"Sailing after Lunch" (Stevens) **6**:297, 338; **110**:142, 215
Sailing Alone Around the Room: New and Selected Poems (Collins) **68**:203, 205-6, 208, 212, 214-16, 219, 221, 223
"Sailing Home from Rapallo" (Lowell) **3**:205, 220, 245
"The Sailing of Hell Race" (Masefield) **78**:62
"Sailing of the Swallow" (Swinburne) **24**:356-57
"The Sailing of the Swan" (Swinburne) **24**:313, 349, 357
"The Sailing of the Sword" (Morris) **55**:279, 302
"Sailing or Drowning" (Curnow) **48**:4
Sailing or Drowning (Curnow) **48**:3, 11-12, 23
"Sailing to Byzantium" (Yeats) **20**:308, 310, 316, 329, 333, 335, 346, 349; **51**:67-153
"Sailor Ashore" (Merwin) **45**:7, 31
"A Sailor in Africa" (Dove) **6**:110
"Sailor in Moscow" (Pasternak)
See "Matros v Moskve"
"Sailors' Hospital" (Thomas) **99**:270
"The Sailor's Mother" (Wordsworth) **4**:398, 402
"Sailors with the Clap" (Kennedy) **93**:152
"Saint" (Graves) **6**:141, 144, 151
"Saint" (Merrill) **28**:240-41
"The Saint" (Shapiro) **25**:268, 286
"A Saint about to Fall" (Thomas) **2**:408-09
"Saint Anthony and the Rose of Life" (Smith) **12**:308
"St. Augustine-by-the-Sea" (Swenson) **14**:288
"Saint Bernadette and All That" (Berrigan) **103**:30
"Saint Cadoc" (Betjeman) **75**:26
"Saint Catherine Street" (Cohen) **109**:17
"Saint Catherine of Siena" (Meynell) **112**:166, 176
"Saint Clare" (Erdrich) **52**:186, 188
"Saint Escolastica" (Castro)
See "Santa Escolástica"
"Saint Francis" (Corso) **108**:16, 41
"Saint Francis and Lady Clare" (Masters) **1**:325, 333; **36**:175
"Saint Francis and the Sow" (Kinnell) **26**:259-60, 292
"Saint Graal" (Duncan) **75**:216
"Saint Judas" (Wright) **36**:295-96, 302-4, 306, 315-16, 324, 344, 360-62, 379, 387, 399
Saint Judas (Wright) **36**:281-82, 292-94, 296, 299, 314-17, 337-38, 341, 349, 353, 358, 360, 373-74, 380, 385-87, 390, 396
"Saint Monica" (Smith)
See "St. Monica"
"Saint Nicholas" (Moore) **49**:119-20, 143, 146
"Saint Nightingale" (Longfellow) **30**:46
"The Saint of the Uplands" (Merwin) **45**:33
Saint Peters Complaint, with Other Poems (Southwell) **83**:229, 232, 236-37, 245, 249, 252-53, 265, 279, 281, 284, 287, 298, 311-12, 315, 325
"Saint Senan's Well" (Melville) **82**:5, 35, 37, 39
"Saint Simeon Stylites" (Tennyson)
See "St. Simeon Stylites"
"Sainte" (Mallarmé) **4**:201; **102**:53, 101, 108
"La Sainte Alliance des Peuples" (Béranger) **112**:19
"Une Sainte enson auréole" (Verlaine) **32**:393
"Sainte Lucie" (Walcott) **46**:233, 237, 240-41, 262, 290
"Sainte-Nitouche" (Robinson) **1**:460
"Saints" (Brown) **55**:80
"Saints" (Corso) **33**:3
"Saints and Singing" (Stein) **18**:346
"Saipan" (Ciardi) **69**:26
La Saisiaz (Browning) **2**:66, 68, 71-2, 74
"La Saison des amours" (Éluard) **38**:87
Une saison en enfer (Rimbaud) **3**:249, 252-53, 260-66, 268, 270, 279, 286; **57**:174, 177-78, 183-85, 188-91, 193-95, 197, 199, 224, 227, 229, 235-36, 243, 246-51, 254, 260, 273, 276-77, 279-80, 299-301
"Sais-tu" (Péret) **33**:216
"Un sajón" (Borges) **22**:98; **32**:96
"Sakyamuni Coming Out from the Mountain" (Ginsberg) **4**:49
"Sal" (Mistral) **32**:161
"Sal" (Tagore) **8**:416
"Sala vacía" (Borges) **32**:82
"La Salade" (Ronsard) **11**:240
Salamán and Absál (FitzGerald) **79**:72, 94, 99, 110, 115, 129, 133, 140-41, 149, 175-77
The Salamander (Paz)
See *Salamandra*
"Salamandra" (Paz) **48**:235-40
Salamandra (Paz) **1**:353, 357, 360-62, 369
"Salamater" (Paz)
See "Salamandra"
"Salamis in Cyprus" (Seferis) **66**:172, 194, 207, 211-12
"S'alcun se stesso al mondo ancider lice" (Michelangelo) **103**:243
"Sale" (Rimbaud)
See "Solde"
"Sale of a Historian's Library" (Shvarts) **50**:140-41, 143
"The Salesman" (Ignatow) **34**:273
"Saleswoman of Ties" (Yevtushenko) **40**:345
"La salida" (Guillén) **35**:160
"Saliences" (Ammons) **16**:6, 23
Salisbury Plain (Wordsworth) **4**:429; **67**:276-78, 280
"Sallie Chisum/Last Words on Billy the Kid. 4 a.m." (Ondaatje) **28**:338-39
"The Sallow Bird" (Smith) **12**:326
"El salmo de la pluma" (Darío) **15**:93
"Salmon" (Graham) **59**:152, 184
"Salmon Eggs" (Hughes) **89**:135-36, 152, 156
"The Salmon Fisher to the Salmon" (Heaney) **18**:225
"The Salmon Leap" (MacDiarmid) **9**:153
"Salmon-Fishing" (Jeffers) **17**:131
Salmos (Cardenal) **22**:103, 117-19, 125, 129-31
Salmos Psalms of Struggle and Liberation (Cardenal) **22**:118
"Salome" (Ai) **72**:24
"Salome" (Cavafy) **36**:103
"Salomé" (Laforgue) **14**:69, 72
"Salome's Dancing-lesson" (Parker) **28**:351, 363
"Salomons good housewife" (Deloney) **79**:55
Salon de 1845 (Baudelaire) **106**:88
Salon de 1846 (Baudelaire)
See *Salon de 1845*
"Salon des indépendents" (Szirtes) **51**:156
"Salsa Con Crackers" (Alurista) **34**:23
"Salt" (Stone) **53**:215-16
"Salt" (Thomas) **99**:270-71, 273, 276, 308-10
Salt (Szymborska)
See *Sól*
"The Salt Garden" (Nemerov) **24**:261
The Salt Garden (Nemerov) **24**:260-61, 264, 288-89
"Salt Lick" (Sarton) **39**:349, 369
"The Salt Marsh" (Dickey) **40**:156, 257
"The Salt Pond" (Merwin) **45**:97
"Saltfish and Akee" (Birney) **52**:16
"Saltimbanque Elegie" (Rilke)
See "Saltimbanques"
"Saltimbanques" (Rilke) **2**:278, 295
"Les Saltimbanques" (Tzara) **27**:224
"Salts and Oils" (Levine) **22**:224
Salt-Water Ballads (Masefield) **78**:5, 20, 44, 55-56, 67-68, 70, 74, 88-89, 93-97
"Saludo a León Felipe" (Paz) **48**:181
"Saludo al hombre" (Storni) **33**:280, 305
"Salus populi, suprema lex" (Michelangelo) **103**:220
"Salut" (Mallarmé) **102**:33
"Salut au Monde!" (Whitman) **91**:207, 327-28
"Salutación al águila" (Darío) **15**:77, 90, 107, 115
"Salutación del optimista" (Darío) **15**:81, 115
"Salutamus" (Brown) **55**:70-71, 110
"Salutation" (Montague) **106**:298
"The Salutation" (Traherne) **70**:183-86, 190, 194, 197, 265, 268, 273, 288, 303, 312-16, 330
"Salutation to the Eagle" (Darío)
See "Salutación al águila"
"Salutations" (Waldrop) **109**:173
"Salutatory" (Howe) **81**:12, 19, 21, 46
"Salute" (MacLeish) **47**:188
"Salute" (Schuyler) **88**:189, 201, 203
"Salute Sweet Deceptions" (Kennedy) **93**:152-53
"Salute to Guinea" (Césaire) **25**:32
"Salute to Our Allies" (Brutus) **24**:119
Salutes and Censures (Brutus) **24**:118-20
"Saluto d'autunno" (Carducci) **46**:87
"Saluto Italico" (Carducci) **46**:52
"Salvación de la primavera" (Guillén) **35**:180, 181, 182, 183
"Salvador Díaz Mirón" (Darío) **15**:118
"Salvage" (Sandburg) **41**:226, 360
"Salvation of Springtime" (Guillén) **35**:219
Salve Deus Rex Judæorum (Lanyer) **60**:2, 4, 9, 15-16, 18, 20, 22, 24, 26, 29, 31, 33, 39-40, 44-45, 47-48, 52-54, 58-60, 62-65, 67, 69-70, 76-81, 88-90, 92-93, 95-99, 101, 103, 105-14, 118-22, 124-26
"Salviour, suppois" (Dunbar) **67**:22
Salz. Gedichte (Szymborska) **44**:268
"Sam" (Hughes) **89**:177
"Sam Hookey" (Masters) **36**:170
"Sam Smiley" (Brown) **55**:71, 73, 140, 150
"Sam Yancey" (Brown) **55**:1120
Samá láska (Seifert) **47**:315, 331-33
"Sambhashan" (Tagore) **8**:417
"The Same Again" (Kavanagh) **33**:73, 76, 96
"The Same Fault" (Montague) **106**:3258
"The Same Gesture" (Montague) **106**:277, 303
"Same in Blues" (Hughes) **53**:120, 123, 158
"The Same Moon Above Us" (Stern) **115**:263
"Sammy Lou of Rue" (Walker) **30**:352
"Samos" (Merrill) **28**:233
"Samothrake" (Ekeloef) **23**:76
"Samoubiistvennoe more" (Shvarts) **50**:163
"A Sample of Coffee Beans" (Tuckerman) **85**:319
"A Sampler" (MacLeish) **47**:182
"Sam's Three Wishes" (de la Mare) **77**:73, 113
"Samson" (Blake) **12**:31
"Samson" (Hecht) **70**:108
"Samson" (Péret) **33**:201, 217
Samson Agonistes (Milton) **29**:212, 227, 232, 244
Samson's Anger (Vigny)
See "La colère de Samson"
Sämtliche Werke (Heine) **25**:172
"The Samuel Pie" (Belloc) **24**:42
"Samuel Sewall" (Hecht) **70**:69, 89
"A San Diego Poem: January February 1973" (Ortiz) **17**:226, 233
"San Fernando Road" (Soto) **28**:369, 377, 384-85
"A San Francesco le soir" (Bonnefoy) **58**:155, 158
"San Francisco Beat" (Kaufman) **74**:240, 268, 274
"San Francisco Poems" (Oppen) **35**:295
"San Fruttuoso: The Divers" (Tomlinson) **17**:349
"San Giorgio di Donatello" (Carducci) **46**:52
"San Ildefonso Nocturne" (Paz)
See "Nocturno de San Ildefonso"
"A San Juan de la Cruz" (Fuertes) **27**:14
"San Lorenzo's Mother" (Meynell) **112**:157, 165, 184, 229, 245
San Martín Copybook (Borges)
See *Cuaderno San Martín*

San Martin Notebook (Borges)
See *Cuaderno San Martín*
"San Martino" (Carducci) **46**:48, 56, 58, 78
"San Onofre, California" (Forché) **10**:141, 152-53, 155, 158
"San Sebastian" (Hardy) **92**:268-69, 277
"San Sepolcro" (Graham) **59**:139, 146, 149, 152, 178
"Sancta Maria Dolorum" (Crashaw) **84**:9, 15, 32-33, 53, 96-98, 109, 112-15, 153
"Sanctity" (Kavanagh) **105**:154
"Sanctuary" (Randall) **86**:289
"Sanctuary" (Reese) **29**:335
"The Sanctuary" (Teasdale) **31**:360, 370
"Sanctuary" (Wright) **14**:343
"Sanctuary" (Wylie) **23**:323, 329
Sanctuary (Carman) **34**:205, 210-11
"Sand" (Guest) **55**:212
"The Sand Altar" (Lowell) **13**:95
Der Sand aus den Urnen (Celan) **10**:95, 121
"Sand Dabs, Three" (Oliver) **75**:330
"Sand Drift" (Teasdale) **31**:334
"Sand Dunes" (Frost) **1**:203, 218
Sand from the Urns (Celan)
See *Der Sand aus den Urnen*
"Sand Martin" (Clare) **23**:5
"The Sand Roses" (Hogan) **35**:252, 272
"Sandalphon" (Longfellow) **30**:27
"The Sand-Diggrers' Twilight" (Pavese)
See "Crepuscolo di sabbiatori"
"Sandhurst" (Douglas) **106**:187
Sandhya sangit (Tagore) **8**:405-6
"Sandle's Wave" (Hunt) **73**:134
Sandover (Merrill)
See *The Changing Light at Sandover*
"Sandpiper" (Bishop) **3**:53-4
"Sands" (Cassian) **17**:11
"The Sandy Hole" (Kenyon) **57**:17
"Sandy Star" (Braithwaite) **52**:107
"Sandy's Sunday Best" (Berrigan) **103**:4
"Le Sang, la note si" (Bonnefoy) **58**:167-68
Le sanglot de la terre (Laforgue) **14**:57, 64, 68-71, 74, 80-1, 95
"Sanglot perdu" (Laforgue) **14**:86, 88
Sangre (Quintana) **36**:249, 252-58, 260-66, 266-71
"La sangre numerosa" (Guillén) **23**:128-29
Sangschaw (MacDiarmid) **9**:151, 158, 166, 187, 190-91, 196
"Sans âge" (Éluard) **38**:63
"Sans chercher à savoir" (Char) **56**:185
"Sans musique" (Éluard) **38**:69
"Sans rancune" (Éluard) **38**:70
"Sans toi" (Éluard) **38**:74
"Sans tomates pas d'artichauts" (Péret) **33**:202
Sant Kabīr (Kabīr) **56**:344
"Santa" (Sexton) **2**:365; **79**:199, 207
"Santa Barbara Road" (Hass) **16**:217
"Santa Claus" (Nemerov) **24**:267
"Santa Cruz Propositions" (Duncan) **2**:116
"Santa Escolástica" (Castro) **41**:104
"Santa Fe" (Harjo) **27**:66, 70
"The Santa Fe Trail" (Lindsay) **23**:264, 268, 273, 278, 286-87, 294
"Santa Filomena" (Longfellow) **30**:27, 46
"Santa Lucia" (Hass) **16**:211
"Santa Maria a Monte" (Carducci) **46**:4
"Santa Maria degli Angeli" (Carducci) **46**:49, 76
"Santarém" (Bishop) **3**:64-5; **34**:79, 99, 191, 193
"Santorini" (Seferis) **66**:90, 109, 148, 167
"Santorini: Stopping the Leak" (Merrill) **28**:267-69
"Santos" (Bishop) **34**:52
Saōgi (Yosano) **11**:310
"The Sap" (Vaughan) **81**:367
"The Sap is Gone Out of the Trees" (Ammons) **16**:39
"Sapho" (Lamartine) **16**:277
"Sapho to Philaenis" (Donne) **43**:166, 168, 170
"Sapo y mar" (Storni) **33**:246
"Sapobsidiana" (Alurista) **34**:42
"Sapphics" (Swinburne) **24**:320
"Sappho" (Teasdale) **31**:379
"Sappho" (Wright) **36**:299, 335-36
Sappho: One Hundred Lyrics (Carman) **34**:205, 210-12, 214, 226, 231-35
The Sar (Castro)
See *En las orillas del Sar*
"Sara" (Nishiwaki) **15**:241
"Sara Cynthia Sylvia Stout Would Not Take the Garbage Out" (Silverstein) **49**:313, 344
"Sara in Her Father's Arms" (Oppen) **35**:308, 310
"Saraband" (Lovelace)
See "A Loose Saraband"
"Sarah and Tobias" (Gower) **59**:72
"Sarajevo" (Nemerov) **24**:291
"el sarape de mi personalidad" (Alurista) **34**:12, 36
"sarape of my personality" (Alurista)
See "el sarape de mi personalidad"
Sarashina kikō (Matsuo Basho) **3**:26
"Sarastro" (Werfel) **101**:301, 319
"Sarcophagi I" (Montale) **13**:116
Sardanapalus (Byron) **16**:91, 103, 109-10
"Sardegna" (Quasimodo) **47**:302
The Sargeantville Notebook (Strand) **63**:171
Sarir al-Ghariba (Darwish) **86**:23
"Sarmiento" (Borges) **32**:60
"Sarn Rhiw" (Thomas) **99**:266
"Sarum Plain" (Patmore) **59**:228-29
Sarumino (Matsuo Basho) **3**:3, 4, 29
"Sarvaneshe" (Tagore) **8**:414
"Sashes and bearskins in the afternoon" (Davie) **29**:107
"Sashka" (Lermontov)
See *Sashka*
Sashka (Lermontov) **18**:278
"Satan in Westmount" (Cohen) **109**:17
"Satan Says" (Olds) **22**:319
Satan Says (Olds) **22**:307, 310, 312, 315, 317, 319-20, 322, 327-28
"A Satana" (Carducci)
See *Inno a Satana*
"Satanic Form" (Swenson) **14**:252
Satin-Legs Smith (Brooks)
See "The Sundays of Satin-Legs Smith"
"Satire" (Surrey) **59**:297
Satire (Crabbe) **97**:119
Satire II, i (Pope)
See *Satires and Epistles of Horace, Imitated*
"Satire III" (Wyatt) **27**:342
Satires (Donne)
See *Satyres*
Satires (Horace) **46**:97, 99-100, 102, 104, 114, 117-19, 126, 140, 145-46, 170-71, 190-95, 197-98, 212-14, 220-22
Satires and Epistles of Horace, Imitated (Pope) **26**:321
"Satires of Circumstance" (Hardy) **8**:124
Satires of Circumstance (Hardy) **8**:91, 97
Satires of Circumstance, Lyrics and Reveries (Hardy) **92**:286, 290-91, 370-71
Satires of Dr. Donne Versified (Pope) **26**:324-25
Satires of Horace (Pope) **26**:359
"A Satirical Elegy on the Death of a Late Famous General" (Swift) **9**:256, 294, 307
Satirical Poems (Sassoon) **12**:258
"The Satirist" (MacNeice) **61**:141, 185
"The Satisfactions of the Mad Farmer" (Berry) **28**:43
"Satori" (Kennedy) **93**:138
"The Satrapy" (Cavafy) **36**:52, 57, 84
"Satsujin jiken" (Hagiwara) **18**:177, 180
"Satturday: The Small Pox: Flavia" (Montagu) **16**:349
Satura (Montale) **13**:131-34, 138, 143, 148, 152, 161, 167
"A Saturday" (Borges)
See "Sábado"
"Saturday" (Elliott) **96**:163, 174-75
"Saturday" (Storni)
See "Sábado"
"Saturday Evening in Jerusalem" (Douglas) **106**:186, 203
"Saturday Market" (Mew) **107**:51
Saturday Market (Mew) **107**:4, 55
"Saturdays" (Borges)
See "Sábados"
Saturnine Poems (Verlaine)
See *Les Poèmes saturniens*
"Saturn's Rings" (Wakoski) **15**:369
"A Satyr" (Montagu) **16**:338
A Satyr against Mankind (Wilmot) **66**:237, 244, 250, 260, 262-65, 267-68, 273-74, 276, 285-89, 293, 295-97, 321-22, 324, 328-30, 332, 336-37, 339-41, 353
A Satyr Against Reason and Mankind (Wilmot)
See *A Satyr against Mankind*
"The Satyr in the Periwig" (Sitwell) **3**:294
"A Satyr on Charles II" (Wilmot) **66**:234, 269-70, 329-30
"Satyr on Dr. Dryden" (Behn) **88**:107
"Satyr on the Modern Translators" (Prior) **102**:311-12
"Satyr on the Poets. In Imitation of the Seventh Satyr of Juvenal" (Prior) **102**:311-12
"Le satyre" (Hugo) **17**:62, 65, 85, 87, 89
"Satyre II" (Donne) **1**:144; **43**:132, 134, 137
"Satyre III" (Donne) **1**:125, 143, 147; **43**:137, 139
"Satyre IV" (Donne) **43**:137, 141
Satyres (Donne) **1**:140-42, 145; **43**:112, 115, 138, 140-41
"Satyric Complaint" (Winters) **82**:324
"Saudade" (Dalton) **36**:129
"Saul" (Browning) **2**:36, 67-8, 72, 75
"Saul and David" (Hecht) **70**:108
La Saulsaye, Eglogue de la vie solitaire (Scève) **111**:163-66, 168-69, 171-72
"The Sausages" (Corso) **108**:39
"Sausages" (Stein) **18**:353
"De Sauty" (Holmes) **71**:95
"La sauvage" (Vigny) **26**:368-70, 372, 382, 402, 412
"Saved" (Dylan) **37**:72
"Saved by Faith" (Harper) **21**:189, 208
"The Saving" (Pinsky) **27**:159
"Saving My Skin from Burning" (Stern) **115**:271
"The Saving Quality" (Corso) **108**:8
Savings (Hogan) **35**:256, 257
"The Savior Is Abducted in Puerto Rico" (Espada) **74**:124-25
"Saviours" (Cohen) **109**:49
Le Savon (Ponge) **107**:78-82, 96, 102-3, 112-13, 121-26, 138, 148, 174, 191, 200, 226, 231
"Sawmill, Limekiln" (Montague) **106**:246
"A Saxon" (Borges)
See "Un sajón"
"Say Goodbye to Big Daddy" (Jarrell) **41**:185
"Say, Lad, Have You Things to Do" (Housman) **2**:179, 192
"Say not the struggle nought availeth" (Clough) **103**:54, 71
"Say Pardon" (Ignatow) **34**:317-18, 327
Say Pardon (Ignatow) **34**:270-72, 275-76, 281, 283, 285, 311, 313, 316-17, 324
"Saying Dante Aloud" (Wright) **36**:311
"Saying 'good morning' becomes painful" (Spender) **71**:179, 216
"Saying It to Keep It from Happening" (Ashbery) **26**:136
"Saying No" (Enright) **93**:8
Sayings of Kabir (Kabīr) **56**:341-42, 346
"Scale" (Silverstein) **49**:340
"A Scale in May" (Merwin) **45**:15-16, 20, 27, 34, 61, 83-4
"The Scales" (Empson) **104**:91
"The Scales of the Eyes" (Nemerov) **24**:261-62

"The Scanning" (Graham) **59**:183
"Scapegoats and Rabies" (Hughes) **7**:137; **89**:102, 104-6, 108
"The Scar" (Boland) **58**:62
"Scar" (Lorde) **12**:139
"Scarab" (Brutus) **24**:111
"Scarcity of Corn" (Deloney) **79**:55
"Scarecrow" (Borges)
See "Espantapájaros"
"Scarecrow" (Stryk) **27**:197
"Scarecrow Colloquy" (Chappell) **105**:22
"Scarlet Tanager" (Schuyler) **88**:197-98
"The Scarred Girl" (Dickey) **40**:226
"Scars on Paper" (Hacker) **47**:117
"The Scattered Term" (Char)
See "Le Terme épars"
"Scattering As Behavior Toward Risk" (Howe) **54**:52, 57
A Scattering of Salts (Merrill) **28**:281-82, 284-87
"Scenario for a Little Black Movie" (Hughes) **53**:114
"Scenarios" (Mueller) **33**:193
"The Scene" (Curnow) **48**:11, 28
"Scene" (Hugo) **68**:267
"Scene" (Mallarmé) **102**:19-23
"Scene intermediaire" (Mallarmé) **102**:20, 23-24
"Scene of War" (Southey) **111**:254
"A Scene on the Banks of the Hudson" (Bryant) **20**:14, 46
"Scènes" (Rimbaud) **57**:175, 177
"Scenes" (Thomas) **99**:260
"Scenes from the Fall of Troy" (Morris) **55**:258
"Scenes of Childhood" (Merrill) **28**:248
"Scented Herbage of My Breast" (Whitman) **91**:245
"The Scepter Lampoon" (Wilmot) **66**:267
"Schädelstätten" (Benn) **35**:75, 76
"Ein Schatten an der Mauer" (Benn) **35**:68
"Schattenbild" (Enzensberger) **28**:139
"schaum" (Enzensberger) **28**:136
"Scheherazade" (Ashbery) **26**:127, 150
"Scheherazade Is Mailed and Nailed in Five Days" (Stone) **53**:225
"Der Scheidende" (Heine) **25**:178-80
"Scherzo" (Berryman) **64**:95
"Die Schildkröte" (Enzensberger) **28**:165
"Schir, for Your Grace" (Dunbar) **67**:7
"Schir, Lat it Nevir in Toun be Tald" (Dunbar) **67**:4, 8
"Schir, Ye Have Mony Servitouris" (Dunbar) **67**:3, 6, 44
"Schizophrene" (MacNeice) **61**:141
"Schlacht" (Stramm) **50**:178, 208-9
"Schlachtfeld" (Stramm) **50**:173, 198, 216-17
Schlaf und Erwachen (Werfel) **101**:308, 319, 350, 360
"schläferung" (Enzensberger) **28**:139
"Schneebett" (Celan) **10**:114
Schneepart (Celan) **10**:96, 98
"The Scholar" (Baraka) **4**:23
"The Scholar" (Clarke) **112**:35, 71
"The Scholar Gypsy" (Arnold)
See "The Scholar-Gipsy"
"The Scholar-Gipsy" (Arnold) **5**:7, 13, 18-24, 33-5, 37, 47, 51, 53, 53, 59
"Scholars at the Orchid Pavillion" (Berryman) **64**:76, 78
"Scholia" (Berryman) **64**:161
"A Scholium" (Borges)
See "Un escolio"
"Schon" (Sachs) **78**:164
"Schön" (Stramm) **50**:189
"Schon vom Arm des himmlischen Trostes umfangen" (Sachs) **78**:167
"Schöne Jugend" (Benn) **35**:30
"Der schöne strahlende Mensch" (Werfel) **101**:345
"The School Boy" (Blake) **63**:15, 68, 103, 114, 132
"The School Children" (Glück) **16**:128, 132, 149
"School Days" (Ashbery) **26**:137
School Figures (Song) **21**:341, 347
"School Lesson Based on Word of Tragic Death of Entire Gillum Family" (Warren) **37**:296
"School Nights" (Soto) **28**:399
"The School of Babylon" (Sarton) **39**:344
"The School of Desire" (Swenson) **14**:276, 284
"The School of Night" (Hope) **56**:288, 305
"A School of Prayer" (Baraka) **4**:10, 18; **113**:17, 76
School of Udhra (Mackey) **49**:15, 17, 25, 29-33, 35-36, 39-40, 42, 51-53, 57, 59-60, 64-66, 68, 72, 75-78
"The School-Boy" (Blake) **12**:7, 34
"The Schoolboy" (Holmes) **71**:75
Schoolboy Lyrics (Kipling) **3**:190, 193
"School-Days" (Whittier) **93**:267
"The Schoolgirl" (Tuckerman) **85**:302
"Schoolgirl at Seola" (Hugo) **68**:235
"Schoolgirl's Company" (Char) **56**:162
"Schoolmaster" (Larkin) **21**:234, 241
"The Schoolmaster at Spring" (Winters) **82**:314
"The Schoolmistresses" (Pavese)
See "Le maestrine"
"Schooner" (Brathwaite) **56**:65
"The Schooner Flight" (Walcott) **46**:260, 312, 322-23
"Schoonermen" (Thomas) **99**:270-71, 308
"Schopenhauer's Crying" (Zagajewski) **27**:384
"Schöpfung" (Benn) **35**:34
"Schrapnell" (Stramm) **50**:170, 202, 222
"Schrei" (Stramm) **50**:175, 188
"Schutt" (Benn) **35**:33, 50, 73, 75, 76, 77
Schutt (Benn) **35**:8
"An Schwager Kronos" (Goethe) **5**:245, 247, 251
"Schwermut" (Stramm) **50**:176, 195
"Schylek wieku" (Szymborska) **44**:288, 295, 297, 319
"La Scie rêveuse" (Char) **56**:138
"Science" (Jeffers) **17**:113
"Science Fiction Water Letter" (Chappell) **105**:35, 42, 70, 72
"Science has looked" (Owen) **19**:371
"The Science of the Night" (Kunitz) **19**:153, 170, 182
"Scientists" (Stafford) **71**:315, 330
"Scilla" (Glück) **16**:169
"Scirocco" (Graham) **59**:146, 176, 179
"Scirocco" (Montale) **13**:105, 125
"The Scissors and their father" (Éluard) **38**:90-91
"Scoglio di Quarto" (Carducci) **46**:52
"Scorn Not the Least" (Southwell) **83**:281
"Scorpio, Bad Spider, Die" (Sexton) **79**:199
"Scorpion" (Smith) **12**:301, 319, 333
Scorpion and Other Poems (Smith) **12**:299, 315
"Scotch Drink" (Burns) **114**:75
Scotch Nationality: A Vision (Elliott) **96**:181, 187
"A Scotch Song" (Behn)
See "Song. To a New Scotch Tune"
"Scotland, 1941" (Muir) **49**:212, 214, 254-55, 299
"Scotland's Winter" (Muir) **49**:253-54, 299
The Scots Musical Museum (Burns) **114**:50, 94, 113, 161-62, 164, 186-92
"Scots Ode" (Burns) **114**:162
"Scots Prologue, for Mrs. Sutherland's Benefit Night" (Burns) **114**:116
"Scots Song" (Behn)
See "Song. To a New Scotch Tune"
Scots Unbound and Other Poems (MacDiarmid) **9**:158, 175-76, 196
"Scots Wha Hae wi' Wallace Bled" (Burns) **6**:78; **114**:47, 56-58, 94, 116, 162-63, 165
"The Scotsman's Return from Abroad" (Stevenson) **84**:301, 329
The Scottish Musical Museum (Burns)
See *The Scots Musical Museum*
"Scottsboro" (Hughes) **53**:148
Scottsboro Limited: Four Poems and a Play in Verse (Hughes) **53**:111, 148, 181
"Scotty Has His Say" (Brown) **55**:155
"The Scout toward Aldie" (Melville) **82**:71, 93, 101, 196, 206
"Scouting" (Levine) **22**:220-21, 228, 231-32
"The Scream" (Hughes) **89**:198-99
"Screaming Tarn" (Bridges) **28**:68
The Screech Owl (Jaccottet)
See *L'Effraie et autres poésies*
"The Screen of Distance" (Guest) **55**:185
"A Screened Porch in the Country" (Dickey) **40**:155, 182, 185, 212
"Screvo meu livro à beira-mágoa" (Pessoa) **20**:155-56
"Screw: A Technical Love Poem" (Wakoski) **15**:332
"Screw Guns" (Kipling) **3**:158
"The Scribe" (de la Mare) **77**:142
"Scripts for the Pageant" (Merrill) **28**:233-38, 243, 260-64, 276-78, 281
Scritti e interventi (Ungaretti) **57**:333
"Scroll" (Noyes) **27**:130
"Scrub" (Millay) **6**:235
"Scrutinie" (Lovelace) **69**:181, 194
"The Sculptor" (Plath) **1**:388-89; **37**:188-89
"Sculptor from Tyaneia" (Cavafy)
See "Sculptor of Tyana"
"Sculptor of Tyana" (Cavafy) **36**:46, 73
"Sculpture Musicale" (Cage) **58**:219
"Scurry" (Swenson) **14**:254
"Scuttle up the workshop" (Niedecker) **42**:150
"Scyros" (Shapiro) **25**:268, 279
"Scythe Lifted Again" (Char)
See "La Faux relevée"
The Scythians (Blok)
See *Skify*
"Se acabó" (Guillén) **23**:117, 125
"Se ben concetto ha la divina parte" (Michelangelo) **103**:182, 344
"Se canta al mar" (Parra) **39**:299
"Se 'l foco fusse alla bellezza equale" (Michelangelo) **103**:217
"Se 'l mie rozzo martello i duri sassi" (Michelangelo) **103**:188, 342
"Se me ocurren ideas luminosas" (Parra) **39**:286
"Sé, mujer, para mí" (Martí) **76**:106
"Se réchauffer l'ardeur" (Char) **56**:148
"Se rencontrer paysage avec Joseph Sima" (Char) **56**:146
"A se stesso" (Leopardi) **37**:92, 102, 121, 123-24, 134, 142-43
"Se vuelve a yo" (Neruda) **4**:287
"The Sea" (Borges)
See "El mar"
"The Sea" (Hall) **70**:31
"The Sea" (Oliver) **75**:284, 303, 305-6, 308
"The Sea" (Parker) **28**:351
"The Sea" (Swenson) **14**:288
"The Sea" (Thomas) **99**:272-73
"The Sea" (Williams) **7**:385, 387; **109**:293-94
"Sea and land are but his neighbors" (Thoreau) **30**:203
"Sea and Night" (Aleixandre)
See "Mar y noche"
The Sea and the Bells (Neruda)
See *El mar y las campanas*
The Sea and the Honeycomb (Bly) **39**:68-69
The Sea and the Mirror (Auden) **92**:19, 23-24, 33, 44, 88, 95, 127, 129
"The Sea and the Mirror: A Commentary on Shakespeare's Tempest" (Auden) **1**:22, 34
"The Sea Battle" (Cavafy) **36**:84
"The Sea Bird" (Douglas) **106**:199
"Sea-Blue and Blood-Red" (Lowell) **13**:60, 64, 66, 72, 81, 83
"Sea Burial from the CruiserReve" (Eberhart) **76**:40, 59
"Sea Calm" (Hughes) **1**:236; **53**:85

"Sea Canes" (Walcott) **46**:236, 279
"Sea Change" (Tomlinson) **17**:321
"Sea Change" (Wagoner) **33**:359
"Sea Changes" (Montague) **106**:327
"Sea Changes" (O'Hara) **45**:130
"Sea Chanty" (Corso) **33**:43; **108**:30, 38, 40
"A Sea-Chantey" (Walcott) **46**:231, 248, 259, 272-73
"A Sea Child" (Carman) **34**:210, 216
"Sea Children" (Carman) **34**:225
"A Sea Dialogue" (Holmes) **71**:68, 94
"Sea Dirge" (Carroll) **18**:46
"A Sea Dream" (Whittier) **93**:197, 252
"Sea Dreams" (Tennyson) **6**:360; **101**:215
"A Sea-Drift" (Carman) **34**:216
"Sea-Drift" (Whitman) **91**:207
"The Sea-Elephant" (Williams) **7**:360; **109**:193
"The Sea-Fairies" (Tennyson) **6**:348, 359; **101**:121
"Sea Fever" (Masefield) **78**:68, 89, 95, 97
"Sea Flesh" (Cernuda) **62**:171
"The Sea Fog" (Jacobsen) **62**:306
Sea Garden (H. D.) **5**:266-67, 288-90, 303
"Sea Grapes" (Walcott) **46**:272, 279
Sea Grapes (Walcott) **46**:233, 236-37, 240, 248, 259, 274-75, 278-79, 289-91, 323-24
"The Sea Horse" (Graves) **6**:154
"Sea hymn" (Borges)
See "Himno del mar"
"The Sea in Winter" (Mahon) **60**:142-43, 147, 155, 171, 179, 186-88, 192, 196, 198, 200, 203, 205-9, 215, 220, 233
"Sea Iris" (H. D.) **5**:289
"Sea Lily" (H. D.) **5**:288
"Sea Love" (Mew) **107**:56, 58
"Sea Lullaby" (Wylie) **23**:332
"Sea Monster" (Merwin) **45**:7
"The Sea of Death" (Hood) **93**:58, 66, 117, 119
"Sea of Forgetfulness" (Guillén) **35**:218
"The Sea of Suicide" (Shvarts)
See "Samoubiistvennoe more"
"Sea Poppies" (H. D.) **5**:288
"Sea Surface Full of Clouds" (Stevens) **6**:304, 332
"Sea Unicorns and Land Unicorns" (Moore) **4**:233; **49**:94, 161
"The Sea Urchins of Pégomas" (Char) **56**:162
"The Sea View" (Smith) **104**:166, 213
"Sea Violet" (H. D.) **5**:289
"Sea Voyage" (Empson) **104**:84, 92, 97-98
"The Sea Was Asleep" (Zagajewski) **27**:394
"The Sea Wife" (Kipling) **91**:144
"Seafarer" (MacLeish) **47**:155, 165
"The Seafarer" (Pound) **4**:317, 331, 364
"The Sea-Hawk" (Eberhart) **76**:13, 29, 50, 59
"Seal" (Sexton) **79**:240
"The Seal Boy" (Barker) **77**:5
"The Sealchie's Son" (Snodgrass) **74**:334
"Seals, Terns, Time" (Eberhart) **76**:13, 26, 51-53, 59
"A Seamark, a Threnody for Robert Louis Stevenson" (Carman) **34**:220
Seamarks (Perse)
See *Amers*
"The Seamless Garment" (MacDiarmid) **9**:177
"The Seamstress" (Song) **21**:331, 333-34, 336, 341, 350
"Séan an Dimas, 1562" (Montague) **106**:343
"The Sean Bhean Vocht" (Montague) **106**:215, 250, 275, 284-86, 294, 312
"Séance" (Szymborska) **44**:269
"Seans" (Szymborska) **44**:308
"Sea-Nymph's Prayer to Okeanos" (Zukofsky) **11**:368
"The Search" (Abse) **41**:3
"The Search" (Herbert) **4**:101
"The Search" (Masters) **1**:343-44
"The Search" (Merwin) **45**:48
"Search" (Montague) **106**:240, 287
"Search" (Silverstein) **49**:324
"The Search" (Vaughan) **81**:270, 295
Search for the Base and the Summit (Char)
See *Recherche de la base et du sommet*
"Searching for the Canto Fermo" (Wakoski) **15**:362
"Searching, Not Searching" (Rukeyser) **12**:224
"Searchlight Practice" (Wright) **14**:354
"Sea-Reverie" (Sandburg) **41**:360
"Sea-Rose" (H. D.) **5**:288, 303
"Seascape" (Bishop) **3**:37; **34**:116
"Seascape" (Spender) **71**:139, 153, 188
Seascape: Needle's Eye (Oppen) **35**:293, 294, 324, 331, 332, 334, 336 338, 340
"Sea-Serpent" (MacDiarmid) **9**:193
The Seashell Game (Matsuo Basho)
See *Kai oi*
"The Seashore" (Emerson) **18**:76, 80, 89, 91
"Seashores" (Ponge)
See "Bords de mer"
"Seaside" (Brooke) **24**:58, 76, 84, 86, 88
"Seaside" (Thomas) **99**:272
The Seaside and the Fireside (Longfellow) **30**:27
"Seaside Golf" (Betjeman) **75**:103
"A Sea-Side Meditation" (Barrett Browning) **6**:20
"Seaside Postcard" (Szirtes) **51**:169
"The Season" (Stone) **53**:216
A Season in Hell (Rimbaud)
See *Une saison en enfer*
"The Season of Phantasmal Peace" (Walcott) **46**:247
The Season of Violence (Paz)
See *La estación violenta*
Season Songs (Hughes) **7**:157, 162, 171; **89**:125, 232
"Seasonal" (Ashbery) **26**:166
"Seasonal Woman" (Tapahonso) **65**:258
Seasonal Woman (Tapahonso) **65**:223-24, 226, 240, 257-59
"The Seasonless" (Wright) **36**:303, 336
"Seasons" (Bradstreet)
See "The Four Seasons of the Year"
"The Seasons" (Koch) **80**:339
"Seasons" (Tomlinson) **17**:326
The Seasons (Kālidāsa)
See *Rtusamhāra*
"The Seasons of the Soul" (Tate) **50**:245, 252-54, 256-57, 259, 266-67, 276-77, 280, 290-95
Seasons on Earth (Koch) **80**:303, 309, 319, 328, 333-35
"Seaspin" (Corso) **33**:48; **108**:16, 24
"Seat Belt Fastened?" (Stone) **53**:219
"Seated Figure" (Chappell) **105**:37
"Seated Figure" (Glück) **16**:153
Seaton Prize Odes (Smart) **13**:329
"Seaton's Aunt" (de la Mare) **77**:99
"Seattle 7 May 72" (Brutus) **24**:123
"Seattle, 1987" (Alexie) **53**:14
Seaven Bookes of the Iliades (Chapman) **96**:36
"A Sea-Voyage from Tenby to Bristol" (Philips) **40**:298
"Sea-Watching" (Thomas) **99**:358
"Seaweed" (Longfellow) **30**:27, 31
"Sea-Wind" (Mallarmé) **4**:187
Sebastian im Traum (Trakl) **20**:236, 241, 244, 250
"Sebastian in Traum" (Trakl) **20**:228, 230-31
"Sécheresse" (Perse) **23**:255, 257
"Second Air Force" (Jarrell) **41**:154, 160, 173-74, 201
"The Second Angel" (Levine) **22**:213
The Second Anniversarie. Of the Progres of the Soule. Wherein, By Occasion Of the Religious death of Mistris Elizabeth Drury, the incommodities ofthe Soule in this life, and her exaltation in the next, are Contemplated (Donne) **1**:122, 145-51, 155-57; **43**:128, 131-32
Second April (Kaufman) **74**:194, 199, 207, 218, 240, 268
Second April (Millay) **6**:211-12, 214-15, 233, 242-44; **61**:243
"Second Avenue" (O'Hara) **45**:130, 135, 148, 160, 175-76, 191, 219, 224, 242
"The Second Best" (Arnold) **5**:42
"Second Best" (Brooke) **24**:59, 60, 76, 84
"Second Best Bed" (Shapiro) **25**:316
The Second Birth (Pasternak) **6**:253-54, 268, 281
A Second Book (Mandelstam)
See *Vtoraya kniga*
The Second Booke of Ayres (Campion)
See *Light Conceits of Lovers*
"The Second Chambermaid's Song" (Yeats) **20**:332
"Second Chance" (Wakoski) **15**:347
"Second Chances" (Hugo) **68**:303-4
"The Second Coming" (Abse) **41**:9, 19
"The Second Coming" (Yeats) **20**:308, 312-13, 319-20, 349; **51**:107
"Second Diptych" (Yau) **61**:332
"Second Elegy" (Rilke) **2**:273-4, 286
"Second Epistle to John Lapraik" (Burns) **6**:68-70, 78; **114**:41
"A Second Epistle, To my Honoured Friend Mr. E. S." (Barker) **91**:26
"Second Fig" (Millay) **6**:227
"Second Generation: New York" (Hughes) **53**:116
"Second Georgic" (Vergil) **12**:359, 365
"Second Glance at a Jaguar" (Hughes) **7**:136-37; **89**:103, 207
"Second Hymn to Lenin" (MacDiarmid) **9**:158, 177, 180-81, 197
Second Hymn to Lenin, and Other Poems (MacDiarmid) **9**:156, 179, 196
The Second Jungle Book (Kipling) **3**:162, 185, 188-89; **91**:83-84, 135
"Second Language" (Gallagher) **9**:60
Second Language (Mueller) **33**:176, 189-91
Second livre des poemes (Ronsard) **11**:282
"A Second Meeting with my Father" (Amichai) **38**:27
"The Second Night" (Hardy) **92**:277
"Second Night in N.Y.C. After Three Years" (Corso) **33**:11, 25; **108**:8
"The Second Night in the Week" (Duncan) **75**:228
"Second Nun's Tale" (Chaucer) **19**:13, 15
"The Second Nuptials" (Elliott) **96**:157, 181
"Second Oldest Story" (Parker) **28**:362
Second Olympian (Pindar)
See *Olympian 2*
"Second Poem" (Duncan) **75**:265-67
Second Poetic Anthology (Jiménez)
See *Segund antolojía poética*
"Second Populist Manifesto" (Ferlinghetti)
See "Adieu á Charlot"
"The Second Prologue at Court to 'The Empress of Morocco,' Spoken by the Lady Elizabeth Howard" (Wilmot) **66**:329, 343
"Second Psalm" (Sexton) **79**:220
"A Second Psalm of Life" (Longfellow)
See "The Light of Stars"
Second Pythian (Pindar)
See *Pythian 2*
"The Second Rapture" (Carew) **29**:10
"The Second Sermon on the Warpland" (Brooks) **7**:63
"A Second Siege" (Montague) **106**:236
"Second Song" (Bogan) **12**:90, 129
"Second Song" (Kinsella) **69**:100
"Second Song" (Rilke)
See "Second Elegy"
"Second Song for the Worship of the Goddess at Yü Mountain: 'Bidding the Godeess Farewell'" (Wang Wei) **18**:369
"The Second Spring" (Sarton) **39**:337, 365
The Second Symphony (Bely)
See *Vtoraia simfoniia: Dramaticheskaia*

"Second Thoughts on the Abstract Gardens of Japan" (Sarton) **39**:339
Second Voronezh Notebook (Mandelstam) **14**:133-34, 149, 152-53
"The Second Voyage" (Ní Chuilleanáin) **34**:360
The Second Voyage (Ní Chuilleanáin) **34**:349-50, 359, 361
"Second Wind" (Chappell) **105**:26, 31, 44, 58, 72, 75, 81
Second Year of Chang-ho (Li Ho) **13**:42
"Secondary Epic" (Auden) **92**:66
"The Second-Best Bed" (Nemerov) **24**:291
"Second-Class Constable Alston" (McKay) **2**:205
Second-Hand Coat (Stone) **53**:220, 226, 229-39, 242-46, 251-55, 258
"Secrecy" (Clarke) **112**:83
"Le Secret" (Jaccottet) **98**:174
"The Secret" (Kenyon) **57**:45
"The Secret" (Merton) **10**:348
"The Secret" (Ní Chuilleanáin) **34**:384
"A Secret" (Plath) **37**:255
"The Secret" (Simic) **69**:306-7
"Secret Festival; September Moon" (Levertov) **11**:177
"The Secret Garden" (Kinsella) **69**:101-2
"A Secret Gratitude" (Wright) **36**:368
"Secret History of the Dividing Line" (Howe) **54**:124, 126, 130, 134
Secret History of the Dividing Line (Howe) **54**:36-37, 40, 65, 107, 109, 140-47
"Le secret humain" (MacLeish) **47**:129, 156, 186
"The Secret Life of Ford Madox Ford" (Berrigan) **103**:32, 43
"A secret love" (Campion) **87**:57, 67, 92, 118-20, 122, 126
The Secret Meaning of Things (Ferlinghetti) **1**:173-74, 176, 186-87
"The Secret Miracle" (Borges)
See "El milagro secreto"
"Secret Music" (Sassoon) **12**:247
Secret: New Poems (Akhmadulina)
See *Taina: novye stixi*
"The Secret of Light" (Wright) **36**:311, 356, 370, 376
"The Secret of Machu Pichhu" (Cardenal)
See "El Secreto de Machu-Picchu"
"The Secret of the Legal Secretary's Cigarette Smoke" (Espada) **74**:126
"The Secret of the Sea" (Longfellow) **30**:27
"The Secret of the Stars" (Holmes) **71**:94
"Secret Treasure" (Teasdale) **31**:380
"Secretary" (Hughes) **7**:140; **89**:137
A Secretary to the Spirits (Reed) **68**:340
"El Secreto de Machu-Picchu" (Cardenal) **22**:132
Secrets from the Center of the World (Harjo) **27**:65, 68
The Secrets of the Heart (Gibran) **9**:72
"Secrets of the Trade" (Akhmatova) **2**:5
Section: Rock-Drill, 85-95 de los cantares (Pound) **4**:352, 357; **95**:80, 164, 168, 171, 198
"Sects and Professions in Religion" (Crabbe) **97**:118
Secular Hymn (Horace) **46**:122
Secular Love (Ondaatje) **28**:314-17, 340
"Security" (Stafford) **71**:371
"Sed de Correr" (Clampitt) **19**:100
"Sediment" (Ignatow) **34**:320-21
"Seduction" (Giovanni) **19**:111, 113, 117
"See Los Angeles First" (Winters) **82**:319
"See Naples and Die" (Hecht) **70**:80, 92, 100
"See Venice and Die" (Hecht) **70**:81
"See where she flies" (Campion) **87**:64
"Seed and Bran" (Tzara) **27**:242
"The Seed Cutters" (Heaney) **18**:203; **100**:210-11
"The Seed growing secretly" (Vaughan) **81**:306, 325, 367
"Seed Journey" (Corso) **33**:49
"Seed Leaves" (Wilbur) **51**:270, 287-88, 305, 310, 312
"The Seed Picture" (McGuckian) **27**:79, 97
"Seed Pods" (Snyder) **21**:305
Seeds and Bran (Tzara)
See *Grains et issues*
Seeds for a Hymn (Paz)
See *Semillas para un himno*
Seeds for an Anthem (Paz)
See *Semillas para un himno*
"Seeds of Revolution" (Randall) **86**:328-29, 335, 337
Seedtime (Jaccottet)
See *La Semaison*
"Seed-Time" (Meredith) **60**:298, 327
"Seeing a Friend Off" (Li Po) **29**:146
"Seeing and Perceiving" (Stafford) **71**:324, 355
"Seeing in the Dark" (Komunyakaa) **51**:41
Seeing Is Believing (Tomlinson) **17**:302, 306, 317-18, 321, 323-24, 332-33, 335, 338, 341-42, 346, 352, 359
"Seeing the Bones" (Kumin) **15**:207, 209
"Seeing the Moon Rise" (Hardy) **92**:235
"Seeing the Sick" (Heaney) **100**:241; **100**:235, 245-46
"Seeing the Wind" (Wagoner) **33**:360
"Seeing Things" (Nemerov) **24**:302
Seeing Things (Heaney) **18**:254-61; **100**:231, 234-35, 243-49, 251-53, 287-88
Seeing through the Sun (Hogan) **35**:244, 245, 247, 255, 256, 259
"Seeing You Have" (Snodgrass) **74**:285, 304
"Seeke flowers of heaven" (Southwell) **83**:295
"Seeke the Lord" (Campion) **87**:55-56, 66, 97
The Seeker (Sachs)
See *Die Suchende*
"The Seekers" (Masefield) **78**:7
"Seeking Religion" (Brown) **55**:156
"The Seekonk Woods" (Kinnell) **26**:278, 293
"Seele im Raum" (Jarrell) **41**:139, 171, 177, 182, 189, 194-95, 208, 211
"Seen by the Waits" (Hardy) **8**:130
"S'egli è che 'n dura pietra alcun somigli" (Michelangelo) **103**:344
"Segments of a Bamboo Screen" (Chin) **40**:3
Segund antolojía poética (Jiménez) **7**:178, 201
"Sehnen" (Stramm) **50**:168, 170, 208
"Le Seigneur habite en toi" (Gautier) **18**:144
"Les Seigneurs de Maussane" (Char) **56**:154
"La Seine" (Ponge) **107**:97, 146
La Seine (Ponge) **107**:176, 191
"Seizure" (Sappho)
See "Ode to Anactoria"
A Seizure of Limericks (Aiken) **26**:24
Šel malíř chudě do světa (Seifert) **47**:323, 326, 335
"Selah" (Thomas) **99**:276
"Ein Selbstmörder" (Benn) **35**:48
"Seldom Yet Now" (Graves) **6**:156
A Select Collection of Original Scottish Airs for the Voice (Burns) **114**:50, 94, 113, 162, 186
Select Meditations (Traherne) **70**:280-81, 283, 305-8, 312, 333
Selected Failings (Neruda)
See *Defectos escogidos: 2000*
Selected letters (Williams) **7**:374
"A Selected Life" (Kinsella) **69**:72
A Selected Life (Kinsella) **69**:126
"Selected Poems" (Ignatow) **34**:309
Selected Poems (Abse) **41**:9, 11, 13-14, 16-17
Selected Poems (Amichai) **38**:32, 44
Selected Poems (Ashbery) **26**:158
Selected Poems (Auden) **92**:19, 51
Selected Poems (Berrigan) **103**:3-7, 15, 42
Selected Poems (Betjeman) **75**:61, 63, 66, 68
Selected Poems (Bly) **39**:72, 82-5, 87, 98, 100-02, 104
Selected Poems (Breton) **15**:57
Selected Poems (Brooks) **7**:81, 102
Selected Poems (Ciardi) **69**:48-50, 52-55
Selected Poems (Clarke) **112**:129
Selected Poems (Corso) **33**:38, 53; **108**:40, 47
Selected Poems (Creeley) **73**:102
Selected Poems (Davie) **29**:127
The Selected Poems (Dickey) **40**:262
Selected Poems (Dorn) **115**:218
Selected Poems (Douglas) **106**:182, 199-200
Selected Poems (Duncan) **2**:102; **75**:227-28
Selected Poems (Eberhart) **76**:8, 48, 50, 53
Selected Poems (Frost) **1**:195
Selected Poems (Goodison) **36**:154
Selected Poems (Guest) **55**:185, 187, 196, 206, 209-11, 213, 221, 224, 227
Selected Poems (H. D.) **5**:274
Selected Poems (Hayden) **6**:176, 178-79
Selected Poems (Herbert)
See *Wybór wierszy*
Selected Poems (Hope) **56**:289
Selected Poems (Hugo) **68**:270-71, 280-82, 285-86
Selected Poems (Jarrell) **41**:143, 145, 173, 179-80, 185, 193, 196, 205, 207-09, 213, 217
Selected Poems (Justice) **64**:266-68, 272, 277-78, 280
Selected Poems (Kinnell) **26**:261-62, 288
Selected Poems (Levine) **22**:220
Selected Poems (Lowell) **3**:226-27
Selected Poems (MacNeice) **61**:173-74
Selected Poems (Mahon) **60**:175, 184, 187, 191, 195, 198, 204-5, 220
Selected Poems (McKay) **2**:207, 228
Selected Poems (Meredith) **28**:207
Selected Poems (Milosz) **8**:174
Selected Poems (Montague) **106**:275, 290, 302-5, 317
Selected Poems (Montale) **13**:135
Selected Poems (Moore) **4**:240, 242, 253; **49**:88, 96, 98, 113-14, 159, 161
Selected Poems (Muir) **49**:286
Selected Poems (Niedecker) **42**:102
Selected Poems (Pasolini) **17**:289
Selected Poems (Philips) **40**:300
Selected Poems (Pound) **95**:112
Selected Poems (Ransom) **61**:267, 271-72, 274-76, 279, 288, 304-5, 308, 320, 323
Selected Poems (Rukeyser) **12**:210
Selected Poems (Schuyler) **88**:174, 185-86, 190
Selected Poems (Senghor) **25**:238, 241, 245
Selected Poems (Sexton) **2**:347-48; **79**:248, 336
Selected Poems (Shapiro) **25**:315
Selected Poems (Sitwell) **3**:320
Selected Poems (Smith) **12**:293, 309, 350
Selected Poems (Spender) **71**:229
Selected Poems (Strand) **63**:150, 156-58, 175, 181-82, 189-90, 192-93
Selected Poems (Stryk) **27**:185, 187-89, 191, 197-98, 201-3
Selected Poems (Tate) **50**:230, 246, 337
Selected Poems (Tomlinson) **17**:327, 345
Selected Poems (Very) **86**:102, 104
Selected Poems (Walcott) **46**:238, 247-48
Selected Poems (Williams) **109**:197, 290, 301
Selected Poems by Anna Wickham (Wickham) **110**:293, 300, 308, 310
Selected Poems, 1923-1943 (Warren) **37**:286, 300, 308, 318, 324-25, 330-31, 335, 339, 350, 354, 356, 359-60, 363-64, 372, 382
Selected Poems, 1923-1967 (Borges) **32**:93-5, 99, 135-36, 138
Selected Poems, 1928-1958 (Kunitz) **19**:148, 155, 157, 159, 161-63, 168-70, 173-76
Selected Poems, 1930-1965 (Eberhart) **76**:45, 50, 53
Selected Poems (1938-1958): Summer Knowledge (Schwartz)
See *Summer Knowledge: New and Selected Poems, 1938-1958*
Selected Poems, 1940-1966 (Birney) **52**:6, 20, 22-24, 37, 47, 51, 55, 80
Selected Poems, 1940-1989 (Curnow) **48**:43, 53, 59, 62-63
Selected Poems, 1946-1968 (Thomas) **99**:248, 250-51, 272, 353

Selected Poems, 1950-1975 (Gunn) **26**:206
Selected Poems, 1951-1974 (Tomlinson) **17**:325
Selected Poems, 1956-1968 (Cohen) **109**:19, 29, 82, 88
Selected Poems 1956-1968 (Kinsella) **69**:115, 117-22
Selected Poems, 1957-1967 (Hughes) **7**:163
Selected Poems 1957-1981 (Hughes) **89**:156, 187
Selected Poems, 1963-1983 (Simic) **69**:292, 294, 310-11, 318
Selected Poems 1965-1975 (Atwood) **8**:23
Selected Poems, 1965-1990 (Hacker) **47**:104, 115, 119
Selected Poems 1965-1975 (Heaney)
See *Poems: 1965-1975*
Selected Poems 1966-1987 (Heaney)
See *New Selected Poems: 1966-1987*
Selected Poems: 1976-1996 (Szirtes) **51**:171
Selected Poems and New (Villa) **22**:349, 351, 353-54
Selected Poems and Prose of John Clare (Clare) **23**:3-8, 11, 13-14
Selected Poems: Beyond Even Faithful Legends (Bissett) **14**:27-30, 34-5
Selected Poems: German-English Bilingual Edition (Enzensberger) **28**:166
Selected Poems: In Five Sets (Jackson) **44**:7, 9, 52, 84, 96-97
Selected Poems, Joseph Brodsky (Brodsky) **9**:8
The Selected Poems of David Ignatow (Ignatow) **34**:303-05, 307-10, 323
The Selected Poems of Frank O'Hara (O'Hara) **45**:127, 205, 221
The Selected Poems of Langston Hughes (Hughes) **1**:248, 258; **53**:94, 108-9, 111, 113, 116-19, 138, 144, 146-50, 153, 158, 182
The selected poems of Lizette Woodworth Reese (Reese) **29**:334-335, 339, 347, 352
Selected Poems of Pierre Reverdy (Rexroth) **95**:251
Selected Poems of Yvor Winters (Winters) **82**:347
Selected Poems, Revised and Enlarged (Ransom) **61**:267
Selected Poetry (Amichai) **38**:26, 33, 35, 42, 45
Selected Poetry of Amiri Baraka/LeRoi Jones (Baraka) **4**:31; **113**:29, 41, 48, 52
Selected Poetry of Andrea Zanzotto (Zanzotto) **65**:272-73, 321
The Selected Poetry of Hayden Carruth (Carruth) **10**:84
The Selected Poetry of Robinson Jeffers (Jeffers) **17**:111, 123, 130, 133, 136-37, 141
The Selected Poetry of Yehuda Amichai (Amichai) **38**:53
Selected Shorter Poems (Schwerner) **42**:204
Selected Translations, 1948-1968 (Merwin) **45**:21, 30-1
Selected Verse (Gilmore) **87**:286, 289
Selected Works. Poems (Akhmadulina)
See *Izbrannoe. Stikhi*
Selected Works of Stephen Vincent Benét (Benét) **64**:21, 49-53, 55-57
Selected Writings (Olson) **19**:268, 276-77, 305, 316-17
Selected Writings of Juan Ramon Jimenez (Jiménez)
See *Antolojía poética (1898-1953)*
A Selection from the Poems (Blunden) **66**:44
Selection of the Poems of Laura Riding (Jackson) **44**:101, 103, 106
A Selection of the Shorter Poems (Blunden) **66**:44
Selections from the Sibylline Leaves (Coleridge)
See *Sibylline Leaves: A Collection of Poems*
"Selections From Unpublished Verse" (Service) **70**:140
"Selective Service" (Forché) **10**:137, 144, 146, 157, 165
"Selene Afterwards" (MacLeish) **47**:167, 185
"Self" (Hacker) **47**:88
"Self Analysis" (Wickham) **110**:263, 277
"Self and Life" (Eliot) **20**:136
"The Self and The Other" (Borges)
See "El otro, el mismo"
The Self and the Other (Borges)
See *El otro, el mismo*
"Self in 1958" (Sexton) **2**:351; **79**:314
"Self Portrait" (Wylie) **23**:321
Self Portrait (Dylan) **37**:60, 63
"The Self Unsatisfied Runs Everywhere" (Schwartz) **8**:285
"The Self-Abuser and the Suicide" (Viereck) **27**:279
"The Self-Banished" (Waller) **72**:322, 371
"The Self-Betrayal Which Is Nothing New" (Schwartz) **8**:294
"Self-Criticism and Answer" (Day Lewis) **11**:128, 144
"Self-Criticism in February" (Jeffers) **17**:123, 132
"Self-Dependence" (Arnold) **5**:19, 42-3, 49
"Self-Employed" (Ignatow) **34**:326
"The Self-Hatred of Don L. Lee" (Madhubuti) **5**:337
"The Selfish One" (Neruda)
See "El egoísta"
"Self-Knowledge" (Graham) **59**:166
"Self-Pity Is a Kind of Lying, Too" (Schuyler) **88**:189
"Self-Portrait" (Cassian) **17**:7
"Self-Portrait" (Cervantes) **35**:117
"Self-portrait" (Parra)
See "Autoretrato"
"Self-Portrait" (Stern) **115**:248, 281
"Self-Portrait" (Thomas) **99**:260, 267
"Self-Portrait as a Bear" (Hall) **70**:13, 25
"Self-Portrait as Apollo and Daphne" (Graham) **59**:133, 157
"Self-Portrait as Demeter and Persephone" (Graham) **59**:158, 173
"Self-Portrait as Hurry and Delay" (Graham) **59**:157-58
"Self-Portrait as Still Life" (Justice) **64**:261
"Self-Portrait as the Gesture between Them" (Graham) **59**:152, 157-58, 184
"A Self-Portrait: David" (Tomlinson) **17**:346, 348
"Self-Portrait in a Convex Mirror" (Ashbery) **26**:109, 119-21, 123-24, 126, 134, 140, 142-43, 147-50, 159, 171-72, 174
Self-Portrait in a Convex Mirror (Ashbery) **26**:115-16, 118, 124, 126-27, 130, 145, 148-50, 160, 169, 171, 174
"Self-Portrait in Tyvek (tm) Windbreaker" (Merrill) **28**:287
"The Self-Portrait of Ivan Generalić" (Schnackenberg) **45**:337
"Self-Portrait on a Summer Evening" (Boland) **58**:6
"Self-Portrait with Max Beckmann" (Yau) **61**:358
"Self-Portraits" (Graham) **59**:138, 157-58, 171, 174
"Self-Praise" (Graves) **6**:139
"Self's Despite" (Muir) **49**:206
"The Selfsame Song" (Hardy) **92**:255, 326
"The Self-slaved" (Kavanagh) **33**:63
"The Self-Unseeing" (Hardy) **8**:88, 129; **92**:340-42, 358-59, 361, 367, 371
"Selige Sehnsucht" (Goethe) **5**:248
"Selim; or, The Shepherd's Moral" (Collins) **72**:57
"Selina, Countess of Huntingdon" (Davie) **29**:115-16
"Selinda and Cloris" (Behn) **13**:30
"Selinda and Cloris, made in an Entertainment at Court" (Behn) **88**:16, 39, 71
"Sella" (Bryant) **20**:15
"La Selle, & les deux hommes" (Scève) **111**:5
"A Seltzer Bottle" (Stein) **18**:334
"Selva austral" (Mistral) **32**:166
"Selva Oscura" (MacNeice) **61**:186
"Selvas de mi ciudad" (Storni) **33**:239, 246
"The Selves" (Page) **12**:198
"La semaine pâle" (Péret) **33**:202
"La semaine Sainte" (Lamartine) **16**:277, 299
"La Semaison" (Jaccottet) **98**:159
La Semaison (Jaccottet) **98**:148, 150, 157, 161-64, 172-73, 178-79, 184, 186, 190, 192-96, 198, 200, 209
"The Semblables" (Williams) **7**:360
"A Semblance" (Ignatow) **34**:313
"Seme" (Quasimodo) **47**:302
"Semele Recycled" (Kizer) **66**:79
"Semi-Detached" (Thomas) **99**:358
Semillas para un himno (Paz) **1**:353, 366; **48**:244
"Semiotics" (Montague) **106**:313
"Semper eadem" (Baudelaire) **1**:61, 72
"Semper eadem" (Verlaine) **32**:385
"Semplicità" (Pavese) **13**:229
"Sen" (Mickiewicz) **38**:196-97
"Senaida" (Quintana) **36**:274
"The Sence of a Letter Sent Me, Made into Verse; to a New Tune" (Behn) **13**:31
"Sence You Went Away" (Johnson) **24**:132, 141, 151, 154, 162
"Send Back My Heart to Me, Relentless One" (Stampa) **43**:296
"Send No Money" (Larkin) **21**:234, 242, 248
"Sending to the War" (Morris) **55**:338
"The Send-Off" (Owen) **19**:347; **102**:167, 171-72, 263
Seneca Unmasqued (Behn)
See *Reflections on Morality, or Seneca Unmasqued*
Senlin: A Biography (Aiken) **26**:4, 6, 12, 22, 29, 70-2
"Señor Diego Valverde" (Juana Inés de la Cruz) **24**:186
"Señor, para responderos" (Juana Inés de la Cruz) **24**:187
"Señora doña Ros" (Juana Inés de la Cruz) **24**:211
"Sens" (Milosz) **8**:215
"Sensation" (Rimbaud) **3**:275, 283; **57**:191, 234, 241, 244, 248, 252, 255, 284
"Sensation Time at the Home" (Merton)
See "A Song: Sensation Time at the Home"
"Sensational Disclosures! (Kavanagh Tells All)" (Kavanagh) **33**:76, 87, 96
"Sense and Conscience" (Tennyson) **6**:372-73
"The Sense Comes Over Me, and the Waning Light of Man by the 1st National Bank" (Dorn) **115**:120
"The sense of a Letter sent me, made into Verse" (Behn) **88**:148, 152
"The Sense of an Ending" (Graham) **59**:132, 149, 155-56, 179
The Sense of Movement (Gunn) **26**:181, 184-185, 188-189, 200-201, 206-207, 210, 212, 218-220, 230
"The Sense of the Sleight-of-Hand Man" (Stevens) **110**:202
A Sense of Time (Ungaretti)
See *Sentimento del tempo*
"Sensemayá" (Guillén) **23**:131-32, 134
"The Senses Loosely, or the Married Woman" (Waldrop) **109**:179
"Sensibility! O La!" (Roethke) **15**:257, 278, 299, 301
"The Sensitive Knife" (Stern) **115**:248
"The Sensitive Plant" (Shelley) **14**:167, 171, 175, 193, 196, 198
"The Sensualists" (Roethke) **15**:275
sent på jorden (Ekeloef) **23**:62, 75, 77, 88
"Sent to My Two Little Children in the East of Lu" (Li Po) **29**:146
"Sentado sobre un golfo de sombra" (Cernuda) **62**:238

"The Sentence" (Akhmatova)
See "Prigovor"
"The Sentence" (Creeley) **73**:108
"The Sentence" (Graves) **6**:157
"A Sentence for Tyranny" (Hass) **16**:248
Sentenced He Gives a Shape (Raworth) **107**:291
Sentenced to Death (Raworth) **107**:285, 290-91, 302, 304-10
"Sentences" (Milosz) **8**:189
"Sentences" (Parra)
See "Frases"
Sentences (Nemerov) **24**:288
"The Sententious Man" (Roethke) **15**:272, 278
"Les sentiers de la création" (Ponge) **107**:238
Les sentiers et les routes de la poésie (Éluard) **38**:78
"Le Sentiment de la nature" (Éluard) **38**:96
Sentiment of Time (Ungaretti)
See *Sentimento del tempo*
"Sentimental Colloquy" (Verlaine)
See "Colloque sentimental"
"The Sentimental Surgeon" (Page) **12**:176
"The Sentimentalist" (Moore) **49**:104, 109
"Sentimentalist's Song, or Answers for Everything" (Kennedy) **93**:144
Sentimento del tempo (Ungaretti) **57**:334, 338-39, 347, 358, 360, 375-76
"Sentiments for a Dedication" (MacLeish) **47**:165
"Sentries" (Masefield) **78**:100
"The Sentry" (Borges)
See "El centinela"
"The Sentry" (Owen) **102**:145, 150, 167, 246, 263
"Separate Lives" (Hacker) **47**:87
"The Separate Notebooks" (Milosz)
See "Osobny zeszyt"
The Separate Notebooks (Milosz) **8**:182, 195-97
The Separate Rose (Neruda)
See *La rosa separada: obra póstuma*
"The Separation" (Cowley) **90**:15
"Separation" (Merwin) **45**:8
"Separation" (Montague) **106**:240, 287-88, 311
"Separation" (Spender) **71**:186-87, 210, 227
Separations (Hacker) **47**:80, 104
"Les sept epées" (Apollinaire) **7**:46
"Les Sept poémes d'amour en guerre" (Éluard) **38**:79
"Les sept vieillards" (Baudelaire) **1**:45, 65, 70; **106**:97, 147, 156, 158-59
"September" (Belloc) **24**:29
"September" (Benn) **35**:9, 34, 66
"September" (Hughes) **7**:113, 118
"September" (Snodgrass) **74**:292
"September" (Zagajewski) **27**:396
"September 1, 1939" (Auden) **1**:14, 25; **92**:37, 58, 65, 105, 113-14, 129
"September 17" (Herbert) **50**:12-13
"September 22nd" (Kumin) **15**:190
"September, 1903" (Cavafy) **36**:41, 42
"September 1913" (Yeats) **20**:324-25
"September Afternoon in the Abandoned Barracks" (Zagajewski) **27**:391
"September Gale" (Holmes) **71**:68, 85
"September Garden Party" (Kenyon) **57**:40
"September in Great Yarmouth" (Mahon) **60**:134
"September in the Park" (Snodgrass) **74**:285, 300
"September Ode" (Hall) **70**:30
"September on Jessore Road" (Ginsberg) **4**:59
"September Salmon" (Hughes) **89**:135
"September Shooting" (Nemerov) **24**:288
"September Song" (Heaney) **100**:334
"September Twelfth, 2001" (Kennedy) **93**:154
"September Twilight" (Glück) **16**:170
"Septet for the End of Time" (Mackey) **49**:2, 77
Septet for the End of Time (Mackey) **49**:4-6, 17, 22
"Le Septiesme livre des poemes" (Ronsard) **11**:246
Le septiesme livre des poemes (Ronsard) **105**:244, 269, 274
Septimi Gadis (Horace) **46**:94
"Sepulchre" (Herbert) **4**:120
"The Sepulchre of the Books" (Very) **86**:57
Sequel to Drum-Taps (Whitman) **3**:418, 422
"A sequence" (Scalapino) **114**:275, 284
"Sequence" (Snodgrass) **74**:330
"Sequence" (Wylie) **23**:310, 315, 322
A Sequence for Francis Parkman (Davie) **29**:96, 98, 109
"A Sequence of Poems for H. D.'s Birthday" (Duncan) **75**:188, 198, 230, 239, 245
The Sequence on the Virgin Mary and Christ (Southwell) **83**:344
"Sequence, Sometimes Metaphysical" (Roethke) **15**:311
Sequences (Sassoon) **12**:247-48, 255, 257-60, 271
"Sequentia de Septem Doloribus Beatæ Virginis: A Patheticall Descant upon the Devout Plainsong of Stabat Mater Dolorosa. Sancta Maria Dolorum" (Crashaw)
See "Sancta Maria Dolorum"
"Sequoia" (Herbert) **50**:15
"La sera del dí di festa" (Leopardi) **37**:83, 102, 111, 124, 126-27, 130-31, 142
"Un Sera in San Pietro" (Carducci) **46**:49
"Sera nella valle del Màsino" (Quasimodo) **47**:279, 303
"The Seraphim" (Barrett Browning) **6**:6, 20, 22, 26-7
The Seraphim, and Other Poems (Barrett Browning) **6**:14-15, 19, 26, 29, 31-2; **62**:62
"Serata romana" (Pasolini) **17**:265
"Serenade" (Carducci)
See "Serenata"
"Serenade" (Chappell) **105**:50-52
"Sérénade" (Verlaine) **32**:388
"Serenade" (Viereck) **27**:263
"Serenade: Any Man to Any Woman" (Sitwell) **3**:309, 311, 314
"Serenata" (Carducci) **46**:50
"Serenata indiana" (Montale) **13**:107, 128
"Serene Words" (Mistral)
See "Palabras serenas"
"The Serepta Scold" (Masters)
See "Serepta the Scold"
"Serepta the Scold" (Masters) **36**:177, 181
"The Sergeant's Weddin'" (Kipling) **3**:164, 192
"Serious Reflections" (Prior) **102**:315
"A Serious Step Lightly Taken" (Frost) **1**:203
"Seriously Comma" (Cage) **58**:207
"Sermon for Our Maturity" (Baraka) **4**:19; **113**:21, 78
"A Sermon on Swift" (Clarke) **112**:60-61, 94
"A Sermon on the Warpland" (Brooks) **7**:63
Sermones (Horace) **46**:114
Sermones y prédicas del Cristo de Elqui (Parra) **39**:289-90, 292, 298-99, 303, 313
Sermons (Donne) **43**:115-17, 162, 173
Sermons and Homilies of the Christ of Elqui (Parra)
See *Sermones y prédicas del Cristo de Elqui*
"Le serpent" (Valéry)
See "Ébauche d'un serpent"
"Le serpent qui danse" (Baudelaire) **1**:62
"Le Serpent qui danse" (Char) **56**:197
The Serrated Wheel (Guillén)
See *La rueda dentada*
"Servant" (Thomas) **99**:237, 242
"Servant Boy" (Heaney) **100**:193-95, 297
"A Servant to Servants" (Frost) **1**:193, 228
"La servante au grand coeur" (Baudelaire) **1**:67-68; **106**:77
"Service" (Thomas) **99**:241
"Service Songs" (Kipling) **91**:69-70, 72, 171, 175-76
"Ses purs ongles très haut dèdiant leur onyx" (Mallarmé)
See "Sonnet en -yx"
"Sesenheimer Lyrik" (Goethe) **5**:245
"Śesh lekhā" (Tagore) **8**:424, 426-27
"A Session of the Poets" (Suckling) **30**:118, 121, 134, 144, 149, 155
"Sestina" (Bishop) **34**:58-59, 61, 76, 91, 120, 160, 165, 190, 192
"Sestina" (Curnow) **48**:29
"Sestina" (Eberhart) **76**:11
"Sestina" (Rukeyser) **12**:232
"Sestina" (Schuyler) **88**:180
"Sestina: Altaforte" (Pound) **4**:356;
"Sestina at 34" (Barker) **77**:10, 13
"Sestina for the Ladies of Tehuántepec" (Birney) **52**:41, 79, 98
"Sestina from the Home Gardener" (Wakoski) **15**:360
"Sestina of the Tramp Royal" (Kipling) **3**:160; **91**:88
"Sestina on Six Words by Kees" (Justice) **64**:253
Sestra moia zhizn (Pasternak) **6**:250-51, 254-55, 260, 263-65, 268-69, 271-72, 278-80, 282, 285
"Set by Mr. H. Lawes / A Dialogue between Lucasia and Orinda" (Philips) **40**:318
"Set of Country Songs" (Hardy) **8**:127
"A Set of Romantic Hymns" (Duncan) **2**:103
"Setting a Snare" (Wagoner) **33**:352
"The Setting Forth" (Masefield) **78**:90
"The Setting of the Moon" (Leopardi)
See "Il tramonto della luna"
"The Setting Sun" (Clare) **23**:40
"The Setting Sun. To Silvia" (Leapor) **85**:250
"The Settle Bed" (Heaney) **18**:259; **100**:253, 260, 322
"The Settler" (Kipling) **91**:143, 175
"The Settlers" (Atwood) **8**:12
"Seuil" (Char) **56**:106, 137-38, 141, 155, 190-91, 193-95, 200
"Un seul corps" (Éluard) **38**:61
"Le seul savant, c'est encore Moïse" (Verlaine) **2**:416
"Le seul témoin" (Bonnefoy) **58**:133, 173, 175
"Seule" (Éluard) **38**:75
"La seule, rose" (Bonnefoy) **58**:154
"Seulete suy et seulete vueil estre" (Christine de Pizan) **68**:18, 35, 81, 192
Seuls demeurent (Char) **56**:112, 131, 184-89
"Seurat's Sunday Afternoon along the Seine" (Schwartz) **8**:289-99, 317-18
"VII" (Joyce) **22**:136, 144, 167
"Seven" (Kinsella) **69**:130-31
"The Seven Ages" (Auden) **1**:39
"The Seven Arts" (Frost) **71**:24
"Seven Days for Eternity" (Elytis) **21**:123
"The Seven Deadly Sins" (Hecht) **70**:108
"7.IV.64" (Snyder) **21**:287
"Seven Lakes Canto" (Pound)
See "Canto 49"
"Seven Laments for the Fallen in the War" (Amichai) **38**:43
"Seven Laments for the War-Dead" (Amichai)
See "Seven Laments for the Fallen in the War"
"Les 7 500 000 oui (Publie en Mai 1870)" (Hugo) **17**:98
"Seven Moments of Love" (Hughes) **53**:99, 101
"Seven Moments of Love: An Un-Sonnet Sequence in Blues" (Hughes)
See "Seven Moments of Love"
"The Seven Old Men" (Baudelaire)
See "Les sept vieillards"
"Seven Poems" (Strand) **63**:177
Seven Poems and a Fragment (Yeats) **51**:108
"Seven Poems for Marthe, My Wife" (Rexroth) **20**:181
"Seven Poems for the Vancouver Festival" (Spicer) **78**:312
"The Seven Sages II" (Auden) **92**:65

"Seven Seals" (Lawrence) **54**:168
The Seven Seas (Kipling) **3**:159-62, 164, 167, 192-93; **91**:62-63, 66, 81, 84, 86-88
"Seven Songs for a Journey" (Wright) **14**:369
"Seven Songs Written during the Ch'ien-yüan Era while Staying at T'ung-ku-hsien" (Tu Fu) **9**:322
"Seven Sonnets" (Clough) **103**:99
"Seven Strophes" (Brodsky) **9**:22
"The Seven Swords" (Apollinaire)
See "Les sept epées"
"Seven Things" (Carman) **34**:210
"Seven Times" (Sexton) **79**:193
"Seven Years from Somewhere" (Levine) **22**:219
Seven Years from Somewhere (Levine) **22**:218-19, 234
"7.40 PM. JUNE 29th. 1970" (Raworth) **107**:275
The Seven-League Crutches (Jarrell) **41**:139, 194, 216-17
"Sevens (Version 3): In the Closed Iris of Creation" (Bell) **79**:32, 35
"XVII" (Joyce) **22**:136, 144, 164, 167
"Seventeen" (Zagajewski) **27**:389
"A Seventeen Morning" (Ammons) **16**:44
"1777" (Lowell) **13**:78, 84
"Seventeen Years" (Berry) **28**:9
"A Seventeenth Century Suite" (Duncan) **2**:115-16, 127
"Seventeenth Floor: Echoes of Singapore" (Creeley) **73**:93
"A Seventeenth-Century Suite in Homage to the Metaphysical Genius in English Poetry, 1590-1690" (Duncan) **75**:145, 171, 190, 223, 261
The Seventh and Last Canto of the Third Book of Gondibert, Never Yet Printed (Davenant) **99**:170, 173
"The Seventh Angel" (Herbert) **50**:3, 34
"Seventh Birthday of the First Child" (Olds) **22**:318
"Seventh Elegy" (Rilke) **2**:281, 286
"Seventh Gift of the Holy Ghost" (Melville) **82**:46
Seventh Isthmian (Pindar)
See *Isthmian 7*
Seventh Nemean (Pindar)
See *Nemean 7*
"Seventh Psalm" (Sexton) **2**:367; **79**:220, 232
"The Seventh Summer" (Levine) **22**:220
77 Dream Songs (Berryman) **64**:71, 121, 126, 128, 130-33, 141, 147, 164, 190, 192
73 Poems (Cummings) **5**:109-11
"Seven-year-old Poets" (Rimbaud)
See "Les poètes de sept ans"
Several Poems Compiled with Great Variety of Wit and Learning, Full of Delight (Bradstreet) **10**:43-5, 51
"Several Voices Out of a Cloud" (Bogan) **12**:100, 107, 124
A Severed Head (Montague) **106**:251, 266-67, 318, 340-42, 345-46
Severnaia simfoniia: Pervia geroicheskaia (Bely) **11**:3, 12-15, 21
"The Sévignés" (Spencer) **77**:326
"A Sewerplant Grows in Harlem or I'm a Stranger Here Myself When Does the Next Swan Leave?" (Lorde) **12**:158
"Sewing a dress" (Niedecker) **42**:100, 121
"Sex, like Desire" (Baraka) **113**:12
"Sex Manual" (Kennedy) **93**:131
"Sex without Love" (Olds) **22**:328-29, 339
"El sexo" (Aleixandre) **15**:34
"Sexsmith the Dentist" (Masters) **36**:233
"Sext" (Auden) **1**:23; **92**:16-18, 43
"Sextet" (Brodsky) **9**:19, 22
"Sexual Water" (Neruda)
See "Agua sexual"
"Sh, This Poem Wants to Say Something" (Ignatow) **34**:306
"ShááÁko Dahjinĺleh Remember the Things They Told Us" (Tapahonso) **65**:257
"Shack Dye" (Masters) **36**:183
Shackles (Césaire)
See *Ferrements*
"The Shad-Blow Tree" (Glück) **16**:126-27, 142
"Shade of Fonvizin" (Pushkin) **10**:408
"The Shade of the Queen Teaches Her Noblemen, What Is to be Thought of These Fleeting Things below" (Southwell) **83**:230
"The Shade-Catchers" (Mew) **107**:6, 22
Shades (McHugh) **61**:201
"The Shade-Seller" (Jacobsen) **62**:277, 320
The Shade-Seller: New and Selected Poems (Jacobsen) **62**:277, 286-87, 301, 304, 308-9, 317, 320
"Shadow" (de la Mare) **77**:115
"The Shadow" (Lowell) **13**:60-1, 83
"Shadow" (Stryk) **27**:201
"The Shadow" (Thomas) **99**:353-54
"Shadow and Shade" (Tate) **50**:231, 280
"The Shadow and the Light" (Whittier) **93**:347
"Shadow March" (Stevenson) **84**:312, 345
"Shadow: 1970" (Wright) **14**:371
The Shadow of Cain (Sitwell) **3**:320, 327
"The Shadow of Death" (Lawrence) **54**:244
"The Shadow of Fire" (Wright) **14**:376
The Shadow of Night: Containing Two Poeticall Hymnes (Chapman) **96**:7-8, 32-34, 55-57, 60-61, 67, 74-75, 77, 114, 120, 132
Shadow of Paradise (Aleixandre)
See *Sombra del paraíso*
"A Shadow Play for Guilt" (Piercy) **29**:309
"Shadow Suite" (Brathwaite) **56**:64
"The Shadow That Is Born with Us" (Howe) **81**:49
Shadow Train: Fifty Lyrics (Ashbery) **26**:151-152, 154, 166-167
"Shadow Wash" (Silverstein) **49**:347
"Shadow-Maker" (Swenson) **14**:261
"Shadows" (Duncan) **75**:232
"Shadows" (Stafford) **71**:275, 277-78, 280, 291
"Shadows" (Thomas) **99**:356
"Shadows" (Williams) **109**:275
"Shadows" (Winters) **82**:344
Shadows (Lawrence) **54**:203, 251
"Shadows in the Water" (Traherne) **70**:182, 185, 241, 245, 248-50, 253, 258, 288, 293, 320
"Shadows of Myself" (Cernuda) **62**:173
"Shadows of Taste" (Clare) **23**:14
"Shadows on the Wall" (Blok) **21**:14
The Shadowy Waters (Yeats) **20**:303, 353
"Shad-Time" (Wilbur) **51**:249, 310, 331
"The Shaft" (Tomlinson) **17**:342
The Shaft (Tomlinson) **17**:325-27, 334-36, 338, 342-43, 347, 350, 353-54
"Shah Akbar" (Whittier) **93**:176
"Shaker, Why Don't You Sing?" (Angelou) **32**:26-27
"Shakespeare" (Arnold) **5**:49
"Shakespeare" (Hardy) **92**:256, 322
"Shakespeare" (Pasternak) **6**:252
"Shakespeare in Harlem" (Hughes) **1**:239, 242, 246-47, 254-56, 268, 270; **53**:99-100, 171-73
Shakespeare in Harlem (Hughes) **53**:94, 98-100, 119, 137, 139, 173
"Shakespeare Say" (Dove) **6**:109
"A Shakespearean Sonnet: To a Woman Liberationist" (Knight) **14**:46
Shakespeare's Sonnets (Shakespeare)
See *Sonnets*
"Shaking" (Silverstein) **49**:333
"Shall I come, sweet love, to thee?" (Campion) **87**:13
"Shall I then hope" (Campion) **87**:59, 69-71
Shall We Gather at the River (Wright) **36**:294, 296, 299-300, 302, 304-6, 314, 317, 319, 325, 327, 329-30, 341, 342, 344-47, 350-51, 353-55, 358, 360, 363, 365-66, 368, 375, 391-92, 396, 399-400, 403
"The Shallot" (Wilbur) **51**:246, 282
"Shalom" (Levertov) **11**:170
Shalvah gedolah: She'elot utshuvot (Amichai) **38**:10, 19, 25-8, 36
"Shaman Mountain is High" (Li Ho) **13**:51
"Shame" (Mistral)
See "Desvelada"
"Shame" (Wilbur) **51**:266
"Shame Mi Lady" (Goodison) **36**:142, 150
"Shame on You" (Hughes) **53**:162
"The Shampoo" (Bishop) **34**:105, 146
"Shancoduff" (Kavanagh) **33**:70, 73, 77, 81, 83, 91, 99, 102, 147, 150; **105**:99, 108, 111, 134, 144-45
"Shango" (Brathwaite) **56**:61
"Shanna in the Sauna" (Silverstein) **49**:342
"Shantung, Or the Empire of China Is Crumbling Down" (Lindsay) **23**:265, 280
"Shape and Tonal Equilibrium" (Komunyakaa) **51**:62
"Shape of Boeotia" (Elytis) **21**:116
"The Shape of Death" (Swenson) **14**:286
"The Shape of the Fire" (Roethke) **15**:248, 254, 272, 274, 277, 282, 284-85, 287, 298
"Shape of the Invisible" (Randall) **86**:289
"The shapers: Vancouver" (Birney) **52**:36
"The Shapes of Death" (Spender) **71**:219
Shar (Brathwaite) **56**:43, 46, 71
"Sharecroppers" (Brown) **55**:167-69
"Shared Nights" (Éluard)
See "Nuits partagées"
"Sharing Eve's Apple" (Keats) **1**:311
"The Shark" (Oliver) **75**:293
"Shark Meat" (Snyder) **21**:292, 308
"The Shark: Parents and Children" (Wakoski) **15**:356
"The Shark's Parlor" (Dickey) **40**:183, 186, 213, 216, 221, 241, 254
"The Sharp Ridge" (Graves) **6**:156
"Sharpeville" (Brutus) **24**:117
Sharps and Flats (Tagore)
See *Kari o komal*
"Shatabdir surya" (Tagore) **8**:412
"Shatter Me, Music" (Rilke) **2**:275
"A Shattered Lute" (Meynell) **112**:162, 287, 295
"A Shawl" (Stein) **18**:328, 348
"She" (Roethke) **15**:275
"She" (Strand) **63**:161
"She" (Wilbur) **51**:235, 312
"She at His Funeral" (Hardy) **92**:250, 285
"She Being Brand-New" (Cummings) **5**:95
"She Belongs to Me" (Dylan) **37**:54
"She Bitches about Boys" (Hacker) **47**:79
"SHE CALLS ME ADONIS" (Bissett) **14**:32
"She Carries a 'Fat Gold Watch'" (Ondaatje) **28**:292
"She Cries" (Montague) **106**:282
"She Daydreams, By the Blue Pool" (Montague) **106**:241
"She Didn't Even Wave" (Ai) **72**:6
"She Does Not Fear Amorous Pain, But Rather Its End" (Stampa) **43**:296
"She Dreams" (Montague) **106**:241, 288
"She Had Some Horses" (Harjo) **27**:64-65
She Had Some Horses (Harjo) **27**:56-8, 60, 64-5
"She had tumult of the brain" (Niedecker) **42**:151
"She Has Given Me the Bullet" (Cohen) **109**:26
"She Hid in the Trees from the Nurses" (Wright) **36**:279, 335
"She Is Away" (Rexroth) **95**:258, 260, 273
"She Looks Back" (Lawrence) **54**:186
"She of All Time, All" (Éluard)
See "Celle de toujours, toute"
"She of the Dancing Feet Sings" (Cullen) **20**:63
"She Remembers the Future" (Harjo) **27**:56
"She Said . . ." (Smith) **12**:326
"She Said as Well to Me" (Lawrence) **54**:185-87, 239

"She Said Bread, Fred" (Raworth) **107**:274
"She Shall Be Called Woman" (Sarton) **39**:318-19, 325, 335, 337, 342, 354-56, 358
She Steals My Heart (Li Ho) **13**:44
"She Tells Her Love while Half Asleep" (Graves) **6**:144
"She Thinks of Him" (Li Po) **29**:176
"She, to Him" (Hardy) **8**:90
"She, to Him I" (Hardy) **92**:241, 248-50, 342
"She, to Him II" (Hardy) **92**:241, 248-50, 342
"She, to Him III" (Hardy) **92**:241, 248-50, 342
"She, to Him IV" (Hardy) **92**:241, 248-50, 342
"She Walks Alone" (Montague) **106**:241, 280, 288
"She Walks the Lady of My Delight" (Meynell) **112**:167
"She Was a Sinner" (Mew) **107**:11, 35
"She Weeps over Rahoon" (Joyce) **22**:137
"She Wept, She Railed, She Spurned the Meat" (Kunitz) **19**:151
"She Will Be One Day Free; He, Too Late, Repentant" (Stampa) **43**:296
"she won't ever forgive me" (Clifton) **17**:25
"She Writes" (Montague) **106**:311
"A Sheaf for Chicago" (Stryk) **27**:187, 195, 210, 214
"She'at ha-Hesed" (Amichai) **38**:19, 23-24
"The Sheaves" (Robinson) **1**:478
"Shee is admir'd" (Campion) **87**:35
"Sheela na Gig" (Montague) **106**:289
"Sheep" (Francis) **34**:255-56
"Sheep" (Sandburg) **41**:249
"The Sheep and the Dog" (Henryson) **65**:9, 17, 54, 61-62, 65, 81, 110
"The Sheep Child" (Dickey) **40**:153, 171-72, 176, 183, 221, 232, 248, 259
"A Sheep Fair" (Hardy) **8**:101
"Sheep in a Fog" (Plath) **1**:408-09; **37**:258, 260
"Sheep in the Rain" (Wright) **36**:378
"Sheep Trails Are Fateful to Strangers" (Spicer) **78**:242
"The Sheep Went On Being Dead" (Hughes) **7**:149
Sheepfold Hill: Fifteen Poems (Aiken) **26**:24
"Shell" (Sarton) **39**:368
"Shell" (Zagajewski) **27**:403
"Shelley" (Simic) **69**:278
"Shelley's Skylark" (Hardy) **92**:236, 255
"Shells" (Nemerov) **24**:299
"Shelter" (Erdrich) **52**:178
"Shelter from the Storm" (Dylan) **37**:55
"The Sheltered Edge" (Montague) **106**:226
"Sheltered Garden" (H. D.) **5**:269, 303
"Shem el Nessim" (Cavafy) **36**:53
"Shemselnihar" (Meredith) **60**:309
"Shenandoah" (Sandburg) **41**:270
"Shenendoah" (Shapiro) **25**:284-85
The Shepheardes Calender (Spenser)
See *The Shepheardes Calender: Conteyning Twelve Æglogues Proportionable to the Twelve Monethes*
The Shepheardes Calender: Conteyning Twelve Æglogues Proportionable to the Twelve Monethes (Spenser) **8**:326-28, 335, 385-87; **42**:266
"The Shepheards" (Vaughan) **81**:313
The Shepheards Garland (Drayton)
See *Idea. The Shepheards Garland, Fashioned in Nine Eglogs. Rowlands Sacrifice to the Nine Muses*
The Shepheards Sirena (Drayton) **98**:51, 77
"The Shepherd" (Blake) **12**:7, 32; **63**:6-7, 14-15, 49, 68, 70-71, 99-100, 113, 123-24
"The Shepherd" (Blunden) **66**:5
"Shepherd" (Brathwaite) **56**:74-75, 86
"The Shepherd" (H. D.) **5**:305
"The Shepherd" (Soto) **28**:371
"Shepherd and Goatherd" (Yeats) **51**:110
The Shepherd and Other Poems of Peace and War (Blunden) **66**:7, 17
"Shepherd Bound for Mountain Pass" (Aleixandre) **15**:12, 18
"A Shepherd in Lesbos" (Carman) **34**:208-09
"The Shepherdess" (Meynell) **112**:159-60, 164, 167, 190-91, 193, 202, 288, 295, 299
The Shepherdess and Other Verses (Meynell) **112**:159
The Shepherdess' Tale (Christine de Pizan)
See *Le dit de la pastoure*
"The Shepherd's Brow, Fronting Forked Lightning, Owns" (Hopkins) **15**:168
The Shepherd's Calendar, with Village Stories, and Other Poems (Clare) **23**:10, 16-21, 37-8, 40, 44
Shepherd's Home (Vigny) **26**:371
"The Shepherd's Praise of Diana" (Raleigh) **31**:260
"Sheridan at Cedar Creek" (Melville) **82**:117
Sherwood (Noyes) **27**:123
"She's All My Fancy Painted Him" (Carroll) **74**:69
"She's Awake" (Wright) **36**:304
"She's Free" (Harper) **21**:204
"She's Your Lover Now" (Dylan) **37**:66
"Shesh katha" (Tagore) **8**:407
Shesh saptak (Tagore) **8**:417
"The She-Wolf" (Spark) **72**:263
"Shiberia no uta" (Ishikawa) **10**:213
"The Shield of Achilles" (Auden) **1**:23; **92**:14-15, 17, 38, 43, 66, 129
The Shield of Achilles (Auden) **92**:66
"Shiftless" (Carver) **54**:32
"The Shih-men Monastery in the Lan-t'ien Mountains" (Wang Wei) **18**:378
"Shillin' a Day" (Kipling) **3**:191
"Shiloh" (Melville) **82**:99, 133, 135
"The Shimmer of Evil" (Roethke) **15**:278
"Shine" (Knight) **14**:49
"Shine, Perishing Republic" (Jeffers) **17**:107, 117-19, 132
"Ship" (Merwin) **45**:48
"Ship Near Shoals" (Wickham) **110**:311
"The Ship of Death" (Lawrence) **54**:172-73, 176, 178, 181, 187, 197-99, 201-3, 218, 226-27, 234, 250
"Ship of Fools" (MacLeish) **47**:246
"The Ship of the World" (Crane) **80**:69
"Shipbored" (Updike) **90**:350
"The Shipbuilders" (Whittier) **93**:172
"Shipbuilding Office" (Page) **12**:173, 176
"Shipman's" (Chaucer)
See "Shipman's Tale"
"Shipman's Tale" (Chaucer) **19**:13, 26; **58**:352
Shipovnik tsevetyot (Akhmatova) **2**:9
"Ships" (Masefield) **78**:11, 31, 90
Ships and Other Figures (Meredith) **28**:171, 173, 186-87, 189, 210, 217
"The Ships of Yule" (Carman) **34**:208
"Ships That Pass in the Night" (Dunbar) **5**:121
"The Shipwreck of Idomeneus" (Meredith) **60**:245, 293
"Shiraha no toribune" (Ishikawa) **10**:214
"Shiraz" (Hafiz) **116**:24
The Shires (Davie) **29**:116
Shirim, 1948-1962 (Amichai) **38**:23, 26-28, 32-33, 35-36, 44
"Shirley & Auden" (Berryman) **64**:75, 103
"The Shirt" (Kenyon) **57**:12, 46
"Shirt" (Pinsky) **27**:158, 164-65, 176
"Shirt" (Simic) **69**:269
"The Shirt Poem" (Stern) **115**:251
"Shit" (Bell) **79**:3
"Shit" (Serote) **113**:293-94
"Shitsurakuen" (Nishiwaki) **15**:237, 239
"Shiv and the Grasshopper" (Kipling) **3**:183
"Shizumeru kane" (Ishikawa) **10**:214
"The Shoals Returning" (Kinsella) **69**:66, 68, 73, 80, 84-85, 88-89, 91, 102-3
"The Shoemakers" (Whittier) **93**:172
"Shoes" (Raworth) **107**:275
"The Shoes of Wandering" (Kinnell) **26**:243, 249, 266, 272-73
"Shoot It Jimmy" (Williams) **7**:383
"Shoot the Buffalo" (Momaday) **25**:214
"A Shooting Incident" (Smith) **12**:318, 346
"The Shooting of Dan McGrew" (Service) **70**:115, 139, 148, 155, 163-66
"Shooting Script" (Rich) **5**:366-67, 378, 383, 396-97
"Shooting the Girl" (Dafydd ap Gwilym)
See "Saethu'r Ferch"
"Shootings of the Third of May" (Heaney) **18**:205; **100**:225
"Shop" (Browning) **2**:59
"Shopping and Waiting" (Schuyler) **88**:200
"Shopping at Oxford" (Masefield) **78**:91
"The Shore" (Clampitt) **19**:90
"Shore Piece" (Ciardi) **69**:34
"Shore Woman" (Heaney) **100**:202
"Shoreline" (Heaney) **18**:201, 203
"Shoreline Horses" (Ríos) **57**:323
"Shores" (Montale)
See "Riviere"
"The Shorewatchers' House" (Montale) **13**:150
"The Short End" (Hecht) **70**:67, 75, 79, 86
"A Short Film" (Hughes) **89**:162
"A Short History of Bill Berkson" (O'Hara) **45**:142
"The Short Life of Kazuo Yamamoto" (Enright) **93**:5, 18
"A Short Note to My Very Critical and Well-Beloved Friends and Comrades" (Jordan) **38**:117
"Short Ode" (Benét) **64**:14-15
"A Short Ode to a Philologist" (Auden) **92**:69
"Short Poem" (Sanchez) **9**:212, 223
Short Poems (Berryman) **64**:81-90
Short Prose Poems (Baudelaire)
See *Le spleen de Paris, petits poèmes en prose*
"A Short Recess" (Milosz) **8**:183, 186
"A Short Song of Congratulation" (Johnson) **81**:116, 235, 241, 246-48
Short Songs of Pure Feelings (Hagiwara)
See *Junjo shokyoku shu*
"A Short Speech to My Friends" (Baraka) **113**:136, 139
"Short Summary" (Bogan) **12**:101
Short Talks (Carson) **64**:210, 216, 236
"Short Thoughts for Long Nights" (Warren) **37**:380
"Short Version of Ecstasy" (Bell) **79**:35
"Short Views in Africa" (Jacobsen) **62**:308, 317
Short Wave (Szirtes) **51**:158-59
Shorter Poems (Bridges) **28**:52-3, 67, 69, 82-3
Shorter Poems (Rexroth)
See *The Collected Shorter Poems*
Shorter Poems (Schwerner)
See *Selected Shorter Poems*
"The Shorter View" (Kennedy) **93**:139-40, 149
"Shorts" (Auden) **92**:66
"The Shot" (Graves) **6**:143-44
"The Shot" (Hughes) **89**:271
"The Shot" (Pushkin)
See "Vystrel"
Shot of Love (Dylan) **37**:65
"Should lanterns shine" (Thomas) **52**:237
"Should the Wide World Roll Away" (Crane) **80**:80
"Should We Legalize Abortion" (O'Hara) **45**:226
"A Shout after Hard Work" (Kinsella) **69**:116
"The Shovel Man" (Sandburg) **2**:332; **41**:226, 296, 321, 365
"The Show" (Owen) **19**:327, 336-37, 341, 343-44, 347, 353, 355, 359; **102**:167, 169-72, 203, 263
"The Shower" (Riley) **48**:293
"Shower" (Swift)
See "A Description of a City Shower"
"The Shower" (Vaughan) **81**:274-75
"A Shower in War-Time" (Dobell) **100**:139
"The Shower of Secret Things: 3" (Mackey) **49**:3
"Showing How to Make the Right Kind of a Man Out of the Right Kind of a Boy"

(Riley) **48**:304
"The Showings; Lady Julian of Norwich, 1342-1416" (Levertov) **11**:210
"The Shrike" (Thoreau) **30**:184
"The Shrine" (H. D.) **5**:270
"The Shrivers" (Jacobsen) **62**:323
A Shropshire Lad (Housman) **2**:159-67, 171-78, 180-81, 183-84, 186-88, 191-95, 197, 199-200; **43**:210-17, 219, 222-23, 225-28, 231-47, 249-53, 256, 258-62, 264-68, 271-74
"The Shroud" (Millay) **6**:205
"The Shroud of Color" (Cullen) **20**:52, 54-55, 57, 62, 64, 67, 69, 73, 84
"Shrubs Burned Away" (Hall)
See "Shrubs Burnt Away"
"Shrubs Burnt Away" (Hall) **70**:19-21
"Shūchō" (Ishikawa) **10**:212
Shukumei (Hagiwara) **18**:176
"Shun Not the Strife" (Service) **70**:153
"The Shunamite" (Duck) **89**:11, 35, 66-67, 86
"The Shunammite" (Duck)
See "The Shunamite"
Shundeishū (Yosano) **11**:305
"Shun'ya" (Hagiwara) **18**:181
"Shut, Bellada" (Bely) **11**:24
"Shut Nad ney" (Bely) **11**:24
"Shut Out" (Rossetti) **7**:280
"Shut Out That Moon" (Hardy) **92**:295
"Shut out That Moon" (Winters) **82**:337
"Shut: Plamen" (Bely) **11**:24
"Shutka" (Bely) **11**:24
"The Shutter, Followed by Its Explication" (Ponge)
See "Le Volet, suivi de sa scholie"
"Shuttles" (Swenson) **14**:273
Shyamali (Tagore) **8**:417
"Shylock" (Shapiro) **25**:283
"Si acaso, Fabio mío" (Juana Inés de la Cruz) **24**:180, 184, 187
"Si al mecer las azules campanillas" (Bécquer)
See *see "Rima 16"*
"Sì, ancora la neve" (Zanzotto) **65**:266-67, 276, 310, 314, 316-17, 321
"Si come leuar, donna, si pone" (Michelangelo)
See "Si come per levar, donna, si pone"
"Si come nella penna e nell'inchiostro" (Michelangelo) **103**:190, 192, 293-94
"Si come per levar, donna, si pone" (Michelangelo) **103**:189, 344
"Si daros los buenos años" (Juana Inés de la Cruz) **24**:180
"Si el desamor o el enojo" (Juana Inés de la Cruz) **24**:186, 234
"Si el Papa no rompe con el USA" (Parra) **39**:275, 311
"Si es amor causa productiva" (Juana Inés de la Cruz) **24**:189
"Si . . . Genuflexion comme à l'eblouissant" (Mallarmé) **102**:20, 22
"Si j'étais petit oiseau" (Béranger) **112**:11
"Si los riesgos del mar cpmsoderara" (Juana Inés de la Cruz) **24**:225
"Si Quisquam Mutus Gratum Acciptumve Sepuleris" (Carson) **64**:224
"Si tu aimes" (Éluard) **38**:74
"Si tú supiera" (Guillén)
See "Ay negra, si tu supiera"
"Si yo fuera presidente de Chile" (Parra) **39**:272
"Siberian note" (Char)
See "Note sibérienne"
"Siberian Wooing" (Yevtushenko) **40**:366
"Sibir" (Tsvetaeva) **14**:326
"Sibling Mysteries" (Rich) **5**:373, 384
"Sibrandus Schafnaburgensis" (Browning) **2**:59
"A Sibyl" (Atwood) **8**:25
"Sibyl of the Wall" (Jones) **116**:118
"Sibyl Warns Her Sister" (Spencer)
See "Letter to My Sister"
Sibylline Leaves (Coleridge) **11**:57, 60, 97, 115; **100**:20-24, 26, 56, 65
"Sibyl's Leaves" (Hopkins)
See "Spelt from Sibyl's Leaves"
"Sibyl's Morning" (Montague) **106**:314
"Sic Transit" (Lowell) **3**:213
"Sic Vita" (Thoreau) **30**:188-89, 258, 275, 293
"Siccome nella penna e nell'inchiostro" (Michelangelo)
See "Si come nella penna e nell'inchiostro"
"Sicilia e la Rivoluzione" (Carducci) **46**:5, 51, 56
"Sicilian Cyclamens" (Lawrence) **54**:187
"The Sick" (Page) **12**:176
"Sick" (Silverstein) **49**:310
"Sick African" (Williams) **109**:259
"Sick at Summer's End" (Kenyon) **57**:29, 34
"A Sick Bed" (Bryant) **20**:17, 46
"Sick Call" (Montague) **106**:310
"The Sick Child" (Glück) **16**:132, 136, 138
"A Sick Child" (Jarrell) **41**:171, 174
"The Sick King in Bokhara" (Arnold) **5**:6, 39, 49
"Sick Leave" (Sassoon) **12**:267, 288
"Sick Love" (Graves) **6**:136-37, 142, 144, 151, 169
"The Sick Muse" (Baudelaire)
See "La muse malade"
"The Sick Rose" (Blake) **12**:7; **63**:16, 24-26, 68, 70, 106, 120
"The Sick Wife" (Kenyon) **57**:21, 25-26, 44, 48
"The Sick-Bed of Cuchulain" (Clarke) **112**:78
"Sickly Face at the Bottom of the Ground" (Hagiwara) **18**:175
"Sickness" (Akhmadulina)
See "Bolezn"
"Sickness" (Ransom) **61**:294
"Sickness and Schooling" (Jackson) **44**:63
"The Sickness of Kleitos" (Cavafy) **36**:34, 75, 79, 109
"The Sickness unto Death" (Sexton) **2**:372; **79**:216, 221-22, 237
"Side by Side" (Brown) **55**:168
"Sideboard" (Rimbaud)
See "Le buffet"
Sidestreets (Tsvetaeva)
See *Pereulochki*
Siding with Things (Ponge) **107**:245
"Sie erlischt" (Heine) **25**:178
"Sie haben wegen der Trunkenheit" (Heine) **25**:162
"Siede" (Stramm) **50**:168, 176, 194, 202
"The Siege of Mullingar" (Montague) **106**:277, 279, 293, 307, 337
"Siegfried" (Jarrell) **41**:169, 178, 203, 218
"Siegmund Freud" (Parra) **39**:274-75, 287
"Siempre aguarda mi sangre" (Guillén) **35**:229
"Siena mi fe'; disfecemi Maremma" (Pound) **4**:319
"Sierra" (Guillén) **35**:231
"Sierra" (Storni) **33**:270
"Sierra Nevada" (Cardenal) **22**:125, 131
"Siesta" (Storni) **33**:254-55
"Siesta: Barbados" (Kenyon) **57**:45
Siete poemas (Borges) **32**:61-2
"A Sigh" (Finch) **21**:141
"The Sigh" (Hardy) **8**:104
"Sigh" (Mallarmé)
See "Soupir"
"Sigh No More" (Lawrence) **54**:184
"The Sigh That Heaves the Grasses" (Housman) **2**:183, 191
"Sighs and Groans" (Herbert)
See "Sighs and Grones"
"Sighs and Grones" (Herbert) **4**:120, 133-34,
"Sighs are my food, drink are my tears" (Wyatt) **27**:369
"Sight" (Parker) **28**:365
"Sight of the Hills from the Kozłowa Steppes" (Mickiewicz)
See "Widok gór ze stepów Kozłowa"
"The Sight of the Ocean" (Very) **86**:54
"Sightseeing on a Winter Day" (Wang Wei) **18**:373
"Sigma" (Tolson) **88**:241-42, 257, 277, 281, 304, 324-25
"Sign" (Apollinaire)
See "Signe"
"A Sign" (Enright) **93**:25
"A Sign" (de la Mare) **77**:64
"The Sign" (Masters) **1**:333, 337
"The Sign in My Father's Hands" (Espada) **74**:147
"The Sign of Saturn" (Olds) **22**:324
"The Sign of the Golden Shoe" (Noyes) **27**:124
Sign towards the long way round (Char)
See *Placard pour un chemin des écoliers*
"The Signal" (MacLeish) **47**:197
"Signal" (Silverstein) **49**:334
"Signal" (Stramm) **50**:176
"Signal" (Tzara) **27**:229-31
"The Signal from the House" (Kunitz) **19**:172-73
"The Signature" (Jackson) **44**:74
"Signature for Tempo" (MacLeish) **47**:127, 156, 185, 197
"The Signature of All Things" (Rexroth) **20**:196, 217; **95**:260, 262-63, 292, 321, 324-26, 347
The Signature of All Things: Poems, Songs, Elegies, Translations, and Epigrams (Rexroth) **20**:181, 183-84, 192-94, 203; **95**:254, 257-58, 272, 332-33
"Signe" (Apollinaire) **7**:44, 48
"The Significance of Veteran's Day" (Ortiz) **17**:226, 232
"The Signifying Monkey" (Knight) **14**:49
"Signing the Pledge" (Harper) **21**:191
"Signior Dildo" (Wilmot) **66**:234, 329
"A Signiture. A Herold. A Span" (Brooks) **7**:90
"La Signorina Felicita" (Gozzano) **10**:176-77, 180-83
"Signpost" (Jeffers) **17**:129, 131, 145
"The Sign-Post" (Thomas) **53**:270, 332
"Signs" (Merwin) **45**:16
"Signs and Tokens" (Hardy) **8**:111
"Signs of Winter" (Clare) **23**:28
"A Sign-Seeker" (Hardy) **92**:289
"Sigue" (Guillén) **23**:142
"Sigurd rideth with the Niblungs, and wooeth Brynhild for King Gunnar" (Morris) **55**:334
Sigurd the Volsung (Morris) **55**:260, 262, 273, 277, 324, 328-30, 332-35, 337-41, 262261
"Silas Dement" (Masters) **36**:231
"Die silbe schmerz" (Celan) **10**:102, 105
"The Silence" (Berry) **28**:5, 7, 43
"Silence" (Eliot) **5**:217
"Silence" (Hood) **93**:78, 117, 119
"Silence" (Lawrence) **54**:167, 250
"Silence" (Masters) **1**:325, 333, 342
"Silence" (Moore) **49**:100
"The Silence" (Sarton) **39**:328, 369
"Silence" (Traherne) **70**:222, 259, 268-69, 315
"Silence" (Wright) **14**:342
"Silence, and stealth of days" (Vaughan) **81**:306, 326
"Silence and Tears" (Smith) **12**:341
"The Silence Answered Him Accusingly" (Schwartz) **8**:293
"Silence de l'Evangile" (Éluard) **38**:70
Silence in the Snowy Fields (Bly) **39**:3, 5-6, 8-15, 17, 19, 22, 24, 37, 42, 48-9, 52-3, 64, 67, 69-71, 73-6, 78-87, 89-91, 94, 98-100, 102-03, 115
Silence: Lectures and Writings (Cage) **58**:193-95, 198, 203-4, 221, 224
"The Silence Now" (Sarton) **39**:369
The Silence Now (Sarton) **39**:347-50, 360, 362-63, 368-69
"The Silence of Plants" (Szymborska)
See "Milczenie roslin"
The Silence of the Sea (Mickiewicz) **38**:158
"The Silence of Tudor Evans" (Ackerley) **41**:19, 25
A Silence Opens (Clampitt) **19**:100-01

"Silence Wager Stories" (Howe) **54**:87-88, 106-7
"Silences: Lament of the Silent Sisters" (Okigbo) **7**:225, 228, 234, 244-47, 251
"¡Silencio!" (Castro) **41**:115
"The Silent Angel" (Wright) **36**:311, 369
"The Silent Battle" (Teasdale) **31**:360
"Silent Faces at Crossroads" (Okigbo) **7**:255
"Silent in America" (Levine) **22**:212, 222
"Silent Love" (Mistral)
See "El amor que calla"
"Silent Noon" (Rossetti) **44**:174
"Silent Poem" (Francis) **34**:244, 249, 252
"Silent Service" (Sassoon) **12**:252
"Silent Sisters" (Okigbo)
See "Silences: Lament of the Silent Sisters"
"The Silent Slain" (MacLeish) **47**:186, 197
Silex Scintillans; or, Sacred Poems and Private Ejaculations; by Henry Vaughan, Silurist (Vaughan) **81**:258-59, 262, 264, 272, 286, 294-98, 300, 304-5, 308, 310, 312-14, 317, 320-25, 330, 332, 335-43, 346-49, 351, 353-55, 357, 359-60, 364-70
"Silhouette of a Serpent" (Valéry)
See "Ébauche d'un serpent"
"Silk of a Soul" (Herbert)
See "Jedwab duszy"
"The Silken Tent" (Frost) **1**:196, 214
"Silly boy" (Campion) **87**:58, 69, 71-72
"Silly Sallie" (de la Mare) **77**:112
"Silly Song" (García Lorca)
See "Canción tonta"
"Silos" (Dove) **6**:120
"Silver" (Ammons) **16**:5
"Silver" (de la Mare) **77**:112
"Silver and Gold" (Clarke) **112**:83
"The Silver Bird of Herndyke Mill" (Blunden) **66**:5
"Silver Filigree" (Wylie) **23**:314, 322, 332
"The Silver Flask" (Montague) **106**:319
"The Silver Lily" (Glück) **16**:170
"Silver Star" (Hugo) **68**:250
"The Silver Swan" (Rexroth) **20**:221;
"The Silver Tassie" (Burns) **6**:97
"A Silvia" (Carducci) **46**:63
"A Silvia" (Leopardi) **37**:102, 109, 120-21, 123-24, 141
"Silvia and the Bee" (Leapor) **85**:250-51
"Silvio's Complaint" (Behn) **88**:150, 163-64
"Simaetha" (H. D.) **5**:266
"Simeon" (Cavafy) **36**:40, 104
Simfonija (1-aga) (Bely)
See *Severnaia simfoniia: Pervia geroicheskaia*
Simfonija (2-aja) (Bely)
See *Vtoraia simfoniia: Dramaticheskaia*
"Simile" (Prior) **102**:306
"A Simile for Her Smile" (Wilbur) **51**:188, 193, 209
"Simkin, Tomkin and Jack" (Masefield) **78**:45
"Simon" (Wright) **36**:313
"Simon Lee" (Wordsworth) **4**:374, 416-17, 425-26, 428; **67**:277-78, 282, 300, 310, 328, 330, 340, 359, 367-68
"Simon Lee, the Old Huntsman" (Wordsworth)
See "Simon Lee"
"Simon Legree" (Lindsay) **23**:264, 269, 273, 287
"Simon Surnamed Peter" (Masters) **1**:325, 342
"Simon the Cyrenian Speaks" (Cullen) **20**:56, 65
"Simple agonie" (Laforgue) **14**:73
"Simple Autumnal" (Bogan) **12**:87-8, 106, 121
"Simple Frescoes" (Verlaine)
See "Simples Fresques"
A Simple Lust: Selected Poems Including Sirens, Knuckles, Boots; Letters to Martha; Poems from Algiers, Thoughts Abroad (Brutus) **24**:113-16, 118
"A Simple Recipe" (Riley) **48**:304
"Simple Sonatina" (Gallagher) **9**:60
"A Simple Tale" (Clarke) **112**:62
The Simple Truth (Levine) **22**:228, 232-33
"Simple Twist of Fate" (Dylan) **37**:56
"Simples Fresques" (Verlaine) **32**:402
"Simple-Song" (Piercy) **29**:309
"Simplex Munditiis" (Winters) **82**:326, 336-37
"Simplicity" (Pavese)
See "Semplicità"
"Simplicity" (Stone) **53**:224
Simplicity (Stone) **53**:220-21, 223-25, 243, 251-54, 256, 258
"Simplify Me When I'm Dead" (Douglas) **106**:198
"Simposio" (Parra) **39**:272
"Sin" (Herbert)
See "Sinne"
Sin (Ai) **72**:21-25
"Sin I" (Herbert)
See "Sinne (1)"
"Sin lamento" (Guillén) **35**:174
"Sin nido" (Castro) **41**:113, 116
"Sinaloa" (Birney) **52**:36-37, 44, 46, 97
"Since 1619" (Walker) **20**:275, 283
"Since Death Brushed Past Me" (Teasdale) **31**:372
"Since I am comming" (Donne)
See "Hymne to God my God, in my sicknesse"
"Since Nine O'Clock" (Cavafy) **36**:109
"Since she whom I loved" (Donne) **43**:160
"Since Then" (Enright) **93**:32
"Since There is no Escape" (Teasdale) **31**:360
"Since Volume One" (Waldrop) **109**:179
"Since we loved" (Bridges) **28**:86
"Since ye delight to know" (Wyatt) **27**:353
"Since You've Come" (Baca) **41**:47
"Sindhu-taranga" (Tagore) **8**:407
"Sinew" (Carver) **54**:14
"Sinfonía en gris mayor" (Darío) **15**:93, 96
"Sinful City" (Seifert)
See "Hříšné město"
"Sing" (Raworth) **107**:276
"Sing a Song o' Shipwreck" (Masefield) **78**:68, 70
"Sing a song of joy" (Campion) **87**:55, 65
"Sing the Rat" (Hughes) **89**:189
"Singapore" (Gilmore) **87**:303
"Singapore" (Oliver) **75**:295-96
"The Singer" (Guillén) **35**:158
"The Singer" (Levertov) **11**:183
"The Singer" (Tsvetaeva)
See "Pevitsa"
"The Singer" (Whittier) **93**:215
"The Singer" (Wickham) **110**:263, 277
"A Singer Asleep" (Hardy) **8**:125; **92**:233-34, 238, 255
"The Singer in the Prison" (Whitman) **91**:214
"Singers" (Hughes) **7**:123
"The Singers" (Longfellow) **30**:103
"Singers of Provence" (Ignatow) **34**:314, 323
"Singers to Come" (Meynell) **112**:192, 228, 230, 285-86
"Singing" (Stevenson) **84**:314, 342
"Singing Aloud" (Kizer) **66**:70, 74, 79-80
"Singing Nigger" (Sandburg) **2**:316
"Singing School" (Heaney) **18**:205; **100**:224-25, 266-67, 272, 351
"Singladura" (Borges) **32**:125
"Single Sonnet" (Bogan) **12**:90, 107
"Single Vision" (Kunitz) **19**:154
"Singling & Doubling Together" (Ammons) **16**:63-4
Sing-Song: A Nursery Rhyme-Book (Rossetti) **7**:291
Singularities (Howe) **54**:79, 81-82, 84, 88, 92-93, 95, 97, 100, 110-14, 124-28, 130-31, 133-34, 136-37
"Sinistre" (Valéry) **9**:359, 381, 399-401
The Sinking of the Titanic (Enzensberger)
See "Der Untergand der Titanic"
"The Sinking Ship" (Rimbaud)
See "L'eclatante victoire de Saarebrück"
"Sinne" (Herbert) **4**:100
"Sinne (1)" (Herbert) **4**:130
"Sinners" (Lawrence) **54**:187
"Sinners in the Hands of an Angry God" (Lowell) **3**:203
"Sinnsear: Kindred" (Montague) **106**:357
"Sin's Heavy Load" (Southwell) **83**:239, 284-85, 326
"The Sins of Kalamazoo" (Sandburg) **2**:308; **41**:246, 254, 298, 314
"Sin's Round" (Herbert) **4**:114
"Sion" (Herbert) **4**:100
"Siostra" (Herbert) **50**:37
Sir Eustace Grey (Crabbe) **97**:90, 102, 119
"Sir Federigo's Falcon" (Longfellow)
See "The Falcon of Ser Federigo"
"Sir Galahad" (Masters) **1**:330, 333
"Sir Galahad" (Tennyson) **6**:359
"Sir Galahad: A Christmas Mystery" (Morris) **55**:238, 240, 300, 302, 348-51
"Sir Gawain and the Green Knight" (Anonymous)
See *Sir Gawain and the Green Knight*
Sir Gawain and the Green Knight (Anonymous) **76**:146-335
"Sir Hubert" (Patmore)
See "The Falcon"
"Sir James South Side" (Cisneros) **52**:157
"Sir Jhon Sinclair Begowthe to Dance" (Dunbar) **67**:4, 8
"Sir John Herschel Remembers" (Noyes) **27**:129
"Sir, more then kisses" (Donne) **43**:108
"Sir Peter Harpdon's End" (Morris) **55**:238, 258, 301
Sir Proteus: A Satirical Ballad (Peacock) **87**:333, 351
"Sir Richard's Song" (Kipling) **91**:109
"Sir Thopas" (Chaucer)
See "The Tale of Sir Thopas"
"Sir William Herschel's Long Year" (Hope) **56**:291
"Sir William Treloar's Dinner for Crippled Children" (Blunden) **66**:26
"Sire" (Merwin) **45**:8, 24
"Siren" (Birney) **52**:83
"Siren Limits" (Okigbo) **7**:240-46
"Siren Song" (Atwood) **8**:23, 25-6, 41
"La sirena" (Storni) **33**:294
"The Sirens" (Kennedy) **93**:147, 149
"Sirens, Knuckles, Boots" (Brutus) **24**:98-9, 112-13, 119
"The Sirens' Welcome to Cronos" (Graves) **6**:144, 146
"Sirius" (Tuckerman) **85**:309
"Sirmione" (Carducci) **46**:52
"Sirocco" (Montale)
See "Scirocco"
"Sister Act" (Jacobsen) **62**:325
"A Sister by the Pond" (Hall) **70**:10, 34
"Sister Helen" (Rossetti) **44**:167, 202
"Sister Lou" (Brown) **55**:108, 115, 153, 176
"Sister Maude" (Rossetti) **7**:260, 270, 272-3, 276, 280
"A Sister on the Tracks" (Hall) **70**:16, 34
"Sister Water" (Warren) **37**:313
"The Sisters" (Crabbe) **97**:123
"The Sisters" (Jacobsen) **62**:320, 324
"The Sisters" (Lowell) **13**:67
"The Sisters" (Whittier) **93**:248-49
The Sisters: A Tragedy (Swinburne) **24**:348-50, 352
"Sisters in Arms" (Lorde) **12**:141, 151-53
"Sisters in the Fog" (Baraka) **113**:20
The Sisters: New and Selected Poems (Jacobsen) **62**:307-9, 315-19
"Sisters of Charity" (Rimbaud)
See "Les soeurs de charité"
"Sitcom on the Greyhound in Rutland, Vermont" (Stone) **53**:258
"Site of Ambush" (Ní Chuilleanáin) **34**:360, 381

Site of Ambush (Ní Chuilleanáin) **34**:350, 359, 381
"Sit-Ins" (Walker) **20**:276
"The Sitter" (Silverstein) **49**:333
"The Sitting" (Day Lewis) **11**:147
"The Sitting" (McGuckian) **27**:101
"Sitting Alone" (Masefield) **78**:92
"Sitting Alone on an Autumn Night" (Wang Wei) **18**:388
"Sitting on a Gulf of Shadow" (Cernuda) See "Sentado sobre un golfo de sombra"
"The Situation in the West Followed by a Holy Proposal" (Ferlinghetti) **1**:172
The Situation of Poetry: Contemporary Poetry and Its Traditions (Pinsky) **27**:143, 153, 160, 162, 173
"Situations" (Raworth) **107**:276
"S.I.W." (Owen) **19**:354, 357, 369, 371; **102**:148, 181, 188, 202, 230, 265
"VI" (Joyce) **22**:136, 138, 145, 160, 167, 173
"The Six" (Randall) **86**:291
Six and One Remorses for the Sky (Elytis) **21**:118, 122, 124, 133
Six Books of Latin Verse (Cowley) See *Poemata Latina*
"Six Brothers" (Cisneros) **52**:160
"Six Casually Written Poems" (Wang Wei) **18**:388
"Six Days" (Raworth) **107**:273-74, 324
Six Epistles to Eva Hesse (Davie) **29**:99-100, 102, 104, 109
"Six Lectures in Verse" (Milosz) **8**:199-200, 202-03, 211
Six Moral Tales from Jules Laforgue (Laforgue) See *Moralités légendaires*
"Six O'Clock in Princes Street" (Owen) **19**:342; **102**:203
Six Odes (Auden) **1**:8
Six Plays (MacLeish) **47**:208, 211
Six Poems (Muir) **49**:239-40
"Six Poems Matching Poems Expressing Kumagori's Feelings" (Yakamochi) See "Tsutsushimite Kumagori no tame ni sono kokorozashi wo noburu uta ni kotauru rokushu"
"Six Poems to Tamar" (Amichai) **38**:14-15
"Six Poets in Search of a Lawyer" (Hall) **70**:31
Six Quatrains Composed in Jest (Tu Fu) **9**:327
"Six Religious Lyrics" (Shapiro) **25**:320
"Six Sentences" (Clarke) **112**:78
"Six Songs for Chloe" (Hope) **56**:302, 305
"Six Variations" (Levertov) **11**:183
"Six Views from the Same Window of the Northside Grocery" (Dorn) **115**:126
"The Six Who Were Hanged" (Melville) **82**:9, 28-29, 34, 38, 44, 53-54
"Six Winter Privacy Poems" (Bly) **39**:27, 71-2
"Six Years Later" (Brodsky) **9**:7, 8, 19, 26
"Six Years Later" (Wilbur) **51**:249
"Six Young Men" (Hughes) **7**:113
"Six-Bit Blues" (Hughes) **1**:256
"The 6:40 from Amiens Street" (Kavanagh) **105**:164
Le sixiesme livre des poemes (Ronsard) **105**:274
"Six-Sided Square: Actopan" (Birney) **52**:28, 36, 79, 95-96
"XVI" (Joyce) **22**:145, 162, 170
"1614 Boren" (Hugo) **68**:281-82, 285
"Sixteen Haiku" (Seferis) **66**:206
"Sixteen Months" (Sandburg) **41**:296
Sixteen Poems (Justice) **64**:249
"16.ix.65" (Merrill) **28**:220
"The Sixteenth Floor" (Lowell) **13**:97
"Sixth Elegy" (Rilke) **2**:273
"Sixth Elegy. River Elegy" (Rukeyser) **12**:231-32
Sixth Isthmian (Pindar) See *Isthmian 6*
Sixth Olympian (Pindar) See *Olympian 6*
"Sixth Psalm" (Sexton) **79**:220
Sixth Pythian (Pindar) See *Pythian 6*
65 Poems (Celan) **10**:120
"61 and Some" (Updike) **90**:359
Sixty-Two Mesostics re: Merce Cunningham (Cage) **58**:182-83, 218
"The Size" (Herbert) **4**:100, 108
"Size and Tears" (Carroll) **18**:46
"The Size of a Fist" (Stafford) **71**:372
"S.K." (Thomas) **99**:321, 324
"Skateboard" (Gunn) **26**:215
"The Skaters" (Ashbery) **26**:107, 114, 129, 143, 151, 154-156
"The Skaters" (Jarrell) **41**:127, 158
Skazka dlya detey (Lermontov) **18**:282, 303
"Skazka o dozhde" (Akhmadulina) **43**:2-11, 13-16, 33
"Skazka o Mertvoy Tsarevne" (Pushkin) **10**:382
"Skazka o Pope i o Rabotnike Yego Balde" (Pushkin) **10**:382
"Skazka o Rybake i Rybke" (Pushkin) **10**:382
"Skazka o Tsare Sultane" (Pushkin) **10**:381-83
"Skazka o Zolotom Petushke" (Pushkin) **10**:382-83
"Skazki" (Pushkin) **10**:408
Skazki (Pushkin) **10**:381-86
"Skeats and the Industrial Revolution" (Berrigan) **103**:26
Skeeters Kirby (Masters) **36**:188
"Skeleton Crow" (Szirtes) **51**:158
"The Skeleton in Armor" (Longfellow) **30**:12, 21, 26, 48, 99, 103
"The Skeleton of the Future" (MacDiarmid) **9**:176, 179
"The Skeleton of the Great Moa in the Canterbury Museum, Christchurch" (Curnow) **48**:27
"Skeptic" (Frost) **39**:233
"The Skeptic" (Spencer) **77**:332
"Sketch" (Sandburg) **2**:303, 335; **41**:238, 259, 364
"A Sketch" (Wilbur) **51**:237, 281
"Sketch for a Landscape" (Swenson) **14**:246, 262
"A Sketch in the Manner of Hogarth" (Patmore) **59**:240
"Sketches for a Portrait" (Day Lewis) **11**:148
"Sketches for a Summer" (Seferis) **66**:209
"Sketches from Edgewater" (Dorn) **115**:233-34
Sketches of Southern Life (Harper) **21**:185, 187, 189, 191-93, 197-98, 200-01, 211, 213-14
"Sketching a Thatcher" (Hughes) **89**:189
"Skier" (Francis) **34**:243, 255
"The Skier and the Mountain" (Eberhart) **76**:37, 57
"Skiers" (Warren) **37**:299
"The Skies" (Aleixandre) See "Los cielos"
Skify (Blok) **21**:9, 17, 21-2, 26, 28-9, 31, 35, 41
"The Skilled Man" (Sarton) **39**:348
"Skin" (Larkin) **21**:229
"Skin Canoe" (Forché) **10**:134
"Skin Dreaming" (Hogan) **35**:277, 278
"the skinny voice" (Cummings) **5**:99
"Skipper Ireson's Ride" (Whittier) **93**:167, 173-74, 228-29, 234-36, 239-40, 245, 266, 281, 346
"Skizze zu einem Sankt Georg" (Rilke) **2**:267
"The Skull beneath the Skin of the Mango" (Espada) **74**:137
"Skullshapes" (Tomlinson) **17**:340, 357
"The Skunk" (Heaney) **18**:244; **100**:321
"Skunk Hour" (Cunningham) **92**:157
"Skunk Hour" (Lowell) **3**:209-11, 213-14, 221, 223, 227, 235, 243-46
"Skunk Hour" (Sexton) **2**:350
"Sky" (Szymborska) See "Niebo"
"A Sky Beyond Sky for Me" (Darwish) **86**:27
"The Sky Falling" (Soto) **28**:370
"Sky Furnance" (Hughes) **89**:212
"Sky House" (McGuckian) **27**:78
"The Sky Is Blue" (Ignatow) **34**:273, 291, 312, 327-28
"The Sky Lark" (Clare) **23**:6
Sky Sea Birds Trees Earth House Beasts Flowers (Rexroth) **95**:281
"Skykomish River Running" (Hugo) **68**:287
"Skylarks" (Hughes) **7**:121-22, 136-37; **89**:110-11, 216-17, 259-64
"Skylarks" manuscript (Hughes) **89**:259, 261-62, 264
"The Skylarks of Mykonos" (Clampitt) **19**:87
Skylight One: Fifteen Poems (Aiken) **26**:24
"Skylights" (Gallagher) **9**:45
"Skyscraper" (Sandburg) **41**:226, 295
"The Skyscraper Loves Night" (Sandburg) **41**:327
"Slabs of the Sunburnt West" (Sandburg) **2**:306, 308, 310-11, 314, 323, 330; **41**:346
Slabs of the Sunburnt West (Sandburg) **2**:306, 308, 311, 314, 323; **41**:249-52, 255, 260-61, 263, 271, 274, 277, 314, 319, 325, 329-30
"The Slacker Apologizes" (Viereck) **27**:273
"The Slacker Need Not Apologize" (Viereck) **27**:263
"Slam, Dunk, & Hook" (Komunyakaa) **51**:23
The Slant Door (Szirtes) **51**:156
"The Slanting Rain" (Pessoa) See "Chuva Oblíqua"
"Slapstick" (Szymborska) See "Komedyjki"
"The Slate Ode" (Mandelstam) See "Grifel' naja oda"
"Slave" (Storni) See "Esclava"
"The Slave" (Thomas) **99**:241, 303-4, 306, 309-10
"The Slave Auction" (Harper) **21**:190, 194, 205-06, 216-17
"slave cabin sotterly plantation maryland 1989" (Clifton) **17**:30
"Slave Castle" (Randall) **86**:339, 341
"The Slave Mother" (Harper) **21**:192, 194, 197, 203-04, 216
"The Slave Mother, A Tale of Ohio" (Harper) **21**:197, 204-05, 210, 218
"Slave on the Block" (Hughes) **53**:150
"Slave Quarters" (Dickey) **40**:151, 154, 158, 178, 197, 209, 212, 214-16, 259
"The Slave Ships" (Whittier) **93**:312-15
"The Slaves of Martinique" (Whittier) **93**:317
"Slaves on the Block" (Hughes) See "Slave on the Block"
Slavík zpívášpatně (Seifert) **47**:316, 324, 332-33
"Sled Burial, Dream Ceremony" (Dickey) **40**:155
"The Sleep" (Barrett Browning) **6**:21
"Sleep" (Cowley) **90**:114
"Sleep" (Hope) **56**:268
"Sleep" (Hughes) **1**:240
"Sleep" (Johnson) **24**:145, 159
"Sleep" (de la Mare) **77**:148
"Sleep" (Mickiewicz) See "Sen"
"Sleep" (Pushkin) **10**:407
"The Sleep" (Strand) **63**:175
Sleep and Awakening (Werfel) See *Schlaf und Erwachen*
"Sleep and Poetry" (Keats) **1**:280, 289, 291-92, 313; **96**:193, 215-16, 221-23, 228, 264, 341, 343-45, 347, 350
"Sleep at Sea" (Rossetti) **7**:293, 296-7
"Sleep Brings No Joy to Me" (Brontë) **8**:74
"Sleep defends my Don drowsiness" (Mandelstam) See "Oboroniaet son moiu donskuiu son"
"Sleep Is a Suspension Midway" (Sandburg) **41**:332
"Sleep of the Valiant" (Elytis) **21**:123
"The Sleep of the Valiant (Variation)" (Elytis) **21**:116
"The Sleep Worker" (Hardy) **8**:129; **92**:229
"The Sleeper" (Bly) **30**:43, 44

"The Sleeper" (Poe) **1**:434, 443-44; **54**:270
"The Sleepers" (Carman) **34**:213
"The Sleepers" (Whitman) **3**:391, 396-97, 401; **91**:207-8, 230-31, 256, 258
"Sleepers in Jaipur" (Kenyon) **57**:20, 44
"Sleepers Joining Hands" (Bly) **39**:22, 26, 71, 79, 95, 103
Sleepers Joining Hands (Bly) **39**:15, 18, 22, 24-5, 27-8, 37, 43, 45, 52, 55, 64, 67, 70-1, 84, 90, 92, 94-5, 102-03
"Sleeping at Last" (Rossetti) **7**:287
"Sleeping Beauty" (Clifton) **17**:29
"The Sleeping Beauty" (Owen) **19**:358
"Sleeping Beauty" (Sexton)
See "Briar Rose"
"The Sleeping Beauty" (Tennyson) **101**:245
"Sleeping Beauty" (Wylie) **23**:321
The Sleeping Beauty (Carruth) **10**:75-8, 83-4, 86, 91
The Sleeping Beauty (Sitwell) **3**:292-94, 298, 300-01, 303, 307-08, 310, 316-17, 320, 324-25
"Sleeping Beauty IV" (Stone) **53**:223
"The Sleeping Beauty: Variation of the Prince" (Jarrell) **41**:173, 177, 186, 196
"A Sleeping Black Boy" (Serote) **113**:292
"The Sleeping Fury" (Bogan) **12**:100, 104
The Sleeping Fury (Bogan) **12**:88-90, 105, 109, 111, 120, 122-25, 131
"The Sleeping Giant" (Hall) **70**:30, 32
"The Sleeping God" (Sarton) **39**:327, 341
"Sleeping in the Forest" (Oliver) **75**:282-83, 285
"Sleeping in the Woods" (Wagoner) **33**:347-48
Sleeping in the Woods (Wagoner) **33**:334, 344, 348, 353
"The Sleeping Lord" (Jones) **116**:95-96, 118, 162-65, 180, 185, 215, 228
The Sleeping Lord and Other Fragments (Jones) **116**:77, 83, 85, 88, 96-97, 100, 107-8, 110-16, 125-26, 129, 132-33, 141-43, 158-61, 163, 165, 167-69, 185, 198-99, 214-16, 218, 221, 227-28, 238
Sleeping on Fists (Ríos) **57**:312
"Sleeping on Stones" (Wagoner) **33**:356-57, 361
"Sleeping on the Ceiling" (Bishop) **3**:37; **34**:120, 123, 156
"Sleeping Out at Easter" (Dickey) **40**:154, 189, 212, 240, 258
"Sleeping Out Full Moon" (Brooke) **24**:57
"Sleeping out in College Cloister" (Empson) **104**:100
"The Sleeping Palace" (Tennyson) **101**:245
"The Sleeping Rocks" (Mackey) **49**:4, 6
"Sleeping Standing Up" (Bishop) **34**:66, 79, 86, 123, 156
"Sleeping Well" (Cunningham) **92**:160
Sleeping windows and door on the roof (Char)
See *Fenêtres dormantes et porte sur le toit*
"Sleeping with Animals" (Kumin) **15**:209, 211, 215, 223
Sleeping with One Eye Open (Strand) **63**:140, 144, 159-60, 167, 172, 174, 176, 178-79
"Sleeping with One Eye Open" (Strand) **63**:151, 160, 175
"Sleeping with Women" (Koch) **80**:318
"Sleepless at Crown Point" (Wilbur) **51**:246, 279
"A Sleepless Night" (Levine) **22**:214
"Sleepless Night" (Paz) **48**:273
The Sleepless Night of Eugene Delacroix (Yau) **61**:328, 340
"Sleepwalker Ballad" (García Lorca)
See "Romance sonámbulo"
"Sleepyhead" (de la Mare) **77**:95, 129
"Sleet Storm on the Merritt Parkway" (Bly) **39**:89
"Sleigh Ride" (Very) **86**:45, 58
"The slender wire above the sea of oats" (Tsvetaeva)
See "U tonkoi pnovoloki nad volnoi ovsov"
"Slender's Love Elegy" (Peacock) **87**:321
Slick But Not Streamlined: Poems and Short Pieces (Betjeman) **75**:24-25, 38
"A Slight Fragrance" (Montague) **106**:320
"The Slighted Lady" (Wickham) **110**:277
"Slim Greer" (Brown) **55**:71-73, 75, 110, 120, 156
"Slim Hears 'The Call'" (Brown) **55**:112, 121, 156
"Slim in Atlanta" (Brown) **55**:120-21, 140, 156
"Slim in Hell" (Brown) **55**:112, 115-16, 121, 156
"Slim Lands a Job?" (Brown) **55**:110, 112, 120, 156
Slinger (Dorn) **115**:51, 69, 74-77, 85-89, 92-100, 103-4, 108-9, 119-20, 124, 129-33, 135, 137-42, 156, 180, 202-3, 205-6, 220-22, 227
"Slipped Quadrant" (Mackey) **49**:20-21, 25, 62, 68
"The Slippers of the Goddess of Beauty" (Lowell) **13**:67
"Slips" (McGuckian) **27**:97
"Slip-Shoe Lovey" (Masters) **1**:333, 336; **36**:176
"Sliver" (Alurista) **34**:27
"Slough" (Betjeman) **75**:7, 12, 24
"Slovo" (Akhmadulina) **43**:6, 17, 49, 52
"Slow Coon" (Brown) **55**:110
A Slow Dance (Montague) **106**:217-19, 228, 237-39, 242, 244-46, 279-81, 283, 289, 298, 313, 317, 327-29, 353
"Slow News from Our Place" (Stafford) **71**:375
"The Slow Pacific Swell" (Winters) **82**:342-43, 346
"The Slow Rain" (Mistral)
See "La lluvia lenta"
"The Slow Sounding and Eventual Emergence Of" (Graham) **59**:175
"The Slow Sting of Her Company" (Erdrich) **52**:178
"Slow through the Dark" (Dunbar) **5**:131
"Slowly I Married Her" (Cohen) **109**:23-24
"Slowly You Spoke" (Seferis) **66**:118, 124, 126
"Slowness of the Future" (Char) **56**:137-38
"Slug" (Roethke) **15**:274
"Slug in Woods" (Birney) **52**:6, 8, 33, 64-65, 85
"The Sluggish Smoke Curls Up from Some Deep Dell" (Thoreau) **30**:181, 216, 227, 235, 257
"Sluggishness" (Akhmadulina) **43**:11
"Sluicegates of Thought" (Tzara) **27**:235
"A Slumber Did My Spirit Steal" (Wordsworth) **4**:420
"Slump Sundays" (Hughes) **89**:146
"Small Action Poem" (Tomlinson) **17**:325
"The Small Bird to the Big" (Empson) **104**:86, 88
"The Small Blue Heron" (Wright) **36**:341-42, 345
"Small Comment" (Sanchez) **9**:224
"A Small Death" (Montague) **106**:314, 316
A Small Desperation (Abse) **41**:9-10, 15, 28, 30
"Small Elegy" (Ciardi) **69**:56
"Small Frogs Killed on a Highway" (Wright) **36**:366
"Small Garden near a Field" (Gallagher) **9**:62
"A Small Grove" (Wright) **36**:311
"The Small Hours" (Parker) **28**:359
"Small Hours" (Plath) **1**:391
Small Hours of the Night: Selected Poems of Roque Dalton (Dalton) **36**:135-37
"Small Items" (Stafford) **71**:293
"The Small Lady" (Smith) **12**:295
"A Small Light" (Song) **21**:344
"Small Moment" (Nemerov) **24**:293
"Small Ode to a Black Cuban Boxer" (Guillén)
See "La Pequeña oda a un negro boxeador cubano"
"Small Perfect Manhattan" (Viereck) **27**:263, 278
"A Small Piece of Wood" (McGuckian) **27**:107, 110-111
"Small Poems for the Winter Solstice" (Atwood) **8**:44
"small port in the outer Fijis" (Birney) **52**:36, 38
"Small Role Felicity" (Berrigan) **103**:42
"A Small Room with Large Windows" (Curnow) **48**:7-8, 10, 61
A Small Room with Large Windows: Selected Poems (Curnow) **48**:3
"Small Secrets" (Montague) **106**:298
"Small Song for Crossing a Big River" (Césaire) **25**:32
Small Testament (Villon)
See *Les Lais*
"Small White House" (Warren) **37**:305
"A Small Will" (Montale)
See "Piccolo testamento"
"Small Woman on Swallow Street" (Merwin) **45**:8
The Smallest Muscle in the Human Body (Ríos) **57**:327, 329
"Smalltown Dance" (Wright) **14**:378-79
Smashing the Piano (Montague) **106**:325, 328-29
"The Smell of Gasoline Ascends in My Nose" (Amichai)
See "Reah habenzin 'oleh be'api"
"Smelt Fishing" (Hayden) **6**:196
"Smert" (Lermontov) **18**:302
"Smert' poeta" (Lermontov) **18**:277, 281, 285
"The Smile" (Blake) **12**:35, 43
"The Smile" (Merrill) **28**:248
"Smile" (Silverstein) **49**:349
"Smile, Smile, Smile" (Owen) **19**:354, 357, 359; **102**:146, 167, 171, 181, 263
"The Smile Was" (Abse) **41**:11, 22, 30
"The Smitten Purist" (Riley) **48**:340
"Smoke" (Mahon) **60**:236
"Smoke" (McGuckian) **27**:97
"Smoke" (Reese) **29**:340
"Smoke" (Thoreau) **30**:168, 126, 190, 204, 294
"Smoke & Cinders: Some Thoughts on the Truckers" (Dorn) **115**:161, 201
"Smoke and Earth" (Aleixandre) **15**:18-19
"Smoke and Steel" (Sandburg) **2**:304, 316
Smoke and Steel (Sandburg) **41**:243-44, 248, 250, 254-56, 260-62, 267, 270, 274, 277, 284, 286, 297-98, 302, 313-14, 318, 325, 327, 329-30
"Smoke in Colombo" (Das) **43**:83
"The Smokers" (Shapiro) **25**:323
"Smokers of Cheap Cigarettes" (Pavese)
See "Fumatori di carta"
"Smokey the Bear Sutra" (Snyder) **21**:291
"Smoky the Bear Bodhisattva" (Rexroth) **95**:340, 343
"Smooth Gnarled Crape Myrtle" (Moore) **49**:128
"Smothered by the World" (Bly) **39**:12
"Smudging" (Wakoski) **15**:331, 364
Smudging (Wakoski) **15**:332, 345, 364
"The Smug Never Silent Guns of the Enemy" (Dorn) **115**:127
"Snail" (Hughes) **1**:241; **53**:122
"Snail" (Sexton) **79**:240
"The Snail's Road" (Wright) **36**:313, 355
"The Snake" (Abse) **41**:25
"The Snake" (Berry) **28**:25
"Snake" (Hughes) **1**:241
"Snake" (Lawrence) **54**:176-77, 179, 181, 187, 189, 223-24, 236
"Snake" (Roethke) **15**:272
"Snake Eyes" (Baraka) **113**:150
"Snake Hunt" (Wagoner) **33**:336
"Snake Hymn" (Hughes) **7**:159
"Snake River" (McKay) **2**:216
"Snakebite" (Dickey) **40**:152, 158, 160, 188, 192
"Snakecharmer" (Plath) **1**:388-89; **37**:188, 207, 238

"The Snake-man" (Tapahonso) **65**:259
"Snakes, Mongooses, Snake-Charmers, and the Like" (Moore) **49**:97, 161
"Snakeskin and Stone" (Douglas) **106**:203
"Snakeskin on a Gate" (Wright) **14**:356
"Snap-Dragon" (Lawrence) **54**:163-64, 221
"Snapping the Fringe" (Alexie) **53**:11
Snaps (Cruz) **37**:3, 5, 10-14, 17, 25, 30
"Snaps of Immigration" (Cruz) **37**:35
"A Snapshot of 15th S. W." (Hugo) **68**:252
"A Snapshot of the Auxiliary" (Hugo) **68**:260
"A Snapshot of Uig in Montana" (Hugo) **68**:288
"Snapshots" (Kennedy) **93**:140
"Snapshots" (Winters) **82**:344
"Snapshots for Boris Pasternak" (O'Hara) **45**:156
"Snapshots of a Daughter-in-Law" (Rich) **5**:370-72, 396
Snapshots of a Daughter-in-Law: Poems, 1954-1962 (Rich) **5**:354, 358, 363, 369-72, 374, 382, 388, 392
The Snark (Carroll)
See *The Hunting of the Snark: An Agony in Eight Fits*
"Snarley-Yow" (Kipling) **3**:158
"Snatch of Sliphorn Jazz" (Sandburg) **41**:287
"The Snayl" (Lovelace) **69**:171, 229, 239, 243-44, 250, 256-57
Snezhnye maski (Blok) **21**:20, 24
"Sniper" (Randall) **86**:336, 341
"The Snob" (Shapiro) **25**:295
"The Snobs" (Das) **43**:85
"Snoqualmie" (Hugo) **68**:238
"Snorri Sturluson, (1179-1241)" (Borges) **32**:95
"The Snow" (Creeley) **73**:7
"Snow" (Frost) **1**:195, 215
"Snow" (Hayden) **6**:193, 196
"Snow" (Hughes) **7**:155; **89**:98, 107
"Snow" (de la Mare) **77**:110
"Snow" (Levine) **22**:225
"Snow" (MacNeice) **61**:115, 130, 137, 146, 160
"Snow" (Mueller) **33**:174
"Snow" (Rich) **5**:366
"Snow" (Sexton) **79**:222
"Snow" (Stone) **53**:228
"Snow" (Thomas) **53**:274
"The Snow" (Very) **86**:165
"Snow. Christine sick" (Niedecker) **42**:121
"Snow Country Weavers" (Welch) **62**:340, 370, 374
"snow cummin" (Bissett) **14**:20
"Snow Day" (Collins) **68**:207
"The Snow Fairy" (McKay) **2**:228
"The Snow Fences" (Tomlinson) **17**:341
"Snow in Tokyo: A Japanese Poem" (Yevtushenko) **40**:370
"Snow Jobs" (Merrill) **28**:284-85
"The Snow King" (Dove) **6**:108
"Snow King Chair Lift" (Merrill) **28**:222, 257
"The Snow Lamp" (Hayden) **6**:189, 192
"The Snow Leopard" (Jarrell) **41**:174
"The Snow lies sprinkled on the beach" (Bridges) **28**:89
"Snow Line" (Berryman) **64**:171
"Snow Maiden" (Blok) **21**:9
"The Snow Man" (Stevens) **110**:153, 173, 208, 227
"The Snow Man" (Winters) **82**:316
The Snow Mask (Blok)
See *Snezhnye maski*
"Snow Melting" (Schnackenberg) **45**:338
"Snow Mountains" (Berssenbrugge) **115**:8
"Snow on a Southern State" (Dickey) **40**:182
"The Snow Party" (Mahon) **60**:135, 139, 155, 184, 211
The Snow Party (Mahon) **60**:132, 134, 136, 138-41, 144, 154, 158, 183-84, 198-202, 205-11
The Snow Poems (Ammons) **16**:23-6, 42-7, 49-51, 54, 61-2, 65
"The Snow Queen" (Hacker) **47**:81-82
"Snow) Says! Says" (Cummings) **5**:106
"Snow Shower" (Bryant) **20**:15-16
"Snow Signs" (Tomlinson) **17**:342, 345
"Snow, snow" (Piercy) **29**:315
"Snow Songs" (Snodgrass) **74**:331
"The Snow Storm" (Emerson) **18**:79-80, 88, 98, 107
"Snow Upon Paris" (Senghor)
See "Neige sur Paris"
"Snow White" (Sexton) **2**:368
"Snow White and the Seven Dwarfs" (Sexton) **79**:191, 205, 241
"Snowbanks North of the House" (Bly) **39**:65
"Snowbed" (Celan)
See "Schneebett"
"The Snow-Bird" (Very) **86**:69
Snow-Bound: A Winter Idyl (Whittier) **93**:167, 170, 173, 176, 194, 215, 225, 235-40, 253-54, 257, 267-71, 273-75, 281, 285-87, 289, 293, 298, 304-10, 341, 348, 350
"Snowdrop" (Hughes) **7**:169; **89**:150
"The Snow-drop in the Snow" (Dobell) **100**:182
"Snowed In" (Austin) **39**:43-44
"Snowfall" (Carducci)
See "Nevicata"
"Snowfall" (Gunn) **26**:203
"The Snowfall" (Justice) **64**:279
"Snowfall" (Teasdale) **31**:334
"Snowfall" (Vigny)
See "La neige"
"Snowfall" (Warren) **37**:377-78
"Snowfall in the Afternoon" (Bly) **39**:76, 78, 85
"Snowfield" (Montague) **106**:287
"The Snowflake" (de la Mare) **77**:110
"Snowflakes as Kisses" (Schwarzweller) **8**:314
"Snow-Ghost" (Winters) **82**:322, 325-26
"The Snowman" (Page) **12**:167-68, 183
"Snows" (Perse)
See "Neiges"
"Snows" (Stryk) **27**:202-3
"The Snow's Perfection" (Zanzotto)
See "La perfezione della neve"
"A Snowshoe" (Heaney) **100**:322
Snowstorm (Akhmadulina)
See *Metel'*
"Snowy Heron" (Ciardi) **69**:10, 40, 55
Sny o Gruzii (Akhmadulina) **43**:12-13, 15-17, 32-33, 46, 52
"So" (Dorn) **115**:133
"So-and-So Reclining on Her Couch" (Stevens) **110**:93
"So Be It" (Stone) **53**:239-40, 252
"So crewell prison" (Surrey) **59**:316, 327, 330, 338, 352-58
"So Far As the Future Is Concerned" (Moore)
See "The Past Is the Present"
"So Frost Astounds" (Warren) **37**:331
"So Going Around Cities" (Berrigan) **103**:5
So Going Around Cities: New and Selected Poems, 1958-1979 (Berrigan) **103**:4, 6, 14-15, 20-21, 31-32, 34-35, 41
"So Good" (Schuyler) **88**:189, 194
"So I Said I Am Ezra" (Ammons) **16**:39
"So Intricately Is This World Resolved" (Kunitz) **19**:170
"So It Would Seem" (de la Mare) **77**:142
"So Long!" (O'Hara) **45**:192
"So Long Charlie Parker" (Brathwaite) **56**:45
"So many loves have I neglected" (Campion) **87**:57, 67, 90
"So Many Things Terrify, So Many" (Cisneros)
See "Tantas Cosas Asustan, Tantas"
"So Mexicans Are Taking Jobs from Americans" (Baca) **41**:37
"So Much Depends" (Williams) **7**:362
"So Old" (Snyder) **21**:307
"So quicke, so hot, so mad" (Campion) **87**:25, 58, 71-72, 120
"So Slight" (Jackson) **44**:29
"So, so breake off this last lamenting kisse" (Donne)
See "The Expiration"
"So sweet love seemed that April morn" (Bridges) **28**:86
"So There" (Creeley) **73**:81
"So, Time" (Hardy) **92**:212
"So To Fatness Come" (Smith) **12**:326
"So trust me . . ." (Rimbaud)
See "Fiez-vous donc à moi . . ."
"So tyr'd are all my thoughts" (Campion) **87**:58, 69-70
"So We Grew Together" (Masters) **1**:326-26, 328; **36**:175
"So What" (Stone) **53**:258
"So What's Wrong" (Stone) **53**:256
"The So-and-So's" (Cisneros) **52**:163
Soap (Ponge)
See *Le Savon*
"Soap" (Stern) **115**:252, 279
"Soap Suds" (MacNeice) **61**:176-77
Sobranie sochinenij (Mandelstam) **14**:113, 117, 123
"Sobrera" (Castro) **41**:89
Sochineniia (Akhmatova) **55**:25
Social Credit, An Impact (Pound) **4**:328
Social Ironies (Abse) **41**:3
"The Social Muse" (MacLeish) **47**:134, 151
"Social Revolution in England" (Abse) **41**:7
"Social Work" (Kinsella) **69**:133, 135, 137
"Sociedad de amigos y protectores" (Fuertes) **27**:16
"Socrates' Ghost Must Haunt Me Now" (Schwartz) **8**:302, 315
"Soeur Monique" (Meynell) **112**:156
"Les soeurs de charité" (Rimbaud) **57**:174, 177, 245, 251
"The Sofa" (Cowper) **40**:45, 51, 58, 127, 130
"The Sofa" (McGuckian) **27**:98
"A Sofa in the Forties" (Heaney) **100**:247-49, 285-87
"The soft lights, the companionship, the beer" (Cunningham) **92**:168-69
"Soft Snow" (Blake) **63**:26
"Soft to Your Places" (Kinsella) **69**:117
"Soft Toy" (Kinsella) **69**:78, 98, 103
"Soft Wood" (Lowell) **3**:211
"Softer-Mother's Tale" (Wordsworth) **4**:373
"Softly" (Jacobsen) **62**:325
"Il Sogno del prigioniero" (Montale) **13**:104
"Sogno d'estate" (Carducci) **46**:50, 63, 65-66
"Sograzhdánam" (Akhmatova) **55**:16
Söhne (Benn) **35**:29, 30, 45, 46
"Soho Cinema" (Lorde) **12**:140
"Soho: Saturday Night" (Abse) **41**:3
"Sohrab and Rustum" (Arnold) **5**:9, 12-13, 33, 35, 37, 45, 52, 62
"Soil" (Szirtes) **51**:172
"Soiled Dove" (Sandburg) **41**:336
"The Soil-Map" (McGuckian) **27**:97
"Un soir" (Apollinaire) **7**:46
"Le Soir" (Baudelaire) **106**:88
"Le Soir" (Bonnefoy) **58**:167-68
"Le soir" (Lamartine) **16**:275-76, 298-99, 302
"Soir d'août" (Ponge) **107**:73
"Soir de carnaval" (Laforgue) **14**:92
"Soir historique" (Rimbaud) **57**:239-40, 247, 283
"Le soir qu'amour vous fist en la salle descendre" (Ronsard) **11**:264-66
"Le Soir Tombe" (Borges) **32**:103
"Une soirée perdue" (Gautier) **18**:136-37
"Soissons" (Douglas) **106**:186, 197
"Soissons 1940" (Douglas) **106**:197
"Sojourn in the Whale" (Moore) **49**:100-101, 112, 116, 122, 161
"Sokolinya slobodka" (Tsvetaeva) **14**:326
"El sol" (Aleixandre) **15**:25
"Sol" (Tolson) **88**:331, 341
Sól (Szymborska) **44**:268
"Sol e amore" (Carducci) **46**:48
"Sol en la boda" (Guillén) **35**:182, 188

"Sol perche tuo' bellezze al mondo sieno" (Michelangelo) **103**:196, 198
"Sol pur col focoil fabbro il ferro stende" (Michelangelo) **103**:192
"El sol victorioso" (Aleixandre) **15**:19
"Sola con esperanza" (Fuertes) **27**:8, 29
Sola en la sala (Fuertes) **27**:17-8, 21, 38
"Solace" (Eberhart) **76**:73
"SOLACE IN WORDS" (Bissett) **14**:33
"Solar" (Larkin) **21**:250-51
"Solar Ode to the People's Army" (Neruda) See "Oda solar al ejérito del pueblo"
"Un soldado de Lee" (Borges) **32**:87
"Soldati" (Ungaretti) **57**:359
"Solde" (Rimbaud) **3**:261, 264; **57**:194, 228, 248, 271
"The Soldier" (Brooke) **24**:54, 59, 63-4, 71, 74, 80, 86-7, 89
"Soldier" (Herbert) See "Zolnierz"
"The Soldier" (Hopkins) **15**:144
"The Soldier" (Jarrell) **41**:179
The Soldier (Aiken) **26**:24
The Soldier; and Other Poems (Elliott) **96**:181
"Soldier Asleep at the Tomb" (Schnackenberg) **45**:334
"A Soldier Dreaming of White Lilies" (Darwish) See "A Soldier Dreams of White Lilies"
"A Soldier Dreams of White Lilies" (Darwish) **86**:16, 28, 33
"A Soldier Dreams of White Tulips" (Darwish) See "A Soldier Dreams of White Lilies"
"Soldier from the wars returning" (Housman) **43**:245
"Soldier, Soldier" (Kipling) **3**:163, 188-89
"A Soldier under Lee" (Borges) See "Un soldado de Lee"
"The Soldier Walks under the Trees of the University" (Jarrell) **41**:180
"The Soldiers" (Duncan) **2**:104, 116; **75**:114-15, 118, 158, 254, 276
"Soldiers" (Ungaretti) See "Soldati"
"Soldier's Dream" (Owen) **19**:341, 356; **102**:148, 207
"Soldier's Farm" (Wright) **14**:340
"A Soldier's Son" (Boland) **58**:42
"Soldier's Song" (Burns) **6**:78
"The Soldier's Wife" (Southey) **111**:193
"De Sole" (Tomlinson) **17**:336
"Soledad" (Hayden) **6**:194, 196
"Soledad" (Storni) **33**:235, 239, 271
Soledad (Paz) **1**:366
"Soledades of the Sun and Moon" (Hope) **56**:268, 273, 307
"Le Soleil" (Baudelaire) **106**:136
Soleil Cou-Coupé (Césaire) **25**:15, 23, 30-2, 35, 44
Le soleil des eaux (Char) **56**:181
"Soleil d'Hiver" (Jaccottet) **98**:174
"Soleil et chair" (Rimbaud) **3**:251, 280, 283, 285; **57**:174, 202, 208, 244-46, 248, 250-51, 284
"Soleil était encore chaud . . ." (Rimbaud) **57**:243-45, 248, 253
"Le Soleil placé en abîme" (Ponge) **107**:71, 73, 90-91, 95, 173-75, 239
"Soleil route usée" (Péret) **33**:230
"Soleils couchants" (Verlaine) **32**:362-63, 382, 387
"Soliloquio del farero" (Cernuda) **62**:213
"Soliloquio del individuo" (Parra) **39**:261, 288
"Soliloquy" (Jeffers) **17**:132
"Soliloquy" (Muir) **49**:224, 227, 229, 233
"Soliloquy" (Thomas) **99**:257, 317
"Soliloquy for Cassandra" (Szymborska) **44**:300
"Soliloquy of a Misanthrope" (Hughes) **7**:116
"Soliloquy of the Spanish Cloister" (Browning) **2**:37; **97**:4, 9, 42
"Soliloquy on a Southern Strand" (Montague) **106**:257, 275
"The Solipsist" (Cunningham) **92**:173
"Le solitaire" (Lamartine) **16**:281
"The Solitary" (Teasdale) **31**:323, 333, 371, 380, 389
"Solitary Confinement" (Kennedy) **93**:131, 137-38
"The Solitary Life" (Leopardi) See "La vita solitaria"
"The Solitary Place" (Muir) **49**:242, 288
"The Solitary Reaper" (Wordsworth) **4**:399, 404
"The Solitary Sparrow" (Leopardi) See "Il Passero Solitario"
"La Solitude" (Baudelaire) **106**:88
"Solitude" (Carroll) **74**:64
"Solitude" (Ishikawa) See "Kyoko"
"La solitude" (Lamartine) **16**:277
"A Solitude" (Swinburne) **24**:327
"Solitude" (Traherne) **70**:241-44, 268, 302
"Solitude Late at Night in the Woods" (Bly) **39**:82
"The Solitude of Glass" (Winters) **82**:323
"Solitudes at Sixty" (Sassoon) **12**:259
Solitudes Crowded with Loneliness (Kaufman) **74**:175, 179-83, 185, 188, 194-95, 200, 207, 212, 216-17, 234, 240, 252, 268-70, 273, 275
"Solo de lune" (Laforgue) **14**:74-6
"Solo de piano" (Parra) **39**:264, 299
Solo na raskalennoi trube (Shvarts) **50**:162
Solo on a White-Hot Trumpet (Shvarts) See *Solo na raskalennoi trube*
"Sólo por juego, nunca" (Guillén) **35**:198-99
"Solominka, The Straw" (Mandelstam) **14**:111-12, 124
"Solomon and the Witch" (Yeats) **51**:151
Solomon on the Vanity of the World (Prior) **102**:281-83, 293, 296-300, 310, 317-21, 332, 334, 337
"Solonique" (Apollinaire) **7**:48
"Solstice" (Jeffers) **17**:111, 127, 141
"Solstice" (Lorde) **12**:153
"Solstice" (Williams) **109**:284
Solstice and Other Poems (Jeffers) **17**:111, 125, 135
Solstices (MacNeice) **61**:125, 176, 182
"Solution" (Oppen) **35**:331
"The Solution" (Stone) **53**:221
"Som de escalina" (Eliot) **5**:201
Sombra del paraíso (Aleixandre) **15**:6, 8, 10-11, 15-16, 18, 21, 22-5, 33-4, 37-8, 40-1
"Sombre Figuration" (Stevens) **6**:298, 318, 320; **110**:191-92
Some (Ashbery) **26**:167, 172
"Some Answers Are Cold Comfort to the Dead" (Schwartz) **8**:293
"Some Are Born" (Smith) **12**:316
"Some Beasts" (Neruda) **64**:328
"Some Brilliant Sky" (Wakoski) **15**:336
Some Changes (Jordan) **38**:114, 118-20, 122
"Some Contemporary Poets of the Negro Race" (Braithwaite) **52**:118
"Some Dreams They Forgot" (Bishop) **34**:190
"Some Echoes" (Creeley) **73**:53
"Some Extensions on the Sovereignty of Science" (Ríos) **57**:327
"Some Eyes Condemn" (Thomas) **53**:271
"Some Foreign Letters" (Sexton) **2**:350, 361, 363; **79**:187
"Some Foreign Wife" (Sexton) **2**:359
"Some Frenchmen" (Updike) **90**:357
"Some Friends from Pascagoula" (Stevens) **6**:337; **110**:101, 103-4
"Some General Instructions" (Koch) **80**:303
"Some Greek Writings" (Corso) **33**:33-34, 38, 44; **108**:8, 25
"Some Last Questions" (Merwin) **45**:9, 21-2, 42
"Some Last Words" (Strand) **63**:199
"Some Like Poetry" (Szymborska) See "Niektórzy lubia poezje"
"Some Lines" (Viereck) **27**:280
"Some Lines in Three Parts" (Viereck) **27**:263, 278, 280, 282
Some Memories of W. B. Yeats (Masefield) **78**:41
Some Men Are Brothers (Enright) **93**:4, 9, 13
"Some Moroccan Writings" (Corso) **108**:8
"Some Negatives: X at the Chateu" (Merrill) **28**:242
"Some Notes on Organic Form" (Levertov) **11**:160-62
"Some of Satans Sophestry" (Taylor) **63**:217, 284
"Some People" (Jordan) **38**:127, 145
"Some People Like Poetry" (Szymborska) See "Niektórzy lubia poezje"
"Some Place" (Creeley) **73**:43-44, 48
"Some Quadrangles" (Swenson) **14**:273
"Some Questions You Might Ask" (Oliver) **75**:318, 342
"Some Reflections of His upon the Several Petitions in the Same Prayer" (Waller) **72**:364
"Some San Francisco Poems" (Oppen) **35**:285, 335, 337, 340, 342
"Some Science Fiction" (Frost) **71**:26
"Some Shadows" (Stafford) **71**:265, 279-80, 290-91, 318
"Some South American Poets" (Koch) **80**:319
"Some Things" (Crane) **80**:40
"Some Things You'll Need to Know Before You Join the Union" (Stone) **53**:220, 229, 243, 253
Some Time (Zukofsky) **11**:343
"Some Trees" (Ashbery) **26**:118
Some Trees (Ashbery) **26**:111, 113, 118, 129, 135, 137, 143, 162, 164
"Some Verses Upon the Burning of Our House, July 18th, 1666" (Bradstreet) **10**:8, 19, 21, 27, 29-30, 34, 36-7, 42
"Some Years" (Ríos) **57**:325
"Somebody" (Borges) **32**:58
"Somebody Blew Up America" (Baraka) **113**:102-11
"Somebody's Song" (Parker) **28**:351
"Someday, Maybe" (Stafford) **71**:321
Someday, Maybe (Stafford) **71**:271-72, 275-76, 280, 282-83, 287-88, 299, 320-21, 333, 336, 340, 342, 349
"Somehow It Doesn't Write Itself" (Ignatow) **34**:310
"Someone Is Harshly Coughing as Before" (Schwartz) **8**:301
"Someone Talking to Himself" (Wilbur) **51**:208, 223, 232, 308
"Someone's got to say Williams ..." (Bell) **79**:18
"Somersault" (Sarton) **39**:325, 332
"Something" (Creeley) **73**:37, 120
"Something A Direction" (Tomlinson) **17**:312
"Something Amazing Just Happened" (Berrigan) **103**:34
"Something Borrowed" (Piercy) **29**:302
"Something Else" (Akhmadulina) See "Drugoe"
"Something for Hope" (Frost) **1**:200
"Something Like a Sonnet for Phillis Miracle Wheatley" (Jordan) **38**:125
"Something Missing" (Silverstein) **49**:324
"Something Tapped" (Hardy) **92**:206
"Something That Happens Right Now" (Stafford) **71**:374
"Something that sounded like Good-bye" (Mew) **107**:26
"Something There Is" (Corso) **33**:38, 44
"Something to Wear" (Levertov) **11**:165-66, 168
"Something Was Happening" (Hughes) **7**:154
"Something We Can All Agree On" (Dorn) **115**:163
Sometimes (Yau) **61**:333
"Sometimes Even Now" (Brooke) **24**:62
"Sometimes I Am Very Happy and Desperate" (Amichai) **38**:46
"Sometimes I Breathe" (Stafford) **71**:374

"Sometimes I fled the fire that me brent" (Wyatt) **27**:368
Sometimes Like a Legend (Stafford) **71**:315, 332, 337-38
"Somewhat Delayed Spring Song" (Parker) **28**:355
"Somewhere" (Abse) **41**:31
"Somewhere" (Nemerov) **24**:262
Somewhere among Us a Stone Is Taking Notes (Simic) **69**:262
"Somewhere East o' Suez" (Kipling) **3**:189
"Somewhere I Have Never Travelled, Gladly Beyond" (Cummings) **5**:88
"Somewhere in Africa" (Sexton) **2**:364, 371
"Somewhere in America" (Sexton) **79**:284
"Sommarnatten" (Ekeloef) **23**:76
"Sommation" (Hugo) **17**:98, 100
"Sommeil aux Lupercales" (Char) **56**:123, 157
"Le Sommet de la tour" (Gautier) **18**:143, 146
"Somnambulisma" (Stevens) **110**:151
"Somnambulent Ballad" (García Lorca)
See "Romance sonámbulo"
"Somnambulist Ballad" (García Lorca)
See "Romance sonámbulo"
"Son" (Brathwaite) **56**:51
"The Son" (Very) **86**:43, 117, 119, 132-33, 135, 151, 158, 166
"Son and Mother" (Blok) **21**:14
"Son del bloqueo" (Guillén) **23**:126
El son entero (Guillén) **23**:100, 108, 131, 139, 142
"Son más en una mazorca" (Guillén) **23**:125
Son Motifs (Guillén)
See *Motivos de son*
"Son numero 6" (Guillén) **23**:127, 130, 132, 139
"The Son of Croesus" (Morris) **55**:305
"Son of Judas" (Wright) **36**:377
"The Son of Lir" (Clarke) **112**:84
"Son of Spiders" (Empson) **104**:97
Son of the People (Quintana)
See *Hijo del pueblo: New Mexico Poems*
"Soñador que camina" (Guillén) **35**:230
"Soñando la muerte" (Cernuda) **62**:252-53
"Soñar" (Storni) **33**:319
"Sonar tari" (Tagore) **8**:408
Sonar tari (Tagore) **8**:409, 418, 427
"Sonata" (Schnackenberg) **45**:330, 337
"Sonata for Methylated Prose" (Ekeloef) **23**:85
"sonatform denaturerad prosa" (Ekeloef) **23**:75
"Sonatina" (Darío) **15**:79-80, 95, 107-08, 110, 119-20
"Sonatina in Green" (Justice) **64**:266, 274-75
"Sonatina in Yellow" (Justice) **64**:275
"Son-dayes" (Vaughan)
See "Sun-dayes"
"Sonet 1" (Drayton) **98**:123
"Sonet 2" (Drayton) **98**:122-23
"Sonet 3" (Drayton) **98**:121-23
"Sonet 57" (Drayton) **98**:122
"Sonet 58" (Drayton) **98**:122
Sonetos de la muerte (Mistral) **32**:143, 149-50, 152, 154, 161, 164-65, 176, 200
"Sonetos de la poda" (Mistral) **32**:188-89
Sonetos espirituales (Jiménez) **7**:191-92, 194-96, 202, 211
Sonette (Goethe) **5**:248, 250
Die Sonette an Orpheus (Rilke) **2**:267-68, 277, 280-81, 283, 290, 293, 295
Sonette an Orpheus (Rilke)
See *Die Sonette an Orpheus*
Die Sonette an Orpheus/Sonnets to Orpheus (Rilke)
See *Die Sonette an Orpheus*
"Sonetto del Linneo e Dioscoride" (Zanzotto) **65**:298-99
"(Sonetto di furtività e traversie)" (Zanzotto) **65**:282
"Sonetto di sterpi e limiti" (Zanzotto) **65**:299-300
Sonety Krymskie (Mickiewicz) **38**:158, 166, 191, 194, 215, 221, 223-25
"Song" (Abse) **41**:6
"Song" (Barker) **91**:26, 31
"Song" (Behn)
See "Love Arm'd"
"Song" (Berry) **28**:7-8
"Song" (Blake)
See "Bard's Song"
"Song" (Bogan) **12**:86, 90, 103
"Song" (Brontë) **8**:62
"Song" (Burns) **114**:96
"Song" (Cage) **58**:220
"A Song" (Carew) **29**:19
"Song" (Corso) **108**:38-39
"A Song" (Crashaw) **84**:52, 69
"Song" (Creeley) **73**:7, 29, 31, 33, 40, 89
"Song" (Cummings) **5**:109
"Song" (Dorn) **115**:109, 126, 155-56
"Song" (Duncan) **75**:243-44
"Song" (Elliott) **96**:166, 175
"Song" (H. D.) **5**:304
"Song" (Hafiz) **116**:44
"Song" (Hughes) **89**:140, 211
"The Song" (Ignatow) **34**:312
"Song" (Justice) **64**:279
"Song" (Kenyon) **57**:14, 36
"Song" (Kinsella) **69**:122
"Song" (Mackey) **49**:66, 68, 78
"song" (MacNeice) **61**:171
"Song" (Meredith) **60**:245
"Song" (Mew) **107**:56, 58
"Song" (Montague) **106**:280
"Song" (Muir) **49**:205, 226, 245, 250
"Song" (Nemerov) **24**:256
"Song" (O'Hara) **45**:158, 219
"Song" (Poe) **1**:432
"The Song" (Roethke) **15**:269
"Song" (Rossetti) **7**:273, 276, 289
"Song" (Sarton) **39**:325
"Song" (Sitwell) **3**:313
"Song" (Snodgrass) **74**:285, 303-4
"Song" (Spender) **71**:148
"Song" (Stern) **115**:254
"Song" (Suckling) **30**:127, 130, 139, 158
"Song" (Tennyson) **101**:243
"The Song" (Very) **86**:42, 80-81, 102, 137, 151
"Song" (Waller) **72**:339, 361
"Song" (Wickham) **110**:277
"Song" (Williams) **7**:408
"Song" (Wright) **14**:338, 342, 347
Song (Schuyler) **88**:225-26
"Song about a Woman" (Dorn) **115**:179
"A Song about Girls" (Seifert) **47**:340
"Song About Love" (Seifert)
See "Píseň o lásce"
"The Song and Dance of" (Olson) **19**:273
Song and Idea (Eberhart) **76**:28, 36, 38, 40-42, 58
"Song and Praise" (Very) **86**:98
Song and Sonnets (Longfellow) **30**:27
"Song: Aske me no more" (Carew) **29**:73
"Song at Capri" (Teasdale) **31**:340
"Song at Fifty" (Kavanagh) **33**:81; **105**:100
"Song at the End of Winter" (Wagoner) **33**:370-71
"A Song at the Winepresses" (Rexroth) **95**:264, 281
"Song at the Year's Turning" (Thomas) **99**:245
Song at the Year's Turning: Poems 1942-1954 (Thomas) **99**:235, 268-69, 284, 334, 348
"Song Before Drinking" (Li Po) **29**:142
"The Song before Sailing" (Carman) **34**:213
Song Books (Cage) **58**:218
"Song by an Old Shepherd" (Blake)
See "The Shepherd"
"Song Coming toward Us" (Forché) **10**:132
"Song, Composed in August" (Burns) **114**:95
"Song for a Banjo Dance" (Hughes) **53**:91-92
"Song for a Dancer" (Rexroth) **95**:256
"Song for a Dark Girl" (Hughes) **1**:238, 243
"Song for a Hypothetical Age" (Muir) **49**:280
"Song for a Lady" (Sexton) **2**:352
"Song for a Lyre" (Bogan) **12**:90, 92
"Song for a Phallus" (Hughes) **7**:132, 159, 171; **89**:137-38, 141
"Song for a Red Night Gown" (Sexton) **2**:352-53
"Song for a Slight Voice" (Bogan) **12**:90, 92
"Song for a Small Boy Who Herds Goats" (Winters) **82**:323
"Song—For A' That and A' That" (Burns)
See "For A' That and A' That"
"Song for a Viola d'Amore" (Lowell) **13**:88, 97
"Song for Abraham Klein" (Cohen) **109**:52, 54, 56
"Song for Billie Holiday" (Hughes) **53**:114
"Song for Bird and Myself" (Spicer) **78**:253
"The Song for Colin" (Teasdale) **31**:330, 332, 338
"Song for Gwydion" (Thomas) **99**:285-86
"A Song for J. H." (Behn) **13**:19
"A Song for Kenneth Burke" (Stern) **115**:272
"Song for Music" (Hood) **93**:62, 78
"Song for Myself" (Tolson) **88**:231, 329-30, 343
"A Song for New-Ark" (Giovanni) **19**:143
"Song for Nobody" (Merton) **10**:349
"A Song for Occupations" (Whitman) **3**:385, 401-02; **91**:230, 249-51, 285-86
"SONG FOR OOLJAH" (Bissett) **14**:33
"A Song for Rosemarie" (Villa) **22**:354
"A Song for Simeon" (Eliot) **5**:194, 196-97, 203, 205, 209
"A Song for Soweto" (Jordan) **38**:130-31
Song for St Cecilia's Day (Dryden) **25**:75-8
"Song for Stalingrad" (Neruda)
See "Canto a Stalingrado"
"Song for Sunsets" (Birney) **52**:74
"Song for Synge" (Montague) **106**:297
"Song for the Death of Averroës" (Merton) **10**:343
"Song for the Last Act" (Bogan) **12**:124
"A Song for the Middle of the Night" (Wright) **36**:335, 373
"Song for the Mothers of Dead Militiamen" (Neruda)
See "Canto a las madres de los milicianos muertos"
"Song for the Next River" (Gallagher) **9**:35
"Song for the Pockets" (Soto) **28**:375
"A Song for the Ragged Schools of London" (Barrett Browning) **6**:7, 23
"Song for the Rainy Season" (Bishop) **3**:67; **34**:91, 105
"Song for the Renewal of Power" (Wagoner) **33**:353
"Song for the Saddest Ides" (Nash) **21**:263
"Song for the Season" (Welch) **62**:371
"Song for the Squeeze Box" (Roethke) **15**:256
"A Song for the Time" (Whittier) **93**:321
"A Song for the Year's End" (Zukofsky) **11**:349
"A Song from Shakespear's Cymbeline" (Collins) **72**:60, 62, 82, 125, 129
"Song from the HIghest Tower" (Rimbaud)
See "Chanson de la plus haute tour"
"Song from the Second Floor" (Wagoner) **33**:357, 367
"A Song from the Structures of Rime Ringing as the Poet Paul Celan Sings" (Duncan) **2**:117
"Song. 'Goe, and catche a falling starre'" (Donne) **1**:125
"Song: Great Chain of Being" (Kennedy) **93**:143
"Song: Heat" (Dorn) **115**:126
"Song I" (Rilke) **2**:273
"Song in a Wine-Bar" (Wright) **14**:333
"Song in a year of Catastrophe" (Berry) **28**:43
"A Song in the Front Yard" (Brooks) **7**:69
"A Song in the same Play by the wavering Nymph" (Behn) **88**:148-49
"Song in the Songless" (Meredith) **60**:327
"A Song Inscribed to the Fremont Clubs" (Whittier) **93**:212
"Song: Lift-Boy" (Graves) **6**:142, 144

"Song: Love a woman? You're an ass!" (Wilmot)
See "Love a woman? You're an ass!"
"The Song Maker" (Teasdale) **31**:321
"Song Making" (Teasdale) **31**:351, 359-60, 379
"Song: Not There" (Jarrell) **41**:174
"Song of a camera" (Gunn) **26**:212
"Song of a Dream Visit to T'ien-mu: Farewell to Those I Leave Behind" (Li Po) **29**:147
"Song of a Hebrew" (Abse) **41**:6
"Song of a Man Who Has Come Through" (Lawrence) **54**:182-83, 216-17
"Song of a Man Who Is Loved" (Lawrence) **54**:183
"Song of a Man Who Is Not Loved" (Lawrence) **54**:183
"Song of a Prisoner" (Spicer) **78**:271
"The Song of a Rat" (Hughes) **7**:142, 155-56, 159; **89**:99, 112-13, 216
"Song of a Second April" (Millay) **6**:206
"Song of a Young Lady to Her Ancient Lover" (Wilmot) **66**:266, 269, 344, 347
"The Song of Absinthe Granny" (Stone) **53**:228-29, 237-38, 258
"Song of Another Tribe" (Rukeyser) **12**:217
"Song of Autumn in Spring" (Darío)
See "Canción de otoño en primavera"
"Song of Color" (Walker) **30**:352
"Song of Corinna" (Wilmot)
See "What cruel pains Corinna takes"
"The Song of Courtesy" (Meredith) **60**:294, 308
"Song of Days" (Meredith) **60**:331
"Song of Death" (Mistral)
See "Canción de la Muerte"
"Song of Defeat" (Tagore)
See "Parajaya sangīt"
"A Song of Derivations" (Meynell) **112**:192, 286
"Song of Despair" (Carducci)
See "Desperata"
"Song of Despair" (Neruda) **4**:301
"The Song of Diego Valdez" (Kipling) **3**:182
"Song of Enchantment" (de la Mare) **77**:109
"The Song of Finis" (de la Mare) **77**:124
"The Song of God's Child" (Li Ho) **13**:52
The Song of Hiawatha (Longfellow) **30**:16, 20-2, 25, 28-30, 34-5, 38-40, 44, 55-57, 59-61, 65, 73-4, 77-80, 82-4, 87-8
"Song of Indian Women" (Whittier) **93**:171
"Song of Invisible Boundaries" (Glück) **16**:166
"A Song of Joys" (Whitman) **3**:402
"The Song of Lamech" (Clough) **103**:138
"Song of Li Ling" (Wang Wei) **18**:389
"A Song of Liberty" (Blake) **12**:33
"A Song of Life" (Werfel) **101**:346
"Song of Longsight" (Hughes) **89**:129
"The Song of Love" (Carducci)
See "Il canto dell' amore"
"Song of Love" (Lamartine)
See "Chant d'amour"
"Song of Love" (Seferis)
See "Erotikos Logos"
"A Song of my heart" (Bridges) **28**:69
"Song of Myself" (Berryman) **64**:110
"Song of Myself" (Whitman) **3**:370, 394, 396-97, 399, 401-03, 405, 411-12, 414-17; **91**:201, 206-8, 216, 218, 225-27, 229-30, 232, 245, 257, 260-61, 270-72, 277, 281, 295, 298, 309, 316, 329
"The Song of Nature" (Emerson) **18**:88
"Song of Occupations" (Whitman)
See "A Song for Occupations"
"Song of Opposites" (Keats) **1**:312; **96**:241, 309-10
"Song of P'eng-ya" (Tu Fu) **9**:321, 332
"Song of Praise" (Cullen) **20**:52, 63
"A Song of Praise" (Sanchez) **9**:243
"The Song of Rahéro" (Stevenson)
See "The Tale of Rahéro"
The Song of Roland (Anonymous)
See *La Chanson de Roland*
"The Song of Safe Conduct" (Bonnefoy)
See "Le Chant de sauvegarde"
"The Song of Seven" (de la Mare) **77**:109-10
"The Song of Shadows" (de la Mare) **77**:73
"A Song of Sherwood" (Noyes) **27**:136-137
"Song of Siberia" (Ishikawa)
See "Shiberia no uta"
"Song of Slaves in the Desert" (Whittier) **93**:265, 268, 343
"A Song of Sojourner Truth" (Jordan) **38**:125
"The Song of Soldiers" (de la Mare) **77**:112
"Song of Songs" (Owen) **102**:143
"Song of Spain" (Hughes) **53**:115
"A Song of Swans" (Gilmore) **87**:299
"Song of Taurus" (Mistral)
See "Canción de taurus"
"Song of the Andoumboulou: 1" (Mackey) **49**:37
"Song of the Andoumboulou: 3" (Mackey) **49**:31, 37-38, 43
"Song of the Andoumboulou: 4" (Mackey) **49**:6
"Song of the Andoumboulou: 5" (Mackey) **49**:3, 39, 71, 74
"Song of the Andoumboulou: 6" (Mackey) **49**:4, 31, 42-44
"Song of the Andoumboulou: 7" (Mackey) **49**:4, 37, 42
"Song of the Andoumboulou: 10" (Mackey) **49**:39
"Song of the Andoumboulou: 11" (Mackey) **49**:71
"Song of the Andoumboulou: 14" (Mackey) **49**:39
"Song of the Andoumboulou: 15" (Mackey) **49**:30, 40, 70
"Song of the Andoumboulou: 16" (Mackey) **49**:42, 54-55, 61, 64, 68, 70
"Song of the Andoumboulou: 1-7" (Mackey) **49**:30, 55-7
"Song of the Andoumboulou: 18" (Mackey) **49**:57, 63, 77-79
"Song of the Andoumboulou: 19" (Mackey) **49**:68
"Song of the Andoumboulou: 20" (Mackey) **49**:57
"Song of the Andoumboulou: 23" (Mackey) **49**:42, 74
"Song of the Andoumboulou: 24" (Mackey) **49**:42
"Song of the Andoumboulou: 26" (Mackey) **49**:57, 67
"Song of the Andoumboulou: 27" (Mackey) **49**:58
"Song of the Andoumboulou: 30" (Mackey) **49**:80
"Song of the Andoumboulou: 31" (Mackey) **49**:58
"Song of the Andoumboulou: 34" (Mackey) **49**:68, 76
"Song of the Andoumboulou: 35" (Mackey) **49**:58, 64, 80
"Song of the Andoumboulou: 8-15" (Mackey) **49**:30
Song of the Andoumboulou: 18-20 (Mackey) **49**:2-3, 17, 25, 29, 31-36, 38-42, 45, 47, 51-53, 56, 58-59, 61-62, 65-68, 71-72, 74-75, 77-78
"Song of the Answerer" (Whitman) **3**:386, 390
"Song of the Banjo" (Kipling) **3**:160-61; **91**:104
"Song of the Bard" (Blake)
See "Bard's Song"
"Song of the Beasts" (Brooke) **24**:59, 82
"Song of the Beasts" (Hecht) **70**:93
"Song of the Beautiful Ladies" (Tu Fu) **9**:320
"Song of the Bird" (Tagore)
See "Vihanger gan"
"Song of the Blind Artificer" (Schwerner)
See "Tablet XXVI"
"Song of the Body Electric" (Whitman)
See "I Sing the Body Electric"
"The Song of the Bongo" (Guillén)
See "La canción del bongo"
"Song of the Books" (Clarke) **112**:93-94
"Song of the Borderguard" (Duncan) **75**:180
"The Song of the Bower" (Rossetti) **44**:165
"Song of the Broad-Axe" (Whitman) **91**:207, 209
"The Song of the Chattahoochee" (Lanier) **50**:77-78, 98-99; **50**:56, 92
"The Song of the Children" (Chesterton) **28**:100
"Song of the Children in Heaven" (Brooke) **24**:76
"The Song of the Cities" (Kipling) **3**:162; **91**:66, 85
The Song of the Cold (Sitwell) **3**:320, 326
"Song of the Columns" (Valéry)
See "Cantique des colonnes"
"Song of the Crows roosting at night" (Li Po) **29**:143
"Song of the Day to the Night" (Meynell) **112**:156
"Song of the Dead" (Kipling) **3**:160, 162
"A Song of the Dust" (Sitwell) **3**:327
"A Song of the English" (Kipling) **3**:160-62, 164; **91**:64, 84-86, 89-90
"The Song of the Exiles" (Kipling) **3**:194
"The Song of the Final Meeting/Song of the Last Meeting" (Akhmatova)
See "Pesnia poslednei vstrechi"
"The Song of the Galley Slaves" (Kipling) **3**:170
"The Song of the Happy Shepherd" (Yeats) **20**:354; **51**:149
"Song of the Heavenly Horse" (Li Po) **29**:159, 161
"Song of the Hen's Head" (Atwood) **8**:41
"Song of the Highest Tower" (Rimbaud) **3**:259
"The Song of the Ill-beloved" (Apollinaire)
See "La chanson du mal-aimé"
"Song of the Little Square" (García Lorca)
See "Ballada de la Placeta"
The Song of the Love and Death of Cornet Christopher Rilke (Rilke)
See *Die Weise von Liebe und Tod des Cornets Christoph Rilke*
"The Song of the Low-Caste Wife" (Wickham) **110**:270-71
"Song of the Mad Prince" (de la Mare) **77**:73
"Song of the Man Forsaken and Obsessed" (Berryman) **64**:87
The Song of the Merchant Kaláshnikov (Lermontov)
See *Pesnya pro tsarya Ivana Vasilievicha, molodogo oprichnika i undalogo kuptsa Kalashnikova*
"Song of the Native Land" (Seifert) **47**:326
"Song of the Negro Boatmen" (Whittier) **93**:315, 318
"Song of the Night" (Kinsella) **69**:130
Song of the Night (Leopardi)
See "Canto notturno di un pastore errante dell'Asia"
Song of the Night and Other Poems (Kinsella) **69**:77, 140
"Song of the Night at Daybreak" (Meynell) **112**:156, 189
"Song of the Ogres" (Auden) **92**:70
"Song of the Open Road" (Whitman) **3**:387; **91**:214, 216
"The Song of the Pacifist" (Service) **70**:133
"Song of the Peach Fountainhead" (Wang Wei) **18**:389
"The Song of the Pilgrims" (Brooke) **24**:76
"The Song of the Poorly Beloved" (Apollinaire)
See "La chanson du mal-aimé"
"The Song of the Red War-Boat" (Kipling) **3**:183
"Song of the Redwood Tree" (Whitman) **91**:278-82
"Song of the Rescued" (Sachs)
See "Chor der Geretteten"
"A Song of the Rolling Earth" (Whitman) **91**:270

"A Song of the Rosy Cros" (Yeats) **51**:103
"The Song of the Shirt" (Hood) **93**:44, 47, 60-62, 69, 81-82, 84-85, 87, 101-5, 108, 116, 118-19
The Song of the Six Bards (Macpherson) **97**:194
"The Song of the Social Failure" (Service) **70**:152-53
"Song of the Soldiers" (Hardy) **92**:200
"Song of the Son" (Toomer) **7**:310, 317, 319, 334
"The Song of the Sons" (Kipling) **3**:162
"A Song of the Soul of Central" (Hughes) **1**:268
"Song of the Sower" (Bryant) **20**:14
"Song of the Stars" (Bryant) **20**:4
"Song of the Taste" (Snyder) **21**:297
"A Song of the Time" (Whittier) **93**:212
"The Song of the Tortured Girl" (Berryman) **64**:186, 191
"Song of the Trees" (Winters) **82**:319
Song of the Tsar Ivan Vasilievich, the young oprichnik and the bold Merchant Kalashnikov (Lermontov)
See *Pesnya pro tsarya Ivana Vasilievicha, molodogo oprichnika i undalogo kuptsa Kalashnikova*
"Song of the Worms" (Atwood) **8**:19, 25
"The Song of the Young Hawaiian" (Berryman) **64**:89
"Song of Theodolinda" (Meredith) **60**:250
The Song of Tzar Ivan Vasiljevich, His Young Life-Guardsman, and the Valiant Merchant Kaláshnikov (Lermontov)
See *Pesnya pro tsarya Ivana Vasilievicha, molodogo oprichnika i undalogo kuptsa Kalashnikova*
"The Song of Vermonters" (Whittier) **93**:243
The Song of Viktorka (Seifert)
See *Píseň o Viktorce*
"Song of Virgo" (Mistral)
See "Canción de virgo"
"Song of Women" (Masters) **1**:330, 333
Song Offerings (Tagore)
See *Gitanjali*
"A Song on Gazing at Chung-nan Mountain For Hsü of the Secretariat" (Wang Wei) **18**:369
"A Song on Greife" (Finch) **21**:150, 152, 179
"Song: On Her Loving Two Equally" (Behn) **88**:87, 149
"Song over Some Ruins" (Neruda)
See "Canto sobre unas ruinas"
"A Song: Sensation Time at the Home" (Merton) **10**:345
"A Song Sparrow Singing in the Fall" (Berry) **28**:7
"Song. 'Sweetest love, I do not goe'" (Donne) **1**:130
"Song: The Rev. MuBngwu Dickenson Ruminates behind the Sermon" (Brooks) **7**:94
"A Song to a Negro Wash-woman" (Hughes) **53**:169-70
"Song. To a New Scotch Tune" (Behn) **88**:111, 163-65
"Song to a Scotish tune" (Behn)
See "Song. To a New Scotch Tune"
"A Song to a Scotish Tune (Come My Phillis Let Us Improve)" (Behn) **13**:18
"Song to a Scotish Tune (When Jemmy First Began to Love)" (Behn) **13**:4, 7, 18, 32; **88**:111, 148, 150, 152
"Song to Alfred Hitchcock and Wilkinson" (Ondaatje) **28**:291
"Song: To Amarantha" (Lovelace)
See "To Amarantha, That She Would Dishevell Her Hair"
"A Song to Amoret" (Vaughan) **81**:358
"Song to an Old Burden" (Hardy) **92**:240
"Song to Awaken a Little Black Child" (Guillén) **23**:132
"Song . . . to be Sung at the Class-Supper of the Sophomore Class of 1834" (Very) **86**:123
"Song to Celia" (Jonson) f **17**:170, 180
"Song to Ceres, in the wavering Nymph or Mad Amyntas" (Behn) **88**:148-49
"Song to Chloris" (Wilmot) **66**:278, 329, 336
A Song to David (Smart) **13**:328-34, 336-46, 352-54, 358, 360-65, 367-69
"Song to Ishtar" (Levertov) **11**:169
"A Song to No Music" (Brodsky) **9**:4, 9, 12
"Song: To Pesibles Tune" (Behn) **88**:149
"Song to the Men of England" (Shelley) **67**:214
"Song to the Mothers of Dead Loyalists" (Neruda)
See "Canto a las madres de los milicianos muertos"
"Song to the Tune of 'Somebody Stole My Gal'" (Kennedy) **93**:138, 144, 148
"Song to the Young John" (Wickham) **110**:308
"Song. To Two Lovers Condemn'd to die" (Davenant) **99**:176
"Song to Woody" (Dylan) **37**:67
"Song upon the Bleeding Crucifix" (Crashaw) **84**:15, 33, 102-3, 155
"A Song Untitled" (Hagiwara) **18**:173
"Song: Venceremos" (Dorn) **115**:127
"Song (Where I Walk Out)" (Winters) **82**:319
"Song Winds of Downhill" (Oppen) **35**:340
"Song without Music" (Brodsky)
See "A Song to No Music"
"Songe D'Athalie" (Smith) **12**:331
"Songe toe Ella" (Chatterton) **104**:19
"Songin Black Armor" (Wylie) **23**:308, 310, 332
"Songless" (Walker) **30**:348
Sóngoro cosongo: Poemas mulatos (Guillén) **23**:98-100, 105-106, 111, 114, 131, 139, 142-44
"Songs" (Benn) **35**:54
Songs (Blake)
See *Songs of Innocence and of Experience: Shewing the Two Contrary States of the Human Soul*
"Songs" (Hughes) **1**:241; **53**:134
"Songs" (Lawrence) **54**:183
"Songs" (Mistral)
See "Coplas"
Songs (García Lorca)
See *Canciones*
Songs (Wickham) **110**:258, 273, 308
"Songs: 65° N" (Larkin) **21**:226
Songs and Little Odes (Stevenson) **84**:335
Songs and Satires (Masters) **1**:328, 335, 342; **36**:174, 176, 183
Songs and Sonets (Donne) **1**:130, 139, 145; **43**:102, 132, 163, 166, 168, 180, 188
Songs and Sonnets (Donne)
See *Songs and Sonets*
Songs and Sonnets (Masters) **36**:221
Songs and Sonnets (Surrey) **59**:290, 310
Songs and Sonnets of Pierre de Ronsard, Gentleman of Vendomois (Ronsard)
See *See Les œuvres de P. de Ronsard, gentilhomme vandomois*
Songs and Sonnets, second series (Masters) **1**:321, 325, 332
Songs before Sunrise (Swinburne) **24**:312
"Songs for a Colored Singer" (Bishop) **3**:37, 46-7; **34**:69, 78, 137-38, 160, 188, 190
Songs for a Summer Day (MacLeish) **47**:182
Songs for Eve (MacLeish) **47**:175-80, 192, 197, 208, 214
"Songs for My Father" (Komunyakaa) **51**:36
"Songs For My Son" (Goodison) **36**:148
Songs for My Supper (Service) **70**:140, 144, 161
"Songs for Myself" (Teasdale) **31**:333, 358, 360, 370, 379
Songs for Naëtt (Senghor)
See *Chants pour Naëtt*
Songs for Sale (Christine de Pizan)
See *Jeux à vendre*
Songs for Soldiers and Tunes for Tourists (Guillén)
See *Cantos para soldados y sones para turistas*
"Songs for the Dream Catchers" (Wagoner) **33**:348
"Songs for the People" (Harper) **21**:189
Songs for the Republic (Cassian) **17**:6
Songs from a Northern Garden (Carman) **34**:205, 210, 225
"Songs from Cyprus" (H. D.) **5**:304
Songs from down there (Jaccottet)
See *Chants d'en bas*
"Songs from the Plays" (Koch) **80**:326-27
Songs from Vagabondia (Carman) **34**:198, 200, 205-08, 214, 218-20, 229, 231, 237-38
"Songs in a Cornfield" (Rossetti) **7**:275
"Songs in Many Keys" (Holmes) **71**:66
Songs of a Sourdough (Service) **70**:114, 127, 129, 139, 143-44, 150-53, 155-59, 161
Songs of a Sun-Lover (Service) **70**:140-41, 161
Songs of Bhanusigh Thakur (Tagore)
See *Bhanusingh Thakurer padāvali*
Songs of Bhanusingh Thakur (Tagore)
See *Bhanusinga Thakurer Padavali*
Songs of Childhood (de la Mare) **77**:58, 73, 81, 86-87, 94, 97, 118, 120, 128-29, 133, 142
"Songs of Education" (Chesterton) **28**:99
Songs of Experience (Blake)
See *Songs of Innocence and of Experience: Shewing the Two Contrary States of the Human Soul*
Songs of Innocence (Blake)
See *Songs of Innocence and of Experience: Shewing the Two Contrary States of the Human Soul*
Songs of Innocence and of Experience: Shewing the Two Contrary States of the Human Soul (Blake) **12**:8-11, 19, 21-25, 31-35, 42-47, 51, 61-62; **63**:1-136
Songs of Jamaica (McKay) **2**:208, 210, 216, 221, 223-27
Songs of Kabir (Kabīr) **56**:316
Songs of Labor, and Other Poems (Whittier) **93**:170, 172, 266, 277
Songs of Leonard Cohen (Cohen) **109**:29, 81
Songs of Life and Hope (Darío)
See *Cantos de vida y esperanza*
Songs of Many Seasons (Holmes) **71**:74
"The Songs of Maximus" (Olson) **19**:282-83
Songs of Mourning: Bewailing the Untimely Death of Prince Henry. Worded by Tho. Campion. And Set Forth to Bee Sung with One Voyce to the Lute, or Violl: by John Coprario (Campion) **87**:7, 12, 48, 68
"Songs of Release" (Goodison) **36**:152
"The Songs of Selma" (Macpherson) **97**:185, 206, 319, 324
Songs of the High North (Service) **70**:161
"Songs of the Ingenues" (Verlaine)
See "La chanson des ingénues"
"songs of the old frogs" (Alurista) **34**:32
"Songs of the Pixies" (Coleridge) **39**:212
"Songs of the Psyche" (Kinsella) **69**:131
Songs of the Psyche (Kinsella) **69**:133, 135
"Songs of the Runaway Bride" (Gallagher) **9**:37
Songs of the Sea Children (Carman) **34**:205, 209-11, 224-26
"Songs of the Shade" (Senghor)
See *Chants d'ombre*
Songs of the Springtides (Swinburne) **24**:322
"Songs of the Transformed" (Atwood) **8**:23, 25-6
Songs of the Yukon (Service) **70**:160
Songs of Three Centuries (Whittier) **93**:216
Songs of Travel and Other Verses (Stevenson) **84**:324-27, 331-32
"Songs out of Sorrow" (Teasdale) **31**:322, 355-56
Songs: Set 2 (Dorn) **115**:119, 221

"Songs to Survive the Summer" (Hass) **16**:199, 201, 210-16
Songs without Words (Verlaine)
See *Romances sans paroles*
"sonik prayr" (Bissett) **14**:27
"The Sonne" (Herbert) **4**:109
"The Sonne hath twyse" (Surrey) **59**:312
"Sonnet" (Meynell) **112**:255, 257, 287, 291
"Sonnet 1" (Duncan) **75**:200
"Sonnet 1" (Shakespeare) **98**:231, 233, 240, 243, 246, 271, 276, 278-79, 287, 300-301, 304, 313, 318; **101**:106
"Sonnet 1" (Smith) **104**:160
"Sonnet 2" (Shakespeare) **98**:271, 275, 287, 315; **101**:105-6
"Sonnet 2" (Smith) **104**:194
"Sonnet 2" (Suckling)
See "Sonnet II"
"Sonnet 3" (Shakespeare) **98**:275-76, 278, 301, 313
"Sonnet 3" (Smith) **104**:286-87
"Sonnet 4" (Barker) **77**:3
"Sonnet 4" (Shakespeare) **98**:262, 276, 278-79, 287, 313, 315; **101**:105-7
"Sonnet 4" (Smith) **104**:268, 281, 319
"Sonnet 5" (Shakespeare) **98**:276, 278, 313
"Sonnet 5" (Smith) **104**:162-63, 281, 286, 289, 320
"Sonnet 6" (Barker) **77**:3
"Sonnet 6" (Ronsard) **105**:346
"Sonnet 6" (Shakespeare) **98**:262, 272, 276, 278, 287-88, 313, 315, 335; **101**:106
"Sonnet 6" (Smith) **104**:286
"Sonnet 7" (Milton) **19**:214, 256
"Sonnet 7" (Shakespeare) **98**:262, 266, 272, 276
"Sonnet 7" (Smith) **104**:287, 319
"Sonnet 8" (Barker) **77**:3
"Sonnet 8" (Shakespeare) **98**:242, 255, 273-74, 313
"Sonnet 8" (Smith) **104**:162, 281, 343
"Sonnet 9" (Barker) **77**:3
"Sonnet 9" (Shakespeare) **98**:240, 242, 262, 270, 287, 313
"Sonnet 9" (Smith) **104**:160, 186, 190
"Sonnet 10" (Shakespeare) **98**:242, 287, 313
"Sonnet 11" (Shakespeare) **98**:242, 276, 288; **101**:106
"Sonnet 12" (Shakespeare) **98**:240, 242, 268, 271, 275-76, 302
"Sonnet 12" (Smith) **104**:164, 197, 212, 300, 320-21
"Sonnet 13" (Shakespeare) **98**:239, 287, 313
"Sonnet 13" (Smith) **104**:245, 287
"Sonnet 14" (Shakespeare) **89**:333; **98**:247, 266, 276-77
"Sonnet 14" (Smith) **104**:189, 287
"Sonnet 15" (Shakespeare) **98**:271, 275, 313
"Sonnet 15" (Smith) **104**:245, 287
"Sonnet 16 (On his blindness)" (Milton) **19**:214
"Sonnet 16" (Shakespeare) **98**:287, 313; **101**:106
"Sonnet 16" (Smith) **104**:246, 287
"Sonnet 17" (Shakespeare) **98**:239, 273, 276, 293, 299, 313
"Sonnet 18" (Ronsard) **105**:343, 345
"Sonnet 18" (Shakespeare) **89**:338; **98**:241, 248, 255, 262, 272-73, 275, 293, 304, 313
"Sonnet 19" (Shakespeare) **98**:239, 241, 246, 273, 275, 313
"Sonnet 20" (Shakespeare) **98**:243, 250, 256, 260, 278-79, 304, 314-15, 318, 329, 345-46
"Sonnet 21" (Shakespeare) **89**:335; **98**:239, 242, 264, 288, 294, 298, 304-5
"Sonnet 21" (Smith) **104**:161, 243, 245-46, 268, 276
"Sonnet 22" (Berryman) **64**:107
"Sonnet 22" (Shakespeare) **98**:242, 254, 290, 316
"Sonnet 23" (Shakespeare) **98**:242-43, 298
"Sonnet 23" (Smith) **104**:224, 268, 276
"Sonnet 24" (Shakespeare) **98**:272, 277, 286, 302, 325
"Sonnet 24" (Smith) **104**:269
"Sonnet 25" (Shakespeare) **98**:262, 290, 302, 312, 316, 318
"Sonnet 25" (Smith) **104**:246
"Sonnet 26" (Shakespeare) **98**:298, 302, 319
"Sonnet 26" (Smith) **104**:163, 246, 320
"Sonnet 27" (Shakespeare) **98**:227-28, 277, 315
"Sonnet 27" (Smith) **104**:163
"Sonnet 28" (Shakespeare) **98**:227-28, 315
"Sonnet 29" (Shakespeare) **98**:260, 271, 277, 312-13, 316, 318; **101**:73
"Sonnet 29" (Smith) **104**:247
"Sonnet 30" (Shakespeare) **98**:243, 260, 271, 277-78, 316
"Sonnet 30" (Smith) **104**:163
"Sonnet 31" (Shakespeare) **98**:277, 316; **101**:81
"Sonnet 32" (Shakespeare) **98**:277, 298, 305, 316
"Sonnet 32" (Smith) **104**:163, 194, 246-47, 249
"Sonnet 33" (Shakespeare) **98**:215-16, 265, 277, 316
"Sonnet 34" (Shakespeare) **98**:215-16, 265, 272, 316
"Sonnet 35" (Shakespeare) **98**:214-15, 241, 250, 277, 316; **101**:38-39, 91
"Sonnet 36" (Shakespeare) **98**:237, 253, 272, 277, 311, 316-17
"Sonnet 36" (Smith) **104**:319
"Sonnet 38" (Shakespeare) **98**:255, 298-99, 305-6
"Sonnet 38" (Smith) **104**:163, 244
"Sonnet 39" (Shakespeare) **98**:277, 298
"Sonnet 39" (Smith) **104**:269
"Sonnet 40" (Shakespeare) **98**:217-20, 263-64, 273, 277, 314, 317
"Sonnet 40" (Smith) **104**:163, 319
"Sonnet 41" (Shakespeare) **98**:218-20, 317
"Sonnet 42" (Shakespeare) **98**:218-20, 254, 272, 277, 317
"Sonnet 43" (Shakespeare) **98**:241, 265, 271, 277
"Sonnet 44" (Shakespeare) **98**:247, 290
"Sonnet 44" (Smith) **104**:186, 281, 319
"Sonnet 45" (Ronsard) **105**:303-7
"Sonnet 45" (Shakespeare) **98**:290
"Sonnet 45" (Smith) **104**:163, 225
"Sonnet 46" (Shakespeare) **98**:265, 277, 286
"Sonnet 47" (Shakespeare) **98**:240, 265, 277
"Sonnet 47" (Smith) **104**:235, 244, 254, 286
"Sonnet 48" (Shakespeare) **98**:253, 286
"Sonnet 48" (Smith) **104**:245, 253
"Sonnet 49" (Shakespeare) **98**:271, 289
"Sonnet 49" (Smith) **104**:280
"Sonnet 50" (Shakespeare) **98**:254, 277
"Sonnet 51" (Shakespeare) **98**:254, 271
"Sonnet 52" (Shakespeare) **98**:240
"Sonnet 53" (Shakespeare) **89**:339; **98**:274, 276, 278-79, 317
"Sonnet 54" (Shakespeare) **98**:233-34, 254, 261, 266, 298
"Sonnet 54" (Smith) **104**:164, 186, 319
"Sonnet 55" (Shakespeare) **98**:256, 273-74, 277, 279, 298, 345
"Sonnet 56" (Ronsard) **105**:346
"Sonnet 56" (Shakespeare) **98**:241, 272, 274, 279, 345
"Sonnet 57" (Shakespeare) **98**:220, 253, 265, 271, 274, 311, 330-32
"Sonnet 57" (Smith) **104**:196, 252
"Sonnet 58" (Shakespeare) **98**:220-21, 253, 274
"Sonnet 59" (Shakespeare) **98**:273-74, 298, 300
"Sonnet 60" (Shakespeare) **98**:233, 242, 260, 267, 274, 326
"Sonnet 61" (Shakespeare) **98**:242, 263, 277
"Sonnet 61" (Smith) **104**:229
"Sonnet 62" (Shakespeare) **98**:242, 265, 271
"Sonnet 62" (Smith) **104**:196, 300
"Sonnet 63" (Shakespeare) **89**:337-39; **98**:242-43, 254, 275, 277
"Sonnet 64" (Shakespeare) **98**:242, 271
"Sonnet 64" (Smith) **104**:338-39, 348
"Sonnet 65" (Shakespeare) **98**:242, 271
"Sonnet 65" (Smith) **104**:274, 339
"Sonnet 66" (Shakespeare) **98**:230, 242, 261-62, 265-66, 277
"Sonnet 66" (Smith) **104**:195
"Sonnet 67" (Shakespeare) **89**:337; **98**:229-33, 254, 272, 287
"Sonnet 67" (Smith) **104**:195
"Sonnet 68" (Shakespeare) **98**:229-33, 286-87
"Sonnet 69" (Shakespeare) **98**:230-33
"Sonnet 70" (Berryman) **64**:89
"Sonnet 70" (Shakespeare) **98**:230, 232-33
"Sonnet 70" (Smith) **104**:190, 222, 244-45, 285, 299
"Sonnet 71" (Shakespeare) **98**:277, 289, 304-5
"Sonnet 72" (Shakespeare) **98**:289, 304-5
"Sonnet 73" (Shakespeare) **89**:337; **98**:243, 247-48, 262, 267, 271, 277, 305, 312, 316; **101**:3
"Sonnet 74" (Shakespeare) **98**:247, 289, 298, 305
"Sonnet 74" (Smith) **104**:165, 274-75
"Sonnet 75" (Shakespeare) **98**:241, 277, 315
"Sonnet 76" (Berryman) **64**:82
"Sonnet 76" (Shakespeare) **98**:241, 254, 261, 264, 268-70, 274, 293, 302-3, 305
"Sonnet 77" (Shakespeare) **98**:289
"Sonnet 78" (Shakespeare) **98**:264-65, 279, 302, 304-5, 311
"Sonnet 78" (Smith) **104**:274
"Sonnet 79" (Shakespeare) **98**:272, 292, 305-6
"Sonnet 79" (Smith) **104**:167, 197-98, 340, 344-45, 347
"Sonnet 80" (Shakespeare) **98**:277, 305
"Sonnet 81" (Shakespeare) **98**:247, 274, 277, 304-5
"Sonnet 82" (Shakespeare) **98**:277, 288, 292, 299, 305
"Sonnet 82" (Smith) **104**:166, 280
"Sonnet 83" (Shakespeare) **98**:288, 299, 301, 305
"Sonnet 83" (Smith) **104**:224
"Sonnet 84" (Shakespeare) **98**:264, 289, 299-301, 305-6
"Sonnet 85" (Shakespeare) **98**:247, 264, 299, 301, 305-6; **101**:42
"Sonnet 86" (Shakespeare) **98**:277, 293, 301, 305-6, 311; **101**:42
"Sonnet 87" (Berryman) **64**:168
"Sonnet 87" (Shakespeare) **98**:252, 277, 306, 311, 316-18; **101**:42
"Sonnet 88" (Berryman) **64**:90
"Sonnet 88" (Shakespeare) **98**:289, 306-7; **101**:42
"Sonnet 89" (Shakespeare) **98**:289, 307; **101**:42
"Sonnet 89" (Smith) **104**:195, 274
"Sonnet 90" (Shakespeare) **98**:271-72, 307; **101**:42
"Sonnet 90" (Smith) **104**:190, 195, 274-75, 281
"Sonnet 91" (Shakespeare) **98**:236, 273; **101**:42
"Sonnet 91" (Smith) **104**:183, 188-89, 195, 274, 339
"Sonnet 92" (Shakespeare) **98**:272-73; **101**:42
"Sonnet 92" (Smith) **104**:195
"Sonnet 93" (Shakespeare) **98**:233, 243-44, 279, 307, 317, 343; **101**:42
"Sonnet 94" (Shakespeare) **98**:215, 233-37, 245, 252, 263-64, 277, 307, 317; **101**:42, 63
"Sonnet 95" (Shakespeare) **98**:233-37, 264, 307; **101**:42
"Sonnet 96" (Shakespeare) **98**:234, 236-37, 241, 253, 272, 306-7, 317; **101**:42
"Sonnet 97" (Shakespeare) **98**:248, 265, 277, 307-8; **101**:42
"Sonnet 98" (Shakespeare) **98**:248, 273, 276-77, 279, 306-8; **101**:42
"Sonnet 99" (Berryman) **64**:107
"Sonnet 99" (Shakespeare) **98**:251, 253, 287, 308; **101**:42
"Sonnet 100" (Shakespeare) **98**:275, 279, 306, 308; **101**:42

"Sonnet 101" (Shakespeare) **98**:241, 308, 318; **101**:42
"Sonnet 102" (Shakespeare) **98**:248, 279, 326; **101**:42
"Sonnet 103" (Shakespeare) **89**:339; **98**:288, 308; **101**:42
"Sonnet 104" (Shakespeare) **89**:338-39; **98**:240, 261-62, 273-74, 276-77, 279, 302, 316, 318; **101**:42
"Sonnet 105" (Shakespeare) **98**:247, 260-61, 264, 273, 293, 302-3; **101**:42
"Sonnet 106" (Shakespeare) **98**:260, 262, 271, 277; **101**:42
"Sonnet 107" (Shakespeare) **98**:247, 275, 308; **101**:42
"Sonnet 108" (Shakespeare) **98**:241, 247, 264; **101**:42
"Sonnet 109" (Shakespeare) **98**:315; **101**:42
"Sonnet 110" (Shakespeare) **98**:273, 277, 315-16; **101**:42
"Sonnet 111" (Shakespeare) **98**:277; **101**:42
"Sonnet 112" (Shakespeare) **98**:279; **101**:42
"Sonnet 113" (Shakespeare) **98**:241, 276-77; **101**:42
"Sonnet 114" (Shakespeare) **98**:279; **101**:42
"Sonnet 115" (Shakespeare) **101**:42
"Sonnet 116" (Shakespeare) **98**:221, 248, 252, 260-61, 264, 272, 316, 339; **101**:42
"Sonnet 117" (Shakespeare) **98**:261; **101**:42
"Sonnet 118" (Shakespeare) **98**:277; **101**:42
"Sonnet 119" (Shakespeare) **98**:272, 277, 279; **101**:42
"Sonnet 120" (Shakespeare) **101**:42, 47
"Sonnet 121" (Shakespeare) **98**:252, 262, 266, 272; **101**:42
"Sonnet 122" (Shakespeare) **98**:241, 264; **101**:42
"Sonnet 123" (Shakespeare) **98**:318, 345; **101**:42
"Sonnet 124" (Shakespeare) **98**:221, 248, 262, 279, 327; **101**:42
"Sonnet 125" (Shakespeare) **89**:337; **98**:241, 260, 279; **101**:42
"Sonnet 126" (Shakespeare) **89**:337; **98**:241, 250-55, 276-77, 279, 311, 318, 344; **101**:42
"Sonnet 127" (Shakespeare) **89**:339; **98**:242, 280, 283, 290-91, 343-44; **101**:42
"Sonnet 128" (Shakespeare) **98**:242, 255-56, 277, 280, 330-32, 335; **101**:42
"Sonnet 129" (Shakespeare) **89**:316; **98**:233, 242, 252, 255, 257, 260, 262, 264, 266, 274, 277, 285, 315, 318, 341-43; **101**:11, 42, 59
"Sonnet 130" (Shakespeare) **89**:316, 336; **98**:242, 260, 264, 277, 284, 341; **101**:42
"Sonnet 131" (Shakespeare) **98**:242, 272, 277, 281, 339; **101**:42
"Sonnet 132" (Shakespeare) **98**:242, 262, 272, 280-81; **101**:42
"Sonnet 133" (Shakespeare) **98**:217, 277, 281, 286; **101**:42
"Sonnet 134" (Shakespeare) **98**:217, 281, 317; **101**:42
"Sonnet 135" (Shakespeare) **98**:221, 279, 281, 335-36, 338; **101**:42
"Sonnet 136" (Shakespeare) **98**:221, 279, 281; **101**:42
"Sonnet 137" (Shakespeare) **98**:221, 277, 332, 335-36; **101**:42
"Sonnet 138" (Shakespeare) **98**:239, 242, 262, 265, 284, 344; **101**:42
"Sonnet 139" (Shakespeare) **98**:273, 281; **101**:42
"Sonnet 140" (Shakespeare) **98**:272, 277, 338; **101**:42
"Sonnet 141" (Shakespeare) **98**:239, 277
"Sonnet 142" (Shakespeare) **98**:277, 281, 336
"Sonnet 143" (Shakespeare) **98**:255, 264, 273, 279
"Sonnet 144" (Shakespeare) **98**:217, 239, 242, 257, 264, 280-81, 317, 338, 342-43; **101**:62
"Sonnet 145" (Shakespeare) **98**:262
"Sonnet 146" (Shakespeare) **98**:246-47, 271, 280, 336; **101**:63
"Sonnet 147" (Shakespeare) **98**:255, 262, 264, 272, 277, 284, 336
"Sonnet 148" (Shakespeare) **98**:260, 264, 284, 337
"Sonnet 150" (Shakespeare) **98**:336-37
"Sonnet 151" (Shakespeare) **98**:271, 279-80, 323, 329, 337-38, 342, 345
"Sonnet 152" (Shakespeare) **98**:260, 284, 335, 339, 345
"Sonnet 153" (Shakespeare) **98**:262, 279; **101**:93
"Sonnet 154" (Shakespeare) **89**:339; **98**:262; **101**:93
"Sonnet I" (Berrigan) **103**:12-14
"Sonnet I" (Clough) **103**:100
"Sonnet I" (Meredith) **60**:310, 313, 315, 317-18, 320
"Sonnet I" (Patmore) **59**:257
"Sonnet I.9" (Tuckerman) **85**:322
"Sonnet I.10" (Tuckerman) **85**:336, 338-39, 342
"Sonnet I.11" (Tuckerman) **85**:319
"Sonnet I.23" (Tuckerman) **85**:321, 328, 342
"Sonnet I.24" (Tuckerman) **85**:305
"Sonnet I.25" (Tuckerman) **85**:328
"Sonnet I.26" (Tuckerman) **85**:328
"Sonnet I.27" (Tuckerman) **85**:329
"Sonnet I.28" (Tuckerman) **85**:319, 331
"Sonnet II" (Berrigan) **103**:12, 15, 39
"Sonnet II" (Clough) **103**:100
"Sonnet II" (Meredith) **60**:265, 272, 310, 313, 315, 319-20
"Sonnet II" (Suckling) **30**:129
"Sonnet II" (Thomas) **2**:388
"Sonnet II.7" (Tuckerman) **85**:341
"Sonnet II.12" (Tuckerman) **85**:319
"Sonnet II.14" (Tuckerman) **85**:335
"Sonnet II.15" (Tuckerman) **85**:340
"Sonnet II.16" (Tuckerman) **85**:340-41
"Sonnet II.17" (Tuckerman) **85**:336, 340
"Sonnet II.18" (Tuckerman) **85**:321, 340
"Sonnet II.19" (Tuckerman) **85**:321, 340
"Sonnet II.20" (Tuckerman) **85**:321, 340
"Sonnet II.23" (Tuckerman) **85**:320
"Sonnet II.24" (Tuckerman) **85**:322
"Sonnet II.37" (Tuckerman) **85**:305
"Sonnet III" (Berrigan) **103**:12
"Sonnet III" (Clough) **103**:100
"Sonnet III" (Meredith) **60**:266, 310-11, 315, 319-20
"Sonnet III" (Suckling) **30**:140
"Sonnet III" (Thomas) **2**:388
"Sonnet III.1" (Tuckerman) **85**:305
"Sonnet III.8" (Tuckerman) **85**:336
"Sonnet III.10" (Tuckerman) **85**:319
"Sonnet IV" (Berrigan) **103**:5, 12
"Sonnet IV" (Clough) **103**:100
"Sonnet IV" (Meredith) **60**:264-65, 274, 311, 313-15, 319-2
"Sonnet IV.2" (Tuckerman) **85**:320
"Sonnet IV.3" (Tuckerman) **85**:320
"Sonnet IV.4" (Tuckerman) **85**:320-21
"Sonnet IV.5" (Tuckerman) **85**:321
"Sonnet IV.7" (Tuckerman) **85**:321
"Sonnet IV.8" (Tuckerman) **85**:321
"Sonnet IV.9" (Tuckerman) **85**:321
"Sonnet IV.10" (Tuckerman) **85**:321, 336
"Sonnet V" (Berrigan) **103**:12
"Sonnet V" (Clough) **103**:100
"Sonnet V" (Meredith) **60**:272, 311, 315, 319-20, 342
"Sonnet V" (Wylie) **23**:304
"Sonnet V.3" (Tuckerman) **85**:335
"Sonnet V.8" (Tuckerman) **85**:305
"Sonnet V.14" (Tuckerman) **85**:319
"Sonnet V.15" (Tuckerman) **85**:319
"Sonnet V.16" (Tuckerman) **85**:319, 329, 337
"Sonnet VI" (Berrigan) **103**:12, 34
"Sonnet VI" (Clough) **103**:101
"Sonnet VI" (Meredith) **60**:265, 271, 309, 311, 315, 318-20, 342
"Sonnet VII" (Meredith) **60**:265, 272, 274-75, 310-11, 342
"Sonnet VII" (Pound) **95**:119
"Sonnet VIII" (Meredith) **60**:310-11, 314, 320-21, 323, 342
"Sonnet VIII" (Thomas) **2**:388
"Sonnet IX" (Meredith) **60**:265, 271-72, 274, 311, 313, 315, 317, 320-21, 323, 342-43
"Sonnet X" (Meredith) **60**:311, 320-21
"Sonnet X" (Thomas) **2**:388
"Sonnet XI" (Meredith) **60**:313, 321, 344
"Sonnet XII" (Meredith) **60**:313, 323
"Sonnet XIII" (Meredith) **60**:271, 301, 344
"Sonnet XIV" (Meredith) **60**:273, 312, 322
"Sonnet XV" (Berrigan) **103**:11-12
"Sonnet XV" (Meredith) **60**:266, 271, 312, 342
"Sonnet XVI" (Barrett Browning) **6**:17
"Sonnet XVI" (Meredith) **60**:266, 313, 321, 323
"Sonnet XVII" (Meredith) **60**:300, 306, 312-13, 321
"Sonnet XIX" (Meredith) **60**:271, 312, 314, 321-22
"Sonnet XX" (Meredith) **60**:265, 312
"Sonnet XXI" (Meredith) **60**:313, 321
"Sonnet XXII" (Meredith) **60**:311, 313, 342
"Sonnet XXIII" (Meredith) **60**:267, 311, 313-14, 317, 321, 323-24, 343
"Sonnet XXIV" (Meredith) **60**:267, 311, 313, 341, 344
"Sonnet XXV" (Meredith) **60**:266, 271, 312-13, 322
"Sonnet XXVI" (Meredith) **60**:275, 310
"Sonnet XXVII" (Berrigan) **103**:43
"Sonnet XXVII" (Meredith) **60**:266, 273, 310, 312-13, 321-22
"Sonnet XXVIII" (Meredith) **60**:266, 269, 310, 312-14, 345
"Sonnet XXIX" (Meredith) **60**:273, 312-14, 345
"Sonnet XXX" (Meredith) **60**:273, 313-14, 344-45
"Sonnet XXXI" (Berrigan) **103**:39
"Sonnet XXXI" (Meredith) **60**:272-73, 311, 314, 324
"Sonnet XXXII" (Meredith) **60**:273, 313, 344-45
"Sonnet XXXIII" (Meredith) **60**:266, 273, 275, 310, 313-14, 324
"Sonnet XXXIV" (Meredith) **60**:267, 310, 312, 322, 343
"Sonnet XXXV" (Meredith) **60**:267, 312
"Sonnet XXXVI" (Berrigan) **103**:16-17, 39
"Sonnet XXXVI" (Meredith) **60**:273
"Sonnet XXXVII" (Meredith) **60**:312
"Sonnet XXXVIII" (Meredith) **60**:267, 271, 312, 314
"Sonnet XXXIX" (Berrigan) **103**:32
"Sonnet XXXIX" (Meredith) **60**:267, 273-74, 314, 321, 343
"Sonnet XL" (Meredith) **60**:267, 312, 314, 322, 324
"Sonnet XLI" (Meredith) **60**:275, 312, 314
"Sonnet XLII" (Meredith) **60**:267, 275, 312, 343
"Sonnet XLIII" (Meredith) **60**:267, 270, 276, 303-4, 312, 314, 324, 343-44
"Sonnet XLIV" (Meredith) **60**:272, 276, 280, 313-14, 323
"Sonnet XLV" (Meredith) **60**:267, 310, 314
"Sonnet XLVI" (Meredith) **60**:267, 314, 344
"Sonnet XLVII" (Meredith) **60**:276, 303-5, 313-14, 324, 344
"Sonnet XLVIII" (Meredith) **60**:268, 272, 304-5, 310, 313-14, 323, 344
"Sonnet XLIX" (Meredith) **60**:268, 273, 303-05, 313, 314-15, 317, 320
"Sonnet L" (Meredith) **60**:275-76, 305, 313, 315, 317, 345
"Sonnet LV" (Berrigan) **103**:17, 44
"Sonnet LXXIV" (Berrigan) **103**:9
"Sonnet LXXV" (Berrigan) **103**:5, 16
"Sonnet LXXVII" (Berrigan) **103**:11, 16
"Sonnet LXXXVIII" (Berrigan) **103**:14-15

"Sonnet No. 1" (Surrey) **59**:285
"Sonnet No. 4" (Surrey) **59**:285
"Sonnet No. 6" (Surrey) **59**:285
"Sonnet No. 8" (Surrey) **59**:285
"Sonnet No. 9" (Surrey) **59**:285
"Sonnet No. 11" (Surrey) **59**:285
"Sonnet No. 12" (Surrey) **59**:285
"Sonnet No. 13" (Surrey) **59**:285
"Sonnet No. 14" (Surrey) **59**:285
"Sonnet No. 16" (Surrey) **59**:285
"Sonnet No. 18" (Surrey) **59**:285
"Sonnet No. 19" (Surrey) **59**:285
"Sonnet No. 20" (Surrey) **59**:285
"Sonnet No. 21" (Surrey) **59**:285
"Sonnet No. 40" (Surrey) **59**:285
"Sonnet No. 44" (Surrey) **59**:285
"Sonnet No. 45" (Surrey) **59**:285
"Sonnet No. 47" (Surrey) **59**:285
"Sonnet No. 91" (Surrey) **59**:286
"Sonnet" (Bishop) **34**:55, 63, 69, 90-91
"Sonnet" (Bogan) **12**:98, 110
"Sonnet" (Collins)
See "When *Phoebe* . . ."
"Sonnet" (Collins) **68**:215
"Sonnet" (Empson) **104**:89
"Sonnet" (Justice) **64**:279
"Sonnet" (Lovelace) **69**:198
"A Sonnet" (Raleigh) **31**:297
"Sonnet" (Rimbaud) **57**:271-72
"Sonnet" (Tennyson) **101**:244
"Sonnet" (Wilbur) **51**:300
"Sonnet" (Winters) **82**:339-40
"Sonnet à elle-même" (Ronsard) **105**:219
"Sonnet à Madame P." (Sainte-Beuve) **110**:56
"Sonnet à Sinope" (Ronsard) **105**:198-99
"Sonnet allégorique de lui-même" (Mallarmé) **102**:93, 95, 98
"Sonnet at Christmas" (Tate) **50**:234
"Sonnet. Aux Champs-Élysées" (Sainte-Beuve) **110**:45
"Sonnet boiteux" (Verlaine) **32**:375, 401, 406
"Sonnet de Baptême" (Mallarmé) **102**:30
"Sonnet (Death. Nothing is simpler. One is dead.)" (Winters)
See "The Realization"
"Le Sonnet des voyelles" (Rimbaud) **57**:226
"Sonnet: Chi è questa?" (Pound) **95**:119-20
"Sonnet du trou du cul" (Rimbaud) **57**:203
"Sonnet en -yx" (Mallarmé) **4**:214-15, 218; **102**:9-15, 69-72, 93, 97-98, 100-101
"Sonnet Entitled How to Run the World)" (Cummings) **5**:106
"Sonnet for Hélène" (Kennedy) **93**:145
"Sonnet for the Seventh of August" (Belloc) **24**:43-4
"A Sonnet from the Stony Brook" (Jordan) **38**:125
"Sonnet: *Homage to Ron* " (Berrigan) **103**:36
"Sonnet héroïque" (Verlaine) **2**:416
"Sonnet in Polka Dots" (Villa) **22**:351
"Sonnet in time of Revolt" (Brooke) **24**:62, 82
"Sonnet. L'Amant antiquaire" (Sainte-Beuve) **110**:47
"Sonnet: O City, City" (Schwartz) **8**:302, 316
"Sonnet of the Blood" (Tate) **50**:245, 255
"Sonnet of the Vowels" (Rimbaud)
See "Le Sonnet des voyelles"
"Sonnet on an Alpine Night" (Parker) **28**:351
"Sonnet on Beauty" (Tate) **50**:228-29
"Sonnet on Rare Animals" (Meredith) **28**:172, 188
"Sonnet on the Death of Mr. Richard West" (Gray) **80**:180, 187-88, 192, 235, 238
"Sonnet on the Nile" (Hunt) **73**:137
"Sonnet Reversed" (Brooke) **24**:56, 64
"Sonnet (Suggested by some of the Proceedings of the Society for Physical Research)" (Brooke) **24**:58, 73
"Sonnet (The fact that offers neither cause nor gain)" (Winters) **82**:338
"Sonnet: The Ghosts of James and Peirce in Harvard Yard" (Schwartz) **8**:302
"Sonnet (The Table Softly Flames)" (Winters) **82**:320
"Sonnet To a Child" (Owen) **19**:343
"Sonnet to an Ox" (Carducci)
See "Il bove"
"Sonnet: To Fancy" (Hood)
See "To Fancy"
"Sonnet to My Friend with an Identity Disc" (Owen)
See "With an Identity Disc"
"Sonnet to My Father" (Justice) **64**:278
"Sonnet to My Mother" (Barker)
See "To My Mother"
"Sonnet—to My Mother" (Poe) **1**:439, 445-46
"Sonnet to Satan" (Plath) **37**:207-8
"Sonnet To Sleep" (Keats) **96**:209
"Sonnet, to the Rev. James Flint, D. D., on Reading His Collection of Poems" (Very) **86**:57
"Sonnet with the Compliments of the Season" (Chesterton) **28**:114
"Sonnet Written in Keats's 'Endymion'" (Hood) **93**:67
The Sonnets (Berrigan) **103**:4-20, 23, 29-33, 35, 37-46
Sonnets (Smith)
See *Elegiac Sonnets, and Other Essays*
"Sonnets 1-17" (Shakespeare) **98**:239, 275
"Sonnets 1-36" (Shakespeare) **98**:311
"Sonnets 1-125" (Shakespeare) **98**:245
"Sonnets 1-126" (Shakespeare) **89**:314
"Sonnets 18-125" (Shakespeare) **98**:239
"Sonnets 20-126" (Shakespeare) **98**:283
"Sonnets 22-23" (Shakespeare) **98**:319
"Sonnets 33-35" (Shakespeare) **98**:215
"Sonnets 40-42" (Shakespeare) **98**:217, 311
"Sonnets 55-59" (Shakespeare) **98**:274
"Sonnets 56-58" (Shakespeare) **98**:274
"Sonnets 67-70" (Shakespeare) **98**:227-28
"Sonnets 69-74" (Shakespeare) **98**:304
"Sonnets 71-74" (Shakespeare) **98**:305
"Sonnets 76-86" (Shakespeare) **98**:298
"Sonnets 78-86" (Shakespeare) **89**:335; **98**:305
"Sonnets 83-85" (Shakespeare) **98**:299
"Sonnets 87-96" (Shakespeare) **98**:245
"Sonnets 87-99" (Shakespeare) **98**:307
"Sonnets 94-96" (Shakespeare) **98**:227
"Sonnets 100-08" (Shakespeare) **98**:298
"Sonnets 109-11" (Shakespeare) **98**:315
"Sonnets 127-52" (Shakespeare) **98**:251
"Sonnets 127-54" (Shakespeare) **98**:217, 283
"Sonnets 133-35" (Shakespeare) **98**:311
"Sonnets 133-36" (Shakespeare) **98**:281
"Sonnets 147-52" (Shakespeare) **98**:277
"Sonnets, Part I" (Tuckerman) **85**:306
"Sonnets, Part I, V" (Tuckerman) **85**:307
"Sonnets, Part I, XIII" (Tuckerman) **85**:308-9
"Sonnets, Part I, IX" (Tuckerman) **85**:307
"Sonnets, Part I, X" (Tuckerman) **85**:307, 310
"Sonnets, Part I, XIV" (Tuckerman) **85**:308, 310
"Sonnets, Part I, XV" (Tuckerman) **85**:308, 310
"Sonnets, Part I, XXII" (Tuckerman) **85**:308
"Sonnets, Part I, XXVIII" (Tuckerman) **85**:308, 319
"Sonnets, Part II" (Tuckerman) **85**:306
"Sonnets, Part II, XI" (Tuckerman) **85**:308
"Sonnets, Part II, XVI" (Tuckerman) **85**:309
"Sonnets" (Suckling) **30**:118
Sonnets (Berryman)
See *Berryman's Sonnets*
Sonnets (Carruth) **10**:91
Sonnets (Mickiewicz)
See *Sonety Krymskie*
Sonnets (Rilke) **2**:280-82
Sonnets (Shakespeare) **84**:255; **89**:292, 333, 335, 338-39; **98**:213-350; **101**:18, 29-30, 38-39, 41-43, 51, 54, 56, 60, 71, 75, 81, 89-91, 93-94, 96, 107-8
The Sonnets and Ballate of Guido Cavalcanti (Cavalcanti) **114**:255-58, 260
Sonnets and Poems (Masefield) **78**:44, 71
Sonnets and Verse (Belloc) **24**:11, 31-3, 36, 38, 40
"Sonnets at Christmas" (Tate) **50**:252, 255-56
Sonnets at Christmas (Tate) **50**:231, 251
"Sonnets by Nehemiah Higginbottom" (Coleridge) **67**:333
Sonnets et madrigals pour astrée (Ronsard) **11**:250
Sonnets for Hélène (Ronsard)
See *Sonnets pour Hélène*
"Sonnets from an Ungrafted Tree" (Millay) **6**:224-25, 228, 230-32, 235, 239
"Sonnets from Hellas" (Heaney) **100**:238, 240, 243, 321
Sonnets from the Crimea (Mickiewicz)
See *Sonety Krymskie*
Sonnets from the Portuguese (Barrett Browning) **6**:4-6, 15-8, 22, 32, 36-9, 41-2, 46; **62**:83, 160
Sonnets of Death (Mistral)
See *Sonetos de la muerte*
The Sonnets of Frederick Goddard Tuckerman (Tuckerman) **85**:307, 324, 326, 334, 337
Sonnets of Good Cheer (Masefield) **78**:73
"Sonnets of Pruning" (Mistral)
See "Sonetos de la poda"
"Sonnets of the Blood" (Tate) **50**:230, 244, 255, 275, 293
"Sonnets of the Triple-Headed Manichee" (Barker) **77**:14-15
"Sonnets of the Twelve Months" (Belloc) **24**:29
Sonnets on the War (Dobell) **100**:152, 160, 163, 176
Sonnets pour Hélène (Ronsard) **11**:218, 220-22, 239, 242, 250, 254, 275-76, 278, 283; **105**:198, 213, 303, 306
"Sonnets That Please" (Stein) **18**:341
"Sonnets to Baudelaire" (Hope) **56**:281, 289, 298, 300, 304
Sonnets to Chris (Berryman)
See *Berryman's Sonnets*
"Sonnets to Duse" (Teasdale) **31**:340
Sonnets to Duse, and Other Poems (Teasdale) **31**:321, 324, 329, 335, 337, 344, 346, 378
Sonnets to Orpheus (Rilke)
See *Die Sonette an Orpheus*
"Sono pronto ripeto, ma pronto a che?" (Montale) **13**:139
"sonora desert poem" (Clifton) **17**:27
"The Son's Sorrow: From the Icelandic" (Morris) **55**:340
"Soon to be a National Geographic Special" (Alexie) **53**:24
"Soonest Mended" (Ashbery) **26**:125-126, 134, 138, 141, 149
"The soote season" (Surrey) **59**:285, 297, 311-12, 319-20
"Sophist Leaving Syria" (Cavafy) **36**:76, 80, 104, 106
"Sophocles Says" (Stafford) **71**:285
"Sopra il monumento di Dante" (Leopardi) **37**:79, 98-100, 150
"Sorapis, 40 anni fa" (Montale) **13**:138
Sordello (Browning) **2**:26-30, 34, 42, 50, 65-6, 73-6, 82, 92-6; **97**:6
"Sore Fit" (Bradstreet)
See "From Another Sore Fit"
Sorgen och stjärnan (Ekeloef) **23**:76
"La Sorgue" (Char)
See "La sorgue: Chanson pour Yvonne"
"The Sorgue: a song for Yvonne" (Char)
See "La sorgue: Chanson pour Yvonne"
"La sorgue: Chanson pour Yvonne" (Char) **56**:173
"Sorrow" (Millay) **61**:213
"Sorrow" (Muir) **49**:205, 245-46, 249-50
The Sorrow Dance (Levertov) **11**:175-77, 191-94
"Sorrow Home" (Walker) **20**:281-83
"Sorrow of Mydath" (Masefield) **78**:95-96
"Sorrowful Moonlit Night" (Hagiwara)
See "Kanashi Tsukio"

"The Sorrowing Girl" (Seferis) **66**:119, 124
"Sorry" (Thomas) **99**:280, 282
"Sort of an Apocalypse" (Amichai) **38**:35-37
"Sortes Vergilianae" (Ashbery) **26**:149
"Sorting It Out" (Stone) **53**:257
"Sorting, wrapping, packing, stuffing" (Schuyler) **88**:179
"SOS" (Baraka) **4**:20; **113**:75
"Sosedka" (Lermontov) **18**:291
"Sospetto d'Herode" (Crashaw) **84**:7-8, 31
"Soto. A Character" (Leapor) **85**:248
"Sotto la pioggia" (Montale) **13**:122
"(Sotto l'alta guida)" (Zanzotto) **65**:277
"(Sotto l'alta guida), (Abbondanze)" (Zanzotto) **65**:277
"(Sotto l'alta guida)(traiettorie, mosche)" (Zanzotto) **65**:277
"Sotto Voce" (de la Mare) **77**:138
"Sought by the World, and Hath the World Disdain'd" (Raleigh) **31**:201
"The Soul" (Cowley) **90**:14, 115
"The Soul" (Pasternak)
See "Dusha"
"The Soul admiring the Grace of the Church Enters into Church Fellowship" (Taylor) **63**:278, 284
"Soul, Be Calm" (Ishikawa)
See "Tama yo shizume"
A Soul for Sale (Kavanagh) **33**:61-62, 71-75, 77, 81, 85-86, 93-95, 97, 102, 146; **105**:89-90, 93-94, 99-100, 127, 140, 144
"A Soul, Geologically" (Atwood) **8**:3, 8, 19
"The Soul Has Bandaged Moments" (Dickinson) **1**:94
"Soul in Space" (Rilke) **2**:275
"The Soul Longs to Return Whence It Came" (Eberhart) **76**:5, 14, 29, 32, 49, 58
"The Soul of a Schoolboy" (Enright) **93**:24
"The Soul of the World" (Rumi) **45**:251
"The Soul on Weekdays" (Herbert)
See "Codziennosc duszy"
"Soul Says" (Graham) **59**:136, 157
"A Soul that out of Nature's Deep" (Tuckerman) **85**:304, 319, 321
"The Souldier going to the Field" (Davenant) **99**:200
"The Soule Bemoning Sorrow rowling upon a resolution to seek Advice of Gods people" (Taylor) **63**:216
"The Soule Seeking Church-Fellowship" (Taylor) **63**:278, 283
"Soulful Sam" (Service) **70**:131
"Souls Admiration" (Taylor)
See "The Soul admiring the Grace of the Church Enters into Church Fellowship"
"Soul's Adventure" (Kunitz) **19**:148
"Soul's Beauty" (Rossetti) **44**:255
"Soul's Desire" (Masters) **1**:342
"The Soul's Expression" (Barrett Browning) **6**:20, 26, 30
"The Soul's Freedom" (Very) **86**:113
"The Souls of Old Men" (Cavafy) **36**:95
"The Souls of the Slain" (Hardy) **8**:120-21; **92**:269
Souls of Violet (Jiménez)
See *Almas de violeta*
"The Soul's Season" (Thoreau) **30**:281, 282, 295
"A Soul's Tragedy" (Browning) **2**:30, 37
"A Sound from the Earth" (Stafford) **71**:334
The Sound I Listened For (Francis) **34**:245, 259
"A Sound in the Night" (Hardy) **92**:266-67
"The Sound of a Wound" (Montague) **106**:278, 326
"The Sound of the Sea" (Longfellow) **30**:31
"The Sound of the Trees" (Frost) **1**:197, 202; **39**:232, 237, 239, 246-47; **71**:55
"The Sound of Trees" (Frost)
See "The Sound of the Trees"
"Sound of War" (Aleixandre) **15**:4-6
"Sound Poem I" (Toomer) **7**:333
"Sound Poem II" (Toomer) **7**:333
"Sound Sleep" (Rossetti) **7**:267, 280
"Soundings" (Baraka) **113**:36
"Sounds" (Barrett Browning) **6**:20
"The sounds begin again" (Brutus) **24**:114, 116
Sounds, Feelings, Thoughts: Seventy Poems (Szymborska) **44**:274, 295
"Sounds of Rain" (Heaney) **18**:260
"Sounds of the Resurrected Dead Man's Footsteps" (Bell) **79**:37, 39-40, 42
"Sounds of the River Naranjana" (Schwerner) **42**:196, 202, 204
Sounds of the River Naranjana and The Tablets I-XXIV (Schwerner) **42**:202-4
"Sounds Out of Sorrow" (Masters) **1**:333
"Soup" (Sandburg) **41**:252
"Soup of the evening beautiful Soup" (Carroll) **18**:49
"La Soupe et les Nuages" (Baudelaire) **106**:90
"Soupir" (Mallarmé) **4**:187; **102**:110
Sour Grapes (Williams) **7**:344, 349, 367, 377, 381, 399-400, 409-10
"Sour Swan" (Melville) **82**:33-34, 38, 47, 50, 58, 62
"Source" (Doty) **53**:70
"Source" (Hughes) **89**:146
"The Source" (Olds) **22**:338
"Source" (Péret) **33**:231
"The Source" (Wagoner) **33**:360
Source (Chappell) **105**:6, 9, 16-19, 26, 30, 37-38, 65
Source (Doty) **53**:69
"La source dans les bois" (Lamartine) **16**:292
"Source de plour, riviere de tristece" (Christine de Pizan) **68**:189-92
"Sources" (Levine) **22**:224
Sources (Rich) **5**:389-90, 397
"Le Sourcil" (Scève) **111**:75
"La sourd et l'aveugle" (Éluard) **38**:70
"Sous la menace rouge" (Éluard) **38**:71, 84
"Sous le feuillage" (Char) **56**:155
"Sousa" (Dorn) **115**:57, 125, 138, 219
"South" (Brathwaite) **56**:64, 83
"The South" (Hughes) **53**:85
"South" (Stryk) **27**:181, 200
"South Africa" (Kipling) **91**:174-75
"South America" (Raworth) **107**:336
South and East (Masefield) **78**:51, 62, 73
"South Cottage" (Wang Wei) **18**:367
"The South Country" (Belloc) **24**:8, 10, 30
"South of My Days" (Wright) **14**:340, 349, 351, 360, 378
"South Sangamon" (Cisneros) **52**:160
"South Sea Island" (Benn) **35**:49
"The South Wind" (Bridges) **28**:66
"Southampton Winter" (Berrigan) **103**:34
"Southeast Corner" (Brooks) **7**:58, 69, 80
"Southern Mammy Sings" (Hughes) **53**:120
"A Southern Night" (Arnold) **5**:8
"Southern Pacific" (Sandburg) **2**:302; **41**:240, 316
"Southern Road" (Brown) **55**:73-75, 80, 110, 113, 149, 158, 160-61, 174
"The Southern Road" (Randall) **86**:287, 301, 305, 315, 343
Southern Road (Brown) **55**:73-77, 80-81, 86-87, 89, 93-94, 96, 98, 100-101, 109-17, 120-21, 124-26, 128-29, 131, 134-35, 143, 148, 154, 156-59, 164, 166-67, 175, 178
"Southern Song" (Walker) **20**:272, 281-83
"The Southerner" (Shapiro) **25**:283, 296, 313
"Southpaw" (Mueller) **33**:191
"South-West Wind in the Woodland" (Meredith) **60**:287, 294-95
"The South-Wester" (Meredith) **60**:278, 280, 283
"Le Souvenir" (Bonnefoy) **58**:156, 158
"Souvenir d'Avignon" (Ponge) **107**:110
"Souvenir de Monsieur Poop" (Smith) **12**:313
"Le souvenir d'enfance; ou, La vie cachée" (Lamartine) **16**:276, 300, 302
"Souvenirs" (Randall) **86**:338
"Souvent sur la montagne" (Lamartine) **16**:302
"Sovente una riviera" (Quasimodo) **47**:303
The Sovereign Sun: Selected Poems (Elytis) **21**:118-19
"Sovereign Thought" (Leopardi)
See "Il Pensiero Dominante"
"Soviet Souvenir" (Berrigan) **103**:41
"Soviet Union" (Guillén)
See "Unión Soviética"
"Sow" (Plath) **1**:388, 404; **37**:254
Soweto (Brathwaite) **56**:42, 90
"The Sowing" (Teasdale) **31**:323
"Sowing" (Thomas) **53**:328
"The Sowing of Meaning" (Merton) **10**:332
"The Sowtar and the Tailyouris War" (Dunbar) **67**:128
"Soy" (Borges) **32**:58, 76, 90
"Soy como un árbol florido" (Guillén) **23**:125
"Soy Sauce" (Snyder) **21**:300
"Soy sólo una mujer" (Fuertes) **27**:7
Soyti na tikhoy stantsiy Zima, Otkuda vy? (Yevtushenko) **40**:363
Space (Aleixandre)
See *Ambito*
Space (Jiménez)
See *Espacia*
"The Space Spiders" (Hall) **70**:33
space travl (Bissett) **14**:34
"The Space We Live" (Levine) **22**:215
"Spaces We Leave Empty" (Song) **21**:343
"Spade" (Brathwaite) **56**:99
"The Spades" (Brathwaite) **56**:82
Spain (Auden) **1**:22; **92**:58, 64, 73-74, 77-78, 102-4, 129
Spain (Gautier)
See *España*
Spain at Heart (Neruda)
See *España en el corazón: himno a las glorias del pueblo en la guerra (1936-1937)*
Spain in My Heart (Neruda)
See *España en el corazón: himno a las glorias del pueblo en la guerra (1936-1937)*
Spain in the Heart (Neruda)
See *España en el corazón: himno a las glorias del pueblo en la guerra (1936-1937)*
Spaltung (Benn) **35**:8, 33
The Spanish Gypsy (Eliot) **20**:90-100, 104-6, 111-15, 122-23, 126, 128-31, 137-39, 141-48
"Spanish Harlem" (Dylan) **37**:54
"The Spanish Ladies Love" (Deloney) **79**:57
"The Spanish Needle" (McKay) **2**:228
"The Spanish of Our Out-Loud Dreams" (Espada) **74**:112, 114, 117, 120, 123, 141
"Spanish School" (Smith) **12**:316
The Spanish Student (Longfellow) **30**:23, 25, 34-5, 52, 63-4, 68
"Spare Us from Loveliness" (H. D.) **5**:273
"spark" (Bukowski) **18**:20
"The Spark" (Cullen) **20**:58
"A Spark in the Tinder of Knowing" (Rexroth) **20**:221; **95**:264, 281
"A Sparkler" (Ashbery) **26**:137
"Sparrow" (Benét) **64**:14
"Sparrow Hawk" (Hughes) **89**:150
"A Sparrow Hawk" (Hughes) **89**:169
"Sparrow Hills" (Pasternak) **6**:258
"Sparrow Nights" (Carver) **54**:18
"A Sparrow Sheltering Under a Column of the British Museum" (Merwin) **45**:6
"The Sparrow Sky" (Dorn) **115**:120
"Sparrow Song" (Li Po) **29**:140
"The Sparrows" (Cohen) **109**:108
"The Sparrow's Fall" (Harper) **21**:189
The Sparrow's Fall and Other Poems (Harper) **21**:187, 189
"Spasskoye" (Pasternak) **6**:252, 259
"Spät" (Benn) **35**:36
"Spät II" (Benn) **35**:72
"Spät, V" (Benn) **35**:67
Späte Gedichte (Sachs) **78**:111-12
"Das späte Ich" (Benn) **35**:8, 75

"Spätherbst in Venedig" (Rilke) **2**:267, 277, 282, 288-90
"Spätlese" (Hope) **56**:278
"Speak" (Wright) **36**:305-6, 317, 344, 350
Speak, Parrot (Skelton)
See *Speke, Parot*
"Speak roughly to your little boy" (Carroll) **74**:24, 29-30, 32, 63-64
"Speak, You Also" (Celan) **10**:99
"La Speakerine de Putney" (Smith) **12**:354
Speaking for Scotland (MacDiarmid) **9**:159
"Speaking of Love (of" (Cummings) **5**:105
"speaking speaking" (Bissett) **14**:31
"Speaking to the Dead in the Language of the Dead" (Spender) **71**:189
"Specchio" (Quasimodo) **47**:301
"Special Pleading" (Lanier) **50**:55
"Special Starlight" (Sandburg) **2**:331
"Specimen of an Induction to a Poem" (Keats) **1**:313; **96**:221, 265
"Un Spectacle interrompu" (Mallarmé) **102**:114-15, 119-21
"The Spectacles" (Snodgrass) **74**:324
Spectacula (Martial)
See *Liber Spectaculorum*
"Spectacular Blossom" (Curnow) **48**:6-7
Spectaculorum Liber (Martial)
See *Liber Spectaculorum*
"Spectral Lovers" (Ransom) **61**:267, 272, 306, 311
"The Spectre Pig" (Holmes) **71**:68, 91-92, 96
Spectrum (Nishiwaki) **15**:228, 237
Speculum Meditantis (Gower) **59**:113
"The Speech at Soli" (Oppen) **35**:294
"Speech for the Repeal of the McCarran Act" (Wilbur) **51**:226, 228
"Speech to a Crowd" (MacLeish) **47**:147, 190, 242
"Speech to Scholars" (MacLeish) **47**:147, 256
"Speech to the Detractors" (MacLeish) **47**:190
"Speech to the Young. Speech to the Progress-Toward" (Brooks) **7**:91, 94
"Speech to those who say Comrade" (MacLeish) **47**:145, 147, 190, 242
Speeches (Parra)
See "Discursos"
"Speeches at the Barriers" (Howe) **54**:63
"Speeches for Doctor Frankenstein" (Atwood) **8**:11
"Speech-Grille" (Celan)
See "Sprachgitter"
Speech-Grille, and Selected Poems (Celan)
See *Sprachgitter*
"Speed" (Traherne) **70**:272-73, 312, 315-16
The Speed of Darkness (Rukeyser) **12**:216, 222, 228, 230
Speke, Parot (Skelton) **25**:329-31, 336, 341, 348, 351-52, 360, 374, 377-78, 380-85
Speke Parott (Skelton)
See *Speke, Parot*
Speke, Parrot (Skelton)
See *Speke, Parot*
Spektorsky (Pasternak) **6**:253, 265, 283, 285
"Spel Against Demons" (Snyder) **21**:291-92, 297
"Speleology" (Warren) **37**:337
"The Spell" (Kumin) **15**:192
"Spell" (Montale)
See "Incantesimo"
"The Spell of the Rose" (Hardy) **8**:93, 136
"The Spell of the Yukon" (Service) **70**:114, 116, 125, 139-40, 152-53
Spell of the Yukon and Other Verses (Service) **70**:113-15, 156
"Spell-Bound" (Morris) **55**:238, 279-80, 282
"Spelling" (Duncan) **2**:104
"Spelling Bee" (Silverstein) **49**:324
"Spelt from Sibyl's Leaves" (Hopkins) **15**:128, 132-33, 138, 144
"A Spending Hand" (Wyatt)
See "A spending hand that alway poureth out"
"A spending hand that alway poureth out" (Wyatt) **27**:371
"Spenser's Ireland" (Moore) **4**:258; **49**:100, 128, 161
"Sperm" (Kumin) **15**:202
"The Sperm and Egg" (Stone) **53**:254
"Sphere" (Ammons) **16**:31, 53
Sphere: The Form of a Motion (Ammons) **16**:23, 25, 27-30, 33, 46-7, 54, 60-1
Sphericity (Berssenbrugge) **115**:8, 13-15, 18, 28
"Sphericity" (Berssenbrugge) **115**:14
"The Sphinx" (Emerson) **18**:71, 84, 88, 93, 102, 110
"Le Sphinx" (Gautier) **18**:141
"The Sphinx" (Hayden) **6**:186
Sphinx: A Poem Ascrib'd to Certain Anonymous Authors: By the Revd. S—t (Swift)
See "Ode to the Athenian Society"
"Le Sphynx vertébral" (Breton) **15**:51
The Spice-Box of Earth (Cohen) **109**:4-5, 7, 11, 13-15, 17-19, 28-29, 31, 34, 43, 51-52, 54-55, 57, 68, 81-82, 88, 111
"The Spice-Tree" (Lindsay) **23**:268
"Spicewood" (Reese) **29**:330
Spicewood (Reese) **29**:335, 339, 347-348, 351
"Spider Blues" (Ondaatje) **28**:320, 327, 333
"Spiders" (Cervantes) **35**:104, 117
"Spider's Song" (Zagajewski) **27**:389
"Spiel" (Stramm) **50**:189-91, 201, 209
"Spight hathe no Powre" (Wyatt) **27**:315
Spik in glyph? (Alurista) **34**:15, 23, 26, 31, 43
"Spilt Milk" (Yeats) **20**:314
Spin a Soft Black Song: Poems for Children (Giovanni) **19**:136
"Spindrift" (Kinnell) **26**:257
"The Spinner" (Valéry)
See "La fileuse"
"The Spinning Heart" (Berryman) **64**:83
"Spinning Tops" (Reese) **29**:330
"Spinoza" (Borges) **32**:60, 68, 71
"Spinoza's Bed" (Herbert) **50**:45
"Spinster" (Plath) **1**:388
"Spirals" (Niedecker) **42**:145-48
"The Spire Cranes" (Thomas) **2**:408
"Spirit" (Corso) **33**:50; **108**:20
"Spirit" (Soto) **28**:370
"The Spirit" (Very) **86**:45
"The Spirit" (Werfel)
See "Der Geist"
Spirit (Corso) **33**:50
"A Spirit Haunts the Year's Last Hours" (Tennyson) **101**:247
"The Spirit Land" (Very) **86**:43, 166
The Spirit Level (Heaney) **100**:231, 234, 237, 240, 242-45, 247-49, 275, 278, 285, 287, 299, 304, 306, 338-44
"The Spirit Medium" (Yeats) **20**:314
"The Spirit of Earth in Autumn" (Meredith) **60**:298
"The Spirit of Fire: A Mythological Ode" (Peacock)
See "Mythological Ode to the Spirit of Fire"
"Spirit of History" (Milosz) **8**:204
"The Spirit of Lake Switzez" (Mickiewicz)
See "Switezianka"
"The Spirit of Place" (Rich) **5**:386
"The Spirit of Poetry" (Longfellow) **30**:33
The Spirit of Romance (Pound) **4**:352
Spirit Reach (Baraka) **4**:19-20, 26; **113**:55, 73, 77-78, 80
"The Spirit's Epochs" (Patmore) **59**:205
"Spirit's House" (Teasdale) **31**:355
"Spirit's Song" (Bogan) **12**:90, 92, 100, 124
"Spirits Summoned West" (Lawrence) **54**:245
"A Spiritual" (Dunbar) **5**:123
"Spiritual" (Pasolini) **17**:253
"The Spiritual Birth" (Very) **86**:113
"Spiritual Diary" (Cowper) **40**:48, 51
"Spiritual Laws" (Emerson) **18**:94
"A Spiritual Manifestation" (Whittier) **93**:252
"Spiritual Navigation" (Very) **86**:102
Spiritual Sonnets (Jiménez)
See *Sonetos espirituales*
"Spirituals" (Hughes) **53**:91, 109, 118
"Spirto ben nato, in cu' si spechia e uede" (Michelangelo) **103**:196, 216-17
"Spit in my face ye Jewes, and pierce my side" (Donne) **43**:148, 160
"Spite" (Bukowski) **18**:5
"Spleen" (Baudelaire)
See *Le spleen de Paris, petits poèmes en prose*
"Le spleen" (Baudelaire)
See *Le spleen de Paris, petits poèmes en prose*
"Spleen" (Eliot) **31**:100, 138
"The Spleen" (Finch)
See "Ode to the Spleen"
"Spleen" (Laforgue) **14**:84-5, 89
"Spleen" (O'Hara) **45**:223
"Spleen" (Verlaine) **2**:415
Le spleen de Paris (Baudelaire)
See *Le spleen de Paris, petits poèmes en prose*
Le spleen de Paris, petits poèmes en prose (Baudelaire) **1**:48-49, 55, 58-59; **106**:9, 147, 152
The Splendid Village (Elliott) **96**:161, 170, 181-82
"Splendour of the Sun and Moon" (Hope) **56**:302
"Split, Conjugate, Whatever" (Stone) **53**:254
"The Split Lyre" (Montague) **106**:271
"Splitting Wood at Six Above" (Kumin) **15**:206, 219
"The Spoiler's Return" (Walcott) **46**:247, 322
"Spoke Joe to Jack" (Cummings) **5**:88
"Sponsa Dei" (Patmore) **59**:210, 223, 265, 268
"Spontaneous Combustion" (Hogan) **35**:256
"Spontaneous Me" (Whitman) **3**:387
"Spontaneous Poem" (Corso) **108**:15
"Spontaneous Requiem for the American Indian" (Corso) **33**:44, 49; **108**:10, 44-45
"The Spoon" (Simic) **69**:314, 340
The Spoon River Anthology (Masters) **1**:321-42, 344-49; **36**:161-245
"The Spooniad" (Masters) **1**:327; **36**:169, 172, 182, 195-96, 212, 220, 223, 228
The Spooniad (Masters) **36**:243
"Spor" (Lermontov) **18**:291
"Sport" (Hughes) **1**:270
"Sporting Beasley" (Brown) **55**:72, 75, 155
"Sporting Life" (Spicer) **78**:288
"Sports Field" (Wright) **14**:362
"Sports Page" (MacNeice) **61**:177
"Sportsmen" (Douglas) **106**:198, 200-201
"Spot in Space and Time" (McHugh) **61**:200
"S.P.Q.R." (Ciardi) **69**:49
"Sprachgitter" (Celan) **10**:112, 115, 129-30
Sprachgitter (Celan) **10**:95-6, 121
"Sprawozdanie z raju" (Herbert) **50**:9
"Spraying the Potatoes" (Kavanagh) **33**:62, 81, 94, 99, 118, 145-6, 152, 154, 157, 162; **105**:99, 126, 140, 142-45
"Spread of Mrs. Mobey's Lawn" (Jacobsen) **62**:301
"Sprich zu dir selbst, dann sprichst du zu den Dingen" (Benn) **35**:70
"A Sprig of Rosemary" (Lowell) **13**:64
"Sprightly Old Age" (Hunt) **73**:138
"Spring" (Baca) **41**:47
"Spring" (Blake) **12**:7, 32; **63**:14, 66, 119-20, 123-24
"The Spring" (Carew) **29**:8-9, 19
"Spring" (Ciardi) **69**:25
"The Spring" (Cowley) **90**:115
"Spring" (Darío)
See "Primaveral"
"Spring" (Gray)
See "Ode on Spring"
"Spring" (Hass) **16**:209
"Spring" (Hopkins) **15**:152
"Spring" (Koch) **80**:339

"Spring" (McGuckian) **27**:96
"Spring" (Millay) **6**:236
"Spring" (Oliver) **75**:294, 343
"Spring" (Pasternak) **6**:251
"Spring" (Rexroth) **20**:209
"Spring" (Simic) **69**:319
"Spring" (Sitwell) **3**:311
"Spring" (Teasdale) **31**:321
"Spring" (Williams) **7**:345, 399
"Spring 1942" (Curnow) **48**:12
"Spring, A. D." (Seferis) **66**:95, 167
"Spring, Ages Ago, Home" (de la Mare) **77**:74
Spring and All (Williams) **7**:349, 351, 353, 355, 373-78, 381-83, 387-88, 400-02, 405-06, 409-11; **109**:192, 194, 206-8, 257, 260, 262, 264, 267, 271, 273-75, 277-79, 282-87, 289-96, 298, 315, 319, 336-37
"Spring and All" (Williams) **109**:223-24, 248, 286
"Spring and Fall" (Hopkins) **15**:144
"The Spring and the Fall" (Millay) **6**:225
"Spring and Tyranny" (Lanier) **50**:106
"Spring Azures" (Oliver) **75**:322
"Spring Blades" (Brathwaite) **56**:34
"Spring Cleaning" (MacNeice) **61**:176
"Spring, Coast Range" (Rexroth) **95**:287-88
"Spring Comes to Murray Hill" (Nash) **21**:266
"Spring Day" (Ashbery) **26**:124
"Spring Day" (Lowell) **13**:79
"Spring Day" (Sarton) **39**:325
"Spring Drawing" (Hass) **16**:215, 221
"Spring Drawing 2" (Hass) **16**:216
"Spring Ecstasy" (Reese) **29**:331
"Spring Evening" (Kenyon) **57**:18, 28
"Spring Flood" (Pasternak) **6**:266
"Spring for All Seasons" (Welch) **62**:340, 372
Spring Garden: New and Selected Poems (Chappell) **105**:52-53, 67
"Spring goeth all in white" (Bridges) **28**:66-7
"Spring Images" (Wright) **36**:316, 359, 374, 398
"Spring in Belfast" (Mahon) **60**:235
"Spring in Hellas" (Carducci)
See "Primavere elleniche"
"Spring in New Hampshire" (McKay) **2**:228
Spring in New Hampshire, and Other Poems (McKay) **2**:213, 228
"Spring in the Garden" (Millay) **6**:215
"Spring in These Hills" (MacLeish) **47**:197
Spring Is a Season and Nothing Else (Waldrop) **109**:167
"Spring Lake" (Masters) **1**:343
"Spring Lament" (Surrey) **59**:291
"Spring Magic" (Carman) **34**:223
"Spring Nature Notes" (Hughes) **89**:125
"Spring Night" (Hagiwara)
See "Shun'ya"
"Spring Night" (Teasdale) **31**:378
"Spring Night in Lo-yang-Hearing a Flute" (Li Po) **29**:145
"Spring Oak" (Kinnell) **26**:237-38, 257
"Spring Ode I" (Bridges) **28**:84
"Spring Ode II" (Bridges) **28**:84
"Spring Offensive" (Owen) **19**:334, 337, 341-42, 344, 347, 353-55; **102**:152, 167-68, 170-72, 181, 186, 208, 222, 225, 232, 242, 246, 248-49, 252-53, 263
"Spring on the Alban Hills" (Meynell) **112**:190, 289
"Spring Pastoral" (Wylie) **23**:321-22
"Spring Poem" (Atwood) **8**:24
"A Spring Poem-Song" (Tapahonso) **65**:213
"Spring Pools" (Frost) **1**:206; **39**:239
"Spring Prospect" (Tu Fu) **9**:322
"Spring Rain" (Hass) **16**:221-22
"Spring Rain" (Pasternak) **6**:251
"Spring Rains" (Teasdale) **31**:356
"Spring, Says the Child" (Jacobsen) **62**:321, 323-24
"Spring Season of Muddy Roads" (Brodsky) **9**:2
"Spring, Sierra Nevada" (Rexroth) **95**:287-88
"Spring Snow" (Kenyon) **57**:45
"Spring Song" (Amichai) **38**:25
"Spring Song" (Baraka) **4**:39; **113**:25
"Spring Song" (Ciardi) **69**:5, 25
"Spring Song" (Clifton) **17**:16
"Spring Street in '58" (Walcott) **46**:237
"Spring Suite" (Snodgrass) **74**:329-30
"Spring Sunshine" (MacNeice) **61**:129, 134
Spring Thaw (Yosano)
See *Shundeishū*
"Spring Thunder" (Rich) **5**:383
"The Spring to the Summer" (Meynell) **112**:156, 158, 192, 228, 230, 289
"Spring Torrents" (Teasdale) **31**:360
"Spring Uncovered" (Swenson) **14**:247, 250, 268
"The Spring Vacation" (Mahon) **60**:153, 171, 182-85, 190, 193
"Spring Warning" (Larkin) **21**:259
"A Spring Wooing" (Dunbar) **5**:145
"The Springboard" (MacNeice) **61**:160
Springboard (MacNeice) **61**:140, 142
"Springer Mountain" (Dickey) **40**:163-64, 166
"Springfield Magical" (Lindsay) **23**:284
"Springs" (Montague) **106**:327
Spring's Bedfellow (Morris) **55**:325
"Springs Near Hagerman" (Stafford) **71**:267
"The Springs of Guilty Song" (Crane) **99**:43
"The Springs of the Clitumnus" (Carducci)
See "Alle fonti del Clitumno"
"Spring's Saraband" (Carman) **34**:208
"The Sprinter at Forty" (Dickey) **40**:229
"The Sprinter's Sleep" (Dickey) **40**:175
"Spruce Woods" (Ammons) **16**:45
"Sprüche" (Goethe) **5**:248
"Spuk" (Benn) **35**:72
"Spunyarn" (Masefield) **78**:69
"Spur" (Yeats) **51**:120
"The Spur of Love" (MacDiarmid) **9**:189-90
"The Spy" (Francis) **34**:264-65
"Squabblings and Reconcilation" (Akhmadulina)
See "Prepiratel'stva i primirenija"
"Squarcia 'l vel tu, signor . . ." (Michelangelo) **103**:286
"The Square Peg and the Round" (Gilmore) **87**:301
"Squares and Angles" (Storni)
See "Cuadros y angulos"
"Squares and Courtyards" (Hacker) **47**:118-19
Squares and Courtyards (Hacker) **47**:117, 120
"Squarings" (Heaney) **18**:254, 257-58; **100**:245-47, 287-88, 298, 312
Squarings (Heaney) **100**:246
"Squash in Blossom" (Francis) **34**:242
"The Squatter on Company Land" (Hugo) **68**:287
"Le squelette laboureur" (Baudelaire) **1**:45
"Squieres Tale" (Chaucer)
See "Squire's Tale"
"Squince" (Mahon) **60**:174
"The Squire and the Priest" (Crabbe) **97**:104, 106
"Squire Hawkins's Story" (Riley) **48**:288
"Squire Leech" (Elliott) **96**:163
"Squire Thomas" (Crabbe) **97**:104
"Squire's Tale" (Chaucer) **19**:13
"The Squirrel" (Stryk) **27**:189, 203
"Squishy Touch" (Silverstein) **49**:336
"Srishti-sthiti-pralaya" (Tagore) **8**:406
"Śroczość" (Milosz) **8**:187
St. Agnes (Keats)
See *The Eve of St. Agnes*
"St. Barnabas, Oxford" (Betjeman) **75**:98
"St. Barthomomew's On the Hill" (Carman) **34**:225
"St. Botolph's" (Hughes) **89**:180, 235
"St. Brandan" (Arnold) **5**:12
"St. Catherine of Siena" (Meynell)
See "Saint Catherine of Siena"
"St. Catherine's Clock" (Kinsella) **69**:135-36
St. Catherine's Clock (Kinsella) **69**:80-81, 107
"St Eustace" (Mahon) **60**:202
"St. George and the Dragon" (Masefield) **78**:64
"The St. James Phenomenon" (Hunt) **73**:152
"St. John" (Lawrence) **54**:194
"St. Launce's Revisited" (Hardy) **8**:136
"St. Louis Blues" (Hughes) **53**:81
"St. Lucies Day" (Donne)
See "A Nocturnal upon S. Lucies day, Being the shortest day"
"St. Luke the Painter" (Rossetti) **44**:227-28, 232, 250
"St. Lukes, Service for Thomas" (Corso) **33**:46; **108**:15
"St. Mark" (Lawrence) **54**:170
St. Martin's (Creeley) **73**:91
"St. Mary Magdalen, Old Fish Street Hill" (Betjeman) **75**:94
"St. Mary Magdalene Preaching at Marseilles" (Ní Chuilleanáin) **34**:350, 360
"St. Matthew" (Lawrence) **54**:224
"St. Monica" (Smith) **104**:170-71, 227, 229-30
St. Patrick's Purgatory (Marie de France)
See *L'Espurgatoire Saint Patrice*
"St. Paul and All That" (O'Hara) **45**:151, 216, 218-19
"St. Peter Relates an Incident of the Resurrection Day" (Johnson) **24**:133, 141, 144, 153, 161, 170
St. Peter Relates an Incident: Selected Poems (Johnson) **24**:130, 159, 162
St. Peters Complaint (Southwell)
See *Saint Peters Complaint, with Other Poems*
"St. Peter's Remorse" (Southwell) **83**:280, 297, 326
"St. Praxed's Church" (Browning) **2**:30
"St. Saviour's, Aberdeen Park, Highbury, London, N." (Betjeman) **75**:20, 31, 66, 81, 99-100
"St. Senan's Well" (Melville)
See "Saint Senan's Well"
"St. Simeon Stylites" (Tennyson) **6**:411; **101**:225, 257
"St. Thomas's Ruins" (Curnow) **48**:29
"St Valentine Is Past" (Birney) **52**:22
"St. Valentine's Day" (Patmore) **59**:208-9, 224
"St. Vincent's" (Merwin) **45**:63-4
"Stabat Mater" (Crashaw)
See "Sancta Maria Dolorum"
"The Stable" (Kinsella) **69**:79, 133, 137
"Stadium High, Tacoma" (Stafford) **71**:315, 332, 335, 343
"The Staff of Aesculapius" (Moore) **49**:126, 136, 138
"Stafford Country" (Hugo) **68**:314
"The Stag" (Hughes) **89**:125
"Stag Skull Mounted" (Raworth) **107**:275, 324
"Stage Directions" (Niedecker) **42**:101, 148
"Stages" (Ignatow) **34**:326
"Stages" (Meredith) **28**:180
"Stages of a Journey Westward" (Wright) **36**:288, 340
"Stagirius" (Arnold) **5**:38
"Staircase" (Tsvetaeva)
See "Poèma lestnitsy"
Staische Gedichte (Benn) **35**:4, 5, 6, 8, 42
"Stalin" (Lowell) **3**:223
"Stalin Epigram" (Mandelstam) **14**:149, 153
"Stalin's Heirs" (Yevtushenko) **40**:343, 346, 350, 352, 368, 370
Stalin's Heirs (Yevtushenko) **40**:365
"The Stalker" (Momaday) **25**:212-13
"Stan" (Tagore) **8**:407
"Stances" (Gautier) **18**:163
"Stances de la fontaine de'Helene" (Ronsard) **11**:241
"Stanchion Roots" (Spencer) **77**:339
"Stand who so list upon the slipper top" (Wyatt) **27**:331, 362, 367
Stand with Me Here (Francis) **34**:241, 244
"The Standard Oil Co." (Neruda)
See "La Standard Oil Co."

"La Standard Oil Co." (Neruda) **4**:296
"Standardization" (Hope) **56**:266, 284, 306
"Standards and Paradise of the Blacks" (García Lorca)
See "Norma y paraíso de los negros"
"A Standing Ground" (Berry) **28**:43
"Standing in the Middle of a Desert" (Wagoner) **33**:352
"Standing Is Stupid" (Silverstein) **49**:330
Standing Still and Walking in New York (O'Hara) **45**:154, 163
"The Stand-Ins" (Sexton) **79**:240
"Standomi un giorno solo a la fenestra" (Petrarch) **8**:253-57
"The standstillness of unthought" (Villa) **22**:354
"The Stand-To" (Day Lewis) **11**:146
"Stand-to: Good Friday Morning" (Sassoon) **12**:241, 251, 262, 280
"Stand-Up Comedy Routine" (Berrigan) **103**:37
"Stand-up Comic" (Chappell) **105**:52
"Stanley Kunitz" (Ignatow) **34**:345
Stantsiya Zima (Yevtushenko) **40**:359, 363-65
"Stanza" (Bogan) **12**:103
"Stanza and Strophe" (Ponge)
See "Strophe"
"Stanza from Epistle to Mr. Tytler of Woodhouslee, Author of the Defence of Mary Queen of Scots" (Burns) **114**:116
"Stanzas" (Brodsky) **9**:4
"Stanzas" (Hood) **93**:121-22
"Stanzas" (Mandelstam) **14**:151
"Stanzas for the Times" (Whittier) **93**:206, 315
"Stanzas from the Grande Chartreuse" (Arnold) **5**:18, 24, 33, 35, 52-3, 58
Stanzas in Love with Life and August Again Again (Viereck) **27**:265
"Stanzas in Meditation" (Stein) **18**:309-316, 335-37, 339-41, 343, 345-48
Stanzas in Meditation (Stein) **18**:309-316, 335-37, 339-41, 343, 345-48
"Stanzas in Memory of Edward Quillinan" (Arnold) **5**:52
"Stanzas in Memory of the Author of 'Obermann'" (Arnold) **5**:42, 50, 52
"Stanzas on a Visit to Longleat House in Wiltshire, October, 1953" (Barker) **77**:20
"Stanzas on Peele Castle" (Wordsworth) **4**:394, 410-11
"Stanzas to Bettine" (Barrett Browning) **6**:15
"Stanzas to Tolstoi" (Pushkin) **10**:409
"Stanzas Written at Night in Radio City" (Ginsberg) **4**:55
"Stanzas Written at Sea" (Peacock) **87**:326, 347
"Stanzas Written on Battersea Bridge during a South-Westerly Gale" (Belloc) **24**:30-1, 36
"Stanzas wrote in a Country Church-Yard" (Gray) **80**:131-32, 148-52, 163, 166, 244, 249
"Stanze in lode della vita rusticale" (Michelangelo) **103**:188
"Star" (Bedier) **46**:236
"A Star" (Kavanagh) **33**:117, 120
"The Star" (Masters) **1**:326, 333, 337, 342
"The Star" (Vaughan) **81**:347, 349
The Star (Bely)
See *Zvezda*
"The Star and the Water-Lily" (Holmes) **71**:91
"The Star Field" (Berssenbrugge) **115**:10
"A Star in a Stone-Boat" (Frost) **1**:194, 221; **39**:233, 235
"Star Rats" (Raworth) **107**:276
"Star Suite" (Goodison) **36**:152
"Star Woman Falling" (Wagoner) **33**:354
The Star-Apple Kingdom (Walcott) **46**:259, 322-23, 325
stardust (Bissett) **14**:30
"The Stare of the Man from the Provinces" (Nemerov) **24**:268
"A Stared Story" (Stafford) **71**:292, 295
"Star-Fall" (Warren) **37**:312, 337
"Starfish" (Cervantes) **35**:104, 114, 117
"The Starfish" (Jacobsen) **62**:320
"Starfish" (Oliver) **75**:293
"Star-Gazer" (MacNeice) **61**:177
"Staring at the Sea on the Day of the Death of Another" (Swenson) **14**:288
"Staring into a River Till Moved by It" (Kennedy) **93**:151
"Starinnyi portret" (Akhmadulina) **43**:3
"Staritsa" (Shvarts) **50**:137, 143
"Starlight" (Meredith) **28**:171
"Starlight like Intuition Pierced the Twelve" (Schwartz) **8**:290-91
"The Starlight Night" (Hopkins) **15**:144, 152, 160, 162
"Starlight Scope Myopia" (Komunyakaa) **51**:26-27, 30, 37-38
"The Starling" (Lowell) **13**:61
"The Starling" (Smith) **12**:326
"The Starling" (Soto) **28**:375
"Starlings on the Roof" (Hardy) **92**:228
The Starlit Eye (Kinsella) **69**:115
"The Starred Coverlet" (Graves) **6**:156
"The Starry Flower" (Tuckerman) **85**:333
"The Starry Night" (Sexton) **2**:350, 371-72
"Starry Night" (Sexton) **2**:350, 371-72; **79**:253
"Stars" (Hayden) **6**:184-85, 190, 194, 196
"The Stars Are with the Voyager" (Hood) **93**:78
"Stars, Songs, Faces" (Sandburg) **41**:313
"Stars Which See, Stars Which Do Not See" (Bell) **79**:21
Stars Which See, Stars Which Do Not See (Bell) **79**:22-23, 28, 32, 39-40
"The Star-Song: A Carroll to the King; Sung at White Hall" (Herrick) **9**:118, 119
"The Star-Splitter" (Frost) **1**:194; **39**:233, 235
"Start Again Somewhere" (Gallagher) **9**:58
"Star-Talk" (Graves) **6**:166
"Starting Back" (Hugo) **68**:253
"Starting from Paumanok" (Whitman) **91**:314
"Starting from San Francisco" (Ferlinghetti) **1**:187
Starting from San Francisco (Ferlinghetti) **1**:166, 172-76, 187
Starting Point (Day Lewis) **11**:129
"Starting Therapy" (Kenyon) **57**:46
"Starting with Little Things" (Stafford) **71**:353
"Starvation" (Ai) **72**:29
"Starvation" (Brathwaite) **56**:34
"Starvation Camp Near Jaslo" (Szymborska)
See "Obóz glodowy pod Jaslem"
"Starved Lovers" (MacLeish) **47**:192
Starved Rock (Masters) **1**:332, 335, 338, 342-44
"Stary Prometeusz" (Herbert) **50**:39
"Stasis" (Stone) **53**:228
"The State" (Jarrell) **41**:172, 195, 198
"The State of Age" (Meredith) **60**:255
"State of Siege" (Guillén) **35**:218
State of Siege (Darwish)
See *Halat hisar*
"The State of World Affairs from a Third Floor Window" (Bukowski) **18**:3
"State/meant" (Baraka) **113**:11
"Statement" (Curnow) **48**:44
"Statement" (Francis) **34**:251
"Statement" (Hughes) **53**:101-2
"Statement of the Times" (Ignatow) **34**:323
"Statement on Poetics" (Hayden) **6**:198
Statements After an Arrest Under the Immorality Act (Brutus) **24**:119
"The Staten Island Ferry" (Clampitt) **19**:100
"The State's claim that it seeks in no way to deprive Indians of their rightful share of water, but only to define that share, falls on deaf ears" (Ortiz) **17**:233
"The Statesman's Secret" (Holmes) **71**:94
"Stati maggiori contrapposti, loro piani" (Zanzotto) **65**:281
"Static Landscape" (Sarton) **39**:320
Static Poems (Benn)
See *Staische Gedichte*
"The Station" (Merwin) **45**:18
"Station" (Olds) **22**:307, 328
"Station Island" (Heaney) **18**:220, 240; **100**:235, 243, 268, 278, 328
Station Island (Heaney) **18**:211-12, 214-16, 218, 226, 228, 232, 237; **100**:221, 226, 230, 237, 239, 273, 299, 322
Station Zima (Yevtushenko)
See "Zima Station"
"The Stationary Journey" (Muir) **49**:239, 289, 297
"Stations" (Hughes) **7**:137; **89**:103-4, 106
"Stations" (Lorde) **12**:140
Stations (Heaney) **100**:224, 231, 286-87
"The Stations of King's Cross" (Enright) **93**:28
"Statische Gedichte" (Benn) **35**:33
"Statistics" (Cunningham) **92**:184
"Statistics" (Sandburg) **41**:235, 269
"The Statue" (Belloc) **24**:9
"The Statue" (Berryman) **64**:73, 82-83, 90
"La Statue" (Hugo) **17**:64
"Statue and Birds" (Bogan) **12**:94, 101, 127
"The Statue and the Bust" (Browning) **61**:96; **97**:33
"The Statue at the World's End" (Stevens)
See "Mr. Burnshaw and the Statue"
"Statue at Tsarskoye Selo" (Akhmatova) **2**:12
The Statue Guest (Pushkin)
See *Kamennyi gost'*
"The Statue in Stocks-Market" (Marvell) **10**:276
"The Statue in the Garden" (Lowell) **13**:61
"A Statue in the Silence" (Neruda)
See "Una estatua en el silencio"
"The Statue of Liberty" (Hardy) **8**:99
"The Statues" (Yeats) **20**:324, 334
"Status Quo," (Birney) **52**:39
"Status Quo" (Curnow) **48**:25
"A Statute of Wine" (Neruda)
See "Estatura del vino"
"A Stave of Roving Tim" (Meredith) **60**:262, 294-95
"Stay, Phoebus! Stay" (Waller) **72**:334
"Stay With Me" (Hongo) **23**:203
"Staying Alive" (Levertov) **11**:178-79, 195-96
"Staying Alive" (Wagoner) **33**:333, 348, 359
Staying Alive (Wagoner) **33**:329, 332-33, 352, 359, 373
"Staying at Grandma's" (Kenyon) **57**:40-41
"Steak" (Snyder) **21**:292-93
"Steal Away to Jesus" (Johnson) **24**:170
"Stealing Trout on a May Morning" (Hughes) **7**:120, 170
"The Stealthy School of Criticism" (Rossetti) **44**:206
"Steam Shovel Cut" (Masters) **1**:343
"The Steamboat Whistle" (MacLeish) **47**:197
"Lo steddazzu" (Pavese) **13**:229
"Steele" (Quintana) **36**:272
"Steelhead" (Jeffers) **17**:141
"Steely Silence" (Wakoski) **15**:332
Steeple Bush (Frost) **1**:200, 205-06, 217; **39**:233
"The Steeple-Jack" (Bishop) **34**:106
"The Steeple-Jack" (Moore) **4**:256; **49**:100-101, 108
"Steering Wheel" (Graham) **59**:152, 177
"Stein Imitations" (Duncan) **75**:224, 228
"Der Steinsammler" (Sachs) **78**:200
"Stele for a Northern Republican" (Montague) **106**:325, 355
"Stella's Birthday, March 13, 1718-19" (Swift) **9**:255, 297
"Stella's Portrait" (Howe) **54**:130
"Stellenbosch" (Kipling) **3**:176
"Stellenbosh" (Kipling) **91**:70, 144, 172
"The Stenographers" (Page) **12**:163, 173
"A Step Away from Them" (O'Hara) **45**:115, 127, 141, 145, 147, 170, 178, 184, 216, 243
"Stepchild" (Hongo) **23**:197
"Stephen A. Douglas" (Masters) **1**:334
"The Steppes of Akkerman" (Mickiewicz)
See "Stepy Akermańskie"
"Stepping Backward" (Rich) **5**:352
"Stepping Outside" (Gallagher) **9**:35
Stepping Outside (Gallagher) **9**:35

"Stepping Stones" (Heaney) **100**:252
"Stepping Westward" (Wordsworth) **4**:395; **67**:248
"Steps for Three" (Ignatow) **34**:321
"The Steps of the Commander" (Blok) **21**:6
Steps to the Temple. Sacred Poems With Other Delights of the Muses (Crashaw) **84**:9-10, 12, 14, 20-21, 24, 48-49, 69-70, 77, 102, 109-10, 113, 127, 151, 153, 167, 171
"Stepy Akermańskie" (Mickiewicz) **38**:158
"Sterben im Walde" (Werfel) **101**:345
"Sterling, Colorado" (Quintana) **36**:249, 270
"Stern" (Heaney) **100**:331
Sternverdunkelung (Sachs) **78**:110, 121, 128, 130, 157, 163-64, 170-71, 173-74, 176, 187, 219, 225
"The Stethoscope" (Abse) **41**:22, 25, 29-30
"The Stethoscope Song" (Holmes) **71**:68, 93
Stevie Smith: A Selection (Smith) **12**:331, 348
"Stifled cries" (Péret)
See "Des cris étouffés"
"The Stigmata of Fact" (Rexroth) **95**:276
Stikhi (Akhmadulina) **43**:33
Stikhi (Shvarts) **50**:134, 142, 145
"Stikhi K Akhmatovoi" (Tsvetaeva) **14**:321
Stikhi K Blok (Tsvetaeva) **14**:299, 311-12
"Stikhi k Chekhii" (Tsvetaeva) **14**:325, 327
"Stikhi k Pushkinu" (Tsvetaeva) **14**:324-25
"Stikhi k synu" (Tsvetaeva) **14**:328
"Stikhi o neizvestnom soldate" (Mandelstam) **14**:145, 148-49, 152, 155
Stikhi o prekrasnoi dame (Blok) **21**:13, 18, 24, 30
Stikhi raznykh let (Yevtushenko) **40**:341
Stikhotvoreniia (Akhmadulina) **43**:33, 49-50
Stikhotvoreniia i poemy (Akhmatova) **55**:26
Stikhotvoreniia i poemy (Shvarts) **50**:162
Stikhotvoreniya (Bely) **11**:29
"still" (Birney) **52**:83
"Still at Annecy" (Montale)
See "Ancora ad Annecy"
"The Still Centre" (Spender) **71**:209
The Still Centre (Spender) **71**:138-39, 146, 166-69, 180, 182, 186, 188-91, 202, 209, 211-12, 223-29
"Still, Citizen Sparrow" (Wilbur) **51**:187, 221
"Still Do I Keep My Look, My Identity" (Brooks) **7**:71
"Still Falls the Rain" (Sitwell) **3**:310, 323, 326
"Still Here" (Hughes) **53**:150-51
"Still Life" (Glück) **16**:128, 136, 139, 142
"Still Life" (Graham) **59**:175
"Still Life" (Hecht) **70**:65, 96-98, 100-101
"Still Life" (Hughes) **7**:121, 137; **89**:150, 166, 169
"Still Life" (Sandburg) **41**:297
"Still Life in Snowstorm" (Sarton) **39**:328
"Still Life with Window and Fish" (Graham) **59**:179
"Still Night" (Smith) **12**:317
"Still Night Thoughts" (Li Po) **29**:145
"Still on Water" (Rexroth) **20**:206, 216
"The Still Small Voice" (Winters) **82**:344-45
"The Still Time" (Kinnell) **26**:260, 281
"Still Will I Strive to Be" (Thoreau) **30**:128
"Stillborn" (Plath) **1**:391, 405
"Stillborn Love" (Rossetti) **44**:169
"Stilleben" (Benn) **35**:69
"Stillness" (Pasternak)
See "Tishina"
"Stillpoint Hill That Other Shore" (Chappell) **105**:45
"Stimme des Heilegen Landes" (Sachs) **18**:147, 156; **78**:202
"Stimme des Volks" (Hölderlin) **4**:166
"Die Stimme hinter dem Vorhang" (Benn) **35**:32, 34
"Stinging" (Cummings)
See "Sunset"
"Stings" (Plath) **1**:394, 410, 412-14; **37**:239, 241, 262
"Stirling Street September" (Baraka) **113**:18
"The Stirrup-Cup" (Lanier) **50**:56, 77
"Stixi na smert T. S. Èliota" (Brodsky) **9**:2, 4
Sto pociech (Szymborska) **44**:268
"I' sto rinchiuso come la midolla" (Michelangelo) **103**:199, 257-60
"Stockings in the Farm-House Chimney" (Melville) **82**:154
"Stoic Poet" (Chappell) **105**:21
"Stokely Malcolm Me" (Hughes) **53**:111, 151
"Stol" (Tsvetaeva) **14**:318
Stolen Apples (Yevtushenko) **40**:365
"The Stolen Child" (Yeats) **20**:337, 346
"Stolen Trees" (Hogan) **35**:250
"Stolen Waters" (Carroll) **74**:65
"Stone" (Brathwaite) **56**:43
"The Stone" (Carruth) **10**:71
"Stone" (Simic) **69**:314
"The Stone" (Soto)
See "Piedra"
Stone (Mandelstam)
See *Kamen'*
"The Stone Age" (Das) **43**:74, 91
"A Stone Age Figure Far Below" (Mahon) **60**:214
The Stone Bridge (Seifert)
See *Kammený most*
"A Stone Church Damaged by a Bomb" (Larkin) **21**:259
"Stone from Delphi" (Heaney) **100**:342
"The Stone Fleet" (Melville) **82**:92, 204
"The Stone from the Sea" (Celan) **10**:112
"The Stone Garden" (Sarton) **39**:327, 339
"The Stone Garden (Kyoto)" (Blunden) **66**:45
The Stone Guest (Pushkin)
See *Kamennyi gost'*
"A Stone Knife" (Schuyler) **88**:189, 207
"Stone, Paper, Knife" (Piercy) **29**:315-16, 318-19, 321-22
Stone, Paper, Knife (Piercy) **29**:312-13, 316-17, 321
"The Stone Sermon" (Brathwaite) **56**:76, 100
"The Stone Verdict" (Heaney) **18**:229, 233; **100**:241
"Stone Walls" (Hall) **70**:9, 27-28, 34, 36
"Stone Works" (Ciardi) **69**:31
"The Stonecarver's Poem" (Levertov) **11**:169
"Stone-Head" (Plath) **37**:188
"The Stones" (Plath) **1**:389-90; **37**:190-91
"Stones" (Zagajewski) **27**:389
The Stones of the Field (Thomas) **99**:239-40, 268, 309
"Stonewall Jackson" (Melville) **82**:93, 206
"Stony, Fifteen Years in the Joint" (Baca) **41**:37
"Stony Grey Soil" (Kavanagh) **33**:62, 75, 86, 93, 102, 127, 129, 150, 154-7; **105**:93, 103, 144, 176
"Stony Limits" (MacDiarmid) **9**:156, 176
Stony Limits and Other Poems (MacDiarmid) **9**:156, 158, 172-73, 175-76, 179-80, 182-84, 196, 200
"Stony Lonesome" (Hughes) **53**:119
"Stool" (Herbert) **50**:4
"Stop All the Clocks" (Auden) **92**:51, 54-56
"Stop That Clowning at Once If Not Sooner" (Enright) **93**:14
"Stopped Dead" (Plath) **37**:256
"Stopping by Woods on a Snowy Evening" (Frost) **1**:194, 197, 208, 213-14, 221, 225; **39**:230-57; **71**:17, 43
"Stop-Short" (Belloc) **24**:39
"A Stopwatch and an Ordnance Map" (Spender) **71**:155, 206, 226
"La storia" (Montale) **13**:134
"Storie dell'Arsura I" (Zanzotto) **65**:290
"Storie dell'Arsura II" (Zanzotto) **65**:290
"The Storie of William Canynge" (Chatterton) **104**:6
Stories and Storms and Strangers (Stafford) **71**:331
"Stories from Kansas" (Stafford) **71**:276, 288, 295
"Stories of Snow" (Page) **12**:164, 167-69, 172, 190, 197
"Stories of the Drought II" (Zanzotto)
See "Storie dell'Arsura II"
Stories of the Sioux (Chief Standing Bear) **10**:333, 341-42
Stories that Could Be True: New and Collected Poems (Stafford) **71**:302-7, 320-22, 325-34, 336-43, 349, 363, 368-69
"Stork Story" (Silverstein) **49**:341
"The Storm" (Bly) **39**:115
"The Storm" (Mickiewicz)
See "Burza"
"The Storm" (Montale)
See "La bufera"
"Storm" (Owen) **19**:353-54
"The Storm" (Peacock) **87**:320
"Storm" (Stryk) **27**:195, 212
"Storm" (Wright) **14**:342
The Storm and Other Things (Montale)
See *La bufera e altro*
"Storm at Hoptime" (Blunden) **66**:4
"The Storm Came" (Kipling) **3**:171, 183
"Storm Ending" (Toomer) **7**:317, 330-32
"Storm Fear" (Frost) **39**:244, 246-47
"A Storm in April" (Wilbur) **51**:278
"The storm is over" (Bridges) **28**:83
"Storm of Love" (Aleixandre) **15**:19
"Storm Warnings" (Rich) **5**:392, 396
"Storm Windows" (Nemerov) **24**:264-67, 270-71
"Story" (Boland) **58**:24
"The Story" (Chappell) **105**:38
"Story" (Ignatow) **34**:270
"A Story" (Jarrell) **41**:127, 168, 213
"The Story" (Mueller) **33**:179
"A Story" (Stafford) **71**:295
"Story" (Wakoski) **15**:365
"Story Between Two Notes" (McGuckian) **27**:91
"A Story for a Winter Night" (Stafford) **71**:331
"The Story of a Citizen" (Gallagher) **9**:60, 62
"A Story of a Cock and a Bull" (Smart) **13**:348
"Story of a Love" (Dalton) **36**:122
"The Story of a Well-Made Shield" (Momaday) **25**:189, 213
"The Story of Adrastus" (Morris) **55**:305
"The Story of Aristomenes" (Morris) **55**:306-7, 309
"A Story of Courage" (Ortiz) **17**:246
"The Story of Cupid and Psyche" (Morris) **55**:242, 249
"The Story of Dorothea" (Morris) **55**:305-6
"A Story of How a Wall Stands" (Ortiz) **17**:225
"The Story of Margaret" (Wordsworth)
See "The Ruined Cottage"
"The Story of Orpheus and Eurydice" (Morris) **55**:306-7
"The Story of Ossian" (Masefield) **78**:84
The Story of Our Lives (Strand) **63**:144-46, 152, 160-61, 163, 165-66, 169, 173, 198
"The Story of Our Lives" (Strand) **63**:143, 147, 154-55, 160-62
"The Story of Phœbus and Daphne Applied" (Waller) **72**:330-31, 345
"The Story of Rhodope" (Morris) **55**:308
"The Story of Richard Maxfield" (Wakoski) **15**:346, 355, 361
"The Story of Rimini" (Hunt) **73**:181, 183, 203, 210
The Story of Rimini (Hunt) **73**:135-36, 145-51, 153, 157, 162, 166, 177, 180-83, 195-97, 202-12, 218-20, 223-29, 235
"The Story of Solomon and the Hoopoe" (Rumi) **45**:312
"The Story of the Churn" (Stone) **53**:217
The Story of the Great War (Braithwaite) **52**:106
The Story of the Heart (Aleixandre)
See *Historia del corazón*
"The Story of Tommy" (Kipling) **3**:194
"Story of Two Gardens" (Paz)
See "Cuento de dos jardines"

"The Story of Ung" (Kipling) **91**:86
"The Story's Ending" (Morris) **55**:339
"Stotras to Kali Destroyer of Illusions" (Ginsberg) **47**:21, 39
"Stra" (Mackey) **49**:25, 53, 57
"(Stracaganasse o castagne secche)" (Zanzotto) **65**:271, 282
"La strada" (Pasolini) **17**:253
"Strada di Agrigentum" (Quasimodo) **47**:279, 288
"Stradivarius" (Eliot) **20**:123, 125
"Straight from Your Prejudice" (Amichai) **38**:19
"Straight Talk" (Giovanni) **19**:112
"Straight Talk from a Patriot" (Randall) **86**:291, 335
"Straight-Creek—Great Burn" (Snyder) **21**:297
The Straightening (Celan)
See *Sprachgitter*
Strains (Brutus) **24**:121-22, 124
"The Strait" (Ammons) **16**:4
The Strait of Anian (Birney) **52**:11, 39, 45, 49, 52, 67, 92
"The Straitening" (Celan)
See "Engführung"
The Straitjacket (Parra) **39**:310
Straits (Koch) **80**:325-28, 339-40
"Strand" (Benn) **35**:49, 75
"The Strand" (MacNeice) **61**:110, 128, 186
"The Strand at Lough Beg" (Heaney) **100**:259, 274
"Strands" (Stone) **53**:249, 257
"Strands" (Thomas) **99**:275, 310
"The Strange and True Story of My Life with Billy the Kid" (Momaday) **25**:221
"The Strange Case" (Ondaatje) **28**:329
"Strange Fits of Passion Have I Known" (Wordsworth) **4**:420
"Strange Fruit" (Harjo) **27**:71
"Strange Fruit" (Heaney) **18**:196
Strange Histories, of Kings, Princes, Dukes, Earles, Lords, Ladies, Knights, and Gentlemen (Deloney) **79**:56-57
"The Strange House" (Hardy) **92**:275, 329
The Strange Islands (Merton) **10**:331, 342, 347, 349, 351
"Strange Legacies" (Brown) **55**:71, 76, 79-80, 95
"Strange Meeting" (Owen) **19**:325-27, 329, 332, 335-37, 341-45, 347, 353, 355, 359, 370-71; **102**:167-68, 171-73, 181, 188, 192, 194-95, 197-200, 203, 206, 208, 216-17, 225-26, 232, 258, 263, 265, 267
"Strange People" (Erdrich) **52**:192
"A Strange Song" (Wylie) **23**:324
"A Strange Story" (Wylie) **23**:307, 310
"Strange Victory" (Teasdale) **31**:372
Strange Victory (Teasdale) **31**:326, 330, 333, 339, 341-42, 346, 349, 364, 370, 372-73, 380, 389-90
"Strangeness of Heart" (Sassoon) **12**:254
"The Stranger" (Kinsella) **69**:82, 133-35
"The Stranger" (de la Mare) **77**:116
"The Stranger" (Rich) **5**:384
"The Stranger" (Tuckerman) **85**:302
The Stranger (Blok)
See *Neznakomka*
Stranger Music: Selected Poems and Essays (Cohen) **109**:67, 69-70
"The Stranger: Poverty of an Anti-Hero" (Merton) **10**:349
"The Stranger Song" (Cohen) **109**:66
"The Strangers" (Berry) **28**:7
"The Strangers" (Very) **86**:113, 158
"The Stranger's Gift" (Very) **86**:46, 81
"Strategy" (Gallagher) **9**:59
"Stratford on Avon" (Davie) **29**:102
"Strathallan's Lament" (Burns) **114**:161
"Stratis Thalassinos among the Agapanthi" (Seferis) **66**:144, 148, 150, 178
"Stratis Thalassinos on the Dead Sea" (Seferis) **66**:179
"Stratis the Sailor Describes a Man" (Seferis)
See "Mr. Stratis Thalassinos Describes a Man"
"Strato in Plaster" (Merrill) **28**:258
"Stratton Water" (Rossetti) **44**:202-3
"Strauss Park" (Stern) **115**:249
"Stravinsky's Three Pieces "Grotesques", for String Quartet" (Lowell) **13**:77
"Straw Hat" (Dove) **6**:110, 114
"Strawberries" (Merwin) **45**:97
"Strawberry Hill" (Hughes) **7**:119, 148
"Strawberrying" (Swenson) **14**:273
"Stray Animals" (Song) **21**:332
"The Strayed Reveller" (Arnold) **5**:5, 12, 39, 50
The Strayed Reveller, and Other Poems (Arnold) **5**:8, 31, 38-9, 42, 48
"The Straying Student" (Clarke) **112**:30, 36, 50, 80, 90, 139
"Stream and Sun at Glendalough" (Yeats) **20**:328
"The Stream of the Golden Honey was Pouring So Slow . . ." (Mandelstam) **14**:141
"The Stream's Secret" (Rossetti) **44**:164, 194-95, 203, 210-11, 259-60
"Street" (Ní Chuilleanáin) **34**:352, 382-84
"The Street" (Paz)
See "La calle"
"The Street" (Soto) **28**:378, 383, 386
"Street" (Storni)
See "Calle"
"Street Car Gang" (Brown) **55**:114
"Street Entertainment" (Szirtes) **51**:169, 171-72
"A Street Game" (Clarke) **112**:64
"The Street Has Changed" (Jarrell) **41**:169
A Street in Bronzeville (Brooks) **7**:52-4, 56-8, 60-1, 67, 70, 75, 79-80, 85-7, 95, 102, 105
"Street Moths" (Kennedy) **93**:153
"Street Scene" (MacNeice) **61**:115
"Street Scene" (Simic) **69**:320-21
"Street Scenes" (Hacker) **47**:107
"Street Song" (Hughes) **53**:162
"Street Song" (Sitwell) **3**:311
Street Songs (Sitwell) **3**:308, 320
"The Street Ventriloquist" (Simic) **69**:306
"Street Window" (Sandburg) **2**:309
"Street with a pink store" (Borges)
See "Calle con almacén rosado"
"Streetcorner Man" (Borges)
See "El Hombre de la esquina rosada"
"Streets" (Borges)
See "Las Calles"
"Streets" (Verlaine) **2**:415; **32**:371
"The Streets" (Winters) **82**:316, 320
Streets Enough to Welcome Snow (Waldrop) **109**:120-21, 179, 186
"The Streets Grow Young" (Wright) **36**:307
Streets in the Moon (MacLeish) **47**:126-27, 165, 183, 185-86, 188, 190, 192, 212, 215, 222
"The Streets of Laredo" (MacNeice) **61**:140, 157-61
"Streets of Pearl and Gold" (Kizer) **66**:73-74
"The Strength of Fields" (Dickey) **40**:222, 258
The Strength of Fields (Dickey) **40**:219, 222, 229, 232
"Strength out of Sweetness" (Winters) **82**:318, 326
"Strength through Joy" (Rexroth) **95**:259, 271, 288-89, 312-13
"Strengthening the Spirit" (Cavafy) **36**:39, 41, 74, 107
"Strephon and Chloe" (Swift) **9**:257-58, 262, 270, 274, 286, 288, 294, 298, 301
"Strephon to Celia. A Modern Love-Letter" (Leapor) **85**:201, 211, 250, 293
"Strephon's Song" (Belloc) **24**:6
"Stretcher Case" (Sassoon) **12**:242, 262
"The Stretcher-bearer" (Service) **70**:130
Strick: Song of the Andoumboulou: 16-25 (Mackey) **49**:17, 25, 33, 41-42, 53
Strike (Viereck) **27**:280-82, 284
Strike Through the Mask! (Viereck) **27**:262-63, 278
"Strine Authors Meet" (Birney) **52**:63
String (Akhmadulina)
See *Struna*
"The String" (Dickey) **40**:175, 179, 192
"The Stripping of the River" (Dorn) **115**:110, 122
"Stripping the vista to its depth" (Tomlinson) **17**:342
"Striptease-Tänzerinnen" (Enzensberger) **28**:165
"Strive Not With Love" (Surrey) **59**:353
"The Stroke" (Dove) **6**:111
"Stroke" (Jacobsen) **62**:333
"The Stroke" (Smith) **12**:314
"Stroll" (Borges)
See "Caminata"
"The Stroller" (Kenyon) **57**:11, 13, 44
"A Strolling Minstrel's Ballad of the skulls and Flowers" (Snodgrass) **74**:324, 334
"Strong Men" (Brown) **55**:70-71, 77, 82, 95-96, 110, 113-14, 152, 178
"Strong Men, Riding Horses" (Brooks) **7**:106
"A Strong New Voice Pointing the Way" (Madhubuti) **5**:346
"The Strong Woman" (Mistral)
See "La mujer fuerte"
"Strophe" (Ponge) **107**:225, 236-37, 239-40
"Strophe" (Seferis) **66**:117-18, 121-22, 125-27
Strophe (Seferis) **66**:89, 92, 101, 105, 110-11, 117-18, 120, 124-25, 142-44, 181-82, 184, 214
Strountes (Ekeloef) **23**:59-61, 63, 76-8
"The Structure of Rime" (Duncan) **2**:116, 124-25, 126; **75**:145, 147, 161, 171, 176, 232, 261, 265
The Structure of Rime (Duncan) **2**:126
"The Structure of Rime I" (Duncan) **75**:161, 230
"The Structure of Rime II" (Duncan) **2**:125; **75**:230
"The Structure of Rime XIV" (Duncan) **75**:223, 265
"The Structure of Rime XVI" (Duncan) **75**:199
"The Structure of Rime XX" (Duncan) **75**:161, 231
"The Structure of Rime XXIII" (Duncan) **75**:232
"The Structure of Rime XXVI" (Duncan) **75**:133
"The Structure of Rime XXVIII" (Duncan) **2**:114
"The Structure of the Plane" (Rukeyser) **12**:202
"Struggle" (Hughes) **7**:165-66
"The Struggle between the Statistical Mentality and Eros" (Ignatow) **34**:304-05
"The Struggle Staggers Us" (Walker) **20**:289, 294
"Struggling Sea" (Guillén) **35**:221
"Strumpet Song" (Plath) **1**:388
Struna (Akhmadulina) **43**:2, 11, 33
Struna swiatła (Herbert) **50**:4, 7, 18-19, 24
"Stubborn Hope" (Brutus) **24**:112
Stubborn Hope: New Poems and Selections from "China Poems" and "Strains" (Brutus) **24**:112, 116, 118, 122
"Stuck Inside of Mobile with the Memphis Blues Again" (Dylan) **37**:52, 54-56
"The Student" (Moore) **4**:260; **49**:100, 119
Studi letterari (Carducci) **46**:55
"Studies by the Sea" (Smith) **104**:178
"Studies in Secrecy" (Graham) **59**:164
Studies in Song (Swinburne) **24**:322
"The Studies of Narcissus" (Schwartz) **8**:311
"The Studio" (Mahon) **60**:178-79, 188, 190-91, 201-2
Studium przedmiotu (Herbert) **50**:4-5, 7, 18, 20, 25
"A Study" (Masters) **1**:342
"A Study" (Meynell) **112**:156-57, 271, 278-80
"The Study of History" (Rich) **5**:365

Study of the Object (Herbert)
See *Studium przedmiotu*
The Study of the Object (Herbert)
See *Studium przedmiotu*
"Study of Two Pears" (Stevens) **110**:201
"Study Peace" (Baraka) **113**:78
"Study to Deserve Death" (Smith) **12**:318
"Studying the Language" (Ní Chuilleanáin) **34**:356, 384-85
Stuff and Nonsense and So On (de la Mare) **77**:74
"Stumbling" (Montale)
See "Incespicare"
"The Stump" (Hall) **70**:31
"Stump" (Heaney) **18**:202
Stunden-Buch (Rilke)
See *Das Stundenbuch*
Das Stundenbuch (Rilke) **2**:277, 282, 288-90
Stundenbuch/Das Stundenbuch/A Book for the Hours of Prayer (Rilke)
See *Das Stundenbuch*
Das Stundenbuch enthaltend die drei Bücher (Rilke)
See *Das Stundenbuch*
"Stupid" (Carver) **54**:12
"The Stupid Pencil Maker" (Silverstein) **49**:347
"Stupid Piety" (Goethe) **5**:229
"Les stupra" (Rimbaud) **57**:203
Les Stupra (Rimbaud) **57**:252
"The Sturgeon" (Carver) **54**:18
"Sturmangriff" (Stramm) **50**:218-19
"Stutgard" (Hölderlin) **4**:147
"Style" (Baraka) **4**:9
"Style" (Cohen) **109**:18, 58
"Style" (Moore) **4**:259; **49**:126, 133, 139
"Style" (Sandburg) **41**:234, 359, 361
"Styx" (Duncan) **2**:119
"Su l'Adda" (Carducci) **46**:27, 42, 54, 84
"Su Monte Mario" (Carducci) **46**:9, 54, 87
"Su persona" (Guillén) **35**:188
"La suave agonie" (Valéry) **9**:391-92
"Suavidades" (Mistral) **32**:201
"Sub Contra" (Bogan) **12**:120
Sub Specie Aeternitatis (Hayden) **6**:194
"Sub Terra" (Williams) **7**:377; **109**:207, 287
"A Subaltern" (Sassoon) **12**:242
"The Subalterns" (Hardy) **8**:111, 119
"A Subaltern's Love Song" (Betjeman) **75**:75, 84, 86-87, 105
"Sub-entries" (Niedecker) **42**:148, 150
"Submission" (Philips) **40**:271
"The Submission" (Wilmot) **66**:339
"Sub-Post Office" (Thomas) **99**:273
"The Substance" (Herbert) **50**:19
"A Substance In A Cushion" (Stein) **18**:321, 328, 349
"Substitution" (Spencer) **77**:346
"Subterranean Homesick Blues" (Dylan) **37**:54, 59, 71
"Subtexts & Nazdaks" (Dorn) **115**:160
"Suburb" (Borges)
See "Arrabal"
"Suburb" (Smith) **12**:317
"Suburb. Evening. Autumn" (Abse) **41**:8
"Suburb in which the country lies heavily" (Borges)
See "Arrabal en que pesa el campo"
"Sub-Urban" (Stafford) **71**:337-38
"Suburban Dream" (Muir) **49**:245
"Suburban Woman" (Boland) **58**:13, 43-44
"Suburban Woman: A Detail" (Boland) **58**:15, 47-48
"Suburbia Mad Song" (Corso) **33**:25, 49; **108**:7
"The Subverted Flower" (Frost) **1**:198; **39**:246
"The Subway" (Tate) **50**:231, 246, 280, 288, 309, 312-14
"Subway No Way" (Alurista) **34**:22
"Subway Rush Hour" (Hughes) **53**:193
"Success" (Brooke) **24**:56-7
"Success" (Empson) **104**:117
"Succory" (Reese) **29**:336
"The Succubus" (Graves) **6**:163
"Such a Parcel of Rogues in a Nation" (Burns) **114**:61, 91, 116
Such Counsels You Gave to Me and Other Poems (Jeffers) **17**:135
"Such is the Sickness of Many a Good Thing" (Duncan) **75**:258
"Suche Happe as I ame Happed in" (Wyatt) **27**:317, 352
Suche nach Lebenden (Sachs) **78**:209, 211-12
Die Suchende (Sachs) **78**:187-88, 190-91, 197, 199-201, 209
"Suchness" (Rexroth) **95**:282
"Suctorial" (Dorn) **115**:134
"Sudden Death" (Alexie) **53**:39
"Sudden Frost" (Wagoner) **33**:324, 367
"Sudden Journey" (Gallagher) **9**:50
"Sudden Light" (Rossetti) **44**:173
"Sudden Things" (Hall) **70**:33
"Suddenly" (Thomas) **99**:299-300
"Suddenly Where Squadrons Turn" (Ciardi) **69**:25
"The Sudder Bazaar" (Kipling) **3**:190, 194
"El sueño" (Storni) **33**:262, 296, 313
El Sueño (Juana Inés de la Cruz) **24**:182-83, 189, 191-94, 198, 207, 209, 211-15, 217, 220, 224-27, 235
"Suenos" (Parra) **39**:261
"Suffer the Children" (Lorde) **12**:157
"Suffering" (Page) **12**:190
Suffering (Ungaretti)
See *Il dolore*
"The Sufficient Place" (Muir) **49**:230, 242, 265
Suffised not, Madam (Wyatt) **27**:317
"Suffryng in sorow in hope to attayn" (Wyatt) **27**:310
"Sugar" (Stein) **18**:320, 322-23, 328, 334
"Sugar Loaf" (Hughes) **7**:121; **89**:103, 109, 111, 166, 169
"Sugar Town" (Alexie) **53**:24
"Sugestión de un sauce" (Storni) **33**:262, 296
"Sugestión de una cuna vacía" (Storni) **33**:261
"Suggested by Reading an Article" (Tennyson) **101**:194
"Suggestion from a Friend" (Kenyon) **57**:28
"Suggestiones de un canto de pájaro" (Storni) **33**:295
"Suggestions by Steam" (Hood) **93**:102
"Sui Campi di Marengo" (Carducci) **46**:11, 53
"El suicida" (Borges) **32**:90, 140
"The Suicide" (Ai) **72**:29
"The suicide" (Borges)
See "El suicida"
"Suicide" (Bukowski) **18**:5
The Suicide (Das) **43**:79
"The Suicide" (Das) **43**:74, 80, 85, 90
"Suicide" (Hughes) **1**:255
"The Suicide" (Millay) **6**:206; **61**:212, 225, 245
"Suicide Blues" (Rukeyser) **12**:228
"The Suicide in the Copse" (Graves) **6**:142, 144
"Suicide in the Trenches" (Sassoon) **12**:267, 285
"Suicide in Two Voices" (Ignatow)
See "Two Voices"
"Suicide off Egg Rock" (Plath) **1**:389
"The Suicides" (Justice) **64**:269-70, 276
"Suicide's Note" (Hughes) **1**:236; **53**:85
"Suis-je" (Laforgue) **14**:85
"The Suit" (Levine) **22**:225
"A Suite of Appearances" (Strand) **63**:188, 195
"A Suite for Augustus" (Dove) **6**:106
"A Suite for Love" (Ciardi) **69**:41
"A Suite for Marriage" (Ignatow) **34**:320
"Suite furlana" (Pasolini) **17**:281-82
Suite furlana (Pasolini) **17**:252, 256, 279, 281
"Suite I" (Éluard) **38**:69
"Suite ii" (Éluard) **38**:69
"Suite in Prison" (Eberhart) **76**:14, 57
Suite logique (Brossard) **80**:3, 5-6
"The Suitor" (Hughes) **89**:107
"The Suitor" (Kenyon) **57**:19, 43
"Sukher vilap" (Tagore) **8**:405
"Sulla colonna più alta" (Montale) **13**:109, 111
"Sulla Greve" (Montale) **13**:152
"Sulle rive del Lambro" (Quasimodo) **47**:279, 303
"Sullen Bakeries of Total Recall" (Kaufman) **74**:181-82, 259-60
"Sulmalla of Lumon" (Macpherson) **97**:233
"Sultry" (Lowell) **13**:95-6
"Sultry Rain" (Pasternak) **6**:257
"The Sumac in Ohio" (Wright) **36**:393, 400
Summa poética 1929-1946 (Guillén) **23**:104
"Summary" (Sanchez) **9**:224, 232
"Summary" (Sarton) **39**:335
"Summer" (Ashbery) **26**:124-125
"Summer" (Bryant) **20**:12
"Summer" (Darío)
See "Estival"
"Summer" (Glück) **16**:156, 166
"Summer" (Koch) **80**:328
"Summer" (Rossetti) **7**:280
"Summer" (Stryk) **27**:196, 208
"The Summer" (Trakl) **20**:226
"Summer" (Wright) **14**:377, 379
"The Summer Anniversaries" (Justice) **64**:266, 280
The Summer Anniversaries (Justice) **64**:248-49, 252-53, 257, 266-67, 273, 275-76, 278, 280, 287, 289-90
"Summer between Terms I" (Lowell) **3**:241
"A Summer Commentary" (Winters) **82**:334
"Summer Dawn" (Morris) **55**:238, 258
"A Summer Day" (Riley) **48**:333
"Summer Day in the Mountains" (Li Po) **29**:145
"Summer Fog" (Carver) **54**:19
"Summer Haiku" (Cohen) **109**:53-54
"Summer Holiday" (Jeffers) **17**:132
"Summer Home" (Heaney) **18**:203
"Summer Idyll" (Cunningham) **92**:140
Summer in Calcutta (Das) **43**:71-72, 74, 76, 80, 85, 90-91, 93, 95
"Summer in Calcutta" (Das) **43**:85
"Summer in England, 1914" (Meynell) **112**:168, 174, 177, 218, 223
"'Summer Is Over" (Cummings) **5**:108-09
"Summer Knowledge" (Schwartz) **8**:297-98, 312-19
Summer Knowledge: New and Selected Poems, 1938-1958 (Schwartz) **8**:289-91, 296, 301-02, 305, 309, 311
"Summer Landscape" (Doty) **53**:69
"Summer Landscape" (Eberhart) **76**:13
"Summer Lightning" (Clarke) **112**:48, 50, 67
"Summer Morning" (Simic) **69**:262
"A Summer Morning Walk" (Kavanagh) **33**:87
"Summer Mornings" (Cernuda)
See "Mañanas de verano"
"Summer Music" (Sarton) **39**:323, 332
"A Summer Night" (Arnold) **5**:36, 42, 49, 50
"Summer Night" (Cohen) **109**:3
"Summer Night" (Hughes) **53**:201
"A Summer Night" (Jarrell) **41**:169
"Summer Night Piece" (Lowell) **13**:64, 67
"Summer 1961" (Levertov) **11**:165
"Summer 1969" (Heaney) **18**:205
The Summer of Black Widows (Alexie) **53**:15, 25, 34
"The Summer People" (Merrill) **28**:224-25, 230-31, 235
"A Summer Pilgrimage" (Whittier) **93**:239-40
"Summer Place" (Ammons) **16**:23, 47
"Summer Poem" (Enzensberger) **28**:141, 147-48
"Summer Rainstorm" (Blunden) **66**:28
"A Summer Ramble" (Bryant) **20**:37, 39
"Summer Resort" (Page) **12**:173
"Summer Sequence" (Snodgrass) **74**:329
"Summer Session" (Ammons) **16**:50
"Summer Solstice" (Seferis) **66**:196
"Summer Sonatina" (Chin) **40**:36
"Summer Song I" (Barker) **77**:11
"Summer Sun" (Stevenson) **84**:299, 347
"Summer time T. V. (is witer than ever)"

(Sanchez) **9**:210-11, 213, 225
"The Summer Tree" (Sarton) **39**:367
"The Summer We Almost Split" (Piercy) **29**:311
"The Summer We Didn't Die" (Stafford) **71**:370-71
"Summer Will Rise" (Stafford) **71**:268
"Summer Wind" (Bryant) **20**:40
"Summer Wish" (Bogan) **12**:94-5, 98, 100, 106, 121-22
"Summer Words of a Sistuh Addict" (Sanchez) **9**:225
"Summer-end in the Sharon" (Amichai) **38**:33-34
"A Summer's Dream" (Bishop) **3**:47; **34**:160
"Summer's Elegy" (Nemerov) **24**:291
"A Summer's Wish" (Leapor) **85**:248-49
"Summertime and the Living..." (Hayden) **6**:194, 196
"Summing It Up" (Stone) **53**:258
"Summit Beach, 1921" (Dove) **6**:121
Summits Move with the Tide (Berssenbrugge) **115**:3, 7-9, 28, 37, 46
Summoned by Bells (Betjeman) **75**:13, 25-26, 42, 47-49, 55, 58, 64, 66, 71, 75, 80-81, 83, 108
"The summoner" (Hughes) **89**:194, 233
"Summoner's Tale" (Chaucer) **19**:13
A Summoning of Stones (Hecht) **70**:62, 65, 69-70, 77-78, 80-83, 85, 87, 89, 91, 93, 105
"The Summons" (Auden) **1**:38
"The Summons" (Dickey) **40**:150, 184-85, 228
"A Summons" (Whittier) **93**:206, 314-15
"The Summons in Indiana" (Stafford) **71**:267
"A Summons to Town" (Suckling) **30**:148-49, 150
Summonses of the Times (Bely)
See *Zovy vremen*
"Sumptuous Destitution" (Wilbur) **51**:293
"The Sun" (Baudelaire)
See "Le Soleil"
"Sun" (Corso) **33**:40, 47
"Sun" (Dickey) **40**:158, 160, 181
"The Sun" (Hall) **70**:31
"Sun" (Kennedy) **93**:147
"The Sun" (Milosz) **8**:192, 207
"Sun" (Moore) **4**:243; **49**:113-14, 122, 136, 149
"The Sun" (Nishiwaki)
See "Taiyo"
"The Sun" (Noyes) **27**:129
"The Sun" (Piercy) **29**:305
"The Sun" (Sexton) **2**:351, 372; **79**:212-13
"The Sun" (Trakl) **20**:226
"Sun and Flesh" (Rimbaud)
See "Soleil et chair"
"Sun and Love" (Carducci)
See "Sol e amore"
"Sun and Moon" (Kenyon) **57**:43
"Sun and Rain" (Merwin) **45**:97
"The Sun Burns" (Thomas) **52**:290, 293-95
"S'un casto amor, s'una pietà superna" (Michelangelo) **103**:218, 307
"The Sun Does Not Move" (Bissett) **14**:5
"Sun Dog" (Wagoner) **33**:353-54
"The Sun Is near Meridan Height" (Brontë) **8**:73
"The Sun of the Waters" (Char)
See *Le soleil des eaux*
"The Sun on the Letter" (Hardy) **8**:97
Sun out: Selected Poems, 1952-1954 (Koch) **80**:341
Sun Poem (Brathwaite) **56**:34-35, 41, 43-44, 51, 60-62, 71, 90-92, 100
"The Sun Rising" (Donne)
See "The Sunne Rising"
"The Sun Says His Prayers" (Lindsay) **23**:281
"Sun Stone" (Paz)
See *Piedra de sol*
Sun Stone (Paz)
See *Piedra de sol*
"Sun the First" (Elytis) **21**:131
Sun the First (Elytis)
See *Ílios o prótos*
"The Sun This March" (Stevens) **110**:153
"The Sun Travels" (Stevenson) **84**:314, 342, 344
Sun Tries to Go On (Koch)
See *When the Sun Tries to Go On*
"The Sun Was Still Warm . . ." (Rimbaud)
See "Soleil était encore chaud . . ."
"Sun, Wind" (Wagoner) **33**:365-66, 368
"Sunbathing on a Rooftop in Berkeley" (Kumin) **15**:203
"Sunday" (Ai) **72**:29-30
"Sunday" (Chappell) **105**:65, 69
"Sunday" (Herbert) **4**:100; **66**:163, 186
"Sunday" (Hughes) **1**:255; **89**:107, 113
"Sunday" (Nemerov) **24**:277
"A Sunday" (Soto) **28**:397-98, 400
"Sunday" (Stone) **53**:230, 235
"Sunday" (Williams) **7**:351; **109**:286
"Sunday, 4 a.m." (Bishop) **34**:116
"Sunday Afternoon near the Naval Air Base" (Ciardi) **69**:6
"Sunday Afternoon Service in St. Enodoc Church, Cornwall" (Betjeman) **75**:8, 10, 66-67, 79, 83, 89, 98-99
"Sunday at Key West" (Bishop) **34**:65, 123
"Sunday Evening" (Abse) **41**:26
"A Sun-Day Hymn" (Holmes) **71**:63
"Sunday in Ireland" (Betjeman) **75**:9-10, 66
"Sunday in the Country" (Swenson) **14**:247, 250, 264
"Sunday in the Park" (Williams) **109**:311
"Sunday Lemons" (Walcott) **46**:240, 278
"Sunday Morning" (Hall) **70**:9
"Sunday Morning" (MacNeice) **61**:130-34
"Sunday Morning" (Stevens) **6**:292, 301, 304, 306, 327, 336; **110**:85, 93, 114-16, 146, 153, 169, 200, 229, 234-36, 242
"Sunday Morning" (Whitman) **3**:391
"Sunday Morning" (Wilbur) **51**:237
"Sunday Morning Apples" (Crane) **3**:83, 90, 100; **99**:66
"Sunday Morning, High Tide" (Oliver) **75**:303-4, 307-8
"Sunday Morning, King's Cambridge" (Betjeman) **75**:68, 76, 91-92
"Sunday Morning Prophecy" (Hughes) **53**:117
"A Sunday Morning Tragedy" (Hardy) **8**:99
"Sunday New Guinea" (Shapiro) **25**:269, 286, 295
"Sunday Night" (Hacker) **47**:98
"A Sunday with Shepherds and Herdboys" (Clare) **23**:13
sunday work(?) (Bissett) **14**:5, 16
"Sun-dayes" (Vaughan) **81**:264, 295
"Sundays before noon" (Bukowski) **18**:23
"Sundays Kill More Men than Bombs" (Bukowski) **18**:4
"The Sundays of Satin-Legs Smith" (Brooks) **7**:69, 79-80, 85
"Sundays, Too" (Alexie) **53**:26, 31
"The Sundering U. P. Tracks" (Dorn) **115**:54, 129
"Sunderland" (Nemerov) **24**:295
"Sundew" (Atwood) **8**:13
Sundry Phansies (Kipling) **3**:193
"Sunflower" (Breton)
See "Tournesol"
"The Sunflower" (Montale) **13**:138, 141, 149
"Sunflower" (Updike) **90**:351
"Sunflower Possessed" (Goodison) **36**:142
"Sunflower Sonnets" (Jordan) **38**:122
"Sunflower Sutra" (Ginsberg) **4**:48, 50, 92; **47**:5, 37-38
"Sung beneath the Alps" (Hölderlin) **4**:142
Sung into the Rotary Press (Seifert) **47**:325
"Sunk Lyonesse" (de la Mare) **77**:62, 65
"The Sunken Bell" (Ishikawa)
See "Shizumeru kane"
"Sun-King" (Hope) **56**:307
"Sunlight" (Gunn) **26**:204, 214, 219
"Sunlight" (Heaney) **18**:203
"Sunlight and Flesh" (Rimbaud)
See "Soleil et chair"
"Sunlight Is Imagination" (Wilbur) **51**:235, 266
"The Sunlight on the Garden" (MacNeice) **61**:117, 119, 131-32, 137, 139, 147
"The Sunlit House" (Mew) **107**:35
"The Sunlit Vale" (Blunden) **66**:60
"The Sunne Rising" (Donne) **1**:125, 134, 145, 147, 152, 154; **43**:131, 169-70, 176, 184-86, 198
"Sunny Prestatyn" (Larkin) **21**:229
"Sunrise" (Corso) **33**:44, 50; **108**:3, 48
"Sunrise" (Lanier) **50**:54-56, 62, 82-84, 86, 93, 98, 100-101
"Sunrise" (Reese) **29**:330
"Sunset" (Corso) **33**:44
"Sunset" (Cummings) **5**:70, 94
"Sunset" (Dunbar) **5**:138-39
"Sunset" (Glück) **16**:170
"Sunset" (Ransom) **61**:291
"Sunset, Blue Bird" (Das) **43**:92-93
"Sunset from Omaha Hotel Window" (Sandburg) **41**:297
Sunset Gun (Parker) **28**:347-48, 351, 353, 362-63
"The Sunset Maker" (Justice) **64**:281
The Sunset Maker (Justice) **64**:279-81, 288
The Sunset Maker: Poems/Stories/A Memoir (Justice)
See *The Sunset Maker*
"Sunset of the Century" (Tagore)
See "Shatabdir surya"
"A Sunset of the City" (Brooks) **7**:68-9, 96
"Sunset on the Bearcamp" (Whittier) **93**:193
"Sunset on the Spire" (Wylie) **23**:324, 328
"Sunset Over Villa Ortuzar" (Borges)
See "Ultimo sol en Villa Ortúzar"
"The Sunset Piece" (MacLeish) **47**:158
"Sunset Piece: After Reaching Rémy De Gourmont" (Cummings) **5**:71
"Sunset: Southwest" (Stafford) **71**:276, 295
"Sunset Walk in Thaw-Time in Vermont" (Warren) **37**:305, 379
"Sunsets" (Abse) **41**:25
"Sunstruck" (Hughes) **89**:122
"Sunsum" (Brathwaite) **56**:7-8, 11, 30
"Sunthin' in the Pastoral Line" (Riley) **48**:298
"Super" (Dorn) **115**:133
"Superexistences" (Zanzotto) **65**:277
"Superfluous Advice" (Parker) **28**:362
"Superiorities" (Wilbur) **51**:266-67
"Superman" (Updike) **90**:352
"A Supermarket in California" (Ginsberg) **47**:4, 38
"Supernatural Love" (Schnackenberg) **45**:330, 334, 338, 341, 346-47
Supernatural Love Poems (Schnackenberg) **45**:341, 343, 348
The Supernaturalism of New-England (Whittier) **93**:267, 277
"A Superscription" (Rossetti) **44**:255-56
"The Superseded" (Hardy) **92**:295
"Superstition" (Whittier) **93**:193
"Superstitions" (Hughes) **89**:234-35
"Suplication" (Sidney) **32**:247
"Supper" (de la Mare) **77**:113
"The Supper after the Last" (Kinnell) **26**:238, 257, 279
"Supper Time" (Hughes) **1**:255; **53**:99-100
"The Supplanter" (Hardy) **92**:264-65, 277
"A Supplication for Love" (Barrett Browning) **6**:31
"Supplication to Venus" (Gower) **59**:20
"Supposed Confessions of a second-rate sensitive mind not in unity with itself" (Tennyson) **6**:406, 409; **101**:270
"Supposed to be Written by Werter" (Smith)
See "Sonnet 21"
"Supposed to Have been Written in a Church-Yard, over the Grave of a Young Woman of Nineteen" (Smith)
See "Sonnet 49"

"Supposed to Have been Written in America" (Smith)
See "Sonnet 61"
"Supreme Fiction" (Ammons) **16**:23
"Supreme Kinship" (Werfel)
See "Hohe Gemeinschaft"
"Supreme Surrender" (Rossetti) **44**:169
"Supuesto, discurso mío" (Juana Inés de la Cruz) **24**:180, 184
Sur la poésie (Char) **56**:126, 129, 137, 142-44
"Sur l'eau" (Valéry) **9**:391-92
"Sur les lagunes" (Gautier) **18**:125
"Sur l'herbe" (Verlaine) **2**:430; **32**:348, 350, 385, 390-91
"Sur un front de quinze ans" (Sainte-Beuve) **110**:65, 67
"Sur une nuit sans ornement" (Char) **56**:120, 179
"Sura" (Corso) **33**:25, 49
"Sure, there's a tie of bodies!" (Vaughan) **81**:327-28
"Los Sures" (Espada) **74**:118, 120
"The Surface" (Graham) **59**:177
"The Surface" (Swenson) **14**:261, 282
"The Surface as Object" (Guest) **55**:185
"Surf-Casting" (Merwin) **45**:45
"The Surfer" (Wright) **14**:345
"The Surgeon" (Sexton) **79**:244
"Surgi de la croupe et du bond . . ." (Mallarmé) **102**:98, 101
"The Surname" (Guillén)
See "El apellido"
"Surprise" (Collins) **68**:211
"La Surprise" (Éluard) **38**:96-97
"The Surprise" (Masefield) **78**:91
"Surprise" (Parker) **28**:362
"Surprise" (Silverstein) **49**:326
"Surprise, Surprise!" (Abse) **41**:3, 6
"Surprises" (Kumin) **15**:210, 223
"The Surprize" (Behn) **88**:149
Surrealist Poetry (Aleixandre)
See *Poesía superrealista*
"The Surrender at Appomattox" (Melville) **82**:132, 202, 206
"Surrexit Dominus" (Dunbar) **67**:98, 100
"Surrey Poems" (Mahon) **60**:141, 192, 199
"The Surround" (Dickey) **40**:211, 236, 238
"Surrounded by Wild Turkeys" (Snyder) **21**:326
"A Survey" (Stafford) **71**:259, 297
"Survey of Literature" (Ransom) **61**:300, 308
"Surview" (Hardy) **92**:208, 320
Survival (Raworth) **107**:314
"Survival as Tao, Beginning at 5:00 a.m." (Carruth) **10**:88
"Survival in Missouri" (Ciardi) **69**:31, 34
"Survival: Infantry" (Oppen) **35**:284
"Survival of the Fittest" (Gozzano) **10**:183
"Surviving" (Welch) **62**:338-39, 370, 374
"Surviving Love" (Berryman) **64**:89
"Survivor" (Goodison) **36**:145
"The Survivor" (Graves) **6**:137, 142, 144
"A Survivor" (Merwin) **45**:46
"The Survivor" (Wagoner) **33**:335
"The Survivors" (Chappell) **105**:67
"Survivors" (Sassoon) **12**:267-68, 285
"The Survivors" (Snodgrass) **74**:290
"The Survivors" (Thomas) **99**:270, 308
"Survivor's Ballad" (Jacobsen) **62**:323-24
"Susan Bathing" (Chappell) **105**:24-25, 27, 30-31, 41, 44, 59, 71-73, 75
"Susan Tichy, a Poet from Colorado" (Amichai) **38**:22
"Susan's Morning Dream of Her Garden" (Chappell) **105**:44, 46, 81
"Suspenders" (Carver) **54**:15, 18, 28
"Suspension" (Lorde) **12**:158
"The suspicion" (Cavafy) **36**:53
"Suspicor Speculum: To Sisyphus" (Merwin) **45**:19
"Sussex" (Kipling) **3**:167, 192; **91**:109
"Sustainment" (Dickey) **40**:158
"Suzanne" (Cohen) **109**:9, 18, 82
"Svalka" (Shvarts) **50**:146, 160
"Svapna" (Tagore) **8**:410-11
"Svarga" (Tagore) **8**:414
"Svarga ha'ite biday" (Tagore) **8**:409
Svecha (Akhmadulina) **43**:11, 33
Světlem oděná (Seifert) **47**:316, 335
"Svoe muchenie nochnoe" (Shvarts) **50**:134
"The Swallows Return" (Eberhart) **76**:54
"The Swamp" (Das) **43**:92
"The Swamp Angel" (Melville) **82**:198, 271
"Swamp Plant" (Wright) **14**:374
"The Swan" (Baudelaire)
See "Le cygne"
"The Swan" (Berssenbrugge) **115**:9
"The Swan" (Oliver) **75**:310
"The Swan" (Roethke) **15**:275, 288
"Swan Dive" (Hecht) **70**:65
"Swan, Elemental" (Lawrence) **54**:187
"The Swan of Usk" (Vaughan) **81**:356, 364
"The Swans" (Darío)
See "Los cisnes"
"The Swans" (Lowell) **13**:86
"The Swans" (Sarton) **39**:323
"Swans" (Stone) **53**:218, 228
"The Swans" (Storni)
See "Los Cisnes"
"Swans" (Teasdale) **31**:322
The Swans' Encampment (Tsvetaeva)
See *Lebediny stan*
"The Swarm" (Graham) **59**:166
"The Swarm" (Plath) **1**:410, 412
Swarm (Graham) **59**:184-90
"Swathed round in mist" (Meredith) **60**:287
"Swaziland" (Giovanni) **19**:141
"Swedes" (Thomas) **53**:329
"Sweeney" (Montague) **106**:328
"Sweeney" (Sexton) **79**:284, 287
"Sweeney among the Nightingales" (Eliot) **5**:184; **31**:121; **90**:208, 291, 313
Sweeney Astray: A Version from the Irish (Heaney) **18**:215-18, 235
"Sweeney Redivivus" (Heaney) **18**:215, 228, 233
"The Sweeper of Ways" (Nemerov) **24**:282
"The Sweep's Complaint" (Hood) **93**:100
"Sweet Afton" (Burns) **6**:77
"Sweet Ar the Thoughtes" (Raleigh)
See "Sweete Are the Thoughtes Wher Hope Persvadeth Happe"
"Sweet Boy, Give me Yr Ass" (Ginsberg) **4**:90
"Sweet Breathed Celia" (Randall) **86**:344
"Sweet, exclude me not" (Campion) **87**:25, 56, 67
"A Sweet Flying Dream" (Ferlinghetti) **1**:183, 188
The Sweet Harm (Storni)
See *El dulce daño*
"Sweet Hopes" (Pushkin)
See "Nadezhdoi Sladostnoi"
"Sweet like a Crow" (Ondaatje) **28**:338
"The Sweet Little Man" (Holmes) **71**:66, 68, 75
Sweet Machine (Doty) **53**:60-61, 63
"Sweet Mary Dove" (Clare) **23**:25
"Sweet Meat Has Sower Sauce or, the Slave-Trader in the Dumps" (Cowper) **40**:119
"Sweet Michel" (Browning) **2**:30
A Sweet Nosgay, or Pleasant Posye: Contayning a Hundred and Ten Phylosophicall Flowers (Whitney) **116**:250-51, 253-54, 256, 261, 264-65, 268, 270-71, 273, 276-78, 281-84, 286-88, 290-91, 295, 308, 310-11, 316
"The Sweet o' the Year" (Noyes) **27**:114
"The Sweet Primroses" (Hardy) **8**:130
"Sweet Rois of Vertew" (Dunbar) **67**:3, 25
"Sweet Susan" (Clare) **23**:25
"Sweet Things" (Gunn) **26**:209, 211
"Sweet Violets" (Parker) **28**:351
Sweet Will (Levine) **22**:221, 224, 226
"Sweete Are the Thoughtes Wher Hope Persvadeth Happe" (Raleigh) **31**:284, 294-95, 309, 312
"Sweetened Change" (Ammons) **16**:63
"Sweetest love, I do not goe" (Donne)
See "Song. 'Sweetest love, I do not goe'"
"Sweetness" (Mistral)
See "Dulzura"
"The Sweetness of Life" (Stern) **115**:249
Swellfoot (Shelley)
See *Oedipus Tyrannus; Or Swellfoot the Tyrant*
Swellfoot the Tyrant (Shelley)
See *Oedipus Tyrannus; Or Swellfoot the Tyrant*
"Swells" (Ammons) **16**:32, 63
"The Swerve" (Stafford) **71**:280, 290
"Swete were the sauce" (Raleigh) **31**:294
"Świadomość" (Milosz) **8**:209
"Swiat umielismy kiedys..." (Szymborska) **44**:318-19
"The Swift" (Char) **56**:131
"Swiftly walk over the western wave" (Shelley) **14**:177
"Swimmer" (Francis) **34**:243, 250
"The Swimmer" (Olds) **22**:323, 325
"The Swimmer" (Oliver) **75**:303, 305-6, 308
"The Swimmer at Lake Edward" (Hugo) **68**:287, 293
"Swimmers" (Swenson) **14**:265, 276, 287
"The Swimmers" (Tate) **50**:268, 281, 290-96, 307, 325, 329, 331-34, 336
"A Swimmer's Dream" (Swinburne) **24**:313, 325
"Swimming Chenango Lake" (Tomlinson) **17**:316, 319, 321, 328
"The Swimming Race" (Noyes) **27**:116
"Swinburne & Watts-Dunton" (Berrigan) **103**:41
"Swineherd" (Ní Chuilleanáin) **34**:351-52
"The Swing" (Stevenson) **84**:344, 347
"Swit" (Herbert) **50**:5
"Switchback" (Parra)
See "La montaña rusa"
"Switchboard Girl" (Niedecker) **42**:102, 123
"Switezianka" (Mickiewicz) **38**:153
"Switzerland" (Arnold) **5**:12-13
"The Switzer's Song" (Whittier) **93**:198
Sword Blades and Poppy Seed (Lowell) **13**:69-70, 76, 93
"A Sword in a Cloud of Light" (Rexroth) **20**:190
"Sword Land" (Montague) **106**:321
The Sword of the West (Clarke) **112**:27, 29, 33, 40, 43-44, 72, 74, 78, 89
"Swords" (Borges)
See "Espadas"
Swords Like Lips (Aleixandre)
See *Espadas como labios*
"The Sycamore" (Berry) **28**:25
"The Sycamore" (Moore) **49**:126, 135, 138
"The Sycamores" (Whittier) **93**:252
"Sydney Bridge" (Shapiro) **25**:269
"Sygil" (H. D.) **5**:306
"The Syllable Pain" (Celan) **10**:102
"Le sylphe" (Valéry) **9**:387, 391, 393
"Les Sylphides" (MacNeice) **61**:138
Sylva (Cowley)
See *Poeticall Blossomes*
Sylvae (Dryden) **25**:80
Sylvan Moon (Paz)
See *Luna silvestre*
"Sylvia" (Stern) **115**:272
"Sylvia's Death" (Sexton) **2**:364, 370
Symbiosis (Guest) **55**:211, 221-23
"Symbolism in Painting" (Yeats) **20**:299
"The Symbolism of Poetry" (Yeats) **51**:147
The Symbolism of Poetry (Yeats) **20**:336
"Symbols" (Yeats) **51**:148
"Symmetrical Companion" (Swenson) **14**:274, 284
"Sympathetic Portrait of a Child" (Williams) **7**:349; **109**:236, 323

"Sympathy" (Dunbar) **5**:134
"Sympathy" (Thoreau)
See "Elegy"
"Symphonie en blanc majeur" (Gautier) **18**:124-27, 129-30
"Symphonie en blanc mineur" (Pound) **95**:95
"The Symphony" (Lanier) **50**:55-56, 61-62, 72-74, 84, 90, 98, 106-8
"Symposium" (Boland) **58**:15
"The Symposium" (Cunningham) **92**:135, 167
"Symposium" (Parra)
See "Simposio"
"Symptoms of Love" (Graves) **6**:155
"The Synagogue" (Shapiro) **25**:263, 269, 283, 296, 299-300
"Synamism" (Niedecker) **42**:148
"Syngrou Avenue, 1930" (Seferis) **66**:144-45
"Synopsis" (Thomas) **99**:274, 310
"Synthese" (Benn) **35**:50
"The Sypres curten of the night" (Campion) **87**:64, 98
"Syra" (Melville) **82**:77, 151
"Syria" (Douglas) **106**:186
"Syrinx" (Merrill) **28**:223, 256
"The Syrophenician Woman" (Harper) **21**:208, 215-16
"The System" (Ashbery) **26**:108, 130
"System" (Stevenson) **84**:299
"The System" (Stone) **53**:223
"The Szechwan Road" (Li Po) **29**:140
Szomoru beres (Illyés) **16**:238, 247
T & G: The Collected Poems (1936-1966) (Niedecker) **42**:94, 96, 101-2, 106, 133, 135
T. S. Eliot, The Waste Land: A Facsimile and Transcript of the Original Drafts Including the Annotations of Ezra Pound (Eliot) **90**:207-8, 221, 295, 301, 317, 320
T. V. Baby Poems (Ginsberg) **4**:47
"Ta bouche au lèvres d'or" (Éluard) **38**:71
"Ta chevelure d'oranges" (Éluard) **38**:71
Ta eleýa tis Oxópetras (Elytis) **21**:134-35
"Ta foi" (Éluard) **38**:70
"Ta Lettre sur le Drap" (Senghor) **25**:233-34, 249
"Tabacaria" (Pessoa) **20**:166, 169
Taberna otros lugares (Dalton) **36**:120, 129
"Tabibito" (Nishiwaki) **15**:229
Tabibito Kaerazu (Nishiwaki) **15**:229-36
"The Tabill of Confession" (Dunbar) **67**:86
"Las tablas" (Parra) **39**:284-85
"The Table" (Hall) **70**:32
"The Table" (Hughes) **89**:179
"A Table" (Stein) **18**:320-22, 324, 328, 330, 350
"Table I" (Milosz) **8**:210
"Table II" (Milosz) **8**:210
"The Table and the Chair" (Lear) **65**:152-53, 157
"Table Talk" (Mahon) **60**:146, 148, 178-79
Table Talk (Cowper) **40**:101
"Tableau" (Cullen) **20**:64
"Tables of Longevity" (Char) **56**:138
"The Tables of the Law" (Yeats) **51**:76, 101-3, 106-7
"The Tables Turned" (Wordsworth) **67**:277, 282, 285-86, 301-2, 310, 312, 330, 365, 370
"Tablet XVIII" (Schwerner) **42**:202-3
"Tablet XV" (Schwerner) **42**:201-2
"Tablet V" (Schwerner) **42**:202
"Tablet IV" (Schwerner) **42**:188, 192
"Tablet IX" (Schwerner) **42**:203
"Tablet I" (Schwerner) **42**:192, 202-3
"Tablet VII" (Schwerner) **42**:192, 204
"Tablet XVII" (Schwerner) **42**:203
"Tablet VI" (Schwerner) **42**:190, 202
"Tablet XVI" (Schwerner) **42**:202
"Tablet XIII" (Schwerner) **42**:204
"Tablet III" (Schwerner) **42**:192, 203
"Tablet XII" (Schwerner) **42**:190
"Tablet XXVII" (Schwerner) **42**:193, 196, 205, 208
"Tablet XXVI" (Schwerner) **42**:192-93, 196
"Tablet II" (Schwerner) **42**:192, 203
"Table-Talk" (Cowper) **40**:47-50, 56-7, 71, 104, 116, 142
The Tablets (Schwerner) **42**:187-96, 198, 200-209
"Tablets Journals" (Schwerner) **42**:194, 202, 205
"Tachycardia at the Foot of the Fifth Green" (Wagoner) **33**:335
"Tact and the Poet's Force" (Snodgrass) **74**:305
"Tag" (Hughes) **53**:192
"Tag och skriv" (Ekeloef) **23**:51, 76, 78
"Tagore's Last Poems" (Tagore)
See "Śesh lekhā"
"Tahirassawichi en Washington" (Cardenal) **22**:131
"The Taill of the Lyoun and the Mous" (Henryson)
See "The Lion and the Mouse"
Taina: novye stixi (Akhmadulina) **43**:17, 33-37, 40, 48, 54
"Taipei Girl" (Quintana) **36**:266, 271
"Taith i Garu" (Dafydd ap Gwilym) **56**:241
"Taiyo" (Nishiwaki) **15**:240-41
"Tak durno zhit,' kak ia vchera zhila" (Akhmadulina) **43**:7
"Take" (Hagiwara) **18**:179
"Take a whole holiday in honour of this" (Day Lewis) **11**:130
"Take Anguish for Companion" (Sarton) **39**:324
"Take Back the Bowl!" (Whittier) **93**:260
"Take from My Palms" (Mandelstam) **14**:117
"Take heed of loving mee" (Donne)
See "The Prohibition"
"Take Something Like a Star" (Frost)
See "Choose Something like a Star"
"Take Them Out!" (Jordan) **38**:127
"Take This Hammer" (Brown) **55**:159
"Take This Waltz" (Cohen) **109**:67
"Take Wine" (Li Po) **29**:161
"take you down" (Alurista) **34**:39
"Taken Aback" (McKay) **2**:221
"Take-Off Over Kansas" (Ciardi) **69**:26
"Taking" (Ondaatje) **28**:327, 332
"Taking a Walk with You" (Koch) **80**:312, 317
"Taking In Wash" (Dove) **6**:111
"Taking justice into one's own hands" (Castro)
See "La justicia por la mano"
"Taking Leave of Zenka" (Hacker) **47**:118
"Taking Notice" (Hacker) **47**:105
Taking Notice (Hacker) **47**:81, 104
"The Taking of Helen" (Masefield) **78**:47, 91
"Taking Off Emily Dickinson's Clothes" (Collins) **68**:216
"Taking Off My Clothes" (Forché) **10**:133, 135
"Taking the Forest" (Howe) **54**:64, 69, 113-14
"Taking the Hands" (Bly) **39**:69
"Taking the Lambs to Market" (Kumin) **15**:216
"Takkakaw Falls" (Birney) **52**:22, 35, 58
"Tal vez porque te quiero" (Alurista) **34**:25, 40-41
Tala (Mistral) **32**:147, 149-50, 159-62, 164, 166, 168-71, 173, 179-83, 185, 208, 210
"Talbot Road" (Gunn) **26**:220, 229
"A Tale" (Bogan) **12**:85, 111, 127
"A Tale" (Coleridge) **11**:101
"A Tale" (Finch) **21**:166
"Tale of Apollonius" (Gower) **59**:76-78, 80, 84
The Tale of Balen (Swinburne) **24**:348, 350-54, 357
"A Tale of Bananas" (Cruz) **37**:18
"Tale of Ceix and Alceone" (Gower) **59**:107
"A Tale of Country Things" (Masefield) **78**:90-91
"The Tale of Custard the Dragon" (Nash) **21**:265
"Tale of Deianira, Hercules, and Nessus" (Gower) **59**:14, 41, 98-99
"Tale of Diogenes" (Gower) **59**:4
The Tale of Fatumeh (Ekeloef)
See *Sagan om Fatumeh*
"Tale of Florent" (Gower) **59**:108
"Tale of Hercules and Faunus" (Gower) **59**:102
"Tale of Iphis and Ianthe" (Gower) **59**:98, 100, 102, 108
Tale of Joan of Arc (Christine de Pizan)
See *Le Ditié de Jehanne d'Arc*
"The Tale of Me" (Ní Chuilleanáin) **34**:385
"Tale of Melibee" (Chaucer) **19**:26, 33, 47
"Tale of Nectanabus" (Gower) **59**:15
"Tale of Orestes" (Gower) **59**:109
Tale of Orpheus and Erudices his Queene (Henryson)
See *Here Begynnis the Traitie of Orpheus Kyng . . .*
A Tale of Paraguay (Southey) **111**:212, 224-25, 227-28, 231-33, 236, 261-62
The Tale of Poissy (Christine de Pizan)
See *Le Dit de Poissy*
"The Tale of Rahéro" (Stevenson) **84**:306, 332
"Tale of Rosiphelee" (Gower) **59**:106
"The Tale of Sir Thopas" (Chaucer) **19**:25, 33-4, 37, 47, 50-1; **58**:368
"A Tale of Starvation" (Lowell) **13**:60, 84
The Tale of Sunlight (Soto) **28**:371, 384, 386
"Tale of Tereus, Progne, and Philomene" (Gower) **59**:5, 109
"A Tale of the Airly Days" (Riley) **48**:284, 315, 319
"The Tale of the Cock and the Jasp" (Henryson)
See "The Cock and the Jasp"
"The Tale of the Cock and the Jasper" (Henryson)
See "The Cock and the Jasp"
"The Tale of the Dead Princess and the Seven Heroes" (Pushkin)
See "Skazka o Mertvoy Tsarevne"
"Tale of the False Bachelor" (Gower) **59**:15
"The Tale of the Fisherman and the Fish" (Pushkin)
See "Skazka o Rybake i Rybke"
"The Tale of the Fox, the Wolf, and the Husbandman" (Henryson)
See "The Fox, the Wolf, and the Husbandman"
The Tale of the Golden Cockerel (Pushkin)
See "Skazka o Zolotom Petushke"
"The Tale of the Lion and the Mouse" (Henryson)
See "The Lion and the Mouse"
"The Tale of the Parson and His Man Balda" (Pushkin)
See "Skazka o Pope i o Rabotnike Yego Balde"
The Tale of the Shepherdess (Christine de Pizan)
See *Le dit de la pastoure*
"A Tale of the Thirteenth Floor" (Nash) **21**:270-71
"The Tale of the Tsar Sultan" (Pushkin)
See "Skazka o Tsare Sultane"
"The Tale of the Wolf and the Lamb" (Henryson)
See "The Wolf and the Lamb"
"Tale of Time" (Warren) **37**:307, 380
A Tale of Time: New Poems, 1960-1966 (Warren) **37**:355
"Tale of Tobias and Sara" (Gower) **59**:110
Tale of Troy (Masefield) **78**:91
"Tale of Two Cities" (Kavanagh) **33**:86
"A Tale of Two Gardens" (Paz)
See "Cuento de dos jardines"
A Tale of Two Gardens: Poems from India, 1952-1995 (Paz) **48**:264
"Tale of Ulysses and Telegonus" (Gower) **59**:15
Tales (Chaucer)
See *Canterbury Tales*
Tales (Crabbe) **97**:71, 75, 85-86, 90, 94-96, 98-101, 103-5, 107, 110-13, 116-17, 120, 125, 130, 135, 148-50, 153
"Tales from a Family Album" (Justice) **64**:266, 278

Tales from Ovid (Hughes) **89**:159, 171, 178-79, 181, 189-90, 243, 251
Tales in Verse (Crabbe)
See *Tales*
"Tales of a Wayside Inn" (Noyes) **27**:129
Tales of a Wayside Inn (Longfellow) **30**:18-19, 24-5, 36, 40-1, 43, 47-8, 61, 63, 65, 68, 75, 99, 107
Tales of Canterbury (Chaucer)
See *Canterbury Tales*
"Tales of Ireland" (Clarke) **112**:87
"Tales of Shatz" (Abse) **41**:19
Tales of the Hall (Crabbe) **97**:78, 83, 88, 90, 94, 101, 107, 113-14, 116-17, 119-20, 123, 132
"Tales of the Islands" (Walcott) **46**:272
"Tales of the Madwoman" (Mistral)
See "Historias de loca"
Tales of the Mermaid Tavern (Noyes) **27**:123-4, 126, 129, 134, 137
Talifer (Robinson) **1**:475, 477, 479, 483
"A Talisman" (Moore) **4**:232; **49**:89, 108
"Talismanes" (Borges) **32**:58, 90
"Talismans" (Borges)
See "Talismanes"
Talismatic Night (Char)
See *La nuit talismanique*
"Talk 1" (Cage) **58**:205
"A Talk with Friedrich Nietzsche" (Zagajewski) **27**:389, 392
"The Talking Back of Miss Valentine Jones" (Jordan) **38**:125, 127, 138-39
"Talking Back (to W. H. Auden)" (Meredith) **28**:216
"Talking Dirty to the Gods" (Komunyakaa) **51**:61
Talking Dirty to the Gods (Komunyakaa) **51**:50, 57, 60, 64-65
"Talking in the Woods with Karl Amorelli" (Knight) **14**:43
"Talking Late with the Governor about the Budget" (Snyder) **21**:300, 326
"Talking Myself to Sleep in One More Hilton" (Ciardi) **69**:47-48
"Talking Oak" (Tennyson) **6**:356; **101**:220
"Talking to Air in Words of Flame" (Sachs)
See "Die Kerze"
"Talking to Myself" (Ignatow) **34**:309
"Talking to Sheep" (Sexton) **79**:240, 296
"Talking to the Dead" (Stone) **53**:223-24
"Tall Ambrosia" (Thoreau) **30**:182, 232-36
"The Tall Girl" (Ransom) **61**:271, 307
"A Tall Man" (Sandburg) **41**:321
"Tall Nettles" (Thomas) **53**:280, 317, 329
"The Tall Sailing Ship" (Quasimodo)
See "L'alto veliero"
"A Tally" (Creeley) **73**:44
"Talu Dyled" (Dafydd ap Gwilym) **56**:247
"Tam Glen" (Burns) **6**:59
"Tam o' Shanter" (Burns) **6**:55-8, 73-4, 76, 78, 81, 89, 96; **114**:3-6, 8-9, 39, 41, 50, 62, 72, 76-77, 80, 92, 120-21, 155, 181
"Tam Samson's Elegy" (Burns) **114**:101, 120
"Tama yo shizume" (Ishikawa) **10**:213
"Tamar" (Jeffers) **17**:106-07, 111, 116, 130-32, 135, 138, 141, 146
Tamar and Other Poems (Jeffers) **17**:122, 124, 128, 135, 138, 146
"Tamara" (Lermontov) **18**:291-92, 298
Tamarind Season (Goodison) **36**:140-43, 150, 158
"Tamarisk" (Herbert) **50**:3
"Tamarlane" (Poe) **1**:428, 436-38, 442, 444-45, 448
Tamarlane, and Other Poems, By a Bostonian (Poe) **1**:428, 432, 437, 449
"Tambourine Life" (Berrigan) **103**:5-6, 20, 33, 40-42, 45
"Tambourines" (Hughes) **53**:91
The Tambov Treasurer's Wife (Lermontov)
See *Tambovskaya kaznacheysha*
Tambovskaya kaznacheysha (Lermontov) **18**:278, 282
"Tamer and Hawk" (Gunn) **26**:200, 221
"Tamerton Church-Tower" (Patmore) **59**:237, 239-40, 244, 257
Tamerton Church-Tower, and Other Poems (Patmore) **59**:205, 218-19, 239-40
"Tampa Robins" (Lanier) **50**:62, 77
"Tan Tien" (Berssenbrugge) **115**:7, 46
"Tanghi-Garu Pass" (Paz) **1**:361
"Tangible Disaster" (Césaire) **25**:18
"Tangled Up in Blue" (Dylan) **37**:56-9
"Tango" (Glück) **16**:151, 154
The Tango (Scalapino) **114**:283, 331, 336, 338, 340-41
"Tankas" (Borges) **22**:78
"Tanks in the Snow" (Masefield) **78**:81
"Tano" (Brathwaite) **56**:8, 75, 100
"Tantas Cosas Asustan, Tantas" (Cisneros) **52**:152
"Tanto e Amara" (Olson) **19**:320
"Tantsuiushchii David" (Shvarts) **50**:137
Tantsuiushchii David (Shvarts) **50**:134-36, 141-45, 147, 159
"Tanu" (Tagore) **8**:407
"Tanz" (Stramm) **50**:171, 201, 206
"Die Tänzerin" (Sachs) **78**:186, 188-89, 192
"Die Tänzerin (D.H.)" (Sachs) **18**:162
"The Tao and the Art of Leavetaking" (Chin) **40**:27
"Tao in the Yankee Stadium Bleachers" (Updike) **90**:346, 350, 353
"Tap Dance: W. D. Escapes from Miss Treavle" (Snodgrass) **74**:333
"Tape for the Turn of the Year" (Ammons) **16**:31
Tape for the Turn of the Year (Ammons) **16**:3-4, 6, 21-4, 28, 35, 42-3, 47-50, 59-61, 64-5
"Tapestries of Time" (Tolson) **88**:329, 344
"The Tapestry" (Bridges) **28**:79
"Tapestry" (Cassian) **17**:5
The Tapestry (Bridges) **28**:76, 80-1
"Tapestry and Sail" (Dickey) **40**:236
"Taproot" (Forché) **10**:142
Taproot (Stryk) **27**:191, 197-98, 215, 218
"Taps" (Quintana) **36**:253
"Tara" (Kinsella) **69**:66
"Tarakar atmahatya" (Tagore) **8**:405
"Tarantella" (Belloc) **24**:7, 22, 31
"A Tarantula in the Bananas" (Espada) **74**:158
"Tarantula or The Death of Death" (Hecht) **70**:93
"Tarde" (Mistral) **32**:203-05
"Tarde fresca" (Storni) **33**:251
"Tarde mayor" (Guillén) **35**:233, 234
"The Tarentinians carouse" (Cavafy) **36**:55
Tares (Thomas) **99**:232, 235-36, 269
"Targe" (Dunbar)
See "The Golden Targe"
Target Study (Baraka) **4**:38; **113**:12-13, 16-17, 24, 74-75
"Tarkington Thou Should'st Be Living in This Hour" (Nash) **21**:273
"th tarot match covr uv th lovrs" (Bissett) **14**:33
"Tarquin, Aruns, and Lucrece" (Gower) **59**:7, 58, 60, 61, 63
"Tarquins" (Gower) **59**:60-61, 63
"Tarrant Moss" (Kipling) **3**:183
"The Tarsier" (Szymborska)
See "Tarsjusz"
"Tarsjusz" (Szymborska) **44**:312
"Tartary" (de la Mare) **77**:58, 118
"Tartuffe's Punishment" (Rimbaud)
See "Le châtiment de Tartuff"
"Taruse" (Akhmadulina) **43**:63
"tarzan collage" (Bissett) **14**:31
"A Task" (Milosz) **8**:206
The Task (Cowper) **40**:39, 42-43, 45, 50, 56-60, 64-68, 70, 72-74, 76-77, 79, 81-93, 96, 99, 101, 104-7, 109-11, 113-14, 116-20, 122-23, 125, 127, 129-31, 133-35, 137, 139-43
The Tasking (Sassoon) **12**:271
"The Taste" (Oppen) **35**:285, 331
"Tata Juan" (Alurista) **34**:25
"La Ta'tadir Amma Fa'alt" (Darwish) **86**:33
"Tatinir katha" (Tagore) **8**:406
"Tattooed City" (Simic) **69**:299
"The Tattooed Man" (Hayden) **6**:195
"Tattooed Man" (Snodgrass) **74**:328, 332, 334
"Tattooing Ruth" (Silverstein) **49**:342
"Tau" (Tolson) **88**:241-42, 277, 304, 324
"Tavern" (Dalton) **36**:121, 136
"Tavern" (Millay) **6**:205
The Tavern and Other Places (Dalton)
See *Taberna otros lugares*
The Tavern and Other Poems (Dalton)
See *Taberna otros lugares*
"Tavern by the Hellespont" (Birney) **52**:22
"The Taxi" (Lowell) **13**:93
"The Taxis" (MacNeice) **61**:177, 184-85
"Taylor Street" (Gunn) **26**:213, 231
"T-Bar" (Page) **12**:177, 183, 188
"TCB" (Sanchez) **9**:225
"Te quiero" (Cernuda) **62**:203
"Tea" (Berryman) **64**:102
"Tea at My Shetland Aunt's" (Birney) **52**:79
"Tea at the Palaz of Hoon" (Stevens) **6**:304
"Tea Ceremony" (Enright) **93**:19-20
"The Tea Party" (MacLeish) **47**:187
"Teacher" (Kenyon) **57**:45
"Teacher" (Walker) **20**:273, 286
"Teaching a Dumb Calf" (Hughes) **7**:166
"Teaching in Belfast" (Mahon) **60**:140, 143, 182-83
"The Teamster" (Pavese) **13**:218
"A Teamster's Farewell" (Sandburg) **41**:234, 273
"Teamsters Union" (Shapiro) **25**:316
Teapots and Quails, and Other New Nonsenses (Lear) **65**:168
"Tear" (Hogan) **35**:259
"Tear" (Kinsella) **69**:73
"The Tear" (Pushkin) **10**:407
A Tear and a Smile (Gibran)
See *Dam 'ah wabitisāmah*
"A Tear for Cressid" (Wylie) **23**:314
"Tear Gas" (Rich) **5**:393, 396
"The Teare" (Crashaw) **84**:49, 77, 176, 179
The Teares of Peace (Chapman)
See *Euthymicæ Raptus: Or The Teares of Peace*
"Tearing" (Montague) **106**:311
"Tears" (Jacobsen) **62**:320
"Tears" (Reese) **29**:330, 332-333, 335, 346-347, 352-353
"Tears" (Sitwell) **3**:326
"Tears" (Thomas) **53**:290
"Tears" (Whitman) **3**:379; **91**:207
"Tears and Laughter" (Gibran)
See *Dam 'ah wabitisāmah*
"Tears, Idle Tears" (Tennyson) **101**:147, 150, 152, 219, 239, 249-51, 270
"Tears of an Excavator" (Pasolini) **17**:258, 289
The Tears of the Blind Lions (Merton) **10**:339
"The tears of the sisters of Phäethon" (Cavafy) **36**:53
"The Teasers" (Empson) **104**:91-92
"Teasing the Nuns" (Shapiro) **25**:286, 300
"Teatro Bambino" (Lowell) **13**:94
"Techiman" (Brathwaite) **56**:29, 85
Technical Supplement (Kinsella) **69**:76-77, 81, 107, 128, 139, 141
"The Technique of Perfection" (Graves) **6**:128
"Technologies" (Oppen) **35**:308, 348-53
"Tecumseh" (Oliver) **75**:285, 299, 301
"Teddungal" (Senghor) **25**:255
"Teddy Bears" (Swenson) **14**:273
"Tedio Invernale" (Carducci) **46**:23, 50, 78
"A Teen-Ager" (Snodgrass) **74**:333
"The Teeth-Mother Naked at Last" (Bly) **39**:12-16, 18, 22, 24-5, 37, 92-4
"TeeVeePeople" (Kaufman) **74**:194
"Tegnér's Drapa" (Longfellow) **30**:49, 91-5
"Tehran 3 May 68" (Brutus) **24**:123

Teile dich Nacht (Sachs) **78**:175
"Tejedores viejos" (Mistral) **32**:181, 191
"Telegramas de urgencia escribo" (Fuertes) **27**:16
"The Telegraph Operator" (Service) **70**:116, 145
"Telemachus Remembers" (Muir) **49**:220, 279-80
"The Telephone" (Angelou) **32**:27
"The Telephone Call" (Yau) **61**:337, 340, 342-44
"The Telephone Number of the Muse" (Justice) **64**:261, 279
Telephone Poles, and Other Poems (Updike) **90**:348, 353, 357-58
"Telephoning God" (Soto) **28**:375
"Telescopic" (Frost)
See "A Loose Mountain Telescopic"
"Televangelist" (Chappell) **105**:50
"Television Is a Baby Crawling Toward That Death Chamber" (Ginsberg) **4**:51, 76
"Television Poem" (Sanchez) **9**:210
"Tell It Like It Is" (Randall) **86**:340
"Tell Me" (Hughes) **1**:244; **53**:123, 191
"Tell Me" (Silverstein) **49**:342
"Tell Me" (Toomer) **7**:335
"Tell Me a Story" (Warren) **37**:380
Tell Me Again How the White Heron Rises and Flies Across the Nacreous River at Twilight Toward the Distant Islands (Carruth) **10**:86-7
"Tell Me Some Way" (Reese) **29**:333
"Tell Me, Tell Me" (Moore) **49**:148
Tell Me, Tell Me: Granite, Steel, and Other Topics (Moore) **4**:242, 259; **49**:113, 144, 146-47, 149
"tell me what attackd yu" (Bissett) **14**:32
"Telling the Bees" (Reese) **29**:333
"Telling the Bees" (Whittier) **93**:166-67, 173, 234-36, 239-40, 247, 250, 265-70, 344, 347
"Telos" (Hughes) **89**:275
"Temas candentes Agricultura" (Fuertes) **27**:28
"The Temeraire" (Melville) **82**:84, 270
Temora, an Ancient Epic Poem, in eight books; together with several other poems, composed by Ossian, the son of Fingal; translated from the Galic language by James Macpherson (Macpherson) **97**:173, 182, 187-89, 196, 200, 202-3, 207, 218, 230-33, 236, 239-40, 243, 245, 248-51, 253-54, 256, 264-65, 273, 279, 283, 292-93, 297, 305-16, 330, 334, 343-51
"The Temper" (Herbert) **4**:100, 118
"The Temper I" (Herbert) **4**:101, 111
"Temperance" (Crashaw) **84**:69
The Tempers (Williams) **7**:344, 348, 367, 378, 395, 398, 405; **109**:290
"The Tempest" (Vaughan) **81**:332, 340
The Tempest (Gibran)
See *Al-'awāsif*
"Tempest and Music" (Viereck) **27**:278, 280
"Tempid: Bellosguardo" (Montale) **13**:126
"The Temple" (Brown) **55**:82, 114
"The Temple" (Herrick)
See "The Fairie Temple: or, Oberons Chappell. Dedicated to Mr. John Merrifield, Counsellor at Law"
"Le temple" (Lamartine) **16**:277
"The Temple of Fame" (Pope) **26**:318-19, 331
"The Temple of Love" (Leapor) **85**:259
The Temple: Sacred Poems and Private Ejaculations (Herbert) **4**:99-102, 106, 110, 114-18, 120-21, 123, 126, 129, 132-33
"Il tempo passa" (Pavese) **13**:209, 226
"Tempora Mea in Manibus Tuis" (Werfel) **101**:350
"The Temporary the All" (Hardy) **92**:206, 224
"Le Temps" (Char) **56**:146
Le temps déborde (Éluard) **38**:75, 78
"Le Temps et les Cités" (Hugo) **17**:88
"Temps Perdu" (Parker) **28**:365
"Temptation" (Cassian) **17**:4
"Temptation in Harvest" (Kavanagh) **33**:71, 94, 102, 117, 121, 127, 131, 137; **105**:93-94, 109-10, 119, 156
"Temptation of a Poet" (Thomas) **99**:232
"The Temptation of St. Joseph" (Auden) **1**:38-39
"Tempyo gannen tsuchinoto mi, Settsu no kuni no handen no shisho Hasetsukabe no Tatsumaro mizukara wanaki mimakarishi toki, hangan Otomo no Sukune Minaka no tsukuru uta" (Yakamochi) **48**:132
Temy i variatsi (Pasternak) **6**:252, 255, 261, 264-65, 269, 271, 275, 277-81, 283
Temy i var'iatsii (Pasternak)
See *Temy i variatsi*
"X" (Joyce) **22**:136, 138, 145, 153, 160, 162, 168
"10" (Seferis) **66**:118
"10 April 67" (Brutus) **24**:122
Ten Burnt Offerings (MacNeice) **61**:181
"Ten Days Leave" (Snodgrass) **74**:284, 295-96, 300
"1080" (Stafford) **71**:334
"Ten Greatest Books" (Berrigan) **103**:36
Ten New Songs (Cohen) **109**:79-80
"The Ten-Penny Nail" (Leapor) **85**:257
"Ten Poems for Downbeat" (Spicer) **78**:294
"Ten Thousand Leaping Swords" (Melville) **82**:37, 45
The Ten Thousand Leaves (Yakamochi)
See *Man'yōshū*
"Ten Years Ago When I Played at Being Brave" (Ciardi) **69**:40, 55
"A Tenancy" (Merrill) **28**:249-50, 268
"The Tenant" (Brodsky) **9**:2
Tenants of the House (Abse) **41**:2-4, 7, 9-11, 13, 15-16, 19, 27
"Ten-Day Leave" (Meredith) **28**:180, 186
Tender Buttons: Objects, Food, Rooms (Stein) **18**:316-34, 336, 341-42, 344, 349-54
Tender only To One (Smith) **12**:292, 326, 340, 343, 349
"Tenderness" (Ignatow) **34**:270
Tenderness (Mistral)
See *Ternura*
Tenderness (Yevtushenko)
See *Nezhnost*
"Tenderness toward Existence" (Kinnell) **26**:251
"Tenders of Objects" (Dorn) **115**:75
"Tenebrae" (Celan) **10**:101-02, 118
"Tenebrae" (Clarke) **112**:36, 47, 49
"Tenebrae" (Levertov) **11**:176
"Ténèbres" (Brossard) **80**:25
"The Tenements of Death" (Barker) **77**:4
"Tengo" (Guillén) **23**:106, 115
Tengo (Guillén) **23**:124-25, 127, 130-31, 133
"Tengo que deciros" (Fuertes) **27**:4
"Tenjō Ishi" (Hagiwara) **18**:178-79
"Tenki" (Nishiwaki) **15**:228
"The Tennessee Hero" (Harper) **21**:206, 218
"Tennessee June" (Graham) **59**:150, 181
"Tennis" (Pinsky) **27**:144, 162
"The Tennis Court Oath" (Ashbery) **26**:113
The Tennis Court Oath (Ashbery) **26**:108, 112-13, 118, 129, 137-38, 143, 163
"Tenor" (Guillén) **23**:122, 124
"The Tent on the Beach" (Whittier) **93**:167, 170, 172, 176, 232, 238-39, 262, 339
The Tent on the Beach, and Other Poems (Whittier) **93**:224, 346
"Les Tentations" (Baudelaire) **106**:100
Tentativa del hombre infinito (Neruda) **4**:276
"Tentative Description of a Dinner to Promote the Impeachment of President Eisenhower" (Ferlinghetti) **1**:167
"Tentative Gardening" (Hacker) **47**:118
"Tentative orale" (Ponge) **107**:104, 143-44
"Tenth Elegy" (Rilke) **2**:273, 286-87
"Tenth Muse" (Lowell) **3**:213
The Tenth Muse Lately Sprung up in America (Bradstreet) **10**:2-3, 6-8, 12, 18, 20-1, 25-7, 29-31, 34, 37, 40-1, 43, 46, 51-2, 59
Tenth Nemean (Pindar)
See *Nemean 10*
Tenth Olympian (Pindar)
See *Olympian 10*
"Tenth Psalm" (Sexton) **2**:372; **79**:222, 231
Tenth Pythian (Pindar)
See *Pythian 10*
"Tenuous and Precarious" (Smith) **12**:312, 337
"Tenzone" (Ciardi) **69**:7, 14, 54
"Teodoro Luna's Two Kisses" (Ríos) **57**:316
Teodoro Luna's Two Kisses (Ríos) **57**:325
"Tequila Jazz" (Kaufman) **74**:195, 245
"Terce" (Auden) **92**:17, 43, 47
Tercera residencia, 1935-1945 (Neruda) **4**:291, 306; **64**:305, 308
"Tercero antolojía poética" (Jiménez) **7**:195
"Teremteni" (Illyés) **16**:235, 249
"Terence, This Is Stupid Stuff" (Housman) **2**:193; **43**:240, 259, 261, 271
"Teresa" (Wilbur) **51**:284
"A Term" (Aleixandre) **15**:4
"The Term" (Williams) **109**:192
"Le Terme épars" (Char) **56**:137
"Terminal" (Shapiro) **25**:324
"The Terminal Bar" (Mahon) **60**:172
"Terminal Day at Beverly Farms" (Lowell) **3**:219
"Terminal Resemblance" (Glück) **16**:158
"Terminus" (Emerson) **18**:75-77, 113
"Terminus" (Heaney) **18**:227
"Terms" (Hecht) **70**:80, 88, 106-7
"Terms of Surrender" (Stafford) **71**:318, 336-37
Ternura (Mistral) **32**:147, 149, 164, 171, 179-80, 183, 208
"Terorysta, on patrzy" (Szymborska) **44**:270, 283
"Terpsichore" (Holmes) **71**:115-16
"Terra" (Quasimodo) **47**:272, 302
"Terra" (Ungaretti) **57**:342
La terra impareggiabile (Quasimodo) **47**:287, 289, 304
La terra promessa (Ungaretti) **57**:339-40, 376-77
"The Terrace" (Wilbur) **51**:188
"The Terrace at Berne" (Arnold) **5**:12, 19, 49
"The Terraced Valley" (Graves) **6**:135, 139, 143-44, 172
"La Terre" (Bonnefoy) **58**:168-69
"Terre bianche" (Quasimodo) **47**:278
"Terrestrial" (Jacobsen) **62**:324
"The Terrestrial Paradise" (Morris) **55**:306
The Terrible Shears: Scenes from a Twenties Childhood (Enright) **93**:16-17, 22-23, 28-29, 33
"Territory" (Kumin) **15**:207
"The Territory Is Not the Map" (Spicer) **78**:242
"Terror" (Levertov) **11**:169
"Terror" (Warren) **37**:284, 287, 289, 323-24, 332, 380
"The Terror" (Very) **86**:97, 138-39
"Terror and Decorum" (Viereck) **27**:267, 271
Terror and Decorum (Viereck) **27**:258-63, 277-84
"A Terror Is More Certain" (Kaufman) **74**:185, 254
"The Terror of Existing" (Montale)
See "Il terrore di esistere"
"Il terrore di esistere" (Montale) **13**:139
"The Terrorist, He Watches" (Szymborska)
See "Terorysta, on patrzy"
"The Terrorist, He's Watching" (Szymborska)
See "Terorysta, on patrzy"
Terze Odi Barbare (Carducci) **46**:8
"The Tesment of Maister Andro Kennedy" (Dunbar) **67**:101, 103-5
"Tess's Lament" (Hardy) **8**:85; **92**:243, 265
"The Test" (Emerson) **18**:77
"Test" (Parra) **39**:271, 277, 302, 307, 310
"Test Case" (Kinsella) **69**:116-17
"The Test of Atlanta 1979" (Jordan) **38**:144
"The Test of Manhood" (Meredith) **60**:262
"A Testament" (Lermontov) **18**:278

"Testament" (Sandburg) **41**:256, 270
"Testament" (Stryk) **27**:215
Le Testament (Villon) **13**:374-75, 377, 379, 387-90, 393-418
The Testament (Villon)
See *Le Testament*
"Testament Coran" (Pasolini) **17**:262, 279
The Testament of Beauty (Bridges) **28**:48-50, 54-6, 59, 62, 65, 70-3, 76-8, 81
The Testament of Cresseid (Henryson) **65**:11, 14, 20, 29-30, 38, 42, 58, 69-70, 73-74, 84, 89, 92-99, 104, 109-12, 114, 116-20, 124-25
"The Testament of Love" (Bridges) **28**:65
Testament of Love (Chaucer)
See *Legend of Good Women*
"Testament of the Thief" (Kinnell) **26**:240
Testimonies (Dalton) **36**:120
"Testimony" (Komunyakaa) **51**:55, 63
"Testimony of a Canadian Educational Leader" (Birney) **52**:17
"The Testing Tree" (Kunitz) **19**:175, 178, 180, 183
The Testing-Tree (Kunitz) **19**:157, 161, 163, 168, 172-74, 176, 185-86
"Tête de faune" (Rimbaud) **3**:271; **57**:175, 191, 236
"Têtes du serail" (Hugo) **17**:75
"Tetrameter Ode" (Kenyon) **57**:46
Teuila (Stevenson)
See *R. L. S. Teuila*
"Teurer Freund" (Heine) **25**:161
"Tewksebury Road" (Masefield) **78**:56
"Texas" (Berssenbrugge) **115**:10, 47
"Texas" (Lowell) **13**:86
"Texas" (Whittier) **93**:208
"The Text" (Riley) **48**:300
"Text" (Thomas) **99**:272
"Text on Electricity" (Ponge)
See "Texte sur l'électricité"
"Le Texte interdit" (Éluard) **38**:83, 87
"Texte sur l'électricité" (Ponge) **107**:127, 220, 224
"Th' Ambrosia of the God's A Weed On Earth" (Thoreau) **30**:226
"th lonliness of literacy" (Bissett) **14**:34
Thalaba the Destroyer (Southey) **111**:199-200, 216, 220, 225, 233, 241-42, 254, 256, 260-61, 276, 279
"Thalamus" (MacDiarmid) **9**:168, 176-77
"Thalassa" (MacNeice) **61**:113, 166
"Thalassius" (Swinburne) **24**:312-315
"Thalerò" (Sikelianos) **29**:373
Thalia Rediviva: The Pass-Times and Diversions of a Countrey-Muse, in Choice Poems on Several Occasions. With Some Learned Remains of the Eminent Eugenius Philalethes. Never Made Publick Till Now (Vaughan) **81**:346, 349, 355, 357, 363, 366
"Thamár y Amnón" (García Lorca) **3**:120, 131-32, 134, 146
Thames (Peacock)
See *The Genius of the Thames: A Lyric Poem, in Two Parts*
"Thamesfontein" (Kipling) **91**:176
"Thammuz" (Mahon) **60**:135
"Thanatopsis" (Bryant) **20**:10, 12, 14, 16-19, 21-3, 26-30, 32, 34, 41, 43, 47
"Thank God for Little Children" (Harper) **21**:197
"Thank You" (Koch) **80**:314, 322
Thank You and Other Poems (Koch) **80**:290, 309, 318, 321
"Thank You, Christine" (Berryman) **64**:102-3
"Thank You, Fog" (Auden) **1**:31; **92**:5
"Thank You for Love" (Duncan) **75**:223
"Thank You, Thank You" (Kavanagh) **33**:96, 138; **105**:177
"Thanking My Mother for Piano Lessons" (Wakoski) **15**:325, 347
"Thanks" (Benét) **64**:14
"A Thanksgiving" (Auden) **1**:31; **92**:41
"Thanksgiving" (Glück) **16**:124, 129, 150
"Thanksgiving at Snake Butte" (Welch) **62**:339
"Thanksgiving: Detroit" (Berryman) **64**:81, 84
"Thanksgiving for a Habitat" (Auden) **1**:24; **92**:67
"Thanksgiving Ode" (Wordsworth) **4**:399
Thanksgivings (Traherne) **70**:171, 228, 287, 289, 308
"Thanksgivings and Prayer for the NATION" (Traherne) **70**:280-82, 285, 306, 333
"Thanksgivings for the Beauty of his Providence" (Traherne) **70**:285, 327
"Thanksgivings for the Glory of God's Works" (Traherne) **70**:229
"Thanksgiving's Over" (Lowell) **3**:206
"Thank-you Note" (Szymborska)
See "Podziekowanie"
"Thar's More in the Man Than Thar Is in the Land" (Lanier) **50**:91
"Th'Assyryans king" (Surrey) **59**:303
"That April night's menu" (Enzensberger) **28**:155
"That Blessed Hope" (Harper) **21**:189, 208, 217
"That Bright Chimeric Beast" (Cullen) **20**:67
"That Day" (Sexton) **2**:353
"That Day" (Stone) **53**:256
"That Day That Was That Day" (Lowell) **12**:85
"That Force" (Zagajewski) **27**:385
"That Intrinsic Old Man of Peru" (Lear) **65**:171, 184-85
"That is sufficient" (Guillén)
See "Eso Basta"
"That Kind of Thing" (Gallagher) **9**:61
"That Mendacious Old Person of Gretna" (Lear) **65**:171, 184
"That Mighty Flight" (Baraka) **113**:17
"That Moment" (Hardy) **8**:94
"That Moment" (Wagoner) **33**:364
"That Morning" (Hughes) **89**:133
"That None Beguiled Be" (Suckling) **30**:143
"That Ombliferous person of Crete" (Lear) **65**:171, 184-85
"That Oracular Lady of Prague" (Lear) **65**:171, 184
"That Pheaton of Our Day" (Thoreau) **30**:268
"That Swan's Way" (Aleixandre) **15**:5
"That the Night Come" (Yeats) **20**:351
"That the Science of Cartography Is Limited" (Boland) **58**:18, 25, 59-60
"That there are powers above us I admit" (Clough) **103**:85
that they were at the beach (Scalapino) **114**:275, 284, 291-92, 319
"That Weather" (Stafford) **71**:290
"That Which is Now Behind, Previous Condition: The Eight of Swords" (Piercy) **29**:324
"That which is one they shear and make it twain" (Belloc) **24**:37-8
"That Which is White" (Storni)
See "Lo blanco"
"That Which Opposes the Overthrowing of the Tower: The Nine of Cups" (Piercy) **29**:324
"That Winter" (Stone) **53**:252
"That Woman There" (Stryk) **27**:203
"That women are but men's shadows" (Jonson)
See *The Forest VII*
"That Year" (Olds) **22**:308, 320, 322
"That-Air Young 'Un" (Riley) **48**:340, 362
"The Thatcher" (Heaney) **18**:200
"That's the Man" (Cavafy) **36**:106
"That's the Place Indians Talk About" (Ortiz) **17**:228, 230-31, 234
That's What We Live For (Szymborska)
See *Dlatego zyjemy*
That's Why We Are Alive (Szymborska)
See *Dlatego zyjemy*
"Thaw" (Thomas) **53**:328
"The Thaw" (Thoreau) **30**:192, 194, 234, 241, 245
"The" (Zukofsky)
See "Poem Beginning 'The'"
"Theater Impressions" (Szymborska) **44**:278
"Théâtre" (Bonnefoy) **58**:130, 132, 134
"Theatre of Sidon A.D. 400" (Cavafy) **36**:66, 76
"Thébaide" (Gautier) **18**:146
Theban Dithyramb (Pindar) **19**:423
"The,bright,Centipede" (Villa)
See "Centipede Sonnet"
"The,caprice,of,canteloupe,is,to,be" (Villa) **22**:356-57
Thee (Aiken) **26**:24, 29
"Their Beginning" (Cavafy) **36**:69, 76, 78, 81, 91
"Their Behaviour" (Brutus) **24**:99
"Their Camp" (Wagoner) **33**:359
"Their Canvases Are" (Thomas) **99**:266
"Their Frailty" (Sassoon) **12**:267
"Their Mouths Full" (Ignatow) **34**:310
"Their Poem" (Cruz) **37**:5
"Their Shelter" (Wagoner) **33**:359
"Their Very Memory" (Blunden) **66**:59
"Their Week" (Merwin) **45**:34
"Thekla's Answer" (Arnold) **5**:50
"thel" (Clifton) **17**:30
Thel (Blake)
See *The Book of Thel*
"Them, Crying" (Dickey) **40**:196, 215
"Theme and Variation" (Hayden) **6**:186, 197
"Theme and Variations" (Pasternak) **6**:251
"Theme for English B" (Hughes) **53**:94, 126, 128, 163, 192-93
Themes and Variations (Pasternak)
See *Temy i variatsi*
Themes & Variations (Cage) **58**:200-201, 205-6
"Then" (Hacker) **47**:88
"Then" (de la Mare) **77**:112
"Then" (Muir) **49**:231, 249
"Then" (Stone) **53**:240, 258
"Then" (Wilbur) **51**:223
"Then and Now" (Kennedy) **93**:153
"Then Follows" (Jackson) **44**:13
"Then I Saw What the Calling Was" (Rukeyser) **12**:223
"Then It Is a Prison" (Alurista) **34**:22
"Then It Was" (Jordan) **38**:120
"Then the Ermine" (Moore) **49**:126, 130-31, 137
"Thence is my grief" (Campion) **87**:35
"Theodore Dreiser" (Masters) **1**:343
"Theodore the Poet" (Masters) **1**:345; **36**:201
"Theodotos" (Cavafy) **36**:8
"Theogonien" (Benn) **35**:8
"Theological Cradle Songs" (Viereck) **27**:262
"Theology" (Dunbar) **5**:120, 125, 127
"Theology" (Hughes) **7**:123, 159; **89**:113-14
"The Theology of Cockroaches" (Alexie) **53**:25
"Theophilos Palaiologos" (Cavafy) **36**:40
"Theophilus" (Robinson) **35**:368
"Theory" (Simic) **69**:301
"Theory of Art" (Baraka) **4**:9
"Theory of Evil" (Hayden) **6**:194, 196
"Theory of Flight" (Rukeyser) **12**:207, 218, 225
Theory of Flight (Rukeyser) **12**:202-03, 206, 209-10, 226-27, 235-36
"Theory of Maya" (Tagore)
See "Mayavada"
"Theory of Numbers" (Rexroth) **95**:260, 271
"A Theory of Prosody" (Levine) **22**:227
"A Theory of Truth" (Dorn) **115**:109
"Theory of Truth" (Jeffers) **17**:131, 142, 144
"ther may have been a tunnel thru which my train rolld" (Bissett) **14**:34
"There" (Creeley) **73**:12
"There" (Verlaine) **2**:416
"There Are Birds" (Shapiro) **25**:294
"There Are Blk/Puritans" (Sanchez) **9**:218
"There Are Courtesies That Make You Want to Kill" (Parra)
See "Hay cortesías que merecen palos"
"There Are Delicacies" (Birney) **52**:32, 82
"There are Lime Trees in Leaf on the Promenade" (Raworth) **107**:274

"There Are No Gods" (Lawrence) **54**:185, 187
"There Are Orioles in Woods and Lasting Length of Vowels" (Mandelstam) **14**:141
"There Are Silent Legends" (Welch) **62**:339, 372
"There Are So Many Houses and Dark Streets without Help" (Bukowski) **18**:15
"There Are Some Men" (Cohen) **109**:52
"There Are Things I Tell to No One" (Kinnell) **26**:258, 260-61, 280, 292
"There Came a Day" (Hughes) **89**:125
"There Can Be No Other Apple for Me" (Corso) **33**:36; **108**:8
"There Exists the Eternal Fact of Conflict" (Crane) **80**:52
"There Has to Be a Jail for Ladies" (Merton) **10**:341
"There Have Been Nights" (Tapahonso) **65**:224
"There he is!" (Cavafy) **36**:57
"There I Could Never Be a Boy" (O'Hara) **45**:132, 142, 165
"There is a Garden in her face" (Campion) **87**:32-33, 71, 99
"There is a Happy Day" (Parra)
See "Hay un día feliz"
"There is a hill beside the silver Thames" (Bridges) **28**:66-7, 83
"There is a joy in footing slow across a silent plain" (Keats) **96**:207
"There Is a Right Way" (Welch) **62**:370
"There Is an Inner Nervousness in Virgins" (Spicer) **78**:302
"There is none, O none but you" (Campion) **87**:12
"There Is Nothing Quite Like This" (Tapahonso) **65**:227
"There Is Only One of Everything" (Atwood) **8**:23, 28
"There *Must* Be a Lone Ranger" (Baraka) **113**:4-5, 15
"There Never Yet Was Woman Made" (Suckling) **30**:139
"There Once Lived a Poor Knight" (Pushkin)
See "Zhil Na Svete Rytsar' Bednyi"
"There Shines the Moon, at Noon of Night" (Brontë) **8**:75
"There Should be No Despair" (Brontë) **8**:68-9
"There Was a Boy" (Wordsworth) **67**:331
"There Was a Child Went Forth" (Whitman) **3**:392, 396, 415; **91**:230
"There Was A Dance Sweetheart" (Harjo) **27**:69
"There Was a Lad Was Born in Kyle" (Burns) **6**:76
"There Was a Lass" (Burns) **114**:19
"There Was a Man Who Lived a Life of Fire" (Crane) **80**:82
"There Was a Poor Knight" (Pushkin)
See "Zhil Na Svete Rytsar' Bednyi"
"There Was a Saviour" (Thomas) **2**:390; **52**:258
"There Was a Time" (Thomas) **53**:286-87
"There Was an Old Man of Apulia" (Lear) **65**:170
"There Was an Old Man of Coblenz" (Lear) **65**:168, 171
"There was an Old Man of the Coast" (Lear) **65**:144
"There Was an Old Person in Gray" (Lear) **65**:184
"There was an Old Person of Crowle" (Lear) **65**:182
"There was an Old Person of Filey" (Lear) **65**:183
"There Was an Old Person of Prague" (Lear) **65**:171
"There Was an Old Person of Rhodes" (Lear) **65**:171
"There Was Glass and There Are Stars" (Jarrell) **41**:169
"There was Never Nothing" (Wyatt) **27**:318
"There Was One" (Parker) **28**:362
"There Was One I Met upon the Road" (Crane) **80**:52
"There Was Set Before Me Mighty Hill" (Crane) **80**:82
"There Will Be Rest" (Teasdale) **31**:336, 341, 390
"There You Were" (Sexton) **79**:245
Therefore (Mallarmé)
See *Igitur*
"There's a Better Shine" (Niedecker) **42**:150-51, 167, 169
"There's a Grandfather's Clock in the Hall" (Warren) **37**:304-5
"There's a Thread You Follow" (Stafford) **71**:374
There's a Trick with a Knife I'm Learning to Do: Poems, 1963-1978 (Ondaatje) **28**:327-40
"There's Me" (Baca) **41**:38
"There's Nothing Here" (Muir) **49**:298
"There's Something I Often Notice" (Yevtushenko) **40**:341
"There's the sound of rain" (Akhmadulina)
See "Vot zvuk dozhdia"
"Theresa's Friends" (Creeley) **73**:80
"Thermopylae" (Carver) **54**:28
"Thermopylae" (Cavafy) **36**:28, 56, 57, 89
"These" (Williams) **7**:360, 362-63
"These Are the Young" (Lindsay) **23**:281
"These Fellowing Men" (Gilmore) **87**:302
"These grasses, ancient enemies" (Douglas) **106**:199
"These Green-Going-to-Yellow" (Bell) **79**:21-22
These Green-Going-to-Yellow: Poems (Bell) **79**:25, 28
"These Heroics" (Cohen) **109**:14, 49
"These I Singing in Spring" (Whitman) **91**:247-48, 251
"These Images Remain" (Sarton) **39**:324, 345
"These Mornings" (Stafford) **71**:382
"These Mornings of Rain" (Walker) **30**:343
"These Pure Arches" (Sarton) **39**:322
"These States: To Miami Presidential Convention" (Ginsberg) **4**:82
"These Streets" (Levine) **22**:224
"These Things that Poets Said" (Thomas) **53**:291
"These Trees Stand" (Snodgrass) **74**:281, 284-86, 307, 323
"These Were Her Nightly Journeys" (Sarton) **39**:333
"Theseus and Ariadne" (Graves) **6**:136-37, 144, 146
"Thesis" (Dorn) **115**:54, 57, 220
"Theta" (Tolson) **88**:237-38, 272, 275, 277, 280, 304, 316
"Thetis" (H. D.) **5**:267-68
"Thetis" (Meynell) **112**:291
"They" (Corso) **108**:8
"They" (Cunningham) **92**:175
"They" (Sassoon) **12**:241, 249, 263, 275, 277-78, 286
"They" (Thomas) **99**:246, 359
"They All Want To Play Hamlet" (Sandburg) **41**:276
"They are all gone into the world of light!" (Vaughan) **81**:268, 272, 280, 370
"They Are More on a Corncob" (Guillén)
See "Son más en una mazorca"
"They Are Not Missed" (Toomer) **7**:338-39
"They Are Not Ready" (Madhubuti) **5**:338
"They Are Silent and Quick" (Tapahonso) **65**:252
"They came at a pace" (Niedecker) **42**:151
"They Clapped" (Giovanni) **19**:141
"They Eat Out" (Atwood) **8**:6
"They Feed They Lion" (Levine) **22**:216, 221, 227
They Feed They Lion (Levine) **22**:211, 213, 215, 217, 223
"They fle from me" (Wyatt) **27**:300, 302, 309, 314, 316, 329-31, 338, 343, 347-48, 355, 357, 362
"They Flee from Me" (Wyatt)
See "They fle from me"
"They Folded the Scene" (Darwish)
See "Aghlaqu al-Mashhad"
"They Have Come" (Storni)
See "Han venido"
"They Have Put Us on Hold" (Walker) **20**:294
"They Led You Away at Dawn" (Akhmatova)
See "Uvodili tebya na rassvete"
"They Never Were Found" (Jacobsen) **62**:313
"They Say I Have..." (Silverstein) **49**:342
"They Say it Snowed" (Ammons) **16**:44
"They Say the Sea Is Loveless" (Lawrence) **54**:197
"They Say This Isn't a Poem" (Rexroth) **20**:195-96; **95**:250, 258, 260, 274
"They shall not pass" (Paz)
See "¡No pasarán"
"They Should Have Provided" (Cavafy) **36**:51
"They Take A Little Nip" (Walker) **30**:338
"They told me you had been to her . . ." (Carroll) **74**:29
"They (2)" (Creeley) **73**:46
"They Went Home" (Angelou) **32**:27, 29
"They Who Feel Death" (Walker) **30**:345
"They Will Say" (Sandburg) **41**:239, 243, 327, 334, 337, 350, 364, 367-68
"They'd Never Know Me Now" (Masters) **1**:344
"They'll Never be Peace till Jamie Comes Hame" (Burns) **114**:116, 163
"They've Put a Brassiere on the Camel" (Silverstein) **49**:313, 324
"A Thicket in Lleyn" (Thomas) **99**:264-65, 267
"Thick-Lipped Nigger" (Guillén)
See "Negro bembón"
"The Thief" (Kunitz) **19**:150-51, 172, 175
"The Thief and the Cordelier, A Ballad" (Prior) **102**:314
Thieves of Paradise (Komunyakaa) **51**:33, 50, 52, 54-57, 63
"The Thimble" (Kenyon) **57**:23, 43
"Thin Air" (Hass) **16**:215, 217
"Thin Breast Doom" (Berrigan) **103**:36
"The Thin Edge of Your Pride" (Rexroth) **95**:256-57, 260, 262, 269
"The Thin People" (Plath) **1**:388, 406; **37**:184
"Thin Strips" (Sandburg) **41**:298
"The Thing about Crows" (Jacobsen) **62**:323
"The Thing I Am" (Borges) **32**:58
"Thing Language" (Spicer) **78**:326
"Things" (Borges) **32**:58, 140
"The Things" (Borges) **32**:58
"Things" (Kenyon) **57**:5, 17, 33
"Things" (Reese) **29**:336
"Things Are What They Seem" (Moore) **49**:105, 110, 134
"Things Ended" (Cavafy) **36**:80
"Things I Learned Last Week" (Stafford) **71**:310
"Things I Say to Myself While Hanging Laundry" (Stone) **53**:224
"Things I Took" (Bell) **79**:28
"Things of August" (Stevens) **6**:313; **110**:97, 229
Things of This World (Wilbur) **51**:231, 237, 272-73, 293, 299, 322, 330, 333
"Things Seen" (Jaccottet)
See "On voit"
"Things Seen" (Sarton) **39**:342
Things Taking Place (Swenson)
See *New and Selected Things Taking Place*
"Things That Are Worse Than Death" (Olds) **22**:313
"Things That Come" (Stafford) **71**:376
"Things That Happen" (Stafford) **71**:328
Things that Happen Where There Aren't Any People (Stafford) **71**:330, 340, 342
Things That I Do in the Dark: Selected Poetry (Jordan) **38**:112, 120-22, 127
"Things That Might Have Been" (Borges) **32**:46, 58, 66, 90
"Things to Do" (Schuyler) **88**:189

"Things to Do in Anne's Room" (Berrigan) **103**:4-5, 20
"Things to Do in New York City" (Berrigan) **103**:20
"Things to Do in Providence" (Berrigan) **103**:4, 7-8, 30, 34-35, 42, 45
"Things to Do on Speed" (Berrigan) **103**:20
"Things to do with Moonlight" (Curnow) **48**:15-17, 19, 34
"Things We Did That Meant Something" (Stafford) **71**:262, 293
Things We Dreamt We Died For (Bell) **79**:23, 39
"Think" (Cunningham) **92**:163
"Think No More, Lad: Laugh, Be Jolly" (Housman) **2**:179, 183, 185
"Think of It" (Celan) **10**:98
"Think Tank" (Merrill) **28**:267
"The Thinker" (Williams) **7**:353
"Thinking" (Creeley) **73**:13
"Thinking about El Salvador" (Levertov) **11**:198
"Thinking about Shelley" (Stern) **115**:263
"Thinking about the Past" (Justice) **64**:273
"Thinking for Berky" (Stafford) **71**:257, 320, 323, 378
"Thinking of Inishere in Cambridge, Massachusetts" (Mahon) **60**:143, 170, 198
"Thinking of Madame Bovary" (Kenyon) **57**:5, 15
"Thinking of Mr. D" (Kinsella) **69**:75-77, 121-22
"Thinking of Old Tu Fu" (Matsuo Basho) **3**:10
"Thinking of the Lost World" (Jarrell) **41**:162, 164, 180-81, 189, 208, 217-18
"Thinking of Wallace Stevens" (Creeley) **73**:96
"Think'st thou to seduce me then" (Campion) **87**:32, 34, 71, 92, 120
"Thinness" (Schuyler) **88**:212
"Thir Ladyis fair that in the Court ar kend" (Dunbar) **67**:25
"Thir Ladyis Fair that Makis Repair" (Dunbar) **67**:3, 7
The Third and Fourth Bookes of Ayres (Campion) **87**:7, 12, 50, 67-68, 72
"Third Base Coach" (Chappell) **105**:34, 67
Third Book of Odes (Ronsard)
See *See Les quatre premiers livres des odes de Pierre de Ronsard, ensemble son bocage*
The Third Booke of Ayres (Campion) **87**:12, 25, 32, 47, 50, 57, 59, 69-72, 74
"Third Degree" (Hughes) **1**:248; **53**:119
"The Third Dimension" (Levertov) **11**:159
"Third Elegy" (Rilke) **2**:271, 273
"Third Georgic" (Vergil) **12**:361
"Third Hymn to Lenin" (MacDiarmid) **9**:180-81, 197
"Third Memory" (Yevtushenko) **40**:347
Third Nemean (Pindar)
See *Nemean 3*
"The Third of February" (Tennyson) **101**:194
Third Olympian (Pindar)
See *Olympian 3*
"Third Psalm" (Sexton) **2**:367; **79**:220
"Third Psalm of Life" (Longfellow) **30**:109
Third Pythian (Pindar)
See *Pythian 3*
The Third Residence (Neruda)
See *Tercera residencia, 1935-1945*
Third Residence (Neruda)
See *Tercera residencia, 1935-1945*
"The Third Retainer" (Raworth) **107**:274
"Third Sermon on John 1.8" (Donne) **43**:162
"The Third Sermon on the Warpland" (Brooks) **7**:88-9
Third Snow (Yevtushenko) **40**:341
"Third Song" (Rilke)
See "Third Elegy"
"Third Street" (Stafford) **71**:374
The Third Symphony (Bely)
See *Vozvrat: Tretiia simfoniia*
Third Voronezh Notebook (Mandelstam) **14**:149, 152, 155
"The Third World" (Ferlinghetti) **1**:186
"Third World Calling" (Ferlinghetti) **1**:183
Third World Express (Serote) **113**:286-87, 297, 299
Third World Poems (Brathwaite) **56**:92
"Third Ypres" (Blunden) **66**:36, 39
"XIII" (Joyce) **22**:145, 168
"13/16" (Alexie) **53**:34
"13 settembre 1959 (Variante)" (Zanzotto) **65**:266
"Thirteen Ways of Looking at a Blackbird" (Stevens) **6**:293, 326-27; **110**:123, 170
"The Thirteens (Black and White)" (Angelou) **32**:28
Thirteenth Olympian (Pindar)
See *Olympian 13*
"The Thirties Revisited" (Kumin) **15**:202
"XXX" (Joyce) **22**:138, 144-45, 164, 173
"Thirty Delft Tiles" (Doty) **53**:60-61
"The 34th Chapter of Isaiah" (Cowley) **90**:104
38 Variations on a Theme by Alison Knowles (Cage) **58**:196-97
31 Letters and 13 Dreams (Hugo) **68**:267, 271, 277-78, 281, 286, 293, 311
Thirty Poems (Merton) **10**:338-39, 350-51
Thirty Preliminary Poems (Barker) **77**:2, 4, 8, 26
"Thirty Rhymes to Hermit Chang Piao" (Tu Fu) **9**:326
"36 Mesostics Re and not Re Duchamp" (Cage) **58**:195
Thirty Spanish Poems of Love and Exile (Rexroth) **95**:251
Thirty Things (Creeley) **73**:41, 91, 117
"Thirty Years Under" (Yamada) **44**:330, 333, 345
"XXXV" (Joyce) **22**:138-39, 144, 154, 157, 161, 164
"XXXIV" (Joyce) **22**:139, 145, 157, 161-62, 164-65, 170
"XXXI" (Joyce) **22**:152, 164, 170
"XXXVI" (Joyce) **22**:136, 138, 144-45, 157, 161, 163-64
Thirty-Six New Poems (Wickham) **110**:262, 284-85, 312
Thirty-Six Poems (Warren) **37**:279, 319, 321, 324, 331, 354, 376, 380-81
"XXXIII" (Joyce) **22**:145, 164, 166, 168, 173
"XXXII" (Joyce) **22**:145, 164, 167, 173
"XXXII" (Larkin) **21**:242
"* * * this in a Letter I sent to my schoolfellow. W.M." (Taylor) **63**:281
"This" (Housman) **43**:240
"This" (Stone) **53**:259
"This Afternoon Was Unholy" (Dorn) **115**:122
"This Black Rich Country" (Ammons) **16**:40
This Body Is Made of Camphor and Gopherwood (Bly) **39**:29, 37-41, 43, 45, 99-100
"This Bread I Break" (Thomas) **2**:379, 389; **52**:295-97, 299
"This Bridge" (Silverstein) **49**:323-24
"This Cold Man" (Page)
See "Now This Cold Man"
"This Compost" (Whitman) **3**:410; **91**:270
"This Configuration" (Ashbery) **26**:141
"This Corruptible" (Wylie) **23**:304-305, 308, 311, 316
"This Day" (Levertov) **11**:198-99, 201
"This Dove & Olive Branch to you" (Taylor) **63**:274
"This Do, in Remembrance of Me" (Bryant) **20**:45
"This Fevers Me" (Eberhart) **76**:48, 57, 67, 69, 73
"This Florida: 1924" (Williams) **7**:369
"This Foolish Wing" (Ciardi) **69**:24
"This Frieze of Birds" (Page) **12**:168
"This Grievous Pain" (Storni)
See "Este grave daño"
"This Hinder Nycht, Halff Sleiping as I Lay" (Dunbar) **67**:7
"This Humanist" (Cunningham) **92**:158
"This Hyndir Nycht in Dumfermeling" (Dunbar) **67**:5
"This in Which" (Oppen) **35**:301
This in Which (Oppen) **35**:308, 309, 310, 311-17, 321, 322-23, 333, 336, 340, 343, 348-50, 353
"This Is" (Ammons) **16**:54
"This Is A Hymn" (Goodison) **36**:148
"This Is a Photograph of Me" (Atwood) **8**:12, 23
"This Is Disgraceful and Abominable" (Smith) **12**:293, 309
"This Is How They Were Placed for Us" (Tapahonso) **65**:257
"This Is It" (Stern) **115**:247-48
"This Is Just to Say" (Williams) **7**:363, 399, 401
"This Is My Carnac" (Thoreau) **30**:192, 235-36
This Is My Century: New and Collected Poems by Margaret Walker (Walker) **20**:293
"This Is My Father's Country" (Goodison) **36**:158
"This is my playes last scene, here heavens appoint" (Donne) **43**:160
"This Is No Case of Petty Right or Wrong" (Thomas) **53**:306-7, 350
"This Is Noon" (Graves) **6**:166
"This Is Not For John Lennon (And This Is Not a Poem)" (Giovanni) **19**:142
"This is the Life" (MacNeice) **61**:178
"this is the tale" (Clifton) **17**:25, 27
"This Is the Track" (Owen) **19**:342
"This Is Their Fault" (Forché) **10**:142
"This is Who I Am" (Akhmadulina)
See "Eto ja"
This Journey (Wright) **36**:333, 342, 347-48, 358, 364-66, 368, 370-71, 378, 387, 393, 399-400
"This Lang Lentern Makis Me Lene" (Dunbar) **67**:3, 5, 7
"This Last Pain" (Empson) **104**:84, 90, 101, 119, 121, 124, 132
"This (Let's Remember) day Died Again and" (Cummings) **5**:107
"This Life" (Dove) **6**:108
"This Lime-Tree Bower My Prison" (Coleridge) **11**:51, 53, 72, 83, 88-9, 97, 104, 107; **39**:127, 161; **67**:281
"This love lost to all" (Char)
See "Cet amour à tous retiré"
"This Marriage" (Cohen) **109**:23
"This Moment" (Boland) **58**:18
"This Morning" (Carver) **54**:21-22
"This Morning" (Cervantes) **35**:118
This Music Crept by Me upon the Waters (MacLeish) **47**:175, 210
"This, My Song, is Made for Kerensky" (Lindsay) **23**:269
"This Near-At-Hand" (Rossetti) **7**:276
This Neutral Realm (Montague) **106**:319-22
"This Night Only" (Rexroth) **95**:254
"This nycht, befoir the dawning cleir" (Dunbar) **67**:13, 18
"This nycht in my sleip I wes agast" (Dunbar) **67**:14, 16
"This Occurs To Me" (Ortiz) **17**:225
"This Ol' World" (Alurista) **34**:22
"This Old Woman" (Serote) **113**:292
"This Page My Pigeon" (Birney) **52**:22
"This Place Rumord to Have Been Sodom" (Duncan) **2**:127
"This Pleasing Anxious Being" (Wilbur) **51**:332-33, 336
"This poetry anthology i'm reading" (Reed) **68**:348
"This Praying Fool" (Kumin) **15**:180
"This Room and Everything in It" (Lee) **24**:243
"This Side of the Truth" (Thomas)
See "This Side of Truth"

"This Side of Truth" (Thomas) **2**:390; **52**:316
"This Summer and Last" (Hardy) **92**:324
"This sun on this rubble after rain" (Brutus) **24**:113
"This, That, and the Other" (Nemerov) **24**:298, 303
"This To Do" (Thomas) **99**:328-30, 334-36, 340
This Tree Will Be Here for a Thousand Years (Bly) **39**:46, 53, 69, 85-7, 99
"This Urn Contains Earth from German Concentration Camps" (Lorde) **12**:136
"This Was a Poet" (Dickinson) **1**:96, 102
"This Was My Meal" (Corso) **33**:5, 41, 43; **108**:24, 39
"This waverand warldis wretchidnes" (Dunbar) **67**:11, 67
"This Way Is Not a Way" (Snyder) **21**:310
"This Will Be Her Shining Hour" (Berrigan) **103**:37, 42-43
"This Winter" (Mueller) **33**:193
"Thistledown" (Merrill) **28**:228
"Thistles" (Hughes) **7**:121, 137; **89**:103, 218-19, 228
"Tho I cannot your crueltie constrain" (Wyatt) **27**:321
Thomae Campiani Poemata. Ad Thamesin. Fragmentum Umbra. Liber Elegiarum. Liber Epigrammatum (Campion) **87**:4, 12, 96
Thomas and Beulah (Dove) **6**:104, 107, 110-20, 122
"Thomas at the Wheel" (Dove) **6**:111
Thomas Campiani Epigrammatum Libri II. Umbra. Elegiarum liber unus (Campion) **87**:13
"Thomas Jefferson" (Niedecker) **42**:107-9
Thomas Kinsella: Collected Poems 1956-1994 (Kinsella) **69**:115, 125-46
"Thomas Mann" (Szymborska) **44**:294
"Thomas Rhodes" (Masters) **36**:230, 232
Thomas Traherne: Centuries, Poems, and Thanksgivings (Traherne) **70**:170, 173-76, 216-17, 221-25
"Thomas Trevelyn" (Masters) **36**:190
"Thompson's Lunch Room" (Lowell) **13**:79
"Thor" (Tennyson) **101**:194
"Thorkild's Song" (Kipling) **3**:183
"The Thorn" (Wordsworth) **4**:381, 402, 412, 416-17, 426, 428; **67**:261-62, 269, 276, 278, 280, 282-83, 296-98, 304-5, 311-14, 317-22, 324, 328, 346-48, 357, 359-62, 368
"A Thorn Forever in the Breast" (Cullen) **20**:63
"Thorn Piece" (Lowell) **13**:85
"Thoroughgo" (Char)
See "La minutieuse"
"Thorow" (Howe) **54**:38, 40, 48, 52, 58, 95, 97, 112, 125, 130, 135-36
"Those Being Eaten by America" (Bly) **39**:9, 12, 48, 50
"Those Dancing Days Are Gone" (Yeats) **20**:328
"Those eies which set my fancie on a fire" (Raleigh) **31**:201, 219, 249-50, 253
"Those Eyes Which Set My Fancy on a Fire" (Raleigh)
See "Those eies which set my fancie on a fire"
"Those fireballs, those ashes" (Spender) **71**:189, 220
"Those Others" (Thomas) **99**:269-70
"Those Times" (Sexton) **2**:362-63, 370
"Those Various Scalpels" (Moore) **4**:263-64, 270; **49**:93, 113, 118, 172, 174-76
"Those Who Do Not Dance" (Mistral)
See "Los que no danzan"
"Those Who Fought For the Achaean League" (Cavafy) **36**:8, 17, 58, 60, 84
"Those Who Lost" (Herbert) **50**:17
"Those Who Love" (Teasdale) **31**:379
"Those Who Pass Between Fleeting Words" (Darwish) **86**:3
Those Who Ride the Night Winds (Giovanni) **19**:126-27, 137-38, 142-43
"Those who through their tears" (Castro)
See "Los que a través de sus lágrimas"
"Those Winter Sundays" (Hayden) **6**:194-95
"The Thou" (Montale)
See "Il tu"
"Thou Art Indeed Just, Lord" (Hopkins) **15**:171
"Thou art not faire" (Campion) **87**:64
"Thou blindmans marke" (Sidney) **32**:239
"Thou Camest to Thy Bower, My Love" (Tennyson) **101**:246
"Thou canst read nothing" (Crane) **99**:134, 138
"Thou didst delight my eyes" (Bridges) **28**:85
"Thou Dusky Spirit of the Wood" (Thoreau) **30**:223
"Thou Famished Grave, I Will Not Fill Thee Yet" (Millay) **6**:242
"Thou has made me, And shall they worke decay?" (Donne) **43**:160
"Thou joy'st, fond boy" (Campion) **87**:72
"Thou Shalt Not Kill" (Rexroth) **20**:181, 187, 193, 205, 218
Thou Shalt Not Kill: A Memorial for Dylan Thomas (Rexroth) **95**:247, 249-50, 254, 258, 263, 273-74, 306, 314-15, 333-34, 338, 349
"Thou that knowst for whom I mourn" (Vaughan) **81**:325
"Thou Unbelieving Heart" (Kunitz) **19**:155
"Though I regarded not" (Surrey) **59**:297
"Though you are yoong" (Campion) **87**:25
"Though your strangenesse frets my heart" (Campion) **87**:32-33, 56, 67
"Thought" (Corso) **108**:18
"A Thought" (Stevenson) **84**:341
"Thought and Image" (Muir) **49**:300
"Thought for a Sunshiny morning" (Parker) **28**:362
A Thought Is the Bride of What Thinking (Hejinian) **108**:253, 288, 291-92
"The Thought Machine" (Stafford) **71**:262
"A Thought of Columbus" (Whitman)
See "A Prayer of Columbus"
"The Thought of Heaven" (Stern) **115**:270
"The Thought-Fox" (Hughes) **7**:120, 158, 166, 168-69; **89**:142-43, 149, 156, 186, 206, 211, 221-24, 228, 240, 263
"A Thought Revolved" (Stevens) **110**:93, 97
"Thoughts" (Howe) **81**:22, 47
"Thoughts" (Teasdale) **31**:357, 360
"Thoughts" (Traherne) **70**:194-96, 198, 204, 253, 275-77, 317-18
"Thoughts about the Christian Doctrine of Eternal Hell" (Smith) **12**:301, 325, 333
"Thoughts about the Person from Porlock" (Smith) **12**:293, 330, 350
"Thoughts During an Air Raid" (Spender) **71**:202, 204, 226
"Thoughts fer the Discuraged Farmer" (Riley) **48**:288, 333, 335
"Thoughts I" (Traherne) **70**:194-95, 198-99, 201, 203-4, 317-18
"Thoughts II" (Traherne) **70**:194-95, 289, 318
"Thoughts III" (Traherne) **70**:183, 194-95, 318
"Thoughts IV" (Traherne) **70**:183, 277, 318
"Thoughts I-IV" (Traherne) **70**:317
"Thoughts in 1938" (Sassoon) **12**:252
"Thoughts in Bed upon Waking and Rising" (Hunt) **73**:154
"Thoughts in Separation" (Meynell) **112**:153, 157, 162, 189
"The Thoughts of an Old Artist" (Cavafy) **36**:94-95
"Thoughts of Death / Crowd Over My Happiness" (Brown) **55**:74, 110, 114
"Thoughts on a Breath" (Ginsberg) **4**:76
"Thoughts on His Excellency Major General Lee" (Wheatley) **3**:337
"Thoughts on Looking into a Thicket" (Ciardi) **69**:10, 33, 38, 55
"Thoughts on One's Head" (Meredith) **28**:174, 211
"Thoughts on Saving the Manatee" (Kumin) **15**:211
"Thoughts on 'The Diary of a Nobody'" (Betjeman) **75**:15, 20
"Thoughts on the Shape of the Human Body" (Brooke) **24**:56-7
"Thoughts on the Works of Providence" (Wheatley) **3**:332, 339, 358, 361, 363
Thoughts under the Clouds (Jaccottet)
See *Pensées sous les nuages: Poèmes*
"Thoughts While Driving Home" (Updike) **90**:348, 358
"Thou-poems" (Stramm)
See "Du-Gedichte"
"The Thousand and One Nights" (Borges) **32**:58
"The Thousand and Second Night" (Merrill) **28**:222, 225-26, 228, 230-32, 234, 250, 252-53
A Thousand Kisses Deep (Cohen) **109**:79-80
"Thousand League Pool" (Tu Fu) **9**:333
"A Thousand Thousand Times" (Breton) **15**:73
"The Thraldom" (Cowley) **90**:13
"Thrawn Janet" (Burns) **114**:8
Thread-Suns (Celan)
See *Fadensonnen*
"The Threatened Man" (Borges)
See "The Threatened One"
"The Threatened One" (Borges) **32**:58
"Three" (Corso) **33**:41; **108**:19
"Three" (Gunn) **26**:208
"III" (Joyce) **22**:144, 160, 162, 164, 166
"Three Airs" (O'Hara) **45**:219
"3 a.m. in the High Street" (Abse) **41**:9
"3 A.M. Kitchen: My Father Talking" (Gallagher) **9**:53
"Three Angels" (Dylan) **37**:56
"Three Bushes" (Yeats) **20**:332; **51**:139
"Three Cantos" (Pound) **95**:158-65, 167
"Three Cantos II" (Pound) **95**:158
"The Three Captains" (Kipling) **3**:157
"The Three Children" (Jacobsen) **62**:320
"The Three Conspirators" (Nemerov) **24**:293
"Three Crows" (Kenyon) **57**:45
"Three Darknesses" (Warren) **37**:365-66, 377-81
"Three Days" (Spender) **71**:225
"Three Days' Ride" (Benét) **64**:19, 52, 55
"The Three Decker" (Kipling) **3**:161
"Three Desk Objects" (Atwood) **8**:2, 13
"Three Dollars Cash" (Walker) **30**:367
"Three Eggs Up" (Ciardi) **69**:6
"Three Elegiac Poems" (Berry) **28**:15
"Three Faces" (Swinburne) **24**:329
"Three Floors" (Kunitz) **19**:178
"Three Gardens" (Schuyler) **88**:217
"The Three Gatekeepers of the Jealous Husband" (Dafydd ap Gwilym)
See "Tri Phorthor Eiddig"
"Three Ghosts" (Sandburg) **2**:309
"Three Glimpses of Irish Life" (Kavanagh) **33**:157
"The Three Graves" (Coleridge) **11**:117; **67**:280, 354
"Three Green Windows" (Sexton) **2**:363
"The Three Gunners" (Gilmore) **87**:303
"Three Hearts" (Stern) **115**:271
Three Hundred and Sixty Degrees of Blackness Comin at You (Sanchez) **9**:222
"Three Implements" (Bell) **79**:33
"Three Italian Pictures" (Loy) **16**:313
"Three Kinds of Pleasures" (Bly) **39**:3, 7, 76-8, 82
"Three Kings" (Spark) **72**:226
"The Three Kings" (Zagajewski) **27**:396
Three Legendary Sonnets (Kinsella) **69**:115
"3 Local Men Vanquish Monster in Fight" (Rexroth) **95**:257
"Three Loves" (Corso) **33**:25; **108**:34
Three Material Cantos (Neruda)
See *Homenaje a Pablo Neruda de los poetas espanoles: Tres cantos materiales*

Three Material Songs (Neruda)
See *Homenaje a Pablo Neruda de los poetas espanoles: Tres cantos materiales*
"Three Meditations" (Levertov) **11**:169
"The Three Mirrors" (Muir) **49**:246-47, 249-50
"Three Modes of History and Culture" (Baraka) **4**:16; **113**:16
"Three Moments in Paris" (Loy) **16**:312, 327-28
"Three Monologues" (Meynell)
See "A Study"
"Three Mountebanks" (Ransom) **61**:289
"Three Movements and a Coda" (Baraka) **4**:9, 19, 24; **113**:14
"Three Nuns" (Rossetti) **7**:277
"The Three Oddest Words" (Szymborska)
See "Trzy slowa najdziwiniejsze"
"3 of Swords—for dark men under the white moon" (Wakoski) **15**:362, 367
"Three old men" (Illyés)
See "Harom oreg"
"Three Palms" (Lermontov)
See "Tri palmy"
"Three Palm-Trees" (Lermontov)
See "Tri palmy"
"Three Pieces on the Smoke of Autumn" (Sandburg) **41**:313
"Three Poems" (Niedecker) **42**:147, 152
"Three Poems" (Parra)
See "Tres Poesías"
"Three Poems" (Thomas) **52**:316, 322, 324
Three Poems (Ashbery) **26**:108-9, 114-16, 118, 123, 126, 130, 135, 143, 149, 167, 169-71, 173-74
Three Poems (Curnow) **48**:25-26
"Three Poems about Children" (Clarke) **112**:31, 38, 52
"Three Poems after Jaccottet" (Mahon) **60**:188
"Three Poems Apart" (MacNeice) **61**:138
"Three Poems from Memory" (Herbert) **50**:18
Three Poems under a Flag of Convenience (Elytis) **21**:131
"Three Poets" (Oppen) **35**:341
"The Three Porters of Eiddig" (Dafydd ap Gwilym)
See "Tri Phorthor Eiddig"
"Three Postcards from the Monastery" (Merton) **10**:332
"3 Prophetic Visions of Egyptian Downfall" (Corso) **108**:12
"Three Questions" (Gower) **59**:88
"Three Romances" (Hope) **56**:269, 271, 287
Three Secret Poems (Seferis)
See *Tria Krilka Poema*
"Three Sentences for a Dead Swan" (Wright) **36**:328, 341, 345-46, 363
"Three Sheets in the Wind" (Chappell) **105**:32, 40, 44, 69-70, 75, 81
"The Three Silences of Molinos" (Longfellow) **30**:51
"Three Skies" (Stern) **115**:268, 271
"Three Small Oranges" (Kenyon) **57**:12, 41, 44
"Three Songs" (Crane) **3**:106; **99**:70
"Three Songs at the End of Summer" (Kenyon) **57**:45
"Three Songs for a Colored Singer" (Bishop) **34**:160
"Three Sonnets" (Sarton) **39**:322
"Three Sonnets for the Eyes" (Bishop) **34**:94, 160-61
"Three Sons Had Abraham" (Amichai) **38**:50
"Three Speeches in a Sick Room" (Wright) **36**:336
"Three Spring Notations on Bipeds" (Sandburg) **41**:285
"Three Stanzas from Goethe" (Wright) **36**:331, 338
"Three Stops to Ten Sleep" (Hugo) **68**:253
"Three Street Musicians" (Abse) **41**:28
"Three Studies on the Subject of Realism" (Herbert) **50**:3, 25, 31
"Three Sunsets" (Carroll) **74**:65
Three Sunsets (Carroll) **74**:3, 64, 66
"The Three Susans" (Kenyon) **57**:14-15
The Three Taverns (Robinson) **1**:465-66, 468
"Three Tears" (Stern) **115**:249
Three Tenors, One Vehicle (Kennedy) **93**:144-45
"Three Things" (Sarton) **39**:367
"Three Things" (Yeats) **20**:328
"Three Times in Love" (Graves) **6**:172
"Three Times the Truth" (Elytis) **21**:123
"The Three Tommies" (Service) **70**:132
"Three Travellers Watch a Sunrise" (Stevens) **6**:295
"Three United States Sonnets" (Cummings) **5**:94
"Three Valentines" (Bishop) **34**:161
"Three Versions of Judas" (Borges)
See "Tres versiones de Judas"
"Three Voices" (Abse) **41**:3
"3 Voices" (Carroll)
See "The Three Voices"
"The Three Voices" (Carroll) **74**:7, 69
"Three Voices" (Plath) **37**:210
"The Three Voices" (Service) **70**:114
"Three White Vases" (Swenson) **14**:273
"Three Women: A Poem for Three Voices" (Plath) **37**:209-10
"Three Woodchoppers" (Francis) **34**:246
"The Threefold Place" (Muir) **49**:265
"Threefold Time" (Muir) **49**:229
"Threes" (Atwood) **8**:21
"Three-year-old" (Tagore)
See "Tritiya"
Threnodia Augustalis (Dryden) **25**:88-9
"A Threnodiall Dialogue between The Second and Third Ranks" (Taylor) **63**:279
"Threnody" (Emerson) **18**:69, 81, 84, 86, 90, 102-3, 112-3
"Threnody" (Parker) **28**:360
"Threnody for a Brown Girl" (Cullen) **20**:57-58, 62, 66
The Thresher's Labour (Duck) **89**:6, 10-11, 20-21, 27-28, 34-35, 37-43, 46, 48-50, 52-53, 56-63, 66-70, 72-74, 76-77, 83-85, 88-89
"The Threshing Machine" (Meynell) **112**:154
"Threshold" (Char)
See "Seuil"
"Threshold" (Thomas) **99**:274, 360
"Thrice toss these oaken ashes in the air" (Campion) **87**:13
"The Thrissill and the Rois" (Dunbar) **67**:12, 18, 25, 34, 38, 46-50, 92, 109, 128
The Throne of Labdacus (Schnackenberg) **45**:339-43, 345, 347-50
Thrones, 96-109 de los cantares (Pound) **4**:337-38, 352, 353, 357; **95**:128-29, 168, 171, 178-79, 188, 192, 198
Through an Orchard (Jaccottet)
See *À travers un verger*
"Through Corralitos under Rolls of Cloud" (Rich) **5**:401
"Through Nightmare" (Graves) **6**:137, 173
"Through the Boughs" (Carver) **54**:19
"Through the Fences that Surround You, Grita" (Alurista) **34**:23
"Through the Inner City to the Suburbs" (Angelou) **32**:3
"Through the Looking Glass" (Ferlinghetti) **1**:173
"Through the Mouth of the Whippoorwill" (Char)
See "Par la bouche de l'engoulevent"
"Through the Round Window" (McGuckian) **27**:83
"Through the Smoke Hole" (Snyder) **21**:292
"Through These Lashed Rings" (Thomas) **52**:290, 293, 295
"Throughout Our Lands" (Milosz) **8**:187, 194, 214
"Throw Away Thy Rod" (Herbert) **4**:103, 121
A Throw of the Dice Never Will Abolish Chance (Mallarmé)
See *Un coup de dés jamais n'abolira le hasard*
A Throw of the Dice Will Never Abolish Chance (Mallarmé)
See *Un coup de dés jamais n'abolira le hasard*
"Throwing the Apple" (Eberhart) **76**:47
"Thrush" (Seferis) **66**:90, 92, 94-96, 98, 113-14, 119-20, 122, 128, 132, 136, 138-39, 141, 148-52, 179, 194-95, 197, 206-9, 216
"The Thrush" (Thomas) **53**:294, 330
"A Thrush before Dawn" (Meynell) **112**:155, 159, 168
"The Thrush in February" (Meredith) **60**:256, 280, 299, 301, 319
"Thrush Song at Dawn" (Eberhart) **76**:13
"Thrushes" (Hughes) **7**:119, 169; **89**:130, 188, 223
"Thrushes" (Sassoon) **12**:253
"Thrust and Riposte" (Montale)
See "Botta e riposta"
"Thum Ku Klux" (Lanier) **50**:92
"Thunder Can Break" (Okigbo)
See "Come Thunder"
"Thunder in the Garden" (Morris) **55**:340
"Thunder in Tuscany" (Tomlinson) **17**:349-50
"Thunder, Momentarily Instantaneous" (Pasternak) **6**:251
"Thunderhead" (MacLeish) **47**:192
"A Thunder-Storm" (Dickinson) **1**:79
"The Thunderstorm" (Trakl)
See "Das Gewitter"
"Thursday" (Millay) **6**:208, 211
"Thursday" (Schuyler) **88**:212
"Thursday" (Seferis) **66**:186
"Thursday: The Bassette Table: Smilinda, Cardelia" (Montagu) **16**:338, 349
"Thurso's Landing" (Jeffers) **17**:141-42
Thurso's Landing, and Other Poems (Jeffers) **17**:122, 124-25, 135, 142
"Thus I resolve" (Campion) **87**:71
"Thus Truly" (Ignatow) **34**:324
"Thy Beauty Fades" (Very) **86**:46, 58, 79-80
"Thy Brother's Blood" (Very) **86**:88
"Thy Neighbor" (Very) **86**:97, 113
"Thy Will Be Done" (Whittier) **93**:181, 213
"Thyestes" (Davie) **29**:107
"Thyme Flowering Among Rocks" (Wilbur) **51**:235
"Thyrsis" (Arnold) **5**:7-8, 18-19, 21, 23-4, 33, 36, 45, 47, 52, 55-6
"Ti" (Tolson) **88**:331
"Ti svelerà" (Ungaretti) **57**:344
"Tiara" (Doty) **53**:72
"Tiare Tahiti" (Brooke) **24**:53, 64, 66, 73-4, 78, 86
"Tiburón" (Espada) **74**:116, 123, 139
"Tic Tac Toe" (Stone) **53**:229
"Tick Tock" (Ignatow) **34**:213, 277
"Ticonderoga" (Stevenson) **84**:331-32
"Tidal Friction" (Kaufman) **74**:241
Tide and Continuities (Viereck) **27**:292, 294-96
Tide and Continuities Last and First Poems 1995-1938 (Viereck) **27**:295
"The Tide at Long Point" (Swenson) **14**:247, 249
"Tide Ratio" (Char) **56**:138
"The Tide Rises, The Tide Falls" (Longfellow) **30**:36, 47
"Tidemark" (Ní Chuilleanáin) **34**:349
Tides (Montague) **106**:215, 218, 232-33, 244-46, 277-78, 285-86, 298, 313, 328
"Tides" (Teasdale) **31**:336
"Tiempo" (Storni) **33**:244, 302-03
"Tiempo de esterilidad" (Storni) **33**:261, 294-95, 299, 302, 305
"Tiempo libre" (Guillén) **35**:228, 229
"Tienanmen, the Aftermath" (Chin) **40**:9
Tiepolo's Hound (Walcott) **46**:302, 322
"Tierra de azules montañas" (Guillén) **23**:125

"Tierra del Fuego" (Zagajewski) **27**:396, 400
"Tierra en la sierra y en el llano" (Guillén) **23**:127
"La tierra se llama Juan" (Neruda) **4**:294; **64**:316
"The Tiger" (Belloc) **24**:24
"The Tiger" (Blake)
See "The Tyger"
"The Tiger" (Borges)
See "El tigre"
Tiger Joy (Benét) **64**:19
"Tiger-psalm" (Hughes) **89**:129, 152
"Tightrope Walker" (Goodison) **36**:143
"El tigre" (Borges) **32**:64
"The Tigress" (Wickham) **110**:266
"Till de folkhemske" (Ekeloef) **23**:76
"Till Other Voices Wake Us" (Oppen) **35**:301
"Tillie" (de la Mare) **77**:73, 113
The Tilted Cart (Gilmore) **87**:298-99, 301
"Tilting Sail" (Hass) **16**:251
"Tim Turpin" (Hood) **93**:52
"The Timber" (Vaughan) **81**:341
"Timber Waggons" (Masefield) **78**:30
"Timbuctoo" (Tennyson) **6**:358, 389, 407-08, 413, 415-18; **101**:140, 245-46
"Timbuctu" (Brathwaite) **56**:29
"Time" (Char)
See "Le Temps"
"Time" (Peacock) **87**:326
"Time" (Stafford) **71**:293
"Time" (Very) **86**:157
"Time" (Wright) **36**:378
Time (Amichai)
See *Ha-Zeman*
"Time and Life" (Swinburne) **24**:323
"Time and the Garden" (Winters) **82**:333, 341
"The Time and the Place" (Carman) **34**:208
"Time and Violence" (Boland) **58**:23, 27
"Time as Hypnosis" (Warren) **37**:366
"The Time before You" (McGuckian) **27**:82
"Time Blonde" (Dorn) **115**:155
"Time Does Not Bring Relief" (Millay) **6**:205
"Time Eating" (Douglas) **106**:197
"Time Flies" (Tapahonso) **65**:224, 258
"Time Goes By" (Pavese)
See "Il tempo passa"
Time in Armagh (Montague) **106**:306, 315
"Time in Our Time" (Spender) **71**:189
Time in the Rock (Aiken)
See *Time in the Rock: Preludes to Definition*
Time in the Rock: Preludes to Definition (Aiken) **26**:6, 12, 19, 23, 29, 52, 57
"Time Is an Inclusion Series Said McTaggart" (Rexroth) **95**:255, 260, 269
"Time Is Fleeting" (Carducci)
See "Ruit hora"
"Time is Mute" (Ungaretti) **57**:360
"Time Is the Mercy of Eternity" (Rexroth) **20**:181, 208-09, 216-18; **95**:250, 260, 273, 290, 295, 326
"Time Lapse with Tulips" (Gallagher) **9**:37
"A Time of Day" (Curnow) **48**:53
"Time of Disturbance" (Jeffers) **17**:141
The Time of History (Guillén)
See *Clamor*
"Time on Main" (Doty) **53**:69
"Time Out" (Montague) **106**:327
Time Overflows (Éluard)
See *Le temps déborde*
"Time Passes" (de la Mare) **77**:71, 116
"Time Passing, Beloved" (Davie) **29**:94, 100, 108
"Time Spirals" (Rexroth) **20**:195, 217-18; **95**:293-94, 321
"A Time to Dance" (Day Lewis) **11**:126
A Time to Dance and Other Poems (Day Lewis) **11**:126-27, 129
"Time to Kill in Gallup" (Ortiz) **17**:240
"Time to Rise" (Stevenson) **84**:346
"Time unhinged the gates" (Tolson) **88**:231
"The Time Was Aeon" (Owen) **102**:146, 149
"A Time Zone" (Koch) **80**:301
"Time-Bomb" (Birney) **52**:7-8, 101
"Timehri" (Brathwaite) **56**:75
"The Time-Piece" (Cowper) **40**:48-9, 51-2, 66, 117, 123
"A Timepiece" (Merrill) **28**:225, 234
"Times" (Whittier)
See "Stanzas for the Times"
"The Times" (Whittier) **93**:201
"Times at Bellosguardo" (Montale) **13**:147, 152
"Time's Betrayal" (Melville) **82**:154
"Time's Dedication" (Schwartz) **8**:305, 307, 314
"Time's Exile" (Stafford) **71**:262
"Times Go by Turns" (Southwell) **83**:281
Time's Laughingstocks and Other Verses (Hardy) **8**:93, 123; **92**:241-42, 247, 287, 290
"Time's Long Ago" (Melville) **82**:204
"Times Passes" (Pavese)
See "Il tempo passa"
"Time's Revenges" (Browning) **2**:33
"Time's Reversals: A Daughter's Paradox" (Meynell) **112**:153
"Times Square Water Music" (Clampitt) **19**:81, 88
"The Times Table" (Frost) **1**:205
Timespace Huracán (Alurista) **34**:4, 15, 26-28, 31
"Timesweep" (Sandburg) **41**:303-4
"Time-Travel" (Olds) **22**:322
"Timoleon" (Melville) **82**:74, 104, 145, 147
Timoleon (Melville) **82**:74-75, 77, 86, 90, 97-98, 104-6, 141, 143, 145-48, 151, 156, 182, 185, 199, 211
"Timon" (Leapor) **85**:213
"Timon" (Wilmot) **66**:235, 240, 263-64, 267-68, 310, 321
"Timor dei" (Cunningham) **92**:135, 160, 166, 173, 177, 186, 188
"Timor mortis conturbat me" (Dunbar) **67**:46, 48-49, 101, 103-6
"Tin Roof" (Ondaatje) **28**:314
"Tin Roof Blues" (Brown) **55**:70, 110, 153, 156
"Tin Roof Blues" (Chappell) **105**:65, 69
"Tin Wedding Whistle" (Nash) **21**:268
"Tinder" (Heaney) **18**:202
"The Tingling Back" (Shapiro) **25**:317, 320
"The Tinker Camp" (Hugo) **68**:290
"Tinker's Wife" (Kavanagh) **33**:74
"Tinseltown" (Szirtes) **51**:172
"Tintern Abbey" (Wordsworth)
See "Lines Composed a Few Miles above Tintern Abbey, on Revisiting the Banks of the Wye during a Tour, July 13, 1798"
"Tippoo's Tiger" (Moore) **49**:149
"Tirade for the Lyric Muse" (Boland) **58**:48, 98
"Tirade for the Mimic Muse" (Boland) **58**:4-5, 12, 29, 44
"Tired" (Silverstein) **49**:329-30
"The Tired Man" (Wickham) **110**:277, 311
"Tired Memory" (Patmore) **59**:223
"Tired Old Whore" (Ai) **72**:29
"Tiresias" (Tennyson) **6**:361; **101**:121-24, 241
Tiresais, and Other Poems (Tennyson) **101**:119
Tiresias: A Poem (Clarke) **112**:76, 89, 125-27, 129, 131-33, 136-39
Tiriel (Blake) **12**:61; **63**:98, 104
"Tirzey Potter" (Masters) **1**:338
"'Tis April and the morning, love" (Clare) **23**:23
"'Tis Now, Since I Sate Down Before" (Suckling) **30**:141
"'Tis said, that some have died for love . . ." (Wordsworth) **67**:329, 331
"Tishina" (Pasternak) **6**:286
"Tit for Tat" (de la Mare) **77**:73, 114
"Tithon" (Tennyson) **101**:220
"Tithonus" (Mahon) **60**:177, 192, 194; **101**:119, 121, 123-24, 127, 219-20, 224, 250
"Tithonus" (Tennyson) **6**:366, 411
"Title Divine Is Mine the Wife without the Sign" (Dickinson) **1**:93
"Titmouse" (Emerson) **18**:79, 103-4, 113
"tizoc left us his hair" (Alurista) **34**:34
"Tizzic" (Brathwaite) **56**:10, 15, 76, 88, 100
"Tlön, Uqbar, Orbis Tertius" (Borges) **32**:60, 69
"To—" (Owen) **19**:352
"T—" (Poe) **54**:264
"To—" (Poe) **1**:436, 445
"To * * * * * *" (Keats) **96**:348
"To a Babe Smiling in Her Sleep" (Harper) **21**:197
"To a Black Dancer in 'The Little Savoy'" (Hughes) **53**:79
"To a Blackbird" (Kavanagh) **33**:83, 92
"To a Blossoming Pear Tree" (Wright) **36**:308, 314, 321, 358, 369, 372, 377, 381-82, 384, 403
To a Blossoming Pear Tree (Wright) **36**:310-11, 314, 318, 320, 322, 347, 354, 356, 358, 363-64, 368-70, 377-78, 381-83, 392, 399, 403
"To a Book" (Wylie) **23**:303
"To a Brother in the Mystery" (Davie) **29**:96, 102
"To a Brown Boy" (Cullen) **20**:52, 62
"To a Brown Girl" (Cullen) **20**:52, 62
"To A Butterfly" (Merrill) **28**:247
"To a Butterfly" (Wordsworth) **67**:248
"To a Captious Critic" (Dunbar) **5**:125, 127, 135
"To a Certain Lady, in Her Garden" (Brown) **55**:110, 114
"To 'A Certain Rich Man'" (Meynell) **112**:231
"To a Chameleon" (Moore) **49**:89, 114, 118-19, 134, 140
"To a Child" (Kavanagh) **33**:92, 97, 156; **105**:155
"To a Child" (Longfellow) **30**:48
"To a Child" (Snodgrass) **74**:291, 312
"To a Child Dancing in the Wind" (Yeats) **20**:338
To a Child Embracing his Mother (Hood) **93**:62
"To a Child in Death" (Mew) **107**:56, 61
"To a Child of Quality of Five Years Old" (Prior) **102**:316
"To a Child Running with Outstretched Arms in Canyon de Chelly" (Momaday) **25**:219
"To a Clergyman on the Death of His Lady" (Wheatley) **3**:357
"To a Cold Beauty" (Hood) **93**:48
"To a Comet" (Thoreau)
See "To the Comet"
"To a Common Prostitute" (Whitman) **3**:416; **91**:347
"To a Contemporary Bunkshooter" (Sandburg)
See "To a Contemporary Bunk-Shooter"
"To a Contemporary Bunk-Shooter" (Sandburg) **2**:317, 330; **41**:238, 242, 246, 251, 255, 272, 295, 335, 351
"To a Critic" (Hood) **93**:80
"To a Cuckoo at Coolanlough" (McGuckian) **27**:103
"To a Daisy" (Meynell) **112**:153, 156, 190-91, 245, 290-91, 295
"to a dark moses" (Clifton) **17**:34
"To a Dead Beggar" (Smith) **104**:166
"To a Dead Child" (Bridges) **28**:57
"To a Dead Poet" (Cernuda) **62**:174
"To a Defeated Savior" (Wright) **36**:318, 335-36
"To a Dog Injured in the Street" (Williams) **109**:259, 261-63
"To a Downfallen Rose" (Corso) **33**:40
"To a Dreamer" (Pushkin) **10**:407
"To a Face in a Crowd" (Warren) **37**:287, 319, 330
"To a Fair Lady, Playing with a Snake" (Waller) **72**:334
"To a Fellow Scribbler" (Finch) **21**:168
"To a Fish Head Found on the Beach Near Malaga" (Levine) **22**:215
"To a Freedom Fighter" (Angelou) **32**:28
"To a Friend" (Arnold) **5**:12, 49

"To a Friend" (Cunningham) **92**:156, 166-68, 170
"To a Friend" (Herrick) **9**:90
"To a Friend" (Waller) **72**:323
"To a Friend" (Yeats) **20**:321
"To a Friend and Fellow-Poet" (MacDiarmid) **9**:183-84
"To a Friend in the Making" (Moore) **49**:115
"To a Friend in Time of Trouble" (Gunn) **26**:215
"To a Friend Parting" (Warren) **37**:284, 288, 354
"To a Friend who sent me some Roses" (Keats) **96**:346
"To a Friend Whose Work Has Come to Triumph" (Sexton) **2**:370
"To a Fringed Gentian" (Bryant) **20**:12, 45
"To a Fugitive" (Wright) **36**:335, 373
"To a Gardener" (Stevenson) **84**:303-4
"To a Gentleman at his uprising" (Davenant) **99**:165-66
"To a Gentleman on His Voyage to Great Britain for the Recovery of His Health" (Wheatley) **3**:358
"To a Gentleman Who Had Sent Him a News-Paper, and Offered to Continue It Free of Expense" (Burns) **114**:145
"To a Gentleman, who requested a Copy of Verses from the Author" (Duck) **89**:67, 75
"To a Gipsy Child by the Sea-shore" (Arnold) **5**:38, 49-50
"To a Giraffe" (Moore) **4**:242-43; **49**:145
"To a Guinea Pig" (Shapiro) **25**:269
"To a Highland Girl" (Wordsworth) **4**:404
"To a High-Toned Old Christian Man" (Stevens) **110**:90
"To a High-Toned Old Christian Woman" (Stevens) **110**:90, 174
"To a Husband" (Angelou) **32**:29
"To a Husband" (Lowell) **13**:74
"To a Japanese Poet" (Stryk) **27**:203-4
"To a Jealous Cat" (Sanchez) **9**:223, 232
"To a Lady and Her Children, On the Death of Her Son and Their Brother" (Wheatley) **3**:363
"To a Lady, from Whom He Received a Silver Pen" (Waller) **72**:361
"To a Lady in a Garden" (Waller) **72**:336-37, 372, 376
"To a Lady in a Letter" (Wilmot) **66**:307-8, 311
"To a Lady in Retirement" (Waller) **72**:337
"To a Lady on Her Remarkable Preservation in an Hurricane in North Carolina" (Wheatley) **3**:354
"To a Lady on the Death of Three Relations" (Wheatley) **3**:343, 348
"To a Lady, Quhone He List to Feyne" (Dunbar)
See "Quhone He List to Feyne"
"To a Lady Singing" (FitzGerald) **79**:69
"To a Lady that desired I would love her" (Carew) **29**:3-4
"To A Lady the Forbade to Love Before Company" (Suckling) **30**:130
"To a Lady Who Made Posies for Rings" (Cowley) **90**:13
"To a Lady with child that asked an Old Shirt" (Lovelace) **69**:199
"To a Lady's Countenance" (Wylie) **23**:321
"To a Little Child in Death" (Mew) **107**:35
"To a Little Girl, One Year Old in a Ruined Fortress" (Warren) **37**:295, 297, 300, 307, 347, 360
"To a Louse, on Seeing One on a Lady's Bonnet at Church" (Burns) **6**:65, 79; **114**:42, 59, 90, 103
"To a lovely woman" (Lermontov) **18**:303
"To a Man" (Angelou) **32**:14-17, 29
"To a Man Working His Way Through the Crowd" (Moore) **49**:114
"To a Mountain Daisy, on Turning One Down with the Plough in April, 1786" (Burns) **6**:50, 74; **114**:80, 94, 98
"To a Mouse, on Turning Her Up in Her Nest with the Plough, November, 1785" (Burns) **6**:50, 65, 74, 80, 96; **114**:42, 51, 90, 92, 101, 103-5
"To a Nightingale" (Smith)
See "Sonnet 3"
"To a Painter in England" (Walcott) **46**:271
"To a Passing Woman" (Baudelaire)
See "À une passante"
"To a Poet" (Jiménez) **7**:183
"To a Poet" (McKay) **2**:206
"To a Poet" (Meynell) **112**:192, 247, 290-91, 295
"To a Polish Mother" (Mickiewicz) **38**:158
"To a Poor Old Woman" (Williams) **7**:390, 399
"To a Portrait" (Lermontov) **18**:297
"To a Portrait in a Gallery" (Page) **12**:168
"To a Prize Bird" (Moore)
See "To Bernard Shaw: A Prize Bird"
"To a Pupil" (Whitman) **91**:313, 320
"To a Red haired Beggar Girl" (Baudelaire) **106**:4
"To a Republican Friend" (Arnold) **5**:49
"To a Romantic" (Tate) **50**:285, 306
"To a Romantic Novelist" (Tate) **50**:306
"To a Romanticist" (Tate) **50**:228, 285
"To a Sad Daughter" (Ondaatje) **28**:316
"To a Saxon Poet" (Borges) **32**:95
"To a Screen-Maker" (Moore) **49**:104-5, 107
"To a Seamew" (Swinburne) **24**:313, 328
"To a Shade" (Yeats) **20**:348
"to a Sinister Potato" (Viereck) **27**:259, 262, 279
"To a Skylark" (Meredith) **60**:332
"To a Skylark" (Shelley) **67**:180
"To a Sky-Lark" (Wordsworth) **67**:248
"To a Snail" (Mew) **107**:57
"To a Solitary Disciple" (Williams) **7**:357, 378
"To a Southern Statesman" (Whittier) **93**:209
"To a Sower" (Mistral)
See "A un sembrador"
"To a Spanish Poet (for Manuel Altolaguirre)" (Spender) **71**:187, 202, 204, 228
"To a Spider" (Southey) **111**:252
"To a Steam Roller" (Moore) **49**:114-15, 119-20, 126, 155
"To a Stranger" (Whitman) **91**:311, 342
"To a Strategist" (Moore) **4**:266; **49**:114
"To a Stray Fowl" (Thoreau) **30**:235
"To a sword in York" (Borges)
See "A una espada en York"
"To a Teacher" (Cohen) **109**:52-54
"To a Ten-Months' Child" (Justice) **64**:279
To a Tense Serenity (Char)
See *À une sérénité crispée*
"To a Town Poet" (Reese) **29**:333
"To a Very Young Lady" (Waller) **72**:297, 374
"To a War Poet" (Enright) **93**:33
"To a Waterfowl" (Bryant) **20**:5-6, 14, 18, 35, 42
"To a Waterfowl" (Hall) **70**:26, 32
"To a Western Bard Still a Whoop and a Holler Away from English Poetry" (Meredith) **28**:174, 187, 207
"To a Winter Squirrel" (Brooks) **7**:82
"To a Woman Passing By" (Baudelaire)
See "À une passante"
"To a Wreath of Snow" (Brontë) **8**:67, 73
"To a Young Actress" (Pushkin) **10**:407
"To a Young American the Day after the Fall of Barcelona" (Ciardi) **69**:24
"To A Young Friend" (Burns)
See "Epistle to a Young Friend"
"To a Young Girl" (Millay) **6**:217
"To a Young Girl" (Yeats) **20**:330
"To a Young Lady Netting" (Peacock) **87**:321
"To a Young Lady on her Birthday" (Johnson) **81**:115, 241
"To a Young Man Entering the World" (Smith) **104**:166
"To a Young Mother" (Jaccottet) **98**:199
"To a Young Poet" (Thomas) **99**:280
"To A.D., unreasonable distrustfull of her owne beauty" (Carew) **29**:29
"To Adversity" (Gray)
See "Ode to Adversity"
"To Ailsa Rock" (Keats) **96**:284
"To A.L. Perswasions to Love" (Carew) **29**:10, 23-24, 66-68
"To Alchymists" (Jonson) **17**:197
"To Alexander" (Pushkin)
See "Aleksandru"
"To Alexis, in Answer to His Poem against Fruition" (Behn) **13**:26
"To Alexis in Answer to his Poem against Fruition. Ode by Mrs. B" (Behn) **88**:74, 87, 104
"To Alexis, On his saying I lov'd a Man that talk'd much. By Mrs. B." (Behn) **88**:74, 105
"To All Brothers" (Sanchez) **9**:221, 224, 232
"To All Gentleness" (Williams) **7**:354
"To All Sisters" (Sanchez) **9**:224, 231-32
"To all vertuous Ladies in generall" (Lanyer) **60**:5, 17, 52, 90-92, 97, 111-12
"To Althea: From Prison" (Lovelace) **69**:156-57, 159, 166, 169, 172, 179, 181-85, 203, 206, 208-9, 217, 219, 223, 229, 249
"To Amarantha" (Lovelace)
See "To Amarantha, That She Would Dishevell Her Hair"
"To Amarantha, That She Would Dishevell Her Hair" (Lovelace) **69**:156, 181, 191-93, 196-97, 199, 226, 238, 243-44, 249
"To America" (Johnson) **24**:131, 142, 148, 158, 160
"To Amintas, upon Reading the Lives of Some of the Romans" (Behn) **13**:32
"To Amoret" (Waller) **72**:338
"To Amoret Walking in a Starry Evening" (Vaughan) **81**:306, 308
"To Amoret Weeping" (Vaughan) **81**:357-58
"To an Actress" (Hardy) **92**:241-42, 245-46
"To an Alexandrian Poet" (Enright) **93**:7
"To an American Poet Just Dead" (Wilbur) **51**:192, 219
"To an Ancestor" (Stone) **53**:215
"To an Ancient" (Frost) **1**:200
"To an Apple" (Ignatow) **34**:305
"To an Athlete Dying Young" (Housman) **2**:180, 183, 185, 191-94, 198, 201; **43**:214, 217, 248-49, 254, 261, 273
"To an Earth of Dawn" (Bonnefoy)
See "À une Terre d'aube"
"To an Impersonator of Rosalind" (Hardy) **92**:241, 245-46
"To an Insect" (Holmes) **71**:91
"To an Intra-Mural Rat" (Moore) **49**:114, 119
"To an Old Lady" (Empson) **104**:83-84, 88, 90, 100, 118, 122
"To an Old Man" (Randall) **86**:291, 297, 346-47
"To an Old Philosopher in Rome" (Stevens) **6**:304, 324, 328; **110**:226
"To Ann Scott-Moncrieff (1914-1943)" (Muir)
See "For Ann Scott-Moncrieff (1914-1943)"
"To Another Housewife" (Wright) **14**:356
"To Antenor on a Paper of mine which J J threatens to publish to prejudice him" (Philips) **40**:273, 297
"To Anthea" (Herrick) **9**:145
"To Anthea Lying in Bed" (Herrick) **9**:137
"To Anthea, Who May Command Him Any Thing" (Herrick) **9**:102
"To Antiquity" (Meynell) **112**:231
"To Any Dead Officer" (Sassoon) **12**:268, 277
"To Any Poet" (Meynell)
See "To a Poet"
"To Any Reader" (Stevenson) **84**:328, 347
"To Aphrodite, with a Talisman" (Wylie) **23**:320, 324
"To Art" (Reese) **29**:354
"To Artemisia" (Leapor)
See "An Epistle to Artemisia. On Fame."

—*To Augustus* (Pope)
See *Epistle to Augustus*
"To Autumn" (Ashbery) **26**:160
"To Autumn" (Glück) **16**:142, 149
"To Autumn" (Keats)
See "Ode to Autumn"
"To Autumn" (Kinsella) **69**:67, 69, 96-97
"To Autumn" (Wilbur) **51**:237
"To Bake the Bread of Yearning" (Amichai) **38**:54
"To Bargain Toboggan To-Woo!" (Nash) **21**:265
To Bathurst (Pope)
See *An Epistle to Bathurst*
"To B— E—" (Berryman) **64**:102-3
"To Be a Jew in the Twentieth Century" (Rukeyser) **12**:234
To Be a Poet (Seifert)
See *Býti básníkem*
"To Be Carved on a Stone at Thoor Ballylee" (Yeats) **20**:346, 348
"To Be Dead" (Jarrell) **41**:214
"To Be Hungry Is To Be Great" (Williams) **109**:286
"To Be in Love" (Brooks) **7**:81-2
"To Be in Love" (Randall) **86**:345
"To Be Liked by You Would Be a Calamity" (Moore) **4**:250; **49**:114, 120, 122
To Be of Use (Piercy) **29**:302, 309-10, 323
"To Be of Use" (Piercy) **29**:309
"To Be Quicker for Black Political Prisoners" (Madhubuti) **5**:330, 346
"To be Sung" (Viereck) **27**:265
"To Be Sung on the Water" (Bogan) **12**:90, 124
"To Be Written on the Mirror in Whitewash" (Bishop) **34**:67, 109
To Bedlam and Part Way Back (Sexton) **2**:345-47, 349-50, 353, 355, 357-58, 360, 363, 367; **79**:187, 189-90, 195, 202-4, 208, 214-15, 226-27, 231, 236, 248, 257-58, 271, 275, 302, 310
"To Beethoven" (Lanier) **50**:77-78
"To Begin" (Strand) **63**:145, 147
"To Begin With" (Guillén)
See "Por de pronto"
"To Ben Jonson Upon occasion of his Ode of defiance annext to his play of the new Inne" (Carew) **29**:7, 32, 82
"To Bennie" (McKay) **2**:221
"To Bernard Shaw: A Prize Bird" (Moore) **49**:114, 116, 134
"To Billy Sunday" (Sandburg)
See "To a Contemporary Bunk-Shooter"
"To Blk/Record/Buyers" (Sanchez) **9**:209, 217
"To Blossom in Winter" (Char)
See "Eclore en hiver"
"To Blossoms" (Herrick) **9**:145
"To Bobbie" (Creeley) **73**:11
"To Bring the Dead to Life" (Graves) **6**:143
"To Brooklyn Bridge" (Crane) **99**:15, 30
"To Browning" (Moore) **49**:114
To Burlington (Pope)
See *An Epistle to Burlington*
"To C. W. Stoddard" (Stevenson) **84**:331
"To Call up the Shades" (Cavafy) **36**:75
"To Camden" (Jonson)
See "Epigram XIV"
"To Carl Sandburg" (Lowell) **13**:67
"To Carry the Child" (Smith) **12**:320
"To Cedars" (Herrick) **9**:91
"To Celia" (Jonson) **17**:170, 196
"To Celimena" (Philips) **40**:284
"To Certain Censors" (Carducci)
See "A certi Censori"
"To Certain Critics" (Cullen) **20**:66, 83
"To Certain Journeymen" (Sandburg) **41**:313, 338, 365
"To Chaadaev" (Pushkin)
See "Chaadayevu"
"To Change in a Good Way" (Ortiz) **17**:234
"To Charis" (Jonson)
See *A Celebration of Charis in Ten Lyric Pieces*
"To Charles Cowden Clarke" (Keats) **96**:291
"To Charles Baudelaire" (Barker) **77**:12
"To Christ Our Lord" (Kinnell) **26**:239
To . . . Christopher Duke of Albemarle (Behn) **13**:8
"To Chuck" (Sanchez) **9**:224, 233
"To Cipriano, in the Wind" (Levine) **22**:225
To Circumjack Cencrastus; or, The Curly Snake (MacDiarmid) **9**:151-53, 158, 171, 175-77, 197
"To Clarendon Hills and H.A.H." (McKay) **2**:222
"To Claudia Homonoea" (Wylie) **23**:324
"To Clio Muse of History" (Nemerov) **24**:262
"To Cole, the Painter, Departing For Europe" (Bryant) **20**:34, 44-5
"To Columbus" (Darío)
See "A Colón"
"To Conclude" (Montale) **13**:146
"To Confirm a Thing" (Swenson) **14**:247, 252, 278
"To Conscripts" (Meynell) **112**:177
"To Constantia Singing" (Shelley) **14**:177; **67**:231
"To Cooke-ham" (Lanyer) **60**:31, 45, 107
"To Countess Rostopchina" (Lermontov) **18**:297
"To Daddy" (Lowell) **3**:226
"To Daffadills" (Herrick) **9**:101
"To Damon. To Inquire of Him If He Cou'd Tell Me by the Style, Who Writ Me a Copy of Verses That Came to Me in an Unknown Hand" (Behn) **13**:30-1
"To Dante Gabriel Rossetti" (Braithwaite) **52**:107
"To Daphnie and Virginia" (Williams) **7**:360, 363, 392
"To Deal with You" (Cohen) **109**:25
"To Dean Swift" (Swift) **9**:295
"To Death" (Akhmatova) **55**:9, 38, 43, 56-57, 60, 62
"To Death" (Finch) **21**:179-80
"To Death—An Irregular Ode" (Duck) **89**:37
"To Delaware" (Whittier) **93**:208
"To Delmore Schwartz" (Lowell) **3**:219, 222
"To Dependence" (Smith)
See "Sonnet 57"
"To Desire" (Behn) **13**:24
"To Dianeme" (Herrick) **9**:145
"To Dick" (O'Hara) **45**:157
"To Die in Milltown" (Hugo) **68**:250
"To Die Laughing" (Corso) **108**:18
To Disembark (Brooks) **7**:84, 93
"To Dispel My Grief" (Tu Fu) **9**:326
"To Disraeli on Conservatism" (Moore) **49**:114, 118
"To *** Do not think I deserve regret" (Lermontov) **18**:301, 304
"To Doctor Alabaster" (Herrick) **9**:142
"To Don at Salaam" (Brooks) **7**:84, 92
"To Dorothy on Her Exclusion from the Guinness Book of World Records" (Kennedy) **93**:129
"To Dr. F . . . in a Letter to Beverley Disswading Him from Drinking Waters" (Prior) **102**:311
"To Dr Parry of Bath" (Smith)
See "Sonnet 65"
"To Dr. Sherlock, on His Practical Discourse Concerning Death" (Prior) **102**:329
To Dream of A Butterfly (Hagiwara)
See *Chō o yumemu*
"To E. Fitzgerald" (Tennyson) **101**:121-22
"To E. T.: 1917" (de la Mare) **77**:138
"To Earthward" (Frost) **1**:197; **39**:246
"To Edith" (Thoreau) **30**:187
"To Electra" (Herrick) **9**:94
"To Elizabeth Ward Perkins" (Lowell) **13**:90
"To Elsie" (Williams) **7**:382, 384, 411; **109**:260, 296
"To E.M.E." (McKay) **2**:223
"To Emily Dickinson" (Winters) **82**:338, 340, 342
"To Endymion" (Cullen) **20**:67, 86
"To Enemies" (Bely) **11**:24
"To Enter That Rhythm Where the Self is Lost" (Rukeyser) **12**:227
"To Eros" (Owen) **19**:352; **102**:149
"To Eros" (Storni)
See "A Eros"
"To E.T." (Frost) **71**:34
"To Ethelinda" (Smart) **13**:331, 347
"To Evalyn for Christmas" (Shapiro) **25**:286
"To Eve, Man's Dream of Wifehood As Described by Milton" (Lindsay) **23**:281
"To Evoke Posterity" (Graves) **6**:143, 152
"To Fancy" (Hood) **93**:65, 78, 117
"To Fancy" (Smith)
See "Sonnet 47"
"To Faneuil Hall" (Whittier) **93**:208
"To Fanny Ann" (Elliott) **96**:166
"To Father Gerard Manley Hopkins, S. J." (Barker) **77**:11, 36-37
"To Fausta" (Arnold) **5**:49
"To F.C. in Memoriam Palestine" (Chesterton) **28**:97
"To Find God" (Herrick) **9**:109
"To Fine Lady Would-bee" (Jonson) **17**:197
"To Flavia" (Waller) **72**:340
"To Flood Stage Again" (Wright) **36**:341
"To Flowers" (Herrick) **9**:102
"To Flush My Dog" (Barrett Browning) **6**:6-7
"To Ford Madox Ford in Heaven" (Williams) **7**:370; **109**:195
"To Forget Self and All" (Curnow) **48**:3-4
"To Fortitude" (Smith) **104**:163
"To Fortuna Parvulorum" (Hecht) **70**:94
"To France" (Cullen) **20**:66
"To Francis Jammes" (Bridges) **28**:76
"To Free Nelson Mandela" (Jordan) **38**:132
"To Friendship" (Smith) **104**:163
"To Galich" (Pushkin) **10**:407
"To George Felton Mathew" (Keats) **96**:222, 291, 293-94, 343, 348, 353
"To George Sand: A Recognition" (Barrett Browning) **6**:26
"To Gerhardt" (Olson) **19**:307
"To Go By Singing" (Berry) **28**:3-4
"To Go to Lvov" (Zagajewski) **27**:381-82, 383-85, 387
"To God" (Herrick) **9**:94-5, 109, 118
"To God, His Good Will" (Herrick) **9**:118
"To God in Affliction: An Elegy" (Southwell) **83**:231
"To God, on His Sicknesse" (Herrick) **9**:144
"To Grammaticus" (Leapor) **85**:213
"To Gurdjieff Dying" (Toomer) **7**:338
"To Gwendolyn Brooks, Teacher" (Randall)
See "For Gwendolyn Brooks, Teacher"
"To Hafiz of Shiraz" (Wright) **14**:356, 366
"To Have Done Nothing" (Williams) **7**:383, 389, 410
"To Have Without Holding" (Piercy) **29**:311
"To Harold Monro" (Wickham) **110**:277, 294
"To Hayley" (Smith) **104**:163
"To Heaven" (Jonson)
See *The Forest XV*
"To Hedli" (MacNeice)
See "Dedicatory Poem to Collected Poems, 1925-1948, To Hedli"
"To Helen" (Poe) **1**:420, 424, 426, 428, 431, 438-39, 441, 443-45, 447; **54**:264, 278
"To Helen" (Simic) **69**:289
"To Helen" (Stryk) **27**:204
"To Helen (of Troy NY)" (Viereck) **27**:294
"To Hell With Commonsense" (Kavanagh) **33**:103; **105**:153
"To Hell With It" (O'Hara) **45**:128
"To Help" (Stein) **18**:313
"To Henry Higden, Esq.; on his Translation of the Tenth Satyr of Juvenal" (Behn) **88**:141
"To Henry Jarmin" (Davenant) **99**:179
"To Henry Purcell" (Jaccottet) **98**:197, 199
"To Her" (Pushkin) **10**:408-09

"To Her Ancient Lover" (Wilmot)
See "Song of a Young Lady to Her Ancient Lover"
"To her Brother. B. W." (Whitney) **116**:254, 284
"To her Brother. G. W." (Whitney) **116**:254, 265, 284
"To her Cosen [kinsman] F. W." (Whitney) **116**:312
"To Her Father with Some Verses" (Bradstreet) **10**:27, 35
"To Her Most Honoured Father Thomas Dudley" (Bradstreet) **10**:2
"To Her Royal Highness, the Duchess of York, on Her Commanding Me to Send Her Some Things I Had Written" (Philips) **40**:268, 295
"To Her Sister Misteris A. B." (Whitney) **116**:254, 267, 284, 312
"To Her, Too Merry" (Baudelaire)
See "À celle qui est trop gaie"
"To Her Who is Too Gay" (Baudelaire)
See "À celle qui est trop gaie"
"To him who Prophecy'd a Succesles end of the Parliament" (Davenant) **99**:177
"To himselfe and the Harp" (Drayton) **98**:66
"To His Book" (Herrick) **9**:106, 109
"To his Books" (Vaughan) **81**:338
"To His Children in Darkness" (Dickey) **40**:176, 178, 184, 187
"To His Closet-Gods" (Herrick) **9**:88
"To His Countrymen" (Cernuda) **62**:173
"To His Coy Love" (Drayton) **98**:69
"To His Coy Mistress" (Marvell) **10**:259, 265, 269, 271, 273-74, 277-79, 281-82, 290-94, 297, 304, 310-11, 313; **86**:171-282
"To his Dear Brother Colonel F. L." (Lovelace)
See "Immoderately Mourning My Brother's Untimely Death"
"To His Excellency General George Washington" (Wheatley) **3**:337, 341
"To His Father" (Jeffers) **17**:131
"To His Friend on the Untuneable Times" (Herrick) **9**:89
"To His Girles" (Herrick) **9**:107
"To His Girles Who Would Have Him Sportfull" (Herrick) **9**:107
"To His Grace, Gilbert, Lord Archbishop of Canterbury, July 10, 1664" (Philips) **40**:270
"To His Honor the Lieutenant Governor on the Death of His Lady" (Wheatley) **3**:340
"To his lady" (Leopardi)
See "Alla sua donna"
"To his Love when hee had obtained Her" (Raleigh) **31**:274
"To His Majesty at His Passage into England" (Philips) **40**:271
"To His Mistress Going to Bed" (Donne) **43**:130, 191, 200
"To His Mistresses" (Herrick) **9**:128, 146
"To his more than Meritorious Wife" (Wilmot) **66**:343
"To His Paternall Countrey" (Herrick) **9**:108
"To his retired friend, an invitation to Brecknock" (Vaughan) **81**:258, 324, 368
To His Royal Highness the Duke of Cumberland, on His Birth-Day, April the 15th, 1732 (Duck) **89**:37
"To His Royal Highness, the Prince of Wales, on his birth day" (Barker) **91**:4
"To His Savior, a Child; a Present, by a Child" (Herrick) **9**:120, 143
"To His Saviour, the New Yeers Gift" (Herrick) **9**:95
"To His Saviours Sepulcher: His Devotion" (Herrick) **9**:122
"To His Skeleton" (Wilbur) **51**:283
"To his Son" (Raleigh) **31**:203
"To his sweet Lute Apollo sang the motions of the Spheares" (Campion) **87**:70
"To His Watch" (Hopkins) **15**:167
"To Homer" (Keats) **1**:279, 314
"To Hope" (Hood) **93**:62, 65
"To Hope" (Keats) **96**:221
"To Hope" (Smith) **104**:162
"To I. C. Rob'd by his Man Andrew" (Davenant) **99**:192
"To Ianthe in Heaven" (Poe) **54**:273
"To Iceland" (Borges) **32**:58, 66
"To Imagination" (Brontë) **8**:54
"To Imagination" (Wheatley)
See "On Imagination"
"To Indianapolis 17 Nov 71" (Brutus) **24**:123
"To Insure Survival" (Ortiz) **17**:225
"To Introduce the Landscape" (Curnow) **48**:12-13
"To I. P. L." (Cohen) **109**:17, 48
"To Ireland in the Coming Times" (Yeats) **20**:324, 347, 353
"To Ishtar" (Wilbur) **51**:208, 301
"To Ivor Gurney" (Tomlinson) **17**:354-55
"To J. F. H. (1897-1934)" (Muir) **49**:272
"To J. M." (Meredith) **60**:295
"To J. S." (Tennyson) **101**:244
"To Jewishness, Paris, Ambition, Trees, My Heart and Destiny" (Koch) **80**:330
"to joan" (Clifton) **17**:18
"To John C. Fremont" (Whittier) **93**:213
"To John Goldie, August 1785" (Burns) **6**:70, 78
"To John I Ow'd Great Obligation" (Prior)
See "Another"
"To John Keats, Poet: At Spring Time" (Cullen) **20**:62, 66, 86
"To Jos: Lo: Bishop of Exeter" (Herrick) **9**:146
"To Joseph Joachim" (Bridges) **28**:88
"To Joseph Sadzik" (Milosz)
See "Do Jōzefa Sadzika"
"To Joy" (Blunden) **66**:7-10
"To Juan at the Winter Solstice" (Graves) **6**:137, 144, 146, 168, 171-72
"To Judith" (Ciardi) **69**:36
"To Judith Asleep" (Ciardi) **69**:6, 10, 41, 52
"To Julia" (Herrick) **9**:128, 143
"To Julia, in Her Dawne, or Day-breake" (Herrick) **9**:143
"To Julia, the Flaminica Dialis, or Queen-Priest" (Herrick) **9**:143
"To Julia Walking Away" (Hope) **56**:295
"To . . . K. Charles" (Jonson)
See *The Under-Wood LXIV*
"To K. Charles . . . 1629" (Jonson)
See *The Under-Wood LXII*
"To Kenya Tribesmen, the Turkana" (Eberhart) **76**:54
"To Keorapetse Kgositsile (Willie)" (Brooks) **7**:83, 92, 105
"To Kevin O'Leary Wherever He Is" (Levertov) **11**:189
"To Kidding Around" (Koch) **80**:331
"To King Henry IV, in Praise of Peace" (Gower)
See *In Praise of Peace*
"To King Henry the Fourth, in Praise of Peace" (Gower)
See *In Praise of Peace*
"To King James" (Jonson)
See "Epigram IV"
"To L. with a Few Violets" (Cernuda) **62**:174
"To Lady Arabella" (Lanyer) **60**:17
"To Lady Crew, upon the Death of Her Child" (Herrick)
See "To the Lady Crew, upon the Death of Her Child"
"To Landrum Guy, Beginning to Write at Sixty" (Dickey) **40**:182
"To Laurels" (Herrick) **9**:127
"To Leigh Hunt, Esq." (Keats) **96**:223, 266
"To Let Go or to Hold On" (Lawrence) **54**:226
"To Liberty, On Rereading the Works of Vittorio Alfieri" (Cannan)
See "Alla Libertà rileggendo le opere di Vittorio Alfieri"
"To Licinius" (Pushkin)
See "K Liciniju"
"To Life" (Koch) **80**:330
"To Like, To Love" (Sexton) **79**:244
"To Live" (Bly) **39**:86
"To live as foolishly as I lied yesterday" (Akhmadulina)
See "Tak durno zhit,' kak ia vchera zhila"
"To Live Merrily, and to Trust to Good Verses" (Herrick) **9**:96, 103-05, 107, 114
"To Live With Such Men" (Char)
See "Vivre avec de tels hommes"
"To Lord Byron" (Keats) **1**:313
"To Lord Harley, on His Marriage" (Swift) **9**:254
"To Lose the Earth" (Sexton) **2**:363
"To Louise" (Dunbar) **5**:121
"To Love" (Aleixandre) **15**:19, 21
"To Love" (Reese) **29**:331
"To Lu Chi" (Nemerov) **24**:257
"To Lucasta, About That War" (Ciardi) **69**:12
"To Lucasta: From Prison" (Lovelace) **69**:159, 167, 181, 183, 197, 203, 206, 208, 215, 218, 236, 238-39, 251
"To Lucasta: Going beyond the Seas" (Lovelace) **69**:158, 197
"To Lucasta: Going to the Warres" (Lovelace) **69**:156, 159, 164-65, 167, 179, 197, 206, 223, 226-27, 229, 235-36
"To Lucia at Birth" (Graves) **6**:137
"To Lucy, Countesse of Bedford, with Mr. Donnes Satyres" (Jonson)
See "Epigram XCIV"
"To Lyce" (Smart) **13**:348
"To Lycomedes on Scyros" (Brodsky)
See "K Likomedu, na Skiros"
"To Lysander at the Musick-Meeting" (Behn) **13**:30; **88**:150, 152
"To Lysander, on Some Verses He Writ, and Asking More for His Heart than 'Twas Worth" (Behn) **13**:30; **88**:16, 150, 152
"To Lysander, who made some Verses on a Discourse of Loves Fire" (Behn) **88**:150, 152-53
"To M" (Teasdale) **31**:368
"To M. L. S." (Poe) **54**:264
"To M.A. at parting" (Philips) **40**:296, 300
"To Madam Fitz James, on the day of her profession, at Pontoise, she taking the name of St. Ignace" (Barker) **91**:50
"To Madonna Poetry" (Storni)
See "A Madona Poesía"
"To Make a Poem in Prison" (Knight) **14**:48
"To Make Much" (Oppen) **35**:300
"To make seen" (Éluard)
See "Donner à voir"
"To Marcus Aurelius" (Herbert) **50**:30
"To Marguerite" (Arnold) **5**:19, 64
"To Marina" (Koch) **80**:290-91
"To Mark Anthony in Heaven" (Williams) **7**:367
"To Mary" (Cowper) **40**:99
"To Mary" (Shelley) **14**:234-36
"To Mary Lady Wroth" (Jonson)
See "Epigram CIII"
"To Mary Wollstonecraft" (Southey) **111**:193
"To Massachusetts" (Whittier) **93**:209
"To Master Baudelaire" (Duncan) **75**:208, 232
"To Matilda Betham" (Coleridge) **11**:58
"To Mæcenas" (Wheatley)
See "Ode to Mæcenas"
"To Melancholy" (Smith)
See "Sonnet 32"
"to merle" (Clifton) **17**:18
"To Minnie" (Stevenson) **84**:347
"To Mira" (Crabbe) **97**:76
"To Miss C— on Being Desired to Attempt Writing a Comedy" (Smith)
See "Sonnet 29"

"To Miss Carpenter, on her playing upon the Harpsichord in a Room Hung with some Flower-Pieces of her own Painting" (Johnson) **81**:115, 242
"To Miss Macartney" (Cowper) **40**:45, 48
"To Mistress Isabel Pennell" (Skelton) **25**:336
"To Mistress Margaret Hussey" (Skelton) **25**:345
To Mix with Time: New and Selected Poems (Swenson) **14**:249-50, 254-55, 257, 260, 266, 268, 274, 278, 281-82, 285
"To Moses Risson: A Glasgow Literateur" (Service) **70**:152
"To Mr. Congreve" (Swift) **9**:250
"To Mr. Creech" (Behn)
See "A Letter to Mr. Creech"
"To Mr. Creech (under the Name of Daphnis) on His Excellent Translation of Lucretius" (Behn) **13**:8, 31
"To Mr. Delany, Nov. 10, 1718" (Swift) **9**:255
"To Mr. F. Now Earl of W." (Finch) **21**:153, 164
"To Mr. Henry Lawes" (Philips) **40**:268, 296-97
"To Mr. Henry Lawes" (Waller) **72**:347
"To Mr. Hobbes" (Cowley) **90**:45, 51, 105, 128, 139, 141
"To Mr. Hobs" (Cowley)
See "To Mr. Hobbes"
"To Mr. M. L. upon his reduction of the Psalms into Method" (Vaughan) **81**:262
"To Mr R. W. 'If as mine is'" (Donne) **1**:124
"To Mr. Rowland Woodward" (Donne) **43**:131
"To Mr. Scarborough" (Cowley) **90**:52
"To Mrs. G." (Smith) **104**:163
"To Mrs. Harriet Beecher Stowe" (Harper) **21**:201, 205
"To Mrs. Harsenet, on the Report of a Beauty, which she went to see at Church" (Behn) **88**:40
"To Mrs. Hickman Playing on the Spinet" (Johnson) **81**:115
"To Mrs. King" (Cowper) **40**:49
"To Mrs. Thrale, on her completing her Thirty-fifth Year" (Johnson) **81**:115
"To Mrs. W." (Behn) **88**:73, 148, 151
"To Mrs. W. on Her Excellent Verses (Writ in Praise of Some I Had Made on the Earl of Rochester)" (Behn) **13**:8, 31
"To Muscovite Friends" (Mickiewicz)
See "Do przyjaciól Moskali"
"To Musicke bent" (Campion) **87**:12, 25, 54
"To My Adopted Brother, Mr. G. P. On my frequent Writing to Him" (Barker) **91**:27
"To My Barrio, the Four Twenty-One" (Paredes)
See "A mi barrio, El Cuatro Veintiuno"
"To My Bones" (Herbert) **50**:4
"To My Brother" (Cervantes) **35**:113
"To My Brother" (Sassoon) **12**:261, 278
"To My Brother George" (Keats) **96**:293
"To My Brother; Killed: Chaumont Wood, October, 1918" (Bogan) **12**:117
"To My Cup-Bearer" (Moore) **49**:104
"To My Daimon" (Cunningham) **92**:186, 191
"To My Daughter the Junkie on a Train" (Lorde) **12**:146-47, 154
"To My Dead Red-Haired Mother" (Stone) **53**:224
"To My Dear and Loving Husband His Goeing into England" (Bradstreet) **10**:13, 36, 40, 63
"To My dear cosen Coll—" (Barker) **91**:17
"To My Dear Cousin Mrs. M.T. after the Death of her Husband and Son" (Barker) **91**:24-25
"To my Dear Friend Mr. E. R. On his Poems Moral and Divine" (Lovelace) **69**:238
"To My Dear Sister Mrs CP on Her Marriage" (Philips) **40**:297
"To my dearest Antenor on his Parting" (Philips) **40**:296
"To my Excellent Lucasia on our Friendship" (Philips)
See "Friendship in Embleme or the Seal To My Dearest Lucasia"
To My excellent Lucasia, on our Friendship (Philips) **40**:281
"To My Fairer Brethren" (Cullen) **20**:52
"To My Father" (Ciardi) **69**:37
"To My Father" (Olds) **22**:325
"To My Father's Business" (Koch) **80**:330
"To My Father's Violin" (Hardy) **92**:207, 317
"To My Friend" (Owen)
See "With an Identity Disc"
"To my Friend Exillus, on his persuading me to Marry Old Damon" (Barker) **91**:28
"To my friend G.N. from Wrest" (Carew)
See "Letter to G.N. from Wrest"
"To My Friend Jerina" (Clifton) **17**:29
"To my Friend Mr. Ogilby" (Davenant) **99**:172, 179
"To My Friend Whose Parachute Did Not Open" (Wagoner) **33**:326, 369, 371-73
"To My Friend with an Identity Disk" (Owen) **19**:334, 358
"To My Friends" (Barker)
See "An Invitation of my learned Friends at Cambridge"
"To My Friends against Poetry" (Barker) **91**:28, 42
"To My Friends, the Cambro-Britans" (Drayton)
See "To the Cambro-Britans, and their Harpe"
"To My Greek" (Merrill) **28**:220, 262-63
"To My Heart at the Close of Day" (Koch) **80**:342
"To My Honored Friend, Dr. Charleton" (Dryden) **25**:95
"To my Honoured friend, Master Thomas May, upon his Comedie, The Heire" (Carew) **29**:53
"To My Ill Reader" (Herrick) **9**:89
"To my Inconstant Mistress" (Carew) **29**:3-4, 9, 18, 32-34
"To My Lady Moreland at Tunbridge" (Behn) **13**:8, 29-30
"To my Lady Morland at Tunbridge" (Behn) **88**:16, 40, 148, 152
"to my last period" (Clifton) **17**:29, 36
"To my lord Ignorant" (Jonson)
See "Epigram X"
"To my Lucasia in defence of declared Friendship" (Philips) **40**:313
To my Lucasia, in defence of declared friendship (Philips) **40**:281
"To My Lyre" (Smith) **104**:161, 184
"To My Master" (Howe) **81**:12
"To My Mirtle" (Blake) **63**:26
"To My Mother" (Barker) **77**:38, 41
"To My Mother" (Montale) **13**:112, 149, 152
"To my much honoured Friend, Henry Lord Carey of Lepington, upon his translation of Malvezzi" (Carew) **29**:65, 81
"To My Muscovite Friends" (Mickiewicz)
See "Do przyjaciól Moskali"
"To My Muse" (Jonson)
See "Epigram LXV"
"To My Name-Child" (Stevenson) **84**:314
"To My Old Familiars" (Stevenson) **84**:333
"To My Old Friend, William Leachman" (Riley) **48**:288, 334
"To My Old Readers" (Holmes) **71**:94
"To My Old Schoolmaster" (Whittier) **93**:172, 252, 266-68
"To My Playmate" (Viereck) **27**:263, 278, 281
"To My Prince's Command" (Wang Wei) **18**:366
"To My Readers" (Holmes) **71**:83
"To My Rivall" (Carew) **29**:72
"To My Sister" (Roethke) **15**:275
"To My Sister" (Whittier) **93**:266-67, 306
"To My Sister" (Wordsworth) **67**:301
"To My Son" (Barker) **77**:10-11, 13, 35
"To My Wife" (Cunningham) **92**:163, 169
"To My Wife" (Stevenson) **84**:332
"To my worthy Friend, M. D'Avenant, Upon his Excellent Play, The Just Italian" (Carew) **29**:83
"To my Worthy Friend Master George Sandys, on his Translation of the Psalms" (Carew) **29**:7, 17-18
"To my Worthy Friend Mr. Peter Lilly: on that excellent Picture of his Majesty, and the Duke of Yorke, drawne by him at Hampton-Court" (Lovelace) **69**:232-33
"To My Young Lover: A Song" (Barker) **91**:26, 31
"To My Young Lover On His Vow" (Barker) **91**:26
"To Myself in an Album" (Zagajewski) **27**:389
"To Nahant" (Whittier) **93**:193
"To Nannette Falk-Auerbach" (Lanier) **50**:79
"To Natal'ia" (Pushkin) **10**:404
"To Natasha" (Spender) **71**:188
"To Nature" (Hölderlin)
See "An die Natur"
"To Ned" (Melville) **82**:104, 142
"To Nichori" (Cavafy) **36**:108
"To Night" (Shelley) **14**:171, 177
"To Night" (Smith)
See "Sonnet 39"
"To Oblivion" (Smith)
See "Sonnet 90"
"To Odoardo Corazzini, killed by the French in the Campaign of Rome, 1867" (Carducci) **46**:5
"To Old Age" (Chappell) **105**:52
"To Old Age" (Koch) **80**:330
"To Old Cavafy from a New Country" (Enright) **93**:34
"To Oliver Wendell Holmes" (Whittier) **93**:275, 345
"To Olivia, of Her Dark Eyes" (Meynell) **112**:177
"To One in Despair" (Carman) **34**:226
"To One in Paradise" (Poe) **1**:432-33, 437, 444, 446; **54**:273
"To One 'Investigated' by the Last Senate Committee, or the Next" (Ciardi) **69**:5, 24
"To One Poem in a Silent Time" (Meynell) **112**:192, 228, 231
"To One Who Died Young" (Reese) **29**:335
"To One Who Died Young" (Trakl)
See "An einen Frühverstorbenen"
"To One Who Was With Me in the War" (Sassoon) **12**:246
"To Orgasm" (Koch) **80**:330
"To Orlov" (Pushkin)
See "Orlovu"
"To Our Friends" (Szymborska) **44**:301
"To Our Friends of the Tiber Valley" (Carducci)
See "Agli amici della Valle Tiberina"
"To Our Mocking Bird Died of a Cat" (Lanier) **50**:79
"To Outer Nature" (Hardy) **92**:298-301
"To Ovid's Heroines in his Epistles" (Barker) **91**:30
"To Paint a Water Lily" (Hughes) **89**:139
"To Paolo and Francesca in Purgatory" (Wylie) **23**:326
"To pay for his keep" (Thomas) **99**:251
"To P'ei Ti" (Wang Wei) **18**:362-63, 373-74
"To Penshurst" (Jonson)
See *The Forest II*
"To Perenna" (Herrick) **9**:136-37
"To Perilla" (Herrick) **9**:127-28
"To Phyllis" (Waller) **72**:336
"To Pile Like Thunder to Its Close" (Dickinson) **1**:102
"To Pliuskova" (Pushkin) **10**:409
"To Poesy" (Owen) **102**:262
"To Poesy" (Tennyson) **101**:270

"To Poet Bavius; Occasion'd By His Satyr He Writ in his Verses to the King, Upon the Queens Being Deliver'd of a Son" (Behn) **88**:101
"To Poetry" (Carducci)
See "Alla rima"
"To Posterity" (MacNeice) **61**:183
"To Professor Jebb, with the Following Poem" (Tennyson) **101**:122, 125
"To R. B." (Hopkins) **15**:157
"To Raja Rao" (Milosz) **8**:195, 200
"To Remain" (Cavafy) **36**:42
"To Remember" (Ekeloef) **23**:87
"To Remember is a Kind of Hope" (Amichai) **38**:43
"To Return to the Trees" (Walcott) **46**:237, 278, 291
"To Rhea" (Emerson) **18**:102
"To Rich Givers" (Whitman) **91**:249
"To Richard Wagner" (Lanier) **50**:77-78
"To Robert Burns" (Bridges) **28**:65
"To Robert Earle of Salisburie" (Jonson)
See "Epigram XLIII"
"To Robert Southey" (Coleridge) **11**:106
"To Robinson Jeffers" (Milosz) **8**:184, 199, 208
"To Roger Blin" (Stryk) **27**:203, 213
"To Ronge" (Whittier) **93**:166
"To Roosevelt" (Darío)
See "A Roosevelt"
"To Rosa Parks of Montgomery who started it all" (Hughes) **53**:150
"To Rosemary" (Benét) **64**:21-22
"To S. M., A Young African Painter, on Seeing His Works" (Wheatley) **3**:336, 338, 344, 362
"To Saint Catherine, Virgin and Martyr" (Southwell) **83**:231
"To Saxham" (Carew)
See "Address to Saxham"
"To Science" (Poe) **1**:437
"To Secretary Ling-hu" (Wang Wei) **18**:373
"To See a World in a Grain of Sand" (Blake) **12**:36
"To See Him Again" (Mistral)
See "Volverlo a ver"
"To See the Heron" (Tomlinson) **17**:348
"To Sensual Pleasure" (Cavafy) **36**:74
"To Shape a Song" (Snodgrass) **74**:334
To Shape a Song (Snodgrass) **74**:326
"To Share the Way with . . ." (Char)
See "Faire du chemin avec . . ."
"To Silence" (Hood) **93**:59
"To Silvia" (Leopardi)
See "A Silvia"
"To Simplicity" (Coleridge) **67**:306, 329
"To Sing a Song of Palestine" (Jordan) **38**:127
"To Sir Anthony Cooke" (Drayton) **98**:122
"To Sir Edward Dering (the Noble Silvander) on His Dream and Navy" (Philips) **40**:296
"To Sir Horace Vere" (Jonson)
See "Epigram XCI"
"To Sir Joshua Reynolds" (Cowper) **40**:103
"To Sir Robert Wroth" (Jonson)
See *The Forest III*
"To Sir Walter Aston, Knight of the honourable order of the Bath, and my most worthy patron" (Drayton) **98**:126
"To Sir William Davenant. Upon his two first Books of Gondibert, finished before his voyage to America" (Cowley) **90**:53, 55
"To Skin the Hands of God" (Espada) **74**:124
"To Sleep" (Graves) **6**:137
"To Sleep" (Smith) **104**:162
"To Solitude" (Smith) **104**:162
"To Some Ladies" (Keats) **96**:221
"To Some Winter Is Arrack" (Mandelstam) **14**:155
"To Speak of Woe That Is in Marriage" (Lowell) **3**:221, 245
"To Spring" (Smith)
See "Sonnet 8"
"To Spring or Concerning the Antique Fables" (Leopardi)
See "Alla primavera o delle favole antiche"
"To Stand (Alone) in Some" (Cummings) **5**:110
"To Statecraft Embalmed" (Moore) **49**:90, 114-15, 120
To Stay Alive (Levertov) **11**:178-80, 195
"To Stella, Visiting Me in My Sickness" (Swift) **9**:297
"To Stella, Who Collected and Transcribed His Poems, 1720" (Swift) **9**:255
"To Susan Countesse of Montgomerie" (Jonson)
See "Epigram CIV"
"To Swindon From London by Britrail Aloud" (Birney) **52**:33, 79
"To Sylvia" (Herrick) **9**:97
"To T. A." (Kipling) **3**:191
"To T. A. R. H." (Spender) **71**:157, 181, 183, 219-20, 243
"To T. L. H." (Hunt) **73**:211
"To The Airport" (Rich) **5**:382
"To the American Negro Troops" (Senghor) **25**:238
"To the Balloil Men Still in Africa" (Belloc) **24**:3, 11
"To the Beloved" (Meynell) **112**:157, 190, 237-38, 243, 287
"To the Bitter Sweet-Heart: A Dream" (Owen) **19**:352
"To the Body" (Patmore) **59**:223
"To the Boy Elis" (Trakl)
See "An den Knaben Elis"
"To the Cambro-Britans, and their Harpe" (Drayton) **98**:59, 65
"To the Canary Bird" (Very) **86**:40, 69-70, 73, 89-90, 127, 158
"To the Cicada" (Wright) **36**:368, 378
"To the Clouds" (Wordsworth) **67**:269
"To the Comet" (Thoreau) **30**:266
"To the Countess of A—" (Smith) **104**:163
"To the Countess of Anglesie upon the immoderately-by-her lamented death of her Husband" (Carew) **29**:60-61
"To the Countess of Bedford" (Lanyer) **60**:17
"To the Countesse of Bedford. 'Madame, reason is'" (Donne) **1**:123
"To the Countesse of Bedford. 'This twilight of'" (Donne) **1**:124
"To the Countess of Huntington" (Donne) **43**:131
"To the Countess of Salisbury" (Donne) **43**:105
"To the Creature of the Creation" (Wright) **36**:346-47
"To the Cross of Savoy" (Carducci)
See "Alla croce di Savoia"
"To the Crucified" (Winters) **82**:325
"To the Cuckoo" (Wordsworth) **4**:403
"To the Daisy" (Wordsworth) **4**:376
"To the Dawn" (Carducci)
See "All'Aurora"
"To the Dead Poets" (Herbert) **50**:18
"To the Dean, when in England, in 1726" (Swift) **9**:255
"To the De'il" (Burns)
See "Address to the De'il"
"To the Diaspora" (Brooks) **7**:84
"To the Dog Belvoir" (Smith) **12**:317
"To the Driving Cloud" (Longfellow) **30**:78
"To the Duchess" (Waller) **72**:344
"To the Duke of Wellington" (Arnold) **5**:49
"To the Earl of Egremont" (Smith) **104**:163
"To the Earle of Portland, Lord Treasurer; on the mariage of his Sonne" (Davenant) **99**:175
"To the East and to the West" (Whitman) **91**:248
"To the Eleven Ladies" (Holmes) **71**:96
"To the Empire of America Beneath the Western Hemisphere. Farewell to America" (Wheatley) **3**:341
"To the Endimion Porter" (Davenant) **99**:193
"To the Etruscan Poets" (Wilbur) **51**:278
"To the Evening Star" (Blake) **12**:31
"To the Evening Star: Central Minnesota" (Wright) **36**:316
"To the Excellent Mrs Anne Owen upon receiving the Name of Lucasia and Adoption into our Society December 28 1651" (Philips) **40**:272
"To the excellent Orinda" (Philips) **40**:302
"To the Fair Clarinda Who Made Love to Me, Imagin'd More than Woman" (Behn) **13**:10, 13-14, 20, 22-3, 29; **88**:33, 39, 73-74, 87, 95-96, 124-26, 130, 132, 138, 153
"To the Film Industry in Crisis" (O'Hara) **45**:138, 147, 171, 174, 189, 204-8
"To the Fossil Flower" (Very) **86**:42, 152
"To The Fringed Gentian" (Bryant) **20**:10, 35, 45
"To the Generall Reader" (Drayton)
See "To the Reader"
"To the German Language" (Mandelstam) **14**:109
"To the Ghost of Marjorie Kinnan Rawlings" (Williams) **109**:195
"To the Girl Who Lives in a Tree" (Lorde) **12**:154
"To the Glorious Epiphany" (Crashaw) **84**:9, 15, 97, 108
"To the Goddess of Botany" (Smith)
See "Sonnet 79"
"To the Governor and Legislature of Massachusetts" (Nemerov) **24**:262, 279
"To the Grasshopper and the Cricket" (Hunt) **73**:136, 162
"To the Hawks" (Justice) **64**:251, 270
"To the high and mighty Prince, James, King of Scots" (Drayton) **98**:124
"To the Holy Bible" (Vaughan) **81**:338-39
"To the Holy Ghost" (Skelton) **25**:339
"To the Holy Nativity" (Crashaw) **84**:9, 15, 48, 96, 108-9, 130, 147
"To the Honorable Charles Montague, Esq." (Prior) **102**:300, 304-5, 311
"To the Honorable Edward Howard" (Behn) **13**:8
"To the Honorable the Lady Worsley at Longleat" (Finch) **21**:167, 176
"To the Honourable Edward Howard, on his Comedy called The New Utopia" (Behn) **88**:150-51
"To the honoured Lady E.C." (Philips) **40**:296
"To the House" (Jeffers) **17**:131
"To the Humming Bird" (Very) **86**:40
"To the Immaculate Virgin, on a Winter Night" (Merton) **10**:339
"To the Immortal Memory of the Halibut on which I dined This Day" (Cowper) **40**:125
"To the Insect of the Gossamer" (Smith) **104**:167
"To the Italians" (Carducci)
See "Agli Italiani"
"To the King" (Smart) **13**:342
"To the King On His navy" (Waller) **72**:305, 307-8, 312
"To the King on New-yeares day 1630" (Davenant) **99**:175, 199
"TO THE KING, upon His Comming with His Army into the West" (Herrick) **9**:109
To the King, Upon His Majesty's Happy Return (Waller) **72**:304, 354
"TO THE KING, upon His Welcome to Hampton-Court" (Herrick) **9**:109
"To the Lacedemonians" (Tate) **50**:231, 235, 243-45, 250-51, 255-56, 274, 280, 288, 301
"To the Ladie Anne, countesse of Dorcet" (Lanyer) **60**:33, 112
"To the Ladie Lucie, Countesse of Bedford" (Lanyer) **60**:26, 112
"To the Ladie Susan, Countesse Dowager of Kent, and daughter to the Duchesse of Suffolke" (Lanyer) **60**:15, 52, 82, 112
"To the Lady" (Yamada) **244**:333, 348

"To the Lady Bridget Kingsmill; sent with Mellons after a report of my Death" (Davenant) **99**:179
"To the Lady Crew, upon the Death of Her Child" (Herrick) **9**:104, 131, 143
"To the Lady E. Boyl" (Philips) **40**:312
"To the Lark" (Herrick) **9**:98
"To the Living" (Sarton) **39**:322
"To the Lord B. in performance of a vow, that night to write to him" (Davenant) **99**:192-93
"To the Lord Cary of Lepington" (Davenant) **99**:179
"To the Lord D. L. upon his Mariage" (Davenant) **99**:193
"To the Lord Falkland. For his safe Return from the Northern Expedition against the Scots" (Cowley) **90**:63
"To the Maiden" (Crane) **80**:40, 52
To the Majestie of King James (Drayton) **98**:124
"To the Man after the Harrow" (Kavanagh) **33**:73, 77, 117, 127, 130-2, 147; **105**:151
"To the Master of Balliol" (Tennyson) **101**:125, 127
"To the Master of Sea Bird of Friday Harbor" (Wagoner) **33**:328
"To the Memory of Chatterton, Who Died Aged 17" (Whittier) **93**:193
"To the Memory of David Sands" (Whittier) **93**:194
To the Memory of . . . George Duke of Buckingham (Behn) **13**:9
"To the Memory of My Dear Daughter in Law, Mrs. Mercy Bradstreet" (Bradstreet) **10**:31
"To the Memory of the most Ingenious and Vertuous Gentleman Mr. Will Cartwright, my much valued Friend" (Philips) **40**:273
"To the Mercy Killers" (Randall) **86**:291, 339-40
"To the Merrimack" (Whittier) **93**:201
"To the Moon" (Hardy) **92**:208
"To the Moon" (Leopardi)
See "Alla Luna"
"To the Moon" (Smith) **104**:160-62, 170, 286
"To the Moon from a Jealous Person" (Akhmadulina)
See "Lune ot revnivtsa"
"To the Most Illustrious and Most Hopeful Prince, Charles" (Herrick) **9**:133
"To the Most Noble Gentleman, William Percy" (Campion) **87**:75
"To the Mother of Christ the Son of Man" (Meynell) **112**:186, 216, 232
"To the Mothers of the Dead Militia" (Neruda)
See "Canto a las madres de los milicianos muertos"
"To the Mountains" (Thoreau) **30**:293
"To the Muse" (Blok)
See "K Muze"
"To the Muse" (Wright) **36**:319, 324, 327-30, 341, 346, 354, 372, 375
"To the Muse of the North" (Morris) **55**:340
"To the Muses" (Blake) **12**:31
"To the Mutable Fair" (Waller) **72**:323
"To the Name above Every Name" (Crashaw) **84**:9, 15, 20, 25, 38, 92, 128
"To the New World" (Jarrell)
See "For an Emigrant"
"To the New Year" (Cowley) **90**:104, 106
"To the Nightingale" (Finch) **21**:141, 144, 157-61, 175
"To the Nile" (Keats) **96**:206, 255
"To the Noble Palæmon Jeremy Taylor on His Incomparable Discourse on Friendship" (Philips) **40**:267, 296, 300
"To the Noblest and Best of Ladyes, the Countesse of Denbigh" (Crashaw) **84**:9, 69
"To the North" (Sarton) **39**:325
"To the Not Impossible Him" (Millay) **6**:211, 235
"To The, O Mercifull Salviour" (Dunbar) **67**:7, 21
"To the One of Fictive Music" (Stevens) **110**:92, 94
"To the Outer World" (Williams) **109**:236
"To the Painted Columbine" (Very) **86**:41, 152, 163
"To the Painter of an Ill-Drawn Picture of Cleone, the Honorable Mrs. Thynne" (Finch) **21**:164
"To the Painter Polelonema" (Winters) **82**:322
"To the Peacock of France" (Moore) **4**:261; **49**:114
"To the Pious Memory of C. W. Esquire who Finished His Course Here, and Made His Entrance into Immortality upon the 13 of September, in the Year of Redemption 1653" (Vaughan) **81**:349
"To the Pious Memory of the Accomplisht Young Lady Mrs. Anne Killigrew" (Dryden) **25**:69
"To the Poem" (O'Hara) **45**:178
"To the Poet Who Happens to Be Black and the Black Poet Who Happens to Be a Woman" (Lorde) **12**:136
"To the Poets in New York" (Wright) **36**:301, 341
"To the Poets: To Make Much of Life" (Oppen) **35**:324
"To the Postboy" (Wilmot) **66**:276, 310, 326
"To the Pure All Things Are Pure" (Very) **86**:81, 137
"To the Pushkin House" (Blok)
See "Pushkinskomu domu"
"To the Queen" (Duck) **89**:26
"To the Queen" (Tennyson) **101**:210
"To the Queen of Italy" (Carducci)
See "Alla Regina d'Italia"
"To the Queene" (Herrick) **9**:116
"To the Queene on her arivall at Portsmouth. May. 1662" (Philips) **40**:318
"To the Queene, presented with a suit" (Davenant) **99**:191-92
"To the Queenes most Excellent Majestie" (Lanyer) **60**:4, 37, 49, 54
To the Quick (McHugh) **61**:199-200
"To the Rain" (Merwin) **45**:97
"To the Reader" (Baudelaire)
See "Au lecteur"
"To the Reader" (Campion) **87**:65
"To the Reader" (Cunningham) **92**:134-35, 137, 155, 163
"To the Reader" (Drayton) **98**:6, 68, 104, 106, 127
"To the Reader" (Merrill) **28**:283
"To the Reader" (Southwell) **83**:251, 278-79, 325
"To the Reader" (Werfel)
See "An den Leser"
"To the Reader of Master William Davenant's Play" (Carew) **29**:84
"To the Reader Who Should Love Me" (Meynell) **112**:287
"To the Rev. F. D. Maurice" (Tennyson) **101**:122
"To the Rev. John M'Math" (Burns) **114**:17, 20
"To the Right Honorable William, Earl of Dartmouth, His Majesty's Principal Secretary of State for North America" (Wheatley) **3**:337, 341, 343, 347, 350, 352
"To the Right Person" (Frost) **1**:200
"To the River Arun" (Smith)
See "Sonnet 26"
"To the River Isca" (Vaughan) **81**:306
"To the Road" (Dunbar) **5**:139
"To the Romantic Traditionists" (Tate) **50**:255, 289
"To the Rose upon the Rood of Time" (Yeats) **20**:343; **51**:149
"To the Royal Society" (Cowley) **90**:44, 46, 48, 136-37
"To the Sad One" (Borges) **32**:58
"To the Same" (Montagu) **16**:338
"To the Same Party Council Concerning Her Choice" (Crashaw) **84**:24, 69, 73-75, 98-99
"To the Sea" (Larkin) **21**:238, 240
"To the Sea" (Pushkin)
See "K moriu"
"To the Sea" (Teasdale) **31**:341
"To the Season" (Zanzotto)
See "Alla stagione"
"To the Second Person" (Skelton) **25**:339
"To the Servant of a Fair Lady" (Waller) **72**:344
"To the Shade of Burns" (Smith)
See "Sonnet 82"
"To the Shore" (Swenson) **14**:263
"To the Sister" (Trakl) **20**:248
"To the Small Celandine" (Wordsworth) **67**:248
"To the Snake" (Levertov) **11**:205
"To the Soul of 'Progress'" (Moore) **49**:113-14, 120
"To the South" (Dunbar)
See "To the South: On Its New Slavery"
"To the South Downs" (Smith)
See "Sonnet 5"
"To the South: On Its New Slavery" (Dunbar) **5**:131
"To the Statue" (Swenson) **14**:264
"To the Statues of the Gods" (Cernuda) **62**:171
"To the Stone-Cutters" (Jeffers) **17**:117
"To the Sun" (Smith)
See "Sonnet 89"
"To the Thirty-Ninth Congress" (Whittier) **93**:213
"To the True Romance" (Kipling) **91**:86
"To the truly noble Mr. Henry Lawes" (Philips) **40**:318
"To the Tune of the Coventry Carol" (Smith) **12**:316, 330
"To the Unborn" (Mahon) **60**:177-78
"to the unborn and waiting children" (Clifton) **17**:19
"To the Union Savers of Cleveland" (Harper) **21**:190
"To the University of Cambridge, in New England" (Wheatley) **3**:337, 340-41, 344-45, 353
"To the Unknown Daphnis on his Excellent Translation of Lucretius" (Behn) **88**:114, 118
"To the Unknown Eros" (Patmore) **59**:259, 262, 276
"To the Unknown God" (Hardy) **8**:121; **92**:230
"To the Unseeable Animal" (Berry) **28**:26
"To the Virgin of the Hill" (Mistral)
See "A la Virgen de la colina"
"To the Virginian Voyage" (Drayton) **98**:59, 61-63, 128, 141-42
"To the Virgins, to Make Much of Time" (Herrick) **9**:100, 145
"To the Vision Seekers, Remember This" (Rose) **13**:241
"To the Warsaw Critics" (Mickiewicz)
See "O Krytykach i Recenzentach"
"To the Water Nymphs Drinking at the Fountain" (Herrick) **9**:97
"To the White Fiends" (McKay) **2**:212, 216, 218, 229
"To the Wife of a Sick Friend" (Millay) **6**:217
"To the World" (Zanzotto)
See "Al mondo"
"To the World. A Farwell for a Gentlewoman, Vertuous and Nobel" (Jonson) **17**:172, 212
"To the Worthy . . . Sir Henry Goodere" (Drayton) **98**:69
"To the Young Poets" (Hölderlin)
See "An die jungen Dichter"
"To Thee" (Darío)
See "A ti"
"To Think of Time" (Whitman) **91**:229
"To Thos. Floyd" (Bridges) **28**:88
"To Those Grown Mute" (Trakl) **20**:258

"To Those of My Sisters Who Kept Their Naturals" (Brooks) **7**:86
"To Thyrza" (Byron) **95**:28-29
"To Time" (Clare) **23**:44
"To Tintoretto in Venice" (Meynell) **112**:177, 233
"To Tirzah" (Blake) **12**:7, 34-35; **63**:52, 54, 91-92, 105, 110, 112, 116-17
"To Tizengauzen" (Lermontov) **18**:284-85
"La tourterelle turque" (Jaccottet) **98**:181
To Transfigure, To Organize (Pasolini)
See *Trasumanar e organizzar*
"Le travail du poète" (Jaccottet) **98**:174, 176, 181
"La Traversée" (Jaccottet) **98**:172
"To Uffington Ringers" (Betjeman) **75**:83
"Under Clouded Skies" (Jaccottet)
See "Pensées sur les nuages"
Under Clouded Skies (Jaccottet)
See *Pensées sous les nuages: Poèmes*
"To Urania" (Brodsky) **9**:25, 27
To Urania: Selected Poems 1965-1985 (Brodsky) **9**:20, 23-4, 26, 29, 30
"To Us, All Flowers Are Roses" (Goodison) **36**:154
To Us, All Flowers Are Roses: Poems (Goodison) **36**:154
"To V. L. Davydovu" (Pushkin)
See "V. L. Davydovu"
"To Vandyck" (Waller) **72**:332
"To Victor Hugo of My Crow Pluto" (Moore) **4**:255, 259; **49**:133, 147, 161
"To Victory" (Carducci)
See "Alla Vittoria"
"To Victory" (Sassoon) **12**:261, 263, 276
"To Virgil" (Tennyson) **6**:370
"La Voix" (Jaccottet) **98**:176
"To Waken an Old Lady" (Williams) **7**:345, 353, 360, 363
"To Walk on Hills Is to Employ Legs" (Graves) **6**:143
"To W.G.G." (McKay) **2**:226
"To What Listens" (Berry) **28**:9
"To What Serves Mortal Beauty" (Hopkins) **15**:144
To What Strangers, What Welcome: A Sequence of Short Poems (Cunningham) **92**:140-42, 144, 150-51, 160-61, 164, 167, 177, 182, 191
"To William Butler Yeats on Tagore" (Moore) **49**:114, 116
"To William Dinsmore Briggs" (Winters) **82**:338, 340, 347
"To William E. Channing" (Longfellow) **30**:48
"To William H. Seward" (Whittier) **93**:212
"To William Simpson of Ochiltree, May 1785" (Burns)
See "Epistle to William Simpson of Ochiltree, May 1785"
"To William Wordsworth Composed on the Night after His Recitation of a Poem on the Growth of the Individual Mind" (Coleridge) **11**:52-3, 58, 92, 106
"To Willie and Henrietta" (Stevenson) **84**:347
"To Winkey" (Lowell) **13**:64
"To Winter" (Blake) **12**:32
"To Wisshe and Want" (Wyatt) **27**:316-317, 319
"To You" (Koch) **80**:314
"To You" (O'Hara) **45**:150
"To You" (Whitman) **3**:381
"To You, Out There (Mars? Jupiter?)" (Wright) **36**:377
"To You that Build the New House" (Sachs)
See "An euch, die das neue Haus bauen"
"To You Who Read My Book" (Cullen) **20**:55
To Your Scythe's Content (Char)
See *A Faulx contente*
"Toad and Spyder" (Lovelace) **69**:181, 186, 240-46, 250
"Toad dreams" (Piercy) **29**:297
"Toads" (Larkin) **21**:229, 234, 238
"Toads Revisited" (Larkin) **21**:229, 234, 237-38, 244
"The Toadstool" (Holmes) **71**:68
"A Toast" (Burns) **114**:22
"A Toast" (MacNeice) **61**:138
"Toast" (Thomas) **99**:253
"Toast for a Golden Age" (Hope) **56**:266, 306
"Toast funèbre" (Mallarmé) **102**:50, 98
"Tobacco Shop" (Pessoa)
See "Tabacaria"
"The Tobacconist's" (Pessoa)
See "Tabacaria"
"The To-Be-Forgotten" (Hardy) **92**:295
"A Toccata of Galuppi's" (Browning) **2**:37, 88
"A Toccatta of Galuppi's" (Browning) **61**:89
"Todas les efes tenía la novia que yo quería" (Fuertes) **27**:37
"Today" (Baraka) **4**:30; **113**:24
"Today" (Hughes) **53**:149
"Today" (O'Hara) **45**:160, 178, 183-84, 199
"Today" (Reese) **29**:346, 353
"To-Day" (Very) **86**:97
"Today and Tomorrow" (Rossetti) **7**:275, 277
"To-day I Climbed" (Thoreau) **30**:236
"Today I Was So Happy, So I Made This Poem" (Wright) **36**:327, 330, 364
"today is a day of great joy" (Cruz) **37**:21
"To-day, this Insect" (Thomas) **52**:228, 230-32
"Todesfuge" (Celan) **10**:96, 102, 115-17, 120-21
Todo asusta (Fuertes) **27**:10, 12
"Todo soy canas ya" (Martí) **76**:104, 108
"Todos" (Dalton) **36**:130
"Todtnauberg" (Celan) **10**:98
"Toenails" (Borges) **32**:94
"The Toes" (Carver) **54**:26
"Together" (Kipling) **91**:110
"Token Drunk" (Bukowski) **18**:15
"Told" (Levine) **22**:214, 224
"Tolerance" (Hardy) **8**:93
"Tolerance" (Pavese) **13**:205
"The Tollund Man" (Heaney) **18**:195, 202, 204, 210-11
"Tom" (Brathwaite) **56**:49, 82, 99-100
"Tom Deadlight" (Melville) **82**:73, 97, 141, 144, 160, 162
"Tom Fool at Jamaica" (Moore) **49**:126, 128, 134, 136-37, 145, 149
"Tom May's Death" (Marvell) **10**:276
"Tom Merrit" (Masters) **1**:324
"Tom Snooks the Pundit" (Smith) **12**:333
"Tom, Tom the Piper's Son" (Ransom) **61**:279
"th tomato conspiracy aint worth a whol pome" (Bissett) **14**:23, 34
"Tomatoes" (Francis) **34**:242
"Tomb" (Paz) **48**:274
"The Tomb at Akr Çaar" (Pound) **95**:96, 159
"The Tomb of Edgar Poe" (Mallarmé)
See "Le tombeau d'Edgar Poe"
"Tomb of Eurion" (Cavafy)
See "Tomb of Evrion"
"Tomb of Evrion" (Cavafy) **36**:8, 66
"Tomb of Iases" (Cavafy)
See "Tomb of Iasis"
"Tomb of Iasis" (Cavafy) **36**:8, 13, 65, 75
"Tomb of Ignatios" (Cavafy)
See "Tomb of Ignatius"
"Tomb of Ignatius" (Cavafy) **36**:8, 75
"Tomb of Lanes" (Cavafy)
See "Tomb of Lanis"
"Tomb of Lanis" (Cavafy) **36**:8, 75
"Tomb of Lysias Grammaticus" (Cavafy) **36**:8
The Tomb of Secrets (Char)
See *Le tombeau des secrets*
"The Tomb of Stuart Merrill" (Ashbery) **26**:145
"The Tomb of the Abbess of Tours" (MacLeish) **47**:131
"Tombeau d'Anatole" (Mallarmé) **102**:135
"Tombeau de Charles IX" (Ronsard) **11**:243-44
Le Tombeau de Manuel (Béranger) **112**:9
"Le Tombeau de tres illustre Marquerite de France, duchesse de Savoye" (Ronsard) **11**:243-44
"Le tombeau d'Edgar Poe" (Mallarmé) **4**:203, 209; **102**:50, 52
"Le tombeau d'Edgard Poe" (Mallarmé)
See "Le tombeau d'Edgar Poe"
Le tombeau des secrets (Char) **56**:127
"Le tombeau d'une mère" (Lamartine) **16**:264, 293
"Tombeaux" (Mallarmé) **102**:98, 129
"Tombstone Blues" (Dylan) **37**:51
"The Tombstone-Maker" (Sassoon) **12**:242, 263
"Tom-Dobbin" (Gunn) **26**:226
Tome premier (Ponge) **107**:78, 89-91, 100, 103, 108, 111, 114-18, 120, 122-23, 128-35, 138-39, 142-44, 146-48, 161, 163, 184-87, 222-25
"Tomes" (Collins) **68**:221
"Tomlinson" (Kipling) **3**:167, 182
"Tommy" (Kipling) **3**:187; **91**:68
"Tommy" (Service) **70**:122
"Tomorrow" (Hughes) **53**:191
"To-Morrow" (Masefield) **78**:7
"Tomorrow Is My Birthday" (Masters) **36**:195
"Tomorrow's Song" (Snyder) **21**:298
"Tom's Garland" (Hopkins) **15**:134, 138, 171
"Ton portrait" (Césaire) **25**:31
"Ton Soir Mon Soir" (Senghor) **25**:249
"A Tone Poem" (Ashbery) **26**:132
"Tone Poem" (Baraka) **113**:145-46, 152
"Tongue" (Herbert) **50**:4
"Tonight slippers of darkness fall" (Abse) **41**:25
"Tonight the Woods Are Darkened" (Warren) **37**:330
Tonight This Savage Rite: The Love Poems of Kamala Das and Pritish Nandy (Das, Nandy) **43**:93
"Tonique" (Tzara) **27**:230-31
"Tonu Soy" (Mackey) **49**:66
"Tony Went to the Bodega but He Didn't Buy Anything" (Espada) **74**:139
"Too Blue" (Hughes) **1**:243
Too Great a Vine: Poems and Satires (Clarke) **112**:31, 34, 37, 47, 50-51, 54, 62, 80
"A Too Hopefully Bold Measure" (Dorn) **115**:125
"Too Late" (Arnold) **5**:43, 56
"Too Late" (Thomas) **99**:236
"The Too Late Born" (MacLeish) **47**:186
"Too Young for Love" (Holmes) **71**:96
"The Tool" (Thomas) **99**:257, 262, 286, 290-94
"Tools" (Mistral)
See "Herramientas"
"Toome" (Heaney) **18**:202, 204, 210, 241
"The Toome Road" (Heaney) **18**:246
"To—One word is too often profaned" (Shelley) **14**:233
"A Tooth" (Storni)
See "Un diente"
"Top Rock" (Stern) **115**:248
Topoemas (Paz) **1**:363
"Topographical Map" (Hugo) **68**:253
Topography and Other Poems (Stone) **53**:215-18, 220, 227-28, 239, 242
"Topsfield Fair" (Updike) **90**:356
"Torch Procession" (Celan)
See "Fackelzug"
The Torch-Bearers (Noyes) **27**:128, 130, 133, 137-8
"The Torch-bearer's Race" (Jeffers) **17**:107
"La Torche du prodigue" (Char) **56**:147
"Torero" (Stryk) **27**:187, 203, 214
"Torero nuestro de cada día" (Fuertes) **27**:38
"La Tormenta" (Espada) **74**:113-14, 139, 142-43
"La tormenta" (Guillén) **35**:154
"The Torn Sky: Lesson #1" (Jordan) **38**:127
"Tornado" (Stafford) **71**:287
"Tornado Blues" (Brown) **55**:71, 74, 151, 160
"Tornado Warning" (Shapiro) **25**:306
"Tornant al pais" (Pasolini) **17**:252, 265
"Tornasol" (Guillén) **35**:158
"Toronto Board of Trade Goes Abroad" (Birney) **52**:16

"Torquemada" (Longfellow) **30**:41, 107
"La torre" (Olson) **19**:268, 293, 309-10
"Torre" (Storni) **33**:239
The Torrent and the Night Before (Robinson) **1**:459, 474, 484-85
"Torres d' Oeste" (Castro) **41**:95
"Torso" (Brodsky) **9**:8
"The Torso" (Duncan) **75**:126, 131, 212-13, 215-17, 220-21
"Tortilla Host" (Alurista) **34**:40
"Tortoise Gallantry" (Lawrence) **54**:225
"The Tortoise in Eternity" (Wylie) **23**:301, 309
"Tortoise Shout" (Lawrence) **54**:177, 212, 236
Tortoises (Lawrence) **54**:189, 198
"La tortuga de oro..." (Darío) **15**:99
"Torture" (Walker) **30**:343
"The Tortured Heart" (Rimbaud)
See "La coeur volé"
"Tortures" (Szymborska)
See "Tortury"
"Tortury" (Szymborska) **44**:281
"Toscani" (Carducci) **46**:50
Tossing and Turning (Updike) **90**:346
"The Total Influence or Outcome: The Sun" (Piercy) **29**:305-06
Total Song (Éluard)
See *Chanson complète*
"Totem" (Césaire) **25**:21-2
"Totem" (Hughes) **89**:177
"Totem" (Plath) **1**:391, 393, 399, 412; **37**:258
"Totem" (Senghor) **25**:224, 230
"The Totem" (Swenson) **14**:249-50
"Totò Merùmeni" (Gozzano) **10**:184-88, 190
Tottel's Miscellany (Surrey) **59**:284, 290, 319, 321, 341
Tottering State: Selected and New Poems 1963-1984 (Raworth) **107**:278, 281-82, 297, 300, 305, 308, 310-11, 326, 339-40
Tottering State: Selected Poems 1963-1987 (Raworth)
See *Tottering State: Selected and New Poems 1963-1984*
"Tou Wan Speaks to Her Husband, Liu Sheng" (Dove) **6**:107, 109
"Touch" (Gunn) **26**:195, 202, 207, 217, 219
"The Touch" (Sexton) **2**:352
Touch (Gunn) **26**:192, 196-197, 202-203, 207-209, 211-214, 219, 223, 225-226, 231
"Touch Me" (Kunitz) **19**:187
"A Touch of the Hand" (Curnow) **48**:18, 35
"Touches" (Stafford) **71**:333
"Touching" (Thomas) **99**:304, 310, 312
"Touching the River" (Kinsella) **69**:72
"Touch-Me-Nots" (Oliver) **75**:342
"Touch-up Man" (Komunyakaa) **51**:53
"Tough Cookies" (Berrigan) **103**:26
Toujours je la connus (Sainte-Beuve) **110**:39
"Toujours Miroirs" (Senghor) **25**:251
"Toulouse-Lautrec 'Jane Avril Dancing'" (Thomas) **99**:305-6
"Toulouse-Lautrec 'Justine Dieuhl'" (Thomas) **99**:306
"The Tour" (Plath) **1**:399-401; **37**:257
"Tour" (Wakoski) **15**:359
"Tour 5" (Hayden) **6**:189, 194
"A Tour of London" (Spark) **72**:218, 226
"A Tour Song" (Owen) **102**:151
"Touring for Trujillo" (Guillén) **23**:126
"The Tourist and the Town" (Rich) **5**:353, 362
"Tourist Death" (MacLeish) **47**:130, 188
"The Tourist from Syracuse" (Justice) **64**:270
"Tourists" (Amichai) **38**:19, 41, 54
"The Tournament" (Chatterton) **104**:69
"Tournament" (Dunbar)
See "Nixt that a turnament wes tryid"
"Tournesol" (Breton) **15**:61-2
"Tous partis" (Char) **56**:146
"Toussaint l'ouverture" (Whittier) **93**:312, 316-18, 343
"De tout ce que j'ai dit de moi que rest-t-il" (Éluard) **38**:68
"Tout entière" (Baudelaire) **106**:128
"Tout Entouré de Mon Regard" (Tomlinson) **17**:321, 339
"Le tout, le rien" (Bonnefoy) **58**:154
"Tout Orgueil fume-t-il du soir" (Mallarmé) **102**:95, 98, 101
A toute épreuve (Éluard) **38**:67
Toute la lyre (Hugo) **17**:65, 86
"Toute une vie" (Péret) **33**:208, 213
"Toward a City That Sings" (Jordan) **38**:119
"Toward a Personal Semantics" (Jordan)
See "Towards a Personal Semantics"
"Toward an Organic Philosophy" (Rexroth) **20**:215, 217, 221; **95**:257, 259, 270, 287-88
"Toward Dawn" (Welch) **62**:338, 362-63
"Toward Finestère" (Montale)
See "Vento sulla mezzaluna"
"Toward His Malaise" (Duncan) **75**:259
"Toward Nightfall" (Simic) **69**:285, 287
"Toward Rationality" (Warren) **37**:284, 288
"Toward Siena" (Montale)
See "Verso Siena"
Toward the Cradle of the World (Gozzano)
See *Verso la cuna del mondo*
"Toward the Earth" (Cernuda)
See "Hacia la tierra"
"Toward the Empty Earth" (Mandelstam)
See "K pustoi zemle nevol'no pripadaia"
Toward the Gulf (Masters) **1**:330, 332, 335, 342-44; **36**:179, 183
"Toward the Interior" (Wagoner) **33**:364, 367
"Toward the name" (Guillén)
See "Hacia el nombre"
"Toward the Piraeus" (H. D.) **5**:268, 304
"Toward the Shaman" (Duncan) **75**:224-25
"Toward the Solstice" (Rich) **5**:374
Towards a New Poetry (Wakoski) **15**:359
"Towards a Personal Semantics" (Jordan) **38**:119-21
Towards a tense serenity (Char)
See *À une sérénité crispée*
"Towards Autumn" (Hacker) **47**:81, 105
"Towards Byzantium" (Yeats) **51**:89, 91-92
"Towards the Slave Quisqueya" (Guillén)
See "Hacia la esclava Quisqueya"
"The Tower" (Yeats) **20**:310, 318, 320, 329, 334, 342; **51**:98, 120, 135-37, 139, 143, 152
The Tower (Yeats) **20**:307, 311, 333, 335; **51**:74, 108, 120, 134-35
"The Tower beyond Tragedy" (Jeffers) **17**:106, 108, 110, 112, 135, 144-46
The Tower of Babel (Merton) **10**:344, 349
Tower of Ivory (MacLeish) **47**:165, 182, 251
"The Tower of Pisa" (Song) **21**:344
"The Tower of Siloam" (Graves) **6**:133
"Tower of Song" (Cohen) **109**:32, 112
"The Tower of Sun" (Cunningham) **92**:182
"The Tower Struck by Lightning Reversed; The Overturning of the Tower" (Piercy) **29**:324
"The Towerer" (Masefield) **78**:98
"Towers of the West" (Castro)
See "Torres d' Oeste"
"The Town" (Cavafy) **36**:52, 57
"The Town" (Masefield) **78**:30
"The Town" (Pushkin)
See "Gorodok"
"Town" (Soto) **28**:378, 385
"Town and Country" (Brooke) **24**:56
"The Town Betrayed" (Muir) **49**:264, 289
The Town down the River (Robinson) **1**:462-63, 467, 474, 478, 490
"The Town Dump" (Nemerov) **24**:257, 261, 291-92
"A Town Eclogue" (Swift) **9**:278
Town Eclogues (Montagu)
See *Court Poems*
"The Town Fathers" (Tolson) **88**:343
Town in Tears (Seifert)
See *Město v slzách*
"Town Marshal" (Masters) **36**:230
"Town of Bathsheba's Crossing" (Carson) **64**:206
The Town of Hill (Hall) **70**:9, 14, 26, 33, 3232
"Towns in Colour" (Lowell) **13**:79
"The Towns We Know and Leave Behind, the Rivers We Carry with Us" (Hugo) **68**:292
"The Toys" (Patmore) **59**:209, 222, 264
Toys in a Field (Komunyakaa) **51**:20, 33, 63
"Tracé sur le gouffre" (Char) **56**:153
"Traces of Living Things: Shelter" (Niedecker) **42**:138
"Tracking" (Raworth) **107**:300
"Tracking" (Wagoner) **33**:338-39, 345
"Tracks" (Montague) **106**:287, 298, 303
"Tract" (Williams) **7**:348, 362, 378
"Tractatus" (Mahon) **60**:189, 217-19
"Tractor" (Hughes) **7**:166
"The Trade of an Irish Poet" (Heaney) **18**:201
"The Trade-Off" (Stone) **53**:259
"Tradimento" (Pavese) **13**:202, 226
"Tradition" (Niedecker) **42**:100, 109
"Traditions" (Heaney) **18**:252
"Trafferth mewn Tafarn" (Dafydd ap Gwilym) **56**:208, 220-21, 224, 232, 245, 249
"Traffic" (Hall) **70**:9, 34
"Trafficker" (Sandburg) **41**:336
"Traficante" (Cisneros) **52**:158-60, 164
"Tragedy" (Graham) **59**:179
"Tragedy" (Spencer) **77**:330
"Tragedy of Teeth" (Kipling) **3**:194
"The Tragedy of the Leaves" (Bukowski) **18**:6, 21
"Trägheit des Herzens" (Werfel) **101**:349
"Tragic Architecture" (Simic) **69**:280, 317
"Tragic Books" (Reese) **29**:333, 335
"Tragic Destiny" (Aleixandre) **15**:10
"Tragic Love" (Winters) **82**:314
Traherne's Poems of Felicity (Traherne) **70**:183, 198, 241
"Traigo conmigo un cuidado" (Juana Inés de la Cruz) **24**:188
"The Trail" (Mistral)
See "La huella"
"Trail Creek, Aug. 11, the Reason of Higher Powers" (Dorn) **115**:125
"The Trail into Kansas" (Merwin) **45**:45
"The Trail of Ninety-Eight" (Service) **70**:115
"Train" (Erdrich) **52**:176
Train Ride (Berrigan) **103**:33, 40
"Train Time" (Bogan) **12**:107
"Train to Dublin" (MacNeice) **61**:108, 111, 114-20, 136, 145, 164
"Train Wreck" (Corso) **108**:13
"Training" (Owen) **19**:336
"The Training" (Whittier) **93**:269
"Trainor the Druggist" (Masters) **1**:347
"Trains in the Distance" (MacNeice) **61**:126
Traité du pianiste (Bonnefoy) **58**:150
"A Traitor to France" (Tolson) **88**:348-50, 353
Traktat poetycki (Milosz) **8**:198-99, 204
"Tramontana" (Montale) **13**:105, 126
"Tramontana at Lerici" (Tomlinson) **17**:342
"Tramp" (Thomas) **99**:237
"The Tramp Transfigured" (Noyes)
See "The Tramp Transfigured: An Episode in the Life of a Corn-Flower Millionaire"
"The Tramp Transfigured: An Episode in the Life of a Corn-Flower Millionaire" (Noyes) **27**:121, 134
"La trampa" (Parra) **39**:268-69, 282-83
"Las Trampas USA" (Tomlinson) **17**:353
"A Trampwoman's Tragedy" (Hardy) **8**:99; **92**:267, 277, 287
"Trams" (Sitwell) **3**:301
"The Trance" (Muir) **49**:239
Transbluency (Baraka) **113**:96, 126, 131, 133, 136, 138-40
"A Transcendental Idealist Dreams in Springtime" (Chappell) **105**:67, 72
"Trane" (Brathwaite) **56**:54-55
"Transaction" (Ammons) **16**:22
"Transcedental Etude" (Rich) **5**:381
"Transcontinental" (Birney) **52**:47-48, 50-52, 58, 92

A Transcript of Edward Taylor's Metrical History of Christianity (Taylor) **63**:285
"Transcription of Organ Music" (Ginsberg) **47**:21, 39
"Transfer" (Brown) **55**:89-90
"Transfer of the the Remains of Ugo Foscolo to Santa Croce" (Carducci)
See "Per il Trasporto delle Relique di Ugo Foscolo in Santa Croce"
"The Transfiguration" (Muir) **49**:198, 229, 233, 262, 264, 274, 284
"Transfigured Life" (Rossetti) **44**:169-70
"Transformation & Escape" (Corso) **33**:37; **108**:21
The Transformation/Transformations (Ovid)
See *Metamorphoses*
"Transformations" (Hardy) **8**:113
"Transformations" (Seifert)
See "Proměny"
"Transformations" (Wright) **14**:339
Transformations (Sexton) **2**:349, 354-55, 362, 364-65, 368; **79**:190, 202, 204-6, 213, 241, 250, 252, 266, 281, 310, 320-29
"The Transformed One" (Olds) **22**:326
"The Transformed Twilight" (Chappell) **105**:37
"Transfusión" (Storni) **33**:250
"Transgressing the Real" (Duncan) **2**:104; **75**:117
"Transient Barracks" (Jarrell) **41**:172, 189, 203
"Transients and Residents" (Gunn) **26**:220
"Transients in transient words" (Darwish)
See "Abiruna fi Kalamin 'Abir"
"Transistors" (Birney) **52**:97
"Transit" (Berryman) **64**:100
"Transit" (Wilbur) **51**:335
"Transition" (Niedecker) **42**:143
"Transition" (Sarton) **39**:320, 323
"Transitional" (Williams) **7**:392
Transitional Poem (Day Lewis) **11**:123-25, 128-31, 133-35, 137, 143-45, 148, 151
"Tránsito" (Guillén) **35**:154
"Translated from the American" (Alexie) **53**:10, 40
"Translating the Birds" (Tomlinson) **17**:348, 350
"A Translation" (Behn) **88**:150
"Translation" (Sarton) **39**:321
"Translation from Chopin (Prelude Number 7 in A Major, Opus 28)" (Randall) **86**:292, 344
"Translation of the Latin Epitaph on Sir Thomas Hammer, written by Dr. Freind" (Johnson) **81**:214
A Translation of the Psalms of David, Attempted in the Spirit of Christianity, and Adapted to the Divine Service (Smart) **13**:330-32, 341-42, 362
"Translations" (Rich) **5**:397
"Translations" (Stone) **53**:230
Translations, 1915-1920 (H. D.) **5**:304
The Translations of Ezra Pound (Pound) **4**:331
"Translations of the Psalms" (Wyatt) **27**:359
"Translucence" (Erdrich) **52**:186
"The Transmutation" (Muir) **49**:239
Transparence of the World (Merwin) **45**:31
"Transparency" (Kennedy) **93**:141
"Transparent Garments" (Hass) **16**:199, 210
"The Transparent Man" (Hecht) **70**:80-81
The Transparent Man (Hecht) **70**:80-81, 86-88, 92
Les Transparents (Char) **56**:166, 173, 176
"Transplanting" (Roethke) **15**:295
"Transport" (Meredith) **28**:174
"The Transport of Slaves from Maryland to Mississippi" (Dove) **6**:108
Transport to Summer (Stevens) **6**:301-03; **110**:150, 183, 227
"Transylvania" (Szirtes) **51**:171
"The Trap" (Parra)
See "La trampa"
"The Trap" (Wright) **14**:356
"Trapped" (Hughes) **89**:134
"Trapped Dingo" (Wright) **14**:345
"Trappings" (Das) **43**:90
"The Trappist Abbey: Matins" (Merton) **10**:332
"The Trappist Cemetery, Gethsemani" (Merton) **10**:332-33, 342
"Le Trappiste" (Vigny) **26**:401-402, 404
"Trappists, Working" (Merton) **10**:332-33
Trasumanar e organizzar (Pasolini) **17**:273, 286
"Der Traum" (Benn) **35**:69
"Traum" (Stramm) **50**:170-71, 175, 189, 204
"Traum und Umnachtung" (Trakl) **20**:239, 268
"Träumerei am Abend" (Trakl) **20**:239
"Traumig" (Stramm) **50**:171, 173, 188
"Traumstadt eines Emigranten" (Werfel) **101**:350
"Travel" (Brooke) **24**:66
"Travel" (Stevenson) **84**:340-42, 344
"Travel Note" (Empson) **104**:119
"The Traveler" (Apollinaire)
See "Le voyageur"
"The Traveler" (Cernuda) **62**:173
"The Traveler" (Jarrell) **41**:146
"The Traveler" (Tate) **50**:230, 243, 256
"A Traveler at Night Writes His Thoughts" (Tu Fu) **9**:324
The Traveler Does Not Return (Nishiwaki)
See *Tabibito Kaerazu*
"Travelers in Erewhon" (Rexroth) **95**:255, 268
"TRAVELERS: Lake Superior region" (Niedecker) **42**:110-11, 114-16
"Traveling" (Alexie) **53**:40
"Traveling through Fog" (Hayden) **6**:194
"Traveling through the Dark" (Stafford) **71**:259, 275-76, 278, 282, 294, 299, 306, 325, 330, 350, 368, 371, 379
Traveling through the Dark (Stafford) **71**:259-60, 266-67, 269-70, 275-76, 281, 287-88, 291-92, 298, 320-21, 325, 327-28, 330, 332, 349, 368-69, 377-78
"The Traveller" (Berryman) **64**:80, 88
"The Traveller" (Curnow) **48**:46
"Traveller" (Kinsella) **69**:84-85, 89, 93, 100
"The Traveller" (de la Mare) **77**:78-80, 82, 84-85, 92-93, 95, 116
"The Traveller and the Angel" (Wright) **14**:339, 346
The Traveller; or, A Prospect of Society (Goldsmith) **77**:160, 162-63, 166, 172, 174-75, 178, 180-85, 188-89, 191, 194-98, 201-3, 214, 216, 218, 221, 230-31, 233-34, 237-40, 250-53, 255, 266-67, 270, 274, 278-82, 286, 314-15, 317-18
"Traveller's Curse after Misdirection" (Graves) **6**:137
"Traveller's Palm" (Page) **12**:181
"Travelling" (Merwin) **45**:48
"Travelling Light" (Wagoner) **33**:337, 344
"Travelling on an Amtrak Train Could Humanize You" (Sanchez) **9**:234
"Travelogue for Exiles" (Shapiro) **25**:269, 279, 290
"Travels" (Thomas) **99**:339
"Travels in the South" (Ortiz) **17**:227, 231
"Travels of a Latter-Day Benjamin of Tudela" (Amichai)
See "Mas'ot Binyamin ha'aharon mitudela"
"Travels of the Last Benjamin of Tudela" (Amichai)
See "Mas'ot Binyamin ha'aharon mitudela"
"Traversando la Maremma Toscana" (Carducci) **46**:50, 58, 65, 77, 80
"Traverse" (Char) **56**:120
"A través de los sueños" (Alurista) **34**:28
"Tre donne intorno al cor mi son venute" (Dante) **21**:87
"Treachery" (Cavafy) **36**:56
Tread the Dark (Ignatow) **34**:324-25, 330
"The Treasure" (Brooke) **24**:87-9
"The Treasure" (Jeffers) **17**:117
"The Treasure" (Meynell) **112**:165
"Treaty" (Jacobsen) **62**:277, 320
"Trebetherick" (Betjeman) **75**:9, 26
"The Treble Recorder" (Seifert) **47**:327
"Trébol" (Darío) **15**:89
"Trech a Gais nog a Geidw" (Dafydd ap Gwilym) **56**:232
"The Tree" (Aleixandre)
See "El árbol"
"The Tree" (Cowley) **90**:33-34, 115
"The Tree" (Finch) **21**:149
"Tree" (Hope) **56**:292
"A Tree" (Hughes) **89**:121
"Tree" (Rukeyser) **12**:224
"The Tree" (Stone) **53**:229
"The Tree" (Teasdale) **31**:360, 370
"The Tree" (Very) **86**:42, 70, 90-92, 158, 161
"Tree and Sky" (Williams) **109**:286
"The Tree and the Cloud" (Hall) **70**:31
"Tree at My Window" (Frost) **1**:197, 205; **39**:232
"Tree Burial" (Bryant) **20**:14, 17
"Tree Disease" (Hughes) **7**:120
"Tree House" (Silverstein) **49**:331
"Tree of Fire" (Chappell) **105**:45
"The Tree of Knowledge" (Cowley) **90**:44, 46, 51
"The Tree of Knowledge" (Graham) **59**:155
"The Tree of Liberty" (Burns) **114**:47, 78
"Tree of Song" (Teasdale) **31**:322, 356
"Tree Planting" (Tagore)
See "Vriksha-ropan"
"A Tree Telling of Orpheus" (Levertov) **11**:177
"Tree Trimming" (Ciardi) **69**:10
The Tree Witch (Viereck) **27**:275-76, 278-80, 282
A Tree Within (Paz)
See *Arbol adentro*
The Tree Within (Paz)
See *Arbol adentro*
"The Trees" (Carruth) **10**:71
"Trees" (Hughes) **7**:120
"Trees" (Nemerov) **24**:266-67
"The Trees" (Sarton) **39**:323, 332
"Trees" (Tsvetaeva)
See "Derev'ya"
"Trees" (Williams) **7**:351
"Trees and Cattle" (Dickey) **40**:162-63, 181, 189, 191
"The Trees Are Down" (Mew) **107**:56, 61
Trees, Effigies, Moving Objects (Curnow) **48**:13, 23, 46-48, 59
"Trees in a Grove" (Meredith) **28**:170
"The Trees in the Garden Rained Flowers" (Crane) **80**:52
"Trees in the Open Country" (Simic) **69**:287-88
"treez" (Bissett) **14**:24, 33
"Tregardock" (Betjeman) **75**:26, 32
"La Treizieme" (Nerval) **13**:196; **67**:360
"Trelawnys Dream" (Meredith) **28**:215
"A Trellis for R." (Swenson) **14**:267, 280
"Tremayne" (Justice) **64**:280
The Trembling of the Veil (Yeats) **20**:330
"Tremor" (Zagajewski) **27**:395
Tremor (Zagajewski) **27**:380-81, 383-84, 389, 395, 397, 399
"Tren Fortynbrasa" (Herbert) **50**:36
"Trench Poems" (Owen) **19**:350
"Trenches" (Borges) **32**:121
"Tres Poesías" (Parra) **39**:272, 307
"Tres versiones de Judas" (Borges) **32**:48
"Trespass Into Spirit" (Baraka) **4**:24
The Trespasser (Stryk) **27**:191, 194, 197-98, 215-16, 218
"Trestles by the Blackfoot" (Welch) **62**:371
"The Tretis of the Tua Mariit Women and the Wedo" (Dunbar) **67**:3-4, 6-7, 17, 25-26, 30, 33-34, 39, 41, 84-86, 95, 101-4, 106, 109, 114, 117, 128
"Trevenen" (Davie) **29**:103, 109
"Trew Luve" (Dunbar) **67**:26
"Tri palmy" (Lermontov) **18**:268, 290-91, 293
"Tri Phorthor Eiddig" (Dafydd ap Gwilym) **56**:208, 225, 227-33, 249

Tria Krilka Poema (Seferis) **66**:118, 149, 152, 171, 195-97, 206, 212
Tria poiemata me simea efkerias (Elytis)
See *Three Poems under a Flag of Convenience*
"A Triad" (Rossetti) **7**:272-73, 275, 291
"Tríada" (Borges) **32**:91
"Triage" (Mueller) **33**:192-93
"The Trial" (Abse) **41**:6, 8, 22
"The Trial" (Berryman) **64**:83
"The Trial" (Sassoon) **12**:260
Trial Balances (Bishop) **34**:161
"The Trial by Existence" (Frost) **71**:6-7
"Trial of a City" (Birney) **52**:8-9, 46-47
Trial of a City and Other Verse (Birney) **52**:7-8, 11, 21-22, 36, 40, 43, 45, 67
"Trial of a Poet" (Shapiro) **25**:277-79
Trial of a Poet and Other Poems (Shapiro) **25**:273-74, 285, 290, 296, 319, 322, 324
"The Trial of Robert Emmet" (Clarke) **112**:54
"The Trial of the Dead Cleopatra in Her Beautiful and Wonderful Tomb" (Lindsay) **23**:280, 286
"The Trial of the Fox" (Henryson) **65**:18, 28, 54-55, 61, 79, 81-82
"Trial Run" (Jacobsen) **62**:319
"Trial-Pieces" (Heaney) **18**:246
"Tribal Memories" (Duncan) **75**:120, 189, 215
"Tribal Scenes" (Song) **21**:345
"Tribe" (Dorn) **115**:230-31, 235
"Tribe" (Song) **21**:336, 343
"Tribulación" (Mistral) **32**:155, 176
Tribunals: Passages 31-35 (Duncan) **2**:106, 116, 127; **75**:204, 232, 248, 275
The Tribune's Visitation (Jones) **116**:61, 100, 105, 108, 110, 115-16, 159, 199-200, 224, 227
"Tribute" (Brutus) **24**:111
"The Tribute" (H. D.) **5**:298, 304
"Tribute" (Merwin) **45**:5
"The Tribute" (Patmore) **59**:231-32
Tribute to Ballet in Poems (Masefield) **78**:62, 80
Tribute to the Angels (H. D.) **5**:272, 274-75, 283-84, 286-87, 293-97, 308-09, 313, 315
"Tribute to the Nursing Staff" (Wickham) **110**:269, 286
"Tribute to the Painters" (Williams) **109**:275
"The Trick" (Borges)
See "El truco"
"The Trick Was" (Yamada) **44**:347
"Trickle Drops" (Whitman) **3**:406
"Tricks with Mirrors" (Atwood) **8**:21-6
"Trickster 1977" (Rose) **13**:232
"Trieb" (Stramm) **50**:189, 201, 208
"Triebkrieg" (Stramm) **50**:168
"The Triennial" (Very) **86**:57, 61
"Trillium" (Glück) **16**:171
Trilogie der Leidenschaft (Goethe) **5**:250
Trilogy (H. D.) **5**:281, 283-86, 292-93, 2960-98, 304-07, 310-15
Trilogy (Wakoski) **15**:365
"Trilogy for X" (MacNeice) **61**:127, 138
"Trinchera" (Borges) **22**:92
"Trinitas" (Whittier) **93**:239
"The Trinity" (Stone) **53**:257
"Trinity Churchyard" (Rukeyser) **12**:225
"Trinity Peace" (Sandburg) **2**:304
"Trinket" (Bell) **79**:6
"Trio for Two Cats and a Trombone" (Sitwell) **3**:303, 306
"Triolet" (Brooke) **24**:54
Trionfi (Petrarch) **8**:224-26, 238, 240, 243, 246, 252, 254, 257, 260, 273-78
"Trip" (Schuyler) **88**:188
"The Trip" (Stafford) **71**:267, 294
"Trip to Brundisium" (Horace) **46**:190, 193
"The Triple Fool" (Donne) **1**:125
"Triple Time" (Larkin) **21**:227, 236, 242
"Triptych" (Heaney) **18**:246
"A Triptych" (Ignatow) **34**:323
"Triptyque" (Mallarmé) **102**:98, 101
"Tristan and Isolt" (Masefield) **78**:47
"Tristan's Singing" (Masefield) **78**:47, 51
"El triste" (Borges) **22**:80
"Triste, triste" (Laforgue) **14**:86, 88-9
"Los tristes, IV" (Castro) **41**:112
"Tristesse" (Benn) **35**:67
"Tristesse" (Lamartine) **16**:293
"Tristesse d'Olympio" (Hugo) **17**:64, 76-77, 82, 97
"Tristesse d'un étoile" (Apollinaire) **7**:3
"Les tristesses de la lune" (Baudelaire) **1**:44-5
"Tristia" (Mandelstam) **14**:106
Tristia (Mandelstam)
See *Vtoraya kniga*
Tristia (Ovid) **2**:233, 240-42, 244-45, 252-53, 255-59
Tristibus (Ovid)
See *Tristia*
"Tristitia" (Patmore) **59**:262
Tristram (Robinson) **1**:470-72, 474-75, 481, 489; **35**:368
Tristram and Iseult (Arnold) **5**:9, 12, 33-34, 42, 49, 64
"Tristram Crazed" (Muir) **49**:239
Tristram of Lyonesse (Swinburne) **24**:307, 309, 310, 313-14, 316, 319, 321-23, 348-50, 352, 355-57
"Tristram's Journey" (Muir) **49**:230, 270, 288
"Tritiya" (Tagore) **8**:415
"Triton" (Douglas) **106**:186
"Triumph" (Reese) **29**:332
"Triumph" (Winters) **82**:325
The Triumph of Achilles (Glück) **16**:149, 151-52, 155-57, 159, 163
"Triumph of Charis" (Jonson)
See *A Celebration of Charis in Ten Lyric Pieces*
"The Triumph of Life" (Shelley)
See *The Triumph of Life*
The Triumph of Life (Shelley) **14**:174, 188, 193, 211; **67**:138, 233
"The Triumph of Life: Mary Shelley" (Mueller) **33**:175, 197
"the triumph of the will" (Schwerner) **42**:196
"The Triumph of Time" (Swinburne) **24**:308, 322, 325, 337-38, 342-43
"The Triumph of Woman" (Southey) **111**:193
Triumphal March (Eliot) **5**:168, 185
"Triumphal Ode" (Barker) **77**:38, 40
"Triumphalis" (Carman) **34**:229
"The Triumphs" (Lovelace) **69**:168, 181
Triumphs (Petrarch)
See *Trionfi*
"The Triumphs of Bacchus" (Pushkin) **10**:407
"The Triumphs of Owen" (Gray) **80**:207
"Trivial Breath" (Wylie) **23**:310
Trivial Breath (Wylie) **23**:302, 307-309, 324-25
Trivial, Vulgar, and Exalted: Epigrams (Cunningham) **92**:175
"Trofeo" (Borges) **22**:93; **32**:82
Troilus (Chaucer)
See *Troilus and Criseyde*
Troilus and Criseyde (Chaucer) **19**:6-7, 11, 13, 15, 23, 36-9, 42-3, 60-1, 63, 73-5; **58**:265-6, 363
Troilus and Cryseide (Chaucer)
See *Troilus and Criseyde*
"Trois Ans après" (Hugo) **17**:83
Trois jugemens (Christine de Pizan)
See *Le Livre des Trois jugemens*
Les trois livres du recueil des nouvelles poesies (Ronsard) **11**:248
"Trois respirations" (Char) **56**:191
"Les Trois Sœurs" (Char) **56**:150, 190-91, 193-95
Troisime livre des odes (Ronsard) **11**:283
The Trojan Horse: A Play (MacLeish) **47**:164, 211
"A Trojan Slave" (Muir)
See "Troy II"
"Trojans" (Cavafy) **36**:7, 28, 57, 73
"Trolling for Blues" (Wilbur) **51**:249, 261, 310-11
"Trompeten" (Trakl) **20**:250, 254-55
"Troop Train" (Shapiro) **25**:263, 268, 288, 295, 297, 324
Tropfblut (Stramm) **50**:204, 208, 214, 221-24
"Trophies of Peace" (Melville) **82**:153
"Trophy" (Borges)
See "Trofeo"
"The Trophy" (Hope) **56**:268
"The Trophy" (Muir) **49**:246
"Tropic Rain" (Stevenson) **84**:332
Tropicalization (Cruz) **37**:12, 16, 36
"Trópico" (Storni) **33**:239, 269
"trópico de Ceviche" (Alurista) **34**:28
"The Tropics in New York" (McKay) **2**:228
"Trostnik" (Lermontov) **18**:304
"Troth with the Dead" (Lawrence) **54**:175, 244
"Troths" (Sandburg) **41**:242, 255
"A troubadour I traverse all my land" (Brutus) **24**:113
Troubadour Songs (Snodgrass) **74**:323
"Trouble in a Tavern" (Dafydd ap Gwilym)
See "Trafferth mewn Tafarn"
"Trouble in De Kitchen" (Dunbar) **5**:146
"The Trouble is with No and Yes" (Roethke) **15**:277
"The Trouble with 'In'" (McHugh) **61**:200
"The Trouble with Intellectuals" (Randall) **86**:290, 299, 336
"The Trouble with Women Is Men" (Nash) **21**:268, 274
"The Troubled Bay" (Cassian) **17**:11, 13
"Troubled Woman" (Hughes) **53**:119
"The Trout" (Char)
See "La Truite"
"Trout" (Hugo) **68**:287-88
"The Trout" (Montague) **106**:296, 298, 327
"Troy" (Muir)
See "Troy I"
"Troy I" (Muir) **49**:214, 230, 243, 255, 258, 264, 278
"Troy II" (Muir) **49**:214, 243, 255-56, 264, 278
Troy Park (Sitwell) **3**:293-94, 298, 301, 303, 307-08, 320
"Troy Town" (Rossetti) **44**:202, 204-5
Troylus and Criseyde (Chaucer)
See *Troilus and Criseyde*
"Trozos del poema" (Mistral) **32**:166
"The Truce of Piscataqua" (Whittier) **93**:172, 267
"The Truce of the Bear" (Kipling) **3**:171, 182; **91**:91
"Las truchas" (Forché) **10**:134
"Truck-Garden-Market Day" (Millay) **6**:232
"Truco" (Borges)
See "El truco"
"El truco" (Borges) **32**:82
Trudy i dni Lavinii monakhini iz ordena obrezaniia serdtsa (Shvarts) **50**:133-37, 142-43, 159-60
"A True Account of Talking to the Sun at Fire Island" (O'Hara) **45**:117, 133, 141, 164, 189, 229
"The True Beatitude" (Brooke) **24**:57
"The True Confession" (Barker) **77**:24, 31
The True Confession of George Barker (Barker) **77**:9, 39
"True Confessional" (Ferlinghetti) **1**:187
"The True Import of Present Dialogue, Black vs. Negro" (Giovanni) **19**:107, 114-15, 139
"The True Light" (Very) **86**:88
"True Love" (Olds) **22**:338
"True Love" (Warren) **37**:375
"True Love at Last" (Lawrence) **54**:185
"True Love Leaves No Traces" (Cohen) **109**:68
"The True Lover" (Housman) **43**:214, 260-61
"True Night" (Snyder) **21**:300
"True Pearl—Belle of the Lo" (Li Ho) **13**:54
"True Place" (Bonnefoy) **58**:123

"True Recognition Often Is Refused" (Schwartz) **8**:292
"The True Religion" (Cunningham) **92**:191
"True Romance" (Kipling) **3**:161
True Stories (Atwood) **8**:43
"The True Story of Mortar and Pestle" (Chin) **40**:36
"True Story of the Pins" (Ríos) **57**:311
"True Tenderness" (Akhmatova) **2**:14
"The True, the Good, and the Beautiful" (Schwartz) **8**:292
"True Vine" (Wylie) **23**:303, 305, 323
"Truganinny" (Rose) **13**:240
"The Truisms" (MacNeice) **61**:112
"La Truite" (Char) **56**:182
"Trump of Death" (Gower) **59**:88, 91-92, 94, 108-9
"The Trumpet" (Thomas) **53**:266
"Trumpet Player: 52nd Street" (Hughes) **1**:241, 247, 249; **53**:90, 205
"Trumpets from the Islands of Their Eviction" (Espada) **74**:116, 133
Trumpets from the Islands of Their Eviction (Espada) **74**:113, 115, 121-22, 128, 133-34, 139, 141-42, 145, 149-52, 154-55, 158, 168
"The Trumpets of Dollkarnein" (Hunt) **73**:201
"The Truncated Bird" (Eberhart) **76**:54
"Trunks the forest yielded" (Clough) **103**:52
"Ein Trupp hergelaufener Söhne schrie" (Benn) **35**:46, 47
"Trust" (Whittier) **93**:239
"The Trusting Heart" (Parker) **28**:362
"Truth" (Brooks) **7**:61
"The Truth" (Cowper) **40**:47, 50-1, 70-1
"The Truth" (Jarrell) **41**:190, 192, 198
"The Truth" (Jiménez)
  See "Paisaje del corozon"
"Truth" (McKay) **2**:215
"The Truth" (Montale) **13**:156
"Truth" (Thomas) **99**:237
"The Truth about God" (Carson) **64**:207, 228, 233
"Truth and Error" (Goethe) **5**:228
Truth and Falshood (Duck) **89**:88
"Truth and Falsehood. A Tale" (Prior) **102**:314
"Truth and Ignorance" (Deloney) **79**:55, 57
"The Truth at Last" (Chappell) **105**:49
"The Truth Is" (Hogan) **35**:245, 255
"Truth is a golden thread" (Clough) **103**:81
"Truth Is Not the Secret of a Few" (Ferlinghetti) **1**:186
"Truth Kills Everybody" (Hughes) **7**:160
"The Truth of the Matter" (Hogan) **35**:271
"The Truth of the Matter" (Nemerov) **24**:290
"'Truth,' Said a Traveller" (Crane) **80**:79
"The Truth the Dead Know" (Sexton) **2**:346, 361
"Try On" (Graham) **59**:187
Tryflings (Ekeloef) **23**:63
"Tryin' on Clothes" (Silverstein) **49**:325, 332
"Trying to Hold It All Together" (Eberhart) **76**:60
"Trying to Pray" (Wright) **36**:287
"Trying to Sing in the Rain" (Wagoner) **33**:357
"The Tryst" (de la Mare) **77**:59
"A Tryst that Failed" (Meynell) **112**:156-57, 287
"Trzy slowa najdziwiniejsze" (Szymborska) **44**:298
"Tsar Sultan" (Pushkin)
  See "Skazka o Tsare Sultane"
Tsar-devitsa (Tsvetaeva) **14**:313, 325-26
The Tsar-Maiden (Tsvetaeva)
  See *Tsar-devitsa*
Tsetlo (Serote) **113**:297
Tsuki ni hoeru (Hagiwara) **18**:169, 172-73, 175-82
"Tsung-wu's Birthday" (Tu Fu) **9**:324
"Tsurugai Bridge" (Ishikawa)
  See "Tsurugaibashi"
"Tsurugaibashi" (Ishikawa) **10**:213
"Tsutsushimite Kumagori no tame ni sono 'kokorozashi wo noburu uta ni kotauru rokushu" (Yakamochi) **48**:137, 139
"Tsvety" (Akhmadulina) **43**:3, 5
"Tsyganskie stikhi" (Shvarts) **50**:160
Tsygany (Pushkin) **10**:357-61, 365-66, 369, 371, 386-89, 391-92, 398, 410
"Tú" (Borges) **32**:90, 138
"Tú" (Guillén) **23**:134-37
"Il tu" (Montale) **13**:132
"Tu Do Street" (Komunyakaa) **51**:9, 20-21, 39, 42
"Tú me quieres blanca" (Storni) **33**:243, 248-50, 297-98, 305, 318
"Tú no sabe inglé" (Guillén) **23**:142
"Tu Parles" (Senghor) **25**:250
"Tu pequeña figura" (Cernuda) **62**:220
"tú sabes" (Alurista) **34**:37
"tu Te Languis" (Senghor) **25**:249-50
"Tu ti spezzasti" (Ungaretti) **57**:338
"The Tua Mariit Wemen and the Wedo" (Dunbar)
  See "The Tretis of the Tua Mariit Wemen and the Wedo"
Tucky the Hunter (Dickey) **40**:233-34
"Tuesday: St. James's Coffee-house: Silliander and Patch" (Montagu) **16**:348
Tuft by Puff (Stafford) **71**:315, 318, 330, 338
"Tulip" (McGuckian)
  See "Tulips"
"Tulips" (McGuckian) **27**:79-80, 102, 278
"Tulips" (Page) **12**:176
"Tulips" (Plath) **1**:390, 395, 399-401, 405, 407, 409, 414; **37**:196, 203
Tulips and Chimneys (Cummings) **5**:74-5, 77-8, 86, 91, 93-4, 104
"Tulpen" (Celan) **10**:122-23
"Tumba de Amir Khusrú" (Paz) **48**:232
"La Tumba de Buenaventura Roig" (Espada) **74**:124-25, 130, 162
"Tumblers, Pouters and Fantails" (Moore) **49**:116
"Tumbling-Hair" (Cummings) **5**:104
"Tumi o ami" (Tagore) **8**:414
"A Tune for Festive Dances in the Nineteen Sixties" (Merton) **10**:345
"Tune, in American Type" (Updike) **90**:351
"The Tune of Seven Towers" (Morris) **55**:279-80, 282, 302-3
"Tune thy Musicke to thy heart" (Campion) **87**:12, 25, 54, 65
"El túnel" (Parra) **39**:283
"Tunica Pallio Proprior" (Moore) **49**:105, 121, 134
"tuning flower tones" (Alurista) **34**:28
"Tunk: A Lecture of Modern Education" (Johnson) **24**:141, 163
"The Tunnel" (Crane) **3**:86, 88-90, 106-07, 110-11
"The Tunnel" (Creeley) **73**:7
"The Tunnel" (Strand) **63**:152, 176-79
"Tunnels" (Komunyakaa) **51**:40
The Tunning of Eleanor Rumming (Skelton)
  See *The Tunnynge of Elynour Rummynge*
Tunning of Elinor Rumming (Skelton)
  See *The Tunnynge of Elynour Rummynge*
The Tunning of Elynour Rummyng (Skelton)
  See *The Tunnynge of Elynour Rummynge*
The Tunnying of Elynour Rummyng (Skelton)
  See *The Tunnynge of Elynour Rummynge*
The Tunnyng (Skelton)
  See *The Tunnynge of Elynour Rummynge*
The Tunnyng of Elynour Rummyng (Skelton)
  See *The Tunnynge of Elynour Rummynge*
The Tunnynge of Elynour Rummynge (Skelton) **25**:330, 332, 338, 342, 347-49, 361-62, 364, 367, 386-88, 390-93
"Il tuo volo" (Montale) **13**:111
Turbine (Dorn)
  See *The North Atlantic Turbine*
"Turbonave Magnolia" (Birney) **52**:34, 97
"Turin" (Gozzano) **10**:177, 180
"The Turk of Shiraz" (Hafiz) **116**:15, 17, 24, 43
"The Turkey in the Straw" (Williams) **7**:400
"Turkey Villas" (Guest) **55**:219
"Turkeys Observed" (Heaney) **18**:189, 200
"Turkish Verses" (Montagu) **16**:338
The Türler Losses (Guest) **55**:217, 220-21
"Turlupin" (Béranger) **112**:20
Turn (Paz)
  See *Vuelta*
"The Turn of the Century" (Szymborska)
  See "Schylek wieku"
"The Turn of the Moon" (Graves) **6**:154, 156
Turn of the Offended (Dalton) **36**:120, 124
Turn Off the Lights (Seifert)
  See *Zhasněte světla*
"Turn on Your Side and Bear the Day to Me" (Barker) **77**:13
Turn Out the Lights (Seifert)
  See *Zhasněte světla*
Turn Thanks (Goodison) **36**:158
"Turn Thanks to Miss Mirry" (Goodison) **36**:158
"Turnbridge Wells" (Wilmot) **66**:237, 240, 263-64, 267-68, 329, 342
"The Turncoat" (Baraka) **4**:5, 14; **113**:4-5, 7
"Turne backe, you wanton flyer" (Campion) **87**:63-64
"turning" (Clifton) **17**:21
"The Turning" (Graham) **59**:167
"The Turning" (Levine) **22**:212
"Turning" (Rilke) **2**:280-81
"Turning a Moment to Say So Long" (Ammons) **16**:39
"Turning Away from Lies" (Bly) **39**:51
"Turning Away: Variations on Estrangement" (Dickey) **40**:187-88, 199, 202-3
"Turning Fifty" (Wright) **14**:355
"The Turning of the Tide" (Masefield) **78**:6, 68
"Turning Point" (Seferis)
  See "Strophe"
Turning Point (Seferis)
  See *Strophe*
"Turning To" (Kumin) **15**:182
"A Turning Wind" (Rukeyser) **12**:213
A Turning Wind: Poems (Rukeyser) **12**:211-12
Turns and Movies and Other Tales in Verse (Aiken) **26**:21, 50, 53
"Turquoise Skies Above, and Below" (Quintana) **36**:250
"The Turtle" (Bly) **39**:24
"The Turtle" (Nash) **21**:278
"The Turtle" (Oliver) **75**:287-88
"The Turtle and the Sparrow" (Prior) **102**:314-15
Turtle Island (Snyder) **21**:290-300, 306-08, 310, 316-17, 320, 324-25
"Turtle Lake" (Hugo) **68**:252
"Turtle Mountain Reservation" (Erdrich) **52**:176, 178, 183, 192
"The Turtle Overnight" (Wright) **36**:367, 378
"Turtle Soup" (Chin) **40**:12, 16, 27
Turtle, Swan (Doty) **53**:47, 60, 62
"Tus ojos" (Paz) **48**:183
"Tutecotzimí" (Darío) **15**:92
"The Tutelar of the Place" (Jones) **116**:100, 108, 110, 113-16, 126, 137-39, 159-60, 227-28
"Tutto é sciolto" (Joyce) **22**:136
"TV Men" (Carson) **64**:221, 223
"TV Men: Antigone (Scripts 1 and 2)" (Carson) **64**:222
"TV Men: Hektor" (Carson) **64**:221
"TV Men: Lazarus" (Carson) **64**:222
"TV Men: Sappho" (Carson) **64**:201, 226
"TV Men: Tolsroy" (Carson) **64**:222
"TV Off" (Hughes) **89**:156
"Tvoi dom" (Akhmadulina) **43**:3-4
"The Twa Cummeris" (Dunbar) **67**:17, 38
"The Twa Dogs" (Burns) **6**:51, 78, 83-4, 88; **114**:5, 17-19, 22, 33, 42, 59, 80, 87-88, 117, 135-36, 138-42, 145-46
"The Twa Herds" (Burns) **6**:85

"Twa Myis" (Henryson)
See "The Two Mice"
"The Twelfth Day of March" (Akhmadulina)
See "Den' 12 marta"
"Twelfth Morning; or, What You Will" (Bishop) **34**:191
"Twelfth Night" (Belloc) **24**:49
"Twelfth Night, Next Year, a Weekend in Eternity" (Schwartz) **8**:294
"XII" (Joyce) **22**:136, 138, 145, 164, 169, 171
"The Twelve" (Tate) **50**:231, 256
The Twelve (Blok)
See *Dvenadsat*
"Twelve Articles" (Swift) **9**:260
"The 12 boock" (Raleigh) **31**:302, 304
"The Twelve Dancing Princesses" (Sexton) **2**:365; **79**:190, 205
"Twelve Dead, Hundreds Homeless" (Kennedy) **93**:150
"1200 South / 2100 West" (Cisneros) **52**:157
"Twelve Months After" (Sassoon) **12**:288
Twelve Moons (Oliver) **75**:283-85, 287, 293-94, 300, 302, 305
"Twelve O'Clock News" (Bishop) **34**:68, 158
"12 O'Clock News" (Bishop)
See "Twelve O'Clock News"
"Twelve Years Old" (Stafford) **71**:290
The Twelve-Spoked Wheel Flashing (Piercy) **29**:311, 313
"A Twelve-Step Treatment Program" (Alexie) **53**:30
Twentieth Century Harlequinade and Other Poems (Sitwell) **3**:299-300, 302
"20th-century Fox" (Baraka) **4**:11
"XX" (Joyce) **22**:145, 168
Twenty Love Poems and a Despairing Song (Neruda)
See *Veinte poemas de amor y una canción desesperada*
Twenty Love Poems and a Desperate Song (Neruda)
See *Veinte poemas de amor y una canción desesperada*
Twenty Love Poems and a Song of Despair (Neruda)
See *Veinte poemas de amor y una canción desesperada*
Twenty Love Poems and One Song of Despair (Neruda)
See *Veinte poemas de amor y una canción desesperada*
"The 21th: and last booke of the Ocean to Scinthia" (Raleigh) **31**:218, 237, 246, 252, 286, 290
"Twenty Poems" (Berryman) **64**:81-84, 87, 90, 154, 168
XX Poems (Larkin) **21**:226, 229
Twenty Poems (Neruda)
See *Veinte poemas de amor y una canción desesperada*
Twenty Poems (Spender) **71**:146, 179-80, 186, 216-18
Twenty Poems (Trakl) **20**:227
Twenty Poems of Anna Akhmatova (Kenyon) **57**:13, 22
"27 June 1906, 2 p.m" (Cavafy) **36**:53
"26 Points à préciser" (Péret) **33**:203
"XXVIII" (Joyce) **22**:145, 154, 159, 162, 169, 172
"28" (Levine) **22**:224
"Twenty-fifth of Vaisakh" (Tagore)
See "Panchishe vaisakh"
"The Twenty-fifth Year of his Life" (Cavafy) **36**:75, 78
"XXV" (Joyce) **22**:139, 160, 173
"25¢ Song" (Snodgrass) **74**:324
"25 Mesostics Re and not Re Mark Tobey" (Cage) **58**:219
Twenty-Five Poems (Thomas) **2**:378, 389; **52**:271
25 Poems (Walcott) **46**:259
"XXIV" (Joyce) **22**:136, 139, 170, 172-73
"Twenty-Four Hokku on a Modern Theme" (Lowell) **13**:66
Twenty-Four Love Songs (Dorn) **115**:57, 105, 108, 119, 123, 205, 221
24 Love Songs (Dorn)
See *Twenty-Four Love Songs*
"Twenty-four Poems" (Schwartz) **8**:302
"2433 Agnes, First Home, Last House in Missoula" (Hugo) **68**:251
"Twenty-four Years" (Ciardi) **69**:27
"Twenty-Four Years" (Thomas) **2**:383; **52**:264
"XXIX" (Joyce) **22**:145, 167, 170, 173
"XXI" (Joyce) **22**:146, 166-68, 170
Twenty-One Love Poems (Rich) **5**:384, 395
"XXVII" (Joyce) **22**:145, 156, 170, 172-73
"XXVII" (Smith)
See "Sonnet 27"
"XXVI" (Joyce) **22**:136, 139, 168, 171, 173
"Twenty-Third Flight" (Birney) **52**:22-23
"XXIII" (Joyce) **22**:145, 170
"XXII" (Joyce) **22**:138, 145, 170-71, 173
"XXII" (Williams)
See "The Red Wheelbarrow"
"Twenty-two Rhymes" (Tu Fu) **9**:326
"Twice" (Rossetti) **7**:267, 275
Twice or thrice had I loved thee (Donne)
See "Aire and Angels"
"Twice-Done, Once-Done" (Muir) **49**:245, 250-51
"Twicknam Garden" (Donne) **1**:124, 130, 134
"Twilight" (Apollinaire)
See "Crépuscule"
"Twilight" (Clare) **23**:47
"Twilight" (Kunitz) **19**:147
"Twilight" (Masefield) **78**:8, 69
"Twilight" (Teasdale) **31**:323, 334
"Twilight: After Haying" (Kenyon) **57**:5, 13
"The Twilight Bell" (Ishikawa)
See "Kure no kane"
The Twilight Book (Neruda)
See *Crepúsculario*
"Twilight in Eden" (Carman) **34**:202
"The Twilight of Freedom" (Mandelstam) **14**:106, 147
"The Twilight of the Gods" (Melville)
See "Crón Tráth na nDéithe"
"Twilight of the Outward Life" (Viereck) **27**:263
"Twilight Reverie" (Hughes) **1**:255
Twilight Songs (Hugo) **17**:45
"Twilights" (Wright) **36**:305, 340, 398
The Twin In the Clouds (Pasternak)
See *Bliznets v tuchakh*
"Twine" (Brathwaite) **56**:96
"Twinkle, twinkle little Bat" (Carroll) **74**:24, 63
"The Twins" (Bukowski) **18**:4, 22
"The Twins of Lucky Strike" (Service) **70**:144
"Twister" (Stryk) **27**:211
"Two" (Hughes) **89**:122
"II" (Joyce) **22**:138, 165-66
"Two American Haikus" (Stern) **115**:259
"Two Amsterdams" (Ferlinghetti) **1**:183
"Two Apparitions" (Kennedy) **93**:141
"The Two April Mornings" (Wordsworth) **4**:374; **67**:287
"The Two Armies" (Holmes) **71**:66, 68
"Two Armies" (Spender) **71**:138, 202-3, 226
"Two Astrological Conundrums" (Hughes) **89**:145
"Two Bad Things in Infant School" (Enright) **93**:24
"The Two Bobbies" (Carman) **34**:207, 219
"Two Bodies" (Paz)
See "Dos cuerpos"
Two Bookes of Ayres: The First Contayning Divine and Morall Songs: The Second, Light Conceits of Lovers (Campion) **87**:6-7, 12, 25, 31-32, 42, 50, 65, 67-68, 71, 84, 100
Two Books of Airs (Campion)
See *Two Bookes of Ayres: The First Contayning Divine and Morall Songs: The Second, Light Conceits of Lovers*
"Two Boyhoods" (Meynell) **112**:232
"Two Brothers" (Ai) **72**:23
"The Two Brothers" (Carroll) **74**:64, 67-70
"The Two Brothers" (Lermontov) **18**:299
"Two Cantos of Mutabilitie" (Spenser) **8**:344, 346, 375, 396; **42**:340-41, 343-44
"Two Children" (Graves) **6**:156
"Two Children" (Guillén)
See "Dos niños"
"Two Cigarettes" (Pavese)
See "Due sigarette"
Two Citizens (Wright) **36**:304, 306-9, 313-14, 317-18, 346-48, 354-56, 358, 363, 367-68, 370, 376-77, 392, 397-98
"Two Conceits for the Eye to Sing, If Possible" (Tate) **50**:290, 293
"Two days of fever" (Pasolini) **17**:279
"Two Deaths" (Olds) **22**:317
"The Two Deserts" (Patmore) **59**:262, 275-77
"Two Drops" (Herbert)
See "Dwie krople"
"Two Easter Stanzas" (Lindsay) **23**:282
"Two Egrets" (Ciardi) **69**:40, 56
"Two Egyptian Portrait Masks" (Hayden) **6**:185
"2/18/97" (Graham) **59**:188
"Two English Poems" (Borges) **22**:95; **32**:58, 85
"Two Eskimo Songs" (Hughes) **7**:153, 159
"Two Evenings" (Stafford) **71**:288
Two Figures (Momaday) **25**:201
"Two Figures from the Movies" (Meredith) **28**:187, 210
"Two Figures in Dense Violet Night" (Stevens) **110**:93
"The Two Fires" (Atwood) **8**:37
The Two Fires (Wright) **14**:341-49, 353-55, 369
"Two for the Festival" (Welch) **62**:339, 346, 359-60
The Two Foscari (Byron) **16**:103
"Two Generations" (Wright) **14**:344, 354
"Two Gentlemen in Bonds" (Ransom) **61**:308, 311
Two Gentlemen in Bonds (Ransom) **61**:267, 274, 289, 305-6, 315
"Two Girls" (Nemerov) **24**:291
"The Two Good Sisters" (Baudelaire) **106**:5
"The Two Graves" (Coleridge) **67**:276
"2 Gulls Sittin on the Richmond Bridge" (Dorn) **115**:160
"Two Gun Buster and Trigger Slim" (Walker) **20**:273
"Two Hands" (Sexton) **2**:371
"Two Hangovers" (Wright) **36**:326, 340, 396, 398
"Two higher mammals" (Piercy) **29**:303
"Two Horses Playing in the Orchard" (Wright) **36**:326, 338
"Two Hours in an Empty Tank" (Brodsky) **9**:2, 4
"The Two Houses" (Hardy) **92**:275, 295
"200 B.C." (Cavafy) **36**:35
"Two Hymns" (Ammons) **16**:4
"Two Implements" (Bell) **79**:33
"Two in August" (Ransom) **61**:288
"Two in the Campagna" (Browning) **2**:68
"Two in the Twilight" (Montale)
See "Due nel crepuscolo"
"Two Kinds of Deliverance" (Oliver) **75**:299
"Two Kisses" (Spender) **71**:161, 211, 228
"Two Leading Lights" (Frost) **39**:345
"Two Legends" (Hughes) **7**:159
"Two Little Boots" (Dunbar) **5**:122, 129
"Two Look at Two" (Frost) **1**:194, 229, 231
"Two Lovers" (Eliot) **20**:123
"The Two Lovers" (Marie de France)
See "Les Dous Amanz"
"Two Lyrics from Kilroy's Carnival: A Masque" (Schwartz) **8**:311
"Two Masks Unearthed in Bulgaria" (Meredith) **28**:182

"Two Meditations on Guanajuato" (Yau) **61**:333
"The Two Men" (Hardy) **92**:241, 245
"Two Men" (Service) **70**:141
"Two Mexicanos Lynched in Santa Cruz, California, May 3, 1877" (Espada) **74**:161
"The Two Mice" (Henryson) **65**:4, 25, 27, 54
"Two Moments in Venice" (Wright) **36**:321
"Two Neighbors" (Sandburg) **41**:360
"Two Night Pieces" (Sitwell) **3**:293
"Two of Hearts" (Hogan) **35**:257
"The Two Offers" (Harper) **21**:194
"The Two Old Bachelors" (Lear) **65**:146
"Two Old Crows" (Lindsay) **23**:281
"Two or Three Angels" (Crane) **80**:40, 68
"Two Organs" (Berryman) **64**:93
"2 Pages, 122 Words on Music and Dance" (Cage) **58**:204
"Two Paintings by Gustav Klimt" (Graham) **59**:140, 143-44
"Two Pair" (Nemerov) **24**:302
"The Two Parents" (MacDiarmid) **9**:156, 176
"The Two Peacocks of Bedfont" (Hood) **93**:42, 58, 66, 77, 117
"Two Pendants: For the Ears" (Williams) **7**:360, 364, 394
"Two Pewits" (Thomas) **53**:289
"Two Phases" (Hughes) **89**:138
"Two Poems" (Madhubuti) **5**:321
"Two Poems" (Niedecker) **42**:148
"Two Poems about President Harding" (Wright) **36**:340, 396
"Two Poems Ending with the Word Blind" (Shvarts) **50**:133
"2 Poems for Black Relocation Centers" (Knight) **14**:46-8
"Two Poems of Going Home" (Dickey) **40**:220
Two Poems to Harriet Beecher Stowe (Holmes) **71**:96
"Two Poets" (Cullen) **20**:68
"The Two Poets" (Meynell) **112**:161, 192, 228-29
"Two Postures beside a Fire" (Wright) **36**:341, 393
"Two Preludes" (Swinburne) **24**:323
"The Two Presences" (Bly) **39**:53
"Two Presentations" (Duncan) **75**:197, 200, 203, 231
"The Two Questions" (Meynell) **112**:165
"Two Red Roses across the Moon" (Morris) **55**:299, 301
"Two Riddles from Aldheim" (Wilbur) **51**:301
"Two Rivers" (Emerson) **18**:76, 88-89
"The Two Roads" (Gozzano) **10**:177-78
"Two Rondeaus" (Szirtes) **51**:167
"The Two Rosalinds" (Hardy) **92**:245
"Two Saints" (Ciardi) **69**:31, 34
"Two Scavengers in a Truck, Two Beautiful People in a Mercedes" (Ferlinghetti) **1**:183, 188
"Two Scenes" (Berrigan) **103**:13
"Two Shakespeare Tercentenaries" (Meynell) **112**:177, 230
"Two Sisters" (Ní Chuilleanáin) **34**:373
"Two Sisters of Persephone" (Plath) **37**:202
"Two Songs" (Mahon) **60**:138
"Two Songs" (Rich) **5**:365
"Two Songs" (Sarton) **39**:323, 341
"Two Songs for Solitude" (Teasdale) **31**:323
"Two Songs from a Play" (Yeats) **20**:315, 319
"Two Songs of a Fool" (Yeats) **20**:304
"Two Sonnets: Harvard" (Holmes) **71**:96
"Le Sonneur" (Mallarmé) **102**:100
"Two Speak Together" (Lowell) **13**:96-7
"Two Stories" (Gallagher) **9**:36
"The Two Swans" (Hood) **93**:62, 66-67
"Two Tales of Clumsy" (Schnackenberg) **45**:337
"The Two Thieves" (Wordsworth) **4**:374, 388
"2527th Birthday of the Buddha" (Komunyakaa) **51**:6, 8
"The Two Towers" (Carducci)
See "Le due Torri"
"Two Tramps in Mud Time" (Frost) **1**:198, 221; **39**:246; **71**:9, 11-12, 43, 49
"The Two Travellers" (Bryant) **20**:10, 16
"The Two Trees" (Yeats) **20**:317
"221-1424 (San Francisco suicide number)" (Sanchez) **9**:211, 224-25
"221-1424 (San/francisco/suicide/number)" (Sanchez)
See "221-1424 (San Francisco suicide number)"
"Two Versions of 'Ritter, Tod und Teufel'" (Borges)
See "Dos versiones de 'Ritter, Tod und Teufel'"
"Two Views of a Cadaver Room" (Plath) **1**:389; **37**:177, 185-86
"Two Views of Rhyme and Meter" (Kennedy) **93**:149
"Two Voices" (Blunden) **66**:55-57
"Two Voices" (Ignatow) **34**:277, 324
"The Two Voices" (Tennyson) **6**:360
"Two Voices in a Meadow" (Wilbur) **51**:196, 289
"2 Weird Happenings" (Corso) **108**:21
"Two Who Crossed a Line (He Crosses)" (Cullen) **20**:86
"Two Women Talking" (MacLeish) **47**:195
Two Women, Two Shores (McGuckian) **27**:95
"Two Wrestlers" (Francis) **34**:242
"Two Years Later" (Yeats) **20**:338
"Two Young Men, 23 to 24 Years Old" (Cavafy) **36**:50, 76, 78-79, 80
"Two-an'-Six" (McKay) **2**:208-09
"2Cor.: 5.19 God was in Christ reconciling the World to himself" (Philips) **40**:298
"The Two-Days-Old Baby" (Blake)
See "Infant Joy"
Two-Headed Poems (Atwood) **8**:43
Two-Headed Woman (Clifton) **17**:17-18, 23-24, 26-27, 34-35
"Two-Part Pear Able" (Swenson) **14**:247
2000 (Neruda) **4**:287
"Two-Volume Novel" (Parker) **28**:352, 359, 352
"Tyaroye" (Senghor) **25**:235
"Tydingis fra the Sessioun" (Dunbar) **67**:13
"The Tyger" (Blake) **12**:6-7, 10, 25, 30, 34-5, 59-64; **63**:4, 17-18, 54, 57-60, 62, 68, 105, 107, 116, 119, 134-35
"Tying One On in Vienna" (Kizer) **66**:66, 68
"The Typical American?" (Masters) **1**:343
"Typists" (Page) **12**:173
"Typists in the Phoenix Building" (Wright) **14**:348
Tyrannus Nix? (Ferlinghetti) **1**:174
"Tyranny" (Lanier)
See "Spring and Tyranny"
"Tyrant of the Syracuse" (MacLeish) **47**:193
"Tyrian Businesses" (Olson) **19**:280, 283
Tzingal (Chappell)
See *See Castle Tzingal*
"Tzu-yeh Song #3" (Li Po) **29**:144
"U nog drugikh ne zabyval" (Lermontov) **18**:302
U samovo morya (Akhmatova) **2**:15
"U tonkoi pnovoloki nad volnoi ovsov" (Tsvetaeva) **14**:319, 321, 323
"Uber Das Werden im Vergehen" (Hölderlin) **4**:147
"Über Gräber" (Benn) **35**:45
"Überall Jerusalem" (Sachs) **78**:157
"Überlebende" (Sachs) **78**:114
"Uccello" (Corso) **33**:41, 43, 47; **108**:19
"Ucieczka" (Mickiewicz) **38**:151-53
"Uffington" (Betjeman) **75**:26, 82, 95-96
"Ugliness" (Mistral)
See "Lo feo"
"Ugolino" (Heaney) **18**:240
"Uh, Philosophy" (Ammons) **16**:6, 13, 36-7
"Ulalume" (Poe) **1**:425-26, 428, 431, 434, 436, 439-40, 442-43, 447, 453; **54**:273, 276, 330-31
"Ulster" (Kipling) **91**:133
"An Ulster Prophecy" (Montague) **106**:216, 251, 263-67
"Ultima canto di Saffo" (Leopardi) **37**:102, 110, 142, 169
"A Ultima Nau" (Pessoa) **20**:162
"Ultima Ratio Reagan" (Nemerov) **24**:290
"Ultima Ratio Regum" (Spender) **71**:202, 226
Ultima Thule (Longfellow) **30**:26
"Ultimate Birth" (Aleixandre) **15**:3
"The Ultimate Infidelity" (Gozzano) **10**:180
"Ultimate Motel" (Kennedy) **93**:144
"The Ultimate Poem Is Abstract" (Stevens) **6**:314; **110**:116-18, 229
"Ultimate Reality" (Lawrence) **54**:185
"Ultimatum" (Cullen) **20**:57
"Ultimatum" (Larkin) **21**:224-25
"Ultimátum" (Parra) **39**:273
"Ultimatum" (Sassoon) **12**:259
"Ultimi cori per la Terra Promessa" (Ungaretti) **57**:339
"L'Ultimo" (Quasimodo) **47**:297
"El último amor" (Aleixandre) **15**:38
"Ultimo árbol" (Mistral) **32**:183
"Ultimo canto di Saffo" (Quasimodo) **47**:297
"Ultimo sol en Villa Ortúzar" (Borges) **32**:83
"Ultra Crepadarius" (Hunt) **73**:136, 150-51
"Ultraísmo" (Borges) **22**:93
Ultramarine (Carver) **54**:3, 11, 13, 20-23
"Ultrasons" (Brossard) **80**:22
"Ultrateléfono" (Storni) **33**:261, 295
"Ulysses" (Birney) **52**:8, 39
"Ulysses" (Graves) **6**:130, 137
"Ulysses" (Tennyson) **6**:354, 359, 366, 381, 383-84, 398, 409, 411; **101**:119, 121, 123-24, 127, 142, 219-21, 224, 226, 270, 272-73, 281
"Ulysses by the Merlion" (Thumboo) **30**:310, 312-13, 314, 320-21, 329
"Umarli" (Herbert) **50**:6-7
"Umbra" (Campion) **87**:63
"Umbra reginae nobiles viros docet, quid sit de rebus hisce fluxis sentiendum" (Southwell)
See "The Shade of the Queen Teaches Her Noblemen, What Is to be Thought of These Fleeting Things below"
"An Umbrella" (Stein) **18**:334
Umbrella from Piccadilly (Seifert)
See *Deštník z Piccadilly*
The Umbrella from Piccadilly (Seifert)
See *Deštník z Piccadilly*
An Umbrella from Piccadilly (Seifert)
See *Deštník z Piccadilly*
"Umi no ikari" (Ishikawa) **10**:215
"L'umile Itallia" (Pasolini) **17**:294
"Umirajushchij gladiator" (Lermontov) **18**:302
"A un heiniano d'Italia" (Carducci) **46**:73
"A un poeta'" (Guillén) **35**:230
"A un poeta del siglo XIII" (Borges) **22**:82, 85
"A un poeta futuro" (Cernuda) **62**:197
"A un riche" (Hugo) **17**:94
"A un sembrador" (Mistral) **32**:145
"A un vincitore nel pallone" (Leopardi) **37**:102, 118
"A una Bottiglia di Valtellina del 1848" (Carducci) **46**:52
"A una espada en York" (Borges) **32**:87, 95
"Unable to Create Carrier" (Raworth) **107**:301
"Unable to Hate or Love" (Page) **12**:175
"Unable to Wake in the Heat" (Bell) **79**:9
"The Unacknowledged Legislator's Dream" (Heaney) **18**:205
"Un'altra risorta" (Gozzano) **10**:185
"Un-American Investigators" (Hughes) **1**:252; **53**:111
"Unanimity Has Been Achieved, Not a Dot Less for Its Accidentalness" (Kaufman) **74**:185, 216
Unattainable Earth (Milosz)
See *Niobjeta ziemia*
"The Unattained Place" (Muir) **49**:230, 265
"Das Unaufhörliche" (Benn) **35**:66

"The Unauthorized Autobiography of Me" (Alexie) **53**:23
"Unbelief" (Pushkin)
See "Bezverie"
"The Unbeliever" (Bishop) **3**:48; **34**:52-53, 156
"The Unborn" (Wright) **14**:352
"An Unborn Child" (Mahon) **60**:138, 181, 186, 192
"Unclassified Poem" (Wang Wei) **18**:387
"Unclassified Poems of Ch'in-chou" (Tu Fu) **9**:332
"Uncle" (Niedecker) **42**:119-22
"Uncle Ananias" (Robinson) **35**:362
"Uncle Arly" (Lear)
See "Incidents in the Life of My Uncle Arly"
"Uncle Bullboy" (Jordan) **38**:127
"Uncle Cal" (Stone) **53**:258
"Uncle Cal on Fashions" (Stone) **53**:258
"Uncle Isidore" (Abse) **41**:25
"Uncle Jim" (Cullen) **20**:64
"Uncle Ool's Song against the Ill-Paid Life of Poetry" (Kennedy) **93**:144
Uncle Shelby's Story of Lafcadio, the Lion Who Shot Back (Silverstein) **49**:348
"The Uncle Speaks in the Drawing Room" (Rich) **5**:359, 392
"The Unclean Start" (Cohen) **109**:23, 27
"Unclench Yourself" (Piercy) **29**:310
"Uncle's First Rabbit" (Cervantes) **35**:104, 108, 113, 116, 134
"Uncle's Journey" (Tapahonso) **65**:259
"Uncollected Poems" (Crane) **3**:90
Uncollected Poems (Betjeman) **75**:81
The Uncollected Verse of Aphra Behn (Behn) **88**:22
"The Uncreating Chaos" (Spender) **71**:166-67, 186, 208, 225, 229
"The Uncreation" (Pinsky) **27**:164
"Und Drang" (Pound) **95**:112, 120-23
Und Niemand weiss weiter (Sachs) **78**:111, 140, 156-57, 167, 169-71, 173-74, 219, 225
"Undenominational" (Betjeman) **75**:75
"Under" (Guest) **55**:213
"Under" (Sandburg) **2**:300; **41**:225, 314
"Under a Certain Little Star" (Szymborska)
See "Pod jedna gwiazdka"
"Under a Hat Rim" (Sandburg) **41**:313
"Under a Patched Sail" (Moore) **49**:109
Under a Soprano Sky (Sanchez) **9**:238-39, 245
"Under Ben Bulben" (Yeats) **20**:312, 324, 333
"Under Black Leaves" (Merwin) **45**:39-40
"Under Libra" (Merrill) **28**:223, 256
"Under One Small Star" (Szymborska)
See "Pod jedna gwiazdka"
"Under Peyote" (Corso) **33**:22
"Under Rain" (Winters) **82**:316
"Under Saturn" (Yeats) **20**:342
"Under Sedation" (Hope) **56**:276
"Under Sirius" (Auden) **1**:23
"Under St. Paul's" (Davie) **29**:94
"Under Stars" (Gallagher) **9**:37, 58, 60
Under Stars (Gallagher) **9**:37, 42, 54, 58-60
"Under the Bamboo Tree" (Johnson) **24**:151, 170
"Under the Canals" (Wright) **36**:311
"Under the Cupola" (Merrill) **28**:251-52
"Under the Earth" (Aleixandre) **15**:20-2
"Under the Hanger" (Schuyler) **88**:194
"Under the Hazel Bough" (Birney) **52**:22
"Under the L.A. Airport" (Ortiz) **17**:229
"Under the Locusts" (Ransom) **61**:294
"Under the Maud Moon" (Kinnell) **26**:247-52, 255, 257, 264, 272
"Under the Migrants" (Merwin) **45**:48-9
"Under the Mistletoe" (Cullen) **20**:85
"Under the Moon's Reign" (Tomlinson) **17**:336, 349
Under the North Star (Hughes) **89**:149-50
"Under the Oak" (Lawrence) **54**:168
"Under the Old One" (Merwin) **45**:8
"Under the Olives" (Graves) **6**:155-56
"Under the Rose" (Rossetti)
See "The Iniquity of the Fathers upon the Children"
"Under the Rowans" (Carman) **34**:208
"Under the Skin of the Statue of Liberty" (Yevtushenko) **40**:369
Under the Skin of the Statue of Liberty (Yevtushenko) **40**:369
"Under the Viaduct" (Dove) **6**:110
"Under the Violets" (Holmes) **71**:67-68, 92
"Under the Waterfall" (Hardy) **8**:118
"Under the Weather" (Hope) **56**:277
Under the Wilgas (Gilmore) **87**:283, 299, 301-2
"Under the Window: Ouro Prêto" (Bishop) **34**:138-39, 141
"Under the Wood" (Thomas) **53**:303-5
"Under the World's Wild Rims" (Hughes) **89**:123
"Under Three Lower Topsails" (Masefield) **78**:90
"Under Willows" (Rossetti) **7**:285
Under Your Clear Shadow and Other Poems about Spain (Paz)
See *Bajo tu clara sombra y otros poemas sobre España*
Undercliff: Poems, 1946-1953 (Eberhart) **76**:5, 37, 42, 48, 59
"The Underdog" (Tolson) **88**:254
"The Underground Stream" (Dickey) **40**:175, 180, 185, 192
"Underkill" (Birney) **52**:28, 43
"The Undermining of the Defense Economy" (Wright) **36**:340
"Underneath 8" (Graham) **59**:186
"Underneath 9" (Graham) **59**:188
"Underneath 13" (Graham) **59**:189
"Underneath (Upland)" (Graham) **59**:184
Undersong: Chosen Poems Old and New (Revised) (Lorde) **12**:153-58
"Understanding" (Cavafy) **36**:91
"Understanding but not Forgetting" (Madhubuti) **5**:337-38, 340
"Understood Not" (Cavafy) **36**:33
"The Undertaking" (Glück) **16**:126, 128, 142
Undertones of War (Blunden) **66**:12, 14, 17, 21, 33-34, 36-40, 44-45, 48-49, 51, 54, 58
"Undertow" (Sandburg) **41**:267
"Underwear" (Ferlinghetti) **1**:183
The Under-wood (Jonson) **17**:169, 180, 191
The Under-Wood II (Jonson) **17**:171, 194-95, 214
The Under-Wood III (Jonson) **17**:195
The Under-Wood IV (Jonson) **17**:194
The Under-Wood LVI (Jonson) **17**:194
The Under-Wood LVIII (Jonson) **17**:194
The Under-Wood LXII (Jonson) **17**:156
The Under-Wood LXIV (Jonson) **17**:156
The Under-Wood LXIX (Jonson) **17**:153
The Under-Wood LXVIII (Jonson) **17**:156
The Under-Wood LXX (Jonson) **17**:164
The Under-Wood LXXI (Jonson) **17**:162
The Under-Wood LXXII (Jonson) **17**:193
The Under-Wood LXXVI (Jonson) **17**:156
The Under-Wood LXXXVI (Jonson) **17**:191
The Under-Wood XIII (Jonson) **17**:154, 157-59, 211
The Under-Wood XL (Jonson) **17**:194
The Under-Wood XLII (Jonson) **17**:180
The Under-Wood XLIV (Jonson) **17**:194
The Under-Wood XLV (Jonson) **17**:181, 189
The Under-Wood XLVII (Jonson) **17**:153-54, 208
The Under-Wood XV (Jonson) **17**:153, 158, 161-62, 164, 208
The Under-Wood XVI (Jonson) **17**:191
The Under-Wood XXIX (Jonson) **17**:189
The Under-Wood XXVI (Jonson) **17**:153, 172, 192
The Under-Wood XXXI (Jonson) **17**:193
The Under-Wood XXXVII (Jonson) **17**:153-54
Underwoods (Stevenson) **84**:299, 302-4, 306, 308, 321, 324-26, 328-32, 338
"The Underworld" (Hongo) **23**:199
"Undraped Beauty" (Tagore)
See "Vivasana"
"L'Une et l'autre" (Char) **56**:120
"A une femme" (Hugo) **17**:68
"A une robe rose" (Gautier) **18**:125, 129
À une sérénité crispée (Char) **56**:108-9, 112, 169, 173
"À une Terre d'aube" (Bonnefoy) **58**:126
"Uneasiness in Fall" (Bly) **39**:85
Unedited Books of Poetry (Jiménez)
See "A Horrible Religious Error"
"Unemployment Monologue" (Jordan) **38**:125
Unending Blues (Simic) **69**:282-83, 287, 289, 291, 297, 302, 311, 318-19, 337
"The Unending Rose" (Borges) **22**:97; **32**:140
The Unending Rose (Borges) **32**:66
"Unendurable Love" (Tagore)
See "Asahya bhalobasa"
"The Unequal Fetters" (Finch) **21**:154, 181
"Unequalled Days" (Pasternak)
See "Edinstvennye dni"
"Unerwidert" (Stramm) **50**:172
"Unexpected Joy" (Blok) **21**:3
"An Unexpected Meeting" (Szymborska)
See "Niespodziane spotkanie"
"The Unexpected Peril" (Meynell) **112**:165, 191
"The Unexplorer" (Millay) **6**:235
"The Unfaithful Married Woman" (García Lorca)
See "La casada infiel"
"The Unfaithful Servants" (Very) **86**:96
"The Unfaithful Wife" (García Lorca)
See "La casada infiel"
"Unfaithfulness" (Cavafy) **36**:80, 86
"The Unfamiliar Place" (Muir) **49**:230, 242, 288
"Unfinished Ballad" (Wylie) **23**:321
"Unfinished Book of Kings" (Merwin) **45**:18, 22, 28, 49
Unfinished Poems (Southwell) **83**:294
"Unfinished Portrait" (Wylie) **23**:318, 322, 324
"Unflushed Urinals" (Justice) **64**:273, 279
"Unfold! Unfold!" (Roethke) **15**:248, 254, 276, 300-03
"Unforeseen" (de la Mare) **77**:148
"Unforgotten" (Service) **70**:150
"Unfortunate Coincidence" (Parker) **28**:360
"The Unfortunate Lover" (Marvell) **10**:265-66, 271, 300, 302; **86**:178, 198, 257, 263
"The Unfortunate One" (Marie de France)
See "Le Chaitivel"
Unfortunately It Was Paradise: Selected Poems (Darwish) **86**:33
"'Ung 'Imself Alright" (Gilmore) **87**:295
"Ungathered Apples" (Wright) **36**:279, 336
Ungathered Verse (Jonson) **17**:161
"The Ungrateful" (Stone) **53**:256
"The Ungrateful Garden" (Kizer) **66**:73
The Ungrateful Garden (Kizer) **66**:72
"Ungratefulnesse" (Herbert) **4**:119, 133-34
"Unhappy Dighton" (Crabbe) **97**:112
"Unhappy Man, Why Wander There" (Tennyson) **101**:244
"Unheard" (Char)
See "Ne s'entend pas"
"Unheroic" (Boland) **58**:38, 40, 62
"The Unhistoric Story" (Curnow) **48**:4, 25, 27-29
"Unhistorical Events" (Kaufman) **74**:216, 231, 259, 271
"The Unicorn" (Silverstein) **49**:319, 346
"Unidad" (Alurista) **34**:42
"Unidentified Flying Object" (Hayden) **6**:196
L'Union libre (Breton) **15**:51, 62
"Unión Soviética" (Guillén) **23**:123, 127
"Union Square" (Teasdale) **31**:363, 379
"Union Street: San Francisco, Summer 1975" (Carver) **54**:29
"The Unions at the Front" (Neruda)
See "Los Grernios en el frente"
"L'unique" (Éluard) **38**:69

"A Unison" (Williams) **7**:360
"The United Fruit Company" (Neruda)
See "La United Fruit Company"
"La United Fruit Company" (Neruda) **4**:296
"University Days" (Raworth) **107**:309
U.S. 1 (Rukeyser) **12**:203-04, 211
"U.S. 1946 King's X" (Frost) **1**:200
"The Unity" (Stern) **115**:277
"Unity of Hearts" (Baca) **41**:37
"L'univers solitude" (Éluard) **38**:67, 85
"The Universal Andalusia" (Jiménez)
See "El andaluz universal"
"The Universal Dream" (Leapor) **85**:259
Universal Prayer (Pope) **26**:311
"Universal Sorrow" (Tagore)
See "Vishvashoka"
"The Universe" (Swenson) **14**:258, 268, 281
"Universe Is One Place" (Stafford) **71**:288-89, 360
"UNIVERSITY" (Birney) **52**:76-77
"University" (Shapiro) **25**:279, 283, 290, 297-300, 311, 313, 318
"The Unjustly Punished Child" (Olds) **22**:307
"The Unknown" (Masters) **36**:181, 221, 242
"The Unknown" (Thomas) **53**:271
"The Unknown" (Williams) **7**:369
"The Unknown Bird" (Thomas) **53**:300
The Unknown Eros (Patmore)
See *The Unknown Eros, and Other Odes I-XXXI*
The Unknown Eros, and Other Odes I-XXXI (Patmore) **59**:204-10, 212-15, 218, 222-25, 259, 261-62, 264-68, 273, 275-77
"Unknown Girl in the Maternity Ward" (Sexton) **2**:349, 355; **79**:258
"The Unknown God" (Meynell) **112**:152, 221-22
"The Unknown Neighbor" (Stryk) **27**:201
"Unknown Soldier" (Hughes) **89**:102
"Unknown Soldiers" (Masters) **36**:210
"Unknown to Mr. Colburn" (Hood) **93**:91, 105
"The Unknown War" (Sandburg) **41**:303
"Unknown Water" (Wright) **14**:341, 353
"The Unknown Woman" (Blok) **21**:14
"Unlawful Assembly" (Enright) **93**:21
"Unless" (Warren) **37**:312
"Unless It Was Courage" (Bell) **79**:35
"Unlinked" (Meynell) **112**:191, 228, 291
"The Unlived Life" (Boland) **58**:48
"Unlucky Soldier" (Sarton) **39**:322
"An Unmarked Festival" (Meynell) **112**:157, 165, 230
"Unmarried Mothers" (Clarke) **112**:62, 122
"Unmeasured Tempo" (Angelou) **32**:29
"Unmut" (Werfel) **101**:323
"Unnatural Love" (Tate) **50**:274, 300
"Unnatural Powers" (Jeffers) **17**:118
"Unnatural State of the Unicorn" (Komunyakaa) **51**:52-53, 55-56
"Uno" (Storni) **33**:238, 306
"The Unpardonable Sin" (Lindsay) **23**:280
"Unpredicted Particles" (Waldrop) **109**:141, 178
"Unprofitableness" (Vaughan) **81**:275, 332
"The Unquiet Grave" (Hardy) **92**:269
"Unregierbarkeit" (Enzensberger) **28**:150
"Unresolved" (Levertov) **11**:198
"Unrest" (Bly) **39**:4, 83, 90
"The Unreturning" (Carman) **34**:210, 216
"The Unreturning" (Owen) **19**:343; **102**:226
"Unrhyming Poems" (Lawrence) **54**:184
"Unromantic Love" (Cunningham) **92**:134, 140
"Les uns et les autres" (Verlaine) **2**:416
"An Unsaid Word" (Rich) **5**:359, 393
"Unscratchable Itch" (Silverstein) **49**:336
"The Unseen" (Pinsky) **27**:163
"The Unseen Hunter" (Shvarts) **50**:131, 144-45
"Unsere Marine" (Heine) **25**:134
"The Unsettled Motorcyclist's Vision of His Death" (Gunn) **26**:185, 207
"Unsleeping City" (García Lorca)
See "Ciudad sin sueño"
"Unsleeping City (Brooklyn Bridge Nocturne)" (García Lorca)
See "Ciudad sin sueño"
"Unsounded" (Rich) **5**:359
"Unspeakable" (McHugh) **61**:205
"Unspeakable" (Stone) **53**:257
"An Unstamped Letter in Our Rural Letter Box" (Frost) **39**:233
"The Unsung Heroes" (Dunbar) **5**:131
"Unsuspecting" (Toomer) **7**:336
"The Untamed" (Thomas) **99**:272-73, 275, 309
"The Untelling" (Strand) **63**:143-48, 154-56, 161-65
"Der Untergand der Titanic" (Enzensberger) **28**:149-51, 158, 160, 164-66
"Untergang" (Trakl) **20**:234, 264-65, 267, 269
"Untergrundbahn" (Benn) **35**:25, 30, 46
"Until Volume One" (Waldrop) **109**:179
"Untitled" (Graham) **59**:169
"Untitled" (Kaufman) **74**:219
"Untitled" (Strand) **63**:188
"Untitled" (Swenson) **14**:274, 285
"Untitled Blues" (Komunyakaa) **51**:33
"Untitled Lines Written Extempore in a Lady's Pocket-Book" (Burns) **114**:96
"Unto a caitife wretch" (Sidney) **32**:235
Unto Dyvers People (Skelton) **25**:374
"Unto the Whole—How Add?" (Dickinson) **1**:103
"Unto Us a Son Is Given" (Meynell) **112**:232, 299
"Untreu" (Stramm) **50**:172, 175, 189, 202, 209
"Untrimmed Mourning" (Chin) **40**:3
"The Untrustworthy Speaker" (Glück) **16**:157
"The Unvert Manifesto" (Spicer) **78**:255
"Unwilling Admission" (Wylie) **23**:310
"The Unwritten" (Merwin) **45**:77
The Unwritten (Sikelianos)
See "Agraphon"
"Unylyi kolokola zvon" (Lermontov) **18**:302
"Gli uomini che si voltano" (Montale) **13**:133
"L'uomo di pena" (Pasolini) **17**:261
"Up and Down" (de la Mare) **77**:73
"Up and Down" (Merrill) **28**:222
"Up and Down" (Smith) **12**:316
"Up at a Villa-Down in the City, as Distinguished by an Italian Person of Quality" (Browning) **2**:38
"Up at La Serra" (Tomlinson) **17**:311, 325-26, 341
"Up Branches of Duck River" (Snyder) **21**:297
Up Country: Poems of New England (Kumin) **15**:181-83, 187, 189, 194, 208
"up her can nada" (Birney) **52**:74
"Up Hill" (Rossetti) **7**:261, 298
"Up in the Wind" (Thomas) **53**:291, 327
"Up Rising" (Duncan) **2**:25, 104; **75**:114-15, 118, 120, 132-33, 158, 254-55, 273, 276
"Up So Doun" (Montague) **106**:327
"Up There" (Stone) **53**:259
"Upahar" (Tagore) **8**:407
"The Upas Tree" (Pushkin)
See "Anchar"
"An Upbraiding" (Hardy) **8**:93; **92**:235
"Uplands" (Ammons) **16**:31
Uplands (Ammons) **16**:22, 28, 46, 61
"Upon a Beautiful Young Nymph Going to Bed" (Swift)
See "A Beautiful Young Nymph Going to Bed. Written for the Honour of the Fair Sex"
"Upon a Child. An Epitaph" (Herrick) **9**:129-31
"Upon a Child That Died" (Herrick) **9**:130-31
"Upon a Comely and Curious Maide" (Herrick) **9**:129
"Upon a Confessional Poet" (Chappell) **105**:50
"Upon a Dead Man's Head" (Skelton)
See *Uppon a Deedmans Hed*
"Upon a fit of Sickness, Anno 1632" (Bradstreet) **10**:20, 26, 34, 59
"Upon a Foreign Verse" (Seferis)
See "Reflections on a Foreign Line of Verse"
"Upon A.M." (Suckling) **30**:129, 143
"Upon A moale in his mistris face" (Davenant) **99**:165-66
"Upon A Mole in Celia's Bosom" (Carew) **29**:43
"Upon a Ray of Winter Sun" (Seferis) **66**:206
"Upon a Ribband" (Carew) **29**:9
"Upon a Spider Catching a Fly" (Taylor) **63**:315
"Upon a Wasp Child with Cold" (Taylor) **63**:297
"Upon Abhorrence" (Traherne) **70**:320
"Upon Abilitie" (Traherne) **70**:320
"Upon Appleton House" (Marvell) **10**:260, 265-67, 269, 271-73, 289-91, 294, 298, 303-04, 314-15, 318; **86**:178, 184, 198, 239-42, 244, 263
"Upon Ben Jonson" (Herrick) **9**:86
"Upon Dr. Harvey" (Cowley) **90**:46, 53-54
"Upon Her Blush" (Herrick) **9**:143
"Upon Her Majesty's New Buildings at Somerset House" (Waller) **72**:327
"Upon Himself" (Herrick) **9**:89, 109
"Upon Himselfe Being Buried" (Herrick) **9**:128, 131
"Upon His Drinking a Bowl" (Wilmot) **66**:237, 306, 308, 329
"Upon His Kinswoman Mistris Elizabeth Herrick" (Herrick) **9**:131
"Upon His Last Request to Julia" (Herrick) **9**:108
"Upon his leaving his Mistriss" (Wilmot) **66**:339
"Upon His Majesty's Repairing of St. Paul's" (Waller) **72**:328, 340
"Upon His Returning Home to Pei-hai, I Respectfully Offer a Farewell Banquet to Reverend Master Kao Ju-Kuei, Gentleman of the Tao after He Transmitted to Me a Register of the Way" (Li Po) **29**:171
"Upon Julia's Clothes" (Herrick) **9**:135-36
"Upon Julia's Recovery" (Herrick) **9**;102
"Upon Julia's Washing Her Self in the River" (Herrick) **9**:143
"Upon Meeting Don L. Lee, in a Dream" (Dove) **6**:104-05, 108
"Upon Mr. Abraham Cowley's Retirement" (Philips) **40**:270, 328
"Upon My Daughter Hannah Wiggin Her Recovery from a Dangerous Fever" (Bradstreet) **10**:34
"Upon My Dear and Loving Husband His Goeing into England" (Bradstreet)
See "To My Dear and Loving Husband His Goeing into England"
"Upon my Lady Carlile" (Suckling)
See "Upon My Lady Carlisle's Walking in Hampton Court Garden"
"Upon my Lady Carliles walking in Hampton-Court garden" (Suckling)
See "Upon My Lady Carlisle's Walking in Hampton Court Garden"
"Upon My Lady Carlisle's Walking in Hampton Court Garden" (Suckling) **30**:138
"Upon My Lord Broghill's Wedding" (Suckling)
See "Upon My Lord Brohall's Wedding"
"Upon My Lord Brohall's Wedding" (Suckling) **30**:143, 148, 152-53
"Upon My Lord Winchilsea's Converting the Mount in His Garden to a Terras" (Finch) **21**:176
"Upon My Refusal to Herald Cuba" (Corso) **108**:6, 22, 34-35
"Upon My Son Samuel His Going to England" (Bradstreet) **10**:26, 34, 36, 63
Upon Nothing, A Poem (Wilmot) **66**:237, 257, 259-62, 264-65, 285-87, 289, 339

"Upon occasion of his Ode of defiance annext to his Play of the new Inne" (Carew)
See "To Ben Jonson Upon occasion of his Ode of defiance annext to his play of the new Inne"
"Upon Our B. Saviours Passion" (Crashaw)
See "The Office of the Holy Cross"
"Upon St. Thomas's Unbelief" (Suckling) **30**:156
"Upon the Annunciation and Passion" (Donne) **1**:139
"Upon the Bank at Early Dawn" (Thoreau) **30**:181, 194, 223, 254-55, 267
"Upon the Bleeding Crucifix" (Crashaw)
See "Song upon the Bleeding Crucifix"
"Upon the Body of our Blessed Lord, Naked and Bloody" (Crashaw) **84**:15
"Upon the Crown of Thorns taken down from the Head of our Blessed Lord, all Bloody" (Crashaw) **84**:15
"Upon the Curtaine of Lucasta's Picture" (Lovelace) **69**:233-34
"Upon the Death of King James the Second" (Finch) **21**:170
"Upon the Death of my Lady Rich" (Waller) **72**:347
"Upon the Death of O.C." (Marvell)
See "Poem upon the Death of O. C."
"Upon the Death of Sir William Twisden" (Finch) **21**:144
"Upon the Death of the Lord Protector" (Marvell)
See "Poem upon the Death of O. C."
"Upon the Dolorous Death and Much Lamentable Chance of the Most Honourable Earl of Northumberland" (Skelton) **25**:339, 372
"Upon the Earl of Roscommon's Translation of Horace" (Waller) **72**:355
"Upon the Feast of St. Simon and St. Jude" (Johnson) **81**:220
"Upon the Graving of her Name Upon a Tree in Barnelmes Walk" (Philips) **40**:297
"Upon the Hill and Grove at Billborow" (Marvell) **10**:269
"Upon the Image of Death" (Southwell) **83**:239, 279
"Upon the Lonely Moor" (Carroll) **74**:70, 73
"Upon the Marriage of the Lady Jane Cavendish with Mr. Cheney" (Davenant) **99**:179
"Upon the Much Lamented, Master J. Warr" (Herrick) **9**:129
"Upon the Nipples of Julia's Breast" (Herrick) **9**:143
"Upon the Priorie Grove, His usuall Retyrement" (Vaughan) **81**:363
"Upon the Roses in Julias Bosome" (Herrick) **9**:143
"Upon the Sweeping Flood" (Taylor) **63**:297, 319
"Upon This Bank at Early Dawn" (Thoreau)
See "Upon the Bank at Early Dawn"
"Upon Wedlock, and Death of Children" (Taylor) **63**:296-97, 316-17
"Upon Your Held-Out Hand" (Thomas) **2**:406
"An upper chamber in a darkened house" (Tuckerman)
See "Sonnet I.10"
"Upper Lambourne" (Betjeman) **75**:20, 77
"The Upper Meadows" (Winters) **82**:313
"Upper Voight's, To All the Cutthroat There" (Hugo) **68**:249, 292
Uppon a Deedmans Hed (Skelton) **25**:344
"Uprawa filozofii" (Herbert) **50**:5
"Uprooting" (Montague) **106**:303
"Upsilon" (Tolson) **88**:233, 241-43, 255, 262, 277, 304, 316, 320, 324, 333
"Upstream" (Montague) **106**:289, 319
"Upstream" (Sandburg) **41**:330
"Uptown" (Ginsberg) **4**:47
"The Urals" (Pasternak) **6**:268
"Urania" (Arnold) **5**:43
"Urania" (Holmes) **71**:69
Urania (Wroth)
See *The Countesse of Mountgomeries Urania*
"Urban Cemetery" (Cernuda) **62**:169, 172
"An Urban Convalescence" (Merrill) **28**:226, 234, 249, 273
"An Urban Guerrilla" (Curnow) **48**:49
Urbasi (Tagore) **8**:403
"Uriah Heap" (Yevtushenko) **40**:344
"Uriel" (Emerson) **18**:69, 79, 88
Urizen (Blake)
See *The Book of Urizen*
"Urlied" (Chappell) **105**:26, 38
"The Urn" (Olds) **22**:324
The Urn (Bely)
See *Urna*
Urna (Bely) **11**:3-4, 6-7, 24, 32-3
"Urodziny" (Szymborska) **44**:269
Uroki muzyki (Akhmadulina) **43**:2, 33, 48
"Uroki muzyki" (Akhmadulina) **43**:64
"Urtod" (Stramm) **50**:172-73, 198, 205-6, 209
"Urvashi" (Tagore) **8**:409
"Urwanderung" (Stramm) **50**:175
"Úryvek z dopisu" (Seifert) **47**:336
"Us" (Sexton) **2**:352
"U.S.A." (Birney) **52**:58
"The Use of 'Tu'" (Montale) **13**:145
"The Used Side of the Sofa" (Ríos) **57**:325
"Used Up" (Sandburg) **2**:303; **41**:225, 336
"Useless" (Atwood) **8**:27
"Uses" (Sexton) **79**:245
"Usignolo VI" (Pasolini) **17**:266
"Usignolo VII" (Pasolini) **17**:266
L'usignuolo della Chiesa Cattolica (Pasolini) **17**:252, 262, 264-67, 270, 272, 275, 277, 285, 287
Ustep (Mickiewicz)
See *The Digression*
"Ustica" (Paz) **1**:355, 360-61
"A Usual Prayer" (Berryman) **64**:96
"Usufruct" (Clarke) **112**:55
"The Usurpers" (Muir) **49**:197, 229, 233, 256, 283, 294-95
"Uswetakiyawa" (Ondaatje) **28**:338
"A Utilitarian View of the Monitor's Fight" (Melville) **82**:80, 84, 93, 196-97, 202-4, 270
"Utopia" (Enzensberger) **28**:159
"Utopia" (Szymborska) **44**:282, 298
"A Utopian Journey" (Jarrell) **41**:145
"Utopias" (Eliot) **20**:123
"Utopie" (Lamartine) **16**:263, 284
"Utro posle luny" (Akhmadulina) **43**:36, 43-44
"Utsarga" (Tagore) **8**:409
"Uvodili tebya na rassvete" (Akhmatova) **55**:25, 41, 55
"Uznik" (Lermontov) **18**:304
"V Al'bom" (Lermontov) **18**:302
"V bol'nitse" (Pasternak) **6**:266, 269, 286-87
"V den' Blagoveshchen'ia" (Tsvetaeva) **14**:322
"V dushe pustynnoi mnogo-mnogo" (Shvarts) **50**:134
"V. Jahrhundert" (Benn) **35**:9, 10, 70
"V. L. Davydovu" (Pushkin) **10**:412
"V lesu" (Pasternak) **6**:280
"V ony dni, ty mne byla kak mat'" (Tsvetaeva) **14**:321
"V opustevshem dome otdykha" (Akhmadulina) **43**:7
"V. R. 1819-1901" (Hardy) **92**:217, 310
"V starinny gody zhili-byli" (Lermontov) **18**:288
"V tot mesiats Mai" (Akhmadulina) **43**:3-4
"V tot mesjac maj, v tot mesjac moj" (Akhmadulina) **43**:3, 17
"vaalee daancers" (Bissett) **14**:33
"The Vacant Farmhouse" (de la Mare) **77**:149
"The Vacant Lot" (Brooks) **7**:69
"Vacant Lot" (Randall) **86**:334
"Vacant Lot" (Winters) **82**:319
"Vacation" (Shapiro) **25**:310, 316
"Vacation" (Stafford) **71**:287-88
"Vacation" (Zagajewski) **27**:389
Vacation Time: Poems for Children (Giovanni) **19**:138
"Vacation Trip" (Stafford) **71**:377
"La Vache" (Hugo) **17**:76, 91
"Les Vaches" (Clough) **103**:133, 155
"Vacillation" (Yeats) **20**:333; **51**:84, 147, 152
"The Vagabond" (Stevenson) **84**:309, 311
"The Vagabonds" (Carman) **34**:197, 218
"Vagabonds" (Rimbaud) **3**:261; **57**:229
"Vagg Hollow" (Hardy) **92**:274
"Vaguedás" (Castro) **41**:88
Vägvisare till underjorden (Ekeloef) **23**:62, 68-9, 77-8
"Vaile, love, mine eyes" (Campion) **87**:72
"Vain and Careless" (Graves) **6**:141, 150
"Vain, vain love" (Cavafy) **36**:52
"Vain wits and eyes" (Vaughan) **81**:317, 320
"Vain Word" (Borges)
See "Vanilocuencia"
"Vaine men" (Campion) **87**:53, 56, 67, 111
"Les vaines danseuses" (Valéry) **9**:392
"Vaishnava kavita" (Tagore) **8**:408
"Vaishnava Poetry" (Tagore)
See "Vaishnava kavita"
"Vaivén" (Paz) **1**:359
Vala (Blake)
See *The Four Zoas: The Torments of Love and Jealousy in the Death and Judgement of Albion the Ancient Man*
"Vale" (Ciardi) **69**:4
Vale (Viereck) **27**:259, 278
Vale Ave (H. D.) **5**:282
"The Vale of Esthwaite" (Wordsworth) **4**:417; **67**:354
"A Vale of Tears" (Southwell) **83**:281, 289-90, 296-97, 302-4, 307-8
"The Valediction" (Cowper) **40**:46
"Valediction" (Heaney) **18**:207
"Valediction" (MacNeice) **61**:106-7, 109, 111, 126, 133, 135, 137, 170-71
"Valediction" (Thomas) **99**:240, 243-44
"A Valediction: forbidding mourning" (Donne) **1**:124, 126, 130, 135; **43**:132, 177-78
"A Valediction Forbidding Mourning" (Rich) **5**:371, 395
"A Valediction: of my name, in the window" (Donne) **1**:152
"A Valediction: of the booke" (Donne) **1**:128, 130; **43**:166, 170
"A Valediction: of weeping" (Donne) **1**:124, 130, 153
"Valedictions" (Donne) **43**:163
"A Valedictory to Standard Oil of Indiana" (Wagoner) **33**:333
"Valentine" (Ashbery) **26**:145
"Valentine" (Creeley) **73**:95
"A Valentine" (Poe) **1**:445
"Valentine" (Wylie) **23**:332
"Valentine" (Zukofsky) **11**:349
"Valentine Delivered by a Raven" (Gallagher) **9**:63
"Valentine I" (Bishop) **3**:36
"A Valentine's Song" (Stevenson) **84**:326
"Valerik" (Lermontov) **18**:283
"Valery as Dictator" (Baraka) **113**:9
"Valhalla" (Francis) **34**:244, 246, 259-60
Valhalla and Other Poems (Francis) **34**:241, 244, 258-59, 261
"Valiant Love" (Lovelace) **69**:239
Vallée close (Char) **56**:115-16
"Valley Candle" (Stevens) **6**:338
Valley of Decision (Curnow) **48**:23-25, 29
"The Valley of the Shadow" (Robinson) **1**:490
"The Valley of the Shadow of Death" (Carroll) **74**:64-65
"The Valley of Unrest" (Poe) **1**:438
"Le vallon" (Lamartine) **16**:268, 276, 283, 290, 298-301
"Valparaiso" (Cisneros) **52**:163

"El vals" (Aleixandre) **15**:8, 14
"Valse d'Automne" (Benn) **35**:26, 66
"Valse triste" (Benn) **35**:8, 25, 26, 27
"Valuable" (Smith)
See "Valuable (After Reading Two Paragraphs in a Newspaper)"
"Valuable (After Reading Two Paragraphs in a Newspaper)" (Smith) **12**:296
"Value in Mountains" (Rexroth) **95**:271
"Value is in Activity" (Empson) **104**:92, 122
"Values" (Blunden) **66**:31, 44-45, 51, 53-55
"Values in Use" (Moore) **4**:261; **49**:132, 140
"Valvins" (Valéry) **9**:392
"The Vampire" (Baudelaire)
See "Les métamorphoses du vampire"
"Le Vampire" (Baudelaire)
See "Les métamorphoses du vampire"
"The Vampire" (Kipling) **3**:166
"Van der Lubbe" (Spender) **71**:181, 219, 221
"Van Gogh" (Niedecker) **42**:152
"Van Gogh among the Miners" (Mahon)
See "A Portrait of the Artist"
"Van Gogh in the Borinage" (Mahon) **60**:140, 149, 199
"Van Winkle" (Crane) **3**:100, 109
"Vanaspati" (Tagore) **8**:415
"Vancouver" (Davie) **29**:109
"Vancouver Lights" (Birney) **52**:4-6, 8, 38, 44, 46-47, 49, 66-67, 71-72, 74
"Vanilocuencia" (Borges) **22**:72; **32**:82
"The Vanishers" (Whittier) **93**:270-72
"Vanishing Point: Urban Indian" (Rose) **13**:232
"Vanitie" (Herbert) **4**:120
"Vanitie I" (Herbert) **4**:132
"Vanity" (Ungaretti) **57**:359
"The Vanity of All Worldly Things" (Bradstreet) **10**:2, 6, 21
The Vanity of Human Wishes: The Tenth Satire of Juvenal, Imitated by Samuel Johnson (Johnson) **81**:68-73, 78, 83, 85-89, 92, 95, 98, 103-8, 111-14, 126-29, 133-34, 138-44, 146-47, 150, 157, 163-66, 174, 178-81, 184, 186-87, 193-201, 203-4, 207-8, 210-11, 216, 227-30, 232-34, 236-39, 241-42, 248
"Vanity of Spirit" (Vaughan) **81**:277, 280-81, 306, 369
"Vanna's Twins" (Rossetti) **7**:291
"The Vantage Point" (Frost) **39**:231
"The Vanytyes of Sir Arthur Gorges Youthe" (Raleigh) **31**:238
"Vapor Trail Reflected in the Frog Pond" (Kinnell) **26**:263, 290
"Vaquero" (Dorn) **115**:109
"Varia" (Castro) **41**:88
"Variable" (Péret) **33**:220
Variaciones sobre tema mexicano (Cernuda) **62**:215-16, 220-21, 223
"Variation 1" (Cage) **58**:197
"Variation 4" (Cage) **58**:197
"Variation 5" (Cage) **58**:197
"Variation 6" (Cage) **58**:197
"Variation 7" (Cage) **58**:197
"Variation 9" (Cage) **58**:197
"Variation 10" (Cage) **58**:197
"Variation 12" (Cage) **58**:197
"Variation 15" (Cage) **58**:197
"Variation 16" (Cage) **58**:197
"Variation 19" (Cage) **58**:197
"Variation 21" (Cage) **58**:197
"Variation 25" (Cage) **58**:197
"Variation 26" (Cage) **58**:197
"Variation 29" (Cage) **58**:197
"Variation 30" (Cage) **58**:197
"Variation 31" (Cage) **58**:196
"Variation 32" (Cage) **58**:197
"Variation 34" (Cage) **58**:199
"Variation 36" (Cage) **58**:197-98
"Variation and Reflection on a Poem by Rilke" (Levertov) **11**:206
"Variation and Reflection on a Theme by Rilke (The Book of Hours Book I Poem 7)" (Levertov) **11**:203
"Variation: Ode to Fear" (Warren) **37**:284, 287, 289
"Variation on a Sentence by Laura (Riding) Jackson" (Yau) **61**:335
"Variation on a Theme by Rilke" (Levertov) **11**:202
"Variation on Heraclitus" (MacNeice) **61**:125
"Variations" (Creeley) **73**:11, 44, 48
"Variations" (Jarrell) **41**:127, 169
"Variations Calypso and Fugue on a Theme of Ella Wheeler Wilcox" (Ashbery) **26**:137, 155
"Variations for Two Pianos" (Justice) **64**:274
"Variations IV" (Jarrell) **41**:179
"Variations on a Generation" (Corso) **33**:45
"Variations on a Summer Day" (Stevens) **110**:150, 199
Variations on a Sunbeam (Elytis) **21**:120
"Variations on a Text by Vallejo" (Justice) **64**:252, 266, 272
"Variations on a Theme" (Cullen) **20**:58, 85
"Variations on a Theme by Rilke (The Book of Hours Book I Poem 4)" (Levertov) **11**:203
"Variations on a Theme by William Carlos Williams" (Koch) **80**:322
"Variations on a Theme of the Seventeenth Century" (Hope)
See "The Elegy"
"Variations on a Time Theme" (Muir) **49**:196, 200
Variations on a Time Theme (Muir) **49**:197, 229, 240-42, 269, 276, 288
"Variations on an Original Theme" (Ashbery) **26**:140
"Variations on Estrangement" (Dickey)
See "Turning Away: Variations on Estrangement"
"Variations on Intuition" (Spark) **72**:263
"Variations on My Life" (Spender) **71**:210
"Variations on My Life: The First" (Spender) **71**:228
"Variations on My Life: The Second" (Spender) **71**:228
"Variations on Two Dicta of William Blake" (Duncan) **2**:103; **75**:123, 199
"Variations on Variety" (Jacobsen) **62**:325, 333
"Variations sur le carnaval de Venise" (Gautier) **18**:130
"Vari-Colored Song" (Hughes) **53**:111
"Variorum" (Dorn)
See "Languedoc Variorum: A Defense of Heresy and Heretics"
Variorum (Yeats)
See *The Variorum Edition of the Poems of W. B. Yeats*
The Variorum Edition of the Poems of W. B. Yeats (Yeats) **51**:87, 143
Variorum Poems (Yeats)
See *The Variorum Edition of the Poems of W. B. Yeats*
"Various 1930s Love Songs" (Snodgrass) **74**:333
Various Poems of All Periods (Valéry)
See *Poésies*
Various Positions (Cohen) **109**:29
"Various Protestations from Various People" (Knight) **14**:52
"Varsha-mangal" (Tagore) **8**:411
"Varshashesh" (Tagore) **8**:411
"The 'Varsity Students' Rag" (Betjeman) **75**:9, 13
"Vasanter Kusumer mela" (Tagore) **8**:406
"The Vase of Life" (Rossetti) **44**:169
"The Vase of Tears" (Spender) **71**:161
"Vashti" (Harper) **21**:185, 191, 209
"El vaso" (Mistral) **32**:176
"Vasundhara" (Tagore) **8**:408
"Vater und Sohn" (Werfel) **101**:302, 339
"Vaticinio" (Storni) **33**:239
Vaudeville for a Princess, and Other Poems (Schwartz) **8**:285, 292-94, 318
"Vaudracour and Julia" (Wordsworth) **4**:399
"Vaunting Oak" (Ransom) **61**:301
"Vecchi versi" (Montale) **13**:108, 157
"La vecchia ubriaca" (Pavese) **13**:214
"A veces me sucede" (Fuertes) **27**:3
Vecher (Akhmatova) **2**:3, 5-6, 11, 17
Vecherny albom (Tsvetaeva) **14**:305
"Vechernyaya progulka" (Bely) **11**:22
"Veer-Voices: Two Sisters Under Crows" (Dickey) **40**:210-12, 236
"Vegetable Island" (Page) **12**:178
"The Vegetable King" (Dickey) **40**:165, 175-76, 189, 230, 246, 258
"Vegetables I" (Stone) **53**:228, 254
"Vegetables II" (Stone) **53**:229
"A Vegetarian" (Hughes) **89**:102, 109
"Vegetation" (Neruda) **64**:329
"Vegetation" (Tagore)
See "Vanaspati"
"Veggio co' be ' vostr'occhi un dolce lume" (Michelangelo) **103**:307
"Veggio negli occhi della donna mia" (Cavalcanti) **114**:210, 223, 234
"Veggio nel tuo bel viso, signor mio" (Michelangelo) **103**:194, 306
"Veglia" (Ungaretti) **57**:361-64
"Vegnerà el vero Cristo" (Pasolini) **17**:254
"Vehi tehillatekha" (Amichai) **38**:6, 14
"Veía sentado" (Cernuda) **62**:240
"The Veil" (Graham) **59**:130
The Veil, and Other Poems (de la Mare) **77**:58, 63, 71, 73-74, 77, 83, 94
La Veillée (Sainte-Beuve) **110**:39-40
"Veillées" (Rimbaud) **57**:173, 243, 250, 253
The Vein (Raworth) **107**:305, 325, 341
Veinte poemas de amor y una canción desesperada (Neruda) **4**:276, 282, 284, 291, 299-305, 307; **64**:297, 318-19, 347
"Veinte siglos" (Storni) **33**:252
"The veïzades to his love" (Cavafy) **36**:52
Vějíř Boženy Něcové (Seifert) **47**:335
Ve-Lo al Menat Lizkor (Amichai) **38**:17-18, 23
"Velorio" (Cisneros) **52**:158-60, 164
"Velvet Shoes" (Wylie) **23**:301, 305, 307, 314-15, 318-20, 322-23, 330-32
"Vendanges" (Verlaine) **32**:400
"El vendedor de papeles" (Fuertes) **27**:11
"Vendémiaire" (Apollinaire) **7**:10, 36, 44-6
"Vendette della luna" (Carducci) **46**:42, 48
"vending machine" (Enzensberger) **28**:147
"The Vending Machine" (Ignatow) **34**:273
"Venerabile Viro" (Vaughan) **81**:363
"The Venetian Blind" (Jarrell) **41**:168
Venetian Epigrams (Goethe) **5**:223
The Venetian Glass Nephew (Wylie) **23**:322, 330
"The Venetian Vespers" (Hecht) **70**:67, 72, 75, 79, 81, 92, 109
The Venetian Vespers (Hecht) **70**:65-66, 77, 79, 86-88, 92, 94
"La venganza del minero" (Parra) **39**:303
The Vengeance of Fionn (Clarke) **112**:27-29, 33, 40-43, 66, 72-74, 76, 78, 81, 89, 115-16
"Veni Creator" (Meynell) **112**:156, 165-66, 298-99
"Veni Creator Spiritus" (Werfel) **101**:347, 357
"Veni vidi vixi" (Hugo) **17**:64
"Venice" (Longfellow) **30**:20
"Venice" (Melville) **82**:97, 106, 149
"Venice" (Pasternak) **6**:276
"Venice" (Tomlinson) **17**:331, 334
"Venice, an Italian Song" (Longfellow)
See "Venice"
"The Venice Poem" (Duncan) **2**:105-6; **75**:112, 126, 129, 174, 176-77, 179-81, 227-29, 261, 273
"Venom" (Dickey) **40**:199
"Il ventaglio" (Montale) **13**:108, 128-29
"La ventana" (Cernuda) **62**:214-15, 222
"Ventas" (Guillén) **23**:111
"Vento a Tindare" (Quasimodo)
See "Vento a Tíndari"

"Vento a Tíndari" (Quasimodo) **47**:273-74, 276, 290, 297, 301-2
"Vento e bandiere" (Montale) **13**:164
"Vento sulla mezzaluna" (Montale) **13**:110
"Ventriloquist" (Stone) **53**:257-58
Vents (Perse) **23**:209, 211, 213-18, 221, 223, 232, 234-35, 238-40, 242-43, 247-53, 255, 257
Venture of the Infinite Man (Neruda)
See *Tentativa del hombre infinito*
"Venus" (Darío) **15**:87
"Vénus anadyomène" (Rimbaud) **3**:255; **57**:202-4, 210-11, 243, 257, 292-94
Venus and Adonis (Shakespeare) **84**:229, 233, 254, 257, 260, 263, 292; **89**:281-364; **98**:241, 283, 311, 318; **101**:15, 42, 45-46, 56-58, 65, 71, 91
Venus and Adonis (Shakespeare)
"Venus and the Ark" (Sexton) **2**:355
"Venus and the Lute Player" (Snodgrass) **74**:330, 334
Venus and the Rain (McGuckian) **27**:77-78, 80-81, 93, 95, 100-104
"Venus and the Sun" (McGuckian) **27**:97
"Venus Transiens" (Lowell) **13**:66, 96
"Venus Tying the Wings of Love" (McGuckian) **27**:103
"Venusberg" (Barker) **77**:40
"Venus's-flytraps" (Komunyakaa) **51**:12, 58
"Veracruz" (Hayden) **6**:193-94
"Verandah" (Walcott) **46**:275, 285, 287
"Le Verbe Être" (Breton) **15**:51
"Le verbe marronner à René Depestre" (Césaire) **25**:29, 33
"Vercingetorix" (Melville)
See "Homage to Vercingetorix"
"La verdad" (Jiménez) **7**:202
"Verdade, Amor, Razão, Merecimento" (Camões) **31**:24
"Verde deriva" (Quasimodo) **47**:302
"Vereda del cuco" (Cernuda) **62**:174, 183, 196-97, 201, 222
"Vergissmeinnicht" (Douglas) **106**:199-201, 203-4, 206
"Verhalten" (Stramm) **50**:189
"Verifying the Dead" (Welch) **62**:339, 343, 370-71
"Verlaine Villanelle" (Spark) **72**:256
"Verlorenes Ich" (Benn) **35**:8, 34
"Vermächtnis" (Goethe) **5**:248
"Vermeer" (Nemerov) **24**:262, 266, 299
"Vermillon" (Char) **56**:156
"Vermont" (Carruth) **10**:73-4, 83
"Vermont Ballad: Change of Season" (Warren) **37**:341, 379
"Vermont Nature" (Stone) **53**:258
"Vernal Equinox" (Lowell) **13**:64
"Vernal Sentiment" (Roethke) **15**:246
The Vernal Walk: A Poem (Elliott) **96**:156-57, 181
"Vernichtung" (Stramm) **50**:170, 205
"Le verre d'eau" (Ponge) **107**:80, 118-19, 129, 173, 195
Vers de circonstance (Mallarmé) **102**:97-98
"Les Vers d'Eurymédon et Callirée" (Ronsard)
See *See "Les Amours d'Eurymédon et Callirée"*
"Vers dorés" (Nerval) **13**:181
"Vers dorés" (Verlaine) **32**:386
Vers et prose (Mallarmé) **4**:207; **102**:135
"Vers l'Arc en ciel" (Breton) **15**:49
"Vers minuit" (Éluard) **38**:67
"Vers nouveaux et chansons" (Rimbaud) **3**:285
"Versaglia" (Carducci) **46**:71
"The Versatile Historian" (Welch) **62**:338, 370, 374
Verschiedene (Heine) **25**:129-131
"Verse" (Corso) **108**:23
"Verse" (Cunningham) **92**:171
Verse (Benn) **35**:6
"Verse about a Red Officer" (Tsvetaeva) **14**:313
"Verse From Prose Writings" (Service) **70**:140
"Verse Forms" (Randall) **86**:291, 346-47
"A Verseman's Apology" (Service) **70**:140
"Verses about Russia" (Blok) **21**:9
"Verses about the Beautiful Lady" (Blok) **21**:2-3, 23
The Verses about the Beautiful Lady (Blok)
See *Stikhi o prekrasnoi dame*
Verses Address'd to the Imitator of the First Satire of the Second Book of Horace (Montagu) **16**:338-41
Verses and Sonnets (Belloc) **24**:28-9, 34, 38
"Verses design'd by Mrs. A. Behn to be sent to a fair Lady, that desir'd she would absent herself to cure her Love. Left Unfinished" (Behn) **88**:40
"Verses for a Centennial" (MacLeish) **47**:156
"Verses for a Certain Dog" (Parker) **28**:360
"Verses for a Nursery Wall" (Barker) **77**:3
"Verses for the 60th Birthday of Thomas Stearns Eliot" (Barker) **77**:12-13
Verses from a Tapestry (Seifert)
See *Býti básníkem*
Verses Humbly Address'd to Sir Thomas Hanmer on his Edition of Shakespear's Works 1743 (Collins) **72**:44, 48, 56-57, 78, 80-82, 118, 126, 146, 178, 193, 198
"Verses in Reply to an Invitation to dinner at Dr Baker's" (Goldsmith) **77**:223
"Verses in the Night" (Parker) **28**:362
Verses Intended for Lock and Montaigne (Prior) **102**:288
Verses, Lately Written upon Several Occasions (Cowley) **90**:7, 46, 118
"Verses on His Own Death" (Swift)
See "Verses on the Death of Dr. Swift"
"Verses on the Death of Dr. Swift" (Leapor) **85**:184
"Verses on the Death of Dr. Swift" (Swift) **9**:258, 265, 279-82, 294-95, 304, 306-08, 310
"Verses on the Death of T. S. Eliot" (Brodsky)
See "Stixi na smert T. S. Èliota"
"Verses on the Unknown Soldier" (Mandelstam)
See "Stikhi o neizvestnom soldate"
"Verses to Czechoslovakia" (Tsvetaeva)
See "Stikhi k Chekhii"
"Verses to Hanmer" (Collins) **72**:120, 122
"Verses to Lord Mulgrave" (Wilmot) **66**:262
Verses to the Imitator of Horace (Montagu)
See *Verses Address'd to the Imitator of the First Satire of the Second Book of Horace*
"Verses Turned" (Betjeman) **75**:93
"Verses Upon the Burning of Our House" (Bradstreet)
See "Some Verses Upon the Burning of Our House, July 18th, 1666"
"Verses written at Bath on Finding the Heel of a Shoe" (Cowper) **40**:70, 122
"Verses Written on a Paper which contained a Piece of Bride-Cake" (Collins) **72**:59
"Verses Wrote in a Lady's Ivory Table-book" (Swift)
See "Written in a Lady's Ivory Table-book, 1698"
Versi (Leopardi) **37**:123
"Versi del testamento" (Pasolini) **17**:259
Versi prosaici (Pound) **95**:171
Versification of Donne's Fourth Satire (Pope)
See *Satires of Dr. Donne Versified*
Versifications of Donne (Pope)
See *Satires of Dr. Donne Versified*
"Versilian Shore" (Montale)
See "Proda di Versilia"
"Version I" (Niedecker) **42**:124-25
"Version II" (Niedecker) **42**:124-25
"Verso decorativo" (Storni) **33**:246
"Verso Finistère" (Montale)
See "Vento sulla mezzaluna"
Verso la cuna del mondo (Gozzano) **10**:177, 184
"Verso la fede" (Gozzano) **10**:184
"Verso Siena" (Montale) **13**:109
"Versos de catorce" (Borges) **32**:57
Versos de salón (Parra) **39**:260, 270-73, 277, 285-87, 292, 295-96, 300-2
Versos libres (Martí) **76**:81-82, 88, 90, 96-97, 101, 103-6, 108, 116, 133, 140
"Versos para ti mismo" (Cernuda) **62**:265
Versos sencillos (Martí) **76**:76-77, 81-85, 90, 96, 99-103, 105-9, 117, 127, 135
Versts (Tsvetaeva)
See *Vyorsty I*
Versty I (Tsvetaeva)
See *Vyorsty I*
Versty II (Tsvetaeva)
See *Vyorsty II*
Versus (Nash) **21**:267, 269
Verteidigung der Wölfe (Enzensberger) **28**:133-38, 140, 143
Vertical Man (Kinsella) **69**:126
"Vertigo" (Graham) **59**:130, 138, 151-52, 193-94
"Vertigo" (Rich) **5**:360
"Vertue" (Herbert) **4**:100-01, 110, 113, 132-34
"Vertueux solitaire" (Éluard) **38**:84
A Very Heroical Epistle from My Lord All-Pride to Dol-Common (Wilmot) **66**:246, 266, 284-86, 321, 329, 342, 347-48
"Very late July" (Piercy) **29**:315
"Very Old Are the Woods" (de la Mare) **77**:99
"A Very Short Song" (Parker) **28**:346
"A Very Stretched Sennett" (Stone) **53**:222
"Very Tree" (Kunitz) **19**:147, 160
"Very Veery" (Niedecker) **42**:94
"Der Verwundete" (Werfel) **101**:348
"Verzeiht ihr meine Schwestern" (Sachs) **78**:211
"Verzweifelt" (Stramm) **50**:209
"Verzweiflung" (Stramm) **50**:204
"Verzweiflung" (Werfel) **101**:346
"Vespers" (Auden) **92**:43-49
"Vespers" (Glück) **16**:170
"Vespers" (Lowell) **13**:64, 67, 97
"Vespertine River" (Cernuda)
See "Río Vespertino"
"The Vestal in the Forum" (Wright) **36**:333
The Vestal Lady on Brattle. (Corso) **33**:2, 8, 14, 35-6, 42, 46-7; **108**:30-31, 38-39
"Vestigia" (Carman) **34**:229
"Vestigia nulla retrorsum (In Memoriam: Rainer Maria Rilke 1875-1926)" (MacDiarmid) **9**:156, 176
"Vesuvius" (Tolson) **88**:344
"The Veteran" (Blunden) **66**:60
"Vétérance" (Char) **56**:157
"Les veuves" (Baudelaire) **1**:44, 58-9; **106**:89
"Veve" (Brathwaite) **56**:68, 73-75, 88
"Vexilla Regis: the Hymn of the Holy Cross" (Crashaw) **84**:15, 19, 33, 37, 95, 98
"Via Crucis" (Noyes) **27**:136
La via del refugio (Gozzano) **10**:179, 184-85, 188
"Via et Veritas et Vita" (Meynell) **112**:166
"Via Felice" (Howe) **81**:49-50
"Via Negativa" (Thomas) **99**:359
"Via Portello" (Davie) **29**:95
"Viaje finido" (Storni) **33**:248-50
"The Vial of Attar" (Melville) **82**:78
"La víbora" (Parra) **39**:268-69, 277, 279, 282-84, 287
"Vibratory Description" (McGuckian) **27**:105
"Vice" (Baraka) **4**:15; **113**:7
"Vice Versa to Bach" (Hughes) **53**:192
"The Vices of the Modern World" (Parra)
See "Los vicios del mundo moderno"
"Los vicios del mundo moderno" (Parra) **39**:268-69, 287-89
"Vicissitude" (Gray)
See "Ode on the Pleasure Arising from Vicissitude"
"Vicolo" (Quasimodo) **47**:274
"A Victim" (Curnow) **48**:29
"The Victim of Aulis" (Abse) **41**:8-9

"The Victims" (Olds) **22**:310, 312, 319, 321, 323
"The Victor" (Winters) **82**:315
"The Victor Dog" (Merrill) **28**:230
"The Victor of Antietam" (Melville) **82**:138, 206
A Victorian Village (Reese) **29**:339
"Victoria's Secret" (Collins) **68**:216
"Victoria's Tears" (Barrett Browning) **6**:14, 29
The Victories of Love (Patmore) **59**:205-6, 210-11, 221, 226, 234-35, 240, 242-45, 258-61, 273-74
"The Victorious Sun" (Aleixandre)
See "El sol victorioso"
"Victory" (Dickey) **40**:242, 246-50
Victory: Celebrated by Thirty-eight American Poets (Braithwaite) **52**:106
"Victory in Defeat" (Patmore) **59**:262
Victory Odes (Pindar) **19**:378, 386, 390
"Vida" (Aleixandre)
See "Life"
"La Vida a veces es un río frío y seco" (Fuertes) **27**:16
"Vida de la expresión" (Guillén) **35**:227
"Vida de perros" (Parra) **39**:285-86
"Vida extrema" (Guillén) **35**:230
"Viday" (Tagore) **8**:415
Video Poems (Collins) **68**:203, 208, 217
Vides ut alta...Soracte (Horace) **46**:94
"Videshi phul" (Tagore) **8**:415
"La vie" (Éluard) **38**:69
"La Vie antérieure" (Baudelaire) **106**:65-71, 73, 127, 134
"La Vie dans la mort" (Gautier) **18**:131-32, 155
"La Vie de Chateau" (Hacker) **47**:80
"La vie immédiate" (Éluard) **38**:67, 73
La vie immédiate (Éluard) **38**:68
Vie, poésies et pensées de Joseph Delorme (Sainte-Beuve) **110**:3, 9, 12-13, 15, 17-18, 36-41, 43, 46, 48, 50-59, 61-69, 74
"Vieira de Silva, chère voisine, multiple et une . . ." (Char) **56**:146
"Los viejos" (Paz) **48**:179-80, 183
"Viele Herbste" (Benn) **35**:69
"Die vielen Dinge" (Werfel) **101**:317
Vienna (Spender) **71**:138, 171, 173-77, 181-84, 189, 191, 196, 199, 222-23
"Viennese Waltz" (Wylie) **23**:314, 333
"Viento entero" (Paz) **48**:207-8, 211, 213-14, 274
Viento entero (Paz) **1**:353, 356, 362-63, 369
"El vientre" (Aleixandre) **15**:34
"La Vierge folle" (Rimbaud) **57**:236, 277
"Le vierge, le vivace et le bel aujourdhui" (Mallarmé) **4**:202, 206; **102**:101
"Vierge Ouvrante" (Ní Chuilleanáin) **34**:362, 367, 373
"Les Vierges de Verdun" (Hugo) **17**:62, 74
"Vies" (Rimbaud) **3**:261-62; **57**:174, 247, 249, 251, 275
"Vies I" (Rimbaud) **57**:284
"Vietnam" (Montague) **106**:357
"Viet-Nam Addenda" (Lorde) **12**:155
"Vieux de la vieille" (Rimbaud) **57**:252
"Le Vieux Drapeau" (Béranger) **112**:12
"Le vieux saltimbanque" (Baudelaire) **1**:44, 58; **106**:89
"The View" (Hölderlin) **4**:178
"The View" (Milosz) **8**:198
"The View" (Strand) **63**:189
"A View across the Roman Campagna" (Barrett Browning) **6**:23
The View from a Blind I (Barker) **77**:40
"View from a Train" (Spender) **71**:225
"The View from an Attic Window" (Nemerov) **24**:270-71
"View from an Empty Chair" (Gallagher) **9**:50
"View from Charles Bridge" (Seifert) **47**:327
"The View from Here" (Stafford) **71**:263
"The View from Kandinsky's Window" (Guest) **55**:185
"View from Rosehill Cemetery: Vicksburg" (Walker) **30**:352
"View from the screen" (Bukowski) **18**:22
"The View from the Window" (Thomas) **99**:235
"View mee, Lord" (Campion) **87**:56, 65
"View of a Lake" (Williams) **109**:324
"View of a Pig" (Hughes) **7**:136, 140; **89**:188
"A View of Cracow" (Zagajewski) **27**:381, 385
"A View of Delft" (Zagajewski) **27**:385
"A View of Fujiyama After the War" (Dickey) **40**:175
"View of Pasadena from the Hills" (Winters)
See "On a View of Pasadena from the Hills"
"View of Teignmouth in Devonshire" (Lowell) **13**:67
"A View of the Brooklyn Bridge" (Meredith) **28**:182, 190
"A View of the Burning" (Merrill) **28**:239
"View of the Mountains from the Kozlov Steppes" (Mickiewicz)
See "Widok gór ze stepów Kozłowa"
"View of the Wilds" (Tu Fu) **9**:332
"View to the North" (Swenson) **14**:288
"View with a Grain of Sand" (Szymborska) **44**:314
View with a Grain of Sand: Selected Poems (Szymborska) **44**:286, 293, 295, 303-9, 317
"Views" (Montague) **106**:327
"Viewing the Body" (Snodgrass) **74**:290
"Viewing the Waterfall at Mount Lu" (Li Po) **29**:145
"Views of Myself" (Berryman) **64**:102
"Vigil" (Montague) **106**:215
"The Vigil" (Roethke) **15**:263
"Vigil" (Ungaretti) **57**:374
"Vigil" (Wagoner) **33**:366
"The Vigil" (Winters) **82**:320, 326
"Vigil Strange I Kept on the Field One Night" (Whitman) **3**:378
"Vigilance" (Breton) **15**:50-1
"Vigils" (Rimbaud)
See "Veillées"
"The Vigils of Fancy" (Peacock) **87**:326
"La vigne et la maison" (Lamartine) **16**:268
"Le vigneron champenois" (Apollinaire) **7**:22
"Vignetta" (Carducci) **46**:49
"Vignette" (Kumin) **15**:224
Vignettes (Tolson)
See *Harlem Vignettes*
"Vignettes Overseas" (Teasdale) **3**:330-311
"Vihanger gan" (Tagore) **8**:406
VIII (Wylie) **23**:305
"Viking Dublin: Trial Pieces" (Heaney) **18**:204
Viktorka (Seifert)
See *Píseň o Viktorce*
"Le Vilain" (Béranger) **112**:21
"Villa Adriana" (Rich) **5**:362
"La Villa Adriana" (Sainte-Beuve) **110**:56
"Villa on Chung-nan Mountain" (Wang Wei) **18**:368
"The Villa Restaurant" (Vulliamy) **46**:266
"Villa Serbelloni, Bellaggio" (Teasdale) **31**:338
"The Village" (Carruth) **10**:71
"The Village" (Pushkin) **10**:408-09
"The Village" (Thomas) **99**:269
"The Village" (Walcott) **46**:280
The Village: A Poem. In Two Books (Crabbe) **97**:69-75, 78, 82, 100, 135, 145, 148, 150, 153, 162, 167
"The Village Atheist" (Masters) **1**:335
"The Village Blacksmith" (Longfellow) **30**:12, 21, 34, 36, 48, 99, 103, 107
"A Village Edmund" (Gunn) **26**:183
"Village Girl" (Randall) **86**:339
"Village in Late Summer" (Sandburg) **41**:284
"The Village Inn" (Betjeman) **75**:18, 79
"A Village Life" (Walcott) **46**:283
The Village Minstrel, and Other Poems (Clare) **23**:25, 38, 42-4
"Village Mystery" (Wylie) **23**:301
The Village Patriarch: A Poem (Elliott) **96**:158, 160-61, 181-83
"A Village Tale" (Sarton) **39**:328
"The Village Wedding" (Sikelianos) **29**:359, 367-68, 373
"Villager" (Hugo) **68**:287
"The Villagers and Death" (Graves) **6**:142
"Villains" (Smith) **12**:339
"Villa-Lobos" (Stern) **115**:263
"Villanelle" (Empson) **104**:122
"Villanelle" (Hacker) **47**:79
"Villanelle for Fireworks" (Sarton) **39**:323
"Ville" (Rimbaud) **57**:234
"A Villequier" (Hugo) **17**:64, 82-83
"Villes" (Rimbaud) **3**:261, 264-65; **57**:173, 241, 284
"Villes III" (Rimbaud) **57**:241
"Vilota" (Pasolini) **17**:252
"Le Vin de l'assassin" (Baudelaire) **106**:104
"Le Vin des chiffonniers" (Baudelaire) **106**:146
"Le vin perdu" (Valéry) **9**:388, 390, 396
"The Vindictives" (Frost) **1**:206
"Vine" (Herrick) **9**:100, 109, 137
"Vine en un barco negre" (Guillén) **23**:120, 127
"The Vineyard" (Kipling) **3**:182
"The Vineyard" (Merwin) **45**:55
Vingt-cinq poèmes (Tzara) **27**:223, 227, 233
"Víno a čas" (Seifert) **47**:333
"Vino, primero, puro" (Jiménez) **7**:187
"Il vino triste" (Pavese) **13**:224
"Vintage" (Hass) **16**:216
"The Vintage to the Dungeon" (Lovelace) **69**:167, 181-82, 204, 206-8
"Vinus sai no zenban" (Nishiwaki) **15**:238
Violence (Boland)
See *In a Time of Violence*
"Violences" (Char) **56**:154, 156
Violent Pastoral (Merrill) **28**:253
The Violent Season (Paz)
See *La estación violenta*
"The Violent Space (or when your sister sleeps around for money)" (Knight) **14**:39, 41, 43-4, 52
"Violent Storm" (Strand) **63**:176
"The Violet" (Very) **86**:41
"Violetas" (Cernuda) **62**:222-23
"Las violetas" (Guillén) **35**:203
"Violets" (Cernuda)
See "Violetas"
"Violets" (Lawrence) **54**:161
"The Violets" (Patmore) **59**:228-29, 232
"The Viper" (Parra)
See "La víbora"
"Le Vipereau" (Char) **56**:152
"Viper-Man" (Davie) **29**:110
"Virgen de plástico" (Fuertes) **27**:23, 30
"Una virgen espléndida" (Martí) **76**:105
"A Virgile" (Hugo) **17**:94-95
"Virgilio" (Carducci) **46**:49, 52, 76
"The Virgin" (Jackson) **44**:7, 11-12
"The Virgin" (Philips) **40**:297
"The Virgin" (Thoreau) **30**:180, 198
"The Virgin Carrying a Lantern" (Stevens) **6**:310
"A Virgin Life" (Barker) **91**:17, 31-33, 42-44
"The Virgin Mary to the Child Jesus" (Barrett Browning) **6**:29-30
"The Virgin Mary's Conception" (Southwell) **83**:254, 278-79, 282, 284
"The Virgin Rides on Venice, and I on Her Back" (Shvarts) **50**:141-43
"The Virgin to Christ on the Cross" (Southwell) **83**:279
"Virgin Youth" (Lawrence) **54**:163-65, 174, 220, 231, 233-35
"Virginia" (Eliot) **5**:166
"Virginia" (Lindsay) **23**:280
"Virginia Britannia" (Moore) **49**:91, 98, 128, 134, 141
"Virginia Portrait" (Brown) **55**:108, 112-13, 152
"Virginia Woolf" (Schuyler) **88**:193
"The Virginians Are Coming Again" (Lindsay) **23**:280, 285
"The Virgins" (Voss) **46**:278

"The Virgins paradise: a dream" (Barker) **91**:6-7, 52
"Virgins Plus Curtains Minus Dots" (Loy) **16**:333
"The Virgin's Salutation" (Southwell) **83**:254, 283
Virgyne (Chatterton) **104**:18
"Virtue" (Herbert)
See "Vertue"
"Virtue" (Wheatley)
See "On Virtue"
"Virtue" (Williams) **109**:236, 323
"The Virtues" (Chappell) **105**:19
"Virtuosi" (Mueller) **33**:193
"Virtuoso Literature" (Wakoski) **15**:346-47
Virtuoso Literature for Two and Four Hands (Wakoski) **15**:346, 355, 361, 365-66
"Le visage mortel" (Bonnefoy) **58**:125
Le visage nuptial (Char) **56**:141, 171, 201
"Vishvashoka" (Tagore) **8**:417
"Visibile, invisibile" (Quasimodo) **47**:288
"Visible Export" (Montague) **106**:357
Visible Shivers (Raworth) **107**:291
"The Visible the Untrue" (Crane) **99**:70
The Visibility Trigger (Brathwaite) **56**:71
"The Visible World" (Graham) **59**:151
"A Vision" (Berry) **28**:8-9
"The Vision" (Brathwaite) **56**:64
"Vision" (Bridges) **28**:63, 88
"The Vision" (Burns) **6**:50; **114**:31, 42, 77, 81, 90, 135-38
"A Vision" (Clare) **23**:22, 25
"Vision" (Gibran)
See "Ru'ya'"
"The Vision" (Masters) **1**:342
"Vision" (Rimbaud) **3**:263
"Vision" (Sassoon) **12**:245
"The Vision" (Southey) **111**:184-85
"The Vision" (Traherne) **70**:169, 174, 176, 188-89, 228, 230, 243, 256-57, 270-71, 276, 314
"A Vision" (Winters) **82**:346
"Vision (2)" (Alexie) **53**:5-7
"Vision And Prayer" (Thomas) **2**:382, 387-88, 390; **52**:279, 290-91, 299, 301, 303-5
"Vision by Sweetwater" (Ransom) **61**:269, 271, 274, 279, 307
"A Vision, concerning his late Pretended Highnesse Cromwell, the Wicked" (Cowley) **90**:106
"La Vision des montagnes" (Hugo) **17**:66
"Vision Epizootic" (Corso) **108**:39
"Vision: From the Drum's Interior" (Alexie) **53**:11
"Vision in the Repair Shop" (Graves) **6**:143
A Vision of Beasts and Gods (Barker) **77**:14, 19-20
"Vision of England, '38" (Barker) **77**:38
"A Vision of India" (Kipling) **3**:190
"Vision of Jubal" (Eliot) **20**:123
"Vision of Kubla Khan" (Coleridge)
See "Kubla Khan"
"A Vision of Poets" (Barrett Browning) **6**:7, 26, 38, 41
"Vision of Rotterdam" (Corso) **33**:7, 41; **108**:20
A Vision of Sappho (Carman) **34**:232
"The Vision of Sin" (Tennyson) **6**:359-60, 366, 378
"The Vision of the Archagels" (Brooke) **24**:62, 75-6
"A Vision of the Last Judgment" (Blake) **63**:49
A Vision of the Last Judgment (Blake) **12**:40-42
"Vision through Timothy" (Eberhart) **76**:60
"Vision under the October Mountain: A Love Poem" (Warren) **37**:304
"A Vision upon this Conceit of The Fairy Queen" (Raleigh) **31**:204, 217, 298
"The Visionary" (Brontë) **8**:52
"Visione" (Carducci) **46**:49, 77, 86
"Visions" (Cervantes)
See "Visions of Mexico While at a Writing Symoposium in Port Townsend, Washington"
"Visions" (Howe) **81**:31
Les visions (Lamartine) **16**:266, 269, 287
"Visions of Johanna" (Dylan) **37**:47-49, 54-55
"The Visions of Love" (Peacock) **87**:321-22
"Visions of Mexico While at a Writing Symoposium in Port Townsend, Washington" (Cervantes) **35**:108, 118, 123, 124, 125, 126, 127, 130, 131, 135
Visions of the Daughters of Albion: The Eye Sees More Than the Heart Knows (Blake) **12**:35, 46, 57, 61, 63; **63**:16, 112
"The Visions of the Maid of Orleans" (Coleridge)
See "Joan of Arc"
"Visit" (Ammons) **16**:54
"The Visit" (Baraka) **4**:17; **113**:14
"Visit" (Hughes) **89**:270
"The Visit" (Leapor) **85**:198, 213
"The Visit" (Nash) **21**:274
"Visit" (Paz)
See "Visita"
"A Visit" (Spark) **72**:226, 259
"A visit from the ex" (Piercy) **29**:313
"A Visit from the Sea" (Stevenson) **84**:300
"A Visit Home" (Stafford) **71**:377
A Visit to Sarashina Village (Matsuo Basho)
See *Sarashina kikō*
"The Visit to the Immortals' Dwelling" (Yakamochi) **48**:105
A Visit to the Kashima Shrine (Matsuo Basho)
See *Kashima kikō*
"A Visit to the Ruins" (Hope) **56**:278, 285
"Visit to Toronto, with Companions" (Atwood) **8**:40
"Visita" (Paz) **48**:246-49, 251
"La visita de Dios" (Cernuda) **62**:203, 249, 253
"Visitation" (Dorn)
See "An Idle Visitation"
"The Visitation" (Graves) **6**:172
"The Visitation" (Hafiz) **116**:15-16, 20-23, 26
"A Visitation" (Snodgrass) **74**:291, 313, 323
"The Visitation" (Southwell) **83**:256
Visitations (MacNeice) **61**:176, 182
"Visiting a Dead Man on a Summer Day" (Piercy) **29**:307
"Visiting Flannery O'Connor's Grave" (Kumin) **15**:215
"Visiting Hour" (Kinsella) **69**:138, 141
"Visiting Hsiang-chi Monastery" (Wang Wei) **18**:378-80
"Visiting Monk Hsüan" (Wang Wei) **18**:388
"The Visiting Sea" (Meynell) **112**:190-91
"Visiting the Ho Family Again" (Tu Fu) **9**:319
"Visiting the Temple of Gathered Fragrance" (Wang Wei) **18**:383, 386
"The Visitor" (Forché) **10**:144, 153
"Visitor's Day at the Fort" (Ciardi) **69**:24
"Visits to St. Elizabeths" (Bishop) **3**:47, 56; **34**:119
"A vista de hombre'" (Guillén) **35**:228
"Vita" (Herbert) **50**:25
"Vita" (Stafford) **71**:371-72
Vita d'un uoma (Ungaretti) **57**:337, 343, 350-7
Vita d'un uomo: Saggi e interventi (Ungaretti)
See *Vita d'un uoma*
"La vita fugge" (Stampa) **43**:285
"La vita non è sogno" (Quasimodo) **47**:286
La vita non è sogno (Quasimodo) **47**:284, 286, 289
"Vita Nuova" (Kunitz) **19**:148, 176, 179
La vita nuova (Dante) **21**:48-53, 55, 62, 66, 72-6, 86-92, 94; **108**:92, 115, 133, 147-48, 162, 166, 199, 202
"La vita solitaria" (Leopardi) **37**:82, 102, 113-17, 124-25, 138-40, 143
"Vital Lightning" (Shvarts) **50**:148
"Vitam quae faciunt beatiorem" (Martial) **10**:243
"Vitzliputzli" (Heine) **25**:167, 170
ViVa (Cummings) **5**:100, 104-07, 110-11
"Viva la Cordillera de los Andes" (Parra)
See "Viva la cordillera de los Andes / Muera la cordillera de la Costa!"
"Viva la cordillera de los Andes / Muera la cordillera de la Costa!" (Parra) **39**:261, 299
"Viva Stalin" (Parra) **39**:311
"Vivaldi, Bird and Angel" (Hope) **56**:301-2
"Vivaldi Years" (Stern) **115**:273
"Vivamus" (Bridges) **28**:59, 63
"Vivasana" (Tagore) **8**:407
Vivir sin estar viviendo (Cernuda) **62**:172, 200, 203, 214-15, 221, 224, 256
"Vivre avec de tels hommes" (Char) **56**:131
"V-J Day" (Ciardi) **69**:5
V-Letter and Other Poems (Shapiro) **25**:262-67, 269, 285, 288, 292, 295, 297, 307, 309, 316, 319, 322
"Vlez besenok v mokroi sherstke" (Mandelstam) **14**:153-54
"Vmesto predisloviia" (Akhmatova) **55**:13-15, 17-19, 28-29
"Vnov' Ia Posetil" (Pushkin)
See "Vnov' Ya Posetil"
"Vnov' Ya Posetil" (Pushkin) **10**:384, 414-15
"Vnutri gory bezdeistvuet kumir" (Mandelstam) **14**:153
"Vocation" (Levertov) **11**:198
"Vocation" (Stafford) **71**:352, 377
Vocative (Zanzotto)
See *Vocativo*
Vocativo (Zanzotto) **65**:263, 274-75, 278, 287-89, 295, 309, 311
"Voce giunta con le folaghe" (Montale) **13**:112
"Vœu" (Sainte-Beuve) **110**:18
"Voeu à Phebus" (Ronsard) **11**:256
"The Voice" (Arnold) **5**:49
"A Voice" (Atwood) **8**:14
"The Voice" (Brooke) **24**:56, 76
"The Voice" (Hardy) **8**:88, 117-18, 135; **92**:312-14
"The Voice" (Levine) **22**:225
"A Voice" (Ní Chuilleanáin) **34**:372
"The Voice" (Roethke) **15**:275
"A Voice" (Sarton) **39**:368
"The Voice" (Silverstein) **49**:343
"The Voice" (Teasdale) **31**:326
"Voice Arriving with the Coots" (Montale) **13**:146, 149
"The Voice as a Girl" (Snyder) **21**:289
"Voice Coming with the Moorhens" (Montale)
See "Voce giunta con le folaghe"
"A Voice from a Chorus" (Blok) **21**:15
"Voice from the Tomb" (Smith) **12**:349
"A Voice from under the Table" (Wilbur) **51**:221, 231, 293
"The Voice of a Bird" (Meynell) **112**:230
"The Voice of God" (Very) **86**:72
"The Voice of Nature" (Bridges) **28**:67
"The Voice of Rock" (Ginsberg) **4**:55
"The Voice of the Ancient Bard" (Blake) **12**:7; **63**:114, 121, 132
Voice of the Forest (Tagore)
See *Banabani*
"The Voice of the Holy Land" (Sachs)
See "Stimme des Heilegen Landes"
"Voice of the Past" (Bely)
See "Golos proshlogo"
"The Voice of the People" (Belloc) **24**:42
"Voice of the People" (Hölderlin)
See "Stimme des Volks"
The Voice of Things (Ponge)
See *Le Parti pris des choses*
"The Voiceless" (Holmes) **71**:82-83, 86
"Voices" (Cavafy) **36**:73
"Voices" (Szymborska) **44**:279, 284, 289
"Voices about the Princess Anemone" (Smith) **12**:298, 348-49
"Voices Between Waking and Sleeping in the Mountains" (Wright) **36**:355
"Voices from Kansas" (Kumin) **15**:215
Voices from the Forest (Mueller) **33**:197

"Voices from the Other World" (Merrill) **28**:235, 259
Voices of Freedom (Whittier) **93**:182, 318
"Voices of the elements" (Enzensberger) **28**:143
"Voices of the Night" (Longfellow) **30**:21-2, 26, 28, 47, 63, 96, 103, 105-06, 108-09
"Voices under the Ground" (Ekeloef) **23**:71, 73, 75
"Voici" (Char) **56**:127
"Voicy le temps, Hurault, qui joyeux nous convie" (Ronsard) **11**:250
"Void in Law" (Barrett Browning) **6**:28, 32
"Void Only" (Rexroth) **20**:221; **95**:282
"Voie" (Tzara) **27**:229-31
Les voisinages de Van Gogh (Char) **56**:163, 177, 186-87
"La Voix" (Baudelaire) **1**:73
"Une voix" (Bonnefoy) **58**:119, 131, 167-68, 174
"Voix basses et Phénix" (Bonnefoy) **58**:132, 174
Les Voix intérieures (Hugo) **17**:42, 45, 52, 63, 74, 76, 80, 83, 91-92, 96-97
"Volcanic Holiday" (Merrill) **28**:283, 285
"Volcano" (Walcott) **46**:237, 279
Volcano a Memoir of Hawaìi (Hongo) **23**:204-206
"Le Volet, suivi de sa scholie" (Ponge) **107**:225
"Völker der Erde" (Sachs) **78**:124, 163
"An vollen Büschelzweigen" (Goethe) **5**:247
"Vollmondnacht" (Goethe) **5**:247
"Vol'nost': Oda" (Pushkin) **10**:408-9
"Volontairement" (Éluard) **38**:69
Volshebny fonar (Tsvetaeva) **14**:318
"Volt" (Tzara) **27**:229-31
"Volta" (Brathwaite) **56**:7, 29, 50
"Voltaire" (Jackson) **44**:7, 11
"Voltaire at Ferney" (Auden) **92**:104
Volume Two (Villa) **22**:347, 353
"Voluntaries" (Emerson) **18**:76-77, 88, 113
The Voluntary Insane (Crabbe) **97**:165
"The Volunteer" (Service) **70**:119, 130
"La volupté" (Baudelaire) **1**:71
"Volved" (Castro) **41**:84
"Volverán las oscuras golondrinas" (Bécquer) See "Rima 12"
"Volverlo a ver" (Mistral) **32**:176
"Von diesen Stauden" (Celan) **10**:122
"Von Flüchtlingen und Flucht" (Sachs) **78**:114
Von Schwelle zu Schwelle (Celan) **10**:95, 121
"Voodoo Cucumber" (Espada) **74**:113, 139
"Vooruzhennyi zren'em uzkikh os" (Mandelstam) **14**:154
"Vor einem Kornfeld sagte einer" (Benn) **35**:8, 68
"Voracities and Verities Sometimes Are Interacting" (Moore) **4**:261; **49**:102, 126-27, 129-30, 134
"Vorfrühling" (Stramm) **50**:199, 201, 204, 206
"Vorobyev Hills" (Pasternak) **6**:251-54
Voronezh Notebooks (Mandelstam) **14**:123, 149-50
"Vorrei voler" (Michelangelo) **103**:184, 282-83, 286
"Vorstadt im Föhn" (Trakl) **20**:261
"Vosled 27 dnju fevralja" (Akhmadulina) **43**:19, 40
"Vosled 27 dnju marta" (Akhmadulina) **43**:19, 40, 42
"Vospominanie o strannom ugoshchenii" (Shvarts) **50**:136-37
"Vospominanie v Tsarskom Sele" (Pushkin) **10**:409, 421
"Vostok pobledneuskii, vostok onemesvshii" (Bely) **11**:32
"Vot zvuk dozhdia" (Akhmadulina) **43**:3-4
"A Vote" (Cowley) **90**:16
"Voto" (Mistral) **32**:159, 173-74
"Vous Êtes Plus Beaux que Vous ne Pensiez" (Koch) **80**:325-26
"A Vow" (Ginsberg) **4**:56
"The Vow" (Hecht) **70**:78, 91
"The Vow" (Kinnell) **26**:286
"The Vow" (Lowell) **13**:86-7
"Vowel Sonatas" (Yau) **61**:337
"Vowels 2" (Baraka) **4**:24
"vowl man" (Bissett) **14**:15
Vox Clamantis (Gower) **59**:17, 25, 44, 62, 99, 113-19
"Vox Corporis" (Teasdale) **31**:368-691
"Vox Humana" (Gunn) **26**:200
"Voy a dormir" (Storni) **33**:236, 261, 300
"Voy hasta Uján" (Guillén) **23**:128
"Le voyage" (Baudelaire) **1**:50, 60, 70, 73-4; **106**:6, 22-23, 28, 101
"Le Voyage" (Char) **56**:197-98
"The Voyage" (Hughes) **89**:139-40
"The Voyage" (Jonson) **17**:207
"Voyage" (MacLeish) **47**:190
"The Voyage" (Muir) **49**:233
"Le voyage à Cythère" (Baudelaire) **1**:65, 72-3; **106**:6, 23-24, 26-29, 77, 103, 154
"Un Voyage à Cythère" (Char) **56**:198
The Voyage, and Other Poems (Muir) **49**:210, 224, 229, 232-33, 245, 247, 250-51, 255, 270, 289
"Voyage de découverte" (Péret) **33**:202
"Le Voyage de Tours, ou les amoureus Thoinet et Perrot" (Ronsard) **11**:260-61, 264
"Voyage Imaginaire" (Béranger) **112**:22
"The Voyage of Maeldune" (Tennyson) **6**:359, 369
"Voyage to Cythera" (Baudelaire) See "Le voyage à Cythère"
Voyage to the Island of Love (Behn) See *Poems upon Several Occasions, with a Voyage to the Island of Love*
"Voyage to the Moon" (Pinsky) **27**:157
"The Voyage Up River" (Walcott) **46**:322
"Voyage West" (MacLeish) **47**:164, 167, 260
"Voyager" (Mueller) **33**:190
"Voyagers" (Chappell) **105**:20
"Voyagers" (Kaufman) **74**:175
"Voyagers" (Page) **12**:199
"Voyages" (Clampitt) **19**:87, 91
"Voyages" (Crane) **3**:90, 97, 104; **99**:14, 17, 27, 29-30, 49-50, 55, 59-60, 68, 71, 75-77, 79, 89-95, 100-101, 107, 135, 139
"Voyages: A Homage to John Keats" (Clampitt) See "Voyages"
"Voyages II" (Crane) **3**:80, 83, 96, 102
"Voyages III" (Crane) **3**:83
"Voyages IV" (Crane) **3**:83
"Voyages V" (Crane) **3**:83
"Le voyageur" (Apollinaire) **7**:48
"Voyant" (Rimbaud) **57**:193
"Les Voyelles" (Rimbaud) **3**:249, 268, 274; **57**:175, 177, 216, 235, 247
"Vozdushnyi korabl" (Lermontov) **18**:291
Vozmezdie (Blok) **21**:10, 17, 25-6, 39, 44
Vozvrat: Tretiia simfoniia (Bely) **11**:3, 8-9, 14-17, 22
"Vpon a Ribband" (Carew) See "Upon a Ribband"
"Vpon the Image of Death" (Southwell) See "Upon the Image of Death"
"Vrai Corps" (Bonnefoy) **58**:173
"Le vrai de la chose" (Laforgue) **14**:76
"Vrai Lieu" (Bonnefoy) **58**:132
"Vrai lieu du cerf" (Bonnefoy) **58**:133-34
"V.R.I." (Mew) **107**:35
"Vriksha-ropan" (Tagore) **8**:416
"Vriksha-vandana" (Tagore) **8**:416
Vrindaban (Paz) **1**:361-63
"Vrindavan" (Das) **43**:73
"Vse Povtoryayv pervyi stikh" (Tsvetaeva) **14**:329
"Vse ushli, i nikto ne vernulsia" (Akhmatova) **55**:52
"Vstrecha" (Pasternak) **6**:280
"Vstuplenie" (Akhmatova) **55**:4, 8, 16, 27, 29, 41, 43, 51
"Vsye eto bylo bylo bylo" (Blok) **21**:15
Vtoraia simfoniia: Dramaticheskaia (Bely) **11**:3-4, 8-11, 13-16, 21, 27, 33
Vtoraya kniga (Mandelstam) **14**:106, 113-18, 121-22, 129, 135, 141, 150, 153, 155
"Vue" (Valéry) **9**:392
"Vuelta" (Paz) **1**:370-72, 374
Vuelta (Paz) **1**:370-71, 374, 376; **48**:188, 192, 228, 233, 245
"La vuelta a America" (Cardenal) **22**:110
"La vuelta a Buenos Aires" (Borges) **22**:94
"Vuelta de paseo" (García Lorca) **3**:139
"Vulcan" (Oppen) **35**:305, 307, 312
"Vulnerant omnes ultima necat" (Cavafy) **36**:53
"Vultures" (Oliver) **75**:287, 293
VV (Cummings) See *ViVa*
"Vykhozhu odin ja na dorogu" (Lermontov) **18**:303
Vyorsty I (Tsvetaeva) **14**:310, 318
Vyorsty II (Tsvetaeva) **14**:322
"Vysokaya bolesn" (Pasternak) **6**:265
"Vystrel" (Pushkin) **10**:414
Vzmakh Ruki (Yevtushenko) **40**:344, 350
"W. D. and Cock Robin Discuss the Dreaded Interrogation" (Snodgrass) **74**:328
"W. D. Assists in Supporting Cock Robin's Roost" (Snodgrass) **74**:328
"W. D. Creates a Device for Inverting Mr. Evil" (Snodgrass) **74**:327
"W. D. Sees Himself Animated" (Snodgrass) **74**:333-34
"W drodze do Delf" (Herbert) **50**:5
"W. D.'s Carnival Friends" (Snodgrass) **74**:330, 334
W. D.'s Midnight Carnival (Snodgrass) **74**:323-25, 328, 332
"W. E. B." (Randall) See "Booker T. and W. E. B."
"W. Lloyd Garrison Standard" (Masters) **36**:231
"W. S. Landor" (Moore) **4**:242, 259; **49**:145
"Wacht" (Stramm) **50**:172, 175
"Wachusett" (Thoreau) See "A Walk to Wachusett"
"Wadin' in de Crick" (Dunbar) **5**:144
"Wading at Wellfleet" (Bishop) **3**:49, 57; **34**:117
"Wading in a Marsh" (Wagoner) **33**:361
"Waga Uta" (Yosano) **11**:302, 306
"The Wage Slave" (Service) **70**:117
"The Wager" (Crabbe) **97**:97, 112
"The Wage-Slaves" (Kipling) **91**:70-73
"The Waggoner" (Blunden) **66**:26
The Waggoner (Wordsworth) **67**:269
"The Waggon-Maker" (Masefield) **78**:101
"Wagner" (Brooke) **24**:53, 56, 64, 83
"Wagon Wheels" (Dorn) **115**:125
"The Wagoner" (Pavese) **13**:205
"Waialua" (Song) See "Easter: Wahiawa, 1959"
The Waif: A Collection of Poems (Longfellow) **30**:46
"Waikiki" (Brooke) **24**:56, 67, 86
"Wail" (Parker) **28**:360
"The Wail" (Simic) **69**:278-79
"Wailing Wall, Night" (Sachs) See "Klagemauer Nacht"
"The Wait" (Borges) See "La espera"
"Wait" (Hughes) **53**:115
"Wait" (Kinnell) **26**:292-93
"Wait for Me, and I'll Return" (Randall) **86**:317
"The Waiting" (Borges) See "La espera"
"Waiting" (Creeley) **73**:10, 51-52
"WAITING" (Kaufman) **74**:241
"Waiting" (Kenyon) **57**:45
"Waiting" (Montague) **106**:215, 280, 296
"The Waiting" (Olds) **22**:330, 332, 334, 337, 340
"Waiting" (Raworth) **107**:308-9
"Waiting" (Reese) **29**:333
"Waiting" (Sandburg) **41**:339
"Waiting" (Thomas) **99**:256, 274, 353-54, 357

"Waiting" (Warren) **37**:313
"The Waiting" (Whittier) **93**:239
"Waiting" (Wright) **14**:341
"Waiting by the Gate" (Bryant) **20**:8
"Waiting for Breakfast" (Larkin) **21**:226-27
"Waiting for Father in Pawling, N.Y." (McHugh) **61**:198
"Waiting for It" (Swenson) **14**:263
"Waiting for the Barbarians" (Cavafy) **36**:29, 31, 39, 50, 51, 55, 56-57, 84
Waiting for the King of Spain (Wakoski) **15**:366
"Waiting for the Miracle" (Cohen) **109**:64
Waiting for the Yeti (Szymborska)
See *Wołanie do Yeti*
"The Waiting Head" (Sexton) **2**:350
"Waiting in a Rain Forest" (Wagoner) **33**:337, 342
"Waiting Inland" (Kumin) **15**:208
"The Waiting-Maid" (Cowley) **90**:15, 35
"Wake" (Brathwaite) **56**:74, 87
"Wake Island" (Birney) **52**:22
"The Wake of the Books" (Kavanagh) **33**:62, 118; **105**:143, 173
"Wake Up" (Carver) **54**:18-19
"The Wakening" (Merwin) **45**:18
"Wake-Up Niggers" (Madhubuti) **5**:329, 338
"The Waking" (Kinnell) **26**:279
"The Waking" (Roethke) **15**:278, 286
"Waking Alone" (Sexton) **79**:241
"Waking an Angel" (Levine) **22**:213
"Waking Early Sunday" (O'Hara) **45**:133
"Waking from Drunkenness on a Spring Day" (Li Po) **29**:143
"Waking from Sleep" (Bly) **39**:6-7
"Waking in a Newly-Build House" (Gunn) **26**:201
"Waking in a Newly-Built House" (Gunn) **26**:211
"Waking in the Blue" (Lowell) **3**:209, 221
"Waking in the Dark" (Rich) **5**:370, 392, 395
The Waking: Poems, 1933-1953 (Roethke) **15**:249, 261, 263, 282, 284, 309
"Waking this Morning" (Rukeyser) **12**:230
"Waking Up in Streator" (Stryk) **27**:214
"Waking Who Knows" (Oppen) **35**:300, 303
"Walcourt" (Verlaine) **32**:411
"Waldeinsamkeit" (Emerson) **18**:76, 88
Walden; or, Life in the Woods (Thoreau) **30**:207-08, 220, 242, 265
"Wales Visitation" (Ginsberg) **4**:74, 93-4; **47**:17
"The Walgh-Vogel" (Wilbur) **51**:295
"The Walk" (Hardy) **8**:93; **92**:226, 315, 327
"The Walk" (Walcott) **46**:237
"A Walk in Kyoto" (Birney) **52**:23, 34, 45-46, 67-69
"A Walk in Late Summer" (Roethke) **15**:274
"A Walk in the Country" (Kinnell) **26**:257
"A Walk in the Country" (Stafford) **71**:297
"A Walk in the Shrubbery" (Smith) **104**:152
"Walk Near False Creek Mouth" (Birney) **52**:25
"A Walk on Snow" (Viereck) **27**:260, 277, 282
"Walk on the Moon" (Momaday) **25**:188
"Walk There" (Ignatow) **34**:279
"A Walk to Wachusett" (Thoreau) **30**:246
"A Walk with Tom Jefferson" (Levine) **22**:225-27
"The Walker" (Hope) **56**:270
"Walking" (Creeley) **73**:10-11, 43, 48
"Walking" (Ignatow) **34**:313
"Walking" (Traherne) **70**:180, 182, 238
"Walking among Limnatour Dunes" (Bly) **39**:23
"Walking Around" (Neruda) **64**:297, 320, 324
"Walking Down Park" (Giovanni) **19**:140-41, 143
"Walking in a Swamp" (Wagoner) **33**:336-38
"Walking in Broken Country" (Wagoner) **33**:350, 352, 362
"Walking in Paris" (Sexton) **2**:363; **79**:187
"Walking in the Blue" (Sexton) **2**:350
"Walking in the Breakdown Lane" (Erdrich) **52**:178
"Walking in the Snow" (Wagoner) **33**:333
"Walking in the Swamp" (Wagoner)
See "Walking in a Swamp"
"Walking into Love" (Piercy) **29**:308, 311
"Walking into the Wind" (Wagoner) **33**:360
"The Walking Man of Rodin" (Sandburg) **2**:334; **41**:296
"Walking My Baby Back Home" (Thumboo) **30**:328
"Walking on the Prayerstick" (Rose) **13**:233
"Walking Parker Home" (Kaufman) **74**:174, 208, 240, 261-62, 268
"Walking Swiftly" (Bly) **39**:38, 42
Walking the Black Cat (Simic) **69**:300, 303, 305-6, 308-9
"Walking the Wilderness" (Stafford) **71**:361
"Walking Through Broken Country" (Wagoner)
See "Walking in Broken Country"
"Walking to Bell rock" (Ondaatje) **28**:336-37
"Walking to Sleep" (Wilbur) **51**:236, 249, 276, 278, 280, 307, 335
Walking to Sleep: New Poems and Translations (Wilbur) **51**:231, 235, 249, 259, 276, 288, 301, 305
"Walking to the Next Farm" (Bly) **39**:44-45
"Walking to Work" (O'Hara) **45**:227
Walking under Water (Abse) **41**:3, 6, 9-10
"Walking West" (Stafford) **71**:258, 276, 278, 295-96
"Walking Where the Plows Have Been Turning" (Bly) **39**:58, 63, 103
"Walking-Sticks" (Moore) **49**:129
"The Wall" (Brooks) **7**:82
"The Wall" (Herbert) **50**:26
"The Wall" (Jones) **116**:108, 111, 114, 159, 224
"The Wall" (Jordan) **38**:121
"The Wall" (Komunyakaa) **51**:54-55
"The Wall" (Montale) **13**:148
"The Wall" (Raworth) **107**:274
"The Wall" (Sexton) **79**:216, 238
"A Wall in the Woods: Cummington" (Wilbur) **51**:336
"Wall Songs" (Hogan) **35**:245, 252
Wallenrod (Mickiewicz)
See *Konrad Wallenrod*
"Die Wallfahrt nach Kevlaar" (Heine) **25**:145
"The Walls" (Cavafy) **36**:46, 52, 53, 54, 56, 73, 74, 112
"Walls" (Hughes) **7**:149
The Walls Do Not Fall (H. D.) **5**:272, 274-76, 293-95, 307, 309, 312, 314-15
"Walls, Nothing Else" (Cernuda) **62**:170
"The Walrus and the Carpenter" (Carroll) **18**:51-52; **74**:11, 63, 76, 107
"Walsingham" (Deloney) **79**:57
"Walt" (Hughes) **89**:146, 189
"Walt Whitman" (Whitman)
See "Song of Myself"
Walt Whitman Bathing (Wagoner) **33**:373-74
Walt Whitman's Blue Book: The 1860-61 Leaves of Grass Containing His Manuscript Additions and Revisions (Whitman) **91**:313-14, 316-20
Walt Whitman's Leaves of Grass: The First (1855) Edition (Whitman)
See *Leaves of Grass*
"Walter Bradford" (Brooks) **7**:92
"Walter Jenks' Bath" (Meredith) **28**:178, 182, 213
"Walter Llywarch" (Thomas) **99**:236
"Walter Rawley of the Middle Temple, in Commendation of the Steele Glasse" (Raleigh) **31**:309, 312-13
"Walter Simmons" (Masters) **36**:182
"The Waltz" (Aleixandre)
See "El vals"
"The Waltzer in the House" (Kunitz) **19**:155
"Wanda" (Vigny) **26**:369, 402
"The Wanderer" (Auden) **92**:62
"The Wanderer" (Masefield) **78**:9, 71-72, 90, 101
"The Wanderer" (Pushkin) **10**:409
"The Wanderer" (Smith) **12**:326, 349-50, 354
"The Wanderer" (Teasdale) **31**:363, 378-79
"The Wanderer" (Williams) **7**:374, 382, 394; **109**:232, 240-41, 287
"A Wanderer" (Zagajewski) **27**:381
"Wanderer and Wonderer" (Masefield) **78**:90
"Der Wanderer kniet" (Werfel) **101**:345
"The Wanderers" (de la Mare) **77**:65
"The Wanderers" (Morris) **55**:260-61, 306
"The Wanderer's Song" (Hagiwara)
See "Hyōhakusha no uta"
"The Wandering Islands" (Hope) **56**:266, 279-81, 305
"The Wandering Islands" (Walcott) **46**:273
The Wandering Islands (Hope) **56**:265-66, 268-70, 273, 288-89
"The Wandering Jew" (Robinson) **1**:487
"Wandering on Mount T'ai" (Li Po) **29**:166
"The Wandering Scholar's Prayer" (Cunningham) **92**:133, 162
"Wandering Willie" (Stevenson) **84**:332
"The Wanderings of Cain" (Coleridge) **11**:89, 91
"The Wanderings of Oisin" (Yeats) **20**:353; **51**:75, 101, 103
The Wanderings of Oisin, and Other Poems (Yeats) **20**:298, 302, 344, 346
"Wanderlied" (Werfel) **101**:345
"Wanderschaft" (Trakl) **20**:241
"Wandrers Sturmlied" (Goethe) **5**:237-39, 245, 247
Wang Stream Collection (Wang Wei) **18**:367, 370, 385
"Wang-ch'uan Garland" (Wang Wei) **18**:374
"Wankelmut" (Stramm) **50**:189, 195, 208
"The Want" (Olds) **22**:321, 325-26, 340
The Want Bone (Pinsky) **27**:156, 160, 163-64, 169, 172, 174
"Want of Wyse Men" (Henryson) **65**:10
"Wantage Bells" (Betjeman) **75**:98
"Wanted: An American Novel" (Updike) **90**:350
"Wanting a Child" (Graham) **59**:132, 178
"Wanting to Die" (Sexton) **2**:364; **79**:196-97, 228, 253, 286
"Wants" (Larkin) **21**:227, 242, 252
"Wapentake" (Longfellow) **30**:51
"War" (Birney) **52**:44, 58
"War" (Gilmore) **87**:302
"War" (Herbert)
See "Wojna"
"War" (Levine) **22**:218
"War" (Niedecker) **42**:99
"War" (Rimbaud)
See "Guerre"
"War" (Simic) **69**:277, 340
"The War" (Werfel)
See "Der Krieg"
"The War Against the Trees" (Kunitz) **19**:175
War All the Time: Poems, 1981-1984 (Bukowski) **18**:15, 18-19
"War and Memory" (Jordan) **38**:126, 128
"War and Peace" (Kavanagh) **105**:130
"War Cemetery" (Blunden) **66**:60
"The War Horse" (Boland) **58**:42, 46
The War Horse (Boland) **58**:12-13, 42-44, 91
"War in Ethiopia" (Bishop) **34**:136
"The War in the Air" (Nemerov) **24**:290
"War Is Kind" (Crane) **80**:46, 52-54
War Is Kind (Crane) **80**:44, 46-47, 51, 53, 56, 65, 68, 74-85, 93, 96-97, 99, 108
"War Machine" (Ondaatje) **28**:327-28, 331
"War Memoir: Jazz, Don't Listen To At Your own Risk" (Kaufman) **74**:175, 195, 275-76
"The War of Caros" (Macpherson) **97**:175, 230, 265
"The War of Inis-thona" (Macpherson) **97**:183, 230, 310
"War Photograph" (Spender) **71**:202, 204, 226
"War Pictures" (Lowell) **13**:76
"War Poems (1914-1915)" (Sandburg) **41**:235-36, 294, 348
"War Song" (Parker) **28**:356
"War Sonnet" (Meredith) **28**:209

War Stories Poems about Long Ago and Now (Nemerov) **24**:287, 289-90
War Trilogy (H. D.)
See *Trilogy*
"War Winters" (Birney) **52**:21, 27, 39, 46, 62
"The War Wound" (Dickey) **40**:181
"The Warden of the Cinque Ports" (Longfellow) **30**:50
"The Wards" (Rukeyser) **12**:225
Ware the Hauke (Skelton) **25**:335, 338, 354, 377, 377-78, 380-81
Ware the Hawk (Skelton)
See *Ware the Hauke*
"Waring" (Browning) **2**:26
"A Warm Place to Shit" (Bissett) **14**:10
"Warm Protest" (Enright) **93**:34
"A Warm Small Rain" (Zagajewski) **27**:394
"Warmhearted" (Silverstein) **49**:340
"The Warning" (Creeley) **73**:87, 90, 122
"Warning" (Hughes) **1**:252; **53**:150-52, 161
"Warning" (Meredith) **60**:263
"A Warning" (Randall) **86**:345
"Warning" (Wagoner) **33**:325, 367
"Warning: Children at Play" (Nemerov) **24**:255
"Warning to Children" (Graves) **6**:139, 143-44, 150
"A Warning to Those Who Live on Mountains" (Day Lewis) **11**:144
"Warnings" (Parra) **39**:310
"Warnings to the Reader" (Parra)
See "Advertencia al lector"
"Warnung" (Goethe) **5**:250
"The Warriors" (Alexie) **53**:23
"The Warriors of the North" (Hughes) **7**:132, 148; **89**:114
"The Warrior's Prayer" (Dunbar) **5**:134
"Wars" (Lovelace) **69**:181
"The Wars" (Ondaatje) **28**:338
"Wars" (Sandburg) **41**:249, 269
"War's People" (Blunden) **66**:30
"A Warsaw Gathering" (Zagajewski) **27**:381
"Warum gabst du uns die tiefen Blicke" (Goethe) **5**:246
"Warum mein Gott?" (Werfel)
See "Why, My Lord and God?"
"Was He Married?" (Smith) **12**:333, 352
"Was I never yet" (Wyatt) **27**:356
"Wash" (Ní Chuilleanáin) **34**:349
"Washerwoman" (Sandburg) **2**:329
"Washington" (Updike) **90**:357
"Washington Cathedral" (Shapiro) **25**:286, 318
"Washington McNeely" (Masters) **36**:183
"Washington Monument at Night" (Sandburg) **41**:251
"Washyuma Motor Hotel" (Ortiz) **17**:227
"A WASP Woman Visits a Black Junkie in Prison" (Knight) **14**:42, 53
"The Wassaile" (Herrick) **9**:104
"Waste" (Masefield) **78**:63, 92
The Waste Land (Eliot) **5**:155-62, 165-67, 173-74, 176, 178-79, 183-89, 191-93, 198, 206-18; **31**:99, 116-17, 120-21, 123-24, 133-34, 137-38, 144, 156, 165, 169, 190; **90**:201-342
The Waste Land (Pound) **4**:353
The Waste Land Facsimile (Eliot)
See *T. S. Eliot, The Waste Land: A Facsimile and Transcript of the Original Drafts Including the Annotations of Ezra Pound*
"Waste Paper Basket" (Tagore) **8**:417
"Waste Sonata" (Olds) **22**:325
"Wasted Energy" (Niedecker) **42**:97, 136-37, 143
The Wat It Is (Stafford) **71**:374
Wat Tyler. A Dramatic Poem (Southey) **111**:213
Watakushi no Oitach (Yosano) **11**:309-11
"The Watch" (Swenson) **14**:250
"Watch" (Ungaretti)
See "Veglia"
"Watch Out, Papa" (Hughes) **53**:115
"The Watcher" (Borges)
See "El centinela"
"The Watcher" (Hope) **56**:285-86
"The Watchers" (Braithwaite) **52**:106
"Watchers" (Merwin) **45**:23
"The Watchers" (Thomas) **53**:327
"The Watchers" (Whittier) **93**:314, 317
"Watchers of the Sky" (Noyes) **27**:127-28
"Watchful" (Mistral)
See "Desvelada"
"Watchful" (Smith) **12**:303-05, 337
"Watching Crow Looking South Towards the Manzano" (Harjo) **27**:64
"Watching Football on TV" (Nemerov) **24**:284
"The Watching of the Falcon" (Morris) **55**:250, 287, 305, 308
"Watching Shoah in a Hotel Room in America" (Zagajewski) **27**:388, 391
"Watching Television" (Bly) **39**:9
"Watching the Dance" (Merrill) **28**:254
"Watching the Jet Planes Dive" (Stafford) **71**:289, 298
"Watching the Needleboats at San Sabra" (Joyce) **22**:137
"The Watchman" (Chappell) **105**:21
"The Water" (Carruth) **10**:71
"Water" (Creeley) **73**:10
"Water" (Larkin) **21**:244
"Water" (Lee) **24**:247
"Water" (Lowell) **3**:212, 215
"Water" (Wright) **14**:366
"Water and Marble" (Page) **12**:178
"Water Color" (Verlaine)
See "Aquarelles"
"The Water Diviner" (Abse) **41**:2-3, 12
"Water Drawn Up Into the Head" (Bly) **39**:28
"The Water Drop" (Elytis) **21**:130
"Water Element Song for Sylvia" (Wakoski) **15**:345
"the water falls in yr mind nd yu get wet tooo" (Bissett) **14**:16, 33
"A Water Glass of Whisky" (Kennedy) **93**:138
"The Water Hyacinth" (Merrill) **28**:247
"The Water Journey" (Ní Chuilleanáin) **34**:358
"The Water Lady" (Hood) **93**:66
Water Lilies (Jiménez)
See *Ninfeas*
"Water Music" (MacDiarmid) **9**:154, 156, 158, 171, 176
"Water Music for the Progress of Love in a Life-Raft down the Sammamish Slough" (Wagoner) **33**:330, 361
"The Water Nymph" (Lermontov)
See "Rusalka"
"Water of Life" (MacDiarmid) **9**:197-98
"Water Picture" (Swenson) **14**:261, 263; **106**:351
"Water Raining" (Stein) **18**:334, 349
"Water Sign Woman" (Clifton) **17**:29
"Water Sleep" (Wylie) **23**:301
Water Street (Merrill) **28**:220, 225, 228, 234, 238, 240, 244, 247-49, 281
"Water under the Earth" (Bly) **39**:18
"Water Walker" (Wilbur) **51**:188, 192, 224, 279-80
"Water, White Cotton, and the Rich Man" (Espada) **74**:113, 122
"The Water-Carrier" (Montague) **106**:284, 354
"Watercolor of Grantchester Meadows" (Plath) **1**:388; **37**:185
"Watercolors" (Rose) **13**:238
"The Watercourse" (Herbert) **4**:114
"Watered-Down Love" (Dylan) **37**:66
"Waterfall" (Heaney) **18**:200
"The Waterfall" (Oliver) **75**:321-22
"The Water-fall" (Vaughan) **81**:283, 307, 330, 335, 342
"The Waterfall and the Eglantine" (Wordsworth) **67**:328
"The Waterfall at Powerscourt" (Davie) **29**:110
"Watergate" (Baraka) **4**:30
"The Watergaw" (MacDiarmid) **9**:156, 160, 196
"Watering the Horse" (Bly) **39**:7, 70, 79
"Waterlily Fire" (Rukeyser) **12**:221
Waterlily Fire: Poems, 1935-1962 (Rukeyser) **12**:215-16
"A Waterloo Ballad" (Hood) **93**:116
"Watermaid" (Okigbo) **7**:232, 239
"The Watershed" (Meynell) **112**:191
"Watershed" (Warren) **37**:376
"Watteau" (Walcott) **46**:242
"The Wattle-tree" (Wright) **14**:344, 353
"A Wave" (Ashbery) **26**:159
"The Wave" (MacLeish) **47**:192
"The Wave" (Merwin) **45**:22
"Wave" (Snyder) **21**:304-06, 308
A Wave of the Hand (Yevtushenko)
See *Vzmakh Ruki*
"Wave of the Night" (Benn)
See "Welle der Nacht"
A Wave: Poems (Ashbery) **26**:169-170
"Wave Song" (Ekeloef) **23**:53-4
"The Wave the Flame the Cloud and the Leopard Speak to the Mind" (Swenson) **14**:247
"The Waves" (Oliver) **75**:303, 305-8
Waving from Shore (Mueller) **33**:191-92
"The Waving of the Corn" (Lanier) **50**:56, 105
"Wawóz Malachowskiego" (Herbert) **50**:5
"Waxwings" (Francis) **34**:242
"The Way" (Braithwaite) **52**:107
"The Way" (Creeley) **73**:5
"The Way" (Lowell) **13**:60, 83
"The Way" (Muir) **49**:198, 284, 296
way (Scalapino) **114**:267-68, 273-77, 284-85, 288, 303-4, 307, 309-12, 333-34
"The Way a Ghost Dissolves" (Hugo) **68**:242
"The Way Ahead" (Thumboo) **30**:301
"The Way Down" (Kunitz) **19**:149, 155, 178
"Way down the Ravi River" (Kipling) **3**:194
"The Way In" (Tomlinson) **17**:319-20, 326
The Way In and Other Poems (Tomlinson) **17**:327, 336, 349, 351-52, 354
"The Way It Is" (Strand) **63**:142, 145
"The Way It Is" (Tapahonso) **65**:259
"The Way it Was" (Clifton) **17**:23
Way of All the Earth (Akhmatova) **2**:16
"The Way of It" (Thomas) **99**:312
The Way of It (Thomas) **99**:359
"The Way of Parents" (Guillén) **35**:221
"The Way of Refuge" (Gozzano)
See "The Road to Shelter"
The Way of Refuge (Gozzano)
See *La via del refugio*
"The Way of the Wind" (Swinburne) **24**:329
Way Out in the Centre (Abse) **41**:19, 21-2, 31
"Way Out West" (Baraka) **113**:5
"The Way the Cards Fall" (Komunyakaa) **51**:36
"The Way Things Are in Franklin" (Kenyon) **57**:20
"The Way Things Work" (Graham) **59**:132-33, 170-71, 176, 181
"The Way through the Woods" (Kipling) **3**:171, 183, 186, 192; **91**:154
"A Way to Love God" (Warren) **37**:309, 363-64, 378
"Way to the West" (Birney) **52**:37-38
"The Way West, Underground" (Snyder) **21**:296
"The Wayfarer Kneels" (Werfel)
See "Der Wanderer kniet"
"The Wayfarer/Perceiving the Pathway to Truth" (Crane) **80**:52
"The Wayfarers" (Baraka) **113**:69
"The Wayfarers" (Brooke) **24**:57
"Way-Out Morgan" (Brooks) **7**:63
"The Ways of Daughters" (Stone) **53**:241, 244
"The Wayside Inn" (Longfellow) **30**:62
Wayside Inn (Longfellow)
See *Tales of a Wayside Inn*
A Wayside Lute (Reese) **29**:330, 335, 339, 346, 349, 352-353
"The Wayside Station" (Muir) **49**:197, 231, 273
"A Wayside Weed" (Melville) **82**:77

The Wayward and the Seeking: A Collection of Writings by Jean Toomer (Toomer) **7**:341
"W.C.W., the lovely man" (Berryman)
See "Dream Song 324"
"We" (Ignatow) **34**:345
"We" (Wilbur) **51**:209
"We a BaddDDD People" (Sanchez)
See "We a BaddDDD People (for gwendolyn brooks/a fo real bad one)"
We a BaddDDD People (Sanchez) **9**:204, 206-08, 210-13, 216, 218-20, 224-27, 229, 234, 237-38, 240, 242
"We a BaddDDD People (for gwendolyn brooks/a fo real bad one)" (Sanchez) **9**:209, 225, 237
"We and They" (Kipling) **91**:152
"We Are" (Éluard)
See "Nous sommes"
"We Are" (Kumin) **15**:183
We Are (Werfel)
See *Wir sind*
"We are Alive" (Harjo) **27**:57
"We Are All Particles of This" (Stone) **53**:251
"We Are Always Too Late" (Boland) **58**:48
"We Are Getting to the End" (Hardy) **92**:222
"We Are Human History. We Are Not Natural History" (Boland) **58**:8, 13-14, 48, 84
"We Are Muslim Women" (Sanchez) **9**:228
"We Are Seven" (Wordsworth) **4**:374, 415, 420, 428; **67**:277, 282, 300, 313-17, 323, 338, 347-48, 368
"We Are the Only Animals Who Do This" (Boland) **58**:21
"We Are the Women" (Goodison) **36**:142, 153-54
"We Are Transmitters" (Lawrence) **54**:239
"We become new" (Piercy) **29**:301
"We began together: the workers, winter and I" (Akhmadulina)
See "My nacali vmeste: rabocie, ja i zima"
"We Call Them the Brave" (Moore) **49**:126, 134
"We can work it out. Raza" (Alurista) **34**:29, 45
"We Cannot Hold onto the World" (Spender) **71**:189
"We Cannot Parallel" (Barker) **77**:3
"We Come Back" (Rexroth) **20**:217-18; **95**:259, 271
"We Did It" (Amichai) **38**:13
"We Encounter Nat King Cole as We Invent the Future" (Harjo) **27**:65, 72
"We English" (Loy) **16**:320
"We Exist" (Graham) **59**:189
"We Fought South of the Ramparts" (Li Po) **29**:176
"We Free Singers Be" (Knight) **14**:40, 46
"We Got out of the Walls" (Seferis) **66**:170
"We Have Been Believers" (Walker) **20**:272-74, 283, 289
"We knew the world backwards and forwards" (Szymborska)
See "Swiat umielismy kiedys..."
"We know him — Law and Order League—" (Niedecker) **42**:136
"We Let the Boat Drift" (Kenyon) **57**:27
"We Live by What We See at Night" (Espada) **74**:123
"we live in a hundrid yeer old house" (Bissett) **14**:25
"We Lying by Seasand" (Thomas) **2**:404; **52**:243, 334
"We Must Call A Meeting" (Hogan) **35**:266
"We Need th Setting" (Bissett) **14**:10
"We Never Know" (Komunyakaa) **51**:25-26, 35
"We Pray Most Earnestly" (Jacobsen) **62**:323
"We Real Cool" (Brooks) **7**:62, 85, 90
"We Shall Gather Again in Petersburg" (Mandelstam) **14**:116, 121, 157
we sleep inside each other all (Bissett) **14**:6
"We Stood There Singing" (Kumin) **15**:213
"We that ar Heir" (Dunbar) **67**:5
"We Too" (H. D.) **5**:268
"We Walk on Pebbled Streets" (Alurista) **34**:48
We Walk the Way of the New World (Madhubuti) **5**:326-27, 336, 343, 345-46
"We Watch the Love Balloon" (Spicer) **78**:302
"We Wear the Mask" (Dunbar) **5**:124, 130, 132, 135, 140, 142, 144
"We Were Not Expecting the Prince Today" (Spark) **72**:218
"We Were without a Present" (Darwish) **86**:32
"We Who Are Playing Tonight" (Lindsay) **23**:286
"We Would Have Been Relieved with Death" (Alurista) **34**:23, 47
"The Weak Monk" (Smith) **12**:333
Weapon Man (Raworth) **107**:285
"A Wearied Pilgrim" (Herrick) **9**:108
"Weariness" (Longfellow) **30**:27
"The Wearing of the Green" (Davie) **29**:107, 109, 120
"The Weary Blues" (Hughes) **1**:236, 246, 248, 261, 269; **53**:80-82, 85-86, 94, 114, 117, 143, 200-203, 205
The Weary Blues (Hughes) **1**:236-37, 242, 244-46, 248, 258, 260, 262-64, 268-70; **53**:79, 85-86, 94, 105-6, 108, 117, 127, 140, 147, 156, 164, 170, 181-82, 189
"Weary in Well-Doing" (Rossetti) **7**:268
"Weary of the Bitter Ease" (Mallarmé)
See "Las de l'amer repos"
"The Weary Pund o' Tow" (Burns) **6**:78; **114**:19
Weather (Stafford) **71**:288, 292
Weather Forecast for Utopia and Vicinity (Simic) **69**:311
"The Weather in Tohunga Crescent" (Curnow) **48**:13, 20, 29
"The Weather of the World" (Nemerov) **24**:287, 302
"Weather Report" (Stafford) **71**:288
"The Weather-Cock Points South" (Lowell) **13**:96
"Weathering Out" (Dove) **6**:111
"Weathers" (Hardy) **8**:124
"Weauers Song" (Deloney) **79**:56
"The Weaver" (Melville) **82**:74, 147
"The Web One Weaves of Italy" (Moore) **49**:128-29, 137-38
"Webern's Mountain" (Chappell) **105**:20
"Webster Ford" (Masters) **1**:344, 346, 348
"The Wedding" (Eberhart) **76**:54
"The Wedding" (Patmore) **59**:204, 230, 234
"Wedding Day" (Raworth) **107**:275
A Wedding in Hell: Poems (Simic) **69**:299, 304-6, 308-9, 338
"The Wedding Night" (Sexton) **79**:227
"A Wedding on Cape Rosier" (Eberhart) **76**:59
"Wedding Party" (Hall) **70**:32
"The Wedding Photograph" (Smith) **12**:316, 323
"The Wedding Sermon" (Patmore) **59**:221, 245, 274
"Wedding Speeches" (Hall) **70**:30
"A Wedding Toast" (Wilbur) **51**:279
"Wedding Wind" (Larkin) **21**:227, 247
"Weddings" (Yevtushenko) **40**:341
Weddings (Yevtushenko) **40**:354
The Wedge (Williams) **7**:370, 402; **109**:195, 273, 279, 282, 301
"Wedlock" (Lawrence) **54**:183
"The Wedlock" (Sexton) **79**:241
"Wednesday" (Seferis) **66**:151, 206
"Wednesday at the Waldorf" (Swenson) **14**:267, 276
"Wednesday: The Tete a Tete" (Montagu) **16**:348-49
"The Weed" (Bishop) **3**:37, 45, 75; **34**:52, 144, 160, 162-63, 181, 191
"Weed Puller" (Roethke) **15**:278, 295, 297
"Weeds" (Stafford) **71**:296
"The Weeds" (Stern) **115**:248
"Weeds and Peonies" (Hall) **70**:55
Weeds and Wildings (Melville) **82**:77, 100, 106-8, 141, 151-56
"Weekend Glory" (Angelou) **32**:29
"The Weekend Is Over" (Tapahonso) **65**:259
"Weeknight Service" (Lawrence) **54**:175
"Weep, Girl, Weep" (Spender) **71**:161, 163
"The Weeper" (Crashaw) **84**:9, 38, 48-49, 73-74, 76-78, 80, 82-83, 89, 96, 103, 106, 108-9, 116, 128, 130-32, 141, 151-54, 157, 169-72, 176-77, 180
"The Weepers in the Sacred Tree" (Barker) **77**:11
"Weeping" (Cowley) **90**:115
"Weeping and Wailing" (Stern) **115**:251
"The Weeping Garden" (Pasternak) **6**:268
"The Weeping Saviour" (Barrett Browning) **6**:14
"Weggebeizt" (Celan) **10**:106, 111
"Weiß sind die Tulpen" (Celan) **10**:123
"The weight" (Piercy) **29**:313
"Weight" (Tagore)
See "Bhar"
"A Weightless Element" (Benn) **35**:7
"Die Weihe" (Heine) **25**:157-61, 163-64
"Weinhaus Wolf" (Benn) **35**:34
"Weird Tales" (Chappell) **105**:33, 67
Die Weise von Liebe und Tod des Cornets Christoph Rilke (Rilke) **2**:266, 268
"Weitere Gründe dafür daB Dichter lügen" (Enzensberger) **28**:165
"weiterung" (Enzensberger) **28**:135
"The Welcome" (Cowley) **90**:14, 32
"Welcome Aboard the Turbojet Electra" (Swenson) **14**:268
"Welcome and Parting" (Goethe)
See "Willkommen und Abschied"
"Welcome Back, Mr. Knight: Love of My Life" (Knight) **14**:46
"Welcome joy, and welcome sorrow" (Keats) **96**:309-14
"Welcome Morning" (Sexton) **2**:372; **79**:222, 238
"Welcome" (Thomas) **99**:251
"The Welcome to Sack" (Herrick) **9**:88, 94, 102
"Welcome to the Caves of Arta" (Graves) **6**:153
"A Welcoming Party" (Montague) **106**:314
"The Well" (Levertov) **11**:168, 205-06
"The Well" (Merwin) **45**:32
"The Well" (Tomlinson) **17**:341-42
"Well" (Walker) **30**:343
"The Well Dreams" (Montague) **106**:271, 321
"The Well Rising" (Stafford) **71**:286, 288, 330
"Well Said Old Mole" (Viereck) **27**:259
"Well, Then, I Hate Thee" (Crane) **80**:69
"We'll to the Woods No More, the Laurels Are Cut Down" (Sarton) **39**:328
"Well Water" (Jarrell) **41**:189
Well Well Reality (Waldrop) **109**:179
"Well, What Are You Going to Do?" (Wright) **36**:359
"Welland River" (Morris) **55**:301-2
"The Well-Beloved" (Hardy) **8**:91
The Well-Beloved (Hardy) **92**:264, 328
"The Well-Beloved" (Montague) **106**:282, 290, 302, 305
"Welle der Nacht" (Benn) **35**:7, 27, 28, 36
"Wellfleet: The House" (Wilbur) **51**:326
"The Wellspring" (Olds) **22**:338
The Wellspring (Olds) **22**:330, 338-39
"A Well-to-Do Invalid" (Jarrell) **41**:172
"Welsh" (Thomas) **99**:252
Welsh Airs (Thomas) **99**:251-54, 270, 311
"Welsh Incident" (Graves) **6**:143, 150
"Welsh Landscape" (Thomas) **99**:258
"The Welsh Marches" (Housman) **2**:159, 179
Welsh Retrospective (Abse) **41**:32-3
"A Welsh Testament" (Thomas) **99**:241
"A Welshman at St. James' Park" (Thomas) **99**:253
"A Welshman to Any Tourist" (Thomas) **99**:251
Der Weltfreund (Werfel) **101**:299, 313-14, 316-17, 321, 330, 336, 344-47, 352-58

"Weltwehe" (Stramm) **50**:173, 175-76, 207, 214
"wer they angels i didnt know" (Bissett) **14**:34
"Werben" (Stramm) **50**:166-68, 189, 194
"We're at the Graveyard" (Ondaatje) **28**:327, 331, 334
"Were but my Muse an Huswife Good" (Taylor) **63**:281
"We're Extremely Fortunate" (Szymborska) See "Wielkie to szczeście"
"We're few" (Pasternak) **6**:252
"Were my hart" (Campion) **87**:58, 69, 71
"We're Not Learnen to Be Paper Boys (for the young brothas who sell Muhammad Speaks)" (Sanchez) **9**:229
"The Wereman" (Atwood) **8**:36
"The Werewolf" (Marie de France) See "Bisclavret"
Das Werk (Stramm) **50**:181-85, 198-99, 201-2, 204-9
"Wersja wydarzen" (Szymborska) **44**:308
"An Werther" (Goethe) **5**:250-51
"Werttod" (Stramm) **50**:207
"Wessex Heights" (Hardy) **92**:336, 338, 369-75
Wessex Poems, and Other Verses (Hardy) **8**:114, 123; **92**:206, 224, 241, 248, 254, 269, 284-85, 289, 291-92, 333, 341, 346, 353-54, 371
"The West" (Housman) **2**:167, 191, 199; **43**:250
"West" (MacNeice) **61**:113
"West" (Oppen) **35**:286, 341
"West and Away the Wheels of Darkness Roll" (Housman) **2**:162
"West Coast" (Thomas) **99**:265
"West Coast Sounds—1956" (Kaufman) **74**:195
West Indies, Ltd.: Poemas (Guillén) **23**:98-99, 106-107, 114, 133, 137-39
"The West Main Book Store chickens" (Piercy) **29**:315
"West Marginal Way" (Hugo) **68**:234, 274, 298-300, 309-11
"West of Your City" (Stafford) **71**:276, 278, 295-97
West of Your City (Stafford) **71**:257, 275-78, 281, 286-87, 296, 320, 325-26, 328, 330-31, 333-34, 337, 349-50, 355, 377
"West Somerville, Mass." (Kennedy) **93**:132, 139
"The West Wind" (Bryant) **20**:4, 40
"The West Wind" (Masefield) **78**:56, 63
"West Wind" (Raworth) **107**:280, 299-300, 310, 317-21, 325-28, 332, 336
"West Wind" (Wright) **14**:342, 354
"West Wind in Winter" (Meynell) **112**:191, 229, 255-57
West Wind: Poems and Prose Poems (Oliver) **75**:321, 329-30
"Westering" (Heaney) **18**:203
The Western Approaches: Poems, 1973-1975 (Nemerov) **24**:275, 284-86, 303
The Western Borders (Howe) **54**:45
"Western Country" (Merwin) **45**:46
"Western Elegies" (Hope) **56**:292
"The Western Front" (Bridges) **28**:77, 81
"Western Landscape" (MacNeice) **61**:109, 111-12
"Western Purdah, Inc." (Stone) **53**:257
"Western Song" (Trakl) See "Abendländisches Lied"
Western Star (Benét) **64**:9, 17, 36, 60
"The Western View" (Masefield) **78**:30
"Westgate-on Sea" (Betjeman) **75**:106
West-Östlicher Divan (Goethe) **5**:223, 225, 229, 239, 247, 250
"Westport" (Kinnell) **26**:238, 252
"West-Running Brook" (Frost) **1**:203, 218, 220; **39**:365
West-Running Brook (Frost) **1**:195, 203, 205, 213; **39**:232-33, 253
"Westward" (Clampitt) **19**:95-8
Westward (Clampitt) **19**:93, 95-6
"Westward Haut" (Dorn) **115**:223, 233
"A Wet August" (Hardy) **92**:235
"Wet Casements" (Ashbery) **26**:155
"The Wet Litany" (Kipling) **91**:86
"We've Played Cowboys" (Alurista) **34**:16
"Wha Is That at My Bower-Door" (Burns) **6**:77
"The Whale, His Bulwark" (Walcott) **46**:274
"The Whaleboat Struck" (Ammons) **16**:39
"Whales Weep Not" (Lawrence) **54**:198-201
"Wham Will We Send to London Town?" (Burns) **114**:51
"The Wharf" (Merwin) **45**:48
what (Bissett) **14**:15
" *What a Dump*, or, Easter" (Berrigan) **103**:23
What a Kingdom It Was (Kinnell) **26**:236, 238-39, 252-53, 255, 257, 279, 289
"What a Pretty Net" (Viereck) **27**:259, 179
"What a Sad Sound" (Cernuda) See "Qué ruido tan triste"
"What a woman! — Hooks men like rugs" (Niedecker) **42**:102, 123
"What Am I without Thee?" (Lanier) **50**:91
"What Are Cities For?" (Jeffers) **17**:132
"What Are Years" (Moore) **4**:243; **49**:100-101, 116, 134
What Are Years (Moore) **49**:98-99, 126
"What Became of What-Was-His-Name?" (Enright) **93**:21
"What Came to Me" (Kenyon) **57**:14
"What Can I Do" (Carver) **54**:12
"What Can I Tell My Bones?" (Roethke) **15**:264, 274
"What Can You Do?" (Stone) **53**:229-30, 234
"What Clings like the Odor of a Goat" (Ignatow) **34**:304
"What cruel pains Corinna takes" (Wilmot) **66**:329, 343
"What Declaration" (Jordan) **38**:119
"What Did?" (Silverstein) **49**:311, 344
"What Did You Buy" (Wylie) **23**:330
"What Do I Care" (Teasdale) **31**:323, 359, 379
"What Do I Know of the Old Lore?" (Duncan) **75**:124, 195
"What Does Mr. Cogito Think About Hell" (Herbert) See "Co robia nasi unmarli"
"What Does the Bobwhite Mean?" (Wright) **36**:312
"What Does the King of the Jungle Truly Do?" (Wright) **36**:313
"What else is hell, but losse of blisfull heauen?" (Raleigh) **31**:201
"What faire pompe have I spide of glittering Ladies" (Campion) **87**:62
"What, For Us, My Heart . . ." (Rimbaud) See "Qu'est-ce pour nous"
What For? Verses, 1938-1942 (Zanzotto) See *A che valse? Versi, 1938-1942*
"What Gives" (Eberhart) **76**:15
"What God Is" (Herrick) **9**:94, 141
"What God Is Like to Him I Serve" (Bradstreet) **10**:34
"What goes up" (Piercy) **29**:315, 317-19, 322
"What Happened" (Duncan) **2**:103
"What Happened Here Before" (Snyder) **21**:298, 325
What Happened When the Hopi Hit New York (Rose) **13**:239
"What harvest half so sweet is" (Campion) **87**:12
"What Has Happpened to These Working Hands?" (Hogan) **35**:257
"What Have I Learned" (Snyder) **21**:318
"What He Thought" (McHugh) **61**:201
"What I Am" (Tapahonso) **65**:259
"What I Am Doing Here" (Cohen) **109**:8, 76
"What I Did in Paris in the Twenties" (Bell) **79**:23
"What I Expected" (Spender) **71**:133, 171, 221, 240-41
"What I Heard Whispered at the Edge of Liberal, Kansas" (Stafford) **71**:276, 288
What I Love (Elytis) **21**:131
"What I Saw" (Herbert) **50**:13-14
"What I Should Have Said" (Harjo) **27**:56
What Is a Welshman? (Thomas) **99**:249, 251
"What is Blind" (McHugh) **61**:196
"What Is Called Thinking" (Graham) **59**:151
"What is it all" (Campion) **87**:58, 69
"What is it, Dear?" (Patmore) **59**:248
"What Is Left to Say" (Mueller) **33**:191
"What is Life?" (Clare) **23**:40
"What is Most Hoped and/or Most Feared: The Judgement" (Piercy) **29**:326
"What Is Said to the Poet About Flowers" (Rimbaud) See "Ce qu'on dit au poète à propos de fleurs"
"What Is This Thing Called Contemplation" (Dorn) **115**:133
"What It Cost" (Forché) **10**:166
"What It Was" (Strand) **63**:188
"What It's Like" (Kenyon) **57**:44
"What Joy to Live" (Southwell) **83**:239, 249, 280
"What Language Did" (Boland) **58**:50
"What Lips My Lips Have Kissed" (Millay) **6**:225
"What Love Intended" (Boland) **58**:49
"What may it availl me" (Wyatt) **27**:324
"What menythe this?" (Wyatt) **27**:316, 322, 324
What Moon Drove Me to This? (Harjo) **27**:64
"What Must" (MacLeish) **47**:191, 196, 210
"What no perdy" (Wyatt) **27**:304, 328
"What of the Night?" (Kunitz) **19**:175-76, 178
"What One Says to the Poet on the Subject of Flowers" (Rimbaud) See "Ce qu'on dit au poète à propos de fleurs"
"What Our Dead Do" (Herbert) See "Co robia nasi unmarli"
"What Ovid Taught Me" (Walker) **30**:350
what poetiks (Bissett) **14**:15
"What rage is this?" (Wyatt) **27**:304
"What Says the Sea, Little Shell?" (Crane) **80**:40, 53
"What Shall I Give My Children?" (Brooks) **7**:76
"What? So Soon" (Hughes) **1**:266; **53**:159-60
"What Stillness Round a God" (Rilke) **2**:275
"What the Bird with the Human Head Knew" (Sexton) **2**:372; **79**:222
"What the Brand New Freeway Won't Go By" (Hugo) **68**:290
"What the Child Sees" (Corso) **33**:50
"What the Dead Man Said About Himself" (Parra) See "What the Deceased Had to Say About Himself"
"What the Deceased Had to Say About Himself" (Parra) **39**:278, 308, 311
"What the Doctor Said" (Carver) **54**:15, 19
"What the Dog Perhaps Hears" (Mueller) **33**:180
"What the Earth Asked Me" (Wright) **36**:337
"What the End Is For" (Graham) **59**:130, 133-34, 156-57
"What the Fox Agreed to Do" (Bly) **39**:67
What the Grass Says (Simic) **69**:262, 299
"What the Light Was Like" (Clampitt) **19**:102
What the Light Was Like (Clampitt) **19**:85-7, 90-1, 93
"What the Moon Saw" (Lindsay) **23**:268
"What the Old Women See" (McHugh) **61**:191
"What the Rattlesnake Said" (Lindsay) **23**:286
"What the Voice Said" (Whittier) **93**:166
"What the Women Said" (Bogan) **12**:110
"What Then?" (Yeats) **20**:342
"What This Mode of Motion Said" (Ammons) **16**:20
What Thou Lovest Well, Remains American (Hugo) **68**:252, 254, 260, 262, 271, 281, 288, 306
"What vaileth trouth" (Wyatt) **27**:366
"What 'vaileth truth" (Wyatt) See "What vaileth trouth"

"What vain, unnecessary things are men!" (Wilmot) **66**:329
"What Virginia Said" (Tomlinson) **17**:353
"What Voice at Moth-Hour" (Warren) **37**:337
"What Was the Promise that Smiled from the Maples at Evening" (Warren) **37**:348
"What was the Thought" (Warren) **37**:341
"What We Come To Know" (Ortiz) **17**:246
"what we dew if thrs anything" (Bissett) **14**:33
"What We Leave Behind" (Wagoner) **33**:363
"What We Lost" (Boland) **58**:12, 15, 48, 88, 92-93
"What We Take With Us" (Wagoner) **33**:363
"What Were They Like?" (Levertov) **11**:176
"What Why When How Who" (Pinsky) **27**:164
"What Will Be Historically Durable" (Dorn) **115**:160
"What Will Remain" (Mahon) **60**:134
What Work Is (Levine) **22**:220-21, 227-28, 231-32
"What Would I Do White" (Jordan) **38**:127
"What Would Tennessee Williams Have Said" (Wakoski) **15**:368
"What Wourde is That" (Wyatt) **27**:314, 342
"What You Might Answer" (Hacker) **47**:98
"What You Need for Painting" (Carver) **54**:21
"What you say . . ." (Cage) **58**:220-22, 224
"Whatever Happened?" (Larkin) **21**:235-36
"Whatever You Now Are" (Warren) **37**:379
"Whatever You Say Say Nothing" (Heaney) **18**:189, 205
"Whatever You Wish, Lord" (Jiménez) **7**:184
"Whatif" (Silverstein) **49**:326, 339
What's for Dinner? (Schuyler) **88**:201
"What's Good for the Soul Is Good for Sales" (Wilbur) **51**:245
"what's happening" (Alurista) **34**:34, 38
"WHATS HAPPNING OZONE CUM BACK WE STILL LOV YU" (Bissett) **14**:32
"What's in My Journal" (Stafford) **71**:371
"What's Meant by Here" (Snyder) **21**:300
What's O'Clock (Lowell) **13**:66, 76, 84-5, 91, 93-4, 97-8
"What's Real and What's Not" (Baca) **41**:47
"what's so big about GREEN" (Birney) **52**:36, 43, 82, 101
What's So Big about Green? (Birney)
See "what's so big about GREEN"
"What's That" (Sexton) **2**:359
"What's the matter with her?" (Castro)
See "¿Qué tiene?"
"What's the Railroad to Me?" (Thoreau) **30**:236
"What's the Riddle . . ." (Jarrell) **41**:178, 180-81
"What's wrong with marriage?" (Niedecker) **42**:136
"What's Wrong with People" (Serote) **113**:292-93
Whatsaid Serif: Song of the Andoumboulou: 16-35 (Mackey) **49**:51-61, 63-65, 67-69, 75-80
"Whe' Fe Do?" (McKay) **2**:222-23
"Wheat-in-the-Ear" (Lowell) **13**:96
"The Wheel" (Césaire) **25**:17
"The Wheel" (Hayden) **6**:194-95
The Wheel (Berry) **28**:16
"The Wheel of Being II" (Carruth) **10**:71
"The Wheel Revolves" (Rexroth) **20**:195; **95**:255-56, 259, 269
"The Wheeling Gospel Tabernacle" (Wright) **36**:376
"Wheels Slowly Turning" (Montague) **106**:246-47
"Wheesht, Wheesht, My Foolish Heart" (MacDiarmid) **9**:156, 160
"When" (Stone) **53**:259
"When a Boy..." (Corso) **33**:44
"When a People Reach the Top of a Hill" (Crane) **80**:41
"When All My Five and Country Senses See" (Thomas) **2**:392; **52**:247
"When April Comes" (Masefield) **78**:63
"When Black Is a Color Because It Follows a Grey Day" (Wakoski) **15**:348
"When Coldness Wraps This Suffering Clay" (Byron) **16**:89
"When de Co'n Pone's Hot" (Dunbar) **5**:117, 122
"When De Folks Is Gone" (Riley) **48**:340
"When de Saints Go Ma'ching Home" (Brown) **55**:102, 108, 110-11, 115, 152, 160, 175-76, 178
"When Death Came April Twelve 1945" (Sandburg) **2**:333; **41**:301-2
"When Death Comes" (Oliver) **75**:317
"When Ecstasy is Inconvenient" (Niedecker) **42**:98, 144-45
"When First" (Thomas) **53**:266
"When First I Saw" (Burns) **6**:78
"When Forth the Shepherd Leads the Flock" (Melville) **82**:77, 154
"When from Afar" (Hölderlin) **4**:174, 178
"When God Lets My Body Be" (Cummings) **5**:99
"When Golda Meir Was in Africa" (Walker) **30**:343
"When Golden Flies upon My Carcass Come" (Eberhart) **76**:14, 50
"When Guilford Good" (Burns) **6**:78
"When Hair Falls Off and Eyes Blur and" (Cummings) **5**:105
"When he was at sea" (Waller) **72**:272
"When He Would Have His Verses Read" (Herrick) **9**:87, 96, 102, 109, 139, 145
"When I Am Asked" (Mueller) **33**:197
"When I am Not With You" (Teasdale) **31**:335
"When I Banged My Head on the Door" (Amichai) **38**:41, 53-4
"When I Buy Pictures" (Moore) **4**:251, 266; **49**:96, 160
"When I Came from Colchis" (Merwin) **45**:9
"When I Come" (Francis) **34**:251
"When I consider how my light is spent" (Milton)
See "Sonnet 16 (On his blindness)"
"When I Die" (Brooks) **7**:68
"When I Die" (Giovanni) **19**:113
"When I Drink" (Cohen) **109**:101
"When I Have Fears That I May Cease to Be" (Keats) **1**:314; **96**:205
"When I Have Reached the Point of Suffocation" (Stern) **115**:246, 289
"When I Nap" (Giovanni) **19**:112
"When I or Else" (Jordan) **38**:119-20
"When I Paint My Masterpiece" (Dylan) **37**:56
"When I Read the Book" (Whitman) **91**:311
"When I Roved a Young Highlander" (Byron) **16**:86
"When I Set Out for Lyonesse" (Hardy) **8**:92, 112, 115; **92**:225-26, 317
"When I Think About Myself" (Angelou) **32**:14, 28
"When I was a Child" (Amichai) **38**:22
"When I Was One-and-Twenty" (Housman) **2**:161, 192; **43**:261
"When I Was Young, the Whole Country Was Young" (Amichai) **38**:53
"When I Watch the Living Meet" (Housman) **2**:184
"When in Rome-Apologia" (Komunyakaa) **51**:18
"When in the Gloomiest of Capitals" (Akhmatova)
See "Kogda v mrachneyshey iz stolits"
"When is the Question" (Raworth) **107**:276
"When Jemmy First Began to Love" (Behn)
See "Song to a Scotish Tune (When Jemmy First Began to Love)"
"When Let by Rain" (Taylor) **63**:296
"When Like a Running Grave" (Thomas) **52**:243, 245
"When, like the cloud before the sun" (Whittier) **93**:200
"When Like the Sun" (Hope) **56**:301, 306-7
"When Lilacs Last in the Dooryard Bloom'd" (Whitman) **3**:378, 382, 396-97, 410, 418-19, 422; **91**:207-8, 215, 218, 278-79
"When Lilacs Last in the Dooryard Bloomed" (Whitman)
See "When Lilacs Last in the Dooryard Bloom'd"
"When Love Becomes Words" (Jackson) **44**:8, 11, 43-4
"When Malindy Sings" (Dunbar) **5**:117, 119-21, 134, 146
"When Mrs. Martin's Booker T." (Brooks) **7**:67, 69
"When News Came of His Death" (Ignatow) **34**:310
"When on my night of life the Dawn shall break" (Brooke) **24**:72
"When Once the Twilight Locks No Longer" (Thomas) **2**:402; **52**:227, 237
When One Has Lived a Long Time Alone (Kinnell) **26**:285-87, 293
"When *Phoebe* . . ." (Collins) **72**:78-79, 82, 116
"When ragyng love" (Surrey) **59**:314-15, 330
"When Rain Whom Fear" (Cummings) **5**:105
"when raza?" (Alurista) **34**:5-6, 32, 38
"When Satan Fell" (Lawrence) **54**:250
"When Serpents bargain for the Right to Squirm" (Cummings) **5**:90, 107
"When She Comes Home Again" (Riley) **48**:290
"When She Wears Red" (Hughes)
See "When Sue Wears Red"
"When Sir Beelzebub" (Sitwell) **3**:303
"When Smoke Stood Up from Ludlow" (Housman) **2**:184
"When Songs Become Water" (Espada) **74**:138
"When Sue Wears Red" (Hughes) **53**:84, 86, 91
"When Summer's End Is Nighing" (Housman) **2**:165, 181
"When the Armies Passed" (Hughes) **53**:149
"When the Dead Ask My Father about Me" (Olds) **22**:323, 326
"When the Dumb Speak" (Bly) **39**:13, 52
"When the Frost Is on the Punkin" (Riley) **48**:288, 314-15, 317-19, 331, 333-34, 340, 350
"When the Glass of My Body Broke" (Sexton) **79**:241
"When the God of merrie love" (Campion) **87**:63, 101
"When the Guelder Roses Bloom" (Carman) **34**:210, 216
"When the Horizon is Gone" (Merwin) **45**:79, 100-1
"When the Hulk of the World" (Curnow) **48**:45-46
"When the Lamp Is Shattered" (Shelley) **14**:177, 207
"When the Light Falls, It Falls on Her" (Kunitz) **19**:151, 155
"When the Night Comes Falling from the Sky" (Dylan) **37**:61
"When the Shy Star" (Joyce)
See "IV"
When the Skies Clear (Pasternak)
See *Kogda razglyaetsya*
When the Sun Tries to Go On (Koch) **80**:290, 292-93, 299, 308-9, 317
"When the Tooth Cracks - Zing!" (Warren) **37**:313
"When the Trees Grow Bare on the High Hills" (Muir) **49**:263
"When the Vacation is Over for Good" (Strand) **63**:156, 175
"When the War Is Over" (Merwin) **45**:23
"When the Watchman Saw the Light" (Cavafy) **36**:39, 54, 86
"When the Wheel Does Not Move" (Bly) **39**:43
"When the Year Grows Old" (Millay) **61**:213, 222
"When the Yellowing Fields Billow" (Lermontov) **18**:281

"When They Come Alive" (Cavafy) **36**:107
"When They Have Lost" (Day Lewis) **11**:144
When They Have Senses (Waldrop) **109**:127, 179
"When thou must home" (Campion) **87**:7, 12, 54, 63-64, 77
"When to her lute Corinna sings" (Campion) **87**:32, 36, 44, 64, 85-86
"When to my deadlie pleasure" (Sidney) **32**:235
"When to the King I bid good morrow" (Wilmot) **66**:329
"When Under the Icy Eaves" (Masters) **1**:328; **36**:174
"When Unto Nights of Autumn Do Complain" (Cummings) **5**:104
"When We All..." (Corso) **33**:50; **108**:20
"When We Got to Chitina" (Stafford) **71**:288
"When We Two Parted" (Rossetti) **7**:276
"When We Two Walked" (Thomas) **53**:291
"When We with Sappho" (Rexroth) **20**:203, 216; **95**:257, 260, 347
"When We'll Worship Jesus" (Baraka) **4**:29, 39; **113**:25
"When Will I Return" (Brutus) **24**:116
"When Windesor walles" (Surrey) **59**:352-53, 355-57
"When Winter Fringes Every Bough" (Thoreau) **30**:214, 220, 293
"When Wishes Were Fishes" (Stone) **53**:227
"When You Are Old" (Yeats) **20**:355
"When You Asked for It" (Rexroth) **95**:262, 269
"When You Go Away" (Merwin) **45**:9, 18
"When You Have the Earth in Mouthful" (Alurista) **34**:24, 28, 41
"When You Lie Down, the Sea Stands Up" (Swenson) **14**:261
"When you pass the doorway" (Ní Chuilleanáin) **34**:382
"When You Speak to Me" (Gallagher) **9**:36
"When Your Body Brushed against Me" (Spicer) **78**:302
"When You've Forgotten Sunday" (Brooks) **7**:53, 68
"Whenever I Go There" (Merwin) **45**:22, 42, 49
"Where Am I Now?" (Crabbe) **97**:91
"Where are all thy beauties, now, all hearts enchaining?" (Campion) **87**:12, 66
"Where Are the Snows of Yesteryear" (Kennedy) **93**:137
"Where Are the War Poets?" (Day Lewis) **11**:131
"Where Are We?" (Shvarts) **50**:132
Where Are We Eating? and What Are We Eating? (Cage) **58**:196, 199
"Where Are You From?" (Yevtushenko) **40**:349
"Where can I go, now it's January?" (Mandelstam)
See "Kuda mne det'sia v etom Ianvare?"
"Where Chance Meets Necessity" (Simic) **69**:300
"Where Charity Begins" (Enright) **93**:6
"Where Dream Begins" (Sarton) **39**:324
Where Forgetfulness Lives (Cernuda)
See *Donde habite el olvido*
"Where Gleaming Fields of Haze" (Thoreau) **30**:182
"Where Go the Boats?" (Stevenson) **84**:315, 342
"Where He's Staying Now" (Meredith) **28**:179
"Where Is the Moralizer, Your Mother?" (Chin) **40**:9
"Where Is the Real Non-Resistant?" (Lindsay) **23**:281-82
"Where It Appears" (Duncan) **75**:189-90, 192
"Where It Was Back Then" (Sexton) **79**:240
"Where Knock Is Open Wide" (Roethke) **15**:251, 261, 272, 275-76, 278, 298, 300
"Where Mission Creek Runs Hard for Joy" (Hugo) **68**:251
"Where nothing grows" (Piercy) **29**:313
"Where Nothing Is Hidden" (Ignatow) **34**:278
"Where, O Where?" (Wylie) **23**:324
Where Oblivion Dwells (Cernuda)
See *Donde habite el olvido*
"Where Once the Waters of Your Face" (Thomas) **52**:245, 335
"Where Potchikoo Goes Next" (Erdrich) **52**:193
"Where Purples Now the Fig" (Warren) **37**:302
"Where shall I have at myn owne will" (Wyatt) **27**:332, 351-352
"Where Shall the Lover Rest" (Scott) **13**:304
"Where, Tall Girl, Is Your Gypsy Babe" (Akhmatova)
See "Gde, vysokaya, tvoy tsyganyonok"
"Where the Groceries Went" (Carver) **54**:12
"Where the Guelder Roses Bloom" (Carman)
See "When the Guelder Roses Bloom"
"Where the Hayfields Were" (MacLeish) **47**:164-65
"Where the Hell Would Chopin Be?" (Bukowski) **18**:4
"Where the House Was" (Hugo) **68**:291
"Where the light" (Ungaretti)
See "Dove la luce"
"Where the Peacock Cried" (Sarton) **39**:321
"Where the Picnic Was" (Hardy) **8**:136
"Where the Rainbow Ends" (Lowell) **3**:200, 207
Where the Sidewalk Ends (Silverstein) **49**:306, 309-13, 319, 322-24, 327, 331, 335-36, 338-41, 343, 346-49
"Where the Slow Fig's Purple Sloth" (Warren) **37**:301, 361
"Where the Tennis Court Was" (Montale)
See "Dov'era il tennis"
"Where the Track Vanishes" (Kinnell) **26**:238, 252
Where the Wolves Drink (Tzara) **27**:250
"Where There's a Will There's Velleity" (Nash) **21**:265
"Where They So Fondly Go" (Bukowski) **18**:5
Where Water Comes Together with Other Water (Carver) **54**:20-21
"Where We Live Now" (Levine) **22**:214
"Where We Must Look for Help" (Bly) **39**:42, 82, 85
"Where Were Cast Down" (Cernuda) **62**:206-7, 209-10
"Wherefore" (Howe) **81**:27-28
"Where's Agnes?" (Barrett Browning) **6**:24
"Where's the Poker" (Smart) **13**:348
"Wherever Home Is" (Wright) **36**:348
"Whether on Ida's Shady Brow" (Blake) **12**:11
"Whether or Not" (Lawrence) **54**:161
"Whether There Is Sorrow in the Demons" (Berryman) **64**:88
"Which" (Thomas) **99**:318
"Which Ane" (Riley) **48**:340
"Which, Being Interpreted, Is as May Be, or, Otherwise" (Lowell) **13**:91
"Whiffs of the Ohio River at Cincinnati" (Sandburg) **41**:288
"While Blooming Youth" (Prior) **52**:205
"While Drawing in a Churchyard" (Hardy) **8**:120-21
"While I Live" (Ignatow) **34**:305
"While in the Park I sing, the listning Deer" (Waller)
See "At Penshurst"
"While Love Is Unfashionable" (Walker) **30**:340, 365
"While She Chews Sideways" (Hughes) **89**:125
"While Sitting in the Tuileries and Facing the Slanting Sun" (Swenson) **14**:261, 285
"While Someone Telephones" (Bishop) **34**:89
"While the Record Plays" (Illyés) **16**:249, 251
"While We Were Arguing" (Kenyon) **57**:6
"whilst waiting for" (Bissett) **14**:32
"Whimper of Sympathy" (Meredith) **60**:289
Whims and Oddities (Hood) **93**:42, 45, 51-55, 72-74, 80, 89, 117
Whimsicalities: A Periodic Gathering (Hood) **93**:47, 82-83, 89, 99
"The Whinnying Mare of Bronte" (Gilmore) **87**:287
"The Whip" (Creeley) **73**:30, 123, 125, 127-28
"The Whip" (Robinson) **35**:368
The Whip (Creeley) **73**:3, 40
"Whip the World" (MacDiarmid) **9**:187
Whipperginny (Graves) **6**:127-28, 131
"The Whipping" (Hayden) **6**:194-96
"Whip-poor-will" (Hall) **70**:19, 34
"The Whirligig of Time" (Hecht) **70**:94
"Whirligigs" (Kenyon) **57**:45
"The Whirlwind" (Lindsay) **23**:281
"Whiskers, A Philosophical Ode" (Pushkin) **10**:407
Whisper to the Earth (Ignatow) **34**:324-25
"Whispered into the Ground" (Stafford) **71**:338
"whispered to lucifer" (Clifton) **17**:30
Whispering to Fool the Wind (Ríos) **57**:311-12, 319, 322-25
"Whispers" (Oliver) **75**:292
"Whispers of Heavenly Death" (Whitman) **3**:378
"Whistle and I'll Come tae Ye, My Lad" (Burns) **6**:59
"The Whistle Cockade" (Burns) **6**:82
"The Whistle of Sandy McGraw" (Service) **70**:131
"Whistle of the 3 A.M." (Warren) **37**:379
Whistle or Hoot (Ignatow) **34**:270
Whistles and Whistling (Ishikawa)
See *Yobuko to kuchibue*
"A Whistling Girl" (Parker) **28**:353, 362
"Whistling Sam" (Dunbar) **5**:122, 146
"Whit Monday" (MacNeice) **61**:140, 144
"Whit Sunday" (Dorn) **115**:54, 57
White (Paz)
See *Blanco*
White (Simic) **69**:265-73, 299-300, 328, 330-37, 339, 341, 348-51, 353-58
"White" (Strand) **63**:192, 194
"White and Green" (Lowell) **13**:60, 69
"White and Violet" (Jiménez) **7**:183
"White April" (Reese) **29**:339
White April (Reese) **29**:335-336, 339, 348, 351
"White Arrow" (Toomer) **7**:336
"White Ash" (Sandburg) **41**:357
"The White Birds" (Yeats) **51**:149
White Buildings (Crane) **3**:81, 84, 87, 90; **99**:3, 11-12, 14, 27-29, 32, 55-56, 59, 62, 74-75, 89, 93, 100, 104, 107, 113, 133-34, 136, 139
"White Center" (Hugo) **68**:304
The White Center (Brossard)
See *Le Centre blanc*
White Center (Hugo) **68**:271, 294
"White Christmas" (Service) **70**:141
"The White City" (McKay) **2**:211
"White Coat, Purple Coat" (Abse) **41**:33
White Coat, Purple Coat (Abse) **41**:32
"The white doe" (Borges)
See "La cierva blanca"
"The White Doe of Rylstone" (Wordsworth)
See *The White Doe of Rylstone; or, The Fate of the Nortons*
The White Doe of Rylstone; or, The Fate of the Nortons (Wordsworth) **4**:394, 402, 407; **67**:264-65
"White Dwarf" (Ammons) **16**:45
"White Dwarfs" (Ondaatje) **28**:314, 317, 327, 331-32, 334, 336, 338
"White Feather" (Berryman) **64**:81
White Flock (Akhmatova)
See *Belaya staya*
"White Flowers" (Oliver) **75**:322
"White Goat, White Ram" (Merwin) **45**:32
"The White Gull" (Carman) **34**:203-04
"White Hawthorn in the West of Ireland" (Boland) **58**:58
"The White Horse" (Very) **86**:96
"White Horses" (Kipling) **3**:183

"The White House" (McKay) **2**:210, 221, 229
"White Kimono" (Doty) **53**:60
"White Lady" (Clifton) **17**:28
"The White Lilies" (Glück) **16**:170-71
"White Lotus Ode" (Hughes) **89**:113
"The White Man's Burden" (Kipling) **3**:192; **91**:65, 91, 93, 95-96, 111, 127, 155-59, 166, 173, 178-79, 181-85
"White Men Can't Drum" (Alexie) **53**:15
"White Night" (Oliver) **75**:285
"White Night" (Wright) **14**:372
"White Notes" (Justice) **64**:274
"The White Ones" (Hughes) **53**:85
White Pine: Poems and Prose Poems (Oliver) **75**:310, 312-13
"The White Porch" (Song) **21**:331-32, 334, 338, 340-41, 350
"White Rabbit" (Dorn) **115**:231
"White road, old road" (Castro)
See "Camino blanco, viejo camino"
"White Shoulders" (Sandburg) **2**:303
"White Shroud" (Ginsberg) **4**:86, 90
White Shroud, Poems 1980-1985 (Ginsberg) **4**:86-7, 89-90; **47**:30
"The White Snake" (Sexton) **2**:365; **79**:191
"White Sunday" (Vaughan) **81**:335-36, 340, 349
"White Things" (Spencer) **77**:324-25, 327-28, 330, 345-46
"The White Thought" (Smith) **12**:292, 341, 354
"The White Tiger" (Thomas) **99**:260, 356, 358
"The White Troops" (Brooks) **7**:73
"The White Van" (Tomlinson) **17**:333
"White Wines" (Stein) **18**:341
"The White Witch" (Johnson) **24**:127, 142, 161, 166
"Whitehaired Girl" (MacLeish) **47**:206
White-Haired Lover (Shapiro) **25**:316, 321-22
The White-Haired Revolver (Breton)
See *Le revolver á cheveux blancs*
"The White-Tailed Hornet" (Frost) **1**:221
"Whitman in Black" (Berrigan) **103**:30, 41
"The Whitsun Weddings" (Larkin) **21**:228, 230, 238-39, 255
The Whitsun Weddings (Larkin) **21**:224, 227-28, 230, 233, 235, 240, 244, 253, 255, 259
"Whitsunday" (Herbert) **4**:118
"Whitsunday in the Church" (Howe) **81**:29
"Who" (Kenyon) **57**:13, 15, 40
"Who Among You Knows the Essence of Garlic" (Hongo) **23**:196-97
"Who & Where" (Bell) **79**:35
Who Are We Now? (Ferlinghetti) **1**:187-88
"Who are We? Somos Aztlán" (Alurista) **34**:45
"Who Burns for the Perfection of Paper" (Espada) **74**:132
"Who But the Lord" (Hughes) **1**:241
"Who Cares, Long as It's B-Flat" (Carruth) **10**:85
"Who Emptied the Sand from Your Shoes" (Sachs) **78**:226-27, 232
"Who ever comes to shroud me do not harme" (Donne)
See "The Funerall"
"Who has not walked" (Bridges) **28**:83
"Who Hath Ears to Hear Let Him Hear" (Very) **86**:45
"Who Hath Herd" (Wyatt) **27**:317
"Who Is Alienated from What?" (Rexroth) **95**:340
"Who Is My Proper Art" (Kinsella) **69**:118
"Who Is the God of Canongate" (Owen) **102**:149
"Who Is the Widow's Muse?" (Stone) **53**:258
Who Is the Widow's Muse? (Stone) **53**:220, 224
"Who is this Who Howls and Mutters?" (Smith) **12**:313, 336
"Who Killed James Joyce?" (Kavanagh) **33**:81, 86; **105**:100
"Who Knew" (Spicer) **78**:276
"Who Knows" (Dunbar) **5**:130
"Who Know's If the Moon's" (Cummings) **5**:88
"Who list his wealth and ease retain" (Wyatt) **27**:368
"Who Live Under the Shadow" (Spender) **71**:180
Who Look at Me (Jordan) **38**:111, 114
"Who Made Paul Bunyan" (Sandburg) **2**:327
"Who on Earth" (Kinnell) **26**:287
"Who Ordered the Broiled Face?" (Silverstein) **49**:323
"Who Said It Was Simple" (Lorde) **12**:153, 157
Who Shall Be the Sun? (Wagoner) **33**:353
"Who Shall Doubt" (Oppen) **35**:299
"Who Shot Eugenie?" (Smith) **12**:333
"Who so list to hount, I knowe where is an hynde" (Wyatt) **27**:300-01, 303, 309-10, 323, 329-30, 342-44, 348, 356, 358, 360, 363, 367
"Who so list to hounte" (Wyatt)
See "Who so list to hount, I knowe where is an hynde"
"Who Wakes" (Sarton) **39**:358
"Who Was Mary Shelley?" (Niedecker) **42**:134
"Who Watches from the Dark Porch" (Graham) **59**:135
Who Will Know Us?: New Poems (Soto) **28**:402
"Who Will Remember the Rememberers" (Amichai) **38**:56
"Who Will Survive America?/Few Americans/Very Few Negroes/No Crackers at All" (Baraka) **4**:14, 19
"Whoever Finds a Horseshoe" (Mandelstam)
See "Nashedshij podkovu"
"Whoever You Are: A Letter" (Mueller) **33**:174
"Whoever You Are Holding Me Now in Hand" (Whitman) **91**:245-46
"A Whole Day Without Debate" (Char) **56**:146
"Whole Duty of Children" (Stevenson) **84**:344
"The Whole Mess . . . Almost" (Corso) **108**:4, 22, 25
"The Whole Question" (Warren) **37**:376, 378
"The Whole Story" (Stafford) **71**:282, 284, 293
"The Whole Story" (Strand) **63**:178, 180
The Whole Works of Homer; in His Iliads, and Odysses (Chapman) **96**:37
"Wholesome" (Meredith) **28**:208
"Whom I Write For" (Aleixandre)
See "¿Para quién escribo?"
"Whooping Cranes" (Erdrich) **52**:183, 191
"The Whore of Babylon" (Chatterton) **104**:4, 68
"Whorls" (Meredith) **28**:198
"Who's in the Next Room" (Hardy) **92**:262
"Who's Out" (Stone) **53**:228
"Whose" (Boland) **58**:38
"Whoso List" (Wyatt)
See "Who so list to hount, I knowe where is an hynde"
"Whoso list to hount, I knowe where is an hind" (Wyatt)
See "Who so list to hount, I knowe where is an hynde"
"Whoso List To Hunt" (Wyatt)
See "Who so list to hount, I knowe where is an hynde"
"Whuchulls" (MacDiarmid) **9**:197-98
"Why" (Carman) **34**:210
"Why Animals Stay Away" (Ríos) **57**:323
"Why Boy Came to Lonely Place" (Warren) **37**:378
"Why Can't I Live Forever?" (Viereck) **27**:258, 276
"Why Come Ye Nat to Courte?" (Skelton)
See *Why Come Ye Nat to Courte?*
Why Come Ye Nat to Courte? (Skelton) **25**:336-37, 342, 348, 350, 356, 374, 379
Why Come Ye Not to Court? (Skelton)
See *Why Come Ye Nat to Courte?*
"why dew magazines lie" (Bissett) **14**:32
"Why Did I Laugh Tonight" (Keats) **1**:279, 305; **96**:260-61
"'Why Did I Sketch'" (Hardy) **8**:137; **92**:257
Why Did You Leave the Horse Alone? (Darwish)
See *Limadha Tarakta al-Hisana Wahidan*
"Why do I" (Smith) **12**:337
"Why Do You Sing My Bird" (Ekeloef) **23**:87
"Why does he pace? I like to alone" (Akhmadulina)
See "Zachem on khodit? Ia liubliu odna"
"Why do'st thou shade thy lovely face?" (Wilmot) **66**:265
"Why East Wind Chills" (Thomas) **2**:379
Why Have You Left the Horse Alone? (Darwish)
See *Limadha Tarakta al-Hisana Wahidan*
"Why I Am a Liberal" (Browning) **2**:66
"Why I Am Not a Painter" (O'Hara) **45**:121, 127, 176, 190
"why i often allude to osiris " (Reed) **68**:323-24, 335, 338, 348
"Why I Voted the Socialist Ticket" (Lindsay) **23**:267, 282, 296
"Why I write not of love" (Jonson)
See *The Forest I*
"Why Indian Men Fall in Love with White Women" (Alexie) **53**:24
"Why, My Lord and God?" (Werfel) **101**:347
"Why Kid Yourself" (Stone) **53**:252
"Why Not More Than One Husband?" (Das) **43**:84
"Why presumes they pride on that" (Campion) **87**:69
"When Guilford Good" (Burns) **114**:51-52, 54, 189
"When She Cam Ben She Bobbed" (Burns) **114**:167
"Why She Moved House" (Hardy) **92**:328
"Why Should Na Poor Folk Mowe" (Burns) **114**:129-30
"Why So Pale and Wan, Fond Lover" (Suckling) **30**:119, 122, 132-34, 156-59
"Why Some Look Up to Planets and Heroes" (Merton) **10**:334
"Why Sorrow?" (Kavanagh) **33**:144, 150, 152, 160; **105**:153, 172
"Why the Classics" (Herbert) **50**:30
"Why We Die" (Swenson) **14**:247
"Why We Tell Stories" (Mueller) **33**:198
"Why Wilt Thou Chide?" (Meynell) **112**:165-66, 174
"Why Write About" (Kaufman) **74**:241, 269
"Why You Climbed Up" (Warren) **37**:377
"Whys/Wise" (Baraka) **4**:40; **113**:26-27
"Wichita Vortex Sutra" (Ginsberg) **4**:50, 53, 66, 82, 85; **47**:48
Wickham (Wickham)
See *The Writings of Anna Wickham: Free Woman and Poet*
"Widdop" (Hughes) **89**:121, 123
"The Widdowes Solace" (Deloney) **79**:56
"The Wide Mouth" (Snyder) **21**:292
"Widok gór ze stepów Kozłowa" (Mickiewicz) **38**:221-22
"The Widow" (Merwin) **45**:20, 22, 25, 34, 43
"Widow" (Mueller) **33**:190
"The Widow" (Southey) **111**:193
"The Widow at Windsor" (Kipling) **3**:161, 186-87, 191; **91**:93, 97
The Widow in the Bye Steet (Masefield) **78**:21, 30, 51, 56, 58-60, 63, 74, 92, 104
"Widow La Rue" (Masters) **1**:330, 333
"The Widow o' Windsor" (Kipling)
See "The Widow at Windsor"
"The Widow of Windsor" (Kipling)
See "The Widow at Windsor"
"The Widow Who Taught at an Army School" (Stafford) **71**:272
"Widower's Tango" (Neruda) **4**:306
"Widowhood or the Home-Coming of Lady Ross" (Smith) **12**:351-52
"Widows" (Baudelaire)
See "Les veuves"

"The Widow's Lament in Springtime" (Williams) 7:345, 353, 360, 363; **109**:261
"Widows of the Living and of the Dead" (Castro)
See "As viudas d'os vivos e as viudas d'os mortos"
"The Widow's Party" (Kipling) **3**:160
"The Widow's Resolution" (Smart) **13**:347
"The Widow's Tale" (Crabbe) **97**:95, 97, 114
"Wie wenn am Feiertage ..." (Hölderlin) **4**:162, 165-66, 169
"Wielka liczba" (Drew) **44**:269, 271-73, 294, 300, 317
Wielka liczba (Szymborska) **44**:268-69
"Wielkie to szczeście" (Szymborska) **44**:309
Wiersze zebrane (Herbert) **50**:5-6, 8
"The Wife" (Creeley) **73**:11, 31
"The Wife" (Service) **70**:132
"The Wife" (Wickham) **110**:270
"A Wife at Daybreak I Shall Be" (Dickinson) **1**:93
"Wife of Bath's Prologue" (Chaucer)
See "Prologue to the Wife of Bath's Tale"
"Wife of Bath's Tale" (Chaucer) **19**:13, 15, 29, 33, 60, 63; **58**:230-40, 242-4, 250, 252, 255-63, 270, 272-6, 280-4, 299-300, 302-3, 307, 321, 324-8, 334, 336, 342, 354-5, 362-3
"Wife to Husband" (Rossetti) **7**:267
"The Wife's Song" (Wickham) **110**:276
"Wife's Tale" (Chaucer)
See "Wife of Bath's Tale"
"Wife-Woman" (Spencer) **77**:341
"The Wild" (Berry) **28**:14, 37
"Wild Blessings" (Clifton) **17**:29
"The Wild Bougainvillea" (Das) **43**:85
"Wild Boys of the Road" (Ashbery) **26**:163
"Wild Cherries" (Zagajewski) **27**:389
Wild Cherry (Reese) **29**:335-336, 339, 347-348, 351
"The Wild Common" (Lawrence) **54**:163, 165-66, 175, 179, 188, 191, 221, 231-36
The Wild Dog Rose (Montague) **106**:215, 233, 243, 245, 249-50, 262, 273, 277-79, 285-86, 298, 304, 311, 318, 321, 340
Wild Dreams of a New Beginning (Ferlinghetti) **1**:188
"Wild Ducks, People and Distances" (Stevens) **110**:224
"Wild Flower" (Tagore)
See "Banaphul"
"WILD FLOWRS ABOVE TH TREE LINE" (Bissett) **14**:20
Wild Garden (Carman) **34**:205, 211
"Wild Gardens Overlooked by Night Lights" (Guest) **55**:185
"Wild Geese" (Oliver) **75**:293
"Wild Grapes" (Frost) **1**:215; **39**:235
The Wild Iris (Glück) **16**:168, 170-71
"Wild Iron" (Curnow) **48**:11, 29
"Wild Life Cameo, Early Morn" (Ferlinghetti) **1**:182-83, 188
"Wild Oats" (Larkin) **21**:230, 234, 244, 247
"The Wild Old Wicked Man" (MacLeish) **47**:214
"A Wild Old Wicked Man" (Yeats) **51**:152
The Wild Old Wicked Man (MacLeish) **47**:193, 197, 214
"Wild Orchard" (Williams) **7**:345; **109**:287
A Wild Patience Has Taken Me This Far: Poems, 1978-1981 (Rich) **5**:385, 389
"Wild Peaches" (Wylie) **23**:301, 305, 314, 329, 333-34
"Wild Plums" (Erdrich) **52**:188
"Wild Rock" (Hughes) **89**:123
The Wild Rose Flowers (Akhmatova)
See *Shipovnik tsevetyot*
"The Wild Sky" (Rich) **5**:362
"Wild Sports of the West" (Montague) **106**:276
"Wild Sunflower" (Winters) **82**:319, 322
"The Wild Swan" (Masefield) **78**:43, 45
The Wild Swan: Poems (Gilmore) **87**:283, 299, 301
"The Wild Swans at Coole" (Yeats) **20**:303, 327; **51**:334
The Wild Swans at Coole (Yeats) **20**:304, 310-11, 314, 326, 328
"Wild Water" (Swenson) **14**:283
"Wild Without Love" (McGuckian) **27**:83
Wild Writing of the Recent Past (Shvarts)
See *Dikopis' poslednego vremeni*
"The Wildebeest" (Bly) **39**:117
"The Wilderness" (Merwin) **45**:23
"Wilderness" (Niedecker) **42**:101
"The Wilderness" (Robinson) **1**:459
"Wilderness" (Sandburg) **2**:302; **41**:240, 251, 270, 296, 303
"The Wildflower" (Williams) **7**:382, 386; **109**:294
"Wildflower Plain" (Wright) **14**:342
"Wildwest" (MacLeish) **47**:146, 189
"Wilfred Owen's Photographs" (Hughes) **7**:133
"Wilia" (Mickiewicz) **38**:149
"Wilk i owieczka" (Herbert) **50**:9
"Will" (Chatterton)
See "The Last Will and Testament of Thomas Chatterton"
"The Will" (Donne) **1**:126
"The Will" (Merrill) **28**:272
"Will" (Walker) **30**:339
"Will Be" (Pasternak) **6**:252
"Will Boyden Lectures" (Masters) **1**:343
"Will Not Come Back" (Lowell) **3**:226-27
"Will Out of Kindness of Their Hearts a Few Philosophers Tell Me" (Cummings) **5**:93
"Will They Cry When You're Gone, You Bet" (Baraka) **4**:18; **113**:139
The Will to Change: Poems, 1968-1970 (Rich) **5**:365-67, 370-72, 383, 387-89, 391, 399
"Will Waterproof's Lyrical Monologue" (Tennyson) **6**:360; **101**:220
"Will You Perhaps Consent to Be" (Schwartz) **8**:305
"Willful Homing" (Frost) **1**:197
"Willful-Missing" (Kipling) **91**:174
"William and Cynthia" (Simic) **69**:289
"William Bailey" (Crabbe) **97**:114
William Blake's Prophetic Writing (Blake) **12**:25
"William Bond" (Blake) **12**:35, 43
William Carlos Williams: Selected Poems (Williams) **7**:357
"William H. Herndon" (Masters) **1**:334; **36**:221
"William Leachman" (Riley) **48**:284
"William Marion Reedy" (Masters) **1**:325, 333, 342
"William McKinley" (Riley) **48**:326
"William Sycamore" (Benét) **64**:8, 20
"Williams' influence: Some Social Aspects" (Ignatow) **34**:205
"Willie" (Angelou) **32**:2
"Willie" (Brooks)
See "To Keorapetse Kgositsile (Willie)"
"Willie Brew'd a Peck o' Maut" (Burns) **6**:76
"Willie Fingers" (Espada) **74**:139
"Willie Wastle" (Burns) **6**:78, 81; **40**:97
"The Willing Mistress" (Behn) **13**:4, 14-16, 18-20, 29
"The Willing Mistriss" (Behn) **88**:29-30, 148, 152
"Willingly" (Gallagher) **9**:58
Willingly (Gallagher) **9**:42-4, 50-1, 53, 56, 58-62
"Willkommen und Abschied" (Goethe) **5**:247, 251
"The Willow" (Akhmatova)
See "Iva"
"The Willow" (de la Mare) **77**:63
"Willow Waves" (Wang Wei) **18**:364
"Willows" (Stryk) **27**:212-13
"Willowwood" (Rossetti) **44**:166, 203, 238, 256-7, 260, 622
"Willowwood (II)" (Rossetti) **44**:257
"Willowwood (III)" (Rossetti) **44**:257
"Willowwood (IV)" (Rossetti) **44**:257
"Willy Lyons" (Wright) **36**:324, 328, 345, 366, 400
"Wilt thou forgive" (Donne)
See "A Hymne to God the Father"
"Wind" (Carver) **54**:13, 22
"The Wind" (Dafydd ap Gwilym) **56**:215
"Wind" (Hughes) **7**:118, 165; **89**:188
"A Wind" (Kavanagh) **33**:74
"The Wind" (Morris) **55**:238, 279-80, 282
"The Wind" (Simic) **69**:263, 369
"Wind" (Soto) **28**:370, 373-75, 377-78, 384
"The Wind" (Stevenson) **84**:316, 344
"The Wind" (Teasdale) **31**:356
"Wind" (Tomlinson) **17**:328
The Wind among the Reeds (Yeats) **20**:303, 330; **51**:101
"Wind and Flags" (Montale)
See "Vento e bandiere"
"Wind and Gibbon" (Warren) **37**:379
"Wind and Glacier Voices" (Ortiz) **17**:232
"Wind and Mist" (Thomas) **53**:285-88, 290, 292, 341
"Wind and Silver" (Lowell) **13**:94-5
"The Wind and Stream" (Bryant) **20**:15
"The Wind and the Rain" (Frost) **1**:196
"Wind and Water and Stone" (Paz) **48**:190
"Wind and Wave" (Patmore) **59**:208, 212, 271
"Wind at Night" (Zagajewski) **27**:394
"The Wind at Penistone" (Davie) **29**:94, 108, 110
"The Wind Bloweth Where It Listeth" (Cullen) **20**:58
"Wind Chimes in a Temple Ruin" (Birney) **52**:25
"The Wind Coming Down From" (Ammons) **16**:5
"A Wind Flashes the Grass" (Hughes) **89**:100, 103, 109
"The Wind-Flower" (Very) **86**:41, 72, 158
"Wind from All Compass Points" (Paz)
See "Viento entero"
"Wind in Florence" (Brodsky) **9**:14
"The Wind in the Dooryard" (Walcott) **46**:237, 240, 289
"Wind in the Hemlock" (Teasdale) **31**:360
"The Wind Increases" (Williams) **109**:283
"The Wind Is Blind" (Meynell) **112**:261
"Wind is the wall of the year" (Piercy) **29**:314
Wind Mountain (Chappell) **105**:26, 28, 30-31, 34-36, 39-40, 42, 44, 47, 53, 61, 67-68, 72
"Wind on the Crescent" (Lewis)
See "Vento sulla mezzaluna"
"The Wind Over the Chimney" (Longfellow) **30**:103, 110
"Wind Subsides on the Earth River" (Chappell) **105**:42, 44
"The Wind, the Clock, the We" (Jackson) **44**:73-4, 78
"Wind through St. John's" (Birney) **52**:57-58
"Wind World" (Stafford) **71**:340
"Wind-Clouds and Star-Drifts" (Holmes) **71**:94, 109-10
"Windfalls" (Kenyon) **57**:45
"A Windflower" (Carman) **34**:210, 216
"Windflower Leaf" (Sandburg) **41**:255
"Windharp" (Montague) **106**:329
"The Windhover" (Hopkins) **15**:125, 127, 132-33, 144, 160, 168, 169, 171
"Windigo" (Erdrich) **52**:192
The Winding Stair (Yeats) **20**:307, 311, 326-28, 330, 333, 335
The Winding Stair, and Other Poems (Yeats) **51**:73, 94
"Winding Up" (Walcott) **46**:240
Windings (Duncan) **75**:230
"The Windmill" (Bridges) **28**:67
"The Window" (Cernuda)
See "La ventana"
"Window" (Corso) **108**:19-20
"The Window" (Creeley) **73**:59-60, 62, 96-98, 100, 102
"Window" (Hass) **16**:222

"The Window" (MacNeice) **61**:115, 117, 160
"The Window" (Mahon) **60**:134, 155, 187
"A Window" (Merton)
See "The Blessed Virgin Mary Compared to a Window"
"The Window" (Muir) **49**:197, 245, 247, 252
"Window" (Pinsky) **27**:157, 164, 172
"Window" (Sandburg) **41**:228, 234
"The Window" (Sarton) **39**:321, 358
"A Window Frame" (Curnow) **48**:13, 33
Window in My Face (Dalton) **36**:120
"The Window of the Tobacco Shop" (Cavafy) **36**:74, 81
"Window Poems" (Berry) **28**:5, 39
"The window-pane" (Char)
See "Le carreau"
"The Windows" (Apollinaire) **7**:36
"Windows" (Chappell) **105**:17
"The Windows" (Herbert) **4**:119, 131
"Windows" (Jarrell) **41**:170
"The Windows" (Mallarmé)
See "Les fenêtres"
Windows (Creeley) **73**:86, 91-92, 118
"Windows in th Straw" (Bissett) **14**:8
"The Windows of the Tobacco Shop" (Cavafy) **36**:53, 56, 57, 73, 112
"Windows to the Fifth Season" (Elytis) **21**:118
"Windröschen" (Celan) **10**:122
"Winds" (Auden) **1**:23
"The Winds" (Williams) **7**:369
Winds (Perse)
See *Vents*
"The Winds of Downhill" (Oppen) **35**:332
"The Winds of Orisha" (Lorde) **12**:155
"The Wind's Prophecy" (Hardy) **8**:115-17; **92**:362-63, 367
"The Wind's Way" (Swinburne) **24**:327
"Windshield" (Berrigan) **103**:27
"Wind-Song" (Lanier) **50**:101
Windsor Forest (Pope) **26**:315, 319, 321
"The Windy City" (Sandburg) **2**:306, 308, 314; **41**:249, 252, 271, 319-20, 329, 346
"Windy Nights" (Stevenson) **84**:316
"The Wine" (Ashbery) **26**:135-136
"The Wine" (Teasdale) **31**:360
"Wine and Time" (Seifert)
See "Víno a čas"
Wine from These Grapes (Millay) **6**:214, 217, 232
"The Wine Menagerie" (Crane) **3**:81, 90; **99**:11, 14, 16-17, 19, 33, 37, 50, 74
"Wine: Passages 12" (Duncan) **2**:108
Wine Press (Mistral)
See *Lagar*
"Winged Abyss" (Mackey) **49**:5-6
Winged Chariot (de la Mare) **77**:84, 116, 118
Winged Chariot and Other Poems (de la Mare) **77**:92, 95-96
"The Winged Horse" (Belloc) **24**:11
"Wingfoot Lake" (Dove) **6**:112
"The Wings" (Doty) **53**:53, 63
"Wings" (Hughes) **7**:132, 137; **89**:114
"Wings of a Dove" (Brathwaite) **56**:75-76, 83
"Wings of a God" (Levertov) **11**:176
"Wings of Prophecy" (Sachs) **78**:220
"Winkel im Wald" (Trakl) **20**:232
"Der Winkel von Hahrdt" (Hölderlin) **4**:148
"The Winning Argument" (Piercy) **29**:309
"Winning His Way" (Stein) **18**:312-14, 316
"Winning of Cales" (Deloney) **79**:57
"The Winnowers" (Bridges) **28**:66-7
"Wino" (Hughes) **7**:123, 132, 137
"Winston Prairie" (Masters) **1**:343
"Winter" (Celan) **10**:129
"Winter" (Clare) **23**:44-5
"Winter" (Darío)
See "Invernal"
"Winter" (Giovanni) **19**:116
"Winter" (Hagiwara) **18**:168
"Winter" (Koch) **80**:328
"Winter" (Melville) **82**:37
"Winter" (Milosz) **8**:210
"Winter" (Morris) **55**:325
"Winter" (Patmore) **59**:227, 271
"Winter" (Wright) **14**:376
"Winter, a Dirge" (Burns) **6**:52
"A Winter and Spring Scene" (Thoreau) **30**:220
"Winter and Summer" (Spender) **71**:154
"The Winter Bird" (Very) **86**:69-70
"Winter Boredom" (Carducci)
See "Tedio Invernale"
"Winter Bouquet" (Snodgrass) **74**:285, 302, 311
"Winter Bulletin" (Cohen) **109**:89
"Winter Castle" (Jacobsen) **62**:311, 320
"A Winter Daybreak above Vence" (Wright) **36**:360, 370
"Winter Dreams" (Goodison) **36**:158
"Winter Dusk" (de la Mare) **77**:94
"Winter Encounters" (Tomlinson) **17**:333, 344, 352
"The Winter Evening" (Cowper) **40**:45, 48-9, 52, 77, 140, 142-43
"Winter Evening" (Pushkin)
See "Zimniy Vecher"
"Winter Event" (Cassian) **17**:5
"Winter Festivities" (Pasternak) **6**:266
"Winter Fields" (Clare) **23**:45
"Winter Garden" (Neruda)
See "Jardín de invierno"
"Winter Grace" (Sarton) **39**:323
"Winter Holding off the Coast of North America" (Momaday) **25**:219
"A Winter Holiday" (Carman) **34**:211
"Winter Honey" (Jordan) **38**:44
Winter Idyl (Whittier)
See *Snow-Bound: A Winter Idyl*
"Winter in Dunbarton" (Lowell) **3**:218-19
"Winter in Leeds" (Kavanagh) **105**:111, 175, 177
"Winter in the City" (Mickiewicz)
See "Zima miejska"
Winter Insomnia (Carver) **54**:3
"Winter Lambs" (Kenyon) **57**:11, 25, 42
"Winter Landscape" (Berryman) **64**:79, 86-88, 90, 159
Winter Light (Jaccottet)
See *À la lumière d'hiver*
"Winter Love" (Duncan) **75**:248
Winter Love (H. D.) **5**:299-300
"Winter Mask" (Tate) **50**:241, 244, 254, 256-57, 259, 295, 336
"Winter Moon" (Hughes) **53**:85
"Winter Morning's Walk" (Cowper) **40**:46, 49, 61, 132
"Winter: My Secret" (Rossetti) **7**:281
"A Winter Night" (Burns) **114**:101
"Winter Night" (Sarton) **39**:360
"The Winter Night" (Smith)
See "Sonnet 74"
"Winter Night Song" (Teasdale) **31**:365
Winter Numbers (Hacker) **47**:105-8, 112, 115-17
"Winter on the River" (Meredith) **28**:198
"A Winter Piece" (Bryant) **20**:18, 35-7, 39
"Winter Piece" (Tomlinson) **17**:325
"A Winter Poem For Tony Weinberger Written on the Occasion of Feeling Very Happy" (Wakoski) **15**:331
"Winter Privacy Poems at the Shack" (Bly) **39**:115
"Winter Quiet" (Williams) **109**:323
"A Winter Scene" (Bryant) **20**:15
"The Winter Sea" (Tate) **50**:246
The Winter Sea (Tate) **50**:239-41, 252, 257, 259
"A Winter Ship" (Plath) **1**:389; **37**:176, 180
"Winter Sleep" (Oliver) **75**:284, 300
"Winter Sleep" (Wylie) **23**:309, 329, 332
"Winter Sleepers" (Atwood) **8**:12
"Winter Song" (Owen) **19**:336, 343
"Winter Spring" (Wilbur) **51**:266
"Winter Stars" (Teasdale) **31**:360
Winter Station (Yevtushenko)
See "Zima Station"
"Winter Sunset" (Williams) **109**:239
"Winter Swan" (Bogan) **12**:95, 106, 122
"Winter Syntax" (Collins) **68**:220
A Winter Talent and Other Poems (Davie) **29**:93-96, 100, 106, 108-09, 112, 117
"Winter Thunder" (Kennedy) **93**:151
Winter Thunder (Kennedy) **93**:150-51
"Winter-Time" (Stevenson) **84**:344
"Winter Trees" (Oliver) **75**:285, 293
Winter Trees (Plath) **1**:396; **37**:184
"Winter Trees on the Horizon" (Meynell) **112**:192
"The Winter Twilight Glowing Black and Gold" (Schwartz) **8**:295
"Winter Verse for His Sister" (Meredith) **28**:213
"A Winter Visit" (Abse) **41**:21
"The Winter Walk at Noon" (Cowper) **40**:49-51, 132
Winter Words in Various Moods and Metres (Hardy) **92**:208, 210, 221, 225-26
Winter Words: Various Moods and Metres (Hardy) **8**:89, 96, 124
"Wintergreen Ridge" (Niedecker) **42**:94, 96, 100, 104, 106-7, 109, 132
"Wintering" (Plath) **1**:410, 412-13; **37**:239-41
Wintering Out (Heaney) **18**:188, 192-95, 199, 202-5, 209-11, 215, 238, 241, 252
Wintermarchen (Heine)
See *Deutschland: Ein Wintermärchen*
"Winternacht" (Trakl) **20**:229
"A Winter-Piece to a Friend Away" (Berryman) **64**:89
"Winterreise" (Hope) **56**:277
"A Winter's Day" (Dunbar) **5**:126
"Winter's gone the summer breezes" (Clare) **23**:23
"The Winter's Night" (Merton) **10**:340, 351
"Winter's Tale" (Jacobsen) **62**:320, 323
"The Winter's Tale" (Jarrell) **41**:169
"A Winter's Tale" (Lawrence) **54**:168
"A Winter's Tale" (Plath) **37**:254
"A Winter's Tale" (Thomas) **2**:382, 385, 402; **52**:218-19, 221-22, 224, 272, 279, 286, 312, 314, 322
Winter's Tale (Heine)
See *Deutschland: Ein Wintermärchen*
"Winterward" (Stafford) **71**:361
Winterward (Stafford) **71**:276, 279, 287
"Wintry" (Gozzano)
See "A Wintry Scene"
"A Wintry Scene" (Gozzano) **10**:177-78, 180
"Wintry Sky" (Pasternak) **6**:250
"Wir gerieten in ein Mohnfeld" (Benn) **35**:30, 68
Wir sind (Werfel) **101**:299-300, 302, 314, 317-18, 322, 329-31, 336, 339, 345-46, 355-58
"Wir ziehn einen großen Bogen" (Benn) **35**:70
"Wire Walker" (Snodgrass) **74**:334
"Wirers" (Sassoon) **12**:267, 285
"Wires" (Tsvetaeva)
See "Provoda"
"Wiretapping" (Montale)
See "Intercettazione telefonica"
"Das wirkliche Messer" (Enzensberger) **28**:159-61, 165
"Wisdom" (Corso) **33**:44; **108**:35
"Wisdom" (Parker) **28**:362
"Wisdom" (Teasdale) **31**:323, 333, 340, 355, 364, 389
"Wisdom" (Yeats) **51**:86
Wisdom (Verlaine)
See *Sagesse*
"Wisdom Cometh with the Years" (Cullen) **20**:52, 62
"The Wisdom of Insecurity" (Eberhart) **76**:69
"The Wisdom of the Eld" (Meredith) **60**:261
"The Wise" (Cullen) **20**:54-55
"The Wise Delights of Love" (Patmore)
See "Deliciae Sapientiae de Amore"
"Wise Men" (Hughes) **53**:115
"The Wise Men from the East" (Carman) **34**:208

"Wise Men in Their Bad Hours" (Jeffers) **17**:129
"The Wise Woman" (Teasdale) **31**:389
"The Wish" (Cowley) **90**:16, 113, 179
"The Wish" (Lermontov) **18**:277, 295
"Wish" (Merwin) **45**:22
"Wish" (Mistral)
See "Voto"
"A Wish for Unconsciousness" (Hardy) **92**:209
"Wish: Metamorphosis to Hearldic Emblem""Wish: Metamorphosis to Heraldic Emblem" (Atwood) **8**:32, 39
"The Wish of To-day" (Whittier) **93**:169
"The Wish to be Generous" (Berry) **28**:43
"The Wish to Escape into Inner Space" (Swenson) **14**:250
"Wishbones" (Wakoski) **15**:332
"Wishes" (Wright) **14**:355
"wishes for sons" (Clifton) **17**:29, 36
"Wishes to His *Supposed* Mistresse" (Crashaw) **84**:99, 107, 127
"The Wishing Box" (Plath) **37**:209
"The Wishing Tree" (Heaney) **18**:229, 232
"The Wishing-Gate Destroyed" (Wordsworth) **67**:269
"Wistful" (Sandburg) **41**:298
"The Witch" (de la Mare) **77**:74
"Witch Burning" (Plath) **1**:394
"Witch Doctor" (Hayden) **6**:186, 196
"Witch Hazel" (Reese) **29**:330
"The Witch of Atlas" (Shelley) **14**:174, 193, 196, 198; **67**:233
"The Witch of Coös" (Frost) **1**:197, 209, 220; **39**:235
"The Witch of Endor" (Hecht) **70**:108
"The Witch of Wenham" (Whittier) **93**:173, 226, 239, 247-48
"Witches" (Hughes) **89**:137
"Witches are Flying" (Shapiro) **25**:316
"Witching" (Boland) **58**:37, 44-45
"The Witch's Daughter" (Whittier) **93**:166-67, 173, 239, 267
"The Witch's Life" (Sexton) **2**:373; **79**:237
"Witch-Woman" (Lowell) **13**:61, 64
"With a Copy of Stevens' Harmonium" (Cunningham) **92**:185
"With a Gift of Silver Candlesticks" (Benét) **64**:22
"With a Guitar, to Jane" (Shelley) **14**:177, 189; **67**:228
"With a Picture sent to a Friend" (Crashaw) **84**:123
"With a Rose to Brunhilde" (Lindsay) **23**:286
"With All Deliberate Speed" (Madhubuti) **5**:346
"With an Identity Disc" (Owen) **102**:227
With But a Few Hours Left (Cernuda)
See *Con las horas contadas*
"With Eyes At The Back of Our Heads" (Levertov) **11**:168
With Eyes at the Back of Our Heads (Levertov) **11**:168, 205
"With Eyes Veiled" (Simic) **69**:279, 300, 302, 316
"With Frontier Strength Ye Stand Your Ground" (Thoreau) **30**:194, 215, 217, 219, 267, 293
"With Garments Flowing" (Clare) **23**:23
"With Happiness Stretch's across the Hills" (Blake) **12**:36
"With Her Lips Only" (Graves) **6**:151
"With His Pistol in His Hand": A Border Ballad and Its Hero (Paredes) **83**:10-11, 14-20, 22-23, 26, 35, 43
"With Kathy in Wisdom" (Hugo) **68**:261
"With Kit, Age 7, At the Beach" (Stafford) **71**:328
"with liberty and justice for all" (Alurista) **34**:37
"With me" (Guillén) **35**:219
"With Mercy for the Greedy" (Sexton) **2**:346, 348, 351, 370; **79**:288, 299
"With Muted Strings" (Verlaine) **32**:371
"With Official Lu Hsiang Passing Hermit Hsiu-Chung's Bower" (Wang Wei) **18**:358
"With One Launched Look" (Stafford) **71**:293
"With Pale Women in Maryland" (Bly) **39**:14, 103
"With Pencil" (Guillén) **35**:211
"With Rue My Heart Is Laden" (Housman) **2**:180, 184, 192
"With Scindia to Delhi" (Kipling) **3**:182
"With Seed the Sowers Scatter" (Housman) **2**:180
"With the Caribou" (Kumin) **15**:212, 223
"With the deep voice of a prophet" (Akhmadulina)
See "Glubokim golosom proroka"
"With the Dog at Sunrise" (Kenyon) **57**:27, 35
"With the Door Open" (Ignatow) **34**:276, 305, 327
"With the Gift of a Feather" (Wright) **36**:396
"With the Gift of an Alabaster Tortoise" (Wright) **36**:378
"With the Persuader" (Meredith) **60**:263
"With the Shell of a Hermit Crab" (Wright) **36**:312
"With the World in My Bloodstream" (Merton) **10**:345
With Time Running Out (Cernuda)
See *Con las horas contadas*
"With Trumpets and Zithers" (Milosz)
See "Natrabach i na cytrze"
"With Vengeance Like a Tiger Crawls" (Bukowski) **18**:5
"A Withered Leaf—Seen on a Poet's Table" (Very) **86**:69
"Within the Circuit of the Plodding Life" (Thoreau) **30**:234, 267
"Within These Caverned Days" (Birney) **52**:8
"Within this mindless vault" (Cunningham) **92**:137
"Without" (Snyder) **21**:297
Without (Hall) **70**:55
"Without a Counterpart" (Gunn) **26**:218
"Without a Nest" (Castro)
See "Sin nido"
"Without a Sough of Wind" (Simic) **69**:290, 319
"Without Benefit of Declaration" (Hughes) **1**:252; **53**:111
"Without Ceremony" (Hardy) **8**:134-35; **92**:328
"Without End" (Zagajewski) **27**:383
"Without Faith" (Aleixandre) **15**:5
"Without Fear" (Ignatow) **34**:313
"Without that once clear aim, the path of flight" (Spender) **71**:221
"Witness" (Boland) **58**:40
"Witness" (Montague) **106**:327
"Witness" (Stafford) **71**:282, 297
"The Witness" (Tomlinson) **17**:344
A Witness Tree (Frost) **1**:196-97, 203, 205-06; **39**:234
"The Witnesses" (Auden) **1**:22
"The Wits" (Suckling) **30**:148-53, 155
"The Wives" (Hall) **70**:31
"Wives in the Sere" (Hardy) **8**:90
"A Wizard Considers a Lady" (Wickham) **110**:265
"The Wizard in Words" (Moore) **49**:161
"Wizards" (Noyes) **27**:135
"Wm. Brazier" (Graves) **6**:143
"Wodwo" (Hughes) **7**:127-28, 155; **89**:111, 150, 168, 264
Wodwo (Hughes) **7**:120-23, 133-34, 136-38, 140-42, 150, 157-60, 163, 171-72; **89**:98-104, 106, 108, 110-11, 114-15, 119-21, 123, 137, 140-42, 150, 155-57, 166, 210-11, 216-19, 233-34, 259
"Woefully arrayed" (Skelton) **25**:330
"Wohin" (Sachs) **78**:115
Wohnungen des Todes (Sachs)
See *In den Wohnungen des Todes*
"Wojna" (Herbert) **50**:5, 7, 9
Wołanie do Yeti (Szymborska) **44**:268, 280, 285, 292, 294, 298, 311, 318
"Wolf" (Mandelstam) **14**:149
"The Wolf and the Lamb" (Henryson) **65**:8, 17, 27, 54, 64-65, 81, 110-11
"The Wolf and the Sheep" (Herbert) **50**:8
"The Wolf and the Wether" (Henryson) **65**:18, 27, 54, 64, 81
"Wolf Knife" (Hall) **70**:9, 27, 33
"The Wolf Screamed" (Rimbaud)
See "Le loup criait"
"Wolfe Tone" (Clarke) **112**:55
"Wolfe Tone" (Heaney) **18**:228, 232
Wolfwatching (Hughes) **89**:145, 150, 169, 217
"The Wolves" (Tate) **50**:231, 259, 303, 306-7
"Wolves Defended against the Lambs" (Enzensberger) **28**:147, 165
"The Woman" (Carruth) **10**:71
"The Woman" (Creeley) **73**:46
"Woman" (Howe) **81**:4
"Woman" (Jarrell) **41**:142, 168-69, 171, 173, 179, 217
"The Woman" (Levertov) **11**:213-14
"A Woman" (Mistral)
See "Una mujer"
"A Woman" (Pinsky) **27**:176
"The Woman" (Thomas) **99**:310
"A Woman Alone" (Levertov) **11**:210
"The Woman and the Sea" (Yevtushenko) **40**:345
"Woman and Tree" (Graves) **6**:149
"The Woman at Banff" (Stafford) **71**:277
"The Woman at the Washington Zoo" (Jarrell) **41**:171, 185, 188-89, 191, 194-95, 205, 210
The Woman at the Washington Zoo (Jarrell) **41**:146, 159, 215
"The Woman Changes Her Skin" (Boland) **58**:45, 98
"A Woman Dead in Her Forties" (Rich) **5**:379-80, 394
"The Woman Hanging from the Thirteenth Floor" (Harjo) **27**:64-5
"A Woman Homer Sung" (Yeats) **20**:329
"Woman, I Got the Blues" (Komunyakaa) **51**:33
"The Woman I Met" (Hardy) **92**:276
"A Woman in Heat Wiping Herself" (Olds) **22**:316
"Woman in Kitchen" (Boland) **58**:45
"Woman in Orchard" (Wright) **14**:373
"Woman in Rain" (Kennedy) **93**:150
"The Woman in the Ordinary" (Piercy) **29**:309
"The Woman of Five Fields" (Gilmore) **87**:302
"Woman of Strength" (Tagore)
See "Sabala"
"The Woman on the Stair" (MacLeish) **47**:190
"A Woman Painted on a Leaf" (Boland) **58**:50, 96
"Woman Poem" (Giovanni) **19**:108
"A Woman Resurrected" (Gozzano) **10**:177-78
"A Woman Speaks" (Lorde) **12**:160
"The Woman Speaks to the Man Who Has Employed Her Son" (Goodison) **36**:154
"Woman to a Philosopher" (Wickham) **110**:271
"Woman to Child" (Wright) **14**:337, 341, 349, 352, 360, 362, 364
"Woman to Man" (Wright) **14**:333, 336-39, 349, 358-60, 363
Woman to Man (Wright) **14**:334, 336-38, 341, 345-47, 349, 352, 358, 363, 365-66, 369
"The Woman Turns Herself into a Fish" (Boland) **58**:45
"A Woman Unconscious" (Hughes) **89**:140, 145
"A Woman Waits for Me" (Whitman) **3**:372, 387; **91**:329
"Woman! when I behold thee" (Keats) **96**:346, 352, 354
"The Woman Who Blamed Life on a Spaniard" (Stevens) **110**:94-95
"The Woman Who Forgot Everything" (Sachs)
See "Die alles Vergessende"
"The Woman Who Lived in a Crate" (Stryk) **27**:187

"The Woman Who Raised Goats" (Gallagher) **9**:35-6, 59
"A Woman Whose Movements Are a River's" (Paz)
See "Una mujer de movimientos de rio"
"Woman With a Blue-Ringed Bowl" (McGuckian) **27**:102
"Woman with Girdle" (Sexton) **2**:346, 350
"Woman Work" (Angelou) **32**:29
"A Woman Young and Old" (Yeats) **20**:327
"Woman—and Man" (Gilmore) **87**:301
"The Womanhood" (Brooks) **7**:54
"Woman's Constancy" (Donne) **1**:125; **43**:133
"Woman's Honor" (Wilmot) **66**:267, 342
"Woman's Song" (Wright) **14**:349, 352, 364
"Women" (Bogan) **12**:101
"The Women" (Boland) **58**:7, 15, 80, 92-94
"Women" (Parra) **39**:289
"Women" (Randall) **86**:291, 343-44
"Women" (Rich) **5**:370
"Women" (Swenson) **14**:279
"The Women" (Walker) **30**:338, 341, 367
"Women" (Yevtushenko) **40**:345
"Women and Poets" (Randall) **86**:348
The Women and the Men (Giovanni) **19**:114, 124, 128, 130, 137
"The Women at Point Sur" (Jeffers) **17**:130
The Women at Point Sur (Jeffers) **17**:107, 109-11, 116, 124, 135, 144-4
The Women at Point Sur and Other Poems (Jeffers)
See *The Women at Point Sur*
"Women Laughing" (Stone) **53**:230
"Women like You" (Ondaatje) **28**:314
"Women Looking for Lice" (Rimbaud)
See "Les chercheuses de poux"
"The Women of Dan Dance With Swords in Their Hands to Mark the Time When They Were Warriors" (Lorde) **12**:159-60
"Women of Four Countries" (Douglas) **106**:187, 191
"The Women Speaking" (Hogan) **35**:247
"Women We Never See Again" (Bly) **39**:47, 86
"the women you are accustomed to" (Clifton) **17**:30
"Women's Shuttles" (Das) **43**:82
"Women's Tug of War at Lough Arrow" (Gallagher) **9**:37
"Wonder" (Hughes) **53**:162
"Wonder" (Traherne) **70**:173, 184-86, 216, 255, 262, 265-68, 273, 275, 288, 290-91, 314
"The Wonder Castle" (Illyés) **16**:234, 250
"The Wonder Woman" (Giovanni) **19**:107, 110, 112
"The Wonderful Musician" (Sexton) **2**:365
Wonderings (Masefield) **78**:27-30, 56, 74, 81, 88-90
"Wonderment" (Szymborska)
See "Zdumienie"
"Wonga Vine" (Wright) **14**:348
"Woo/Dove" (Brathwaite) **56**:89
"A Wood" (Wilbur) **51**:283
"The Wood Dove at Sandy Spring" (MacLeish) **47**:192
"The Wood Pewee" (Francis) **34**:261, 265
"Wood Song" (Teasdale) **31**:325, 340, 356
"The Wood Thrush" (Carman) **34**:229
"Wood-Cock" (Yevtushenko) **40**:347
"Woodcuts for America" (Tolson) **88**:329-30, 343
"The Woodcutter" (Service) **70**:116
"Woodcutting on Lost Mountain" (Gallagher) **9**:60
"The Wooden Bird" (Herbert) **50**:4
"Wooden Die" (Herbert)
See "Drewniana kostka"
The Wooden Pegasus (Sitwell) **3**:301-02
"Wooden Steeds" (Verlaine)
See "Chevaux de bois"
"Woodland Peace" (Meredith) **60**:289
"The Woodlot" (Clampitt) **19**:89
"The Woodman" (Clare) **23**:13
"The Woodman" (Stevenson) **84**:332
"Woodman and Echo" (Meredith) **60**:299
"The Woodman's Daughter" (Patmore) **59**:218, 225, 240, 258
"Woodnotes" (Emerson) **18**:79, 87-88, 99, 102-3, 108-10
"A Woodpath" (Carman) **34**:208
"The Wood-Pile" (Frost) **1**:220, 222, 226, 228; **39**:253; **71**:22, 44, 50
"The Woodpile Skull" (Kennedy) **93**:150-51
"Woodrow Wilson (February, 1924)" (Jeffers) **17**:107
"Woods" (Berry) **28**:43
"The Woods" (Erdrich) **52**:174-75, 192
"The Woods" (Jacobsen) **62**:320
"Woods" (MacNeice) **61**:118, 126
"The Woods" (Mahon) **60**:145-47
"The Woods of Westermain" (Meredith) **60**:246, 256-57, 262, 287-88, 290-91, 2967-97, 327, 320-30, 333, 339
"The Woodspurge" (Rossetti) **44**:173, 224-29, 231-32
"Woof of the Sun, Ethereal Gauze" (Thoreau) **30**:194, 208, 235, 257, 267, 287, 294
"Wooing" (Bridges) **28**:63, 86
"The Wooing of Hallbiorn" (Morris) **55**:340
"The Wooing of Swanhild" (Morris) **55**:306-8, 331
The Wooing of Swanhild (Morris) **55**:309
"Wooing the Muse" (Hughes) **53**:96-97
"Woolworth's" (Hall) **70**:32
"The Word (Akhmadulina)
See "Slovo"
"The Word" (Brathwaite) **56**:32
"Word" (Chappell) **105**:20, 39
"A Word" (Chesterton) **28**:100
"The Word" (Dorn) **115**:116
"The Word" (Smith) **12**:354
"The Word" (Thomas) **53**:313, 319, 328
The Word as Archipelago (Char)
See *La parole en archipel*
"The Word at St. Kavin's" (Carman) **34**:225
"Word Basket Woman" (Snyder) **21**:326
"The Word 'Beautiful'" (Swenson) **14**:250
"The Word Crys Out" (Ammons) **16**:25
"A Word for Summer" (Seferis) **66**:206, 209
"A Word for the Hour" (Whittier) **93**:212, 348
"A Word from Hart Crane's Ghost" (Kennedy) **93**:147
"The Word in the Beginning" (Carman) **34**:223
"The Word Joy" (Jaccottet)
See "Le mot joie"
Word Making Man: A Poem for Nicolas Guillen (Brathwaite) **56**:55, 90
"A Word on the Quick and Modern Poem-Makers" (Bukowski) **18**:5
Word over All (Day Lewis) **11**:144, 148
"A Word to the Wise" (Patmore) **59**:204
"Words" (Creeley) **73**:10, 53
"Words" (Douglas) **106**:209
"Words" (Gunn) **26**:212
"Words" (de la Mare) **77**:114
"Words" (Levine) **22**:219
"The Words" (Montale)
See "Le parole"
"Words" (Plath) **1**:409; **37**:258
"Words" (Reese) **29**:336
"Words" (Sexton) **2**:372-73; **79**:237
"Words" (Stone) **53**:246, 248
"Words" (Thomas) **53**:271, 330, 332
"Words" (Thumboo) **30**:300, 334
"Words" (Yeats) **20**:329, 331
Words (Creeley) **73**:8, 11-13, 15, 26-27, 36-39, 41-49, 51-54, 64, 89, 104, 115
"Words Above a Narrow Entrance" (Wagoner) **33**:333, 372
"Words for a Wall-Painting" (Shapiro) **25**:304
Words for Dr. Y.: Uncollected Poems With Three Stories (Sexton) **79**:199-201, 210, 212, 215, 217-18, 242-45, 251-52
"Words for Hart Crane" (Lowell) **3**:219, 222
"Words for Love" (Berrigan) **103**:4, 6, 33, 46
"Words for Maria" (Merrill) **28**:224, 231, 264, 277
"Words for Music Perhaps" (Yeats) **20**:326-29, 331, 333
Words for Music Perhaps, and Other Poems (Yeats) **20**:328, 334
"Words for the Hour" (Harper) **21**:190
Words for the Hour (Howe) **81**:8, 49-50, 52, 62-63
"Words for the Wind" (Roethke) **15**:263
Words for the Wind: The Collected Verse of Theodore Roethke (Roethke) **15**:257, 262-64, 267, 282, 284, 286, 288, 309
"Words from a Totem Animal" (Merwin) **45**:34-5
"Words heard, by accident, over the phone" (Plath) **37**:262
Words in Stone (Bonnefoy)
See *Pierre écrite*
Words in th Fire (Bissett) **14**:13-14
"Words in the Mourning Time" (Hayden) **6**:197-98
Words in the Mourning Time (Hayden) **6**:179, 181-83, 193, 195
"Words Like Freedom" (Hughes) **53**:150
"Words of Comfort" (Ammons) **16**:25, 43
"Words of Comfort to the Scratched on a Mirror" (Parker) **28**:361
"The Words of the Mute Are Like Silver Sollars" (Espada) **74**:124
"The Words of the Poet" (Aleixandre) **15**:6
"The Words of the Preacher" (Kunitz) **19**:149, 170
"Words on a Windy Day" (Stryk) **27**:212
"The Words on Magnet" (Seifert) **47**:332
"Words Rising" (Bly) **39**:67
"Words, Roses, Stars" (Wright) **14**:378-79
"Words to Frank O'Hara's Angel" (O'Hara) **45**:120
"A Word with José Rodriguez-Feo" (Stevens) **110**:80, 82, 85
"Words Without Songs" (Enright) **93**:15
"Words, Words, Words" (Randall) **86**:340
"Work" (Hass) **16**:249
"Work" (Komunyakaa) **51**:35
"the work" (Schwerner) **42**:196
"Work Gangs" (Sandburg) **2**:304, 308
"Work in Progress" (MacDiarmid) **9**:199
"Work in Progress" (Williams) **109**:217
Work Is Tiresome (Pavese)
See *Lavorare stanca*
"The Work of Creation" (Lawrence) **54**:250
"The Work of Happiness" (Sarton) **29**:332
"Work Song and Blues" (Brathwaite) **56**:38, 82
"Work Wearies" (Pavese)
See "Lavorare stanca"
Work Wearies (Pavese)
See *Lavorare stanca*
"The Workbox" (Hardy) **92**:363-64
"Worker in Mirror, at his Bench" (Kinsella) **69**:75, 78
"A Worker Reads History" (MacDiarmid) **9**:181
"Workers" (Rimbaud)
See "Ouvriers"
"Worker's Hands" (Mistral)
See "Manos de obreros"
"Worker's Song" (Angelou) **32**:30
"The Workhouse Clock" (Hood) **93**:87, 99, 102, 119
"Working Against Time" (Wagoner) **33**:332
"Working for a Living" (Ignatow) **34**:305
"A working man appeared in the street" (Niedecker) **42**:151
"Working on the '58 Willys Pickup" (Snyder) **21**:300
"A Working Party" (Sassoon) **12**:257, 261-62, 277-78, 284
"The Workingman's Drink" (Baudelaire) **1**:47
"The Workman" (Storni)
See "El obrero"
Works (Longfellow) **30**:68
Works (Philips) **40**:280

Works (Poe)
See *The Collected Works of Edgar Allan Poe*
Works (Pope) **26**:359-60
Works (Sidney)
See *Complete Works of Philip Sidney*
Works (Tennyson) **101**:268-69
Works (Wilde)
See *Collected Works*
Works, 1735—Poems on Several Occasions (Swift) **9**:256
The Works and Days of Lavinia, a Nun of the Order of the Circumcision of the Heart (Shvarts)
See *Trudy i dni Lavinii monakhini iz ordena obrezaniia serdtsa*
Works II (Pope) **26**:360
The Works of Aphra Behn (Behn) **13**:16, 18; **88**:22, 141-42
The Works of Charlotte Smith (Smith) **104**:325, 340, 343, 345-52
The Works of George Herbert (Herbert) **4**:107
The Works of Henry Vaughan (Vaughan) **81**:258, 260-66, 296, 325, 330
The Works of Horace, Translated into Verse (Smart) **13**:361-62
The Works of Michael Drayton (Drayton) **98**:41, 61-64
The Works of Mirabai (Mirabai) **48**:150-69
The Works of Mr. Abraham Cowley (Cowley) **90**:63, 112, 118-19, 151
The Works of Ossian, the Son of Fingal, in two volumes. Translated from the Galic language by James Macpherson. The third Edition. To which is subjoined a critical dissertation on the poems of Ossian. By Hugh Blair, D.D. (Macpherson) **97**:241-43, 245-56, 289-90, 298
The Works of Robert Burns (Burns) **114**:123-24
The Works of Sir John Suckling (Suckling) **30**:120, 125
The Works of Sir William D'avenant, Knight; Consisting of Those Which Were Formerly Printed, and Those Which He Design'd for the Press; Now Published out of the Authors Originall Copies (Davenant) **99**:165, 179
The Works of the Rev. George Crabbe (Crabbe) **97**:124
The Works of Thomas Campion: Complete Songs, Masques, and Treatises with a Selection of the Latin Verse (Campion) **87**:38-41, 43-45, 48, 62, 65, 71
The Works of Thomas Chatterton (Chatterton) **104**:12, 65
The Works of William Blake, Poetic, Symbolic, and Critical (Blake) **12**:51
"The World" (Herbert) **4**:100
"The World" (Milosz) **8**:187, 192, 194, 207, 209
"The World" (Rossetti) **7**:277
"The World" (Smith) **12**:328
"The World" (Tagore)
See "Vasundhara"
"The World" (Traherne) **70**:237, 245-50, 254
"The World" (Vaughan) **81**:306, 308, 342
"The World" (Very) **86**:162
World Alone (Aleixandre)
See *Mundo a solas*
"The World and I" (Jackson) **44**:86, 97, 99, 104
"The World and the Child" (Merrill) **28**:249
"The World and the Child" (Wright) **14**:352
"The World and the Quietist" (Arnold) **5**:38, 49
"The World as Meditation" (Stevens) **110**:230-31
"The World between the Eyes" (Chappell) **105**:65
The World between the Eyes (Chappell) **105**:33-34, 37, 47, 64-67, 69
"The World Box-Score Cup of 1966" (Dorn) **115**:109, 119, 140, 204, 216
The World Doesn't End (Simic) **69**:291-95, 299-300, 304-5, 311, 318-19, 339-41
"A World in Crystal" (Illyés) **16**:249
"The World Is a Beautiful Place" (Ferlinghetti) **1**:180, 182-83
"The World Is a Wedding" (Schwartz) **8**:303
"A World Is Everyone" (Ekeloef) **23**:80
"The World Is Full of Remarkable Things" (Baraka) **4**:23-4; **113**:19
A World of Difference (McHugh) **61**:190, 200, 205
"The World of Dreams" (Crabbe) **97**:90, 102, 156
"The World of Fantasy the Buddha Saw" (Hagiwara) **18**:178
The World of Gwendolyn Brooks (Brooks) **7**:64, 66, 105
"The World of Seven Wells" (Storni)
See "El mundo de siete pozos"
World of the Buddha (Stryk) **27**:181, 194, 198
"The World Outside" (Levertov) **11**:168, 193
"The World Situation" (Eberhart) **76**:23
"World Soul" (Bely) **11**:24
"The World State" (Chesterton) **28**:100
"World Telegram" (Berryman) **64**:78, 84
"World War" (Eberhart) **76**:8
"World War Two" (Koch) **80**:330
"A World without Objects Is a Sensible Emptiness" (Wilbur) **51**:188, 206-8, 211, 237, 296, 303, 314, 323
"World without Peculiarity" (Stevens) **110**:95
"World World" (Oppen) **35**:317
Worldly Hopes (Ammons) **16**:45-6
"Worlds" (Masters) **1**:333
"Worlds Back of Worlds" (Masters) **1**:343
"The World's Desire" (Masters) **1**:333
"World's End" (Ashbery) **26**:166
"The World's End" (Empson) **104**:94, 122-24, 134
"World's Fair" (Berryman) **64**:88
"The World's faire Rose" (Drayton) **98**:127
"The World's Homage" (Holmes) **71**:96
"The World's Instability" (Dunbar)
See "This waverand warldis wretchidnes"
"The World's Only Corn Palace" (Welch) **62**:340, 346, 371
"The World's Wonders" (Jeffers) **17**:141
"The World-Soul" (Emerson) **18**:86
Worleys (Reese) **29**:339
"The Worm Turns" (Lawrence) **54**:229
"The Worms of History" (Graves) **6**:137, 142, 144
"Wormwood" (Kinsella) **69**:100-101, 127
Wormwood (Kinsella) **69**:66, 76, 83, 89, 101, 108-9, 120, 122
"The Wormwood Star" (Milosz) **8**:201, 204
"Worsening Situation" (Ashbery) **26**:124
"Worship" (Kavanagh) **33**:120
"Worship" (Ransom) **61**:267
"The Worst Of It" (Sassoon) **12**:248
"Das Wort" (Benn) **35**:35, 58, 61, 62, 63
"Ein Wort" (Benn) **35**:34
"Die Wortemacher des Krieges" (Werfel) **101**:348
"Wortermelon Time" (Riley) **48**:286, 333-34
Worthy It Is (Elytis)
See *The Axion Esti*
"Would Jacob Wrestle with a Flabby Angel?" (Viereck) **27**:286
"Would You Wear My Eyes?" (Kaufman) **74**:205, 208, 216
"Woulda-Coulda-Shoulda" (Silverstein) **49**:343
"The Wound" (Glück) **16**:124, 138, 154
"The Wound" (Gunn) **26**:199, 206-207
"The Wound" (Hardy) **8**:93
"The Wound" (Soto) **28**:375
The Wound (Hughes) **7**:155
"A Wound Does Not Make a Dead Man" (Cernuda) **62**:169
"The Wounded Soldier" (Werfel)
See "Der Verwundete"
"The Wounded Soldier" (Whittier) **93**:193
"The Wounded Wilderness of Morris Graves" (Ferlinghetti) **1**:165
"The Wounds of Fodhla" (Clarke) **112**:64
"The Wounds of our Crucified Lord" (Crashaw) **84**:4, 25, 102, 152-53
Woven Stone (Ortiz) **17**:244
"Wovoka in Nevada" (Stafford) **71**:343
"Wovoka's Witness" (Stafford) **71**:343
"The Wraith" (Roethke) **15**:256, 272
"The Wraith Friend" (Barker) **77**:5-6, 44-45
"Wrapt in my carelesse cloke" (Surrey) **59**:315
"The Wrath of Lester Lame Bull" (Welch) **62**:345, 367
"The Wrath of Samson" (Vigny)
See "La colère de Samson"
"A Wreath" (Herbert) **4**:127, 130
"Wreath" (Illyés) **16**:250
"Wreath for the Warm-Eyed" (Merrill) **28**:234
"A Wreath for Tom Moore's Statue" (Kavanagh) **33**:75, 86, 90, 94, 121, 156; **105**:93, 143
"The Wreck of Rivermouth" (Whittier) **93**:176, 242, 247, 249
"The Wreck of the Deutschland" (Hopkins) **15**:129, 131-32, 134, 136-38, 144, 146, 151-52, 156, 170, 172-73
"The Wreck of the Hesperus" (Longfellow) **30**:12, 21, 26, 39, 47-8, 64, 99, 103
"The Wreck of the Nordling" (Corso) **33**:43
"The Wreck of the Thresher" (Meredith) **28**:178, 181, 193-94, 200, 206, 213, 215
The Wreck of the Thresher (Meredith) **28**:175, 178, 191-95, 209, 211, 213, 215
"Wreckage" (Momaday) **25**:221
"The Wrestlers" (Owen) **102**:236
"The Wrestler's Heart" (Soto) **28**:394, 399
"The Wretched One" (Marie de France)
See "Le Chaitivel"
"The Wrights' Biplane" (Frost) **71**:24
"Writ in Horace Greeley Square" (Corso) **33**:34-5, 49; **108**:5
"Writ on the Eve of My 32nd Birthday" (Corso) **33**:16, 35; **108**:8, 21, 25
"Writ on the Steps of Puerto Rican Harlem" (Corso) **33**:34; **108**:6, 23
"Write It Down" (Ekeloef) **23**:86
"The Writer" (Wilbur) **51**:236, 250-52, 278, 308-9
"Writer Waiting" (Silverstein) **49**:340
"The Writhing, Imperfect Earth" (Lindsay) **23**:281
"Writin' Back to the Home-Folks" (Riley) **48**:302
"Writing" (Cage) **58**:218
"Writing" (Nemerov) **24**:259
"Writing" (Paz)
See "Escritura"
Writing (Raworth) **107**:278, 281, 285-87, 290-91, 299, 302, 307, 309-10, 321-22, 325, 327-28, 336, 341
"Writing Again" (Bly) **39**:53, 86
Writing for the Fifth Time through Finnegans Wake (Cage) **58**:189
Writing for the First Time through Finnegans Wake (Cage)
See *Writing through 'Finnegans Wake'*
Writing for the Second Time through Finnegans Wake (Cage) **58**:192, 205
Writing for the Third Time through Finnegans Wake (Cage) **58**:189, 191
"Writing in a Time of Violence" (Boland) **58**:18, 51, 59, 61
"Writing in the Dark" (Levertov) **11**:199
Writing Is an Aid to Memory (Hejinian) **108**:253, 255-56, 261-67, 288, 310
"Writing My Feelings" (Li Po) **29**:179
"The Writing on the Image" (Morris) **55**:262, 329
"Writing on the Sand" (Rossetti) **44**:173
Writing through 'Finnegans Wake' (Cage) **58**:183, 189-90
"Writing to Aaron" (Levertov) **11**:208

Writing Writing (Duncan) **2**:106
Writings and Drawings (Dylan) **37**:59
Writings and Interviews (Ungaretti)
See *Scritti e interventi*
"The Writings Depart" (Breton) **15**:73
The Writings of Anna Wickham: Free Woman and Poet (Wickham) **110**:269-70, 272, 292, 294, 296-97, 303-4, 308-12
Writings through Finnegans Wake (Cage) **58**:183-84, 189, 195
Writings to an Unfinished Accompaniment (Merwin) **45**:30, 33-35, 40, 48-49, 63, 71-72, 75, 77, 79, 83-84, 86, 92, 97
"Written aboard a Boat on the Day of Little Cold Food" (Tu Fu) **9**:320
"Written after Long Rains at My Villa by Wang Stream" (Wang Wei) **18**:392
"Written at Bignor Park in Sussex, in August, 1799" (Smith)
See "Sonnet 92"
"Written at Bristol in the Summer of 1794" (Smith)
See "Sonnet 64"
"Written at Mule Hollow, Utah" (Bly) **39**:65
"Written at the Close of Spring" (Smith) **104**:194
"Written by Dr. Swift on His Own Deafness" (Swift) **9**:295
"Written by the Sea Shore—October, 1784" (Smith)
See "Sonnet 12"
"Written during a Remarkable Thunderstorm" (Smith)
See "Sonnet 54"
"Written for the Benefit of a Distressed Player, Detained at Brighthelmstone for Debt, November 1792" (Smith) **104**:227-29, 247, 325
"Written in a Hotel" (Szymborska)
See "Pisane w hotelu"
"Written in a Lady's Ivory Table-book, 1698" (Swift) **9**:251, 295
"Written in a Lady's Prayer Book" (Wilmot) **66**:322
"Written in Bristol" (Smith)
See "Sonnet 64"
"Written in Disgust of Vulgar Superstition" (Keats) **96**:204
"Written in Emerson's Essays" (Arnold) **5**:38, 49
"Written in Imitation of a Greek Epigram" (Prior) **102**:306
"Written in March" (Wordsworth) **67**:269, 271
"Written in Nostalgia for Paris" (Corso) **108**:30
"Written in October" (Smith) **104**:165
"Written in the Beginning of Mezeray's History of France" (Prior) **102**:311
"Written in the Church-Yard at Middleton in Sussex" (Smith)
See "Sonnet 44"
"Written in the Mountains in Early Autumn" (Wang Wei) **18**:392
"Written in the Sand at Water Island and Remembered" (O'Hara) **45**:172
"Written Off" (Enright) **93**:7
"Written on a Big Cheap Postcard from Verona" (Wright) **36**:356, 377
"Written on Passing by Moonlight through a Village" (Smith)
See "Sonnet 62"
"Written on The Door" (Perse) **23**:229
"Written on the Sea Shore—October, 1784" (Smith)
See "Sonnet 12"
"Written on the Stub of the First Paycheck" (Stafford) **71**:267
Written on Water (Tomlinson) **17**:321-23, 327, 333
"Written September 1791, during a Remarkable Thunderstorm" (Smith)
See "Sonnet 54"
Written Stone (Bonnefoy)
See *Pierre écrite*
"Written While Watching the Yankees" (Corso) **108**:22
"Written Whilst Walking Down the Rhine" (Spender) **71**:180, 217
"The Wrong Kind of Insurance" (Ashbery) **26**:134
"Wrong Number" (Bukowski) **18**:4
"Wszelki wypadek" (Szymborska) **44**:270
Wszelki wypadek (Szymborska) **44**:268
"Wunder" (Stramm) **50**:168-69, 189, 199, 201, 208, 217-18
"die würgengel" (Enzensberger) **28**:134
"Wuthering Heights" (Hughes) **89**:162
"Wyatt resteth here" (Surrey) **59**:317, 320-21, 326-27, 329-30, 340
Wybór wierszy (Herbert) **50**:39-40
"Wyeth's Milk Cans" (Wilbur) **51**:301, 324, 327
"The Wykehamist" (Betjeman) **75**:68-69
"Wyll and Testament" (Whitney) **116**:250-51, 253-54, 264-65, 272-73, 276, 284, 286, 294, 312
"Wystan Auden" (Schuyler) **88**:190
X/Self (Brathwaite) **56**:34-35, 54, 61-62, 71, 92-94
X: Writings, '79-'82 (Cage) **58**:202, 204-6, 208
Xaipe: Seventy-One Poems (Cummings) **5**:82-3, 86, 107-08
"Xango" (Brathwaite) **56**:61, 71
"XCI" (Carman) **34**:228
"XCIII" (Carman) **34**:211
Xenia (Martial) **10**:230
Xenia (Montale) **13**:132-33, 135-36, 138, 165, 167
"Xenia I" (Montale) **13**:144
"Xenia II" (Montale) **13**:144
"Xenion" (Montale) **13**:133-34
"Xenion" No. 7 (Montale) **13**:134
Xénophiles (Breton) **15**:53-4
"Xi" (Tolson) **88**:238-40, 258, 260, 273, 304, 312, 314-16, 324-26, 332
"XL" (Carman) **34**:224
"XLV" (Carman) **34**:234
"XLVII" (Carman) **34**:209
"Xoanon" (Ekeloef) **23**:67
"X-Ray Photograph" (Hope) **56**:266, 285-86, 294
"XV" (Carman) **34**:211
"XVI" (Shapiro) **25**:285
"XVIII" (Carman) **34**:234
"XXIII" (Carman) **34**:211, 227-28
"XXXII" (Carman) **34**:224
"XXXIV" (Carman) **34**:211, 224
Y and X (Olson) **19**:318
"Y Bardd a'r Brawd Llwyd" (Dafydd ap Gwilym) **56**:211-12
"Y Cariad a Wrthodwyd" (Dafydd ap Gwilym) **56**:246
"Y Cwt Gwyddau" (Dafydd ap Gwilym) **56**:247
"Y Cyffylog" (Dafydd ap Gwilym) **56**:230, 254
"Y Deildy" (Dafydd ap Gwilym) **56**:233, 247, 254-55
"Y Ffenestr" (Dafydd ap Gwilym) **56**:225, 227-30, 233
"Y la cabeza comenzó a arder" (Storni) **33**:270, 282
Y Otros poemas (Guillén) **35**:188, 189, 227, 229, 230, 231, 232, 234
"Y Rhew" (Dafydd ap Gwilym) **56**:225, 227, 229-30, 233
"Y Rhugl Groen" (Dafydd ap Gwilym) **56**:247
"Y Wawr" (Dafydd ap Gwilym) **56**:232
"Ya que para despedirme" (Juana Inés de la Cruz) **24**:180
Yabloko (Yevtushenko) **40**:343
"Yacht for Sale" (MacLeish) **47**:143
"The Yachts" (Williams) **7**:360, 368; **109**:284-85, 287
"Yad elohim ba'olam" (Amichai) **38**:5
The Yaddo Letter (Mahon) **60**:203, 205
"Yadwigha, on a Red Couch, Among Lilies; A Sestina for the Douanier" (Plath) **37**:188-89
Yakhal'inkomo (Serote) **113**:282, 290-91, 293-94, 296-97
"Yalluh Hammer" (Walker) **20**:273, 275-76, 286, 292
"Yam" (Merrill) **28**:259
"Yama no ugoku hi" (Yosano) **11**:321
"Yamanote Sen" (Hongo) **23**:197
"The Yankee Girl" (Whittier) **93**:291
"Yankee Nocturne" (Cernuda) **62**:173
"Yardley Oak" (Cowper) **40**:122
"The Yarn of the Loch Achray" (Masefield) **78**:70
"Los yaruros" (Cardenal) **22**:132
Ya—sibirskoy porody (Yevtushenko) **40**:364
"Yauvan-svapna" (Tagore) **8**:407
"Yawm mawlidi" (Gibran) **9**:78
"Ye Are Na Mary Morison" (Burns) **6**:99; **114**:41, 87
"Ye Goatherd Gods" (Sidney)
See "Yee Gote-heard Gods"
"Ye Have Hoarded Up Treasure in the Last Days—James 5:3" (Very) **86**:140
"Ye hidden Nectars" (Traherne) **70**:194
"Ye Jacobites by Name, Give an Ear ..." (Burns) **114**:61
"Ye Know My Herte" (Wyatt) **27**:314-15
"Ye old mule" (Wyatt) **27**:362
"yeah man?" (Bukowski) **18**:14
"The Year" (Melville) **82**:154
"The Year" (Patmore) **59**:240
"The Year" (Sandburg) **41**:296
"The Year 1812" (Davie) **29**:109
"The Year 1905" (Pasternak)
See "Devyatsat pyaty god"
"Year at Mudstraw" (Forché) **10**:133
A Year from Monday: New Lectures and Writings (Cage) **58**:182, 194-95, 199, 204, 219
"The Year I Was Diagnosed with a Sacrilegious Heart" (Espada) **74**:132
"The Year of 1812" (Mickiewicz) **38**:186
"The Year of Mourning" (Jeffers) **17**:141
"The Year of the Double Spring" (Swenson) **14**:267, 275
"The Years" (Aleixandre) **15**:4
"The Years After" (Quintana) **36**:272
"The Years as Catches" (Duncan) **75**:173-74
The Years as Catches (Duncan)
See *The Years as Catches: First Poems, 1939-1946*
The Years as Catches: First Poems, 1939-1946 (Duncan) **2**:104, 109; **75**:130, 157, 168, 173-75, 214, 225, 243-44, 252, 254
"The Year's Awakening" (Hardy) **8**:105
"Year's End" (Borges) **32**:139
"Year's End" (Hacker) **47**:104
"Year's End" (Wilbur) **51**:188, 212-13, 257-58, 261
"Year's End, 1970" (Berryman) **64**:96
"The Years Go By" (Niedecker) **42**:99
"Years of Indiscretion" (Ashbery) **26**:115, 124
"The Year's Sheddings" (Meredith) **60**:299
"A Year's Spinning" (Barrett Browning) **6**:32
"A Year's Windfalls" (Rossetti) **7**:262
"Yeats in Civil War" (Boland) **58**:42
"Yee Bow" (Masters) **1**:327; **36**:168
"Yee Gote-heard Gods" (Sidney) **32**:245, 260, 303
Yehuda Amichai: A Life of Poetry 1948-1994 (Amichai) **38**:54
"Yell'ham Wood's Story" (Hardy) **8**:91
"Yellow" (Jacobsen) **62**:300
"Yellow" (Sexton) **79**:201
"Yellow Afternoon" (Stevens) **110**:142
The Yellow Book (Mahon) **60**:230, 235-36
"Yellow Cars" (Stafford) **71**:323
"The Yellow Flower" (Williams) **109**:259, 261, 263
"Yellow Flowers" (Schuyler) **88**:187

The Yellow Heart (Neruda)
See *El corazón amarillo*
The Yellow House on the Corner (Dove) **6**:104-09, 116, 118, 122
"Yellow Light" (Chappell) **105**:42
"Yellow Light" (Hongo) **23**:203
Yellow Light (Hongo) **23**:195, 197, 202-204
Yellow Lola (Dorn) **115**:109-10, 113, 116, 120, 133-34, 157, 160-62, 222-23
"Yellow Ribbons, Baghdad 1991" (Rose) **13**:241
The Yellow Room (Hall) **70**:9, 26, 33
"Yellow Vestment" (Kavanagh) **33**:96; **105**:96
"The Yellow Violet" (Bryant) **20**:4, 35, 40
"The Yellow-Hammer" (Hardy) **92**:322
"Yellowhammer's Nest" (Clare) **23**:5
"Yes" (Ferlinghetti) **1**:187
"Yes" (Gallagher) **9**:64-5
"Yes" (Stafford) **71**:371
"Yes and It's Hopeless" (Ginsberg) **4**:76, 85
"Yes and No" (Jackson) **44**:70
"Yes, But" (Wright) **36**:349
"Yes, I am lying in the earth, moving my lips" (Mandelstam)
See "Da, ia lezhu v zemle . . ."
"Yes! No!" (Oliver) **75**:320
"Yes, the Snow Again" (Zanzotto)
See "Sì, ancora la neve"
"Yes, Think" (Stone) **53**:241, 252, 258
"Yesterday" (Aleixandre) **15**:5
"Yesterday" (Sitwell) **3**:293
"Yesterday" (Thumboo) **30**:328
"Yesterday I Was Called Nigger" (Guillén)
See "Ayer me dijeron negro"
Yesterday the Desert Reigning (Bonnefoy)
See *Hier régnant désert*
"Yesterdays" (Borges) **32**:58
"Yestreen I Had a Pint o' Wine" (Burns) **6**:75
"Yet Do I Marvel" (Cullen) **20**:63, 76
"the yeti poet returns to his village to tell his story" (Clifton) **17**:30
"Les yeux des pauvres" (Baudelaire) **1**:58
Les yeux fertiles (Éluard) **38**:68, 73, 86
"Yeux Glauques" (Pound) **4**:319; **95**:122
Yevgeny Onegin (Pushkin) **10**:357-62, 366, 368-69, 371, 374-83, 386, 391, 400-04, 406, 409
"The Yew Tree" (Wordsworth)
See "Lines Left upon a Seat in a Yew-tree"
"The Yew-berry" (Patmore) **59**:239-40, 258, 271
"Yew-tree Seat" (Wordsworth)
See "Lines Left upon a Seat in a Yew-tree"
"YgUDuh" (Cummings) **5**:98
"Yin and Yang" (Rexroth) **95**:255-57, 259, 269
Yin: New Poems (Kizer) **66**:75
"Ylang-Ylang" (McGuckian) **27**:83
"Yo" (Borges) **32**:58, 76
"Yo" (Fuertes) **27**:26, 49-50
"Yo cantar, cantar, canté" (Castro) **41**:107, 110-11
"Yo Jehová decreto" (Parra) **39**:275
"Yo no he nacido para odiar" (Castro) **41**:118
"Yo persigo una forma" (Darío) **15**:103-04, 119
"Yo soy aquél" (Darío) **15**:97
"Yo tengo un amigo muerto" (Martí) **76**:101
Yobuko to kuchibue (Ishikawa) **10**:211
"Yogisha" (Hagiwara) **18**:168, 179, 183
"Yonder Comes Sin" (Dylan) **37**:59
"Yonder See the Morning Blink" (Housman) **2**:179
"Yonec" (Marie de France) **22**:241-45, 258, 260-66, 269-72, 274-75, 299-300, 302-03
"The Yonghy-Bonghy-Bò" (Lear)
See "The Courtship of the Yonghy Bonghy Bo"
"York: In Memoriam W. H. Auden" (Brodsky) **9**:12
The York Road (Reese) **29**:339
"You" (Borges)
See "Tú"
"You" (Cummings) **5**:105
"You All Are State I Alone Am Moving" (Viereck) **27**:258
"You All Know the Story of the Other Woman" (Sexton) **2**:352-53
"You Also, Gaius Valerius Catullus" (MacLeish) **47**:197
"You and I Are Disappearing" (Komunyakaa) **51**:7, 10, 15, 17
"You and Me" (Tagore)
See "Tumi o ami"
"You, Andrew Marvell" (MacLeish) **47**:125-26, 130, 137, 143, 164, 167, 188, 196, 213, 253
"You Are" (Swenson) **14**:274, 283-84
"You are Gorgeous and I'm Coming" (O'Hara) **45**:150, 157
"You Are Happy" (Atwood) **8**:25, 27
You Are Happy (Atwood) **8**:20-4, 29, 31, 33, 41-2
"You Are Like the Realistic Product of an Idealistic Search for Gold at the Foot of the Rainbow" (Moore) **49**:118
"You are old Father William" (Carroll) **18**:49; **74**:63, 73
"You Are Waiting" (Aleixandre) **15**:6
"You Asked About My Life; I Send You, Pei Di, These Lines" (Wang Wei) **18**:391
"You Be Like You" (Celan)
See "Du sei wei du"
"You Bet Travel Is Broadening" (Nash) **21**:273
"You Came Last Season" (Corso) **108**:38
"You Can Have It" (Levine) **22**:223
"You Can Keep the Sun out of Your Eyes with Just One Hand" (Bell) **79**:25
"You Can Take It with You" (Jacobsen) **62**:323
You Can't Get There from Here (Nash) **21**:274
"You Cramp My Style, Baby" (Cervantes) **35**:109
"You, Doctor Martin" (Sexton) **79**:187, 190, 195, 203, 274-75, 281
"You, Dr. Martin" (Sexton) **2**:359, 365
"You Drive in a Circle" (Hughes) **7**:137; **89**:113
You, Emperors, and Others: Poems, 1957-1960 (Warren) **37**:300, 332, 361, 373, 380-81
"You Frog!" (Hagiwara)
See "Kaeru yo"
"You Get What You Pay For" (Curnow) **48**:14, 20
"You Gote-heard Gods" (Sidney)
See "Yee Gote-heard Gods"
"You Gotta Have Your Tips on Fire" (Cruz) **37**:31
"You Had to Go to Funerals" (Walker) **30**:338
"You Hated Spain" (Hughes) **89**:208, 217
"You Have a Name" (Aleixandre) **15**:5
"You Have Pissed Your Life" (Williams) **109**:286-87
"You Have the Lovers" (Cohen) **109**:4, 15
"you know" (Alurista)
See "tú sabes"
"you know that i would be untrue" (Alurista) **34**:39
"You luminous person of Barnes" (Lear) **65**:171, 184
"You may not see the Nazis" (Brutus) **24**:118
"You Old Mule" (Wyatt)
See "Ye old mule"
"You, Reader" (Stafford) **71**:372
"You say that I should not weep" (Akhmadulina) **43**:51
"You Shattered" (Ungaretti)
See "Tu ti spezzasti"
"You sit in the shade of the bare rocks" (Castro)
See "A la sombra te sientas de las desnudas rocas"
"You Speak No English" (Guillén)
See "Tú no sabe inglé"
"You Talk on Your Telephone; I Talk on Mine" (Gallagher) **9**:59
"You Tell Me This Is God?" (Crane) **80**:41
"You Think of the Sun That It" (Ammons) **16**:43
"You want me white" (Storni)
See "Tú me quieres blanca"
"You Were Wearing Blue" (Raworth) **107**:282
You WIll Know When You Get There: Poems, 1979-81 (Curnow) **48**:13, 15, 18, 20
"You Would Know" (Bell) **79**:32
"The Young" (Aleixandre) **15**:5
"Young" (Sexton) **2**:350
Young Adventure: A Book of Poems (Benét) **64**:19, 21
"Young Africans" (Brooks) **7**:65, 91, 93
"Young and simple though I am" (Campion) **87**:32, 34, 71-72, 90
"Young and Old" (Thomas) **99**:275
Young and Old (Thomas) **99**:272-73
"The Young and the Old" (Eberhart) **76**:54
"A Young Birch" (Frost) **1**:200
"Young Blood" (Benét) **64**:21
"The Young British Soldier" (Kipling) **3**:158
Young Cherry Trees Secured Against Hares (Breton) **15**:47
"A Young Child and His Pregnant Mother" (Schwartz) **8**:282, 302, 304
"The Young Cordwainer" (Graves) **6**:144
"Young Damon of the vale is dead" (Collins) **72**:44
"The Young Dead Soldiers" (MacLeish) **47**:212, 259
"Young Don't Want to Be Born" (Wright) **36**:310
The Young Fate (Valéry)
See *La jeune parque*
"Young Gal's Blues" (Hughes) **53**:135-36, 140
"The Young Girl at the Ball" (Hope) **56**:301
"Young Girls" (Page) **12**:176
"The Young Good Man" (Wright) **36**:306-7
"A Young Greek, Killed in the Wars" (Eberhart) **76**:16
"Young Heroes" (Brooks) **7**:92-3, 105
"The Young Highland Rover" (Burns) **114**:190
"Young Household" (Rimbaud)
See "Jeune ménage"
"The Young Housewife" (Williams) **7**:348, 363, 378, 409; **109**:262, 322
"Young Jemmy" (Behn)
See "Song to a Scotish Tune (When Jemmy First Began to Love)"
"Young Lady of Tyre" (Lear) **65**:168
"The Young Lady of Welling" (Lear) **65**:172, 185
"The Young Lord and the Maiden" (Mickiewicz)
See "Panicz i dziewczyna"
"Young Love" (Marvell) **10**:303-04; **86**:221, 223-24, 263-64
"Young Love" (Williams) **7**:382, 410
"The Young Lovers" (Aleixandre) **15**:4-6
"The Young Mage" (Bogan) **12**:100
"Young Man" (Seferis) **66**:144
"Young Man with Letter" (Ashbery) **26**:125
"A Young Man's Epigram on Existence" (Hardy) **92**:241, 247
"A Young Man's Exhortation" (Hardy) **8**:108; **92**:241, 245, 247, 250
"Young Man's Song" (Yeats) **20**:331, 333
"Young Maples in Winter" (Graham) **59**:169, 177
"Young Mothers" (Olds) **22**:328
"Young Mothers I" (Olds) **22**:308
"The Young Neophyte" (Meynell) **112**:153, 190, 232, 301
"The young night" (Borges)
See "La joven noche"
"Young Night-Thought" (Stevenson) **84**:317
"A Young Pan's Prayer" (Carman) **34**:222
"A Young Poet, in His Twenty-Fourth Year" (Cavafy) **36**:68, 75, 76, 79
"The Young Princess" (Meredith) **60**:251, 256, 263
"Young Prostitute" (Hughes) **53**:79
"The Young Queen" (Kipling) **91**:89, 142
"Young Romance" (Williams) **109**:283, 285

"Young Singer" (Hughes) **1**:236, 246
"Young Sorrows" (Heine)
See "Junge Leiden"
"Young Soul" (Baraka) **4**:9
"Young Sycamore" (Williams) **7**:372-77
"The Young Warrior" (Johnson) **24**:127, 166
"The Young Woman of Beare" (Clarke) **112**:34-35, 79, 81, 90
"Youngest Daughter" (Ransom) **61**:274
"The Youngest Daughter" (Song) **21**:331-32, 350
"The Youngest Son" (Service) **70**:115
"Youngsters" (Parra)
See "Jóvenes"
"Your Animal" (Stern) **115**:270
"Your Birthday in the California Mountains" (Rexroth) **20**:204; **95**:290
"Your Body Is Stars Whose Million Glitter Here" (Spender) **71**:181, 221
"Your eyes" (Paz)
See "Tus ojos"
"Your Face on the Dog's Neck" (Sexton) **2**:363; **79**:228
"Your faire lookes enflame my desire" (Campion) **87**:64, 68, 71, 119
"Your Flight" (Montale)
See "Il tuo volo"
Your Hours Are Numbered (Cernuda)
See *Con las horas contadas*
"Your House" (Akhmadulina)
See "Tvoi dom"
"Your Last Drive" (Hardy) **8**:134; **92**:314, 358-59, 361, 367
"Your Life" (Stafford) **71**:371
"Your Life and Death My Father" (Amichai) **38**:26, 28
"Your Name in Arezzo" (Wright) **36**:378-79
Your Native Land, Your Life (Rich) **5**:387-89
"Your Paris" (Hughes) **89**:270
"Your Slip's Showing" (Raworth) **107**:277
"Your Small Form" (Cernuda)
See "Tu pequeña figura"
"Your Tired, Your Poor" (Mueller) **33**:189
"Your Wound" (Sexton) **79**:211
"You're" (Plath) **1**:389-90; **37**:256
"You're a Big Girl Now" (Dylan) **37**:56
"Yourself" (Very) **86**:97, 118
"You's Sweet to Yo' Mammy jes de Same" (Johnson) **24**:141
"Youth" (Akhmatova) **2**:8
"Youth" (Cernuda)
See "Juventud"
"Youth" (Rimbaud)
See "Jeunesse"
"Youth" (Zukofsky) **11**:368
"Youth and Age" (Coleridge) **39**:175
"Youth and Age on Beaulieu River, Hants" (Betjeman) **75**:37, 79, 86
"Youth and Calm" (Arnold) **5**:42, 51
"A Youth in Apparel That Glittered" (Crane) **80**:52, 96
"Youth in Heaven" (Harper) **21**:209
"The Youth of Man" (Arnold) **5**:19, 49
"The Youth of Nature" (Arnold) **5**:19, 42, 49, 51, 59
"Youthful Picnic Long Ago: Sad Ballad on Box" (Warren) **37**:379
"Youthful Religious Experiences" (Corso) **108**:35
"The Youth's Magic Horn" (Ashbery) **26**:162
"Yr Adfail" (Dafydd ap Gwilym) **56**:231-32
"Ys It Possyble" (Wyatt) **27**:317, 324
Ysopet (Marie de France) **22**:258-59
yu can eat it at th opening (Bissett) **14**:17
"yu know th creaturs ar ourselvs" (Bissett) **14**:34
"yu sing" (Bissett) **14**:30
"yu want th music" (Bissett) **14**:34
"Yube no kane" (Ishikawa) **10**:214
"Yūbe no umi" (Ishikawa) **10**:213, 215
"Yugao" (Rexroth) **95**:272
"Yugel'skii baron" (Lermontov) **18**:288
"The Yule Guest" (Carman) **34**:202, 213
"Yule-Song: A Memory" (Braithwaite) **52**:106
"Yvonne" (Char) **56**:157
"Za Ki Tan Ke Parlay Lot" (Lorde) **12**:155
"Zachem on khodit? Ia liubliu odna" (Akhmadulina) **43**:37, 45
"Zagen" (Stramm) **50**:170, 178, 188, 209
Zahme Xenien (Goethe) **5**:223
"Zakinuv golovu i opustiv glaza" (Tsvetaeva) **14**:319, 322-23
"Zaklinanie" (Akhmadulina) **43**:8
"Zambesi and Ranee" (Swenson) **14**:277
Zapadno-Vostochnyi Veter (Shvarts) **50**:147
"Zaporogue" (Apollinaire) **7**:48
"Ein zärtlich jugendlicher Kummer" (Goethe) **5**:247
"Zarublennyi sviashchennik" (Shvarts) **50**:159
"Zasha" (Randall) **86**:345
"Zauberspruch" (Celan) **10**:124-25
"Zaveshchanije" (Lermontov) **18**:303
"Zaydee" (Levine) **22**:223
"Zazhigaia svechu" (Shvarts) **50**:163
"Zdumienie" (Szymborska) **44**:270
"Zea" (Wilbur) **51**:332
The Zea Mexican Diary (Brathwaite) **56**:71
"Zebra Question" (Silverstein) **49**:327, 335
"Żeglarz" (Mickiewicz) **38**:231
"Zeitgedichte" (Heine) **25**:131, 134
Zeitgedichte (Heine) **25**:129
Zeitgehöft (Celan) **10**:96, 111
"Der Zeitgeist" (Hölderlin) **4**:166
"Zen Poems of China and Japan: The Crane's Bill" (Stryk) **27**:181
"Zen Poetry" (Stryk) **27**:188
"Zennor Idyl I" (Barker) **77**:10
"Zennor Idyl II" (Barker) **77**:10
"Zennor Idyls" (Barker) **77**:13
"The Zeppelin Factory" (Dove) **6**:110
"Zero" (Berry) **28**:6
"Zero" (Gallagher) **9**:58
"Zero Hour" (Cardenal)
See "La hora O"
Zero Hour and Other Documentary Poems (Cardenal) **22**:117
"0015 hours Mayday CQ Position 41°46' N orth 50°14' West" (Enzensberger) **28**:155
"Zeroing In" (Levertov) **11**:205
"Zeta" (Tolson) **88**:237, 243, 257, 270-71, 304, 316-17, 332
"Zeus over Redeye" (Hayden) **6**:183, 194
"Zeusian toy" (Corso) **33**:46
"Zharenyi anglichanin v Moskve" (Shvarts) **50**:159, 162
Zhasněte světla (Seifert) **47**:316, 325-26, 334
"Zhil Na Svete Rytsar' Bednyi" (Pushkin) **10**:411
"Zhong feng" (Li Po) **29**:188
"Zikade" (Enzensberger) **28**:139
"Zilos' mne veselo i sibko" (Akhmadulina) **43**:60
"Zima Junction" (Yevtushenko)
See "Zima Station"
"Zima miejska" (Mickiewicz) **38**:153, 162, 219
"Zima Station" (Yevtushenko) **40**:349, 340-41, 352-53, 365, 367, 370
Ziminiskaya ballada (Yevtushenko) **40**:363
"Zimniji den'" (Akhmadulina) **43**:17
"Zimniy Vecher" (Pushkin) **10**:381
"Zim-Zizimi" (Hugo) **17**:59
Zither and Autobiography (Scalapino) **114**:283
"Znayu" (Bely) **11**:32
"The Zodiac" (Dickey) **40**:174
The Zodiac (Dickey) **40**:176-77, 181, 183-84, 207-9, 217, 219, 221-22, 232, 239, 256, 262
"Zoetropes" (Curnow) **48**:46
"Zokudo no, kari ni ai sunawachi hanare, sariyasuku todomarigataki koto wo kanashiburu shi" (Yakamochi) **48**:137
"Zola" (Robinson) **35**:367
"Zolnierz" (Herbert) **50**:5, 7
Zoloto v lazuri (Bely) **11**:3-6, 22, 26, 31-2
"Zone" (Ammons) **16**:6, 28
"Zone" (Apollinaire) **7**:6, 10-12, 14-15, 21, 41, 44-8
"Zone" (Bogan) **12**:126
"Zoo de verbena" (Fuertes) **27**:16
"Zoo Keeper's Wife" (Plath) **1**:399
"A Zorro Man" (Angelou) **32**:29
"Zov" (Akhmatova) **55**:49
Zovy vremen (Bely) **11**:31-2
"Zueignung" (Goethe) **5**:257
"Zuleika" (Goethe) **5**:228
"Zver'-tsvetok" (Shvarts) **50**:134, 159
Zvezda (Bely) **11**:7, 24, 30, 32
"Zwist" (Stramm) **50**:189, 198, 202, 207
"Zvuk ukazuiushchii" (Akhmadulina) **43**:37, 45